Nashua Public Library

Enjoy this book!
Please remember to return it on time
so that others may enjoy it too.

Manage your library account and
discover all we offer by visiting us
online at www.nashualibrary.org

Love your library? Tell a friend!

CRITICAL COMPANION TO

Henry James

Henry James

A Literary Reference to His Life and Work

ERIC HARALSON AND KENDALL JOHNSON

Facts On File
An imprint of Infobase Publishing

Facts On File, Inc.
An imprint of Infobase Publishing
132 West 31st Street
New York NY 10001

Library of Congress Cataloging-in-Publication Data

Haralson, Eric L.
Critical companion to Henry James : a literary reference to his life and work /
Eric Haralson and Kendall Johnson.
p. cm.
Includes bibliographical references and index.
ISBN 978-0-8160-6886-9 (acid-free paper) 1. James, Henry, 1843–1916—
Handbooks, manuals, etc. I. Johnson, Kendall, 1969– II. Title.
PS2123.H37 2009
813'.4—dc22   2008036451

Facts On File books are available at special discounts when purchased in bulk
quantities for businesses, associations, institutions, or sales promotions. Please call
our Special Sales Department in New York at (212) 967-8800 or (800) 322-8755.

You can find Facts On File on the World Wide Web at http://www.factsonfile.com

Text design by Erika K. Arroyo
Cover design by Cathy Rincon/Takeshi Takahashi

Printed in the United States of America

VB Hermitage 10 9 8 7 6 5 4 3 2 1

This book is printed on acid-free paper and contains 30 percent
postconsumer recycled content.

CONTENTS

ACKNOWLEDGMENTS

At the heart of this book are the very fine contributors from throughout the world whose dedication to the scholarly study of Henry James has broadened our understanding and remains an inspiration.

Thank you to our editor, Jeff Soloway, for his steady guidance and patience throughout each stage of this endeavor. Kyoko Miyabe's careful editing and keen-eyed substantive queries improved the final product. The collections at the Butler Library of Columbia University and the McCabe Library of Swarthmore College were rich resources without which this book would not be possible.

The Hungerford Fund from Swarthmore College helped bring this project to completion. Our thanks go out to Connie Hungerford, the provost of Swarthmore College, who supported our work, and to Eugene Lang for his kind generosity.

INTRODUCTION

Critical Companion to Henry James takes its place in a series of volumes designed to introduce readers to a major writer and to provide a resource for exploring further the rich themes and historical contexts implicit in an author's literary style. Henry James was a particularly prolific and well-connected writer whose literary criticism and narrative techniques have influenced generations of subsequent writers and inspired generations of literary scholars to interpret and reinterpret the meaning of his work. His writing career begins in the midst of the Civil War and ends with his death during World War I. His productivity is astonishing. The published oeuvre includes more than 100 short stories, 20 novels, many articles of literary criticism, several book-length travel accounts, a multivolume autobiography, and two biographies, one of Nathaniel Hawthorne and another of the expatriated American sculptor William Wetmore Story. Add to this his vast correspondence, and it is hard to imagine that he had time to do anything but write.

James's career presented a unique challenge to us as editors of this companion. It is simply impossible to cover all of James's work within a single binding. We therefore decided to focus on those works of the most importance to scholars and most interest to students. Contemplating the task, we sought counsel from a network of exceptional scholars who have demonstrated the dynamic relevance of Henry James to the contemporary world. We are deeply grateful to all those who evaluated our list of entries and suggested additions, as well as, at our prompting, ways of tidying up the offerings.

The process of selection was difficult, but we can say with confidence that what appears here is the result of many hours' consideration and conversation during which we weighed the advice of many, including: Martha Banta, Nancy Bentley, Gert Buelens, Sharon Cameron, Tamara Follini, Wendy Graham, Susan Griffin, Richard Lansdown, Jesse Matz, David McWhirter, Michael Moon, Elsa Nettels, Lee Person, Adrian Poole, Ross Posnock, Julie Rivkin, Eric Savoy, Sheila Teahan, Pierre Walker, Percy Walton, Kenneth Warren, and Greg Zacharias. Even if we could not follow all of their suggestions, their advice fundamentally shaped the design of the companion. Herein the reader will encounter more than 60 avid James critics who are based in three continents and reside in 10 countries. It is fitting that James, who was so mightily invested in the international contexts of his literary calling, would attract such a wide-ranging group of diverse and rigorous scholars as contributors.

Of the companion as a whole, there are two major parts: Part II, dedicated to his fiction and nonfiction, and Part III, with entries on 62 people, places, and themes that are important to understanding the life and work of Henry James. Each Part II entry begins with a short summary of a work's publication history and is divided into three main parts, including a plot synopsis, a critical analysis, and a character summary. The plot synopsis offers an overview of the novel or short story and complements the reading of James's actual text—the truth of which is definitely in its telling. For those entries dealing with nonfiction and travel writing, the contributors have adapted the plot synopsis section to summarize James's literary theories or to provide the biographical and historical narrative behind James's observations. The critical analysis section offers an interpretation of James's work as informed by the century-long heritage of scholarly interpretation that James has inspired. The character summaries focus on the major characters in a particular work in order to provide a brief description of the personalities involved in the drama. Finally, each entry includes a list of stage or screen adaptations (wherever apropos) and a further reading section that lists those texts to which the contributors refer in the critical analysis sections. Part III entries are meant to supplement those of Part II. As a set of 62, they provide an awareness of the people, places, and themes important to James and to readings of his writing.

Within this general design, the companion's contributors have each rendered their treatment of James's work and associated topics with distinctive style and insights. This collaborative approach means that a vast coverage of James's work never settles into the tone of either of the editors;

instead, readers are able to enjoy the fresh variations among contributors and yet not sacrifice an overall structure that ensures a referential clarity for even casual users. References to other entries are given in small capital letters the first time they appear in an entry.

In compiling and editing the companion, it was hard not to marvel again at earlier reference works that were designed to be comprehensive. Robert L. Gayle's *A Henry James Encyclopedia* (1989) remains the most extensive and thorough guide to the author's life and work; Daniel Fogel's *A Companion to Henry James Studies* (1993) is a collection of essays that provides a dazzling overview of James's writing and its scholarly reception; and Glenda Leeming's *Who's Who in Henry James* (1976) is a handy reference in factoring through the dramatis personae of James's major novels. Finally, any attempt to address James's life and work owes an immense debt to the varied biographical enterprises of Leon Edel, Lyndall Gordon, Fred Kaplan, R. W. B. Lewis, Sheldon Novick, and Jean Strouse.

Eric Haralson and Kendall Johnson

PART I

Biography

Henry James

(1843–1916)

When first considering the life of Henry James, it may be difficult to sort through the many names of correspondents and friends. How could anyone have had the time to lead such a vibrant social life among writers, sculptors, musicians, painters, and actors, to travel extensively throughout Europe and the United States, and, on top of it all, to write 20 novels, well over 100 short stories, influential essays in literary CRITICISM, copious book reviews, and many more articles on travel and art? And then there are the hundreds of people to whom he wrote thousands of letters, only a fraction of which has yet been published. THEODORA BOSAN-QUET, the secretary to whom he dictated in the last decade of his life, noted in her retrospective book that "Henry James was a voluminous letter-writer and exhaustively communicative in his talk upon every subject but one, his own work, which was his own real life" (25).

Reading about James's life affords a window into the influential literary circles of the 19th century, when the United States and Europe were undergoing massive economic and political changes brought on by industrialization and new technologies of travel and communication. For James, as for many of his contemporaries, these changes made the world feel at times more coordinated and connected, and at other times more fragmented and isolating. James's intense commitment to the literary arts earned him the title of "the Master" to a generation of younger admirers. There is a pompous ring to the phrase but also a poignant measure of irony in the way his mastery derived from striving after the impossible literary standards that he set for himself as he dedicated his personal life to the craft of writing. To his disappointment, James's works were only infrequently popular, and his best efforts were underappreciated by a public thrilled with what he considered sensationalist plot-driven fiction and by publishers who reduced reading to its entertainment value. When James tried to write for more popular audiences, particularly for the theater, he was forced to live down the embarrass-ments of substantial public failures. Furthermore, in his later years he selected and revised his short stories and novels in the definitive NEW YORK EDI-TION (1907–09), which he hoped would stand as a literary edifice comparable to Balzac's massive *La comédie humaine* (1830–56) and would win him comparable respect. Yet the New York Edition sales were a great disappointment. Nevertheless, James did enjoy remarkable esteem among fellow writers and a dedicated set of readers who recognized in the subtlety and complexity of his writing the poignancy of life's ambiguities. In the 20th century, literary critics and readers paid increasingly more attention to the challenges and rewards of his work.

There have been a number of excellent biographies of James, but the most influential have been those written by Leon Edel (a five-volume work published from 1953 to 1972), Fred Kaplan, and, more recently, Sheldon Novick. These life stories highlight the fulfillment that James derived from his devotion to writing, along with the insecurity and loneliness with which he wrestled, as borne out in his letters and notebooks. There is disagreement about certain aspects of James's life, particularly the nature of his SEXUALITY, his political convictions, his seeming prejudices, and his sense of national affiliation. Nevertheless, Edel's work provides a solid blueprint from which to organize periods of James's life into an overall story. The following sections borrow from Edel's chronology.

1843–1870

Henry James, Jr., was born in 1843 in NEW YORK CITY, the son of HENRY JAMES, SR., and Mary Walsh, whose Calvinist grandparents had emigrated from Scotland and Ireland to the city during the volatile Revolutionary War era. Henry, Sr.'s father, William James, emigrated from Ireland a few years later, in the late 1780s, and flourished in the sale of dry goods and land speculation, taking prosperous advantage of the development of the Erie Canal; speculating successfully on western land in Syracuse, New York, Michigan, and Illinois; and establishing an impressive estate in Albany, New York. At his death in 1832, his worth was estimated at $3 million, making him one of the wealthiest men in early 19th-century New York.

However, Henry James, Sr., had to rescue this inheritance from his father's peculiar will, which granted each of his 12 children a solid annuity but put the fortune's greatest share into a trust to be protected for 21 years and subsequently apportioned by managers who assessed the heirs' professional accomplishments. Henry, Sr.'s rambunctious adolescent years had alarmed his father, who had expected his son's adherence to the strict moral standards of a Presbyterian upbringing and his pursuit of a conventional career in business or the law. Henry, Sr.'s teenage years had been particularly challenging; at 13, he lost a leg as a result of an accident during a school science experiment gone awry (he tried stamping out a barn fire). He spent several years nursing the wounds resulting from the amputation before attending Union College, where he eventually graduated with warnings from the college president about his drinking and gambling.

After his father's death, Henry, Sr., challenged the will in court. He also enrolled at the Princeton Theological Seminary. In 1837, the lawyers managed to win a complete division of the James estate. The resulting influx of capital enabled Henry James, Sr., to live unconventionally and comfortably without a money-making profession, traveling throughout Europe in search of the optimal educational curriculum for his precocious sons William and Henry, Jr. Early in his marriage to Mary Walsh in the 1840s, Henry, Sr., dedicated his life to the pursuit of his spiritual convictions, writing philosophical tracts and lecturing in favor of liberalized marriage, against slavery, in defense of the Union of the United States, and on other social issues, inspired by the tenets of the theologian Robert Sandeman, the socialist Charles Fourier, and, most influential, the Christian mystic EMANUAL SWEDENBORG. Henry, Sr., published such works as *Moralism and Christianity; or Man's Experience and Destiny* (1850), *The Social Significance of Our Institutions* (1861), and *The Secret of Swedenborg, Being an Elucidation of His Doctrine of the Divine Natural Humanity* (1869). In the course of his career, Henry, Sr., corresponded and socialized with many famous writers of his day in LONDON, Boston, and New York, including Thomas Carlyle, RALPH WALDO EMERSON, and Margaret Fuller.

Henry James, Jr., was born on April 15, 1843, in New York City at 21 Washington Place. He was the second oldest of the five James children: from eldest to youngest, WILLIAM JAMES, Henry, Garth Wilkinson (Wilky), Robertson (Bob), and ALICE JAMES. His older brother, William, became a major American philosopher as a professor of psychology at Harvard University and, with Charles Sanders Peirce, one of the primary theorists of the tenets of PRAGMATISM. His two younger brothers, Wilky and Bob, were shaped by their courageous service in the Massachusetts black regiments during the CIVIL WAR. Both died relatively young, in late middle age, never finding a true vocation and troubled by bouts with alcohol and depression. The youngest of the five was Alice, who faced the constrained gender roles of conventional Victorian (see VICTORIANISM and WOMEN'S ISSUES) womanhood, fought against depression as a young adult, and wrote a fascinating diary, copies of which she gave to her brothers upon her death from cancer in the early 1890s. In the last years of her adult life, she lived near Henry in England with her companion, Katharine Loring. The James family also included Mary's older sister, Katherine or Aunt Kate, who helped raise the children.

For much of his early childhood, Henry, Jr., grew up in Manhattan, first on Washington Square and then near Union Square at 14th Street and Sixth Avenue. He frequently visited his cousins in Albany, where his grandfather had amassed his fortune. From very early in life, he was on the move, traveling with his parents through England, France, and other parts of continental Europe. In his autobiography, *A Small Boy and Others* (1913), he reports his first memory as being in PARIS at the Place Vendôme, gazing at a distinctive obelisk erected by Napoleon to commemorate the Battle of Austerlitz. In Manhattan, Henry's childhood was filled with outings to theaters, lecture halls, vaudeville shows, and P. T. Barnum's Great American Museum. Henry was an avid reader, which helped him cope with the unpredictability of being shuffled between schools and from tutor to tutor as his father grew impatient with each successive phase of instruction.

Young Henry James, Jr., with his father, Henry James, Sr., a daguerreotype from the studios of Matthew Brady, frontispiece to *A Small Boy and Others (Charles Scribner's Sons, 1913)*

Perpetually restless, Henry, Sr., became convinced that New York was too provincial to promote the education of his sons, whom he hoped would speak French and German. For the next three years, from 1855 to 1858, Henry, Jr., was a teenager living between SWITZERLAND, Paris, and London with his family or at school. In 1858, the James family returned to the United States and spent a year in NEWPORT, Rhode Island, where Henry became good friends with THOMAS SERGEANT PERRY and JOHN LA FARGE, who recommended the novels of Balzac, a primary and enduring influence on James's writing and career. Much to their father's chagrin, Henry and William joined their friend La Farge in committed study of landscape painting under the direction of William Morris Hunt. Henry had little talent and lost interest, but William was convinced that painting was his vocation. In 1859, Henry, Sr., and Mary uprooted the

family, taking them back to Europe—specifically to Geneva, where Henry enrolled in the engineering school at Institute Rochette. Soon disenchanted with the curriculum, he joined his brother William at what would become the University of Geneva. There he attended whichever lectures caught his eye. He continued to read with a passion, absorbing William Thackeray and Anthony Trollope, Charles Dickens and GEORGE ELIOT, and he began to write in earnest, rarely showing his work to anyone.

In 1860, after just a year in Switzerland and Germany, the family returned to Newport as the nation hovered on the brink of civil war. William reconfirmed his commitment to painting and returned to Hunt's studio before changing his mind, much to his father's relief, and enrolling in the Lawrence Scientific School at Harvard University. Meanwhile, Henry continued to read extensively and to write. The Newport scene became even more interesting with the arrival of the six Temple children, Henry's cousins on his father's side, whose parents had died, leaving them orphaned. MARY (Minny) TEMPLE captivated Henry and his friends, but she would later die young of tuberculosis. Her vibrant spirit and determination to speak her mind made her a favorite correspondent of Henry's during his first accompanied European tour in 1869. She helped to inspire some of James's famous characters, including Isabel Archer of The PORTRAIT OF A LADY (1881) and Milly Theale of The WINGS OF THE DOVE (1902).

As the Civil War began, Henry James, Sr., protected his two older sons from soldiering. In 1862, the younger brothers, Wilky and Bob, who had been attending Frank Sanborn's school in Concord, pushed to enlist; Wilky joined the Massachusetts 44th and later served in the Massachusetts 54th, the first black army regiment, under the command of Colonel Robert Gould Shaw. The following year, 17-year-old Bob lied about his age to join the black regiment of the Massachusetts 55th. Meanwhile, during the summer of 1862, Henry, Jr., injured himself in an accident oddly like his father's while pumping water to fight a stable fire in Newport. This "obscure hurt," as Henry, Jr., later referred to it in his autobiography, eluded a professional diagnosis and has been the source of much biographical speculation. In August of 1863, Wilky suffered more ennobling albeit life-threatening injuries in the battle for Fort Wagner, South Carolina, under Colonel Shaw. Wilky was found unconscious in a hospital by Cabot Russell, a family friend searching in vain for his own son who had been killed in the battle. As Wilky recovered and returned to his regiment within the year, Henry tried to study law at Harvard. He found it dull and uninspiring and dedicated himself to literary writing, becoming determined to trust his pen as the source of his vocation.

In 1864, the family moved from Newport to Boston's Ashburton Place. Henry's literary efforts began to bear fruit when New York's the *Continental Monthly* published without attribution his first story, "A Tragedy of Error." In May, Henry wept upon hearing of the death of Nathaniel Hawthorne, who represented to him an example of an American writer earning international respect. Henry continued to write reviews for the *Nation* and the *North American Review*. In March 1865, the *Atlantic Monthly* published James's first signed story, "The

STORY OF A YEAR," about the disillusioning effects of war and injury on a youthful romance. Even at the start of his career, Henry's productivity was quite astonishing. Fred Kaplan notes that between 1864 and 1866, when in his early 20s, James "published six of his stories and twenty-nine reviews" (65), making enough money to support himself as he lived at home. He was thrilled by the experience of making an impression on the literary scene. (See PERIODICALS and PUBLISHERS.)

On the morning of Henry's 23rd birthday in 1865, President Abraham Lincoln died from an assassin's bullet in the immediate aftermath of the Civil War. William heard the news upon arriving in Brazil as an assistant to the famous paleontologist and Harvard professor Louis Agassiz on the yearlong Thayer Expedition. William collected specimens in the Amazon rain forest, did some sketching, kept a diary, and endured illness that made him quite miserable. After returning to Harvard in early 1866, William suffered another vocational crisis, retreating for a time to Germany to recover his health and mental energy, and breaking away from Agassiz's mentorship. Upon his return to Harvard, he decided to pursue psychology after graduating from medical school. Absorbed by his own self-doubts, William was not particularly encouraging of his brother's writing efforts. Meanwhile, the younger brothers followed up their rather heroic soldiering with an ill-fated attempt to run a plantation in Florida, backed by their father's and Aunt Kate's financial support. The venture had failed rather spectacularly by 1870, and thereafter Wilky and Bob struggled to find fulfilling careers or happiness as either husbands or fathers.

Between 1865 and 1868, James moved with his family to CAMBRIDGE, MASSACHUSETTS, where he continued to deepen friendships that he would cherish throughout his transatlantic life and that would inspire certain characters in his fiction. As he worked up the courage and capital to go abroad on his own, he spent his days with Minny Temple, the young Oliver Wendell Holmes, Jr. (the future United States Supreme Court justice who had served and been wounded in the Civil War), and WILLIAM DEAN HOWELLS (whose eventual editorship of the *Atlantic Monthly* would guide many of

"William James" (self-sketch, ca. 1866), frontispiece to *Notes of a Son and Brother* (*Charles Scribner's Sons, 1914*)

James's stories into print). He also cultivated professional relationships with Charles Eliot Norton, a distinguished family friend who served as editor of the *North American Review* from 1864 to 1868, and with James T. Fields, editor of the *Atlantic Monthly* from 1862 to 1870. During this period, Henry also met Minny's friend Elizabeth (Lizzy) Boott, an inspiring painter who was studying under William Morris Hunt and whose father, Francis, was a composer. James would later meet them in Italy and follow their tumultuous story over the coming two decades. These friends encouraged James's literary aspirations as they read his many reviews.

In the aftermath of the Civil War, Henry set his sights on Europe, where he hoped to learn about the world and develop an international perspective and appeal as an author. In February 1869, with a line of credit and introductions from his father, he embarked on his first independent tour of England and the Continent. In England, he visited many famous landmarks and enjoyed the social connections of Charles Eliot Norton, who had moved with wife and sisters (including Grace Norton) to London. Norton helped James meet intellectual luminaries such as George Eliot, William Morris, John Ruskin, and Leslie Stephen. Insisting in letters home that travel was necessary to improve his health, he went to Germany, Paris, Switzerland, and Italy. He gathered his initial impressions of FLORENCE, ROME, and VENICE, all important settings in his subsequent fiction. While still in England, he learned of Minny's death, which if not wholly unexpected was nonetheless heartbreaking.

1870–1881

In May 1870, Henry returned to Cambridge, Massachusetts, mourning the loss of Minny and yet invigorated by his Old World travels. While abroad, he had remained in close touch with William Dean Howells, who had succeeded James T. Fields as the editor of the *Atlantic Monthly*. For the next two years, James continued to write avidly and to divide his time between New York, Newport, and Vermont. The *Atlantic Monthly* serialized his first novel, *Watch and Ward* (August–December 1871); despite this regular income, New York proved

expensive, and Henry plotted his return to Europe, where he hoped to remain for a longer period.

In May 1872, James again crossed the Atlantic, this time with his sister, Alice, and Aunt Kate. They toured England, France, Germany, Switzerland, Austria, and Italy, where James wrote travel sketches, some of which appeared in the *Nation.* He would later collect and revise these articles into a substantial part of *Italian Hours* (1909). In Paris, he befriended James Russell Lowell, the elder American poet who had been the first editor of the *Atlantic Monthly* starting in 1857. He also met up with Ralph Waldo Emerson, with whom he would later tour St. Peter's Basilica in Rome. In Italy, James was thrilled to meet the famous British actress FANNY KEMBLE and her daughter, Sarah Butler Wister, with whom he rode through the Italian countryside on horseback. Kemble and James would renew their friendship in London, remaining close until her death in 1893. In Rome, Henry befriended fellow American expatriates, including the sculptor William Wetmore Story, whose biography (*William Wetmore Story and His Friends*) he would publish in 1903. He reunited with Francis and Lizzy Boott, who were living in a villa in Bellosguardo, just outside of Florence. Lizzy eventually married the American painter Frank Duveneck, and like Minny, she died tragically young. When William joined Henry, the two brothers traveled together, and Henry stayed on in Europe until September 1874, writing RODERICK HUDSON (1875) before returning to the United States. To manage living in Europe, he committed himself to the goal of making about $3,000 dollars a year through writing (Kaplan 151).

As *Roderick Hudson* was being serialized in the *Atlantic Monthly,* James spent 1875 in New York. The $200 a month he earned for the novel's year-long run was not enough to stabilize him financially. He left for France in November 1875, hoping to become part of the Parisian literary scene; however, its salon culture proved unsatisfying. Initially, he was thrilled to make acquaintance with influential writers, including Ivan Turgenev, Alphonse Daudet, Émile Zola, Guy de Maupassant, Ernest Renan, and Gustav Flaubert, who held weekly salon gatherings. In April 1876, Turgenev introduced

James to Paul Joukowsky, a young aristocratic painter and intellectual from Russia, with whom he became deeply infatuated. James's attraction faltered in 1880, when he visited Joukowsky, who had gone to Naples to live near the German composer Richard Wagner. According to Fred Kaplan, James "was appalled by the openly homosexual and adulterous activities of the Wagner entourage" (223). Joukowsky was one of several men with whom James seems to have fallen in love in his lifetime. To what degree, if at all, James's feelings of intellectual and emotional intimacy extended to sexually physical affection remains a point of controversy among his biographers. In his letters, he expresses fondness, warmth, and excitement in strikingly passionate language. (See MASCULINITY.)

During this time in the French capital, Henry wrote journalistic letters about life in Paris as a correspondent for New York's *Tribune*, the newspaper formerly edited by Horace Greeley until his death in 1872. The bloom on this arrangement quickly faded as the *Tribune* pressed him to reveal more personal anecdotes in his reporting. Rather than risk being thought a gossip, and since he was already feeling alienated from authentic Parisian society, James resigned. He frequently attended plays at the Comédie Française and dedicated himself to his novel *The* AMERICAN (1877), which features Christopher Newman, a wealthy American businessman whose romantic designs of marrying a French aristocrat are thwarted by a haughty family that ultimately rejects him as a suitable husband in spite of his millions. The ending was unpopular for readers who followed the novel's *Atlantic Monthly* serialization beginning in June 1876, orchestrated by editor Howells to coincide with the Centennial Exhibition in Philadelphia. By December 1876, James had grown decidedly weary of Paris and plotted his escape. He moved to Bolton Street, Piccadilly, in London, where he finished the novel's final installments. London and Rye became his home bases for the rest of his career; as he recalls in a journal entry from November 1881, when he first "took up [his] abode in Bolton Street": "I had very few friends, the season was of the darkest and wettest; but I was in a state of deep delight. I had complete liberty, and the prospect of profitable work; I used to take long walks in the rain. I took possession of London; I felt it to be the right place" (Edel 218).

In 1877, James traveled through Paris to Italy and overheard an anecdote that would grow into the novella "DAISY MILLER: A STUDY" (1878). After the Philadelphia publisher Lippincott rejected the story, it appeared in Leslie Stephen's *Cornhill Magazine* and proved very popular. James regretted not securing the American copyright but followed up the novella with the respectfully received *The* EUROPEANS (1878). He enjoyed his skyrocketing reputation in London, where he often dined out, befriending the British critic, librarian, and poet EDMUND GOSSE and the *Punch* illustrator GEORGE DU MAURIER, who would later confide to an encouraging James the "germ" for Du Maurier's smash-hit novel *Trilby* (1894). James became friends with JOHN ADDINGTON SYMONDS after admiring his seven-volume *Renaissance in Italy*; Symonds, though married, wrote openly about love and sex between men. James would later use anecdotes about Symonds related to him by Gosse to write the story "The AUTHOR OF 'BELTRAFFIO'" (1884). James also enjoyed his conversations with Fanny Kemble, who affirmed the necessity of ending *The American* with Newman's failure and who gave to him the kernel of what would become WASHINGTON SQUARE (1880), which James recorded in his notebook (Edel 11). When his critical literary biography HAWTHORNE (1879) appeared in *Scribner's*, the reaction from the American press was "unfavorable" (Edel 219). Readers resented James's portrayal of American society as shallow and meager. Meanwhile, in Cambridge, Massachusetts, William married Alice Howe Gibbens in July 1878. Henry visited Florence, where for the next year he worked on *The Portrait of a Lady* (1881). He befriended the writer CONSTANCE FENIMORE WOOLSON, the grandniece of the famous American novelist James Fenimore Cooper.

1882–1895

In November 1881, as the last installment and the book editions of *The Portrait of a Lady* appeared, James returned to the United States. He had been gone for six years and received a warm welcome from those who had followed his developing career.

He spent Christmas with his family at Quincy Street in Cambridge, and as the New Year began, he went to Washington D.C., meeting President Chester A. Arthur and visiting Henry Adams (grandson of John Quincy Adams and editor of the *North American Review*), whom James had first met in Rome. On January 29, 1882, James's mother died, and he returned to Cambridge to attend the funeral, where the family was reunited in their grief. Afterward, a fatalistically resigned Henry, Sr., moved with Alice to Boston. Henry, Jr., returned to England in May 1882 and managed to travel in France and write *A Little Tour in France* (1884). (See TRAVEL WRITINGS.) His father's death in December brought him back to the United States. Sorting through his father's will as its executor, he insisted on giving his brother Wilky a full share of inheritance, against the protests of William. Sadly, Wilky died in the fall of 1883 after suffering from chronic illness. By the late fall of 1883, James had returned to London, and Constance Fenimore Woolson arrived to spend a few months. James continued to publish, including *The Siege of London* (1883) and the essays *Portraits of Places* (1883), and to think seriously about writing for the theater. Turgenev died as the year ended, and James published an appreciation of his work in the *Atlantic Monthly*.

In the winter of early 1884, James returned to Paris and reassuringly concluded that moving to London in 1876 had been for the best. During this stay, he visited Zola; he also met the American painter JOHN SINGER SARGENT, who would become a close friend, and Paul Bourget, a French writer who would dedicate his novel *Cruelle Enigma* (1885) to James. James maintained a friendship with Bourget, despite Bourget's ANTI-SEMITISM, especially troublesome to James during the DREYFUS AFFAIR. James returned to London as the essay "The ART OF FICTION" (1884) and his collection of stories *Tales of Three Cities* (1884) appeared. Alice's illness, diagnosed finally as breast cancer, was intensifying, and she voyaged to England, where she, Henry, and her companion, Katharine Loring, moved to Bournemouth in 1885. While there, Henry became good friends with ROBERT LOUIS STEVENSON, whose novel *Treasure Island* (1883) enjoyed immense popularity, and he enjoyed conversations with the popular Brit-

"Henry James," from a photograph by Elliot and Fry, frontispiece to *The Middle Years* (Charles Scribner's Sons, 1917)

ish writer MRS. MARY HUMPHRY WARD, the niece of Mathew Arnold. James concentrated on writing, producing over the next year two long novels: *The BOSTONIANS* (1886), first serialized in *The Century*, and *The PRINCESS CASAMASSIMA* (1886), first serialized in the *Atlantic Monthly*. Moving to London in the spring of 1886, James rented an apartment at 34 De Vere Gardens in Kensington. Disappointed with the sales of his novels, he plotted his popular success as a dramatist, eventually rewriting *The American* for the stage to include a happy ending in which Newman wins his wife.

James traveled through Italy from late 1886 until the spring of 1887, residing in Venice and Florence, where he stayed with Woolson and visited with Violet Paget, a writer of fiction and criticism who used the masculine "Vernon Lee" as her pseudonym. He wrote "The ASPERN PAPERS" (1888) and began thinking about *The TRAGIC MUSE* (1890), a novel he worked on after returning to London in the summer of 1887. In 1888, the tragic and unexpected death of Elizabeth (Lizzy) Boott Duveneck from pneumonia unnerved him. He saw a few more books into print (*The Reverberator*, "The Aspern Papers," *Louisa Pallant*, *The Modern Warning* [1888], and *Partial Portraits* [1888]). His friend Robert Louis Stevenson left for the United States and eventually settled on a Samoan island. James spent the rest of the year traveling, including a visit with Woolson in Geneva. He continued to write fiction, publishing "A LONDON LIFE" (1889; a collection of stories) and "The PUPIL" during the same year. He met Rudyard Kipling and spent the summer of 1890 in Italy. His literary agent, Wolcott Balestier (whose sister Kipling later married), fed James's enthusiasm for the stage. In 1889, James learned of his Aunt Kate's death. This was also when he developed deep friendships with the young American writer-journalists Jonathan Sturges and MORTON FULLERTON.

In 1891, as his brother William enjoyed the acclaim of his work *Principles of Psychology* (1890), Henry eagerly anticipated the theatrical debut of *The American* by the Compton Comedy Company. Meanwhile, Alice's health grew worse. After initial success in the countryside theater circuit, *The American* opened in London in late September to lukewarm reviews. A disappointed James recommitted himself to writing new plays. His sister died on March 6, 1892, and left her diary in the trust of Loring, who printed four copies, one of which she gave to Henry in 1894. After her funeral, he traveled to Italy and then to Switzerland, meeting his brother William and his family. The collection *The Real Thing and Other Tales* (1893) appeared, but James remained dedicated to the theater, and in 1893 he started writing *Guy Domville* (1894). (See DRAMA.) He was greatly saddened by the death of Fanny Kemble, whose funeral he attended and whom he eulogized in the magazine *Temple Bar*. John Addington Symonds also died of tuberculosis, having always suffered from poor health. And then, in early 1894, Constance Fenimore Woolson was found dead in Venice, after having apparently jumped to her death from a window of her villa. James went to Venice to help sort through her estate. Meanwhile, Robert Louis Stevenson died in Samoa at the age of 44, another victim of chronic illness.

In 1894, James pinned great hopes on the success of *Guy Domville*. On the night of its London premier at the St. James Theater, he bided his time by attending the smash hit by OSCAR WILDE, *An Ideal Husband*. When he showed up as his own play ended, James made an unfortunate curtain call, encouraged by the principal actor George Alexander. James was greeted by the rowdy boos and jeers of the audience. Tepid reviews sealed the fate of the production, which lasted just five weeks and was a significant financial disappointment. James's hopes for theatrical success were dealt a severe blow, and afterward he never more than fiddled with writing plays, finishing small ones here and there, and enjoying only modest theatrical successes. He tried to shake his depression by rededicating himself to fiction, hoping to apply lessons that he had learned about drama in his ensuing novels.

1895–1901

In his notebook entry on January 23, 1895, James rallied his forces: "I take up my own old pen again—the pen of all my old unforgettable efforts and sacred struggles. To myself—today—I need say no more. Large and full and high the future still opens. It is now indeed that I may do the work of my life. And I will" (Edel 109). By the year's end, Wilde had gone from celebrity to public infamy, sentenced to hard labor for acts of "gross indecency," the legal phrase naming sexual acts between men. James, while no fan of Wilde, thought the business of his trial was sordid, cruel, and unfair. James published the collection of stories *Terminations* (1895) and started to write *The SPOILS OF POYNTON*, which appeared in the *Atlantic Monthly* beginning in the spring of 1896. His collection *Embarrassments* appeared later that year, and he started working on the novel *WHAT MAISIE KNEW*. Meanwhile, George Du Maurier died, leaving James to mourn another close friend. He hired a stenographer, hoping to remain productive despite increasing pain in his wrist. Dictation became his preferred method of composition, first to William MacAlpine, to Mary Weld in 1901, and starting in 1911 to Theodora Bosanquet. In 1897, James made another major move, signing a long lease for LAMB HOUSE in Rye, which would become his home until the end of his life. He wrote a biography of his expatriate friend, the sculptor William Wetmore Story, whose studio in Rome had been a vibrant intersection of artists and intellectuals.

In 1898, "The TURN OF THE SCREW" began a run from January through April in *Collier's*. The story was much discussed and highly regarded. James settled into Lamb House and began to host his friends, including Oliver Wendell Holmes, Mrs. James T. Fields ("Annie," whose husband had passed away in 1881), the Bourgets, Edmund Gosse, and the novelist Howard Sturgis. He also met the young American writer Stephen Crane and H. G. WELLS, who was beginning to enjoy popularity as a novelist and had written a fairly positive review of *Guy Domville* three years before. James began work on *The AWKWARD AGE* before leaving for a tour of the Continent, including Paris, Venice, and Rome, where he met the young Norwegian-American sculptor HENDRIK C. ANDERSEN, of whom he would grow very fond. In France, Zola published the famous letter "J'Accuse!," damning France for the injustice of fraudulently convicting and imprisoning the Jewish captain Alfred Dreyfus in 1894; in private correspondence, James expressed his sympathy with the Dreyfusards. In July 1899, James returned to Lamb House to host his brother William and his family in the autumn. By year's end, he had purchased Lamb House and taken on a professional literary agent named James B. Pinker. He continued working on *The SACRED FOUNT* (1901) and *The AMBASSADORS* (1903), one of his three great later-phase novels, along with *The WINGS OF THE DOVE* (1902) and *The GOLDEN BOWL* (1904). He met JOSEPH CONRAD, whose novels he admired, and the young writer Ford Maddox Hueffer (later Ford). James's collection of stories *The Soft Side* (1900) appeared in print.

1901–1916

Queen Victoria died in 1901, ending a reign that had started more than a decade before James's birth and affecting him, like the rest of his cohorts, as a watershed in British history. James finished *The Ambassadors* and began *The Wings of the Dove*, which was published in the summer of 1902. Meanwhile, his brother William delivered the prestigious

Gifford Lectures at Edinburgh University, the basis of what would become *The Varieties of Religious Experience: A Study in Human Nature* (1902). Henry fired his servants Mr. and Mrs. Smith when their heavy drinking became unmanageable. He also hired as a houseboy the young Burgess Noakes, who would eventually travel with James as his assistant and serve on the front lines in WORLD WAR I. James grew fond of his visiting nephew William James, Jr. At this time, he wrote his memorable "The BEAST IN THE JUNGLE" (1903). As *The Ambassadors* made its debut in 1903, first as a serial in the *North American Review* and then as a book, James began writing *The Golden Bowl*. In December 1903, he met the admiring EDITH WHARTON, an emerging novelist who would become a very close friend. A year later, in November 1904, *The Golden Bowl* was published.

In the late summer of 1904, James embarked for the United States, arriving in New Jersey in late August. He toured the United States, writing travel sketches that appeared in *Harpers Weekly* and that he later collected as *The AMERICAN SCENE* (1907). He visited Manhattan, his brother and his family in New Hampshire, Edith Wharton in Lenox, Massachusetts, and the places where he had once lived: Boston, Cambridge, and Newport. In Philadelphia, he delivered the public lecture "The Lesson of Balzac" and stayed with Sarah Wister, the daughter of Fanny Kemble. He traveled south through Richmond, Virginia; North Carolina (where he stayed at the Vanderbilt estate Biltmore); and Charleston, South Carolina, ending up in Florida (St. Augustine and Palm Beach), where he visited his niece and his sister-in-law, the widow of Wilky. James returned to New York and delivered the commencement address "The Question of Our Speech" at Bryn Mawr College outside Philadelphia in the late spring of 1905. During his tour of the East Coast, he visited in Washington, D.C., his longtime friend John Hay (now secretary of state) and met President Theodore Roosevelt, whose expansionist, bellicose vision of America's future James and his brother William condemned. Having completed visits to cities on the East Coast and gathered impressions that he would publish, he took a three-week rail journey through Chicago to

California, which he would recall as a particularly rich experience in his life. In July 1905, he left the United States, embarking for England, where he began to select and revise his novels for Scribner's New York Edition (1907–09) of his work. In 1906, he finished *The American Scene,* wrote "The JOLLY CORNER" (1908) (a story influenced by his reaction to New York City), and composed new prefaces to the novels he selected for inclusion in the New York Edition, leaving out *Watch and the Ward* (serialized in 1871; book publication 1878), *Confidence* (1879), *The Bostonians,* and even the more popular works *Washington Square* and *The Europeans.* In London, James engaged the Boston-born photographer ALVIN LANGDON COBURN, who had photographed him in New York in 1905, to work with him in assembling 24 photographs to serve as frontispieces for the edition.

In the spring of 1907, he rendezvoused with Edith Wharton in Paris and enjoyed touring the

Henry James, 1912 photo portrait by E. O. Hoppe, frontispiece to *Letters of Henry James,* volume 2 *(Charles Scribner's Sons, 1920)*

Midi region of southwest France in her automobile. James returned to England in 1908, meeting his brother William, who delivered the Hibbert Lectures at Oxford University. The sales of the New York Edition were meager, a very serious disappointment to James. In a letter to Edmund Gosse in 1915, he looked back on the New York Edition as being "from the point of view of profit either to the publishers or to myself, practically a complete failure; vulgarly speaking, it doesn't sell . . . [and] has never had the least intelligent critical justice done it—or any sort of critical attention at all paid to it . . ." (Edel, *The Master* 777). James's health began to deteriorate with attacks of gout, while he also became deeply depressed.

In 1909, *Italian Hours* appeared in book form. (See TRAVEL WRITINGS.) As if facing the inevitability of his death, James burned thousands of pages of CORRESPONDENCE and notes in a fire at Lamb House. The new year of 1910 found James depressed and feeling increasingly ill. He was eventually confined to his bed, although doctors were unable to diagnose a physical cause. William and his wife, Alice, traveled to England, attempting to get him back on his feet and rejuvenate his spirits. Alice cared for Henry as William headed to Germany's Bad Nauheim, where he got evidence of his failing heart in the form of an X-ray. Alice and Henry joined him as he looked for relief in the spas. In June, the three headed off to Switzerland, where William hoped to hike the mountains for the last time. Sadly, they learned that their brother Robertson had died of a heart attack. In August 1909, James, William, and Alice returned to the United States. Shortly upon arriving, on August 26, William died at his family home in Chocorua, New Hampshire. A heartbroken Henry stayed with Alice and her family through the winter, visited New York, Cambridge, and Boston, and took solace in his friendships with Grace Norton (whose brother Charles Eliot Norton had passed away in 1908), William Dean Howells, and Edith Wharton, whose motorcar was a happy vehicle of diversion through the New England countryside. In the spring, Harvard University conferred an honorary degree upon James. The collection of stories *A Finer Grain* (1910) and his last completed novel, *The Outcry* (1911), appeared.

On July 30, 1911, James left the United States for the last time. He relocated to London, staying at the Reform Club, and he worked with Theodora Bosanquet, dictating his autobiography, *A Small Boy and Others* (1913). (See AUTOBIOGRAPHIES.) Amid faltering health, he began to enjoy public awards in England, receiving an honorary doctorate from Oxford University, and delivered a lecture at the Royal Society of Literature in honor of the centenary of the poet Robert Browning's birth. Edith Wharton spent the summer of 1912 in England, visiting James at Lamb House. Aware of his financial concerns and in hope of cheering him further, she secretly arranged for Scribner's to deposit $8,000 in his account, ostensibly for the sales of the New York Edition. To commemorate Howells's 75th birthday, he wrote an essay taking appreciative measure of his friend's accomplishments as a writer and editor. In 1913, James turned 70. John Singer Sargent painted his portrait, sponsored by more than 250 subscribers. For his birthday, James received this portrait and a bowl and dish once owned by King Charles II, a reference to *The Golden Bowl*. Sargent dedicated the proceeds of the subscription to fund the sculpting of a bust of James by Derwent Wood.

With the outbreak of the Great War in 1914, James felt that he was in "a nightmare from which there is no waking" as civilization crashed around him (Edel, *The Master* 511). He directed his energy to relocation efforts for Belgian refugees and visits of the war wounded in the hospital, reminiscent of the bedside comfort provided by Walt Whitman to soldiers during the Civil War. James became the chairman of the American Volunteer Motor Ambulance Corps in France. He continued to work on his fiction, starting the unfinished novel *The Ivory Tower* and collecting his essays on Balzac, Flaubert, and Zola in *Notes on Novelists* (1914). As the war dragged on, James continued to work on behalf of the wounded, meeting with England's prime minister Herbert Asquith, whom he asked to cosponsor his application for British citizenship. He received his Certificate of Naturalization on July 26, 1915. In December, his health took a fatal turn when he suffered a

series of strokes and developed pneumonia. His sister-in-law Alice arrived from the United States in mid-December to care for him. On January 1, 1916, although confined to his bed in Chelsea, James received the Order of Merit from King George V. Henry James died on February 28 at age 72. His funeral service was held in London. He was cremated, and his ashes were taken to the United States, where they were buried in the James family plot in Cambridge Cemetery.

FURTHER READING

Anesko, Michael. *"Friction with the Market": Henry James and the Profession of Authorship*. New York: Oxford University Press, 1986.

Bell, Millicent. *Edith Wharton & Henry James: The Story of Their Friendship*. New York: G. Braziller, 1965.

Bosanquet, Theodora. *Henry James at Work*. Edited and introduced by Lyall H. Powers. Ann Arbor: University of Michigan Press, 2006.

Brooks, Peter. *Henry James Goes to Paris*. Princeton, N.J.: Princeton University Press, 2007.

Edel, Leon. *Literary Biography*. Toronto: University of Toronto Press, 1957.

———. *Henry James*. Minneapolis: University of Minnesota Press, 1960.

———. *Henry James: The Untried Years, 1843–1870*. Philadelphia: Lippincott, 1953.

———. *Henry James: The Conquest of London, 1870–1881*. Philadelphia: Lippincott, 1962.

———. *Henry James: The Middle Years, 1882–1895*. Philadelphia: Lippincott, 1962.

———. *Henry James: The Treacherous Years, 1895–1901*. London: Hart-Davis, 1969.

———. *Henry James: The Master, 1901–1916*. Philadelphia: Lippincott, 1972.

———, ed. *Henry James, Selected Letters*. Cambridge, Mass.: Belknap Press of Harvard University, 1987.

Edel, Leon, and Lyall H. Powers, eds. *The Complete Notebooks of Henry James*. New York and Oxford: Oxford University Press, 1987.

Gunter, Susan E., and Steven H. Jobe, eds. *Dear Beloved Friends: Henry James's Letters to Younger Men*. Ann Arbor: University of Michigan, 2002.

Habegger, Alfred. *The Father: A Life of Henry James, Sr.* New York: Farrar, Straus & Giroux, 1994.

Hayes, Kevin J. *Henry James: The Contemporary Reviews.* Cambridge: Cambridge University Press, 1996.

Horne, Philip. *Henry James: A Life in Letters.* New York: Viking, 1999.

Hyde, H. Montgomery. *Henry James at Home.* New York: Farrar, Straus & Giroux, 1969.

Kaplan, Fred. *Henry James: The Imagination of Genius: A Biography.* Baltimore: Johns Hopkins University Press, 1999.

Matthiessen, F. O. *Henry James: The Major Phase.* New York: Oxford University Press, 1944.

Lewis, R. W. B. *The Jameses: A Family Narrative.* New York: Doubleday, 1991.

Novick, Sheldon M. *Henry James: The Young Master.* New York: Random House, 1996.

———. *Henry James: The Mature Master.* New York: Random House, 2007.

Richardson, Robert D. *William James: In the Maelstrom of American Modernism.* Boston: Houghton Mifflin, 2006.

Simon, Linda. *Genuine Reality: A Life of William James.* New York: Harcourt Brace, 1998.

Strouse, Jean. *Alice James.* New York: HarperCollins, 1980.

Zorzi, Rosella Mamoli. *Beloved Boy: Letters to Hendrik C. Andersen, 1899–1915.* Charlottesville: University of Virginia Press, 2004.

Eric Haralson and Kendall Johnson

PART II

James's Works

NOVELS

The Ambassadors (1903)

Henry James wrote *The Ambassadors* in 1900–01. It was serialized in 12 installments in the *North American Review* during 1903 and was published later in the same year by Methuen in Great Britain and by Harper's in the United States. It was lightly revised for the NEW YORK EDITION of James's work (Scribner's Sons, 1909). James added the preface for this edition, and *The Ambassadors* appeared in two volumes, 21 and 22. The break between the volumes was placed at the end of Book Sixth. In Book Eleventh of both the Harper's and the Scribner's editions, sections 1 and 2 were mistakenly reversed. This error is corrected in most modern reprints of the novel, which generally follow the New York Edition. (See also prefaces to the NEW YORK EDITION.)

SYNOPSIS

Book First

(Chapter 1) The novel opens in Chester, an old Roman medieval town in the northwest of England.

The story is told in third-person narrative from the perspective of Lewis Lambert Strether, a quiet yet observant middle-aged American from Woollett, Massachusetts. He has recently arrived at Liverpool and is due to meet his friend Waymarsh at the hotel in Chester. However, Strether arrives early and falls into the company of Maria Gostrey, an American in her mid-thirties who has lived in Europe most of her life and is adapted to its tastes and customs. She agrees to show Strether around town, and by the end of their walk it has been agreed that she will show him around Europe too. Strether is conscious of new possibilities opening up to him, but he doubts that Waymarsh will approve.

(Chapter 2) Later that evening, Strether and Waymarsh stay up and talk, allowing the reader a closer look at their contrasting personalities. Waymarsh represents his New England hometown of Milrose and its moral code. He is a rigorous, hardworking, financially successful American lawyer who views Europe as something of an ordeal. After three months of traveling, he wants nothing more

"By Notre-Dame," by A. L. Coburn, frontispiece to the first volume of *The Ambassadors*, Volume 21, the New York Edition

than to go home. Strether, however, is already warming to Europe in general and Miss Gostrey in particular. In the course of the conversation, Waymarsh learns that Strether is in Europe to conduct some business for a friend, the widowed Mrs. Newsome.

(Chapter 3) Strether, Maria Gostrey, and Waymarsh spend a day in Chester together shopping and looking around. This sets a pattern for the rest of the novel, in which the American tourists do a great deal of shopping and looking around. Maria describes herself as an unofficial guide for Americans and admits that she is expert at "putting them through" so thoroughly that they will never want to come back (78). She also admits that Strether is an exception to this rule, and their friendship is cemented. Strether and Maria analyze Waymarsh's dislike of all things European and find a name for it, "the sacred rage" (85). Waymarsh expresses this rage by running into a jeweler's shop to spend his hard-earned American money, but Strether never finds out what, if anything, he buys there.

Book Second

(Chapter 1) After introducing several key characters, James uses this important section to establish the scenario of the novel. Strether and Maria Gostrey, now staying separately in London, meet to spend an evening together at a restaurant and at the theater. Strether explains that his assignment from Mrs. Newsome is to rescue her son, Chad, from a romantic entanglement in PARIS. Maria's questions draw more from Strether about himself and the Newsome family. The Newsomes are the economic magnates of Woollett but have made their money through sharp practice and through the manufacture of a commodity so common and embarrassing that Strether refuses to say what it is. Strether, however, has no contact with business. He has lived quietly, has lost a wife and a young son, and has rescued his "one presentable little scrap of identity" through his editorship of the *Woollett Review*, a journal funded by Mrs. Newsome (101). Mrs. Newsome emerges as a formidable personality, rich, fastidious and coercive, bearing a visual resemblance to Queen Elizabeth I. She plans to marry Strether on his return to Woollett.

Maria, who looks more like Mary Stuart, challenges Strether's view of his assignment. She suggests that Chad may have been refined rather than corrupted by Paris. She also pledges to help Strether the best she can.

(Chapter 2) Now in Paris, Strether collects his letters from Mrs. Newsome but finds that despite these missives his errand loses urgency as he strolls around the city, admiring the parks and the people and recalling his visit with his young wife many years before. Strether is aware of a sense of youth and escape, and of the aesthetic possibilities presented by Paris. He wonders how he will square his attraction to these with his mission to reclaim Chad. He walks round to Chad's home, a third-floor apartment on the Boulevard Malesherbes, where he sees and is seen by a young man smoking on the balcony. Intrigued and reluctant to rejoin Waymarsh at the hotel, Strether goes in to visit.

Book Third

(Chapter 1) Strether dines with Waymarsh and confesses that he has met Chad's friend John Little Bilham and agreed to eat with him the next day. However, Chad himself is out of town, visiting Cannes. Strether describes Bilham as "pleasant and curious" (132). He is another expatriate American living in Paris. He had hoped to learn painting but has given up studying in favor of simply enjoying the lifestyle of the city. Strether also admits that Bilham confuses many of his ideas and assumptions about Chad and his social circle. Waymarsh gruffly advises Strether to quit the whole errand for the Newsomes. However, he comes the next day to have lunch with Bilham in Chad's apartment. Bilham has also invited Miss Barrace, who takes an instant liking to Waymarsh as an American "type." Miss Barrace's talk and social freedom confuse Strether's moral categories more than ever. Nevertheless, he finds that he very much enjoys smoking with her on the balcony.

(Chapter 2) Maria Gostrey arrives in Paris, and Strether goes to visit her. Her apartment is crammed with interesting and stylish possessions, which make him deeply aware of the "empire of 'things'" (141). She agrees to meet Bilham to help Strether make up his mind about him. After a visit to the Louvre and a tea at Bilham's own modest and bohemian house, Maria invites Strether, Waymarsh, and Bilham to the theater. Bilham fails to arrive, and Maria notes that for the past few days he has probably been acting on instructions from Chad, but she suspects that this evening he is working on Strether's behalf. As the play resumes after the interval, a man steps into the box. Initially Strether does not recognize him, but it is Chad himself.

Book Fourth

(Chapter 1) After the play, Strether tells Chad that his purpose in Paris is to make him break with everything and bring him home to Woollett. However, Strether is disconcerted by how much Chad has aged and altered. At first Strether suspects that he has become a "Pagan" but comes round to wondering whether he is, after all, a "gentleman." Chad asks for some time to commit to Strether's proposal, but he assures him that he is not entangled with any woman to the extent that he cannot go home whenever he chooses.

(Chapter 2) Strether writes home, but his letters reflect his uncertainty about the cause of Chad's transformation. Maria Gostrey remains convinced that Chad has been improved by a close connection with a clever woman but that perhaps he now wishes to shake her off. Strether asks Bilham directly if Chad is involved in a romance and is told that there is a "virtuous attachment" (187). Subsequently, Chad tells Strether that he would like him to meet two friends of his, a mother and daughter. When Strether reports this to Maria, she points out that the virtue of the attachment will depend on the age, position, and character of the woman concerned. Strether, she says, must find out for himself if Chad's attachment is virtuous or not.

Book Fifth

(Chapter 1) Chad invites Strether to an afternoon party at the house of the great sculptor Gloriani, where Madame de Vionnet and her daughter will also be present. In the old garden, Strether discusses Chad's friends with Bilham, who advises him to rely on the "vain appearance" when trying to judge them (204). Miss Barrace joins the conversation and affirms that in Paris what matters is not

so much what things are but what they resemble. Both advise Strether to make up his own mind about Chad's friends.

(Chapter 2) Strether is introduced to Madame de Vionnet, who strikes him as remarkably correct and respectable, almost worthy of Woollett itself. But she is called away by other friends, and Strether finds himself once more with Bilham, who tells him that Madame de Vionnet's husband is still living. She is therefore not free to marry Chad. Bilham wants to introduce Strether to more of Gloriani's guests, but Strether replies that it is "too late" for him to enter the great world of the glamorous. However, he says that it is not too late for Bilham. He tells him, "Live all you can; it's a mistake not to" (215). As they talk, Chad brings Madame de Vionnet's daughter, Jeanne, out to meet them. Charmed by her innocence and prettiness, Strether decides that he has misread the situation. It must be Jeanne, he thinks, whom Chad wishes to marry.

(Chapter 3) Chad sees his female friends home, leaving Strether in Gloriani's garden. He is rescued by Maria, who knows Madame de Vionnet's history because the two had been schoolmates in Geneva. Madame de Vionnet married young to a comte who was a brute, and the couple have lived apart for many years. She has carried herself with style and has brought up her daughter for society. Maria conjectures that recently she has brought up Chad for her daughter. However, the following day Chad denies that there is any engagement. Moreover, he states that it is his gratitude to Madame de Vionnet that is the hitch preventing him from leaving Paris. He persuades Strether to go and visit her to judge her for himself.

Book Sixth

(Chapter 1) The following day, Strether calls on Madame de Vionnet in her distinguished old home. He is impressed by the sense of history and by Madame de Vionnet's civility. Strether is still confused about Chad's relationship to Jeanne, but Madame de Vionnet makes it clear that she does not wish them to marry. However, she does ask Strether to find out if Jeanne is in love with Chad. Madame de Vionnet argues that because she has done so much to improve Chad, Strether ought to help her. He agrees to report well of her to Mrs. Newsome in his letters.

(Chapter 2) Strether meets Jeanne again at a gathering at Chad's home. He finds her delightfully unspoiled and well bred. Later, Strether finds himself in conversation with Gloriani and then Miss Barrace, whom he asks about the possibility of Madame de Vionnet divorcing in order to marry Chad. Miss Barrace replies that what is remarkable is the power of their relationship without MARRIAGE. She also discusses her friendship with Waymarsh, who escorts her around Paris and buys her flowers. Strether finds this amusing until Miss Barrace questions him about his friendship with Maria Gostrey.

(Chapter 3) At the same party, Madame de Vionnet wants to know from Strether why Maria has suddenly left Paris. He is able to tell her that Maria has gone to stay with a sick friend in the south, but he is disconcerted again by the implication that he and Maria are closely connected. They discuss Jeanne, and he warns her to leave the girl's feelings alone, so as not to spoil her. Later, Strether asks Bilham why he does not ask Jeanne to marry him. Bilham replies that he is not rich enough, and they discuss Chad's situation once more. It becomes clear to Strether that Chad cannot marry Madame de Vionnet while her husband is alive; nor can he marry Jeanne after being "in love with her mother," as Bilham phrases it (267). Strether and Bilham agree that it would be a torment for the couple to carry on as they are without marriage or for them to part. Strether marks the midpoint of the novel with a dramatic volte face. Abandoning his original remit from Mrs. Newsome altogether, he concludes that Chad and Madame de Vionnet should "face the future together." Strether feels that after all that she has done to improve him, Chad "ought to be ashamed of himself" if he goes back to Woollett (268).

Book Seven
(Chapter 1) Twelve days later, Strether encounters Madame de Vionnet in Notre-Dame Cathedral. Strether has watched her meditating without realizing who she is, but then she comes to speak to him, interrupting his less devout thoughts about Victor Hugo. Having concluded that her visit to

the church must vouch for her innocence, Strether feels able to invite her out for lunch. They eat together at an intimate café and discuss Chad more openly than ever before. Strether asserts that he is ready to go home and that Chad probably is too. Madame de Vionnet is sure that if Chad goes home his mother will want to marry him off. Strether pledges to help Madame de Vionnet and Chad the best he can.

(Chapter 2) Three days later, Strether receives a telegram from Mrs. Newsome. After a strained, silent dinner with Waymarsh, Strether writes a long reply home, only to tear it up later the same night. Early the next morning, Chad calls at Strether's hotel and declares that he is ready to sail. However, Strether holds him back—even though this will mean that Mrs. Newsome is likely to send out Chad's sister, Sarah, and her husband, Jim, to complete the task of bringing Chad home.

(Chapter 3) Later the same day, Strether goes to visit Maria Gostrey, newly returned to Paris. He tells her about Mrs. Newsome's telegram: "Come back by the first ship" (296). He also says he is sure that it must have been prompted by a secret report by Waymarsh on Strether's apparent lack of progress. Maria and Strether discuss the likely arrival of the Pococks and Jim's sister, Mamie, the girl to whom the Newsomes hope to marry Chad. Strether privately reflects that everything is changing. His letters home are becoming more and more evasive, and even his friendship with Maria is shifting balance. He can now, as she says, "toddle alone" in the act of perception (299).

Book Eighth
(Chapter 1) Strether analyzes how his feelings toward Waymarsh have changed after his secret communication with Woollett, but he recognizes that his friend has acted with serious and earnest motives. Strether also reflects that his relationship with Madame de Vionnet will be on a new footing as soon as the Pococks arrive. He goes to visit her, but is disappointed to find her away from home for a few days. While he fears Sarah's arrival, he feels that if he is to be censured, he might as well enjoy himself. He resolves to see Madame de Vionnet as often as he likes. Subsequently, he goes to the

station with Chad to meet the Pococks. On the way, they discuss what Sarah, Jim, and Mamie will make of Paris and whether Strether is really in disgrace with Mrs. Newsome.

(Chapter 2) The Pococks arrive. Strether is relieved to find himself greeted by Sarah as a trusted friend, which makes him realize how much he hopes to avoid a split with her mother. He also finds Mamie as attractive as ever. Going back across town in a cab with Jim, a plain American businessman who has come over for a "good time," Strether tries to find out how he stands with Mrs. Newsome at home. Jim assures him that she is "sitting up" for Strether and that therefore he should not go home (334). Strether is not sure if this advice is flippant or not.

(Chapter 3) Strether calls on Sarah the following morning, but both Waymarsh and Madame de Vionnet are there before him. Madame de Vionnet offers to show Sarah around the city, but Sarah asserts that she already knows Paris. Strether is a little embarrassed that Madame de Vionnet makes him look like an intimate friend of hers. He is even more embarrassed at her repeated references to his friendship with Maria Gostrey. But having pledged to back Madame de Vionnet, he decides that he may as well make things look worse than they really are. So he escorts her down to her carriage.

Book Ninth

(Chapter 1) Strether visits Madame de Vionnet in her old house, and they discuss whether the Pococks are likely to notice the transformation in Chad or not. Strether is on the point of leaving when Madame de Vionnet informs him that she and Chad have arranged a marriage for Jeanne to a Monsieur de Montbron. Strether is troubled by this news, which strikes him as the outcome of "something ancient and cold" (364). However, he also sees that Madame de Vionnet tells him this to demonstrate her faith in Chad.

(Chapter 2) Strether calls on Maria Gostrey to let her know how the Pococks are getting on. He reports that Sarah is quite smitten with Waymarsh, Chad is escorting Mamie around the city, and Jim is getting the good time he desired. Maria tells Strether about Jeanne's engagement and

is surprised to find that he already knows. The two friends explore Chad's motives in arranging it, and they conclude that he has done this to assure Madame de Vionnet that he cares for her more than her daughter. Strether also reports that the Pococks are having a mixed effect on Chad, reminding him of both the wholesome and tasteless elements of Woollett. Jim, in particular, is awful, but Strether is amused that Mamie is aware of just how awful he is.

(Chapter 3) Strether calls at Sarah's hotel and finds her out for the day. However, as Strether enters the empty salon, he realizes that Mamie is out on the balcony, watching the street below. Strether has been aware for several days of a growing affinity with Mamie, so he goes out to speak to her. He discovers that she is expecting Mr. Bilham. Strether stays to talk and hears about Mamie and Sarah's visit to Madame de Vionnet's house, where they meet both Jeanne and Monsieur de Montbron. Mamie appears to have grasped many of the subtleties of the situation, and Strether feels that he can now count on her to help him.

Book Tenth

(Chapter 1) Chad throws a lavish party to introduce his sister to his Paris circle of friends. In a side room, Strether chats with Bilham, to whom he has something particular to say. He suggests that Bilham should marry Mamie. Strether also tells Bilham that he intends to leave him his inheritance to provide him with the funds to marry. Bilham is touched but noncommittal in his response and leaves Strether to return to the crowd. As he goes, Miss Barrace comes to speak to Strether. She reports that Sarah is almost suffocated by the party but is nevertheless still breathing. Meanwhile, Madame de Vionnet is busy being charming to Jim Pocock, which they both find funny. Both Miss Barrace and Strether recognize that some kind of climax is approaching and that all of Chad's friends and acquaintances are watching to see what will happen.

(Chapter 2) Waymarsh, who has been on an early morning trip to the flower market with Sarah, delivers a message from her to Strether. She wishes to visit Strether at the hotel to inform him that the

Pococks along with Waymarsh intend to leave for SWITZERLAND at once. Strether asks if this has been commanded by one of Mrs. Newsome's cables. Waymarsh replies that he knows "nothing about Mrs. Newsome's cables," which Strether suspects to be far from true (411). He reflects on the irony that Waymarsh is now having the time of his life in Europe, but that this is eroding the "sacred rage," the gruff, direct element of his personality, which is what Strether likes best in his friend.

(Chapter 3) Sarah visits Strether as arranged to announce her departure from Paris. She also challenges him to take Chad home immediately. When Strether stalls for more time to discuss the matter with Chad, she berates him for his failure to follow Mrs. Newsome's instructions and for his collusion with Madame de Vionnet, which Sarah sees as a direct insult to her mother. When Strether asks if Sarah is not impressed by the "fortunate transformation" that Madame de Vionnet has caused in Chad, Sarah responds that the change in her brother is "hideous" (421). She marches out of the hotel, leaving Strether feeling that everything is at an end.

Book Eleventh
(Chapter 1) Strether goes to visit Chad on the evening of the day of Sarah's visit. Finding that he is not at home, Strether waits in the empty apartment, watching over the balcony and sitting in the dark until Chad returns. The two men discuss Sarah's ultimatum and agree that she, to all intents and purposes, has become Mrs. Newsome in Paris. Strether explains that he defers to Chad's decision about returning home. Chad admits that the previous day he had deferred to Strether's final decision. It is clear neither wishes to force the other to return to Woollett. Chad admits that he wants to break with Madame de Vionnet and Parisian life, but he commits no further. He feels that as his family hates his "good friend" Madame de Vionnet, they must really dislike him too (436). Chad cannot see what Strether has to gain by defying Mrs. Newsome and staying in Paris. Strether replies that this merely shows that Chad lacks imagination.

(Chapter 2) This is the chapter James misplaced in the Harper's edition of the novel when restoring sections that had been omitted from the abridged serialization in the *North American Review*. The mistake was repeated in the New York Edition. In both of these editions, this chapter was placed before the preceding chapter. However, it is clear from the content of the chapter that it belongs in this position. Strether calls on Maria Gostrey the day after his late-night visit to Chad. He reports that the Pococks have left town, taking Waymarsh for Sarah, and Bilham for Mamie. Chad and Madame de Vionnet remain in Paris. Maria tells Strether that she, too, has been invited out of town but will stay if he wants her. He tells her that he does. He also reports that the Pococks will sail home from Liverpool in five or six weeks, and it is still open to Chad and himself to join them there. Maria and Strether discuss whether Chad is likely to go, and they openly discuss Strether's changed relationship with Mrs. Newsome. He admits that while she is doubtless disappointed in him, he is also disappointed in her failure, and that of Sarah, to understand the beauty of what has happened to Chad in Paris. Mrs. Newsome, he reflects, has no ability for feeling or change. She is "all fine cold thought" (447).

(Chapter 3) A few days later, Strether takes a train out from Paris into the countryside for a day trip. The landscape strikes him as very like that of a painting by E. C. Lambinet, which he had once seen in an exhibition in Boston but was unable to afford to buy. All day Strether feels himself to be walking about within the frame of the picture. As he explores the countryside and villages, he muses on two recent visits to Madame de Vionnet in which they have not discussed Chad but have spoken of other matters and have formed a friendship based on her adaptability and the many things they have in common. Strether is aware of the "danger of one's liking such a woman too much" (455). Toward the end of the afternoon, Strether finds a country inn by the river where he orders some dinner.

(Chapter 4) As Strether waits for his meal, he sees a boat containing a couple come round the bend in the river. The man is rowing, and the lady, sitting with a parasol. They look young, happy, and familiar. They appear to have been through this routine before. As they draw closer, Strether realizes that it is Chad and Madame de Vionnet. After their own momentary shock in recognizing Strether, the couple realize they have been seen and wave and greet him enthusiastically. The three friends dine together and then take the train home to Paris. But Strether is aware throughout the meal of tension and evasion in their conversation, and as the evening wears on he notices that Madame de Vionnet and Chad are not dressed for travel. Eventually, he understands that they have been staying together at a country hotel rather than day-tripping from Paris as they claim. He realizes also the implication of this fact: that the couple's relationship is more physically intimate than he wanted to imagine. Strether is distressed that his friends have lied to him. However, the change in his own set of values has been so complete that he can accept the SEXUALITY in their intimacy. It fires his imagination, and he finds himself "supposing innumerable and wonderful things" (468).

Book Twelfth

(Chapter 1) The next morning, Strether receives a telegram from Madame de Vionnet asking him to visit her that evening. Strether accepts, aware that he is now mixed up in "the typical tale of Paris" (472). However, he finds that he is rather enjoying it and spends the day lounging in the city streets. When the evening comes and he presents himself at Madame de Vionnet's beautiful old house, he finds her simple and natural, but the scene also reminds him of the nobility and the tragedy of revolutionary France. Strether is not sure how she will handle the matter of the previous day's encounter, but he trusts her to "make deception right" and to take the ugliness out of the situation (477).

(Chapter 2) Still at Madame de Vionnet's house, Strether realizes that she wished to see for herself how he has taken the knowledge about the actual nature of her attachment to Chad. Strether also realizes that she has come to rely on him and that she is terrified with the prospect of losing Chad. Strether is astonished to discover how much Chad has been "transcendently prized." Improved he may be, but Strether knows that at root he is "none the less only Chad" (482). To Madame de Vionnet,

however, Chad represents something more, and she weeps as she confesses her fear of losing him. As Strether leaves, she admits that she has wanted him too. "Ah, but you've *had* me" (485), he ambiguously replies as he exits, suggesting both that she has deceived him and that he has loved her.

(Chapter 3) Chad disappears from Paris for a few days, and Strether fills his time escorting Maria to lunches and outings around the city. One evening he visits her at home to find that Madame de Vionnet has just left the apartment. She has told Maria about the encounter with Strether in the country. She is also looking for Chad, who has not communicated with her for days. Maria admits that she knew all along about Chad and Madame de Vionnet's affair, but that she left Paris (as narrated in Book Sixth) so as not to have to lie about it. Maria is also impressed to see that this new knowledge has not catapulted Strether back into the values of Woollett. However, she herself does not expect to gain anything from the situation, especially as she begins to grasp the depth of Strether's attraction to Madame de Vionnet.

(Chapter 4) Strether is aware that it is time to go home in order to avoid being drawn into a relationship with Madame de Vionnet. He also wishes to do what he can to ensure that Chad stays behind with her. Passing Chad's apartment late one night, he realizes someone is watching from the balcony. It is Chad, newly returned from England. Strether goes up to talk and tells him that if he leaves Madame de Vionnet he would be a brute. Chad declares that he is not tired of her and that he will stay. However, as he walks Strether back to his hotel, Chad admits that he has been finding out about advertising and the money it brings into a business. He claims to want only to know the size of the bribe he is giving up, but Strether understands that Chad is now "restless" in Paris (506).

(Chapter 5) Strether goes to say good-bye to Maria Gostrey. Both agree that it is likely Chad will give up Madame de Vionnet and go home in the end. Maria asks if this will help repair Strether's relationship with Mrs. Newsome, but he rejects this possibility. He has changed too much for her, and although she has not changed, he now

"The Luxembourg Gardens," by A. L. Coburn, frontispiece to the second volume of *The Ambassadors,* Volume 22, the New York Edition

sees her more clearly than before. Maria makes it apparent that she will do anything in the world for Strether, but he refuses her offer. To come out of the whole affair with Maria as a prize would, he argues, make him wrong, and she prefers him when he is right.

CRITICAL ANALYSIS

The Ambassadors was Henry James's favorite among his own novels. In the preface for the New York Edition he boasted that on rereading the work for revision it struck him as "quite the best 'all round', of all my productions" (35). It is not hard to see why. *The Ambassadors* is a novelist's novel. It is carefully designed and confidently executed. The narrative structure of the text is closely connected to its thematic content. Also, this thematic content is concerned with the things that novelists in general, and Henry James in particular, like best: language, perception, social systems, and personal relationships. James develops this material into a complex exploration of the nature of human experience and consciousness, and of the ability of art to represent and shape them.

The Ambassadors is one of the great novels of the English language. However, it is not to everyone's taste. F. R. Leavis disqualifies it from his "great tradition" of literature on the grounds that the novel's values are not substantial enough to support the "subtleties and elaborations" that James builds upon them (161). E. M. Forster admires the beauty of the plot's symmetry but finds the characters childish and unreal, formed only for show, like costume dolls. He complains that "their clothes will not take off" and that they have no personalities (162). These judgments tell us as much about Leavis and Forster as they do about James. Nevertheless, the observations are in many ways valid. *The Ambassadors* is constructed around a remarkably simple scenario, and most of the action is social or emotional. Also, James does limit what the reader can see of the characters, and he works hard to conceal their passions and motives—but whether these are flaws or strengths of the novel is a matter of perspective. Indeed, most aspects of *The Ambassadors* are matters of perspective. The profound possibilities for observation in mundane, even in sordid situations, and the hidden depths of personality and desperation beneath the presentable exterior of the individual in society lie at the heart of the novel. *The Ambassadors* is all about the process of learning to see from a new point of view, but this process is rarely straightforward. Nor does it always reveal what one most wants to see, which is perhaps why Leavis and Forster find the novel so disappointing. However, for Strether, the process of seeing becomes inseparable from the business of living itself.

James highlights the importance of vision in *The Ambassadors* in his preface. Here he recounts "the story of one's story" (38), the chain of events that set the novel in motion within his own imagination. As with many of James's novels, the idea for *The Ambassadors* was sparked by an anecdote told to him by a friend. James gives the outline of the incident in the preface without the names of those involved, but these are clearly recorded in James's notebooks (140–142). Jonathan Sturges, a young American living in Europe, recounted his meeting with James's old friend and editor, WILLIAM DEAN HOWELLS, in the garden of Whistler's house in Paris. Howells gave Sturges the advice that is repeated as Strether's speech to Bilham in chapter 2 of Book Fifth: "Live all you can; it's a mistake not to. It doesn't so much matter what you do in particular, so long as you have your life. If you haven't had that what *have* you had?" (215). In both the preface and the novel, this speech develops into a consideration of vision and illusion. In Book Fifth, Strether explains to Bilham that the illusion of life is better than nothing at all, and later Bilham paraphrases Strether's advice as a call "to see, while I've a chance, everything I can" (262). Similarly, in the preface, James connects the desire to "live" with the newfound ability of the older man to observe: "He now at all events *sees*; so that the business of the tale and the march of my action, not to say the precious moral of everything, is just my demonstration of this *process* of vision" (34).

The idea of vision is also closely tied to James's narrative method. Much of the preface to *The Ambassadors* explores the relationship between fiction and visual images, either painted on canvas or projected onto "the white sheet suspended for the figures of a child's magic-lantern" (37). James also explains that the construction of the novel demonstrates this link. He aims to show the reader what Strether sees, while avoiding the "terrible *fluidity* of self-revelation" that comes with first-person narrative (46). James therefore presents the novel in third-person narrative but focalized through Strether's point of view. *The Ambassadors* was not the first novel in English to attempt this technique. James himself had done something similar in WHAT MAISIE KNEW (1897), and other writers on both sides of the Atlantic had started to experiment with the use of a detached narrative voice that nevertheless gave privileged access to the thoughts and feelings of central characters. For example, OSCAR WILDE's *The Picture of Dorian Gray* (1891) and Theodore Dreiser's *Sister Carrie* (1900) employ similar narrative strategies with dramatically different results. However, *The Ambassadors* is often seen as the first narrative in English to present a consistently limited point of view through the eyes of one character. James's choice of narrative standpoint allows him to probe deeply into Strether's psychological experience while retaining an element of authorial judgment and control. In truth, it is hard to see how the novel could have worked with any other narrative structure. The whole focus of the plot is on the evolving realization within Strether's consciousness of the variety and intensity of life. If the reader were to see more or less than Strether at any point in the novel, the balance of the story would collapse, and the sense of epiphany that surrounds the final chapters would vanish into banality. *The Ambassadors* is a pioneering work of literary technique. It is the finest early example of a novel in which the controlled use of this limited perspective is integral to the plot and to the overall reading effect of the text. The "process of vision" unfolds for the reader at exactly the same pace as it does for Strether himself, demonstrating James's control of both content and form.

James appears to feel that naming the theme of vision amply explains the novel. "Nothing," he writes at the opening of the preface, "is more easy to state than the subject of *The Ambassadors*" (33). However, the idea of "the process of vision" does not help the reader unravel the plot as much as one might hope. On reading the novel itself, the clarity that James offers is quickly obscured by contingent questions and problems, the most obvious being: What is it exactly that Strether sees? In the first instance, Strether sees Europe, particularly Paris—and on one level this vision is remarkably superficial. Of all James's novels, *The Ambassadors* contains the strongest sense of everyday objects and the most passionate curiosity about their appearance. Books, paintings, clothes, accessories, houses, galleries, churches, shops, carriages, food, and furniture all crowd into Strether's conscious perception with an intensity that appears

not to have troubled him in Woollett. The other characters, too, devote much of their time and conversation to the process of vision—sightseeing, shopping, hanging over balconies, watching the passersby, or closely observing friends and relations. As Miss Barrace says, "I dare say . . . that I do, that we all do here, run too much to mere eye. But how can it be helped? We're all looking at each other—and in the light of Paris one sees what things resemble" (207).

Miss Barrace with her long-handled, tortoiseshell lorgnette is one of several characters in *The Ambassadors* who make use of spectacles of some sort. Maria Gostrey, Gloriani, and Strether also wear "aids to vision" as James often calls them. James himself started wearing glasses for reading in the late 1890s, and his own deteriorating eyesight is probably one of the causes of his growing fascination with vision in his later novels. In *The Ambassadors*, however, these apparently trivial accessories appear to be carefully coded; Miss Barrace and Gloriani wear convex lenses for long-sightedness, as did James himself, while the Americans, Strether and Maria Gostrey, wear concave lenses for the shortsighted (Hutchison 87). These spectacles alert the reader to the fact that these characters are seeing the world quite differently from one another. Strether's shortsightedness also leads to several key moments of delayed recognition in the novel. Every time he encounters Chad or Madame de Vionnet unexpectedly, he does not immediately realize who they are. It takes a few moments for them to swim into focus. These small delays mirror Strether's suspended recognition of the nature of Chad and Madame de Vionnet's affair, which in turn provides a metaphor for the late flowering of perception and experience in Strether's own life.

James's use of spectacles to underscore the theme of visual distortion is only part of his more general method of employing material objects to widen a text's frame of reference and to map its underlying agenda. In *The Ambassadors*, the items most useful to James all appear to be connected to vision in some way: windows, balconies, lights, lenses, and, especially, pictures. Charles Anderson points out that through this experience of the material culture of Paris, Strether grows emotionally until he can recognize the operation of different moral and aesthetic systems of value from those that have governed his experience in Woollett (223). Therefore, Strether's new vision is social as well as material.

Critical readings of *The Ambassadors* often map the novel on a grid of binary opposites based on such social systems: American innovation versus European tradition, innocence versus experience, morality versus style, New England Puritanism versus 1890s aestheticism (see the AESTHETIC MOVEMENT), idealism versus realism (see also ROMANCE/REALISM/NATURALISM). These studies are fascinating and illuminating, highlighting important aspects of James's work and the contemporary surrounding culture. It is proof, if proof were needed, of the richness of the text that it can support so many crisscrossing patterns of reading. The difficulty for the reader is in choosing which of these lines to follow and in which direction. That this is no easy business is demonstrated by the conflicting conclusions that many readers draw about Strether's adventures in Paris, particularly at its close. For example, John Carlos Rowe and Merle Williams both read the novel as an exploration of the relation between art and reality. However, Rowe concludes that the use of paintings as referents and narrative devices within the novel obscures Strether's view of reality and creates in him "a certain blindness, an inability to see beneath the surface of events" (194). In contrast, Williams argues that the novel's paintings are the means through which Strether's vision is heightened; the Lambinet scenes effect a moment of phenomenological insight that allows him to reestablish his relationship with reality. Similarly, William Righter and Tessa Hadley both offer readings of the novel along the lines of social and sexual codes. On the one hand, Righter concludes that Strether is unable to stomach the sexual freedoms of Paris, and that in the end he must return home because he remains "the mental prisoner of a law of Woollett that is not his law" (87). On the other hand, Hadley argues that *The Ambassadors* reveals to the reader a Henry James at last comfortable with writing about sexuality, and a Strether developing toward the acceptance of physical as well as emotional intimacy. Both Alan W. Bellringer and Rich-

ard A. Hocks read the novel as a development and demonstration of the cultural ideology of its period. However, Bellringer identifies Matthew Arnold's high culture and Walter Pater's aestheticism as the governing ideas in the novel, while Hocks reads it as an early experiment in PRAGMATISM. For every critic propelling Strether toward a particular set of values, there is another waiting in the wings to escort him back in the opposite direction.

The difficulty of providing a single reading of the novel clearly reflects some plurality within the text itself. The conflict of critical viewpoints is obviously symptomatic of Strether's own hesitation about the course of his own life and his uncertainty about the shape of reality. It also reflects James's unwillingness to offer simple solutions in his later fiction. Right from the start of the novel, James is careful to establish complex and contradictory elements that resist classification and which make it impossible to read the plot neatly. Take the places, for example. Strether's hometown of Woollett, which can be read as a locus for respectability and moral probity, is also quickly shown to have made its money through the swindling of Chad's grandfather and through the manufacture of a material object so vulgar that Strether refuses ever to say what it is. The reader is presented with the plotting and maneuvering of Mrs. Newsome and Sarah, and the awfulness of Jim Pocock, as part of the character of the town. However, Woollett is also shown to be capable of style, perception, and taste in the representative figure of Mamie—and for that matter in Chad and Strether. Conversely, Paris, originally seen as a "vast bright Babylon" (118) of decadence, reveals virtues and politenesses that come as a surprise to Strether, who had obviously braced himself for something more lurid. In the end, ironically, it is the adulterous Parisian *femme du monde*, Madame de Vionnet, who voices the principle of self-sacrifice as a governing rule. "What it comes to is that it's not, that it's never, a happiness, any happiness at all, to *take*. The only safe thing is to give. It's what plays you least false" (482). For Strether, who is attempting to navigate his way between these multifaceted people and places, there is little chance of charting a clear course to a single thematic destination. The answer to the question about what Strether sees is both simpler and more complex than any one option. Strether sees life in Paris. However, life is presented in *The Ambassadors* as pluralistic, changeable, and subjective, a splendid and terrible mystery not to be solved by neat choices between binary opposites.

Strether's observations are further complicated through his encounters with art. Almost as soon as he arrives in Paris, he finds himself surrounded by paintings and art objects both in public galleries and private homes. As Anderson and Adeline Tintner point out, even the street scenes in *The Ambassadors* are designed to look like impressionist paintings. However, it is Strether's encounter with the real-life Lambinet scene in chapters 3 and 4 of Book Eleventh that fuses art and reality and gives Strether a fuller understanding of his situation. Riding out on a train from Paris into the countryside, Strether recalls a painting by Lambinet, which he once saw at an art exhibition in Tremont Street, Boston, but could not afford to buy. He feels that he is now walking around inside the picture with "the poplars, the willows, the rushes, the river, the sunny silvery sky, the shady woody horizon" (453). However, the arrival of Chad and Madame de Vionnet in a rowing boat and Strether's subsequent realization that the couple's relationship is not what he has been led to believe crystallizes his perception. This moment of lucidity draws together many of the novel's opposed elements: New England and France, art and reality, imagination and action, past and present. But Strether's sense of cohesion and control is short-lived. No sooner has he understood the physical nature of Chad's relationship with Madame de Vionnet than he finds himself troubled by new questions and problems of perception. As the three friends dine together by the riverbank, Strether is bewildered by Madame de Vionnet's fluent and evasive French. Later in the railway carriage as they travel back to Paris, communication breaks down entirely and they sit in silence while Strether takes note of all the little details that confirm that the couple were not day-tripping as they claim but staying together at a country inn. Finally, in Strether's hotel room, during the night he abandons the attempt to make sense of the situation and escapes

into his imagination. His new knowledge strikes him not as a triumph but as a failure: "He recognised at last that he had really been trying all along to suppose nothing. Verily, verily, his labour had been lost. He found himself supposing innumerable and wonderful things" (468). This is, as Julie Rivkin notes, in line with the logic of delegation at work throughout the novel, in which everything and everybody are represented by something or somebody else in an endless chain of referrals of meaning and responsibility. Thus the climax of the novel does not deliver a moment of completeness or possession, but a series of absences, suggestions, and contingencies.

Strether's journey toward knowledge breaks down at the very point of success. The truth he sets out to uncover unravels into a series of questions, evasions, and suppositions—as the concluding chapters of the novel demonstrate. As Nicola Bradbury argues, *The Ambassadors* is not structured as a linear plot but as a picture composed around a "vanishing point" of perspective that eludes and transcends a "rigid two-dimensional structure of meaning" (Bradbury 38). The novel therefore resists any system of values but shows the difficulty of attempting to catalog or explain the fluidity of reality. This places the novel at an interesting pivot point between Victorian realism and modernist fiction (see MODERNISM AND MODERNITY). Elements of both traditions are at work in the novel, which can be seen as testing the conventions of one while providing a route-map for the other. Although *The Ambassadors* explores familiar realist territory in terms of its subject matter—the relationship of the individual to the community and the operation of sexual and social constraints—James's decision to present this material through the lens of Strether's evolving consciousness produces a narrative that contributes to the growing trend in fiction in the early 1900s toward internalizing and problematizing reality. *The Ambassadors* is not a "stream of consciousness" novel, in the sense that this term is often applied to the work of James Joyce or Virginia Woolf. However, it is worth noting that this term, which would become the distinctive hallmark of modernist fiction, was coined by James's brother, psychologist and philosopher WILLIAM JAMES, to describe the constant yet constantly changing nature of experience. Henry James, too, was fascinated by the problem of expressing the internal and ever-shifting workings of the mind and the means by which the mind makes sense of the world around through language. *The Ambassadors* demonstrates the inadequacy of language to mediate truth completely by showing the misunderstandings and half-truths communicated between characters and by testing the ability of the narrative to represent fully Strether's experience.

James's abstract language and complex sentence structure can cause readers of his late fiction to complain that it is difficult to work out what is really happening. It *is* difficult, but this difficulty is deliberate and reflects James's sense of the difficulty of perceiving reality itself. In his late novels, James attempts to recreate the process of experience, with all its halts, hitches, and contradictions, through the very language that he uses. Many studies of *The Ambassadors,* both old and new, point out that the language of the novel is intrinsically bound to its theme of perception. For example, Ian Watt's classic analysis of the opening paragraph of the novel explores how both the desire to correlate reality to abstract ideas and the contradictory, roundabout process of acquiring knowledge are dramatized through the reading experience of the first few sentences of the book. Also, Collin Meissner's work *Henry James and the Language of Experience* (1999) demonstrates how James's linguistic structures reflect his underlying ideas about the politics of perception and experience. Clearly this is a novel concerned as much with sensation and expression as with cultural and social mores. Indeed, the exploration of the means of perception is probably what James has in mind when he draws the reader's attention to the *process* of vision. The reader of *The Ambassadors* should not merely ask *what* Strether sees—a question that treats the text as a realist depiction of culture and society presented through the transparent medium of language. The reader also needs to ask *how* Strether sees—a question that reveals the novel's modernist agenda as a text that asks questions about the nature of language and reality.

The dual realist-modernist personality of *The Ambassadors* is also demonstrated by the ending of the text, which resists the traditional patterns of closure for the novel: marriage or death. This is in many ways dissatisfying, because the original impetus of the plot has been Mrs. Newsome's desire to persuade Chad to come home and get married, and initially Strether's involvement is due to his wish to please Mrs. Newsome in order to be able to get married himself. The many liaisons and flirtations among the characters in Paris, as well as the novel's exploration of the admissible boundaries of behavior within marriage, all point toward a conclusion in which marriage will figure largely. However, no one actually gets married at the end of *The Ambassadors*—although Mamie and Bilham appear to be thinking about it. Strether simply decides to return home to satisfy his curiosity about what Mrs. Newsome will have to say about the whole incident. Indeed, the ending of the novel is left fairly open. The reader is never quite certain whether Strether or Chad really do make it back to Woollett, as there is the suggestion at the end of the novel of Chad taking up with another woman in London and the possibility of the whole tale repeating itself endlessly. What is apparent is that Strether's ambassadorial mission has not been a success on its original terms. Strether abandons the Woollett principles of business and respectability, but he does not convert to Parisian values of passion and style either. He takes home his "wonderful impressions" and leaves with the sense of having seen and understood. He has mastered the process of vision, and he values this new perception beyond other possible prizes.

CHARACTERS

Barrace, Miss A member of Chad and Bilham's social set, Miss Barrace grew up in the diplomatic quarter of Paris, and her name and manners imply that she had American parents. However, she is completely naturalized as a Parisian and understands all the French social customs. She dresses brilliantly, smokes cigarettes, and talks without restraint or embarrassment. She is amused by Waymarsh as an American "type" and likes to drive him around the city in her carriage. Miss Barrace was probably based on the figure of the elegant American expatriate Henrietta Reubell, whom James first met in Paris in 1876 (James, *Notebooks* 70).

Bilham, John Little A young American living in Paris, Bilham is one of Chad's closest friends. He originally came to Paris to learn to paint but quickly realized that he lacked the talent. Although he has little money, he stays on in Paris, living in a sparse apartment in a backstreet, while appreciating the cultural and social life of the city. Strether quickly grows fond of Bilham and offers to leave him his inheritance so that he can afford to marry.

Gloriani The great sculptor Gloriani also appears in James's early novel *RODERICK HUDSON* (1875). In *The Ambassadors,* his main role is to host the garden party at which Strether meets Madame de Vionnet and advises Bilham to "live all you can." Gloriani lives in a house in the Faubourg Saint-Germain, which was inspired by the home of the painter James McNeill Whistler.

Gostrey, Maria Maria Gostrey is an expatriate American who has lived most of her life in Europe. She has an apartment in Paris, where she displays her collection of interesting objects and ornaments. She is in her mid-thirties, but strikes Strether as young, despite her spectacles and a few gray hairs. She is well connected in Paris and knows most of the other characters, including Madame de Vionnet, with whom she attended school many years ago in Geneva. She is a shrewd observer and becomes Strether's closest friend and confidante during his time in Paris.

Newsome, Chad Mrs. Newsome's son, Chad, is the reason for Strether's visit to Paris. For three years he has lived in Paris on his family's wealth, but now the Newsomes want him to return home to Woollett to run the advertising side of the family business. Strether's task is to persuade him to leave his glamorous social circle and head home. However, Chad has been dramatically altered by his time in Paris. Although only 28, he now looks older and more sophisticated, which is the result of his relationship with Madame de Vionnet.

Newsome, Mrs. Although she never appears "on stage" in the novel, Mrs. Newsome is a large presence in *The Ambassadors*. She is the widow of a Woollett industrialist, and she plans to marry Strether if he succeeds in bringing her son, Chad, home from Paris to help run the family business. The reader gains a vivid picture of Mrs. Newsome through Strether's mental images of her and through the letters and telegrams by which she sends her instructions to her "ambassadors"—initially Strether and later her daughter, Sarah Pocock. Mrs. Newsome is proud, respectable, manipulative, and used to having her own way.

Pocock, Jim Sarah's husband, Jim, is a manager within the Newsome's family business. He is a tasteless man of business who has come out to Paris for a "good time." He largely leaves his wife and sister to entertain themselves, while he socializes with Strether or Chad.

Pocock, Mamie Jim's sister, Mamie, is the girl the Newsomes hope Chad will marry when he comes home to Woollett. She is beautiful, sociable, and intelligent. She also proves to be perceptive enough to realize that Chad has been changed by his time in Paris and that she no longer wants to marry a man who has been so profoundly changed by another woman.

Pocock, Sarah Chad's sister and Mrs. Newsome's daughter, Sarah is married to Jim Pocock. She has many of her mother's redoubtable qualities; she is forceful, perceptive, and direct. However, she lacks charm or humor. She dislikes the social scene in Paris and is disappointed in both Strether and Chad for enjoying it so much. However, she sees no discrepancy between her disapproval of Chad's behavior and her own infatuation with Waymarsh.

Strether, Lewis Lambert The central character of *The Ambassadors* is a quiet American gentleman in his fifties. In the opening chapter, the reader learns that he was named after Louis Lambert, a minor novel by Honoré de Balzac about a young intellectual who slides into mysticism and insanity. Strether has previously been married and visited Paris once before with his wife. However, both his wife and young son have died. He has lived mostly in Woollett, where he edits the *Woollett Review*, and he is engaged to be married to the formidable widow Mrs. Newsome. The character of Strether was originally inspired by James's friend and fellow writer William Dean Howells, but Strether also has many characteristics of other Jamesian protagonists. He has a receptive mind and a quick imagination. He also has "the oddity of a double consciousness," which makes for "detachment in his zeal and curiosity in his indifference" (56). The novel is narrated from his perspective throughout, and as the story progresses, Strether's psychological development becomes the main focus of the novel.

Vionnet, Jeanne de Madame de Vionnet's daughter, Jeanne, is just approaching marriageable age. She is pretty, charming, and timid and is secretly in love with Chad.

Vionnet, Madame de Separated from her husband for many years, Madame de Vionnet lives in Paris in a beautiful old house with her daughter, Jeanne. She is in her late thirties and is in love with Chad. She is beautiful, charming, and elegant in an old-fashioned Parisian style, and Strether is strongly attracted to her. However, the Pococks perceive her as a decadent and dangerous *femme du monde*.

Waymarsh Strether has planned to visit Europe with his old friend Waymarsh from the New England town of Milrose. Waymarsh is a rich, patriotic American lawyer, separated from his wife, who regards Europe as an ordeal. Strether labels this dislike of Europe "the sacred rage," but he still finds Waymarsh endearing and appreciates his friendship and good nature until Waymarsh joins forces with the Pococks.

ADAPTATIONS

The Ambassadors was adapted for television in 1977. It was directed for the BBC by James Cellan Jones. It starred Paul Scofield as Strether and Lee Remick as Maria Gostrey.

FURTHER READING

Anderson, Charles. *Person, Place and Thing in Henry James's Novels.* Durham, N.C.: Duke University Press, 1977.

Bellringer, Alan. *The Ambassadors.* London: Allen and Unwin, 1984.

Bradbury, Nicola. *Henry James: The Later Novels.* Oxford, U.K.: Clarendon Press, 1979.

Forster, E. M. *Aspects of the Novel.* 1927. Reprint, Harmondsworth, England: Penguin, 1968.

Hadley, Tessa. *Henry James and the Imagination of Pleasure.* Cambridge: Cambridge University Press, 2002.

Hocks, Richard A. *Henry James and Pragmatist Thought.* Chapel Hill: University of North Carolina Press, 1984.

Hutchison, Hazel. *Seeing and Believing: Henry James and the Spiritual World.* New York: Palgrave, 2006.

James, Henry. *The Ambassadors.* 1903. Reprint, Harmondsworth, England: Penguin, 1986.

———. *The Complete Notebooks.* Edited by Leon Edel and Lyall H. Powers. New York and Oxford: Oxford University Press, 1987.

Leavis, F. R. *The Great Tradition: George Eliot, Henry James, Joseph Conrad.* London: Chatto & Windus, 1948.

McGann, Jerome. "Revision, Rereading; or, 'An Error [Not] in the Ambassadors.'" *American Literature* 64, no. 1 (1992): 95–110.

Meissner, Collin. *Henry James and the Language of Experience.* Cambridge: Cambridge University Press, 1999.

Righter, William. *American Memory in Henry James: Void and Value.* Burlington, Vt.: Ashgate, 2004.

Rivkin, Julie. *False Positions: The Representational Logics of Henry James's Fiction.* Palo Alto, Calif.: Stanford University Press, 1996.

Rowe, John Carlos. *The Theoretical Dimensions of Henry James.* London: Methuen, 1985.

Tintner, Adeline. *Henry James and the Lust of the Eyes.* Baton Rouge: Louisiana State University Press, 1993.

Watt, Ian. "The First Paragraph of *The Ambassadors*: An Explication." 1960. In *Henry James: Modern Judgements,* edited by Tony Tanner. London: Macmillan, 1968.

Williams, Merle. *Henry James and the Philosophical Novel: Being and Seeing.* Cambridge: Cambridge University Press, 1993.

Hazel Hutchison, *University of Aberdeen*

The American (1877)

Henry James started writing his third novel in 1875 at age 33 while living in PARIS. *The American* first appeared in the *Atlantic Monthly* in 12 installments, from June 1876 to May 1877. It was then published as a book by J. R. Osgood in 1877. In 1905, James revised the novel and wrote a new preface. It became Volume 2 of the NEW YORK EDITION (1907), published by Charles Scribner's Sons. (See also PREFACES TO THE NEW YORK EDITION.)

SYNOPSIS

(Chapter 1) The novel is set in Paris, May 1868. Christopher Newman, the very wealthy 36-year-old American protagonist sits on a divan in the Salon Carré of the Louvre Museum. He stares at a painting by Murillo of the Madonna that mystifies him, and he takes interest in an attractive young lady, Mademoiselle Noémie Nioche, who is clumsily copying Murillo's work. He approaches her and abruptly asks *Combien?*—"how much?" Although he is referring to the painting, he could be misinterpreted as making an advance. Noémie quotes him a very high price and promises to send the picture to his address when it is finished. Her meek father arrives to chaperone her home. Newman hires him as a French tutor for a month. For an afternoon at the Louvre, the Nioches have made out well, but Noémie has grander designs.

(Chapter 2) Left to himself, Newman notices an old acquaintance from the United States and reintroduces himself to Tom Tristram. The two retire to a café in the Palais Royal to catch up. Newman explains he has made enough money "to rest awhile . . . to look about me, to see the world, to have a good time, and, if the fancy takes me, to marry a wife" (30). Newman began his fabulously successful business career without a penny but

with an abundance of energy and health. Moving through the West, he ended up in San Francisco, where he made a lot of money. Newman tells Tristram about his recent and sudden renunciation of business. A couple of months before in NEW YORK CITY, he passed up the opportunity to exact revenge on an adversary, sacrificing $60,000 of stock investments. Tristram, who loves to gossip, soaks up Newman's story. He tells Newman of his fabulous life of playing cards with clever expatriates at the Occidental Club and plans to introduce Newman to his wife.

(Chapter 3) Newman visits the Tristrams at their apartment near the Arc de Triomphe. Mrs. Lizzie Tristram is a rather plain-looking American woman with a sharp wit and a "tendency to irony" (36). She takes Newman under her wing and finds out that Newman is shopping for a wife and "want[s] to possess, in a word, the best article in the market" (44). Mrs. Tristram challenges Newman to consider her former school friend Claire de

"The Faubourg Saint-Germain" by A. L. Coburn, frontispiece to *The American,* Volume 2, the New York Edition

Cintré, a widowed French aristocrat with a severe English mother and the esteemed name of de Bellegarde. Tom raises a dissenting alarm, but Mrs. Tristram insists that she is quite beautiful and a perfect woman. Mrs. Tristram introduces Newman to Claire and is impressed that he so quickly wins an invitation to the Bellegarde address. Late in the afternoon, Newman walks the "silent streets of the Faubourg St. Germain" (50), whose blank-faced houses impress upon him the privacy of the French elite. Newman presents his card to two men but is told that Claire is not at home. As he leaves, he learns that the men are her brothers. He had mistaken them for the family butlers.

(Chapter 4) Monsieur Nioche delivers his daughter's outlandish painting to Newman. It has a very thick coat of varnish, a comically broad frame, and now costs even more. Newman is quite pleased with his acquisition. They discuss pretty Noémie. Her father sighs over the world's unscrupulous men, and Newman comes to the rescue by offering a dowry in the form of a commission for six more pictures. Over the next month of French lessons, M. Nioche confides that he fears for Noémie's virtue. Like her dead mother, she is a coquette. M. Nioche implores Newman to respect her innocence. Newman is amused. He meets Noémie at the Louvre to choose the paintings, requesting something "bright and gay" (59) from the solemn gallery. She humors him as they select six masterpieces whose copying would require the work of 10. She admits to being an awful painter, but Newman sticks to their bargain. Noémie does not seem grateful and pouts to gain his attention. Newman leaves.

(Chapter 5) Newman travels around Europe to improve his mind. In Holland, he meets a young American named Benjamin Babcock who is a Unitarian minister and native of Dorchester, Massachusetts. His travels are funded by his congregation. They begin an awkward friendship. Babcock secretly detests Europe, and he resents Newman's seeming lack of a moral standard by which to evaluate art. In VENICE, Newman enjoys himself grandly, strolling aimlessly and buying many bad pictures. Babcock broods and finally takes leave of Newman. In a subsequent letter, he warns Newman to take life more seriously and to consider art from a moral

perspective; Newman replies by sending back "a grotesque little statuette" of an "ascetic-looking monk" in tattered clothing (73). Newman writes to Mrs. Tristram, announcing his return and his determination to learn more about Claire.

(Chapter 6) In Paris, Newman establishes himself on the Boulevard Haussmann in an expensive apartment that, according to Tom Tristram, matches his social position. Mrs. Tristram relates Claire de Cintré's predicament. Her father is dead. Her older brother and mother are pushing her to marry (see MARRIAGE) a rich aristocrat to support their flagging capital. Having weathered one unhappy marriage, Claire is distraught. Mrs. Tristram urges Newman to swoop in like an eagle to rescue Claire. One dusky afternoon, he finds her at home on the rue de l'Université. He meets her younger brother, the playful, charming, and slightly impudent Count Valentin. Newman also meets the older brother's wife, the chatty and bored young Marquise, who questions Newman about his life in America. Newman wins an invitation to visit again, if he is brave.

(Chapter 7) At his sister's request, Valentin visits Newman, and the two fast become friends. Valentin admires Newman's sense of self-possession and confidence, complaining that he has grown up as a Bellegarde and under the scrutiny of his demanding mother. Newman does not understand Valentin's resentment but is flattered by his attention. They spend hours talking. Newman is a bit shocked by Valentin's perverse curiosity in the demise of Madame Dandelard, a divorced Italian émigré. Newman visits Claire twice more. Surrounded by visitors, she throws him vague smiles, which seem enough to stoke the burning fire of his affection.

(Chapter 8) Newman questions Valentin about Claire as they spend the evening at Newman's fireside. When Claire's disreputable husband died, she angered her mother and older brother by renouncing claims to his much diminished property. To appease them, she vowed to do anything they requested for 10 years—anything except marry again. Newman optimistically announces his intention of marrying Claire and asks Valentin to speak highly of him. Valentin is taken utterly aback. Not knowing whether to laugh or take offense, he embraces the opportunity to be amused. He reassures Newman that he thinks him a fine man but warns him that the Bellegardes are one of the "old races" with "strange secrets" (109).

(Chapter 9) Newman visits Claire and finds her alone. He tells her of his intention to marry her. Claire declares that it is impossible for her to marry. Newman convinces her to reconsider, under the condition that he refrains from mentioning the proposal for a period of six months. That night he discloses the agreement to Valentin, who declares that he will now present Newman to his older brother.

(Chapter 10) The Tristrams playfully reproach Newman for neglecting them as he wins Claire. But when Newman meets the Bellegarde family, things do not go very well. Valentin presents him to his mother, the Bellegarde matriarch, who seems guarded and inscrutable. The Marquis Urbain de Bellegarde, Valentin's older brother, icily takes measure of Newman, who tries to hold his own in a conversation that is full of awkward moments and double entendres. Newman tells of his rise from poverty to wealth and outlines his project of finding a wife. Valentin interrupts to announce that Claire has unexpectedly decided to accompany her brothers to the evening's ball. Without her mourning attire, she raises the brows of her mother and the Marquis. Before leaving, Newman tells Claire's mother of his intention to propose. The Marquise bluntly asks how much he is worth. Impressed with Newman's answer, she nevertheless seems offended by his presumptuous design.

(Chapter 11) M. Nioche manages to track Newman down at his new apartment and expresses concern over his daughter's behavior and progress on the paintings. Newman goes to the Louvre to check up on her and coincidentally encounters Valentin, who is waiting for a British cousin whom he will dutifully escort through the museum. The two men find Noémie halfheartedly making Newman's copies. Valentin confirms that she is a bad painter. She responds by marking her picture with a large red cross. Newman is horrified, but Valentin claims that the work is much improved for the story it now tells. Noémie mentions that it, and everything else she has, is for sale. Valentin's fas-

cination with her mystifies Newman. Valentin suggests that M. Nioche is not the concerned father he seems. Newman marvels at Valentin's cynicism. With a poke of an umbrella, the British cousin appears.

(Chapter 12) Three days after the formal introduction, the Bellegardes accept Newman's plan to woo Claire. However, throughout the evening's dinner, Urbain and Valentin both seem agitated and the conversation is awkward. Newman is surprised when Urbain informs him of his mother's positive decision. On the way to speak with her, Newman encounters the elderly Count Rochefidèle and his wife, who appraises him as an American and recalls having met Benjamin Franklin. Madame Bellegarde then informs Newman that she will not interfere with Claire's consideration. Newman does not register any offense as the Marquise and Marquis emphasize the favor they are bestowing. He is happy to establish a verbal "contract" that gives him range on the "open field" of his marriage prospects. As Newman leaves, Valentin reports with a laugh that Noémie has left her father's home. Newman is disgusted, but Valentin savors the opportunity to visit her.

(Chapter 13) Newman's frequent visits to rue de l'Université make him very happy with Madame de Cintré. He does complain to Mrs. Tristram of the Marquis and Marquise's chilly disposition. In all events, Newman maintains his "friendly style of communication" (152) as the Marquis holds "his breath as not to inhale the odour of democracy" (153). Newman suspects that the family's secrets are quite dreadful. He meets Mrs. Catherine Bread, an English servant who has been with the family for many years and encourages Newman never to give up his plans of marrying Claire. Newman also learns of Claire's deep affection and concern for her younger brother, Valentin. When Newman admits to not liking all of her family, Claire is troubled. In the middle of their conversation, Urbain interrupts to introduce the wealthy Lord Deepmere, who is rather unattractive but holds an English title and land. As Newman leaves, he cannot resist thanking Urbain for not only living up to his side of the bargain but for helping Newman win Claire's heart. Urbain stares blankly after him.

(Chapter 14) As agreed, Newman does not mention marriage to Claire for six months. On this visit, he revives his proposal. He reassures Claire that she would be safe as his wife, "as safe . . . as in your father's arms" (163). Claire breaks into tears. A befuddled Newman asserts that she loves him. He returns the next day and encounters Mrs. Bread, who urges him to marry Claire without delay. Newman and Claire announce their engagement. Urbain and his mother receive the news coldly. Newman continues to offend the Bellegardes by revealing he has already telegraphed America with the news. Valentin extends his blessing but seems troubled by the affairs of his own heart. Relishing his success, Newman announces a grand celebration in Paris. Madame de Bellegarde counters by announcing her own.

(Chapter 15) Newman catches up with the Nioches. Noémie has reportedly taken up with an old and wealthy man. Concerned for M. Nioche, Newman seeks him out. He finds him at home with his daughter visiting. She confronts Newman about his strange offer to provide her with a meager dowry and accuses him of not truly caring about her. Newman insists that he had hoped she would marry a respectable young fellow, but Noémie laughs dismissively. After she leaves, Newman faces M. Nioche, who seems resigned to his daughter's plans. Newman is disgusted at his philosophical tone and takes his leave with a handshake. A week later, he learns, much to his chagrin, that Valentin is taken with Noémie. Valentin quizzes Newman about his plans to marry his sister, and he inspects with some amusement his mother's party invitation, which Newman proudly displays.

(Chapter 16) Newman blissfully spends the days with Claire, who even invites the Tristrams to meet her mother. However, Newman's fortune is about to change drastically. When the Bellegardes' grand fête begins, Urbain manages the stage, chaperoning Newman through introductions to a throng of French aristocrats, including a very large countess who reminds Newman of the "Fat Lady at a fair" (189). Suddenly, Newman feels the tone of the event shift as she gently mocks his bizarre career. As the introductions continue, Newman feels more and more insecure as the "object of exhibition"—

as a "bear" being judged "a very fair imitation of humanity" (191); as a "terrier" stepping about "on his hind legs"; and the "strange American" whom Claire de Cintré was to marry. Newman shakes off his embarrassment. He thanks his future mother-in-law for the event and asks that she walk with him through the crowd. She stiffly agrees. Newman then comes upon Claire and Lord Deepmere in hushed conversation. She halfheartedly attests to being happy. Mrs. Bread brings Claire a shawl, and Newman invites her to live with them.

(Chapter 17) Newman attends the opera *Don Giovanni* and notices Urbain and his wife in a separate box. He also spies Noémie with a new man. During intermission, he heads over to greet Urbain and runs into Valentin, who is desperately brooding over Noémie. Newman encourages him to go to America and make some money. When talking with Urbain and his wife, Newman wonders aloud how the opera will end. Urbain's wife pleads with Newman to take her after his marriage to the Bal Bullier, a student party in the Latin Quarter. During the next intermission, Valentin seems to embrace the American adventure. However, Newman later learns of his impending duel with M. Stanislas Kapp, the son of a rich brewer.

(Chapter 18) The next morning, everything falls apart. Newman visits Claire but discovers that she is on the verge of bolting to the family castle in Fleurières near Poitiers. Newman interrupts a meeting between Claire, her mother, and Urbain. Deeply distressed, Claire tells Newman that she cannot marry him. Newman demands an explanation. Urbain softly replies, "It's impossible"; Madame de Bellegarde follows with, "It's improper" (214). A shocked Newman appeals to Claire but to no avail. She leaves, and Newman accuses the Bellegardes of going against their word not to interfere. Madame de Bellegarde responds by insisting that she has held to the bargain; they have not persuaded Claire but ordered her through their *authority* not to marry him. Furthermore, they intervened only *after* she had accepted the proposal. In the end, they simply could not let her marry a dreadful "commercial person" (218). Newman vows to change Claire's mind. He retreats to Mrs. Tristram, who explains the plan of marrying Claire off to Lord Deepmere. Newman suddenly remembers Valentin's duel. At his apartment, there is a telegram urging him to rush to SWITZERLAND, where Valentin is dying. Newman dashes off a note to Claire and catches the night express.

(Chapter 19) Newman arrives outside Geneva after a long train ride. MM. de Grosjoyaux and Ledoux watch over their wounded friend, and the doctor and curé hold no hope for recovery. Newman is disgusted by the whole affair. The next day, he meets with a weak Valentin, who senses something is very wrong. Newman tells him of the ruined engagement. Deeply saddened on Claire's behalf, he urges Newman not to give up, and he reveals that there is a devastating secret that Newman can use: There was foul play in the death of the Bellegarde patriarch. Valentin urges Newman to seek out Mrs. Bread.

(Chapter 20) Valentin dies, and Newman travels to attend his funeral at Fleurières. Claire answers his letter and thanks him for being at Valentin's side. She instructs him to notify her after the funeral and before attempting a rendezvous. After three days, he meets with her in the family castle. She holds firm, trying to dash his hopes by revealing her plan to enter a convent.

(Chapter 21) Confused and angry, Newman takes stock of his situation. The next morning, he demands an interview with Madame de Bellegarde and Urbain. Mrs. Bread intercepts him to say that Claire has left for Paris. Mrs. Bread is anxious to hear about Valentin's final moments, and they set up a rendezvous at dusk. Newman then faces Urbain and Madame de Bellegarde. He tells them of Valentin's apology on their behalf. As Urbain and his mother turn to leave, Newman accuses them of having a terrible secret that Valentin all but revealed. Urbain hangs fire, declaring that his brother was probably delirious. Newman threatens disclosure if he is not allowed to marry Claire. He demands a response by three o'clock at his inn. In a punctual letter, Urbain dismisses Newman's threat. In the secluded ruin of a nearby church, Newman meets Mrs. Bread.

(Chapter 22) After Newman relates Valentin's final moments, Mrs. Bread divulges her long-held grudge against Madame de Bellegarde. Initially reticent, Mrs. Bread recalls how she had scolded her many years before for wearing a red ribbon to attract the wandering eye of the Marquis Henri-Urbain de Bellegarde. On top of this embarrassment, Madame de Bellegarde had once declared that Mrs. Bread was only fit to be a pen-wiper for her children. Newman promises to pension Mrs. Bread for life. She tells him of the patriarch's final days of intense stomach pains and of his unflagging support for Claire in refusing to marry M. de Cintré. One night, Urbain and his mother instructed Mrs. Bread to leave the patriarch's bedside. Suspicious, Mrs. Bread tried to relieve them in the middle of the night. She encountered Urbain pacing the hall as his mother emerged from the sickroom to announce her husband's death. While Urbain went for the doctor, Mrs. Bread stole some moments alone with the old man, whose eyes suddenly opened; he gasped that his wife had murdered him. Mrs. Bread helped him write a deathbed accusation, which she hid in her apron. Newman convinces her to give it to him. From the French, Newman translates Henri-Urbain's accusation.

(Chapter 23) Newman returns to Paris with his instrument of revenge. Mrs. Bread visits with news that Claire is in the convent of the stern Carmelite order and will soon vow no contact with the outside world. When moving to Newman's apartment, Mrs. Bread must insist that the Bellegardes' porter unlock the door. Newman takes this as a sign that Madame de Bellegarde is scared. Worried over Newman's erratic behavior, Mrs. Tristram nevertheless agrees to get him into the Carmelite chapel on the following Sunday.

(Chapter 24) In excruciating frustration, Newman listens to the sisters' hymns. Upon leaving the chapel, he encounters the arriving Madame de Bellegarde and Urbain, who seem surprised and disconcerted. Outside, he meets Urbain's chatty wife, who agrees to help arrange a confrontation in the nearby Parc Monceau. The ensuing conversation is intense, and Newman gives them a copy of Henri-Urbain's deathbed note. The next day, Urbain condescends to visit Newman but refuses to retract the marriage sanction. With nothing to offer, Urbain nevertheless argues that circulating the note would only damn Newman himself and rake up the dishonorable behavior of Henri-Urbain. Urbain admits that disclosure would be very disagreeable but insists that is all it would be. No one would believe that Madame de Bellegarde had killed her husband. Would Claire want her father's poor reputation spread like a nasty rumor? Newman shows Urbain out. When the doors close, Newman says to himself, a bit unconvincingly, "Well, I ought to begin to be satisfied now!" (288).

(Chapter 25) Intending to reveal the Bellegardes' secret, Newman visits Madame d'Outreville, the grand lady from the fête. Realizing that she has no sympathy for him, he abruptly leaves without relating his story. In subsequent dinners with the Tristrams, he tries to recover while enduring Tom's assurances that everything turned out for the best. Mrs. Tristram urges Newman to leave Paris for a spell. He heads for LONDON. One afternoon in Hyde Park, he is unpleasantly surprised to see Lord Deepmere with the exquisitely dressed Mademoiselle Nioche. Her father is there too, walking her lapdog and playing the part of the honorable father. More surprising is Lord Deepmere's relationship with Noémie. He tells Newman that the public explanation for his cousin Valentin's duel was an argument over the pope.

(Chapter 26) Newman tries to pull himself together. Seeing himself as "a good fellow wronged" (303), he returns to the United States but cannot take an interest in business or any of his former pursuits. He feels like "[a] hopeless, helpless loafer, useful to no one and detestable to himself" (303). From Mrs. Tristram, he receives a long letter that reports that Claire has taken the veil and is now Sister Veronica. Impulsively, he returns to Paris, where lonely Mrs. Bread keeps his empty apartment. Staring at the blank walls of the convent in the rue d'Enfer, he has a change of heart. In an epiphany that recalls his renunciation of business, he loses his thirst for revenge. He returns to his apartment and tells Mrs. Bread to pack his things. In the final conversation with Mrs. Tristram, he tosses Henri-Urbain's deathbed accusation into the fire. Mrs. Tristram wonders at his boldness. Newman concludes that the Bellegardes' months of uncertainty is revenge enough. Mrs. Tristram concludes that Newman cannot be sure that the

Bellegardes were ever very upset. Perhaps they had anticipated his "good nature." As if registering her point, Newman glances back at the fire, but the document is gone.

CRITICAL ANALYSIS

When monthly installments of *The American* first appeared in the *Atlantic Monthly* 10 years after the CIVIL WAR, there were many questions about what it meant to be "an American." Looking back on Nathaniel Hawthorne's life in HAWTHORNE (1879), James enumerated the "items of high civilization" that "exist in other countries" but were "absent from the texture of American life":

> No State, in the European sense of the word, and indeed barely a specific national name. No sovereign, no court, no personal loyalty, no aristocracy, no church, no clergy, no army, no diplomatic service, no country gentlemen, no palaces, no castles, nor manors, nor old country-houses, nor parsonages, nor thatch cottages nor ivied ruins; no cathedrals, nor abbeys, nor little Norman churches; no great universities nor public schools—no Oxford, nor Eton, nor Harrow; no literature, no novels, no museums, no pictures, no political society, no sporting class—no Epsom nor Ascot! (351–352)

James marvels that Hawthorne was able to write anything at all about the United States. America in the 1870s seemed little better than in Hawthorne's time. The nation's war on Native Americans for the West suffered a setback in June 1876 with General George Armstrong Custer's defeat at the Battle of the Little Bighorn. And in the wake of Ulysses S. Grant's scandal-ridden presidency, the country endured the controversial presidential election of 1876, which ended in a disturbing compromise. In exchange for the presidency, the Republican Party agreed to roll back the federal policy of Reconstruction, tacitly sanctioning Jim Crow laws that restricted the voting rights and economic opportunities of African Americans.

Meanwhile, the Centennial Exhibition in Philadelphia exuberantly celebrated the nation's 100th birthday with displays of art and commerce that proclaimed the United States to be a cultural peer of Europe. The name Christopher Newman echoes America's promise to have improved on the Old World by rejecting aristocratic convention for the commercial opportunities of a democratic republic. Looking back on the novel from 1951, literary critic F. W. Dupee characterized Christopher Newman as a "mythic American," a "*novus homo, social upstart,*" and "the new humanity produced by American democracy" (84). Newman's immense wealth suggests that democracy has served his business interests very well. However, he fails to win Claire as his wife, and he misunderstands much of what happens in the Old World.

The language with which the narrator introduces this "new man" as a "powerful specimen of an American" (18) implies the broader quandaries over American identity. As Constance Rourke remarked in *American Humor: A Study in National Character* (1931), "Who ever heard of a significant English novel called *The Englishman* or an excellent French novel called *Le Français*? The simple and aggressive stress belonged to an imagination perennially engaged by the problem of the national type" (245). Figuring out "the American type" was a difficult matter. James playfully assumes that the reader is an "observer" with "an eye for national types" who would recognize Newman's "local origin" and infer his "American type" (17–18). In the first scene, as Newman stares at the artwork in the Louvre, the narrator asks the reader to consider his "physiognomy" (his facial features, the size and shape of his head) and to infer a "shrewd and capable fellow" (17). James is being ironic, and Newman is not a tidy American specimen. In 1950, Irving Howe commented that the notion of an abstract national type is absurd, especially in the United States of 1876, when New England was very different from San Francisco. James would have very much agreed. Newman's facial features are not objective attributes of cultural form. Instead, they imply a "vagueness which is not vacuity" and a "blankness which is not simplicity" (18). This ironic "physiognomy" asks the reader to interpret Newman through his attitudes and interactions with those around him and through the way he sees the world. As Leon Edel put it, Newman is "rich in national ambiguities" (Tuttleton 418).

Literary critics have often considered cultural confrontation to be the crux of James's novels with an INTERNATIONAL THEME. In "The First International Novel" (1958), Oscar Cargill avers that although James was not the first to write a novel in which different European cultures interact, *The American* makes cultural conflict a fundamental basis of the plot to an extent never before seen. Cargill's claim is disputable, but with *The American* in mind he defines the "international novel" as one:

> In which a character, usually guided in his actions by the mores of one environment, is set down in another, where his learned reflexes are of no use to him, where he must employ all his individual resources to meet successive situations, and where he must intelligently accommodate himself to the new mores, or, in one way or another, be destroyed. It is the novelist's equivalent of providing a special medium in a laboratory for studying the behavior of an organism, only here it is a device for the revelation of character. (419)

Accordingly, Newman's American "freeness" and the Bellegardes' old world "fixedness" are the very premise of dramatic action. In 1954, Isadore Traschen's "An American in Paris" compared the two versions of the novel, the first published in 1877 and the second in 1907, when James revised it for the New York Edition. Traschen focuses on the tension of melodrama, a type of story in which good and evil stand in conflict, and in which good triumphs in the end. Traschen concludes that the revisions emphasize the confrontation between the "innocence" of Newman and the "poor effete" corruptness of the old world Bellegardes, who become Newman's "lesson in evil" (77). However, subsequent critics are more circumspect about establishing such clear distinctions between Newman and the Bellegardes.

Whereas Traschen ratchets up the opposition between America and France, Richard Poirier's *The Comic Sense of Henry James: A Study of His Early Novels* (1960) alerts readers to the comedic elements that lessen a "tendency toward moral strictures" in the novel's first half (28). With humor,

James develops Newman's capacity to see potential where those fixed in aristocratic convention do not. James's extravagant metaphors promote a humor that "absorbs the morally serious implications in moral absurdity" (34). This gives readers the room to consider the characters as "representatives of certain kinds of social conduct" (39). For example, when Newman brags that one of his sisters is married to the owner of the "largest india-rubber house in the west," Madame de Bellegarde responds by taking him literally, remarking for all to hear: "Ah, you make houses also of india-rubber?" (125–126). Newman assumes that she has misunderstood and has fallen for a rather tall tale. He laughs too loudly. Actually, she is making fun of him, suggesting that America's lax standards of familial association require such inventive architecture. Madame de Bellegarde does not seem "evil" here. By allowing us to smile, James endears us to the characters while laying the dramatic groundwork for the Bellegardes' ultimate betrayal. With comedy, James also demonstrates the centrality of art, manner, and style in negotiating social respectability.

James stands with Newman in the readers' spotlight as a representative American. Oscar Cargill along with Leon Edel, Peter Brooks, and Martha Banta considers the novel in the context of James's own biographical struggle to adapt to Paris, where he moved in the autumn of 1875 and pledged to make a living by writing. He met famous writers (including Gustave Flaubert, Ernest Renan, Ivan Turgenev, and Émile Zola) and reviewed books by Hippolyte Taine, who examined a writer's race, time, and milieu to discern a national category. James also frequented the Paris theater and borrowed certain popular plot devices such as the duel and the all-important "scrap of paper." How well did James rework these melodramatic set pieces? The novel's mixed reviews appraise his potential to develop into an American author who deserves international respect. They also imply the precarious state of American literature more generally. For example, in September 1877, the *North American Review* judged "the perfection of [James's] literary style" to be "almost beyond cavil" but found the novel's character development to be chilly, appealing "almost entirely" to the "reader's intel-

lectual side" (Tuttleton 38). Meanwhile, the *British Quarterly Review* in 1879 noticed a "strong relentless realism which leaves a large amount of failure and continuing unhappiness"—a "fine tonic" to "jaded novel-readers" (Tuttleton 41). James was challenged to write in a style that was recognizably literary yet innovative to present characters that engaged a reader's interest and affection and to present a credible "American" while showing that he knew something about French society.

The plot of the novel is a key feature of James's artistic innovation. Readers, along with James himself, have carefully considered the novel's shift from a relatively lighthearted comedy of manners into a melodramatic showdown that expires in the unhappy ending. Newman's failure definitely provoked a reaction, drawing criticism even from WILLIAM DEAN HOWELLS, James's good friend and the editor of the *Atlantic Monthly*. In a letter to Howells (March 30, 1877), James defended himself, insisting that, although readers "have a right to their entertainment," he does not "believe it is in me to give them, in a satisfactory way, what they require" (Tuttleton 348–349). He seems to imply that the frustration of a fairy-tale ending is true to the real world in which Newman and Claire would have been an "impossible couple" and, "to speak very materially," had no place to live. Is James chiding the American public for the easy terms of their entertainment? It would be wrong to take his stand too far. When trying to win popularity as a playwright with British audiences in 1890, he rewrote the ending so that Claire reclaims Newman. Alas, the *Atlantic Monthly* (December 1891) panned it, declaring that the play "sacrific[ed] all of the distinction of the original tale" (848).

But is the novel's rejection of Newman truly more realistic? By 1907, James did not think so. In the new preface for the New York Edition, he admits that the Bellegardes "would positively have jumped . . . at my rich and easy American"; their course of action "would have been to haul him and his fortune into their boat under the cover of the night" and accommodate him with a "safe and convenient seat" (12). James rationalizes the Bellegardes' unrealistic "tergiversation" (12), or abrupt turnabout, by weighing the difference between romance and realism. In the process, he admits to the novel's romantic spirit, as if in 1876 he had thought romance to be "vulgar." James recalls brainstorming the Bellegardes' "affront" to Newman and discounting an offense "done by his mistress herself, since injuries of this order are the stale stuff of romance" (4). He also discounts portraying Newman as "successfully vindictive." Both options would have been "too vulgar a type" of literary expression with which to introduce the American. What was wrong with romance? (See ROMANCE/REALISM/NATURALISM.)

Etymologically, the term *romance* derives from the word *Rome*. In the phrase *romance languages,* it designates those vernacular or common languages that sprang up on the edge of the Roman Empire. Eventually, these languages stood on their own for a group of people (in France, Spain, Portugal, etc.) whose local elite developed specifically national networks of print publication outside the Latin pale. As a literary form, the "romance" is a sort of mini-epic with a hero who stands against the conventional powers to assert a new center of communal identification. The literary historian and critic Robert Spiller defined "the romantic movement in western European literatures" as "the literary expression of the revolutionary political, social, religious, and other ideas which attempted to overthrow traditional patterns of society and thought" (344). When the United States won its independence, writers asked if older European models of romance could convey a sense of American distinctiveness. What kind of society would grow out of the promise of democratic republicanism, and what kind of literature would result? What kind of hero would appeal to a people who had rejected the principle of aristocracy?

Romance promised escape and innovation from "traditional patterns," but it could easily seem trite, a melodramatic simplification of good and evil. In the early part of his career, James did not want to be just a "vulgar" romance writer for a fledgling nation that European sophisticates considered young, rough, and undeveloped. He wanted a reputation as a substantial author concerned with a "highly civilized" society (to borrow his phrase from *Hawthorne*). As a literary genre, realism promised to bring the romantic quests of princes and prin-

cess down to the misadventures, disappointments, mundane experiences, and the modest victories of everyday life. Some of the first realistic novels were Daniel Defoe's *Robinson Crusoe* (1719) and Samuel Richardson's *Pamela* (1741), which focused on the ordinary lives of a commercially savvy sailor and a domestic serving girl. In 19th-century France, Honoré de Balzac attempted in *La comédie humaine* (1799–1850) to classify in taxonomy all of the social types that comprise French society, including laborers, shopkeepers, lawyers, and courtesans. The mostly French writers (Turgenev was Russian) with whom James associated in Paris were committed to the disciplined observation of actual society and to a *réalisme* that portrayed the world in the messy details of peoples' struggle to survive. James's novel gives us "an American" millionaire who tells Mrs. Tristram that he wants "to possess, in a word, the best article on the market" (44). This attitude may defy Europe's aristocratic convention, but there is little romance in purchasing a wife as one might a new suit of clothes. In his essay "Physical Capital: *The American* and the Realist Body" (1987), Mark Seltzer accounts for Newman's commercial mindset by arguing that American "culture" was a result of business transactions that are impossible to transcend, thereby dooming the very premise of romance.

When in 1907 James admitted to having written an "arch-romance," he was at a late point in his career when he had earned an international reputation and could claim the license to redefine the terms of romance and realism. He differentiates romance from realism by characterizing the romantic as the "unknown" and the "real" as representing:

> the things we cannot possibly *not* know, sooner or later, in one way or another; it being but one of the accidents of our hampered state, and one of the incidents of their quantity and number, that particular instances have not yet come our way. The romantic stands, on the other hand, for the things that, with all the facilities in the world, all the wealth and courage and all the wit and all the adventure, we never *can* directly know; the things that can reach us only

through the beautiful circuit and subterfuge of our thought and our desire. (9)

In asserting his authorship, James deconstructs the opposition between the romantic and real by recovering the accident and uncertainty behind what we know as "the real" and by emphasizing the sense of reality to which people cling through the emotional circuitry of their fantasies. Obviously, the line between the genres of romance and realism is blurry. Terminological consistency aside, the confusion between the "romantic" and "realistic" is James's opportunity to outline the method of his writing craft.

With the term *arch-romance*, James recasts the novel as his adaptation of literary form to the idea of American type. Peter Brooks's essay "The Turn of *The American*" (1987) considers the novel's many elements of melodramatic romance. The ending is ostensibly antiromantic in the way it frustrates a happy marriage, but it is romantic in the sense that it conveys the integrity of Newman's point of view. Both the Bellegardes' refusal to accept the marriage and Newman's renunciation of revenge suggest the elemental cores of their respective cultural identities. Brooks argues that the novel demonstrates how James wrestled with literary form to assert the respectability of American type. In the preface, James recalls overhearing an anecdote while "seated in an American 'horse-cart'" (2)—not a very auspicious start to a literary classic. Having learned of a "situation, in another country and an aristocratic society, of some robust but insidiously beguiled and betrayed, some cruelly wronged compatriot" (2), James transforms Newman into "a strong man indifferent to his strength and too wrapped in fine, too wrapped above all in *other* and intenser, reflexions for the assertion of his 'rights'" (2–3). The meaning of the *arch-romance* lies in Newman's realization of these "other and intenser" reflections. In the vague fascination with a sense of value beyond commercial success or the vulgar satisfaction of melodramatic revenge, James captures his readers' interest in *The American.*

What of the novels' readers? Might the book be testing them? James Tuttleton's "The Supersti-

tious Valuation of Europe" (1978) explains many of the novel's allusions to art, literature, mythology, and opera. Readers are supposed to catch Newman's mistakes and appreciate the deeper history of what he initially engages superficially as churches to be visited and images to be copied and owned. In 1983, William Stowe emphasized the novel's "superimposed interpretations" (37), which comprise an elaborate structure of dramatic irony that calls on readers to interpret Newman as he interprets his surroundings. For example, when Newman introduces himself to Mme Nioche, he proudly claims Christopher Columbus as his patron saint. This links Newman to a history of imperial conquest that he overlooks, even as he stands in the Louvre Museum, which had been a royal palace until 1793. It matters that Newman lacks any self-consciousness in invoking Columbus. John Carlos Rowe recasts Newman's supposed "innocence" as a *relationship* to European history rather than a mere ignorance of it (1,987 and 1,998). In *The Other Henry James* (1998), Rowe states that "historical innocence is by no means an advantage, but instead an American fatality from which [James] is usually at pains to save us" (58). Not knowing history dooms one to repeat it, and in Newman's ignorance of everything from the Bellegardes' family history to the plot of *Don Giovanni*, readers sense that this "new man" is not so free as earlier critics had implied. James shows "how profoundly Americans are involved in history and how little we are justified in claiming the 'uniqueness' . . . that comes of forgetting the past" (58).

Race, Gender, and the "Newman"

James's Newman is a representative type whose civil rights and social standing as a white person facilitate his rise from rags to riches. Imagine how different the story would have been if in 1875 James had presented Newman as African American or Native American. Despite the intense cultural frictions, the novel's international scene does not include anyone who is not white. It is true that the expatriated Americans might not feel "white" in France, and that they resent being looked down upon by the aristocratic Parisians. To cope with the Old World's condescension, the novel's Americans often refer to and joke about racial groups who have been marginalized in the United States. At one point, Mrs. Tristram quips that Newman is a barbarian. When he objects, she clarifies: "I don't mean that you are a Comanche chief, or that you wear a blanket and feathers. There are different shades" (42). Newman replies that he is a "highly civilized" man. At another deeply ironic moment, Newman tries to befriend Urbain de Bellegarde by assuming their mutual interest in the collection of "negroes' skulls" (124). Urbain has nothing to say to this and most likely considers Newman the "specimen" of greater interest. These references suggest that being respectably American depended on disassociating oneself from African Americans and Native Americans, who were significantly barred from participating in the national community as full citizens.

Women were also second-class citizens, and Newman's economic attitudes are full of assumptions about the role women should play in supporting his conquests. On a literal level, Newman seems the epitome of rugged MASCULINITY as a "muscular Christian" who never exercises (18). One reason that Newman feels he can approach Mme Nioche in the Louvre is because he regards her as an available resource—a copying hand that he can employ to acquire the gallery's images. Furthermore, he arranges her payment in the form of a dowry, suggesting that her proper place is with a husband in a respectable middle-class family. Mme Nioche rejects his offer and plays by different rules.

In terms of social power, the women in the novel trump Newman's commercial manhood. Carolyn Porter notices in "Gender and Value in *The American*" (1987) that Newman's ostensible manliness—his combination of physical strength, capital, and forthright manner—is not enough to win Claire's hand. This man of action loses out to the Bellegarde matriarch, who rejects his terms of commerce and thereby undercuts his source of social power. To appreciate Newman's loss of masculine privilege, Porter considers his misunderstanding of Mme Nioche's and Claire's relations to the public world. Mme Nioche defies his sense of sexual propriety to embrace a commercial attitude, selling anything to succeed as a courtesan. Newman's disgust is not

due to a Puritanical sensitivity but because Noémie cuts him out of the deal. Claire defies Newman in a different sense, ultimately overlooking his wealth for the security of a convent. Along these lines, Cheryl Torsney's essay "Translation and Transubstantiation in *The American*" (1996) considers the novel as a crisis in translation that centers on the incompatibility of Newman's economic worldview with the Bellegardes' sacred sense of aristocratic blood.

Finally, Eric Haralson's "James's *The American*: A (New)man Is Being Beaten" (1992) understands Newman's "corporal and capitalist energies" (478) as James's complex psychological reaction to the vigorous masculinity exemplified in Charles Kingsley's novels, which James admired as a young reader and reviewed while writing *The American*. Through Sigmund Freud, Haralson reads Newman as James's attempt "to limn a male character who is virile enough to succeed in his bid for a patriarchal stature, and yet (crucial caveat) whose avenue must bypass the anxiety-ridden area of genitality" (487). In other words, James fails to make Newman credible as a passionate lover; in trying to win Claire from her mother, Newman speaks the language of paternal affection and ends up looking like a frustrated child being punished, both by the Bellegardes and the author. By embarrassing Newman so thoroughly, James initiates a "critique of hypermasculinity" (Haralson 490) that foreshadows the more passive, aesthetic, and observant styles of manhood undertaken by subsequent leading men in James's fiction, such as Ralph Touchett of *The PORTRAIT OF A LADY* (1881) and Lambert Strether of *The AMBASSADORS* (1903).

CHARACTERS

Babcock, Mr. Benjamin (a.k.a. "Dorchester") A Unitarian minister from Dorchester, Massachusetts, Babcock travels with Newman through Europe on funds provided by his congregation. Newman nicknames him "Dorchester" and tries to enjoy his company. Secretly despising Europe, Babcock grows tired of Newman for his seeming lack of a "moral reaction" (69) to art, and the two part ways in Venice.

Bellegarde, Blanche de   The wife of the severe Urbain de Bellegarde, she is self-absorbed but always prettily dressed. She sees Newman as a possible ally in staving off the boredom of her marriage. She pleads that he accompany her, after his marriage, to a student ball in the Latin Quarter. She mischievously arranges his showdown with the Bellegardes in Monceau Park.

Bellegarde, Claire de (a.k.a. Mme Claire de Cintré, Sister Veronica)   A tragic figure who must endure her mother's treasure-hunting marriage plots, she is tall with "thick fair hair" and "clear gray eyes" that are "strikingly expressive" (85). Her first marriage to a scandalous older man mercifully ended with his death. She made a deal with her mother to remain under her authority as long as she is not required to marry again.

Claire lives with her family in Paris at a very exclusive address that keeps her sheltered from Newman's world. She remains a bit of an enigma throughout the novel, signaling the extent to which she is a symbol for Newman, and perhaps for James. The narrator describes her as a "rare and precious—a very expensive article," who has been shaped by "mysterious ceremonies and processes of culture" (110). At times she seems ready to break from her mother's authority, but ultimately she pleads weakness and fear. She seeks refuge in the Carmelite sisterhood as Sr. Veronica.

Bellegarde, Comte Valentin de   The handsome, "gallant, expansive" and "amusing" (95) younger brother of Urbain and Claire, he uses humor to cover a sense of purposeless and spends his time appreciating social scandals from his basement apartment in the rue d'Anjou St. Honoré. He cares greatly for Claire but is not able to protect her from his mother and brother. He befriends Newman, partly to rankle his older brother and partly because Newman amuses him. Valentin is killed in a duel, staged in Switzerland, with Stanislas Kapp, a rival for Mme. Nioche's affection. He is genuinely disappointed by his family's double cross of Newman, and in his dying hours he urges him to seek out a family secret through Mrs. Bread.

Bellegarde, Marquis de (Henri-Urbain, Junior)   Along with his mother, the Marquis is Newman's archrival. His "long lean face," "high-bridged nose," and "small opaque eyes," combined with a dimpled chin and fair whiskers, suggest a very "distinguished" person of "British origin" (123). The polish of his nails and the perpendicularity of his posture convey nobility that fascinates Newman, who grows to resent the Marquis's condescension.

Bellegarde, Marquis de (Henri-Urbain, Senior)   The deceased Bellegarde patriarch was a lusty aristocrat with a penchant for servant girls. His wandering eye greatly embarrassed his wife and provoked the resentment of his oldest son. A loving father to Claire, he did his best to prevent her marriage to M. de Cintré, but he died a painful death before he could save her. In his final moments of life, he wrote a note that accused his wife of murdering him and gave it to Mrs. Bread.

Bellegarde, Marquise de (a.k.a. Lady Emmeline Atheling)   The English daughter of Lord St. Dunstans now transplanted to Paris, she is the matriarch of the Bellegarde family and Newman's main adversary. Newman finds her "a formidable, inscrutable little woman" (120), who resembles her daughter, Claire, but with a pinched mouth and an imposing austerity. The Marquise has endured a philandering husband and now seems dedicated to securing a fortune by marrying her daughter to a wealthy aristocrat. She rejects Newman and Claire's marriage as "improper" (214) and impossible, despite his vast wealth. To her, he will always be a dreadful "commercial person" (218) and unfit to be a member of the Bellegarde family.

Bread, Mrs. Catherine   A longtime servant to the house of de Bellegarde, having accompanied the Marquise from England, Mrs. Bread harbors a grudge against Madame de Bellegarde for accusing her of trying to attract the amorous attention of the elder marquis. Nevertheless, she virtually raises Claire and Valentin and is at the elder marquis's bedside when he dies. To save Claire from the convent, she gives Newman a note that the patriarch had written before breathing his last—a note in which he accuses his wife of murder. At the novel's end, Mrs. Bread has left the Bellegardes and is the lonely housekeeper of Newman's vast and empty apartments in Paris.

Cintré, M. de   Claire's first husband is an odious man who treats her badly and wastes nearly all his money before dying. Much older than Claire, he seems to enjoy the scandal his behavior provokes.

Deepmere, Lord   A small man of 33, Deepmere is the not very attractive cousin of Claire. He is bald with a short nose, lacks upper front teeth, and has pimples on his chin. He is also very wealthy. Urbain and Marquise de Bellegarde suggest him as Claire's future husband. He loves Dublin but possesses an English manor and title. His "round, candid, blue eyes" match his direct and sympathetic approach with Claire about her mother's machinations. By novel's end, he takes up with Mme Nioche, despite Valentin's death.

D'Outreville, Duchess   A "grand lady" of aristocratic Paris, she turns the tables on Newman at the Bellegardes' grand party. After learning the Bellegardes' secret, Newman intends to tell her of the sordid event in his vendetta against the Bellegardes. He changes his mind and keeps the secret.

Grosjoyaux, M. de   One of Valentin's two friends who served with him in the Pontifical Zouaves, he stands with Valentin at the duel and watches over him as he dies in the Alps. To Newman, Grosjoyaux seems generally aloof and oddly resigned to Valentin's death.

Kapp, Stanislas   A young Alsatian man who is Valentin's rival in the affections of Mme Nioche, he is the "son and heir of a rich brewer of Strasbourg, a youth of sanguineous—and sanguinary—temperament" (210). He kills Valentin in a duel.

Ledoux, M.   One of Valentin's friends who served with him in the Pontifical Zouaves, he is the "nephew of a distinguished Ultramontane bishop" (225). Like M. de Grosjoyaux, he watches Valentin die with a grim fatalism that bothers Newman.

Newman, Mr. Christopher   An energetic, healthy, and formidable businessman of 36, he is presented by the narrator as the novel's "powerful specimen of an American" (18). He is "long, lean, and muscular" (33), with a brown complexion, and "a rather abundant mustache" (18). The narrator gives a paradoxically detailed but allusive description of Newman's appearance and demeanor, hoping to typify "the American" in the look of Newman's "clear, cold gray" eye, "in which innocence and experience were singularly blended" (18). His character balances contrary traits of personality; he is "frigid and yet friendly, frank yet cautious, shrewd yet credulous, positive yet skeptical, confident yet shy, extremely intelligent and extremely good-humoured" (18–19). He seems a formidable hero for a novel but ultimately fails in his quest to marry Claire.

As a young boy, Newman is left to fend for himself. He becomes eminently capable in the competitive world of business and eventually makes a fortune in San Francisco from the manufacture of washtubs and leather. He dabbles less successfully in oil and rail. One day in New York he abruptly retires from business, renouncing the hard-nosed rivalries that underpin his success. Instead, he travels Europe to improve his mind. Despite wanting to leave his commercial attitudes behind, he cannot help but bring them to Europe.

When in an unfamiliar place like the Louvre or the Bellegardes' home, he has a habit of "extending his legs" as a "symbol of his taking mental possession of the scene" (82). As he moves through Europe to see the art and architecture of the Old World, he quantifies his experience, tallying the number of places he has visited and purchasing a great number of copied pictures. When explaining to the Tristrams his "programme" of finding a wife, he declares "I want to posses, in a word, the best article in the market" (44). In the early stages of the novel, Newman seems to portray "the American" as overly confident in the power of money to purchase experience and respect. The Bellegardes frustrate him thoroughly.

By the novel's end, Newman seems transformed by his failure into a man who wrestles with what James terms in his 1907 preface "*other* and intenser, reflexions" (3). His renunciation mirrors his earlier disavowal of business and suggests his growing sense of culture as irreducible to material wealth.

Nioche, M.   A crestfallen father with a story of marital strife involving a fickle and unfaithful wife, he struggles to maintain the pretense of gentility and makes an elaborate show of protecting his daughter Noémie's virtue. Newman hires him as a French tutor and initially sympathizes with him. Later, Newman learns that M. Nioche puts on a good show and is probably a conspirator in his daughter's career as a courtesan.

Nioche, Mme Noémie   A pretty and bright young French woman, she is determined to climb her way up the social ladder by selling what she has to men with money and power. Newman meets her in the Louvre as she copies a Murillo painting. She flirts with him but is frustrated when he does not seem to register her flirtation. She later captivates Valentin, who is killed over her in a duel with a rival. By the novel's end, she appears in Hyde Park (London) with Lord Deepmere and her father, who now minds her little dog.

Rochefidèle, Comte and Comtesse de la   They are guests of the Bellegardes when Newman announces his proposal. They are elderly relics from the Bourbon monarchy, and the countess, whose French Newman cannot understand, remembers having once met Benjamin Franklin as a young girl.

Tristram, Mrs. Lizzie   An American woman expatriated in Paris with a "very plain face" (36) and a "marked tendency to irony" (36), who, in order to punish a clever man who had spurned her, married a foolish man, Tom Tristram, whom she despises. Lacking good looks as a girl, she cultivated "charming manners" (37) and an intelligence that make her a very interesting woman:

"restless, discontented, visionary, without personal ambitions" (38). Tom is a standing audience to her social experiments, one of which is introducing Newman to her old school friend Claire. She is a bit surprised when things initially go well, disappointed when it ends badly, and entertained throughout.

Tristram, Tom   An affable but doltish American husband who spends his Parisian life gossiping and playing cards with other expatriates, he sees nothing to admire in the stiff, allusive beauty of Claire, whom he describes as "a great white doll of a woman who cultivates a quiet haughtiness" (48). Newman must suffer through his counsel in the depth of his despair.

ADAPTATIONS

A play adaptation was produced in 1890.

A television version, *The American* (2001), was directed by Paul Unwin for PBS. Matthew Modine played Christopher Newman.

FURTHER READING

The interpretive work on James's novel is extensive. James W. Tuttleton's Norton Critical Edition is an excellent source for sorting through the different versions of the novel, and it includes excerpts from relevant letters by James, contemporary reviews, and important readings of the novel from 20th-century critics. Martha Banta's critical anthology (1987) is an excellent source for further contemporary analysis.

Banta, Martha, ed. *New Essays on The American.* Cambridge: Cambridge University Press, 1987.

Brook, Cleanth. "The American Innocence." *Shenadoah* 16 (1964): 21–37.

Brooks, Peter. "The Turn of *The American*," in Banta.

Cargill, Oscar. "The First International Novel." *PMLA* 73 (1958): 418–425.

Dupee, F. W. *Henry James: His Life and Writings.* 1951. New York: Doubleday Anchor Books, 1956.

Edel, Leon. "The American." In *Henry James: the Conquest of London, 1870–1881,* 245–260. Philadelphia: Lippincott, 1962.

Gettman, Royal A. "Henry James's Revision of *The American*." *American Literature* 16 (1945): 279–295.

Haralson, Eric. "A New(man) is being beaten." *American Literature* 64, no. 3 (1992): 475–495.

Howe, Irving. "Henry James and the Millionaire." *Tomorrow* 9 (January 1950): 53–55. In Tuttleton.

James, Henry. *The American*. Edited by James W. Tuttleton. New York: W.W. Norton, 1978.

———. *Hawthorne*. In *Literary Criticism: Essays on Literature, American Writers, English Writers*. 1879. Reprint, New York: Library of America, 1984.

Johnson, Kendall. "Rules of Engagement: The Archromance of Visual Culture in *The American*." In *Henry James and the Visual*, 85–122. Cambridge: Cambridge University Press, 2007.

Poirier, Richard. *"The American."* In *The Comic Sense of Henry James: A Study of His Early Novels*, 44–94. New York: Oxford University Press, 1960.

Porter, Carolyn. "Gender and Value in *The American*." In Banta, 99–130.

Rourke, Constance. *American Humor: A Study of National Character*. New York: Harcourt, Brace, 1931.

Rowe, John Carlos. "A Phantom of the Opera: Christopher Newman's Unconscious in *The American*." In *The Other Henry James*. Durham, N.C.: Duke University Press, 1998.

———. "The Politics of Innocence in Henry James." In Banta, 69–98.

Seltzer, Mark. "Physical Capital: *The American* and the Realist Body." In Banta, 131–168.

Spiller, Robert E. "Critical Standards in the American Romantic Movement." *College English* 8, no. 7 (1947): 344–352.

Stowe, William. "Interpretation: *Le Père Goriot* and *The American*." In *Balzac, James and the Realistic Novel*, 21–55. Princeton, N.J.: Princeton University Press, 1983.

Teahan, Sheila. "*The American*'s Double-Cross." *Arizona Quarterly* 53, no. 4 (1997): 147–160.

Torsney, Cheryl B. "Translation and Transubstantiation in *The American*." *Henry James Review* 17, no. 1 (1996): 40–51.

Traschen, Isadore. "An American in Paris." *American Literature* 26, no. 1 (1954): 67–77.

Tuttleton, James W. "Rereading *The American*: A Century Since." *Henry James Review* 1, no. 1 (1980): 139–153.

Kendall Johnson, *Swarthmore College*

The Awkward Age (1899)

James first noted the idea for *The Awkward Age* in his notebook in an entry dated March 2, 1898, and wrote it swiftly between September and December 1898 for serialization in the American journal *Harper's Weekly* (October 1898–January 1899). It was published in book form in England by William Heinemann and by Harper and Brother in America a month later. In 1908, it was published with a new preface and some minor corrections, as Volume 9 of Charles Scribner's Sons' NEW YORK EDITION of the collected works. (See also PREFACES TO THE NEW YORK EDITION.)

SYNOPSIS

Book 1. Lady Julia

(Chapter 1) Mr. Longdon, recently returned to LONDON after an absence of some 30 years, shares a cab home with Vanderbank (called Van) after meeting at a dinner party. They decide to extend their evening at the latter's apartment, where they discuss the social circle that meets every Sunday in the parlor of Mrs. Brookenham (called Mrs. Brook).

(Chapter 2) The focus of their conversation turns to Mrs. Brook's daughter, Nanda, who is of an age to make her social debut and find a husband according to the custom of the time. Vanderbank hints that she has already been out and unmarried for too long and risks being perceived as spoiled goods. This bemuses Longdon.

(Chapter 3) As Longdon prepares to leave, Vanderbank abruptly guesses that the older man had been in love with Nanda's deceased grandmother, Lady Julia, and had been refused by her. Longdon admits this is true. Exit Longdon.

Book 2. Little Aggie

(Chapter 4) Mrs. Brook enters her parlor to find her eldest son, Harold, asleep on the sofa. Awakening, he candidly admits to having pilfered some money from her unlocked bureau. Exit Harold. Enter the Duchess Jane.

(Chapter 5) The women discuss the duty of mothers to their unmarried daughters. Comparing Nanda unfavorably to her own niece, little Aggie, the Duchess accuses Mrs. Brook of neglect in permitting an improper friendship to develop between Nanda and a young unhappily married woman, Tishy Grendon. She insists on the need to marry the girls off early, and they discuss Van and Mr. Mitchett (known as Mitchy) as the principal potential suitors within their social circle. Exit the Duchess.

(Chapter 6) Enter Edward Brookenham. His wife insinuates that the Duchess is having an affair with Lord Petherton. They discuss their responsibility toward the probable fact that Harold is borrowing heavily to sustain his high life. They agree that it is time for Nanda to "sit downstairs" at their social evenings (59). Mrs. Brook reveals her hopes that Mr. Longdon will like them out of loyalty to the memory of her mother, Lady Julia. Enter Petherton and Mitchy.

(Chapter 7) Mitchy instantly asks after Nanda, whom he admits to liking, but whom he does not think likes him in return. He in fact believes her to be in love with Van. Mrs. Brook denies this and does not think that Van would ever marry her daughter. Enter the Duchess and little Aggie.

(Chapter 8) Aggie's striking beauty and "emphasized virginity" impress the group deeply (68). The Duchess makes much of the need to protect her from their conversation, which hinges on Nanda's risk of degradation in her relationship with Tishy and her sister, Mrs. Carrie Donner. Enter Mrs. Donner, prompting the Duchess to order Edward to retreat with Aggie into a far corner. Enter Lady Fanny Cashmore.

(Chapter 9) The Duchess outlines to Mitchy the gossip about an adulterous affair between Mrs. Donner and Mr. Cashmore. She describes how the details of the affair have been reported by Nanda to Mrs. Brook through her friendship with Tishy. Exit Mrs. Donner. The Duchess permits Mitchy to sit with Aggie. She tells Petherton that she "must have" Mitchy for Aggie (80).

"Mr. Longdon's" by A. L. Coburn, frontispiece to *The Awkward Age,* Volume 9, the New York Edition

Book 3. Mr. Longdon

(Chapter 10) Arriving early for a small gathering at Van's, Mitchy meets Longdon while they wait for their host to dress. They discuss Van, his popularity with women, his good looks, and his apparent reluctance to marry, which Mitchy puts down in part to his lack of a private fortune. Enter, to both men's great surprise, an unescorted Nanda.

(Chapter 11) Nanda's presence discomposes Longdon considerably. Enter Van. They discuss why Mrs. Brook has insisted that her daughter attend the evening alone. Longdon abruptly leaves the room. Van attends to Longdon, then returns to ask Nanda to go and talk with him.

(Chapter 12) The scene skips to Longdon's retreat, where Van enters to see him standing in tears by the window. Longdon confesses to being overwhelmed by Nanda's close physical similarity to Lady Julia. Exit Van. Enter Nanda, whose open and astute opinions dominate the conversation, reinforcing his sense of the incredible disparity of manner, despite the physical resemblance between the girl and her grandmother.

Book 4. Mr. Cashmore

(Chapter 13) Mr. Cashmore enters the Brookenham parlor, where Harold promptly taps him for five pounds. Harold exits as Mrs. Brook enters. Cashmore denies any relationship with Mrs. Donner and confesses to liking Nanda after meeting her at Tishy's. His suggestion that Mrs. Brook might assist him in getting to know her daughter is highly improper. Enter Van and Longdon.

(Chapter 14) Sending Longdon to talk to Cashmore, Mrs. Brook pulls Van away to ask his advice on how to try to make Longdon like her, convinced that he currently does not. She is somewhat flirtatious with him. They discuss Longdon's probable wealth.

(Chapter 15) Swapping places with Cashmore, Mrs. Brook proceeds to try to charm Longdon. He struggles with his ambivalence toward her. But she seems to win him over. He agrees to "never let her go" (120). She announces her triumph to the group, and further conversation ensues contrasting Nanda's exposed upbringing to Aggie's conservative education. A telegram from Nanda arrives, announcing she is staying out to attend the opera with Tishy. All three men decide to leave to go there also.

Book 5. The Duchess

(Chapter 16) The scene is set in July, three months later, at a country house rented by Mitchy for the weekend. Van encounters Nanda on a bench in the park. They discuss both their old friendship and the new one developing between Nanda and Longdon. Departing the park for the terrace, they encounter Longdon. Exit Van.

(Chapter 17) Longdon and Nanda return to the bench, where he reflects on how he feels incredibly out of touch with the times. Their talk turns to his repeated invitation for Nanda to stay at his home in Suffolk and then to her possible marriage. Longdon wishes Nanda to marry Mitchy, but she is not interested, believing that she will never marry and insisting Mitchy ought instead to marry Aggie.

(Chapter 18) The next day, the Duchess accosts Longdon to sit with Aggie, while she finds Mitchy and Petherton. Aggie sweetly and innocently outlines the narrow limits of her world to him. Petherton and the Duchess rejoin them. Exit Aggie on the Duchess's orders under Petherton's protection.

(Chapter 19) Puzzling over this arrangement, Longdon remains with the Duchess. She tells him of her wish for Nanda to marry Van, hinting that Longdon should make a financial settlement for her. She claims that Mrs. Brook only favors Mitchy for her daughter because "she wants 'old Van' for herself," a desire that she does not think is reciprocated (153).

(Chapter 20) Later that evening, Van and Longdon talk in the smoking room. Longdon expresses his desire that Van should marry Nanda and tells him of his plans to make her a financial settlement to accommodate this. Van seems charmed by Longdon's confidence in him but asks for time to think about what he will do.

Book 6. Mrs. Brook

(Chapter 21) Three days later, Van visits Mrs. Brook. They discuss his repeated expressions of interest in Nanda these past three months, which Mrs. Brook greets with disdain, and he finally confides to her the nature of Longdon's offer. She repeatedly insists that he will not follow through on it. Enter Mitchy.

(Chapter 22) Much to Van's discomfort, Mrs. Brook instantly and indiscreetly announces Longdon's offer to Mitchy. Van, feigning humorous detachment, insinuates that she is motivated by jealousy of her daughter. She retorts by suggesting it is his own fancy that she wants him for herself, and she further outlines her belief that he will not follow through for fear of seeming to be taking a bribe. Yet she piles on this dilemma by suggesting to him that Longdon will give Nanda an even larger sum by way of compensation if she does not marry at all. They all agree to keep this information from Nanda. Exit Van and Mitchy.

(Chapter 23) Enter Nanda, half an hour later. Her mother questions her whether Longdon intends either to marry or adopt her, which Nanda deflects. On hearing that he has extended an indefinite invitation for her to join him in Suffolk sometime, Mrs. Brook instructs her to go down with him immediately the following Saturday.

Book 7. Mitchy

(Chapter 24) At Longdon's house in Suffolk, Nanda is sitting in the garden with Van, who is visiting for the weekend. They discuss the freedom Longdon has granted her to his home and the fact that she represents a new type of modern girl who "understands" things (204). There is a prolonged pause in which it seems as if Van really might propose to her, but it passes. Longdon calls them to lunch.

(Chapter 25) The next day, Van escorts Longdon to church while Nanda speaks privately to Mitchy, who is also visiting, in the drawing room. Despite Mitchy's repeated declaration of interest in her, she persuades him to marry Aggie to "save her" from the Duchess's life (208).

(Chapter 26) Later, after Longdon and Nanda have retired for the evening, Van and Mitchy remain in the library, speculating on Longdon's proposed settlement. Mitchy informs Van that he is renouncing Nanda, at her request, to marry Aggie, thus clearing the way for Van's proposal, which he still has not decided to offer.

Book 8. Tishy Grendon

(Chapter 27) January: Van arrives early for a gathering at Tishy's, where he encounters Nanda, who is now staying there. They discuss Mitchy and Aggie's marriage and the massive transformation it has effected in the latter's character. Van asks why a French book has his name on it, written in Nanda's hand. She admits it is one she believes he lent to her mother, which she had borrowed to read for Tishy. His concern at being associated with it indicates that its subject matter is somewhat salacious. Enter the rest of the party.

(Chapter 28) After dinner, the Duchess corners Longdon. To his discomfort, she congratulates him on arranging Mitchy and Aggie's marriage before turning her attention to the second part of this alleged plan: how to get Van to marry Nanda. She believes Mrs. Brook is still an obstacle, and she directs him to watch her at the gathering.

(Chapter 29) They are joined by Van and Mrs. Brook, who launches into a sardonic update on the affairs of the various scandalous figures in the group. Longdon struggles to follow. Abruptly, she tells him that they want Nanda back, a demand that is farcically undermined when the Duchess appeals to Edward Brookenham, just then joining them. He retorts: "'Want' her Jane? We wouldn't *take* her" (243).

(Chapter 30) Attempting to pass off Edward's faux pas as a joke, Mrs. Brook endeavors to rally her position. The deliberate nature of her public exposure of the issue is underscored by Longdon's repeated request that this topic be preserved for a "private half hour" they have previously arranged (244). She turns to provoking Mitchy by drawing attention to the fact that his wife is playing a flirtatious game of hide-and-seek with Petherton and the French book in the next room. The couple rejoins the group, still with the book, and Mr. Brook draws attention to Van's name on it in Nanda's hand. She turns to challenge her daughter on having read it. After an attempt at denial, the girl is forced to confess that she has. Exit Longdon.

Book 9. Vanderbank

(Chapter 31) Some months later, Van visits Mrs. Brook and Nanda. Meeting with the mother first, they discuss the collapse of the circle, which Van blames on her behavior at Tishy's party. He asks her for further news of the group, and she directs him to ask Nanda, who is now meeting her own circle in her own drawing room, which includes Mr. Cashmore. Exit Van.

(Chapter 32) Enter Edward, who has just been with Nanda. Mrs. Brook realizes this means Van has left without seeing the girl after all. On hearing that Longdon is due later, she asks him to tell their daughter of Van's change of heart, insisting he should do so before Longdon arrives. They both know she will see it as a sign of his having given her up, and Mrs. Brook expects the knowledge will secure her to Longdon. Exit Edward. Enter Mitchy.

(Chapter 33) On hearing of what has just occurred, Mitchy also insists that Van's actions are a direct result of Mrs. Brook's machinations. She asks him to inform Longdon, who has just arrived and is waiting in another room, of Van's retreat, admitting in the process that she believes Van now hates her. Exit Mrs. Brook. Enter Longdon.

(Chapter 34) Longdon and Mitchy discuss the affair, agreeing that it was at Tishy's that Nanda was finally and fully "spoiled" for Van (279). They discuss their continued liking for him, despite all. Exit Longdon.

Book 10. Nanda

(Chapter 35) Two weeks later, Van visits Nanda in her room in response to a note he has received from her. He babbles nervously while she sits still and then gets up to leave almost immediately. Nanda realizes they have "changed places" and "that it is he—not she—who should be let down easily" (286).

(Chapter 36) Stalling his exit, she asks him to make up to her mother and not abandon her, as he seems to have done. He agrees, but he asks her in return to make a "bargain" with him by apologizing for him to Longdon for having "been a brute" (292). Exit Van.

(Chapter 37) Enter Mitchy. They talk of Van's visit, and Nanda also asks him to continue visiting her mother, who has taken up Aggie as her latest study. Nanda restates their differences: Aggie kept in such perfect ignorance and innocence that she can only now begin to learn who she is and herself as someone who knows everything. Exit Mitchy.

(Chapter 38) Enter a nervous Longdon, who has given her a few days to reply to his proposal to live with him permanently. They discuss Van's visit, and Longdon is both shocked at his behavior and deeply sympathetic to Nanda's loss. She denies she is in love with him and then bursts into tears. He hears her consent to his proposal. She insists he must accept her for who she is. They admit that Van should have married Aggie, but Nanda still insists that, even then, she would never have married Mitchy. Exit Longdon till "tomorrow."

CRITICAL ANALYSIS

Contrary to his usual verbosity, James is reported to have had one short word to describe the reception of *The Awkward Age* when it was first published in book form in 1899: "flat" (Clarke 300). Most of the early reviews concurred that there was some-

thing terribly sordid going on in this novel, with one describing it as a "delineation of the detestable," comprising a "whispering gallery of ignoble souls," and another accusing James of having "done a delicate thing to death" (Clarke 265, 274). Critics were uncertain of the intrinsic merits of presenting readers with such a vicious landscape and were even more reluctant to embrace the novel's experimental form, which was based, as James would later outline in his 1908 preface, on the dramatic form of the stage play and of the *roman dialogué* (dialogue novels) developed by French satirists such as Gyp. Its form also reflects James's early efforts, beginning with WHAT MAISIE KNEW (1897), at dictating his works to a stenographer, William McAlpine. James would dictate all his subsequent novels.

Ambivalence has continued to haunt the reception of this novel, strongly dividing those critics who have not simply passed it over entirely. Indeed, one might even say it is a novel haunted by its own subject matter. Critics have often treated the work as something of a transition novel in the trajectory of James's writing career, something like Nanda Brookenham, the girl on the cusp of womanhood who forms its focus. It has been read as representing his emergence from his own professional "awkward age" in the wake of the *Guy Domville* fiasco of 1895; most notably by Leon Edel, who writes of it as signaling the author's readiness to "shed the protective disguises of girlhood that he had assumed" (through characters such as Maisie Farange) and "to take his own shape in his fiction—that of the elderly and fastidious observer of his world" (236). Others have seen it as a kind of practice experiment in form, which would ultimately yield riper fruit in James's final major phase. This is an idea that is central to the Jamesian myth: "'The Master' is born from the death of the playwright" (Kurnick 109).

Similarly, the novel evokes the flatness for which its harshest critics have condemned it. The dominance of dialogue strips it of the more familiar convention of narrative comment used to signal depth. The extent of dialogue forces the reader to work harder in constructing the inner lives of the characters from their verbal exchanges and gestures. Consequently, "[t]he experience James recreates for his readers is . . . less of witnessing a performance than of *reading a play*—one that has not yet been cast with the actors who will give these names and actions bodily density." This reading process is rendered even more difficult through the "complicated notation" of directions and a "descriptive thinness" that makes it a "play marked with the caveat *never to be performed*" (Kurnick 113–114). This point is all the more evident when one considers the fact that a novel James himself likened to a script for a play is not known to have been adapted to the stage or screen.

This dramatic quality has a notable further effect of seeming to distance the characters from their own actions. Susan L. Mizruchi notes how the characters seem to find themselves "blurting out invitations they are conscious of only retrospectively" and "subject to actions toward which they feel no direct motivation" (107). Vanderbank, for example, in his first meeting with Longdon in their shared cab, "*became conscious* of having proposed his own rooms as a wind-up to their drive" (19, emphasis added). It is a device that underscores the vacuity and hypocrisy of the social scene the novel describes, where the appearance of virtue is held in higher esteem than ethical substance. As Mrs. Brook says of the Duchess's careful cultivation of her daughter Aggie's innocence: "Aggie, don't you see? is the Duchess's morality, her virtue: which by having it, that way, outside of you . . . you can make a much better thing of it" (184).

This emphasis on surface over depth also seems to signal an epistemological crisis in British society at the turn of the century. Epistemology, as the theory of how we come to know things, is here driven by the need to interpret increasingly elaborate social codes that are no longer supported by any recognizable social values. As Margaret Walters observes:

> The [eighteen] nineties themselves come to figure as an awkward age, a period in which the forms of the past are less and less relevant to the present realities. Yet because social status is divorced from social function, style from meaning, morality from convention, the outer forms and codes of social behaviour are more and more elaborately articulated. They take on a

life of their own, in which appearance is everything. So many scenes depend for their impact on what it means, say, for a girl to smoke, or to visit a man alone, or to read French novels. And we have to discern further the meaning of that meaning; the fact that in this wholly exploitative society, callous and promiscuous, manners determine respectability. (192)

Consequently, the problematic nature of "knowing" becomes articulated in the convolutions of such observations as: "She knows I know *she* knows" (54) or "I know you know what I've known" (276). Bouncing around with all the frantic chaos of a catapulted pinball, the verb *to know* no longer delivers clarity of knowledge for the reader but instead yields even greater obscurity.

Despite all this talk of who knows and what is known, *The Awkward Age* is also structured around failures of *action*. This is most evident in Van's constant deferral and ultimate retreat from proposing to Nanda. "He won't do it," says Mrs. Brook repeatedly of Van on hearing of Longdon's attempt to secure this end by agreeing to make a financial settlement for Nanda (178). Similarly, Nanda believes herself to be "one of those people who don't. I shall be in the end . . . one of those who haven't" (142).

In addition to these failures to act, there is an even greater problem of how inaction nevertheless generates negative judgments from others. Nanda never *does* anything wrong, as far as we can definitely know, yet she is nevertheless perceived as having been corrupted through her mere association with depraved conversation. Today's reader is left to puzzle over just how corrupting, for example, it can be to read a novel, however salaciously French, which is here presented for the social circle as the final proof of the extent of Nanda's depredation. Does reading about sex equate to the deflowering deed that would, traditionally, make a girl unsuitable for marriage?

If the leap from thought to deed seems somewhat large, one would also have to note that *none* of the seemingly adulterous crew in Mrs. Brook's circle are actually *shown* stepping outside the bounds of propriety. If the novel is something of a script for a play, then it is one in which all the action seems to occur offstage. Cashmore denies there is anything in his liaison with Mrs. Donner; his wife, Lady Cashmore, is always on the verge of running off with her suitor but never does; Mrs. Brook constantly rebuffs allegations that she wants Van for herself; and readers can only guess at the affair between Petherton and the Duchess, and later Aggie herself, through the gossip of others. In a world where surface counts more than substance, allusion and innuendo are sufficient to turn speculation into fact, and inaction consequently becomes subject to as great a degree of suspicion as action.

What is more, the denials of wrongdoing that this gossip provokes from the characters seem to have a reverse effect to their intent. This is demonstrated most cogently in the Duchess's reply to Longdon's question: "What is it [Van] hasn't done with Mrs. Brook?"

> He hasn't done the thing that *would* be a complication. He hasn't gone beyond a certain point. You may ask how one knows such matters, but I'm afraid I've not the receipt for it. A woman knows, but she can't tell. They haven't, as it's called, done anything wrong. (234)

The use of the conditional tense, *would,* which James emphasizes, undercuts the confirmation of their ostensibly innocent relationship with the ever-present possibility of future guilt. They have not done anything wrong *yet.* In addition, even if they never do anything wrong, the erotic charge lent to inaction in sexual relations throughout the novel suggests that even a nonsexual relationship poses as high a threat to any possible marriage between Nanda and Van as an overtly sexual affair. The most powerful relationships are always, in *The Awkward Age,* the ones that are not sexually consummated. Longdon's unsuccessful suit of Lady Julia, or Nanda's insistence that she would prefer to sustain her unrequited love for Van than to accept the compromise of MARRIAGE to Mitchy, or even the final platonic pairing of Nanda and Longdon, are all represented as purer, more "beautiful" romances than the sordid and unhappy relations of actual married or otherwise sexually entangled couples (see, for example, 92 and 210).

For Walter Isle, this "peculiar form of action, in which no one 'does' anything, points to the deepest concern of the novel. James is examining a static social situation in which nothing can be done" (193). It is an observation that supports a large critical consensus that the novel describes a certain sterility and impotence arising from the commodification of SEXUALITY at the turn of the century. For Mizruchi, "The novel's final word, 'tomorrow,' echoes tensely in a society that offers little grounds for generational continuity" (101). Michael Trask has argued that the novel examines "the lapse from the timeless innocence of the nursery to the initiatory rigor of the adult drawing room," which brings with it the need to negotiate "the pressures of a marriage market conspicuously modeled on the futures market" (187). The historical context that each provides to the novel indicates a twofold burden on sexual relationships: the scandal of OSCAR WILDE's trial of 1895 and the increasing popular concern for the "race suicide" of Anglo-Saxon peoples in the late 19th century (Stanley Hall qtd. in Mizruchi 111).

As many others have also observed, the "exposure" of Wilde as a homosexual generated an increased level of suspicion toward even ostensibly celibate men such as James. No longer secure in the previously tolerated public role of the eternal bachelor, the increasingly sexualized climate made it seem as if "any exposure of erotic privacy [was] inevitable stigmatising" (Trask 115). Hence, in *The Awkward Age,* even inaction and denial risk signaling and reinforcing suspicions of perversity. Yet the novel also signals a fundamental problem within the now more tightly policed and heavily romanticized heterosexual relationships; namely, that marriages were neither functioning nor, at least within the elite classes, successfully reproducing the next generation. Furthermore, the anxieties surrounding marriage in *The Awkward Age* reveal the culture's belated awareness of the institution's instability as guarantor of sexual order. Wilde was, after all, Trask adds, "a husband and father" (117). Consequently, as best demonstrated by innocent Aggie's dramatically swift descent into debauchery after her marriage to Mitchy, "marriage is figured as heightening erotic energies and desires" rather than controlling them (Trask 118).

This problem of an obstacle in the path of generational continuity rests not only on the apparent biological sterility of the final pairings but also on the "problem" of childhood itself. *The Awkward Age* develops James's thoughts on the social status of children and the "impossibility" of adult/child relationships (see Honeyman). Indeed, Shine argues that the figure of Nanda represents the culmination of an even more prolonged interest in childhood on James's part, which extends back to his first full-length novel, *Watch and Ward* (first serialized in 1871). *The Awkward Age* in particular, she argues, radically reworks the subject of this early novel about an older man raising an orphaned child to be the perfect wife after having been similarly rebuffed by his first love. The novel also expatriates to England James's insights into the troubling American girl from stories such as "DAISY MILLER: A STUDY" (1878). This interest reaches its peak with *The Awkward Age,* which seems to complete a sequence of stories on childhood beginning with "The AUTHOR OF 'BELTRAFFIO'" (1884) and "The PUPIL" (1891), and developed through *What Maisie Knew* (1897) and "The TURN OF THE SCREW" (1898).

Central to James's studies of childhood was the question of how children come to know anything about the world when faced with the conventional expectation that they remain in splendid, isolated innocence. In *The Awkward Age,* this ideal is figured through little Aggie, who seems to attain the "blankness of mind" that Mrs. Brook believes is a "preposterous fiction" in Nanda's case (*The Awkward Age* 170). Yet Aggie's role as the "real old thing" that "the books [are] full of" proves to be something of a charade as she collapses into debauchery within weeks of her marriage (201). In comparison, the knowledge Nanda gains through "a hundred little chinks of daylight" means that she is conscious of the false performance that this ideal demands of her, and she refuses to acquiesce to it (302). This is also reflected in her resistance to modeling herself on yet another nostalgically idealized figure, Lady Julia. To adapt to these models, she explains to Longdon, would merely "be arranging to keep myself back from you, and so being nasty and underhand, which you naturally don't want, and neither do I" (141).

The hypocritical intolerance to Nanda's impulse to be herself, however apparently flawed, signals an even deeper problem than that of racial and class continuity. For it raises a fundamental question about the roots of this intolerance in nostalgic and moribund fictions: fictions of idealized lost loves long deceased or of beatific, innocent children who have only existed in books. The "sad but loving sterility" of the closing relationship between Longdon and Nanda testifies to James's critical reaction to this impulse (Walters 218). For it challenges the dynamics of what Lee Edelman in *No Future: Queer Theory and the Death Drive* (2004) has called reproductive futurism, as the empty rhetoric of a perpetually deferred future for our children, leaving the question of what *kind* of future they can be expected to have when their actual lives in the present are so agonizingly determined by these fictions.

CHARACTERS

Brookenham, Edward   A stock character of many of James's books, this dignified yet colorless and apparently socially clueless individual is nevertheless a reliable source for unwitting humor in the novel. Ostensibly a minor character, he nevertheless serves the important function of dramatizing the superior wit and intelligence of his wife, Mrs. Brook. He persistently fails to follow her train of thought or catch her allusion. Isle notes him as an acute example of the idea that "the mark of stupidity in the novel is the inability to follow rapid transitions" in conversation (183).

Brookenham, Fernanda (Mrs. Brook)   Forty-one at the start of the novel, she is described as having a trick of seeming young, but there is something of the actress in the account of how "her head, her figure, her flexibility, her flickering color, her lovely, silly, eyes, her natural, quavering tone all played together towards this effect by some trick that had never been exposed." She has the air of "an innocence tragically dimmed," of "disenchanted" boredom, and of "pretty pathos" (40–41).

The Duchess believes her to be negligent and self-interested in her treatment of her daughter, insinuating that she sees the girls as a rival for

Van's affections. However, as Walters notes, she is in fact "always an enigma," and the reader can never be wholly certain of her motives (201). She herself roundly denies any capacity for petty jealousy, and one might also observe that she is raising her daughter to see the world as it really is and not subjecting her to the hypocrisy of a sheltered innocence. As Mizruchi notes, "there is a tension between Mrs. Brook's desire to destroy her daughter and her desire to liberate her from ultimately debilitating social forms" (121). The novel's close finds her somewhat abandoned and isolated by her former social circle, and particularly Van, but successful in preventing Nanda's marriage to him while securing her to Longdon.

Brookenham, Harold The eldest Brookenham child, this dissolute young man lives richly by pilfering from his family, borrowing from everyone in his vast social circle and by presuming on unconfirmed invitations to stay at the homes of wealthy families. By the novel's close, he is described as having made some ill-defined social success and seems to have begun an affair with Lady Fanny Cashmore.

Brookenham, Nanda Nanda is the "innocent and hapless, yet somehow at the same time, dreadfully damaged and depraved daughter" of the Brookenhams (63). For James, she represents the new type of "modern" girl "who is "not a *jeune fille*" and who is "supposed to know" (*Notebooks* 192). Van claims she lacks the "glaring, staring, obvious, knock-down beauty" that London society demands in their unmarried girls (30–32). Longdon, on the other hand, finds her overwhelmingly striking. Her exact age is a matter of some confusion. Vanderbank initially suggests that she is 17 or 18 years old, before settling on "nearly nineteen," but adds that her mother has been artfully saying that she is 16 "for the last year or two" (27–28). In addition, she is elided with her mother through their shared names Nanda/Fernanda (45) and with her grandmother, Lady Jane, in Longdon's recognition of their physical similarities. Much of her stated impetus in the novel is to try to persuade other people to accept her for herself, a demand that only Longdon seems capable of meeting.

She is frequently described as "serious," or even, at one stage, "tragic" (94). Her apparent seriousness is one of her principal points of contrast to Lady Julia, who Longdon claims was always gay (96), and also to the ever-laughing Van. But it is this capacity for composure that proves to be her best defense against the social machinations within which she is caught. Her composure increases in tandem with the growth of her conscience and ultimately grants her the capacity to treat Van generously despite his rejection of her. For Mrs. Brook, Nanda has "become what we had hoped for—an object of compassion still more marked" (228). But she also insists that she now has in Longdon what every woman wants—"a man of her own" (261). Despite the unconventional nature of this pairing, even Nanda admits to the "extraordinary" fact of having found someone who she says is "taking me as I am" (310).

Duchess, the (Jane) Edward Brookenham's cousin, the Duchess, has gained her aristocratic title through her marriage to a Neapolitan duke who has since died. Vanderbank describes her as "invidiously, cruelly foreign" (24), a woman who has "bloomed in the hothouse of her widowhood" (26). Her relentless determination to secure Mitchy as a husband for her former husband's niece, little Aggie, is a powerful example of the ruthlessness of the marriage market. She is an important agent in the novel as the one who first suggests to Longdon that he make a marriage settlement for Nanda and to persuade Van to marry her. Mrs. Brook insists that her great show of protective, maternal virtue toward Aggie is a sham and a smoke screen for her affair with Petherton.

Grendon, Mrs. Tishy Tishy Grendon is one of the many minor characters whose sorry lives feed the Brookenham circle's appetite for salacious gossip. Much of the expressed concern for Nanda's social exposure centers on her close relationship with this unhappily married woman and the opportunity this relationship affords for the girl to meet figures of scandal. A frequent visitor is her sister, Carrie Donner: another unhappily married woman who is believed to be having an affair with Mr. Cashmore and who is apparently jilted by him when he decides to pursue Nanda. The party that proves so catastrophic to Nanda's reputation, and which prompts Van's final and total retreat, is hosted by Tishy.

Julia, Lady While not a character in her own right, Lady Julia has a significant presence in the novel as Mrs. Brook's deceased mother, and, therefore, Nanda's grandmother. Longdon's unrequited love for her is presented as his prime motivation for involving himself in the affairs of the Brookenham set. He is deeply moved by Nanda's physical resemblance to her, despite their dramatic dissimilarity of manner; and he is as equally appalled by the complete lack of any evident inherited traits in Mrs. Brook. Tessa Hadley argues that Lady Julia is an "an icon of unpolluted femininity" who "burdens the living women in the novel" (75).

Little Aggie (Agnesina) A Neapolitan aristocrat, and the Duchess Jane's niece by marriage, Aggie has been raised in seclusion in a convent according to the European aristocratic tradition of the *jeune fille* (young girl). Even though she has just left school and is also of an age to make her social debut in order to marry, the diminutive "little," or even "ickle," precedes her name right up to her marriage to Mitchy (68). Her sheltered existence is persistently contrasted to Nanda's social exposure. Longdon sees them as "lambs": "one with its neck in a pink ribbon [and] no consciousness but that of being fed from the hand with the small sweet biscuit of unobjectionable knowledge, the other struggling with instincts and forebodings, with the suspicion of its doom and the far borne scent, in the flowery fields, of blood" (146). She seems wholly passive as her marriage to Mitchy is arranged for her but seems to fall dramatically into debauchery once this has been achieved.

Longdon, Mr. Longdon retrieves for this novel something of the characteristics of the naïve innocence that James had previously ascribed to the American type. Van's first impression of him is that "he could not look young, [but] he came nearer—strikingly and amusingly—to looking new" (20). Mrs. Brook sees in him a "narrowness" that she

promises to "broaden," and indeed his increased social consciousness proceeds with many crashes, surprises, and shocks. For all the power his fortune grants him, he seems to be a somewhat passive figure. Even at the novel's close he tells Nanda that she "may dance . . . on the passive thing [she's] made of [him]" (304). The only clue to a possible deeper current of strength lies in his response to Mitchy, calling him an observer: "I am not an observer. I am a hater" (83). For all his passivity, Longdon is the principal agent of action in the novel, even though other characters seem to be working on him for their own ends. While he fails to secure Nanda in marriage to Van, he does succeed in removing her from her family's influence through his adoption of her.

Mitchett, Mr. (Mitchy) Mitchy is initially described by the Duchess as "the son of a shoemaker and superlatively hideous" (49). However, he is also nouveau riche, and it is his wealth that prompts the Duchess to pursue him for Aggie. His preference is for Nanda, and he seems to be the only other character apart from Longdon who can accept her for who she is and who is not perturbed by her apparent social exposure. Despite this, she rejects his attentions and persuades him instead to take what proves to be the unhappy course of marrying Aggie. The close of the novel sees him somewhat disenchanted by the experience. But, secured in his friendship with Longdon and Nanda, there is the suggestion that he has made a start on the slow and painful path of moral growth.

Vanderbank, Gustavus (Van) The "Apollo" of the novel, and the principal love interest according to conventions of the heterosexual romance plot, Van is a professional young man of 34 who has risen to the high rank, for one so young, of deputy chairman of the General Audit in the Civil Service (85). The Duchess, while concurring with the general consensus on his universal attractiveness to women, describes him as "awfully conceited and awfully patronizing but clever and well liked," (150), and Mitchy refers to him as one of the privileged "special cases" who is a "source of the sacred terror" (219).

One of James's "men of the world," he is invariably described as laughing, lolling, and leaning back and smoking (157, 147). Yet there are indications that this debonair manner requires considerable effort. He responds to Mrs. Brook's breach of confidence on the matter of Longdon's settlement by "cultivating his detachment" and laughing once more (179). This ostensible composure is shattered significantly by his failure to act on the general wish that he propose to Nanda. In his final conversations with Mrs. Brook and Nanda, he is considerably more restless: He paces "pointlessly" around the parlor; he then greets Nanda with a "superabundance of interest, inattention and movement," and with a laugh that is now described as distinctly "misapplied" (282). Nanda tolerantly sees his distress as indicative of a vanity bent on an unspoken desire for her to give him "the satisfaction in himself which would proceed in his having dealt with a difficult hour in a gallant and delicate way" (286). The final proof of both his enormous charm and capacity to provoke the "sacred terror" is that Nanda does, finally, decide to "let him off" (286).

FURTHER READING

All references are to the Penguin edition of *The Awkward Age*, Harmondsworth, 1987.

Allen, Elizabeth. *A Woman's Place in the Novels of Henry James*. London: Macmillan, 1984.

Anonymous. Review of "The Awkward Age." *The Spectator* (May 1899). In Clarke.

———. Review of "The Awkward Age." *Bookman* (July 1899). In Clarke.

Bender, Todd K. *A Concordance to Henry James's "The Awkward Age."* New York: Garland, 1989.

Clarke, Graham, ed. *Henry James: Critical Assessments. Vol. 2: The Critical Response: Reviews and Early Essays*. East Sussex, England: Helm Information, 1991.

Davidson, Arnold E. "James's Dramatic Method in *The Awkward Age*." *Nineteenth-Century Fiction* 29 (1974): 320–335.

Edel, Leon. *Henry James: The Treacherous Years 1895–1901*. London: Rupert Hart-Davis, 1969.

Edelman, Lee. *No Future: Queer Theory and the Death Drive*. Durham, N.C., and London: Duke University Press, 2004.

Hadley, Tessa. "'The sacred terror': *The Awkward Age* and James's Men of the World." In *Henry James and the Imagination of Pleasure*, 65–189. Cambridge: Cambridge University Press, 2002.

Honeyman, Susan. "What Maisie Knew and the Impossible Representation of Childhood." *Henry James Review* 22, no. 1 (2001): 67–80.

Isle, Walter. *Experiments in Form: Henry James's Later Novels, 1896–1901*. Cambridge, Mass.: Harvard University Press, 1968.

Krook, Dorothea. *The Ordeal of Consciousness*. Cambridge: Cambridge University Press, 1967.

Kurnick, David. "Horrible Impossible: Henry James's Awkward Age." *The Henry James Review* 26, no. 2 (2005): 109–129.

MacCarthy, Desmond. "James's Isolation." *Portraits*. London: Putnam, 1931. In Clarke.

Mizruchi, Susan L. "Reproducing Women in *The Awkward Age*." *Representations* 38 (Spring 1992): 101–130.

Poole, Adrian. "Nanda's Smile: Teaching James and the Sense of Humor." *Henry James Review* 25, no. 1 (2004): 4–18.

Shine, Muriel G. *The Fictional Children of Henry James*. Chapel Hill: University of North Carolina Press, 1969.

Trask, Michael. "Getting into it with James: Substitution and Erotic Reversal in *The Awkward Age*." *American Literature* 69, no. 1 (1997): 105–138.

Walters, Margaret. "Keeping the Place Tidy for Young Female Minds: *The Awkward Age*." In *The Air of Reality: New Essays on Henry James*, edited by John Goode, 190–218. London: Methuen, 1972.

Wiesenfarth, Joseph. *Henry James and the Dramatic Analogy: A Study of the Major Novels of the Middle Period*. New York: Fordham University Press, 1963.

Williams, Merle A. "Henry James and the Redefinition of 'Awkward' Concepts through Fiction." *Henry James Review* 18, no. 3 (1997): 258–264.

Maeve Pearson, *University of London*

The Bostonians (1886)

After many delays and the death of his father in 1882, Henry James finally began writing *The*

Bostonians in 1884. It first appeared in *Century Magazine* in 13 installments, from February 1885 to February 1886. When the initial publisher J. R. Osgood went bankrupt, Macmillan published the book in both England and United States in 1886. James did not include *The Bostonians* in the NEW YORK EDITION, nor did he ever revise it.

SYNOPSIS

Book First

(Chapter 1) The novel is set in Boston in the late 1870s and opens in the drawing room of Olive Chancellor's Charles Street house, where her widowed sister, Mrs. Adeline Luna, entertains Basil Ransom, their poor but handsome cousin from Mississippi. As he has not yet met Olive, Basil is somewhat anxious for her to appear. Mrs. Luna has just returned from Europe and, like Basil, now lives in NEW YORK, where he works in the courts. She warns Basil that Olive is a radical reformer. When Olive finally comes down, Mrs. Luna leaves for a theater party.

(Chapter 2) Basil can see that Olive is not at all like her attractive and frivolous sister: Olive is exceedingly reserved, serious to the point of morbidity, and not the kind of woman he likes. He sees Olive as a tragic figure and feels sorry for her. Despite having lost her only two brothers in the CIVIL WAR, Olive is fascinated by Basil, who fought to defend the South. As slave owners, Basil's family was ruined, so at nearly 30, he moved to New York to study law. Out of a sense of family duty, Olive wrote to him, asking him to visit. Envious of Basil's having sacrificed everything for a cause, Olive secretly hopes he will respond to the challenge she represents.

(Chapter 3) While Olive gives instructions to the cook, Basil admires the view of the Back Bay and the books, photographs, and watercolors in Olive's drawing room. He grasps that she is a wealthy and cultured young woman, but during dinner he realizes that despite being younger, Olive is a kind of modern-day spinster. After dinner, Olive announces that she is planning to attend a gathering and asks Basil if he would like to accompany her. She explains that a talk on the emancipation of women will be given at the home of the cele-

brated Miss Birdseye, one of the early abolitionists, then teases Basil that he might not like it, which of course piques his interest. (See WOMEN'S ISSUES.) As they prepare to leave, Olive regrets having invited Basil, who is now determined to go.

(Chapter 4) They arrive early, and Olive introduces Basil to the aging Miss Birdseye, whose glory faded with the Civil War. Olives explains that Basil wishes to hear Mrs. Farrinder, who is to lecture on temperance and the vote for women. Miss Birdseye's apartment gradually fills with women and a few working-class men. The mesmeric healer, Selah Tarrant, his wife, and their beautiful red-haired daughter also arrive.

(Chapter 5) A commanding figure, Mrs. Farrinder urges Olive to recruit some working women from the Back Bay. Despite wanting to dedicate herself to the cause, Olive cringes at the suggestion, claiming she could not possibly talk to these women as she is too inarticulate. Inspired by the idea of a contribution, Olive agrees to give money instead.

(Chapter 6) Seeing that Basil is alone, Miss Birdseye introduces him to her downstairs neighbor, Dr. Prance, an independent woman who is a hard-working medical practitioner. Dr. Prance explains who the other guests are, pointing out the journalist Matthias Pardon, who has brought Dr. Tarrant, whom she dislikes because she has had to treat the women he failed to heal with his mesmerism. She informs Basil that Verena, Tarrant's only child, is supposed to be gifted. Basil wishes his cousin was as attractive as Verena. Meanwhile, Mrs. Farrinder declares that she cannot speak as she needs some opposition to stimulate her, so Olive mentions Basil. Mrs. Tarrant suggests that Verena replace the speaker.

(Chapter 7) Olive introduces Basil to Mrs. Farrinder, who asks if he would like to report on the conditions of the South, but Basil begs off. Mr. Pardon steps in to introduce Verena, who gushes over the celebrated spokeswoman, while Mr. Pardon explains to Olive that Verena has already made a name for herself as an inspirational speaker in the West. Miss Birdseye prepares the crowd for the new speaker, and Mrs. Farrinder, who is suddenly put off by the unsavory appearance of Verena's parents, curtly introduces her.

(Chapter 8) Verena sits down in front of her father, who places his hands on her head to provide a channel so that the inspiration can flow. She closes her eyes, and her father begins to assure her that the spirit will come. Although Basil finds Verena pretty, he, too, is repulsed by her father, whom he regards as a "carpet-bagger" (46). Finally, Verena stands up and begins to speak, haltingly at first, as if straining to hear a distant messenger, but she gradually gains confidence and speaks movingly on the oppression of women and the subsequent promise of the women's movement. Verena succeeds in winning over the audience, especially Olive. Everyone agrees that she is gifted. Basil, however, is more impressed by her lovely voice than by her words: He finds her irresistible.

(Chapter 9) Basil joins Mrs. Farrinder and Olive, who is so affected that she is speechless. As Mrs. Farrinder praises Verena, Basil suspects that she plans to exploit the girl. Miss Birdseye asks Mrs. Farrinder to say a few words, and Basil then asks Miss Birdseye to introduce him to Verena. Pleased that he has enjoyed her talk, Miss Birdseye consents, but Olive interrupts, claiming that she is unwell and must leave immediately. Glaring at Basil, she demands that he see her out, so they head toward the door. Before leaving, Olive rushes over to Verena and begs her to visit. As soon as she agrees, Olive whisks Basil away. Once outside, she jumps into the waiting carriage and leaves Basil on the street. He considers going back inside but decides to go for a drink instead.

(Chapter 10) Urged by her mother, who is keenly aware of the social advantages Miss Chancellor can provide, Verena promptly goes to see Olive at her Charles Street home.

(Chapter 11) Olive enthusiastically embraces her new and gifted friend. With her bohemian appearance, Verena represents one of the common folk Olive has longed to know; more important, Verena's speech has so touched Olive that she sees in Verena the soul mate she has been seeking. When Olive asks Verena to come and live with her, Verena naively thinks that this is how wealthy people behave. She simply tells Olive that she must stay with her parents and continue her work, but Olive has grander plans: She wants to be Verena's savior

and protector, and to cultivate her extraordinary talent. Verena tells Olive about her life and the various lectures she has attended with her parents, ranging in topic from miracle cures to new religions to free love, making Olive's desire to rescue Verena all the more intense. When Olive asks Verena how she arrived at such a profound understanding of the suffering of women, Verena responds that, like Joan of Arc, her source was divine. Olive tells Verena that wherever her knowledge came from, she shares the exact same sentiments. Then Olive asks her to swear that the only thing in the world she cares for is the "redemption of women" (67) and that she is willing to give her life to the cause. Verena insists that she wants "to do something great" (68), so Olive assures her that they will work together. At that moment, the maid announces a gentleman caller.

(Chapter 12) Verena recognizes Basil, who is evidently pleased to see her. Thinking it only proper, she gets up to leave. Olive does not introduce her guests but stares angrily at Basil, who mockingly begs Verena to forgive him for being a man. Although she laughs, she can see that Olive is not amused. After getting Verena to sit down again, Basil asks her if she really believes all the nonsense she said the night before. Surprised that Basil does not believe in their cause, Verena nevertheless enjoys the lively exchange that follows, but realizing that Olive does not approve, Verena decides she had better leave. Basil remarks that he would like to see her again, so Verena invites him to visit at her home in CAMBRIDGE. Taking her arm, Olive sees Verena out. While waiting for Olive, Mrs. Luna enters from outside and is surprised to find Basil there. She teasingly asks how he is getting on with her difficult sister. When Olive comes back, Adeline wants to know who Verena is. Basil asks if Olive intends to make her into a public speaker, and they exchange words. Mrs. Luna ushers Basil out. As he is leaving Boston the next day, she is pleased with the idea of having him to herself in New York.

(Chapter 13) Mrs. Tarrant is delighted by the relationship developing between her daughter and Olive. At first, Verena went to see Olive in response to her mother's urging, but after a month,

Verena has really taken to Olive, who cares only about the emancipation of women. Because Olive is too afraid to speak in public, Verena is to be Olive's eloquent mouthpiece. Verena's father is less concerned with the material advantages Olive Chancellor represents than with the promise of publicity his daughter's speeches will bring. To become a celebrity means more to him than anything.

(Chapter 14) Since Olive has not visited Verena at her home in Cambridge, Mrs. Tarrant decides to call on Olive. Besides wanting to see the interior of Olive's home, Mrs. Tarrant also hopes to meet the fashionable and worldly Mrs. Luna, whom Verena has described in fascinating detail. Initially, Verena would have preferred emulating Olive's sister; Olive, however, would like to separate Verena from her deplorable parents. First Olive must go to the Tarrants' for tea. Matthias Pardon has also been invited.

(Chapter 15) Selah Tarrant is on his best behavior. He expresses hope for another evening at Miss Birdseye's, cautiously emphasizing that it is not to promote his daughter but because he values the exchange of new ideas. Taking in the shabby surroundings, Olive concludes that Selah would accept money in exchange for his daughter, although Verena would never desert her parents despite their being "so trashy" (90). Olive wonders how such parents could produce a "gifted being" (90). Whereas Matthias Pardon does not present much of a threat to Olive, she regards the two young Harvard law students who join them with suspicion and worries that Verena might be interested in MARRIAGE. One of the young men, Henry Burrage, is a very rich New Yorker. Olive understands that this social set views Verena as an amusing plaything. Olive is sure that Verena, who has "the consummate innocence of the American girl" (95), is unaware of their insulting attitude.

(Chapter 16) Matthias Pardon sits beside Olive and asks her if she reads magazines. As a successful journalist, Matthias embraces publicity: "everything and every one were one's business" (96). Verena's father thinks Matthias would make an excellent match for his daughter, as he could manage every aspect of her speaking career. Matthias does not understand why Olive is not promoting Verena

more energetically and hopes Olive is not going to hold Verena back. He suggests that Verena lecture in the Boston Music Hall and that she get rid of her father, who only detracts from her performance. Olive is appalled to discover that the two young men Verena has been chatting with now want her to speak. Verena rushes over to Olive, declaring she will speak only if Olive wants her to. Olive suggests that Verena save herself for a more worthy audience. After leaving, Olive draws Verena close to her and begs Verena to promise "not to marry" (105). The group follows them out, so Olive rushes to her carriage. Later, when Selah and his wife have gone to bed, Verena talks with Matthias alone. She realizes he would like to marry her, but she is not attracted to him, so she concludes that it will be easy to make such a promise to Olive.

(Chapter 17) The next time she visits Olive, Verena tells her that she is ready to make the promise. To her surprise, Olive now thinks it is too soon. She lectures Verena on how men cannot possibly understand what she and Verena are trying to accomplish. Although she claims that Verena must be free to learn from her own experience, Olive still wants to be assured that Verena will not let her down. Verena, who longs to please Olive, promises she will not marry any of the young men who were guests at her home. Olive finally suggests that Verena promise not to marry anyone she does not like, mainly because Olive cannot think of any men whom she likes.

Later, Matthias Pardon visits Olive at her home. He wants to know what she intends to do with Verena. He thinks that Verena has improved and finds her "brilliant," the most "attractive female speaker" in America (110). He warns Olive that she should present Verena to the public now or risk losing her. He then proposes they manage Verena together. Matthias claims that he is not after money; rather, he wants to make history. Olive is revolted by the idea of women owing their emancipation to a man.

(Chapter 18) A week later, Verena happily reports to Olive that Matthias promised to make her famous if she married him, but she has turned him down. When Olive asks Verena if she considers fame to be the measure of success, Verena mimics her, stating that changing the law for women is what is needed. Because Olive understands how much Verena is giving up by refusing Matthias, Olive is reassured. However, Henry Burrage has been visiting Verena in Cambridge and has asked her to come and see his art collection. Verena asks Olive to accompany her, but Olive suggests that Mrs. Tarrant go with her daughter instead. They go, and Verena's mother is terribly impressed, as is Verena, but Olive warns her to the effect that "[t]aste and art were good when they enlarged the mind, not when they narrowed it" (117). Upon receiving a personal invitation, Olive goes with Verena to visit Mr. Burrage and his mother. Verena depends on Olive's approval, but ironically Olive cannot find fault with the young man. Before leaving, Mrs. Burrage asks Verena to visit her in New York. Later, at Olive's home, Verena says how she wishes it were always so easy to get along with men and to forget about the vote for women. Olive replies that, on the contrary, she cannot forget about the situation of women; it feels like "a stain that is on one's honour" (121). Once again Verena comes round to Olive's view. Suddenly inspired, they imagine how they will uphold the great cause—together.

(Chapter 19) This ecstatic vision of triumph keeps Olive going all winter. Around Christmas, Olive secretly makes a financial arrangement with Verena's father, permitting her to live with Olive for a year. In the meantime, Mrs. Luna has settled in New York and is planning to hire Basil to look after her legal affairs. Olive wishes they would marry, as she thinks it fitting that her frivolous sister should form a union with the enemy, a southerner who would treat her like a slave. Olive is also relieved that Mrs. Farrinder is off touring the country, as their relationship became quite strained due to petty differences, jealousy, and competitiveness.

(Chapter 20) As Verena remains free to visit her parents, she has promised to live with Olive for as long as it takes to develop her gift. Verena is now passionate about her involvement with the woman's movement, so Olive does not object to Henry Burrage's regular visits. By March, however, Henry begins asking Verena to marry him, but she assures Olive that she will not. To be safe, Olive decides that they will go to Europe for a year in the spring. Besides studying the history of women's oppression,

they spend a lot of time with the aging Miss Birdseye. Olive sees her as "the last link" in "the heroic age of New England life" and is inspired by her faith (139). Before their departure, Olive and Verena attend another of Miss Birdseye's gatherings; this time Verena speaks on her own, without the aid of her father or Mrs. Farrinder, and is more brilliant than ever. In private, Olive has also become quite eloquent in her mastery of the subject.

Book Second

(Chapter 21) A year later, Basil Ransom is living in a shabby boardinghouse in New York. Despite his hard work, he has not succeeded in establishing his career. Because he is so interested in social, economic, and philosophical issues, Basil wonders if law was the right choice. He begins submitting articles to various magazines, but his pieces are all rejected, one editor remarking that Ransom's "doctrines were about three hundred years behind the age" (148). Soon after, Basil receives a note from Mrs. Luna, asking him to visit her, which he does. Since Mrs. Luna's affairs are managed by her legal guardians, Basil can do nothing with them, so he agrees to tutor her son. Unfortunately, Newton proves "insufferable" (150). Basil finds the obligation Mrs. Luna's generosity entails intolerable, so he resigns.

(Chapter 22) A few months later, while Basil is visiting Mrs. Luna, he learns that Olive has returned from Europe and is in Boston with Verena. Because of his desperate situation, Basil considered asking Mrs. Luna to marry him, but the thought of Verena inspires him with renewed hope.

(Chapter 23) Three weeks later, after being summoned to Boston by a former client, Basil decides to visit Mrs. Tarrant in the hope that Verena will be there. On his way to Cambridge, Basil passes in front of Olive's house on Charles Street. Suddenly, Miss Birdseye comes out and signals an approaching omnibus, so Basil quickly offers to see her home. Basil learns that Verena will be visiting her parents that very evening. Miss Birdseye also provides Basil with the name of the street on which the Tarrants live. When Basil asks Miss Birdseye not to mention to Olive that she has seen him, she is taken aback; he then pleads that he is a potential convert, so Miss Birdseye reluctantly agrees.

(Chapter 24) Basil goes directly to the Tarrants' home to see Verena. As he waits in the parlor, Basil takes in the shabbiness of the interior, but when Verena finally comes down, she is even more radiant than he remembers. Although it has been more than a year since Verena invited him, she greets Basil warmly. He disingenuously asks her if she still speaks and says he would very much like to hear her again. As Verena tells Basil about the advances the women's movement has made in Europe, Basil is stunned by her eloquence. When it comes out that he is not going to visit Olive, he admits that he has not been won over to the cause of women. Knowing how much it will upset Olive, Verena worries about telling her of Basil's visit. When she comments on the suffering of women, Basil interrupts, arguing that it is all humanity that suffers and that women's purpose in life is to ease the suffering of men. Not knowing how to respond, Verena offers to give Basil a tour of the university grounds. Although Verena does not know how she will keep this from Olive, she prepares to go out.

(Chapter 25) As they make their way to Harvard, Basil asks Verena if she enjoyed the women's convention the year before. When Verena questions his interest in the progress of the women's movement, Basil admits to fearing it greatly: He thinks Verena is being "ruined" by the company she keeps; instead, she should "make some honest man happy" (186). Upon reaching Harvard Yard, Verena shows Basil the local monuments. Despite its painful association, Basil is drawn to the majestic structure of Memorial Hall, built to honor the Harvard students and graduates who fought for the Union side in the Civil War. Verena argues that it is wrong to build such a beautiful monument to glorify war; in contrast, women will "usher in the reign of peace" (189). When Verena urges Basil to visit Olive, he balks, suggesting that she need not know about their time together. Basil says it is up to her, but he pointedly adds that it will only upset Olive if Verena tells her. Privately, Basil thinks that it will be a minor triumph for him if Verena keeps it from Olive. Verena curtly insists that if she does keep it to herself, "there mustn't be anything more" between them (191). They part ways, leaving Basil wondering how he will find out

whether she tells Olive or not, but then he thinks of Mrs. Luna.

(Chapter 26) Back in New York, Basil receives a written invitation to hear Verena speak at Mrs. Burrage's home. He goes, imagining that he is going to rescue Verena from her ruin. At first, Basil does not recognize anyone but presently he spots Olive, who is sitting by herself, looking terribly uncomfortable. He sits down beside her. When Olive asks Basil what he knows about the speaker, Miss Tarrant, Basil worries that Verena has told Olive about their meeting. Basil reminds Olive that he heard Verena speak at Miss Birdseye's. He is relieved when Olive exclaims that Verena has improved much since then, suggesting to Basil that Verena has said nothing. Henry Burrage comes over to escort Olive to her seat at the front of the room where Verena will lecture. As all the chairs have been taken, Basil remains at the back, where Mrs. Luna joins him.

(Chapter 27) When Basil offers to help Mrs. Luna find a seat, she pulls him back in order to speak to him. Although Basil does not want to miss any of Verena's talk, his southern manners oblige him to follow Mrs. Luna, who is delighted to have him all to herself. Basil is pleased to be informed about the details of Verena's visit to New York: She is to be a guest of Mrs. Burrage while Olive returns to Boston. Mrs. Luna explains how Mrs. Burrage's son wants to marry Verena. When Basil hears Verena begin her talk in the next room, Mrs. Luna succeeds in detaining him when she asks how he obtained his invitation. After determining that she has heard nothing of his meeting with Verena, Basil finally gets up. Suddenly, much applause and cheering can be heard, so he quickly excuses himself despite Mrs. Luna's angry protestations.

(Chapter 28) Basil finds a place to stand behind the crowd from where he can see Verena. In contrast to her performance at Miss Birdseye's, Verena is now "in perfect possession of her faculties, her subject, her audience" (205). Like everyone else, Basil is enthralled. For Verena, the equality of women holds the promise of redemption and the world transformed. Basil realizes he has fallen in love with her. He thinks she is meant for better things than public speaking "—for privacy, for him, for love" (209). As the people file out, Basil is carried along toward the buffet table and sees Verena being led out by Henry. All eyes are on her as the crowd makes room for them to pass. As a couple, Verena and Henry form the picture of success, and Basil realizes that Henry probably wants to marry her. Spotting Basil, Verena graciously extends her hand, asking if he agrees with the new truth. When he says he does not, she jokingly complains to Henry that Basil is her hardest convert. While Henry goes off to get Verena some water, Basil tells her he is convinced she will change her mind about the movement. Verena hopes he will not tell this to Miss Birdseye, who has come to believe that Basil will champion their cause. When Henry returns with a rich and well-known philanthropist, Basil moves away, suddenly feeling very insignificant. He considers going home and looks for Mrs. Burrage, whom he must duly thank. He finds her sitting with Olive, who is not pleased to see Basil again. After thanking Mrs. Burrage, she moves away. Basil asks Olive where they are staying, so she asks why he wants to see Verena when he is not in sympathy with their cause. Basil insists he merely wants to thank Verena, adding that he can get the address from her, so Olive reluctantly gives it to him.

(Chapter 29) The next morning, Mrs. Luna visits her sister at the boardinghouse. She wants to know if Olive invited Basil to Mrs. Burrage's. Taken aback, Olive admits she thought her sister had invited him. Adeline suggests that Verena must have done so and goes on to say that the night before she received the distinct impression that Basil had developed a serious interest in Verena, adding that Mrs. Burrage could not possibly have sent him an invitation as she did not know his address. Olive senses danger but maintains her reserve. She fully understands that her sister has been rebuffed by Basil and wants revenge, but Olive prefers to handle the situation on her own.

(Chapter 30) As Verena is out with Mr. Burrage, Olive returns to her room alone. She prepares to keep Verena busy all afternoon so there will be no time left for Basil, who will undoubtedly call. Olive then considers asking Verena to return to Boston the very next morning. Verena already gave up the plan of staying on at Mrs. Burrage's

for a few extra days when she saw how this worried Olive.

Before lunch, Verena goes to Olive's room to tell her about the wonderful time she had with Henry. Now Olive worries that he is still interested in marrying Verena. Even worse, Olive sees that Verena enjoys the company of men. Olive asks how Mrs. Burrage came to invite Basil Ransom, and Verena replies that she suggested he be sent an invitation when Mrs. Burrage asked her if there were any friends she would like to include. Olive then wants to know *why* Verena invited him. When she replies that it was because he is "so awfully opposed" to the movement (224), Olive wants to know how Verena knows that. Exasperated, Verena exclaims that one can "tell from his appearance! He's the type of the reactionary" (224). Olive begs Verena to leave him alone but then wants to know how she knew his address. Verena lies. She tells Olive he had written to her, but only once. As they go down to lunch, Verena puts her arm around Olive and feels her trembling.

After lunch, they go on their scheduled round of visits. It seems that everyone in New York wants to meet these two Bostonians. Olive is anxious to go home. Verena tells Olive they can leave New York the very next morning; after all, they are still going to dine at Delmonico's and then go to the opera, Wagner's *Lohengrin.*

(Chapter 31) When they get back to the boardinghouse, Verena goes in ahead of Olive and finds two notes lying on the hall table, one for each of them. Verena quickly takes hers and goes up to her room; however, on their way to dinner, she decides to tell Olive about it. This time, Olive insists that it is not her business, but Verena insists she must tell her: Basil wants to see Verena in the morning. When Olive snidely suggests Verena can arrange to see him on the train home, Verena is shocked by her bitterness. That evening at dinner, Olive watches Henry Burrage very closely. When they return to their lodging, Olive draws Verena into her room to show her the letter Olive received earlier from Mrs. Burrage. She wants them to stay in New York and has asked Olive to come to her home the following day so that they can talk privately. Olive thinks she ought to go and asks Verena if she will now consent to their staying a little longer. Verena gaily replies that she will stay as long as Olive wants her to. Then Olive asks if Verena will be spending much time with Basil, so Verena finally loses patience and wants to know why Olive cannot trust her. Verena tells Olive that her suspicious nature is poisoning their relationship.

(Chapter 32) The next day at noon, on her way out to visit Mrs. Burrage, Olive sees Basil, who was expected at 11, alone with Verena in the parlor. At Mrs. Burrage's, Olive considers the large check that Mrs. Burrage gave to Verena for her talk. Olive asks Mrs. Burrage why she wants Verena to stay with her. Of course, Henry still wants to marry Verena, so Mrs. Burrage tries to assure Olive that both she and her son are dedicated to the movement, pointing out that much would be gained from such a union. When Mrs. Burrage asks Olive for her consent, Olive replies that it is entirely up to Verena. Considering all the financial advantages that the Burrages can provide, Olive begins to feel threatened and suggests that Mrs. Burrage meet Verena's parents. Olive remarks that Mrs. Burrage obviously does not understand the bond between Olive and Verena. When Mrs. Burrage suggests that other men may pose a more serious threat, Olive gets up, demanding to know to whom Mrs. Burrage is referring. Although she had not meant anyone in particular, Mrs. Burrage remembers Basil. She also stands and asks Olive how she intends to keep such a charming young woman for herself. When Mrs. Burrage points out that Verena would be much better off with her son than with any other man, Olive is devastated.

Once outside, Olive considers how Verena might be protected from Basil if she stays with the Burrages. What Olive really fears is that Verena will be taken in by them. When Olive reaches Washington Square, she sits down on a bench to think the matter over. After an hour, she realizes that Basil is a greater threat. Olive heads back to the boardinghouse, only to find that Verena has gone out with Basil.

(Chapter 33) Realizing he cannot have Verena, Basil resolves to spend the day with her and then to let her go. He insists that the least he can do for her is show her Central Park, just as she showed him

Harvard. Verena does not want to go but consents as she thinks it the best way to get rid of him. They take the elevated railway to the park, and Verena begins to enjoy herself, forgetting about Olive. Soon, however, Verena tires of Basil's relentless opposition to the country's institutions and "the tendencies of the age" (254). Eventually, Verena stops contradicting him and submits to his powerful will; she lingers on with him even as she worries about Olive, who must now be sick with worry. Verena tells herself that this will be the last time that she sees Basil.

(Chapter 34) Basil thinks that his ideas represent "the slumbering instincts of an important minority" (256) and admits that he would like to be president. In view of his ambition, Verena is surprised to learn that he has not been successful. When Verena suggests he write about his ideas, Basil admits of being unable to find a publisher. Verena realizes that she will never be able to convert such a man. Inwardly, she recoils, yet she presses on, wanting to know where women fit into Basil's scheme of things. At home, not in public, Basil shoots back. He then accuses Verena of not really believing in what she preaches, maintaining that she did it first to please her father and now to please Olive. Pained by this truth, Verena turns away, heading down the path. When Basil catches up to her, she accuses him of not believing in her abilities, but he disarms her by saying she has genius. As they leave the park, Verena insists on going by herself. Despite protesting, Basil does not go after her.

When Verena finally gets back to the boardinghouse, she finds Olive waiting for her "with a face sufficiently terrible" (266). Verena quickly tells Olive everything that happened and wants to know the outcome of Olive's visit with Mrs. Burrage. When Olive tells her that the Burrages "are devoted to the cause, and that New York will be at [her] feet" (266), Verena declares she will not go to them and breaks down sobbing.

Book Third

(Chapter 35) It is now August, and Basil has traveled by train to Marmion on Cape Cod to catch up with the vacationing Bostonians; he has also resolved "to take possession of Verena" (272).

After dinner at his small hotel, Basil walks around the scattered village and meets Dr. Prance, who is out admiring the night sky. Dr. Prance is visiting Miss Chancellor and agrees to show Basil her cottage. The elderly Miss Birdseye is also staying there to rest as her health fails. Basil appreciates that Dr. Prance does not ask why he has come to Marmion, and she readily agrees not to mention having seen him. Before parting ways, Dr. Prance adds that she hopes Miss Birdseye will live to hear Miss Tarrant speak at the Boston Music Hall.

(Chapter 36) The following morning, Basil goes to the cottage, hoping to find Verena alone. The door is wide open, so after knocking, he goes inside. He finds Miss Birdseye dozing on the veranda and sits down beside her. When she wakes up to take her medicine, she is glad that Basil has come to see Olive. Basil tells her that he has actually come to see Verena, and Miss Birdseye assumes he has been converted. Presently, Olive and Verena come back from the post office. Olive is horrified to see Basil, and Verena blushes deeply. When Basil explains that he has come for a much needed holiday and intends to stay for three or four weeks, Olive runs into the house. Basil asks Verena to walk with him, so he can speak to her alone. She silently pleads with him, and he interprets her fear as a sign that he has triumphed over her. Basil requests 10 minutes, so they head off toward the water. He can hardly wait to tell Verena that he has had one of his most important articles published in the *Rational Review*. Verena goes back to the house, anticipating a terrible scene. She finds Olive in her room, seated in a chair by the window. Verena gets down on her knees and takes Olive's hands, confessing to her about the time Basil came to see her in Cambridge. After admitting that she enjoyed it very much, Verena adds that she was afraid to tell Olive because it would upset her—but now Verena wants Olive to know everything: Basil has asked Verena to marry him. At first, Olive remains silent, then demands to know exactly what there is between Verena and Basil. Verena breaks down and begs Olive to help her. When Olive suggests they go back to Boston immediately, Verena does not see how running away again will help. Olive urges Verena to be honest and to tell Basil that she loves

him, but Verena does not know how she can love a man who wants her to give up everything. Verena declares that she must meet with him and overcome the challenge he poses. Bursting into tears, Olive begs Verena not to desert her.

(Chapter 37) As the weeks pass, Basil begins to worry he will not be able to win Verena over to his way of thinking. On her part, Olive is scared that she will not be able to prevent Verena from falling in love with Basil. Of course, Olive cannot believe Basil really loves Verena; rather Olive fears he wants "to crush her, to kill her" by silencing her magical voice (295). In short, Olive understands that he desires Verena for the satisfaction of having her submit to his will, this being the "consummate proof of the fickleness, the futility, the predestined servility, of women" (295). Although Verena spends only an hour a day walking with Basil, both she and Olive spend the entire time in torment.

(Chapter 38) Basil succeeds in converting Verena to her "genuine vocation" (299). Verena's passion has shifted to Basil, but she cannot bring herself to tell Olive, whom she now pities. She also feels that she has let Olive down. Upon learning that Verena is to go on a nationwide tour after speaking on "A Woman's Reason" at the Music Hall, Basil determines to prevent her talk. For Basil, victory lies in stopping her.

One evening when Basil escorts Verena back to the house, they find Dr. Prance waiting outside with the news that Miss Birdseye is dying and wishes to see both Verena and Basil. They find Miss Birdseye on the veranda with Olive, who moves away. Miss Birdseye clings to the belief that Verena has brought the handsome southerner around, an idea that inspires the old abolitionist with hope for the future. She is pleased with the progress women have made and insists that Verena and Olive will live on to see "justice done" (311). Verena is deeply ashamed of herself.

(Chapter 39) The next morning, Basil meets Dr. Prance in the village and learns that Miss Birdseye passed away peacefully. Verena sends Basil a message saying she cannot see him for the next few days and asks him to leave, so he decides to visit Provincetown. Before returning to Marmion, Basil sends Verena a note, requesting to meet with her the following morning. When he sees her, she looks "graver than she had ever been before" (315). Verena tells him that she has thought everything over: Their marriage is simply not possible. As the 10 minutes Verena intended to spend with Basil stretch into a full day, Olive wanders along the shore, feeling it to be the saddest day of her life. She knows that Verena loves Basil and can no longer be trusted, yet Olive pities Verena and so reserves her loathing for Basil, "the author of their common misery" (317). As the afternoon fades, Olive begins to fear they have had an accident. However, when Olive returns to her cottage at nightfall, she finds Verena alone in the darkened parlor, looking "crushed and humbled" (321). The next morning when Basil calls, Olive tells him it will not be possible to see Verena, who has already left.

(Chapter 40) Back in Boston, Basil goes to Olive's house, where he is received somewhat contemptuously by Mrs. Luna. He wants to know where he can find Verena, who is scheduled to speak that very night. Even though Verena's name is posted all over the city, Mrs. Luna has no idea where she is. Matthias Pardon arrives, but all he knows is that Olive promised that Verena will speak on time. Basil leaves.

(Chapter 41) Basil spends the next two hours restlessly walking about, passing in front of the Music Hall over and over again and imagining that he will wrest Verena "from the mighty multitude" (333). Half an hour before her talk is scheduled to begin, Basil enters the theater. When it is almost filled and the organ starts up, Basil slips out of his seat and heads for the lobby, quickly making his way backstage. At the end of a hallway, he enters a vestibule where a policeman is stationed in front of a door. Basil approaches him and asks to see Miss Tarrant as he hands over his business card, but the policeman informs Basil that he is the very man whom Miss Chancellor wishes to keep out. He suggests that Basil take his seat in the hall, but Basil insists on speaking to Verena privately. When the organ stops, Basil checks his watch and sees that it is five minutes past eight. As the minutes continue to slip by, the audience becomes increasingly restless. Matthias Pardon comes bursting in, demanding to know why Verena has not yet gone on. A

burst of applause is heard, and as it subsides, Mr. Filer, Olive's agent, also appears, wanting to know where Miss Tarrant is hiding. When he discovers that their door is locked, he knocks sharply, ordering Verena and Olive to come out.

(Chapter 42) Looking very pale, Verena opens the door. She had spotted Basil in the audience earlier and now needs to talk to him, but Mr. Filer insists that she go on immediately. The three move into her room, where Mrs. Tarrant sits on the couch with Olive stretched out beside her, looking very tragic. Basil closes the door on the reporter and the policeman as Mr. Tarrant enters from the side of the room adjoining the stage. Mr. Filer continues to urge Verena on, but she insists that she must speak to Basil first and looks at him beseechingly. Basil interprets Verena's silent plea as a desire to be saved from speaking; however, she begs him to let her go on for the sake of the others. Bending over her, Basil swears, "not for worlds, not for millions, shall you give yourself to that roaring crowd. . . . You are mine, you are not theirs" (343). When Verena cries that the crowd can have their money refunded, Olive begs Basil to let Verena speak this one time, but he insists that she belongs to him and him alone. Mr. Filer threatens a lawsuit, and Mrs. Tarrant becomes hysterical while Selah circles the room. Verena urges Basil to let her reward the audience, who are impatiently hissing and shouting. As Mr. Tarrant and Mr. Filer go out to try to pacify the crowd, Verena pushes her mother and Olive out of the room and turns to Basil. She tells him that she could not possibly speak after seeing him in the audience and begs him to go away, but Basil ignores her pleas. He grabs a cloak and throws it over her. As he hurries her out of the room, he explains that they will take the night train to New York, where they will be married in the morning. At this point, Olive goes out onto the stage to address the angry crowd, who fall silent in anticipation of her speech. As Basil and Verena reach the street, she is in tears.

CRITICAL ANALYSIS

Following the death of James's beloved mother early in 1882, his sister, ALICE, and HENRY JAMES, SR., moved from their Quincy Street home in Cambridge into a smaller house on Mount Vernon Street in Boston. It was here that James wrote his notebook entry for April 8, 1883. This suggests that the idea for *The Bostonians* occurred to him while he was staying in Boston after the death of his father. Although James did not begin work on the novel during his lengthy stay, he did write "A New England Winter," a short story about an aspiring American artist who lives in Paris but who goes home to visit his mother in Boston, which he soon discovers has been transformed into "a city of women" (113). Life in the state capital was "so completely in the hands of the ladies, the masculine note was so subordinate, that on certain occasions he could have believed himself . . . in a country stricken by a war, where the men had all gone to the army . . ." (113). James's reference to war is no accident. Even though he wrote this story nearly 20 years after the end of the Civil War, the absence of men in the public sphere was still very much in evidence, as more than 600,000 men had lost their lives during that momentous struggle. Consequently, women and the women's movement gained predominance. As James's early biographer Leon Edel points out, this remarkable change provided James with the subject of his novel (Edel 67).

In his *Notebooks*, James transcribed part of a letter he wrote to his publisher J. R. Osgood. James begins by outlining the story and describes the characters as "persons of the radical reforming type who are especially interested in the emancipation of women, giving them the suffrage, releasing them from bondage, co-educating them with men, etc." (18). While James wrote this in 1883, he was actually describing the situation in New England in the 1870s, the decade following the war. The "radical reformers" to whom he refers were effectually carrying on the tradition established by the famous New England transcendentalists, including RALPH WALDO EMERSON, the early American feminist Margaret Fuller, Henry Thoreau, and "the Swedenborgian mystic Bronson Alcott," as well as those who participated in the Brook Farm Experiment (Quebe 94). Once slavery had been abolished, women continued to advance their cause but did not win the right to vote in the United States until 1920, when the Nineteenth Amendment was ratified. It is important to grasp

that throughout the 19th century, married women were still legally regarded as their husband's property, leading many women to perceive marriage as a form of slavery. Sadly, few other options were available; women's seminaries and colleges were founded over the course of the century, but the majority of women were not able to attend. In fact, Henry James, Sr., did not permit his only daughter, Alice, to be educated outside the home. As Edel and others suggest, James was sensitive to the situation of his sister.

Commenting on the plot of his novel, James notes that "it relates an episode connected with the so-called 'woman's movement'" (18). The heroine of the story is a "gifted" inspirational speaker, associated by birth with a circle of "old abolitionists, spiritualists, transcendentalists, etc." (18). This young woman has a friend, a rich and cultured woman, who has devoted herself to the cause of women but is terrified of speaking in public. Her dream is that the two work together to "really revolutionize the condition of women" (19). To complicate matters, the gifted speaker falls in love with a young man of a "hard-headed and conservative disposition, [. . .] resolutely opposed to female suffrage and all similar alterations" (19). The story focuses on the ensuing struggle between the rich young woman Olive Chancellor and her distant cousin Basil Ransom for possession of the charming inspirational speaker Verena Tarrant. James adds that "the relation of the two girls should be a study of one of those friendships between women which are so common in New England" (*Notebooks* 19). Edel remarks that James was able to observe firsthand this type of relation between his sister, Alice James, and Katherine Loring (68), a romantic friendship between women known at the time as a Boston marriage.

In *Surpassing the Love of Men*, Lillian Faderman describes the relationship between Alice and Katherine in sympathetic terms. As a young woman, Alice had

been plagued by psychosomatic illnesses and was a recluse. In 1878, when she was thirty, she suffered a nervous breakdown . . . . A year or two later Alice met Katherine, who was active in Boston charities and betterment organizations, and whose energy and health, in startling contrast to Alice's own condition, immediately attracted Alice.... James observed the difference Katherine made in his sister, who had shown no desire to have serious human contact with any individual before. (195)

From 1881 until Alice's death in 1892, James became more and more grateful for the care and companionship Katherine provided his sister. "Not long after the publication of *The Bostonians*, James wrote his aunt regarding Katherine's love for Alice that 'a devotion so perfect and generous [was] a gift of providence so rare and so little-to-be-looked-for in this hard world that to brush it aside would be almost an act of impiety'" (qtd. in Faderman 196).

Faderman notes that Alice and Katherine's passionate friendship was not entirely a proper Boston marriage, as they did not actually live together, although Katherine sometimes stayed with Alice for extended periods of time. For an example of a model Boston marriage, Faderman comments on the intimate relationship of Annie Fields and the novelist Sarah Orne Jewett, which lasted for almost three decades (197) and which James was also able to observe. When she was 19, Annie Fields married the middle-aged widower James T. Fields, who was the editor of the *Atlantic Monthly* and the publisher of James's first important fiction. The Fieldses had a house on Charles Street and were neighbors of the James family when they first lived in Boston on Ashburton Place. Annie Fields hosted a literary and artistic salon that the young James gratefully attended. After the death of James T. Fields in 1881, "the two women lived together a part of each year, separated for another part of the year so that they could devote complete attention to their work, traveled together frequently, shared interests in books and people, and provided each other with love and stability" (Faderman 197). Jewett believed heterosexual marriage to be destructive to women because they sacrificed their own identities and interests in order to merge with their husbands (Faderman 198). Thus, it seems quite likely that James had Boston marriages in mind when he was deciding on a title for his novel; however, his notebook reference to an episode from the woman's movement has also piqued the curiosity of numerous readers.

In "Feminist Sources in *The Bostonians*," Sara Davis proposes that this episode was the struggle between Susan B. Anthony, one of the founders and leaders of the National Women's Suffrage Association, and Whitelaw Reid, a New York journalist and antifeminist, for possession of Anna Dickinson, "described by newspapers as 'the only pretty, well-shaped, and womanly looking oratorical champion' the suffragettes ever had, her effects being those of 'magic, charm, mesmerism'" (qtd. in Anderson 18). This description fits Verena Tarrant remarkably well, just as the sketch of Reid easily fits Basil Ransom; Anthony, moreover, was described as "hard-featured, guileless, cold as an icicle, fluent, and philosophical" (18), an apt description of Olive Chancellor in the first two books of James's novel. James, of course, would have been aware of this struggle as he was summoned to Boston twice for the successive deaths of his parents during 1881–83, a period when the newspapers were "full of the activities of the Women's Suffrage Association" (18).

James remained in Boston until the end of August 1883, when he returned to LONDON, but he continued to put off work on his novel. After a delay of more than a year, he decided to visit PARIS to renew his connections with French writers Edmond de Goncourt, Alphonse Daudet, and Émile Zola, whose development of the naturalist novel James respected (see ROMANCE/REALISM/NATURALISM). In "The Art of Fiction," James outlined a few criticisms as he presented his theory of the novel. The essay, which first appeared in *Longman's Magazine*, September 1884, was James's response to the publication of a pamphlet based on a lecture of the same title given at the Royal Institution by the English novelist Walter Besant, who maintained that the "laws of fiction may be laid down and taught with as much precision and exactness as the laws of harmony, perspective, and proportion" (qtd. in "The Art of Fiction" 192–193). This prompted James to make one of his most famous statements:

A novel is in its broadest definition a personal, a direct impression of life: that, to begin with, constitutes its value, which is greater or less according to the intensity of the impression. But there will be no intensity at all, and therefore no value, unless there is freedom to feel and say. The tracing of a line to be followed, of a tone to be taken, of a form to be filled out, is a limitation of that freedom and a suppression of the very thing that we are most curious about. (192)

Besant also insisted "that English Fiction should have a 'conscious moral purpose'" (203). For James, "the essence of moral energy is to survey the whole field" (204), meaning "all life, all feeling, all observation, all vision" (200). He found that the "moral purpose" applied to the English and American novel had had a negative, restraining effect, acting as a form of censorship. In defending the writer's freedom to "try and capture the colour of life itself" (206), James invokes Zola, praising his "prodigious effort" (206). What James objected to in Zola's fiction was his pessimistic premises and the relentless sordidness of his subject matter. James would do Boston as Zola had done Paris, only James would illuminate the broader possibilities of the naturalist novel by drawing on the opposition sparked by a southerner and the Boston bourgeoisie. James was finally ready to begin writing *The Bostonians*.

RECEPTION OF *THE BOSTONIANS*

The *Century*'s serialization of *The Bostonians* had preceded *Scribner's Monthly Magazine*'s in 1891, and the editors attempted to make its content more historical in orientation. The very first issue featured a piece by Fredrick Douglass, entitled "My Escape from Slavery," and the magazine soon included the work of other prominent American writers such as the abolitionist Harriet Beecher Stowe and the transcendentalist Ralph Waldo Emerson.

James's novel was not well received; in fact, the editor of *Century Magazine*, R. W. Gilder, "wrote to James that he had never published anything so unpopular" (Rahv vi). To add to James's misfortune, his American publisher J. R. Osgood declared

bankruptcy before James received payment for the serial and book rights, although *Century Magazine* had paid Osgood in full. Macmillan, James's British publisher, stepped in and issued the novel simultaneously in the United States and England in 1886, but at a much reduced royalty. Once again *The Bostonians* did not fare well in the United States, and in the end James excluded it from his prestigious New York Edition (1907–09). Except for the minor changes he made to the original *Century Magazine* text (Habegger 185), James never revised the novel.

In his oft-cited introduction to the Dial's 1945 edition of the novel, Philip Rahv points out that when *The Bostonians* first appeared, it was "the only full-length narrative" in the Jamesian canon in which "the scenes and characters . . . are uniformly American," yet it remained "unavailable in any American edition save the original one of 1886" for some 60 years (v). This gap is all the more remarkable given that *The Bostonians* possesses "none of those difficulties of style and intention associated with the more typical products of James's career" (v). According to Rahv, the failure of the novel in the United States was mainly due to the cultural hegemony of the New England gentility, who found the novel deeply offensive. With the cloud of the Civil War still hovering over the landscape, Bostonians did not approve of James's apparent sympathy for the southerner Basil Ransom, who mocked New England's much revered reformers. They were also offended by James's rendering of Miss Birdseye, whom many readily identified as a caricature of Elizabeth Palmer Peabody, Nathaniel Hawthorne's sister-in-law (see HAWTHORNE). Rahv notes that "James denied any such intention with great vehemence in a letter to his brother William" (vi) (see WILLIAM JAMES). More pointedly, as Rahv adds, it was "the current of Lesbian feeling in the relationship of the arch-feminist Olive Chancellor to her protégé, Verena Tarrant, that proved most disquieting" (vi).

Despite its poor reception, *The Bostonians* has proven to be one of James's more popular novels. It is beautifully written, witty, and offers exquisite impressionistic descriptions of Boston; in addition, James succeeds in capturing the distinctly American character of Boston in the late 1870s. As an example of James's literary realism, the novel has inspired many interpretations by literary critics and scholars. When it was resuscitated in the 1940s, readings tended to privilege Basil Ransom as the hero of the novel, perhaps taking James's claim that he was "the most important personage" in the book at face value (6). At the time, critics such as Rahv and Lionel Trilling defended Ransom "as a conservative hero challenging a culture of triumphant vulgarity and intrusiveness," while Alfred Habegger maintained that James treated Basil with "dignity" (190–191).

THE FEMINIST TURN

With the rise of the second wave of feminism in the 1970s, new readings of *The Bostonians* emerged, perhaps best exemplified by Judith Fetterley's groundbreaking study *The Resisting Reader* (1978), in which she devotes an entire chapter to James's novel. For Fetterley, the resisting reader is one who reads against the grain, who resists the values and underlying "phallic" ideology of the white male literary establishment. *The Bostonians*, Fetterley points out, "is of particular interest to the feminist critic because the critical commentary on it provides irrefutable documentation of the fact that literary criticism is a political act—that it derives from and depends on a set of values, usually unarticulated and unexamined, in the mind of the critic and that it functions to propagate those values" (101).

Before proceeding with her own detailed analysis of the novel, Fetterley provides extracts from 14 prominent "phallic" critics, including Irving Howe, Lionel Trilling, F. W. Dupee, Charles A. Anderson, Philip Rahv, and Leon Edel, to name a few. What strikes Fetterley is the "relentless sameness" of their criticism (107): "Each begins with an attack upon Olive. This attack is followed by a discussion of Ransom, couched in positive terms" (111). Fetterley concludes that the novel threatens the masculinity of these critics as it addresses "the situation of women" in "their relation to society and to each other, and of men's relation to them" (108). Particularly, Olive's desire for equality, freedom, and intimacy with another woman undermines the heterosexual basis that privileges the male and enables his dominant position. Thus, in order to naturalize heterosexuality and thereby maintain male dominance, these "phallic" critics treat as a pathology Olive's love of women. Fetterley elaborates:

> To associate Olive with lesbianism is, in the critic's eye, to define her as odious, perverse, abnormal, unnatural—in a word, evil . . . . From this view of Olive it is but a single, inevitable step . . . to the vision of Ransom as hero, the knight in shining armor, the repository of all that is healthy, sane, and good; and from here it is but another single step to the melodramatic reading of the novel as the rescue of Verena from perversion, exploitation, imprisonment, death—the snow-white maiden saved from the clutches of the wicked witch by the handsome prince. (110)

Robert C. McLean's stunning commentary on the conclusion of the novel readily supports her view. He writes, "The tears Verena is to shed in the future are, after all, a small price to pay for achieving a normal relationship in a society so sick. A spring and summer courtship cannot last forever, but the marriage affirms nature's ability ever to renew itself" (qtd. in Fetterley 105).

Whereas James does set Olive and Ransom against each other in their struggle for the possession of Verena, in Book Third James becomes increasingly sympathetic in his treatment of the suffering Olive and almost ruthless in his exposure of Ransom's antiquated views on women and his intention to silence Verena. Fetterley reminds us that in choosing to write about "the situation of women," James—unlike most male authors—was primarily interested in focusing on women's experience rather than in aligning himself with the male point of view.

Fetterley, however, does not claim that James is a feminist per se but argues that the subject of *The Bostonians* is feminism. As James states in his notebook, "I wished to write a very *American* tale, a tale very characteristic of our social conditions, and I asked myself what was the most salient and peculiar point in our social life. The answer was: the situation of women, the decline of the sentiment of sex, the agitation in their behalf" (20). James, of course, is referring to the women's movement. Fetterley observes that in choosing this "as the crucial American subject rather than the Civil War, in choosing to write about the Bostonians rather than about the great national conflict, James suggests that a war in which men fight one another is of less cultural importance than the struggle between men and women and of less significance than the civil war within women" (117). Precisely because James subordinates the conflict between a southerner and a Bostonian to "the larger sexual one; in his eyes the battle between men and women is the central national issue" (119). However, as Fetterley points out, the two conflicts are interconnected.

> The Bostonians are women, and Boston is representative of that element of reform which had so much to do with bringing the forces behind the Civil War to a head. This implicit connection is made explicit in a character like Miss Birdseye, whose abolitionist activities are the subject of national fame. Thus, it is easy for Ransom to locate the source of the war in the misdirected and aggressive energy of women and to attribute to a female force the responsibility for all his present difficulties. Ransom's struggle with Olive is an outgrowth of his analysis of the national cataclysm and an effort to reverse it. (119)

In other words, Ransom's desire for Verena is not motivated by love. Rather, wresting her from Olive is a means of defeating the Bostonian reformer, the imagined source of his humiliation as a former slave owner. To lose Verena to Olive would mean Basil's further emasculation.

More recently, in *Henry James and the Suspense of Masculinity* (2003), Leland S. Person has shifted the focus to the construction of masculinity in James's fiction. Viewing *The Bostonians* as a Reconstruction novel, Person complicates the "reconstruction" of Ransom's masculinity by considering the racial implications of his being a southerner. Drawing attention to James's description of Ransom, Person suggests that early in the novel, James "subtly confuses" Ransom's racial identity by "noting 'something sultry and vast, something almost African' in the 'rich, basking tone' of his voice—

'something that suggested the teeming expanse of the cotton-field'" (107–108). Thus Ransom's need to reassert his masculinity is fueled by a desperate sense of inhabiting "the abject position of the slave." In order to free himself from this bind and reclaim his position as "master," Ransom makes Verena his slave. Significantly, Person finds that James's highlighting of the "phallocentric, heterosexual economy" provides a critique of the antifeminism Ransom exemplifies (110). For James, "the reconstruction of an archaic masculinity raises more questions than it answers" (111).

Whether or not James was a feminist is a question that continues to fascinate James critics. In *The Theoretical Dimensions of Henry James* (1984), John Carlos Rowe compares the interpretations of Carren Kaston's *Imagination and Desire in the Novels of Henry James* and Suzanne Kappeler's *Writing and Reading in Henry James*. Whereas Kaston argues that "our failure to recognize James's feminism is largely a consequence of our limited perspectives in a patriarchal culture" (qtd. in Rowe 90), Kappeler argues that James's "'feminism' has to be *extracted*" by the reader (qtd. in Rowe 90). Rowe is more inclined toward Kappeler's position, as he finds James ambivalent in his attitude toward feminism. As Rowe aptly puts it, "Henry James, the Master, *uses* feminism, uses 'the other sex' as part of his own literary power for the sake of engendering his own identity as an Author" (91). Nevertheless, James's startling sensitivity and insights into the situation of women and the cultural construction of gender continues to fascinate readers to this day.

CHARACTERS

Birdseye, Miss   A diminutive, elderly lady with kind but weak and tired eyes, she is one of the earliest and most passionate abolitionists, a romantic but faded figure of the Civil War era. She is entirely unselfish and has given all of her capital to her political commitments.

Burrage, Mr. Henry   A wealthy young man from New York, he collects art as a student at Harvard University. He would like to marry Verena, and along with his mother, he is interested in supporting her cause.

Chancellor, Olive The "Chancellors belonged to the *bourgeoisie*—the oldest and the best" (28). When Olive's mother died, she inherited the house on Charles Street. Wealthy, intelligent, and highly cultivated—Olive speaks German—she is also very serious, fearful, and painfully shy, to the point of being considered "morbid," even tragic in her demeanor. As a radical reformer, she has dedicated herself to the women's movement but is terrified of speaking in public. Although she is still in her twenties and younger than Basil, he sees her as "a signal old maid" (16). Olive has vivid green eyes but dresses plainly. She hates men "as a class" (19).

Luna, Mrs. Adeline Olive's older sister and a widow, Mrs. Luna has returned from Europe and now lives in New York. In contrast to the distinctly Bostonian Olive, Adeline is a frivolous social creature, whose main concern is to be fashionably dressed and attractive to men. Even though Basil is penniless, Adeline would like to marry him, as she perceives him as a kind of aristocrat. She has a young son, Newton, who is terribly spoiled.

Pardon, Mr. Matthias A young man, not yet 30, with side whiskers, whose hair is prematurely white, journalist Mr. Pardon is well known in "magazine circles" (35). He believes in the power of publicity; consequently, he has no regard for the private. He would like to marry Verena Tarrant and promote her career. It is not so much love or a belief in the women's movement that motivates him but, rather, the idea of making history, of becoming famous.

Prance, Dr. Mary J. A medical doctor, who lives downstairs from Miss Birdseye, with her short hair and slim physique, Dr. Prance looks like a boy. She is intelligent, independently minded, and hard-working. She hates to waste time. As a woman of action, Dr. Prance thinks women talk too much, but she finds "room for improvement in both sexes" (34).

Ransom, Basil Basil is exceptionally tall, dark, and strikingly handsome with a high and broad forehead, "and his thick black hair, perfectly straight and glossy, and without any division, rolled back from it in a leonine manner." His "magnificent eyes" are like "smouldering fire." James states that Basil is "the most important personage" in his story (6). As a former Mississippi plantation owner, Basil fought on the side of the South in the Civil War. Having lost their slaves, his family was ruined. At 30, Basil moved to New York to study law, but he fails to establish his career successfully. He then attempts to become a writer but cannot find a publisher for his antiquated opinions. Ransom believes women are meant to nurture men as homebound wives.

Tarrant, Mrs. Verena's calculating mother is the daughter of the celebrated (but fictitious) Abraham Greenstreet. She derives from "old Abolitionist stock" (27) and "kept a runaway slave in her house for thirty days" (27). Although she is described as "a flaccid, relaxed, unhealthy, whimsical woman" (56), it was expected that she would do better than to marry Selah Tarrant.

Tarrant, Selah Verena's father began "life as an itinerant vendor of lead-pencils" before achieving "distinction in the spiritualistic world" (56). A mesmeric healer, he is reputed to have performed "miraculous cures" (35). He is a "tall, pale gentleman, with a black moustache and an eye-glass" (35). His huge teeth are emphasized, suggesting a greedy, carnal nature. He craves publicity, which he equates with success, and uses his daughter to get his name in the papers.

Tarrant, Verena The Tarrants' only child, Verena is gifted with a talent for oratory and conversation. She has already made a name for herself in the West as an inspirational speaker. She is pale but very pretty with red hair. Her style is bohemian, although she is easily influenced by others. She generally submits to authority, first to her father, then to Olive, and finally to Basil.

ADAPTATIONS

In 1984, a film version of *The Bostonians* was directed by James Ivory. It starred Vanessa Redgrave, Christopher Reeve, and Jessica Tandy. Ruth Prawer Jhabvala authored the screenplay.

FURTHER READING

Anderson, Charles R. Introduction to *The Bostonians,* by Henry James, 7–30. London: Penguin Books, 1984.

Bell, F. A. Ian. "The Curious Case of Doctor Prance." *Henry James Review* 10, no. 1 (1989): 32–41.

Bell, Millicent. *Meaning in Henry James.* Cambridge, Mass., and London: Harvard University Press, 1991.

Blair, Sara. "Realism, Culture, and the Place of the Literary: Henry James and the Bostonians." In *The Cambridge Companion to Henry James,* edited by Jonathan Freedman, 151–168. Cambridge: Cambridge University Press, 1998.

Castle, Terry. "Haunted by Olive Chancellor." In *The Apparitional Lesbian: Female Homosexuality and Modern Culture,* 150–185. New York: Columbia University Press, 1993.

Dimock, Wai Chee. "Gender, the Market, and the Nontrivial in James." *Henry James Review* 15 (1994): 24–30.

Edel, Leon. *Henry James: The Middle Years, 1882–1895.* New York: Avon Books, 1962.

Faderman, Lillian. *Surpassing the Love of Men: Romantic Friendship and Love between Women from the Renaissance to the Present.* New York: Quill, William Morrow, 1981.

Fetterley, Judith. *The Resisting Reader: A Feminist Approach to American Fiction.* Bloomington and London: Indiana University Press, 1978.

Flannery, Denis. "'A Walking Advertisement': Illusion, Sincerity and Publicity in *The Bostonians.*" In *Henry James: A Certain Illusion,* 61–83. Aldershot, England; Brookfield, Conn.; Singapore; Sydney: Ashgate, 2000.

Fuller, Margaret. *Women in the Nineteenth Century.* New York: W.W. Norton, 1971.

Habegger, Alfred. *Henry James and the "Woman Business."* Cambridge: Cambridge University Press, 1989.

James, Henry. "The Art of Fiction." In *The Critical Muse: Selected Literary Criticism,* edited by Roger Gard, 186–206. London: Penguin Books, 1987.

———. *The Bostonians.* London: Penguin Books, 2000.

———. *The Complete Notebooks of Henry James.* Edited by Leon Edel and Lyall H. Powers. New York and Oxford: Oxford University Press, 1987.

Kaston, Carren. *Imagination and Desire in the Novels of Henry James.* New Brunswick, N.J.: Rutgers University Press, 1984.

Martin, Robert K. "Picturesque Misperception in *The Bostonians.*" *Henry James Review* 9, no. 2 (1988): 77–86.

Moldstad, Mary Frew. "Elizabeth Peabody Revisited." *Henry James Review* 9, no. 3 (1988): 209–211.

Person, Leland S. *Henry James and the Suspense of Masculinity.* Philadelphia: University of Pennsylvania Press, 2003.

Powers, Lyall H. *Henry James and the Naturalist Movement.* Ann Arbor: Michigan State University Press, 1971.

Quebe, Ruth Evelyn. "*The Bostonians:* Some Historical Sources and Their Implications." *The Centennial Review* 25, no. 1 (1981): 80–100.

Rahv, Philip. Introduction to *The Bostonians,* by Henry James, v–ix. New York: Dial Press, 1945.

Rowe, John Carlos. *The Theoretical Dimensions of Henry James.* Madison: University of Wisconsin Press, 1984.

Scudder, Horace Elisha. "*The Bostonians,* by Henry James." *Atlantic Monthly.* June 1886. Available online. URL: http://www.theatlantic.com/unbound/classrev/thebosto.htm. Downloaded on February 16, 2008.

Taylor, Andrew. *Henry James and the Father Question.* Cambridge: Cambridge University Press, 2002.

Warren, Kenneth W. *Black & White Strangers: Race and American Literary Realism.* Chicago and London: University of Chicago Press, 1993.

Elaine Pigeon, *Université de Montréal*

The Europeans (1878)

The Europeans first appeared in four installments in the *Atlantic Monthly* from July to October 1878. It was published in book form by Macmillan in London and by Houghton, Osgood in Boston later that year. James never revised it.

SYNOPSIS

(Chapter 1) It is May 12 in the mid-1840s. Eugenia and her brother, Felix, have arrived in Boston amidst a late snowstorm. Although of American parentage, they have always lived abroad and have come to New England to meet their relatives. Eugenia peers discontentedly out the sleet-battered hotel window at a moldering, snow-covered graveyard and bustling street while Felix blithely sketches. When the storm clears, the two stroll. Eugenia, who has "come to seek her fortune" (43), gloomily contemplates her prospects. Felix's cheery banter provides a counterpoint to her discouraging observations. Eugenia instructs Felix to visit their cousins and report back to her. She will make her appearance in her own time.

(Chapter 2) The following day, a young woman strolls through the garden before a large country house. It is a beautiful morning, and Gertrude Wentworth has decided to skip church. First, her elder sister, Charlotte, and then Mr. Brand, a minister, come to inquire if Gertrude plans to accompany them to church. When Charlotte leaves, Brand announces that he has something to say. Gertrude begs him to desist, and he leaves. Gertrude wanders in the garden before entering the house. Presently, she begins to read *The Arabian Nights*. Lost in a romantic tale, she is surprised when a handsome young man bows low before her. It is Felix. Impressed, Gertrude brings him cake and wine and listens, amazed, as Felix explains that Eugenia, the Baroness Münster, is married unhappily, and perhaps temporarily, to Prince Adolf of Silberstadt-Schreckenstein. When the rest of the family returns, Gertrude, starry-eyed, blunders by introducing Felix as the Prince.

(Chapter 3) That evening, to encourage Eugenia, Felix gleefully describes his visit. The following day, the pair journey to the Wentworths' home. Eugenia impresses the New Englanders with her gracious yet imposing air. Robert Acton, a cousin of the Wentworths, attracts her notice. Charlotte prevails upon her father to invite the Europeans to stay. Genuinely touched, Eugenia yields to a sudden profound emotion and accepts the invitation. Wentworth addresses Eugenia as his "dear niece" (70), while Charlotte reaches out to her and Acton turns aside.

(Chapter 4) That evening, the Wentworths and Actons discuss the visitors. Gertrude believes that

Eugenia would prefer to live with more privacy and pleasure than the Wentworth house affords. Acton suggests that Wentworth offer them a cottage on the property. Wentworth cautiously accedes after warning Gertrude to be careful about the "peculiar influences" of the Europeans (75). A few days later, Felix and Eugenia move into the cottage, which Eugenia adorns with improvised draperies. Felix eagerly anticipates spending time with Charlotte, Gertrude, and Lizzie Acton. Soon Gertrude and Charlotte visit and find Eugenia in Acton's company. Two days later, Acton visits again. This time Mr. Brand is present. Brand marvels at Eugenia's conversation. Acton wonders what has brought the Baroness to this humble American home.

(Chapter 5) A routine is established: Eugenia dines at home, and in the afternoons her uncle visits. In the evenings, she has tea at the Wentworth house. One evening, Felix asks to paint his uncle's likeness. When Wentworth declines, Gertrude suggests that Felix paint her instead. Felix happily agrees. During the sittings, the two discuss her family. Gertrude declares them dreary; Felix observes that they have a melancholy outlook. When Felix reminisces about Europe, Gertrude feels as though she were reading a romance. One afternoon, after visiting Acton's mother, she encounters Brand. Although he believes Gertrude has been avoiding him, he professes his love. Gertrude is not surprised; she has heard his declaration before and is unmoved. Still, Brand has faith in her. After leaving him, Gertrude bursts into tears, composes herself, and does not weep again.

(Chapter 6) On his daily visits, Wentworth frequently finds Acton, a highly eligible bachelor, with Eugenia. Acton is evidently very interested in the Baroness. The pair go for drives together, and their relationship almost seems to become romantic. One day, Eugenia reveals that the reigning prince wishes to annul her MARRIAGE in order to arrange a politically advantageous union for his brother. A "renunciation" document exists that Eugenia has only to sign to dissolve her marriage. A few days later, Acton invites Eugenia to his house. She admires his home and pays her respects to his invalid mother. Eugenia tells Acton that she has almost decided to sign the renunciation. Acton replies that when she has dispatched it, he hopes she will let him know.

(Chapter 7) Felix finishes Gertrude's portrait and paints several others, including one of Wentworth. During a sitting, Wentworth confides that his son, Clifford, has been suspended from college for drunkenness and is now studying with Brand. Felix suggests that a romantic distraction may cure Clifford of this vice. When he recommends that Clifford court Eugenia, Wentworth is shocked. Felix presses the idea upon Eugenia, and a short time later discovers Clifford offering her an ostentatious bouquet. That afternoon, strolling by the pond, Felix and Gertrude observe Charlotte and Brand in the distance. Gertrude reveals that her family hopes that she will marry Brand. Felix declares that if she were engaged, and therefore unattainable, he could profess his love. He wants to encourage a romance between Charlotte and Brand in order to liberate Gertrude from the clergyman's unwanted affections. Although enthusiastic, Gertrude does not take Felix's blandishments seriously. Felix declares that he adores her.

(Chapter 8) That evening, Brand admonishes Gertrude about her friendship with Felix. Gertrude insists that she feels "natural" with Felix (128). In wooing her, she hints, Brand is overlooking something better. After tea, Charlotte reproaches Gertrude with ingratitude. Gertrude retorts that she believes Charlotte loves Brand. Clifford, meanwhile, has taken to visiting Eugenia. Far from being in love, however, he merely considers her amusing. He loves Lizzie Acton and expects to marry her someday. Eugenia is chiefly interested in Acton as a marriage prospect, but she regards Clifford as a potential alternate. When she inquires about Lizzie, Clifford informs her that they are not engaged. Eugenia presses him to visit her in Europe.

(Chapter 9) Conscious that his relationship with Eugenia has changed, Acton wonders if he is in love. After a restless week in Newport, he visits the Wentworths and learns that Eugenia has been absent for several days. Although it is late, Acton calls on Eugenia to discover the reason. He asks about the renunciation. When Eugenia is evasive, Acton impulsively invites her to Niagara Falls. Overcoming her initial shock, Eugenia says

she will tell about the renunciation at Niagara. Moments later, the studio door opens, and Clifford bursts in, makes awkward excuses, and bolts. Eugenia explains that Clifford, cured of drinking, has fallen in love with her. Confused and concerned, Acton leaves at three in the morning. The next day, he questions Clifford about the previous night. Clifford explains that he was visiting Eugenia and mistook Acton for his father. Not wishing to be discovered, he tried to leave through Felix's studio but found the door locked. Asked if he fancies Eugenia, Clifford replies emphatically in the negative.

(Chapter 10) Irritable and weary of New England, Eugenia stays home the next Sunday while the others attend church. She expects Acton, but he does not come. Her vexation increases. When Felix returns, his levity contrasts sharply with her dreariness. She feels ready to leave America, while he would gladly remain. He confides that he and Gertrude are in love, but her father would disapprove of their union. Consequently, Felix intends that Eugenia should marry advantageously. Eugenia asserts that Acton wants to marry her, but she does not care for him. Late that afternoon, Felix informs Brand that Charlotte loves him and will suffer as a result of Brand's misplaced attachment to Gertrude. Although intrigued, Brand recognizes Felix's partiality. Brand leaves in a state of confusion, and Felix feels hopeful.

(Chapter 11) The following day, Eugenia bids farewell to Acton's mother. Aware that she is dying, Mrs. Acton expresses her wish that Eugenia would stay in the cottage and remain her son's companion. When Eugenia spots Acton reclining outside beneath a tree, he springs to his feet and admits that he had been thinking of her. Eugenia announces that she is leaving New England. Acton realizes that he is in love but does not know if he can trust her. He asks whether she has dispatched her renunciation. Eugenia replies in the affirmative, but Acton is uncertain. That evening, Eugenia asks Clifford why his visits have fallen off. Clifford makes excuses, and Eugenia speaks of her impending departure. Walking home, she wonders if she has gained anything by coming to America. Back at the Wentworth house, Felix tells Charlotte that he loves Gertrude and asks her to plead his case with her father. He explains that Gertrude is "a folded flower" (176) who has just awakened. Charlotte leaves in tears. Late that night, Felix affirms his love to Gertrude. Gertrude tells him she will do anything he pleases, even go away with him. She expresses dismay that her family always tries to make one feel guilty. Felix determines to persuade them that he and Gertrude belong together.

(Chapter 12) Three days later, Felix announces to Wentworth that he wishes to marry Gertrude. He believes his uncle considers him frivolous and poor, but Wentworth objects that his reservations spring from moral grounds: What is best for Gertrude and Brand? As Felix remonstrates, Gertrude enters and voices her decision to marry Felix. Before Wentworth can reply, Brand appears. Finally convinced, he urges Wentworth to consent and expresses his desire to perform the nuptials. With Brand's endorsement, Wentworth acquiesces. That afternoon, Felix and Gertrude praise Brand's selflessness and devotion. In the evening, Felix informs Eugenia of his engagement. After dinner, Eugenia pays her compliments to Gertrude and Wentworth. Acton says he hopes Felix's engagement will detain her, especially since she has renounced her own marriage. Detecting his skepticism, Eugenia notes that it is the first time her word has been doubted. Acton then announces the engagement of Clifford and Lizzie. Later, Eugenia tells Felix that she will leave for Germany by the first ship. She says she has refused Acton's marriage proposal and never actually signed the renunciation. She regrets that America is unfavorable to superior women. The night before she embarks, Acton tells her he wishes she would stay. Eugenia says she is sorry to be going. Felix bids her farewell aboard ship. He expects they will meet often abroad, but Eugenia seems doubtful. Shortly thereafter, Felix and Gertrude are married. They are very happy and travel afar. Clifford and Lizzie are married but stay in New England. Gertrude and Felix return for Charlotte and Brand's wedding. Wentworth finds himself listening for the "echo of [their] gaiety" (194). After his mother's death, Acton marries a nice young woman.

CRITICAL ANALYSIS

Newly settled in London, Henry James wrote and published *The Europeans* in 1878, his annus mirabilis (Edel 228). In addition to publishing *French Poets and Novelists* and *The Europeans* in that year, James authored "Daisy Miller: A Study," which created a transatlantic sensation and brought him international fame. Framed by *The American* (1877) and *Hawthorne* (1879), *The Europeans* can be seen as both a direct response to *The American*'s reception and "a preliminary foray into Hawthorne territory" (Lustig 6).

On March 30, 1877, James wrote to William Dean Howells of his initial conception of *The Europeans*. Howells, editor of the *Atlantic Monthly*, had objected to *The American*'s length and somber ending. In response, James promised two significant accommodations: to provide "the brightest possible sun-spot for the four-number tale of 1878" and to "squeeze [his] buxom muse" into a hundred pages for the journal (qtd. in Tanner 7). Although the completed text departs substantially from the plot he initially conceived, James kept his word as to brevity and brightness. Yet in resisting his predilection for intricate articulations of "the tragedies in life" (qtd. in Tanner 7), James created an anomaly within his oeuvre: a comedic novella that concludes with a spate of weddings. Owing in part to these uncharacteristic deviations, *The Europeans* has met with a mixed reception. Pronounced "thin and empty" (qtd. in Tanner 8) by his brother William James and often dismissed as "minor," *The Europeans* has been most highly valued by those who have recognized that James was experimenting with form and theme. The novella's tightness of structure, symmetry, and balance invites comparisons with both Shakespearean comedy (see Nazare) and the well-made play (Ward 95). F. R. Leavis, who dubbed it a "masterpiece" (209), describes it as "extraordinarily dramatic," with dialogue that "is all admirable 'theatre'" (220); while J. A. Ward declares it "a nearly perfect comic performance" (98). Deborah Austin labels *The Europeans* "compassionate comedy" (107), in which James deftly employs understatement and pathos.

Noting its deviation from strict realism (see Romance/Realism/Naturalism)—its "admixture of fantasy with reality" (Fincham 89)—a number of critics have fruitfully explored the mythic, fairy-tale, fablelike, or allegorical aspects of *The Europeans*. Peter Buitenhuis traces various legendary allusions, including links to *The Arabian Nights* and Sleeping Beauty (158–159). Extending the analysis, Edward A. Geary identifies Gertrude as Ugly Duckling—"the dull-eyed family misfit who becomes a creature of beauty and joy" (37)—and to Gail Fincham she is "very much a Cinderella or a Miranda" (89). Robert Emmet Long explores James's use of the Arcadian myth of the Golden Age and the fairy-tale meeting of East and West, while Eben Bass explicates the Acton/Acteon parallel. The effect of this fablelike quality is to imbue the redoubtable New England past of Hawthorne and RALPH WALDO EMERSON with a dreamy, nostalgic, romantic atmosphere and to develop the themes of innocence, experience, and personal transformation. But the fairy-tale elements serve another function as well, one that several critics have explicated eloquently: to satirize the New England ethos and probe the comic paradox of a fallen paradise populated by guilt-ridden innocents.

Austin argues that the vestigial Puritanism of James's New Englanders has become "almost mythical" as they "obey a kind of race-memory" in which "guilt operates rather like a primitive divinity" (109). "The effect on the Baroness and her brother," she elaborates, "is a little as if Adam and Eve, after long exile and much experience, should approach Eden again, and find it tenanted by a new race of careful beings, still worrying about serpents and apples, still chary of the first step to knowledge, still looking nervously over the shoulder for a prohibitive and paternal deity" (108). Geary observes that the New World Eden "is inhabited by a fallen race, though fallen only in possessing a sense of sin, not in having much worldly experience," while "the intruders, who are in the role of tempters in Eden bearing the fruit of the tree of knowledge, either have no sense of sin at all, or else have made an art of worldliness" (38). In *The Europeans*, Austin sums up, "James . . . is acquainting a surprised old world with the sickness of the new" (109). But the fallen Eden of New England is not without redemption. As Ward suggests, "If the pastoral scene [a Forest

of Arden or 'green world'] makes the gloom of the Americans additionally quaint and groundless (they are seen as Calvinists in Eden), it also provides an atmosphere in which young lovers can achieve bliss and in which innocence can never be sullied" (97).

Identifying "distinctly Hawthornean notes in *The Europeans*—echoes, oblique allusions," T. J. Lustig argues that "the novel ultimately stages a curious return of allegory" (6). (For more Hawthornean echoes, see Martin, Kalupahana, and Tuttleton.) To Austin, Felix Young's name is "almost distractingly allegorical" (122), and Ward reads the entire novella as "roughly an allegory, with each of the major characters representing a large aspect of the culture which has produced him" (98). Yet despite the allegorical dimensions of the INTERNATIONAL THEME, most critics agree that the contrast of characters and cultures is neither simple nor straightforward. The "Europeans" are actually expatriate Americans "deracinated from any *patria* or native land" (Tuttleton 487) and "cosmopolitans" rather than representatives of any particular nationality (Ascari 2000). Moreover, they resemble one another so little in temperament that they cannot both broadly represent Europe. As Fincham observes, "Eugenia and Felix represent two utterly different European possibilities" (88). In addition, as Ward points out, "we witness . . . the direct and conscious influence of the Europeans upon the Americans" (100). Critics debate who comes off worse. According to Buitenhuis, "James's bias is clearly in favour of the Europeans": "he loads the dice against his American characters" (162). Others point to the text's affectionate stance toward the New Englanders: Although misguided, they are not unlikable. To Ward, Felix and Eugenia are "essentially different from most of the other Europeans in James's fiction" in that they are "purged of ancestral evil" (100) and are "more archetypically American than the New Englanders" (109). The essential contrast, Ward pursues, is between "a highly refined form of opportunism" and "the contrary quality of discipline" (102). Still other critics emphasize the text's movement toward synthesis, compromise, and hybridity rather than binary oppositions: as Fincham remarks, "New England and Europe need each other" (91).

The question of how Felix and his sister are to be regarded is perennially debated. While some consider Felix to be too insubstantial to sustain one's interest or carry much weight ("the least credible character in the novel," according to Ward [101]), others have seen him as a vital catalyst. Characterizing Felix as "a genial Mephistopheles in whom are met all the graces of European civilization" (91), Fincham argues that "Felix stands in perfect equilibrium" between "eccentric Bohemianism" and stern Puritanism (87). "Surely what *The Europeans* dramatizes," she argues, "is the incompleteness of *both* . . . world-views. It celebrates James's belief . . . that radical differences of outlook between people of intelligence and good will can be resolved, and that this resolution can best be achieved through art. In the character of Felix Young—painter, epicurean, interpreter of life—we have perhaps James's most exuberant example of the creative intelligence which achieves—and through the 'alchemy of art' communicates—a perfect fusion of the aesthetic and the moral" (84).

As for the Baroness, Ward observes that "Eugenia has been judged both a selfish schemer for wealth and position and a charming, graceful woman whose faults are essentially minor" (99). While Fincham maintains that Eugenia's character is "essentially static" (89), "a fully opened exotic bloom that cannot survive transplantation" (88), others, including Tom Petitjean and Merle A. Williams, see her as compelling, complex, and absolutely key. For Poirier, she "is the central figure both in the international theme and in the dramatizations of the theme of art and naturalness" (137). According to Ward, "Eugenia is what Northrop Frye calls the *pharmakos*—the rascal inimical to the well-being of society who is driven out in the comic resolution" (111); nevertheless, "there is a sense of loss and a mood of somberness in her departure. We feel that the society which dismisses her is seriously deficient" (112). Articulating a postcolonial perspective, Chamika Kalupahana locates a submerged Jamesian preoccupation with racial otherness, American expansionism, and imperialism in his portrayal of Eugenia and her relationship with Acton.

For Ward, the Eugenia-Acton relationship develops a crucial tension between sincerity and deception. Observing that "the lie is a regular occasion for moral ambiguity in James," who "nearly always employs the lie to differentiate the rigid moralist from the free spirit" (110), Ward maintains that Eugenia is James's attempt to "represent artfulness as an unequivocal good" (101). Eugenia's "art" proves superior to Mrs. Acton's "artlessness," and, in general, "the Baroness' artificiality is an expansion, not a repression of herself. Her manner, her conversation, even her clothes and her furnishings fully express her" (Ward 106). Williams also explores Acton's (self-)deception and the paradox of Eugenia's "falsehood as truth" and "truth as falsehood" (26), while Ian F. A. Bell places the theme of sincerity and performance within the dual historical contexts of the 1840s and 1870s.

Was *The Europeans* an aberration in James's career or "an eminently successful experiment" (Buitenhuis 162), an inconspicuous milestone on his artistic path or an out-of-the-way cul-de-sac leading nowhere? Subtitled "A *Sketch*," *The Europeans* was, in Lustig's appraisal, "part of a personal artistic trajectory" extending from a "study" ("Daisy Miller: A Study") to a "portrait" (*The* PORTRAIT OF A LADY) that was highly responsive to contemporary debates about literary realism and the transition from romanticism (8). Some consider "its narrative approach . . . old-fashioned, recalling Thackeray and Trollope rather than forecasting the later James" (Ward 97), while for others it "bears traces of James's later manner" (Williams 21). Poirier finds in *The Europeans* evidence that James "began to experiment much earlier than is commonly assumed with a kind of character who could be . . . the artist of her own experience" (124); and Fincham suggests that the text "prefigure[s] . . . a number of central Jamesian themes which are to be explored fully in the major novels," including "the relationship of art to life" (83). Geary considers it "characteristic of James's later fiction, where the plot resides not primarily in outward action but in the interplay of different perspectives, the ironies arising from different attitudes and expectations" (36). In his view, "*The Europeans* is James's first novel to have as its central 'action' this controlled, shifting consciousness of possibilities" (36); Ward, however, pronounces it "the last novel of its type that James wrote" (113).

Given this polarity, perhaps it is safest to say, simply, that it is "unique among James's novels" (Fincham 92), or in Ward's words, *The Europeans* is "*sui generis* in its design" (96).

CHARACTERS

Acton, Lizzie　Lizzie is the younger sister of Robert Acton and sweetheart of Clifford Wentworth, whom she eventually marries. With her dark hair and deep blue eyes, she is "wonderfully pretty," pert, and, in Eugenia's eyes, an American "type" (68).

Acton, Mrs.　Mother of Robert and Lizzie, a 55-year-old invalid in failing health, an admirer of Emerson, she is "very modest, very timid, and very ill" (109). In the end, her death is intimated as a catalyst to her son's marriage.

Acton, Robert　Cousin of Mr. Wentworth, Acton lives with his mother and sister in a large, comfortable house near the Wentworths. "An ornament to his circle" (98) and "man of the world" (98), he has acquired a fortune in the trade with China. He has a slight build, dark hair, a moustache, "a quick, observant, agreeable dark eye" (68), and a "humorous" outlook (99). Fascinated by Eugenia, he falls in love with her, in a matter-of-fact way, yet feels unable to trust her completely. To Felix, he appears to be the one person in the Wentworth circle who is not oppressed by sadness or guilt. After his mother's death, he marries "a particularly nice young girl" (194).

Brand, Mr.　Unitarian minister, friend of the Wentworths, and tutor of Clifford Wentworth, he is tall, fair, and handsome (though stout), with an agreeable smile. He has loved Gertrude for a long time and hoped to marry her. Eventually, he transfers his affections to Charlotte, whom he weds.

Münster, Madame (a.k.a. Eugenia [Eugenia-Camilla-Dolores], née Young, Baroness Münster)　The 33-year-old baroness is the niece of Mr. Wentworth. Her mother, Wentworth's older half sister, went to Europe, converted to Catholicism, married an expatriate American, became estranged from her family, and never returned to New England.

Raised in Europe, Eugenia married Prince Adolf of Silberstadt-Schreckenstein, younger brother of a reigning prince. It is a "morganatic" marriage, which the reigning prince is eager to annul. Having come to New England to "seek her fortune" (43), Eugenia, both clever and ambitious, sets her sights on Robert Acton and (as a possible backup) Clifford Wentworth.

Although not pretty, Eugenia carries herself as though she were. This gives her a graceful, alluring quality. Prone to the use of French phrases and continental flourishes, she seems thoroughly Europeanized. She has "charming," intelligent, and lively grey eyes, earrings, and abundant dark hair, frizzled and braided in a manner that heightens her "exotic," "foreign," or "Oriental" appearance (35). "A woman of sudden emotions" (70), "lively perception," "refined imagination" (77), and "a restless soul" (82), she is also something of an enigma: a stranger in a strange land. She provokes a great deal of ambiguity as "nothing that the Baroness said was wholly untrue," but at the same time "nothing that she said was wholly true" (78).

Wentworth, Charlotte　Eldest of the Wentworth children, like her sister, she is "thin and pale" (47), but shorter, with smooth dark hair and quick, bright eyes. She is prettier, more serious, less imaginative, and more conventional than Gertrude, about whom she constantly worries. She secretly loves Mr. Brand but is determined to sacrifice her own wishes. When Felix proposes to Gertrude, Brand shifts his affections to Charlotte, whom he eventually marries.

Wentworth, Clifford　Younger brother of Gertrude and Charlotte, he has been suspended from Harvard for six months for drunkenness and is now studying with Brand. He is romantically attached to Lizzie Acton, whom he intends to become engaged to once he graduates and whom he does in fact ultimately marry. In the meantime, he amuses himself with Eugenia.

Wentworth, Gertrude　Younger of the Wentworth sisters, Gertrude is 22 or 23, "tall and pale, thin and a little awkward" (46). With her straight, fair hair and "dull and restless" dark eyes (46), she is not considered pretty. Her evident discontent unsettles her sister, father, and Brand. With the approval of her family, Brand has attempted to court her, but Gertrude discourages him. She is fascinated by Felix, who seems to offer the excitement, romance, and imagination she yearns for. Although she can be "a little hard" (97) and sometimes thinks of herself as "wicked" (129), to Felix she is "a folded flower" who only needs to be "pluck[ed] . . . from the parent tree" in order to "expand" (176).

Wentworth, William Father of Charlotte, Gertrude, and Clifford, and uncle of Eugenia and Felix, he is a wealthy man of Puritan stock, sober, earnest, and dutiful with a great deal of "trust-business to transact" in his Devonshire Street (Boston) office (88). He has a large house with a piazza, spacious grounds, a pond, and a smaller house on the property, which he offers to Eugenia and Felix for the summer.

Young, Felix Eugenia's younger brother is 28 years old, slight of build, and although resembling Eugenia, rather handsome. His complexion is clear and fair, his eyes blue with fine arched brows, and he sports an upward-curving moustache that accentuates an impression of smiling benevolence. He is "witty-looking" (37) and "picturesque" (38), and his disposition is aptly reflected in his name, Felix ("happy"), for he has a prodigious "faculty of enjoyment" (79) and "indestructible gaiety" (189). Described as "an obscure Bohemian" (39), Felix is something of a dilettante. He has worked as an itinerant artist, musician, actor, and correspondent for an illustrated newspaper. During his stay on the Wentworth property, he paints portraits and landscapes. Although early on he imagines himself in love with Charlotte, Gertrude, and Lizzie, his affections soon converge upon Gertrude. The two fall in love and in the end marry.

ADAPTATION

The Europeans (1979) was directed by James Ivory with a screenplay by Ruth Prawer Jhabvala. Lee Remick played Eugenia, Tim Woodward played Felix, and Robin Ellis played Robert Acton. The film was nominated for an Oscar and a Golden Globe.

FURTHER READING

Poirier's pioneering essay is considered a benchmark in criticism of *The Europeans*. Austin's and Fincham's critiques are invaluable for their insightful character analyses. Geary's centennial essay offers a useful overview of criticism to 1982, and Tanner's introduction to the Penguin edition is indispensable.

Ascari, Maurizio. "Prince Camaralzaman and Princess Badoura Come to Tea: Cosmopolitanism and the European Identity in *The Europeans*." In *Across the Atlantic: Cultural Exchanges between Europe and the United States,* edited by Luisa Passerini, 59–71. Bruxelles: Peter Lang, 2000.

Austin, Deborah. "Innocents at Home: A Study of 'The Europeans' of Henry James." *Journal of General Education* 14 (1962): 103–129.

Bass, Eben. "James's *The Europeans*." *Explicator* 23, no. 1 (1964): 9.

Bell, Ian F. A. "Sincerity and Performance in *The Europeans*." *Modern Philology* 88, no. 2 (1990): 126–146.

Buitenhuis, Peter. "Comic Pastoral: Henry James's *The Europeans*." *University of Toronto Quarterly* 31 (1962): 152–163.

Edel, Leon. *Henry James: A Life.* New York: Harper & Row, 1985.

Fincham, Gail. "'The Alchemy of Art': Henry James's 'The Europeans'." *English Studies in Africa* 23, no. 2 (1980): 83–92.

Geary, Edward A. "*The Europeans*: A Centennial Essay." *Henry James Review* 4, no. 1 (1982): 31–49.

James, Henry. *The Europeans.* New York: Penguin, 1984.

Kalupahana, Chamika. "'Les beaux jours sont passés': Staging Whiteness and Postcolonial Ambivalence in *The Europeans* by Henry James." *Canadian Review of American Studies* 33, no. 2 (2003): 119–138.

Leavis, F. R. "The Novel as Dramatic Poem (III): 'The Europeans.'" *Scrutiny* 15 (1948): 209–221.

Long, Robert Emmet. *Henry James: The Early Novels.* Boston: Twayne, 1983.

Lustig, T. J. "Sunspots and Blindspots in *The Europeans*." *E-rea Revue d'etudes Anglophones* 3, no. 2 (2005): 6–18.

Martin, Robert K. "Ages of Innocence: Edith Wharton, Henry James, and Nathaniel Hawthorne." *Henry James Review* 21, no. 1 (2000): 56–62.

Nazare, Joseph. "Enter Touchstone: Manners of Comedy in James's *The Europeans*." *Henry James Review* 18, no. 2 (1997): 149–160.

Petitjean, Tom. "James's *The Europeans*." *Explicator* 52, no. 3 (1994): 155–157.

Poirier, Richard. *The Comic Sense of Henry James: A Study of the Early Novels.* New York: Oxford University Press, 1960.

Tanner, Tony. Introduction to *The Europeans*, by Henry James, 7–29. New York: Penguin, 1984.

Tuttleton, J. W. "Propriety and Fine Perception: James's 'The Europeans.'" *Modern Language Review* 73, no. 3 (1978): 481–495.

Ward, J. A. *The Search for Form: Studies in the Structure of James's Fiction.* Chapel Hill: University of North Carolina Press, 1967.

Williams, Merle A. "Traces of James's Later Manner in 'New England's Silvery Prime': A Reading of *The Europeans*." *English Studies in Africa* 36, no. 2 (1993): 21–29.

Sarah Wadsworth, *Marquette University*

The Golden Bowl (1904)

Charles Scribner's Sons first published the novel in two volumes in November 1904. James revised it for the NEW YORK EDITION in which it appeared as Volumes 23 and 24 in 1909.

SYNOPSIS

Book First, The Prince

Part First

(Chapter 1) The novel opens by recording the impressions of Prince Amerigo, an Italian nobleman of modest means, as he strolls through LONDON on a beautiful day in August, having just signed the legal documents that seal his MARRIAGE to a wealthy American girl, Maggie Verver. Although his dark, handsome features mark him as a foreigner, the Prince feels at home in London, where the riches of a modern empire are evident everywhere, especially in the lavish possessions of the Verver household. Amerigo's future father-in-law, Adam Verver, is a fabulously rich American who has retired from business to devote his energies and his massive fortune to art collecting. With his daughter constantly at his side, he wanders the ancient capitals of Europe in search of treasures for his museum in American City. Amerigo declares his admiration for Mr. Verver, but he understands that his marriage to Maggie is another of Adam's acquisitions. Exhilarated by his good fortune, yet troubled by his status as an article of exchange—one of uncertain value—the Prince decides to pay a visit to his confidante and adviser, Fanny Assingham, at her home in Cadogan Place.

(Chapter 2) As her name suggests, Fanny is an "ass," but an earnest and an entertaining one. Her sole occupation in life is to worry about the private lives of other people, whose moods, affections, and amorous relationships she watches and analyzes with obsessive interest. She was responsible for introducing Maggie and Amerigo while the Ververs were in Rome, and since their engagement she has served as his guide through the bewildering emotional landscape of Anglo-American courtship. The Prince confides in Fanny about his fears, explaining that his Italian morality is oddly out of step with that of the modern American Ververs. He worries that he may do something unacceptably "off" without realizing it (23). Fanny tries to reassure him and then mentions, somewhat reluctantly, that Maggie's close friend Charlotte Stant has arrived in London to attend the wedding and will be staying for an undetermined length of time with the Assinghams.

(Chapter 3) Although they were schoolgirls together and remain close, Charlotte and Maggie could not be more different. Unlike Maggie, Charlotte is alone in the world, without family or riches. She is American, but her "strange sense for tongues" makes her seem like a native wherever she goes, and her "perfect felicity in the use of Italian" suggests an extraordinary cosmopolitanism (41). When Fanny disappears from the drawing room to make arrangements for her visitor, the Prince and Charlotte share a moment together, and he advises her to find a wealthy husband. She takes this advice in stride and asks Amerigo if he will, as a favor, join her for an hour before his wedding to shop for a wedding gift for Maggie. He agrees and leaves to join the Ververs for dinner.

(Chapter 4) Later that evening, Fanny and her husband, Bob, a retired colonel, engage in the first of their many long, combative, and thoroughly entertaining conversations about the situation. Fanny is characteristically worried about what may be taking place just beneath the surface of appearances. She wonders why Charlotte has suddenly arrived, unannounced and uninvited, and she speculates that trouble may be brewing. The matter-of-fact Colonel Bob is constitutionally opposed to speculation, and he chides her at every opportunity for her fanciful anxieties. Fanny calls him stupid and elaborates by explaining that Charlotte and the Prince were once passionate lovers in Rome, and that they parted only because neither was wealthy enough to marry. It was after their break that Fanny introduced the Prince to Charlotte's wealthy American friend, a more propitious match for the financially constrained nobleman. Now she worries that the affair may not be over.

(Chapter 5) On the day before the wedding, Charlotte and the Prince keep their appointment to shop for a wedding present for Maggie. As they walk through the park, Charlotte surprises him with her frankness, announcing that she came back to London less for the wedding than for "this," a final hour together before his marriage (67). Their search for the "absolutely *right*" gift is fraught with erotic suggestion, as the former lovers wander through shops together, handling objects, discussing "values and authenticities," collaborating on the purchase of a fit symbol for the marriage that will formalize their separation (69, 75).

(Chapter 6) The couple wanders into a shop in quaint but unfashionable Bloomsbury. The merchant is a small Jewish antique dealer, who strikes Charlotte as an extraordinary figure. Amerigo asks Charlotte if she will accept a gift from him, and she asks him the same question. While they discuss the impropriety of such an exchange, the *antiquario* opens a box and produces his most prized possession, a crystal bowl, entirely gilded according to some ancient forgotten process, "a lost art" from "a

"The Curiosity Shop," by A. L. Coburn, frontispiece to the first volume of *The Golden Bowl,* Volume 23, the New York Edition

lost time" (85). The Prince exits the shop abruptly, while Charlotte discusses the bowl and negotiates over its value. When she cannot afford the asking price of 15 pounds, the dealer promises to save the bowl for her. Outside, the Prince is astounded that she failed to see a crack in the crystal, and he insists that the curious little man in whom she took such interest was a "rascal" (89). The Prince repeats his advice that she must marry, and the two give up the search for an appropriate wedding present.

Part Second

(Chapter 7) Approximately two years later, Adam Verver is at Fawns, his country house in Kent. With a handful of newspapers and unopened letters in his hand, he has retreated to the billiard room in the hope of spending an hour alone. He is pursued there by Mrs. Rance, a crass American visitor whose marital designs are thwarted only by the existence, somewhere in Texas or Nebraska, of a husband. Mrs. Rance is more an annoyance than a danger, but her very presence at Fawns forces Adam to recognize that something has changed in his relation to the social world. Until her marriage, Maggie—always "more than a daughter"—had shielded Adam from fortune-hunting women and other unwanted distractions (99). Now that she has a family of her own, he no longer enjoys her protection, and he reflects that his greatest passion—the pursuit of exquisite objects of great value—may suffer as a result of his vulnerability.

(Chapter 8) While Mr. Verver endures the company of Mrs. Rance, the novel's narrator describes the intellectual and aesthetic awakening that occurred in Adam's life after the death of his meek and somewhat tasteless wife. The material embodiment of this awakened vision will be the "museum of museums" in American City, "a receptacle of treasures sifted to positive sanctity" (107). The narrator reflects that the real meaning of Adam's experience as an art collector is freedom: "his freedom to see" (111). Maggie arrives home from church to find Adam still cornered in the billiard room by the aggressive Mrs. Rance. In an instant and without a word, father and daughter realize that his freedom is in jeopardy. Maggie recognizes that her marriage to the Prince has made room in her father's life "for others" and that others are moving in (114).

(Chapter 9) It is Maggie's routine to spend two hours after luncheon on Sundays with her son, the Principino, and when she arrives in the nursery her father is usually there, playing with his grandson. This intimate family circle—notably lacking the child's father—inspires her to question the nature of her relationship with the Prince, whom she claims to love, but never more dearly than when other women swoon over his good looks. This is an ominous admission, but Maggie is not panicked by her own apparent lack of romantic interest in the Prince. She also wonders about the nature of her affection for her father and decides that they are "right"—that their unusual intimacy is entirely proper (124). But Maggie worries that their "rightness" may not be enough to protect them, for women such as Mrs. Rance will inevitably interfere (123).

(Chapter 10) Adam asserts that he can "hold out" against female pursuers as long as Maggie is there to help, but she cleverly realizes that the right marriage might provide even more security (125). She loses no time in putting her plan into action by suggesting that Adam should invite her old friend Charlotte Stant for a visit. Adam is stunned by this suggestion, but he listens carefully as Maggie extols Charlotte's virtues. Adam seems more impressed by his daughter's beauty and eloquence, which strike him as "mythological and nymph-like," than by the substance of her argument, but he would do anything to please her, including this (139).

(Chapter 11) With Charlotte Stant's arrival at Fawns, her competitors for Adam's affection, Mrs. Rance and the Lutch sisters, immediately flee the scene, vanquished by her irrepressible charisma and "high authenticity" (145). Even the Assinghams, perennial guests in Adam's home, decide that it is time to return to London. Maggie and the Prince remain at Fawns with her father and Charlotte until the Prince is suddenly stricken with a desire to see his ancestral home. The couple departs for Rome, leaving the Principino behind with a corps of doctors and nurses to oversee his care. Adam begins to see Charlotte in a new light as they meet each day in the nursery, where the happy domestic circle is recreated in Maggie's absence. Charlotte plays the piano for him every evening, and it is not long before Adam contemplates marriage, provided that this would make Maggie happy. To marry for his own happiness (or that of Charlotte, for that matter) would be "impossible," but "there was a grand difference in thinking of it for his child" (154).

(Chapter 12) Charlotte and Adam take a three-day holiday on the coast in Brighton, where their relationship flourishes. The season is in full swing, and the resort is crowded with interesting types. While in Brighton, Adam arranges to meet with a Jewish antique dealer, Mr. Gutermann-Seuss, who possesses an extraordinary set of ancient Damascene tiles. Charlotte accompanies Adam to this appointment in the Gutermann-Seuss home, and her presence at his side infuses the transaction with mystical intensity. Adam asks Charlotte to marry him, but she is concerned that Maggie may not approve of her as a stepmother. Charlotte agrees to accept Adam's proposal only if Maggie endorses the marriage.

(Chapter 13) Adam writes to Maggie and then travels with Charlotte to Paris, where they await her decision. Maggie's telegram from Rome, addressed to her father, is apparently encouraging, but its meaning is obscure enough to cause Charlotte further anxiety. She observes that Maggie has written nothing to her directly and speculates that the Prince may be displeased. Adam encourages Charlotte to write them herself. She does so, and when the Prince responds, Charlotte agrees to the marriage. She offers to let Adam read Amerigo's telegram, but he declines.

Part Third

(Chapter 14) Charlotte and Adam are now married and settled in their new home at Eaton Square. At a formal party in London, Charlotte notices Bob Assingham staring at her, and she realizes that the ubiquitous Fanny cannot be far away. The Colonel has observed that Charlotte is there without her husband, and he notices that the Prince is serving as her unusually attentive escort. Maggie is absent from the party, too, having decided at the last minute to minister to her father, who was feeling ill. Sizing up the situation in an instant, Fanny confronts Charlotte to ask why she is not at home with her husband. Charlotte explains that Maggie and her father prefer to be alone together.

(Chapter 15) Still at the party, Charlotte is called away by a distinguished guest, and the Prince takes her place on the sofa beside Mrs. Assingham. He offers his view of the situation, explaining that he and Charlotte are quite naturally and innocently connected by circumstances. They are "in the same boat," and what may look like intimacy is a simple consequence of their common predicament (195). Fanny is skeptical about these rationalizations, but she agrees to think the situation over before giving up on the pair.

(Chapter 16) Riding home from the party in their hired brougham, Fanny and the Colonel argue over how to interpret the evening's developments. Bob wants to "let them alone," whether the relationship between Charlotte and the Prince is virtuous or not, but Fanny feels responsible for setting events in motion and must examine every nuance

of the situation (208). As they enter their house at Cadogan Place, she is convinced that she has orchestrated a terrible "mistake" (210).

(Chapter 17) Fanny continues to reflect on the morally dubious freedom that Adam Verver's marriage has afforded his wife and son-in-law. The Prince, alone on a gray afternoon at his home in Portland Place, is having similar thoughts about his peculiar situation. As he looks out the window, he sees Charlotte arriving in a coach. Surely, he tells himself, she has come to see Maggie, who is out. In fact, she has come to see him.

(Chapter 18) Charlotte explains that she has been to the British Museum, the National Gallery, the Zoo, and the Tower, traversing the city like "a mere wandering woman" (223). Maggie and the Principino have spent the day at Eaton Square with Adam, and her presence there seemed unnecessary. The Prince holds her hand, and they console each other by affirming that their situation is "sacred" (228). Their promise to trust and support each other is sealed with a passionate kiss.

(Chapter 19) The Prince and Charlotte become more brazen about their intimacy, and they decide that Mrs. Assingham's opinion no longer matters. Fanny is a frequent visitor to Eaton Square, where Maggie presides over her father's tea table, and thus she is aware that Charlotte generally vanishes to take her tea with her son-in-law at Portland Place. The arrangement is unconventional, but no public scandal ensues, and it seems to work for all concerned. Under Charlotte's leadership, the Ververs even make a small splash in society by hosting a cheerful, if dull, dinner party for London's elite in a spirit of "Arcadian optimism" (235).

(Chapter 20) The two couples have been invited to a large house party at Matcham, but Maggie and her father are reluctant to attend. To Mrs. Assingham's dismay, the Prince and Charlotte decide to go anyway. The narrator is careful to explain that nothing happens between the two married people at Matcham, but their increasing boldness signals a new level of intimacy.

(Chapter 21) As the house party draws to a close, Amerigo and Charlotte conspire to remain at Matcham until the other guests have left. Fanny is suspicious of this development, but she can do nothing to prevent it. The young people bid farewell to the Assinghams and declare their intention to catch a train to London after luncheon.

(Chapter 22) Only their hostess, Lady Castledean, and a handsome young man named Mr. Blint remain at Matcham, and they are completely preoccupied with each other. The Prince and Charlotte are thus free to do as they please. The Prince declares: "I feel the day like a great gold cup that we must somehow drain together" (263). He is surprised to learn that Charlotte has already consulted the train schedules to be sure they can spend the entire day together. They depart for Gloucester, a nearby village, where they plan to "do" the cathedral. It is unclear what else they "do" in these stolen hours (263).

(Chapter 23) Fanny meanwhile spends the entire journey to London silently contemplating the situation. She goes immediately to Eaton Square, where the behavior of Maggie, Adam, and the Principino gives her a new appreciation for the predicament in which Charlotte and the Prince find themselves "fixed" (269). After much rumination, she announces to Bob: "We were all wrong. There's nothing." The Colonel, as usual, struggles to follow her meaning, but she explains that the "extraordinary relation" between Charlotte and the Prince is something "beautiful" (270).

(Chapter 24) Fanny tells the Colonel that during her visit to Eaton Square she saw "doubt" in Maggie's face for the first time (178). This is a turning point in the novel, which in Book Second will focus on Maggie's awakening consciousness of her situation. Fanny explains that Maggie has begun to experience an illumination and predicts that Maggie will "triumph" (281). In response to the Colonel's crude interpretation of this statement, Mrs. Assingham exclaims that Maggie will succeed by opening her imagination "to what is called Evil . . . to the knowledge of it, to the crude experience of it" (282).

Book Second, The Princess
Part Fourth
(Chapter 25) As she awaits the return of Amerigo and Charlotte from Matcham, Maggie becomes suddenly aware of the complexity of her situation, which rises up like "an outlandish pagoda" occupying "the very centre of the garden of her life" (299). In a beautifully extended metaphor, the narrator explains that for months Maggie had walked around and around this elaborate structure, conducting her life in the space left her for circulation, but that she had never attempted to enter. Now that she has become curious for the first time, she discovers no convenient access from her garden level. Moreover, windows and apertures at the upper levels provide a view from within, and she feels certain that her approach to the structure has "been noted" (300). She decides to wait for Amerigo at their home in Portland Place rather than remain with her father. The Prince arrives home late in the evening and expresses his surprise at Maggie's uncharacteristic decision to leave Eaton Square. Apologizing for his lateness, he explains that his long day of tourism with Charlotte turned into "more of an affair than they expected" (311). Maggie offers to come upstairs to help him bathe and change for dinner, but he leaves her alone downstairs with her troubled thoughts.

(Chapter 26) As she waits for the Prince to arrive for dinner, Maggie thinks about the odd family dynamic she has fostered and reflects that the arrangement is particularly difficult for Charlotte, who was recruited to serve as a fourth wheel when "the family coach lumbered and stuck" (314). The coach now moves more effectively, but Maggie must acknowledge that "Amerigo and Charlotte were pulling it while she and her father were . . . seated inside together, dandling the Principino" (314). The Prince comes downstairs for dinner, and Maggie displays unusual interest in the details of his adventure at Matcham. Amerigo is puzzled by her demeanor and understands that something has changed in her attitude toward their relationship. On the following day, Maggie goes to Eaton Square, where Charlotte is preparing to depart, presumably to be with the Prince. Maggie detains her with questions about her holiday at Matcham. With excellent taste, both the Prince and Charlotte indulge Maggie's curiosity, but their very similar reactions to her unprecedented interest in their affairs leave Maggie feeling lonely and isolated.

(Chapter 27) For a long time, Maggie and her father have planned a trip to the Continent together. Now that her attitude toward her marriage has changed, Maggie worries that to undertake such an adventure might be a mistake. She is reluctant to draw attention to her fears by canceling the trip, but Adam makes this unnecessary by announcing that it would be more pleasant to remain in England for the summer. Maggie suggests to the Prince that he should invite Adam on a sightseeing journey himself. This would give Maggie and Charlotte time to be together.

(Chapter 28) This plan is not immediately adopted. The four characters now spend much of their time together, and Maggie marvels that "it seemed as easy for them to make a quartette as it had formerly so long appeared for them to make a pair of couples" (348). She congratulates herself on having shifted the harmony of the entire group to "a new basis" (352). Nevertheless, she remains troubled and suspects that "a deeper treachery" might perhaps "lurk in recoveries and reassurances" (353). She wonders why her father decided to marry and realizes that it was to guarantee *her* happiness.

(Chapter 29) Maggie and her father, in one of their now rare moments of intimacy, take a walk together in Regent's Park. He mentions that Charlotte has raised the possibility that he and the Prince might travel together. Adam is willing to undertake such a journey, but only if Amerigo seriously wants to go. He tells Maggie that he is very content with the life they are leading, which he compares to "lying like gods together, all careless of mankind" (365). Adam admits that the two interwoven married couples move about "as a selfish mass," and he worries that their happiness may be tinged with immorality (366). Rather than rearrange the group into a new pairing, he proposes that they all return to Fawns for the summer. Maggie agrees to drop the idea of a journey for her father and husband. Instead, she makes plans to invite the Castledeans and the Assinghams to Fawns.

(Chapter 30) Prior to leaving London for Fawns, Maggie has tea with Fanny Assingham at Portland Place. Charlotte and the Prince have left the house to spend the afternoon together. Maggie asks Fanny if she knows of any "awfulness" that may exist between her husband and Charlotte (378). Mrs. Assingham is shocked at this suggestion and tries to convince Maggie that her suspicions are completely unfounded. After a long conversation, Maggie agrees that anything improper between Charlotte and the Prince is "impossible," and yet she throws herself into Fanny's arms "with a sound that had its oddity as a sign of relief" (387). Mrs. Assingham also begins to cry, "sympathetically and perversely" (387).

(Chapter 31) The Assinghams have accepted Adam's invitation for a "good long visit" at Fawns (387). Before departing from Cadogan Place, Fanny and Bob reassess the situation and consider their own role in creating it. As usual, Fanny leads the conversation, while Bob struggles to follow the sequence of her intricate impressions and interpretations. Fanny dreads the visit to Fawns, where she expects to be punished for "the monstrosity of [her] folly" (394). She believes she has injured Maggie and her father unforgivably by encouraging their marriages. Her only "advantage" at Fawns will be Maggie's magnificent tactfulness (395).

(Chapter 32) Adam and Charlotte have departed for Fawns, leaving the Prince and Maggie behind for a week in London. Maggie spends a morning at the British Museum with a curator, Mr. Crichton, who shows her manuscripts, parchments, portraits, and illustrations pertaining to the history of "the Prince's race" (407). Several days later, on the evening before her departure for Fawns, Maggie summons Fanny abruptly to Portland Place, where Fanny suspects that her "impossible hour"—the hour in which Maggie will accuse her of withholding knowledge about the Prince and Charlotte—is at hand (410).

(Chapter 33) Maggie tells Fanny that something strange has happened. On her way home from the museum, while shopping for a birthday present for her father, Maggie wandered into a Bloomsbury shop. There she encountered a "queer little foreign man" whose odd assortment of wares included one that struck her as "a rarity" (414). On the mantel sits the golden bowl, which "has turned witness," Maggie explains, to the fact that Charlotte and the Prince were once "intimate" (416). Maggie has placed the bowl where Amerigo is sure to see it, but she suspects that he has had some premonition of disaster, for he has been absent all afternoon. Fanny tries to convince the distraught Maggie that the Prince and Charlotte both married in good faith and with the highest expectations. After an intense conversation, Fanny smashes the bowl on the marble floor and announces, "whatever you meant by it has ceased to exist" (430). Amerigo, meanwhile, has arrived in the doorway in time to see the bowl destroyed. Fanny quickly exits, leaving the married couple alone.

(Chapter 34) A period of silence ensues as Maggie and the Prince survey the situation. Before anyone speaks, she picks up the three broken pieces of the bowl and places them on the mantel again. The Prince questions the significance of the bowl, but Maggie insists on the testimony it announces and taunts him by suggesting that the pieces might be carried to Fawns for further analysis and discussion. She explains that the queer little antiquarian who sold her the cracked bowl for a large sum repented of the dishonest transaction and asked to visit her in order to make amends. While at Portland Place, he noticed photographs of Charlotte and the Prince, the interesting young couple who had visited his shop four years earlier. The Prince—clearly shaken—announces to Maggie that she was never more sacred to him than at the moment of his transgression, "unless perhaps you've become so at this one" (445).

Part Fifth
(Chapter 35) With the Assinghams in tow, the couples reconvene at Fawns, where they entertain a parade of visitors, including the Castledeans, the Lutch sisters, and Mrs. Rance. In a rare moment of quiet conversation, Maggie tells Fanny that she is certain the Prince has said nothing to Charlotte about the golden bowl or the secret its reappearance has exposed. Amerigo's reluctance to enlighten Charlotte about their new situation constitutes for Maggie the beginning of a new intimacy with her husband. Charlotte is now the character who wanders in darkness and ignorance, and Maggie imagines her as "a prisoner looking through bars" (466).

(Chapter 36) During a lull in their busy social schedule, Adam and Fanny Assingham are playing bridge with the Prince and Charlotte on a warm summer night at Fawns. The Colonel is writing letters at the other end of the room, and Maggie reclines on a sofa with an unopened literary review in her hands. Unable to focus on the review, she walks to the terrace and watches the bridge players through a window. Charlotte excuses herself from the game and, like a "creature who has escaped by force from her cage," follows Maggie to the terrace (474). The two walk arm in arm, and Charlotte asks Maggie if she is angry about anything. Maggie flatly denies that she is in any way displeased with Charlotte. The other players also leave the bridge table and reach the doorway in time to watch Charlotte place a "prodigious kiss" on Maggie's cheek (482).

(Chapter 37) Three days after her confrontation with Charlotte, Maggie speaks with her father about how much has changed in their lives since Mrs. Rance, who is once again a guest at Fawns, caused her to worry about his freedom. Maggie tries to convince Adam that she "sacrificed" him for the sake of her own happiness (493). Adam cannot comprehend her point, but Maggie is careful to speak in abstractions, never directly alluding to Charlotte's dishonesty. In his frustration, Adam threatens to take Charlotte back to American City to live as the happy married couple he believes they are. Maggie says nothing to oppose this new idea.

(Chapter 38) Life at Fawns drags on, the tense silence broken only by a constant stream of unnamed visitors. The Prince refuses to console Charlotte, who feels increasingly helpless and alone. In her desperation, she adopts the role of *cicerone* at Fawns, offering extended tours of the house and collections to their guests. Maggie can hear the cry of despair in Charlotte's voice as she distracts herself by describing Adam's priceless objects for the gawking crowds. Amerigo slips off to London, ostensibly to unpack some books at Portland Place. Maggie understands that he wants to be alone, away from the wrenching sound of Charlotte's voice.

(Chapter 39) On a hot afternoon in August, Maggie sits by the window in her room. She sees

"Portland Place," by A. L. Coburn, frontispiece to the second volume of *The Golden Bowl*, Volume 24, the New York Edition

Charlotte walking alone in the garden. Maggie follows her, and the two once again meet in private, as they did on the terrace in chapter 36. Charlotte says she is tired of the life they are leading and has formed a new plan. She wants to take Adam to America, where for the first time she might really "possess" him as a husband (530). Maggie admits that she has worked against Charlotte by competing for her father's affection and declares that now she has "failed" (531).

Part Sixth
(Chapter 40) Charlotte has taken charge of packing the Verver household for transport to America. The Prince and Maggie return to Portland Place, which seems dismal in late summer. Maggie sug-

gests a trip to the Continent as a distraction, but the Prince wants to remain in London until Charlotte and Adam have departed. Maggie wonders if Amerigo should say good-bye privately to Charlotte. She discusses the situation with Fanny, who marvels at Maggie's quiet manipulation of all the major actors in the drama.

(Chapter 41) The Prince and Maggie are still alone in Portland Place. He is sequestered in his reading room, where Maggie enters with a telegram that has just arrived from Charlotte. She and Adam will arrive at Portland Place for tea at five. As the Prince reads the telegram, Maggie imagines him as a captive animal, much as she once pictured Charlotte. Maggie suggests that her father may wish to take her on a brief excursion after tea, in which case the Prince and Charlotte would have to entertain themselves. A tense moment passes as she waits for his response. He finally says that Charlotte and Adam are doing the best thing. A new intimacy suddenly takes root between Maggie and Amerigo.

(Chapter 42) Adam and Charlotte arrive for tea, a final encounter before their departure for America. The conversation is pleasant, with none of the tension and deception that characterized the talk at Fawns. Adam is impressed with the exquisite furnishings of Portland Place. As he and Maggie survey her many "good things," together they imagine the Prince and Charlotte as "the kind of human furniture required aesthetically by such a scene" (560–561). Father and daughter agree that his marriage to Charlotte has turned out to be a great success. After the guests leave, Maggie watches from her balcony as their coach disappears. Minutes later, as she waits for the Prince to return from putting their son to bed, she understands that this is her reward for the tremendous mental and emotional effort of the months that have passed since the breaking of the bowl. Amerigo enters, and the two embrace.

CRITICAL ANALYSIS

Students encountering *The Golden Bowl* for the first time are apt to be underwhelmed. "These people don't *do* anything," a bright young undergraduate recently complained to me. "It isn't even clear if something *happens* between Charlotte and the Prince when they 'do' the cathedral in Gloucester. I've read over 800 pages in which absolutely nothing takes place!" This is an entirely legitimate response to *The Golden Bowl,* and one that invites reflection on the special quality of Henry James's last major and, in many respects, most extraordinary novel.

Rather than attempt to convince my distressed student that she was wrong, I asked her to reread the following long passage, in which the narrator describes a moment of rare and peculiar intimacy between Charlotte and the Prince. They are at Adam Verver's country house, Fawns, which is crowded with visitors, as usual.

They had found a minute together in the great hall of the house during the half-hour before dinner; this easiest of chances they had already a couple of times arrived at by waiting persistently till the last other loiterers had gone to dress and by being prepared themselves to dress so expeditiously that they might a little later on be among the first to appear in festal array. The hall then was empty, before the army of rearranging cushion-patting housemaids were marshalled in, and there was a place by the forsaken fire, at one end, where they might imitate with art the unpremeditated. Above all, here, for the snatched instants, they could breathe so near to each other that the interval was almost engulfed in it and the intensity both of the union and the caution became a workable substitute for contact. They had prolongations of instants that counted as visions of bliss; they had slow approximations that counted as long caresses. (249)

Novels, like life, unfold in time. Something happens, and then something else happens, either in the next moment or some other one. The tenses that are such an important element in language ensure that our experience of any written narrative is structured in part by our consciousness of time, of the sequence of events being narrated. Some writers, particularly of the 20th century, seek to disorient the reader's temporal awareness by rearranging the sequence in surprising ways, but such experiments are no less thoroughly embedded in our awareness of time. *The Golden Bowl* rates as an unexceptional late-Victorian novel on this score, a relatively straightforward chronicle of events in the lives of its major characters (see VICTORIANISM). Yet, as the passage above begins to suggest, James's novel is less a sequence of moments in time than an attempt to capture something that resides between them.

When Charlotte and the Prince meet in the great hall at Fawns, they do not "do" anything; their meeting is precisely not an event in a chain of events, some of which have come before, some of which will presumably come after. Rather, it is a "prolongation of instants," a moment "snatched" from the sequence and held apart from it. The "intensity" of this encounter, its unexplainable duration, stems from the fact that nothing is going on, no one is kissing or embracing anyone else. Such actions, if they were to occur, would necessarily take place in time and in relation to other actions. By refraining from any activity whatsoever, Charlotte and Amerigo occupy an "interval," a wrinkle in time, and this is where something more exciting to Henry James than actual physical intimacy occurs.

The novel is full of such intervals. Indeed, one can think of *The Golden Bowl*, paradoxically, as consisting of a long series of intervals. Amid the frantic preparations for Maggie's wedding, for example, Charlotte and the Prince enjoy an "exceptional minute" together on the staircase at Portland Place, where she reminds him of his promise to accompany her on a shopping adventure (68). Days later, they spend an exceptional hour together hunting for Maggie's wedding present. These stolen intervals, like the meeting at Fawns, are charged with erotic suggestion because, again, nothing happens. The couple shops but does not buy, and their endless deliberations about values and objects can be understood as another set of "slow approximations that counted as long caresses." Of course, presiding over this extraordinary scene is the odd little antiquarian peddler, proprietor of the golden bowl, whom the narrator suggestively calls "the master," a term James famously conferred on himself at this late stage in his career (78). The antiquarian's prized possession, the gilded crystal bowl that is so rich with interpretive possibilities, itself exists outside of any temporal sequence, the product of "a lost time" (85).

Charlotte and the Prince are not the only characters who occupy the novel's curious intervals. Indeed, to the dismay of my frustrated student, the narrator generally summarizes actual events in the novel (an elaborate dinner party at Eaton Square, a house party at Matcham, a trip to the museum) while offering extended analyses of what takes place in the "interval[s] of calm" that come between them (482). The major characters are constantly socializing in *The Golden Bowl*, but very little of their experience in public makes its way into the novel, which is almost exclusively concerned with gaps that occur after the departure of one set of guests and before the arrival of the next. Maggie and the Prince find themselves alone in the midst of such a gap upon their return to London after the busy social season at Fawns. As they wait for Charlotte and Adam to arrive for a final visit, the uncertain married couple endures an intense interval, a "lingering moment" in which an unprecedented desire for intimacy suddenly flourishes between them (555). This is another of those "prolongations of instants," a moment out of time, as Maggie ironically emphasizes when she tries to cover her embarrassment by invoking the clock: "Then about five, I count on you" (555). She finds it not quite so easy to extricate herself from this sexually charged interval, however, for the Prince moves closer and takes her hand. As they stand "near enough" to kiss, his body "almost" pressing upon her, she chooses the perfect word: "Wait!" (555). And this is what they "do," which is to say *nothing*. Maggie's directive is not simply meant to put him off, as in "don't come any closer." It is also a way of elongating the instant, of stretching this interval between actual social contacts into something almost sublime.

It may seem a peculiar assertion, but the major characters in *The Golden Bowl* are most interesting precisely when they are least active, when they enter a zone of feeling and experience that exists between moments. Surprisingly, it is Adam, the least reflective member of the foursome, who thinks carefully about what it might mean to enter and occupy such a zone. In a conversation with Maggie, he wonders if they have become "lazy, a wee bit languid—lying like gods together, all careless of mankind" (365). Maggie points out that they live in the busiest city on earth, where they are constantly "running about, . . . pursued and pursuing." But Adam insists that there is something vaguely "immoral" about their life of concentrated leisure.

"What it comes to, I dare say, is that there's something haunting—as if it were a bit uncanny—in such a consciousness of our general comfort and privilege. Unless indeed," he had rambled on, "it's only I to whom, fantastically, it says so much. That's all I mean at any rate—that it's 'sort of' soothing; as if we were sitting about on divans, with pigtails, smoking opium and seeing visions. 'Let us then be up and doing'—what is it Longfellow says? That seems sometimes to ring out; like the police breaking in—into our opium-den—to give us a shake. But the beauty of it is at the same time that we *are* doing; we're doing, that is, after all, what we went in for. We're working it, our life, our chance, whatever you may call it, as we saw it, as we felt it, from the first." (366)

This is another remarkable statement about doing and not doing. Adam uses an outlandish orientalist image to suggest the immorality of the group's constant repose, and he invokes Longfellow's version of an American ethic of hard work as a corrective: "Let us then be up and doing." For this brief moment, Adam sounds slightly like the firebrand economist Thorstein Veblen, whose highly critical study of "conspicuous leisure" among people like the Ververs, *The Theory of the Leisure Class* (1899), was published just five years before *The Golden Bowl.* Yet Henry James is a more subtle cultural analyst than Veblen, and he is far too interested in the complex phenomenon of leisure to be merely critical of it. Thus Adam refines his point and reverses its emphasis by explaining to Maggie that the "beauty" of their situation is that they really "*are* doing." In fact, they are doing exactly what they set out to do; more than this, they are "working" it, much as Longfellow might have wished. And what they are doing with such purpose and conviction is, of course, exactly nothing. As Charlotte has said earlier, this nothing they are working at amounts to "taking everything as everything came, and all as quietly as might be" (211). *Everything* and *nothing* become oddly interchangeable terms for what occurs (or does not occur) in the novel's charged intervals, the gaps that open unusually wide in *The Golden Bowl* between points in time.

The idea that some indefinable but tremendous power is accessible to people quiet enough, immobile enough, to occupy and extend such intervals fascinated James throughout his late period. Little Bilham, the unambitious but highly cultured artist of *The Ambassadors,* is another figure who does not "do the least dreadful little thing," as is the lovely Mme. de Vionnet when she sits in "supreme stillness" before the altar at Notre-Dame cathedral (92, 207). Yet *The Golden Bowl* is James's most sustained meditation on the paradoxical notion of a kind of doing that is not doing. This idea permeates the structure of the narrative, and it also operates at the dramatic level, where inaction proves to be the most effective form of action. Consider the way Maggie, after her discovery of the golden bowl and the secret it communicates, succeeds in manipulating each of the other characters in the drama. Her tactics are those of a deft passive-aggressive, for she does absolutely nothing with her new knowledge except hold onto it, and in this way she controls the entire situation. She and the Prince occupy another of the novel's quiet intervals when they remain in London together for a week after Adam and Charlotte have departed early for Fawns. Maggie understands that she must deny Amerigo any consciousness of "the nature of their struggle," for if he recognizes that they are engaged in a "*high* fight," her advantage will be lost.

> She was learning almost from minute to minute to be a mistress of shades . . . but she was working against an adversary who was a master of shades too and on whom if she didn't look out she should presently have imposed a consciousness of the nature of their struggle. To feel him in fact, to think of his feeling himself, her adversary in things of this fineness—to see him at all in short brave a name that would represent him as in opposition—was already to be nearly reduced to a visible smothering of her cry of alarm. Should he guess they were having in their so occult manner a *high* fight, and that it was she, all the while, in her supposed stupidity, who had made it high and was keeping it high—in the event of his doing this before they could leave town she should verily be lost. (403–404)

The week in London passes without a mention of the shattered bowl or even a hint of recrimination. Nothing happens between Maggie and the Prince, and this "occult" silence—which he also maintains—becomes the source of a new intimacy between the married pair, an intimacy that changes the terms of Amerigo's relationship with Charlotte and hastens her decision to leave with Adam for America (401). Maggie's passive aggression, her ability to sit quietly with her knowledge and do nothing about it, transforms each of the major relationships.

Although Maggie eventually masters her situation by discovering the power of passivity, this insight is denied her in the first half of the novel. Throughout volume one, Charlotte and the Prince are the story's "perfectly passive pair," thrown together into a dreary intimacy by the Ververs' incestuous routine (203). Amerigo even congratulates himself by telling Charlotte that "it's precisely boring one's self without relief . . . that takes courage" (221). Although Charlotte is perpetually active, bustling around town like "a mere wandering woman" (233), she understands the meaning of his absurd remark and asks rhetorically: "Isn't the immense, the really quite matchless beauty of our position that we have to 'do' nothing in life at all?" "There has been plenty of 'doing,'" she continues, "and there will doubtless be plenty still; but it's all theirs, every inch of it; it's all a matter of what they've done *to* us" (211). Indeed, as long as Charlotte and the Prince remain "perfectly passive"—as long as they do nothing—their intimacy is what Fanny Assingham repeatedly calls "beautiful" (270). Maggie becomes the heroine only by surpassing Charlotte's authority in the realm of absolute leisure, becoming mistress of the novel's intervals, the quietest character of all.

To read *The Golden Bowl* as a sort of contest over the occult form of authority that attaches to demonstrations of leisure is to return—surprisingly, but inevitably—to Veblen. WILLIAM DEAN HOWELLS, the great novelist and critic of the period, declared that Veblen's 1899 book constituted an "opportunity for American fiction," and while James never read *The Theory of the Leisure Class*, it is difficult to imagine a novel more thoroughly saturated in the spirit of Veblen's bracing analysis (qtd. in Posnock 33). Veblen believed that all humans are naturally inclined to engage in "productive labor" but that, from an early stage of development,

societies attach superior status to "abstention from productive work" (41). In highly evolved societies, where property ownership is well established, an entire class of individuals develops in which prestige is awarded in return for prowess in the various unproductive activities that constitute "leisure." These activities must be conducted conspicuously, according to Veblen, because together they perform "a symbolic pantomime of mastery on the one hand and of subservience on the other" (48). Although the practice of leisure among members of the "superior pecuniary class" might appear like harmless entertainment, Veblen's great insight was to realize that such behaviors actually constitute an implicitly violent contest for status and authority. To display good manners at the dinner table, or to take an extended vacation in Italy, is to claim a certain measure of cultural status by deploying a particular set of signs that very precisely measure one's distance from the realm of productive labor.

Henry James may seem the least likely of all American writers to have participated in Veblen's aggressive critique. But he might also be understood as Veblen's literary counterpart, for *The Golden Bowl* is ultimately a study of the way power is exercised within the most rarified segment of the leisure class. And as Maggie Verver's triumph confirms, James joins Veblen in figuring the practice of leisure as a struggle for authority, a "symbolic pantomime of mastery . . . and of subservience." Veblen's metaphor of the pantomime is uncannily appropriate, for in the fictional world James creates there is little need for noise, much less action. My student was entirely correct in observing that "nothing happens" in *The Golden Bowl*, and yet—as Veblen might have pointed out—it is a highly conspicuous "nothing," a "perfect passivity" that is *more* conspicuous, in its own way, than any overt demonstration of the capacity for leisure. Veblen would not have admired anything about the superrich Ververs and their secretive spouses, but he would have been compelled to admit that *The Golden Bowl* has something important to teach about the "advanced" civilization we inhabit and the symbols through which we describe the inner workings of that civilization to one another.

CHARACTERS

Amerigo (The Prince)   The novel's first volume is called The Prince, and much of its attention is focused on Prince Amerigo's attempt to become a new man through his marriage to Maggie Verver. He comes from a noble but poor Roman family, whose history fills several volumes in the British Museum. The narrator describes the Prince as thoroughly Italian, even to the point that his ancient "race" smells like "some inexpugnable odor in which his clothes, his whole person, his hands and the hair of his head, might have been steeped" (13). Yet as the novel opens, Amerigo desires "some new history that should, so far as possible, contradict, and even if need be flatly dishonour, the old," and he recognizes that "the material for the making" of this new self "had to be Mr. Verver's millions" (13).

Amerigo's first love was Charlotte Stant, but neither he nor Charlotte was rich enough to support a life of leisure. His marriage to Maggie Verver guarantees him a large fortune, but the Prince understands that his name, his title, and his Italian good looks have become articles of exchange, objects in his father-in-law's collection, and he feels like "some old embossed coin, of a purity of gold no longer used" (18).

Assingham, Colonel   Colonel Assingham, or Bob, is Fanny Assingham's sidekick and foil. His principal function in the novel is to listen and scoff at her ongoing analysis of events in the Verver households, where the Assinghams are perpetual guests. He is a retired British military officer who feels that he knows "everything that could be known about life" (50). His American wife finds him hopelessly lacking in "moral" and "intellectual reaction," yet in spite of his limitations he is "a perfectly social creature" (50).

Assingham, Fanny   Fanny Assingham is a childless middle-aged woman who spends most of her time and prodigious mental energy speculating about the private lives of her friends. Never satisfied with what appears on the surface, she is "full of discriminations against the obvious" (25). New York was her birthplace, according to the narrator,

and Europe her "discipline" (26). The Assinghams are not wealthy, and they rely heavily on Mr. Verver's hospitality. Fanny is a matchmaker, having facilitated the marriage between Maggie and the Prince, and she serves as an adviser and confidante to each of the major characters.

Bloomsbury antiquario, the   Charlotte is fascinated by the little man who owns the Bloomsbury shop where she and the Prince first see the golden bowl. In fact, he is "the greatest curiosity" they encounter during their hunt for Maggie's wedding gift (79). According to the narrator, "he was clearly the master" of his business, a phrase that hints at the antiquario's relation to Henry James himself (78). Amerigo calls him "a swindling little Jew" and a "decided little beast," but this curious character is not so easily reduced to a stereotype (263, 443). When he reappears with his golden bowl toward the end of the novel, the antiquario brings information that clarifies Maggie's situation.

Castledeans, the   Lord and Lady Castledean are regular members of the Ververs' social set. They host a house party at their country estate, Matcham, where the relationship between Charlotte and the Prince reaches a new level of intimacy.

Crichton, Mr.   Mr. Crichton is a curator at the British Museum, "the custodian of one of the richest departments of the great national collection of precious things" (406). He escorts Maggie Verver to an archive containing pictures, prints, manuscripts, and historical volumes pertaining to the Prince's ancient family.

Gutermann-Seuss, Mr.   Mr. Gutermann-Seuss is a Jewish antique dealer in Brighton who brokers Adam Verver's purchase of some extraordinarily beautiful Damascene tiles. His household full of children and relatives makes a great impression on Charlotte, for whom the transaction possesses a "touch of some mystic rite of old Jewry" (159).

Principino, the   Maggie's and Amerigo's child makes few appearances in the novel and says absolutely nothing. Although he is ostensibly cherished by all the major characters, he spends surprisingly little time in their presence or in their thoughts.

Rance, Mrs.   Mrs. Rance is a married woman with designs on Adam Verver's millions. The period's social stigma against divorce neutralizes her as an actual threat, but her presence at Fawns is enough to convince Maggie that her father is vulnerable to fortune-hunting women.

Stant, Charlotte   Charlotte is a stunningly beautiful, intelligent, independent young woman, and yet she is poor and unmarried. In her social milieu, these deficiencies potentially trump every other personal characteristic, and Charlotte runs a very real risk of becoming another Lily Bart, the tragic socialite in Edith Wharton's *The House of Mirth* (1905). Once the Prince, her former lover, has found a rich wife for himself, he advises Charlotte to marry well, which she does when she accepts Adam's proposal and becomes the Prince's mother-in-law. Although her marriage brings her great wealth, it comes at a steep emotional cost, and Charlotte's suffering in the second half of the novel is more intense than that of any other major character.

Charlotte is an American by birth, but she has been educated in Europe and no longer thinks of America as home. Her uncertain citizenship seems to "enrich her somehow with an odd, precious neutrality," a cosmopolitan quality that serves as a "small social capital"—the only capital she controls until her marriage (41). Maggie tries to describe Charlotte's curiously appealing aura by explaining, somewhat cryptically, that she "has only to be what she is—and to be it all around," for "it's she who is the real thing" (144). Charlotte's high authenticity catches the attention of Adam—the collector of rare, authentic objects—and he wastes no time in adding her to his collection.

After living like a caged animal through much of her married life, Charlotte prepares for a new life in America at the end of the novel. In American City, she believes, it will be possible "really to possess" her husband, who she has decided is "worth it" (530). This projected shift in their proprietary roles hints that a new intimacy, or at least a new relationship, may be possible for the childless Ververs.

Verver, Adam   Adam Verver is a fabulously rich American capitalist who has moved to England with his daughter, Maggie, in order to pursue his true passion, the accumulation of "costly authenticities" (106). Although he is a "small, spare, slightly stale person, deprived of the general prerogative of presence" (125), his money possesses a charisma of its own and endows Adam with the godlike power to shape destinies. He takes little interest in people, except for his daughter and grandson, the Principino, and he is often in active retreat from social contact.

After thriving in business as a young man, Adam discovered something more enticing than money. His "peak in Darien" was "the hour of his perceiving with a mute inward gasp akin to the low moan of apprehensive passion, that a world was left him to conquer and that he might conquer it if he tried" (104). This unconquered terrain is the world of beautiful objects, "good things," which he collects for his planned "museum of museums" in a place called American City (561, 107). From the novel's beginning to its end, this passion fills Adam to the exclusion of all other passions.

Adam's readiness to treat even people like collectible objects can make him seem quietly sinister, but he has a conscience. Of all the major characters, he is the only one who recognizes their shared life of leisure as absurdly "selfish" (365). Although apparently oblivious to the infidelity of his wife and son-in-law, he senses something "immoral" in the "general comfort and privilege" of their lifestyle, and he compares their lavish home to "an opium den" (366).

Verver, Maggie (The Princess)   Of all the major characters, Maggie is the one who changes most significantly as a result of events in the novel. She is initially little more than Adam Verver's devoted daughter, and her acquisition of a husband does nothing to interfere with their constant intimacy. The arrival of Charlotte as Adam's wife actually fosters even greater filial contact, for Charlotte and the Prince are capable of entertaining each other. Maggie remains fittingly childlike in her role as Adam Verver's little girl, and Fanny Assingham even asserts that, "she wasn't born to know evil. She must never know it" (59).

"Evil" takes root at the center of Maggie's situation, however, in the form of her husband's infidelity and her own incestuous impulses. As her innocence is more and more shaken, Maggie gradually awakens to the truth of her situation, "to the knowledge of it, to the crude experience of it" (282).

With this awakening, Maggie becomes a "much-thinking little person" (312), and the second half of the novel is largely concerned with her troubled thoughts. She becomes masterful at manipulating the nerves of those around her, employing passive-aggressive tactics like "a mistress of shades" (403). She finally succeeds in banishing Charlotte and recovering her husband, not through open persuasion, but through an exceedingly subtle art of emotional diplomacy.

ADAPTATIONS

James Ivory directed a film version of *The Golden Bowl* based on Ruth Prawer Jhabvala's screenplay in 2000. The film starred Uma Thurman, Nick Nolte, Kate Beckinsale, and Jeremy Northam.

A television serial based on the novel, with a screenplay by Jack Pulman, was produced in 1972. This six-part series starred Barry Morse, Jill Townsend, Daniel Massey, and Gayle Hunnicutt and aired on PBS's *Masterpiece Theatre*.

FURTHER READING

Anderson, Quentin. "Why R. P. Blackmur Found James's *Golden Bowl* Inhumane." *English Literary History* 68, no. 3 (2001): 725–743.

Dimock, Wai Chee. "Pre-National Time: Novel, Epic, Henry James." *Henry James Review* 24, no. 3 (2003): 215–224.

Dupee, F. W. *Henry James: His Life and Writings*, 1951. Reprint, New York: Doubleday Anchor Books, 1956.

Freedman, Jonathan. *The Temple of Culture: Assimilation and Anti-Semitism in Literary Anglo-America*. New York: Oxford University Press, 2000.

James, Henry. *The Ambassadors*. 1903. Reprint, New York: Oxford University Press, 1985.

———. *The Golden Bowl*. 1904. New York: Oxford University Press, 1983.

Krook, Dorothea. *The Ordeal of Consciousness in Henry James*. New York: Cambridge University Press, 1962.

Matthiessen, F. O. *Henry James: The Major Phase*. London: Oxford University Press, 1944.

Mitchell, Lee Clark. "Ethics, Aesthetics, and the Case of Late James." *Raritan: A Quarterly Review* 22 (Spring 2003): 71–89.

Person, Leland S. *Henry James and the Suspense of Masculinity*. Philadelphia: University of Pennsylvania Press, 2003.

Peyser, Thomas. *Utopia and Cosmopolis: Globalization in the Era of American Realism*. Durham, N.C.: Duke University Press, 1998.

Posnock, Ross. "Henry James, Veblen, and Adorno: The Crisis of the Modern Self." *Journal of American Studies* 21 (April 1987): 31–54.

Ross, Melanie H. "'The Mirror with a Memory': Tracking Consciousness in the Preface to *The Golden Bowl*." *Henry James Review* 26, no. 3 (2005): 246–255.

Schor, Hilary M. "Reading Knowledge: Curiosity in *The Golden Bowl*." *Henry James Review* 26, no. 3 (2005): 237–245.

Seltzer, Mark. *Henry James and the Art of Power*. Ithaca, N.Y.: Cornell University Press, 1989.

Snediker, Michael. "Stasis & Verve: Henry James and the Fictions of Patience." *Henry James Review* 27, no. 1 (2006): 24–41.

Veblen, Thorstein. *The Theory of the Leisure Class*. 1899. Reprint, New York: Mentor, 1953.

Vidal, Gore. "Return to *The Golden Bowl*." *New York Review of Books*, January 19, 1984.

Wilson, R. B. J. *Henry James's Ultimate Narrative: The Golden Bowl*. St. Lucia: Queensland Press, 1981.

Wollheim, Richard. "Flawed Crystals: James's *The Golden Bowl* and the Plausibility of Literature as Moral Philosophy." *New Literary History* 15 (Autumn 1983): 185–191.

Wonham, Henry B. "Amerigo's Miraculous Metamorphosis: or, the Logic of Ethnic Caricature in *The Golden Bowl*." *Henry James Review* 26, no. 2 (2005): 130–146.

Yeazell, Ruth B. *Language and Knowledge in the Late Novels of Henry James*. Chicago: University of Chicago Press, 1976.

———. "Teaching *The Golden Bowl* as the Last Victorian Novel." *Henry James Review* 17, no. 2 (1996): 275–280.

Henry B. Wonham, *University of Oregon*

The Portrait of a Lady (1881)

In a letter of 1877, Henry James first alluded to a "masterpiece" that he believed he would write. He did not actually begin writing *The Portrait of a Lady* until 1880 while in FLORENCE. The novel initially appeared serially from October 1880 to November 1881 in *Macmillan's Magazine* and from November 1880 to December 1881 in the *Atlantic Monthly*. James secured a book contract shortly thereafter, and by the end of 1881 Macmillan had printed the book. Houghton Mifflin followed with a printing in 1882. *The Portrait of a Lady* was one of a number of James's novels to undergo revision for Charles Scribner's Sons' NEW YORK EDITION, in which it came out in 1908 as Volumes 3 and 4.

SYNOPSIS

(Chapter 1) Mr. Touchett, his son (Ralph Touchett), and their neighbor (Lord Warburton) take their afternoon tea on the lawn of Gardencourt, Mr. Touchett's old English estate. This opening chapter establishes the contrast between England and America, which develops thematically in the novel (see INTERNATIONAL THEME). The theme of MARRIAGE is also introduced through Warburton's character, who claims not to wish to involve himself with anyone. By the end of the chapter, readers learn that the novel's protagonist, Isabel Archer, will soon arrive from America with Mrs. Touchett.

(Chapter 2) When the independent Isabel and her aunt arrive, Mrs. Touchett goes directly to her

"The English Home," by A. L. Coburn, frontispiece to the first volume of *The Portrait of a Lady,* Volume 3, the New York Edition

room, leaving Isabel to introduce herself to her uncle, cousin, and their friend. Mrs. Touchett's ambivalence reflects her character and her relationship to her husband, whom she has not seen for a year. It is clear that Isabel has a romantic view of England based not upon experience but upon her novel reading. She thrills at the idea of meeting a "lord," for example. It exposes her naïveté and also her American brashness and independence. We learn the circumstances of Isabel's past (her mother's early death, her father's recent one, and the quarrel between the Archers and Mrs. Touchett, which kept the cousins from knowing each other). Isabel resists the idea that she has been "adopted" by Mrs. Touchett because she is "very fond of [her] liberty" (74).

(Chapter 3) Structured as a flashback to Isabel's and Mrs. Touchett's first meeting in Albany, this chapter further explains Mrs. Touchett's character and her strained relationship with her husband. She detests England and has been living in Florence. Isabel's unconventional upbringing is noted (she was raised by her father and grandmother) as well as her lack of a formal education. The lack of supervision and conventional guidance in her early years may explain her need for independence now.

(Chapter 4) Isabel's sister and brother-in-law are introduced, and they describe Isabel and her strange ideas as "foreign." The theme of displacement begins here; Isabel seems both out of place in Albany and England. Isabel reflects very favorably upon her father in contrast with others' opinions of him. Caspar Goodwood, one of Isabel's primary suitors, makes his appearance.

(Chapter 5) The narrative returns to Gardencourt, where Ralph, who has not seen his mother for some time, goes to her room at the appointed time, as requested. There is background on how the family got to England with an emphasis on Mr. Touchett's determination to remain "assimilated yet unconverted" (92). This contrasts somewhat with Mrs. Touchett's plan for Isabel: to rescue her from her American destiny and show her opportunity in Europe. Ralph's character is also examined more in depth, with an emphasis on his frailty and sickliness. Ralph and Isabel get to know each other better as they tour the estate's gallery. Though

Ralph is attentive and kind to his cousin, his interest in watching her and looking at her as though she were a painting establishes a theme that will grow in importance as the novel progresses. A bit of foreshadowing occurs as Isabel asks to see Gardencourt's ghost. Ralph replies that she has not suffered enough to see it.

(Chapter 6) This chapter provides a more detailed account of Isabel's character; the narrator tells how she might see herself as superior and is definitely independent. She is different from other women. Henrietta Stackpole, the globe-trotting journalist friend of Isabel is introduced. Though the two are clearly American, Henrietta is travel-tested and holds ideas that seem far more progressive than Isabel, who has relied on books for information about the wide world.

(Chapter 7) Isabel's impropriety is evident when she attempts to stay up alone with her cousin and Lord Warburton, revealing that she does not either understand or care about English conventions. Her behavior highlights the differences between British and American cultures. Lord Warburton visits for several days and is obviously interested in Isabel.

(Chapter 8) Isabel receives an invitation from Warburton to visit his estate, Lockleigh. Warburton holds radical political views although he represents the landed gentry in Parliament. Isabel, who owes her impressions of the world to the novels she has read, is curious about what all of this means and questions Warburton about his views on life.

(Chapter 9) Warburton's sisters, the Misses Molyneux, arrive at Gardencourt to meet Isabel. They are placid and uninteresting, with few original opinions. Isabel, Ralph, and Mrs. Touchett then visit Lockleigh. Isabel tests Warburton's radical resolve by asking his sisters if he would give up property for the cause. The sisters are astounded, again demonstrating the void between the two cultures. Warburton tells Isabel that she has charmed him, and he asks to see her often.

(Chapter 10) A letter from Henrietta Stackpole announces that she is in England and that she plans to visit Gardencourt. By the end of the chapter, she has arrived and initiated what appears to be a contentious relationship with Ralph, who is skeptical of her journalistic habits and intrusive curiosity.

He suspects (correctly) that she will attempt to chronicle her stay at Gardencourt for her "Letters" column.

(Chapter 11) Despite Mrs. Touchett's dislike of her, Henrietta continues her stay at Gardencourt. Henrietta believes that England has changed Isabel for the worse. She informs her that Caspar Goodwood has followed her to England and desires a visit. A letter arrives from Goodwood, echoing Henrietta's announcement. At this point, these characters seem determined to cement Isabel's allegiance to her home country.

(Chapter 12) Lord Warburton visits Gardencourt again. His amorous intentions toward Isabel become clear. In fact, he appears to propose to her. Isabel hesitates and even declares, "I'm not sure I wish to marry any one" (161).

(Chapter 13) Isabel tells her uncle of Lord Warburton's proposal, and Mr. Touchett admits that he had already received a letter from Warburton alerting him to the proposal. Though Mr. Touchett seems surprised and even disappointed that Isabel does not plan on marrying the English lord, Isabel's uncle supports her decision. Caspar Goodwood is examined, both as a suitor and as a character; he is aggressive and decidedly American. Isabel writes a letter to Warburton, declining his marriage proposal. In the meantime, Henrietta and Ralph discuss Isabel. In an attempt to maintain Isabel's American allegiance, Henrietta asks Ralph to invite Goodwood to Gardencourt. Ralph sends an invitation, but Goodwood declines. Henrietta also writes a letter, which he ignores. Henrietta is determined to take Isabel to Goodwood in LONDON.

(Chapter 14) The trip to London is postponed when Lord Warburton decides to visit Gardencourt. He confronts Isabel about her decision, and she cryptically explains that she cannot marry him because she "can't escape [her] fate" (185), which she sees as "unhappiness" (186).

(Chapter 15) Isabel, Henrietta, and Ralph go to London, where Henrietta ostensibly hopes to gather material for her "Letters," but it is September, and most of the aristocracy is away. Ralph introduces them to Mr. Bantling. When Henrietta goes off to meet with some American friends, Isabel and Ralph have a long talk about Warburton, his

proposal, and Isabel's response, all of which greatly intrigue Ralph.

(Chapter 16) With an unannounced visit, Goodwood unpleasantly surprises Isabel as she dines alone. He has come to find out why she has put him off and to press her into marriage. She asks him to wait for a year or two and declares that she needs her "liberty" and "personal independence" (213).

(Chapter 17) Henrietta returns to the hotel to find a relieved yet angry Isabel. Ralph receives a telegram from his mother announcing his father's quickly failing health, and he and Isabel leave for Gardencourt. Ralph learns that Isabel has put off Goodwood's marriage proposal.

(Chapter 18) At Gardencourt, Ralph and Isabel find Mr. Touchett quite ill. Isabel meets Serena Merle, whose piano playing attracts the young woman to the drawing room. Isabel is fascinated by her. Ralph spends much time at his father's deathbed. Mr. Touchett tells Ralph he wants him to do something with his life: marry Isabel. Ralph says he will not marry her, but that he wants her to inherit a substantial portion of the estate so that she will not have to marry.

(Chapter 19) As Isabel and Mme Merle get to know each other better, it becomes clear that Mme Merle envies Isabel and that Isabel adores this new (but dangerous) role model. Mme Merle mentions Gilbert Osmond (the reader's and Isabel's first introduction to him). Mr. Touchett dies.

(Chapter 20) Mme Merle visits Mrs. Touchett as she readies one of the houses for sale. Mrs. Touchett declares that Mr. Touchett has left Isabel a "fortune." Merle is thrilled and calls Isabel a "clever creature," which offends Mrs. Touchett (260). Isabel begins her tour of Europe when Mrs. Touchett takes her to PARIS. While there, Isabel meets Ned Rosier, whom she remembers from her childhood travels with her father.

(Chapter 21) Mrs. Touchett and Isabel visit Ralph in Italy. Isabel asks Ralph if he knew that she would inherit so much money, but his vague response keeps Isabel from knowing the truth.

(Chapter 22) Set in Gilbert Osmond's Florentine villa, this chapter introduces the novel's antagonist. Osmond is difficult to characterize. His country of origin, for example, cannot be determined by his appearance, and many of his features seem vague. He enjoys control over his daughter, Pansy, whose education he entrusts to nuns. Mme Merle arrives, telling Osmond about Isabel and laying out her plan for them to marry. It is clear that Osmond dominates Pansy and that his relationship with Merle is unconventional, which foreshadows later events.

(Chapter 23) Isabel meets and charms Osmond. She discusses him and Mme Merle with Ralph, who dislikes Osmond. However, Isabel has already started showing interest in him.

(Chapter 24) Isabel visits Osmond and meets his sister, the Countess Gemini, who appears flamboyant and vapid. Isabel finds herself drawn to Osmond's discerning taste, his prideful solitude, and his seemingly unconventional views on life.

(Chapter 25) The Countess confronts Merle about her intentions to lure Isabel into a marriage to Osmond and threatens to warn Isabel. Mme Merle argues that Isabel will not listen to the Countess because she does not like her. Pansy is asked what she thinks of Isabel and responds with a vague and noncommittal claim that Isabel is not her guest.

(Chapter 26) Mme Merle notes to Mrs. Touchett that Osmond has visited Mrs. Touchett's villa five times. It becomes clear that Mrs. Touchett disapproves of Osmond, who has no fortune. Ralph, Henrietta, Mr. Bantling, and Isabel make plans to go to ROME. Meanwhile, Osmond and Mme Merle meet at the Countess Gemini's, and Osmond tells Merle that Isabel has invited him to meet her in Rome.

(Chapter 27) Isabel waits for Ralph as he tours some Roman relics. She is startled by the arrival of Lord Warburton, who again proposes to her. Osmond arrives too, and it is clear that Isabel is more interested in him.

(Chapter 28) Lord Warburton calls on Isabel at her hotel only to discover that she has gone to the opera. He follows her there and is disturbed to find Isabel and Osmond alone in the box.

(Chapter 29) Osmond's charms seem to warm even Ralph. But when Isabel receives a telegram from her aunt announcing that she soon will leave Florence for Belaggio, Isabel decides to join her. This inspires Osmond to declare his love for Isabel, and she responds with what seems like her

typical noncommittal response. He also asks her to visit Pansy, who has been staying alone in his villa.

(Chapter 30) Isabel informs Mme Merle that she plans to visit Pansy. Mme Merle says that she, too, was planning to visit, but that there is no need for both of them to go. She warns Isabel about going alone, since others may not know that Osmond is not there (again demonstrating Isabel's naïveté regarding European social customs). Isabel does go, and Pansy is delighted with the visit. In this most detailed sketch of Pansy so far, she appears very obedient and adoring of her father, even in his absence.

(Chapter 31) A year later, Isabel is back at Palazzo Crescentini (Mrs. Touchett's Florence home) after extensive travel. Part of her travel included time with her sister, Lily, and her young children. She also traveled east with Mme Merle and begins to question, ever so subtly, the solidity of their friendship.

(Chapter 32) Though the preceding chapter ends with Isabel expecting Ralph's return, this chapter begins with a visit from Caspar Goodwood. The meeting between the two is intense. Isabel is to marry Osmond.

(Chapter 33) Isabel tells Mrs. Touchett of her marriage plans. Mrs. Touchett disapproves and correctly believes that Merle has orchestrated it. Ralph returns, learns of the engagement, and is deeply disappointed, but he says nothing to an apprehensive Isabel.

(Chapter 34) Isabel encounters Ralph in the garden, and they finally talk about her engagement. He tells her she is "going to be put into a cage" and reminds her that "a year ago you valued your liberty beyond everything" (392). She maintains that she does not mind the loss. The two argue about Isabel's choice and her future.

(Chapter 35) Isabel and Osmond are strolling in the Cascine (a park in Florence) and discussing the public reaction to their engagement. Osmond declares that Isabel's family does not like him because he has no money. Osmond tells Pansy about the engagement, and it is clear that she is delighted. They also visit the Countess Gemini. She likes Isabel and is happy to have her near but warns her about Osmond, saying that someday she will tell Isabel about him.

(Chapter 36) Edward Rosier visits Mme Merle's apartment in Rome. He has met and fallen in love with Pansy and wants Merle to put in a good word for him. She makes him promise not to speak to Pansy. Though their discussion focuses on Pansy, the reader learns much about Osmond and Isabel's relationship too. They apparently differ on everything; Mme Merle tells Rosier that Isabel controls her own money and that while Osmond cannot provide a dowry, he should not expect Isabel to provide one either. Rosier is very fond of Isabel and believes that she will help him. He later goes to Mrs. Osmond's, and the dark and evil description of the architecture reflects the novel's shift in tone.

(Chapter 37) Rosier enters the house and first encounters Osmond, who, Rosier knows, dislikes him. Rosier tries to strike up a conversation about Italian porcelain but fails. Rosier's own interest in acquiring objects becomes more pronounced when he encounters Isabel, whom he classifies as rare, decorative, and authentic. Eventually, he finds and declares his love to a delighted Pansy. Mme Merle arrives, talks with Osmond, and then tells Rosier to visit her tomorrow. Rosier tries to convince Isabel to influence Osmond, but she says she has no influence over him.

(Chapter 38) Rosier visits Merle, who tells him to be patient and cautious—not to visit the Osmonds too much and not to press Gilbert in particular. When Rosier next visits the Osmond household, he first comes across Gilbert. Their exchange is curt and not encouraging. While Rosier is talking to Isabel, Lord Warburton arrives. Warburton has brought Ralph to Rome to convalesce. While there, he sees and admires Pansy, who tells Rosier that her father has forbidden their marriage.

(Chapter 39) Ralph tells of Isabel's wedding; it was very small and took place in Florence. Life has been difficult for Isabel. Ralph believes she has become simply a reflection of Osmond. After several visits with Isabel, Ralph decides to stay in Rome rather than travel to Sicily as he had originally planned. He enjoys the proximity to Isabel. Warburton admits to Ralph that he is smitten with Pansy.

(Chapter 40) Isabel reflects on her decision to marry Osmond and decides that though Mme. Merle was duplicitous, Isabel bears the responsibility for her unfortunate choice. When Isabel and Pansy return from an afternoon walk, Isabel happens upon Osmond and Merle engaged in an intimate conversation. Isabel's suspicions begin to mount. Merle claims to have come to talk about Rosier's devotion to Pansy and to explain that Rosier is jealous of Warburton, who seems to be quite fond of Pansy. Merle tells Isabel to use her influence to make sure Warburton marries Pansy.

(Chapter 41) The chapter opens with Osmond wanting Pansy to marry Warburton and Isabel thinking that if she can orchestrate it, she would be "a good wife" (464). They talk about it and concur. When Isabel suggests that Pansy will protest because she really loves Rosier, Osmond argues that his daughter's main concern in life is to please him.

(Chapter 42) Isabel reflects on the changes in her relationship with Osmond and concludes that "she simply believed he hated her" (475) perhaps because "she had too many ideas" (477). He demands that her own "mind was to be his" (481).

(Chapter 43) While at a dance, Rosier approaches Isabel, who holds Pansy's bouquet, and asks Isabel for a flower. Lord Warburton arrives, and when he finds Pansy occupied, he asks Isabel to dance. Isabel refuses. It is disclosed that although Warburton wants to marry Pansy, he still desires Isabel.

(Chapter 44) Henrietta visits the Countess Gemini, who tells her that Warburton is "making love to Isabel" (502). This enrages Henrietta, who then meets up with Goodwood.

(Chapter 45) Despite Osmond's opposition, Isabel often visits Ralph in Rome. Ralph tells Isabel that Warburton still loves her, not Pansy. Knowing that Pansy loves Rosier puts Isabel in a bind; discouraging Pansy's marriage to Warburton may further raise Osmond's suspicion that she is jealous of her former suitor. Nevertheless, when Isabel returns home, she tells Pansy to obey her father.

(Chapter 46) As Isabel and Osmond discuss Warburton's disappearance, Warburton suddenly appears and announces his plans to return to

England. Ralph will remain behind. It is clear that he is giving up on plans to marry Pansy.

(Chapter 47) Isabel learns that Goodwood is in Rome. Henrietta visits Isabel, who finally admits that she is horribly unhappy. Isabel asks Goodwood to visit Ralph, whose health has continued to deteriorate. She hopes that Goodwood will take Ralph back to England.

(Chapter 48) Ralph decides to return to England, and Henrietta offers to go with him, only to learn that Goodwood has also promised to accompany Ralph. Henrietta visits with the Countess in an attempt to quell the rumor that Isabel and Lord Warburton have been having an affair. Meanwhile, Ralph and Goodwood discuss what they perceive as Isabel's unhappiness. Before leaving for England, Goodwood visits Isabel to profess his continuing love.

(Chapter 49) When Mme Merle expresses disappointment that Pansy will not be marrying Warburton, Isabel becomes suspicious. Are Merle and Osmond collaborating in designing Pansy's marriage? Osmond admits to Mme Merle that part of the problem with Isabel is that she never adored him.

(Chapter 50) While Isabel and the Countess Gemini are out riding, they encounter Rosier and learn that he has sold all of his bibelots in hopes of convincing Osmond that he is a wealthy enough suitor for Pansy. Isabel seems to want to help him, but Pansy is being sent back to the convent by Osmond, presumably to prevent a match with Rosier. Osmond is said to see his daughter "as a precious work of art" (578).

(Chapter 51) Any of Isabel's remaining naïveté now crumbles. First, she receives a telegram from Mrs. Touchett, who reports that Ralph is dying—and implores Isabel to come immediately. Osmond forbids it. Isabel then learns from the Countess that Gilbert in fact did not have a child with his first wife. Pansy is the illegitimate daughter of Osmond and Mme Merle, who arranged Isabel's marriage to Osmond to provide for Pansy.

(Chapter 52) Isabel determines to leave for England but first visits Pansy in the convent. Upon arrival, she finds Mme Merle already there. Their meeting is strained. Isabel asks Pansy to accompany her to England, but Pansy declines, still wanting to please her father. Isabel talks to Merle before she leaves and learns that Ralph orchestrated Isabel's inheritance.

(Chapter 53) Isabel is greeted in London by Henrietta and Mr. Bantling, who have been staying at Gardencourt and who announce their engagement.

(Chapter 54) Isabel arrives at Gardencourt and learns from Mrs. Touchett that Lord Warburton intends to marry an English lady. In Isabel's conversation with the dying Ralph, the two are honest with each other for the first time in many years. She admits her unhappiness, and he acknowledges that the inheritance was his doing. He worries that it has ruined her.

(Chapter 55) Convinced that Ralph will soon die, Isabel goes to her room to think. She falls asleep, and upon awakening she feels that his ghost is watching her. She goes to his room and finds that he has just died. Lord Warburton visits and talks with Isabel, confirming his marriage plans. After Warburton leaves, Isabel wanders the grounds and sees the bench where, six years before, she received the letter announcing that Goodwood had followed her. As she ponders the past, Goodwood suddenly appears and grabs her in a passionate but violent embrace. Her response is ambivalent; she seems simultaneously frightened and aroused. Goodwood reports that Ralph had entreated him to look after her. He begs her to stay with him and not to return to Osmond. She again tells him to leave her alone. He then kisses her passionately and aggressively. Isabel runs away, back into Gardencourt. Later, from Henrietta, Goodwood learns that Isabel is returning to Rome, where she presumably will do her duty to both her stepdaughter and her husband.

CRITICAL ANALYSIS

An analysis of *The Portrait of a Lady* aptly begins with a study of the title. Like many other 19th-century novels, James's work proposes to offer readers an impression of what it means to be a lady in the 19th century. As the title suggests, this impression will be definitive—*the* portrait. The choice of *a* to name the lady, however, suggests that the impression provided, while dealing with the specific

"The Roman Bridge," by A. L. Coburn, frontispiece to the second volume of *The Portrait of a Lady,* Volume 4, the New York Edition

character of Isabel Archer, will also serve as a representation of many women and the difficulties that they face in a capitalist, patriarchal society. Though it may seem more logical to include the lady's name with the more general term, James suggests that Isabel's experience will reflect the class tensions that pervade society's gender roles.

As a *portrait*, the novel entails not just the creation of a character but also an inquiry into the entire artistic process. James begins this inquiry by setting up Isabel as an object. Ralph, for example, observes that "she was better worth looking at than most works of art" (99) and later admits that "she was an entertainment of a high order . . . finer than the finest work of art" (116). Osmond also objectifies Isabel but does so in a much more overtly manipulative way. For him, Isabel functions not so much as a beautiful object worthy of admiration and observation but as "material to work with" (444). Within the context of the novel, it is relatively easy to see these objectifying forces at work; however, James also suggests that both he and his readers participate in the objectification as well. Readers watch Isabel as eagerly as Ralph, and James uses Isabel as the "material" for his novel. These two additional components of the artistic process suggest that art is a participatory endeavor that has the power not only to represent social categories but also to perpetuate stereotypes.

In the preface for the 1908 New York Edition of the novel (see PREFACES TO THE NEW YORK EDITION), James elaborates on the artistic process that eventually led him to create his book. He writes that "The novel is of its very nature an 'ado', an ado about something, and the larger the form it takes the greater of course the ado. Therefore, consciously, that was what one was in for—for positively organizing an ado about Isabel Archer" (48). In constructing this portrait of his main character, James does more than merely provide readers with a literary image of a young woman on the verge of something significant. James's novel probes deeper questions of the human experience, such as marriage, SEXUALITY, gender, family relations, and national differences. That he does so through the character of Isabel reflects a broader late 19th-century interest in what would become known as "the woman question" (see WOMEN'S ISSUES).

Several of these themes emerge more prominently in the revised New York Edition of 1908, where Lyall Powers sees: "first, the increased importance given to Isabel's mind—her imagination or intellect or consciousness—which now dominates the novel; second, the developed erotic element, so salient in Isabel's last encounter with Caspar; third, the enhanced emotional appeal of Ralph Touchett" (105). These changes enhance the "ado" that James creates, and through those changes readers can see James's own development as a writer very much interested in the interiority of his characters. Though external motivation exists in James's novels, the focus most often rests within the recesses of his characters' minds. Further evidence of this tendency is James's response to his contemporary critics in the United States and England.

According to Bonnie Herron, the novel's original reception served as the guiding force behind James's revision. Herron notes that the "The European critic [Margaret Oliphant] calls for a heightened impression of Isabel whereas the American critic [Horace Scudder] is satisfied with James's surface view of Isabel, with her 'missing' physical characteristics and sexual thoughts." The revised portrait combines these seemingly contradictory elements by developing the sexual side of Isabel

not through "physical detail" but through "narrative mode and language" (132).

In the preface, James also articulates his interest in the past, a theme that works its way into many aspects of the novel. He writes that "As for the origin of one's wind-blown germs themselves, who shall say, as you ask, where *they* come from? We have to go too far back, too far behind, to say. Isn't it all we can say that they come from every quarter of heaven" (43–44). In the novel, there exists the past of the characters' lives, those moments that the Jamesian narrator fills in for readers—details about Isabel's upbringing and references to a previous time in British history, for example. The characters' personal history implies a broader national history as James peppers his narrative with references to the CIVIL WAR.

Various critics, such as Charles and Tess Hoffman, have noted the link between James's own experience and the American Civil War. As a result of a mysterious wound, or what James himself referred to in his AUTOBIOGRAPHY as an "obscure hurt," he managed to avoid serving in the war; however, his younger brothers enlisted. Critics have suggested in James's writing a residual guilt over not having served as a soldier and a recurring curiosity in the nature of such violent endeavors. For example, John Halperin argues that "James shared 'the passion and action of his time' in an unusual but no less affecting way, having determined to 'live' through observation rather than through action" (29). James's interest in the Civil War extends beyond the actual conflict and encompasses questions about the war's residual effects on the country and its people. Adrian Poole sees this interest as something that was "for the writing, remembering James no less symbolic than real, a way of insisting that war takes place for bodies off the battlefield as well as on it, and that it assails something other than the body" (292). In this way, James creates characters whose metaphorical use of the event demonstrates its far-ranging impact. Isabel, for example, "was still a very young girl" when the Civil War broke out, "but she passed months of this long period in a state of almost passionate excitement, in which she felt herself at times . . . stirred almost indiscriminately by the valour of either army" (89). Readers also learn that Isabel "had always been fond of history" (336). In this sense, Isabel's portrait may be interpreted as a metaphor for the conflict.

If read as a bildungsroman, as Dorothy Berkson suggests, the novel traces Isabel's development as a young and naive adolescent to a mature, knowledgeable adult. At the start of the Civil War in 1861, the country was also young. Both Isabel and the country confronted their futures with idealistic zeal, buoyed by the principles of independence, freedom, liberty, and equality. The failure of Reconstruction suggests that idealism does not guarantee a more equitable social experience, a lesson echoed in Isabel's misguided choice of Gilbert Osmond as her husband. William Veeder's assessment of Isabel pushes this metaphor even further, to include expatriation. According to Veeder, the image of Isabel as naive and vulnerable links directly to James himself because "young Henry found the truest representation of self in the figures of the orphan and the women" (95). This was not because of a direct connection to war but because of the way orphans and women "respond to the threat of expatriation that James felt menacing him from within his home and throughout society" (95).

With so much importance placed on freedom, liberty, and independence in the novel, and with James's own experience as an expatriate, it is not surprising that the delicate balance between the cultures of America and Europe is a frequent theme of literary criticism. Leon Edel explores the international theme in his essay "The Myth of America in *The Portrait of a Lady*" and observes that James

> had a threefold vision: he was sensitively aware of the myths that Americans—on their great new land mass—were creating about themselves. He equally discerned the myths Europeans were creating about Americans. In turn, he created and explored the myths that emerged from the encounter of the two. (9)

Evidence of these encounters and the subsequent tension that they produce exists throughout the novel. Mr. Bantling, for example, says that "the Touchetts aren't English at all . . . they have their own habits, their own language, their own food—some odd religion even" (196), all of which reflect

Mr. Touchett's loyalty to his American roots despite his financial successes and residency in Europe. Henrietta Stackpole relates her disdain for the British system when she asks if "you call that happiness—the ownership of wretched human beings?" (351). Caspar Goodwood also questions Isabel's allegiance when he disdainfully asks whether she means "to give up [her] country" (213) in announcing her plans to spend a good deal of time in Europe.

Edel and others identify Isabel's unflagging devotion to independence and self-reliance as a nod toward RALPH WALDO EMERSON's transcendental philosophy. However, Isabel's attempt fails. Edel argues that the failure is a result of Isabel's undeveloped knowledge. One cannot be self-reliant if one is naive (Edel 14). Cheryl Torsney contends that whereas Isabel is clearly a student of Emerson's self-reliance, "she is manipulated and invaded by forces eager to bring her under their control." Torsney calls such control "a paradigm of imperialist politics" (86), which links Osmond's controlling behavior to Great Britain's creation of its empire through imperialist and expansionist techniques during the latter part of the 19th century (91). Yet others, such as Kumkum Sangari, argue that Isabel's behavior reflects a shift in class boundaries that occurred in America as a result of industrialization. James's portrait is an attempt to find a new way to define class, particularly as it affects gender distinctions (719). Certainly, Isabel's income appears to offer her the freedom not to marry. Boosted into a new class by her inheritance, Isabel could now support herself and maintain a comfortable lifestyle. It is this very possibility that influences Ralph to ask his father to rewrite his will in Isabel's favor. Ironically, even with this option, Isabel eventually succumbs to marriage with Osmond and lives in a relationship that offers her no liberty.

Indeed, the marriage between Isabel and Osmond proves odd at best. Debra MacComb links the troubling marriage to larger questions of liberty and freedom in the novel. For her, *The Portrait of a Lady* is "James's critique of America's celebrated tendency to elevate individual liberty over obligation or tradition and its faith that radical breaks—for which the American War for Independence is paradigmatic—are sufficient to secure such liberty" (129). MacComb's reading probes the relevance of the ideals that grew out of the country's conflict with England as they relate to subsequent attitudes toward marriage. In her estimation, "Thwarted in her relationship with Osmond, Isabel must re-examine the nature of her much-advertised liberty and her characteristically American belief in the exercise of agency free from external influences" (135). As the relationship between these two expatriates effectively squelches liberty, James questions the plausibility of the nation's revolutionary claims. Can there be such a thing as actual liberty? More specifically, can a woman maintain liberty in a repressive Victorian society? What happens to that liberty (real or perceived) when the woman marries?

Though Isabel and Osmond's marriage receives the most attention, James explores the theme through other characters as well. Robert White calls *The Portrait of a Lady* James's "first extended fictional treatment of marriage after courtship" (62). The novel in fact begins with Mr. Touchett, Ralph, and Lord Warburton taking their tea on the lawn of Gardencourt and musing over the question of falling in love and marrying. Lord Warburton admits that "'I'm not at all keen about marrying . . . but there's no knowing what an interesting woman might do with me'" (66). Isabel arrives shortly thereafter and quickly becomes the "interesting" woman, causing readers to wonder about either Isabel's overwhelming power to charm or Warburton's quickly satisfied desires, both of which continue to grow in pertinence as the novel progresses.

Ultimately, James suggests that though marriage may serve some institutional purpose, it does not foster the type of emotional, psychological, or physical development that many people today expect. Instead, James offers the examples of the Touchetts, who not only live apart from each other but who also maintain separate residences in separate countries (Mr. Touchett's in England and Mrs. Touchett's in Italy). Not surprisingly then, Mrs. Touchett, who might seem like a surrogate mother-figure for the vulnerable Isabel, cannot prevent the doomed marriage between her niece and Gilbert Osmond. This marriage, though also dysfunctional, seems far more dangerous than the Touchetts'

because Osmond not only erodes Isabel's freedoms (which would not have been uncommon during the time period) but also attempts to break her spirit. In this sense, marriage serves as a debilitating social convention, upheld as an institution that not only severely limits women but in some cases actually damages them.

Today sexuality would seem an important theme in a study of the marriage, but many scholars have criticized the novel for its seeming paucity of sex, even going so far as to label Isabel a frigid, asexual character. According to White, the novel does include a study of sexuality, but it does so within the framework of 19th-century mores. Rather than overtly describing the passion that characters feel for one another, James depicts desire through metaphors. Certainly Isabel's quest for freedom includes a type of sexual freedom. Kurt Hochenauer outlines the difficulty of her quest; as a woman in the 19th century, Isabel's sexuality was necessarily depicted as a struggle between the freedom to pursue one's desires and the denial of any type of sexuality in an attempt to "gain equal footing with men," or what Hochenauer calls "the changing sexual ideology among women in the late nineteenth century" (19–20). James best illustrates these oppositional forces through Isabel's response to the characters of Gilbert Osmond and Caspar Goodwood. Her passionless marriage to Osmond contrasts with the passionate kiss she and Goodwood share at the end of the narrative.

According to Annette Niemtzow, the ending of the novel illuminates another important aspect of James's concept of marriage. Though Isabel experiences the passion with Goodwood that clearly seems to be missing in her marriage, she ultimately decides to return to Osmond. Niemtzow argues that this maneuver reflects both James's and his father's published attitude toward marriage—one is responsible for one's own choices (382)—and that while Isabel "once flaunted, 'I don't want to begin life by marrying. There are other things a woman can do,'" she eventually "is transformed into the custodian of domestic organization" (380–381). Another critic, Dorothy Berkson, contends that James's interest in marriage is an attempt to take "us beyond the traditional ending, marriage, and show us the tragedy that can face a young woman whose culture provides her with no serious alternatives to marriage and which expects her to marry before she has experienced life and gained the wisdom necessary for judgment" (68–69). Hochenauer extends his assessment to James himself, arguing that the author also maintained a "divided self" that "both idealized and feared women" and struggled with his alternating allegiance to Europe or America (23).

Though the novel primarily concerns itself with a woman's sense of freedom in the 19th century, James was also interested in societal limitations on men's freedom, especially related to prescribed roles of masculinity. Issues of masculinity pervade both James's fiction and his life and imply James's Civil War experience. Some critics, such as Susan M. Griffin, argue that James's "obscure hurt" or "wound" "marks the space of castration and, therefore, of representation, of writing [and] James uses scars, the traces of past pain, to explore the constructed and changing character of maleness." These "wounds and scars," she further suggests, "serve to represent, and sometimes substitute for, masculine interiority" (62). Ralph's character, for example, and to a lesser degree, Mr. Touchett's, is portrayed as sickly and passive—emasculated. Mr. Touchett wears his wife's shawl over his infirm legs (63), a habit that strikes Lord Warburton as unusual but which aptly represents the familial dynamics. Ralph reflects that "His father . . . was the more motherly; his mother . . . was paternal" (91).

The type of parental inversion presented in the example of the Touchetts highlights yet another of James's themes: familial roles. The absence of strong, successful, and influential role models implies that something has gone wrong. Isabel begins the novel as an orphan who lost her mother early in life and has been raised by a largely uninvolved father. She now claims that she is "not a candidate for adoption" because she is "very fond of [her] liberty" (74). A positive maternal force in her life might have protected her from Mme Merle's and Osmond's advances and helped her to maintain her tenuous freedom. In the early courtship between Osmond and Isabel, Osmond asks Mme Merle if Isabel's mother will be present when he goes to visit her. Mme Merle's responds, "The

mother? She has none—nor father either" (293). This suggests that there will be no obstacles for Osmond as he pursues Isabel. Ironically, though Isabel has rejected her aunt's minor attempts to offer maternal advice, Mme Merle's influence is welcomed. Mme Merle counsels the young Isabel and ultimately orchestrates her doomed union with Osmond. Rather than serving as a protective force in Isabel's life, Mme Merle operates duplicitously: Her ultimate goal is to lure Isabel into a marriage with Osmond so that Pansy will have a wealthy stepmother. Mme Merle may succeed in securing a fortune for Pansy, but instead of identifying Isabel as her new mother, Pansy calls her "a beautiful sister" (404) and recalls that at the convent she had "more than thirty mothers" (287).

Ultimately, *The Portrait of a Lady* leaves readers with an impression of one character's struggle with the sometimes oppositional forces of independence and moral obligation, as well as a sense of the complicated and limiting factors that womanhood faced in the late 19th century. Though many of James's contemporaries explored similar themes in their work, James's ability to use literary realism to move beneath the surface of conventions, institutions, and characters allows readers to comprehend his themes through a multifaceted rather than a singular lens. By the end of the novel, readers have moved with Isabel to a better understanding of the forces that limit and destroy the very ideals that initially propel her actions.

CHARACTERS

Archer, Isabel The novel's young female protagonist and the "lady" referred to in the title, Isabel arrives in England from America, thanks to her long-estranged aunt who has reunited with Isabel following the death of Isabel's father. Though Isabel embodies the elements of liberty, freedom, and independence so often associated with America, it is clear that she is also very naive and shaped by the romantic notions of the novels she has read. This naïveté, along with her unexpected large inheritance from her uncle, set up Isabel as a target for the manipulative strategies of Mme Merle and Gilbert Osmond (whom she eventually marries). Isabel is also sought out by other suitors: the American

Caspar Goodwood and the British Lord Warburton. She refuses their proposals, however, because she claims to value her independence above everything else. Ironically, it is her marriage to Osmond that destroys that very independence.

Bantling, Mr.   An old friend of Ralph Touchett's, Bantling quickly becomes Henrietta Stackpole's companion and eventually proposes to her. As an older bachelor, Bantling should not travel with Henrietta alone throughout Europe. The couple seems to enjoy their transnational match and flaunting of strict conventions.

Gemini, Countess   Gilbert Osmond's sister, who also lives in Italy, she copes with a miserably unhappy marriage. Though she is characterized as silly and annoying, she eventually reveals the truth to Isabel that Pansy is the child of Gilbert and Mme Merle.

Goodwood, Caspar   Isabel Archer's determined American suitor, Goodwood represents the American ideal that hard work and determination lead to success. In Isabel's case, he is never rewarded. Much of the narrative description surrounding Isabel's interactions with Goodwood suggests that he arouses her interest. Often described in hard, stereotypically masculine terms, Goodwood's wooing of Isabel is sometimes threateningly assertive, which substantially qualifies his offer to rescue Isabel from Gilbert's psychological abuse.

Merle, Mme Serena   A widowed American who has lived so long in Europe that she (at least initially) seems to embody none of the characteristics associated with her native land, Mme Merle orchestrates Isabel's marriage to Gilbert in an attempt to provide an inheritance for Pansy, her illegitimate daughter. Mme Merle is characterized as manipulative, opportunistic, and largely alone. She also seems to be at the mercy of Gilbert, who has trained Pansy to look to him as the central authority in her life.

Osmond, Gilbert   An expatriate American living in Italy, Gilbert Osmond defies convention.

During his courtship with Isabel, this unconventionality impresses her as fresh and independent. After their marriage, it becomes clear that his manner has more to do with a need to control those around him. Both his daughter, Pansy, and Isabel fall victim to his domineering obsessions. Both Ralph and Mrs. Touchett dislike him. They see him as a fortune hunter who marries Isabel for her money. Osmond's acquisition of rare objects of art parallels his manipulative control and objectification of both his wife and daughter.

Osmond, Pansy   Gilbert Osmond and Mme Merle's illegitimate daughter, Pansy is young, demure, and very obedient. She has just returned from the convent where she has spent much of her childhood and young adulthood. Pansy eventually falls in love with Edward Rosier and wants terribly to marry him, but she ultimately obeys the wishes of her father: that she not marry someone with so little money. Despite Pansy's obedience to her father, she admires and perhaps even idolizes her stepmother, Isabel.

Rosier, Edward   A friend from Isabel's youth, Edward Rosier is yet another American expatriate now living in Europe. He falls quickly and deeply in love with Pansy Osmond. Though he has a modest income—his bibelots constitute an impressive collection of valuable artifacts—Osmond has larger aspirations for his daughter and forbids her from marrying him. The idea of a genuine love in a novel that seems otherwise devoid of such an affection seems pure and tempting, but Rosier's interest in objects ultimately parallels (though to a lesser degree) Osmond's own objectification of the women in his family. The parallel reminds readers of popular 19th-century attitudes that regarded women as subservient to fathers and husbands.

Stackpole, Henrietta   The independent, unconventional journalist friend of Isabel, Henrietta arrives from America to soak in material for her "Letters" or correspondence column. She quickly becomes disinterested in the stolid life at Gardencourt and convinces Isabel to take her to London, where she meets Mr. Bantling. She and Mr. Bantling quickly become friends and begin traveling together without a chaperon. Though they eventually become engaged, their unconventional relationship places Henrietta far outside of the code of English morals and ethics and reinforces the tension between American and English society. Henrietta's straightforward, often abrasive character contrasts with the conflict between independence and convention that surfaces in Isabel's character. As the prototype for a 19th-century "new woman," Henrietta's unconventional ideas and behavior (she also encourages Isabel to divorce Osmond) offer a sometimes uncomplimentary view of this type of character.

Touchett, Daniel   Isabel's uncle is characterized as infirm but generous. Under the urging of his beloved son, Ralph, Mr. Touchett leaves Isabel a fortune after his death. Though he knows Isabel for only a short time before he dies, the relationship between them is warm and reciprocal. On the other hand, his relationship with his wife defies a similar intimacy. Mr. Touchett also represents the American expatriate who has succeeded financially in Europe but who still holds onto his American ideals, thereby strengthening the thematic tension between the two cultures.

Touchett, Lydia   Isabel's aunt initially seems to take a maternal interest in her niece, but readers quickly learn that Mrs. Touchett is anything but maternal. She maintains a distant relationship with both her husband and her son. Though she disapproves of Isabel's behavior and warns her against marrying Osmond, she does not prevent her from making her own decisions.

Touchett, Ralph   Isabel's cousin is as infirm as his father but much younger. Because of his ill health, his only occupation seems to be watching others—a theme that the novel thoroughly explores. Ralph's reluctance to marry has led some critics to speculate about his ambiguous sexuality. Ralph and Isabel seem to strike a happy balance, which leads Mr. Touchett to recommend that Ralph marry her. Ralph declines and instead asks his father to leave Isabel an impressive inheritance. However, Ralph's impulse does not seem entirely altruistic. Though

he appears generous, kind, and harmless, aspects of his personality parallel that of Gilbert Osmond. He is intrigued by Isabel's reluctance to marry and seems to view her as something of an objectified experiment. With money, he rationalizes, she will be able to be independent. Rather than offering independence, Ralph's misguided action ultimately makes Isabel prey to the predatory intentions of Osmond and Mme Merle.

Warburton, Lord   The closest neighbor to Gardencourt, Lord Warburton immediately takes an interest in Isabel and quickly determines to marry her. She remains aloof, however, despite several occasions when he unexpectedly shows up while she is abroad. He is seen as a parliamentary radical, which suggests that he represents a new kind of England, at the same time as his title and his home represent the older, established order. Eventually, after Isabel marries Osmond, Warburton meets Pansy and decides to pursue her. Pansy's unyielding devotion to Edward Rosier and Warburton's continued interest in Isabel eventually foil that course, and he ends up marrying an English lady of import.

ADAPTATIONS

The BBC produced a television version that was adapted by Jack Pulman in 1968. It featured Richard Chamberlain and Suzanne Neve. A film version of *The Portrait of a Lady* was adapted and directed by Jane Campion in 1996. It starred Nicole Kidman and John Malkovich.

FURTHER READING

Baris, Sharon. "Gender, Judgment, and Presumptuous Readers: The Role of Daniel in *The Portrait of a Lady*." *Henry James Review* 12, no. 3 (1991): 212–230.

Baym, Nina. "Revision and Thematic Change in *The Portrait of a Lady*." *Modern Fiction Studies* 22 (1976): 183–200.

Berkson, Dorothy. "Why Does She Marry Osmond? The Education of Isabel Archer." *American Transcendental Quarterly* 60 (1986): 53–71.

Bloom, Harold. *Henry James's* The Portrait of a Lady. New York: Chelsea House, 1987.

———. *Isabel Archer*. New York: Chelsea House, 1992.

Bollinger, Laurel. "The Ethics of Reading: The Struggle for Subjectivity in *The Portrait of a Lady*." *Criticism: A Quarterly for Literature and the Arts* 44, no. 2 (2002): 139–160.

Budick, Emily Miller. "James's Portrait of Female Skepticism." *Henry James Review* 12, no. 2 (1991): 154–158.

Buelens, Gert, ed. *Enacting History in Henry James: Narrative, Power, and Ethics*. Cambridge: Cambridge University Press, 1997.

Buitenhuis, Peter. "Americans in European Gardens." *Henry James Review* 7, nos. 2–3 (1986): 124–130.

Collins, Martha. "The Narrator, the Satellites, and Isabel Archer: Point of View in *The Portrait of a Lady*." *Studies in the Novel* 8 (1976): 142–157.

Connaughton, Michael E. "American English and the International Theme in *The Portrait of a Lady*." *Midwest Quarterly: A Journal of Contemporary Thought* 22, no. 2 (1981): 137–146.

Edel, Leon. "The Myth of America in *The Portrait of a Lady*." *Henry James Review* 7, nos. 2–3 (1986): 8–17.

Fabi, M. Giulia. "The Reluctant Patriarch: A Study of *The Portrait of Lady*, *The Bostonians*, and *The Awkward Age*." *Henry James Review* 13, no. 1 (1992): 1–18.

Foeller-Pituch, Elzbieta. "Henry James's Cosmopolitan Spaces: Rome as Global City." *Henry James Review* 24, no. 3 (2003): 291–297.

Gilmore, Michael T. "The Commodity World of *The Portrait of a Lady*." *New England Quarterly: A Historical Review of New England Life and Letters* 59, no. 1 (1986): 51–74.

Griffin, Susan M. "Scar Texts: Tracing the Marks of Jamesian Masculinity." *Arizona Quarterly* 53, no. 4 (1997): 61–82.

Habegger, Alfred. "The Fatherless Heroine and the Filial Son: Deep Background for *The Portrait of a Lady*." *New Essays on* The Portrait of a Lady, edited by Joel Porte, 49–93. Cambridge: Cambridge University Press, 1990.

Halperin, John. "Henry James's Civil War." *Henry James Review* 17, no. 1 (1996): 22–29.

Henke, Richard. "The Man of Action: Henry James and the Performance of Gender." *Henry James Review* 16 (1995): 227–241.

Herron, Bonnie L. "Substantive Sexuality: Henry James Constructs Isabel Archer as a Complete Woman in His Revised Version of *The Portrait of a Lady*." *Henry James Review* 16, no. 2 (1995): 131–141.

Hochenauer, Kurt. "Sexual Realism in *The Portrait of a Lady*: The Divided Sexuality of Isabel Archer." *Studies in the Novel* 22, no. 1 (1990): 19–25.

Hoffman, Charles and Tess. "Henry James and the Civil War." *New England Quarterly* 62, no. 4 (1989): 529–552.

Kimmey, John. "London in *The Portrait of a Lady*." *Henry James Review* 5, no. 2 (1984): 96–99.

Kleinberg, Seymour. "Ambiguity and Ambivalence: The Psychology of Sexuality in Henry James' *The Portrait of a Lady*." *Markham Review* 5 (1969): 2–7.

Luciano, Dana. "Invalid Relations: Queer Kinship in Henry James's *The Portrait of a Lady*." *Henry James Review* 23, no. 2 (2002): 196–217.

MacComb, Debra. "Divorce of a Nation: Or, Can Isabel Archer Resist History?" *Henry James Review* 17, no. 2 (1996): 129–148.

Mathews, Carolyn. "The Fishwife in James' Historical Stream: Henrietta Stackpole Gets the Last Word." *American Literary Realism* 33, no. 3 (2001): 189–208.

Miller, Elise. "The Marriages of Henry James and Henrietta Stackpole." *Henry James Review* 10, no. 1 (1989): 15–31.

Niemtzow, Annette. "Marriage and the New Woman in *The Portrait of a Lady*." *American Literature* 47: 377–395.

Poole, Adrian. "Dying before the End: The Reader in *The Portrait of a Lady*." *Yearbook of English Studies* 26 (1996): 143–153.

———. "Henry James, War and Witchcraft." *Essays in Criticism* 41, no. 4 (1991): 291–307.

Porte, Joel. *New Essays on The Portrait of a Lady*. Cambridge: Cambridge University Press, 1990.

Powers, Lyall H. "Visions and Revisions: The Past Rewritten." *Henry James Review* 7, nos. 2–3 (1986): 105–116.

Richmond, Marion. "The Early Critical Reception of *The Portrait of a Lady* (1881–1916)." *Henry James Review* 7, nos. 2–3 (1986): 158–163.

Sabiston, Elizabeth. "Isabel Archer: The Architecture of Consciousness and the International Theme." *Henry James Review* 7, nos. 2–3 (1986): 29–47.

Sangari, Kumkum. "Of Ladies, Gentlemen, and 'The Short-Cut.'" *New Literary History* 19, no. 3 (1988): 713–737.

Sanner, Kristin. "'Wasn't all history full of the destruction of precious things?': Missing Mothers, Feminized Fathers, and the Purchase of Freedom in Henry James's *The Portrait of a Lady*." *Henry James Review* 26, no. 2 (2005): 147–167.

Solomon, Melissa. "The Female World of Exorcism and Displacement: Or, Relations between Women in Henry James's Nineteenth-Century *The Portrait of a Lady*." *Novel Gazing: Queer Readings in Fiction*, edited by Eve Kosofsky Sedgwick, 444–464. Durham, N.C.: Duke University Press, 1997.

Stafford, William T., ed. *Perspectives on James's* Portrait of a Lady: *A Collection of Critical Essays*. New York: New York University Press, 1967.

———. "The Enigma of Serena Merle." *The Henry James Review* 7, nos. 2–3 (1986): 117–123.

Tintner, Adeline R. "'In the Dusky, Crowded, Heterogeneous Back-Shop of the Mind': The Iconography of *The Portrait of a Lady*." *Henry James Review* 7, nos. 2–3 (1986): 140–157.

Torsney, Cheryl B. "The Political Context of *The Portrait of a Lady*." *Henry James Review* 7, nos. 2–3 (1986): 86–104.

Veeder, William. "The Portrait of a Lack." *New Essays on* The Portrait of a Lady, edited by Joel Porte, 95–121. Cambridge: Cambridge University Press, 1990.

Vopat, Carole. "Becoming a Lady: The Origins and Development of Isabel Archer's Ideal Self." *Literature and Psychology* 38, nos. 1–2 (1992): 38–56.

Walton, Priscilla L. *The Disruption of the Feminine in Henry James*. Toronto: University of Toronto Press, 1992.

Weinstein, Philip. *Henry James and the Requirements of the Imagination*. Cambridge, Mass.: Harvard University Press, 1971.

Wexman, Virginia Wright. "The Portrait of a Body." *Henry James Review* 18, no. 2 (1997): 184–186.

White, Robert. "Love, Marriage, and Divorce: The Matter of Sexuality in *The Portrait of a Lady*." *Henry James Review* 7, nos. 2–3 (1986): 59–71.

Kristin N. Sanner, *Mansfield University*

The Princess Casamassima (1886)

James wrote *The Princess Casamassima* in 1885 and 1886 while living in LONDON. The novel was serialized in the *Atlantic Monthly* in 14 installments, from September 1885 to October 1886, and then published in book form in 1886 by Macmillan. James revised the novel and wrote a preface to it in 1907. It became Volumes 5 and 6 of the NEW YORK EDITION (1909), published by Charles Scribner's Sons. The New York Edition has been the version most often reprinted, though both Penguin (1986) and the Library of America (1989) reprinted the 1886 edition. (See also PREFACES TO THE NEW YORK EDITION.)

SYNOPSIS

Book First
(Chapter 1) The novel opens in the home of Amanda ("Pinnie") Pynsent in Lomax Place, in the

"The Dome of Saint Paul's," by A. L. Coburn, frontispiece to the first volume of *The Princess Casamassima*, Volume 5, the New York Edition

Pentonville neighborhood of London. Amanda, a poor dressmaker, has been the guardian of a young boy, Hyacinth Robinson, since his mother, a Frenchwoman named Florentine, was imprisoned for murdering Lord Frederick Purvis. Amanda is being visited by Mrs. Bowerbank, a warden from the prison in which Hyacinth's mother is incarcerated. Mrs. Bowerbank has come with a message that Hyacinth's mother, who is dying, wants to see him. Hyacinth is not at home, and Amanda enlists the help of Millicent Henning, a young girl who lives next door, to bring him back. Mrs. Bowerbank is taken with Hyacinth's refined appearance and hopes that Amanda will let him visit his mother. It is Amanda's firm belief that Hyacinth is the illegitimate son of Lord Frederick, and she has impressed upon the young boy the idea that he is highly born, without specifying her reasons for this belief. Amanda, uncertain about the wisdom of the visit, tells Mrs. Bowerbank she will write to her with her decision in the next couple of days.

(Chapter 2) In a state of agitation about whether to take Hyacinth to visit his mother, Amanda calls in her neighbor Anastasius Vetch, a violinist in a theater orchestra, to advise her. Amanda was a friend of Hyacinth's mother, and she agreed to raise Hyacinth when Florentine was imprisoned. She is reluctant to expose Hyacinth to the disreputable presence of his mother and to the fearsome environment of the prison yet has also been affected by the information that Florentine is crying out for him. Vetch believes that Hyacinth should not be kept in the dark about his mother—that he should know "the worst" (76).

(Chapter 3) Influenced by Mr. Vetch's words, Amanda takes Hyacinth to the prison. She tells Hyacinth they are going to see an old friend of hers who had stolen a gold watch. Both Amanda and Hyacinth are distressed and frightened by the grim environment of the prison. They are taken into the prison infirmary to see Florentine, who, fading away, can only speak French. On overhearing Hyacinth mention the stolen watch, she denies the imputation in English and bursts into sobs. Hyacinth apologizes for making her cry and submits to an embrace from the woman whom he does not yet know is his mother.

(Chapter 4) Ten years later, Amanda answers her door to a strapping, well-dressed, if common young woman, whom at first she does not recognize as Millicent. Millicent's family had been evicted from their house in Lomax Place some years before and suffered penury. Now, though, Millicent is full of her rise in status. She has a "high position" in a haberdashers near Buckingham Palace (96), and she makes clear to Amanda her contempt for her home and her business—or, rather, the lack of her business, for Amanda's dressmaking has all but dried up. The business went into decline after Amanda had a nervous breakdown brought on by what she saw as her mistake in having taken Hyacinth to see his mother, thereby eventually making Hyacinth aware not only of his illegitimacy but also of the fact that his mother was a murderer. Millicent, always keen to wander the streets of London, has come to look up Hyacinth. Amanda gives away as little as possible about the young man, though readers learn that he has become a bookbinder. Eventually, Millicent gets up to leave with a taunt about the mystery of Hyacinth's origins. Amanda, trembling with emotion, cries to Millicent to "leave my room—leave my house!" (100).

(Chapter 5) Just at that moment, Hyacinth comes into the room. Hyacinth is intrigued by the visitor but feels that he would rather talk to her out of sight of Miss Pynsent, who is forever worried that a woman beneath Hyacinth's supposed "station" will get hold of him (105). Much to Amanda's consternation, Hyacinth offers to walk Millicent home. Millicent probes Hyacinth about his parentage, and Hyacinth is evasive in his replies. He walks Millicent to her door, and they arrange to meet again.

(Chapter 6) Hyacinth is perturbed by the unexplained absence from work of his fellow bookbinder and friend Eustache Poupin, and he goes to visit him. Hyacinth got his job at a bookbinding establishment run by a Mr. Crookenden due to Anastasius Vetch's friendship with Poupin. Hyacinth became a protégé of Poupin and adopted the revolutionary politics of his mentor, a political exile from France who was involved in the PARIS Commune of 1871. Hyacinth finds Poupin indisposed in bed. There is a young man, unknown to Hyacinth, sitting by the bedside.

(Chapter 7) Some cryptic exchanges between Poupin, his wife, and their young visitor, who is named Paul Muniment, lead Hyacinth to inquire whether the two men are involved in a political conspiracy. Paul tells him they are members of a kind of society "to which he and I and a good many others belong" (129), and Poupin suggests that Hyacinth might also be asked to join the mysterious organization at some future time. When Poupin's sickness takes a turn for the worse, Mme. Poupin ushers the two young men out. Hyacinth asks to accompany Paul on the walk home. Paul explains that he is very poor and lives with his sister, Rosy, whom he supports financially. The two men arrive at Paul's home in Audley Court, Camberwell, where Rosy is being visited by Lady Aurora Langrish.

(Chapter 8) Hyacinth is charmed by Rosy and fascinated by Lady Aurora, the first aristocrat whom he has ever met. Lady Aurora is a shabby and diffident individual, but Hyacinth thinks he sees in her signs of hereditary refinement. Hyacinth is slightly shocked by the familiarity with which Paul treats Lady Aurora. The discussion turns to politics, with Rosy claiming that Lady Aurora is "a tremendous socialist . . . worse, even, than Paul" (137). Hyacinth ends up claiming strength of political commitment that he is not sure he really feels. Rosy, on the other hand, expresses her conviction about the rightness of social hierarchy and in fact upbraids Lady Aurora for her belief that those in power should make concessions to the working class (141). Paul says that "Rosy's right [. . .] Enjoy your privileges while they last; it may not be for long" (141). Paul shows Lady Aurora out, telling Hyacinth to wait for him.

(Chapter 9) Left alone with Rosy, Hyacinth is intrigued by her account of Lady Aurora. A member of one of the richest aristocratic families in the land, Lady Aurora has turned her back on her privileged life and spends her time visiting the poor and needy. Rosy intimates that Lady Aurora is not only influenced by Paul's revolutionary ideas but is in fact in love with him. Hyacinth is enchanted by her account of Lady Aurora's aristocratic background. Paul returns, and Hyacinth questions him further about his involvement in secret revolutionary activity. Paul is initially evasive and even

dismissively humorous but eventually promises to introduce Hyacinth to some of his confreres.

(Chapter 10) Hyacinth has continued to see Millicent two or three times a week, spending much of the rest of his free time at Audley Court with Paul and his sister. Amanda, who does not know of his new friendship, thinks he is spending all his evenings with Millicent and becoming romantically involved with her. She is distressed at the prospect of Hyacinth marrying beneath him. Hyacinth assures Amanda that Millicent would not marry anyone of such a low social status as himself—that she is socially ambitious and will likely marry "an alderman, or a banker, or a bishop" (156). Also, for his part, he tells Amanda, he would never marry "any one who would marry me" (156)—a comment that Amanda takes to be an allusion to his awareness of his own high social status but that is in fact an indication of his intention to never marry due to what he sees as the hereditary taints of illegitimacy and murder.

(Chapter 11) Millicent wants Hyacinth to take her out on what she calls a "high-class treat," attendance at a play at a West End theater (162). Their time together up to now has been spent mostly in the street, often window-shopping. The displays in the windows of shops in salubrious districts of London bring out acquisitive desire in Millicent and in Hyacinth a sense of melancholy that he is excluded from the world of cultivation and taste that the displayed luxuries suggest. Hyacinth is torn between his commitment to revolutionary change and his desire for connection with the world of the rich, associating his divided impulse with the "extraordinarily mingled current in his blood" (165). Some years earlier, he had confronted Amanda, who told him about his imprisoned mother. Subsequently, Hyacinth researched the report of his mother's trial in newspaper holdings at the British Museum. Although Lord Frederick's family had never admitted Florentine's claim that Hyacinth was Frederick's son, Hyacinth is now no less certain than Amanda that this is the case. Hyacinth's reflection that he is by heritage "a gentleman" at the same time he is "a bastard" has become for him an "article of faith" (168). The revelation that Amanda had kept the secret of his birth from Hyacinth makes him initially very angry with her, so that "he could have beaten her, for grief and shame" (169). He also feels resentment against his supposed father's family for their rejection of him, and this underpins his populist political allegiances. At the same time, he is happy to feel that he has a noble lineage and a refined sensibility.

In response to Millicent's demand, Hyacinth goes to Anastasius, who has contacts in the theater that Millicent wants to attend. Anastasius has learned about Hyacinth's involvement with Paul and the secret society and presses him for further details, but Hyacinth rebuffs him.

Book Second
(Chapter 12) At the play with Millicent, Hyacinth is approached in an interval by Captain Sholto, a gentleman whom Hyacinth has met a couple of times at the Sun and Moon pub meetings of left-wing radicals that he attends with Paul and Poupin. Sholto tells Hyacinth that he is with a lady, the Princess Casamassima (Christina Light), "perhaps the most remarkable woman in Europe" (186), who is "immensely interested" (185) in the political matters discussed at the Sun and Moon and who earnestly wishes to meet Hyacinth. Sholto arranges to take Hyacinth's seat next to Millicent, to whom he is obviously sexually attracted. The attraction is apparently reciprocated in Millicent's flirtatiousness. In some trepidation, Hyacinth goes to Sholto's box to meet the Princess Casamassima.

(Chapter 13) Hyacinth meets the Princess and her companion, Madame Grandoni. The Princess questions Hyacinth about himself and the political movement with which he is associated. The Princess says that she is serious about her interest in revolution despite her own title and riches. She also says that she has not been in London very long and that she sees little of her husband, who lives in Italy. Sholto comes back to the box at the next interval, and Hyacinth returns to Millicent, a little mystified as to what the Princess wants from him. Millicent tells him that Sholto has told her that the Princess has been turned out of her own home by her husband.

(Chapter 14) Hyacinth tells Paul about his meeting with the Princess. Hyacinth is devoted to Paul as a friend and inspired by his political commitments though disconcerted by the lighthearted manner in which Paul often treats the serious matter of revolution and disappointed, too, that Paul has not yet allowed him access to the most guarded parts of the secret society. Paul is dismissive of the Princess's interest in their movement and will not agree to her request, passed on through Hyacinth, to meet with her.

At Rosy's request, Hyacinth brings Amanda to meet her. Lady Aurora is also at the Muniments when Hyacinth and Amanda arrive. It is arranged that Amanda will make Rosy a dressing gown, paid for by Lady Aurora.

(Chapter 15) Paul comes in with Captain Sholto, whom he has met at the Sun and Moon. Paul suspects that Sholto has been sent by the Princess to lure Hyacinth (and possibly Paul) to her. Sholto leaves and asks Hyacinth to go with him. Sholto asks him up to his apartment, and Hyacinth is greatly impressed by the opulence of his quarters and dazzled by his tales of his exploits in Paris and even more far-flung places such as Madagascar and Albania.

(Chapter 16) The Princess's husband arrives in London. Although the Princess refuses to see him, he meets with Madame Grandoni at the Princess's rented house in Mayfair. Madame Grandoni tells the Prince that his marriage to Christina is effectively over. In response to queries about the Princess's future plans, she reminds the Prince that Christina is capricious and perverse and that "she always, at the last moment, d[oes] the . . . thing . . . that had been out of the question" (236). To the Prince's horror, Madame Grandoni also informs him that Christina is preoccupied with the London poor and revolutionary politics, though she thinks this will only be another of her fads. At this moment, the butler announces the arrival of Hyacinth, who has come in response to the Princess's request. The Prince rudely stares at Hyacinth, receives an assent from Madame Grandoni to his request that he see her again, and leaves. Madame Grandoni warns Hyacinth away from the Princess, urging him not to give up his trade as a result of his relationship with Christina.

(Chapter 17) When the Princess comes in, she asks Hyacinth to be her guide to the city and its slums. Hyacinth rather overstates his involvement in secret revolutionary activities, which so far have been limited to discussions at the Sun and Moon. The Princess tells him about her background—she is of mixed Italian and American heritage, was married off by her family to the Prince against her will, then treated badly by his family. In the days after meeting with the Princess, Hyacinth makes an exquisite binding for a volume of Tennyson as a gift for her, but when he goes to give the book to her, the butler informs him that she is away visiting a duke. Shy of sending the book to her while she keeps such company, Hyacinth retains the book, which "seem[s] to create a sort of material link between the Princess and himself" (254).

(Chapter 18) As promised, Madame Grandoni meets with the Prince again. She reiterates to the Prince the hopelessness of his wish that the Princess will come back to him. The Prince questions her about Hyacinth's identity, Christina's interest in the lower classes, and Captain Sholto. Madame Grandoni confirms that Sholto is in love with Christina but adds that he does not have a chance with her, and he knows it. Christina has encouraged him to seek the company of other women. He contents himself with carrying out her whims.

(Chapter 19) Lady Aurora visits Pinnie to look over the final touches to Rosy's dressing gown. Pinnie passes on to Hyacinth the message that Lady Aurora still expects a visit from Hyacinth to pick up some books she had promised to him, and Hyacinth duly goes to see her. Although the books are a little disappointing to someone of Hyacinth's literary discrimination, he finds himself more impressed than ever with Lady Aurora's quietly gracious manner and her saintly work with the poor.

(Chapter 20) Walking toward home through Mayfair one evening, Hyacinth goes into a pub in order to get some change. To their mutual surprise, he sees Captain Sholto. The Captain buys Hyacinth a drink but seems in a hurry to get him to leave the pub with him. Out on the street, they run into Millicent, who at first passes by as if not recognizing them. Hyacinth suspects that Sholto and Millicent were actually planning to meet at the pub, and he accuses Millicent of playing him false. In return, Millicent brings up Hyacinth's relations with the Princess, implying their impropriety and

Christina's lack of respectability. Attesting to his smoothness of manner, Sholto interrupts the budding argument and convinces Hyacinth and Millicent to come with him to a music hall. Afterward, Hyacinth is troubled by the idea that Millicent has probably deceived him regarding her relations with Sholto. His attitude toward Sholto has also changed as a result of the incident and he now "see[s] quite well what Lady Aurora meant by thinking Captain Sholto vulgar" (279).

(Chapter 21) Paul Muniment and Hyacinth attend an unproductive meeting at the Sun and Moon; Hyacinth is nevertheless impressed by a sense of revolutionary purpose. Paul announces the arrival in London of Hoffendahl, a German hero of the revolutionary cause. Although he has never heard of Hoffendahl before, Hyacinth is excited by the news, and, uncharacteristically, he makes a rousing speech to the meeting, asserting his willingness to give up personal safety, even his life, to the cause. To his even greater excitement, after this speech, Paul takes him, along with Poupin and another of the Sun and Moon regulars, Schinkel, to meet with Hoffendahl.

Book Third

(Chapter 22) At the Princess's invitation, Hyacinth visits Medley, a grand country house she is renting for the weekend. Hyacinth is very much impressed by the house, its furnishings, and its artworks. To him, the house embodies the aristocratic world to which he is strongly attracted, even though he is politically opposed to it. Hyacinth is equally impressed by the Princess's command over him. Alarmed, he feels that the demands she might make of him will conflict with the commitment he has made to a scheme of Hoffendahl's.

(Chapter 23) That evening, the Princess is visited by some neighbors, Lady Marchant and her daughters. Hyacinth is somewhat thrilled but also slightly alarmed by the ensuing scene, an example of the Princess's control over him, in which he passes as one of the upper class, conversing with one of the Marchant daughters, who remains ignorant of his true social status. After the Marchants leave, the Princess tells him that she invited him to Medley to observe how he responded to "beautiful, delightful old things," that she is struck by his responsiveness, and that now she wants him to "see more-more-more!" (321). When Hyacinth protests that he must return to London to work, she tells him that she will pay him to bind her books. Hyacinth agrees to stay, though afterward he is still a little afraid that she wants him as a plaything—someone, for instance, she can use to play further tricks on the Marchants. However, he decides that "he [has] simply ceased to care what he [is] in for" and that the important thing is to taste from "the cup of exquisite experience" while he can (325).

(Chapter 24) On another walk through the grounds of Medley, Hyacinth tells the Princess the details of his meeting with Hoffendahl. At some point in the future, Hoffendahl may call on him to carry out an action, the precise details of which are indefinite but which will probably cost him his life. Hyacinth's brief meeting with Hoffendahl has also made clear to him the extent and organization of the revolutionary movement. He tells the Princess there "is an immense underworld, peopled with a thousand forms of revolutionary passion and devotion. . . . In silence, in darkness, but under the feet of each one of us, the revolution lives and works" (330). The Princess then surprises him by revealing that she knows Hoffendahl. She was introduced to him in Europe by two revolutionary acquaintances; her interest in radical politics goes back further, she says, than Hyacinth thinks. She knew Hoffendahl was in England and had written to him, asking to see him, but he had pleaded he was too busy. The Princess is awed by Hyacinth's commitment of his life, though she tries to adopt the air of "accepting for [Hyacinth] everything that he accepted for himself" (335). Hyacinth then surprises her in turn by telling her that, although he has made such a drastic commitment to Hoffendahl's conspiracy, the people he now finds himself pitying are "the rich, the happy" (336). Over the next week, Hyacinth feels his friendship with the Princess deepening, and he eventually tells her of his origins.

(Chapter 25) One day out walking in the countryside around Medley by himself, Hyacinth meets Captain Sholto. Sholto is staying at a nearby town, and he asks Hyacinth to convince the Princess to allow him to come and visit her. He tells Hyacinth

that he is obsessed by the Princess but that he has given up any hope of her reciprocating his feelings; he only desires to be in her presence, "to see her lead her life and act out her extraordinary nature" (344). He implies that Hyacinth owes him assistance here, given that Sholto passed him onto the Princess.

(Chapter 26) When Hyacinth puts Sholto's request to her, the Princess unhesitatingly grants it, inviting Sholto to dinner. Sholto and Madame Grandoni are the first to arrive in the dining room. Madame Grandoni tells Sholto that she is shocked that the Princess has asked Hyacinth to stay with her and meet people of her own class such as the Marchants. Scandal is bound to follow, even if, as Sholto says, Hyacinth can pass himself off as "a poet, or a pianist, or a painter" (350). Meanwhile, before they come into dinner, the Princess tells Hyacinth that she finds Sholto undistinguished and a great faker. Despite his professions of love for her, she also suspects he has taken advantage of the liberty she has given him to pursue other women. Hyacinth does not tell her of his strong suspicions that Sholto has done so with Millicent.

(Chapter 27) Hyacinth returns to Lomax Place to find, to his distress, that Pinnie is gravely ill and near death. Lady Aurora and Anastasius have been caring for her. Pinnie insisted that Hyacinth not be told of her illness. Pinnie was determined that he should enjoy his taste of aristocratic life and remained convinced in some obscure way that the experience of staying with the Princess would lead to his recognition by his aristocratic peers. In talking with Lady Aurora, Hyacinth realizes that she must now know of his supposed parentage due to the way Pinnie has been talking, but he also realizes that he does not care whether anyone knows his secret.

(Chapter 28) During Pinnie's illness, Mr. Vetch harbors feelings of ill-ease about Hyacinth, which he attributes to Poupin "leading the boy too far in the line of social criticism" (366). Mr. Vetch himself has largely abandoned his old radical ideas, having concluded that a reordering of society will not alter human nature, which is characterized by "passions and jealousies and superstitions and stupidities" (367). Lady Aurora, Mr. Vetch, and Hyacinth attend to Pinnie through the last four weeks of her fatal illness. During this period, Hyacinth is made newly aware of the advantages that Pinnie made available to him, an effectively orphaned working-class boy. Pinnie dies, and the funeral is held. Afterward, Mr. Vetch tells Hyacinth that despite the financial struggles of her final years she has left aside some 37 pounds for Hyacinth to travel to Europe.

Book Fourth

(Chapter 29) Hyacinth goes to Paris, using not only his inheritance from Pinnie but also a further 30 pounds impressed upon him by Mr. Vetch. He is dazzled by the glamour and sophistication of Parisian culture. Even though this feeling is occasionally tempered by his reflection that this culture has been built on violence and repression, in general his experience of Paris cements the "transfer . . . of his sympathies" from the downtrodden to the rich (383). Sitting at a café in Paris, Hyacinth thinks about his last days at Medley, when he had become convinced that the Princess was determined to foil his mission for Hoffendahl, despite her claims that she accepted it.

(Chapter 30) During his time in Europe, Hyacinth reflects with dismay on the complacency and stoicism with which Paul has let Hyacinth pledge his life to Hoffendahl's cause. If the positions were reversed, Hyacinth thinks, he could never have let Paul sacrifice himself in this way. Paul's attitude has undermined for Hyacinth his "[dream] of the religion of friendship" (394). Hyacinth goes to VENICE and writes the Princess a letter, in which he tells her of his renunciation of the revolutionary cause represented by Hoffendahl and his new allegiance to the civilization and culture to which only an elite minority has access.

(Chapter 31) Hyacinth returns to London and, rather dispiritedly, returns to work at Crookenden's. Hoping to see the Princess, he discovers that her house in Mayfair is up for sale and that she has relinquished her lease at Medley. He wonders if she really is as capricious as Madame Grandoni claims and whether she has lost interest in him and the revolutionary cause; though when he reflects on her involvement with Hoffendahl, he assures himself this cannot be the case.

Poupin is disappointed that Hyacinth did not meet with any of the radicals in Paris to whom Poupin had written letters of introduction. Hyacinth feels alienated from Poupin, seeing in him the destructive envy of others that now seems to him to characterize revolutionary politics.

(Chapter 32) Hyacinth visits the Muniments and finds the Princess there, along with Lady Aurora. It is obvious to Hyacinth that the Princess has captivated everyone present. She is dressed much less richly than usual, and it soon becomes apparent from her conversation that she has renounced many of the trappings of her wealth. She also says she has sold all her fine things to give the money to the poor and that she has rented a new house in Madeira Crescent, Paddington, a district much less salubrious than Mayfair. Despite these indications of her dedication to the cause of social equality, though, Hyacinth notes that she is wearing a fine pair of gloves. Before leaving, she implores Paul to meet her at her new house. Paul refuses, asking humorously "what good will it do me?" (414). Hyacinth leaves with the Princess, who insists on their walking to her new home rather than taking a cab. She revels in the sights of the lower-class London districts through which they pass.

(Chapter 33) Arriving at the Princess's modest house in the lower middle-class neighborhood where she is now living, Hyacinth is impressed by the spirit she has embraced her change of circumstances. She has made no alteration to the decor of the rented house, which strikes Hyacinth as philistine, and which he perceives must be offensive to a woman of the Princess's refined taste. However, he also notes that the tea Christina serves is as fine as that served at Medley. While Christina is out of the room, Madame Grandoni also tells Hyacinth that the Princess has retained her Italian maid and that she has kept some of her fine possessions. However, Madame Grandoni confirms that Christina's break with the fashionable world has been complete and that she has become deeply involved in correspondence with various Europeans concerning "uprisings and liberations" (423). Hyacinth worries that she might have been trying to intervene with Hoffendahl on his behalf.

(Chapter 34) Hyacinth visits Lady Aurora at her family's home in Belgrave Square and finds her much taken with the Princess. A few days later, he visits the Princess, who tells him she has invited Lady Aurora to tea. Lady Aurora arrives soon afterward and gives flustered responses to the Princess's questions about her charitable work and her political convictions. Despite Lady Aurora's embarrassment at the Princess's probing, Hyacinth senses that the two are "on the point of striking up a tremendous intimacy" and leaves them together (435).

(Chapter 35) One Sunday, Hyacinth visits the Muniments. Conversation centers on the Princess. While Rosy is typically forthcoming in her admiration of Christina, Paul still demurs, querying her interest in people so distant in social rank. Rosy teases that Paul's skepticism is merely a cover for his love for the Princess. Afterward, Hyacinth and Paul go on an excursion to Greenwich. Hyacinth asks Paul whether Rosy is correct about his feelings for the Princess. Paul denies the charge, though rather evasively. Overcome by an impulse he has so far resisted, Hyacinth asks Paul why he gave him up to Hoffendahl, also stating that he thinks Paul may have had more to do with the conception of Hoffendahl's plan than he lets on. Again, Paul is evasive in reply, though Hyacinth senses that he is genuinely puzzled by his questions. Seeking to relieve his discomfort, Hyacinth asks Paul what good will come from Hoffendhal's plan. Paul responds that it will serve as an admonishment to the ruling class and therefore advance the cause of democracy, though it will only be "a detail" in a larger scheme (444). Hyacinth voices his misgivings about the revolutionary cause to Paul, but his doubts about his mission are submerged in his feeling about the great friendship between the two men, though he "[does] not even observe at that moment that [affection] was preponderantly on his own side" (447).

(Chapter 36) One day, to her surprise, the Princess is visited by Paul, who tells her he has come only because of Rosy's constant badgering. The Princess tries to persuade Paul to relieve Hyacinth of his commitment to Hoffendahl, asking if someone less delicate and intellectual might be offered in his place, and even offering to substitute herself. She also asserts that it is unfair for Hyacinth to make such a great sacrifice for a cause in which he

no longer believes. The Princess tells Paul of her involvement with Hoffendahl and other leaders of the revolutionary cause, which have become somewhat difficult. At that moment, she hears Madame Grandoni outside and tells Paul that he must see her again in order to hear about her difficulties. She also impresses upon Paul that she can get money for the cause. Paul, as ever, is noncommittal, but he also, unexpectedly, displays some embarrassment in response to the Princess's entreaties, saying "I don't trust women!" (456). When Paul leaves, Madame Grandoni asks the Princess who he is and whether he is a "successor" to Hyacinth (457).

(Chapter 37) Shortly after Paul's departure, the Princess receives another unexpected visitor—Anastasius Vetch, whom she has never met but whom she has heard of from Hyacinth. Mr. Vetch tells her that he suspects that Hyacinth, under the influence of Paul, has committed himself to a dangerous course of action on behalf of the revolutionary cause, and he implores her to try to dissuade Hyacinth from this course of action. The Princess denies any certain knowledge of Hyacinth's commitment and ushers him out, telling him to argue his case with Paul. At the last moment, however, she implores him not to go to Paul but to leave Paul to her.

Book Fifth

(Chapter 38) Hyacinth becomes the Princess's guide to the very poor neighborhoods of London—though rather reluctantly, as these are districts with which he has no familiarity, and, moreover, he is often appalled by the alcoholism and vice that he sees among the people living there. Immersion in this misery does little to help Hyacinth's doubts about the validity of the revolutionary cause; "annihilation" seems to him the only remedy for the seemingly insurmountable social problems he observes (481). The Princess, however, professes to be deeply affected, giving money to the wretched people whom she visits and inviting them to visit her. Hyacinth is relieved when Lady Aurora takes over the duties of guiding the Princess through the world of London's poor. These expeditions at first intensify the friendship between the two women, but Lady Aurora becomes alarmed at how deeply the Princess is embroiled in revolutionary politics.

(Chapter 39) One day, Paul comes into Rosy's room, dressed in a new hat and necktie, from which Rosy infers that he is going to see the Princess again. The siblings discuss the Princess and Lady Aurora. Rosy opines that Lady Aurora wants to marry Paul and that she visits the Princess to "keep [Paul] off" (493). When Paul arrives at Christina's, it becomes evident that the two have an appointment with an unnamed revolutionary. The conversation turns to Hyacinth, and the Princess unsuccessfully tries to get Paul to agree to help him "out of his scrape" (502). As the two leave the house, they are shadowed by the Prince, who has been waiting in the street.

(Chapter 40) Madame Grandoni, alone in the Princess's house, is visited by the Prince. He has followed the Princess and Paul to their destination and has now returned, assuming that Paul and the Princess are lovers. He tells Madame Grandoni that he followed Christina and Paul to a house in North London, and that after they had gone another two men had gone in. Madame Grandoni says that the Princess is not an adulteress; rather, the assignation indicates her involvement in revolutionary activities. She also tells the Prince that she is planning to leave because she finds Christina's current behavior unconscionable. The Prince declares that he will stop his allowance to her. Hyacinth is ushered into the room. At the Prince's request, Hyacinth leaves the house with him. The Prince excitedly asks him where Paul and the Princess have gone and whether their relationship is based only on their shared political interests or whether they are romantically involved. Hyacinth is shocked by the news of their intimacy but insists he will have no part in spying on or conspiring against his friends. While they are talking in the street, a cab arrives, and Paul and the Princess get out and go into her house. The Prince's agitation increases. Hyacinth leaves the scene in shame at his own involvement in it.

(Chapter 41) One Sunday, Hyacinth visits Millicent. His suspicions about her seeing other men have quieted, and they now have returned to their former friendly relations. Sitting in Hyde Park,

Hyacinth tells her the story of his parents. Millicent is considerably moved, which puts Hyacinth in a newly impressive light. She is also perplexed that he has never taken advantage in some way of his aristocratic lineage. The conversation moves to Hyacinth's suspicion that the Princess and Paul are romantically involved, although he claims not to feel offense. Millicent, on the other hand, is disgusted on Hyacinth's behalf by this betrayal.

(Chapter 42) Feeling lonely and (although he will not admit it to himself) jealous over the behavior of Paul and the Princess, Hyacinth asks Millicent if he can spend the evening with her. Millicent pleads another engagement. Hyacinth considers whether to visit Lady Aurora or the Poupins. Deciding on the former, he goes to Belgrave Square, where Lady Aurora meets him, dressed in uncharacteristic finery. She is going with her family to a party—something, she tells Hyacinth, that she has to do to please her parents. She speaks to Hyacinth volubly and somewhat incoherently, and it becomes apparent to him that she is distressed by the desertion of Paul, just as he is distressed by the desertion of the Princess. Hyacinth leaves her and goes on to the Poupins', where he finds Schinkel also present.

Book Sixth

(Chapter 43) The Poupins and Schinkel are flustered by Hyacinth's appearance and admit they were just talking of him. Hyacinth offers to leave, and Poupin agrees that this would be best. It now becomes clear to Hyacinth that Schinkel has a message for him from Hoffendahl and that Poupin is going to try and relieve him of his responsibility. Hyacinth rebukes Poupin, but Poupin implores Hyacinth to change his mind now that he has altered his political views. Hyacinth insists upon keeping his promise. The Poupins also say they cannot understand why Paul did not do something to change the situation. Hyacinth defends Paul, saying he "walks straight," and, rebuking Poupin once more for his weakness, walks out of the apartment (552).

(Chapter 44) Anxious to receive Hoffendahl's letter, Hyacinth waits in the street outside the Poupins' home for Schinkel to emerge. When Schinkel comes out, he tells Hyacinth that the letter probably releases him from his obligation. Hyacinth asks why Paul was not given the letter, and Schinkel indicates that Paul is no longer trusted. Parting from Schinkel, Hyacinth enters his own apartment, where he finds Mr. Vetch waiting. Vetch tells Hyacinth that he has guessed his commitment to some dire course of action and pleads with him not to go through with it. Hyacinth assures Vetch that he will not. After seeing Vetch into a cab, Hyacinth takes out the letter from Hoffendahl and reads it under a gas lamp on the street.

(Chapter 45) Hyacinth visits the Princess. Discovering that she is not home, he asks to see Madame Grandoni, but the maid tells him she has left for good. When Christina returns, she is as gracious and charming as ever, but a certain detachment in her manner indicates to Hyacinth that he has been definitely "superseded" by Paul (570). She tells Hyacinth that she is distressed by Madame Grandoni's departure and that she left because Christina had become "more and more shocking" (571). The talk turns to Hyacinth's vow; the Princess assures Hyacinth that she knows he will not be called upon and that Paul has told her so. Hyacinth tells her that even though he has relinquished the cause he still cares for the working class. She responds by delivering a highly charged speech about the need for violent revolution, an event that the rich, through their selfishness, will have brought on themselves. Hyacinth is swept up by the fervor of her speech, so that "the vision of a great heroism flashe[s] up again before him, in all the splendour it had lost—the idea of a tremendous risk and an unregarded sacrifice" (574). At the same time, he is concerned about the Princess putting herself in danger. She dismisses this concern impatiently, even contemptuously, and Hyacinth leaves in tears of distress.

(Chapter 46) The next evening, Paul visits the Princess. He tells her he has received a letter from her husband, threatening to cut off support for the Princess. Paul predicts that she will go back to him. Paul then reveals to the Princess that Hyacinth has received the letter from Hoffendahl. The Princess is shocked, as Hyacinth made no mention of it the night before. Paul tells her Hyacinth has been com-

manded to assassinate a duke at a "grand party" (581). The Princess is distressed by this news and implores Paul to let her go in Hyacinth's stead. Paul dismisses the plea. The Princess asks him if he will see Hyacinth before the event, and Paul replies he will "leave him free" (581).

(Chapter 47) Still dwelling on his sense that the Princess has abandoned him, Hyacinth goes to see Millicent in her shop. It seems to him that their relationship had intensified on the Sunday they spent together and that she might even extricate him from his current predicament. On entering her shop, though, he sees her from behind, ostensibly modeling a dress for Captain Sholto. He and Captain Sholto catch each other's eyes, and Hyacinth withdraws before Millicent spots him. That evening, the Princess goes to Hyacinth's lodging. A man standing outside tells her he is also waiting to see Hyacinth; the Princess realizes it is Schinkel, of whom she has heard. Schinkel tells Christina that Hyacinth's door is fastened and that there was no reply when he knocked. They break down Hyacinth's door and find him lying in "a mess of blood" (590) in his bed. He has shot himself through the heart with the pistol with which he was supposed to assassinate the duke. Schinkel puts the pistol on the mantelpiece, thinking that "it would certainly have served much better for the Duke" (591).

CRITICAL ANALYSIS

The Princess Casamassima presents something of an anomaly among James's works. Like *The Bosto-nians*, the novel is exceptional for featuring politics as a central theme. It is the only one of James's novels to treat working-class life (though the shorter fictions "Brooksmith" [1891] and "In the Cage" [1898] also feature working-class protagonists). What appealed to James about working-class discontent and potential revolution? What issues did the novel allow him to explore? The answers that critics have proposed have been diverse, attesting to the semantic richness of this long and, to use James's own term, "panoramic" novel (*Art of the Novel* 90).

Whereas the popular impression of James is that he was unmoved by topical issues, biographical evi-

"Splendid Paris, Charming Paris," by A. L. Coburn, frontispiece to the second volume of *The Princess Casamassima,* Volume 6, the New York Edition

dence indicates that he often had a lively interest in political matters. During the 1880s, for instance, James wrote at length in his letters about the prime minister of England and the issue of Irish home rule (see the IRISH QUESTION). Ireland at this time was in a state of political turmoil caused by discontent with British control of the country, and in 1886 James wrote to his friend THOMAS SERGEANT PERRY that he would like to visit Ireland if he had the time, as "I should like to see a country in a state of revolution" (Edel 170). The idea of revolution was very much in the air in England and elsewhere in the 1880s due to a wave of terrorist acts that seemed to herald an imminent social cataclysm. In Ireland in 1882, the two most senior functionaries in the British colonial government were killed

by nationalists in the so-called Phoenix Park murders. Irish nationalists also dynamited the London underground in 1883 and set off a bomb in the English Parliament building in 1885. Further afield from London, in 1881 both the czar of Russia and President James A. Garfield of the United States were assassinated, and many other terrorists acts caused alarm throughout the period (DeVine 55).

In England, these violent events were linked to a widespread anxiety among the upper and middle classes that the working class would rise up in revolution. John Lucas points out that actually there was in the 1880s "practically no chance of organized revolution in England" and that such fears from a later point in time seem "absurd" (175). Nevertheless, there were good causes for working-class dissatisfaction. Working-class people often lived in wretched conditions, and in the 1880s unemployment was high. The period saw the growth of organized political dissent in the form of a budding labor movement, as well as socialist and anarchist groups that sometimes advocated violent means of advancing their causes. In 1886, working-class discontent flared up in riots at London's Trafalgar Square and Piccadilly. James was himself a witness to the aftermath of the latter riot, which occurred while he was still writing *The Princess Casamassima.* Returning to his home one day in February, he saw mansions boarded up and broken glass strewn across the streets after a day of rioting by the unemployed. James was disappointed to have been away during the event, writing to his brother WILLIAM JAMES, "I should have seen it from my balcony" (Edel 170). James to some extent seems to have shared the widespread feeling among the dominant English classes that the existing social order might be swept away in the 1880s. But although he himself was a social conservative, writing, for instance, to his friend John Clark that "I can't believe in a reform that begins with deforming" (Kaplan 287), he also had a sneaking sense that the upper echelons of English society deserved what seemed to be coming. Sounding not unlike the Princess Casamassima, in a letter to Charles Eliot Norton in 1886, he wrote that the condition of the English upper classes is "in many ways very much the same rotten and *collapsible* one as that of the French aristocracy before the revolution" and that "much of English life is grossly materialistic and wants blood-letting" (Scanlan 385–386).

Despite its topicality, *The Princess Casamassima* was neither a critical nor a commercial success on publication. Lionel Trilling revived interest in this atypical novel with his essay "The Princess Casamassima," first published in 1948 and later collected in his book *The Liberal Imagination* (1950). Arguing against a general critical view that criticized the novel's depiction of the political situation as fanciful, Trilling claimed that *Princess* "is a brilliantly precise representation of social actuality" (71). Trilling also assumed that the shadowy conspiracy headed by Hoffendahl is an anarchist one (even though Trilling conceded that anar-

chism had a negligible presence in 1880s England), and many critics after him have made the same assumption. Trilling's claims initiated a vigorous debate over the accuracy of the novel's representation of revolutionary politics. While James's biographer Leon Edel concurred with Trilling's view about the accuracy of its representation, George Woodcock in "Henry James and the Conspirators" (1952) contended that the kind of authoritarian, hierarchical organization depicted in *The Princess Casamassima* was inconsistent with the doctrines and spirit of anarchism. Subsequently, Maxwell Geismar in his hostile book *Henry James and His Cult* (1964) upbraided James as an antidemocratic conservative who "knew little . . . and cared less" (66) about the actualities of revolutionary politics and who ignored the real concerns of dissidents in the 1880s, such as labor conditions. John Lucas similarly complained that the novel presents a "baffling vagueness" when it comes to the matter of the revolutionary conspiracy: "The ignorance of the characters too often suggests the ignorance of their creator" (208).

More recently, critics have moved away from this concern over the accuracy or inaccuracy of the novel's representation of working-class and revolutionary politics. Christine DeVine maintains that debates over the novel's accuracy miss the point: "While *The Princess Casamassima* has been called James's most political novel because it overtly concerns a political theme, it is not a political analysis or a manifesto" (57). James, DeVine argues, was responding to the general anxiety about revolution in the 1880s, not to actual events (57). Elizabeth Carolyn Miller maintains that James in fact uses the terms *anarchist, nihilist,* and *socialist* interchangeably and indiscriminately, another indication that James was less interested in documenting "social actuality" than he was imaginatively exploiting the political climate of the time (164 n4).

James, in fact, said as much in his 1909 preface to the New York Edition of the novel. Anticipating the accuracy debate, James stated, "There was always of course the chance that the propriety [of Hyacinth's "subterraneous politics"] might be challenged—challenged by readers of a knowledge greater than mine" (*Art of the Novel* 77). His defense of his account is that "the value I most wished to render and the effect I wished most to produce were precisely those of . . . society's not knowing, but only guessing and suspecting and trying to ignore, what 'goes on' irreconcilably, subversively, beneath the vast smug surface" (77–78). James claims in the preface that the only research he carried out in writing the novel was "the habit and the interest of walking the streets" of London over the course of a year (59). It was through his perambulations that he "arrived . . . at the history of little Hyacinth Robinson—he sprang up for me out of the London pavement" (60). James's statements in the preface gesture toward the detail with which James renders 1880s London—one of the most striking features of the book, the significance of which is traced by critics such as Mark Chapman and John Kimmey. But with regard to the inspirations of the novel, James appears to be somewhat disingenuous here.

Although he may not have been concerned with strict accuracy in depicting London's working-class politics, there are indications that he carefully researched some of his material. Wesley H. Tilley shows in his book *The Background of* The Princess Casamassima (1960) that James drew extensively on reports in the London *Times* of dissident groups and terrorist acts. He also seems to have undertaken research into working-class life, writing down in his notebook "Phrases of the People" (Edel 179; *Notebooks* 32). A letter to Tom Perry records that he spent a morning in 1885 at Millbank prison, collecting notes for the novel's first scene (Kaplan 287). And scholars have speculated that there may have been further research, of which there is no extant evidence.

Regarding his visit to the prison, James says, "You see I am quite the naturalist" (Kaplan 287). James had a keen, though ambivalent, interest in naturalism, a literary movement that produced unflinching research-based novels on social problems (see ROMANCE/REALISM/NATURALISM). Influenced by the theories of Darwin and the French writer Émile Zola, naturalism emphasized heredity and environment as determinants of human behavior, and James's novel displays an affinity with naturalism in its suggestions of the shaping force of Hyacinth's upbringing and ancestry upon his character. But scholars have also argued for various other influences upon and models for the novel, including the work of Dickens and Balzac (Kaplan), the contemporary English working-class novel (Jacobson), and Ivan Turgenev's 1877 novel *Virgin Soil* (Lerner).

In the preface, James draws an explicit parallel between Hyacinth and himself. Like the novelist himself in his perambulations, Hyacinth is positioned as an intelligent observer of London life. However, Hyacinth is also "disinherited" (71), shut out from the world of "freedom and ease, knowledge and power, money, opportunity and satiety" (60–61) to which James had access. The conflict that propels the narrative is between Hyacinth's fascination with the world of elite culture and his sense of the iniquity that sustains social hierarchies. Although the novel invokes revolutionary politics and acts of violence, James saw its DRAMA as primarily psychological. The "climax of [Hyacinth's] adventure" is reached, James says, when he arrives at his "tergiversation" (73)—that is, when his attraction to art and culture causes him to turn his back on the revolutionary ideals that have earlier led him to pledge his life to Hoffendahl's conspiracy.

Critics such as Geismar and Lucas interpret this narrative arc as a reflection of James's own cultural conservatism, reading the novel as ultimately endorsing the existing order. But in fact the novel presents a more nuanced and complex account of these issues. Picking up on the preface's analogy of James and Hyacinth, Irving Howe in *Politics and the Novel* (1957) reads James as hesitating over the rival claims of aesthetics and politics. The novel, he writes, "registered [James's] fear that everything he valued was crumbling . . . but it also betrayed his doubt whether, in some ultimate moral reckoning that was beyond his grasp, everything did not deserve to crumble" (145). The novel does not simply ratify Hyacinth's change of heart. Debates between the characters over the issue of social inequality and revolution mean that these issues are explored rather than presented definitively or didactically.

Perhaps the most significant character with regard to the novel's ambivalence about revolutionary ideas is the Princess. Is she simply a dilettante, dabbling in revolutionary politics in a jaded search for sensation or out of vengefulness toward the aristocratic husband who has mistreated her? Certainly, the novel provides plenty of evidence in support of these views. But what about her impassioned speeches on behalf of the revolutionary cause—in particular, the one in Chapter 45 that affects Hyacinth, even after his "tergiversation," with a renewed sense of the worth of "tremendous risk and unregarded sacrifice" (574)?

Some of the most interesting readings of the novel have located it in relation to developments in James's novelistic practice. Again, this line of inquiry is anticipated by James in the preface. As an observer of his situation, Hyacinth is one of what James calls the "intense perceivers" (71) to be found throughout his fiction, from Rowland Mallet in RODERICK HUDSON (1875) to the Prince and the Princess in *The GOLDEN BOWL* (1904). James argues that much of the interest of these novels lies in the keenness and sensitivity of the protagonist's response to his (or her) situation. He also notes the dramatic necessity of making such "perceivers" unaware of key aspects of the various predicaments in which they are involved (hence, for instance, Hyacinth's obliviousness about the relations between the Princess and Paul, and Sholto and Millicent).

Building upon James's observations, in his essay "*The Princess Casamassima*: Its Place in the James Canon" (1966), Walter Dubler argues that the book marks a transition in James's techniques and subject matter—from a more or less conventional style of 19th-century novel-writing, which is largely concerned with social externalities, to one concerned with the complexities of consciousness. Dubler argues that this transition can be traced over the course of the narrative, with Books 1 and 2 largely concerned with relations between characters and the revolutionary conspiracy, and Books 3 through 6 addressing Hyacinth's "internal perception and his growth of consciousness" (45). Thus, this novel exemplifies the concern with psychological realism that comes to dominate James's later novels.

Mark Seltzer, Christine DeVine, and John Carlos Rowe have proposed similar arguments about the place of the novel in the development of

James's style, but they integrate this with discussions of the book's politics. Seltzer argues that in "turning away from the style of omniscient narration towards the technique of the 'central recording consciousness' or 'central intelligence'" (532), James undermines the idea of an objective, all-seeing authority with which late Victorian culture was obsessed and which was manifested in increasing policing and surveillance. The pervasive idea of "supervision" is not so easily disavowed, however, and Seltzer sees in "the deep searching of hearts, of spoken and unspoken words" (532) entailed by the novel's psychological realism another version of the surveillance from which James wants to dissociate himself. Conversely, DeVine argues that in moving away from the authority of the narrator toward the center of consciousness technique, James works against the "all-knowing, middle class, admonitory voice" evident in newspaper reporting of terrorist acts and "writes a fiction that embodies a more democratic worldview" (57). The fact that the novel's final sentence gives us Schinkel's reflection that the gun with which Hyacinth has killed himself "would certainly have served much better for the Duke," DeVine argues, "raises the possibility that this book is indeed advocating the idea of revolution" (69).

Margaret Scanlan, in "Terrorism and the Realistic Novel: Henry James and *The Princess Casamassima*" (1992), also links the novel's political plot to James's development of the "art novel." Both Hyacinth and James are haunted by the possibility that their attempts to change things might simply, pointlessly reproduce what already exists. Contrastingly, Collin Meissner, in "*The Princess Casamassima*: 'A Dirty Intellectual Fog'" (1998), sees the novel as elevating James's perception of himself as an artist at the expense of Hyacinth. The novel "systematically and relentlessly diminishes and ridicules Hyacinth as a parodic version of the Jamesian consciousness" (70 n1). In attempting to confine or reduce the complexity of experience to *either* aesthetic or political terms, Hyacinth falls short of the risky openness to life that James, in his theories of novelistic art, claims for himself.

In recent years, some critics have extended discussion of the novel's ideological dimension by attending not only to class politics but also to the politics of gender and SEXUALITY. Elizabeth Carolyn Miller in "The Inward Revolution: Sexual Terrorism in *The Princess Casamassima*" (2003) contends that "James's employment of the themes of anarchism and terrorism serves predominantly as a means to investigate the book's more pressing concern with gender and the role of women in late-Victorian London" (147) (see WOMEN'S ISSUES). In his representations of Millicent Henning and, particularly, the Princess, James investigates changing aspects of femininity that seem to threaten the social order. Attending to the emphasis in the novel on relations between men, evident for instance in Hyacinth's devotion to Paul Muniment, Wendy Graham in "Henry James's Subterranean Blues: A Rereading of *The Princess Casamassima*" detects a male homosexual narrative shadowing the overt political one: "the novel's anarchist melodrama [is] a screen for the underlying theme of sexual deviance" (193).

CHARACTERS

Casamassima, the Prince An Italian aristocrat and estranged husband of Christina, he first appeared in *Roderick Hudson* (1875). Although the Prince has thrown Christina out of their house in Rome, he wants her back and visits London to try in vain to get her to return. Christina's involvement in the revolutionary cause and her association with lower-class men such as Paul and Hyacinth drive him almost crazy with rage, jealousy, and frustration.

Casamassima, the Princess (Christina) A remarkable woman of dazzling beauty and captivating charm, the Princess first appeared as Christina Light in James's novel *Roderick Hudson* (1875), in which she was the object of the American sculptor Roderick Hudson's unrequited passion. In that novel, the Princess was forced by her unscrupulous mother into marriage with the Prince Casamassima. In the novel that bears her name, it is some years after the events of *Roderick Hudson*. The Princess is separated from her husband and, using the generous allowance with which he provides her, divides her time between London and a country house, Medley. Her husband, she makes clear, has behaved very badly toward her, though readers do not learn the details of his behavior, apart from the fact that he forced her out of their home "by physical violence" (577). Despite her own privileged position, Christina has become obsessed with the possibility of revolution and wants to do anything she can to help the cause. As she reveals to Hyacinth, Christina, like him, is of mixed heritage—in her case, Italian and American. What she does not reveal to Hyacinth, but what we know from *Roderick Hudson*, is that she, too, is illegitimate. It is possible that James is implying that in her case, as in Hyacinth's, a sense of personal injustice has fed into her preoccupation with social injustice? The Princess is talked of by Captain Sholto and Madame Grandoni as capricious and a dilettante. They imply that her interest in revolution is a mere fad. Although the novel gives us evidence of capriciousness—especially when she gives up Hyacinth for Paul—her willingness to involve herself so deeply in the actions of the conspiracy (even offering to kill the duke in Hyacinth's place) raises the strong possibility that her commitment is deeply felt.

Grandoni, Madame The German widow of an upper-class Italian, Madame Grandoni is the Princess's live-in companion. Like Christina, she first appeared in *Roderick Hudson* (1875). A woman of conventional attitudes, Madame Grandoni puts up with the Princess's decidedly unconventional interests and behavior until Christina's involvement with Paul Muniment causes her to leave the house in Madeira Crescent.

Henning, Millicent As a child, Millicent is a neighbor of Hyacinth's in Lomax Place. She moves away with her family and grows up into an attractive young woman, with aspirations to better herself. When she comes back into Hyacinth's life, she works at a store, modeling women's clothes. She and Hyacinth form a close, quasi-romantic relationship, despite their very different temperaments and attitudes. Hyacinth is fascinated by her forceful air and sees her as an embodiment of the spirit of the working class, despite her disdain for "the people" and the politics of equality. Although Millicent has pretensions to respectability, a suggestion of impropriety hangs over her, given her propensity for walking the streets alone. This suggestion is reinforced when Hyacinth discovers her secret involvement with Captain Sholto. Hyacinth's sense that Millicent has betrayed him contributes to his sense of helplessness and his suicide.

Hoffendahl, Diedrich   A German hero of the revolutionary cause, in the early 1860s he was involved in a terrorist action in four European cities, which, although it was unsuccessful, gave the upper classes cause for considerable anxiety. Hoffendahl, the only one of 40 people involved in the action to be captured, was imprisoned and tortured. He is now free and is the head of a shadowy political conspiracy seeking the overthrow of the existing social order. Perhaps appropriately, given the secretive nature of the conspiracy, Hoffendahl is never directly encountered by the reader, who knows about him only through the reports of others.

Langrish, Lady Aurora   An unmarried aristocratic woman in her thirties who lives with her family in Belgrave Square, Lady Aurora has a compassionate interest in the sufferings of the poor, whom she spends a great deal of her time visiting and helping. She is a great friend of Paul and Rosy, whom she has met as a consequence of her work. Although she is firmly convinced of the inequity of the existing social order, she does not share Paul's revolutionary views. Hyacinth becomes her friend after meeting her at the Muniments'. He thinks of her as a kind of saint due to her selfless work with the poor. She seems to be in love with Paul, and it is possible that this romantic attachment plays a key part in her involvement with London's working class. After Paul takes up with the Princess, she feels betrayed. She intimates to Hyacinth that she will renounce her work among the poor and give herself over to the frivolous, fashionable life of a woman of her class, despite the fact that she is temperamentally unsuited to it.

Muniment, Paul   A revolutionary associate of Poupin's, he becomes a friend of Hyacinth's. A son of working-class parents from the north of England,

Paul has come to London to live with his sister, Rosy, and works as a chemist. Paul is intelligent and ambitious—ruthless, even. Hyacinth thinks that he might become prime minister someday—indicating the extent to which Paul's interest in working-class politics is driven by a desire for personal power. It is at Paul's prompting that Hyacinth makes his vow to Hoffendahl. Hyacinth is devoted to Paul and maintains his commitment to Hoffendahl in large part because of their friendship. Paul does not reciprocate this devotion, however, and is quite prepared to sacrifice Hyacinth to the revolutionary cause, despite his knowledge that Hyacinth has changed his views. He is similarly callous in his relations with the Princess.

Muniment, Rosy   Paul's invalid sister, she is permanently confined to her bed. Despite this circumstance, Rosy is spirited and energetically intelligent. She has an almost preternaturally detailed knowledge of the world outside her room—though she has barely seen any of it—and can, for instance, authoritatively discuss with Paul and Hyacinth the particulars of their planned visit to Greenwich in Chapter 35. In contrast to her brother, she is a great believer in the existing social hierarchy. Although initially charmed by Rosy, Hyacinth comes to dislike her, an opinion with which the Princess concurs. There is something hard in Rosy's nature, which is revealed in her sarcasm and lack of compassion for others.

Poupin, M. Eustache and Mme   Eustache Poupin is a bookbinder at Mr. Crookenden's establishment and a member of Hoffendahl's conspiracy, who takes Hyacinth on as his protégé. M. Poupin has revolutionary political views and was involved in the Paris Commune of 1871. He came with his wife, a kind, voluble woman, to England to escape reprisals after the commune fell, and they remain there in spite of French government amnesties. Hyacinth learns French and revolutionary politics from Poupin.

Purvis, Lord Frederick   Possibly Hyacinth's father, this English aristocrat is killed by Florentine Vivier. Lord Frederick had assumed the guise of a

"Mr. Robinson" during his affair with Florentine, hence Hyacinth's surname.

Pynsent, Miss Amanda   Known affectionately as "Pinnie" to Hyacinth, Amanda is a struggling dressmaker. She was a friend of Hyacinth's mother, Florentine. After Florentine was imprisoned for the murder of Lord Frederick, Amanda took the infant Hyacinth into her home and brought him up. Good-hearted but nervous, Amanda undergoes a crisis after taking Hyacinth to see Florentine in prison—a crisis from which she never fully recovers.

Robinson, Hyacinth   An unconventional hero, Hyacinth is small of stature and delicate of feature. Hyacinth achieves an air of cultivation exceptional in his lower-middle-class milieu in part through his avid reading, his experience as a bookbinder, and the knowledge of French he gains from Poupin. Although Hyacinth, like Pinnie, becomes convinced that Lord Frederick was his father, it is worth noting that James never provides any proof of this supposition. It remains unclear whether Hyacinth's refinement is the result of his heredity, his experiences, or a combination of the two.

Once he learns the supposed truth of his parentage, Hyacinth feels that his "inheritance . . . darken[s] the whole threshold of his manhood," and he makes up his mind never to marry at all so as not to pass onto a child the burden of his tragic origins (105). His relations with Millicent and the Princess, two potential objects of romantic desire, are consequently somewhat ambiguous. Although he is at times intensely invested in either or both of these very different women, and although he feels jealousy over their association with other men, there seems to be little sexual charge in his attraction—though possibly, in the case of Millicent, this changes toward the end of the book when Hyacinth fantasizes about running away with her to escape his predicament. In the New York Edition of the novel (1909), James added a final sentence to Chapter 41, in which Hyacinth "passe[s] his arm round [Millicent] and [draws] her closer and closer . . . so close that . . . he felt her yield with a fine firmness . . . and with the full mass of her interest" (*The Princess Casamassima*, v. 2, 556). But Hyacinth seems almost as much invested in his friendship with Paul as he is in his relations with the two women.

Hyacinth associates his conflicted feelings over the revolutionary cause with his supposedly divided heredity (French and English, working-class revolutionary and aristocrat). Even after announcing his renunciation of revolutionary politics in his letter to the Princess from Venice, Hyacinth is liable to vacillation over the issue.

Schinkel   A German cabinetmaker living in London, and a friend of Poupin's, Schinkel is a member of Hoffendahl's conspiracy and a witness to Hyacinth's vow. Schinkel passes to Hyacinth the letter from Hoffendahl instructing Hyacinth to kill the duke.

Sholto, Captain Godfrey   A former captain in the military, Hyacinth first meets Sholto at the political meetings at the Sun and Moon pub. However, Sholto has no interest in social equality and is, in fact, something of a reactionary. He attends the meetings and goes among the poor to collect information for the Princess, with whom he is sexually obsessed. He brings to her specimens of the lower classes with which she has become fascinated. The Princess privately holds him in contempt, and she urges him to occupy himself with other women—which he does with Millicent.

Vetch, Mr. Anastasius   A neighbor and friend of Amanda's, Mr. Vetch is a violinist in a theater orchestra. Despite his humble circumstances, Mr. Vetch has "the nerves, the sensibilities, of a gentleman" (67), and for Amanda he represents culture and social cultivation. Mr. Vetch is indirectly responsible for Amanda's decision to take Hyacinth to see his mother in prison, and he feels guilt about this later on, feeling that he has helped point Hyacinth down the dangerous path of political radicalism. At the beginning of the novel, Mr. Vetch holds republican and democratic political views, though he does not go so far in his radicalism as his friend M. Poupin. Mr. Vetch abandons his views as the years pass, and he becomes concerned about Hyacinth's involvement in revolutionary circles. While

Hyacinth regards Vetch affectionately, he harbors some resentment about Mr. Vetch's responsibility for the visit to the prison.

Vivier, Florentine   Hyacinth's mother is a French-woman who was sexually involved with Lord Frederick Purvis, whom she stabbed to death. Florentine claimed Lord Frederick was Hyacinth's father, and Hyacinth assumes the murder was provoked by Lord Frederick's abandonment of Florentine and himself. Florentine named Hyacinth after her father, who died in Paris "on a barricade, with a gun in his hand" (167), probably in the revolution of 1830.

FURTHER READING

The critical literature on *The Princess Casamassima* is extensive. Dorothy B. Holton's bibliography of the criticism is a useful resource, though now slightly out of date. The editions of the novel from Penguin Classics (edited by Derek Brewer, with notes by Patricia Crick) and the Library of America (edited by Daniel Fogel) are the most detailed critical editions available.

Chapman, Mark. "Physical Mobility as Social Power in *The Princess Casamassima*." *Henry James Review* 9, no. 3 (1988): 165–176.

DeVine, Christine. "Revolution and Democracy in the London *Times* and *The Princess Casamassima*." *Henry James Review* 23, no. 1 (2002): 53–71.

Dubler, Walter. "*The Princess Casamassima*: Its Place in the James Canon." *Modern Fiction Studies* 12 (1966): 44–60.

Edel, Leon. *Henry James: The Middle Years*. Philadelphia: Lippincott, 1962.

Gesimar, Maxwell. *Henry James and His Cult*. London: Chatto & Windus, 1964.

Graham, Wendy. *Henry James's Thwarted Love*. Palo Alto, Calif.: Stanford University Press, 1999.

Holton, Dorothy B. "Henry James's *The Princess Casamassima*: A Bibliography of Primary Material and Annotated Criticism." *Henry James Review* 16, no. 3 (1995): 321–339.

Howe, Irving. *Politics and the Novel*. Greenwich, Conn.: Fawcett, 1967.

Jacobson, Marcia. *Henry James and the Mass Market*. Tuscaloosa: University of Alabama Press, 1983.

James, Henry. *The Art of the Novel*. Boston: Northeastern University Press, 1984.

———. *The Complete Notebooks of Henry James*. Edited by Leon Edel and Lyall H. Powers. New York: Oxford University Press, 1987.

———. *The Princess Casamassima*. Edited and introduced by Derek Brewer. Notes by Patricia Crick. Harmondsworth: Penguin, 1986.

———. *The Princess Casamassima*, 2 volumes. Edited by Leon Edel. London: Bodley Head, 1972.

Kaplan, Fred. *Henry James: The Imagination of Genius*. London: Sceptre, 1992.

Kimmey, John L. "James's London in *The Princess Casamassima*." *Nineteenth-Century Fiction* 41 (1986): 9–31.

Lerner, Daniel. "The Influence of Turgenev on Henry James." *Slavonic and East European Review* 20 (1941): 28–54.

Lucas, John. "Conservatism and Revolution in the 1880s." In *Literature and Politics in the Nineteenth Century*, edited by John Lucas, 173–219. London: Methuen, 1971.

Meissner, Collin. "*The Princess Casamassima*: 'A Dirty Intellectual Fog.'" *Henry James Review* 19, no. 1 (1998): 53–71.

Miller, Elizabeth Carolyn. "The Inward Revolution: Sexual Terrorism in *The Princess Casamassima*." *Henry James Review* 24 (2003): 146–167.

Rowe, John Carlos. *The Theoretical Dimensions of Henry James*. Madison: University of Wisconsin Press, 1984.

Scanlan, Margaret. "Terrorism and the Realistic Novel: Henry James and *The Princess Casamassima*." *Texas Studies in Literature and Language* 34, no. 3 (1992): 380–402.

Seltzer, Mark. "*The Princess Casamassima*: Realism and the Fantasy of Surveillance." *Nineteenth-Century Fiction* 35 (1980–81): 506–534.

Tilley, Wesley H. *The Background of* The Princess Casamassima. Gainesville: University of Florida Press, 1961.

Trilling, Lionel. "The Princess Casamassima." In *The Liberal Imagination: Essays on Literature and Society*, 58–92. New York: Scribner's, 1976.

Woodcock, George. "Henry James and the Anarchists." *Sewanee Review* 60 (1952): 219–229.

Guy Davidson, *University of Wollongong*

Roderick Hudson (1875)

Henry James began work on his first acknowledged novel in 1874 in FLORENCE. Though the novel was yet unfinished, the *Atlantic Monthly* began publishing installments in January 1875. The novel finished its magazine run in December 1875. J. R. Osgood published it in book form in November of that year. In 1878, James revised the novel for an English edition, published by Macmillan. James ultimately revised the novel again, composed a preface for it, and included it as Volume 1 of the NEW YORK EDITION (1907), published by Charles Scribner's Sons. (See also PREFACES TO THE NEW YORK EDITION.)

SYNOPSIS

(Chapter 1) The novel begins in Northampton, Massachusetts, with the American CIVIL WAR in the recent past. Rowland Mallet, a young, wealthy patron of the arts, visits his cousin Cecilia before he sets sail for Europe. Unfit for practical occupation but unable to justify morally his idleness, Rowland needs a project. He declares, "I want to care for something or for somebody" (53). Deciding that no "pretty girl" would serve as an adequate object of attention, Cecilia determines to show Rowland a "pretty boy" (59). She shows him a stunning bronze statuette, given her as a birthday gift by Roderick Hudson. Rowland marvels at the implausibility of any young man from Northampton sculpting a work of such genius.

(Chapter 2) Rowland meets Roderick at Cecilia's house. Roderick's artistic potential exists without direction and without familial support. His elder brother had died in battle during the Civil War, and Roderick is all that his mother, Mrs. Sarah Hudson, has. She desires that he study law, which he does at "the rate of a page a day" (67). His transition from part-time artist to contracted genius-in-the-making occurs at a more fortuitous pace. On a walk with Roderick, Rowland offers to pay for Roderick's immediate relocation to ROME so that the artist might thrive in a classically cultured setting. In return, Roderick must produce 12 sculptures for Rowland. Ecstatic about his impending future, Roderick smashes a bust of his employer, Mr. Striker.

(Chapter 3) News of Roderick's forthcoming departure does not go over well. Mrs. Hudson and Roderick's cousin, Mary Garland, suspect art is the limit of moral depredation, and Mr. Striker declines to take art seriously. Cecilia is displeased to lose an amusement in Roderick, whose eccentricities helped her manage the dullness of Northampton. She warns Rowland that he will be "held to a strict account" (81) for Roderick's personal and professional development, even as Rowland had insisted in his original proposition to Roderick that what he offered was "simply . . . an opportunity" (71). Rowland reassures Roderick's family that Rome will be good for Roderick, who is destined for great success.

"Henry James," by A. L. Coburn, frontispiece to *Roderick Hudson,* Volume 1, the New York Edition

(Chapter 4) Before sailing for Rome, Rowland continues to visit Mrs. Hudson and Mary Garland. Mary "please[s]" him, and he considers not leaving America after all. However, in a significant repetition of language that weakens the credibility of his later insistence that it is Mary whom he desires, Rowland remembers that "[h]e had Roderick to please now" (94–95). Roderick throws a going-away picnic for himself. At the party, Mary and Rowland take a walk and discuss what qualifies as creditable labor. Rowland insists that his occupation is the commitment he has made to Roderick. Mary tells him, "You are very generous" (98), and Rowland responds that his benevolence will have its compensation. Rowland and Roderick set sail for Europe. On the ship, Roderick surprises Rowland with the news that he is engaged to Mary Garland.

(Chapter 5) After three months of absorbing European art, Roderick needs a break. Rowland worries that Roderick's great enthusiasm will lead to burnout. On holiday, Roderick lies in a park. Though it will be another year before he is introduced to her, Roderick is inspired by the beauty of one passerby, Christina Light. She is escorted by her poodle, her mother, and what appears to be the family servant and guide, the Cavaliere Giacosa. The sighting of Christina catalyzes a period of productivity for Roderick. He completes his first sculpture, *Adam,* and begins work on a second, *Eve.*

(Chapter 6) Thankful that Roderick's work is finally under way, Rowland hosts a dinner in honor of the artist. Those invited form an expatriate artist's salon. Gloriani, Sam Singleton, and Augusta Blanchard each lives according to sustainable models of artistic production quite different from Roderick's abstract genius. During dinner, Gloriani insists that Roderick will not be able to "keep" his genius "up" (127). A week after the party, Roderick's work does slow down. Rowland suggests they travel. Oppressed by Rowland's expectations, Roderick prefers to split temporarily from Rowland.

(Chapter 7) Rowland exchanges letters with Cecilia and Mary Garland. Cecilia informs him that Mrs. Hudson did not announce Roderick's engagement to Mary until after they received photographic evidence of Roderick's two early successes, *Adam* and *Eve.* Meanwhile, Roderick spends his summer gambling and carousing with women in Germany. Distressed to hear that Roderick has only "learned . . . to do nothing" (135), Rowland nevertheless bails him out of debt. He hopes Roderick's lapse is only temporary. Once back in Italy, Roderick begins work on a new statue. But his work continues to disappoint. Roderick blames his stagnation on the fits and starts of genius. Rowland contends that Roderick need only apply his will. He is ready to scold Roderick to "Be a man" (144), when a knock at Roderick's studio interrupts him.

(Chapter 8) At the door is Christina Light. She is accompanied by Mrs. Light and Giacosa. Mrs. Light professes that she is touring studios as an art patron, but Christina suggests that her mother is actually interested in finding her a husband. Roderick insists on doing a bust of Christina, who has "spent half her life sitting for her photograph" (150). Rowland advises him not to become involved with these women, whom he suspects are dangerous. Rowland learns through Madame Grandoni that Mrs. Light is a social climber with a sordid and partially mysterious history. Rowland visits the Lights, only to walk in on Christina already sitting for Roderick's bust.

(Chapter 9) Roderick resolves not to leave Rome for six to eight years, and Rowland reminds him of his engagement to Mary Garland. Roderick dismisses the reminder, compelling Rowland privately to compare his feelings for Mary to Roderick's feelings for Mary. The comparison works to Rowland's favor. Christina sits for Roderick for a fortnight, and the bust proves a great success. Rowland marvels at how Roderick can think more of Christina than he does of Mary. He wonders if Roderick has a conscience. Singleton, however, idolizes Roderick as "complete" (171).

(Chapter 10) Augusta Blanchard escorts a prospective patron, Mr. Leavenworth, to Roderick's studio. He commissions Roderick to do a sculpture, but the project amounts to interior decorating. Trading on Christina's beauty, Mrs. Light wins over Roman society in one month's time. Christina's most enthusiastic devotee, Roderick, is seen wherever she is seen. However, at a ball thrown by the Lights, Giacosa informs Roderick that Christina can only marry into a fortune. Roderick is undeterred, and Giacosa laments that his affection will end in folly. Rowland remarks that "He has made a mourner already" (181), referring to either Mary Garland or himself. Christina asks Rowland about Roderick's past, and he reveals that Roderick is engaged. Christina uses Roderick as a dancing partner to avoid her mother's approved suitor, the Prince Casamassima.

(Chapter 11) Roderick holidays in Frascati. Joining him, Rowland recounts his disclosure to Christina of Roderick's engagement. He again cautions Roderick to cease seeing Christina, but Roderick advises Rowland, "Dedicate your nerves to some better cause" (189). Roderick believes genius should have a "long rope" to do what it pleases (191). Rowland cannot endorse this model of "unlimited experimentation" (192) but remains loyal to Roderick.

(Chapter 12) The Lights, Giacosa, the Prince Casamassima, Rowland, and Roderick lunch together in Frascati. Roderick and Christina walk off alone, but Giacosa reassures Rowland that she will choose the Prince over anyone else. Rowland wonders what will compel Christina. Mrs. Light explains her loyalty to her daughter as a lifelong commitment to ensuring Christina's social success. "I have raised money on that girl's face," Mrs. Light contends (209). Rowland admonishes Mrs. Light for "play[ing] a dangerous game" with Christina (211). The next morning, Roderick abruptly announces that he is ready to return to Rome to work.

(Chapter 13) Touring the Colosseum, Rowland inadvertently observes Roderick's attempt to prove his manliness to Christina by scaling the Colosseum's rock face and procuring a blue flower that grows in one of its upper crags. The romantic gesture is ridiculous for its risk, but Roderick believes it will answer Christina's misgivings that he is a failure. Rowland intervenes in time to prevent Roderick from following through with the attempt. He informs Roderick that he thinks Christina toys with him. Roderick continues to work on Leavenworth's statue. Convinced that Christina is the only worthwhile object of attention, Roderick spites Roman society by cultivating a circle of "queer fish" for friends (222). Rowland is provoked by Roderick's behavior, and Roderick asks why Rowland is still interested in him. Rowland answers, "I am wait-

ing" (224). Roderick again disavows his relation to Rowland.

(Chapter 14) Rowland visits Christina to persuade her to stop seeing Roderick. For Rowland, industry is antithetical to passion, and Roderick will resume work only if his emotions are not repeatedly antagonized. Christina admits to being a "horrible coquette" (230). Three days later, she sends Rowland a note, confirming her adherence to his request. Rowland visits Roderick to determine his reaction to Christina's decision, but Roderick has left for Naples.

(Chapter 15) Rowland writes Cecilia a letter, lamenting that he "can only be generous" with Roderick (237). His attempts to keep Roderick from falling into professional and moral ruin seem to have little effect on Roderick's continued stagnation. Roderick spends a riotous month in Naples, recovering from Christina's decision. When he returns to Rome, Leavenworth visits his studio. Piqued by Roderick's inhospitality, Leavenworth discloses Rome's latest gossip: Christina Light's engagement to Prince Casamassima. When Leavenworth asks to see the progress on his commissioned statue, Roderick insists he would rather destroy it than finish it. Rowland appeals to Roderick to finish the statue, and Roderick again disavows his relation to Rowland.

(Chapter 16) Incensed by Roderick's impertinence, Rowland visits Madame Grandoni. There he runs into Christina Light, who informs him that she has not benefited from separating herself from Roderick. Rowland has reached the limit of his benevolent interests in Roderick's personal and professional whimsies. The compensation he imagines for himself is Mary Garland. He considers assisting the destructive behavior of Roderick, even to the point of imagining Roderick's death. However, he repents and advocates instead that Mrs. Hudson and Mary Garland come to Rome. Their presence might redeem Roderick. Roderick consents to their coming but, in an unconscionable lapse of familial hospitality, is not waiting for them when they arrive.

(Chapter 17) Rowland accuses Roderick of missing his family's arrival because of Christina Light. Roderick insists on doing a bust of his mother, who is confused by the motivation behind his request. Roderick and Rowland guide Mrs. Hudson and Mary through Rome. While touring Saint Peter's, they run into Christina Light; Mrs. Hudson and Mary are surprised to discover she is Roderick's acquaintance.

(Chapter 18) As Mrs. Hudson sits for Roderick's bust, Rowland continues to guide Mary through Rome. He attempts to make inroads of intimacy with Mary, but she only expresses interest in learning art history. In an echo of their earlier conversation about creditable labor, Rowland admits he has "no practical occupation" (274). But Mary disagrees, apparently in gratitude for his having remained loyal to Roderick.

(Chapter 19) Roderick completes the bust of his mother. However, he proclaims her attempt to redeem him a failure. He informs Rowland that he plans to break his engagement to Mary since he has no intention of leaving Rome or Christina. Rowland negotiates with Roderick: If Rowland does not oppose Roderick's plan to stay in Rome, Roderick must defer breaking the engagement. Viewing Mrs. Hudson's bust, Gloriani believes Roderick will now manifest genius over a long period of time. The erratic cycles of Roderick's career leave him in no position to trust Gloriani's judgment. Christina defers the date of her wedding to the Prince. Rowland and Madame Grandoni question whether she plans on running off with Roderick. Grandoni wishes to see Mary Garland and throws a party, which Christina crashes. At the party, Christina is impressed with Mary, but the feeling is not reciprocated.

(Chapter 20) Giacosa informs Rowland that Christina has broken her engagement. He enlists Rowland to change her mind. Giacosa warns that if he fails Christina will be forced to marry the Prince. Luxuriating in the news of the broken engagement, Roderick breaks off contact with Mary and his mother. At the Lights' house, the peculiar intensity of Giacosa's anxiety over Christina's MARRIAGE brings Rowland close to inferring what secret would force Christina to marry the Prince. Rowland fails to convince Christina, who claims that she would never marry if only Roderick would be like a brother to her. Giacosa waits for Mrs. Light to privately confer with Christina.

(Chapter 21) At Saint Peter's, Rowland sees Singleton, who has produced more than 900 sketches in the last two years and prepares to return to New York. Grandoni informs Rowland that Christina quietly married the Prince that morning. She and Rowland guess that Giacosa's paternity is the reason for Christina's compulsion. When Rowland visits Mrs. Hudson, she announces that Roderick is ready to leave for America. Depressed by Christina's marriage, Roderick proclaims himself a failure, and much to Mrs. Hudson and Mary's astonishment, Rowland confirms Roderick's evaluation. Details of Roderick's dissolution follow. Crushed, Mrs. Hudson holds Rowland responsible. She asks him about the most economical way to remove Roderick from Rome. Rowland arranges for the Hudsons to go to FLORENCE, but Roderick will not leave without him.

(Chapter 22) In Florence, Roderick remains inert. Rowland determines to never take up another person as an object of benevolence. Mrs. Hudson convinces Roderick to move back to Northampton, but Rowland tries to have him wait at least another year. Mrs. Hudson scolds, "Oh, Mr. Mallet, aren't you satisfied?" (344). Rowland arranges for the Hudsons to remove to an inn in SWITZERLAND and, at Mary's request, accompanies them.

(Chapter 23) En route to Switzerland, Roderick confesses to Rowland, "I know what I have lost, and I think it horrible" (349). Rowland spies a flower in the mountain and ridiculously reenacts Roderick's attempt at chivalry for Christina in the Colosseum. Roderick and Mary reach a new state of intimacy. Rowland is angered by Mary's willingness to pursue Roderick's affection. Rowland presses Roderick to make explicit whether he plans to keep his engagement with Mary. Roderick only declares that he feels nothing for Mary. Rowland discloses his own feelings to Mary. Surprised, Mary disavows all friendship with Rowland.

(Chapter 24) In Engelthal, Roderick and Rowland walk together. Roderick continues the walk alone, while Rowland explores a monastery. There Rowland is surprised to meet Christina and the Prince, who are traveling through Europe. Christina informs Rowland that her fateful marriage has left Mrs. Light triumphant and enabled Giacosa to return to Ancona; his work as Christina's father is complete. Repeatedly, Christina insists that she was sincere in her claim that she would have been devoted to Roderick had he not wished to be her lover. As Christina leaves the monastery, Roderick returns from his walk. They regard each other for a remarkable moment.

(Chapter 25) Rowland once more reaches the limit of his benevolence, which has dwindled to a "residuum of . . . generosity" (369). Roderick asks for 1,000 francs to fund his travel to Interlaken to visit Christina. Rowland complies only when Roderick threatens to ask Mary for the money. But Roderick now refuses Rowland's loan, accusing him of the incapacity to understand passion. Rowland is provoked to confess his love of Mary. The confession genuinely surprises Roderick. Remarkably chastised at the thought of how his actions have affected the range of possibilities for Rowland, Roderick says, "I have been hideous" (379). Roderick resolves to take a walk.

(Chapter 26) A terrific storm surges during Roderick's walk. Rowland takes cover at the inn, and Mrs. Hudson despairs for her son's safety. A search is impossible until the storm clears. At dawn, Rowland enlists Singleton and others to canvass the mountains for Roderick. Three hours' hike from the inn, Singleton discovers Roderick's body; apparently he had fallen from a cliff 50 feet above. While Singleton goes back to the inn to recover help, Rowland sits with the body, not knowing what to do with the future. With Roderick's death, Rowland's "occupation was gone" (387). Mrs. Hudson, Mary, and Rowland return to America, where Rowland often visits Mary and his cousin Cecilia.

CRITICAL ANALYSIS

No interest has informed readings of *Roderick Hudson* more than that in Rowland's relationship with Roderick. Grace Norton, an early reviewer of the novel, judged the relationship "anomalous," arguing that "Americans . . . do not twist themselves into such odd arrangements as these" (14). The arrangements in question are those produced not only by Rowland's first generous offer to Roderick but also by Rowland's patient commitment to seeing that offer through. To call these arrangements

"odd" is to suggest that they exceed the bounds of thinkable relationships between men. On this account, no patron or no friend would last as long as Rowland does in his loyalty to Roderick, for Roderick's delinquency would strain any professional or personal relationship past its breaking point. Mrs. Hudson confirms the expectation of a normal limit to the durability of male-male relations by rebuking Rowland's continued interest in her failed son. When Rowland encourages Roderick to "stay another year" in Europe rather than abort his disastrous career by returning to America, Mrs. Hudson asks, with no slight exasperation, "Oh, Mr. Mallet, aren't you satisfied?" (343, 344).

For readers of the novel, the answer to this question most often has been no. For if Mrs. Hudson presumes that Rowland should be satisfied, it is because she misrecognizes what or who would satisfy Rowland. For critics, what keeps Rowland loyal to Roderick is not his desire for Roderick's success (a desire that, according to Mrs. Hudson, should be all but stamped out by Roderick's unproductiveness) but rather his desire for Roderick himself. Put differently, critical attention to the novel has been motivated by the possibility of explaining what early reviewers wrote off as inexplicable. Rowland's attachment to Roderick is not "anomalous" but rather homosexual. Or, more precisely, it is perceived as "anomalous" because it is homosexual. When Robert Martin argues that *Roderick Hudson* must end tragically "because the situation was homosexual" (101), his theory of the cultural unacceptability of representing happy homosexuality assumes that homosexuality would be culturally recognized as what is represented. For Martin, "Roderick Hudson is indeed a love story, but it is Rowland's [for Roderick] not Roderick's [for Christina Light]" (106). Nor has it been taken seriously as a story of Rowland's love for Mary Garland, as James himself was but the first to notice how Rowland's formal declarations of interest in Mary are not "truly convinc[ing]" (47) alongside the interest he demonstrates in Roderick. While Rowland's attachment to Roderick may end in loss, James's willingness to explore the possibility of such an attachment signals the author's search for an alternative to what Naomi Sofer calls his "profound pessimism about heterosexual relationships" (185). Indeed, the almost hyperbolic incidence of domestic violence within the marriages of *Roderick Hudson* constitutes an ugly joke whose repeated punch line swings just short of endorsing the novel's same-sex relationship as a model alternative.

More recent critics have complicated Martin's characterization of the novel's central erotic attachment as homosexual. To inquire whether Rowland's desire for Roderick might be conceived as something other than homosexual is not to question whether Rowland desires Roderick. It is to question whether the novel is interested in imagining his desire as part of a different, and even more complex, understanding of SEXUALITY than a simple opposition between homosexuality and heterosexuality allows. The identification of persons as either heterosexual or homosexual is traditionally taken to be the signature bequest of late 19th-century medical interventions in Euro-American notions of sexuality. The most familiar story told by historians of sexuality privileges the following development: At the end of the 19th century, sexuality is defined for the first time exclusively by the sex of one's object of desire. More to the point, for the first time this desire for a particular sex is used to define who one is. Since the appearance of the term *homosexual* in medical discourse in Europe in the 1870s (and in America in the 1890s) is generally used to mark the shift toward thinking of same-sex desire as defining a type of human being, critics such as Eric Haralson and Gregory Woods have asked whether it is historically premature to identify Rowland as a homosexual. *Roderick Hudson* (1875), after all, predates the appearance of *homosexual* as a term in America. Sensitive to preserving the potential historical difference between James's understanding of sexuality and later sexual models, Woods and Haralson hedge their claims about James's evolving relation to homosexuality. Woods states that whereas *Roderick Hudson* is "not yet about homosexuality," "it does show signs of an incipient anxiety about homosexual identity" (77). Haralson contends that the novel "is not 'about' homosexuality so much as it is *about* to be about homosexuality" (45).

Hugh Stevens disagrees with the charge that it would be historically inaccurate to think of

Rowland as homosexual. For Stevens, "[sexual] transgression was already seen as demarcative of a certain identity before the terms of such an identity were rigidly categorized" (72). In other words, the appearance of the term *homosexual* in American medical discourse does not precede the wider culture's understanding of same-sex attraction as indicative of an identity. Rather, it actually follows from the wider culture's understanding. Still, while he grants that it is historically possible for James to write a text about a homosexual in 1875, Stevens agrees with Woods and Haralson that James's treatment of same-sex desire is hardly "transparent" (72). Michèle Mendelssohn argues that the opacity of Rowland's desire for Roderick results from that desire's assimilation into the patron/artist relationship. For Mendelssohn, the novel guarantees the acceptability of Rowland's intense commitment to Roderick by having the men share a professional relationship. Rowland's patronage of Roderick affords him a "right to sight," which Mendelssohn describes as a "socially and contractually sanctioned justification for watching his ward" (514). Haralson offers an important variation on this theme, observing that James's emerging anxiety over the expression of homosexuality forces him to redirect any "masculine desire" between Rowland and Roderick into "the channel of a safe and popularly palatable heterosexuality" (45). Thus, Rowland's desire for Roderick is covered over by both men's apparent desire for Mary Garland. For Mendelssohn and Haralson, the most significant aspect of Rowland's desire is not its orientation (Who is its object? A man or a woman?) but its reorientation (How is it transformed into various kinds of relation between Rowland and Roderick? How does it implicate Rowland in relations between other people?).

The constant reorientation of desire in *Roderick Hudson* bears out recent critics' contention that Rowland's desire cannot be comprehended as straightforwardly homosexual. For Leland Person, *Roderick Hudson* "does not simply reflect the closeting or frustration of male desire [for men] but the distribution of desire within a vexing economy of male-male and male-female relationships" (43). This distribution ensures that the novel cannot be about whether a homosexual desire could ever succeed in a culture that sanctions only hetero-sexual love. Rather, the novel persistently refuses to separate male-male desire from male-female desire. As a result of this refusal, it becomes less relevant to classify what kind of desire a given character has for another character. It becomes more relevant to observe how that desire is neces-sarily "entangled," as Person suggests, with other desires (43). Robert Emerick describes the novel's entanglement as a "love rectangle" (353) in which Rowland Mallet loves Mary Garland who loves Roderick Hudson who loves Christina Light who loves Rowland Mallet. Such a network of desire in-dicates how the novel declines to think of desire as that which differentiates one type of person from another type of person, as homosexuals would be differentiated from heterosexuals. The underlying logic of Emerick's rectangle is that all characters have the same desire to the extent that all charac-ters have a desire for what Sharon Cameron calls the "unfulfillable" (45). Stevens also confirms dis-appointment as desire's prevailing quality in the novel, for "each love object is cruel to the lover by turning their attention to another object" (81).

Yet, if cruelty is a charge that might be leveled at every character in *Roderick Hudson,* it is neverthe-less the case that Rowland has received the lion's share of blame. Rowland's cruelty takes a particular shape. It is not so much the cruelty of turning his attention away from someone who loves him so much as it is the cruelty of fixing his attention on someone who does not. Critics have understood Rowland's desire for Roderick to enable control, grant access, produce obligations, and otherwise create a domineering influence over Roderick. Of course, Rowland's desire might be said to lead to his own domination, leaving him at the mercy of Roderick's every whim. In Rowland's words, "I am incapable of giving [Roderick] up" (236). In either case, Roderick bucks at Rowland's watchfulness, declaring, "I resent the range of your vision pre-tending to be the limit of my action" (373). Here Rowland's attention to Roderick—what Mendels-sohn calls his "right to sight"—is also a powerful retention of the artist.

Given this model of desire as power, it is rela-tively unsurprising that Rowland has his detractors.

Peter Conn identifies Rowland's interest in Roderick as "self-serving" (72). Paul Saint-Amour character-izes Roderick's relation to Rowland as "the artist's subjection to his investor" (33). Wendy Graham ups the rhetorical wattage on Roderick's obligation to produce for Rowland by contending that Row-land "traffics in human commodities" (109). Greg Zacharias dismisses Rowland as a "Jamesian tyrant" (122–123). For these critics, Rowland's desire for Roderick, expressed through the form of a self-serv-ing gift, is deeply compromised by Rowland's under-standing of that gift as what he calls a "speculation" (98). For Rowland to place expectations on Rod-erick's development as an artist is to mar the gen-erosity of the original offer of his time and money. Such gifts turn Roderick into a commodity by con-straining his genius to time frames and production schedules. Rowland's flippant guarantee to Cecilia that Roderick will produce "[a] masterpiece a year . . . for the next quarter of a century" (80) stands for these critics as representative of the perversion of Rowland's desire. That desire is perverse for crit-ics not because it is homosexual rather than het-erosexual; it is perverse because it drafts Roderick into a power dynamic that asks of him more than he can consent to. Roderick voluntarily accepts Rowland's original gift, but the strings attached to that gift (the requirement that Roderick produce 12 statues—which, for critics like Graham, is really a cover for the requirement that Roderick reciprocate Rowland's desire) create a debt that Roderick can-not pay off.

But is Rowland's gift actually this grim? The attempt to read Rowland's generosity as an oppres-sive cover for his homosexuality is curiously at odds with the attempt to read sexuality in the novel beyond the terms of heterosexuality and homosexuality. That is, when critics such as Men-delssohn or Graham read the patron/artist rela-tionship as a substitute for Rowland's desire for Roderick, they assume that what Rowland desires is really a particular sex—more specifically, a male; more specifically, Roderick. Yet this risks defining Rowland's sexuality as vectored exclusively toward another person in a way that corresponds to the very categories of heterosexuality and homosexual-ity that critics such as Person or Cameron attempt to complicate. Curiously, however, even critics such as Cameron who argue that sexuality cannot differentiate characters in the novel because all characters desire the "unfulfillable" depend on a restrictive account of desire as only ever vectored toward another person. Put differently, to say that all desire is unfulfilled in the novel is to assume a particular logic by which desire works, and this logic begins to look a lot like that setting up a binary between heterosexuality and homosexuality. Using Emerick's geometry: Rowland cannot have Mary Garland; Mary cannot have Roderick; Roderick cannot have Christina; Christina cannot have Rowland. Nor, of course, can Rowland have Roderick. The unfulfillment of desire requires that desire always be for a person of a particular sex.

But what if Rowland does not want Roderick? This is not to classify Rowland as heterosexual. Rather, it is to consider the implications of Rowland not wanting a specific person at all. If one stops trying to understand Rowland's desire in familiar terms of anxieties over exclusivity and reciprocity, might then the novel not be so bleakly invested in nongratification? If readers respond to Rowland's avowals of "I am waiting" (224) or "I am the most patient" (388) by trying to guess a specific object, then readers foreshorten the potential of these avowals. The question "what is he waiting for" actually prescribes a wrong answer. For as the novel progresses, it becomes clear that Rowland is not waiting for something or someone at all—unless one understands him to be waiting for more time. Rowland's pleas for Roderick to "stay another year" (343) are less convincing as pathetic attempts to usher in a particular kind of future with Roderick—one in which the artist is successful or the artist loves him back. Rowland's persistent attempts to keep Roderick in Europe are, rather, comprehensible as attempts to extend the present, however frustrating that present may be. What does it mean to desire not a different future but the extension of one's present? It is the difference between desiring something other than what one has and desiring what one has. More provocatively, Rowland might be suggesting that the success or failure of his desire does not depend on the unfolding of actual events but rather on there being more time.

For James to end his novel with Rowland's claim, "I am the most patient," is an astonishing rebuke to any theory that Rowland's waiting requires Roderick as its object. Roderick is dead, but Rowland's patience persists. When placed alongside Rowland's mother's "charming patience" (57) or Sam Singleton's "patient industry" (118), Rowland's waiting begins to look less like an eccentric denial of the practicality of waiting and more like part of a potentially extensive engagement on the novel's part in waiting as a mode of being in the world. In *The Europeans* (1878), the Baroness Eugenia Münster distances herself from a life of waiting by declaring, "patience implies suffering" (143). But in *Roderick Hudson*, patience has its pleasures. These pleasures are the pleasures of enduring in a world in which the fulfillment of any desire could not be permanently guaranteed. Waiting in *Roderick Hudson* is not waiting for a substantially different future that could replace the present; waiting is to privilege the very experience of enduring the present.

CHARACTERS

Blanchard, Augusta An American painter whom Rowland befriends in Rome, Augusta's happy "combination of beauty and talent" (120) differs dramatically from Roderick's experience of tortured genius. She primarily serves as a distraction for Rowland, who "cultivates oblivion" (120) with her in order to forget the disappointment of Mary Garland's engagement.

Casamassima, Prince Suitor to Christina Light, the Prince is favored by Mrs. Light and Giacosa for his fortune and title. Rowland considers the Prince "stupid" but acknowledges that the "melancholy nobleman" is at least "serious" about himself (203). Casamassima proposes marriage to Christina, whose attention to Roderick has given little previous encouragement to the Prince. His proposal is accepted, then rejected, then accepted again under coercion.

Cecilia Rowland's cousin and Roderick's friend in Northampton, Cecilia is the first to caution Rowland that he is not the only person who has expectations regarding Roderick's removal from Northampton.

Rowland may expect Roderick to work hard in Rome, but Cecilia expects Rowland to ensure that Roderick does. Rowland describes Cecilia's interest in Roderick as "a flirtation without the benefits of a flirtation" (80). She would prefer that Roderick stay, and her contentment with entertaining Roderick as he is rather than as he could be strikes Rowland as uninspiring and counterproductive.

Garland, Mary Roderick's plain American cousin and fiancée, Mary is "the daughter of a minister, the grand-daughter of a minister, [and] the sister of a minister" (85–86). Rowland spends much of his time trying to understand the specific nature of Mary's morality.

Her family's poverty leaves Mary initially unprepared to grasp the idea of Rowland's offer to Roderick, which she describes as a "fairy tale" (91). She becomes forgettable to Roderick, who in Rome prefers Christina Light's beauty. But she remains unforgettable to Rowland, who cannot account for his early pleasure with her "extreme reserve" (94) and who later imagines that, were he to win her heart, the frustrations of his "wasted kindness" (375) to Roderick would be worth it after all. In his 1907 preface to the novel, James describes Mary as the "antithesis" to Christina Light (47). Where Christina's good looks are the main attraction of her theatrical manipulations, Mary's strength is her moral force. She remains loyal to Roderick, but this loyalty does not preclude her judgment of him.

Giacosa, the Cavaliere A "grotesque-looking personage" (109), he accompanies Mrs. Light and Christina wherever they go. He explains to Rowland that he is not "a hired cicerone, but an ancient Roman gentleman" (157). Though performing menial tasks for the Lights, he is most invested in the much larger project of finding Christina a husband. He is steadfast in his conviction that Christina must marry the Prince over Roderick. Ultimately, the strange intensity of his anxiety over Christina's fate compels Rowland to guess that Giacosa is her father.

Gloriani A 40-year-old American sculptor whom Rowland befriends in Rome, Gloriani has been "obliged to make capital of his talent" (117) after spending his youth irresponsibly. His practical theory of art and popular success thoroughly opposes Roderick's idealism.

Grandoni, Madame An "excessively ugly old lady" (121) whom Rowland befriends in Rome through Augusta Blanchard, Grandoni is a source of wisdom, which the novel credits to her "thirty years' observation of Roman society" (122). These years included a first marriage ending in widowhood and a second marriage beset by domestic violence. Though a self-appointed matchmaker for Augusta, her most significant social service is her gossip about the history of the Light family.

Hudson, Mrs. Sarah Having lost her husband to drink and her eldest son in the Civil War, she is the overprotective mother of Roderick. Her claims on her son are alternately ridiculous and poignant for the persistence with which she asserts them in the face of their inevitable failure.

Hudson, Roderick A young American sculptor with the promise of artistic genius but whose "large capacity for ruin" the novel records (43), Roderick is a man of "insufficient physical substance" but remarkable "nervous force" (64). He is repeatedly described as "picturesque" (64, 311), as though he were the novel's primary art object rather than his statues. His unrelenting commitment to an ideal of beauty is ripe for disillusionment.

As a child, Roderick was transplanted from Virginia to Massachusetts when his mother sold their slaves and lands to pay off her late husband's debts. He grew up "horribly spoiled" (67). In his early twenties, Roderick's southernness is irrepressible. His dress and good-humored idleness strike Rowland as appropriate to the "Virginian or Carolinian of romance" (64). But it is Cecilia who explains why Roderick is out of place in Northampton: "the boy is an artist—an artist to his finger's ends" (67).

Once in Rome, Roderick's stubborn adherence to a "splendid ideal" (115) works to the detriment of the actual persons around him. When that ideal is able to spur him to work, he does so until his models "[drop] with fatigue" (114). When that ideal seems impossible to meet, Roderick settles for a corrupt idleness to which he claims he is entitled. Any attempt to confront Roderick with the consequences of both his failure to work and his resolve to woo Christina Light are met by Roderick with frank disavowals of the relationships that his actions are said to harm.

By the novel's end, Roderick acknowledges the effects of his behavior. But Rowland observes that Roderick's contrition is really only another form of his ideal of beauty. It was "aesthetic disgust at the graceless contour of his conduct, but never a hint of simple sorrow for the pain he had given" (379).

Leavenworth, Mr. A rich American friend of Augusta Blanchard, Leavenworth commissions Roderick to sculpt a representation of *Culture*. Leavenworth's interest in art as ornament irritates Roderick, who agrees to the project only out of financial need.

Light, Christina The novel's femme fatale, she is a self-identified flirt whose beauty she is not alone in manipulating to social advantage. Wearied by her mother's determination to turn her beauty into married fortune, Christina answers her mother with an equal and opposite resolve to play the field. Rowland immediately suspects she is "unsafe" (151) for Roderick. For those who know her, her caprices are at worst a source of tremendous anxiety and at least an object of constant attention.

Christina is hardly villainous, however. She is exhausted by her own egotism and explains her commitment to herself as follows: "I would give all I possess to get out of myself; but somehow at the end I find myself so vastly more interesting than nine-tenths of the people I meet" (182). Rowland perhaps falls into the exceptional 10 percent, for Christina agrees to cease contact with Roderick in order to win Rowland's respect. She reneges on her agreement, but Rowland ultimately considers her an "excellent girl" (312). Her futile, though strenuous, efforts to thwart her mother's wish that she marry the Prince represent for Rowland a form of sympathetic labor.

Light, Mrs. (Miss Savage) Christina's mother, she is an inveterate social climber determined to secure for her daughter a successful marriage. Mrs. Light is the daughter "of an old American painter of very bad landscapes, which people used to buy from charity and use as fireboards" (152). Widow to an American consul, she reappeared pregnant in Rome shortly after her husband's death. Convinced that Christina's "face is her fortune" (154), she uses her daughter's beauty to ascend the ranks of Roman society. But it is ultimately the secret of Christina's illegitimate birth that Mrs. Light exploits to secure her social triumph.

Mallet, Jonas Rowland's father, he is a "chip off the primal Puritan block" (54). He is inexpressive, unloving, and distant. His refusal to allow his business successes to shroud Rowland in comfort leads him to raise his son in contrived severity. As an adult, Rowland's anxiety over having an occupation will be conditioned by the strictness he knew as a child.

Mallet, Mrs. (Miss Rowland) She is Rowland's mother. Her marriage to Jonas Mallet proves an "immitigable error which she had spent her life trying to look in the face" (57). She is worshipped by Rowland for her "charming patience" (57). Her self-determination under adverse conditions becomes an example Rowland will live by or have others live by.

Mallet, Rowland After an austere childhood, Rowland receives an inheritance that has left him comfortable at the age of 30. He served an "obscure" role as a citizen soldier during the Civil War (58). But in postwar America, he is without a "fixed occupation" (58). Nor does he desire one, if work requires "driving a lucrative trade" (58). Unfit for either business or idling, he finds suitable labor in patronizing the arts generally and mentoring Roderick specifically.

Rowland's sense of his own expectations for Roderick evolve from "simply offer[ing]" Roderick "an opportunity" (71) to more patiently desiring a compensation that never comes. His loyalty to Roderick is stretched to its conceivable limit by Roderick's selfishness in Rome but never snaps. Though it afflicts Rowland, that loyalty is Rowland's only genuine reward for his generosity.

Rowland is not so unlike Roderick in that he views the world through his own set of ideals. His generous offer to subsidize Roderick's trip to Rome is also a desire to fashion Roderick after his own wish for what the young artist might be. Rowland ultimately repents of his involvement in Roderick's affairs, resolving that he "must never try it again" (335). But that resolve is at odds with his awareness that he can never "give up" Roderick (236). By the novel's end, Rowland considers the implications of Roderick's death for his own future: "His occupation was gone" (387). In a moment of "transcendent bitterness" (387) over the untimely death of his friend, Rowland's phrasing of his loss as a loss of labor inadequately indicates how his labor for the young artist was also a labor of love.

Singleton, Sam An American painter whom Rowland befriends in Rome. He is "so perfect an example of the little noiseless laborious artist" (119). His work ethic is remarkable for its distinction from Roderick's delinquency. Singleton's "patient industry" (118) wins the respect of Rowland, for whom the evidence of hard work has always had an appeal. At the end of two years in Rome, Roderick is left with only a handful of statues and an enormous sense of indifference about his future. But Singleton is ready to return to America with 900 sketches in tow. In Switzerland, Rowland recruits Singleton to help search for Roderick after the novel's climactic storm. Singleton finds Roderick's body and, in a last act of significant labor, makes the three-hour hike back to Engelberg to enlist others to recover the corpse.

Striker, Mr. An attorney in Northampton and Roderick's first boss. Striker bears the brunt of Roderick's frustration with New England life. While Mrs. Hudson and Mary Garland are eventually won over to Rowland's plan for Roderick, Striker holds out. He is a "plain practical old boy" (89) and considers Europe unnecessary to make a respectable man.

FURTHER READING

Cameron, Sharon. *Thinking in Henry James*, 42–53. Chicago: University of Chicago Press, 1989.

Conn, Peter. "*Roderick Hudson:* The Role of the Observer." *Nineteenth-Century Fiction* 26 (1971): 65–82.

Emerick, Ronald. "The Love Rectangle in *Roderick Hudson:* Another Look at Christina Light." *Studies in the Novel* 18, no. 4 (1986): 353–366.

Graham, Wendy. "Dissipation and Decoration in *Roderick Hudson.*" In *Henry James's Thwarted Love.* Palo Alto, Calif.: Stanford University Press, 1999.

Haralson, Eric. "Indiscreet Anatomies and Protogay Aesthetes in *Roderick Hudson* and *The Europeans.*" *Henry James and Queer Modernity*, 27–53. Cambridge: Cambridge University Press, 2003.

Henke, Richard. "The Embarrassment of Melodrama in the Early James." *Novel* 28, no. 3 (1995): 257–283.

James, Henry. *The Europeans.* 1878. Reprint, New York: Penguin, 1984.

———. *Roderick Hudson.* 1875. Reprint, New York: Penguin, 1986.

Martin, Robert. "'The High Felicity of Comradeship': A New Reading of *Roderick Hudson.*" *American Literary Realism, 1870–1910* 11 (1978): 100–108.

Mendelssohn, Michèle. "Homosociality and the Aesthetic in Henry James's *Roderick Hudson.*" *Nineteenth-Century Literature* 57, no. 4 (2003): 512–541.

Norton, Grace. "*Roderick Hudson.*" 1876. Reprinted in *Henry James: The Contemporary Reviews*, edited by Kevin J. Hayes, 13–15. Cambridge: Cambridge University Press, 1996.

Person, Leland. "Configuring Male Desire and Identity in *Roderick Hudson.*" In *Henry James and the Suspense of Masculinity*, 39–64. Philadelphia: University of Pennsylvania Press, 2003.

Saint-Amour, Paul K. "Transatlantic Tropology in James's *Roderick Hudson.*" *Henry James Review* 18, no. 1 (1997): 22–42.

Saje, Natasha. "'Artful Artlessness': Reading the Coquette in *Roderick Hudson.*" *Henry James Review* 18, no. 2 (1997): 161–172.

Sofer, Naomi. "Why 'Different Vibrations . . . Walk Hand in Hand': Homosocial Bonds in *Roderick Hudson.*" *Henry James Review* 20, no. 2 (1999): 185–205.

Stevens, Hugh. "The Eroticism of Prohibition: Masochism and the Law in *Roderick Hudson.*" In *Henry*

James and Sexuality, 61–89. Cambridge: Cambridge University Press, 1998.

Woods, Gregory. "The Art of Friendship in *Roderick Hudson*." In *Henry James and Homoerotic Desire*, edited by John R. Bradley, 69–77. New York: Macmillan, 1999.

Zacharias, Greg. "James's Morality in *Roderick Hudson*." *Henry James Review* 11, no. 2 (1990): 115–132.

Tony Mick, *Johns Hopkins University*

The Sacred Fount (1901)

Henry James began writing *The Sacred Fount* in the spring of 1900 at LAMB HOUSE, and the completed novel was published by Methuen in England and by Scribners in America in 1901.

SYNOPSIS

(Chapter 1) The unnamed narrator awaits a train from Paddington Station, LONDON, to the country house Newmarch. While waiting, he spies Gilbert Long and seeks to avoid him, fearing Long will not recognize him. Long greets him, however, and arranges to have his luggage moved to the narrator's compartment. He returns with Grace Brissenden, whom the narrator fails to immediately recognize. On the train, Grace informs them that her husband, Guy, will be traveling later with Lady John. While Grace talks to a guest, Long and the narrator discuss her strangely youthful appearance. The narrator then discusses Long's apparent transformation from "stupid" to "clever" with Grace, an improvement she explains through Lady John's recent interest in him.

(Chapter 2) At Newmarch, the narrator accompanies Ford Obert, the painter, and May Server after he senses that Obert wants help. They soon join Long, who again impresses with his talk, and Lady John, whom the narrator doubts has the capacity to improve Long. En route to dinner, Obert claims May Server is flighty and contrasts this with her stillness when he painted her. Entering his room, the narrator fails to recognize the seemingly ancient Guy Brissenden, who is lost. After dinner, the narrator broaches a theory about Guy's aging with both Long and Obert. While Long does not see the change, Obert encourages him when he suggests Guy has been sacrificially tapping "the sacred fount" (34) for his wife's youth.

(Chapter 3) The next day, the narrator suggests to Grace that Lady John is Long's "screen" (38) for another woman, a woman they will recognize as being reduced to idiocy. They soon spy Long talking with a woman, but when he turns round and reveals the woman to be the socialite Mme. de Dreuil, in company with Lady John, they give it up. The pair then stumble on Guy in conversation with May Server. Grace is immediately convinced that May is the woman they are looking for, and the narrator is suddenly ashamed of their theorizing. As Grace leaves the narrator with Guy, the narrator is fearful that May might be "compromised" (45).

(Chapter 4) Entering the house, May informs the narrator that Guy is only interested in Lady John and that Lady John desires Ford Obert. Inside the house, the narrator and May observe Obert and Long viewing a painting. The four gather before a suggestive picture of a man with a mask; the narrator hints that the man resembles a guest, and Long guesses that he means Guy. As Long and May move on, Obert informs the narrator that his account of the Brissendens has offered him an "analogy" (56) for reading May Server's change. Obert is convinced that May's lover is present at Newmarch, but he gives it up as nobody's business.

(Chapter 5) The narrator and Grace discuss May Server. Grace suggests her flightiness is part of a "screen" for her affair and accuses the narrator of both protecting and being in love with May. The narrator does not deny his affection for May and uses this to prove his conviction that she is not their missing woman. They then see May with her back turned in conversation. When May turns, her interlocutor is revealed to be not Long but Guy. Grace claims this as proof that May is using Guy as a screen, and while the narrator agrees he pretends to find Guy's appearance insignificant.

(Chapter 6) The narrator resolves to give up his theorizing, but he remains obsessed. He watches sympathetically as May nervously flits between men, and he deduces that she has become aware that Obert has discovered her secret. The narrator then meets Lady John and Guy Brissenden in silent communion. Lady John's greeting suggests that she is bored with Guy and that she has been using him to mask her love for Long, who at that moment appears. The narrator deduces that Long is using Lady John to mask his real lover, and Lady John is using Long to create the illusion of a lover. The narrator pities Guy and leads him away.

(Chapter 7) Guy declares his irritation with Lady John and, in response to the narrator's questions, tells of May's paucity of conversation. Guy suggests that May has been avoiding the narrator because she fears that he knows why she is "radiant" (90) despite her unhappy circumstances (she has little money and has lost three children). Guy admits to both wanting to be kind to May and being terrified of her. He looks to the narrator to help account for this fear. The narrator concludes their conversation by claiming he has discovered the tie between May and Guy: She wants to conceal something, and he wants to know it.

(Chapter 8) On leaving Guy, the narrator encounters May Server walking alone in the woods. The narrator believes she is looking for Guy, and he senses that May and Guy are connected by a common, unspeakable awareness of their status as victims. In response to May's mute addresses, the narrator makes a casual reference to Guy and finds in May's bemused response evidence of her efforts to conceal this relationship. As May appears to be on the verge of breaking down, Guy appears. The narrator leaves with an excuse that he has to dress for dinner. Guy appears to have again been with Grace, as he looks 10 years older.

(Chapter 9) When Gilbert Long sits beside May Server at dinner, the narrator reads this as the exception that proves their more secret liaisons. The narrator feels that Long is trying to stem his knowledge of the affair. In the drawing room, where a pianist plays, the narrator observes May at peace. The narrator approaches Lady John when Guy seems to silently appeal for saving from her company. He then spies Long and Grace together and assumes that they are conspiring. The narrator is comforted by Lady John's unimaginative theo-

ries: She claims Grace is having an affair with Long and that she arranged the trip in the train from Paddington accordingly.

(Chapter 10) Grace asks to speak with the narrator and then departs. The narrator sees Obert and May conversing comfortably. The narrator escapes the pitiful sight of May and finds himself in a corridor behind the Brissendens; it is this view that makes Guy look "oldest" (140). The narrator turns away, again resolving to leave. He changes his mind when he spies Long through a window, alone and nervously smoking. The narrator returns to the drawing room, hoping to meet Grace, but finds the women already gone. He encounters Obert, and they agree to meet later. The narrator searches again for Grace and then, once more, gives up.

(Chapter 11) In the smoking room, the narrator admits to Obert his ongoing search for May Server's lover (he misleadingly suggests he has just been looking for May). Obert believes May has changed back to being happy. He deduces that May has given up her lover, who is not present at Newmarch. The narrator reveals his idea of Guy's and May's joint sense of victimhood. At the point when he seems to be suggesting that Guy has replaced May's original lover, Guy enters with a message for the narrator to meet his wife. The narrator bids farewell to Obert, leaving him with the mistaken impression that he has been summoned to meet with May.

(Chapter 12) The narrator finds Grace looking more youthful than ever. Grace explains that she postponed their interview with the hope that May would retire before they talked. The narrator asks if there is any new information to support their suspicions about May. Grace announces that she has given up their investigations and that she has decided May is not the woman. The narrator deduces that Gilbert Long instructs Grace and, in order to confirm his suspicions, he presses her to reveal why she changed her mind. He maintains that he has kept his suspicions private, and he asks if she has asked Long himself about his lover.

(Chapter 13) Grace denies speaking with anyone, although the narrator is convinced that she is lying. While Grace encourages the narrator to let it go, he senses that Long and Grace have identified him as a threat. The narrator announces that he will surrender his theory but appeals to Grace to aid him by explaining her abandonment. When he insists, Grace tells him that she thinks he is "crazy" (192). The narrator asks her when she first thought him mad, suggesting it was when she requested this interview. Grace eventually claims that at that time she had discovered Long's stupidity, a claim that, for the narrator, reveals a new level of collusion.

(Chapter 14) Grace announces that the woman they have been searching for is, according to Guy, Lady John. She claims that Guy traveled to Newmarch with Lady John solely to amuse himself. The narrator asks her to explain the scene in which they found Guy and May conversing. Grace refutes the idea that May was depleted, revealing that Guy believes May was making love to him and that she was "awfully sharp" (218) in her conversation. The narrator senses the collapse of his theory, and Grace leaves, reiterating that he is "crazy." The narrator finally seeks escape from Newmarch but closes by claiming his failure is one of "tone" not "method" (219).

CRITICAL ANALYSIS

The Sacred Fount is James's only novel-length example of first-person narration, a technique he decried in his preface to *The Ambassadors* for its "terrible *fluidity* of self-revelation" (*Literary Criticism* 1,316). Its elusive, often frustrating story can, however, be productively read alongside a number of his shorter works, most notably "The Private Life" and "The Turn of the Screw." Each of these works centers on a potentially unreliable narrator, determinedly forming interpretive theories about his or her surroundings while inviting the reader to turn interpretation back on his or her often-complicated "self-revelation[s]."

In a letter responding to a number of comments and queries concerning *The Sacred Fount* by Mrs. [Mary] Humphry Ward, James refers to his short novel as "a *consistent* joke" that has been "taken rather seriously" by the public. The "joke," he claims, lies in the fact that "it has . . . , and applied quite rigorously and constructively, . . . its own little law of composition" (*Letters* 186). What, then,

is the "consistent joke," the secret and ironic key, behind this decidedly earnest narrative?

The key questions that an investigative reader might ask when wading through the text are: Is the narrator reliable? Is the narrator "crazy"? Are the signs of transference between the couples at Newmarch real, or are they only effects of perception? These questions, in turn, might lead to the significance of the narrator's tale: Does the narrator represent James's study of a perversely obsessive voyeur? Or do the narrator's ultimately doomed efforts to construct "a perfect palace of thought" (214) ask readers to understand him as an artist *manqué*, a frustrated artist?

At its heart, James's novel appears vitally concerned with a parasitic vision of intimacy. While James himself never uses the word *vampire*, readers of the time were quick to pick up on the theme in the wake of Bram Stoker's *Dracula* (1897). In *Henry James: A Life* (1985), Leon Edel suggests that *The Sacred Fount* represents James's most morbid exploration of a lifelong "vampire theme"; James writes, Edel argues, from a belief "that men derive strength from the women they marry, and that conversely women can deprive men of both strength and life" (15). But the narrator's interpretive partnership with Grace Brissenden is also described in terms that resemble the very vampirism they seek to analyze: When Grace takes up his model and makes a case for May Server as the missing link, the narrator proclaims "I feel drained—I feel dry!" (67). Interpretation and narration are, in the scheme of James's novel, acts of vampirism and transference. The narrator's claims to creative power in his handling of relations depend upon an emptying out of the subjects of his theories.

In many ways, James's novel asks to be read as a book about art and the interpretation of art. R. P. Blackmur's *"The Sacred Fount"* (1942) reads the narrator as a straight representation of Henry James and suggests that the vampires of the tale are projections of his conscience: "[A]s novelist James is the hidden conscience of his characters, and as conscience he is himself their sacred fount" (67). Poststructuralist scholars in the latter half of the 20th century have tended to read the novel as a "parable" (Blackall 2), with the ever-absent yet central "sacred fount" revealing both the instability of language and the role of the reader in textual play.

Susanne Kappeler in *Writing and Reading in Henry James* (1980) reads the novel as a scene of "infinite production" in which "perceptions are perceived, interpreted, reproduced in discourse, reinterpreted, and where palace is built upon palace, with none at the bottom built upon rock" (173). For Kappeler, James's novel invites the reader into a game where "the pleasure lies in the playing, which is a matter of skill and technique, both of one's own and one's partner" (73). There may be good grounds for reading the narrator's interpretive adventure as James's self-conscious account of his own artistic process. Intriguingly, the narrator's seemingly inescapable obsession with his theory mirrors James's own accounts of his short story as "growing on my hands, to a so much longer thing by a force of its own" (*Letters* 154).

Chapter 4 brings together the novel's concerns with both vampirism and art, as the narrator and others gather before a suggestive portrait of a "young man in black" (50) holding a feminine mask. For the narrator, the painting represents "the Mask of Life" and young man is "Death," who has either removed or is about to put on the mask; for May Server, the mask with its "awful grimace," represents "the Mask of Death" (51). "It's the picture, of all pictures," the narrator proclaims, "that most needs an interpreter" (50). In *Henry James and Henry Adams: The Emergence of a Modern Consciousness* (1976), John Carlos Rowe reads the picture as an attempt "to dramatize the crisis of art itself" (171). The painting, according to Rowe, traces a "paradoxical relationship between definition and free play" (169–170) at the heart of interpretive activity in the novel: On one hand, it "reveals the essential blankness and deathliness beneath the masks we design for our appearances in the world"; on the other, "the mask represents the possibility of creating meaning where there may have been none to begin with" (170).

The enduring critical debates around *The Sacred Fount* suggest that it raises abstract questions about the nature of art, the treachery of intimacy, and the dangers of interpretation. In the last 15 years,

however, scholars have increasingly sought to identify the text's more political concerns with class, the literary marketplace, the public sphere, and the nation. While the physical location of Newmarch is only vaguely suggested (somewhere in the Midlands between London and Birmingham), its social status is clearly indicated. Newmarch is a realm of privilege, a retreat for the wealthy (and white) elite of England. With this in mind, Paul Giles in "Deterritorialization in *The Sacred Fount*" (2004) argues that James's novel foregrounds the leisure class's repression of links between a "protected private sphere" of privilege and "a larger world of commodification" (231). Giles reads the novel's space as being torn by a "double movement": on one hand, turning "social beings into financial and psychosexual commodities" (228) and, on the other, seeking to preserve "social distinction and niceties of taste" (228–229). The narrator's final collapse, according to Giles, shows how the "particular value" of *The Sacred Fount*'s "aristocratic society is locked into a willed ignorance of the intellectual complications and conceptual exchanges which encompass it" (231).

If *The Sacred Fount* deals with the nature of power, knowledge, and privilege for the leisure classes of capitalist society, it also speaks to the place of art in the marketplace. Laurel Bollinger's "'Miracles are Expensive': The Complicated Metaphors of Subjectivity in *The Sacred Fount*" (1999) reads the novel as a tracing of "the economics of literary production" (60). Through the metaphors of capitalist exchange, Bollinger argues, James explores how the "novelistic imagination puts the narrator into the positions of exploiter and exploited" (61), an economic position from which the novel offers no escape.

In *Modernism, Mass Culture and Professionalism* (1993), Thomas Strychacz argues that *The Sacred Fount* asks questions "about the relationship between audience and the constitution of a literary text within a burgeoning (and fragmenting) mass market" (66). Drawing on the narrator's comparison of himself with the "newspaper-man kicked out" of Newmarch, Strychacz suggests that the "playful, self-reflexive, esoteric writing strategies" of James's "modernist" novel works through "an exclusionary process that, by rewriting and defamiliarizing the texts and language of mass culture," such as popular journalism, "achieves a narrow but real authority in our society" (77).

Strychacz's reading of the narrator's identification with the "newspaper man" points to the novel's wider interest in a complicated conflict between privacy and publicity, between private and public identity. While the narrator seeks to read the public movements of others as signs of their private desires, he repeatedly assumes that his own private life is immune to investigation and of little importance for his narrative. *The Sacred Fount's* treatment of the fragile space between private and public locates it in a specific tradition of late 19th-century gothic fictions centered on characters violently split between their public and private selves: for instance, ROBERT LOUIS STEVENSON's *The Strange Case of Dr. Jekyll and Mr. Hyde*, OSCAR WILDE's *The Picture of Dorian Gray*, and Bram Stoker's *Dracula*. Like these works, James's novel traces a pervasive fear of the violence beneath the niceties of elite social manners, a violence that could be traced to repressed histories of colonial oppression behind the public wealth of the British Empire at the end of the 19th century.

Published less than a year after Oscar Wilde's death, *The Sacred Fount's* central concern with concealment and investigation of intimate relations also speaks to its emergence during a period of stringently policed sexual desire. Jonathan Freedman's *The Temple of Culture* (2000) highlights late 19th-century arguments for cultural links between "degeneration, stylistic hypertrophy, nonreproductive sexuality and madness." For Freedman, *The Sacred Fount* represents the climax of James's anxious replies to a debate that threatened his social status as an artist: "The obsessive ravings of the novel's voyeuristic narrator . . . firmly link the enterprise of fiction-making itself to madness, sexual eccentricity, and, ultimately, exhaustion and decrepitude" (128).

A number of recent critics have sought to reread James's novel with an eye to nonheteronormative sexual desires. In "A Gay *Sacred Fount*: The Reader as Detective" (1995), Adeline Tintner claims that James's "consistent joke" is the narrator's misreading of the evidence, his inability to recognize that it is Gilbert Long and Guy Brissenden, May Server and Grace Brissenden, who are, in fact, engaged in affairs. In *The Public Life of Privacy* (2005), Stacey Margolis offers a reading of the narrator's interpretive practices as "homo-formalist." Emphasizing the erotically charged exchanges between the narrator and Ford Obert, Margolis argues that "same-sex desire" figures in James's novel "as a way of both literalizing the analogical relation with others through which individuals come to know themselves and motivating (even more dramatically than vampirism) the terror of these analogies" (192). Both Tintner's and Margolis's approaches foreground the danger of privileging heteronormative readings of James's novel. Indeed, the narrator's elusive and seemingly diverse desires—his intimacy with Obert is matched by his only partly acknowledged feelings for May Server—point to the possibilities for "queer" rereadings of his story of sexual vampires.

CHARACTERS

Brissenden, Grace Grace is both the narrator's principal interlocutor and one of the key targets of his investigations. While details about Grace's age are ambiguous, Gilbert Long believes her to be 42 or 43. Readers are informed that Grace's marriage to Guy was initially joked about as "a case of child-stealing" (19). The narrator becomes convinced that she has grown younger at the expense of her husband. At the end, the narrator believes she looks like she "might have been a large, fair, rich, prosperous person of twenty-five" (167).

Grace initially joins the narrator in his theorizing about Gilbert Long's missing partner, settling on May Server as the key suspect. Grace rejoins the narrator at the close and announces she has given up the question. When pressed by the narrator, she states that the missing woman is Lady John and claims her husband, Guy, as the source of this information. The narrator believes this interpretive shift is due to Grace's communion with Long.

Grace's responses to the narrator at the close do suggest a certain inconsistency. The difficulty lies in knowing whether Grace's inconsistencies signal her attempts to hide an affair with Gilbert Long or indicate her irritation with the narrator's seemingly endless inquiries. When Grace informs the narrator that he is "crazy" (192), she is looking to shut down the conversation because either she has something to hide or she is fed up with the obsessive narrator.

Brissenden, Guy   Guy is first introduced through Gilbert Long's discussion of his MARRIAGE to Grace. Long recalls how Guy had "the face of a baby" and suggests that Grace's seeming youth owes something to the "desperately dull" (20) state of being married to him. Guy makes his first appearance when he mistakes the narrator's room for his own. The narrator's initial inability to recognize Guy's eerily aged form points to a possibly repressed and uncanny doubling of himself in Guy.

Referred to as "poor Briss," Guy Brissenden represents, for the narrator, an object of pity at the mercy of his vampire wife and the machinations of people like Lady John. The narrator believes that May Server and Guy have, by the end, formed an unspeakable "fellowship in misery" (157). Ironically, if readers believe Grace, Guy is the source that depletes the narrator's theories at the end. He reveals to his wife both the identity of Lady John as Long's lover and the sharpness of May Server when she seeks to "make love" to him.

John, Lady   Lady John travels to Newmarch with Guy Brissenden, and the exact reason for her accompaniment of Guy remains a point of contention throughout. The narrator describes Lady John as well versed in public forms but lacking in imagination: "She was pretty, prompt, hard, and, in a way that was special to her, a mistress at once of 'culture' and of slang" (26).

For the narrator, Lady John represents an index of how others at Newmarch are viewing him. When the narrator discusses the subjects of his theories with her, he finds himself fearing the "peril of the public ugliness" (127). Eventually, the narrator discounts Lady John as an interpreter to be feared; he believes her readings of the couples at Newmarch are naive. She does, however, offer some of the novel's most cutting critiques of the narrator. "You can't be a providence," she declares to the narrator, "and not be a bore. A real providence *knows*;

whereas you, . . . have to find out—and to find out even by asking 'the likes of' *me*" (126).

Long, Gilbert   The narrator describes Gilbert Long as a Newmarch regular. He is, according to the narrator, "stupid" but strikingly good-looking: "his six feet and more of stature, his low-growing, tight-curling hair, his big, bare, blooming face" (17). At the start, the narrator believes Long to have undergone a surprising change from "stupid" to "clever." The narrator's initial description of Long as "stupid" is based on Long's having snubbed him during previous stays at Newmarch. The narrator's evaluations of Long's intelligence often seem to depend on whether Long appears to like him or not.

Long, like Grace, is both the target of the narrator's theories and his interpretive partner. The narrator initially looks to Long to confirm his sense of a change in Grace Brissenden. He later appeals to Long for a similar confirmation of his reading of Guy's deterioration, but Long cannot see any change. The narrator later suspects Long of seeking to shut down his theorizing in order to protect his supposedly draining affair with May Server.

Narrator   The narrator reveals very little about his appearance or background. He is "a much older man" (29) than Guy Brissenden. He has been a regular guest at Newmarch and, as such, must move in moneyed circles. Why or for whom the narrator is writing is not revealed.

This withholding of personal information parallels the narrator's efforts to avoid exposure at Newmarch. From early on, he suggests that his theory will benefit from private hoarding: "I had to keep myself in hand in order not too publicly to explain, not to break out right and left with my reflections" (30). But, as he later recognizes, concealment cannot protect him from the attentions of others: his "cogitations," he realizes, "would have made me as stiff a puzzle to interpretative minds as I had suffered other phenomena to become to my own" (74).

The narrator frequently announces his status as the lone intensely conscious observer at Newmarch. "I alone was magnificently and absurdly aware," he proclaims; "everyone else was benightedly out of it" (127). However, when Grace Brissenden informs him that he is "crazy," he hesitates, "wondering if perhaps I mightn't be" (192). Nevertheless, even when Grace appears to dismantle his theory, the narrator announces his surrender as a mere rhetorical defeat: "[I]t wasn't really that I hadn't three times her method. What I too fatally lacked was her tone" (219).

Obert, Ford   Ford Obert is fired by the narrator's theorizing to observe and analyze the couples at Newmarch. He even offers the narrator perhaps the key justification for his "game" of vicariously reading others from a distance: "resting on psychologic signs alone, it's a high application of intelligence. What's ignoble is the detective and the keyhole" (57).

For the narrator, Obert's status as a painter, his "experience of every sort of facial accident, of human sign," makes him "just the touchstone" (33) he wants for testing his observations. The narrator identifies his theorizing with Obert's artistry, proclaiming "I only talk . . . as you paint; not a bit worse!" (34). Obert's earlier painting of May Server offers a key reference point for reading her change from stillness to a state of constant flight. By having the narrator draw on Obert for his reading of May, James's novel points to the way in which the narrator, like a painter, seeks to frame and fix his subjects.

Server, May   May Server is one of the few characters in *The Sacred Fount* to be given a significant backstory. Guy Brissenden informs the narrator that "[s]he has none too much money; she has had three children and lost them; and nobody that belongs to her appears ever to have been particularly nice to her" (90–91). The narrator and Ford Obert read a shift in May's behavior, from appearing "so calm—as if she were always sitting for her portrait" to being "all over the place" (63). The narrator reads her flightiness and her fixed smile as signs of her desire to avoid observation of her depleted state as the victim of Long's parasitic love.

The narrator's responses to May are colored by his repressed affections for her. When the narrator looks finally to escape May's pitiful appearance, he

suggests that her image haunts his writing: "I did see her again; I see her now; I shall see her always; I shall continue to feel at moments in my own facial muscles the deadly little ache of her heroic grin" (140). With this image in mind, the memory of May Server serves as a sort of "sacred fount" from which the narrator draws in reliving his time at Newmarch.

FURTHER READING

Blackall, Jean Frantz. *Jamesian Ambiguity and* The Sacred Fount. Ithaca, N.Y.: Cornell University Press, 1965.

Blackmur, R. P. *"The Sacred Fount."* In *Studies in Henry James*, edited by R. P. Blackmur, 45–68. New York: New Directions, 1983.

Bollinger, Laurel. "'Miracles are Expensive': The Complicated Metaphors of Subjectivity in *The Sacred Fount.*" *Henry James Review* 20, no. 1 (1999): 51–68.

Chapman, Sara S. *Henry James's Portrait of the Writer as Hero.* London: Macmillan, 1990.

Edel, Leon. *Henry James: A Life.* London: Collins, 1985.

Freedman, Jonathan. *The Temple of Culture: Assimilation and Anti-Semitism in Literary Anglo-America.* Oxford and New York: Oxford University Press, 2000.

Giles, Paul. "Deterritorialization in *The Sacred Fount."* *Henry James Review* 24, no. 3 (2004): 225–232.

James, Henry. *Henry James Letters.* Vol. 4. Edited by Leon Edel. Cambridge, Mass.: Belknap Press of Harvard University, 1980.

———. *Literary Criticism: European Writers and the Prefaces.* New York: Library of America, 1984.

———. *The Sacred Fount.* New York: New Directions, 1995.

Kappeler, Susanne. *Writing and Reading in Henry James.* London: Macmillan, 1980.

Margolis, Stacey. *The Public Life of Privacy in Nineteenth-Century American Literature.* Durham, N.C. and London: Duke University Press, 2005.

Rowe, John Carlos. *Henry James and Henry Adams: The Emergence of a Modern Consciousness.* Ithaca, N.Y.: Cornell University Press, 1976.

Strychacz, Thomas. "The Newspaperman Kicked Out: *The Sacred Fount* and Literary Authority." In *Mod-*

ernism, Mass Culture and Professionalism, 62–83. Cambridge: Cambridge University Press, 1993.

Tintner, Adeline. "A Gay *Sacred Fount*: The Reader as Detective." *Twentieth Century Literature* 41, no. 2 (1995): 224–240.

Daniel Hannah, *Lakehead University*

The Spoils of Poynton (1897)

The Spoils of Poynton was first serialized in the *Atlantic Monthly* from April to October 1896 under the title "The Old Things." James changed the title when the novel appeared in book form in February 1897 by Houghton, Mifflin and Company. The novel was included in Volume 10 of the NEW YORK EDITION (1908).

"Some of the Spoils," by A. L. Coburn, frontispiece to *The Spoils of Poynton,* in Volume 10, the New York Edition

SYNOPSIS

(Chapter 1) Mrs. Gereth, a widow, is staying at Waterbath, the home of the Brigstocks, a nouveau riche family. Her son, Owen, is about to become engaged to Mona, one of the daughters of the house. Horrified by the vulgar interior decor of Waterbath, Mrs. Gereth escapes to the garden, where she meets another guest, a young woman called Fleda Vetch, an impoverished artist. Sharing similar aesthetic tastes, the two women become friends. They are joined by Owen and Mona, and it becomes clear that Mrs. Gereth disapproves of her son's choice of fiancée.

(Chapter 2) Mrs. Gereth returns to LONDON, where she is staying with a relative. She is later joined by Fleda, who hears about the Gereths' country house, Poynton, and its beautiful collection of antiques. Although Mrs. Gereth worked with her husband to create the collection, she does not own it because Owen has inherited both Poynton and its contents. Fleda sympathizes with Mrs. Gereth's loss of the beautiful things and her anger that Poynton and its treasures will fall into Mona's hands if she marries Owen.

(Chapter 3) Fleda visits Poynton for the first time and is deeply moved by its beauty. Her friendship with Mrs. Gereth is strengthened. Owen visits, bringing Mona and her mother. Mona, who lacks taste and sensibility, appears unmoved by the beauty of Poynton, and the disapproving Mrs. Gereth tries to draw Owen's attention to Fleda as a more suitable wife, much to Fleda's shame and embarrassment.

(Chapter 4) Fleda then rushes into the garden, where she meets Mona, who is not particularly communicative. The visitors leave, and Fleda reproaches Mrs. Gereth for trying to "offer" her to Owen (27). A week later, Owen arrives, announcing his engagement to Mona. Mrs. Gereth retires to her room, placing Fleda in the position of mediator. Before returning to London, Owen asks Fleda to help him persuade his mother to leave Poynton for her dower-house, Ricks. Fleda agrees to help but is dismayed at the sacrifice that Mrs. Gereth is forced to make. Later, as she walks alone through the house, Fleda can think only of the spectacle of its beauty.

(Chapter 5) The next day, Mrs. Gereth tells Fleda that she will relinquish Poynton if she is allowed to take what antiques she requires. Fleda feels increasingly torn between her loyalty to her friend and her promise to Owen. The following week, Owen returns to Poynton to negotiate a removal date with his mother, with Fleda acting as intermediary because Mrs. Gereth refuses to speak to her son. Mona is clearly pressuring Owen to evict his mother from Poynton. One month later, Mrs. Gereth, accompanied by Fleda, visits Ricks for the first time. While Fleda finds it charming, Mrs. Gereth dislikes it. Fleda is surprised that a dispossessed widow can be so dismissive of so pleasant a house.

(Chapter 6) Mrs. Gereth now plans to move into Ricks but finds it impossible to choose the items she requires from the collection. Fleda, realizing that she loves Owen, now feels obliged to keep up the pretence of hating him. Owen visits Poynton, and Fleda feels herself to be in a false position; she also feels that people will see her as a parasite living off her richer friends. Fleda's sister, Maggie, is shortly to be married to a poor curate, and Fleda departs to stay with her father in London to help prepare her sister's trousseau. In Oxford Street, Fleda unexpectedly meets Owen, who tries to buy her an expensive present; however, she accepts only a cheap pincushion. Fleda is alarmed by Owen's persistence in remaining with her, and she abruptly leaves him, almost bursting into tears.

(Chapter 7) Maggie is now married, and Fleda returns to Mrs. Gereth, who is now installed at Ricks, having brought with her virtually all of the Poynton collection. Fleda, shocked, is unable to express her disapproval. Mrs. Gereth, like a soldier at war, boasts of her triumphant removal of the "spoils." Fleda hates her false position and considers leaving Mrs. Gereth. However, she also fears the exposure of her feelings for Owen and is forced into the hypocritical position of not expressing her disapproval of Mrs. Gereth's actions. Owen arrives at Ricks, demanding the restitution of the antiques, and Fleda is again placed in the difficult position of mediator between mother and son.

(Chapter 8) Owen expresses surprise to find Fleda at Ricks, and she lies to him by saying that she

is only on a short visit. Fleda now sympathizes with Owen completely, even when he threatens to consult his solicitor about the return of the antiques. Owen admits that Mona is angry and is making the return of the "spoils" a condition of their MARRIAGE. Caught between his mother and fiancée, he appears vulnerable, and Fleda determines to help him. Owen confesses that he no longer cares for Mona, and Fleda wonders if he is beginning to feel an attachment toward herself.

(Chapter 9) When Owen has left, Fleda retires to her room and realizes that if she tells Mrs. Gereth of Mona's demands for the restitution of the "spoils" then she will refuse to return them, thus preventing Owen's marriage. Fleda considers such a course of action dishonorable and decides not to say anything that will benefit herself, hoping that Mona will break her engagement. Seeing Mrs. Gereth return from her walk, Fleda joins her in the garden.

(Chapter 10) In the garden, Fleda lets Mrs. Gereth know of her son's demands and the threat of the solicitor. Mrs. Gereth is unmoved and plans to retain the "spoils" unless Owen marries Fleda, arguing that if Fleda becomes mistress of Poynton, then she will happily send them back. Mrs. Gereth guesses that Owen is being bullied by Mona and reasons that if she refuses to send back the things, then Mona will withdraw, defeated. Fleda, however, is deeply unhappy with the idea of profiting in an underhand way and lies to Mrs. Gereth that Mona will never break off her engagement. They return to the house for tea.

(Chapter 11) Fleda is so preoccupied as she makes tea that Mrs. Gereth guesses that she loves her son. Delighted, she reiterates that she will return the "spoils" if Fleda marries Owen. However, Fleda feels vulnerable now that her secret is exposed. She admits that she does not know if Owen reciprocates her feelings and is determined not to divulge his wish to extricate himself from Mona.

(Chapter 12) Mrs. Gereth urges Fleda to meet Owen in London on the pretext of continuing negotiations. Fleda states angrily that she cannot remain with Mrs. Gereth because she disapproves of her tactics. Meanwhile, Owen writes to Fleda, who now realizes that his marriage to Mona will not take place unless the antiques are returned. A fortnight passes, and Fleda, tired of the beauty of the "spoils," leaves for her father's house. As she leaves, Mrs. Gereth urges her to "let herself go" (97) with Owen.

(Chapter 13) In her father's home, Fleda feels isolated, realizing that her intimacy with Mrs. Gereth has made her lose contact with other friends. Now that she is away from the antiques, she misses them and sympathizes once more with Mrs. Gereth's desire to retain possession of them. She thinks that her friend's problem would be solved if Owen married a sensitive woman rather than the aggressive Mona. Fleda once more encounters Owen in the street, and she finds him very attractive but is uneasy when he accompanies her home.

(Chapter 14) As Fleda and Owen have tea, Owen explains that he has not seen Mona for some time, for she will see him only when the "spoils" have been returned to Poynton. Owen is critical of his materialistic fiancée, but Fleda defends her and persuades him to honor his promise. Owen is about to reveal whom he really loves when the maid announces a visitor: Mona's mother, Mrs. Brigstock.

(Chapter 15) Expecting to find Fleda alone, Mrs. Brigstock is outraged at Owen's presence and his apparent intimacy with Fleda. Owen and the visitor exchange angry words while Fleda tries unsuccessfully to smooth things out. Mrs. Brigstock and Owen leave together.

(Chapter 16) Fleda telegraphs to her sister and leaves the next morning to visit her. At Maggie's house, she contrasts its poverty and ugliness with the beauty of Poynton and Ricks. On the second day of her visit, Owen unexpectedly arrives and asks Fleda to marry him. She insists that she will marry him only if Mona definitely ends the engagement. Fleda and Owen embrace before he leaves, but she fears that Mona will never set Owen free.

(Chapter 17) Ten days later, Fleda receives a telegram from Mrs. Gereth asking her to come to her London hotel. Fleda reluctantly visits and finds that her friend presumes that she and Owen are now engaged, Mrs. Brigstock having told her of the intimacy between her son and Fleda. Convinced that Mona has ended her engagement, she has

returned the antiques to Poynton. Fleda realizes that Mona will now marry Owen.

(Chapter 18) Fleda feels despair for her friend's useless sacrifice of her antiques and the shock she will receive when she discovers that Mona will now be mistress of Poynton. The humiliated Fleda admits that she is not engaged to Owen and that Mona will now probably marry him. Mrs. Gereth insults Fleda, arguing that she and Owen (unlike Mona) are weak. Despite her anger, Mrs. Gereth kisses Fleda, and they leave together to send a telegram to Owen, who they guess is staying with the Brigstocks.

(Chapter 19) Fleda sends a telegram to Waterbath, asking Owen to visit her at Maggie's house. Mrs. Gereth also sends a telegram to Poynton in case he is there. Both women visit Owen's London club and discover that he has not been there for a fortnight. Anxious, both women depart for Euston Station, and before Fleda takes her train, Mrs. Gereth asks her to come abroad with her. Fleda agrees.

(Chapter 20) At Maggie's house, Fleda awaits a reply from Owen. Two days pass, and she thinks continuously of the beautiful antiques returned to their "home" at Poynton. She wonders if she will be its mistress. On the third day, she receives a telegram from Mrs. Gereth, and an hour later she arrives, announcing that Owen's marriage to Mona has taken place and that she refuses to see them. Although she blames Fleda for not securing Owen for herself, she says that her friendship is all she has left. The two women weep.

(Chapter 21) Mrs. Gereth leaves for Ricks and later writes to Fleda, inviting her to make a second visit, presuming that she will live with her as her companion. At Ricks, Fleda is surprised by the transformation Mrs. Gereth has wrought, for the house is very beautiful. Her friend has retained four items from the Poynton collection and has arranged everything delightfully. Three days later, they read the official announcement of Owen's marriage to Mona in the *Morning Post*. Mrs. Gereth retires to her room, and Fleda feels at peace. The next day, Mrs. Gereth also feels calm.

(Chapter 22) Mrs. Gereth puzzles why her son's marriage to Mona appears to be a success, and

Fleda explains that his wife is charming. During the summer, the newlyweds honeymoon in Europe, returning briefly to Poynton before travelling to FLORENCE, en route for India. In November, Owen writes to Fleda, offering her a gift from the Poynton collection. Fleda defers choosing one, enjoying the sense of anticipation. She decides to take the "gem" of the collection: the Maltese Cross (179). Just before Christmas, she travels to London, spending the night at her father's house before traveling to Poynton. When she alights, she sees smoke on the horizon and the station master informs her that Poynton has been completely destroyed by fire. Fleda longs to go there, but realizing that there is nothing left to save, asks when the next London train is due. The novel ends with a defeated Fleda waiting on the platform for the return train.

CRITICAL ANALYSIS

The Spoils of Poynton was the first novel published following the period 1890 to 1895, when Henry James devoted much of his time to writing for the theater, although he continued to produce short stories for magazines. His lack of success as a playwright (see DRAMA) was confirmed in 1895, when *Guy Domville* was poorly received and ran for only one month. Deeply depressed by this failure, James returned to novel writing, determined to experiment with new forms. As Kenneth Graham has stated:

> Only a very great writer could make so drastic a mistake about the nature of his own genius as virtually to abandon his proper genre for five years, then out of the effect of that mistake . . . find new, successful ways of releasing into fiction the new sensibility that failure itself had simulated in him. (103–104)

The Spoils of Poynton, begun in the summer of 1895, is much shorter than the novels of the 1880s and is characterized by an economy of style, particularly in relation to dialogue, which suggests that James was employing the techniques of the playwright in a new context. The novel, like his subsequent novels of the 1890s, focuses on the ways in which sensitive and vulnerable individuals are affected by the corrupt values of upper-class British society.

For James, the aesthetic sensitivity of the wealthy was often accompanied by a lack of sensitivity in human relationships, and this dichotomy is central to the novels of his "English phase" of the late 1890s.

The "things" of the earlier title, "The Old Things," refer to the beautiful collection of antiques housed at Poynton, the country home of the Gereth family. By changing "things" to "spoils" in the later title, James emphasizes the dispute over possession of the antiques that forms the basis of the narrative, for the antiques are central to a battle for ownership that rages between a mother and her son. As James stated in his 1908 preface to the New York Edition of the novel (see PREFACES TO THE NEW YORK EDITION), he intended to show the human passions involved in the possession of "the chairs and tables, the cabinets and presses, the material odds and ends" that furnish the homes of the wealthier classes (xliii). In the preface, he explained that the idea for the story came when he heard of a British widow who was being prosecuted by her son for the return of some fine furniture that she had taken to her dower-house, the small house she inherited from her husband. From this "germ" James explores the concept of possession, the nature of aesthetic sensibility, and the ways in which beautiful objects can engender ugly human relationships. Although the story originated in what James describes in the novel as the "the cruel English custom" (9) of primogeniture, whereby widows were dispossessed in favor of the eldest son, James's main focus is not so much on the dispute between Mrs. Gereth and her son, Owen, as on the battle between Mrs. Gereth and her son's fiancée, Mona Brigstock, both of whom want to be mistress of Poynton and its treasures.

Caught up in the battle between these two strong women for the "spoils" is the novel's central figure, or consciousness, Fleda Vetch. For many critics, the complexity of the character of Fleda has made *The Spoils of Poynton*, despite its brevity and comic tone, a particularly rich and complex novel to interpret. Nina Baym, for example, in her 1969 article "Fleda Vetch and the Plot of *The Spoils of Poynton*," has paid close attention to James's own record of the evolution of the character of Fleda in his notebooks. Baym shows how James developed Fleda from a mere background figure into the central "point of view" from which readers gain their understanding of the other characters and events. For Baym, Fleda is a morally frail character, and in this respect she agrees with many earlier critics who focused on Fleda's unsatisfactory relationship with the already engaged Owen, her eagerness for renunciation appearing at odds with her ready acceptance of Owen's gift of the "gem" of the Poynton collection. Among the critics who draw attention to Fleda's contradictory impulses are Patrick F. Quinn in "Morals and Motives in *The Spoils of Poynton*" (1954) and Alan H. Roper in "The Moral and Metaphorical Meanings of *The Spoils of Poynton*" (1960). Yet Fleda's instability as a character, her moral vacillations, her contradictory desires, and her marginal social position as a sensitive but poor artist surrounded by rich and powerful figures—all contribute to the difficulty of this richly experimental novel that points toward the radical techniques of Modernist writers of the early 20th century.

More recently, critical discussion has focused less on the character of Fleda Vetch and more on the function of the "spoils" themselves, particularly Mrs. Gereth's obsessive relationship to her objets d'art. Jean-Christophe Agnew, in an influential essay published in 1983, "The Consuming Vision of Henry James," offers an insight into James's representations of modern consumer culture with its "traffic in commodities, the habit of display, the inclination to theatricality, the worship of novelty and quantity" (76). *The Spoils of Poynton* offers a particularly interesting critique of consumerism. Along with the depiction of the "hideous home" (12) of the Brigstocks, where every new fashionable item of home furnishing is on display, James also depicts a very different type of consumer, the art collector, whose extreme fastidiousness is utterly opposed to the Brigstocks' conspicuous consumption of mass-produced goods. Mrs. Gereth's obsessive acquisition of beautiful and rare antiques means that she resembles more a curator of a museum than a modern consumer. By contrast, Mona Brigstock's materialism—her desire to possess those objects generally believed to be valuable—is presented as

symptomatic of modernity. Fleda's appreciation of beauty for the sake of it, separate from all sense of ownership and possession, is a fragile sensibility doomed to fail against the forces of acquisition at war in the novel. This battle for the "spoils" is in one sense a battle between the exclusivity of the aristocratic art collector and the rapacious acquisitiveness of the modern consumer.

The overriding desire to possess objects, so prominent in *The Spoils of Poynton*, has led a number of critics to explore the notion of fetishism in the novel. Fotios Sarris, in an essay published in 1996, "Fetishism in *The Spoils of Poynton*," discusses the ways in which objects take on a life of their own. He discusses Karl Marx's theory of commodity fetishism, whereby consumers' fantasies about their possessions lead them to lose sight of the fact that they are merely the products of human labor. Sarris argues that "Mrs. Gereth's valorization of Poynton and her own high standards of taste are isolated from the socioeconomic conditions that have made them possible" (56). Her almost religious obsession with her beautiful collection makes her unable to function in the modern world, for when she emerges from her Poynton "museum," she is "condemned to wince wherever she turned" (7). Mrs. Gereth's fetishization of her collection is also intensified by her impression that being separated from her "things" is an "amputation," as though they are part of her own body (46).

The human-object relations depicted in the novel are also the focus of Thomas J. Otten's article "*The Spoils of Poynton* and the Properties of Touch," in which he argues that James "repeatedly focuses on the sense of touch" (263). Otten relates this to the way the "spoils" are handmade (rather than machine-made) objects, and Mrs. Gereth and Fleda's tendency to touch them offers them the illusion of contact with their makers. Drawing upon late Victorian (see VICTORIANISM) advice manuals on interior decoration, Otten argues that James's novel registers the threat to upper-class life from the modern forces of mass production and class mobility, both of which are characteristics of the Brigstock way of life. This link between *The Spoils of Poynton* and the late Victorian obsession with "The House Beautiful" (the title James first considered using for the novel) is also made by Bill Brown in his 2002 essay "A Thing About Things: The Art of Decoration in the Work of Henry James." More recently, Lee Clark Mitchell has explored the novel's preoccupation with human-object relations as evidence of James's "abiding interest in the larger question of possession and possessions, of treating others as things even as things themselves are granted sovereign value" (20–21). Indeed, Mrs. Gereth believes that she compliments Fleda when she says, "you'll at any rate be a bit of furniture. For that, a little, you know, I've always taken you—quite one of my best finds," and Fleda resigns herself to being "a scrap of furniture" (169) in her friend's collection.

Surprisingly few critics have explored *The Spoils of Poynton* specifically from a feminist perspective, which is odd considering how its central theme addresses the way in which patriarchal legal traditions have tended to exclude women from the inheritance of property. John Carlos Rowe, however, has considered the novel in his chapter on feminist issues in his book *The Theoretical Dimensions of Henry James* (1984). Although he concedes that James's feminism is "fundamentally limited" (91), his ability to empathize with powerless women and his depictions of the traditional family as dysfunctional all help to expose the inequalities and tensions symptomatic of patriarchal society. Rowe suggests that James's sympathy with Fleda, who adopts the traditional feminine paths of renunciation and service to others, means that no radical feminist message ever emerges.

Yet Rowe does not explore the emergence in *The Spoils of Poynton* of the New Woman, the late 19th-century feminist toward whom James was singularly ambivalent. While Fleda represents traditional feminine values, Mrs. Gereth and her formidable rival, Mona, can both be seen as New Women: militant, determined to protect what they see as their rights, unintimidated by either Owen or the law. Indeed, Mona even appears to wear men's shoes (19), while Fleda thinks that Mrs. Gereth's shoes resemble Mona's (77). Although the novel presents its New Women as rather unattractive and aggressive characters, James's sympathies lie with the dispossessed Mrs. Gereth, whose loss of her beloved home and its beautiful collec-

tion leaves her "a tired old woman . . . with empty hands" (164), while the new owners, Owen and Mona, do not even bother to live at Poynton. It is fitting that the house and its contents should be destroyed by fire, a fire brought about (one likes to think, although James is never explicit) by its spiritual owner Mrs. Gereth, who had said that rather than allow her antiques to be given to "a woman ignorant and vulgar I think I'd deface them with my own hands" (20). If she is the agent of destruction, then she is asserting her rights of ownership to the very end.

CHARACTERS

Brigstock, Miss Mona   The daughter of Mrs. Brigstock and fiancée (later wife) of Owen Gereth, Mona is described as "the massive maiden of Waterbath" (4). She is tall, beautiful, keen on sports, and wholly uninterested in art and aesthetic beauty. Her interest in Owen is dependent on his ownership of Poynton and its collection. Feeling slighted by the fastidious Mrs. Gereth, Mona engages in a battle with her for possession of the "spoils" of Poynton. She agrees to marry Owen only when they are returned. When Mrs. Gereth mistakenly returns them, her marriage to Owen finally takes place.

Brigstock, Mrs.   Mona's mother, like her daughter, fails to appreciate art and aesthetic beauty. She is a philistine, as her vulgar house and interest in mass-produced commodities signify. Mrs. Brigstock is determined to secure Owen for her daughter and is probably instrumental in misleading Mrs. Gereth and Mona in order to gain this end.

Gereth, Mr.   The husband of Mrs. Gereth and father of Owen dies before the action of the novel takes place. Mr. Gereth has (like his wife) been a collector, yet his decision to bequeath Poynton and its collection to his son brings about the novel's central conflict over possession of the "spoils."

Gereth, Mr. Owen   The weak but handsome son of Mr. and Mrs. Gereth, who inherits Poynton and its treasures, Owen, an active outdoorsman is ignorant about the collection he has inherited, knowing only it is "valuable." His fiancée, Mona Brigstock, has considerable power over Owen and forces him to enter into a dispute with his mother for the return of the "spoils." Owen appears to be attracted to Fleda (although the extent of his attraction remains ambiguous), leading Mrs. Gereth to hope that he will break with Mona and marry Fleda. However, Mona is much stronger than Owen, and she marries him when the "spoils" are returned. Owen recognizes Fleda's help by offering her a gift from the collection.

Gereth, Mrs. Adela A widow, former mistress of Poynton and the mother of Owen, she has spent most of her married life building up with her husband a magnificent collection of antiques, housed in their beautiful country home, Poynton. On her husband's death, Owen inherits the house and its collection, and Mrs. Gereth, to her annoyance, inherits only a small dower-house, Ricks. She befriends the impoverished, like-minded artist Fleda Vetch, who, she realizes, will be the ideal mistress of Poynton. She then tries to arrange a marriage between Fleda and her son. Hating his philistine fiancée, Mona Brigstock, Mrs. Gereth determines to keep her beautiful collection out of her hands by preventing her marriage. Mrs. Gereth is obsessed with her collection and removes it (illegally) from Poynton to Ricks. Only when she wrongly presumes that Owen will marry Fleda does she return the stolen collection. When she realizes her error, she retires from the battle and resigns herself to living at Ricks with Fleda as her companion.

Vetch, Miss Fleda A young penniless artist who has no suitable home of her own because her widowed father does not choose for her to live with him, Fleda becomes friends with Mrs. Gereth; both women are sensitive to beauty and art. Fleda quickly finds herself embroiled in the dispute between mother and son for control of the Poynton collection, and although she sympathizes with both of them, she becomes uneasy when she falls in love with Owen. Fleda does not want to "steal" Owen from Mona, and her moral scruples lead her to eventually lose Owen in the "battle" between Mrs. Gereth and Mona. Fleda is socially vulnerable, fleeing to her newly married sister, Maggie, when

the tension with Mrs. Gereth becomes unbearable. Despite differences of character, Fleda and Mrs. Gereth share a strong love of beauty, and when both women are frustrated in their desires for possession (Fleda for Owen and Mrs. Gereth for the antiques), they decide to live together at Ricks.

Vetch, Miss Maggie Fleda's sister marries a curate (who is never named) largely to provide a home for herself and her sister. Maggie is keen to promote her sister's relations with the rich Gereths because she is herself condemned to live in relative poverty.

Vetch, Mr. The widowed father of Fleda and Maggie lives a bachelor life in West Kensington. Spending most of his time drinking at his club, he has no sense of responsibility as a father, simply wishing to see as little of his daughters as possible.

ADAPTATION

The Spoils of Poynton was adapted for television as part of the BBC series *Masterpiece Theatre*. It was directed by Peter Sasdy and starred Gemma Jones as Fleda Vetch.

FURTHER READING

Agnew, Jean-Christophe. "The Consuming Vision of Henry James." In *The Culture of Consumption: Critical Essays in American History, 1880–1980,* edited by Richard Wightman Fox and T. J. Jackson Lears, 67–100. New York: Pantheon Books, 1983.

Baym, Nina. "Fleda Vetch and the Plot of *The Spoils of Poynton.*" PMLA 84, no. 1 (1969): 102–111.

Brown, Bill. "A Thing About Things: The Art of Decoration in the Work of Henry James." *Henry James Review* 23, no. 3 (2002): 222–233.

Graham, Kenneth. *Henry James: A Literary Life.* Basingstoke, England, and London: Macmillan, 1995.

James, Henry. *The Spoils of Poynton,* edited by Bernard Richards. Oxford: Oxford University Press, 1982.

Lyons, Richard S. "The Social Vision of *The Spoils of Poynton.*" *American Literature* 61, no. 1 (1989): 59–77.

Mitchell, Lee Clark. "'To Suffer Like Chopped Limbs': The Dispossessions of *The Spoils of Poynton.*" *Henry James Review* 25, no. 1 (2005): 20–39.

Otten, Thomas J. "*The Spoils of Poynton* and the Properties of Touch." *American Literature* 71, no. 2 (1999): 264–290.

Quinn, Patrick F. "Morals and Motives in *The Spoils of Poynton*." *Sewanee Review* 61 (1954): 563–577.

Roper, Alan H. "The Moral and Metaphorical Meanings of *The Spoils of Poynton*." *American Literature* 32 (1960): 182–196.

Rowe, John Carlos. *The Theoretical Dimensions of Henry James.* Madison: University of Wisconsin Press, 1984.

Sarris, Fotios. "Fetishism in the *Spoils of Poynton*." *Nineteenth-Century Literature* 51, no. 1 (1996): 53–83.

Deborah Wynne, *University of Chester*

The Tragic Muse (1890)

The *Atlantic Monthly* first serialized *The Tragic Muse* in 1889–90, paying James about $5,000 for the installments. James received more when the novel was published in 1890 by the American firm of Houghton, Mifflin & Company (Anesko 561), and James's English publisher, Macmillan, paid a £250 advance for the novel and brought it out the same year. When preparing his novels and tales for the NEW YORK EDITION, James made significant revisions to *The Tragic Muse,* many of which are detailed in Philip Horne's Penguin edition of the novel (James 1995: 518–534). For ease of reference, the editions most often used today are the Penguin edition (which reprints the 1908 New York Edition text) and the Library of America edition (which reprints the 1890 Macmillan text).

SYNOPSIS

Volume 1

(Chapter 1) The novel begins in PARIS, where Lady Agnes Dormer and three of her children—Biddy, Grace, and Nick—examine French art. Lady Agnes is indifferent to it, but Biddy and Nick wander off together to look at more exhibits.

(Chapter 2) Nick and Biddy encounter Gabriel Nash, a young cosmopolitan man who knows Nick from their student days at Oxford. Nick is glad to have encountered his friend; he is attended by two women who fascinate Biddy. Nash is an aesthete (someone very sensitive to art), though he denies it.

(Chapter 3) Lady Agnes and Grace Dormer go to a buffet where they are joined by Peter Sherringham, Lady Agnes's cousin and a British diplomat. His sister, Julia Dallow, has been touring France's most fashionable locales. Julia wants Nick to run as a liberal Member of Parliament (MP) for the constituency of Harsh because the previous representative has died. Julia is prepared to support the family financially if Nick will run, and Lady Agnes promises he will. Nick arrives for lunch with Nash and Biddy.

(Chapter 4) After some confusion about seating arrangements, Nick is told that Julia wants him to stand for MP. Biddy admires Peter and asks about the two women who were with Nash. They are an aspiring actress, Miriam Rooth, and her mother. Peter, who has a strong interest in the theater, resolves to invite the pair to an artistic tea with the venerable actress Honorine Carré.

(Chapter 5) Lady Agnes wants Nick to go straight to Julia's Paris hotel and wishes Peter had pressed him too. She wonders if Peter is romantically interested in Biddy and speculates that Julia is avoiding the family. Meanwhile, Peter and Nick discuss Nash, whom Peter calls an ass for his views on theater. Since the death of Lady Agnes's husband, Sir Nicholas, the house in which the family lived has been let out to rich Americans, and Lady Agnes and her children now find themselves in an awkward position among their relatives as well as within society. Since Sir Nicholas's death, his friend Mr. Carteret has been sending Nick money and encouraging him to go into politics.

(Chapter 6) At dinner that evening, Julia makes a late entrance. Nick reflects on her rudeness but decides he wants to maintain his illusions about her. Julia arranges for Peter, Biddy, and Grace to go to the Théâtre Français while she and Nick discuss Nick's political prospects. Although attracted to the arts, he feels pressured by his family to stand for MP.

(Chapter 7) In Madame Carré's Paris apartment, Miriam gives a mediocre performance of Tennyson's poems, which the elder actress deems

"The Comédie Française," by A. L. Coburn, frontispiece to the first volume of *The Tragic Muse,* Volume 7, the New York Edition

dreadful. Mrs. Rooth worries that acting is not a morally respectable profession for her daughter; at the time, acting was only slightly more socially acceptable than prostitution. Peter admires Miriam's beauty. He agrees to help her and to ask Nick to paint her portrait.

(Chapter 8) After accompanying the Rooths to their shabby hotel, Peter invites them to his house the next day, where Miriam gives another weak performance. Julia confides to Nash that she finds the actress vulgar. Determined to improve, Miriam presses Peter for criticism of her performance, and he counsels her to quit acting.

(Chapter 9) Nick and Nash meet in a café later that night. They discuss Julia and Nash's artistic attitude to life. They wander around Notre-Dame, and Nick acknowledges that it will be a struggle for him to become a painter (his situation mirrors Mir-

iam's in the preceding chapter), but Nash agrees to support him.

(Chapter 10) Busy with his diplomatic work, Peter feels guilty for dropping Miriam and asks Madame Carré to give the girl acting lessons. He soon learns that Miriam has already been pressing her. He watches Miriam give another mediocre performance, to which Carré responds very critically.

(Chapter 11) Miriam describes the poverty in which she and her mother live. Echoing Nash's speech to Nick in the previous chapter, Peter tells her he wishes contemporary actors had more style; he advises her to study great English authors and not to be a flirt.

(Chapter 12) Peter gives Miriam a box at the theater for the summer and watches her taste evolve. She develops, but a visit to the Louvre leaves him disappointed with her development. He is surprised to find himself in love with her. Carré announces that Miriam's acting has improved; she is sure the girl will go far.

(Chapter 13) Nick wins the seat for Harsh. Lady Agnes is pleased that her son has followed in his father's footsteps. She wishes he would propose to Julia: This would probably motivate Carteret to give Nick more money, which would ensure that Nick's sisters can marry. Nick gives in to his mother.

(Chapter 14) The next morning, Nick reflects on what he has agreed to. He has a double nature: Politics are not his passion; a letter from Nash reminds him that art is. He ponders for the next fortnight.

Volume 2

(Chapter 15) In her garden, Julia is reading a magazine article entitled "The Revision of the British Constitution." Nick teases her for being so political and questions her motives for helping him win the election. He asks her to marry him and denies having any interest in art. She agrees to give Lady Agnes a home, Broadwood.

(Chapter 16) Nick visits Carteret at his house, Beauclere. He finds the guests and the political themes of the dinner conversation quite dull.

(Chapter 17) The next day, Carteret gives Nick advice. When Nick announces his intention to marry the very politically minded Julia, Carteret offers him a settlement to be paid upon his MARRIAGE.

(Chapter 18) Peter considers asking to be transferred from Paris. He has always been sure of his profession and kept his interest in the theater from encroaching upon it, a balance that Nick is not able to strike. Peter worries that his love for Miriam will have a negative effect on his career because she is from a lower social and professional class. When he visits her in Paris, her mother reproaches him for not getting Miriam "an engagement" (James 1995: 306) (which literally means a contract with a theater, but also connotes marriage). Peter suggests they move to LONDON—a suggestion that Basil Dashwood, an actor they know, has already put to the Rooths.

(Chapter 19) Peter goes to Carré's Paris apartments to find Miriam practicing. While discussing the French and English theater, the older actress tells Peter that Miriam has learned far more than she has been taught.

(Chapter 20) Peter takes Biddy and the Rooths to the Théâtre Français to see a performance by Mademoiselle Voisin, an actress Miriam esteems. Backstage, the group marvels at the theater's history.

(Chapter 21) Biddy and Mrs. Rooth leave the theater. Peter asks Miriam to give up acting and marry him, saying that he can offer her a better life than the theater could. Mademoiselle Voisin appears and tells Miriam that she has heard that Miriam will be the theatrical star of the future. Peter and Miriam discuss Voisin's limited social circle and exclusion from polite society. Peter decides that he could not be the husband of an actress.

(Chapter 22) Back in London, Julia is fully committed to political life: She asks parliamentary men and their wives to join her salon at Great Stanhope Street. Nick worries that people will talk because he and Julia are so often seen together but are not married. He confronts Julia, and she is critical of his performance before her political friends, but she agrees to give him her decision in five weeks.

(Chapter 23) While Julia is at her political friends' country house, Nick putters in his artist's studio. He realizes he has not done any work for his constituency or answered his correspondence. On the day before Good Friday, Nash visits him and explains he was away in Sicily for the winter. The meeting proves decisive: Nick recognizes that he is making a mistake in neglecting art in favor of politics.

(Chapter 24) At dinner, the pair discuss art and Nick's desire to make something that will outlast him. He mentions that Julia will not sit for him. Nash suggests that he paint a portrait of Miriam.

(Chapter 25) Nash brings Miriam to Nick's London studio and comments that both the painter and the sitter share an "artistic nature" (James 1995: 295). Miriam is a striking presence, and Nick gladly agrees to paint her.

(Chapter 26) Thanks to Dashwood's help, Miriam gets a principal part in a London play, a remake of a French one. Nick and Nash attend the play and discuss painting between the acts. When

Miriam poses for Nick at his studio the next day, Julia arrives unexpectedly. She is horrified by the scene of the couple alone, and she assumes there has been some impropriety. She quickly leaves as Nash arrives.

(Chapter 27) Nick goes to Julia's to explain. Finding her absent, he waits and vows to give up having models sit for him when he marries. When she finally arrives, they argue about painting. She breaks off their engagement and decides to travel.

(Chapter 28) On their way to FLORENCE, Peter and Julia discuss Nick. Julia suggests that Peter marry Biddy. Back in London, Peter visits Miriam and gets tickets for her performance that evening.

(Chapter 29) Peter then visits Biddy, who has been modeling a clay head, and invites her to the theater. He ponders her attractions while she tells him of her family's situation, and he convinces her to show him Nick's impressive painting of Miriam.

(Chapter 30) Reinvigorated by the theatrical evening, Peter calls on Miriam the next day, only to find Dashwood already with her—much to his annoyance.

(Chapter 31) Peter is critical of Miriam's bohemian friends, though he spends the evening with them. As he watches Nick and Miriam discuss beauty that evening, he wonders if Nick's portrait is not "an act of virtual infidelity" (James 1995: 322).

(Chapter 32) Nick visits Carteret, who is ill, and finds that Julia has told him of their engagement.

Volume 3

(Chapter 33) Nick tells Carteret that the engagement is off and confesses that his artistic temperament makes him unfit for politics, which he will give up. Carteret calls for his solicitor in order for his will to be modified.

(Chapter 34) Nick announces to his mother that he has broken off his engagement. She takes this badly and declares that this will put her and her daughters in a wretched state.

(Chapter 35) Despite his worries about what the gossips of society will make of his decision, Nick goes to dinner with Nash, who reveals that Peter is in love with Miriam.

(Chapter 36) Peter and Nash discuss Miriam's career, with Nash venturing that her next move

should be to marry Nick—a comment that annoys the painter.

(Chapter 37) Peter notices that Nick has changed. Miriam tells Nick she is disappointed that he did not become a statesman, and she sides with Lady Agnes for being heartbroken about her son.

(Chapter 38) Peter considers whether he is jealous of Nick. The next day, he is offered a posting to a small Central American republic, which he takes, and he prepares to leave Europe.

(Chapter 39) In London, Peter calls on Lady Agnes to tell her of his decision. She is in mourning over Nick's choice and complains that her son threw away his chance at Carteret's fortune. Peter considers whether he should marry Biddy in order to offset Nick's decision.

(Chapter 40) Miriam asks Peter to her dress rehearsal, where he finds her in excellent form. She asks him to come see her at six.

(Chapter 41) That evening, the pair discuss the theater and Peter's foreign appointment. Although Miriam claims she only wants to see him fulfilled and happy, Peter doubts her sincerity. He confesses that he is going away to escape his consuming passion for her, but he promises to come to her performance the next evening.

(Chapter 42) In his studio, Nick marvels at Miriam's ambition when he receives a note from her the next morning. He speculates on why Peter has avoided him lately; when Peter arrives, they discuss love and art, and Peter asks to buy Miriam's portrait.

(Chapter 43) Upon her arrival, Biddy accuses Peter of trying to avoid a dinner with the Dormers that evening—to which he protests that he has much to settle before his departure. He asks her to walk with him. Miriam arrives for her sitting as they exit. She taunts Peter and tells him not to come to the theater. Frustrated by Peter's ambivalence, Biddy gets into a cab and leaves him.

(Chapter 44) Meanwhile, Nick paints Miriam, and Mrs. Rooth explores his studio. Nick mentions that Peter wants Miriam's portrait and lets it slip that Peter may be in love with Biddy. Miriam details her career plans but wonders whether Peter would marry her, then decides that she dislikes his ambivalence.

(Chapter 45) At Miriam's magnificent performance that evening, Peter is mutely critical: He refuses to speak to the actress and turns down an invitation to dinner from Dashwood. Instead, he gives a messenger a note in which he proposes marriage to Miriam. She accepts.

(Chapter 46) Miriam and Peter meet alone later that evening. He asks her to give up the theater so that, as his wife, she will be fully devoted to him and his career. She refuses his managerial tactics and declares that she would rather be an actress than a lady of society. She advises Peter to marry Biddy instead. Mrs. Rooth arrives as her daughter departs; she promises she will not let her daughter marry anyone else.

(Chapter 47) Julia returns to London. Biddy receives a proposal from a rich industrialist who does not interest her. Percy Dormer, the eldest of Lady Agnes's children, marries and has a son (a legitimate heir). Nick tells his mother she must give

up Broadwood. To soften the blow, he arranges lodgings for the family at Brighton. Ironically, Julia has invited his family to spend the autumn with her at Broadwood. Carteret dies, and he leaves his fortune to his butler—not to Nick.

(Chapter 48) Miriam continues her social and artistic ascent in London. When she shows Dashwood Nick's portrait of her, he protests that Peter should not have it. Before she leaves on a theatrical tour of the provinces, Nick and Miriam discuss Nash's mysterious appearances and disappearances. She suggests Nick paint Nash.

(Chapter 49) Nick takes up Miriam's suggestion but cannot find Nash since he has no idea where he lives. Fortunately, Nash reappears. He predicts that Julia will ask Nick to paint her portrait. Nick begins Nash's portrait, but his friend disappears again, and in a strange case of art imitating life the portrait begins to fade as well.

(Chapter 50) Six months later, at the end of March, Biddy visits her brother's studio. He shows her Nash's curious metamorphosing portrait. Julia wants him to paint her portrait. Miriam arrives and arranges for Biddy, her friend, and Nick to see her perform the role of Juliet.

(Chapter 51) At the theater that evening, Nick tells the others that Miriam has married Dashwood. Peter leaves because he is so shocked by the news. Days later, Peter visits Biddy and proposes to her. They marry, and she becomes his helpmate, fulfilling the role Miriam refused to play in preferring to become an actress.

CRITICAL ANALYSIS

The Tragic Muse marks an important stage in James's career. It was after writing this novel in which French and English theater figured so prominently that he decided to put his energy into writing plays and short stories rather than novels. Over the next five years, James published two volumes entitled *Theatricals*. Two of his plays were also produced: *The American* (in 1891), based on his earlier novel of the same title (see *The AMERICAN*), and *Guy Domville* (in 1895).

In his preface to *The Tragic Muse*, James explains that "the conflict between art and 'the world'" struck him as one of the great "motives"

"St. John's Wood," by A. L. Coburn, frontispiece to the second volume of *The Tragic Muse,* Volume 8, the New York Edition

for a novel (James 1984: 1,103). Most literary critics still agree with James. The classic reading of *The Tragic Muse* is that it allegorizes the art-life problem, which Horne describes as the conflict of whether or not art can be taken seriously "as an end in itself, as something more like a religious ritual than a means of killing time or spending money" (James 1995: vii).

Both the novel's themes and the plot structure present the conflict between the characters' artistic interests and their real-life responsibilities. Two narrative threads support this reading. The first is Julia Dallow's attempt to coax Nick Dormer into English political life and out of his painting studio. Julia is abetted by the moneyed Mr. Carteret and hindered by the artistic Gabriel Nash. The second plotline that develops the art-life problem is Peter Sherringham's indecisiveness about pursuing his love for the actress Miriam Rooth and his wavering commitment to the diplomatic service. Other important tensions contributing to the structure of this beautiful multifaceted novel are the conflict between personal desires and social responsibilities, between professional calling (what one is born to do) and society's call, between action and passivity, performance and authenticity, seeing and being seen. These themes are not separate from the art-life problem and are actually closely connected to it. The novel's themes are linked by the questions of *how* one should be and *what* one should be.

The DRAMA of *The Tragic Muse* is built around a tension between ways of being. This is a pattern present in James's early fictions—such as *The American* (1877) and *Confidence* (1879)—and it continues to be a focal point in later novels, such as *The AMBASSADORS* (1903). In *The Tragic Muse*, the dualism is not so much a split as an attempt at reconciliation: Nick struggles to figure out *what* he should be—i.e., what type of career will make him happy—and this is resolved when he figures out *how* he should be—i.e., impervious to the temptations of money and popular acclaim in favor of what truly fulfills him, art. Peter Sherringham has already chosen a diplomatic career, but he counterbalances his profession's matter-of-factness with a strong attraction to the theater and the imaginative

freedoms it offers. Nick's and Peter's trajectories intersect in the figure of Miriam Rooth, the heroine of the novel. Crucially, she is also the actress whom Peter loves and whom Nick paints, and these experiences allow them to realize who they really are and what their decisions must therefore be. Miriam enables them to come to terms with themselves and to resolve their inner conflicts.

It is not just the novel's characters and themes that crisscross but the very structure of the novel itself. As Peggy McCormack has pointed out, James plots two opposite courses for Nick and Miriam, and these courses intersect in the middle of the book, when Nick retreats from the public world and Miriam moves into the public eye (35). Both have discovered *what* they should be—artists—but *how* this manifests itself is contradictory: Nick withdraws to his private painter's studio, while Miriam takes center stage as an actress.

These divergent ways of being an artist suggest a disruption of 19th-century gender ideology, as Michael L. J. Wilson argues (107). At the time, men and women were thought to belong to "separate spheres": Each had complementary and separate areas of action in the world. Man held to the public sphere (in politics, the professions, or business) whereas a woman's place was expected to be in the private, domestic sphere. *The Tragic Muse* plays with this idea by giving Nick and Miriam roles opposite to those their sexes would conventionally have held. However, Julia Dallow's dependence on Nick as a means of becoming politically active and Lady Agnes's dominance in domestic affairs suggest that the novel does not completely transgress the ideology of separate spheres.

Many critics have emphasized James's interest in art and, as a result, they have underemphasized his dedication to social issues. The novels James published between 1886 and 1890—among them *The BOSTONIANS* (1886), *The PRINCESS CASAMASSIMA* (1886), and *The Tragic Muse*—all engage with the hot topics of the second half of the 19th century: feminism, anarchism, and the clash between art and politics, respectively. They also show that James was developing a literary style closer to realism (see ROMANCE/REALISM/NATURALISM), a mode of writing dedicated to depicting ordinary, everyday life in all its (un)glorious detail and social complexity. Primarily associated with representations of the middle and lower classes, James's forays into realism in these novels extended the genre's field of application by including the upper classes.

Although *The Tragic Muse* depicts the English upper classes, it also reflects a more general and important question: How should we live our lives? James develops this question in the conflict between art and life, and he answers it by offering the reader an example of the theater world's reproduction of life. The novel requires readers to ask whether the actor's performance is really so different from the everyday performances undertaken in real life. The novel's most histrionic characters, Miriam Rooth and Gabriel Nash, are also those whose real selves are most often likened to theatrical performances. Gabriel is such a talker that he is, paradoxically, considered to be both sincere and a charlatan. Miriam has such an aptitude for metamorphosing into the theatrical characters that she, too, raises suspicions in regard to her sincerity. D. J. Gordon and John Stokes point out that the uncertainties about "who or what Gabriel Nash is . . . who and what are the Rooths? . . . have to do with social identities or roles and with names or signs that define and therefore identify, so limiting and eliminating the uncomfortable realm of the unfamiliar" (82). The novel provides a very willing audience for these performers. Peter Sherringham admits, "I'm fond of representation—the representation of life: I like it better, I think, than the real thing" (James 1995: 62). Nick Dormer is also torn between two kinds of "representation": representing his constituents in Parliament and making representations of people by painting their portraits (64). Yet he is also an actor who is "surprised at the airs he could play" (170) and "conscious of a double nature; there were two men in him . . . each of whom insisted on having an independent turn at life" (169).

The novel's two central problems—*how* one should act and *what* one should do—have significant implications for the way the characters behave toward one another. These issues are developed through the theme of performance. Even those who are not professional actors (virtually everyone except Miriam and her ultimate fiancé) perform, play, and act—as Nick's confession to a double-consciousness suggests. This is not only because James repeats and extends the novel's theater theme by demonstrating that life itself involves a certain amount of art, a certain amount of performance. What Nick, the novel's hero, discovers is that he is, in his everyday life, not really so different from an actor. His driving purpose throughout the novel is to discover which of these performances best approximates what he feels to be a true self. He performs the part of the dutiful eldest son by following in his father's political footsteps and, initially at least, agreeing to a marriage that will ensure his family's financial and social security—though he is not sure he wants to do either of these things. For a time, Nick performs the part of the impatient lover eager to marry Julia—though he is not sure he loves her. Nick performs the part of the bohemian artist with Gabriel Nash—though he is not sure he can give up his sense of familial duty, politics, and his engagement. Nick is not a fake or a fraud: These are just different facets of his life, facets which, James implies, all people have. In other words, all these behaviors are part of human identities, even though these parts do not always fit together very neatly. The novel finally suggests a manner of resolving the tension between life and art. By recognizing that social life involves a certain amount of performance and artistry, James is in complete agreement with Shakespeare's famous adage: "All the world's a stage, and all the men and women merely players. They have their exits and their entrances; and one man in his time plays many parts."

CHARACTERS

Carré, Madame Honorine   This distinguished French actress reluctantly agrees to train Miriam Rooth in Paris.

Carteret, Charles   Wealthy bachelor and friend of the late Sir Nicholas Dormer, he attempts to use his money to persuade Nick to devote himself to politics. When his efforts fail, he removes Nick from his will.

Dallow, George   Julia Sherringham Dallow's late husband.

Dallow, Julia Sherringham (a.k.a Mrs. Dallow) George Dallow's rich widow and Peter Sherringham's sister, Julia is politically savvy and generally gets her way, except with Nick Dormer, whom she loves. Nevertheless, she refuses to marry him unless he gives up painting in order to pursue politics. Confident and self-assured, her behavior borders on arrogance, though she has moments of generosity.

Dashwood, Basil   An actor and man about town who seems slightly suspect at first (especially to Peter Sherringham), Basil introduces Miriam into the London theater world and eventually marries her.

Dormer, Lady Agnes   Sir Nicholas Dormer's widow and cousin to Peter Sherringham, she is preoccupied with finances, society, and setting her children up in life. She tries to force Nick into politics and marrying Julia by emphasizing the benefit that would accrue to his family.

Dormer, Bridget (a.k.a. Biddy)   The youngest of the four Dormer children, Biddy is at different points fascinated, intimidated, and annoyed by Miriam Rooth, who is her rival for Peter's affections.

Dormer, Grace   She is the least attractive of the four Dormer children, and she most resembles her mother.

Dormer, Sir Nicholas   A politician, he is Lady Agnes Dormer's late husband. His death has left the Dormer family less well situated financially than they were during his lifetime.

Dormer, Nick   The son of Lady Agnes and Sir Nicholas Dormer, Nick feels a strong sense of duty toward his family after his father's death. However, when forced to choose between a vocation in art or politics, he prefers painting. As a result, his politically ambitious fiancée, Julia Sherringham Dallow, decides she will not marry him. This proves highly disappointing for his mother. At the suggestion of Gabriel Nash, an artistic friend from his undergraduate days at Oxford, Nick paints Miriam Rooth as the Tragic Muse.

Dormer, Percival   The eldest of Lady Agnes's children, he is a disappointment. Although he has fathered a number of children out of wedlock, he marries a country girl and produces a legitimate heir.

Nash, Gabriel   Oxford-educated, aesthetically inclined friend of Nick Dormer, he travels, talks, and does not seem to do much else. Terrifically opinionated and entertaining, he does not think that Nick should be in politics. He persuades Nick that his true calling is in the arts. It is likely that James modeled Nash on OSCAR WILDE (see Cargill, Powers, Gordon and Stokes, Mendelssohn, Miller).

Rooth, Miriam   An actress of Jewish descent (see Blair 1996), she has lived a rather impoverished café-and-bedsit life with her mother. Her sheer determination allows her to rise to the top of the London theater world. She convinces Mme. Honorine Carré to coach her, and she adamantly refuses Peter Sherringham, who would like her to give up the theater to become his wife. Nick Dormer paints her as the Tragic Muse. She marries a fellow actor, Basil Dashwood. She has several stage names in the novel, including Edith Temple, Gladys Vane, and Maud Vavasour.

Rooth, Mrs. Rudolph   Miriam's mother and the widow of Rudolph Roth, she has changed the spelling of the family name. She pushes for her daughter's success but worries that it will come at a high moral cost.

Sherringham, Peter   A diplomat and theater lover, he is Julia Sherringham Dallow's brother. Like his sister, he is very conscious of conventions and wary of public perceptions of him—particularly with respect to his career. He grows very fond of Miriam Rooth and tries to convince her to give up the theater to become his wife. He ultimately marries Biddy Dormer.

FURTHER READING

Anesko, Michael. "Accommodating Art and the World: The Primary Motive of *The Tragic Muse*." In *Henry James: Critical Assessments*, edited by Graham

Clarke, 555–576. Westfield, England: Helm Information, 1991.

Baker, Robert S. "Gabriel Nash's 'House of Strange Idols': Aestheticism in *The Tragic Muse*." *Texas Studies in Literature and Language* 15, no. 1 (1973): 149–166.

Bellringer, Alan W. "'The Tragic Muse': The Objective Centre." *Journal of American Studies* (Cambridge) 4, no. 1 (1970): 73–89.

Blair, Sara. "Henry James, Jack the Ripper, and the Cosmopolitan Jew: Staging Authorship in *The Tragic Muse*." *ELH: Journal of English Literary History* 63, no. 2 (1996): 489–512.

Brown, Chris. "Satire in *the Tragic Muse*." *Studies in American Fiction* 23, no. 1 (1995): 3–16.

Cargill, Oscar. "Mr. James's Aesthetic Mr. Nash." *Nineteenth Century Fiction* 12, no. 3 (1957): 177–187.

Dellamora, Richard. "The Elusive Queerness of Henry James's 'Queer Comrade': Reading Gabriel Nash of *The Tragic Muse*." In *Victorian Sexual Dissidence*, 191–210. Chicago: University of Chicago Press, 1999.

Ellmann, Richard. "Henry James among the Aesthetes." In *Henry James and Homo-Erotic Desire*, edited by John R. Bradley, 25–44. New York: St. Martin's Press, 1999.

Freedman, Jonathan. *Professions of Taste: Henry James, British Aestheticism, and Commodity Culture*. Palo Alto, Calif.: Stanford University Press, 1990.

Gordon, D. J., and John Stokes. "The Reference of *The Tragic Muse*." In *The Air of Reality: New Essays on James*, edited by John Goode, 81–167. London: Methuen, 1972.

Graham, Wendy. "Henry James and British Aestheticism." *Henry James Review* 20, no. 3 (1999): 265–274.

Greenwood, Chris. *Adapting to the Stage: Theatre and the Work of Henry James*. Aldershot, England: Ashgate, 2000.

Hall, William F. "Gabriel Nash: 'Famous Centre' of *The Tragic Muse*." *Nineteenth-Century Fiction* 21, no. 2 (1966): 167–184.

Haralson, Eric. "The Elusive Queerness of Henry James's "Queer Comrade": Reading Gabriel Nash of *The Tragic Muse*." In *Victorian Sexual Dissidence*, edited by Richard Dellamora, 191–210. Chicago: University of Chicago Press, 1999.

Horne, Philip. "'Where Did She Get Hold of That?': Shakespeare in Henry James's *The Tragic Muse*." *Victorian Shakespeare*, edited by Adrian Poole and Gail Marshall, 100–113. Basingstoke, England: Palgrave, 2003.

James, Henry. *Literary Criticism: French Writers, Other European Writers, the Prefaces to the New York Edition*, vol. 2. Edited by Leon Edel and Mark Wilson. New York: Library of America, 1984.

———. *Novels, 1886–1890: The Princess Casamassima, the Reverberator, the Tragic Muse*. Edited by Daniel Mark Fogel. New York: Library of America, 1989.

———. *The Tragic Muse*. Edited by Philip Horne. London: Penguin, 1995.

Jobe, Steven H. "Representation and Performance in *The Tragic Muse*." *American Literary Realism* 26, no. 2 (1994): 32–42.

Lane, Christopher. "The Impossibility of Seduction in James's *Roderick Hudson* and *The Tragic Muse*." *American Literature* 68, no. 4 (1996): 739–764.

Litvak, Joseph. *Caught in the Act: Theatricality in the Nineteenth-Century English Novel*. Berkeley: University of California Press, 1992.

McCormack, Peggy. *The Rule of Money: Gender, Class, and Exchange Economics in the Fiction of Henry James*. Ann Arbor, Mich.: UMI Research Press, 1990.

Mendelssohn, Michèle. *Henry James, Oscar Wilde and Aesthetic Culture*. Edinburgh: Edinburgh University Press, 2007.

Miller, J. Hillis. "Oscar in *the Tragic Muse*." *Arizona Quarterly* 62, no. 3 (2006): 31–44.

Monteiro, George. "The Manuscript of 'The Tragic Muse'." *American Notes and Queries* 1, no. 5 (1963): 68–68.

Pfitzer, Gregory M. "Sins of Omission: What Henry James Left out of the Preface to *The Tragic Muse* and Why." *American Literary Realism* 25, no. 1 (1992): 38–54.

Powers, Lyall H. "James's *The Tragic Muse*—Ave Atque Vale." In *Henry James: Modern Judgements*, edited by Tony Tanner, 194–203. London: Macmillan, 1968.

Snow, Lotus. "The Prose and the Modesty of the Matter: James's Imagery for the Artist in *Roderick Hudson* and *The Tragic Muse*." *Modern Fiction Studies* 12, no. 1 (1966): 61–82.

Sonstegard, Adam. "Painting, Photography, and Fidelity in *the Tragic Muse*." *Henry James Review* 24, no. 1 (2003): 27–44.

Storm, William. "Henry James's Conscious Muse: Design for a 'Theatrical Case' in *The Tragic Muse*." *Henry James Review* 21, no. 2 (2000): 133–150.

———. "The "Impossible" Miriam Rooth: Performance, Painting, and Spectatorship in *The Tragic Muse*." *Henry James Review* 28, no. 1 (2007): 73–93.

Torgovnick, Marianna. *The Visual Arts, Pictorialism, and the Novel: James, Lawrence, and Woolf*. Princeton, N.J.: Princeton University Press, 1985.

Wilson, Michael L. J. "'To Feel Is Such a Career': Gender and Vocation in *The Tragic Muse*." In *Questioning the Master: Gender and Sexuality in Henry James's Writing*, edited by Peggy McCormack, 104–132. Newark: University of Delaware Press, 2000.

Michèle Mendelssohn, *University of Edinburgh*

Washington Square (1880)

Henry James's sixth novel was serialized in six issues of England's the *Cornhill Magazine*, where it appeared with illustrations by GEORGE DU MAURIER between June and November 1880 and in *Harper's New Monthly Magazine* in the United States. *Washington Square* was then issued in novel form in 1881 by Macmillan (England) and Harper & Brothers (United States). James did not include *Washington Square* in the NEW YORK EDITION. It was collected in Macmillan's *The Novels and Stories of Henry James*, edited by Percy Lubbock (1921–23).

SYNOPSIS

(Chapter 1) The events of *Washington Square* are set in early 19th-century Manhattan, and its action revolves around a shy, repressed, and socially graceless heiress, Catherine Sloper, the daughter of a prominent widowed NEW YORK CITY physician. Dr. Austin Sloper shelters his daughter, providing everything but genuine affection. Embarrassed by what he considers Catherine's lack of intelligence and the social flair for which her late mother was cherished, the patriarchal Sloper rules his trusting, good-hearted daughter and his household with a firmness aimed at protecting her from opportunists seeking her substantial inheritance. Catherine is Sloper's second child (the first, a son, died at age three), and her birth caused her mother's premature death.

(Chapter 2) When Catherine reaches the age of 10, Sloper invites his widowed sister, Lavinia Penniman, to live in his home to provide Catherine with care and domestic education. For Catherine, "Aunt Penniman" becomes a confidante, but Sloper's sister is a foolish, meddlesome woman whose reason is clouded by a penchant for melodrama. Despite this, Lavinia becomes aware that Catherine has more potential than Sloper is able to recognize. He pays little heed to his sister's opinions, preferring the company of his more sophisticated sister, Elizabeth Almond. His only comfort regarding Catherine is that she is an obedient daughter who attempts to please him.

(Chapter 3) As Catherine reaches the age of 16, her debut in society becomes a source of tension, with Sloper disapproving of Catherine's taste in dresses. James initiates a subtle construction of the intricacies of fashionable Washington Square life in the 19th century, as well as Sloper's rigid code of values and taste.

(Chapter 4) When Mrs. Almond gives a party to celebrate her daughter's engagement, Catherine meets Morris Townsend, a handsome young man of considerable charm. Stunned by Morris's ardent attention, Catherine is swept off her feet. Lavinia, aware of Morris's interest in Catherine, engages him in conversation and becomes excited about the possibility of a romantic liaison between Catherine and the dashing young man. Returning home in Sloper's carriage following the party, the doctor quizzes Lavinia and Catherine about Morris, but Catherine says little despite her aunt's obvious enthusiasm.

(Chapter 5) A few days after the Almond party, Morris and his cousin Arthur (fiancé of Mrs. Almond's daughter) pay a call at the Sloper residence. Arthur chats with a self-conscious Catherine while Morris wins over Lavinia, who will become his ally in his ultimate pursuit of Catherine's hand in MARRIAGE. Morris acknowledges that he is presently unemployed and living with a sister. Nevertheless, as the visit ends, Lavinia invites Morris to call again. Catherine is thrilled.

(Chapter 6) Dr. Sloper and Lavinia discuss Morris's interest in Catherine. Sloper insists that the young man see him on his next visit to Washington Square. Defying her brother, Lavinia arranges for Morris to visit Catherine while Sloper is away, leaving the two alone in the parlor. Morris easily charms Catherine before his departure, and Sloper, learning of the visit, teases Catherine by asking if Morris has proposed marriage. Sloper is convinced that Morris is only interested in her fortune. Sharing this concern with his sister Mrs. Almond, the doctor learns that Morris is from a ne'er-do-well branch of the otherwise estimable Townsend family and, more alarming, that he has squandered his pittance of an inheritance and is living off his struggling sister.

(Chapter 7) Dr. Sloper expresses a willingness to give Morris a fair chance to prove his virtue and allows Lavinia to set up a dinner party. Morris is a perfect guest, charming and good-humored, but his subtle machinations fail to win over Sloper. Aware of Sloper's disdain, Morris confesses his fears to Catherine. Convinced that Sloper will not consent to a marriage, Morris is concerned that Catherine has never contradicted her father. For his part, Sloper confides in Mrs. Almond that Morris will not be an appropriate match for Catherine. Sloper determines to set Catherine straight about Morris's less savory characteristics, which his continued research into the young man's background yields.

(Chapter 8) Catherine keeps her feelings about Morris well guarded, even from the sympathetic Lavinia. In conversation with Lavinia, Dr. Sloper lashes out at her for encouraging Morris's intentions. He asserts that Catherine is simply a weak-minded woman of wealth and, as such, easy prey to an opportunist.

(Chapter 9) On their weekly Sunday visit to Mrs. Almond's house, Dr. Sloper, Lavinia, and Catherine find Morris among the callers. Confident in his daughter's loyalty, Sloper presses Morris on his lack of profession and income, which Morris misconstrues as an offer of help in finding a position. Sloper cleverly twists this misunderstanding, indicating that he has nothing to offer except the advice that Morris might find employment away from New York. Attempting to outflank Morris, Sloper prevails upon Mrs. Almond to arrange a meeting with Mrs. Montgomery, Morris's sister. Morris tells Catherine of Sloper's coldness, feeling that the doctor meant to insult him regarding his lack of employment. Catherine, unable to believe her father capable of such an insult, encourages Morris to come to Washington Square again, while Lavinia finds the relationship between Morris and Catherine an exciting diversion.

(Chapter 10) Morris turns up at the Sloper residence the next day. Alone with Catherine, Morris kisses her for the first time. She concludes that she and Morris should confront Dr. Sloper about their future. Deciding that it is best that she explain the situation to Sloper before Morris formally asks for her hand, Catherine otherwise exhibits disinterest in the financial ramifications of a possible marriage. She sees the money as little more than a welcome convenience, but Morris is painfully aware that Sloper regards him as a fortune hunter. Catherine reassures Morris that she will marry him with or without her father's approval.

(Chapter 11) Catherine enters her father's study to announce her engagement. Dr. Sloper takes the news badly, feeling that Catherine should have discussed it with him. Distressed, Catherine asks why Sloper is resistant to Morris, to which he directly replies that Morris has only a mercenary interest in Catherine. She cannot believe this. Sloper states his intention to see Morris the following day.

(Chapter 12) When Morris arrives, Sloper insists that Morris should have approached him before allowing the situation with Catherine to develop. Morris replies that he believed Catherine to be responsible for her own destiny. Abruptly pointing out that Morris has neither an income nor any prospects, Sloper refuses to bless their union. Morris counters that Catherine will marry him anyway, a possibility Sloper finds disturbing.

(Chapter 13) Meeting with Mrs. Almond, who exhibits sympathy for Morris's plight, Sloper concludes he will meet Mrs. Montgomery (Morris's sister) to see if he has misjudged the young man. Confronting Lavinia, who clearly supports Morris,

Sloper states that he will have no familial treason in his house. He begins to realize that the control over his own household is not as secure as he had thought.

(Chapter 14) Following a socially proper exchange of letters, Dr. Sloper visits Morris's sister, Mrs. Montgomery, a single mother struggling to raise her children on limited means. At first wary of Sloper, Mrs. Montgomery cannot bring herself to dispel Sloper's suspicions about her brother's character, thus stiffening Sloper's resolve to end the relationship. When Sloper indicates the vast sum of money Catherine will eventually inherit, Mrs. Montgomery breaks into sympathetic tears and advises Sloper to prevent the marriage.

(Chapter 15) As the situation develops, Sloper becomes concerned by Catherine's reticence to discuss Morris. In the meantime, Catherine exchanges letters with Morris, counseling patience. Lavinia believes that Catherine is too passive and is convinced the lovers should elope at once. Lavinia plans a secret meeting with Morris to encourage his resolve.

(Chapter 16) Lavinia and Morris secretly meet at the Battery, where Morris asks if Catherine has the strength to stand up to Dr. Sloper. Lavinia shares Catherine's belief that Sloper can eventually be won over. She explains that as a man of science, Sloper is guided by facts and that if Morris can prove himself to be a good man, Sloper will give in. For Lavinia, an elopement provides an opportunity for Morris to prove his goodness since the marriage will take place without the guarantee of her father's inheritance (although Catherine already possesses a larger one from her mother). Lavinia's romanticism annoys Morris, but he realizes that she is a valuable ally. He decides the best approach is to do nothing.

(Chapter 17) Later that night, Lavinia confesses her meeting with Morris to an incredulous Catherine, who is angered by her aunt's interference. In a heated exchange, Lavinia expresses frustration with what she regards as Catherine's detachment and unwillingness to take action. Unmoved, Catherine insists that Lavinia schedule no more secret meetings with Morris. Insulted, Lavinia offers a final comment: In her opinion, Catherine's fear of her father is a threat to her future happiness.

(Chapter 18) Distressed by her argument with Lavinia, Catherine turns to her father. She tells him that she wishes to see Morris again. He insists that Catherine trust his judgment and terminate her relationship with Morris. Sloper tells Catherine that she will not inherit his fortune if she marries against his wishes. He cruelly invites her to inform Morris of this fact, which, he is certain, will end the relationship. In tears, Catherine turns to Sloper for comfort, but he abruptly ushers her out of the room.

(Chapter 19) Dr. Sloper confronts Lavinia the following day, insisting that she stay out of Catherine's relationship with Morris. Lavinia insists to Sloper that he is being too severe in dealing with his daughter and that he is risking Catherine's health. Sloper mockingly replies that he is a doctor and can see to her care, but Lavinia cruelly reminds him that the quality of his care has already cost him a wife and a son. Lavinia had eavesdropped on the showdown between Sloper and Catherine the previous evening and offered consolation to Catherine. In the light of the new day, however, Catherine seems able to have put the previous night's conflicts behind her. Lavinia suggests that Catherine take to her bed to inspire some guilt from Sloper, but Catherine intends to prove herself a dutiful daughter.

(Chapter 20) Morris comes to Catherine the following day to ask if she has made up her mind. She pleads for more time as Morris pressures her. Catherine tells Morris of her father's plan to disinherit her, but he insists that she tell Sloper that the money means nothing to him. Despite dreading Sloper's disapproval, Catherine tells Morris she will marry him.

(Chapter 21) Feeling the tension of the standoff, Dr. Sloper visits Mrs. Almond and reveals his fear that Catherine will drag things out in hopes that he will relent. Mrs. Almond agonizes over Catherine's painful dilemma, but Sloper seems only interested in what her next move will be. Sloper raises the idea of taking Catherine on an extended tour of Europe in hopes that she will forget Morris—or that he will move on to another prospect. Despite Catherine's insistence that she stay away from Morris, Lavinia meets him in secret again, although Morris seems less interested in her advice. She withdraws her previous idea of an elopement, suggesting that Morris and Catherine must simply hold firm to their current positions. She also tells Morris that Catherine's love will not be swayed regardless of how much time passes.

(Chapter 22) Morris weighs the relative merits of an immediate elopement or biding his time; Catherine feels uncomfortable remaining in her father's house as she contemplates defying his wishes. She tells this to Sloper, who agrees she should leave his house if she disobeys him, and she adds that the marriage will happen soon. Sloper counters with a suggestion of a six-month European trip before the marriage. She tells him she will discuss this option with Morris as Sloper begins to worry that he has underestimated his daughter.

(Chapter 23) Catherine goes to Europe with her father, who excludes Lavinia from the trip as a punishment for what he considers her familial treason and because she would only remind Catherine of Morris. Lavinia encourages Catherine to go (and to buy her wedding clothes in PARIS), as does Morris, who takes advantage of Sloper's absence to enjoy full access to the comforts of Sloper's home, thanks to Lavinia. A disturbed Mrs. Almond criticizes Lavinia for her close relationship with Morris, but Lavinia posits that Morris might as well enjoy Sloper's largesse now since he will not after the marriage.

(Chapter 24) Dr. Sloper does not talk about Morris during the first months in Europe, and he enjoys the pleasures of continental culture. However, he is disturbed by what he considers Catherine's failure to appreciate the art and scenery they see. Her attention is fixed on letters from Morris and Lavinia. While hiking in the Alps, Sloper abruptly mentions the engagement but is distressed when she makes it clear that she has not changed her mind about Morris. Sloper becomes enraged and for a moment she wonders if he actually intends to do her physical harm. Sloper leaves her to make her way back through a treacherous path to the carriage. They continue their travels for an additional six months, and she continues to insist that she will marry Morris on their return to Washington Square.

(Chapter 25) After a tense return to New York with her father, Catherine does not immediately depart with Morris. Lavinia confesses to a perturbed Catherine that Morris has spent time at Sloper's house. However, Catherine is pleased with news that Morris has taken a position as a commission merchant. A battle of wills continues between father and daughter as Lavinia, reversing her previous position, feels that Catherine and Morris should wait until they can secure Sloper's fortune.

(Chapter 26) When Morris visits the next day, he is disturbed that he no longer has free access to Sloper's house now that the doctor has returned. He is further dismayed to learn from Catherine that Sloper has decided to disinherit her and that they will have to marry without promise of Sloper's fortune. Morris cannot disguise his irritation, but Catherine expresses the hope that they will marry anyway.

(Chapter 27) Dr. Sloper continues to insist that he will disinherit Catherine if she weds Morris. He also confronts Lavinia about Morris's free access to his home during his absence. Sloper is surprised to hear from Mrs. Almond that Morris is making considerable money at his job. Both agree that Catherine is likely to be hurt by the situation, and while Mrs. Almond suggests finding ways to protect Catherine, Sloper pushes for an ultimate reckoning.

(Chapter 28) Lavinia insists on a meeting with Morris to warn him that Dr. Sloper continues to oppose Catherine's marriage plans. She suggests that Morris sue Sloper, but he plans to give up the hope of marrying Catherine and asks Lavinia to prepare her for this turn of events. Morris resolves to tell Catherine that he does not wish to come between her and her father, thus causing her to lose her inheritance.

(Chapter 29) Despite Morris's request, Lavinia is unable to prepare Catherine for his visit. Frustrated that Morris has yet to agree to a date for the wedding, Catherine is shocked when he announces his plans to travel to New Orleans on business. She wants to accompany him, but he lamely warns of the dangers of yellow fever. It slowly dawns on Catherine that Morris is using the trip as an excuse and that he will not return to her. She is overcome with emotion, and he promises that he will come back.

(Chapter 30) Distressed by Morris's departure, Catherine pretends nothing is amiss. Lavinia writes to Morris but receives no reply; Catherine similarly receives no response to her messages. Observing Catherine's behavior, Dr. Sloper concludes that Morris has backed out of the marriage. Lavinia, believing that Morris has definitively ended the relationship, says as much to Catherine, who is devastated. Catherine goes to Mrs. Montgomery's house, seeking Morris, but he has gone.

(Chapter 31) Lavinia advises Catherine to keep up a pretense of the impending marriage in Sloper's presence. Catherine receives a letter from Morris in which he calls off the wedding on the grounds that he would endanger her inheritance, but she believes he is lying. A week after the letter arrives, Sloper asks Catherine about the wedding date, cruelly noting that he looks forward to an empty house. Catherine tells her father that she has broken the engagement, and he mockingly chastises her for toying with Morris's affections for so long.

(Chapter 32) Dr. Sloper's coldness toward Catherine grows over time, and she turns to Mrs. Almond for comfort, feeling betrayed by Lavinia. Sloper convinces himself that Catherine may be tricking him and waiting for his death to marry. Other suitors woo Catherine, all of whom find her genuinely appealing, but she shows no interest. Occasionally news arrives that Morris is in New York, but Catherine does not speak of him nor does she invite him to the house. Sloper finds the lack of information annoying, and his relationships with Catherine, Lavinia, and Mrs. Almond sour.

(Chapter 33) Dr. Sloper recognizes his failing health and retires from medical practice. He invites Catherine and Lavinia to accompany him to Europe and asks Catherine to promise not to marry Morris after his death. Catherine confesses that she rarely thinks of Morris, but she distresses Sloper by refusing to promise. Angered, Sloper calls her obstinate and says he plans to disinherit her after all. A year later, Sloper dies after contracting a cold, and his will provides legacies for Lavinia and Mrs. Almond while reducing Catherine's inheritance to a fifth of his estate (he leaves the rest to various charities). The aunts suggest that Catherine break the will, but she claims to be satisfied.

(Chapter 34) Following Dr. Sloper's death, Catherine goes on living in his house, enjoying the company of younger people who regard her as a benevolent aunt. As the years go by, she establishes a comfortable existence, entertaining frequently and enjoying knitting. She never speaks of Morris or the past.

(Chapter 35) Lavinia announces that she has seen Morris, and Catherine is brought to tears. Lavinia encourages Morris to pay a visit, another act of interference that enrages Catherine. He appears, but his former handsomeness has faded, and Catherine learns that he has failed at both business and love. Catherine makes it clear that she does not wish any sort of relationship with Morris and that he should not come to the house again. Morris insists that she is unfair and that he has merely bided his time until Sloper's death. She replies that she feels warmly toward Morris but cannot forgive his past cruelty. Morris and Lavinia ponder Catherine's rejection as she returns to her comfortable parlor and her knitting.

CRITICAL ANALYSIS

Reviews of *Washington Square* were decidedly mixed, praising the novel's characters and the intensely detailed depiction of a relationship between a father and daughter but criticizing its lack of action. Within a few decades, however, the novel emerged as one of James's most frequently read works. CRITICAL RECEPTION improved, with T. S. Eliot lauding its merits and Graham Greene describing it as reminiscent of Jane Austen's novels. Rich in details of an upper-class American life set in a representative New York neighborhood in a precise historical era, *Washington Square* presents its small, insular world without obvious references to events or cultural issues of greater magnitude in American society. Focusing instead on the relationships of a central quartet—father, daughter, aunt, and suitor—and with a few supporting figures, James critically observes the customs and values inherent in these individuals and their world.

James disliked *Washington Square* and was unable to reread it when considering works to include in the New York Edition. This curious fact has not prevented *Washington Square* from becoming one of his most enduring novels through frequent editions, stage versions, and FILM ADAPTATIONS. Often labeled a tragicomedy, *Washington Square* is more of a domestic DRAMA, although it is possible to experience the novel's outcomes as tragic or, more likely, absurdly, sadly comic. Labels obscure the complex and diverse nature of a work that is deceptively simple in its plot and profoundly complex in the intricate shifting emotions of its characters and in the richness of its atmosphere.

James was supposedly inspired to write the novel based on an anecdote he had heard from the actress FANNY KEMBLE. He resolved to make it a purely American story because his homeland represented to him a unique mixture of optimistic aspiration and stifling provinciality. The setting of *Washington Square* thus becomes both a place of promise, certainly for Morris, who sees it as the land for speculation, and a prison to Catherine, who is confined in a world for which she is ill-suited and in a household where she can only be tolerated. A deeply psychological work, *Washington Square* takes place mostly within the minds of its characters, conveyed by a nameless narrator who recalls events and comments on them.

The novel's triangular interaction among Catherine, Dr. Sloper, and Morris is an early prototype of a structure James employed in such later novels as *The PORTRAIT OF A LADY*, *The WINGS OF THE DOVE*, and *The GOLDEN BOWL*. As in those novels, his protagonist is a complex woman. Catherine seeks fulfillment of the most fundamental human desire—to be loved. She yearns in vain for a sign of her father's genuine affection, but when a prospective suitor appears in the person of Morris Townsend, the floodgates of Catherine's deep-seated need for affection are opened. Sloper, embarrassed by his daughter's social ineptitude, can see her only as victim of fortune hunters. Sloper may well be correct in this assessment, but his conviction is not merely protective. He is overwhelmed by his need not to be outwitted by a calculating predator. Sloper's goal of defeating Morris's pursuit of Catherine ultimately succeeds, but at the unexpected cost of his daughter's trusting affection.

Lavinia, Catherine's middle-aged flibbertigibbety aunt, is captivated by Morris's charms, imag-

ining he would be the sort of husband she would have preferred for herself. She is convinced that Catherine could find happiness with Morris and allows herself to be blinded to the young man's calculation. The level of genuine affection Morris may feel for Catherine is never made clear by James to Catherine or anyone else, although there is little doubt that he is more interested in wealth than in marriage.

Washington Square may be perceived as an intellectualized, ill-fated love story without many of the typical romanticized embellishments of marriage tales. However, James seems less interested in exploring the romantic passions of his characters and directs his attention to the multifarious psychological motivations and familial dysfunction in their lives. Although the novel's conclusion may, in many respects, have a tragic quality, James laces his story with subtly sardonic humor and employs symbolic elements to imbue the experiences of his characters with universal significance.

Jamesian symbols surface in many aspects of the novel, from his description of Catherine's needlework as exemplifying her domesticity to that of the balding, overweight Morris. Irony also comes through in the character of Sloper, who sees himself as an important doctor but who has been unable to save the lives of his wife or infant son. It is similarly ironic that Sloper's chauvinistic view of women blinds him to the very qualities within Catherine's persona most like his own. Catherine's cool resolve in finally rejecting Morris demonstrates that she is indeed her father's daughter. She has grown in moral stature within her community and seems a true heroine who recognizes that, at best, a life with Morris would be little more than a sham. As such, she chooses to sacrifice romantic illusions to embrace reality, becoming a woman much closer to the model her father had espoused.

The style of James's language in *Washington Square* is less elaborate than in his later novels, but its precision, economy, and clarity in each sentence—each phrase—provide shades of meaning, subtle revelation of character, and depths of social observation. As indicated, the narrative of *Washington Square* is presented by an omniscient third-person voice commenting, often critically, on the events and characters. This approach allows James to present the characters at some distance in the initial phases of his plot, moving in closer and more intimately as the action becomes more momentous. The narrator is omniscient but selective in what he chooses to share with the reader, demonstrating reluctance to draw any final conclusions from the comments or actions of the characters. Many qualifying phrases suggest an unwillingness to take a definitive stand on any of his observations, and the narrator also leaves out bits of encounters, assuming that the reader will find them distracting. Following one romantic encounter between Catherine and Morris, the narrator notes "This is all that need be recorded of their conversation" (82), thus eliminating elements that might clear up more compelling ambiguities. James endeavors to retain the ambiguous nature of his story to compel the reader to consider the ethical and moral conundrums.

Critics have praised the novel for an ambiguousness that leaves intriguing questions unresolved. Does Catherine make the correct decisions in dealing with her father and with Morris? Does Sloper truly care for his daughter, or is he merely a chauvinistic narcissist more concerned with appearances than his child's happiness? Is Morris a fraud or does he have true feelings for Catherine? Answers are debatable and central in explaining the novel's enduring popularity.

There are no obvious villains or, for that matter, heroes in *Washington Square* (with the possible exception of Catherine); each character exhibits positive and negative attributes and, as James makes painfully evident, often an individual's presumed strength may also be a weakness and, ironically, lead to her or his undoing. This duality extends to all aspects of the novel; for example, is the charming Morris an amorous grifter or merely a financially challenged suitor unable to better his social position except through a lucrative marital match? Morris and Catherine could make for a good match in the sense that his social skill and easy charm might inspire her potential for genuine warmth, truthfulness, and, as the reader comes to see, steely resolve. Yet, Morris would more likely fail Catherine in marriage, as he may be seen to fail her as a lover. James's sense of irony materializes most tragically in the realization that as Sloper is seemingly proven right about Morris's motives he also ruins his relationship with his daughter. The reader is drawn into the novel less through the transparent evolution of its simple plot than through the intriguing tangle of its characters' minds and hearts.

CHARACTERS

Almond, Elizabeth Mrs. Almond is Dr. Austin Sloper's sister and closest confidante, a warm, assured woman who feels sympathy for the dilemma of her niece, Catherine, and Catherine's suitor, Morris Townsend. Otherwise, Mrs. Almond is a relatively peripheral figure of greatest significance for the engagement party she gives for her own daughter, where Catherine meets Morris.

Penniman, Lavinia Dr. Austin Sloper's widowed sister lives on his charity, sentimentally imagining herself the replacement for the deceased mother of her niece, Catherine. Lavinia has "a passion for little secrets and mysteries" (33). For a time, she serves as Catherine's confidante in promoting the relationship with Morris, but her attempts to manipulate the situation on Morris's behalf costs her Catherine's trust.

Sloper, Dr. Austin Sloper is a clever, witty 50-something intellectual who believes himself a figure of some significance in his elite community of New York. The early death of his wife, a beauty whose social skills were nonpareil, and the loss of a son who died at age three, have hardened Sloper against emotion. The doctor has grown into a rigidly logical man unmoved by romanticism or appeals to feeling; as such, his only surviving child, Catherine, is starved for affection and emotional release. Judging her to lack intelligence and charm, Sloper keeps a tight rein on her activities and becomes the dominant—and domineering—force in her sheltered life. He dies recognizing that his daughter is as capable of firm resolve as he is, although he is never able to fully comprehend the depths of her emotional or intellectual nature.

Sloper, Catherine Twenty-two-year-old Catherine Sloper is the most complex of the novel's characters. At the novel's start, she appears to be an inert doormat who accommodates her father's wishes and derives self-worth from his approval. By the novel's end, she has gained wisdom through suffering and has found in herself the strength to stand alone. She earns the reader's sympathy in her longing for a trusting, caring relationship with both her father and her suitor. Along the way, she discovers that her presumably caring aunt is more interested in her own sentimentalizing view of Morris than her well-being. James chooses not to present her as merely a victim; instead, he slowly reveals her expanding strength of character that results from the blows she suffers. Catherine emerges as a survivor, a woman of unexpected courage able through the arc of the story to accept the realities that have shattered her illusions and to become a more fully realized human being.

Townsend, Morris Townsend is the attractive young man who woos Catherine. Without financial resources of his own, he seeks a life of leisure through a lucrative marriage. Morris fails to win Catherine and, more significant, her fortune, and his prospects for finding the life of comfort he desires are ultimately destroyed by this and his own failure in business. By novel's end, he has aged and endured many disappointments, the last of which is Catherine's rejection of him upon his return after long absence.

ADAPTATIONS

First brought to the movies by director William Wyler in 1949 under the title *The Heiress* (adapted from a 1947 stage adaptation by Ruth and Augustus Goetz), James's story, faithfully recreated, made an affecting cinematic drama, featuring acclaimed performances by Olivia de Havilland, Montgomery Clift, Ralph Richardson, and Miriam Hopkins, and music score by Aaron Copland. Several television productions of the Goetz adaptation appeared, with Julie Harris playing Catherine in a well-received 1961 version. In 1975, a French television adaptation directed by Alain Boudet appeared. The only big-screen challenge to Wyler's version was a generally effective, but far less faithful 1997 production directed by Agnieszka Holland, which featured Jennifer Jason Leigh, Ben Chaplin, Albert Finney, and Maggie Smith.

FURTHER READING

Bloom, Harold, ed. *Henry James*. Broomall, Pa.: Chelsea House, 2002.

Bradley, John R. *Henry James on Stage and Screen*. New York: Palgrave Macmillan, 2000.

Cargill, Oscar. *The Novels of Henry James*. New York: Macmillan, 1971.

Dupee, F. W. *Henry James*. New York: William Sloane, 1951.

Edel, Leon. *Henry James: A Life*. New York: Harper, 1985.

Eliot, T. S. "A Prediction." *Vanity Fair*, February 1924; 55–56.

Fogel, Daniel, ed. *A Companion to Henry James Studies*. Westport, Conn.: Greenwood Press, 1993.

Freedman, Jonathan, ed. *The Cambridge Companion to Henry James*. Cambridge: Cambridge University Press, 1998.

Gale, Robert L. *A Henry James Encyclopedia*. Westport, Conn.: Greenwood Press, 1989.

Gargano, James W. "*Washington Square*: A Study in the Growth of An Inner Self." In *Critical Essays on Henry James: The Early Novels,* edited by James Gargano, 129–136. Boston: G. K. Hall, 1987.

Griffin, Susan M., ed. *Henry James Goes to the Movies*. Lexington: University of Kentucky Press, 2002.

Hardwick, Elizabeth. "On *Washington Square*." *New York Review of Books* 22 (November 1990): 25–28.

Horne, Philip. *Henry James: A Life in Letters*. New York: Viking, 1999.

Howland, Bette. "*Washington Square*, the Family Plot." *Raritan* 15 (1996): 88–110.

Izzo, David Garrett, and Daniel T. O'Hara, eds. *Henry James against the Aesthetic Movement: Essays on the Middle and Late Fiction*. Jefferson, N.C.: McFarland, 2006.

James, Henry. *Washington Square*. Edited with an introduction by Brian Lee. New York: Penguin Classics, 1986.

Kaplan, Fred. *Henry James: The Imagination of Genius*. New York: Morrow, 1992.

Kearns, Michael. "Henry James, Principled Realism, and the Practice of Critical Reading." *College English* 5, no. 7 (1994): 766–787.

Novick, Sheldon. *Henry James: The Young Master.* New York: Random House, 1996.

Rasmussen, Barbara. "Re-producing 'James': Marxism, Phallocentrism and *Washington Square*." *Journal of American Studies* 23, no. 1 (1989): 63–83.

Righter, William, and Rosemary Righter. *American Memory in Henry James: Void and Value.* Burlington, Vt.: Ashgate, 2004.

Yeazell, Ruth, ed. *Henry James: A Collection of Critical Essays.* Englewood Cliffs, N.J.: Prentice-Hall, 1993.

James Fisher, *The University of North Carolina at Greensboro*

What Maisie Knew (1897)

First recorded in James's notebooks in 1892, *What Maisie Knew* initially suggested to James the makings of a short story; soon exceeding that form, *What Maisie Knew* appeared in installments of Chicago's the *Chap-Book* (January–August 1897) and (slightly abridged) in London's *New Review* (February–September 1897). In September 1897, the first book version of *Maisie* was published in England and in the United States a month later. James revised *Maisie* for the NEW YORK EDITION (1908).

SYNOPSIS

(Prologue) Set in turn-of-the-century LONDON, the novel begins with the end of complicated divorce litigation, which first gives custody of a six-year-old Maisie to her father, Beale Farange, but which is then split between Beale and his wife, Ida. Neither is an ideal parent. The divorce intensifies the antagonism between Beale and Ida, and Maisie is caught in the middle as a message and missile.

(Chapter 1) Maisie, reflecting on the divorce and its aftermath, knows something has happened but remains unsure of the event's effect. Her first tenure of custody is with her father, Beale, who saturates Maisie with invectives directed against Maisie's mother. Maisie—as a letter passed from one parent to the other—calls Ida all of the deprecations Beale has told Maisie to call her, even as the narrator nonetheless imagines Maisie's lips as innocent.

(Chapter 2) Maisie's parents collectively embrace the idea of Maisie's stupidity, which coincides with Maisie's own discovery of concealment *as a remedy* for danger. Maisie subsequently "forgets" everything and repeats nothing of what either of her parents communicates to her, ergo earning the epithet "little idiot." Meanwhile, when Maisie returns to Ida's house, she is introduced to her new governess, the pretty Miss Overmore. Even though Miss Overmore is governess at Ida's house, Beale makes his attraction to Overmore clear, and she admits to being susceptible to his charms.

(Chapter 3) Ida decides not to let Miss Overmore travel with Maisie to Beale's in an effort to further inconvenience Beale. Against Ida's orders, Overmore visits Beale's, using Maisie as her cover. Maisie not only adores Overmore but perceives the extent to which her father likes her too.

(Chapter 4) Returning from Beale's house to Ida's, Maisie finds Mrs. Wix as Miss Overmore's replacement. Despite initially finding Mrs. Wix frightening, Maisie revises this appraisal within the hour. Wix has been a mother and lost her daughter, Clara Matilda, in a traffic accident. Wix tells Maisie that Clara Matilda is Maisie's dead little sister. Wix is laughed at and belittled by everyone but Maisie, who finds in Wix something peculiarly (maternally) safe. Wix neglects nearly all aspects of Maisie's curriculum, which Wix is not competent to teach. Instead, she tells Maisie stories that are unwaveringly glorious in detail.

(Chapter 5) There is anguish for Maisie and Wix when Maisie leaves Ida's house for Beale and Miss Overmore, who now serves as sort of governess. En route to Beale's, Maisie innocently asks Overmore (who has come along for the ride) if Beale still likes her (Overmore) as he did when Maisie left. Maisie's query elicits from Beale one of his laughs loud enough to make Maisie jump. Overmore and Beale continue cat-and-mousing around the details of their relationship, leaving Maisie with the sense that she is not being told anything. Maisie, in turn, finds herself treating her doll, Lisette, as adults treat her.

(Chapter 6) Maisie, still with Overmore and Beale, gets the sense that Ida is in no hurry to get Maisie back. Overmore admits to Maisie that she is not being a very good governess. At the same time, Overmore rejects the possibility of hiring another supplemental governess because Beale and Overmore require an alibi for their affair. Maisie learns from Overmore that Ida has gone abroad but is left to wonder with whom. Maisie ingeniously considers whether Ida's gentleman-friend might become her tutor, in effect reversing Overmore's having begun as governess and becoming Beale's mistress. Overmore tells Maisie that she must end her correspondence with Wix.

(Chapter 7) Maisie finds Wix waiting for her in Beale's own hall. Soon after their reunion, however, Overmore appears in a hansom cab. Another tug-of-war ensues between Overmore and Wix, who says she has been sent by Ida in the latter's anticipated return from abroad. Wix thereafter announces Ida's engagement to a certain Sir Claude. Attempting to assuage Maisie's possible resistances to Claude, Wix presents his photograph, and his handsomeness speaks for itself. Maisie and Wix briefly struggle over the Claude photo, suggesting that Wix herself is smitten with Ida's fiancé. Overmore announces—much to Maisie's surprise—that she and Beale have themselves been married several days earlier. Mrs. Wix leaves Beale's house (without Maisie).

(Chapter 8) Maisie moons over Sir Claude's photo, while Overmore asserts Claude's horridness but then suggests they keep the photo on the schoolroom mantel. From here on out, Overmore is now Mrs. Beale. Given Mrs. Beale's busyness as hostess of Mr. Beale's parlor, Maisie spends her days with Susan Ash, the under-housemaid. Upon return from one of her strolls with Ash, Maisie is requested in the drawing room, where she finds Mrs. Beale seated with none other than Sir Claude. Upon seeing Claude, Maisie becomes nearly euphoric but not without noting that Mrs. Beale (contra her earlier criticism of him) likewise seems to have cultivated an esteem for Claude. Claude and Mrs. Beale continue their flirtatious banter.

Mrs. Beale suggests that Maisie has brought her and Claude together.

(Chapter 9) Maisie returns with Claude to Ida's house, which means reunion between Maisie and Mrs. Wix. Ida refuses to see Maisie for three days; Claude insists that Ida will come round. Foreshadowing a subsequent dalliance, Claude impresses on Maisie that Ida is not to know of Mrs. Beale's fondness for him. Maisie is finally summoned by Ida Farange. Although Claude disappears with Ida for days on end, leaving Maisie and Wix to their own devices, he duly returns with gifts for both of them. Maisie and Wix tearfully admit to each other that they are both absolutely in love with Claude. Meanwhile, Claude and Mrs. Beale continue to use Maisie as a cover for their secret meetings.

(Chapter 10) Claude questions Maisie as to whether she thinks Mrs. Beale really cares for her, to which Maisie unequivocally answers in the affirmative. Claude confesses that while Maisie has brought him together with both Mrs. Beale and Wix, there is no hope of repairing the growing estrangement between Claude and Ida.

(Chapter 11) Ida declares Claude unfit for responsibility, a charge that sends Maisie weeping on Wix's bosom. Ida accuses Maisie of hanging about Claude in a manner beyond decency. Ida then thrusts Maisie into the arms of Wix, who exchanges angry looks with Claude. Soon after this scene, Claude leaves for PARIS, and soon thereafter Ida storms into the schoolroom to introduce Maisie to a Mr. Perriam—the ostensible explanation for Ida's having fallen out of love with Claude. Mr. Perriam lacks Claude's charms. Ida and Perriam flee the schoolroom as suddenly as they had entered. Perriam's presence in the house raises Wix's hackles against Ida, and for the first time Wix realizes her potential capacity for sacrificing Ida for the sake of Claude. Claude returns from Paris, bearing gifts for Maisie and Wix. Maisie and Wix keep Perriam a secret from Claude. Upon Maisie's retiring to bed, Wix and Claude discuss his chances of separating from Ida and ending their miserable MARRIAGE.

(Chapter 12) Maisie's perceptiveness continues to quicken, occasioned by the alarm of not knowing—with six protectorates and two homes—where she might next go or finally end up. Wix implores

Claude to jettison Ida altogether, to live with Wix and Maisie as a trio of Ida-refugees. As tensions mount between Wix and Ida, Claude and Maisie take excursions into the city, leaving Wix at home to fend for herself. Meanwhile, Ida increasingly spends her days in London, and Wix dreams of the day when Ida might not return at all, leaving Ida's house as a snug little home for herself, Maisie, and Claude.

(Chapter 13) On one of aforementioned excursions, Claude tells Maisie that Mr. and Mrs. Beale are out of sorts with each other, and that Mrs. Beale has been writing Claude letters. Wix is worried that Claude and Mrs. Beale's arrangement might leave her out. The next day, Claude takes Maisie to her father's house in Regent's Park. The purpose of this visit is not to see Beale, but Mrs. Beale. Maisie and Claude debate the possibility of Mrs. Beale taking Maisie back. It dawns on Maisie that the three of them (Maisie, Claude, Wix) cannot make a happy family, as Claude cannot see himself severing all connections to Ida. Only upon being convinced that if she lives with Mrs. Beale she will see Claude often does Maisie consent to the idea of switching houses. But only too late does Maisie realize that this plan excludes Wix.

(Chapter 14) Maisie is struck by Miss Overmore's transformation into Mrs. Beale—from governess to the "glamour-beauty" that is Beale's wife. When Mrs. Beale tells Maisie that she's "squared" Farange, Maisie promptly amends that the squaring depends on Mrs. Beale's letting Farange do what he wants and vice versa. Maisie all but condones Claude's and Mrs. Beale's affair, exclaiming how beautiful it is to see them side by side. In a shared moment of familial utopia, Claude, Mrs. Beale, and Maisie envision attending lectures together at various art institutes. Maisie feels a touch of guilt in so easily getting along without Wix.

(Chapter 15) Susan Ash announces to Maisie the arrival at Mrs. Beale's house of Sir Claude, who apologizes to Maisie for having reneged on his promise to visit often. Strolling with Claude in Kensington Gardens, Maisie espies her mother with a man she cannot quite make out. Claude delights in his wife's discomfiture. Claude and Ida have it out in front of Maisie, Ida's suitor standing

unembarrassed at some distance. Ida exorbitantly clutches Maisie to her jeweled bosom, then sends her off with the suitor, introduced as the Captain.

(Chapter 16) Maisie immediately is won over by the Captain's bright kindness. The Captain pleads with Maisie not to believe Ida capable of any harm—insists among other things that Ida is *true*. Maisie, moved by the Captain's being the only one who has ever spoken so well of Ida, demands that the Captain admit he loves Ida—for Maisie wants her mother loved by someone so kind. Reunited with Maisie, Claude presses her for what she and the Captain have discussed, but Maisie, in loyalty to the Captain, gives nothing away. Claude angrily sends Maisie off in a cab by herself. But not even this dulls Maisie's love for Claude.

(Chapter 17) Claude has sent Maisie's cab to Mrs. Beale, and Claude does not visit for many days. Despite Claude's absence, Mrs. Beale admits that she continues to see him and that her feelings for him remain as intense as ever. For the sake of Maisie's education, Claude sends Maisie essays and books, which Mrs. Beale and Maisie read together. To further their cultural pursuits, Mrs. Beale tells Maisie they will visit the Great Exhibition at Earl's Court.

(Chapter 18) At the exhibition, Mrs. Beale and Maisie search for Claude in vain. While pausing at a presentation called Flowers of the Forest, Maisie notices a gentleman accompanied by a very brown woman. Mrs. Beale identifies this gentleman as her husband, Beale. Maisie and Mrs. Beale discuss his new mistress with arguably racist vituperation. Soon thereafter, Maisie finds herself alone with her father in a hansom on the way to the quarters of Beale's fabulously wealthy new mistress. Beale tells Maisie that she is an American countess.

(Chapter 19) Awaiting the Countess, Beale and Maisie turn to the topic of Maisie's ever-changing familial situation. Beale asks Maisie if she wishes to join him in America, where he is to look after the Countess's investments. Maisie realizes that he does not want her to say yes and is trying to force Maisie into declining the offer so that he can leave England with the appearance of virtue and honor. When the conversation turns to Claude and Mrs. Beale, Beale tells Maisie that she is useful to them only as pretext. Maisie responds that their needing her, pretext or not, guarantees their kindness *to* her. In the midst of this exchange, the Countess arrives. Before Maisie can say otherwise, Beale informs the Countess of Maisie's rejection of the American invitation. Maisie, disabled by the Countess's terrible ugliness, realizes that she wants to go *nowhere* with this moustached woman, and she asks for a cab to take her home. The Countess gives Maisie a prodigious sum of money, far more than a cab requires.

(Chapter 20) Mrs. Beale chides Maisie for having taken money from so vile a woman and insists it be returned forthwith. Soon thereafter, Maisie travels with Claude from London to the seaside resort of Folkestone. Waiting in the hotel garden before dinner, Claude and Maisie are startled by the unannounced arrival of Ida, who tells them she is heading abroad to Chose, on account of grave illness. Claude is disinclined to leave Ida alone with Maisie—Maisie nonetheless insists on the safety of the situation, holding in mind the Captain's earlier adulation of her mother. Claude exasperatedly relents.

(Chapter 21) Ida reiterates to Maisie the extremity of her vague illness. Maisie infelicitously brings up the Captain, at the mention of whom Ida gives Maisie a look as though a door slammed in her face. Ida leaves. At the sound of the dinner bell, Claude finds Maisie alone and escorts her to dinner on his arm. After dinner, Claude exclaims that he is free, and Maisie repeats his claim verbatim. Claude sends Maisie back to her hotel room with Miss Ash, so he can walk a bit by himself.

(Chapter 22) Claude, Maisie, and Miss Ash take the boat across the channel to Boulogne. Maisie delights in the sense that she is for the first time abroad. Busy with errands and letters, Claude sends Maisie and Ash out for a walk, the first time that Maisie feels herself the guide and not the guided. Later that afternoon, Maisie asks Claude when they will head to Paris. Claude disconcertingly intimates that they are too poor for Paris, and he informs her that Wix is en route. The next morning, Maisie and Claude meet Wix at the Folkestone packet boat. Freshening up back at the hotel, Wix sings Claude's praises unabated.

(Chapter 23) Conversation ensues regarding Ida's various motives and actions. Wix tells Maisie

and Claude that Ida has sent her because Ida does not want Maisie in company with Ash. Claude (to Wix's and Maisie's alarm) offers to take Ash back himself. Further ruminating on Ida's intentions, Claude demands that Wix tell him who was in the cab with her when Ida made her call to Wix. Wix, relenting, offers the name Mr. Tischbein. Wix finally declares that Ida has sent her over to ensure that Claude and Mrs. Beale are not reunited. At this, Claude's face goes pale. Claude equivocates on whether he is returning to England to be with Mrs. Beale, at which Wix accuses Claude of being afraid of her. Claude concurs.

(Chapter 24) Later that night, Claude storms into Maisie and Wix's room, brandishing a letter presumably communicating Mrs. Beale's extrication from Farange. The possibility of Mrs. Beale's having become autonomous infuriates Wix. Claude tells them both that even the minimum of common decency now requires his going to see Mrs. Beale. Wix vehemently protests that if he sees Mrs. Beale, he will be lost. The argument roiling, Claude placates them with the idea of awaiting his return in the hotel's luxe quarters. Claude plans to return to England the next morning.

(Chapter 25) After much wandering and missing of Claude, Maisie puts to Wix the question of why they can't be *four*. Such a possibility promptly is rebuffed by Wix. Wix marches off, and Maisie bursts into sobs.

(Chapter 26) Maisie and Wix reconcile. Sitting the early evening out by the beach, Wix has switched the terms of their conversation—to what Wix denominates the presence or absence of Maisie's moral sense. It strikes Maisie that she is on the road to knowing *everything*. The next morning, there is no letter from Claude, which Wix takes as an ill omen. Wix asks Maisie if it ever occurred to her to be *jealous* of Mrs. Beale, at which Maisie, to her own ostensible surprise, jumps. Upping the ante, Maisie asserts that were Mrs. Beale ever unkind to Claude, Maisie would kill her. In tears, Wix admits the extent to which she adores Claude, and Maisie, also crying, nearly reciprocates with her own adoration, but instead says, "Oh I know!" (218). Returning to the hotel, Maisie discovers in her room none other than Mrs. Beale, radiant from the fact that *she is free*.

(Chapter 27) At the sight of Mrs. Beale, Wix collapses into a chair, while Maisie surrenders to Mrs. Beale's embrace. Maisie notices that among Mrs. Beale's luggage there is no bag belonging to Claude. Maisie and Wix cling together upon hearing that Claude will come, but that it must be *made* to be. Mrs. Beale quickly assumes the role of Maisie's mother, once again demoting Wix to the role of mere governess.

(Chapter 28) At lunch, Mrs. Beale speaks solely to Wix, leaving Maisie to speculate on both Mrs. Beale's beauty and her motives. It strikes Maisie that Mrs. Beale is wooing Wix, and Maisie wonders what Wix is making of it all. In spending the day with Mrs. Beale, Wix and Maisie scarcely have time to confer. Earlier that evening, Mrs. Beale had told Maisie that she was divorcing Farange. Mrs. Beale clarifies that she left Claude in England because he had not yet proceeded with his own divorce. At bedtime, Maisie asks Wix if she has been won over by Beale's wooing. Wix equivocates on whether she accepts Mrs. Beale or not, whereas Maisie unequivocally declares that she does not accept her for a moment—that it is Claude or nobody.

(Chapter 29) Maisie wakes late to find Wix fully dressed. The first words out of Wix's mouth are that Claude has arrived. Parsing outcomes—whether Claude will stay or go, whether Mrs. Beale will stay or go, variations thereof—Wix concludes that Claude, as a slave to his passions, has no strength. Against Wix's injunction, Maisie quits the room to find Claude, who enters his salon from the balcony. To Maisie's alarm, he stands there, without moving to embrace her. Claude admits that he has not yet even seen Mrs. Beale and that he has no idea where she is. As Claude continues, the prospects between him and Mrs. Beale seem ever so much less auspicious. Claude decides that he and Maisie should breakfast alone at a café. Before leaving, Claude orders breakfast for Wix, charming even the French patronne who takes his order.

(Chapter 30) Over coffee and rolls, Maisie realizes that Claude is nervously attempting to replicate a version of their earlier, less complicated relationship. Claude admits he is not even certain if he will go or stay. Maisie girds herself for Claude's potentially telling her that he is giving her

up. Claude instead asks Maisie if she is willing to let go of Wix, conjuring a future in which Maisie lives with Mrs. Beale, and Claude lives separately but nearby. Claude then poses a different question: Would Maisie live with Wix and Mrs. Beale and sacrifice him? Maisie's answers with an emphatic *no*. Claude tells her to think it over for a bit. Maisie tells Claude that before deciding she would like to see Mrs. Wix.

(Chapter 31) After breakfast, Claude and Maisie head to the train station, where Claude buys Parisian newspapers. Maisie exults over the possibility of her and Claude's boarding a Paris train. In the awful velocity of time, however, the train leaves the station just as Claude is discussing tickets with the porter. Maisie then has a revelation: that she would give up Wix if he would give up Mrs. Beale. Claude's single "Oh!" shows Maisie how hopelessly afraid he is. From here, they make their way back to the inn, both of them "grave and tired" (255). They are met by the sight of Wix's luggage in the hotel hallway, at which Maisie insists that she must see her. They enter their rooms to find Mrs. Beale but not Wix. Mrs. Beale informs them that Wix is disgusted by Maisie's lack of moral sense—but before anything else can transpire, Wix appears in the doorway, refuting Mrs. Beale's claim that she had intended to leave the child behind. As a kaleidoscoping of previous questions, Wix asks Maisie if she will come with her. Maisie in turn asks Claude if he will come, "as if she had not already seen that she should have to give him up" (259). Wix asks Maisie if she has again lost it—her moral sense—to which Maisie answers with heartbreaking honesty that she does not know. Claude, Mrs. Beale, and Wix all clamor for Maisie's decision regarding Mrs. Wix. Maisie cannot answer in the affirmative *either way*. Claude, in the midst of the maelstrom, avers that he has not given up Mrs. Beale and never will. At this, Maisie asks Wix if they shall not miss their boat. Maisie says good-bye to Claude; Claude says good-bye to Maisie. Mrs. Beale also says good-bye to Maisie with bitterness in her voice, then disappears into the adjoining room. Claude and Maisie repeat their good-byes, and Maisie follows Wix out the door to catch the steamer back to England. On ship deck, Wix asks Maisie if Claude had been there as they had left. Maisie reports that he was not on the balcony. Wix is left wondering still at what Maisie knew.

CRITICAL ANALYSIS

Interpersonal relations are fundamental to all works by James. What distinguishes *What Maisie Knew* is the absolute minimalism by which relations between persons are construed with an almost mathematical regularity and precision. Maisie's parents, for instance, "made up together . . . some twelve feet three of stature, and nothing was more discussed than the apportionment of this quantity" (37). As the novel's introductory math proliferates into problems more complicated than height, Maisie attempts to solve the problem of having "two fathers, two mothers and two homes, six protections in all . . ." (96). The reduction of persons to the formulas, angles, contact points and nonintersections echoes in the novel's extended conceit of billiards (as observed by Juliet Mitchell) and suggests that human consciousness depends on interactions between persons (as noted by Sharon Cameron). The interpersonal nature of consciousness is the novel's central concern. The dramatic tension of the story depends on the shifting status of Maisie's point of view, which means that the narrator must build a sense of her reality from nearly nothing at all. Unlike Isabel Archer and Maggie Verver, who respond to interpersonal conflict as adults, "[i]t was to be the fate of this patient little girl to see much more than she at first understood . . ." (39). The narrative structure depends on recognizing the vanishing point of Maisie's understanding as her world flashes before her eyes.

Insofar as James singles out the experience of vision as a precursor to understanding, many critical accounts of *What Maisie Knew* parse the novel's reliance on metaphors of vision. Such analyses weigh the importance of Maisie's seeing with the help of Mrs. Wix and her "straighteners" (eyeglasses), of Maisie's looking at the photograph of Sir Claude before she has met him, and of the narrator's own hyperboles of vision (for instance, "the full force of [Ida's] huge painted eyes . . . like Japanese lanterns swung under festal arches" [124]). Many of these critical accounts consider how Maisie's imagina-

tion, a form of internal vision, connects the dots between what she actually, empirically sees and what she eventually processes intellectually and emotionally.

Contemporary reviews of James's 1897 novel defend Maisie's innocence, and later criticism, influenced by Freudian assertions of childhood sexuality, considers Maisie's innocence as a loaded question. With the exception of reviews such as those in the *Saturday Review* and the *New York Times Saturday Review of Books*, early reception of *What Maisie Knew* presents a provocative archive of the tenacity with which readers could sustain Maisie's impeccability against the exposure of her compromising experiences. The Manchester *Guardian*, invoking James's novel as "a credible picture of childish innocence, preserved in the midst of glaring evil," celebrates James to the extent that he supposedly preserves Maisie's so-called innocence. "This is indeed a victory, and of no mean order," the *Guardian* reviewer writes, "for, although largely due to the author's unrivalled skill in the art of . . . skating over thin ice, we are yet conscious that verbal dialectics alone could not have saved from besmirchment the small figure of this helpless toy of chance and evil passions" (283).

Using the novel's title as a springboard, the *Pall Mall Gazette* asks "[w]hat on earth, indeed, *did* Maisie know of all this terrible human imbroglio," and answers, without skipping a beat, "[s]he knew nothing—that is obviously the answer which Mr. James desires us to take from his story" (284). Implying a continuity between moral purity and intellectual imperviousness, the Indianapolis *News* delights that "[t]hrough all this Maisie lives clean and unspotted" (278). The Chicago *Tribune* likewise praises James for "never forget[ting] the blessed innocence of young maidenhood" (290). If such praise seems to overlook the particulars of James's text in its insistence on a virtuous "maidenhood," it threatens to contradict itself by its own inadvertently sensational terms. Consider, for instance, the *Guardian*'s vocabulary of deliciousness and hauntedness: "More even than in some of his other works are we haunted here by the impression that it is the thorny setting of the fruit rather than its succulence which has tempted the author to lay hands on it . . . the book is monotonous and, in spite of the changeful dialogue and the delicious insight into childish character with which every page is full, this monotony presses hard on the reader before the close" (283).

Whereas such accounts of *What Maisie Knew* largely address James's text on the level of content, several other reviews connect the novel's subject to the aesthetic form of how the story gets told. Usually, these reviews strongly criticize James. The *Spectator* writes that James's novel "reminds us of nothing so much as a beautifully dressed child making an elaborate mud-pie in the gutter. The mud-pie is a regular work of art, and the child continues to keep its own hands and dress unsoiled. But when all is said and done, the result is only a mud-pie and nothing more" (285). The *Nation* differently berates James's *lack* of temptation—his keeping his own hands and dress unsoiled, so to speak—for "thrust[ing] the burden of impropriety on the mind of the reader" (297). Interestingly, these reviews treat the reader's immersion in Maisie's point of view as James's unwillingness to declare her situation contemptible: "For, however wide awake a child may be, it is blind as a bat to the cause of certain effects. . . ." The *Nation* goes on to criticize James's ostensible moral project on aesthetic grounds, and its aesthetic project on moral ones: "As we follow [Maisie's] interpretations of marriage and divorce . . . we get to feel that she is an arbitrary, artificial construction, and that the author, fascinated by an experiment, did not realize he was beaten . . ." (297). On a slightly different register, Boston's *Literary World* takes *What Maisie Knew* to task not for what it says or does not say about Maisie but for what it says about James himself: "One feels in the reading that every manly feeling, every possibility of generous sympathy, every comprehension of higher standards, has become atrophied in Mr. James's nature from long disuse, and that all relations between him and his kind has perished except to serve him coldly by way of 'material'" (294). Here we have come full circle from the *Guardian*'s account of James as variously heroic and "tempted" and find in this absence of "manly feeling" the context for recent readings of *Maisie* informed by queer theory.

Later criticism of *Maisie* departs from initial reviews' positing of what the *Pall Mall* denominates Maisie's "virginal spirit," without "stain or shadow." However, certain echoes of her stainlessness resonate in 20th-century appraisals. For example, Muriel Shine's 1969 treatment of *Maisie* destabilizes and reconsolidates Maisie's innocence all at once. Shine notes that *Maisie* constitutes an important progression from "The TURN OF THE SCREW" or "The PUPIL," as a text that takes a child's consciousness as its (more or less) unmediated center. Departing from earlier didactic accounts of Maisie's relation to her parents and stepparents, Shine describes Maisie's affiliations in nondidactic, epistemological terms that emphasize the extent to which consciousness depends on interpersonal relations. "The child's exposure," Shine correctly writes, "becomes her education" (110). Even as Shine's essay attaches value to Maisie's adventures in exposure, it simultaneously couches epistemological insights in familiarly moralistic terms: "[Maisie's] developing awareness becomes a protective armor against the thoughtless cruelty of the adult world" (110). To be exposed while *wearing armor* hardly seems like exposure, per se. Is she exposed or isn't she? On the one hand, Shine views Maisie as "[e]merg[ing] unscathed" from her experiences; on the other hand, Shine claims that the death of Maisie's childhood leads her to "the achievement of maturity" (110). Can one reach adulthood (formulated by Shine as the experience of successive exposures) without being scathed by experience?

Millicent Bell's 1991 feminist account of *Maisie* likewise investigates *Maisie*'s imbrication with forms of innocence. Whereas Shine translates moral innocence to a field of epistemological purity, Bell resuscitates purity as a *textual* phenomenon. Corruption, for Bell, arises not as narrative limitation or extravagance but as synonym for language, against which Bell advances the superior virtues of silence. "Mrs. Wix's inarticulateness, even her poorly written letters, further silenced when kept from Maisie, becomes a language which, like Maisie's silence, is superior to the speech of others" (250). More specifically, Bell locates critical value in what James calls Maisie's sense of wonder, which Bell glosses as

"James's term for Maisie's peculiar form of wordless knowing" (250). In this sense, Bell arguably sentimentalizes textual innocence in ways analogous to early assessments of the novel's purity. Bell's essay productively demonstrates the extent to which innocence itself might be circuited across moral, epistemological, and textual lines. Recalling Shine, Juliet Mitchell (1972) notes that Maisie "has certainly lost her innocence and ignorance, but her 'knowledge' is not corrupt." Scholarship such as Bell's, Mitchell's, and Shine's multiplies the loci of possible innocence, instructively complicating earlier criticism's distortion of innocence as singularly uniform.

Whereas Shine distinguishes Maisie from earlier Jamesian children in terms of the intelligibility of her interiority, Bell calls attention to the distinctiveness of Maisie's *being a girl.* "James seems to value Maisie's femaleness because it guarantees greater sensibility as well as innocence than an equivalent young male consciousness" (243). Bell's essentializiation of what counts as "most representatively a female condition" might seem problematic, given the myriad of sensitive boys in James's oeuvre (not least of all the autobiographical boy in *A Small Boy and Others* [see AUTOBIOGRAPHIES]). Bell's insistence on the fundamental significance of Maisie's femaleness nonetheless makes room for subsequent claims (by Alfred Habegger and John Carlos Rowe) that pivot on the queer possibility of James's having reproduced his boyhood as a fictionalized girlhood.

Charles Samuels (1971) begins his account of *Maisie* with the observation that innocence "will not remain uncompromised" (178). Samuels argues that the novel's non-"accommodata[bility]" of innocence is inseparable from its "indictment" of the "threatening imperiousness" of sex (179). Like Shine, however, Samuels idolizes Maisie as paradigmatically capable of unconditional love—which even if "unviable in the world of the novel . . . remains inspiring to the reader." Like Bell, Samuels distinguishes Maisie's unequivocal relation to love from the amorous energies of those around her. If Bell, then, is interested in ambiguous forms of silence and speech, Samuels is interested in ambiguous forms of relationality. Samuels notes that Claude refers to Maisie as "old man" and "old boy," but only to suggest that such endearments reinforce their relationship as one of "steady, disinterested affection." These "old boy" references will differently resurface in queer readings.

Placing *Maisie* in a historical frame beyond the familial ones, Marcia Jacobsen approaches the novel's innocence as an object of historical and cultural interest. Contra earlier critics such as Edmund Wilson and Leon Edel, Jacobsen argues that James's relation to Maisie was not peculiarly or singularly neurotic but evidence of a culture-wide "common plight" (103). This plight, Jacobsen continues, is evidenced in works by authors such as James Matthew Barrie (who invented the character Peter Pan) and Frances Hodgson Burnett (who wrote *Little Lord Fauntleroy* [1886] and *The Secret Garden* [1909]), which seek "occasion for self-indulgent nostalgia . . . voices of regret for the epic age [of childhood]" (106–107). *Maisie's* subject matter and context, Jacobsen argues, would be familiar to 19th-century readers, from concurrent novels and plays, as well as the time's "surprisingly detailed newspaper accounts of recent divorce trials" (110). Jacobsen suggests that Maisie's history reverses that of the typical child protagonist, turning "from a storybook world to one in which authentic emotion and compassion operate" (119). Jacobsen goes on to claim that the "storybook world" that Maisie outgrows in fact represents James's conception of the contemporary social world of which the novel serves as critique. That the storybook world mirrors a set of lived conventions and restrictions means, in the end, that Maisie's escape from that storybook will always be at best partial and, to that end, unsuccessful.

Following earlier reviews that search for the connections between Maisie's consciousness and that of James, Jacobsen writes that James "blurs [Maisie's] vision with his own" (114). Jacobsen's account of Maisie's vision owes some debt to Juliet Mitchell's argument that *Maisie* is "a process of initiation into vision," and that maturity in Maisie consists of the equivalence of "vision and knowledge" (114). Unlike Jacobsen's alignment of James's vision and Maisie's, Mitchell calls for an understanding of vision routed through Mrs. Wix. More scrupulous than most characterizations of Wix,

Mitchell's essay develops an account of Maisie's governess as correlative to James's own viewpoint. Whereas Mitchell's final assertion of Wix's particular mode of vision as "pornographic" is provocative in the context of earlier reviews' fetishizing of Maisie's besieged but resistant "virgin soul," the distance between pornographic voyeur and the pornographic object structurally recalls the distance between seeing and knowing. Mitchell claims that closing this gap is the novel's governing enterprise.

This distance between experience of vision and the object of vision is usefully understood in terms of Bell's account of "wonder" and, even more so, in Philip Weinstein's account of imagination (1971). For Weinstein, imagination is that faculty which "must develop in order to understand what . . . other characters are doing, and how this affects [one]" (74). Weinstein's essay is a salubrious counterpoint to criticism that indicts those characters who surround Maisie as merely blockish or awful. For Weinstein, the diminution of these characters speaks less to James's indictment of them than the shift in James's enterprise from the stimulus of the empirical world to the minutiae of a world's governing consciousness—in this case, Maisie's. The centrifugal organization of characters and events around this consciousness suggests, for Weinstein, an expansion of the practice by which James earlier conceived of Isabel Archer sitting in thought—an expansion of this single scene's technique into the peregrinations of an entire novel.

Along differently philosophical lines, Paul Armstrong (1983) reads *Maisie* for what it tells us about James's importance to phenomenology (and vice versa). Armstrong advances James's novel as "a kind of paradigm of the relation between consciousness and moral vision in James's fictional universe" (8). A phenomenological approach such as Armstrong's insists on the unity of epistemological and moral questions—the idea that knowledge about the world and ourselves is based on a sense of right and wrong. He leaves readers with the questions: What in fact does Maisie know and has she developed what Wix calls "a moral sense?" Armstrong notes the difficulty of achieving "a coherent understanding of your world's interpersonal structure when that structure refuses to hold together coherently" (10).

Armstrong investigates the necessity of imagination as Maisie's means of producing connections between confounding events. Maisie's pursuits of knowledge are inextricable from the moral concerns of care and compassion to the extent that the limits and fidelities of compassion are precisely the object of her own inquiries (19). Armstrong interestingly reads the nonresolution of *Maisie*'s conclusion as the literalization of Maisie's success in finding freedom from the ways others have been using her. That her future seems unsure is an improvement over being batted back and forth between her incessantly fighting parents. Maisie's morality depends on an openness to experience's sometimes violent and arbitrary nature.

Queer theory has illuminated many of James's texts. Mitchell's account of Claude and Maisie's relationship as "a delicate homosexuality"—to which the nicknames for Maisie of "dear boy" and "chap" allude—occasions Rowe's rigorous redress of *Maisie*'s volatile orchestrations of gender (1998). Rowe resists descriptions of the relationship as homosexual to the extent that homosexuality too quickly presumes Claude's *own* gender stability. As Rowe notes, Claude ceaselessly imagines himself as feminized victim; in calling himself "an old grandmother," Claude can be seen as rewriting his relationship with Maisie not as homosexual but as *differently heterosexual*, conceiving himself as analogue to the "grandmotherly" Mrs. Wix, and Maisie to the chap-like (chapped, clawed) Claude.

Rowe implies that Maisie's attempt to make sense of her volatile world refracts James's attempts to "adapt . . . his own aesthetic values to this new and at times baffling modern world." Invoking Merla Wolk's 1983 essay, Rowe pursues the possibility that Maisie's time in Boulogne not only repeats James's own time in Boulogne (recounted in *A Small Boy and Others*) but that Maisie-as-girl literalizes James's Boulogne-based anxieties about his own inadequacy as a small boy. In being dropped from the "modern" decadence of her parents and stepparents and at best tenuously attached to "the old moral code" of Wix, Rowe reads the equivocal ending of the novel as Maisie's—and James's own—loosening from modernity: less of a return to England than a condition of being suspended in an indeterminacy of knowledge with "a certain *postmodern* potential" (154).

In addition, critical race theory has called attention to the peripheral-seeming figure of the American Countess, one of Beale Farange's mistresses. Toni Morrison (1992) first indicted James criticism for ignoring "the black woman who . . . becomes [in *Maisie*] the agency of moral choice and meaning" (13). Walter Benn Michaels (1995) notes the significant risks of too quickly misreading James's "brown" lady as Morrison's "black woman," arguing that the American definitions of race overlook James's British-centered understanding of black and white as well as public and private. More recently, Kendall Johnson (2001) has called attention to the brown lady's wearing a "scarlet feather," implying an anxiety attending not only the economic and cultural status of African Americans, but "the contradictions at the heart of legislation to . . . assimilate Native Americans in the United States" (130). Johnson's reading illuminates the narrator's previously overlooked description of Maisie herself as an "Indian captive."

While keeping the innovations of Morrison, Michaels, and Johnson in hand, it seems likewise feasible that the Countess posits an ineradicable problem in the familial equation that Maisie has been juggling. The attractiveness and good looks of her parents' paramours give Maisie a rationale for her parents' shifting relationships. In this sense, what matters to Maisie might be the limit to circulation that the Countess's perceived ugliness represents. Overmore had been beautiful enough to snare Beale; Claude had been beautiful enough to snare Overmore. Who, Maisie muses, given the Countess's ugliness, could or would seduce the Countess away from Beale? If the Countess strikes Maisie as a monkey, it may indicate the extent to which the Countess throws a *monkey wrench* into the calculus through which Maisie has charted the survival of her family structure.

CHARACTERS

Ash, Susan The under-housemaid at the home of Beale Farange and a proxy-governess for Maisie.

Beale, Mrs. (née Miss Overmore) Maisie's first governess at Ida's house soon thereafter becomes Beale's mistress. No sooner does Overmore become Beale's wife than Mrs. Beale (née Overmore) grows infatuated with Ida's own suitor, Sir Claude.

Captain, The One of Ida's suitors, following Perriam, boyish and ingenuous-seeming, the Captain presses upon Maisie how truly *good* her mother is, which nearly brings tears to Maisie's eyes, never having heard Ida described as anything approaching beatific. It is thus very much to Maisie's chagrin when Ida later on dismisses the Captain as "the biggest cad in London" (177).

Claude, Sir Ida Farange's second husband, Claude is inexhaustibly charming. As Maisie grows, her relationship with Claude eventually becomes complicated, and by novel's end it is not entirely clear if Maisie and Claude's relationship is not itself on the brink of an unspoken and imminent romantic element.

Cudden, Mrs. (a.k.a the American Countess) Following his estrangement from Mrs. Beale, she became Beale's mistress. Upon first seeing the Countess, Maisie is horrified to think of her father associating with a brown woman so physically grotesque as to seem to Maisie less a lady than a "frizzled poodle" or "human monkey" (156).

Farange, Beale Maisie's biological father was first married to Ida, then to Miss Overmore, and finally attached to a woman he introduces to Maisie as an American countess. Beale's great virtue, as relates to Maisie, might well be his innocuousness.

Farange, Ida Maisie's biological mother, who despite the near imperceptibility of her mouth and the minuteness of her waist (38), is constituted by "some very long lines" (38), including a veritable wingspan that accounts for her remarkable success at billiards. Ida plays romance (and motherhood) with the swift ruthlessness of a billiard player.

Farange, Maisie The heroine of James's novel is first introduced as the six-year-old daughter (and only child) of Beale and Ida Farange. As Maisie is tossed from parent to parent, governess to governess, stepparent to stepparent in the wake of a bitter divorce, she begins to understand more of the world around her.

Moddle Maisie's first nurse at Beale's house, preceding both Overmore and Wix.

Perriam One of Ida's several suitors.

Tischbein, Mr. One of Ida's suitors, he takes Ida to South Africa, and Maisie is left in the hands of Claude and Mrs. Wix.

Wix, Clara Matilda Daughter of Mrs. Wix, she was run over and killed by a hansom in the Harrow Road.

Wix, Mrs. Maisie's governess, following the leave-taking of Miss Overmore for Beale's, Wix serves as Maisie's constant companion and sympathetic sufferer.

ADAPTATIONS

What Maisie Knew was adapted for British television in 1968 and was directed by Derek Martinus.

In 1976, an experimental film called *What Maisie Knew* was directed by Babette Mangolte.

FURTHER READING

Armstrong, Paul. "Consciousness and Moral Vision in *What Maisie Knew*." In *The Phenomenology of Henry James*. Chapel Hill: University of North Carolina Press, 1983.

Beidler, Paul. "*What Maisie Knew*: Domestic Labyrinth and Human Frame." In *Frames in James: The Tragic Muse, The Turn of the Screw, What Maisie Knew, and The Ambassadors*. Victoria: University of Victoria, 1993.

Bell, Millicent. "The Language of Silence: *What Maisie Knew*." In *Meaning in Henry James*. Cambridge, Mass.: Harvard University Press, 1991.

Cornwell, Neil, and Maggie Malone. *The Turn of the Screw and What Maisie Knew*. New York: St. Martin's Press, 1998.

Habegger, Alfred. "*What Maisie Knew*: Henry James's *Bildungsroman* of the Artist as Queer Moralist." In *Enacting History in Henry James: Narrative, Power, and Ethics*, edited by Gert Buelens. Cambridge: Cambridge University Press, 1997.

Hayes, Kevin, ed. *Henry James: The Contemporary Reviews*. Cambridge: Cambridge University Press, 1996.

Jacobsen, Marcia. "*What Maisie Knew*." In *Henry James and the Mass Market*. Tuscaloosa: University of Alabama Press, 1983.

James, Henry. *What Maisie Knew*. Edited by Paul Theroux. New York: Penguin, 1985.

Johnson, Kendall. "The Scarlet Feather: Racial Phantasmagoria in *What Maisie Knew*." *Henry James Review* 22, no. 2 (2001): 128–146.

Michaels, Walter Benn. "Jim Crow Henry James?" *Henry James Review* 16, no. 3 (1995): 286–291.

Mitchell, Juliet. "*What Maisie Knew*: Portrait of the Artist as Young Girl." In John Goode, *The Air of Reality: New Essays on Henry James*. London: Methuen, 1972.

Morrison, Toni. *Playing in the Dark: Whiteness and the Literary Imagination*. Cambridge, Mass.: Harvard University Press, 1992.

Rivkin, Julie. "Undoing the Family in *What Maisie Knew*." In Cornwell.

Rowe, John Carlos. "The Portrait of a Small Boy as a Young Girl: Gender Trouble in *What Maisie Knew*." In *The Other Henry James*. Durham, N.C.: Duke University Press, 1998.

Samuels, Charles. "The Pupils." In *The Ambiguity of Henry James*. Urbana: University of Illinois Press, 1971.

Shine, Muriel. "Maisie." In *The Fictional Children of Henry James*. Chapel Hill: University of North Carolina Press, 1969.

Teahan, Sheila. "*What Maisie Knew* and the Improper Third Person." In Cornwell.

Tucker, Irene. "What Maisie Promised: Realism, Liberalism, and the Ends of Contract." In *A Probable State: The Novel, the Contract, and the Jews*. Chicago: University of Chicago Press, 2000.

Weinstein, Philip. "Resisting the Assault of Experience: *What Maisie Knew*." In *Henry James and the Requirements of the Imagination*. Cambridge, Mass.: Harvard University Press, 1971.

Wilson, Edmund. "The Ambiguity of Henry James." In *The Triple Thinkers.* Harmondsworth, England: Penguin, 1962.

Wolk, Merla. "Narration and Nature in *What Maisie Knew.*" *Henry James Review* 4, no. 3 (1983): 196–206.

Michael Snediker, *Queen's University, Kingston, Ontario*

The Wings of the Dove (1902)

Charles Scribner's Sons published *The Wings of the Dove* in 1902. James revised it for the 1909 NEW YORK EDITION.

SYNOPSIS

Book I

(Chapter 1) Kate Croy is at her father's vulgar, ugly LONDON house for a last visit with him, her only surviving parent. Lionel Croy has assured his daughter that he is very ill and has asked her to stay with him. However, her wealthy aunt, Mrs. Maud Manningham Lowder, will provide for her only if she breaks off contact with him. Lionel dramatically exhorts her to go, but by the chapter's end it is clear that each views the other at best cynically and at worst instrumentally. Lionel discovers that the source of Kate's willingness to risk disinheritance on his behalf is that she has fallen in love with a young man whom her aunt will not allow her to see. Over the course of the novel, Kate very rarely spends time with her family.

(Chapter 2) Kate visits her widowed sister, Marian, in Chelsea. Marian, once a beautiful and accomplished young woman, is now a widow with four young children and barely scraping by. Once Kate is taken in by their Aunt Lowder, she (and her two sisters-in-law) make Kate promise that she will convince their aunt to help to support them all. Kate, who already has given her sister half of her modest inheritance, feels tremendously burdened. Marian confronts Kate and tells her that she has no right to marry (see MARRIAGE) Merton Densher because he is not wealthy enough. Kate

is dismayed but reflects that she can hardly cast off Marian and the children any more than she could cast off Densher.

Book II

(Chapter 1) Kate's lover Densher is an up-and-coming journalist who is "visibly absentminded, irregularly clever, liable to drop what was near and to take up what was far" (WD1 48). Kate had first met him at a gallery, then later, coincidentally, on the London underground, where Merton rode all the way to Kate's stop with her. They began an immediate and intense relationship. By now, they are meeting publicly in the park near Mrs. Lowder's house, risking her disapproval. As they mull over the restricted conditions of their discouraged courtship, Densher asks Kate to marry him in a civil

"The Doctor's Door," by A. L. Coburn, frontispiece to the first volume of *The Wings of the Dove*, Volume 19, the New York Edition

ceremony. Kate resists but nevertheless avers that she will never sacrifice him. She pleads with him to work with her in changing her aunt's opinion about their match.

(Chapter 2) As Densher waits in Mrs. Lowder's London house, Lancaster Gate, he observes the rich, ugly furniture, and he feels the social difference between himself and Mrs. Lowder. Kate has warned him that her aunt is passionate and willful, but unexpectedly, he finds that he likes her and understands her when she tells him that her ambition for Kate is to "see her high, high up—high up and in the light" (*WD1* 82). After their meeting, Mrs. Lowder feels that she has won the day. When recounting this meeting, Densher tells Kate that he is being sent away by his newspaper to America for 15 or 16 weeks in order to write a series of articles about the social aspects of American life. His going away has at least gained them time. Kate agrees to receive Densher's letters at home and further tells him that "I engage myself to you for ever" and shortly after maintains, "I love you as I shall never in my life love anyone else" (*WD1* 95, 98).

Book III

(Chapter 1) Susan Shepherd Stringham, an elderly widowed writer from Boston, gives readers a vision of Milly Theale, the much younger and less experienced woman whom she accompanies to Europe. The narrator presents Milly as a conscious subject, a woman around whom others arrange their lives and desires. In SWITZERLAND, Susan recalls meeting Milly, who had decided to visit friends in Boston after mourning the last of her family. Susan was completely charmed by Milly, who in turn is taken by Susan's New England probity. When Milly invites Susan to her New York home and then to Europe, Susan accedes, feeling completely enthralled with her younger charge. Susan often refers to Milly as a "princess" whose wealth threatens to overshadow her interior character. On this particular day in the Alps, Susan looks for Milly, whom she finds perched alone on a perilous cliff. Initially afraid that Milly is contemplating suicide, Susan realizes that Milly is "looking down on the kingdoms of the earth" (124), seeking not to renounce but rather to embrace and to enjoy them.

(Chapter 2) At dinner, Susan and Milly discuss Milly's health. Milly had seen a doctor in Boston, prompting Susan to suspect Milly's illness. Milly is evasive, hoping that although she will not be able to enjoy everything, she can continue anticipating the great deal that lies before her. Susan suggests that they go to London to be around people and life. She reminds Milly that Merton Densher might well be there and that Milly promised to look him up if in London. Milly appears to only remember Mr. Densher barely (readers will discover that she remembers him very well) but quickly agrees to go. That evening, Susan writes to her old friend Maud Lowder, mildly concerned that she might not wish to renew their friendship. She reassures herself that whatever Maud may have made of her life, she can boast nothing so wonderful as Milly.

Book IV

(Chapter 1) At a dinner party of 20 people at Mrs. Lowder's home, Milly is impressed by the buzz of the London world. She meets Lord Mark and Kate Croy. Lord Mark sizes Milly up and tells Mrs. Lowder that she would profit from knowing Milly. In response to his crude assessment, she charges him with lacking imagination. Milly is especially fascinated by Kate Croy and tells Lord Mark that Kate's kindness to her is much appreciated and unexpected. Lord Mark confides to Milly that he does not understand Kate, who has rebuffed his interest.

(Chapter 2) Milly makes quite an impression on London and develops the confidences of Mrs. Lowder and Kate. Although Kate discloses much to Milly about her background and her sister and father, Milly tells Susan that she feels Kate keeps a secret that weighs heavily on her. As Kate and Milly become fast and close friends, Kate does not mind being swept along in Milly's magisterial financial freedom, and Milly wishes to immerse herself in Kate's vast network of friends. The one sore spot is that Milly realizes that Kate does not like Susan Stringham.

(Chapter 3) Susan Stringham reveals to Milly that Mrs. Lowder and Kate already know Merton Densher. Susan has found this out rather casually, as she and Maud talked about their younger protégées.

Susan wonders why Kate has not mentioned him to Milly; Mrs. Lowder has confided her suspicions that Kate and Merton are involved and has made it clear that she would prefer Kate to marry Lord Mark. Milly is struck by the thought that Kate has been keeping a secret from her. Her suspicion intensifies as she recalls to Susan that Kate's sister (Mrs. Condrip) had revealed Mr. Densher's close attachment to Kate and asked Milly to curb the affair. Mrs. Condrip, who had struck Milly as a character from a novel by Dickens, understands that Mrs. Lowder will cut Kate off financially if she does not give up Mr. Densher. It becomes clear that Susan or Milly do not know how Kate feels. They suspect her of dissimulation. Milly is strongly affected but defends Densher when Susan wonders if he has led Milly on.

Book V

(Chapter 1) Milly, Susan, Kate, Mrs. Lowder, and a crowd of others are at Lord Mark's country house, Matcham, on a beautiful summer afternoon. Milly amuses herself by studying Kate. Milly realizes that she is becoming a factor in other people's plans: in Lord Mark's plan to find a suitable wife; in Mrs. Lowder's plans for Kate's social ascension; and in some unknown way, in Kate's own plans. Milly grasps at understanding the network of unspoken arrangements and friendships slowly unfolding.

(Chapter 2) Lord Mark invites Milly into the house at Matcham to show her a portrait by Bronzino of a slender, pale woman with blazing red hair whom he believes resembles her. As they contemplate the artwork, Milly's eyes fill with tears as she confides that the afternoon has been too beautiful but will not be so again. Kate Croy enters the room with a couple to whom she plans to show the similarity between the portrait and Milly. Sensing that Milly is upset, Kate dispenses of the other three people. Milly asks Kate to accompany her to an appointment with the eminent doctor Sir Luke Strett, an appointment that Milly wants to keep secret from Susan.

(Chapter 3) Milly sees Sir Luke twice and receives a diagnosis that is not revealed even to the reader. In her first 10-minute visit, Kate accompanies Milly, who claims not to be ill, although she must make another appointment. On the way

home, Milly begins to cry and tries to express to Kate how beautiful she finds the world. In her next visit, Milly faces the gravity of the situation as Sir Luke implies the severity of her illness. He directs her to get out of London and assures her that he will visit her wherever she goes. In one of the most important moments in the novel, Sir Luke implores her to see and experience all she can and to worry about nothing. Milly asks him if she will suffer. The doctor reassures her that she will not, reminding her to live all she can in the time that remains.

(Chapter 4) After she has seen the doctor, Milly spends the rest of the day walking around London. She walks through neighborhoods she has never visited, realizing that she has never in her life been anywhere by herself. She becomes determined to keep her illness a secret. Susan Stringham understands that Milly is keeping something back but is willing to let Milly keep the secret. Kate has no such scruples. She arrives at Milly's house and demands to know what the doctor has told her. Milly claims that there is nothing wrong. However, Kate grows to understand that Milly is gravely ill.

(Chapter 5) Maud Lowder and Kate meet Milly and Susan to say good-bye and wish them a good voyage from England. Mrs. Lowder steals a moment alone with Milly in order to ask for her help in determining whether Kate and Densher are still in contact. When she discovers that the two young women have never spoken of him, she is immediately suspicious that the two younger woman may be conspiring. Milly dissembles, claiming that she and Kate do not speak of Densher, but she inadvertently suggests that Densher is in some way important to Kate and to her.

(Chapter 6) Milly and Kate converse freely with each other while their guardians Maud and Susan are out together. Milly's internal dialogue focuses on Kate's inordinate social power and charm. A few central tidbits of conversation are relayed: Kate tells Milly that Milly is better than her new English friends and that she should drop them. She also says that despite Milly's protestations of tenderness for Kate, Milly may learn to loathe her yet. Kate gives Milly the title of *dove* and Milly accepts it. The two women assess each other and come to an unspoken understanding of how much to reveal to the other. Milly infers that Densher is back in town.

(Chapter 7) Milly goes to the National Gallery to avoid being home when Sir Luke visits Susan, whom he will advise about Milly's need to live as much as she can. Sir Luke's visit to Susan happens offstage, and the reader will not know definitively what is wrong with Milly. At the museum, Milly interrupts a secret meeting between Kate and Densher. Although they greet Milly fondly, Milly decides to cover their embarrassment by playing the part of the young American girl, and she takes them to lunch at her hotel. Milly sees that Densher is in love with Kate, and she appears to make up her mind that she does not care one way or the other.

Book VI

(Chapter 1) Densher now becomes the focus. As he and Kate leave Milly's hotel and walk together through the streets, Densher puts himself in Kate's hands. She sees a way to turn their accidental encounter with Milly at the National Gallery into an advantage and promises to arrange for Densher to visit Mrs. Lowder. Densher, while relying on Kate's social deftness, finds himself curious about how Milly has become so central in Kate's world. Densher begins his passive acceptance of Kate's far-reaching plans about their future.

(Chapter 2) Kate and Densher meet at Lancaster Gate with Mrs. Lowder's knowledge and permission. Densher, frustrated with the endless hurdles between himself and Kate, demands that Kate tell him that she still loves him. It is one of the few times he tries to impose his will on Kate, and although she soothes him by telling him how much she cares for him, she also immediately gains the upper hand by managing him again. She tells Densher that Milly is in love with him and asks him to cultivate and encourage Milly's feeling for him. Densher is confused and slightly taken aback. Kate insists that Milly does not know that Kate loves Densher, only that Densher loves Kate, and that Milly is so kind that she will want to help nurse Densher's broken heart. Kate appears to Densher to be playing a deep and unfathomable game, and though he does not understand it, he assents. Sig-

nificantly, Kate hints that she knows very well that Milly is ill and that Densher might profit financially from a friendship with her. Densher chooses not to pursue this hint.

(Chapter 3) Densher finds himself in the odd position of meeting Kate across the table at a dinner party at Lancaster Gate. Susan has come without Milly, who is ill. Densher's observations of the dinner shows that he is mainly interested in how Kate and Milly's personalities are so central to the dinner. Kate seems to him to be playing the part of the beautiful young society woman, and he finds this touching and tragic. Milly, on the other hand, is the subject of most of the evening's discussion, and Densher thus conceives of her as a case study in sudden social success. By the end of the evening, he is aware that he is in a surprisingly close alliance with Susan Stringham to defend the "real" Milly and that he has also been assigned a closer relationship to Milly than the one he had realized. He chooses not to see that Kate has engineered the incipient relationship between Milly and himself.

(Chapter 4) In the drawing room after the dinner, Kate and Densher have a quiet, frank conversation in which Kate tells him that Milly is very ill. She assures him that Milly cares very much for him and that she has stayed in London only because he is there. Kate explains that Milly will never behave like an invalid and that Densher's attention to her will make what is left of her life worth living. Densher feels as though he is caught in a web, but not until he speaks with Mrs. Lowder does he understand how deeply he is enmeshed. Mrs. Lowder tells him frankly that she has smoothed his path to marry the wealthy young American—she has, that is, assured Susan that Kate does not care for Densher.

(Chapter 5) The day after the dinner, Densher visits Milly, whom he finds perfectly natural and easy. Densher sees that Milly really does pity him for what she thinks to be his unrequited love for Kate. Densher and Milly discuss Kate, whom they both profess to admire, and eventually they decide to go out in Milly's carriage. As Milly readies herself for the drive, Kate unexpectedly arrives, and in a few moment's conversation with Densher, she gives him the opportunity to pull out of their plan to deceive Milly. He declines, and she leaves without seeing Milly.

Book VII

(Chapter 1) Susan, having been apprised of Milly's illness by Sir Luke, enlists Mrs. Lowder in the cause of making Milly happy. Although Susan does not know what is wrong with Milly, she understands that it is serious and understands, too, that Sir Luke believes that Milly should be allowed to experience being in love. Susan and Mrs. Lowder thus begin a conspiracy that parallels Kate and Densher's. They decide to encourage Milly and Densher to develop a relationship; Susan wishes to help Milly by asking Mrs. Lowder to keep Densher away from Kate. The only hitch is that Mrs. Lowder must admit that Kate believes that she cares for Densher, but she also assures Susan that Kate has mistaken her own feelings.

(Chapter 2) Milly takes her leave from Sir Luke. Milly, Susan, Mrs. Lowder, and Kate are going to VENICE. Densher will likely follow.

(Chapter 3) Some months have passed, and Milly is ensconced in the Palazzo Leporelli, an ancient and prestigious residence in Venice. Milly has been able to create a luxurious world around herself and her friends; she has, for example, employed Eugenio, a multilingual and well-connected European, to smooth her way. Milly and her retinue are in the center of a social whirl that rivals their time in London, but in the midst of it, Milly and Kate's friendship deepens. The two like to take time away from the crowds to speak about the wearying quality of intense socializing and the sustaining power of their friendship. At the end of the chapter, Lord Mark appears at the Palazzo Leporelli and finds Milly alone.

(Chapter 4) Lord Mark has come to propose to Milly, who feels at once so comfortable with him and so little in love with him that she renounces his proposal by flatly stating that she is very badly ill. She underestimates his interest in her and how cruel her refusal will motivate him to be. After she suggests that he turn his attention to Kate, he obliquely suggests to her that Kate and Densher are in love. When Milly replies that Kate herself has reported herself free of any romantic attachment, Lord Mark suggests that it is possible that Kate is lying to her and is putting her in Densher's way for reasons of her own. Just at this moment, Densher's card is brought up to Milly.

Book VIII

(Chapter 1) Densher has been in Venice for a little over a week and has found himself warmly received at the Palazzo for nearly every meal. In Densher's extraordinary speculations about the meaning of his actions, he wonders if he has bent too much to Kate's will, if he is harming Milly, and whether he has any will of his own left. He consoles himself with the thought that no matter what he does, he genuinely likes Milly and honors Kate by consenting to her every request.

(Chapter 2) On the eighth day of Densher's continuous visits to the Palazzo, Milly is too ill to see him. This allows Kate and Densher an opportunity to speak each other as they stroll in one of the city squares. Densher asks Kate to give him some proof of her love; he asks her to come to his rooms and stay the night with him. It is clear that Densher has made this request before; Kate is not shocked by it.

(Chapter 3) At an evening gathering at the Palazzo, Milly is well enough to come down to her guests, who include Kate and Densher. Milly is uncharacteristically dressed in white (she has worn black, mourning for her family until now), and Densher finds her magnificently beautiful. Kate tells him that she and Mrs. Lowder are going back to England and that she expects Densher to stay on in Venice. He asks Kate whether he ought to propose to a dying girl, admitting to himself that he has known that this was her plan. He sets two conditions. He will marry Milly only if Milly proposes to him, and he will stay in Venice and court Milly only if Kate agrees to come to his hotel that night. Kate accepts.

Book IX

(Chapter 1) Kate and Mrs. Lowder have gone, and Densher is alone in Venice. He is staying in the plain and small rooms where Kate had spent her last night in Venice with him. Although he misses Kate, he also sees Milly often. When she asks him why he has stayed, he finds it difficult to answer. He lets her believe that he stays in order to forget Kate, and he consoles himself by believing that he is not technically lying. The two of them skate around the matter of her health; Milly tells him that she believes she can live if she wishes, but Densher understands that she does not want to discuss her illness.

(Chapter 2) After having had complete access to the Palazzo for more than five weeks, Densher discovers that he is suddenly a pariah. Milly and Susan will not receive him, and Eugenio will not help his cause. When he is turned away, Densher feels that something fateful has happened to damage his standing with the two women. Walking through the crowds in Venice, trying to come to grips with his exclusion, he suddenly sees Lord Mark in a café, and he guesses correctly that Lord Mark has come to Venice to speak to Milly about him. Although Densher surmises that Milly would probably like him to leave Venice, he decides to stay and wait for a sign from her; he believes that his act of waiting purifies his motives. On the evening of the third day of silence, Susan visits his hotel.

(Chapter 3) Susan tells Densher simply that Milly has "turned her face to the wall" (WD2 270), which will become how the characters describe Milly's descent into the final phase of her illness. Susan confirms to Densher that Lord Mark came to see Milly and tells him further that Lord Mark told Milly about Densher and Kate's secret engagement. Densher and Susan piece together a story in which Lord Mark had only wanted Milly's money. Densher cannot decide if he should go to Milly and deny Lord Mark's claim. It is clear to him that Susan knows that Densher has played a false game with Milly. Nonetheless, Susan says frankly that she is prepared to forgive him if he eases Milly's pain.

(Chapter 4) Densher meets Sir Luke, who tells him that Milly has asked for Densher to visit her. Densher does not know if she is better or worse, but he assumes that Milly is in serious danger.

Book X

(Chapter 1) The scene opens in London at Lancaster Gate, where Kate and Densher are meet-ing for tea. Densher has been in London for two weeks, and he tells Kate that he has heard nothing from Milly or Susan Stringham. Kate is surprised to discover that he does not even know if Milly has died and that he has returned to London at Milly's request. She is also alarmed to discover that at their final meeting with Milly in Venice, Densher did not deny that he was engaged to Kate. Densher is appalled that Kate could think he would lie; Kate is amazed that Densher does not understand that had Densher lied, Milly would have known it but treasured him all the more for trying to ease her suffering. Kate guesses that Densher is in love with Milly, and he does not deny it. The two remain engaged, but Milly has come between them in a way that neither could have anticipated.

(Chapter 2) Densher, frazzled from waiting for news of Milly's death, solaces himself by speaking frankly to Mrs. Lowder about the details of Milly's illness, details he has not yet shared with Kate. Alternating between a sense of his own weakness and a desire to take action, Densher demands that Kate marry him immediately so that they can begin their lives without Milly's shadow over them. He is dismayed to find Kate unwilling to do it unless he is absolutely sure that he has inherited Milly's money. This is the beginning of the estrangement between them that will only intensify once Milly dies. It is also the beginning of a chain of actions on Densher's part that show him behaving as a stricken suitor, a role he has told himself he would not play.

(Chapter 3) On Christmas Day, Densher, who has at last discovered that Milly has died, meets Mrs. Lowder at Sir Luke's door. Mrs. Lowder and Densher have come for the same reason; they wish to hear about Milly's last hours, but Sir Luke is not there. Mrs. Lowder asks Densher to dine with her and assures him that she will be alone. Kate has gone to her sister's house, where her dissolute father has suddenly taken up residence. Mrs. Lowder tells Densher that she does not approve of Kate's family feeling but that she understands it and is prepared to let Kate come back when Kate is ready.

(Chapter 4) Densher visits Kate at Mrs. Condrip's house. Densher tells her that he has received

"The Venetian Palace," by A. L. Coburn, frontispiece to the second volume of *The Wings of the Dove,* Volume 20, the New York Edition

a letter from Milly, but that he has not yet opened it. He believes that Milly wrote it long before her last hours but waited to post it until she knew with certainty that she was dying. But before Densher asks Kate to read the letter, he suddenly confronts her, asking her how Lord Mark knew that the two of them were engaged.

(Chapter 5) Kate is outraged that Densher suspects her of having tipped off Lord Mark. She

insists that Lord Mark must have guessed. Kate also realizes that Densher has lost his nerve, and she assures him that Milly will have left him a goodly part of her fortune. Densher cannot bear to open the letter. Kate, on the other hand, is so sure of its contents that she throws the unopened letter into the fire. Thus the two conspirators silence Milly's last words to Densher.

(Chapter 6) As Kate predicted, Milly has left Densher money. Two months after Milly's death—nearly a year after the events of the novel first began—Densher receives his bequest from Milly's New York lawyers. As with his previous letter from Milly, he gives it to Kate without breaking the seal. When she comes to him in his rooms, having read the letter and ascertained the amount Milly has bequeathed to him (he does not wish to know how much, and she will only say that it is "stupendous" [*WD2* 403]), he presents her with a choice. He will marry her tomorrow if she instructs him to renounce the money, but if she does not consent to his renunciation, he will not consent to marry her. Kate understands that Densher is in love with Milly's memory. Kate refuses to make a choice, and as she leaves the room, she asserts that they can never again be as they were before meeting Milly.

CRITICAL ANALYSIS

By the time James was writing *The Wings of the Dove* (1902), a novel conventionally categorized as the first of the three great novels of James's late or major phase, he was in something of an odd situation. On the one hand, he was the most distinguished and accomplished prose stylist of American literature, acknowledged by critics and devotees alike as the master of the novel form. On the other hand, he was not a particularly popular writer. He could not rely on his writing to make money, nor could he even rely on serialization in magazines to introduce his work to a broad audience before a project appeared in book form. There is no doubt that his increasing distance from a popular reading audience vexed him. *Wings,* for example, was not serialized, and James's 1909 preface to the novel's New York Edition reveals that he was only too conscious that the circumstances of its publication had a profound influence on how it was eventually received. (See PREFACES TO THE NEW YORK EDITION.) Paradoxically, James was also convinced that its fraught publication history had influenced its composition. *Wings*, he recalls somewhat mournfully, was "born, not otherwise than a little bewilderedly, into a world of periodicals and editors, of roaring 'successes' in fine, amid which, it was well-nigh unnotedly to lose itself" (9).

Despite the disingenuousness of his claim that *Wings*'s "birth" showed him that the machine of publicity and the business of publication had suddenly become one and the same thing at the turn of the last century, James's account of *Wings*'s composition helps to situate it firmly at a crossroads of his career. It also suggests several ways into the heart of this dense and morally ambiguous novel. In particular, James embraces the refusal of the market as a productive force for the text. He writes that the "cold editorial shoulder" (*WD1* xii) presented to him as he tried to get the novel serialized freed him from market constraints, enabling him to compose the text according to a peculiar logic of its own. He did not, in other words, need to fear that he was compromising his artistic or moral vision to meet a deadline or to please a normative authority, whether that authority was a single editor or a group of readers. This is a fascinating way to explain the development of a novel that is about the very possibilities of plotting both within and against economic constraints, about the wish to be free of those constraints while also recognizing their influence on a person's deepest motives and desires at the turn of the last century.

Wings is a book about delicate plots and counterplots, ethical decisions partially determined by external circumstances, and characters who read other people as instruments to selfish ends. It therefore makes sense to understand how James conceived of his role as an author—a professional maker of plots—in order to understand the powerful role of social, sexual, and economic plotting in the novel itself. Whether or not readers take the preface at its word (it is almost impossible, for example, to believe that James was surprised by the relationship between editors and writers or that he was unaware of the manifold and well-established

practices of publicity that attended the publication of fiction in the United States), it helps to identify a few ways that James was thinking about the social practices of narrative composition and reception. According to his preface, James imagined the writing of *Wings* as the result of a productive, if counterintuitive, series of refusals: a refusal of standard literary form, for he would not produce neat chapters of standard length suitable for serialization, and a refusal of deadlines because he declined to write to meet the publication dates of a periodical. How is James's management of the economic pressure as a writer related to the way in which Densher and Kate Croy manage those around them?

By the time James was composing *Wings*, and certainly by the time he published the New York Edition and its accompanying preface, later 19th-century social and cultural hierarchies were shifting; the rise of the middle classes and their seemingly endless appetite for entertainment, status, and self-improvement meant that the divisions between kinds of people, divisions that had once seemed rigid and all too legible, were softening. The popularity of a book depended on concerted efforts of advertisement to a mass audience, and authors became a sort of brand name that their PUBLISHERS promoted. A rising culture of advertising and celebrity meant that the private lives of authors were of greater interest to a general public. Although James has been charged with writing about only a small group of very wealthy and cultured people—a relatively homogeneous group of the most privileged social actors—a closer look shows us that this is not quite true either. Just as James worried over the conditions of publication of his book—imagining *Wings* as apart from the conditions of other novels—he also worries over the kinds of people who might be drawn to it—who might be drawn to literature itself. *Wings* itself is very much invested in social fragmentation, in the breakdown of standard ways of ordering social value and prestige. It gains its narrative traction because in the world of the novel, it is not possible to place the new people who constantly appeared on the social horizon. The novel is interested in how social groups assimilated or repelled outsiders, how they shaped themselves in accordance to the wills and desires of new people, how they invented pasts and futures based on the introduction of new people and new traditions, and how these new people refused to be known or to know others.

In the case of *Wings*, James is especially interested in how people with very different social backgrounds and expectations could make themselves known to one another. It is about social plotting and social reading that literally becomes a matter of life and death. Characters act on half-known information and traffic in half-understood secrets, forcing them all to act according to external pressures they only half understand as well as on behalf of other people whose motives are not always clear either to themselves or to the readers.

In some ways, then, *Wings* is about interpretation and motive. This might be said of any novel, and any James novel in particular, but is more true of *Wings*. It is a novel that allegorizes novel writing for a public that is not entirely knowable or dependable. The plot of *Wings* is remarkably straightforward. Kate Croy and Merton Densher, unable to marry because Merton does not have enough money to support Kate (who in turn does not have enough money to attain her desired social position), see in their dying friend, Milly Theale, a way to solve their problems. Kate Croy reasons that because Milly is dying and because Milly truly loves Merton Densher, it would not be wrong to arrange circumstances so that Milly might have the experience of a love affair with Merton. It will harm no one, Kate reasons. Milly will not survive long enough to marry, so Densher will never have to tell Milly the truth about his feelings. Indeed, Kate reasons that not only will no one be harmed but also everyone will in fact benefit: She and Merton and Milly will all be made happy because Kate has managed to create a narrative in which everyone's needs will be perfectly met. Although Kate evinces a sophisticated and empathetic ability to read the people around her and displays extraordinary skill at creating an elegant master narrative that can encompass and direct the people and events around her, she ultimately fails. Neither she nor Densher nor Milly is satisfied. Indeed, all of them suffer, and all lose what they most want. Milly dies knowing that Densher and Kate betrayed her; Kate and

Densher part because they cannot bear to profit from Milly's suffering.

Though Kate masterminds the novel's plots and stage-manages even its supposedly most spontaneous events, it is not easy to determine her motives. She is the agent behind many of the actions of other people who act on her behalf and according to her will, but she is not the dominant consciousness or social actor. Like most of James's novels, *Wings* employs a third-person omniscient narrator who occasionally reveals information from the position of various focalizing characters—characters from whose perspective specific events unfold. The early parts of the narrative tend to dip in and out of Kate Croy and Susan Shepherd's consciousness, and although Milly is Kate's quarry and Densher her instrument, the novel does not narrate from Milly's perspective until very late—until she begins to understand that secrets are being kept from her just at the moment when she herself must make peace with the terrible secret of her own illness. Densher, too, is very frequently the focalizing character, especially at the end of the novel, just at the moment he needs to produce a specific effect on Milly but finds his way suddenly blocked by Lord Mark.

As the narrative centers skip from focalizer to focalizer, people's motives and behaviors seem to be out of sync. That is, the narrative tends to foreground the problem of interpreting other people's motives, underscoring those moments when their behavior is out of line with the facts of the case as a character understands them. James takes his characters' drama of consciousness, a staple of realist fiction, to its formal extreme in this novel because although the plot turns on characters' coming to know or finally seeing important facts—that Milly is ill; that Kate and Densher are lovers; that Densher has told Milly the truth; that Milly's letter contains a bequest to Densher—the reader never learns what those important facts are. The novel's revelations and its refusals are mutually confirming. Readers never know, that is, what exactly is wrong with Milly; not a medical proper noun can be found, even in the conversations between Sir Luke and Milly. Neither do readers know, at the end of the book, what Densher says to Milly (although the scene in which Densher reveals to Kate that he has had a final interview with the dying girl is presented with the usual tone of Jamesian or realist fidelity). And readers never know what is in the letter from Milly to Densher; even Densher wants Kate to read it, but Kate is so sure that she knows what is in it that she burns it. The plotting or staging of interpretation—the assembling of particular people in a particular place and concerned with a particular epistemological puzzle—is, in this novel, as important as the interpretations themselves. Just as James narrated the composition of the novel around the refusal to be known and categorized, to be reduced to a mere fact in the circulation of knowledge, so too does he stage the conclusion of *Wings* around the refusal to resolve the plots that Kate has set in motion.

Critics have differed on how to read Kate Croy, in part because while she sets most of the plots in the novel in motion, she achieves her aim by getting others to act on her behalf. For some critics, she is scheming and manipulative, shrewdly willing to gamble with Milly's affections and coolly willing to trade on Densher's own sexual desire for both women. Yet the text also shows that she has the finest sensibilities of anyone in the novel; she can catch the feeling of a moment or a place and conform to it, and perhaps no one but Susan Stringham loves and understands Milly so well. She has, as Densher wonderingly puts it, a talent for life that matches what he understands to be her less estimable talent for plotting and social interpretation. She is really less like an actress or manager and more like a novelist.

This makes it especially remarkable that Kate, who engineers the plots and counterplots regarding Milly and her fortune, and who patiently guides Densher along the way, making subtle interpretive distinctions for him and guiding him as he grows closer to Milly, is rarely the dominant narrative consciousness. This is a striking disjunction between power in the narrative and power over narratives, for if Kate has the power to set plans into motion, she most certainly does not have the power to achieve what she wants without getting others to act on her behalf. Indeed, if Kate is in an odd position in the text, it is in part because of

what she represents for James. She is one of the "new people" with whom he concerned himself by 1902.

Kate is in an odd position socially, for she is the ward of a wealthy aunt but not wealthy herself. She is under obligations to her family, consisting of a demanding sister and an impecunious father, who has put himself beyond the social pale. Her beauty and her intelligence virtually ensure that she can marry well, and her relative poverty in the circle of decayed aristocrats and newly titled pretenders makes it imperative that she do so. All she has is her beauty and her wits. Her skill lies in her ability to manage those qualities and to capitalize on them. In some ways, Kate's is a class DRAMA and a series of class refusals. She cannot ignore the demands of her spoiled sister and manipulative father, but she also cannot refuse her aunt, who wishes to see her marry well. She struggles to refuse Densher but cannot. She finally gives in and sleeps with him so that he in turn will court Milly. She is precisely the new middle-class woman, rich with qualities that have no market for someone of her background.

If Kate's is the drama of the new middle class, especially the new middle class woman, she is caught in the middle of two characters with whom she can make only partial alliances. Densher and Milly are the agents of both her potential success and her final undoing. Densher, too, is a member of the new middle class. A young man with a respectable profession in journalism, he is a young cosmopolitan, having been eccentrically but well educated by his parents, and in possession of a fresh, even a democratic confidence in his power to mix in Kate's world and in his power to make her happy. Densher has all the power of his gender and his solid education to support his strangely tenuous claims to social status. Unlike Kate, he does not need money, for he has the power to earn it. At Kate's other hand is Milly, whom the narrative identifies as so totally *with* and *as* money and capital that it is virtually impossible to imagine her outside of it. The wealthy American Milly seems to transcend the fine class distinctions structuring the English quasi-aristocratic world in which she finds herself. She is new money, as James understood all American millionaires to be, but she is no mere type. On the contrary, she is a singularity. With no family to control her, no scandalous stories about the provenance of her money, she is, as Kate can never be, the master of everything she sees in her short life, for she is, as Kate can never be, unfettered by obligations and commitments.

If Kate and Densher make ethical decisions within economic constraints, feeling at every moment as if the consideration of money taints their values, Milly is apparently able to make ethical decisions outside of economic constraints. But just as James's refusal of the economic constraints of *Wings* could only ever be ideal and not real, so too can Milly's luxurious enjoyment of pure motives only ever be ideal and not real. In part, this is because Milly's decisions are made within a world in which other social actors are measuring all value in material terms; in order to be visible to them, Milly cannot be free of their motives but must be implicated in them. Indeed, when she learns that she is actually ill and dying, she also begins to understand that she will be more valuable dead than alive to her new friends When she discovers that Kate and Densher's tendencies to pet her and metaphorize her (it is Kate who first calls Milly a "dove," for example) are merely a means of converting her into something she is not, she at last understands that her freedom from material constraints has been the very social factor that has separated her from other people.

What should readers make of the ending of the novel, in which the characters try and fail to bring together ethical and material concerns, and in which there are so many refusals of knowledge, action, and responsibility that even the major characters lose track of the plot? There are the obvious refusals: The novel refuses to show Milly and Densher's final meeting; Densher and Kate refuse to read Milly's last letter, and Kate throws it into the fire; Kate refuses to meet Densher's demand that they both refuse to accept Milly's dying gift to him. These refusals are what make *Wings* such a stunning achievement in James's career, for like all of James's refusals, they are charged with a queer sort of labor. They do not just reject knowledge, they rewrite it. They do not deny relationships, they reestablish them along

disquieting lines in which knowledge and ignorance seem oddly constitutive.

Understanding Kate Croy as analogous to James's role as an author provides a particularly rich sense of how class and authorship work together. As Kate refuses to acquiesce to Densher's ultimatum, *Wings* refuses to reward and punish characters in unambiguous terms. When Kate Croy utters the novel's devastating final line: "We shall never be again as we were!" it is not merely a diagnosis. It is a command, and it is at least as applicable to the reader as to Densher. It is James's refusal of the predictable ways of resolving affections in a world where identity and the correlative drama of consciousness are more about circulation in a web of social relations than about any firm commitment to moral certainty.

CHARACTERS

Condrip, Marian Croy   Kate's sister, with whom Kate divides her small income from their mother's estate, is a young widow with four children. Marian made a bad match with a dull parson of a suburb of London. After he dies, she pins all of her hopes on her younger sister, telling her that she must marry for money.

Croy, Kate   A young woman of 25 who lives with her Aunt Maud Lowder at Lancaster Gate, she is in love with Merton Densher. "Handsome," clever, and desirous of a better estate than the one into which she was born, Kate is burdened by her sister and father with their upkeep. A master psychological strategist, Kate is responsible for setting into motion the elaborate emotional and social machinery that she hopes will ensure that she and Merton end up together with Milly's fortune.

Croy, Lionel   Kate's impecunious father, irresponsible and selfish, he has dishonored his family through scandal.

Densher, Merton   A London newspaperman, described as a "longish, leanish, fairish young Englishman" (*WD1* 48), and the child of a chaplain who has been billeted throughout the British Empire, Merton has grown up on the Continent and been eccentrically schooled. He and Kate fall in love in London, and together they agree that he shall promise himself to Milly Theale. An amiable man who trades on his charm and good looks, he is not mentally or emotionally equipped to understand fully the plotting and counterplotting set in motion around him.

Eugenio An impoverished Italian gentleman, Milly and Susan have hired him to accommodate their life in Palazzo Leporelli in Venice.

Lowder, Maud Manningham Kate's late mother's sister, she lives in Lancaster Gate in London and is at the center of a glittering social group. Shrewd, wealthy, passionate, and childless, she has agreed to take on her niece, Kate, and wishes to help her rise in the world. Although she likes Densher personally, she wishes Kate to make a socially brilliant marriage, preferably to Lord Mark.

Mark, Lord An unusually complex secondary character, Lord Mark is a nobleman whose London apartments and country estate strain his finances. He is polished and sophisticated, well-liked and well-seasoned in and by the social world of London. Led to believe by Mrs. Lowder that he has a chance to marry Kate, he also pursues Milly, who rejects him. His revenge is to spoil Kate's deepest plans by telling Milly that Densher and Kate have deceived her.

Strett, Sir Luke An esteemed London physician, he not only diagnoses Milly's terminal illness but also sends her out of London, persuading her that she must live to the fullest in the time she has left.

Stringham, Susan Shepherd An elderly and widowed writer from Boston, she travels with Milly through Europe and is responsible for introducing Milly to her old Vevey school friend, Maud Manningham Lowder. As the book wears on, Susan becomes an important confidante for Milly, as well as for Dr. Luke Strett and Merton Densher. Devoted to Milly in America, England, and Venice, Susan comes to see Milly as a "princess" and schemes with Merton to make her happy.

Theale, Milly A beautiful young American heiress, she is the only surviving member of a family that once numbered six. Sweet, innocent, ready to be pleased, Milly is one of James's favorite characters: the American girl who is ready to experience the world and its wonders without becoming jaded or sated. Milly, though imagined by her friends to be rather unworldly, shows herself to have a keener understanding of the social scene than her best friends—Kate and Merton—initially suspect. Milly suffers from an unspecified illness that eventually claims her life.

ADAPTATION

The novel was filmed in 1997 and starred Helena Bonham Carter as Kate Croy, Allison Elliott as Milly Theale, and Linus Roach as Merton Densher. It was directed by Iain Softley. The film was nominated for a number of awards and is noteworthy for its sympathetic depiction of Kate Croy as well as for its insistence that it is partially sexual passion that keeps Kate and Densher together throughout the novel.

FURTHER READING

Banta, Martha. "'Too Real': Teaching, Reading, Living Henry James." *Henry James Review* 25, no. 1 (2004): 19–32.

Barrish, Phillip. *American Literary Realism, Critical Theory, and Intellectual Prestige 1880–1995.* Cambridge: Cambridge University Press, 2001.

Freedman, Jonathan. *Professions of Taste: Henry James, British Aestheticism, and Commodity Culture.* Palo Alto, Calif.: Stanford University Press, 1990.

Hayes, Kevin, ed. The Wings of the Dove: *Henry James, the Contemporary Reviews.* Cambridge: Cambridge University Press, 1996.

Ingelbein, Raphael. "Reversed Positions: Henry James, Realism, and Sexual Passion." *Henry James Review* 21, no. 1 (2000): 63–71.

James, Henry. *The Wings of the Dove.* 2 vols. New York: Scribner's, 1909. Designated as *WD1* and *WD2.*

Martin, Michael R. "Branding Milly Theale: The Capital Case of *The Wings of the Dove.*" *Henry James Review* 24, no. 2 (2003): 103–132.

McWhirter, David. *Desire and Love in Henry James: A Study of the Late Novels.* Cambridge: Cambridge University Press, 1989.

Otten, Thomas J. *A Superficial Reading of Henry James: Preoccupations with the Material World.* Columbus: Ohio State University Press, 2006.

Rivkin, Julie. *False Positions: The Representational Logics of Henry James's Fiction.* Palo Alto, Calif.: Stanford University Press, 1996.

Salmon, Richard. *Henry James and the Culture of Publicity.* Cambridge: Cambridge University Press, 1997.

Warren, Jonathan. "'A Sort of Meaning': Handling the Name and Genealogy in *The Wings of the Dove.*" *Henry James Review* 23, no. 2 (2002): 105–135.

Yeazell, Ruth Bernard. *Language and Knowledge in the Late Novels of Henry James.* Chicago: University of Chicago Press, 1976.

Stephanie Foote, *University of Illinois at Urbana-Champaign*

SHORT STORIES AND NOVELLAS

"The Altar of the Dead"
(1895)

"The Altar of the Dead" was first published in 1895 in *Terminations*, a collection of Henry James's short stories. It appears in Volume 17 of the NEW YORK EDITION.

SYNOPSIS

George Stransom is a solitary man of 55. His fiancée, Mary Antrim, died soon after they had planned their wedding, and her death has caused an ongoing sense of loss in Stransom. But Mary is not the only dead person who holds significance for the protagonist; in the course of his life, other friends and acquaintances have died, leaving him with a community of "his Dead." Stransom understands himself as a caring and social person to the degree that he remembers these accumulated ghosts. He worships these deceased "Others" with a religious devotion.

On the anniversary of Mary Antrim's death, Stransom encounters Paul, an acquaintance whose wife has recently died. Stransom remembers his friend's wife, Kate Creston, with a protective feeling of fondness just as Paul introduces Stransom to his new wife, an American whom Stransom immediately dislikes. This woman seems a mere imitation of Kate whom Paul has replaced without a decent interval for mourning. Later the same evening, Stransom reads a newspaper account of the death

"The Halls of Julia," by A. L. Coburn, frontispiece to "Julia Bride," in Volume 17, the New York Edition. The vague or Impressionistic qualities of the image are a mark of Coburn's style.

of Acton Hague, a man who had once been his close friend before a permanent falling-out 10 years earlier. Stransom, rather than feeling sadness at the news of Hague's death, feels relieved that their public quarrel is not part of the newspaper story.

The day after visiting Mary Antrim's grave, Stransom enters a church in order to rest from walking. Noticing the altars in the church and the presence of a solitary, somber woman, Stransom is transported by the environment of dedicated mourning. He thinks of his own "silent roll call" of Dead and imagines this church to be a fitting space for an altar for his own Dead. It takes Stransom a year to cultivate enough favor with this church and its bishop to arrange for an undesignated altar to be carefully maintained. Stransom begins to visit "his" altar regularly and gets a great deal of satisfaction, even enjoyment, out of this ritual. He travels to the church each day to light candles and pay his respects. He notes to himself that his altar will never hold a candle for Acton Hague.

The lady whom Stransom saw when he first entered the church two years before begins to worship at his altar. He imagines that she, like him, must have experienced many losses during her life. Later, they see each other at a concert, and Stransom thinks she is pretty. Realizing that he now feels compelled to go to the church in part to see her again, he shudders to think that his feelings for his Dead have mixed with and been tainted by his new attraction. When he next visits his altar, he exchanges words with her. He learns that she mourns only one person and that she is a writer. They become friendly in walks together, and Stransom visits her apartment, where he learns that the person for whom she mourns at his altar is Acton Hague, with whom she was once in love. Stransom finds this very disconcerting, although initially his chief concern about Hague is whether he ever mentioned their quarrel. She implies that Hague did so when she asks Stransom if he has forgiven Hague. Stransom reveals that he had intended that his altar would never memorialize Hague.

The remainder of the story reveals a variety of reasons for the great sense of disturbance occasioned by the revelation that the lady once loved Hague. Stransom realizes that he has been falling

in love with her and, more surprising, that his past feelings for Acton Hague may have resembled love rather than hate. Stransom feels jealous and no longer enjoys spending time with the lady. They argue about Hague and the purpose of Stransom's altar. Stransom stops visiting the altar, and they do not see each other for several months. He eventually returns to the church, motivated by his responsibility to care for his Dead. When he returns, the altar seems somehow incomplete. He is deeply touched by the visiting presence of Mary Antrim's spirit, and he feels that he must add one more candle to the altar's array. Is he ready to forgive Hague? Suffering a serious illness, he again returns to visit his altar, and this time he encounters there the still unnamed lady. They desperately reconcile, but the lady is very concerned with Stransom's state. He calls her attention to the altar and its candles as if he is passing it on to her. He suggests that it lacks one candle, and as she pleads with him not to mention this, he dies. It is unclear to whom exactly Stransom was referring in exhorting the lady to add another flame to the altar of the dead.

CRITICAL ANALYSIS

In the preface to Volume 17 of the New York Edition, Henry James writes: "The sense of the state of the dead is but part of the sense of the state of the living; and, congruously with that, life is cheated to almost the same degree of the finest homage (precisely this our possible friendships and intimacies) that we fain would render it" (1,249).

The central concerns of "The Altar of the Dead" are community and intimacy. In many of his writings, James explores a triangular relationship, with all three people feeling emotionally attached to one another. In "The Altar of the Dead," the two primary characters, Stransom and the unnamed lady, develop a strong emotional connection based in large part on each of their feelings toward the late Acton Hague. While the reader knows each character has been involved with Hague, the precise nature and history of their relationships with him remain a compelling secret.

As Stransom and the lady develop a friendship that may extend to a romantic attachment, they participate in a complicated and rich love triangle.

They channel their powerful feeling for the absent and dead Acton Hague into a structure of feeling for each other. This relationship is fraught with the potentially unparallel nature of their companionate feelings for Hague; the relationship between the lady and Stransom is silently pressured by a comparison between their feelings for Hague. Do they love each other or are they drawn to each other only because they both loved Hague? A reader might believe that Stransom hates Hague since the story indicates that he has had an argument with Hague prior to Hague's death; still, Stransom's feelings about Hague are notably intense and filled with shame to the degree that he hopes Hague has not shared the story of their falling-out with anyone else.

Stransom seems to cultivate the strongest relationships with those who are no longer living. The experience of mourning also enables him to shape and imagine these relationships. The story emphasizes the importance of secrets in building personal connections, dramatizing the negotiation of privacy, and the effects of sharing sensitive information. Stransom feels very defensive about his previous relationship with Hague, and in maintaining its secret he becomes narcissistic. In conversation with the lady, he presses her as to what she has heard from Hague about himself. They never discuss Hague outside the context of Stransom's feelings toward him, and readers do not learn why she has loved Hague. Furthermore, there is no description of Hague himself, suggesting that James's story is primarily concerned with Stransom's patterns of building intimacy. As Stransom grows deeply jealous of the lady's past relationship with Hague, the reader is left to ponder why. Is he jealous of the lady's love for Hague because she may love Hague more than she loves him? Or is he jealous that Hague has loved another besides Stransom himself? The charge of emotion flows in many directions at once in this compelling love triangle, which is a characteristically Jamesian articulation of a structure of desire with the possibility of both heterosexual and homosexual intimacies.

The break or rupture in the otherwise growing attachment between Stransom and the lady seems to occur as a direct result of Stransom's jealousy and causes him to be unable to continue his worship of his dead community of friends. He is dismayed by the prospect of falling in love with her and thereby obscuring his feelings for his dead friends and possibly for Hague. Stransom seems incapable of letting go of his previous attachments. In the first half of the story, Stransom and the lady have developed a friendship that allows them to engage in a rich and mutually affective project. However, by the end, Stransom seems to be in crisis as the friendship reaches a limit. By dying, Stransom joins the community he has represented on his altar as candles.

Stransom's struggle to accept the shifting meanings of the altar, the candles, his dead, and his friendship with the lady implies deeper quandaries about the nature of language and intimacy. Andrzej Warminski interprets "The Altar of the Dead" as an engagement with the project of writing itself. Warminski considers Stransom's altar a version of history written through the symbols of the altar. He suggests that James's story portrays the writing of history as an endless and endlessly revisionary task, always subjecting to the shifting perspectives and competing versions of what has been lost to the passage of time. In this way, James's story functions as an allegory for the act of interpretation itself; we are all like Stransom, visiting the altar James conjures and pondering which attachments those candles represent.

CHARACTERS

Creston, Kate   Paul Creston's deceased wife.

Creston, Paul   An acquaintance of George Stransom, he has remarried too quickly after his wife's death, and to an unsuitable woman, in George Stransom's opinion.

Hague, Acton   A formerly close friend of George Stransom, he died 10 years after the end of their friendship; he is also the former love interest of the unnamed lady to whom Stransom is attracted.

Lady (unnamed)   A woman who worships at Stransom's altar and with whom Stransom forms an attachment.

Stransom, George The protagonist is a middle-aged man who has few living friends and who obsessively cares for his dead friends through the construction of and ritualistic worship at an altar to them.

ADAPTATION

François Truffaut, directed an adaptation of the story and "The Beast in the Jungle" called *La chambre verte* (The green room) in 1978.

FURTHER READING

James, Henry. Preface, vol. 17, *The Altar of the Dead, The Beast in the Jungle, The Birthplace, The Private Life, Owen Wingrave, The Friends of Friends, Sir Edmund Orme, The Real Right Thing, The Jolly Corner, Julia Bride.* In *Literary Criticism: French Writers, Other European Writers, The Prefaces to the New York Edition,* 1,246–1,268. New York: Library of America, 1984.

Stevens, Hugh. "Homoeroticism, Identity, and Agency in James's Late Tales." In *Enacting History in Henry James: Narrative, Power, and Ethics,* edited by Gert Buelens, 126–147. Cambridge: Cambridge University Press, 1997.

Ward, Geoff. "'The Strength of Applied Irony': James' 'The Altar of the Dead.'" In *Henry James: The Shorter Fiction: Reassessments,* edited by N. H. Reeve, 60–76. New York: St. Martin's Press, 1997.

Warminski, Andrzej. "Reading Over Endless Histories: Henry James' Altar of the Dead." *Yale French Studies* 74 (1988): 261–284.

Amanda Berry, *American University*

"The Aspern Papers" (1888)

"The Aspern Papers" was first published in the *Atlantic Monthly* (March–May 1888). That same year it was included in the book *The Aspern Papers, Louisa Pallant, The Modern Warning* (Macmillan and Co.). It was then included in Volume 12 of the NEW YORK EDITION (1908).

"Juliana's Court," by A. L. Coburn, frontispiece to "The Aspern Papers," Volume 12, the New York Edition

SYNOPSIS

(Chapter 1) The novella is set in late 19th-century VENICE. The unnamed narrator suspects that Juliana Bordereau, the former lover of poet Jeffrey Aspern, is in possession of some of the poet's papers. The narrator has traveled to Venice, intent upon retrieving the papers from the reclusive Bordereau. Following the advice of his friend, Mrs. Prest, he proposes to become Juliana and her niece's lodger and travels by gondola to their decrepit palace.

(Chapter 2) The narrator, using a false identity, meets with Tina Bordereau, Juliana's niece, and offers to rent rooms from the two ladies. He attempts to manipulate Tina with promises of refurbishing the rundown garden and filling the house with flowers. The surprised Tina agrees to discuss the matter with her aunt, and the narrator returns the next day for a meeting with Juliana. Recognizing her great age, the narrator contemplates what her death might mean for his quest.

(Chapter 3) Although unable to see her eyes due to the mask she wears, the narrator is bothered by a feeling that Juliana is impenetrable and in possession of a "fuller vision" than he. She agrees to let rooms and names an exorbitant amount of money to which the narrator agrees. Tina guides the narrator to the upper floor so that he may select his rooms. Tina reveals that the money he will pay is for her, as her aunt thinks she will need money after her death.

(Chapter 4) The narrator has lived in the house for six weeks, has had only brief contact with the two women, and has made no progress toward obtaining the papers. He resolves to remedy this situation by returning to his scheme of wooing them with flowers from the garden. As he goes about the work of refurbishing the garden, he speculates concerning the possible history he might uncover about Juliana's past.

(Chapter 5) Returning home early from an outing to the Piazza San Marco, the narrator encounters Tina in the garden. The narrator reveals that he, like Juliana, considers Aspern to be a "god." When pressed by the suspicious Tina, he further reveals that he has written about Aspern and is looking for more material.

(Chapter 6) The narrator is summoned by Juliana and is asked to take Tina to the Piazza. As they tour the sites, Tina reveals that Juliana really does possess many of Aspern's papers. Of particular concern to the narrator is that Juliana might destroy the letters as a last act before her death. The narrator elicits a promise from Tina that she will do what she can to help him.

(Chapter 7) The narrator encounters Juliana in the long room looking out over the garden. She asks him if he would like to take the rooms for six more months. The narrator points out that he is a writer whose means will not allow further extravagance. Juliana shows him a small portrait of Aspern, whom he pretends not to recognize. The narrator helps Tina move Juliana back to her rooms and sees a large secretary that he imagines may contain Aspern's papers. With great restraint, he leaves the room, telling Juliana that he will undertake to find out the value of her portrait.

(Chapter 8) Juliana is now very ill and near death. As the doctor is examining her, the narrator waits anxiously, hoping that she has not destroyed the papers in her final moments. Juliana's condition stabilizes, and the narrator learns from Tina that her aunt has moved the papers to a new hiding place. The narrator reveals his true identity to Tina, and again he asks for her help in securing the papers. Later, he returns from a walk and enters Juliana's rooms. He finds himself alone, facing the secretary that he suspects contains the papers. He imagines that Tina has unlocked it for him, and just as he opens the lid, Juliana appears in her bedroom doorway without the mask covering her eyes. Incensed, she calls him a "publishing scoundrel" and falls into Tina's arms "as if death had descended upon her" (117).

(Chapter 9) Returning to Venice after a 12-day absence, the narrator learns that Juliana has died. Tina tells him that the papers have been saved from Juliana's attempt to destroy them, but she refuses to let him see them. She tells him that if he "were not a stranger" it would be different. The narrator discerns that she is offering to grant him access to the papers if he will marry her (see MARRIAGE). The next morning, he resolves to accept the proposal, but Tina withdraws the offer and tells him that she has burned the papers. The narrator leaves Venice with only the portrait of Aspern.

CRITICAL ANALYSIS

James employs elements from gothic fiction in "The Aspern Papers." The lost manuscript, the hint of a disreputable past, the setting of a decrepit palace, and the shadowy national origins of the Bordereaus all contribute to a sense that the reader is entering a world where the knowledge of events and characters is unstable and changeable. The fact that the first-person narrator remains unnamed highlights the sense that there is something illicit about the events being related. Further, the narrator's anonymity focuses attention on what readers actually know about him: his willingness to go to almost any lengths to gain the object of his obsession.

Whereas knowledge of the narrator's identity is incomplete, readers do know that he is an

American and that "The Aspern Papers" continues James's career-long investigation into the question of national identity. As the story opens, the Bordereaus "were believed to have lost in their long exile all national quality" (53). Further, when the narrator first encounters Tina and asks her if she is an American, she replies, "I don't know; we used to be" (62). While the dangers of living abroad can lead to the adoption of many "strange ways," the "Misses Bordereau formed altogether a new type of the American absentee" (77). The aunt and niece have long since "dropped the local accent and fashion" of the American (77). To enter the "impenetrable regions" of Juliana Bordereau's palace is then to be drawn into an unstable world where even national identity is in danger of being forgotten.

Unlike The AMERICAN or The PORTRAIT OF A LADY, "The Aspern Papers" displaces the question of national identity into the "impenetrable regions" of the reclusive Bordereaus' isolated palace. The thwarted designs of Christopher Newman and the imperfect marriage of Isabel Archer point to the problems of joining the American and European worlds (see INTERNATIONAL THEME). Here, though, the struggle is to recover the lost papers, a seemingly more private quest, which takes on national implications when Aspern's status as an original American poet is taken into account.

Finding the papers becomes an imperative linked to the public memory of Aspern, whose reputation seems crucial to the narrator's own sense of national identity. Considering Aspern's expatriation in Europe, the narrator states that he "should have liked to see what he would have written without that experience" (79). The narrator's romantic desire to return Aspern to an original American context is itself "almost heroic" (79). The narrator confesses that his original love for Aspern came from the fact that Aspern was a product of America when the "native land was nude and crude and provincial" and when it was still possible to "be free and general and not at all afraid" (79). For the narrator, Aspern is representative of an imagined America, free from the "perpetual ferryings of the present hour" and thus where a purer national identity could be constructed (79).

In his preface to the 1908 edition (see PREFACES TO THE NEW YORK EDITION), James relates that the idea for the story came when he discovered that "Jane Clairmont, the half-sister of Mary Godwin, Shelley's second wife and for a while the intimate friend of Byron and the mother of his daughter Allegra, should have been living on in Florence" (404). The longing that the narrator feels for a pure American past then takes on more precision as James reimagines the history of American literature in relation to European romanticism. As James tells the story of this obsessed narrator, he is also retelling the history of American literature. The fictional Aspern thus stands in the tradition of Americans as an analogue of Thomas Jefferson, Washington Irving, or Nathaniel Hawthorne, all of whom attempted to create a unique American literature. Jeremy Tambling, however, points out the incongruous nature of James's fantasy. Tambling claims that it is crucially Walt Whitman, rather than Byron, who "would have enabled in James's mind, a connection between America and American literature, as a New York poet who did not need Europe" (46). This insight leads Tambling to claim that James's "screening out" of Whitman when discussing the tale's origin is mirrored by the narrator's inability to recognize a "particular aspect of an American's dream" having to do with a Whitmanesque vision (47). The failure of the narrator to retrieve the papers then becomes symbolic of James's failure to decipher the Whitmanian nature of American national identity.

"The Aspern Papers" is also haunted by questions concerning SEXUALITY and desire. Aspern is "not a woman's poet," yet the goal of the narrator's research continues to be figured in relation to the women in the poet's life. The narrator seeks the papers in order to dispute the impression that Aspern had "served" Juliana badly (55). In fact, readers learn that both Cumnor (a biographer of Aspern's life and editor of his works) and the narrator have dedicated themselves to acquitting the poet of "shabby behaviour" in his relations with women. Furthermore, the symbolic value of the spaces that the narrator must traverse is linked to the feminine. Jeanne Campbell Reesman points out that through the "metaphorical conquest of the female body and its attendant spaces (the house, the garden, the cabinet) the narrator homoerotically hopes to penetrate the truth about his idol" (148). As in such tales as "The BEAST IN THE JUNGLE" and "The JOLLY CORNER," the exploration of a fractured identity takes on an added sexual significance as the narrator is unable to participate fully in a conventional heterosexual relationship. As Millicent Bell has pointed out, the narrator is a "voyeur" whose "greatest desire is to possess another's love story" (193). And yet, the narrator's desire for Aspern's papers is frustrated by the perpetual displacement of the object he seeks, initially onto the 50-year-old love story between Juliana and Aspern and finally onto Tina. In his desire to possess Aspern, the narrator is driven to possess the intermediary female bodies that never lead to Aspern or his papers.

Critics have considered the narrator's frustrated quest as a commentary on the meaning of history. In the 1908 preface, James probes the relation of the past to the present: "I delight in a palpable imaginable visitable past—in the nearer distances and the clearer mysteries, the marks and signs of a world we may reach over to as by making a long arm grasp an object at the other end of our own table" (406). The narrator is frustrated in that he is unable to "grasp" the object of his obsession, and the question becomes what is actually "visitable" about the past. J. Hillis Miller claims that the narrator's "resurrection" of Juliana and his imaginings about seeing Aspern "face to face" are elements of James's ghost stories, which always deal with an attempt to "recall the dead into being" (18). The use of gothic elements also relates to a structure of history that solicits familiarity with the past but that resists any fundamental intimacy; just as Aspern both fascinates and eludes the narrator, so the past beckons. The narrator's inability to understand "the impenetrable regions" of what has passed leaves him alone, facing a mere portrait of the object, fanning and frustrating his unconventional desire.

CHARACTERS

Bordereau, Juliana   Reclusive and elderly, she is the former lover of the great poet Jeffrey Aspern. In possession of the papers that the narrator seeks, she is skeptical of historians and biographers and intensely protective of her privacy, particularly as it relates to her relationship with Aspern. While the narrator is busy trying to secure the letters, she manipulates him into paying a high price for rent and seems to have designs on him as a companion for her niece. She catches the narrator searching her room, evicts him, and shortly thereafter dies, having failed in her attempt to destroy the papers.

Bordereau, Tina   Originally Tita, renamed Tina in the 1908 edition, she is Juliana's spinster niece. Tina agrees to help the narrator so long as it does not require deceiving her aunt. She eventually finds the papers after her aunt's death but refuses to give them to the narrator unless he marries her. After the narrator changes his mind and agrees to her proposal, she rejects him and burns the papers.

Cumnor, John   The narrator's fellow researcher, Aspern scholar, and biographer, Cumnor sent the initial letters to Juliana, requesting direct access to the Aspern material. His request was denied in a letter written in Tina's hand. His failure sets in motion the plot to send the narrator to Venice.

Narrator   The narrator is an American researcher consumed with locating all material pertaining to the fictional poet Jeffrey Aspern. Suspecting that some of Aspern's papers are in the possession of the great poet's former lover, Juliana Bordereau, he travels to Venice. His obsession motivates him to take on a false identity, to violate the privacy of his hosts, and even to accept a marriage proposal from the unattractive niece of Juliana, who uses the letters as an implicit bribe.

Prest, Mrs.   A lady familiar with Americans living in Venice, she is the narrator's initial source of information about the Bordereaus, and she gives him the idea of seeking lodging in their palace.

ADAPTATION

The Lost Moment was directed by Martin Gabel; the cast included Susan Hayward, Robert Cummings, and Agnes Moorehead. It was released by Universal in 1947.

FURTHER READING

Bell, Millicent. *Meaning in Henry James.* Cambridge, Mass.: Harvard University Press, 1991.

James, Henry. "The Aspern Papers." In *Tales of Henry James: A Norton Critical Edition,* edited by Christof Wegelin and Henry Wonham. New York: Norton, 2003.

Miller, J. Hillis. "History, Narrative, Responsibility: 'The Aspern Papers.'" In *Literature as Conduct: Speech Acts in Henry James,* 12–29. New York: Fordham University Press, 2005.

Reesman, Jeanne Campbell. "The Deepest Depths of the Artificial: Attacking Women and Reality in 'The Aspern Papers.'" *Henry James Review* 19, no. 2 (1998): 148–165.

Tambling, Jeremy. "Monomania and the American Past: 'The Aspern Papers.'" In *Critical Issues: Henry James,* 77–93. New York: St. Martin's, 2000.

———. "Henry James's American Byron." *Henry James Review* 20, no. 1 (1999): 43–50.

William Pore, *State University of New York, Stony Brook*

"The Author of 'Beltraffio'" (1884)

Henry James wrote this short story in 1884 at the age of 44 while living in LONDON. "The Author of 'Beltraffio'" was first published in the June/July issue of the *English Illustrated Magazine* and was subsequently revised for inclusion in Volume 16 of Scribner's Sons' NEW YORK EDITION (1909). Recent scholarship cites the story as it appears in the collection *The Figure in the Carpet and Other Stories* (1986), which follows the New York Edition.

SYNOPSIS

(Part I) An unnamed American man narrates the story based on events that he witnessed three years before. During a visit to England, the narrator solicits an interview with Mark Ambient, the author of a work on aesthetic truth. Ambient invites the narrator to spend several days at his home, along with the author's wife (Beatrice Ambient), his spinster sister (Gwendolyn Ambient), and his beautiful but frail child (Dolcino). Upon arriving, the narrator observes that Beatrice attempts to prevent Dolcino from interacting with his father and avoids reading what her husband writes.

(Part II) Ambient shows the narrator to his room and remarks that his struggle with his wife over access to their son may result in the child's death. Later that evening, Gwendolyn announces that Dolcino is ill and that his mother is tending to him. In a private discussion with the narrator, Gwendolyn explains that Beatrice keeps Dolcino away from Ambient because she believes that her husband's ideas will corrupt the child. Ambient returns and announces that his wife has barred his access to his son's room. He then hands the narrator his book manuscript. Later, the narrator attempts to interest Beatrice in the manuscript, but she dismisses it as immoral.

(Part III) Ambient and the narrator discuss the manuscript. Ambient explains that his wife believes novels ought to be didactic and morally uplifting rather than just aesthetically pleasing, implying an irreconcilability in their domestic life. Gwendolyn tells the narrator that Dolcino needs to see a doctor, although Beatrice claims his condition has improved. In the afternoon, Ambient brings a very pale Dolcino into the drawing room, and his mother holds him possessively on her lap.

(Part IV) At Gwendolyn's suggestion, Ambient goes to fetch the doctor. Meanwhile, Dolcino's inherent sensibility inspires the narrator to suggest that Beatrice read her husband's manuscript. The doctor diagnoses Dolcino with diphtheria-like symptoms and plans to visit the next morning, but Beatrice bars his access. Gwendolyn later tells the narrator that Beatrice read Ambient's manuscript while holding the bedridden child's hand. Although Beatrice bars Ambient from his son's room, Gwendolyn checks in on the sick child and returns, ordering Ambient to fetch the doctor. Gwendolyn tells the narrator that after reading her husband's manuscript, Beatrice allowed her son to die by denying him medical attention. The narrator and Gwendolyn decide to withhold this from Ambient. Dolcino dies that day, and some months later his mother dies also. Five years later, Ambient

"The New England Street," by A. L. Coburn, frontispiece to Volume 16, the New York Edition

himself dies after completing his book, which, he tells the narrator, his wife had read before her own death, in addition to parts of "Beltraffio."

CRITICAL ANALYSIS

"The Author of 'Beltraffio'" is one of Henry James's so-called artist tales, which explore the position of the artist in modern life. The idea of the story grew from a comment made by EDMUND GOSSE concerning the poet and historian JOHN ADDINGTON SYMONDS, who was well known for his aesthetic devotion and for his homosexual encounters. James writes in his notebook that Symonds's moralistic wife inspired him to explore the "opposition between the narrow, cold, Calvinistic wife, a rigid moralist; and the husband impregnated—even to morbidness—with the spirit of Italy, the love of

beauty, of art, the aesthetic view of life, and aggravated, made extravagant and perverse, by the sense of his wife's disapproval" (*Notebooks* 57). The notebook entry touches on two dramatic elements of the story: the AESTHETIC MOVEMENT and the perceived irreconcilability of the artist with the conventions of morality.

As the author of "Beltraffio," a work that the story's narrator refers to as an "aesthetic war-cry" (57), Mark Ambient should be understood in the context of the English Aesthetic movement of the 1880s. As a movement committed to "art for art's sake," aestheticism tried to achieve beauty in art exclusive of moral, political, or social themes. Despite its purely philosophical basis, aestheticism became associated with visual excess, affectation in dress, sensuality, and homosexuality. As Viola

Hopkins Winner points out, the narrator serves as the primary aesthetic character in the story while Gwendolyn functions as the affected and stylized poseur. Ambient, Winner claims, is not an aesthete in these contrived ways but rather resembles James himself, accepting a "theory of art [that] stresses perfection of form almost as an ethical principle" (105). Hana Wirth-Nesher takes a similar view, yet argues that James does not criticize aestheticism per se, but rather the tendency to subordinate life to art or art to life. In this reading, Beatrice overestimates the power of art and becomes a fanatical aesthete by "sacrific[ing] life to preserve form—that of the perfect innocence of childhood" (119). Jonathan Freedman, however, claims that the story and its tragic ending reveal that James was attempting to criticize aestheticism because of its "destabilizing implications" for British culture (145). Regardless of James's opinion about the Aesthetic movement, the narrator's perspective on events functions to stress the centrality of representation to understanding. Can we trust a narrator so invested in metaphors of artistic form? The narrator depicts Gwendolyn as "a symbolic picture" (73), views English scenes as "reproductions of something that existed primarily in art or literature" (61), and describes Dolcino as "'some perfect little work of art'" (71). Even when Dolcino dies, the narrator observes that the boy was "more exquisitely beautiful in death than he had been in life," implying that his beauty is heightened by his sacrifice.

The story has received much critical attention owing to its covert suggestions of homosexuality. The narrator notes how his heart "beat very fast" (59) when he first sees the author and how he felt "happy and rosy, in fact quite transported" by the touch of his hand (60). Reading a homoerotic undercurrent into the story's tragic ending, Leland Monk views "The Author of 'Beltraffio'" as James's repudiation of aestheticism for its "public and flagrant suggestion of a homosexual life" that "threatened to call attention to James's more private and discreet passion for members of his own sex" (247). Avoiding biographical claims, Leland Person reads the story as a coded confrontation between homosexual and heterosexual desire, with Dolcino representing the generative power of heterosexuality, and Ambient's writing as the "creative or recreative potential of homoerotic desire" (113). Person argues that the homoerotic atmosphere in the first half of the story is counteracted by Beatrice's eventual willingness to read her husband's writing, an act that operates as a symbolic heterosexual restoration (114).

Ultimately, "The Author of 'Beltraffio'" is a puzzle that self-consciously resists any resolving of heterosexual desire with aestheticism. As Kevin Ohi argues, this indecipherability may precisely be the story's point because any definite statement about the story's view of aestheticism aligns the reader with one of the characters' flawed mindsets. For example, reading the story as an objection to aestheticism aligns the reader with Beatrice, who kills her son to preserve his supposed innocence. Further, what of the narrator's hasty dismissal of Gwendolyn, who might offer a more balanced sense of the relationship between aesthetic experience and parental responsibility? Ohi argues that the story's indecipherability "enacts the dynamics of aestheticism it describes" (761). Thus, aestheticism, homoerotic desire, and the relationship between a master and his disciple are all issues with not one meaning but instead several conflicting meanings that hang ambiguously—like the meaning of James's story—just beyond the reader's grasp.

CHARACTERS

Ambient, Beatrice   Mark Ambient's beautiful and reserved wife is obsessively devoted to the protection of her son. Her religiosity and moral sensibilities lead her to conclude that her husband's intellectual ideas will pollute her son's character. She avoids reading her husband's work, which she condemns to the narrator as "'most objectionable!'" (83).

Ambient, Dolcino   Beatrice and Mark Ambient's frail seven-year-old child's angelic beauty entrances the narrator. Although he hardly speaks in the story, Ambient, Beatrice, and even the narrator, all long to possess him exclusively. As Dolcino's health deteriorates, his beauty increases for the narrator.

Ambient, Gwendolyn   Mark Ambient's spinster sister spends a month with the Ambients twice a year. She has a number of aesthetic affectations, including her tendency to dress in a medieval style and to strike dramatic poses when speaking. The narrator finds her offensive because "her affectations rubbed off on her brother's renown" (74). Beatrice also dislikes her. After her brother's death, Gwendolyn retires to a nunnery.

Ambient, Mark The renowned English author of "Beltraffio," which the narrator describes as an "aesthetic war-cry" about the "gospel of art" (57), he is working on a book about his impressions of the East, through which he hopes to "'give the impression of life itself'" (87). He remains continually disturbed by his wife's attempt to screen his son from him.

Narrator A young American admirer of Mark Ambient's work, he has read "Beltraffio" five times. During his stay with the Ambients, he devotes himself to two aims: better understanding Mark's character and influences and convincing Beatrice to read her husband's writing. In hindsight, he notes that in convincing Beatrice to read her husband's work he may have contributed to Dolcino's death (99).

FURTHER READING

Freedman, Jonathan. *Professions of Taste: Henry James, British Aestheticism, and Commodity Culture.* Palo Alto, Calif.: Stanford University Press, 1990.

Gardaphe, Fred L. "The Echoes of Beltraffio: Reading Italy in Henry James's 'The Author of Beltraffio'." *RLA: Romance Languages Annual* 1 (1989): 121–127.

James, Henry. *The Notebooks of Henry James.* Edited by F. O. Matthiessen and Kenneth B. Murdock. Chicago: University of Chicago Press, 1981.

Knox, Melissa. "Beltraffio: Henry James' Secrecy." *American Imago: Studies in Psychoanalysis and Culture* 43, no. 3 (1986): 211–227.

Kraver, Jeraldine R. "All about 'Author-ity': When the Disciple Becomes the Master in "The Author of Beltraffio." In *'The Finer Thread, The Tighter Weave': Essays on the Short Fiction of Henry James,* 30–42. West Lafayette, Ind.: Purdue University Press, 2001.

Monk, Leland. "A Terrible Beauty Is Born: Henry James, Aestheticism, and Homosexual Panic." *Bodies of Writing, Bodies in Performance,* 247–265. New York: New York University Press, 1996.

Ohi, Kevin. "'The Author of Beltraffio': The Exquisite Boy and Henry James's Equivocal Aestheticism." *ELH* 72, no. 3 (2005): 747–767.

Person, Leland S. "Homo-Erotic Desire in the Tales of Writers and Artists." In *Henry James and Homo-Erotic Desire,* 111–123. Basingstoke, England; New York: Macmillan; St. Martin's Press, 1999.

———. "James's Homo-Aesthetics: Deploying Desire in the Tales of Writers and Artists." *Henry James Review* 14, no. 2 (1993): 188–203.

Schehr, Lawrence R. "'The Author of Beltraffio' as Theory." *MLN* 105, no. 5 (1990): 992–1,015.

Treitel, Ilona. "Absence as Metaphor in Henry James's 'The Author of "Beltraffio."'" *Studies in Short Fiction* 34, no. 2 (1997): 171–182.

Winner, Viola Hopkins. "The Artist and the Man in 'The Author of Beltraffio'." *PMLA: Publications of the Modern Language Association of America* 83, no. 1 (1968): 102–108.

Wirth-Nesher, Hana. "The Thematics of Interpretation: James's Artist Tales." *Henry James Review* 5, no. 2 (1984): 117–127.

Shalyn Claggett, *Mississippi State University*

"The Beast in the Jungle" (1903)

"The Beast in the Jungle" was written during Henry James's late phase, published just a year before *The GOLDEN BOWL.* The 1903 novella first appeared in *The Better Sort,* a short story collection published simultaneously by Methuen and Company (LONDON) and Charles Scribner's Sons (NEW YORK). James added a preface for the 1909 publication of *The Novels and Tales of Henry James,* Volume 17 of the NEW YORK EDITION.

SYNOPSIS

(Chapter 1) Set in fin-de-siècle London, the novella opens at the Weatherend estate. A group of visitors is wandering around the estate's ancestral halls peering at its treasures, paintings, heirlooms, and collectibles while caught up in "the dream of acquisition" (303). John Marcher, however, feels trapped among all these fine items and fine people, unable to determine the "proper relationship" he is to have with the things that surround him. Soon, though, Marcher happens upon a face he seems to remember from years prior. Marcher is reacquainted with Miss May Bartram, a woman he had met 10 years before in Naples. Just as Marcher begins to be disappointed that there may be no excitement to be found in this reacquaintance, May paralyzes him with a question: had "*the thing*" happened to him yet? Marcher is shocked to be informed that he had confided a secret in May those many years ago in Sorrento, *the* consuming secret of his life: a lurking feeling that some terrible thing would happen to him at some point in his life. By the end of their meeting, May has reassured John that she does not think him delusional for his belief that some unknowable, unnameable "beast in the jungle" is to spring upon him. John pleads with her to stay near to "watch" with him, since it will, he thinks, only be through the observation of *the* thing by another as something "unnatural" that John himself will know the beast has, in fact, sprung. May seems to understand the logic in this and agrees to stand by and "watch."

(Chapter 2) So begins a bizarre, lifelong companionship between Marcher and May that revolves around endless conversations about "*the thing*," whose name cannot be spoken. May's great-aunt—and guardian—passes away. Left without relations (her mother having died years ago), May secures a small estate in London with the help of her recently acquired inheritance. John is thrilled that with the move his meetings with May will be made much more frequent. John reminds himself that he cannot be too selfish in his conversations with May; even though she has invested in his predicament, he must remember that she might over the course of her life have things "happen to *her*" (312). He continues to reflect on the "form" (312) their relationship might take, immediately dismissing the possibility of MARRIAGE since it would be unfair to ask a

woman to share in his misery while waiting for the beast. May continues to "watch," speaking of the secret to John only as "the real truth about you" (315). The pair continues in this way as they grow older, the mention of the "real truth" always lingering explicitly or implicitly in their conversations. John visits May on her birthday and brings her a gift to prove, to himself, that he is not selfish. At the end of an especially dramatic conversation about the beast, John nervously asserts to May, "You know what's to happen . . . You know and you're afraid to tell me" (319).

(Chapter 3) John continues to worry about his selfish investments in his friendship with May as an ongoing opportunity for endless narcissistic psychic reflection. He convinces himself otherwise by extending frequent invitations to the opera, dinner, and other diversions from the primary obsession of his life. He asks May how it is that her reputation has not been harmed by her association with a queer man such as himself. May responds that the two have actually been much talked about because of their suspiciously intimate relations. Apparently, however, this does not bother May since she sees her duty as one of helping John "pass" for an ordinary man. John begins to have a dreaded sense that he might lose May. May tells John that she fears she is ill. In the shock of this statement, John worries that May will not live to see what will happen to him, since it had become the basis of her life. John suddenly looks upon May and seeing how old she has become, recognizes his own age. Full of despair, John hopes his life of waiting will not ultimately be in vain.

(Chapter 4) In the spring, John visits May, who sits with him in front of a fireless hearth with the look of someone waiting for death. John notices how she has aged and feels abandoned and, to some extent, betrayed by the woman who was supposed to be by his side to "watch." Obviously fearing the approaching death of his companion, John anxiously pushes May to help him process his recent thoughts about his "truth." He continues to prod her and again accuses her of knowing what is to happen to him. A traumatized May collapses into the arms of a maid, who is none too pleased to see how John has upset the lady of the house.

(Chapter 5) May is too ill to see John. He continues to worry that her impending death is his "beast in the jungle" and that his destiny is to see her die. On their last meeting, May informs John that the thing has happened without his even knowing it. John is horrified to hear from May that to suffer some grand feeling or "thing" is not necessarily to have known it. May passes away. At her funeral, an already miserable John is even more disappointed to realize that no one in attendance even recognizes the intimacy he had with May. With his exceptional moment passed without his knowledge of it, John resigns himself to living with the tormenting question of an "unidentified past." During May's life, he was obsessed with a future that had not yet come, and in her death he finds himself living in the past, mourning the "lost stuff of his consciousness" (335).

(Chapter 6) John leaves London for East Asia, where he wanders for a year. Back in London, he repeatedly visits May's grave, where he feels most alive since May, under the ground, still "knows." One day, he is struck by the face of a fellow mourner, in whom Marcher sees his own reflection but also sees a man who has genuinely felt something for another, a kind of passion and sympathy never experienced by the almost insufferably egotistical John Marcher. At this moment, John realizes: It was *she* whom he had missed. The terrible thing is that absolutely nothing is to happen to him: "The escape would have been to love her; *then* he would have lived" (339). With this knowledge, John has a hallucinating image of the beast about to lunge. And with that, he flings himself onto May's grave in utter desperation.

CRITICAL ANALYSIS

Scholarship has traditionally characterized James's fiction by narratives that value thick interiority over thin plots and foreground the life of the individual mind over the external actions of a particular character or set of characters. As a text where the inner workings of the egomaniacal protagonist's psyche also serve as the central concern of the plot (a neurotic man obsessed by a nagging, lurking feeling), "The Beast in the Jungle" might be the best example of such an understanding of James's

oeuvre. In fact, critics have often cited the 1903 novella as the author's most finely crafted piece of short fiction, perhaps in part because of the way in which it so artfully dramatizes James's thematic *and* formal concerns.

In his preface to the 1908 edition of "The Beast in the Jungle," James writes, "[Marcher] . . . has indeed been marked and indeed suffered his fortune—which is precisely to have been the man in the world to whom nothing whatever was to happen" (*Tales of Henry James* 417). This is a story in which nothing happens, and that, for the main character, and perhaps also for readers, is the tragedy of his disappointingly mundane life. R. W. B. Lewis notes that the brilliance of James's narrative achievement in "The Beast in the Jungle" derives from the fact that "the story has come to us through the 'consciousness' of a man who has no consciousness, no awareness whatever, within the tight enclosure of his ego, of the reality of other human beings" (xvii). At the same time, however, that Marcher is so alienated and distanced from the world around him, there is something to be sympathized with; in fact, there is a kind of uncomfortable familiarity that readers and critics alike have identified with in their reading, namely the common search for meaning in life and the validation of one's existence in the world. Indeed, in the ego-bound narrative world of "The Beast in the Jungle," James forces his readers into the same kind of proximity to Marcher and the entangling maze of his internal life that May herself possesses throughout the narrative. In other words, readers are, alongside May, asked to "wait" and to endlessly conjecture on the nature of this vague feeling that haunts Marcher. Ultimately, James thwarts narrative expectations, refusing to give a climax and resolution to Marcher's lifelong obsession and perhaps, thus, rejecting a satisfying conclusion for the narrative itself.

Beginning in the 1970s, many female critics started taking James's female characters seriously in their analyses (see, for example, Mary Doyle Springer, *A Rhetoric of Literary Character: Some Women of Henry James* [1978]). Reading outside the obsessions and intricacies of Marcher's psychic life, May is revealed in such criticism as a psychologically complex and important character in her own right. In the mid-1980s, Eve Kosofsky Sedgwick's groundbreaking "The Beast in the Closet: James and the Writing of Homosexual Panic" expanded the critical analysis of gender in "The Beast in the Jungle" beyond a focus on the female body and the limiting lens of feminine subjectivity in the Victorian age (see VICTORIANISM) in order to think in more complicated ways about the intersections of gender, SEXUALITY, MASCULINITY, and femininity in the paranoid world of the novella. Where readings of gender in "The Beast in the Jungle" have traditionally found a deep-seated fear of femininity in the text, viewing Marcher's failure as his inability to love May, Sedgwick places "The Beast in the Jungle" in the context of rampant cultural anxieties over homosexuality in turn-of-the-century England. Rather than thinking in terms of simply male and female, Sedgwick focuses on the new Victorian "categories" of homosexuality and heterosexuality. In 1990, "The Beast in the Closet" was turned into a chapter of Sedgwick's *Epistemology of the Closet,* a foundational text for queer studies.

CHARACTERS

Bartram, May The female protagonist of the story serves as Marcher's confidante in all things related to the dreaded "Beast in the Jungle" lying in wait. May—or Miss Bartram—lives with her great-aunt, her mother having died, until the "ancient" woman passes away herself. May, apparently left without any relations, takes a small estate in London with the help of an inheritance from the great-aunt. She spends the rest of her life receiving visits from Marcher, withers and grays without a consecrated love or marriage, grows ill and dies a spinster, leaving Marcher to agonize over his secret alone.

Marcher, John The egotistical male protagonist spends his life obsessing over a feeling he has that something "exceptional" will occur in his life. He resides in London until after May's death. Having realized that perhaps it was the tragedy of missing her love that was his ultimate

and most terrible destiny, he wanders East Asia for a year before returning to London. The rest of Marcher's life remains quite obscure except for a few details given of the other "forms he went through," including "those of his little office under Government, those of caring for his modest patrimony, for his library, for his garden in the country, for the people in London whose invitations he accepted and repaid . . ." (315).

ADAPTATIONS

La bête dans la jungle (1962) is a play by James Lord.

La chambre verte (1978) was directed by French filmmaker François Truffaut. He combined "The Altar of the Dead," an 1895 short story by James, and "The Beast in the Jungle" in this film adaptation.

La bête dans la jungle (1988) was adapted for French television by Marguerite Duras.

FURTHER READING

The Norton Critical Edition of *The Tales of Henry James,* edited by Cristof Wegelin and Henry B. Wonham, includes the text of the novella along with eight other pieces of short fiction. The second edition also provides relevant background on the origin of "The Beast in the Jungle," a section on James's craft, a preface to the piece by the author, and an excerpt from Eve Kosofsky Sedgwick's article, "The Beast in the Closet: James and the Writing of Homosexual Panic."

Buelens, Gert, ed. *Enacting History in Henry James: Narrative, Power and Ethics.* Cambridge: Cambridge University Press, 1997.

Goodheart, Eugene. "What May Knew in 'The Beast in the Jungle.'" *The Sewanee Review* 111, no. 1 (2003): 116–127.

James, Henry. "The Beast in the Jungle." In *The Tales of Henry James,* edited by Cristof Wegelin and Henry B. Wonham, 2d ed., 303–340. New York: W.W. Norton, 2003.

———. "On 'The Beast in the Jungle.'" In *The Tales of Henry James,* 417–418.

Jones, O. P. "The Cool World of London in *The Beast in the Jungle.*" *Studies in American Fiction* 6 (1978): 227–235.

———. "In Possession of a Secret: Rhythms of Mastery and Surrender in 'The Beast in the Jungle.'" *Henry James Review* 19, no. 1 (1998): 17–35.

Kau, Joseph. "Henry James and the Garden: A Symbolic Setting for 'The Beast in the Jungle.'" *Studies in Short Fiction* 10 (1973): 187–198.

Lewis, R. W. B. Introduction to *The Turn of the Screw and Other Short Fiction*. New York: Bantam Books, 1983.

Lindholdt, Paul J. "Pragmatism and 'The Beast in the Jungle.'" *Studies in Short Fiction* 25, no. 3 (1988): 275–284.

Lucke, Jessie Ryon. "The Inception of 'The Beast in the Jungle.'" *New England Quarterly: A Historical Review of New England Life and Letters* 26, no. 4 (1953): 529–532.

Montgomery, Lomeda. "The Lady Is the Tiger: Looking at May Bartram in 'The Beast in the Jungle' from the 'Other Side.'" In *'The Finer Thread, The Tighter Weave': Essays on the Short Fiction of Henry James*, edited by Joseph Dewey and Brooke Horvath, 139–148. West Lafayette, Ind.: Purdue University Press, 2001.

Perluck, Herbert. "The Dramatics of the Unspoken and Unspeakable in James's 'The Beast in the Jungle.'" *Henry James Review.* 12, no. 3 (1991): 231–254.

Putt, S. Gorley. *Henry James: A Reader's Guide*. Ithaca, N.Y.: Cornell University Press, 1966.

Sedgwick, Eve Kosofsky. "The Beast in the Closet: James and the Writing of Homosexual Panic." In *Sex, Politics and Science in the Nineteenth-Century Novel*, edited by Ruth Bernard Yeazell, 148–186. Baltimore: Johns Hopkins University Press, 1986.

———. "The Beast in the Closet: James and the Writing of Homosexual Panic." In *The Epistemology of the Closet*, 182–212. Berkeley: University of California Press, 1990.

Springer, Mary Doyle. *A Rhetoric of Literary Character: Some Women of Henry James*. Chicago: University of Chicago Press, 1978.

Tompkins, Jane P. "'The Beast in the Jungle': An Analysis of James's Late Style." *Modern Fiction Studies* 16 (1970): 185–191.

Britt M. Rusert, *Duke University*

"Brooksmith" (1891)

James first made a note for the story that was to become "Brooksmith" in 1884, and according to R. W. B. Lewis, it was written in the wake of a long, productive, and consolidating trip to Italy over the winter of 1886–87 (400). The story first appeared in *Harper's Weekly* in the United States and in *Black and White* in Britain. Magazine publication was simultaneous and took place on May 2, 1891. The tale's first book appearance was in the collection *The Lesson of the Master*, published simultaneously in the United States and Britain in 1892. When James assembled his NEW YORK EDITION between 1907 and 1909, a very slightly revised "Brooksmith" appeared in Volume 18 in October 1908.

SYNOPSIS

"Brooksmith" is told in a first-person narration by an unnamed male figure who is on one level external to and on another integral to the events he narrates. Brooksmith is the butler of a retired bachelor diplomat, Mr. Offord, living in LONDON. Key to both Mr. Offord's household and life, Brooksmith is represented by the narrator as both silently running and silently participating in the urbane, civilized, literate and, above all, happy conversation that takes place under his employer's roof. When Mr. Offord falls ill and eventually dies, Brooksmith is obliged to leave his distinguished employer's house. On the day of his departure, Brooksmith's silence breaks, and he makes an astounding speech evidencing his utter devotion to his deceased employer.

After several unsuccessful attempts to gain further employment, unsuccessful either because it is assumed that he has been somehow "spoiled"—a key word in this story and, quite literally, its last word—or because he has worked in an entirely male household, Brooksmith falls ill. The narrator visits him at his aunt's house, a milieu as far away as possible in terms of gender, class, and aesthetics from Mr. Offord's. Subsequently, the narrator is embarrassed to see him working as a waiter for hire at a dinner party. Over the months, the narrator sees less and less of Brooksmith. Three years later, he learns from the aunt that her nephew has disappeared. Both the aunt and the narrator assume that Brooksmith, whose spirit has increasingly become a haunting vision, has committed suicide.

CRITICAL ANALYSIS

"Brooksmith" is a little gem, and it has sat, a bit like its hero, bravely feigning a disregard of the general indifference with which it has been regarded, yet stolidly confident of its place in the world. It was an act of genius on the part of Christof Wegelin to include it in his *Tales of Henry James* for Norton, and when that edition was revised for publication in 2003, it was an act of intelligent reverence on the part of Henry Wonham to keep it there. Leon Edel, in the part of his five-volume biography that covers the years 1884–94, gives "Brooksmith" no attention whatsoever. Fred Kaplan describes it as "a subtle indictment of the British class structure" (367). He situates it in the midst of James's attempts to become a playwright in the 1890s and the writing of "The PUPIL." Picking up on one phrase in the story ("Brooksmith . . . was the artist") R. W. B. Lewis situates it among James's tales of "art and the artist," "art and life," and "art . . . as an analogy for all other modes of conduct" (400). For the most part, critics, whatever their point of interest, have generally disregarded James's story.

In its small, quiet way the tale encapsulates the best and the most complex of what distinguishes James as a writer. Yet it does so with a luminous accessibility and brevity. For those starting to read James or for someone wondering where to begin a consideration of James's oeuvre, "Brooksmith"—a story about the problem of beginning again—is ideal. Several areas make it such an ideal starting place. The first is narration. In "Brooksmith" there is a compressed and clear instance of retrospective, anonymous first-person narration that James would also use in larger and more complex tales such as "The ASPERN PAPERS" (1888) and "The TURN OF THE SCREW" (1898). As with those stories, an unnamed figure—in this case a male guest at Mr. Offord's salon—presents a retrospective view of a situation in which he functions as a kind of liminal figure. A figure, such as guest, lodger, or governess, stands outside the key relationships of the given story and yet also confirms and supports the domestic structure. The domestic status of these kinds of figures has a counterpart in their relation to the events they narrate. If these figures are on one level not *necessary* to the structures they inhabit, how to evaluate their reliability as narrators? There will always be something they do not know, and their way of telling the story may well be a way of disguising this. Furthermore, these narrators do not seem unbiased or disinterested. They often seem to want something out of the situation they are describing.

The narrator of "Brooksmith" is a visitor to Mr. Offord's house. He writes from a position of not knowing. Equally he writes from a position of desire. The house in Mansfield Street has something for him. In "Brooksmith," readers have to be aware of this double position of the narrator, both his involvement in and distance from a situation that greatly interests him. This makes the reader's relationship to "Brooksmith" complex and tricky but also active and rewarding. Readers have to compose, not receive, and James does not provide a means for that process of composition to come to an end. This is a story with a conjectural ending that lacks a firm conclusion, much as it gives the sense of a deeply grim outcome. Not only, then, is "Brooksmith" about beginning again; it is, in itself, a beginning.

So the peculiar *form* of James's first-person narration provokes reading that is active and creative. The peculiarities of style do the same. As a story of the early 1890s, it does not have the complexities of James's post-1897 work (this was the year in which James gave up writing by hand and took to dictation). "Brooksmith" is written with a lean, elegant, and mournful economy. Yet at the same time, James's choice of words, the flow of his sentences, and his distribution of proper names all make reading "Brooksmith" a far more inventive act, something closer to actually *writing* the story than might at first appear. This is a story about a man who temporarily possesses and then loses an imaginative space, a loving bond, and a linguistically delicate, expansive universe. Therefore, the texture and features of James's writing are always keeping that kind of space open to the reader; the textures of the words provide the sense of what is lost.

One striking feature of style is the *interconnectedness* of the tale's sentences, something that echoes and structurally produces the illusion of both imaginative space and linguistically felicitous community. Each sentence responds to, flows from, or bounces off its predecessor so that the whole story, regardless of the content of each sentence, is made of echoes and responses like a room full of conversation. For example: "We felt this, covertly, at the time, without formulating it, and were conscious, as an ordered and prosperous community, of his evenhanded justice, untainted with flunkeyism" (175). The demonstrative *this* and the pronoun *his* refer, respectively, to the feeling of the salon that, in a key phrase, "Brooksmith . . . was the artist!" (175). *His* refers to Brooksmith himself. The placement of both words in the sentence illustrates the earlier point about the stylistic centrality of interconnectedness between sentences. If this is how the sentence provides a sense of felicitous community, how does it provide a sense of imaginative space? Partially because the structure of this sentence, with its frequent but neat subordinations—*covertly, at the time, without formulating it,* and so on—refuses to simply provide the narrative information that Mr. Offord's community implicitly recognized that Brooksmith was the genius behind their collective happiness. The sentence's rhythmic structure, which is both interruptive and cumulative, dips the reader into point after point of nuance, indication, irony, and anxiety in a quiet but intensely provocative way. The reader might, for example, wonder about the occurrence of that word *covertly*. If one imagines the sentence without this word, if one imagines its first clause reading, "We felt this at the time without formulating it," then a whole world of shade, nuance, and possibility slips away. James's inclusion here of the word *covertly* opens up all kinds of questions. Not least of these is the degree to which a communal feeling can, in fact, exist in a covert way. Or is the word *covertly* an act of retrospective supposition on the part of the narrator? Is the narrator using the word *covertly* here to signal that this shared feeling about Brooksmith as artist existed in spite of the fact that he had no evidence for this and so, possibly, never existed at all? And we might think, too, in terms of how the *sound* of the word *covertly* affects this sentence. "We felt

this at the time without formulating it" is nicely alliterative, syntactically neat, yet banal. "We felt this, covertly, at the time without formulating it" maintains that sense of order and structure but introduces—acoustically as well as semantically—elements of disturbance, texture, and possibility. And, of course, the inclusion of such a word keeps the question of "the covert" hauntingly operative in the processes of reading "Brooksmith."

"Brooksmith" can certainly be read, in Kaplan's terms, as indicting class structure. Both the nature of the relationship between Offord and Brooksmith as it is related by the narrator, and the fact of Offord's death, place two kinds of pressure on this system, which the narrator unquestioningly registers without interrogating critically. But if James's choice of first-person narrator—placeless, invited, and desiring—encourages one to read critically in narrative terms, then it trains one to think beyond the narrator in ideological terms—to have a critical edge that the narrator sharply lacks. James's story registers not only the cruelty of the British class system but also the ways in which persons produced by such a system are in a profound sense subjectivized through cruelty.

In terms of class, "Brooksmith" can therefore be read next to The PRINCESS CASAMASSIMA (1886), The SPOILS OF POYNTON (1897), or "IN THE CAGE" (1898). What makes its critique of the class system so intense and valuable, though, is the very reason it has been neglected. This story lacks the dark brooding awkwardness and menace of *The Princess Casamassima,* the crisp, camp comedy of *The Spoils of Poynton,* the interpretive extravagance and audacity of "In the Cage." "Brooksmith" is a small story about a small person (as is repeatedly emphasized, this character has the rare distinction in James of being allocated an exact height, "five feet two" [176]). It is difficult not to conclude that the very diminutive scale of both the story and its hero's fate exposes the class system as determining who is "small" and maintaining them as such.

And if this is true of class, then it is also true of two other categories with which James criticism has been preoccupied in the last decade or so: SEXUALITY and nationality. Denis Flannery's essay concentrates on the vocabulary and practice of devotion in "Brooksmith" and relates this not only to queer theory but, again, to James's critical engagement with a common assumption in 19th-century ideology: that to experience and enjoy same-sex love is in some way a symptom of deficient devotion to powerful categories of loyalty—nation, profession, and family. This is a very particular aspect of the queer legibility of James's tale and is a key part of the legacy of what might be termed "queer narratives of service," of which "Brooksmith" is a part.

"Brooksmith" is one of James's most "English" stories, but in being so it manages to both enact and interrogate a powerful and conflicting set of assumptions about Victorian imperial nationality at the end of the 19th century. The story's representation of Mr. Offord coolly sets out and critiques English suspicion, xenophobia, and simultaneous dependence on "foreign" cultural capital. James's narrative method makes these things intensely *present* to the reader at the same time it enables the reader to gain a critical perspective on them. This simultaneous enactment and critique of widespread (particularly anti-French) xenophobia coexist brilliantly with the story's deployment of queer sexuality. The one cannot exist without the other.

James's stature as a writer resides in many ways in his capacity to articulate, often precisely through nonarticulation, key, forgotten, and troublingly valuable aspects of what constitutes human subjectivity. There is a lot of silence in "Brooksmith," the silence of specific characters and that of the narrator's sleights and evasions. Equally, there is a moment, just over halfway through the story, when silence breaks, when, after Mr. Offord's death, Brooksmith speaks to the narrator of his loss of his employer in rapturous, grief-stricken, and finally lucid terms. "You go back," he says, "to conversation, sir, after all, and I go back to my place" (182). This brief eruption on Brooksmith's part testifies to worlds of feeling, affect, and potential. Like other powerfully silent figures in James, Brooksmith moves out of silence into one vivid moment of the communicative and then back into a (transformed) silence again. These silences point to two key aspects of both James's ethics and James's sense

of the human: first, a practice of intimacy centered on respect for the enigma of identity, and, second, a respect for what cannot be known or captured about others. These strands of James's ethics and his sense of the human are present with luminous concision in "Brooksmith," even as the story traces a social process tantamount to the annihilation of both.

CHARACTERS

Aunt This unnamed person visits the narrator twice, first after Offord's death and, then, at the story's end to suggest the possibility of Brooksmith's own. She lives in a "short, sordid street in Marylebone" (184) and is represented as one of a number of "vague, prying, beery females" who surround Brooksmith as he recovers from his first illness (185). Though sketchily portrayed, she is a crucial conduit of information and embodies the grotesque material and affective consequences of Offord's death on Brooksmith.

Brooksmith The "butler and most intimate friend" of Mr. Offord is the story's central figure and its most physically described and "present" character (173). He is short; his bodily presence amounts to that of a "spare, brisk little person"; he has a "cloistered white face," "extraordinarily polished hair," and "small, clear, anxious eyes." Brooksmith has some sort of a beard ("a permitted, though not exactly encouraged tuft on his chin"), and the narrator gives him an age as exact as his height, describing him as a "sensitive young man of thirty-five" (176). The whole story revolves around Brooksmith's smallness and sensitivity, both of which exist uncomfortably next to his given milieu.

Narrator This unnamed figure is discussed in more detail in the critical analysis above. Readers learn nothing about him other than his gender and his accessibility to a certain milieu in London society. Because of a comment he makes about Brooksmith being a "young man" of 35, one can assume he is older than that. Unlike the experience of the narrators in "The Aspern Papers" or "The Turn of the Screw," no one asks him any questions, so he offers no information or response.

Offord, Mr. Brooksmith's employer is "a retired diplomatist" and "the most delightful Englishman any one had ever known" (173). The narrator's praise of Offord is ambivalent. He manages to insinuate that Offord may have been deficient as a diplomat and possibly even treacherous. These insinuations sit next to a persistent equation in the story between Offord and French culture. He teaches Brooksmith French so that, together, the two of them can read Montaigne's essays and the *Memoirs* of the Duc de Saint Simon. His social gatherings are described in the same terms used to designate the French and feminine practice of the salon. Offord is the story's solid base and the source of its most queer and prevaricating energies. His death signals the demise of Brooksmith.

FURTHER READING

Denis Flannery. "Henry James's 'Brooksmith': Devotion and Its Discontents." *The Yearbook of English Studies* 37, no. 1 (2007): 89–107.

James, Henry. "Brooksmith." In *Tales of Henry James,* edited by Christof Wegelin and Henry B. Wonham, 173–187. New York and London: Norton, 2003.

Kaplan, Fred. *Henry James: The Imagination of Genius: A Biography.* London: Hodder and Stoughton, 1992.

Lewis, R. W. B. *The James's: A Family Narrative.* London: Andre Deutsch, 1991.

Denis Flannery, *University of Leeds*

"Crapy Cornelia" (1909)

One of James's last short stories, "Crapy Cornelia," was originally published in *Harper's* in October 1909. Finished too late for inclusion in the NEW YORK EDITION, it was published in the collection *The Finer Grain* (1910).

SYNOPSIS

White-Mason sits in NEW YORK's Central Park, feeling alienated from the youth around him and debating whether to propose MARRIAGE to the young rich widow Mrs. Worthingham. Each time he had previously tried to propose, something or someone has interrupted. Although irritated by the "gloss of new money" that has taken over his Old New York, White-Mason confidently thinks that he is still young enough to ask for the widow's hand (504). His enthusiastic mood changes when he arrives at her home. Her Louis XIV decor is as overwhelming as usual, and she has a guest. He is struck by the contrast between Mrs. Worthingham's fashionable, sunny style and the visitor's plain, dark appearance. Mrs. Worthingham fails to introduce him but seems nevertheless pleased at his arrival. He suddenly recognizes the visitor as an old associate, Cornelia Rasch. Mrs. Worthingham explains that she has befriended her in Europe, where Cornelia had gone after a series of family deaths, which had left her without resources. Mrs. Worthingham admits her surprise that White-Mason and Cornelia know each other. An embarrassed Cornelia makes a gracious but hasty exit. Mrs. Worthingham's inability to remember what she and Cornelia talked about in Europe, her disinterest in knowing anything of White-Mason's history, and a resurgence of his horror at the possible source of the late Worthingham's "new money" cause him to postpone his proposal yet again.

White-Mason seeks out Cornelia, whom he considers the only other survivor of a "dead and buried society" (518). He admires her home and the history implied by her furniture. They reminisce about a failed relationship that he had with Mary Cardew when he was young. He admits to Cornelia his concerns about Mrs. Worthingham. Cornelia assures him he will be well received. White-Mason insists he would rather enjoy a relationship with someone who would *know* him and the world he comes from. He stresses he would not want to marry Cornelia but would like to enjoy a platonic friendship. Instead of being overwhelmed by the shiny newness of youth, he would rather sit by the fire in an old chair, aging gracefully. The story ends as he basks in the glow of Cornelia's hearth.

CRITICAL ANALYSIS

"Crapy Cornelia" includes two major themes of James's late phase: the decline of Old New York and a middle-aged man's realization of life's lost opportunities. Leon Edel notes that James returned to England particularly agitated after his visit to the United States in 1904. After decades abroad, James was perturbed about the rise of a nouveau riche corrupted by their fabulous wealth. There is perhaps no finer example of James's feelings about the rise of a new set of millionaires than the passage from "Crapy Cornelia" to which most critics point:

> This was clearly going to be the music of the future—that if people were but rich enough and furnished enough and fed enough, exercised and sanitated and manicured, and generally advised and advertised and made 'knowing' enough, *avertis* enough, as the term appeared to be nowadays in Paris, all they had to do for civility was to take the amused ironic view of those who might be less initiated. In his time, when he was young or even when he was only but a little less middle-aged, the best manners had been the best kindness, and the best kindness had mostly been some art of not insisting on one's luxurious differences, of concealing rather, for common humanity, if not for common decency, a part at least of the intensity or the ferocity with which one might be 'in the know.' (513)

The sense of being too much "in the know" is personified in Mrs. Worthingham. White-Mason's attraction to and repulsion from her is a symptom of the push and pull of the modern age on his sense of the past.

The narrator describes Mrs. Worthingham as "so much more 'knowing' in some directions than even [White-Mason], man of the world . . . could pretend to be" (508). She is "'up' to everything" and "surprised at nothing," prepared to "skip by the side of the coming age as over the floor of a ball-room, keeping step with its monstrous stride and prepared for every figure of the dance" (508). Although she often "blinds" him, White-Mason also sees her as a "great square sunny window that hung in assured fashion over the immensity of life" (508). Her modernity does appeal to him, especially as one who admits "he could still enjoy almost anything . . . that might still remind him he wasn't so old" (504). As N. H. Reeve aptly suggests, she

tempts White-Mason "with the prospect of losing himself, forgetting his past, contriving a new identity, pushing the margins of his youthfulness ever further back" (324).

The violent shock of recognizing his old friend Cornelia in Mrs. Worthingham's home destroys this daydream, which "dropped, darkened, disappeared; his imagination had spread its wings only to feel them flop all grotesquely at its sides" (509). He realizes it is too difficult to embrace Mrs. Worthingham's up-to-the-minute fashion and furniture, her inheritance of "new" money from her late husband, her carefree personality, and her lack of formalities. Comparatively, Cornelia is "almost ancient," someone who has shared "no end of things" with him (511). When Cornelia is embarrassed that White-Mason does not initially recognize her, he blames Mrs. Worthingham for not introducing them. Mrs. Worthingham's own response is marked by surprise: "I never supposed you knew her!" (511). Although W. R. Martin and Warren U. Ober use this as evidence that Mrs. Worthingham "meanly and snobbishly disclaim[s] any close or natural friendship with Cornelia" (63), it also implies that White-Mason may be looking for a way to distance himself from Mrs. Worthingham's future "fraught with possibilities" (503). Suddenly, her dazzling newness, her lack of "instinct for any old quality or quantity or identity, a single historic or social value" is unappealing to White-Mason (514).

Mrs. Worthingham is *too* new. She has "no data . . . [for what] the New York of 'his time' had been in his personal life"; conversely, Cornelia is "a massive little bundle of data" (517). His later meeting with Cornelia confirms the contrast. Reeve suggests that "Cornelia restores [White-Mason] to his natural taste, in a quiet room filled with the shared past, where things are done properly" (324). As they talk, White-Mason is aware of "piling up the crackling twigs [of data] as on the very altar of memory," engaging Cornelia in a game of "feeding the beautiful iridescent flame" (521). The accuracy of their memories matters much less than their growing camaraderie in the mutual act of remembering. As White-Mason puts it, "One wants a woman . . . to know *for* one, to know *with* one" (527). As John W. Shroeder asserts, "White-

Mason's quest is for simple escape—an escape, possible only through the meditation of Cornelia, into the temporal and physiological pasts" (428). Maqbool Aziz explains that not having "a definite point of reference in memory and history and tradition, consciousness [is] an unbearable burden" for White-Mason (232). He tells Cornelia she is a kind of anchor for him: "You make me [remember]. You connect me with [the past]. You connect it with *me*" (528). He insists she must have come back, "to help him" navigate the "modern wonders" of New York (529).

White-Mason marvels that Cornelia knows of everyone in their past, including his young love, Mary Cardew, whose photograph he notices in her room. White-Mason notes that Cornelia's opinion on his reaction to Mrs. Worthingham is reminiscent of her expression years ago regarding Mary. Cornelia tells him—perhaps criticizing his overall attitude toward romantic involvement—that he was not fair to Mary, who was hurt by him. Reeve suggests that "White-Mason has always run away from the future—not just now, because it looks garish and common, but whenever it came, in any form that he could not readily control and that threatened his capacity for self-indulgence" (328). Even White-Mason acknowledges that Mary's "charming sad eyes" seem to reproach him these many years later (530). After chiding White-Mason for how he "used to flirt," Cornelia offers him the photograph, perhaps as an appeal for him to see the past, present, and future in a different way.

At the story's conclusion, there is a mixture of peace and resignation in White-Mason. He decides that he is through with Mrs. Worthingham. When Cornelia wonders what he "can do with" *her* instead, since marriage is not an option, White-Mason seems to have an answer: "I can live with you—just this way . . . I can't give you up. It's very curious . . . I know it at last . . . You needn't deny it. That's my taste. I'm old" (532). White-Mason's embrace of himself as a middle-aged man is "a revelation of truth in a final tableau" (Martin and Ober 67). Yet, whereas this scene can look "from one perspective like a salutary return to realism," from another it seems "the prolongation of a sterile self-centeredness, one which has consistently ducked every challenge to open

itself to the differences of others" (Reeve 329). In his criticism of the new New York, James also offers a criticism of his own deeply introspective, critical eye. In a letter he wrote to his friend Henrietta Reubell, he reassures her that she is not Cornelia but admits he was "much White-Mason" (*Letters* 145). James had reserves of personal pity for those who could not keep step with the "monstrous stride" of the "coming age" (*Letters* 145).

CHARACTERS

Cardew, Mary   A young White-Mason flirted with Mary, who confided to Cornelia that he was not fair to her. In the present action of the story, he realizes this is true.

Rasch, Cornelia   An old associate of White-Mason, she has known him since childhood. At the age of 47, she has fallen on hard times financially and has recently returned to New York. Her "frumpy" demeanor masks her deep insight. She remembers much about White-Mason and New York's past, which comforts him.

White-Mason   A 48-year-old American is emotionally torn between two women, Mrs. Worthingham and Cornelia. They represent to him diametrically opposed ideas: forward-rushing modernity and the comfort of the familiar. His character alternates between isolating and potentially selfish introspection and genuine distress regarding the passing of his way of life.

Worthingham, Mrs.   She is a widow whose wealthy husband has left her his "new" money. White-Mason considers proposing to her. Younger than White-Mason, pretty and popular, Mrs. Worthingham is highly "modern" and in the "know."

FURTHER READING

Aziz, Maqbool. "How Long Is Long; How Short Is Short! Henry James and the Small Circular Frame." In *A Companion to Henry James Studies*, edited by Daniel Mark Fogel. Westport, Conn.: Greenwood Press, 1993.

Edel, Leon. *Henry James: The Master. 1901–1916.* New York: Lippincott, 1972.

James, Henry. "Crapy Cornelia." In *The New York Stories of Henry James*, edited by Colm Tóibín. New York: New York Review Books, 2006.

———. *The Finer Grain*. Edited by W. R. Martin and Warren U. Ober. Delmar, N.Y.: Scholars' Facsimiles & Reprints, 1985.

———. *The Letters of Henry James*. Volume 2. Edited by Percy Lubbock. London: Macmillan, 1920.

Martin, W. R., and Warren U. Ober. "'Crapy Cornelia': James's Self-Vindication." *Ariel* 11 (1980): 57–68.

Przybylowicz, Donna. *Desire and Repression*. Tuscaloosa: The University of Alabama Press, 1986.

Reeve, N. H. "Matches and Mismatches in Two Late James Stories." *The Cambridge Quarterly* 11 (1992): 322–339.

Schroeder, John. *The Mothers of Henry James. American Literature* 22 (1951): 424–431.

Tintner, Adeline. "Henry James at the Movies: Cinematograph and Photograph in 'Crapy Cornelia.'" *The Markham Review* 6 (1976): 1–8.

Christine Butterworth-McDermott,
Stephen F. Austin State University

"By Saint Peter's," by A. L. Coburn, frontispiece to *Daisy Miller*, in Volume 18, the New York Edition

"Daisy Miller: A Study" (1878)

Henry James wrote the novella "Daisy Miller: A Study" in LONDON in the winter of 1877–78. It was published in England in the *Cornhill Magazine* in two installments in June–July 1878, and despite having been rejected by *Lippincott's* in Philadelphia, the text was soon pirated in NEW YORK and Boston. It was published in book form by Harper's in the United States (1878) and Macmillan's in England (1879). James revised the story for the NEW YORK EDITION of his work (1909), where "Daisy Miller: A Study" headlines the stories and preface of Volume 18. (See PREFACES TO THE NEW YORK EDITION.)

SYNOPSIS

(Chapter 1) The novella opens one summer in Vevey, SWITZERLAND, on the shore of Lake Geneva. Winterbourne, a young American, is here to visit his aunt, Mrs. Costello, who is staying in a particularly desirable hotel. He studies in Geneva, where he is reportedly involved with an older, foreign woman. Upon hearing that his aunt has one of her headaches, Winterbourne takes breakfast in the hotel.

A small boy wielding a sharp mountaineering stick approaches his table and asks him for a lump of sugar. Winterbourne notes that the boy is a fellow American, and between them they agree that American candy, boys, and girls are "the best" (50). One of these American girls, the boy's pretty older sister, walks into view, wearing a white muslin dress and carrying an embroidered parasol. The girl pauses in front of him, and although Winterbourne remembers that he ought not to approach a young unmarried woman, he proceeds to introduce himself. The young lady, however, merely looks out over the parapet, and only when Winterbourne asks directly whether her family will be going to Italy does she reply in the affirmative. She smooths her dress, and Winterbourne's embarrassment disappears as he realizes that she is quite unflustered. He chats about the view and, as she becomes more engaged, is ever more impressed by her appearance. He corners the boy, whose name is Randolph C. Miller, and discovers that his sister is called Daisy (officially, Annie P. Miller) and that their father is in "big business" (54) back home in Schenectady, New York.

Daisy lowers her parasol and tells Winterbourne about their travels. She likes Europe, apart from the lack of society because she had been used to "a great deal of gentlemen's society" (57) in New York. Winterbourne is "amused, perplexed, and decidedly charmed" (57) by her openness. He cannot decide whether she is morally unscrupulous or disarmingly innocent, and he feels that he has spent too much time in Geneva to be able to read his fellow countrywoman. He concludes that she is just a pretty, unsophisticated flirt and is relieved to have found an appropriate category to put her into.

Daisy asks Winterbourne whether he has visited the Château de Chillon, having not yet been herself. Winterbourne hesitates, then suggests that he would like to take her there, accompanied by her mother, of course. Daisy is eager rather than embarrassed by his boldness, and Winterbourne is stunned by this "almost too agreeable" (60) outcome. At this moment, they are approached by a well-groomed man, whom Daisy addresses familiarly as "Eugenio" even though he is a courier employed by the Millers. He questions their arranged excursion, and Daisy blushes a little. Winterbourne finds Eugenio's tone "impertinent" and offensive and declares that he will introduce Daisy to his aunt so that she may ensure the respectability of his intentions, but Daisy just smiles, saying, "Oh well, we'll go someday" (60). She puts her parasol up and walks back to the hotel.

(Chapter 2) Winterbourne visits his aunt, Mrs. Costello, a widow with great fortune and reputation. After paying his respects, he inquires whether she has come across the American family and is told that she has made a point of avoiding them. She cannot understand how such a common girl has picked up such good taste in dress, and she condemns the family's intimacy with the courier Eugenio. Winterbourne admits that he has already offered to introduce Daisy, but his aunt refuses, shocked that Daisy has agreed to go to the castle with him on such short acquaintance. She warns Winterbourne that he has lived too long abroad and will make a mistake in pursuing Daisy.

Winterbourne is keen to see Daisy again and, by good fortune, finds her walking in the garden that evening, "like an indolent sylph, and swinging to and fro the largest fan he had ever beheld" (65). Daisy remarks on how much she is looking forward to meeting Winterbourne's aunt, and she is obviously affected when she infers her rejection. Winterbourne is embarrassed and blames his aunt's exclusivity on her headaches. Mrs. Miller appears in the distance, and Daisy finds it natural to introduce Winterbourne, although she only now discovers his name. Daisy announces that Winterbourne is going to take her to the castle, and he makes "a few deferential protestations" to Mrs. Miller, worried that she will not approve (70). Unperturbed, Mrs. Miller only comments that they have already seen castles in England.

Daisy, neglected while Winterbourne talks to her mother, regains his attention by asking, rather boldly: "Don't you want to take me out in a boat?" (71). Mrs. Miller's slight initial shock soon dissipates, and Winterbourne is wholeheartedly pleased at the prospect of being ensconced with Daisy in a boat. Eugenio arrives, and Mrs. Miller asks him to persuade Daisy not to go, but although he disapproves, he does not make a fuss. Daisy wishes Winterbourne a good night, saying that she hopes he is "disappointed, or disgusted, or something" (74). He is extremely puzzled at her flippancy.

Two days later, Winterbourne takes Daisy to the Château de Chillon. He is excited, and Daisy is lively, but Winterbourne is disappointed that she is not at all flustered by their "escapade" (75). He wonders whether she is as common as his aunt thinks or whether he has just got used to her manner, and he enjoys her company until she accuses him of being unduly solemn. In the castle, Winterbourne bribes the guard so they are left to themselves. Daisy is animated and flits from one thing to the next, paying little attention to the history of the place, and she asks Winterbourne many questions about his life.

Daisy suggests that Winterbourne could accompany her family on their travels, but he declines, pleading other engagements. In a moment of particular insight, Daisy deduces that Winterbourne has a woman in Geneva. She is upset and openly expresses her displeasure. Winterbourne is again perplexed by her reaction, but he is also charmed and flattered that his departure should affect her so dramatically. Daisy makes him promise to come and see her in ROME—a promise that is easy for Winterbourne to make since he plans to visit his aunt there anyway. That evening, Winterbourne informs his aunt of their excursion, and she sniffs at Daisy's moral laxity, confident in her initial judgment.

(Chapter 3) The following January, Winterbourne goes to Rome, where Mrs. Costello and the Miller family are already in residence. He declares his intention to visit Daisy, and his aunt disapproves but observes that men are able to know whom they like without fear of social rejection. Daisy has been associating with several Italians of dubious repute by the standards of the American colony and is said to be intimate with one particularly charming gentleman. Winterbourne is disappointed, having imagined that Daisy was pining for his own arrival. He delays visiting her and instead calls on Mrs. Walker, an old friend from Geneva, when the Miller family suddenly appears and Daisy berates him for neglecting her. Winterbourne talks to Mrs. Miller, who is disappointed with Rome, and learns that Daisy is happy here because European society finally meets her expectations. Daisy joins their conversation and again complains of Winterbourne's meanness. He is frustrated because he actually rushed to Rome in sentimental expectation of seeing her again.

Daisy asks whether she can bring an "intimate friend" (84) to Mrs. Walker's party. This is the handsome, charming Mr. Giovanelli, with whom Daisy intends to go walking this afternoon on the Pincio (a promenade in Rome). She is warned of the dangers of Roman fever (malaria), and Mrs. Walker pleads with her not to go. Daisy responds to this suggestion of impropriety by asking Winterbourne to accompany her to her rendezvous. Although jealous, he dutifully obliges and enjoys walking through Rome with Daisy on his arm. Winterbourne refuses to lead her to Giovanelli, who meets them with flowers in his buttonhole. Daisy is displeased at Winterbourne's stiff, imperious tone. She tells him that she has never had her actions dictated by a gentleman, implying that neither Winterbourne nor Giovanelli has control over her. Winterbourne is shocked that Daisy cannot tell the difference between a real gentleman (himself) and a fake one (Giovanelli).

The three of them walk together, and Winterbourne is surprised that Giovanelli is not more annoyed at losing his anticipated intimacy with Daisy. Winterbourne admits that Giovanelli is actually quite agreeable, but he is distinctly jealous of the Italian's good looks. This brings him back to his consideration of Daisy's conduct, and he remains puzzled by her "inscrutable combination of audacity and innocence" (90). Mrs. Walker draws up beside them in her carriage and says that they are being gossiped about. Daisy declines to be rescued and states her preference to walk with Giovanelli, mocking Mrs. Walker's lecturing tone. Winterbourne finds the whole scene unpleasant, particularly when Daisy asks his opinion and he finds himself compelled to tell her the only truth he knows—that she should, indeed, get in the carriage with Mrs. Walker. Daisy is clearly hurt, but she simply laughs and says that "If this is improper . . . then I am all improper, and you must give me up" (93). She leaves on the triumphant Giovanelli's arm.

Mrs. Walker orders Winterbourne into her carriage. He criticizes her actions and defends Daisy as being merely "uncultivated" (94), and he again blames Geneva for their own staid morals. Mrs. Walker insists that Daisy had gone too far and needed to be reined in, and she asks Winterbourne to stop seeing Daisy. He refuses, and Mrs. Walker puts him out of the carriage in view of the young couple. Alone, Winterbourne watches as Giovanelli takes Daisy's parasol and opens it to hide them from view. Instead of approaching them, Winterbourne walks in the other direction, back to his aunt.

(Chapter 4) During the next few days, Winterbourne calls on the Millers at their hotel but finds no one at home. At Mrs. Walker's party, Mrs. Miller arrives alone because Daisy and Giovanelli could not be induced to leave their session at the piano in the hotel. Mrs. Walker takes this as a personal slight. Arriving later, Daisy talks loudly through Giovanelli's singing and wishes that she could dance, although not with Winterbourne because he is "too stiff" (98). She questions Mrs. Walker's attempt to get her into the carriage, her own logic being that it would have been rude for her to drop Giovanelli. Winterbourne frowns, calls her a flirt, and Daisy agrees: "Did you ever hear of a nice girl that was not?" (99). He then admits that he would prefer her to flirt only with him, and she questions why it is acceptable for married women to flirt but not unmarried women. Winterbourne is provoked, and he raises the question of love. For him, Daisy's being in love with Giovanelli would make the situation acceptable, but Daisy is embarrassed, and it seems that this is the only thing that can shock her. She retreats to Giovanelli, whom she considers more courteous than Winterbourne because he has at least offered her tea. Daisy leaves with her mother while Mrs. Walker deliberately ignores her. Mrs. Miller does not appear to notice, but Daisy is mortified and confused by the snub.

Winterbourne calls regularly at the Millers' hotel. Whenever he finds them at home, Giovanelli is present but does not seem to mind the intrusions. Winterbourne's aunt deduces that Daisy Miller is on his mind. She predicts that Daisy and her Italian admirer will soon be engaged, but Winterbourne does not believe that Giovanelli intends to marry Daisy.

Daisy, meanwhile, is much talked about, and it pains Winterbourne to hear her prettiness reduced to vulgarity. He meets an unnamed friend, who has seen Daisy with Giovanelli in an art gallery (next to a portrait of Pope Innocent X), and Winterbourne tries to catch her up. He fails and finds only Mrs. Miller, who treats Daisy as though she is engaged. Winterbourne no longer encounters Daisy socially, but one day he sees her by chance in the Palace of the Caesars. She is looking her loveliest, and Winterbourne is briefly at peace in the "mysterious interfusion" (107) of youth and antiquity. Daisy asks if he is lonely, being so constantly by himself, and Giovanelli wanders off, giving them time alone. Daisy again challenges Winterbourne's opinion of her, but he only repeats what other people say, and she toys with him about the question of her engagement.

A week later, Winterbourne is walking home alone after dinner and decides to go to the Colosseum in order to see it by moonlight; he notices an empty carriage on the road. In the great amphitheater, he admires the huge, round space, half of which is in deep shadow, before leaving in a hurry so as not to endanger his health in the "historic atmosphere" (110). But he catches sight of two figures at the base of the cross in the center, whom he recognizes as Daisy and Giovanelli. He is shocked but also relieved to solve the riddle of Daisy's character. In the shadow of the Colosseum, he condemns her: "She was a young lady whom a gentleman need no longer be at pains to respect" (111). He turns away, but just at this moment Daisy recognizes him. He thinks her hurt is an act, but for the sake of appearances he turns back to speak to her, chiding her for ignoring the risk of contracting Roman fever. When Winterbourne tells her that it no longer affects him whether or not she is engaged, Daisy responds by saying "in a little strange tone" (113) that she does not care whether she falls sick.

A few days later, Winterbourne hears that Daisy is seriously ill. He visits her and is told by her mother that she was at no point engaged to Giovanelli (who is now keeping his distance), and that Daisy insisted Winterbourne be told. Mrs. Miller fails to read anything into this, and even Winterbourne remains unmoved. A week later, Daisy dies and is buried in a small Protestant cemetery, surrounded by spring flowers. At her funeral, Giovanelli enigmatically tells Winterbourne that Daisy was "most innocent" (115).

Winterbourne leaves Rome almost immediately. The following summer he meets his aunt again in Vevey, and they talk about Daisy. Winterbourne confesses that he feels he treated her badly, and Mrs. Costello interprets this as meaning that Daisy would have cared for him had Winterbourne been open about his feelings. Winterbourne admits that his aunt was right about his having lived too long abroad, but instead of returning home, he goes back to Geneva—back to his studies and the older, foreign woman with whom he was involved before Daisy.

CRITICAL ANALYSIS

"Daisy Miller: A Study" was Henry James's best-known work during his lifetime, and this is key to the history of its interpretation. James's representation of the demise of a young American girl became a sensation of 19th-century publishing and brought its author fame and notoriety. Argument about the true nature of Daisy's character followed the story's publication on both sides of the Atlantic, as the writer and critic WILLIAM DEAN HOWELLS described in a letter of 1879:

> Henry James waked up all the women with his *Daisy Miller,* the intention of which they misconceived, and there has been a vast discussion in which nobody felt very deeply, and everybody talked very loudly. The thing went so far that society almost divided itself into Daisy Millerites and anti-Daisy Millerites. (qtd. in Stafford 111–112)

Howells was unusual in his response, and most early reviewers reacted angrily to the scandalous behavior of the story's protagonist, in whom they recognized the increasing number of American girls flitting around Europe in the 1870s. This frenzied reaction led James to defend his creation, and he wrote in a letter to a reader in 1880 that "the keynote of her *character* is her innocence" (qtd. in Horne, *A Life in Letters* 122). In the liberal climate of the 21st century, it is easy to read "Daisy Miller: A Study" in the opposite light from how it was first received, and to see Daisy as a naive girl, neglected by her family, left to carve her own way through European society, and finally cruelly sacrificed by expatriated snobs with misogynistic double standards. This is now a more favored reading of the novella, but it, too, turns Daisy into a type, symbolic of innocence rather than vulgarity. Recognizing the limitations of both these interpretations can help unravel the dialectic of type and

individuality that makes "Daisy Miller: A Study" such a success.

Daisy is first and foremost an American girl, and the subject of the novella is the conflict that ensues when she is let loose in an alien European surrounding. In this, James develops the INTERNATIONAL THEME of his earlier work, notably RODERICK HUDSON (1875), *The* AMERICAN (1877) and "Madame de Mauves" (1874). With the success of "Daisy Miller: A Study," the international theme became his signature topic, as PUBLISHERS demanded more work in this vein. Howells wrote in a later introduction to the novella in 1901: "Mr. James is not quite the inventor of the international novel . . . but he is the inventor, beyond question, of the international American girl" (qtd. in Stafford 113). This claim evokes the durable success of "Daisy Miller: A Study," which prefigured several of James's later young American women, notably Isabel Archer of *The* PORTRAIT OF A LADY (1881) and Milly Theale of *The* WINGS OF THE DOVE (1902). Both James's contemporaries and recent critics agree that in Daisy Miller, as Leon Edel writes: "James had discovered nothing less than 'the American girl'—as a social phenomenon, a fact, a type. She had figured in novels before, but never had she stood in fiction so pertly and bravely, smoothing her dress and asking the world to pay court to her" (310). William Wasserstrom identifies this character type as the "*Heiress of All the Ages*"—a free spirit who embodies "both the loveliness and the disorder of the American spirit" (54). This genealogy has been explored by many critics interested in James's development as a writer; for example, in *The Image of Europe in Henry James* (1958), Christof Wegelin links James's young American woman with "the struggle of the individual to protect his integrity and freedom against violation by the world" (58). Daisy's type therefore persisted both in James's work and in a larger social context, but it is her memorable individuality that has made her endure in readers' imaginations. Characteristics such as the appealing syntax of Daisy's speech, the blushes that reveal her hidden feelings, and the twisting of her parasol and fan play off a stereotype but are made so particular to

Daisy that in another setting they would seem but imitation of her.

All the characters in "Daisy Miller: A Study" judge people according to presuppositions of type, but there are subtle differences in their styles of distinguishing appearance from reality. Mrs. Costello cannot understand how Daisy has such perfect taste in dress because this appearance does not match her idea of this "common . . . sort of Americans" (62). Daisy, on the other hand, admires Giovanelli as a perfect gentleman just because he looks and acts like one. James's representation of these two attitudes is complex. There is no doubt that Daisy partially brings about her own downfall because she is blind to the distinction between appearance and reality, but her simplicity is also applauded: Giovanelli *does* behave more courteously toward her than Winterbourne. American society in Rome condemns Daisy for misjudging Giovanelli, but it assumes that she is fitting him into a type. Ironically, this is precisely the kind of judgment that leads them to do Daisy an injustice, and James criticizes its irrationality and insensitivity.

This question of judgment is a key issue in "Daisy Miller: A Study" because Daisy's character is the principal subject of inquiry. In "The Genteel Reader" (1965), John Randall comments that whereas James's contemporaries simply condemned Daisy, "[s]ubsequent critics have recognized the difficulty other characters in the tale have in judging Daisy, but more often than not have gone on to give their own opinions about her" (569). He attributes this critical preoccupation to the fact that Daisy is only ever presented through Winterbourne's own analytical perspective. Winterbourne is undecided whether Daisy is vulgar or naive, but he categorizes people in the same way as his aunt. He is therefore perturbed when Daisy does not fit into either of these boxes, but instead of reassessing his methods, he cuts Daisy down to size. Winterbourne's treatment of Daisy has been variously interpreted as illustrative of patriarchal society, the double standards of gender roles, and class snobbery. His treatment of her has also been seen to symbolize the relationship of fiction to life. Daisy becomes a symbolic character who remains ultimately ambiguous. This illustrates how dogmatic criticism also makes her representative of a type and how her individuality is linked to the ambiguity of the text as something which must be read and interpreted.

This has led many critics to argue that the subject of the novella is not actually the status of Daisy's innocence but the effect of its ambiguity on those around her, particularly Winterbourne (Randall 1965). The observing outsider is a common figure throughout James's work, and the strictness with which Winterbourne's narrative viewpoint frames Daisy's story is an important development in James's narrative technique. The preface to "Daisy Miller: A Study" contains his famous dictum "Dramatize, dramatize!" (40), which is now much quoted in reference to his technique of focalizing the narrative within the consciousness of a single character. This places the DRAMA of the story within Winterbourne's consciousness and implies the possibility of competing interpretations of Daisy's character and conduct. Readers must first evaluate Winterbourne's point of view in order to understand Daisy.

The opening few pages of the novella are narrated by an explicit "I" who sets the scene and introduces Winterbourne to the reader. This detachment from his point of view signals another side to the story: "When his enemies spoke of him they said—but, after all, he had no enemies" (48). The narrator then retreats into the background, but through subtle shifts in Winterbourne's narrative voice, the reader learns to contrast his judgment against this potentially unfavorable view of him. Are the values and prejudices expressed in the text those of Winterbourne or the narrator? The language Winterbourne uses to describe Daisy echoes the vocabulary of his aunt and Mrs. Walker even though he claims to dispute their "categories of disorder" (105). The ironic tone of the narration also seems to mock these attitudes; for example: "[H]e had never yet enjoyed the sensation of guiding through the summer starlight a skiff freighted with a fresh and beautiful young girl" (71). Millicent Bell, in her narratological approach in *Meaning in Henry James* (1991), argues that Winterbourne is "the first of those Jamesian witnesses whose efforts to truly know the Other, to understand the Other's story, are representations of the writer's—and the reader's—bemused efforts to solve the mystery of character and plot" (55). Bell's interpretation thus indicates that readers of the novella should be as suspicious of Winterbourne as he is of Daisy, and that readers should learn from his mistakes as they attempt to interpret her character.

The moral grounds on which Daisy is judged by her fellow Americans can be seen to mirror the thematic structure of the novella. For example, the two settings of Vevey and Rome (and the looming shadow of Geneva) are used to symbolize different systems of values. The Americans Mrs. Costello and Mrs. Walker, who are very much associated with Geneva, expatriate culture, and social distinction, are almost always encountered inside their own quarters. Daisy and her family appear in the open air of Vevey to explore its gardens and shadows. They are less comfortable in an interior situation and are unfamiliar with expatriate social etiquette, which leads Daisy to be talked about when she walks with Giovanelli in public. Appropriately, Vevey is a compromise between the staid morals of Geneva and the moral laxity of Rome. Daisy is most at ease in the garden at Vevey but does not comprehend the dangers of Rome's "historic atmosphere" (110).

For most of the novella, Winterbourne is undecided about Daisy and is therefore suspended above the moral types symbolized by Geneva and Rome. He is a resident of Geneva and so is rooted in the same world as his elder compatriots. Yet, his ease at Vevey indicates that he has potential to be more open-minded. On the one hand, Winterbourne is portrayed as having adopted the staid conventions of his benefactors; "[h]e had imbibed at Geneva the idea that one must always be attentive to one's aunt" (61). On the other hand, he is aware of the negative effects of such rigid values and blames too long a residence at Geneva for his and Mrs. Walker's closed-mindedness. His judgment of Daisy therefore parallels his struggle to negotiate between these moral frameworks.

Winterbourne's language is steeped in the prejudices of his society, but until he sees Daisy in the Colosseum, he disputes the interpretation of this language. He defends Daisy's innocence to his aunt by saying that she is merely "uncultivated" (63). The ambiguity of this word perfectly reflects the contradictions of Daisy's character in its confusion of sophistication and simplicity and carries the suggestion that Daisy is either a fresh bloom or on the verge of wilting. In either case, Daisy lacks appropriate interest in the objects of her Grand Tour—"the dusky traditions of Chillon made but a slight impression upon her" (76). She does not seek to educate herself and appears more interested in the gentlemen who guide her (whether this is Winterbourne, Giovanelli, or Eugenio) than in the art or architecture. Her curiosity is attractive to Winterbourne when it is directed at him, but not when it gets her in trouble with his aunt and her friends.

The relation of culture to innocence also works on both technical and thematic levels of the novella, as James uses European monuments to frame dramatic moments of the story. The section set in Vevey ends with Winterbourne and Daisy's excursion to the Château de Chillon, an event that has been anticipated since their very first meeting. Daisy's fateful moonlit visit to the Colosseum with Giovanelli falls at the end of the Rome section of the story. This parallel draws the reader to make further comparisons between the two scenes. Winterbourne fears that his bold offer to take Daisy to Chillon will offend her, but this sense of impropriety does not curb his own conduct on the trip; he offers to take her out at night alone in a boat, admits that "he should enjoy deucedly 'going off' with her somewhere" (74), bribes the guide that they might be left alone, and is distinctly disappointed at what he perceives as her lack of excitement at being alone with him. The Château de Chillon becomes symbolic of a kind of romantic escapade, but it is crucial that Daisy never actually crosses the line. She may flirt with Winterbourne but never does anything overtly scandalous when alone with him.

A crucial irony of the story is encapsulated in the comparison between Winterbourne's disappointment at Daisy's innocence in this scene and his swiftness to condemn her when he sees her in an equivalent situation with Giovanelli. A simple interpretation concludes that he is merely jealous. However, there is no evidence that Daisy becomes physically intimate with Giovanelli, nor is there an objective sign upon which Winterbourne can base his damning inference. The difference between the appearance and reality of Daisy's innocence depends on the way he sees rather than on what he is looking at, and this is entirely due to the surrounding scene. The frame of the "gigantic circus" (110) of the Colosseum fixes Winterbourne's impression of Daisy and Giovanelli as a philandering couple. The logic of this transformation only works within Winterbourne's perspective, and his view is framed by the limits of his experience. Winterbourne has been longing to categorize Daisy, and as he suddenly sees her as "uncultivated" (in his aunt's sense of the word), he confirms in her the qualities of his preconceived stereotype.

The Colosseum, therefore, seems to become symbolic of reductive judgments made purely on the basis of appearance or manners; culture becomes an affectation and an untrustworthy artifice that blunts perception and understanding. The aesthetic and the moral are linked in a complex double standard in which sensual pleasure is unacceptable unless contained within social convention; Daisy's engagement becomes irrelevant for Winterbourne because he sees her as having flaunted her sexual (see SEXUALITY) attractiveness outside this arena. As John Randall notes, Winterbourne, "like the other Americans in the tale, sees life through the spectacles of the picturesque. What he responds to is a guidebook view of life, not life itself" (575). The frame limits what he sees, and by misreading the frame, Winterbourne makes a false judgment; this warns the reader not to make the same mistake. Paradoxically, it is precisely James's technique of presenting Daisy from Winterbourne's point of view that implies she is an individual who cannot be reduced to a stereotype. The two layers of narrative structure challenge readers to notice the way stereotypes are part of a process of thinking about and evaluating Daisy's innocence.

Through her very name, Daisy is associated with nature and spring, and within this lexicon it is clear on which side Winterbourne falls. The scene at the Colosseum is shortly preceded by an important encounter between Daisy and Winterbourne at the Palace of the Caesars. It is early spring, and as Daisy strolls along one of the ruins, the monument, the fresh grass growing on top of it, and Daisy herself are united in "mysterious interfusion." Daisy is also linked syntactically with Rome through Winterbourne's description: "Rome had never been so lovely"; "Daisy had never looked so pretty" (107). This brief moment reveals the possibility of the resolution of contradictions, but Daisy does not stay long in the shadow of these cultural monuments. She does not mature beyond the spring and remains (as her gravesite is described) a "raw protuberance among the April daisies," a "mystifying" presence to be enjoyed, interpreted, and esteemed (115).

CHARACTERS

Costello, Mrs. Winterbourne's aunt is a moneyed American widow "of much distinction" (61) who is disposed to terrible headaches that help her regulate her social engagements. She has three sons—two married in New York and one traveling in Europe—but none is more attentive than Winterbourne, to whom she is favorably disposed. She has a clear-cut view of the hierarchical levels of society, which leads her to dismiss the Millers as "common" (62) and "hopelessly vulgar" (80), despite Daisy's attractiveness and the mystifying perfection of her dress.

Eugenio The Millers' "ornamental courier" (86), Eugenio is employed to act as their servant, guide, and interpreter while they travel around Europe; a person with such a role was common among tourists of the Grand Tour, particularly unaccompanied ladies. Eugenio is a well-dressed, "tall, handsome man, with superb whiskers" (60) and is only ever identified by his Christian name. Daisy considers him "fastidious" and "splendid" (59), but society frowns on his intimacy with the family and the extent to which he influences their lives. The tone he uses with the family strikes Winterbourne as "impertinent" (60), and Mrs. Costello speculates that it was Eugenio who, in hope of financial reward, introduced Giovanelli to Daisy.

Giovanelli, Mr. Giovanelli is a good-looking Roman with whom Daisy socializes. When Winterbourne arrives in Rome, he learns that she "goes round everywhere" (83) with Giovanelli. First introduced to the reader as "a gentleman with a good deal of manner and a wonderful moustache," he distinguishes himself from among "half a dozen wonderful moustaches" (80) to become Daisy's "intimate friend" (84). The Millers see him as the perfect gentleman—charming, handsome and polite—but the rest of American society in Rome dismisses him as a low-born fortune hunter. He is too polite—obsequious, disingenuously tactful, and a little pompous. When Daisy is dead, Giovanelli tells Winterbourne not only that she was "the most innocent" but that he is sure she "would never have married [him]" (115).

Miller, Daisy (Annie P. Miller)   Daisy Miller is "a beautiful young lady" (50). Her age is never stated, but she is old enough "to be talked about" (92). She is always perfectly dressed, typically in white muslin with "frills and flounces" (51), and habitually carries a parasol or fan. Her face is bright and fresh, and she looks at people openly, but she is not without modesty. Daisy is introduced as "an American girl" (50), which makes her representative of a type. With a father in big business, the family is the newly moneyed class, which the novel's expatriated Americans disparage out of possible insecurity with their own international status.

Daisy is traveling around Europe with her mother (Mrs. Miller), her brother (Randolph), and their courier (Eugenio). She is eager to be noticed, but she is less interested in the cultural and historical monuments. Daisy fails to understand how society could see anything wrong in what she does. Or maybe she enjoys making an impression. Daisy says of herself: "I'm a fearful frightful flirt!" (99), and it is precisely the vivacious spirit of her "uncultivated" chatter that makes her such an appealing character. She prefers weak tea to disagreeable advice and a moonlit walk with a good-looking man to a lecture in a carriage from a staid old lady. The insensitivity of her treatment by the American community, as well as the indications that she had heartfelt feelings for Winterbourne, add a tragic pathos to her untimely death.

Miller, Mr. Ezra B.   Daisy's father is a business mogul in Schenectady, New York, and is significantly absent from his family's European holiday, being, as Randolph describes, "in a better place" (54)—back home in America. This leaves his children unsupervised apart from their ineffectual mother and the hired courier, Eugenio.

Miller, Mrs.   Daisy's mother is the only member of the Miller family without a Christian name and middle initial. She has "a very exiguous nose" and "enormous diamonds in her ears" (68), and she suffers from dyspepsia. She leaves her offspring to their own devices, whether this involves eating sugar, refusing to go to bed, or picking up gentlemen in the hotel gardens. Unlike Mrs. Costello or Mrs. Walker, she seems incapable of being shocked by anything Daisy does. She considers Daisy and Giovanelli to be effectively engaged and makes them promise to tell her if it becomes official so that she can write and inform Mr. Miller of the news. As Daisy lies dying, Mrs. Miller conveys Winterbourne the message that her daughter was never engaged; she is glad to know the truth of the situation but does not see any significance in Daisy's insistence that Winterbourne be told.

Miller, Randolph C.   Randolph is a nine-year-old who is completely uninterested in the cultural heritage of Europe and would far rather be aboard a ship heading back to America, where he could get "the best candy" (50). It is Randolph's forwardness that provides Winterbourne with an introduction to his older sister, Daisy. Ungovernable, Randolph does just what he likes—staying up late, bantering with waiters, and generally rollicking around with his pointed alpenstock, "which he thrust[s] into everything that he approached" (49). Randolph is stereotypically loud and obnoxious in a way that Daisy is not.

Walker, Mrs.   Mrs. Walker is a "very accomplished" (80) American lady who sent her children to school in Geneva and who came to be friends with Winterbourne after spending several winters there. She studies European society and collects "specimens of her diversely-born fellow mortals" (96) for the purposes of her observation. Mrs. Walker is a pillar of American society in Rome, and she pleads with Daisy to act in accordance with expectations. When Daisy walks in public with Giovanelli, Mrs. Walker makes a huge fuss, condemning it as "dreadful" and declaring that Daisy "must not do this sort of thing" (90). Mrs. Walker is concerned about maintaining appearances and hopes to shame Daisy into obedience by telling her that she is being talked about. Mrs. Walker rejects Daisy as soon as her advice is ignored and adopts the same self-righteous tone as Mrs. Costello: "If she is so perfectly determined to compromise herself, the sooner one knows it the better; one can act accordingly" (94).

Winterbourne, Mr. Winterbourne is a 27-year-old American who has lived in Geneva for some years. He is studying—a fact his enemies seem to view as a cover for his devotion to a somewhat shadowy "foreign lady" older than himself (48). Because of his European education, he wonders what it would have been like if he had been raised like Daisy's brother, Randolph. Winterbourne is "stiff" (98) and takes little positive action, which reflects his indecision about Daisy. The tone of his speech is as formal and sterile as that of his aunt, which ensures his social acceptance but frustrates and alienates Daisy.

Winterbourne has "a great relish for feminine beauty" and admires Daisy's appearance rather analytically, praising her nose, ears, eyes, and teeth before accusing the whole "very forgivingly—of a want of finish" (53). He is very attracted to Daisy but is puzzled by her openness and apparent simplicity: Is she straightforwardly innocent or a morally degenerate coquette? Concluding that she is just a "pretty American flirt" (57), Winterbourne defends Daisy against the criticisms of his compatriots, but he is unable to step outside their prejudices. At the end of the novella, Winterbourne concludes: "I have lived too long in foreign parts." The statement indicates his reliance on the moral frame of Geneva, but he chooses to return to his previous life there rather than to learn and change from his experiences.

ADAPTATIONS

James adapted the novella into *Daisy Miller: A Comedy in Three Acts* while living in Boston in early 1882. The play was rejected by the Madison Square Theatre in New York and was not subsequently produced. It was published in England (privately for copyright purposes 1882) and America (*Atlantic Monthly* 1883).

The movie *Daisy Miller* (1974), directed by Peter Bogdanovich, starred Cybill Shepherd as Daisy and Barry Brown as Winterbourne.

FURTHER READING

There is substantial criticism on "Daisy Miller: A Study." A good place to start is William T. Stafford's research guide (1963); this edition contains James's original 1878 text, the 1882 play, contemporary reviews, and an overview of 20th-century criticism. For the changes James made in revising the story for the New York Edition, see Dunbar (1950) and Horne (1990).

Bell, Millicent. "Daisy Miller." In *Meaning in Henry James*, 54–65. Cambridge, Mass.: Harvard University Press, 1991.

Dunbar, Viola R. "A Note on the Genesis of Daisy Miller." *Philological Quarterly* 27, no. 5 (1948): 184–186.

———. "The Revisions of Daisy Miller." *Modern Language Notes* 65, no. 5 (1950): 311–317.

Edel, Leon. "Daisy." In *Henry James: The Conquest of London 1870–1883*, 303–319. London: Rupert Hart-Davis, 1962.

Graham, Kenneth. "*Daisy Miller*: Dynamics of an Enigma." In Pollak.

Horne, Philip, ed. *Henry James: A Life in Letters*. London: Penguin, 1999.

———. "Revised Judgements of Daisy Miller." In *Henry James and Revision: The New York Edition*, 228–264. Oxford, U.K.: Clarendon Press, 1990.

James, Henry. *Daisy Miller*. London: Penguin Books, 1986.

Page, Philip. "Daisy Miller's Parasol." *Studies in Short Fiction* 27, no. 4 (1990): 591–601.

Pollak, Vivian R., ed. *New Essays on* Daisy Miller *and* The Turn of the Screw. Cambridge: Cambridge University Press, 1993.

Randall, John H., III. "The Genteel Reader and *Daisy Miller*." *American Quarterly* 17, no. 3 (1965): 568–581.

Stafford, William T., ed. *James's Daisy Miller: The Story, The Play, The Critics*. New York: Scribner's, 1963.

Wardley, Lynn. "Reassembling Daisy Miller." *American Literary History* 3, no. 2 (1991): 232–254.

Wegelin, Christof. *The Image of Europe in Henry James*. Dallas, Tex.: Southern Methodist University Press, 1958.

Weisbuch, Robert. "Winterbourne and the Doom of Manhood in *Daisy Miller*." In Pollak.

Harriet Carter, *University of East Anglia*

"The Death of the Lion" (1894)

The tale was first published in the periodical the *Yellow Book* in April 1894. It appeared in book form in a collection entitled *Terminations* (London: Heinemann, 1895; New York: Harper, 1895). A revised version of the story appeared in Volume 15 of the NEW YORK EDITION of *The Novels and Tales of Henry James* (New York: Scribner's Sons, 1909). The text used here is that of the 1909 edition.

SYNOPSIS

(Part 1) The anonymous narrator, an "unregenerate" LONDON journalist working for an unnamed "weekly," announces a sudden "change of heart" (99). After proposing an article on the reclusive author Neil Paraday, he has misgivings when the new chief, Mr. Pinhorn, expects him to interview the man. Despite his irreverence, he bristles against the new (equally dubious) journalistic code that replaces "false representations" with "immediate exposure" (101). Yet he is packed off by Pinhorn, who whiffs "the coming glory as an animal smells its distant prey" (102).

(Part 2) The narrator is welcomed by Paraday. On day two of his commission, he sends his article to Pinhorn and transfers his things to Paraday's home. The next day, Paraday's new book comes out, and the narrator reads it rapturously. Pinhorn returns his "finicking feverish study" of Paraday's talent with a demand for "the genuine article, the revealing and reverberating sketch" (105). The narrator recasts his piece and sends it to another journal, where it sinks unnoticed. His change of heart is complete.

(Part 3) The next day, Paraday reads aloud his "written scheme" for a new novel. The narrator is transported by it, likening it to "the overflow into talk of an artist's amorous plan" and "Venus rising from the sea . . . before the airs had blown upon her" (106). He wonders how Paraday, recovering from an illness, will manage it. Just as they agree that his "deadness" (i.e., his obscurity) is what will bring it to life, the newspaper *The Empire* is delivered.

(Part 4) As the notorious newspaper arrives trumpeting Paraday's success, the journalist Mr. Morrow appears. "I was a little fish in the stomach of a bigger one" (113), the narrator half accuses himself, while Morrow presses for Paraday's opinions on "the larger latitude" (the treatment, presumably, of SEXUALITY) in writers Guy Walsingham (the pseudonym of a female) and Dora Forbes (that of a male). The narrator becomes spokesman, allowing Paraday's retreat.

(Part 5) Morrow keeps up his interrogation. The young man heroically assumes his most elevated role: that of a savior. He fetches Paraday's book, promising "revelations." He urges: "The artist's life's his work, and this is the place to observe him" and "the best interviewer's the best reader" (119). When he proposes a reading session, Morrow gets up to leave but notices Paraday's sketch. The narrator seizes it; Morrow flees in disgust.

(Part 6) A week passes, and Paraday's lionization is complete: "he was the king of the beasts of the year" (122). In London, he circulates as his books have never done. He succumbs to "capture" by society hostess Mrs. Weeks Wimbush. Having left Pinhorn, the narrator views his guardianship of Paraday as his vocation. But his program to make himself "odious" to Paraday's fans is complicated by an unexpected arrival on the scene.

(Part 7) On finding Fanny Hurter, a pretty American autograph hunter, lying in wait, the narrator softens his program of deterrence but only to deflect her interest from Paraday onto himself. He pleads: "[h]e's beset, badgered, bothered—he's pulled to pieces on the pretext of being applauded" (130). She renounces her object of meeting Paraday, leaving the autograph book behind, which the narrator promises to return to her himself.

(Part 8) The narrator fulfills his promise. In fact, he returns repeatedly to assist in "weaning" her. Naturally, he continues to foster her desire to *read*, if not see, the great man, and their "communion" on this subject extends to parties and the opera. Paraday surrenders himself to a summer of portrait sitting and "ponderous parties" (137).

(Part 9) The narrator now transcribes events as they occur from his letters to Fanny, who has stayed behind while he and Paraday attend a party at Prestidge, Mrs. Wimbush's country house. What follows is a diatribe against his fellow guests, whose philistinism and posturing reach their pinnacle in "the Princess." The weather worsens ("I've nothing but my acrimony to warm me"), and one of the guests loses Paraday's sketch.

(Part 10) On his contracting a severe chill, Paraday's reading is delayed, and efforts to find the sketch are redoubled. The "larger latitude" of Guy Walsingham, then of Dora Forbes, is embraced by the company, while Paraday lies upstairs in a state of large lassitude. As he worsens, the disgruntled guests disperse. On his deathbed, unaware that it is lost, Paraday asks that his sketch be printed as it stands. The narrator ends by admitting that he is still in search of it and that his partner in this search (Fanny) is now his partner in MARRIAGE.

CRITICAL ANALYSIS

"'So are they all honourable men'," taunts the narrator of "The Death of the Lion," and with this line from Shakespeare's *Julius Caesar*, he borrows the irony and rancor of Antony's wily funeral oration for that other "lion," the Roman emperor. The scene is Prestidge, the country house (or "gilded cage") of Mrs. Wimbush, patron of the "literary lion" Neil Paraday. The occasion is the loss of the outline of Paraday's magnum opus by Lady Augusta Minch, one of his fatuous fans. Self-appointed protector of Paraday, the narrator bitterly reflects

on "the well-meaning ravages of our appreciative circle" (148). This circle fatally constricts Paraday, just as the conspirators encircle and overwhelm the tyrant Caesar. In James's work, too, problems of ambition and duty, popularity and elitism, the artificial division between the public and the private, and personality cults predominate. Through Mrs. Wimbush, culpable and self-interested as she is, James hints at the question the narrator is reluctant to ask, "Who is *not* a parasite?"

"The Death of the Lion" belongs to James's stories of "literary life." These stories stem "from some noted adventure, some felt embarrassment, some extreme predicament, of the artist enamoured of perfection, ridden by his idea or paying for his sincerity" (James, preface viii). In "The Death of the Lion," writer Neil Paraday pays for his wisdom that "success was a complication and recognition had to be reciprocal" (124). His imperial associations—being hailed as "king of the beasts" and enthroned by *The Empire*, a publication that bestows "national glory" on him—invite moral questions of the duty owed to subjects (i.e., readers) and the forms of allegiance these subjects should adopt, as well as the public demand on genius for "personality" and "presence."

Despite the correction of his understanding of "presence," from something that is *embodied* (in the man) to something that is *embedded* (in the text), the narrator's position remains open to revision. James writes in his Notebooks that "the consciousness of the moral should probably reside only in the person telling the story" (87), but James bids the reader of the finished tale to be conscious of a further "moral." When the narrator admonishes Mr. Morrow that "the artist's life's his work, and this is the place to observe him" (119), this is shown to be both an improvement on Morrow's stance and a dangerous abstraction. The coincidence of the loss of Paraday's life with the loss of his manuscript may thus be read as a literalization of the narrator's ironic insistence that he be "dead" (108) to the world in order to write, or of his "interest" in "his absence" (i.e., his work) over "his presence" (124). Furthermore, the interposing of Paraday's book between the writer and his readers effectively "screens" Paraday from them, so that the narrator can monopolize "physical, as well as interpretive, intimacy" (Person 198). Perhaps James's invitation to read *against* the narrator allows for a more *absent* (indirect, ironic) reading, one that deconstructs the narrator's exalted idea of presence (Armstrong 106). It may be argued that James conceives of the problem of reading less as a struggle between an authoritative author and an autonomous text than as an exchange of cultural and political forces (DaRosa 846).

The possibility of an ethics of reading, then, involves even the "right kind" of "enthusiast" (such as Fanny) in the dynamic of taking an "interest" (a frequent word), of having "sympathy," of "guarding" or "saving." In such cases, the object of interest and sympathy is usually overpowered by the subject's "interpretation" of his or her needs; hence the similarity of these impulses to reading. In this view, reading is cast as a perpetual contest or, to put it more positively, as "community building" (Armstrong 107). At one point, the narrator sounds this alarm: "These meagre notes are essentially private, so that if they see the light the insidious forces that, as my story itself shows, make at present for publicity will simply have overmastered my precautions" (103). Maybe this is the narrator being disingenuous; or maybe it is James's way of saying, "*Et tu, Bruté?*"—referring both to his own powers of "mastery" and to his capitulation to the "forces" of appreciation which, for good and ill, have the potential to "overmaster" even The Master.

CHARACTERS

Hurter, Fanny The "ominously" named Miss Fanny Hurter has "a brave face, black hair, blue eyes" (126) and an interest in Paraday that puts the narrator on his guard. Charmed by her combination of American coquetry, naïveté, and abandon, he finds himself caught off-guard by the "romance of her freedom, her errand, her innocence" (128).

Morrow, Mr. As his name implies, the hack Mr. Morrow is a man of tomorrow; his bespectacled gaze is like "the electric headlights of some monstrous modern ship" (112), and his progressive sympathies lie with "the larger latitude" of the gender-swapping new novelists.

Narrator Like Mr. Morrow, the narrator makes the pilgrimage to Neil Paraday "to betray," to expose the man behind the work, but *unlike* his competitor he decides "to save" (114). He is enraged at Mrs. Wimbush's insinuation that his disinterestedness is a cover for a possessiveness and parasitism more insidious than her own.

Paraday, Neil The literary "lion" of the title, Paraday enjoys a vexed distinction. Although his fame and prose style make him "king of the beasts" (122) and a "master," he is also "prey" and "victim" to his readership, a king superseded by new ascensions ("*Le roy est mort—vive le roy*"). Submitting to "periodical prattle" and "ponderous parties" (137), he meets the narrator's histrionic fatalism with resigned pragmatism. Still, he is hunted to extinction.

Pinhorn, Mr. The narrator's "chief," Mr. Pinhorn has professional, if not personal "flair," and a nose for glory. An advocate of the cult of "personality," his "sincerity took the form of ringing door-bells and [his] definition of genius was the art of finding people at home" (101).

Wimbush, Mrs. Weeks The "proprietress of the universal menagerie" (123) and the narrator's nemesis, Mrs. Wimbush is criminally whimsical in her patronage. She has "no more idea of responsibility than . . . the creaking of a sign in the wind" (123).

FURTHER READING

For a readily available edition of the text, see Frank Kermode, ed., *The Figure in the Carpet and Other Stories* (New York: Penguin, 1986), which includes James's other tales of literary life.

Armstrong, Paul B. "Art and the Construction of Community in 'The Death of the Lion.'" *Henry James Review* 17, no. 2 (1996): 99–108.

DaRosa, Marc. "Henry James, Anonymity, and the Press: Journalistic Modernity and the Decline of the Author." *Modern Fiction Studies* 43, no. 4 (1997): 826–859.

James, Henry. *The Complete Notebooks.* Edited by Leon Edel and Lyall H. Powers, 86–87. New York: Oxford University Press, 1987.

———. "The Death of the Lion." In *The Novels and Tales of Henry James*, vol. 15, 97–154. New York: Scribner's, 1909.

Person, Leland S. "James's Homo-Aesthetics: Deploying Desire in the Tales of Writers and Artists." *Henry James Review* 14, no. 2 (1993): 188–203.

Rebekah Scott, *University of Cambridge*

"The Figure in the Carpet" (1896)

Henry James's tale "The Figure in the Carpet," a highly ambiguous literary detective story, first appeared as a serial in the journal *Cosmopolis* from January to February 1896. It was slightly revised for the collection of tales *Embarrassments* published in June 1896. For the NEW YORK EDITION (1907–09), Volume 15, James introduced some further minor changes.

SYNOPSIS

At its outset, the unnamed first-person narrator, a literary critic, welcomes the opportunity to review the latest novel of a famous author named Hugh Vereker. The narrator is certain of having revealed the novel's meaning in his review, until he happens to meet the author at a dinner party, where the latter disparages the review as being quite off the point. In an intimate conversation with the narrator, Vereker reveals that his entire oeuvre is governed by an intricate scheme, like a complex figure in a Persian carpet, which no one has been able to discover. Spurned on by the author's remarks, the narrator makes it his task to reveal the buried treasure of Vereker's works. He is joined in his efforts by his friend and fellow literary critic George Corvick and the writer Gwendolen Erme, Corvick's fiancée. But whereas the narrator tries to wring the secret from Vereker himself and soon even begins to doubt the existence of a "figure in the carpet," Corvick and Gwendolen study Vereker's works, word by word, for more than one year. Even though the couple's attempts to solve the riddle remain as futile as the

narrator's, their common quest strengthens the bond between them.

Later, Corvick sets off for India as a special commissioner for a newspaper, leaving both Gwendolen and Vereker's novels behind. Corvick even declares that he has broken his engagement with Gwendolen, a fact later denied by Gwendolen during his absence. The surprise is great when Gwendolen receives a telegram from India, in which Corvick claims to have finally unearthed Vereker's secret. Withholding this secret from both Gwendolen and the narrator, Corvick goes to Italy to see Vereker, who actually confirms the accuracy of Corvick's theory. Gwendolen has to restrain her curiosity about the "figure in the carpet" until after her MARRIAGE with Corvick, whereas the narrator is left in tantalizing ignorance.

Corvick plans to reveal the figure in Vereker's carpet in a great literary portrait, but he is killed in a road accident during his honeymoon with Gwendolen before he can put his idea on paper. The narrator tries to win Gwendolen's confidence and even considers marrying the young widow in order to obtain the information he so desperately seeks, but he is repulsed in his attempts. The narrator also contemplates turning for help to Vereker again, but he learns of Vereker's death and that of his wife. Gwendolen Erme eventually marries again, this time to the literary critic Drayton Deane. When she dies in childbirth a few years later, the narrator sees his last chance of solving the puzzle in questioning Deane about Vereker's secret. Deane, however, seems totally unaware that such a secret exists, let alone the solution to the riddle. The story closes with the two men left alone in their perplexity concerning Hugh Vereker's "figure in the carpet."

CRITICAL ANALYSIS

When reading "The Figure in the Carpet," one may experience a sense of confusion similar to that of the nameless narrator, who expresses doubts about the existence of the secret figure: "The buried treasure was a bad joke, the general intention a monstrous *pose*" (236). The reason for this kind of bewilderment is that the reader is limited to the point of view of the narrator, whose reliability, however, must be put into question. Without an authoritative narrative voice on which to rely, without a single line from Vereker's works to go by, the obvious question must be put: Is there really a figure in Vereker's carpet, or did the narrator, George Corvick, Gwendolen Erme, Drayton Deane, and finally the reader, fall for a bluff? The latter possibility is rarely taken into account by literary criticism, which apparently refuses to believe in a literary gimmick by Henry James.

What then are readers to make of James's tale and the "figure in the carpet?" Without a clearly discernible autonomous meaning, "The Figure in the Carpet" has frequently been regarded as a parable of some sort. Taking James's PREFACES TO THE NEW YORK EDITION as a point of departure, "The Figure in the Carpet" is often read as a fable of misinterpretation and misreading. In his preface to the 15th volume of the New York Edition, James, in fact, complains about "the odd numbness of the general sensibility, which seemed ever to condemn it, in presence of a work of art, to a view scarce of half the intentions embodied" and hopes to "reinstate analytic appreciation . . . in its virtually forfeited rights and dignities" (xv). The obsessive but futile search for meaning practiced by the narrator, coupled with his rapacity for personal detail, clearly illustrates an erroneous approach to literary texts and constitutes the exact opposite of the "analytic appreciation" cherished by James. If the narrator's approach to literary texts epitomizes the wrong way to read, then it might seem only logical that George Corvick represents the ideal reader. Starting from the supposition that Corvick actually uncovered the secret in Vereker's work (which is again challenged by some critics), Leo B. Levy identifies in his essay "A Reading of 'The Figure in the Carpet'" (1962) the ideal reader as one who "can join in the hunt with both love and intelligence" (465). Levy contrasts the narrator's intellectual and emotional limitations with the humanity of George Corvick. Only those who love—Vereker, Corvick, and Gwendolen—can discern the "figure in the carpet"; those seeking only to acquire knowledge will fail in their endeavor. In a line of reasoning similar to Levy's, Rachel Salmon (1980) argues that James rejected the notion of the act of reading as a "purely intellectual or abstracting activity" (800). Salmon points

out that the secret in James's tale has something to do with physical intimacy and sexual knowledge ("the very mouth of the cave," "the organ of life," "the idol unveiled") and equates the sexual union between Corvick and Gwendolen with the ideal "interaction of text and reader" (801) (see SEXUALITY). A reader of James must embrace the text and "know it"—also in the biblical meaning of the word. In Salmon's view, "The Figure in the Carpet" thus produces an ideal type of reader who does not need to be "told" but shows active involvement and creativity in involvement with the literary text.

J. Hillis Miller (1980) and David Liss (1995) also regard "The Figure in the Carpet" as an allegory of misreading and misinterpretation, denying, however, George Corvick and Gwendolen Erme the satisfaction of having revealed the riddle. For Miller, the highly ambiguous text, with its figure that exists and at the same time does not, "like a Möbius strip which has two sides, but only one side, yet two sides still, interminably" (113), is proof that any attempt to attribute to a work of literature one single meaning must fail. In his essay "The Fixation of Belief in 'The Figure in the Carpet': Henry James and Peircean Semiotics," David Liss takes a similar line: Liss tries to show that James, who was familiar with Charles Sanders Peirce's semiotics, illustrates in his tale the continuous fluidity of meaning. When meaning becomes a never-ending process rather than a product, the attempt to establish a "one-to-one association of text and meaning" (39) must result in failure.

Other approaches to James's tale are less concerned with the act of reading and interpreting: Peter Lock (1981), for example, follows the clearly sexual imagery in the tale and sees the letter V ("Vera, Vishnu, Velasquez, Vandyke, and by immediate suggestion, Virgil, Venus, vulva, victor," [171]) as symbol of Vereker's hidden treasure. Eric Savoy (1999), who also considers the conflation of the textual with the sexual, tries to show underlying homoerotic desires in the relationship between the narrator and Vereker. For Kristin King (1995), "The Figure in the Carpet" is a tale about a struggle between the sexes for literary authority. In her view, the tale can be seen as an expression of James's "anxiety about male privilege in the modern marketplace." Gerard M. Sweeney (1983) finally reads the story less as a literary than a traditional detective story. He even thinks that the "question of whether or not the figure exists" (84) is irrelevant. Sweeney is more interested in the human dimension of the tale (five deaths, serious illnesses, two marriages, and the birth of two children) and tries to prove that Gwendolen Erme is guilty of matricide.

The many different and sometimes contradictory approaches to "The Figure in the Carpet" should not deter students from reading the tale but are proof of its plurality and richness of meanings.

CHARACTERS

Corvick, George A literary critic and friend of the first-person narrator, he is quite condescending to him at the beginning of the tale. When he is told about the "buried treasure" in Hugh Vereker's works, he is determined to solve the riddle of the "figure in the carpet." In his search, he is too proud to resort to external information, relying instead on his own astuteness and literary discernment. When Corvick eventually succeeds in his endeavors, he keeps the narrator and Gwendolen Erme on tenterhooks, promising to tell Gwendolen only after their marriage. He is described as a reckless dogcart driver and dies, fittingly, in a road accident during his honeymoon with Gwendolen. His untimely death prevents him from putting his knowledge about Vereker into writing.

Deane, Drayton A literary critic and the second husband of Gwendolen Erme, he reviews Gwendolen's last novel favorably and eventually marries her. Gwendolen, however, does not reveal to him the secret of Hugh Vereker's works. Realizing that his wife withheld this information from him comes as a painful surprise. The narrator first thinks Deane incompetent and stupid, but he retracts his judgment after a longer conversation with him about the "figure in the carpet."

Erme, Gwendolen She published her first novel at the age of 19. She is described as being "not pretty, but awfully interesting" (220) and as lacking a sense of humor. She avidly aids George Cor-

vick in his search for the literary secret governing Hugh Vereker's works. When Corvick leaves for India, she stays behind. Despite the ensuing uncertainty about their engagement, she readily accepts Corvick's proposal of marriage after he has discovered the "figure in the carpet." After Corvick's death, the young widow changes considerably: Gwendolen seems content with her knowledge, becomes inspired (publishing her second novel), and "incontestably handsome," leading a life of "singular dignity and beauty" (264). Gwendolen eventually marries the literary critic Drayton Deane and gives birth to two children, the second costing her life.

Erme, Mrs. Gwendolen's mother disapproves of the engagement of her daughter with George Corvick, probably because of financial misgivings. She is in poor health and dies somewhat conveniently when Gwendolen and Corvick decide to marry in spite of her.

Narrator Nameless throughout the entire story, he is a literary critic, but it can be inferred that his professional success is limited. After his conversation with Hugh Vereker, he becomes literally obsessed with the idea of solving the mystery of the "figure in the carpet." When he fails to do so, he tries to entice Gwendolen, Vereker, and finally Drayton Deane into letting him in on the secret. Doubts about his reliability as a narrator are justified by his impertinent tone, blatant insensitivity, and monomaniacal behavior.

Vereker, Hugh A renowned author, he claims that there is an undiscovered secret governing his literary works. When he unknowingly offends the narrator by pronouncing his review as the "usual twaddle" (227), he seems sincerely sorry and apologizes profusely. Vereker describes his secret as an "exquisite scheme" (231), a "little trick" (231), and "the loveliest thing in the world" (235). He refuses to drop more than these hints to the first-person narrator and is curious to see whether anyone will be able to discover his secret. He dies shortly after having pronounced George Corvick's theory about the "figure in the carpet" correct.

FURTHER READING

Finch, G. A. "A Retreading of James' Carpet." *Twentieth Century Literature* 14, no. 2 (1968): 98–101.

King, Kristin. "'Lost among the Genders': Male Narrators and Female Writers in James's Literary Tales, 1892–1896." *Henry James Review* 16, no. 1 (1995): 18–35.

Levy, Leo B. "A Reading of 'The Figure in the Carpet'." *American Literature* 33, no. 4 (1962): 457–465.

Liss, David. "The Fixation of Belief in 'The Figure in the Carpet': Henry James and Peircean Semiotics." *Henry James Review* 16, no. 1 (1995): 36–47.

Lock, Peter W. "'The Figure in the Carpet': The Text as Riddle and Force." *Nineteenth-Century Fiction* 36, no. 2 (1981): 157–175.

Miller, J. Hillis. "The Figure in the Carpet." *Poetics Today* 1, no. 3 (1980): 107–118.

Salmon, Rachel. "A Marriage of Opposites: Henry James's 'The Figure in the Carpet' and the Problem of Ambiguity." *ELH* 47, no. 4 (1980): 788–803.

Savoy, Eric. "Embarrassments: Figure in the Closet." *Henry James Review* 20, no. 3 (1999): 227–236.

Sweeney, Gerard M. "The Deadly Figure in James's Carpet." *Modern Language Studies* 13, no. 4 (1983): 79–85.

Arnold Leitner, *University of Salzburg*

"Glasses" (1896)

This story first appeared in the *Atlantic Monthly* in February 1896. It was collected in *Embarrassments*, which was published in June 1896 by William Heinemann in LONDON and by the Macmillan Company in NEW YORK. It was revised in 1916 for *The Uniform Tales,* published in London by Martin Secker.

SYNOPSIS

The narrator, an artist, is on vacation visiting his ailing mother in the English resort town of Folkestone. Through his friend Mrs. Meldrum, a widow who wears very thick glasses and is described as "the heartiest, the keenest, the ugliest of women" (525), he is introduced to the beautiful Flora Saunt, a young woman without a family. According to Mrs. Meldrum, Flora is in danger of losing her fortune to her supposed friends who pretend to be caring for her. Furthermore, her beautiful eyes, Mrs. Meldrum informs the narrator, are "good for nothing but to roll about like sugar balls" (530). The narrator asks Flora, privately, if what he has heard about her vision is true, and she passionately denies it as a lie.

The narrator takes an interest in Flora and begins painting her on a regular basis. He learns that Flora wants to marry Lord Iffield, but that she must overcome his family's disapproval. Meanwhile, a young man named Geoffrey Dawling visits the narrator's studio in search of the beautiful young woman portrayed in the narrator's paintings, with whom he has fallen madly in love. Dawling has a fortune but is neither handsome nor aristocratic; Flora summarily dismisses his proclamations of love.

One day, the narrator sees Flora Saunt and Lord Iffield in a department store and witnesses a telling exchange: Flora, engaged in mysterious gestures before a table of toys, is taken by surprise by Lord Iffield. She wheels around, revealing a hideous pair of glasses "crookedly astride of her beautiful nose" (544). The narrator later discusses the scene with Geoffrey Dawling and speculates that the glasses indicate that Flora's eyesight has started to deteriorate.

These suspicions are confirmed by a visit to the narrator from Flora, who confesses that she risks losing her sight completely if she does not submit to glasses. She knows that the glasses will destroy her beauty, ruining her hopes for future happiness and security, which depend on her ability to secure a wealthy husband. Almost immediately after Flora's confession, Mrs. Meldrum reports to the narrator that Flora is finally engaged to Lord Iffield. Mrs. Meldrum also admits that she herself has fallen in love with Dawling.

The narrator leaves England for America, where he passes a year without any news of his friends. On hearing that his mother's health is failing, he races back to Folkestone. Paying a visit to Mrs. Meldrum, he is shocked to encounter Flora instead, her beauty obliterated by glasses. Lord Iffield has thrown Flora over on the eve of their wedding after learning that her vision was failing. Still unwilling to accept Mr. Dawling, Flora has turned to Mrs. Meldrum and is carrying out what she believes is a cure for her ailments. Without her beauty, the narrator feels that Flora has ceased to exist. He excuses himself to return to London.

The narrator spends the next three years working in America. Upon returning to London, he attends the opera, where he sees an exquisitely beautiful lady. He realizes with a shock that he is looking at Flora, restored to her former glory. He rushes to her box to pay tribute to her, only to realize that she is completely blind. Her recovered beauty and affluence are explained by the entrance of Geoffrey Dawling, now her husband. The narrator congratulates both husband and wife on their MARRIAGE and on Flora's brilliance, but he quickly realizes that neither of them will publicly acknowledge her blindness. He leaves the happy couple and returns to Folkestone to see Mrs. Meldrum, who now refuses to discuss the subject of Flora Saunt altogether. "She simply couldn't bear it" (571).

CRITICAL ANALYSIS

"Glasses" was the only story from *Embarrassments* to have been left out of the NEW YORK EDITION. This may account for what George Bishop has called its "exclusion from the established Jamesian canon" (348). Only a few critics have addressed the story, and those treatments have taken place only in the last 30 years. Yet, thematically and stylistically this "curious tale," as Adrian Poole calls it, has a good deal to offer readers of James. With its untrustworthy artist-narrator, its beautiful and narcissistic heroine, its complex circuits of unrequited love and desire, and its shocking twists of plot, the story is immediately compelling. Further, its meditations on female beauty and the challenges of representation, on glittering surfaces and mysterious depths, on the conflict of the participant-observer, on the "vision" of the artist, and on vision itself make it ripe for analyses from a variety of critical perspectives, including feminist, psychoanalytic, deconstructive, and economic readings.

Most studies of the story have addressed the question of the narrator's trustworthiness. He has been read as "myopic" but largely reliable (Dean);

as suffering from a paralyzing fear of abandonment (Poole); as a voyeur and fetishist (Izzo); and as undermining not only his own authority as a narrator but the very notions of James himself (Bishop). The key to the story seems to lie in the narrator's apparent complicity in the events he claims merely to narrate. He is present at more than one key moment in the narrative and can be credited with bringing Dawling and Flora together in the first place. At some moments, the narrator ostentatiously chooses not to intervene, as when he fails to warn Flora that Lord Iffield is on the verge of discovering her glasses. At other moments, such as his detailed report to the smitten Dawling of Flora's tragic dilemma, his interventions set key events in motion.

Furthermore, his judgment—both aesthetic and moral—is thrown into question throughout the story. On the very first page, he describes Folkestone in surprisingly anti-Semitic (see ANTI-SEMITISM) terms: "there were thousands of little chairs and almost as many little Jews; and there was music . . . over which the little Jews wagged their big noses" (525). Later, he radically misjudges Flora's fate, remarking that "I knew what belonged to my trade well enough to be sure [her beauty] was gone forever" (563). Such a claim, disproven by his very next encounter with Flora, casts doubt on his pronouncement at the conclusion of the story: "Flora was settled for life—nothing could hurt her further" (569). It also throws into question his abilities as a painter; as he says himself, his perceptions of Flora's beauty are directly relevant to his fitness for his trade.

The narrator's moral vision is also flawed. He admits that on his penultimate meeting with Flora, "to put it crudely, I had . . . left poor Flora for dead" (565), emphasizing his objectification of Flora who, no longer a beauty, has ceased to exist for him. He shows an equal want of compassion for the bespectacled Mrs. Meldrum, whom he describes as ugly and whose admission of love for Geoffrey Dawling he all but ignores, and for Dawling himself, whose seemingly fruitless fascination with Flora Saunt he encourages and, indeed, enables in the first place.

George Bishop emphasizes the lack of a definite article in the story's title, suggesting that it can thus be taken to refer not only to Flora's glasses but also to the profusion of related images (including plate-glass windows, opera glasses, and magnifying glasses) that reappear throughout. These images create a sense of fragility and defenselessness that is echoed in repeated references to the saying, "those who live in glass houses shouldn't throw stones" (531). Flora is living in a metaphorical glass house: She is infinitely vulnerable, exposed to the gazes of all the other characters, and imprisoned by her glasses, whether or not she consents to wear them.

A few critics associate "Glasses" with James's own vulnerabilities. The story was composed just after his great theatrical failure, *Guy Domville*, in January 1895, and he had begun to struggle with his own advancing age (James was 52 in 1895). In "James's Spectacles: Distorted Vision in *The Ambassadors*," Hazel Hutchison claims that "in his middle years, James's own eyesight began to alter and deteriorate" and that "James became absorbed not simply by the possibilities of sight, but also by what happens when it fails to function properly" (40). Hutchison argues that the failure of his vision led James to adopt an expanded, proto-modernist treatment of narrative perspective, in which "distorted vision, after all, makes for the better picture" (50).

Vision and visuality figure centrally in James's work, and many critics have taken up these subjects in other contexts (see Griffin, Tintner, and Rivkin). Perhaps a work that is most relevant to an understanding of "Glasses" among them is Carolyn Porter's influential 1981 book *Seeing and Being*, which examines "the seer's complicity in the events he presumes to watch" (xii). More recent readings of "Glasses" emphasize the historical developments of the moment, such as the growing popularity of glasses as a consumer item (Poole) and the development of new technologies of seeing, including the microscope (Armstrong).

Critics have found a wide array of fictional precursors to this story, among them Poe's short story "Spectacles" (Tintner, Izzo); Maupassant's short fiction, to which James refers in a relevant notebook entry (Bishop); Rostand's *La princesse Lointaine* (Tintner, Poole); and E. T. A. Hoffman's "The Sandman," the subject of Freud's famous essay on "The Uncanny" (Izzo).

CHARACTERS

Dawling, Geoffrey Dawling is described as a "long, lean, confused, confusing young man, with a bad complexion and large, protrusive teeth" (535). He is a "worshipper at the shrine of beauty," Flora's chief admirer, and an Oxford-educated man of "tremendous cleverness" and "literary society" (541). Dawling fascinates the narrator, who attempts to sketch him despite his ugliness in order to search "for the buried treasure of his soul" (543).

Iffield, Lord The narrator first describes him as a "small pale youth in showy knickerbockers" (532). The aristocratic son of Lord Considine, Lord Iffield will someday inherit his father's title. He is Flora's primary love interest, though their marriage is opposed by his family. While readers learn little else about him, Mrs. Meldrum states that in the end "he behaved like a regular beast" (560) to Flora when he called off their wedding.

Meldrum, Mrs. A widow of an officer in the Engineers, she befriends the narrator at the beginning of the story. Mrs. Meldrum's physical gracelessness is exacerbated by a pair of conspicuous spectacles, which have the unfortunate effect of magnifying her eyes. Although the narrator spends a significant amount of time explaining how physically unattractive Mrs. Meldrum is, he relies on her sensible, honest, and insightful evaluations of the other characters.

Narrator A successful London artist, he travels frequently to America. Though a devoted son to his aging mother, the narrator is unmarried and seems not to have any other family connections. He drops hints, however, that there may be a few women brightening the unmitigated gloom of his bachelorhood. The narrator assures readers that the story he tells "is all there," likening it to "a row of coloured beads on a string" (525). Still, his trustworthiness as a narrator is questionable. His fascination with Flora's beauty suggests a general affinity for surfaces, and the ease with which he forgets about her when he thinks her beauty is gone forever should perhaps raise questions about his moral and aesthetic judgment.

Saunt, Flora   Completely defined by the stunning beauty of her face, Flora Saunt seems to have little to offer beyond this one asset. Her figure, according to the narrator, is "meager," her intelligence limited, and her inheritance quickly disappearing. Despite all this, or perhaps because of it, she strikes the narrator as "abjectly, divinely, conceited, absurdly, fantastically happy. Her beauty was as yet all the world to her, a world she had plenty to do to live in" (528). Flora has recently lost both her parents and is "extraordinarily alone in the world" (527), a situation made worse by the people who have offered to protect her but are quickly spending her modest inheritance.

Her eventual blindness is presented as both a defeat and a triumph: Though she has lost her vision, she may now be content merely to be beautiful, which has been her greatest talent, and her greatest happiness, all along.

ADAPTATION

Adapted as *Affairs of the Heart: Flora* (October 6, 1974), the film was directed by Michael Ferguson, for UK-TV.

FURTHER READING

Armstrong, Isobel. "The Microscope: Mediations of the Sub-Visible World." In *Transactions and Encounters,* edited by Roger Luckhurst and Josephine McDonagh, 30–54. Manchester, U.K.: Manchester University Press, 2002.

Bishop, George. "Shattered Notions of Mastery: Henry James's 'Glasses.'" *Criticism: A Quarterly for Literature and the Arts* 27, no. 4 (1985): 347–362.

Dean, Sharon. "The Myopic Narrator in Henry James's 'Glasses.'" *Henry James Review* 4, no. 3 (1983): 191–195.

Griffin, Susan. *The Historical Eye: The Texture of the Visual in Late James.* Boston: Northeastern University Press, 1991.

Hutchison, Hazel. "James's Spectacles: Distorted Vision in *The Ambassadors.*" *Henry James Review* 26, no. 1 (2005): 39–51.

Izzo, Donatella. "Woman as Image: 'Glasses.'" In *Portraying the Lady: Technologies of Gender in the Short Stories of Henry James,* 99–126. Lincoln: University of Nebraska Press, 2001.

James, Henry. "Glasses." In *Henry James: Complete Stories, 1892–1898,* edited by John Hollander and David Bromwich. New York: Library of America, 1996.

Poole, Adrian. "Through 'Glasses,' Darkly." In *Henry James: The Shorter Fiction: Reassessments,* edited by N. H. Reeve, 1–16. New York: St. Martin's Press, 1997.

Porter, Carolyn. *Seeing and Being: The Plight of the Participant Observer in Emerson, James, Adams, and Faulkner.* Middletown, Conn.: Wesleyan University Press, 1981.

Rivkin, Julie. *False Positions: The Representational Logics of Henry James's Fiction.* Palo Alto, Calif.: Stanford University Press, 1996.

Tintner, Adeline. "Why James Quoted Gibbon in 'Glasses.'" *Studies in Short Fiction* 14 (1977): 287–288.

———. *The Cosmopolitan World of Henry James.* Baton Rouge: Louisiana State Univeristy Press, 1991.

———. *The Book World of Henry James: Appropriating the Classics.* Ann Arbor: UMI Research Press, 1987.

Lisi Schoenbach, *University of Tennessee*

"The Great Good Place" (1900)

First published in the January 1900 number of *Scribner's Monthly Magazine,* "The Great Good Place" was reprinted later that year in the *Soft Side,* along with "The Real Right Thing," "The Third Person," and "Maud-Evelyn." The tale was also included in Volume 16 of James's 1909 NEW YORK EDITION. James's preface to the story is uncharacteristically brief, somewhat cagey, and even, in its open invitation to "plunge" into the story without critical guidance, a kind of distillation of the mood and meaning of the protagonist's ineffable, revitalizing experience. (See PREFACES TO THE NEW YORK EDITION.) The story is often included in collections of James's supernatural tales.

SYNOPSIS

(Section 1) An enviably successful writer, George Dane wakes to another day overfilled with sunshine and obligations. As he is taxed to the brink of breakdown by his own busy prosperity, the new day's promise is an insistent reminder of his own absolute exhaustion. The previous night's rain had lulled him into a reverie of quiet abstraction in which he imagined his daily pressures washed away in a sympathetic flood. Dane is aware that ever-mounting demands and the ceaseless strain of meeting them are a consequence of his own life-affirming endeavors. He wants, though, to be relieved for an interlude, to be disburdened of all worldly encumbrances, including the exacting requirements of his own writing. His agitation increases when Brown, his efficiently loyal servant, appears with two new additions to his master's unplumbed pile of cares: telegrams warning of impending social contacts and time conflicts. As Brown awaits instructions and attempts to understand Dane's seemingly erratic moodiness, Dane discards the telegrams and opts out of these looming appeals and impositions. He sings a snatch of an old Christian hymn—"'*There* is a happy land—far far away!'"—in response to Brown's half-alarmed question, "'Then where *are* you going?'" (574). Dane wishes for the simple solution of inclement weather to give him a certain respite. Brown then reminds him—not without solicitous hesitation— that a breakfast guest is expected. Dane cannot recall anything about this presumably young guest except that his letter invited response. As Dane goes to meet this unnamed, undescribed man, he is exquisitely sensitive in his nervous state and has all along refused to remove his hands from his pockets, as if to ward off the inevitable deluge of handling his accumulated papers. Yet hospitality calls, and with mannerly spontaneity, he reaches out to shake the hand of his guest. The young man takes Dane's hand and, though the aftermath of this contact is alluded to, time now seems suspended and immeasurable.

(Section 2) Dane is aware that he has been silent for possibly a week in a place apart from the dreary plenitude and paraphernalia of the workaday world, a place of soothing precision and dimensionally suggestive serenity. He sees glimpses of calm water, old statues, a continuous garden, and other silent inhabitants. True to his writerly nature, Dane, muddled but not unpleasantly so, tries to sort

out his surroundings in words and finds the general "absence" of everything (576) to be the peaceful keynote of the place. He is joined on his bench by one of the men—who strangely mirrors Dane's own image. Dane intuits that he and this man are "Brothers" as he sinks into a sense of absorbing tranquility and unchanging, essential stillness. His awareness, freed from daily cares, is heightened. He is in a perfectly proportioned monastery, which he likens to a less austere, more inviting version of the Benedictine abbey Monte Cassino and the Carthusian Grande Chartreuse. This "great good place" offers perfect peace, and when the Brother breaks the silence, he echoes Dane's own thoughts. They muse together on what and where this place might be, on the marvel of discovering it, and on the great, all-encompassing need that led them to its restful precincts. They consider the urgent need for having a place to pause from the day-to-day living and to envision a secular kind of Catholic retreat. Dane recounts his coming to the place and how his breakfast guest—now called his "poor friend," "substitute in the world," and "unutterable benefactor" (582)—appeared just before "the eternal too much" (582) had threatened to engulf him.

(Section 3) The conversation with the Brother continues, with Dane attempting to explain his impressions of the eager young man who came for breakfast. Now able to recall the details of their initial contact, Dane recognizes that what was made as an expedient morning engagement became the catalyst for a soul-saving change. This young writer-turned-savior, brimming with envy and desire, was starved for the kind of success by which Dane was thoroughly sickened. Dane, world-weary and depleted, wished to slough off identity, to become a nobody, and to encounter the great reality of Being, in its purest essence. Their communion is complete and transformative: The younger man assumes Dane's identity at the same time effecting Dane's mysterious effacement. Dane remembers leaning back against the sofa cushions, feeling light now that he has discarded his public, workaday self. His explanation finished, he and the Brother, in silent accord, "as nobody talking with nobody" (586), watch the agreeable scene before them in the softly deepening darkness.

(Section 4) Dane recovers the divine spark of his own original genius, which had been threatened and debased by worldly claims and pursuits. Three weeks may have passed, though time is still hazy, and Dane has a clearer vision of his sanctuary, though he is still uncertain as to where exactly he is. All is regulated with unobtrusive regard for his well-being. He pays for all services in real money as if in an idealized hotel, and he speculates that the place is the bountiful conception of a "wise" (588), like-minded individual consciousness. Away from the bustling contention of the world, he is cured of soul-sickness and reacquainted with his deepest self. The place seems attuned to his vision, as if his innermost needs had determined each scene's perspective and conjured congenial company. He and a new Brother trade unspecified details about their cures when, laying his hand on his Brother's arm, Dane bursts into joyful laughter.

(Section 5) He and a Brother discuss the restorative virtues of the place and consider that the system of payment assures future access. Though the place is built and maintained by love, if payment is exacted, there is a kind of perpetual contract, which permits the place's continued existence and invites return. They liken the place to a great, infinitely interpretable work of art, a "kindergarten" (593), and a kind of earthly maternal deity. As a soothing rain falls, they glimpse again the frightening "front" (594) to which they must return. The Brother, holding Dane's hand, bids him an encouraging farewell and cryptically vows that they will again meet. Dane opens his eyes to find Brown holding his hand, the rain pelting the glass, and the night descending. The young man, radiantly cheerful, is in the same position Dane last remembers. He has finished Dane's chores while Dane slept, and he echoes the parting looks and words of the Brother: "'It's all right!'" (597). Dane believes that this now is so.

CRITICAL ANALYSIS

With characteristic ambiguity and psychological acumen, James offers a place of transcendent utopian perfection that is firmly, if esoterically, grounded on the material plane. "The Great Good Place" is, as many critics have noted, part monas-

tic retreat, part idyllic sanatorium, and part aesthetically refined men's club or resort. Mysterious though it may be, this place of primal refuge is ordered on a recognizably human scale. Though it is arrived at through indirection after an unexplained "tip" (582) and its physicality, though experienced by Dane, is never precisely mapped, its pleasures include perfect human sympathy, harmonious vistas, a limitless library, and the fair purchase of room and board. The autobiographical (see AUTOBIOGRAPHIES) nature of this later-years tale is transparently unmistakable. Dane the artist has been eclipsed but not vanquished by Dane the successful author. He is demoralized—despiritualized—but the real life within him—what he identifies as the "vision and the faculty divine" (from Wordsworth's The Excursion)—remains alight within (586). He and others like him are "victims of the modern madness, mere maniacal extension and motion" (588), no longer authors of themselves. James's dreamworld is less a fantastic parallel universe and more a familiar extension of the world, washed clean of tensions and trivialities. Dane is after authenticity, not just a break from routine work. He wants to feel again the mysterious source of his own creative urges and to experience the real pattern of existence within what Virginia Woolf calls in "Sketch of the Past" as "the cotton wool of daily life" (73).

James's New York Edition preface suggests that the story cannot be comprehended through intellectual deliberation; it—like the place it posits—must be experienced to be known: "There remains 'The Great Good Place' (1900)—to the spirit of which, however, it strikes me, any gloss or comment would be a tactless challenge. It embodies a calculated effect, and to plunge into it, I find, even for a beguiled glance—a course I indeed recommend—is to have left all else outside. There then my indications must wait" (1,242).

Whether dismissing this tale as lesser James (Edgar, Follini) or lauding it as a delicately evocative and moving meditation by the master in his prime (Fadiman), critics have consistently noted the psychospiritual resonance of its dream-symbology, its journey motif, and its penetrating indictment of modern materialism. Leon Edel considers that the "dream-wish" in the story resides in Dane's identification with his young helper. "The great good place," writes Edel, "is the place of youth" (569). Robert E. Whelan, Jr., links the spiritual perceptions in the story to James's 1910 essay, "Is There a Life After Death?" in which James describes being "in communication with sources" that permit artistic "apprehension" and expression ("Life" 224–225). John W. Shroeder concludes that the overt images of cleansing and maternal embracing describe Dane's state of "foetal dependency" and his eventual rebirth (427). Mary Ellen Herx locates James's use of an archetypal "monomyth," which is "symbolic of the primordial experience of a hero's departure from the physical world, his discovery of and initiation into his spiritual realm, and his return, with his boon, to his natural existence" (439). Clifton Fadiman finds "this tiny bit of ordered dreamwork" comparable, in miniature, to *The Pilgrim's Progress* and *The Divine Comedy*. James's "fairy tale" has particular relevance for our time, especially in its thematic exposure of "the essential vacuity of modern living" (413–415).

CHARACTERS

Brother 1   The first fellow-inhabitant of the "Great Good Place" to speak with Dane about their shared experiences, his name for the place is "The Great Want Met." Dane sees himself reflected in the image of this friend, and they muse enthusiastically, attuned to each other's unspecified sufferings, on the place's beneficent effects.

Brother 2   A possible newcomer to the place, he seems tired and perhaps envious of Dane's rediscovered health. He appears in Section 4. See also Brother 3.

Brother 3   Appearing in the fifth and final section, this Brother is distinguished from the Brother in Section 4 because Dane senses that he is in a later stage of developing awareness, though this distinction is somewhat ambiguous. His features transmute into the familiar face of Brown as Dane reinhabits his old identity and returns, altered, from his journey. The young man's words and demeanor reflect those of the Brother.

Brown   Dane's meticulous, efficient, sympathetic servant of 18 years.

Dane, George   An aging, eminently successful writer is overbooked, overworked, and overwhelmed by the life he has made and loved. He wishes for cessation of all things urgent and necessary, of all the daily particulars that require time and attention. He is able—through magical intervention or through a long, nourishing sleep—to transcend the weary grind of the clamoring world and regain his purest self, which had sickened under the assault of his own success. Did he dream himself a place of solace and harmony, or was he actually removed to an alternative world?

Young Man, the   Somewhat of a mystery, the younger man who comes to breakfast is a struggling, failed writer who desperately desires the kind of life Dane has. He assumes Dane's identity and burdens for the length of a day—or for the less time-bound expanse of a dream in an alternative dimension.

FURTHER READING

DeFalco, Joseph. "'The Great Good Place': A Journey into the Psyche." *Literature and Psychology* 6 (1958): 18–20.

Edel, Leon. "Introduction to 'The Great Good Place.'" In *Henry James: Stories of the Supernatural*, edited by Leon Edel, 567–570. New York: Taplinger, 1970.

Edgar, Pelham. *Henry James: Man and Author.* Toronto: Macmillan, 1927.

Fadiman, Clifton. "A Note on 'The Great Good Place.'" In *The Short Stories of Henry James*, edited by Clifton Fadiman, 413–415. New York: Modern Library, 1945.

Follini, Tamara. "Improvising the Past in 'A Small Boy and Others.'" *The Yearbook of English Studies* 30 (2000): 106–123.

Fussell, Edwin Sill. "Protestantizing Catholicity: 'The Great Good Place' (1900)." In *The Catholic Side of Henry James*, 109–111. New York: Cambridge University Press, 1993.

Herx, Mary Ellen. "The Monomyth in 'The Great Good Place.'" *College English* 24, no. 6 (1963): 439–443.

James, Henry. "The Great Good Place." In Edel, 570–597.

———. "Is There a Life After Death?" In *After Days: Thoughts on the Future Life*, edited by William Dean Howells, 99–233. 1910. Reprint, New York: Arno Press, 1977.

———. "Preface to Volume XI of the New York Edition (1909)." In *Literary Criticism: French Writers, Other European Writers, The Prefaces to the New York Edition*, 1,238–1,245. New York: Library of American, 1984.

Shroeder, John W. "The Mothers of Henry James.'" *American Literature* 22, no. 4 (1951): 424–431.

Silverstein, Henry. "The Utopia of Henry James." *New England Quarterly* 35, no. 4 (1962): 458–468.

Tintner, Adeline R. "The Influence of Balzac's *L'Envers d'Histoire Contemporaine* on James's 'The Great Good Place.'" *Studies in Short Fiction* 9 (1972): 343–351.

Veeder, William. "James and the Limitations of Self-Therapy." In *Henry James: The Shorter Fiction, Reassessments*, edited by N. H. Reeve, 170–189. New York: Macmillan/St. Martin's, 1997.

Wagenknecht, Edward. *The Tales of Henry James*, 121–123. New York: Frederick Ungar, 1984.

Ward, J. A. "Silence, Realism, and 'The Great Good Place.'" *Henry James Review* 3, no. 2 (1982): 129–132.

Whelan, Jr., Robert E. "God, Henry James, and 'The Great Good Place.'" *Research Studies of Washington State University* 47 (1979): 212–220.

Woolf, Virginia. "A Sketch of the Past." In *Moments of Being*, edited by Jeanne Schulkind, 61–160. New York: Harcourt Brace Jovanovich, 1985.

Kate Falvey, *New York City College of Technology*

"Greville Fane" (1892)

"Greville Fane" appeared in the *Illustrated London News* (September 17 and 24, 1892) and was reprinted in *The Real Thing and Other Stories* (Macmillan, 1893). It also appears in Volume 16 (1909) of the NEW YORK EDITION.

SYNOPSIS

The story begins as the narrator is asked to write an obituary for an author named Mrs. Stormer. The editor requests that the piece not be overly hard on its subject. The narrator liked Mrs. Stormer as a person but does not admire her as a writer. Mrs. Stormer wrote under a male pseudonym (as did GEORGE ELIOT, George Sand, and originally, the Brontë sisters). She was known to the world as "Greville Fane." For much of the story, the narrator looks back on her life and accomplishments.

The narrator is also a writer of a more highbrow sort and tacitly looks down on the commercial quality of Greville Fane's work, though he admired her industry and productivity and how she quickly adapted to a literary life in her middle age. For the narrator, writing is not only a profession, it is also a vocation. As an artist it does not matter to him that he does not receive much remuneration for his work.

The narrator wonders why Greville Fane, with all her gifts, never aspired to a fine style, attributing its lack as much to her temperament as to her ability. Greville Fane was aware of the limits of her artistic achievement as well as of her mass popularity, which was substantial but not so widespread as to make her financially secure. She was not entirely a populist, having been, for instance, snobbish toward Americans, and seeing herself as sufficiently highbrow to resent literary praise from the wrong sort of people.

In her private life, Mrs. Stormer tried to secure her daughter a good MARRIAGE to Sir Baldwin Luard, a not particularly wealthy politician who was nonetheless more prestigious than any other available match. Mrs. Stormer was greatly disappointed when she was asked to leave her daughter's household after the marriage. Mrs. Stormer's son, Leolin, was the object of her admiration and hope. Instead of giving him a conventional upper-class education, she sent him out into the world to live, with the hope that he would be a greater novelist than she, having really observed life. But Leolin ended up making only a few sales to rather disreputable publications and simply supplying raw material for his mother's fictions. Both children seemed to take their mother's love and talent for granted; her literary legacy has devolved into their bickering over her posthumous publications.

CRITICAL ANALYSIS

As Kristin King points out, "Greville Fane" is one of seven short stories by James that concern female writers. James relies on the Victorian era's (see VICTORIANISM) common stereotype of the woman novelist who produces popular but less artistically rigorous productions. Mrs. Stormer's daughter, Lady Luard, is entirely nonliterary. Her son, Leolin, is a writer of even lower caliber than his mother. Furthermore, he is loathed by the narrator.

Greville Fane is represented as a realistic social novelist, not a sensation writer. She is perhaps an amalgam of women writers from the Victorian era on whom James kept his eye, such as Mrs. Margaret Oliphant, the sober author of *Miss Marjoribanks,* and Mary Elizabeth Braddon, whose productivity, popularity (she authored the sensational best seller *Lady Audley's Secret*), and seeming lack of concern over stylistic assessment resemble those of Fane's. Frederick Wegener has suggested that Greville Fane is partially based on James's friend James Payn; Adeline Tintner has proposed the late Victorian sensation and adventure novelist Ouida as the source. James makes it clear that Greville Fane, despite her fascination with the aristocracy (into which her daughter marries), does not just write late Victorian updates of the so-called silver-fork novels written by earlier 19th-century authors such as the Countess of Blessington.

The name "Greville Fane" sounds aristocratic. Spencer P. Fane was a member of Queen Victoria's court during James's lifetime, and Charles Greville was the great Victorian political diarist. These associations point to one of the subthemes of the story: the intersection of writing and social climbing. But Mrs. Stormer herself is a paradigm of the middle-class writer who succeeds by working industriously, making sure all of her bills are paid on time, and having a keen sense of what the mass audience will appreciate and purchase.

Leolin asks the narrator how far a writer could push the limits of the English novel and wonders if he himself might be the one to expand its boundaries. At one level, Leolin is referring to the novel's recognition of sexual explicitness, recalling the traditional latitude exercised in the French novel. But Leolin is also implying that he wishes to go beyond the conventional mode of his mother's popular formula and that he wishes to be more daring and experimental. Leolin overlooks his mother's own desire to take the English novel in the more passionate direction of Balzac.

The narrator resents the way Leolin uses the specter of radical artistic experiment to promote himself and to imagine a tidy profit. At one point, Leolin asks the narrator if he thinks his writing might injure his mother, implying that she has been too tame and conventional. He also fears dampening her earning power. In disgust, the narrator parrots Leolin's language about the novel form, concluding that it is Leolin himself who goes too far. The narrator finally weighs his respect for "Greville Fane" against his dismissal of her son's character and talent. Conversely, Mrs. Stormer maintained her balancing act of family concerns and artistic production to her death.

"Greville Fane" stands with "The FIGURE IN THE CARPET" and "The LESSON OF THE MASTER" as parables about the elusive qualities of literary merit and with "The MIDDLE YEARS" and "Collaboration" as accounts that address the themes of mortality and literary idealism. Indeed, the story gives a consummate view of the competing challenges that a literary writer faced in working to earn a living in the Victorian marketplace and at the same time believing in art as possessing a transcendent value, irreducible to a paycheck.

CHARACTERS

Fane, Greville   Greville Fane is the pseudonym of Mrs. Stormer, a successful commercial novelist who has entered the literary field in middle age. She lives in the Primrose Hill neighborhood, northwest of Central London. Greville Fane is a friend of the narrator but has disappointed him by her inattentiveness to her craft.

Luard, Lady   The daughter of Mrs. Stormer marries a prominent politician and leads a conventional bourgeois life. Tall, stiff, and cold, she is a stranger to the world of letters.

Narrator   Unnamed throughout, he is also a writer who provides the story's perspective on the Stormer family. He is perhaps a few years older than Leolin.

Stormer, Leolin   The son of Greville Fane cultivates a misguided belief in his extraordinary literary potential. In the narrator's opinion, Leolin is coarse, impudent, and opportunistic. Leolin's corrupt moral viewpoint provides the principal drama of the story.

FURTHER READING

Boyd, Anne E. *Writing for Immortality: Women and the Emergence of High Literary Culture in America.* Baltimore: Johns Hopkins University Press, 2004.

Fussell, Edwin Sill. *The Catholic Side of Henry James.* New York: Cambridge University Press, 1993.

Gay, Peter. *The Cultivation of Hatred (The Bourgeois Experience: Victoria to Freud),* vol. 3. New York: Norton, 1993.

Katz, Tamar. *Impressionist Subjects: Gender, Interiority, and Modernist Fiction in England.* Urbana: University of Illinois Press, 2000.

King, Kristin. "'Lost among the Genders': Male Narrators and Female Writers in James's Literary Tales, 1892–1896." *Henry James Review* 16, no. 1 (1995): 18–35.

Person, Leland S. *Henry James and the Suspense of Masculinity.* Philadelphia: University of Pennsylvania Press, 2003.

Tintner, Adeline. *The Cosmopolitan World of Henry James: An Intertextual Study.* Baton Rouge: Louisiana State University Press, 1991.

Wegener, Frederick. "Henry James on James Payn: A Forgotten Critical Text." *The New England Quarterly* 67, no. 1 (1994): 115–129.

Nicholas Birns, *The New School*

"An International Episode" (1878)

"An International Episode" was serialized in the British *Cornhill Magazine* (December 1878–January 1879). Its second appearance was in the English book collection *Daisy Miller: A Study/An International Episode/Four Meetings* (1879). James then revised it for Volume 14 of the NEW YORK EDITION (1907–09).

SYNOPSIS

(Parts I–III) The story begins in NEW YORK CITY and NEWPORT during the summer of 1874. Two dapper English gentlemen, Lord Lambeth and Barrister Percy Beaumont, try to control their discomfort under the August sun of New York City, where Beaumont is attending to legal business regarding an American railroad company. With a letter of introduction, they seek out Mr. J. L. Westgate, a successful businessman, who, to their relief, undertakes the suit against the railroad company and sends Lambeth and Beaumont off to his hospitable wife in Newport. On the journey to Westgate's seaside home, Lambeth and Beaumont enjoy the scenery as they converse about the United States. Upon their arrival, Mrs. Westgate receives them graciously, and the two Englishmen are taken in by her bright beauty, amiable elegance, and spontaneous nature. To them, she seems unencumbered by a typical British self-restraint. As guests, they defer to Mrs. Westgate's hospitality and enjoy the relaxing atmosphere of her seaside residence. She expresses that she and Mr. Westgate, and Americans in general, very much admire cultured and well-mannered English people.

Lambeth takes an interest in Mrs. Westgate's younger sister from Boston, Bessie Alden, who is more reserved and introspective than her sister. Lambeth and Bessie Alden increasingly spend more quiet times together. He finds it charmingly curious that she is fascinated about the particularities of English life and aristocratic titles and is an avid reader of novels by Thackeray and Kingsley. All the while, Beaumont keeps a keen eye on his infatuated friend. Three weeks later, Beaumont and Lambeth bid the sisters a fond farewell when they leave for England. Lambeth invites Mrs. Westgate and her sister to visit him if they ever travel to LONDON. On the steamer back to England, Beaumont reveals to Lambeth that he has written to Lambeth's mother, the Duchess of Bayswater, about his acquaintance

"On Sundays, now, you might be at home?" by A. L. Coburn, frontispiece to "Lady Barberina," in Volume 14, the New York Edition

with Bessie Alden. He also suspects that this is why the Duchess wrote asking Lambeth to return to England. Lambeth is rather upset.

(Parts IV–VI) The story continues in May 1875. Mrs. Westgate and her sister indeed make it to London. It is Alden's first trip to Europe. They stay in London at a hotel while visiting their friends and run into young Willie Woodley from New York, who escorts Alden around famous and historical sites. Alden wonders why Mrs. Westgate avoids writing to Percy Beaumont about their arrival in England. Their conversation leads Mrs. Westgate to ask Alden whether she is in love with Lambeth; Alden replies, "Not that I know of" (368). Mrs. Westgate adds that she will certainly not send for Lambeth if Alden is. The sisters avoid the subject until Mrs. Westgate informs Alden that she will write to Lambeth so that Alden will learn the reality of how English people behave on their own turf.

On an outing, Woodley spots Lambeth and brings him to Alden. Lambeth is delighted to see Alden and Mrs. Westgate again, and Alden allows

herself to be drawn toward Lambeth again, charmed by what seems to her his picturesque Englishness. The next day, Lambeth and Beaumont call on the sisters. Beaumont warns Lambeth that the Duchess will not approve of his association with the American girls, but despite this Lambeth spends a lot of time with the two. The sisters see many English socialites, attend many dinner parties and balls, and even appear in court at Buckingham Palace. Lambeth invites them to Branches Castle, his country home, along with his mother and sisters. He reproaches Beaumont for only calling upon the sisters twice during their stay in London. Percy replies that there is no need to call upon them because Lambeth's avid attention more than makes up for his neglect. During their conversation, he presses Lambeth on what his intentions are toward Alden.

Meanwhile, the sisters discuss the possibility of Alden marrying Lambeth. Lambeth's mother and sister come to call upon the two sisters; they scrutinize Alden and inquire after her in a rather patronizing and disdainful manner. Toward the end of their visit, the Duchess announces that she will come to Branches Castle after all and will monopolize Alden's company. The visit from Lambeth's mother and sister leaves the sisters feeling very uneasy and disappointed. Later, Alden tells Mrs. Westgate that when Lambeth came she refused his offer to go to Branches Castle. Lambeth laments the end of their association. Wrapping up their affairs in London, the two American sisters travel on to PARIS.

CRITICAL ANALYSIS

There has not been much written on "An International Episode" compared to James's other major novels and works. It paints a sharp contrast between the transatlantic cultures of America and Europe, their people, their attitudes and their sensibilities (see INTERNATIONAL THEME). The story can be read as a counterpart to James's popular international novella "DAISY MILLER: A STUDY" (1878), which was first published in the same magazine. The prose of "An International Episode" can seem flowery, but underneath it lies the dramatic tension of social rejection, hurt feelings, and a class snobbery dressed in the differences of culture.

James is often considered the master of the psychological novel. Though this story seems to lack depictions of internal psychological complexity, there are many clues through which readers can understand the protagonists' states of mind. Through this layered prose, James portrays his characters' prejudices, patterns of thinking, and customary attitudes of the historical period. His works frequently juxtapose characters from two cultures: the Old World of Europe (simultaneously aristocratic and corrupted, emulated but scorned by Americans) versus the New World of America (brash, spontaneous, and openly assertive). In this story, he dramatizes the differences between American and European manners in a courtship drama. The prose dissects how characters yearn for those to whom they are attracted only to have their hopes broken. In these passionate moments, characters find their dreams reorganizing reality in ways that defy class hierarchies and national differences. The layered and complex language of "An International Episode" allows the reader to acknowledge, if not sympathize with, Lambeth's and Alden's personal desires, which are kept in check by their society and cultural moment.

The impediment to their budding romance is Lambeth's "Englishness" and Alden's status as an American girl from Boston. During James's time, what did it mean to be of the upper class in America instead of in England or Europe? In general, class status in England depended on being well-endowed with material capital whose source was less important than the subsequent reputation of a family name and sense of tradition that had accrued to that wealth. The British aristocracy was the symbol of a refined society and a national culture with centuries of tradition behind it. In contrast, to be American, even one with impressive amounts of money and social influence, was to rely on a new type of social prestige. In the story, the Duchess seems to see all Americans as renegades who stand outside England's pretension to a deep history. How can an American establish a family name with claims to intergenerational respect in so short a period?

Americans make up for this apparent lack of roots, antiquity, and history by claiming that development of vast land and other resources will express new democratic ideals of freedom, individualism, and opportunities for all. The typical American establishes social reputation not through a system of peerage or claims to a lineage or title but through the supposed virtues of self-promotion and hard work. In Boston, New York, and Newport, the Westgates and Alden are socialites with an impressive reputation that does not translate to England. The star-crossed lovers of Lambeth and Alden display the trappings of their respective cultural categories. His character is formal and correct, and he is forever a gentleman; Alden's character is a young American who is curious about an England she has encountered through novels. She has a naive sense that British culture must be fine and beautiful because of its lords, royalty, and peerage. She bombards Lambeth with superficial questions on the smallest details about England and its ways of fine living. She very much wants to mold Lambeth into a perfect version of what she fantasizes to be an English gentleman, though in reality the reader realizes that he is relatively dull and not very glamorous.

Lambeth is also naive in his courtship of Alden, believing that love can conquer the prejudices and sensitivities of those with whom he associates. Beaumont reminds Lambeth of proprieties in finding a romantic match and advises him to step back from the transgression of English social norms. When Beaumont proves ineffectual, the Duchess intervenes to put Alden and Lambeth back in their proper place. The Duchess thereby rejects Alden as an appropriate match for her highborn son. By the story's end, Alden seems to have become more sophisticated and less optimistic about the powers of love and attraction. When Alden rejects Lambeth, she does it to prevent his fall from grace, and she quietly acquiesces to the prejudices that make her an unacceptable match. Readers are left to ponder what her acceptance means.

CHARACTERS

Alden, Bessie The sister of Mrs. Westgate, a young beautiful maiden is in love with the idea of "Englishness." She is later disappointed by that very same English reality when her love for and potential union with Lambeth are crushed by English protocol, decorum, and public opinions.

Bayswater, Duchess of A robust and discriminating woman, she monitors her son's friendships, policing him to ensure he does not make an improper match. In facing down the threat of Bessie Alden, she engages the touring Americans in conversation that demonstrates her resolve to handle them without becoming overtly familiar in the necessary association.

Beaumont, Percy Lambeth's friend and a barrister who travels with him to the United States is an Englishman who seems to be critical and skeptical of all things American. He criticizes Lambeth's enthusiasm and love for Bessie Alden and tries to keep Lambeth's feelings in check.

Lambeth, Lord An aristocratic young Englishman is charmed by the spontaneous, unrehearsed, and brash energy of American people. He falls for the story's heroine, Bessie Alden.

Westgate, Mr. J. L. Though he appears very briefly in the story, he provides very well for his wife, Mrs. Westgate. He is an icon of successful business in a young America.

Westgate, Mrs. Kitty A spontaneous, beautiful, and vivacious American lady of high New York society with a summer home in Newport, she is very different from the somber British ladies of comparable class. She has a friendly directness in manner and speaks her mind freely.

Woodley, Willie Bessie Alden's escort in England is a soft-spoken yet friendly American and is known to be a wonderful dancer.

FURTHER READING

James, Henry. "An International Episode." In *Complete Stories, 1874–1884*, 326–400. New York: Library of America, 1999.

Tintner, Adeline R. "'An International Episode': A Centennial Review of a Centennial Story." *Henry James Review* 1 (1979): 24–60.

Van Doren, Carl. "Chapter 8: Henry James." In *The American Novel*, 163–189. New York: Macmillan, 1921.

Hanh Nguyen, *University of Florida*

"In The Cage" (1898)

At more than 30,000 words, "In the Cage" is one of Henry James's longer short works. The novella was one of the first to be dictated to William MacAlpine, a practice James continued for the duration of his career. Published in LONDON by Duckworth and in Chicago and NEW YORK by Stone (both in 1898), it was revised and reprinted in the NEW YORK EDITION of *The Novels and Tales of Henry James*, Volume 11, 1908.

SYNOPSIS

(Chapter 1) The story opens in the post-and-telegraph office, which is a separate cage in the back of Cocker's grocery store, where a Mr. Mudge works.

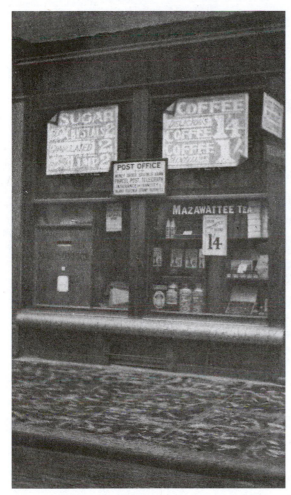

"The Cage," by A. L. Coburn, frontispiece to "In the Cage", in Volume 11, the New York Edition

(Chapter 2) The telegraphist escapes into the "fine print" about "fine folks" that make up the "ha'penny" novels (316). Convinced that she is alone and misunderstood, she retreats into her imagination, much preferable to the reality with her fiancé, Mr. Mudge. She justifies delaying her MARRIAGE in part because it would mean leaving London at the precise moment at which her occupation as a translator of messages has become most engaging. This moment is marked by the appearance of a "memorable" (317) woman, later identified as Lady Bradeen.

(Chapter 3) The girl rushes to receive Lady Bradeen's telegrams, immediately aware of their "entertainment" value (318). She quickly ascertains that the first two telegrams were meant as decoys for the only message with actual significance: a message from Lady Bradeen to her lover, Everard, who is staying in a Parisian hotel. Sensing that she is witnessing the "critical stage" (319) of a personal drama, the girl immerses herself in the world of Lady Bradeen's affair in her imagination.

(Chapter 4) Spying them from within her cage, the girl knows with a "thump" that Everard is accompanied by Lady Bradeen (320). His words consist of "mere numbers," yield no meaning, but leave the girl with a "sweet" impression and desire to know more about the couple's relationship (320). She is so consumed by him that when he returns the following day, she counts his words with a "quick caress" of her pencil (321). She marvels at her privilege of sending his telegrams and at Everard's courtesy; yet she quickly understands that his courtesy is not directed toward her specifically but is parceled out equally to others as a staple of his class.

(Chapter 5) The girl believes that her connection to Everard is natural. She relies more and more on her imagined relations to survive the days at Cocker's. She explains how she reads the telegrams, even changing their words, vainly believing that she could live her clients' lives much better than they do. She thinks her upper-class clientele are like a great herd, indistinguishable from people of her class in every way other than their economic privilege.

(Chapter 6) Mrs. Jordan, a neighbor, proudly tells the girl of her growing stature among "the

Cocker's is located in the higher-class section of Mayfair, London, far from the heroine's poverty-stricken abode, where she resides with her mother and older sister. The unnamed "telegraphist" (314) spends hours in the cage, which serves as the only barrier between her and the clients who can afford frequent correspondence through telegrams. Her use of the "sounder" mechanism contributes something to the "meanness of her function" (314). She distracts herself from the foul smells of the grocery store and distasteful company of two male employees by fantasizing that she *knows* the London elite "without their recognizing the acquaintance" (314).

great people" (326). She realizes the advantages of employing the girl and sending her to their houses to care for their floral arrangements. Mrs. Jordan grossly exaggerates her importance, believing that she brings peace to her clients. Business is growing, which prompts Mrs. Jordan to invite the girl to be her partner, especially since she craves the company of an equal. But the girl feels disadvantaged by the "strange gaps in her learning," which make the idea of working inside the "homes" of the rich intimidating (327). Even though she notes Mrs. Jordan's inflated sense of importance about her occupation, the girl still envies her proximity to the real lives of the upper class.

(Chapter 7) The girl interrogates Mrs. Jordan's ambiguous stories of intimacy with her upper-class employers. As a result, Mrs. Jordan, while not relinquishing the power she possesses over the girl, is forced to concede that her "guests" (328) are almost never home when she is there. The girl wonders if doing flowers might lead to a better match than Mr. Mudge. Mrs. Jordan promises to assign her to wealthy bachelors; she has her own eye on Lord Rye.

(Chapter 8) The girl brags about the "affairs," the "little games and secrets and vices" (330) of the rich. She shocks Mrs. Jordan in claiming to know everything about them and in admitting that she hates them. Mrs. Jordan accuses her of lacking sympathy and imagination and regains her superior footing by explaining the difficulties of navigating a full dining room, maintaining the flower arrangements, and repairing damages done by the "bachelors" (331). The girl doubts that a marriage proposal from Lord Rye is forthcoming, but if it ever does, she will "almost" (332) hate Mrs. Jordan too.

(Chapter 9) The "betrothed of Mr. Mudge" (332) is obliged to take walks with him every Sunday and sometimes to attend the theater. Since both dislike "vulgar" (332) plays, Mr. Mudge imagines they are perfectly suited for each other. Though irritated, the girl still admires his MASCULINITY, as he once overpowered a drunken sailor in Cocker's, and his single-minded ambition to capitalize on the booming London trade. Desperate to continue living the "parallel" (333) existence in and out of the cage, she reveals the many secrets and the possible private liaisons, which she has discovered at work. Mr. Mudge misinterprets her motives for remaining in the cage as business savvy, unaware of her consuming fantasies about Everard or of Mrs. Jordan's plan to identify a rich bachelor in lieu of the grocer.

(Chapter 10) The girl offends Mr. Mudge's staunch Methodism by her unabashed loathing for the upper class. Explaining how she loves to hate the "awful wretches," the girl takes liberties with the rich that seem to Mr. Mudge "vaguely wrong" (334, 336). Nonetheless, he is grateful for the many flirtations she facilitates, which to him amount to "more cheese and pickles" (336). Both share trust in her propriety and fidelity, which have, in part, allowed her to cultivate her private, unspoken, and wholly fabricated intimacy with Captain Everard.

(Chapter 11) Everard always returns to Cocker's, a fact that sustains the girl's interest. She believes there is a "tacit recognition" (337) of their intimacy on his part, suggested by his cordial greetings and polite acknowledgment. She revels in her knowledge of his private affairs and is convinced that he is aware of being at her "mercy" (337). She fears his going to other post offices and having relationships with "other girls" (338). The "queerness" of his words forges their "friendship," forcing his return to Cocker's. (338) She flirts with the idea of what a "bad girl" (339) in a ha'penny novel might do with this power, but she rejects any temptation, not wanting money or impropriety.

(Chapter 12) The girl likens Everard's passion for Lady Bradeen to a steam-wheel spinning him around in bewildered danger, making Mr. Mudge seem a "deluded creature" (340) in comparison. She believes that she is Everard's sole comfort amid his spiraling love affair. Desperately wanting to meet him outside the cage, but knowing that this would be impossible, she follows the porter into his building to determine on which floor he lives. The rush of fear she feels creates the illusion of increasing intimacy, as if they are "face to face" (340). She is conscious of the "small throbbing spot" (341) in her life: the mounting belief that he likes her.

(Chapter 13) Lady Bradeen reappears at Cocker's, looking "distinctly less serene" (341), her manner sharp and impatient. It has been 19 days "counted and checked off" since the girl last saw

Everard. Struck by her beauty, the girl is saddened that Lady Bradeen clearly does not know her; however, she rapidly convinces herself that he, too, has kept his intimacy with her a secret, creating a forbidden love affair. This new possibility emboldens the girl, so that when Lady Bradeen confuses the location assigned to a particular alias of Everard's, she interjects the correct one. The telegraphist feels as if she "alighted on her interlocutress" (343) from on top of her cage, leaving Lady Bradeen dumbstruck by the girl's awareness of their trysts.

(Chapter 14) Summer holidays arrive, which highlight the difference between the "animals in the cage" (344) and those tourists in exotic, faraway locations. Sickened by "chronic resentment" (344), the girl tries to look forward to her short vacation in September, but Mr. Mudge plans it all with "calculation" (344). His care and frugality pale in comparison to Everard, who lives "rapturously" (345). The girl continues to walk past Everard's building and finally spies him. He is slow to recognize her but shows his usual good humor. She imagines him gauging the "properness" (346) involved in asking her up to his rooms.

(Chapter 15) She wonders if he would ask her up to his apartment, and if this would amount to infidelity in his affair with Lady Bradeen; but she quickly realizes that as a mere shopgirl, any relation with her would count "as something else" (347). They walk to a park bench, and she worries he might say something vulgar. She feels "excitement within excitement" (347) about sitting so near to him and playfully tests him (and herself) with her coy responses. When Everard directly questions whether she has taken a "particular interest" in him, the girl is suddenly overcome with embarrassment and a "rush" of emotion that ends in a "flood of tears" (349).

(Chapter 16) The girl claims fatigue, then blurts out: "I shall never see you again" (350). Without going into specifics, she explains that she will leave Cocker's and that she has only stayed for him. Everard cannot hide his shock and embarrassment over this confession, and she is thrilled by her momentary power over him. She also feels a rush of bravery and desire to destroy the fantasy that has kept her in the cage for so long. As she imagines

that they are talking in a "boudoir" (351) rather than on a public park bench, he acknowledges how much she has helped him but disappoints her by not mentioning her role to others. The sting of his omission compels her to point out just how much he and his kind seem to want. She adds that only people like her make such double lives possible.

(Chapter 17) The girl tells him that she is leaving for Chalk Farm for more space, but she is vague about her other motivation, namely her betrothal to Mudge. While claiming he will follow her anywhere, he also protests that she ought to stay so that he will not have to miss her. She reveals her loathing of "his set," their treatment of her as a "letter-box," and the "horrors" to which she is privy (353). He wonders if that is not too strong, and she chastises him for his immorality, his "crimes" (353). Everard's discomfort increases when she claims to feel great pleasure in the knowledge of these indiscretions. After announcing that he is in danger, she repeatedly declares that she will not "give him up" and then leaves him, stupefied, on the park bench to walk home alone (353).

(Chapter 18) The girl vacations with Mr. Mudge and her mother at the seaside town of Bournemouth. While Mr. Mudge manages every hour of every day, and her mother drinks with the landlady in the kitchen of their lodging, the girl looks out at the sea. Her week is "blissfully fine" (355) in part because the "stillness" (355) helps her to convert "melancholy and misery" into "experience and knowledge" (356). While annoyed by Mr. Mudge's incessant financial calculations, she accepts him as she never has before and especially appreciates his gift for chatter so that she can escape into her private reveries. Mr. Mudge surprises the girl by announcing his readiness for marriage: He has been asked to join a business, far extending his fortunes, and has his sights on a "sweet little home" (357) for her, which he intends to show her on the ensuing Sunday.

(Chapter 19) The girl describes Mr. Mudge's concealment of his promotion and plan as a "latent force" (357) that parallels his bravura in subduing the drunken sailor. As a result, she begins to understand him as her future, "distinctly her fate" (357). When she insists that the delay must stand, he insists on the reason, and so she tells him the "whole truth" (358) of her meeting in the park, Everard's affairs, and his "awful danger" (359). Mr. Mudge has confidence in her, but he is surprised that he did not follow her out of the park. While he accepts that the waiting will continue, Mr. Mudge takes her arm with "force" and expects her to resolve her other affairs soon. He calls Everard a "cad" (360).

(Chapter 20) Soon Everard returns to Cocker's but takes his business to Mr. Buckton rather than the telegraphist. From their exchange of glances, she assumes he has understood that the meeting in the park created a pact between them that "could end only with death" (361). Still, she longs for the conversation and attention they formerly shared in Cocker's. After he leaves, she pictures him waiting for her on their park bench. She thinks it might be her last chance to abandon Mr. Mudge and let Everard "make everything up to her" (362). But when he suddenly reenters the shop, she becomes petrified by his prolonged stay and careful avoidance of her. She wonders what he wants and seeks "refuge" (364) in the sounder cubicle.

(Chapter 21) Everard appears three days in a row, illustrating a "tremendous" "rigour" that frightens the girl (364). The cage becomes her only "safety" (364). Instead of passing his apartment, she now goes directly home. She tries to intimate her desire for him to leave, but he instead leaves "redundant money" (365) on the counter. The girl tells herself that the money reflects his respect since he knows she would not take it. When she catches a glimpse of his message to a Doctor Buzzard ("absolutely impossible"), she reads it as a note to Lady Bradeen, especially when he withdraws the form. She thinks he is struggling to give up his lover, the "real mistress of his fate" (366).

(Chapter 22) Everard does not return to Cocker's for 18 days, which the girl interprets as his proper regard for her space and recognition that even the "poor little girl at the P.O." has secrets (366). She waits, wanting to reestablish the proper relations between classes, worker, and client before marrying Mr. Mudge. One day Everard returns, clearly under great anxiety and panic, demanding her to submit his telegram with complete indif-

ference to her. When he returns the next day, he looks even worse. He explains that "we" (369) need to retrieve a telegram sent seven or so weeks prior. She delights in playing the anonymous shopgirl in response to his outrageous and indifferent treatment. Her cold inquiries push him to the point of "terror" and "literal tears" (369), which thrill her. The exchange both reaffirms their original positions *and* gives her the chance to be the "very fountain of fate" on which his life seems to depend (369).

(Chapter 23) She feels real "joy" (370) in his suffering; he looks "splendidly helpless" (370) while she very consciously "dangles" (371) him between hope and despair. Everard explains that Lady Bradeen *may* have made an incriminating mistake, one that was intercepted by an unnamed source, or else a numerical error in their favor. He is impatient and angry with her for not producing the old telegram instantaneously. While she momentarily hesitates to expose the extent of her involvement in his "scandal" (372), her desire to help him and prove her cleverness overrides. She writes, from memory, the all-important number on Everard's card. The number proves that Lady Bradeen has made a mistake. He beams "like a tall lighthouse" (372) at everyone in the cage, then without a word of thanks leaves Cocker's. She is elated; no previous joy had ever come "within miles of it" (373).

(Chapter 24) The thrill of Cocker's has left with Everard's departure; so, too, have Mrs. Jordan's fortunes in the absence of her rich clients from the city. The girl and Mrs. Jordan engage each other in "mystification" and distraction from the "limits of low horizons" (373). Mrs. Jordan calls the aristocracy "a tower of strength" (374) in society, hinting through various references to Lord Rye that she may be engaged. The girl suspects that Mrs. Jordan is not telling her about the impending marriage because Lord Rye would not be interested in a "nonentity" (374) like herself. They attend church together, then arrive at Mrs. Jordan's apartment. "Brown fog" and "acrid smoke" hang in Mrs. Jordan's small parlour, and the girl notices that the room has no flowers (374). She waits for the nervous Mrs. Jordan to make an announcement.

(Chapter 25) Mrs. Jordan reminds the girl of Mr. Drake, a "great and trusted friend" (375) of

Lord Rye's, who is now "separating" (376) from him. The girl realizes then that Mr. Drake, *not* Lord Rye, is the one Mrs. Jordan plans to marry. When the girl asks if he is rich, Mrs. Jordan calls him handsome and frugal. When she explains that Mr. Drake is now "engaged" (377) by Lady Bradeen, the girl's face registers some knowledge of her. She explains how beautiful Lady Bradeen is, and unlike many women who come into Cocker's, she does not "hate" (377) her. They are each confused and suspicious of each other.

(Chapter 26) Mrs. Jordan seems upset, even angry, and neither she nor the girl speaks to the other for a period. Then suddenly the girl realizes that Mr. Drake is a butler. Without confirming this directly, Mrs. Jordan explains that Lady Bradeen's husband has died and that she has asked Mr. Drake to work for her. The girl parades her own access to knowledge of the higher class by naming Everard as the sure fiancé of Lady Bradeen. She is startled, then, to imagine that Mr. Drake will oversee the cleaning of Everard's boots. The girl gets ready to leave, assuming that their new connections would signify the end of their friendship. The girl's coldness toward Mrs. Jordan causes her to give up her resentment. She realizes that Mrs. Jordan's marriage to Mr. Drake merely ensures that she will not "starve" (379). The girl finally grasps how her own "dreams and delusions" have made her unable to see their shared poverty and desperation; though they will forever be separated by their supposedly different class affiliations, the girl sets out to leave without any further bitterness (379).

(Chapter 27) Mrs. Jordan offers information about Everard, explaining that Everard has no say in household affairs and that he brings nothing but debt to the union. The girl replays her fantasies about their tryst in Hyde Park and feels stung by the truth about Everard. Apparently, the affair forced Lord Bradeen to do something, but "luckily . . . he died" (382) before he could intervene. Lady Bradeen has rescued Everard from mysterious crimes and a horrible reputation, but he expresses reluctance to marry her regardless. It becomes clear to the girl that she has played a role in their union. The girl and Mrs. Jordan banter competitively about whose house will be ready for occupancy

first. As she walks through the foggy streets of London, the telegraphist is amazed that so much of her information about her customers has depended on what Mrs. Jordan has heard from Mr. Drake.

CRITICAL ANALYSIS

"In the Cage" was the first of the longer tales that James wrote after leaving London to settle in the country town of Rye. Initially published by Herbert Stone, the "mendacious Chicago publisher [who] claimed indefinite rights over 'In the Cage' and *WHAT MAISIE KNEW*," James revised his tale for the 1908 New York Edition upon discovering no contractual obligation to Stone (Horne 4, 9). "In the Cage" was also one of the first pieces that James dictated to a secretary, the Scotsman William MacAlpine, who translated his words into stenographic code before typing them on a Remington. James, in describing the process to his last secretary, THEODORA BOSANQUET, claimed: "'It all seems to be so much more effectively and unceasingly *pulled* out of me in speech than in writing'" (Bosanquet 248).

Considering how the creation of James's tale depended on the pioneering developments in communication technology, it may be little wonder that the telegraph serves as the controlling image and central plot device of the story. As critics have noted, James's initial anxiety over losing control of his own writing process (there might be an entire day, for example, before MacAlpine would type out a readable copy, making him the sole possessor of the writer's thoughts) helps to explain why his tale would center on the telegraph, a machine that by the turn of the last century had been made part of the nationalized network and placed in local groceries throughout Britain (Rowe 158). Leon Edel suggests that James remained connected to the bustling London in part through telegram; like the high-end clients the telegraphist abhors, James too often "squandered shillings" on "coy" messages such as: "Impossible impossible impossible if you knew what it costs me to say so" (*The Complete Tales* 9).

James's telegrams seem to revel in the playful and paratactic click of the telegraphic mode; indeed, James warned against digging beneath the surface play of his story. In the PREFACE TO THE NEW YORK EDITION, he urges readers not to "speculate" too much about the telegraph girl and what she might "mean." Here James reproaches the "artist" in his "rash" and "idle" imagination, which too often leads to the "vice of reading rank subtleties into simple souls and reckless expenditure into thrifty ones," a critique resonant with the girl's penchant for reading "rank subtleties" into the coded telegrams of her aristocratic clients (*Literary Criticism* 1,169). What allows for such speculation is the "transformation of the scene of writing from a premodern to a modern phenomenon" (Rowe 156). The once private process is figured by the "little public servant" at the culmination of her initial awareness of a "drama at a critical stage," the "high reality" which in a moment "floated to her through the bars of the cage" (319). Once the girl makes her remarkable discovery about the illicit affair between Lady Bradeen (alias Cissy, alias Mary) and Everard, she allows her imagination to take Lady Bradeen "all the way" into the gentleman's home, into his "room": "she had written her missive at his table and with his pen" (319–320) rather than in the cramped space of Cocker's grocery—a public and decidedly less romantic setting.

Private affairs made public and the public's increasing attention to the private lives of the upper classes constitute a central tension in the story. This tension is crystallized by the cage, which acts as a "transparent screen" that "fenced out or fenced in" depending on your "lot." Critics such as Eric Savoy and Hugh Stevens have suggested that sensational scandals like the OSCAR WILDE trials of 1895 and the Cleveland Street Affair of 1889–90—the latter involved young "telegraph boys" in postal offices "going to bed" with aristocratic "gentlemen"—are important events for understanding "In the Cage." Both the Wilde trial and the Cleveland Street Affair penalized homosexuality and the intermingling of people from different socioeconomic classes. This contributed to what Eve Kosofsky Sedgwick has identified as the homosexual panic of late Victorian London, a historical background against which James's uncanny tale demands to be read.

The "queer extension of her experience," that is, the "double life" that the girl leads in the cage,

has been described as a realistic representation of a working-class girl who retreats to her imagination in order to escape from the restrictions of her economic and social conditions (Menke, Brooks). The story of Lady Bradeen's affair with Everard is told through the consciousness of the girl, trapped not only in a cage, where she must "dole out stamps and postal-orders, weigh letters, answer stupid questions, [and] give difficult change," but also by her "contracted future" to the "comparatively primitive" grocer (316, 333). The degree to which a character can work, or play, outside the scrutinizing gaze of the public eye, establishes that character's stature within the economy of James's tale. For example, the girl envies how her friend Mrs. Jordan arranges flowers in "elegant privacy" (329) while she herself holds a humiliatingly public occupation in the cage.

Since Michel Foucault's *History of Sexuality* (1978) (see SEXUALITY), much of Jamesian scholarship has vacillated between deconstructive readings, which mark the "queerness" of the tale as discursive or broadly transgressive, and new historicist readings that place the tale within the sensational and terrifying milieu inspired by Oscar Wilde's trials and the introduction of *homosexuality* into the modern lexicon. These frameworks are used largely by critics who seek to discern a "recognizably gay Henry James"; they also serve those who reject the "depth" model inspired by Freudian psychoanalysis as well as Leon Edel's authoritative, multivolume biography of James for an aesthetically playful, apolitical, or surface model epitomized in the works of Leo Bersani and Eve Kosofsky Sedgwick (Savoy, "'In the Cage' and the Queer Effects of Gay History"). To be sure, Sedgwick's claim in the mid-nineties that "recent work around 'queer' spins the term outward along dimensions that can't be subsumed under gender and sexuality at all" yields some fruitful and rich interpretations of "In the Cage."

It *is* a queer tale when read for ambiguous sexual registers rather than specific sexual referents (Savoy, "Subjunctive Biography," 250). This is perhaps most evident when considering the perspective of the girl, particularly the dual lens through which she interprets the "gaps" in the telegrams exchanged between Lady Bradeen and Everard.

What comes into play here are class desire and "very greasy" romance novels, at a "ha'penny a day" (316). Both encourage a reading of the adulterous affair within a normative heterosexual framework, but in each case, the melodramatic and romantic resolution is dependent upon a performance of masculinity, which Everard fails to produce. The girl's inability to grasp other possible meanings of the oblique telegrams that pass between the couple, or other possible reasons for Everard's frequent, anxious, and increasingly attentive visits to Cocker's after she discloses her knowledge of his affairs on the park bench, is an extension of her deep investment in and admiration of virile masculinity. It is, in fact, the sole attractive quality she attributes to Mr. Mudge: His "air of masterful authority" while subduing a drunken sailor, so impresses her that "she shouldn't soon forget" (333).

Still, from the very start of the story, readers are saturated with the girl's justifications for deferring her marriage to Mr. Mudge. Her imaginative forays into the affairs of her upper-class clients provide not only an escape from her reality but also an excuse for delaying her marriage, one that Mr. Mudge himself accepts because he perceives some monetary benefit (the sale of "cheese and pickles") from her network of relations. The girl loathes his "daily deadly flourishing letters," postpones her transfer to Chalk Farm, and wonders to herself how she might "put up with" a man so "smugly unconscious" and only "practically human" (317, 332). And yet, Mr. Mudge proves to be a respectful and warm companion to the girl, having every "confidence" in her and giving her plenty of "ease and space . . . for telling him the whole truth that no one knew" (358). In fact, the conclusion he draws when learning of her talk with Everard on a park bench at night—an extremely compromising position—is that Everard is a "cad."

When the girl explains to Mr. Mudge that her interest in Lady Bradeen and Everard has been "seen" through, she claims: "I've got them all in my pocket" (358). She is quite aware of the dangers such information poses, so much so that she fantasizes about what she could do with the knowledge: "She quite thrilled herself with thinking what, with such a lot of material, a bad girl would do" (339).

But when Everard returns to Cocker's every day, leaving "redundant money" on the counter, she feels "strangely and portentously afraid of him" (363). The girl's fantasy life has not convinced her that she possesses real power; rather, she claims, she would "do anything" for him. But her knowledge seems to pose a real threat for Everard. The potential for blackmail is signified throughout the tale, marking its participation in the culture of surveillance of fin-de-siècle London.

Finally, if one can read "In the Cage" as a queer tale, it is through the rendering of the girl and Everard as joined by a similarly isolated sensibility. While the girl reads this shared sense as a budding romance akin to her romance novels—the "small throbbing spot" she takes refuge in, "he did like her!"—Everard recognizes her as perhaps the only person who can "help a fellow" (341, 351). When the girl explains to him that people like her must "manage" the secret lives of the upper class, he responds: "'You're awfully clever, you know; cleverer, cleverer, cleverer—!'" (352). The construction implies an absent subject—who is she more clever than? The repetition might suggest the extent of the difference between the girl's own cleverness in inferring how to help Everard in the midst of the love triangle's confusion and Lady Bradeen, who ought to be "cleverer" given what is at stake for her in the affair with Everard.

The tale defies neat resolution; it revolves around intercepted messages, absent words, wrong names, queer feelings, and, ultimately, the wrong numbers recalled by the girl: "'If it's wrong, it's all right!'" (372). The girl's cleverness manifests itself in her recognizing the similitude between herself and Everard: "[S]he was literally afraid of the alternate self who might be waiting outside. He might be waiting; it was he who was her alternate self, and of him she was afraid" (364). Perhaps the queerness in the tale is rooted in their mutual resistance to heterosexual, normative relationships, to marriage, or to the public performance of identity obliterating any possibility for a private, more imaginative one. A tale seemingly impossible to decode entirely, James's "In the Cage" is also about the surface, the pleasure and play of words "as numberless as the sands of the sea" (314).

CHARACTERS

Bradeen, Lady (a.k.a. Mary, Cissy, Juno) A beautiful woman comes to Cocker's with three telegrams, one of which is to Everard. A married woman of the upper class, she once confuses the location for meeting Everard, providing the chance for the girl to divulge that she knows of her affair. Lady Bradeen never returns to Cocker's, but the girl later hears of her husband's death and her impending marriage to Everard.

Buckton, Mr. (a.k.a. one of Mr. Cocker's young men) One of the men with whom the girl works at Cocker's is described as having "cunning hostility" (317). When the girl recites from memory the numbers from the missing telegram for the panicked Everard, Mr. Buckton angrily asks what game she is playing. She believes that he often rushes to intercept the more interesting customers before she can.

Counter Clerk, the The other man with whom the girl works is described as being more generous than Mr. Buckton. He is awestruck by the girl's photographic memory and quite earnestly asks: "But how did you know, dear?" (372).

Drake, Mr. He is a "great and trusted friend" (375) of Lord Rye and his butler for many years. Because of his position, he overhears many details about the secret lives of the upper class. Wishing to marry Mrs. Jordan and live in a separate house, he is forced to leave Lord Rye (who cannot afford to buy him one) and work for Lady Bradeen (who can). In the end, the girl is amazed that her information about Everard comes via Mr. Drake.

Everard, Captain (a.k.a. the Captain, Philip, Phil, the Count, William, "the Pink 'Un'," and Mudge) Everard is first introduced in the tale as the male recipient of a love letter sent by Lady Bradeen to his hotel in Paris. Already the object of romantic intrigue for the girl, she recognizes him instantly when he visits Cocker's with Bradeen. He becomes a regular, living at nearby Park Chambers, and the girl imagines that she shares a secret intimacy with him. He ends up in some trouble, some-thing only the girl can solve, and he is ultimately financially and socially rescued through marriage to Lady Bradeen.

Jordan, Mrs. A widow, and while 10 years older than the girl, she nevertheless is her "only equal" (326). They once lived across the hall from each other. She was a friend of her mother's, a "bereaved" woman without a "penny of provision" (327). She now supports herself by arranging flowers for the upper class in their homes. Her work provides a source of endless stories that seem to belittle the girl's position in the cage. Once hoping to marry Lord Rye, she instead becomes engaged to his former butler, Mr. Drake. Marriage is her only means to avoid starvation.

Mudge, Mr. Mr. Mudge is the girl's fiancé. He meets the girl at Cocker's, where the telegraph-and-post office is located. The girl finds him industrious and more interested in money than in the personal affairs that occupy her. Despite her sense of him as just barely "human" (332), by the end of the tale, he has exhibited great patience (she holds off their marriage), responsibility (he buys a home in which he plans to house her mother also), and interest in her (he listens openly to her tale of meeting Everard in the park).

Telegraphist, the (a.k.a. "the girl") The un-named woman is the center of consciousness in the tale. Her "function" is to operate the sounder, a transmitting device for "words as numberless as the sands of the sea," answer "stupid" questions from her high-class clients, and watch their com-ings and goings from inside a cage (314). The girl feels different from others in her social class in part because of her fantasies, which are fueled by the romance novels she devours. She lives with her mother in relative poverty, is "clever" (318), and spends her time tracking the love affair between Captain Everard and Lady Bradeen through their coded telegrams.

FURTHER READING

Bosanquet, Theodora. *Henry James at Work.* London: Hogarth Press, 1924.

Brooks, Peter. *Realist Vision.* New Haven, Conn., and London: Yale University Press, 2005.

Foucault, Michel. *The History of Sexuality: An Introduction,* vol. 1. Translated by Robert Hurley. New York: Vintage, 1978.

Glavan, Jill. "Class Ghosting 'In the Cage'." *Henry James Review* 22, no. 3 (2001): 297–306.

Horne, Philip. *Henry James and Revision: The New York Edition.* Oxford, U.K.: Clarendon Press, 1990.

James, Henry. *The Complete Tales of Henry James,* vol. 10. Edited by Leon Edel. Philadelphia and New York: Lippincott, 1964.

———. *Literary Criticism: French Writers, Other European Writers, The Prefaces to the New York Edition.* New York: Library of America, 1984.

———. *Henry James: Selected Tales.* Edited by John Lyon. London: Penguin, 2001.

Menke, Richard. "Telegraphic Realism: Henry James's *In the Cage.*" *PMLA* 115 (2000): 975–990.

Rowe, John Carlos. *The Other Henry James.* Durham, N.C., and London: Duke University Press, 1998.

Savoy, Eric. "'In the Cage' and the Queer Effects of Gay History." *Novel* 28 (1995): 284–307.

———. "Subjunctive Biography." *Henry James Review* 27, no. 3 (2006): 248–255.

Stevens, Hugh. *Henry James and Sexuality.* Cambridge: Cambridge University Press, 1998.

Trollope, Anthony. "The Telegraph Girl." In *Later Short Stories,* edited by John Sutherland, 354–385. Oxford, U.K.: Oxford University Press, 1995.

Gretchen Woertendyke, *Stony Brook University*

"The Jolly Corner" (1908)

James began writing "The Jolly Corner" in August 1906. It was first published in the *English Review* in December 1908 and was then revised (though only slightly) for the NEW YORK EDITION (Volume 17), published in 1909, which is considered the standard version. It is often linked with James's "The TURN OF THE SCREW" as one of his ghost stories or with The AMERICAN SCENE as it focuses on the experiences of an American returning home after an extended life abroad.

SYNOPSIS

"The Jolly Corner" is broken into three untitled sections. The title refers to the name that the main character, Spencer Brydon, gives the house where he was born in NEW YORK CITY. For the past 33 years, Brydon has been living in Europe on the proceeds from the rent of the jolly corner house and a second building owned by his family. Now that his two brothers have died, he must personally oversee the renovations and financial responsibilities of the two properties.

(Section 1) The story begins with Spencer Brydon discussing his situation with his old friend Alice Staverton at the site of the second property, which is being renovated into apartments. Alice observes his interactions with some of the workers and is impressed by his head for the job. Her suggestion, that had he remained in New York, he might have "start[ed] some new variety of awful architectural hare and run it till it burrowed in a gold-mine" (344), brings Brydon to think about what might have happened had he stayed in New York rather than lived in Europe.

Together, Staverton and Brydon walk from the apartment house to the house on the jolly corner, where Brydon was born. Brydon has not been keeping tenants here; instead, it remains vacant. He has a woman, Mrs. Muldoon, look in on the place daily to open windows and keep it clean. Although the home is empty and no work is being done on it, Brydon visits the place quite regularly. Brydon and Staverton walk through the vacant house, with Mrs. Muldoon guiding them to show them "how little there was to see" (345). Mrs. Muldoon asks that Brydon never request her to come to the jolly corner house at night, as she fears ghosts may appear. Brydon himself has been visiting the house at night and has in fact kept candles available so that he can lurk in the building whenever he chooses.

Both Staverton and Brydon admire the details of the building; Staverton expresses horror at the thought of destroying it in order to put in ugly (though profitable) apartments. Despite the obvious financial gain that renovating the building would bring him, Brydon wants to keep the jolly corner as it is. Staverton, after listening to his description of his emotional attachment to the building, suggests that he might one day want to live here. He denies this. Together, as they leave, they joke about ghosts.

A few days after their tour of the house together, Brydon confesses to Staverton that he has developed a "morbid obsession" (348) with wondering about how his life might have been if he had stayed in New York rather than leaving for his life in Europe. His specific question—"what would it have made of me?" (348)—torments him. The "it" of this question—whether the city, the house, America—is vague. His thought, however, that by leaving he killed some latent talent within him, troubles his mind. Alice admits that she, too, wonders how Brydon might have been; she imagines his alter ego would have been "splendid, quite huge and monstrous" (349). Brydon agrees but thinks it would have been "quite hideous and offensive" (349). Alice proposes that she, too, might have been something else; Brydon insists that she is "a person whom nothing can have altered," who was "born to be" what she is (350). When Brydon repeats that he wishes to see his alter ego, Alice tells him that she has seen Brydon's alter ego twice in dreams. Brydon presses her for more information about his other, but she puts him off until another time.

(Section 2) Brydon sometimes visits the house three times a day, and he prefers dusky twilight and midnight visitations. He stays in the house for hours at night, and it begins to seem that he is stalking his alter ego. As he hunts through the house for signs of his other self, he develops a familiarity with the house and an increasing ability to see in the darkness.

After staying away from the house for three nights in a row, upon his return he has an uncomfortable feeling of being stalked. He walks into the hall and believes fully that the alter ego is there, for the first time. He continues, slowly, to explore the house. Upstairs, after passing through several rooms, he comes to a closed door, which he is certain he had previously left open. He considers for some time whether or not to open the door, and he wonders what will be behind it. He eventually turns away, wishing to let his obsession rest. He walks to a window and opens it; looking out, he

"Henry James was, I may truthfully say, the only sitter who ever terrified me. I was to do him for publication, and though the time was set for early afternoon, he did not come until nearly four o'clock. It was April, and a warm day, ending in a thunder shower, the sky getting blacker by the minute and the light going. Finally he came; dignified and impressive, with manners almost courtly, and wearing a top hat several sizes too big" (94). Alice Boughton, "Henry James," *Photographing the Famous* (Avondale Press, 1928)

wishes to find another person or a way out of the house without passing back through it, but he finds none. He imagines that the presence of his other self wishes him to leave.

As dawn arrives, he descends through the house and begins to think that it is fine if the builders come and tear out the inside of the house. Arriving downstairs, he realizes with a start that the front door has been left wide open; he is certain that he left it closed. He thinks "wasn't he now in *most* immediate presence of some inconceivable occult activity?" (363). The next thing Brydon sees is the figure of a man. At first, the man has his hands raised and is covering his face; yet he then lowers his hands, one of which is missing two fingers, and reveals a face that Brydon finds hideous. Brydon passes out.

(Section 3) Spencer regains consciousness in the presence of Mrs. Muldoon and Alice Staverton. Alice, initially fearful that Brydon is dead, holds his head in her lap and kisses him. He asks how she found him; she explains that he was to have met her in the afternoon, but he did not arrive or send word. He realizes that he fell or passed out at dawn and had lain unconscious on the floor for the entire day.

Alice admits that she knew Brydon was visiting the house regularly at night and that he was determined to meet his other. She tells him that in the early morning hours she had seen a vision of Brydon's other and took it for a sign that Brydon had met him too. Brydon calls the apparition "brute" and "black stranger," and he cannot accept that it is himself. Alice insists that this apparition was in fact Brydon, as he would have been if he had stayed in New York; she admits that in fact she herself was not horrified by him.

Brydon cannot understand how she could accept this horrible version of himself. She explains that she pitied the alter ego because "he has been unhappy; he has been ravaged" (369). She notes that the alter ego has both ruined vision and a damaged right hand. Brydon points out that although the alter ego may have "a million a year" (369), he does not have Alice, and Brydon finally embraces Alice.

CRITICAL ANALYSIS

"The Jolly Corner" is typically classed among James's best stories. It is a tale of meeting a doppelgänger, or double. The story's plot is set up by Brydon and Alice both wondering what would have become of him if he had remained in New York instead of leaving for Europe. While Alice imagines he would have turned out "splendid," Brydon believes he would have been "hideous." These initial impressions of what remaining in New York would have done to Brydon remain static; from beginning to end, Alice is unafraid of the vision of the other Brydon, while Brydon himself is horrified by the other

version of himself that he encounters. Thus, the doubling of Brydon's character leads to further doubling; Brydon's other is another version of himself, but it evokes two very different reactions.

The theme of doubling recurs throughout. In addition to the two Brydons, there are the two buildings that Brydon now owns, the jolly corner house and another apartment building. The contrast between the two buildings, one that Brydon appreciates for its beauty, and one that he uses for its financial possibilities, also mirrors the two different paths Brydon's life might have taken. Brydon's attitude toward the two buildings is very different; he is very protective of that on the jolly corner, while he is pleased to see the growth of the apartment building, which will provide economic gain. As Alice tells him, "you're to make so good a thing of your sky-scraper that, living in luxury on those ill-gotten gains, you can afford for a while to be sentimental here!" (346). Brydon can afford to keep the jolly corner house vacant because of the financial asset of the apartment building, much as he previously was able to keep himself in Europe, out of the spheres of business, because of his comfortable financial position.

Martha Banta also points to the "double climax" of the story. As she explains, there is a first climax when Brydon almost encounters his ghost upstairs, and then a second climax "when Brydon thinks his adventures are over, he, and we, are led downstairs to a sudden and violent encounter with a second presence" (138). There is repeated doubling in the story line; not only does Brydon have two separate encounters with the ghost (one upstairs and one downstairs), but the ghost has two different reactions to Brydon, first using his hands to cover his face, and then his hands "dropped from the face and left it uncovered and presented" (364).

Yet another doubling can be seen in the two missing fingers of Brydon's alter ego, which, like the alter ego itself, elicit very different reactions from Brydon and Alice. Brydon notices that the two fingers "were reduced to stumps, as if accidentally shot away" (364), while Alice describes only "his poor right hand" (369). While Brydon jumps to conclusions about how his alter ego incurred his injury, Alice immediately pities his injury. While

Brydon uses a "charming monocle" (369), the alter ego requires "dangling double eye-glass" (364) for his ruined eyesight. Even when Brydon first starts to wonder about his other, he asks twice, "what would it have made of me, what would it have made of me?" (348).

Another doubling is the possibility of reading Spencer Brydon as a double for Henry James himself. The story is often read autobiographically since many elements of the character Spencer Brydon seem to mirror James's own life. James's return to New York after living in Europe for 20 years yielded a similar sense of dislocation as that experienced by Brydon. The story is set in the area of the city where James lived as a child.

Most critical commentary has focused on Brydon's encounter with the apparition; there is considerable disagreement on the number of ghosts and whom or what the ghosts represent. Some readers believe that there is just one ghost, who closes the upstairs door and then meets Spencer downstairs. Others believe there are two different ghosts, one upstairs and one downstairs. James himself wrote that the story involved the hero's "turning the tables . . . on a 'ghost' or whatever, a visiting or haunting apparition otherwise qualified to appall him; and thereby winning a sort of victory by the appearance, and the evidence, that this personage or presence was more overwhelmingly affected by him than he by it" (400).

Critics have read Brydon's horror at encountering his alter ego as revealing anxieties about any number of markers of difference, including race, SEXUALITY, and economic class. Stephanie Hawkins draws attention to the fact that Brydon calls his apparition a "black stranger" (368). In her essay "Stalking the Biracial Hidden Self in Henry James's *The Sense of the Past* and 'The Jolly Corner,'" she proposes that the story "betrays a very American preoccupation with racial indeterminacy as it exposes the biracial potentialities that remain unrecognized and deeply threatening within the national psyche" (279). Brydon's return to America forces him to encounter his history, which may include family forebears of unknown racial origins.

Several critics have explored how sexuality figures in understanding the story. C. R. Resetartis claims that "Brydon's nocturnal pursuit of his other self seems, if not at times overtly sexual, then certainly sensual" (63). His repeated nighttime visits to the house, which he takes great pains to hide from everyone, seem to indicate that he knows he is engaged in something forbidden. Eric Savoy, in "The Queer Subject of 'The Jolly Corner,'" reads Brydon's own comments, including his references to his "scandalous" life in Europe, as hidden hints at his homosexuality. From there, Savoy considers the possibility that "Spencer Brydon returns to America as a self-knowing 'gay' bachelor—closeted, to be sure, but with a sexual affiliation richly and connotatively established—whose provisional identity is contested and unraveled by his encounter with his hypothetical and rather differently closeted double" (3). In this reading, the ending, with Brydon literally embracing Alice, represents Brydon's refusal of this earlier, homosexual self and a commitment to a heterosexual life.

Most of the critical focus, just as much of the story itself, is on the character of Spencer Brydon and the ordeal he survives. The role of Alice is only occasionally addressed; Nicola Nixon calls her a "conventional romantic heroine" and explains that "Alice's relationship with Brydon recapitulates the standard, gendered division of commercial and domestic, public and private, that persisted throughout much of nineteenth-century American literature" (822). Alice's role seems to be to wait around for Brydon. Even her attempt to save him at the end requires the assistance of Mrs. Muldoon to open the door.

Other readings take Alice more seriously. Daniel Mark Fogel, for instance, stresses the fact that "the ghost would not have revived, nor would Brydon have encountered it, without Alice's agency" (192). Alice is in fact the one who first proposes the question of what might have happened to Brydon had he remained in New York, and Alice is the one who rescues him at the end, or as Brydon says to Alice after the ordeal, "you brought me literally to life" (366). She is the one who can see and accept both versions of Spencer Brydon.

The ending for many readers is surprisingly optimistic for James; indeed, at least one critic has called it "cloying" (Nixon 821). Ernest Tuveson calls it "one of James's most optimistic, hopeful pictures of the human situation" (271). Barbara Hardy calls it a "grim story with a happy ending" (191).

CHARACTERS

Brydon, Spencer He left New York to live in Europe at 23 and returns at 56 to deal with two properties owned by his family. He is a bachelor, living in a hotel and dining in clubs and restaurants. He is tormented by thoughts of what he might have become had he stayed in New York. He admires Alice, and at key moments he seems wistfully to wonder what might have happened between them. Brydon sees Alice as "a comfort and support" (341). He is terrified by his encounter with what he believes to be his alter ego, after which he awakens in Alice's lap and embraces her.

Muldoon, Mrs. She is described as "a good woman living in the neighborhood" (345) of the house on the jolly corner. Brydon has arranged to have her visit the house for an hour each day to clean and air the house. She is superstitious, loquacious, and speaks with an accent. Mrs. Muldoon's voice is the first thing he hears when he awakens after passing out at the jolly corner house.

Staverton, Alice She has lived in New York all her life and owns her small home in Irving Place. She is unmarried, has one maid, and lives frugally. Her appearance, the narrator explains, "defied you to say if she were a fair young woman who looked old through trouble, or a fine smooth older one who looked young through successful indifference" (344). She is a careful observer of Brydon, a thoughtful listener, and speaks her mind. She believes Brydon's alter ego has come to her in several dreams; she is unafraid of him.

ADAPTATION

A television version of the story, directed by Arthur Barron, was produced in 1975 with Fritz Weaver as Spencer Brydon and Salome Jens as Alice Staverton. A *New York Times* review of a film version of *The PORTRAIT OF A LADY* claimed that "The Jolly Corner" is "unfilmable" (Miller 31).

FURTHER READING

Banta, Martha. *Henry James and the Occult: The Great Extension.* Bloomington: Indiana University Press, 1972.

Edel, Leon. *Henry James: The Master 1901–1916,* 319–324. London: Rupert Hart-Davis, 1972.

Fogel, Daniel Mark. "A New Reading of Henry James's 'The Jolly Corner.'" In *Critical Essays on Henry James: The Late Novels,* edited by James W. Gargano, 190–203. Boston: Hall, 1987.

Hardy, Barbara. "'The Jolly Corner.'" In *Henry James: The Shorter Fiction, Reassessments,* edited by N. H. Reeve, 190–208. New York: St. Martin's Press, 1997.

Hawkins, Stephanie. "Stalking the Biracial Hidden Self in Henry James's *The Sense of the Past* and 'The Jolly Corner.'" *Henry James Review* 25, no. 3 (2004): 276–284.

James, Henry. "The Jolly Corner." In *Tales of Henry James,* 2d edition, edited by Christof Wegelin and Henry B. Wonham, 341–369. New York: W.W. Norton, 2003.

———. "From His Notebooks: Regarding 'The Jolly Corner' in Retrospect." In *Tales of Henry James,* 400.

McCuskey, Brian. "Not at Home: Servants, Scholars, and the Uncanny." *PMLA: Publications of the Modern Language Association of America* 121, no. 2 (2006): 421–436.

Miller, Laura. "Henry James: Losing It at the Movies," *New York Times,* 19 January 1997: pp. 31, 1c.

Nixon, Nicola. "'Prismatic and Profitable': Commerce and the Corporate Person in James's 'The Jolly Corner.'" *American Literature* 76, no. 4 (2004): 807–831.

Resetarits, C. R. "Gore Vidal, Henry James: Turning Another Jolly Corner." *Journal of Gender Studies* 14, no. 1 (2005): 61–64.

Savoy, Eric. "The Queer Subject of 'The Jolly Corner.'" *Henry James Review* 20, no. 1 (1999): 1–21.

Stevens, Hugh. "Homoeroticism, Identity, and Agency in James's Late Tales." In *Enacting History in Henry James: Narrative, Power, and Ethics,* edited by Gert Buelens, 126–147. Cambridge: Cambridge Univeristy Press, 1997.

Tuveson, Ernest. "'The Jolly Corner': A Fable of Redemption." *Studies in Short Fiction* 12, no. 3 (1975): 271–280.

Warren, Kenneth W. "The Jolly Corner." In *Tales of Henry James*, 515–520.

Bridget Marshall, *University of Massachusetts, Lowell*

"The Lesson of the Master" (1888)

This tale was first published in two parts in the *Universal Review* and included later in 1892 as the title story of a collection published by Macmillan. James revised the tale for inclusion in Volume 15 of Scribner's Sons' NEW YORK EDITION. It is one of the best known among the group of stories by James about writers and artists, including "The REAL THING," "The FIGURE IN THE CARPET," and "The MIDDLE YEARS."

SYNOPSIS

(Chapter 1) Paul Overt, a young and ambitious writer, is a guest at Summersoft, the country home of Lord and Lady Watermouth. He is eager to meet one of the other guests, Henry St. George, famous author and the eponymous "Master" of the tale. Paul has greatly admired St. George's first three novels, but he is perturbed by a decline in the writer's later work. Most of the guests—the famous author among them—having gone to church, Paul joins the remaining party, which includes a military gentleman, General Fancourt, and St. George's wife. Paul is rather nonplussed by the appearance and manner of the latter, who shows little reverence on the subject of her husband. He is aghast when she admits to having once persuaded her husband to "burn up a bad book" (219). Soon after this revelation, the churchgoers return, with St. George attentively accompanying General Fancourt's beautiful daughter, Marian. St. George's preoccupation prevents Overt from meeting his idol, and he is left to observe somewhat uncomfortably that the famous writer looks more like a "lucky stockbroker" than a man of letters.

(Chapter 2) Paul is introduced to Marian Fancourt and is quickly charmed by her. As they talk, Paul receives his first intimation that Miss Fancourt may be in love with St. George. Marian introduces the two writers, and Paul notes that St. George is unfamiliar with his work. They embark on a walk with some other guests. St. George and Miss Fancourt soon walk ahead, and Paul is left with Mrs. St. George, whose ill health compels her to return to the house.

(Chapter 3) That evening, the gentlemen assemble after dinner in the smoking room. After one or two cryptic remarks about his wife's control over his social habits, St. George tells Paul that he has read his book, a comment that surprises Paul, as he knows the writer has had barely a free moment all day. St. George praises the young writer and encourages him to forswear the "idols of the market—money and luxury and 'the world'" (239) in favor of his art. St. George invites Paul to visit him in some time; thereafter, the conversation turns to the subject of Marian Fancourt, who, it becomes apparent, is admired by both men.

(Chapter 4) A few days later, Paul meets Marian and St. George at an art exhibition in LONDON, causing Paul to speculate on the nature of their relationship. The following week, Paul visits Marian at her home in Manchester Square. Once more, the main topic of their lively conversation is St. George, his "failure" (250), and the "high theme of perfection" (252) in art. By the end of their meeting, Paul privately concedes that he has fallen in love with Miss Fancourt. As he is leaving, he notices, unobserved, Henry St. George arrive at the Fancourts' door. Later, Marian tells Paul that St. George will not be visiting her again, but she refuses to say why.

(Chapter 5) Paul visits Henry St. George in his writing room, and St. George returns to his advice that Paul ought to abjure the temptations of fame and the domestic in favor of total devotion to his muse. Most significant, he advises Paul (who is both alarmed and thrilled by the conversation) not to marry—specifically, not to marry Miss Fancourt.

(Chapter 6) Paul leaves London and spends two years writing in Europe, during which time he learns of Mrs. St. George's death. St. George's response to Paul's letter of condolence perplexes the young writer, as it seems to contradict the Master's earlier position regarding MARRIAGE as an obstacle to artistic production. Having completed his novel, Paul returns to London to be greeted with the news that Marian is to marry St. George. Stricken, he contemplates whether or not he has been duped by the writer he so admired. St. George remains unrepentant when confronted, arguing that since he no longer writes, his advice does not apply to himself; moreover, his marriage to Miss Fancourt removes her from Paul's life, thereby saving him for art. The story ends with the narrator's speculation that Paul's adoption of the "doctrine of renunciation" (273) was, nevertheless, the right choice.

CRITICAL ANALYSIS

"A bottomless ambiguity" (250)—this is the phrase used by Paul Overt to describe St. George's erratic production. However, for many of James's readers it is also the key term that describes the nature of the tale. Is Henry St. George sincere in his advice to Paul Overt to forgo the demands of the flesh in the interest of art? Or does he have ulterior motives? That is, does he persuade Paul to devote himself exclusively to writing because he recognizes that his young disciple has real promise and that this promise will be tragically compromised if he surrenders to Miss Fancourt's charms? Or does he use his influence over the impressionable young man so as to eliminate him as a sexual rival? And if his motives are indeed selfish, does that necessarily make his advice any less valuable? Is there an argument for the suggestion that St. George saves Paul from his own fate of artistic compromise and decline? These questions point up the intriguing ambiguities that lie at the heart of "The Lesson of the Master" and which, not surprisingly, have been accorded considerable scholarly interest.

On the one hand, St. George's advice to Paul seems sincere and based on painful firsthand experience. There seems to be general consensus that he has written three very fine novels; at the same time, as the enticements of "false gods" (239) and

"Saltram's Seat," by A. L. Coburn, frontispiece to "The Coxon Fund," in Volume 15, the New York Edition

the demands of family convention have overtaken the writer, the quality of his work has suffered. On the other hand, there is a niggling sense that St. George's authority and moral probity are questionable: He seems unimaginatively cowed by his wife's control; his barely concealed, fawning attention to Miss Fancourt—in his wife's presence—is tasteless, at best; and the radical reversal of his attitude at the end of the story toward the role his wife played in his work is certainly inconsistent (what he earlier characterized as interference, he now refers to as the "rarest devotion"). The reader, along with Paul, is suspicious about his claims to have read Paul's book with any attention—thus tainting the sincerity and value of his advice to the young writer.

Shlomith Rimmon set the standard for discussions of ambiguity in James's work in her 1977 study, *The Concept of Ambiguity: The Example of James*. Her chapter on "The Lesson of the Master" is still a touchstone essay about the opposing strands of meaning that run throughout the story. Rimmon's reading has spawned others. Priscilla L. Walton, for example, builds on Rimmon's groundwork in order to offer a poststructural feminist reading of the text wherein the women in the text are seen as foreclosing on productivity *at the same time as* constituting "a space, an absence [which] gives birth to the plurality necessary for the production of art" (74). By contrast, for an entertaining and readable (if iconoclastic) discussion of how the story is not ambiguous *at all*, readers might refer to Adeline Tintner's spirited short essay, in which she argues that the tale is modeled on the English folktale of St. George and the dragon. The anti-aesthetic Mrs. St. George, Tintner claims, is the dragon, vanquisher of all artists, which the knightly St. George must slay on behalf of the "literary glory of England" (150).

The second aspect of the story that invites critical attention is the policy of renunciation that St. George recommends to Paul and which, it would seem, the narrator of the story endorses. This concern is closely bound up with the tale's autobiographical resonances. Not only do the two writers share a first name, but James, like St. George, was frequently alluded to by his contemporaries (such as HUGH WALPOLE and EDITH WHARTON) as "The Master," although not always without irony. And if we take the Master's "lesson" at face value, it sounds remarkably similar to James's own statements about the price of fame and the importance of dedicating one's whole self to art. It is certainly a lesson that the probably celibate and determinedly unmarried, childless James himself seems to have adopted. However, many of James's more astute readers have warned against reading the story too simplistically as reflective of James's own positions as regards to art and the world. Ross Posnock argues persuasively that while "the master's lesson is one with which James would have great sympathy, closer scrutiny reveals that St. George vulgarizes and simplifies his creator's

beliefs. What James would take issue with is the Master's key term—'perfection.' James believed perfection to be a spurious goal" (82). In a similar vein, Sara S. Chapman warns against making too easy an assumption about the tale's autobiographical qualities. She argues astutely that "assigning St. George's views to James is much like the common error of assigning Polonius's opinions to Shakespeare." (Chapman also regards the story as unambiguous; she says that St. George is not deliberately deceptive but simply fallible and unable to live up to his own advice.) Philip Horne offers an especially adroit contemplation on the extent to which the story may be read as a "confessional" piece, showing that the tale contains "many tensions with bearing on James's own life" (294) without forgoing its imaginative and fictional freedoms. In addition to an accomplished reading of the tale and its ambiguities, Horne offers an insightful and comprehensive discussion on James's revisions to the story for the New York Edition.

CHARACTERS

Fancourt, General   A kindly, retired military man with "a pink, smiling face and a white moustache" (215), he has spent a "distinguished" (214) career in India. He is the father of Marian Fancourt.

Fancourt, Marian   The young and beautiful daughter of General Fancourt, she is widely read and possesses a rather naive but enthusiastic and well-intentioned reverence for art and artists.

Overt, Paul   A diffident, idealistic young English author, he has written three or four books, one of which is entitled *Ginistrella*, and none of which has been widely read.

St. George, Henry   A famous and established author, the "Master" of the title, his novel *Shadowmere* is especially well known. His more recent work has enjoyed less acclaim, however, and in the course of the time period of the tale (just over two years) he produces nothing at all. Paul is persistently disconcerted by St. George's conventional rather than bohemian appearance.

St. George, Mrs. The wealthy and fashionable, if physically frail, wife of the Master, she appears to have considerable influence over her husband's domestic and professional life and also seems unfazed by his attentions toward Miss Fancourt. She is a somewhat inscrutable figure.

Watermouth, Lord and Lady They own Summersoft, the country house where the first chapters of the tale are set.

FURTHER READING

Chapman, Sara S. *Henry James's Portrait of the Writer as Hero.* London: Macmillan, 1990.

Horne, Philip. *Henry James and Revision: The New York Edition.* Oxford, U.K.: Clarendon Press, 1990.

James, Henry. "The Lesson of the Master." In *The Complete Tales of Henry James 1888–1891*, vol. 7, edited with an introduction by Leon Edel, 213–284. London: Rupert Hart-Davis, 1963.

Posnock, Ross. *Henry James and the Problem of Robert Browning.* Athens: University of Georgia Press, 1985.

Rimmon, Shlomith. *The Concept of Ambiguity: The Example of James.* Chicago: University of Chicago Press, 1977.

Tintner, Adeline R. *The Pop World of Henry James: From Fairy Tales to Science Fiction.* Ann Arbor, Mich.: UMI Research Press, 1989.

Walton, Priscilla L. *The Disruption of the Feminine in Henry James.* Toronto: University of Toronto Press, 1992.

Karen Scherzinger, *University of Johannesburg*

"A London Life" (1888)

The novella first appeared in *Scribner's Magazine* in four installments, from June to September 1888. In 1889, it was collected in book form by Macmillan with three other 1887–88 stories, "Mrs. Temperly," "The Liar," and "The Patagonia." James then revised it for the NEW YORK EDITION, with few significant changes, and included it in Volume 10 (1908) with *The SPOILS OF POYNTON* (1897) and a shorter tale, "The Chaperon" (1891).

SYNOPSIS

(Chapter 1) The tale is set in England; the first half takes place in the winter on the country estate of Mellows, the home of Lionel Berrington and his American wife, Selina. Selina's sister Laura Wing, has been staying with them for a year. The story opens with Laura conferring with wise old Lady Davenant about her sister's unhappy MARRIAGE and the impending scandal of infidelities. Lady Davenant philosophically advises her to stop fretting and start thinking about getting a husband instead.

(Chapters 2–4) Dispirited, Laura comes back to the deserted Mellows, where her brother-in-law, Lionel, unexpectedly turns up. He informs her that Selina is in PARIS with her lover, Charles Crispin (with her disreputable friend Lady Ringrose acting as a "blind"), and announces his intention to take the case to the divorce courts.

(Chapter 5) A week later, Selina returns and denies to Laura that Crispin had been in Paris with her. Laura does not believe her.

(Chapter 6) Laura expects a row, but nothing happens. The rest of the winter is uneventful, except for the visit by Lady Ringrose, who does not seem so bad to Laura after all.

(Chapter 7) In May, back in LONDON, Laura meets the ingenuous American tourist Mr. Wendover in Selina's drawing room. He walks with her to Lady Davenant's; on the spur of the moment, Laura invites him to come in with her. As they are leaving, Lady Davenant retains Laura and suggests he would do very well for a husband.

(Chapter 8) A few days later, Laura and Wendover go sightseeing; a storm breaks out. As they are visiting the dark basement of the Soane Museum, they chance upon a couple. A ray of lightning illuminates their faces; Laura recognizes Selina and Crispin.

(Chapter 9) Laura tries to confront Selina, but her sister turns the tables by accusing her of indecently roaming about the streets with a young man.

(Chapter 10) Laura challenges her sister again. Selina first reacts indignantly, then collapses in tears, promising she will never see Crispin again. For a month, Laura spends much time with Selina in the attempt to "improve" her; meanwhile, Wendover becomes a regular visitor.

(Chapter 11) At the end of June, Laura and Selina accept Wendover's invitation to share a box with him at the opera. Under the pretext of sitting with Lady Ringrose, who is on the other side of the house, Selina leaves the box—never to return. As Laura realizes that her sister has eloped with Crispin, she frantically determines that now is her last chance to escape disgrace, and she presses Wendover to declare himself and propose marriage. However, she then realizes that he does not love her. Deeply ashamed, she rushes out.

(Chapter 12) On the following day, Laura visits Lady Davenant and confesses everything. She is greatly distressed. Lady Davenant takes her in and secretly sends for Mr. Wendover, to whom she explains the whole situation. He admits that he is not in love with Laura.

(Chapter 13) After three days in bed, Laura gets up, determined to chase after her sister. She twice repulses Wendover's attempts to talk to her, despite his avowal that he has now fallen in love with her after his talk with Lady Davenant. They later learn that Laura has sailed back to America; Wendover follows suit. As the tale concludes, the Berrington divorce trial is about to start, and Wendover is still waiting for Laura to see him.

CRITICAL ANALYSIS

In an age of high divorce rates, this story might not seem all that spicy. However, in 1888, divorce was a social scandal (as illustrated by the much-publicized 1886 Campbell divorce trial) and as a literary topic somewhat risqué. According to James's notebook entry of June 20, 1887, the idea for the tale was given to him by the French writer Paul Bourget. A young friend of Bourget's had jumped out of the window of her hotel and died. Bourget speculated that his friend was horrified by her mother's loose morals and had tried to escape her life by pressing a young man to ask for her hand in marriage. She was then more horrified to learn that the young man had no intention of marrying her. In adapting the anecdote, James dismissed the suicide, which he had already used in another story ("The Modern Warning"), but he retained the motive. He also insisted that he did not want to "depict in an American magazine, a woman carrying on

adulteries under her daughter's eyes" and therefore substituted two sisters for a mother and daughter, concluding, "I think the American magazine can be made to swallow the sister, at least" (38).

The American magazine did swallow it, yet the change was obviously not sufficient to sweeten the plot's flavor. In 1889, a reviewer wrote in the British periodical the *Spectator* that the subject was "intensely disagreeable" and the atmosphere "depressing," while the characters were "repellent" and "unlovable" (Gard 192). Undeniably, James comes very close to dotting his *i*'s in the story's portrayal of infidelity, and there are direct allusions to sex (see SEXUALITY), as when Lionel insists to his young unmarried sister-in-law: "I'll bet you five pounds she's doing it now" (462).

The story's crisis indeed revolves around whether Selina is doing "it" and whether Lionel (who obviously has been doing "it" as well) will dare do the most scandalous "it" of appealing to the divorce courts. Yet, might not Laura be taking things too hard, as Lady Davenant suggests? Is the story meant to convey disapproval of what Robert Gale calls the "out-and-out adulteress?" (395). Or, as Leon Edel suggests, does James take an indulgent view of the married American woman and "a critical view of the inflexible morality of her sister?" (231).

In his 1908 preface, James accentuated the role of the story's central female consciousness through which the plot's events are "richly charged and coloured" (NYE xxii). When accounting for the grouping of the tale with *The Spoils of Poynton* (featuring expropriated Mrs. Gereth as the vindictive version of mild old Mrs. Berrington) and "The Chaperon" (in which the chastised runaway divorcee eventually overcomes her social excommunication, thus providing a lighthearted sequel to "A London Life"), James stressed that all three are "stories about women . . . affected with a certain high lucidity" (xv). The "little law" under which his tale was to be told consequently hinges upon confining the narrative to Laura's point of view (xxi). Providing his own critique of the story, James confesses to a "lapse of artistic dignity" (xxii) in moving outside Laura's impressions to relate the interview between Lady Davenant and Wendover (chapter 12). Unsurprisingly, this is the passage that he revised most extensively, adding many interpretive lines where the original featured comment-free dialogue. The revisions make the breach worse, drawing the reader's attention to the instrumental presence of a third-party observer and indirectly highlighting Laura's very absence.

However, James did not consider the ending a flaw, even though it again strays from the limits of Laura's perspective and consciousness. As his notebooks show, he suspected he would be criticized for the story's lack of closure: "That must be my denouement—it will be vulgarly judged—but it is the only possible one" (40). He still risked it, as he had done a few years before with Isabel Archer in *The PORTRAIT OF A LADY*. Laura is another heroine whose fate James entrusts to the reader's imagination. Although the reviewer for the *Spectator* did find this ambiguity "aggravating," he acknowledged that it "tends to give an air of intense reality" to his writing (Gard 192).

In the preface, James acknowledges one flaw to the story, namely the pseudo-"international" tension (see INTERNATIONAL THEME). He realizes that neither the Wing sisters nor Wendover need have been American. And yet the story seems itself to question the familiar theme of the "young American innocence transplanted to European air" (NYE xix), especially in the relentlessly deterministic terms through which Laura attempts to understand her sister's behavior. Has Selina been corrupted by Europe? Or was she born corrupt in the United States? The harder Laura tries to work out these explanations, the more they fail her. Repeatedly, heredity and the influence of the milieu are put forward, but the successive arguments only succeed in canceling one another out. One way to look at the story's main themes, in short, is to regard it as most critics did in terms of influence (it reflects James's endeavor to emulate the French naturalists [see ROMANCE/REALISM/NATURALISM]) and failure (it makes poor use of the international contrast). Another way would be to consider how the text, grafting naturalism's preferred concepts onto James's own "international" trademark, toys with these constructs and ultimately exposes their hollowness—an analysis that may apply to two other tales of the period, "Lady Barberina" (1884) and "A Modern Warning" (1888).

CHARACTERS

Berrington, Lionel   A boyish red-faced Briton of 35, Lionel Berrington is the owner of the estate of Mellows and the vapid husband of lively Selina. Lady Davenant calls him "as idiotic as a comic song" (444). He puts all of his energy into devising ways of divorcing his adulterous wife, and he is thrilled when she fatally compromises herself by eloping with her lover.

Berrington, Mrs.   Lionel's placid mother never appears in the tale. Very much her son's mother, she is presented as a simple woman, "devoted to birds" and not much given to thinking (438).

Berrington, Selina (née Wing)   A very attractive American woman, she weds Lionel Berrington before her father goes bankrupt, bringing a considerable fortune into the marriage. She comes to despise her husband and conspicuously neglects her home for a social set, which her sister, Laura, deems shallow and immoral. She eventually deserts her husband and children for her lover, Captain Crispin.

Crispin, Captain Charles (a.k.a. Charley)   Selina's impecunious lover, readers only catch a glimpse of his "fine fair beard" at the Soane Museum (494).

Davenant, Lady   Old Mrs. Berrington's close friend and Laura's cynical adviser, she is still terribly quick-witted at nearly 80 years of age. She takes a great liking to Laura, for whom she would like to find a husband. She fails to convince Laura to stop agonizing over her sister's behavior. She is more successful with Mr. Wendover, whom she manages to inspire with genuine love for her protégée by telling him all about Laura's predicament.

Georgie and Ferdy (a.k.a. Scratch and Parson)   The Berringtons' boisterous, chubby sons are aptly endowed with doglike nicknames. Seemingly indifferent to what goes on around them, their unsympathetic conduct does not do much to inspire compassion, despite their tender age and hapless family situation. According to their aunt's damning prophecy, "they would never reflect upon anything in the world" (452).

Ringrose, Lady Selina's ally and a lady reported to have many lovers, she repeatedly covers up for Selina. Laura sees her as "a clever little woman with a single eye-glass and short hair" (478).

Wendover, Mr. A candid New Yorker on a four-month vacation to Europe, he unwittingly becomes entangled in the affairs of the Wing sisters. Through a common acquaintance, he becomes a regular visitor at Selina's, who puts Laura in charge of entertaining him. When Laura pleads that he propose marriage to her, he manages to keep his poise. After Lady Davenant explains everything, he falls in love with Laura, starts pursuing her, and weathers her subsequent rejections.

Wing, Laura An impoverished American "of a serious turn by nature," she travels to England to stay with her wealthy sister after their parents' death (488). After a year, she fears "the odious possibility of her sister's making a scandal" (447). She repeatedly fails to reform Selina; meanwhile, she takes a fancy to the ingenuous Wendover and comes to view him as her only chance to escape disgrace.

FURTHER READING

Edel, Leon. *Henry James: The Middle Years 1882–1895*. New York: Lippincott, 1962.

Gale, Robert L. *A Henry James Encyclopedia*. New York: Greenwood Press, 1989.

Gard, Roger, ed. *Henry James: The Critical Heritage*. New York: Routledge, 1982.

Izzo, Donatella. "Of Shame and Horror: 'A London Life' and the Theatricals of Femininity." In *Portraying the Lady: Technologies of Gender in the Short Stories of Henry James*. Lincoln: University of Nebraska Press, 2001.

James, Henry. *Complete Stories 1884–1891*. New York: Library of America, 1999.

———. *The New York Edition of Henry James, vol. 10: The Spoils of Poynton, A London Life, The Chap-*

eron. 1908. Reprint, New York: Scribner's, 1936. Abbreviated as NYE.

———. *The Complete Notebooks of Henry James*. Edited by Leon Edel and Lyall H. Powers. Oxford: Oxford University Press, 1987.

Moon, Heath. "James's 'A London Life' and the Campbell Divorce Scandal." *American Literary Realism* 13 (1980): 246–258.

Anne-Claire Le Reste, *Université de Rennes 2*

"The Middle Years" (1893)

The tale was first published in *Scribner's Magazine* in April 1893. It was reprinted with minor revisions in book form in 1895 as part of the collection *Terminations* (London: Heinemann, 1895) and with further revisions in Volume 16 of the NEW YORK EDITION. In the preface to that edition, James recalled that he had scarcely ever endured such a difficult "struggle to keep compression rich" (v). (See PREFACES TO THE NEW YORK EDITION.)Leon Edel's collection *The Complete Tales of Henry James* reverts to the first book text, as do most modern editions.

SYNOPSIS

The tale is set at a hotel in the seaside town of Bournemouth, where the aging novelist Dencombe has come to convalesce. As he sits on a bench outdoors, the postman brings him the first published copies of his latest book, itself titled *The Middle Years*. He begins to read his own work, having largely forgotten the plot during his illness, and finds himself pleasantly surprised: It is "extraordinarily good" (56). He hopes to recover so he can reap the fruits of his mature style, achieved only after many years of struggle.

While Dencombe reads, he observes three other residents on the beach below: the "massive" Countess (57), who is also an invalid; her female companion, Miss Vernham; and Doctor Hugh, who is reading a novel. Dencombe puts down his book as they climb the hill and come toward him. Doctor Hugh glances over at it and realizes immediately that Dencombe is reading the same book that he is. He assumes that Dencombe must be a fellow reviewer—rather than the novel's author—and experiences mild jealousy.

The two women go back to the hotel, and Dencombe and Doctor Hugh begin to talk. Dencombe is amused by the game of mistaken identity and enjoys hearing the young man praise his work generously and quote phrases from it. He reflects that it is a happy accident that his "greatest admirer" (61) should be a doctor and wonders if the young man may be able to help him recover. He realizes, however, that Doctor Hugh's freedom is severely limited by the whims of the Countess, who pays him a large salary.

As they discuss Dencombe's work, Doctor Hugh reaches for his copy of *The Middle Years* to illustrate a textual point. Picking up Dencombe's copy instead of his own, he notices pencil marks on the text and sees that these are unmistakably the sign of authorial revision. Even though the novel has just been published, Dencombe feels compelled to keep on revising, unable ever to reach "a form final for himself" (63). Overcome by the situation, Dencombe faints and is carried back to the hotel by Doctor Hugh in a bath chair. When he recovers consciousness in his hotel bedroom, he is mortified.

Later that afternoon, Doctor Hugh comes to visit. He has consulted with Dencombe's own physician and wishes to offer whatever additional medical care he can. Dencombe confesses that he has already "outlived" (his wife and son are dead; 66) but believes that he has only recently begun to realize his literary talent. Now he wants "another go" (67) and believes that Doctor Hugh can cure him. The two men go for a walk, and in a moment of inspiration Dencombe fantasizes about the books he may yet write.

Doctor Hugh leaves for half an hour, and Dencombe waits for him to return. He is interrupted in his reverie by Miss Vernham, who tells him that he should leave Bournemouth and treat Doctor Hugh fairly; the Countess had been planning to make him her heir but is jealous of his friendship with Dencombe and threatening to disinherit him. Dencombe returns in distress to the hotel to pack, but he develops a fever and is told by his physician to rest. The next morning, he receives a telegram from Miss Vernham. She begs him to persuade Doctor Hugh to join the two women in LONDON.

Two days later, Doctor Hugh returns from London with a copy of his review of *The Middle Years*, which has just been published. He explains that the Countess died while he was in London and that she left him nothing; he has chosen to accept the consequences of his "infatuation" (74). Dencombe is now dying himself. He still wishes for another chance and finds Doctor Hugh's praise of his completed work scant solace. In his final moments, he claims that the prospect of a second chance is illusory: "[T]here never was to be but one" (75).

CRITICAL ANALYSIS

"The Middle Years" counts among the group of short stories that James wrote during the 1890s about writers, artists, and their admirers, but it is unique in its apparently autobiographical content and, at times, in the lyricism of its prose style. In the introduction to the New York Edition, James recalled that he had found it difficult to fit the story into the word limit set by *Scribner's Magazine*; the story's form is that of "the concise anecdote," but the subject "would seem one comparatively demanding 'developments'" (v).

The tale is carefully and symmetrically constructed. Over the course of the tale, each of the four characters is paired and contrasted with the others. The ailing and gifted novelist, Dencombe, is paralleled by the sickly and monstrous Countess, the talentless daughter of a famous baritone, while Doctor Hugh finds a foil in Miss Vernham, who is an excellent pianist. The two central characters are male, interested in literature and in art, each for its own sake; the two peripheral characters are female, associated with music and with the corruption of the marketplace. Dencombe and Doctor Hugh are practitioners of art or medicine—writing novels or reviews, curing patients—while the Countess and Miss Vernham are mere consumers: The Countess wastes the money she has inherited from her father and late husband, and Miss Vernham is "hungry" (72) and an "*intrigante*" (66). By the end of the tale, both Dencombe and the Countess are dead.

The story is also framed by two publications. It opens with Dencombe receiving the first copy of his latest book, *The Middle Years,* and closes with Doctor Hugh presenting the dying author with the "great review" (73) of the novel that he has just published in a literary journal. Dencombe is delighted by his own prose when he rereads it, while Doctor Hugh feels childish pleasure in his own work as "something adequate . . . an acclamation, a reparation, a critical attempt to place the author in the niche he had fairly won" (73). In her discussion of the relationship between the two men, Julie Rivkin suggests that Dencombe and Doctor Hugh "supplement one another in needs and talents" (475). As an author, Dencombe has discovered his ideal reader and "greatest admirer" in the young generation, and as an invalid he has met a "bristling young doctor," equipped with all the latest scientific knowledge. Joyce Carol Oates observes that, as in some of James's other stories of writers and artists, there is also more than a hint of homoeroticism in this "strange marriage of artists and 'greatest admirer'" (261). After sacrificing his legacy, Doctor Hugh explains that "I chose to accept, whatever they might be, the consequences of my infatuation" (74). When he tells Dencombe that his life's work has been a success, his voice is tinged with "the ring of a marriage-bell" (75).

By this reading, Dencombe's death at the end of the tale is less than tragic because his legacy as a writer will be preserved by the eager young doctor. His eloquent last words, often quoted in support of James's own views on art, can be understood as an acceptance of this possibility: "We work in the dark—we do what we can—we give what we have. Our doubt is our passion and our passion is our task. The rest is the madness of art" (75). At the same time, the tale can also be read as a more pessimistic assessment of the relationship between writer and admiring critic. Dencombe observes more than once that, despite his intelligence, Doctor Hugh has failed to guess the "deeper meaning" (69) of *The Middle Years,* and he does not willingly yield to the doctor's suggestion that "the second chance has been the public's—the chance to find the point of view, to pick up the pearl!" (74). Moreover, despite his medical ability, Doctor Hugh is unable to cure Dencombe or to make any substantial contribution beyond "guarding him from pain" (74).

In many respects, Dencombe's artistic practice mirrors James's own. He values literary merit over commercial gain; his writing aims at a proto-modernist "rare compression" (56); and he is "a passionate corrector, a fingerer of style" (63), with one eye always turned to the second and revised edition of every text. Whether the complexity of his art and what he has "tried for" (69) can ever be understood by *any* reader is ultimately left ambiguous. Doctor Hugh tries very hard to pin down exactly what makes *The Middle Years* a great novel, but Dencombe can only smile coldly at the review, suggesting that value lies in what he has *not* been able to achieve in his lifetime: "The pearl is the unwritten—the pearl is the unalloyed, the *rest,* the lost!" (74). Publication may be necessary to assure a writer's status *as* an author, but for Dencombe it has also become a dangerous and confusing process, which substitutes readerly for authorial control. He attempts to use post-publication revision as a method to win back control over his own text, but his untimely death illustrates that his dream of finding "a form final for himself" is a futile one. Whether James himself was convinced by his own conclusions is less clear. Despite the overt argument of "The Middle Years" against revision, he was to make substantial changes to it for the New York Edition.

CHARACTERS

Countess, the   A large, wealthy, eccentric woman, she is the daughter of a famous baritone and has inherited "his taste, without his talent" (62). She has traveled to Bournemouth accompanied by Miss Vernham and Doctor Hugh, both of whom she pays handsomely. She dies suddenly after returning to London.

Dencombe   A novelist, he has come to Bournemouth to recover from an illness brought on by the strain of completing *The Middle Years.* He believes that he has wasted much time in life and longs for a second chance to produce his finest work. Despite Doctor Hugh's medical attention, however, his health continues to worsen. He dies at the end of the tale, after an eloquent final speech.

Hugh, Doctor   A "bristling young doctor" (61), he turns out to be a great admirer of Dencombe's writing and publishes a fine review of *The Middle Years*. He is employed by the Countess as her personal physician and must choose between her (and the promise of a large inheritance) and Dencombe (and the seductions of art).

Vernham, Miss   The Countess's humble dependent is an "odd creature" (62) but an excellent pianist. She rebukes Doctor Hugh for neglecting his patron and asks Dencombe to leave him alone.

FURTHER READING

James, Henry. "The Middle Years." In *The Complete Tales of Henry James*, edited with an introduction by Leon Edel. Vol. 9: 1892–1898, 53–76. London: Rupert Hart Davis, 1963.

———. Preface to Volume 16 of the New York Edition, v–xii; and the revised text, 77–106. New York: Scribner's Sons, 1909.

Oates, Joyce Carol. "The Madness of Art: Henry James's *The Middle Years*." *New Literary History* 27, no. 2 (1996): 259–262.

Rivkin, Julie. "Revision and 'The Middle Years.'" In *Tales of Henry James*, edited by Christof Wegelin and Henry Wonham, 470–479. New York and London: Norton, 2003.

Wegelin, Christof. "Art and Life in James's 'The Middle Years.'" *Modern Fiction Studies* 33 (Winter 1987): 639–646.

Hannah Sullivan, *Stanford University*

"The Next Time"   (1895)

The tale was first published in the *Yellow Book* on July 6, 1895. It was reprinted in a slightly revised form in 1896 in the collection *Embarrassments* (London: Heinemann; New York: Macmillan) and with further revisions in Volume 15 of the New York Edition. Leon Edel's collection *The Complete Tales of Henry James* reverts to the first book text, as do most modern editions.

SYNOPSIS

The tale is set in London around 1890. The narrator, a nameless book reviewer, is visited one morning by the successful novelist Mrs. Highmore, who begs him to review her work. Her arrival reminds him of another meeting, 18 years earlier, when she asked him to consider the work of the novelist Ralph (Ray) Limbert. Two more different writers are hard to imagine: Jane Highmore is a best-selling popular novelist; Limbert is an exquisite artist but a commercial failure. Mrs. Highmore hopes that the narrator's review of her latest book will influence public opinion and improve her critical reputation.

(Chapter 1) The narrator remembers his first meeting with Jane Highmore. Her mother, the snobbish Mrs. Stannace, has discouraged him from pursuing Jane's younger sister, Maud, because he lacks connections and money. Maud falls in love with the equally impoverished novelist Ralph Limbert, but their MARRIAGE has to be delayed until he can secure an income. Mrs. Highmore begs the narrator to help, and he graciously finds Limbert a position as London correspondent of *The Blackport Beacon*. However, despite Limbert's best efforts to write to the dictates of the market, his work is pronounced insufficiently "gossipy," and he is sacked. All of his hopes are now vested in his new novel, *The Major Key*.

(Chapter 2) Mrs. Highmore persuades her own PUBLISHER to print *The Major Key* in serial form and to give Limbert a substantial advance. On this promise, Limbert and Maud marry and enjoy a few happy months, despite Mrs. Stannace's decision to move in with the young couple. The novel turns out to be a great critical success and is favorably reviewed by the narrator. Like Limbert's earlier work it also turns out to be commercially weak. Harassed by a growing family, an ailing wife, and a difficult mother-in-law, he vows to try even harder with his next book.

(Chapter 3) There is a turn in Limbert's fortune. He is offered a well-paying position as editor of a "high-class monthly," owned by Mr. Bousefield, and promises to include the narrator's reviews in it. He renounces the idea that "success" is something found inherently in the literary work of art and declares that his future intention is simply to sell. The narrator is doubtful that Limbert will be able to ape his sister-in-law's successes but remains silent and attempts to be supportive. Limbert works alone for a year, afraid that the narrator's comments will be "fatal" (212) to his chance of success. Eventually, the narrator reads an extract from the new work in an American journal. It is "simply superb" (212). This impression is confirmed by the published novel, which turns out, despite Limbert's perverse efforts to the contrary, to be an absolute masterpiece.

(Chapter 4) After rereading the new novel, the narrator goes to Limbert's house to give his verdict. He is met by Mrs. Highmore, who picks him up in her carriage and tells him the bad news: Limbert has quarreled with Mr. Bousefield. Bousefield wants him to make the review more popular, printing no more of the narrator's "deadly" reviews and no more of his own equally unpopular fiction. The case now seems to be hopeless. The reader becomes aware that the narrator is more interested in Limbert's exquisite art than in his personal happiness. He concludes that Limbert will never be satisfied with his present work, given that he invests all hope of success in "the next time." In the end, "you can't make a sow's ear out of a silk purse" (220).

(Chapter 5) The narrator is proven correct: Limbert's novel barely sells a copy; his split with Mr. Bousefield makes him unwelcome in literary circles, and he moves to the country to minimize expenses. Mrs. Stannace moves in with her other daughter, Jane Highmore. Limbert feels guilty about his failure to provide for her, but the narrator suspects she has hidden resources and that she will leave the Limberts money on her death. Limbert's latest novel, *The Hidden Heart*, is modeled as an adventure story "on approved lines" (227), but despite its attempts to be formulaic, it is another brilliant failure. Depressed and in increasingly poor health, Limbert decides to renounce his hopes of attaining commercial success and begins a final novel, *Derogation*. Passionately invested in his theme, he continues writing until his death a few months later. The narrator decides that the book is "a splendid fragment" but that, once again, it would not "wake up the libraries" (229).

CRITICAL ANALYSIS

"The Next Time" is one among the group of dispiriting tales of "writers and artists" that James pro-

duced during the 1890s, while he was struggling to achieve commercial success in the theater. It has received less critical attention than some other tales in this group, which includes "The MIDDLE YEARS" (1893), "The FIGURE IN THE CARPET" (1896), and "The DEATH OF THE LION" (1894), but is similarly acute in its diagnosis: Something is rotten in the state of literature. It was first published in Aubrey Beardsley's *Yellow Book,* which, Leon Edel argues, James saw as a particularly fitting medium for his delicate and ironic subject (7).

At the heart of the tale is a conflict between two different kinds of artistic "value." On the one hand, there are the "shameless, merciless masterpieces" (213) that Ray Limbert naturally and easily produces; on the other, the kind of commercial success enjoyed by his sister-in-law, who is able to translate the profits of her novel writing into an exclusive central London address. The anonymous narrator provides an example of a third kind of literary life: He is a reviewer and critic rather than a creative artist. Like Limbert, however, he is closely allied with failure; his reviews "supply no public want" (217) and are, at one point, even suspected of having been written by Limbert himself. His elevated notions of literary merit are perfectly, and sometimes uncannily, realized in Limbert's literary performances. He begins by attempting to woo the woman whom Limbert marries but in the end finds more consolation in reading Limbert's work. The process is described in sensual and erotic terms as "a long large surrender, the luxury of dropped discriminations" (191).

Ideas of "success" and "failure" weigh heavily, and often paradoxically, on the minds of all the characters in the tale. Limbert's mother-in-law, Mrs. Stannace, is "the second cousin of a hundred earls and a great stickler for relationship" (190); her ambitions are social and financial, and she is frustrated by her inability to engineer a good match for either of her daughters. Mrs. Highmore is a success by the standards of "*le gros public*" (210), as is the publisher Mr. Bousefield; and yet both want to exchange popular acclaim for literary merit. Ralph Limbert is able to knock out masterpieces with facility, yet his only desire is to "cultivate the market," "to sell." Limbert repeatedly attempts, and fails, to discover the art of popularity. He takes on the editorship of a high-minded review and plots to make it popular (it stops selling); he writes his next novel to the formula of the "adventure-story" but produces only "a deep and delicate thing" (228). His struggles seem at times to be modeled after the author's own experiences. During the 1890s, James suffered a series of disasters in the theater and had lost a newspaper position (at the *Herald Tribune*) early in his career, after failing to be sufficiently "gossipy."

Intertwined with the issue of success and failure are questions of gender. The narrator compares Limbert to "an undiscourageable parent to whom only girls kept being born" (228). And yet, as Kristin King has argued, the tale actually stages "the vicissitudes of a modern literary market that brings unwarranted success to the popular female writer and inexplicable failure to the male artist" (25). Both the narrator and Ralph Limbert find themselves repeatedly influenced by Mrs. Stannace and her two daughters; it is, in fact, in response to Mrs. Stannace's belief that he needs something to marry on that Limbert begins his hopeless attempt to woo the market. It is only in the last few months of his life that he once again resumes "doing something for himself," working "in happy mystery, without revelations even to his wife" (229).

The end of the tale suggests that the demands of the market and the demands of art are finally incommensurable. No solution is offered for funding or distributing masterpieces or for reincorporating true art within the confines of the marketplace. In this respect, "The Next Time" is prophetic, looking forward to the severe rupture between the aesthetic and the commercial that marks literary modernism. Nor does Limbert, as one might expect, achieve a paradoxical commercial success with his last novel: It is not a book that "would have waked up the libraries." In the final pages of the tale, his hope that commercial success might be learned is quietly disposed of, and the words *success* and *failure* recover their rightful meanings. The narrator concludes, with the benefit of hindsight: "*Derogation* is a splendid fragment; it evidently would have been one of his high successes."

CHARACTERS

Bousefield, Mr. Proprietor of a "high-class monthly," he offers Limbert the position of editor and hopes he will provide "intellectual power" (215). He is eventually disappointed. Complaining that Limbert has killed the magazine, he sacks him.

Highmore, Mrs. The elder of the Stannace daughters and a popular commercial novelist, she craves some of Limbert's artistic success. She also proposes various schemes to lend him some of her own popularity. She is married to the rather nondescript Cecil Highmore. The narrator ends up wondering if her presence is "the major complication" in Limbert's life.

Limbert, Ralph (Ray) A brilliant novelist, Limbert produces work of the highest artistic quality, but he wants to write commercially successful fiction. His marriage to Maud Stannace increases the financial pressures on him. Eventually, he begins writing something "for himself" but dies shortly afterward of heart failure.

Narrator The anonymous narrator is a book reviewer and man of letters. He has a very high opinion of Limbert's work but wonders if his generous reviews have contributed to Limbert's commercial failure. His own work aims at "delicious irony" but seems to "supply no public want" (217). He equivocates between genuine interest in Limbert's well-being and a more detached concern for his work.

Stannace, Maud "Pretty pink Maud" is wooed by the narrator but marries Limbert, to whom she proves a supportive and tender wife.

Stannace, Mrs. The mother of Maud and Jane, Mrs. Stannace is a social snob who wants her daughters to marry well. She makes her home with the Limberts after their marriage but moves in with Jane Highmore when they begin to suffer severe financial problems.

FURTHER READING

Criticism of "The Next Time" is scant. Frank Kermode's and Leon Edel's introductions do a useful job of placing it within the context of James's other tales of literary life.

Edel, Leon. "Introduction." In *The Complete Tales of Henry James 1892–1898*, vol. 9, 7–12. London: Rupert Hart-Davis, 1964.

James, Henry. "The Next Time." In Edel, 185–229.

Kermode, Frank. Introduction to *The Figure in the Carpet*, by Henry James, 7–30. London: Penguin, 1986.

King, Kristin. "'Lost among the Genders': Male Narrators and Female Writers in James's Literary Tales, 1892–1896." *Henry James Review* 16, no. 1 (1995): 18–35.

Hannah Sullivan, *Stanford University*

"Owen Wingrave" (1892)

James wrote "Owen Wingrave" in the summer of 1892, soon after the death of his sister Alice. It was published at the end of the same year in the Christmas number of *The Graphic*. Subsequently, the tale was included in two 1893 collections published with different titles in NEW YORK (*The Wheel of Time etc.*, Harper's) and in LONDON (*The Private Life etc.*, James R. Osgood, McIlvaine & Co.). A revised text was published in the "ghostly" volume (volume 17) of the NEW YORK EDITION. Leon Edel included it in his 1948 collection *The Ghostly Tales of Henry James*.

SYNOPSIS

The tale is set in London and in the old Wingrave family house of Paramore; it is divided into four sections.

(Section 1) Owen Wingrave announces to his military coach, Spencer Coyle, his decision to renounce his military career. Though Coyle is appalled, he is very fond of Owen and considers him too intelligent to judge him a coward. Coyle enlists Owen's friend Lechmere, an enthusiastic prospective young soldier, to change Owen's mind.

(Section 2) During the dialogue in the Baker Street house of Miss Jane Wingrave, Owen's "remarkable aunt" (19), the reader learns more particulars about the young man's family. Owen's elder brother was relegated to a private asylum, and consequently, the burden of upholding the family name has fallen on Owen, the talented second son. Owen's father died of "an Afghan sabre" (20), and his mother "sank under the multiplication of her woes" (20). The octogenarian Sir Philip, Owen's grandfather, lives in the picturesque but impoverished Jacobean house of Paramore with two other figures. These include Mrs. Julian, a widowed unremunerated housekeeper, and her daughter, Kate, Owen's intended. Miss Wingrave urges Coyle to keep Owen quiet and sees his resistance to the family legacy of soldiering as proof of his uncommon strength. Coyle admires Owen and eventually agrees with Miss Wingrave's estimation. In a subsequent conversation with Lechmere, Coyle learns of Owen's "overwhelming conviction of the stupidity—the 'crass barbarism' he called it—of war" (25).

(Section 3) At Paramore, where Coyle, his wife, and Lechmere have been summoned by the Wingrave family, all attack poor Owen, trying to convince him to give up his decision. Sir Philip and Miss Jane accuse him of dishonoring the family name, speculate that his grandfather will disinherit him, and predict that his sweetheart will think him a coward. At Paramore, there is a haunted room where Owen's great-great grandfather, Colonel Wingrave, "in a fit of passion" (37), had killed one of his children with a blow on the head. The following day, the great-great grandfather was found dead "without a wound, without a mark" (37) on the floor, in the room from which his son had been carried to the grave. Nobody has slept in this room since. A portrait of this tragic ancestor hangs on the wall of a big staircase; ominously, this portrait seems to stir when Owen passes near.

(Section 4) After dinner, almost everyone retreats for the night. However, Spencer Coyle is terribly agitated. He knocks on the door of Lechmere, who has just left Owen and his fiancée quarrelling. According to Lechmere, Kate Julian does not believe that Owen spent the previous night in the haunted room, and she accuses him of deceiving her. The young man answers defiantly: "Take me there yourself, then, and lock me in!" (50). Coyle goes back to his quarters and falls asleep in his chair. He is startled by "a sudden appalling sound" (51) and rushes toward the haunted room. What he sees is indeed appalling: Owen Wingrave lies dead on the very spot where his ancestor had expired. Owen looks finally like "a young soldier on a battle field" (51).

CRITICAL ANALYSIS

In a letter to ROBERT LOUIS STEVENSON (1888) James wrote that he proposed "for a longish period, to do nothing but short lengths" (*Letters* 240). The nineties saw a great explosion in James's short fiction. "Owen Wingrave" is the story of a young man who, trained for a military career, rebels against his family for whom soldiering is an ancient tradition, a vocation more than a profession. As Leon Edel states, "'Owen,' a Scottish name, means 'the young soldier': the title accordingly meant 'The Young Soldier Wins His Grave'" (*A Life* 431). As James makes clear in his *Notebooks*, the first suggestion for the tale came to him from "the fascinated perusal" (66) of the memoirs by Marcelin Marbot, one of Napoleon's generals. However, in the preface to Volume 17 of the New York Edition, James claims to remember almost nothing about the "germ" of the story except that one summer afternoon, while he sat on a penny chair "under a great tree in Kensington Gardens," a young man settled himself with a book on another chair within his "limit of contemplation." He was "a tall quiet slim studious young man, of admirable type" (*Literary Criticism* 1,262), who was to become Owen Wingrave.

Since James included "Owen Wingrave" among his ghost stories, it has been considered mainly as a story of the supernatural. But as Edward Wagenknecht writes, "[T]he supernatural element enters strongly only at the end to resolve the situation" (72). Furthermore, nobody actually sees the ghost. As Edel notes, James's ghostly tales "are not ghost stories in the conventional sense because, in some of them, no ghosts walk; when they do, they usually prefer daylight to moonshine, the open air to the tortuous corridor" ("Henry James's Ghosts" xxvi).

James is less interested in apparitions than in the haunted personalities who see the apparitions and who are victims of unconscious obsessions, like the famous governess of "The TURN OF THE SCREW." At Paramore, Owen is obsessed with ghostly presences that arise from an ancestral past to which his immediate family holds him responsible. Owen remarks to Spencer Coyle: "Oh, the house—the very air and feeling of it. There are strange voices in it that mutter at me—to say dreadful things as I pass. I mean the general consciousness and responsibility of what I'm doing . . . . I've started up old ghosts" (34).

The tale can also be read biographically. Edel maintains that James "tended to translate personal experience constantly into fantasy" ("Henry James's Ghosts" viii) and that the young sensitive pacifist Owen testifies to the writer's own "deep-seated anxieties" (xxxi). The story reaches far back to James's youth and the CIVIL WAR, in which he could not or would not participate because of a "horrid" and "obscure" hurt he had suffered in the spring of 1861 while his younger brothers, Wilkinson and Robertson, sought places in the Union army. This obscurely physical hurt became significantly psychological in time. Like the young Henry, Owen prefers reading literature to preparing himself for the army. Both Owen and Henry muster courage in resisting familial pressures and, in the end, with a typically Jamesian ironical reversal, Owen resembles a hero in his death. As Spencer Coyle remarks to Kate, "to my sense he *is*, in a sense of the term, a fighting man" (43). This is why in *Henry James: A Life* (1987) Edel considers this tale as one of the most deterministic James ever wrote. The young pacifist dies for his ideals, but the ending is ambiguous in raising doubts as to whether the battle has been won by Owen or by the family. It seems as if one can escape neither heredity nor one's soldierly fate; as Owen himself says, "we're tainted—all" (35).

CHARACTERS

Coyle, Mrs. Spencer Coyle's wife, from the very beginning, is on Owen's side. She thinks it a waste for him to become a soldier. Her role is that of the confidante, who provokes the debate and thus dramatizes the story's antagonistic points of view by objectifying them in characters' dialogues.

Coyle, Spencer   A "professional coach," he prepares young people for the army and is "of exactly the stature of the great Napoleon" (14). He is "an artist in his line" and has "taken a particular fancy to Owen Wingrave" (14). Although he says he is disgusted by Owen's sudden decision to renounce soldiering, he gradually becomes convinced that he "after all had a right to his ideas" (25).

Julian, Kate   "A remarkably clever little girl of eighteen" (20), Kate is the daughter of Mrs. Julian, "the widow of an officer and a particular friend of Miss Wingrave" (20). Kate is Owen's sweetheart. She accuses him of being a coward and dares him to spend a night in the haunted room of Paramore.

Lechmere   Wingrave's fellow pupil and supposed best friend, he is "short and sturdy," with a face "from which you could never guess whether he had caught an idea" (16).

Wingrave, Miss Jane   Owen's aunt represents "the genius of a military race" (21). In Coyle's view, she is "almost vulgar about her ancestors" (22). She is unrelenting in her pressure on Owen to change his mind and take up the family profession of soldiering.

Wingrave, Owen   The protagonist of the tale is "a tall, athletic young man" (14) who prefers the "intellectual pleasure" (16) of reading Goethe's poems to the supposed magnificence of a military career. Both Coyle and his aunt regard him as being extraordinarily "intelligent" in contrast with his unhappy brother, who was "literally imbecile and banished from view" (19). Owen rejects the romanticization of war, concluding that "all the great generals ought to have been shot" (26) and that Napoleon Bonaparte was a criminal. Nevertheless, Owen seems to possess the courage to defy his family, even to his death.

ADAPTATIONS

In 1907–08, Henry James converted "Owen Wingrave" into a one-act play titled *The Saloon*, hoping that the Incorporated Stage Society would produce it as a curtain-raiser to his own *The High Bid*. When the script was rejected, James exchanged a number of letters with the society's spokesman, George Bernard Shaw, from which their different assumptions about literature and life clearly emerge.

Benjamin Britten adapted the story to compose an opera for television, first broadcast in May 1971.

In 2001, "Owen Wingrave" was adapted for the screen as a musical by Myfanwy Piper.

FURTHER READING

Edel, Leon. "Henry James's Ghosts—An Introductory Essay." In *The Ghostly Tales of Henry James*, v–xxxii. New Brunswick, N.J.: Rutgers University Press, 1948.

James Henry. "Owen Wingrave." In *The Ghostly Tales of Henry James*, edited by Leon Edel. New Brunswick, N.J.: Rutgers University Press, 1948.

———. "Owen Wingrave." In *The Complete Tales of Henry James*, vol. 9. Edited by Leon Edel. London: Rupert Hart-Davis, 1962–64.

———. *Letters*, vol. 3. Edited by Leon Edel. Cambridge, Mass.: Harvard University Press, 1980.

———. *The Complete Notebooks*. Edited by Leon Edel and Lyall H. Powers. New York and Oxford: Oxford University Press, 1987.

———. "Preface to 'The Altar of the Dead.'" In *Henry James Literary Criticism: French Writers, Other European Writers, The Prefaces to the New York Edition*. 2 Vols. New York: Library of America, 1984.

———. *Henry James. A Life*. London: Collins, 1987.

Wagenknecht, Edward. *The Tales of Henry James*. New York: Frederick Ungar, 1984.

Vittoria Intonti, *University of Bari*

"The Pupil" (1891)

James wrote "The Pupil" in LONDON in the summer of 1890. It was first published in the March and April 1891 issues of England's *Longman's Magazine*. It became part of *The Lesson of the Master* (1892) (see "The LESSON OF THE MASTER"), published by

Macmillan and Co., and appears in Volume 11 of the NEW YORK EDITION (1908), together with *WHAT MAISIE KNEW* (1897) and "IN THE CAGE" (1898).

SYNOPSIS

(Chapter 1) The story is set in 1880s France and Italy in the progressively dingier homes of the Moreens, a cosmopolitan family of adventurers who wander from city to city, with great social pretensions and precarious economic means. They hire Pemberton, a young, impecunious Yale- and Oxford-educated American, to tutor their 11-year-old son, Morgan, a precocious, sensitive boy with a weak heart. The catch: They ultimately deceive Pemberton, hoping that he, like Morgan's previous nurse, will stay on without pay out of affection for the boy.

Pemberton musters the nerve to broach the uncomfortable subject of salary with Mrs. Moreen, whose appearance betrays the shabbiness that exists beneath her excessive display of wealth. Her responses are evasive. Pemberton also meets Morgan and reluctantly takes the job, gradually warming up to his charge.

(Chapters 2 and 3) Pemberton continues to discern the Moreens' facade of wealth and earnestness from their "queerness" (414). As he observes them trying to marry off their daughters, he notes their "topsyturvy" manners and "reversed conventions" (415); the mysterious ventures of Mr. Moreen and his son, Ulick; and their strange social success among the wealthy, given that he had "never seen a family so brilliantly equipped for failure" (415). Pemberton is excited about the Moreens' knowledge of music, food, and foreign cities; their "dazzling sense of culture" (416) suggests that to live with them "would really be to see life" (415). But they also remind him of a "band of gipsies [sic]" (415), a strange "migratory tribe" (418) who speak their own "family language—Ultramoreen" (416). Above all, they neglect Morgan. Pemberton tries to insulate him from the Moreens' neglect, but Morgan knows far more about his family than Pemberton first assumes.

(Chapters 4–7) A year passes. The family's decline becomes obvious: They relinquish their villa in Nice, wander about, and keep up a thin show of affluence. Pemberton has still received no salary. He threatens to leave, but Mr. Moreen mysteriously appears with 300 francs to stall his departure. Pemberton is now too attached to Morgan to abandon him, even though Morgan himself suggests that Pemberton should find a paying job. When Pemberton confronts Mrs. Moreen, she appears in his room with 50 francs. Indignant, she insists he has gained enough by his relationship to Morgan that it is "really too absurd" for him also to "expect to be *paid*" (431). He agrees not to leave on the condition that Morgan be told of his parents' lies. But Morgan, in fact, already knows too much, and begs Pemberton to explain why he must suffer this undeserved "particular blight" (442). Morgan suggests the pair should flee together, like two heroes in a boy's adventure book.

Several years pass. The family moves to VENICE, and Pemberton continues to worry that the 15-year-old Morgan still cannot survive without his support. But when Mrs. Moreen actually approaches Pemberton to borrow 60 francs, it is the last straw. Pemberton accepts a lucrative job in London, tutoring an "opulent youth" (447), hoping to earn enough to retrieve Morgan.

After one year, Mrs. Moreen cables him, falsely claiming that Morgan is ill. Pemberton forfeits his job and returns immediately, only to find the family in worse circumstances than ever. His mother's deception actually *makes* Morgan ill, although with Pemberton's renewed presence he recovers. But the house of cards ultimately collapses. Detained in a dingy PARIS hotel for not paying their bill, the family is publicly exposed. When the parents propose that Pemberton take Morgan off their hands—indeed, the seeming realization of Morgan's dream—Pemberton's response is unclear and is interrupted in any case. Whether from excitement, shame, or anguish at being abandoned, Morgan's weak heart fails, overwhelmed by the emotional upheaval. He collapses and dies.

CRITICAL ANALYSIS

"The Pupil" was written in James's "middle phase," the 1890s, when he turned away from novel writing and toward DRAMA, the short story, and short novel. Although early critics ignored this anomalous period given the dismal theatrical failure of James's play *Guy Domville* (1893), many now consider it the decade of his best short works, culminating with The Spoils of Poynton (1897) and "The Turn of the Screw" (1898). In this work, James transforms his international theme into cosmopolitanism and experiments with a fluid narrative point of view, creating a transition to his "late style."

Like James, himself a cosmopolitan in the 1890s, the characters in "The Pupil" are all Americans living in Europe. According to the Oxford English Dictionary, a "cosmopolitan" is a "citizen of the world"; however, for James this world was European. But what promised freedom for the American abroad was often deplorable to Europeans. Adeline Tintner states in *The Cosmopolitan World of Henry James* (1991) that Europeans are always of some nationality (French, German, etc.): "Only an American can want or hope to be European without belonging to a specific nationality" (2). French writers whom James knew such as Paul Bourget and Maurice Barrès felt that cosmopolitanism was a "disease of modern society," a source of moral corruption, associated with so-called Jewish capitalism, that conflicted with their national pride and anti-Semitism (2).

"The Pupil" features a cosmopolitan American family seen through the eyes of their son and his tutor: "little Morgan's troubled vision of them as reflected in the vision, also troubled enough, of his devoted friend" ("Preface" xviii). As vulgar and selfish as they appear, how do the Moreens concern James? Are they not precisely the kinds of lying and cheating Americans from whom he would wish to distinguish himself? When he first submitted the story to the *Atlantic Monthly*, its new editor, Horace Scudder, rejected it. This was the first refusal James had experienced from the *Atlantic Monthly,* and he expressed his "shock of a perfectly honest surprise" (Edel 100). Why?

In his Preface to the New York Edition (1908), James describes the Moreens as possessing the "special essence of the little old miscellaneous cosmopolite Florence . . . of irrecoverable years" ("Preface" xvi–xvii) (see Florence). They represent, in other words, the first generation of American expatriates. Years earlier, riding in an Italian railway carriage with the expatriated doctor William Wilberforce Baldwin, James heard a story of an American family, "an odd adventurous, extravagant band, of high but rather unauthenticated pretensions, the most interesting member of which was a small boy, acute and precocious, afflicted with a heart of weak action, but beautifully intelligent, who saw their prowling precarious life exactly as it was" (xvii). The resulting story, "The Pupil," illuminates the clash of values and the dangers of confronting the truth but does not decide for readers who is right. As the Moreens wander from city to city, desperately clinging to the social pretensions that exceed them, the cosmopolitan Moreens may seem unfixable in any particular national idiom, but this only better allows them to mirror the superficiality and potentially deadly seductiveness of European high society.

The story's opening presents Pemberton anxious over how to broach the delicate subject of money and introduces the story's central tension. Pemberton cannot resist the emotional manipulations of Morgan's otherwise mendacious parents due to his growing devotion to the sensitive boy. Narrated by a third-person narrator, the story's center of consciousness, or guiding point of view, does seem to be Pemberton's. But the story also offers a double vision, challenging readers to find a stable ground of truth in Pemberton's retrospection, in which the Moreens take on a mysterious, "phantasmagoric" quality, constituting their "queerness" (414).

There is great disagreement as to what this term *queerness* refers. Whether marking the family's vexed relationship to money, moral questions about familial duty, or sexuality, it illustrates what Wayne Booth (1961) describes as the story's unintentional ambiguity, leaving room for a variety of readerly "conventional expectations" (366). Morgan, Pemberton recalls, is "as puzzling as a page in an unknown language"; in fact, the "whole mystic volume in which the story had been bound demanded some practice in translation" (414). "The Pupil" also demands practice in critical "translation."

Whereas in 1951 critic F. W. Dupee read "The Pupil" as an existentialist dilemma about "estranged and solitary men" (153), later readers sought to decipher its moral lesson. Responses to "The Pupil" break down roughly into two categories: those that emphasize Morgan's untimely death and treat the story as a morality tale, and those that emphasize the deep relationship between Pemberton and Morgan to imply a veiled portrait of homosexual intimacy that troubles conventional moral categories. The single greatest point of dispute about the tale's climactic ending hinges on who is responsible for the death of Morgan Moreen. Mrs. Moreen blames Pemberton as she exclaims: "'You walked him too far, you hurried him too fast!'" (460). She may be covering her own deeper responsibility. Upon returning from this vigorous walk in the Bois de Boulogne, Morgan had witnessed again his family's humiliating exposure, their "pile of gaping trunks" strewn about the lobby of the hotel, and "blushed to the roots of his hair" (458). If that were not enough, his parents shove him off onto Pemberton all too hastily. Pemberton counters Mrs. Moreen's accusation by charging that Morgan had grown too ill to stand the "'the shock, the whole scene, the violent emotion'" (460). Without dispute, Morgan has a weak heart. Beyond that, the final tableau hardly clarifies culpability, implying it is shared: Pemberton "pulled him half out of his mother's hands, and for a moment, while they held him together, they looked, in their dismay, into each other's eyes" (460). This final moment is inscrutable.

If the Moreens seem most obviously to deserve blame for neglecting their son, his death allows James to critique their obsession over wealth and status. Charles Hoffman (1957) and Walter F. Wright (1962) share this view, holding the Moreens responsible for effectively murdering their son. Their rapacity, indifference, and devotion to petty luxuries lead them to exploit Pemberton for his parental concern. Others, such as Terence Martin (1959), Elizabeth Cummins (1970), and William B. Stein (1959) see Pemberton as the villain. Seduced by the Moreens' world of appearances, Pemberton is complicit in their parental neglect. He nurtures the fantasy of saving Morgan, teaching him to return to the "'playroom of superstition'" (Cummins 56) then abandoning him, avoiding responsibility when

pressed to act decisively. Stein blames Pemberton's puritanical sensibilities: Prudish, self-renunciating, and self-sacrificing, Pemberton is the real pupil, a figure James casts up for ridicule.

Whereas the Moreens' motivations are evident throughout, the question of Pemberton's culpability depends on the final scene. Most influential is Leon Edel's *Henry James: The Treacherous Years* (1969), according to which Pemberton hesitates to take on Morgan, who is left "betrayed," his life "a void," finding himself "in terror, alone" (100). William Kenney (1971) and John Griffith (1972), however, see no clear sign of hesitation. Kenney attributes Morgan's death to the shock of public exposure (321); for Griffith, it is simply "uncaused," not a murder, but something "nearer suicide," a "providential evil" in a "black high comedy of manners and morals" (267, 268). David Eggenschwiler (1976) goes so far as to call it a "moral tale without a moral" (435), in which the search for causality turns an ending about the "complexities and dangers of the moral life" (444) into a "moral whodunit" (n. 7, 443). Mary Rucker (1976) also resists affixing blame, emphasizing the tension between "Pemberton's radically moral consciousness" and "the narrator's amoral and comic consciousness" (306). Edward Wagenknecht (1984) simply finds the idea of Pemberton rejecting Morgan "an absurd exaggeration" (61).

Whereas Clifton Fadiman (1945), F. W. Dupee (1951), and Maxwell Geismar (1969) noted the homosexual affection between tutor and pupil, more recent studies treat the intimacy between the two main characters as a fundamental theme. Pemberton's unclear response to Morgan becomes an act of what Eve Sedgwick calls "homosexual panic," a concept she popularized in her study *Epistemology of the Closet* (1990). There is no question that Pemberton and Morgan develop a certain flirtatious intimacy, especially in their mutual understanding of the Moreens' lies. The story is triggered in Pemberton's memory by "a lock of Morgan's hair, cut by his own hand, and the half-dozen letters he got from him when they were separated" (415). John R. Bradley, in "Henry James's Permanent Adolescence," claims that this "pederastic yearning of an older man for a younger man or boy" is the form that homosexual expression most consistently takes throughout James's work (55). James repeatedly uses the term *queer* to describe the Moreens, and if Morgan's affection is, indeed, the only form of payment Pemberton receives, their relationship resembles prostitution, as implied by Mrs. Moreen's urging Pemberton to take the job: "He's a genius—you'll love him" (413). John Carlos Rowe's *The Other Henry James* (1998) sees James as a forerunner of queer theorists, arguing that "Morgan understands as well as the other that he is Mr. Pemberton's delayed 'payment'" (22) for services rendered.

But this strand of "queer" reading has not gone unquestioned. Philip Horne (1997) claims that the term *queer* in 19th-century usage is "multiple and ambiguous," referring to a range of conditions without explicit reference to sexuality, though certainly not precluding it. The power of the term *queer* derives from its being "multiple and ambiguous" (121). Looking at textual variations between the first edition and New York Edition of the story, Horne suggests that Morgan's shame may simply be over his dishonest family. Millicent Bell agrees. Her essay, "The Unmentionable Subject in 'The Pupil,'" puts the problem in less controversial terms: The story is about "something considered nearly unmentionable by the genteel—money" (139).

As if in direct response to Horne, Eric Haralson (2003) contextualizes the usage of the term *queer* historically and insists that James's characters can be thought queer "in an anticipatory sense" (23) that intimates a male "effeminate" (24) homosexual figure and implies an abiding, if not necessarily overt, sexual dimension.

CHARACTERS

Moreen, Morgan (a.k.a. "the pupil")   Morgan is the extraordinary, precocious child and the weak heart at the center of his family. The narrator repeatedly describes him in contradictory terms, suggesting both Pemberton and James's fascination with Morgan. Seemingly in need of protection, he ultimately exposes the truth of his parents' lies to his tutor. He matures to age 15, at once a part of, yet apart from, his pretentious family. Upon their public exposure and their attempt to push him off into Pemberton's care, he dies suddenly of heart failure.

Moreen, Mr.   Repeatedly and ironically referred to as a "man of the world," Mr. Moreen is a man of precarious earnings and dubious status. He has the right trappings: a "white moustache" and in his "buttonhole, the ribbon of a foreign order," but for services that remain unnamed (413). "As the parent bird," Mr. Moreen "sought sustenance for the nest" (414), but readers never learn from where. He mysteriously produces 300 francs just when Pemberton threatens to leave. He is present to witness his child's death and expresses nominal grief, but he is otherwise largely absent from the story's action.

Moreen, Mrs.   First seen as a "large, affable lady . . . drawing a pair of soiled *gants de Suède* through a fat, jeweled hand" (409), Mrs. Moreen with her dirty gloves is the perfect picture of greed, excess, and vulgar materialism. Initially seeing in her a genteel sensibility, upon closer inspection Pemberton discovers "that her elegance was intermittent and her parts didn't always match" (414). She is all show. When the family is finally exposed, she rashly urges Pemberton to take Morgan off their hands. But when Morgan dies suddenly, possibly from the shock of her act, possibly from the shame of ruin, she places blame on Pemberton's recklessness.

Pemberton, Mr. (a.k.a. "the tutor")   The tutor is a young American student whom the Moreens "hire" to watch over and educate their son. Educated and gentlemanly, he is also a naive dreamer. He believes in good manners, family duty, and the Puritan values of modesty and self-sacrifice, developing such affection for Morgan that he stays on without pay until Morgan's untimely death. With Morgan's help, he becomes disabused that his values are universally shared, gradually discovering the Moreens' deceptiveness.

FURTHER READING

Bell, Millicent. "The Unmentionable Subject in 'The Pupil.'" In *The Cambridge Companion to Henry James,* edited by Jonathan Freedman. Cambridge: Cambridge University Press, 1998.

Bradley, John R. "Henry James's Permanent Adolescence." In *Henry James and Homo-Erotic Desire,* edited by John R. Bradley, 45–68. New York: St. Martin's Press, 1999.

Cummins, Elizabeth. "The Playroom of Superstition: An Analysis of Henry James's 'The Pupil.'" *Markham Review* 2, no. 3 (1970): 53–56.

Dupee, F. W. *Henry James: His Life and Writings.* 1951. Reprint, Garden City, N.Y.: Doubleday Anchor Books, 1956.

Edel, Leon. *Henry James: The Treacherous Years, 1895–1901.* Philadelphia: Lippincott, 1969.

Eggenschwiler, David. "James's 'The Pupil': A Moral Tale without a Moral." *Studies in Short Fiction* 15 (1976): 435–444.

Fadiman, Clifton. *The Short Stories of Henry James.* New York: Random House, 1945.

Griffith, John. "James's 'The Pupil' as Whodunit: The Question of Moral Responsibility." *Studies in Short Fiction* 9 (1972): 257–268.

Hagopian, James V. "Seeing Through 'The Pupil' Again." *Modern Fiction Studies* 5 (1959): 169–171.

Haralson, Eric. *Henry James and Queer Modernity.* Cambridge: Cambridge University Press, 2003.

Hocks, Richard A. *Henry James: A Study of the Short Fiction.* Boston: Twayne, 1990.

Horne, Philip. "The Master and the 'Queer Affair' of 'The Pupil.'" In *Henry James: The Shorter Fiction: Reassessments,* edited by N. H. Reeve, 114–137. New York: St. Martin's Press, 1997.

James, Henry. "Preface." *The Novels and Tales of Henry James,* vol. 11, v–xxii. New York: Scribner's, 1908.

———. "The Pupil." *The Complete Tales of Henry James,* vol. 7. Edited by Leon Edel. Philadelphia and New York: Lippincott, 1963.

Kaplan, Fred. *Henry James: The Imagination of Genius.* New York: William Morrow, 1992.

Kenney, William. "The Death of Morgan in James's 'The Pupil.'" *Studies in Short Fiction* 8 (1971): 317–322.

Martin, Terence. "James's 'The Pupil': The Art of Seeing Through." *Modern Fiction Studies* 4 (1959): 335–345.

Rowe, John Carlos. *The Other Henry James.* Durham, N.C.: Duke University Press, 1998.

Rucker, Mary E. "James's 'The Pupil': The Question of Moral Ambiguity." *Arizona Quarterly* 32 (1976): 301–315.

Shine, Muriel G. *The Fictional Children of Henry James.* Chapel Hill: University of North Carolina Press, 1968.

Tintner, Adeline. "James Writes a Boy's Story: 'The Pupil' and R. L. Stevenson's Adventure Books." *Essays in Literature* 5 (1978): 61–75.

Wagenknecht, Edward. *The Tales of Henry James.* New York: Frederick Ungar, 1984.

Sharon B. Oster, *University of Redlands*

"The Real Thing" (1892)

James outlined the initial ideas for the story during a visit to PARIS in 1891. "The Real Thing" was published the following year in syndicated form in various American newspapers and most prominently in the British periodical *Black and White.* It was subsequently included in a collection entitled *The Real Thing, and Other Tales* (Macmillan, 1893) and in Volume 18 of the NEW YORK EDITION (Scribner's Sons, 1909).

SYNOPSIS

(Section 1) The tale begins with the entrance of two strikingly attractive guests into an artist's studio. While initially hesitant to reveal the reason for their visit, the guests finally explain to the artist (and narrator) that they are impoverished and seek employment as models for his illustrations. They introduce themselves via calling card as Major and Mrs. Monarch.

(Section 2) The artist finds himself liking the couple in spite of his prejudices regarding amateurs and his preference "for the represented subject over the real one" (38). After the artist agrees to use the Monarchs on a trial basis, one of the artist's regular models arrives. In her social status, irreverence, and ability to lend herself to the artist's transformative skills in her act of modeling, the cockney Miss Churm offers a vivid contrast to the stiff, finished Monarchs.

(Section 3) The Monarchs begin their sittings, but the results are troubling. Meanwhile, tensions develop between the new sitters and Miss Churm.

The Monarchs are particularly shocked when the artist chooses to employ an uneducated Italian immigrant named Oronte as a model.

(Section 4) The artist shows the results of his work to a colleague who tells him that the Monarchs will not do as models. Although the artist realizes that his friend is right, he initially hesitates to dismiss the Monarchs. After telling Major Monarch the truth in an uncontrolled outburst, the artist assumes that he will never see the couple again. However, they return to assist in the studio until the artist gives them money to go away permanently.

CRITICAL ANALYSIS

James offers his most forceful definition of the novel's purposes in his essay "The ART OF FICTION" (1884): "The only reason for the existence of a novel is that it does attempt to represent life" (457). James's close associate WILLIAM DEAN HOWELLS takes up and expands this characterization in 1899: "The novel I take to be the sincere and conscientious endeavour to picture life just as it is" (269).

While 21st-century readers may hardly find these reflections provocative, they were the source of considerable controversy at the end of the 19th century. On the one hand, Howell's and James's emphasis on the representation of life was a rejection of romance and its tendencies to idealization and allegory (see ROMANCE/REALISM/NATURALISM). On the other hand, realism was criticized as "Epidermism" or a practice of art based on external appearance or, literally, the skin (epidermis) that, in the words of an incensed critic, offered nothing more than "filth" and "degradation" (Cady 30).

Such exchanges were part of what has been called the "Realism War." While the novel was central to this conflict, it was not the only form through which artists strove to show life in a nonidealized manner. As Miles Orvell sketches out in *The Real Thing* (1989), many argued that photography was a particularly unbiased and "truthful" medium. Photojournalists ostensibly embraced this claim in the promotion of their documentation of social phenomena such as urban tenements. While readers were shocked at the images of squalid living conditions, reviews tended to emphasize the accuracy of the photographic image. As Ralph F. Bogardus suggests, this seeming exactness made the photographic an "inevitable" symbol of literary realism (122). However, tension arose between literary and photographic claims to capture the real thing. For example, a contemporary reviewer of Jacob Riis's photographic documentation *How the Other Half Lives* (1890) considered the book "enormously more interesting than any novel that ever was written or ever could be" (Orvell 96).

"The Real Thing" takes up questions central to the "Realism War" through its setting (an artist's studio) and narrative perspective (an artist serves as the first-person narrator). Indeed, "The Real Thing" is generally read as "The Realist Thing," that is, as a reiteration of James's own artistic precepts in narrative form. As with so many of James's fictions, an actual life incident provides the inspiration or "germ" of the story. In this case, it was the French-born illustrator GEORGE DU MAURIER, famous for his cartoons in the British humor magazine *Punch,* who related his experiences with a formerly upper-class, but now impoverished couple who sought work as artist's models and found themselves in competition with more proficient working-class models. As the preliminary reflections in James's *Notebooks* stress, the story based on this anecdote must "illustrate" a "*magnificent lesson*" (103–104).

Critics have kept the word *lesson* but have tended to change the adjective. Tzvetan Todorov calls the text a "relatively simple parable" (167) that outlines James's concept of a realism as drawing on, but ultimately transforming, reality. The story's narrator proposes a similar view when he speaks of "the alchemy of art" (42). Whereas the term *alchemy* might refer to the chemical processes that produce a photography image, the narrator reorients the term to connote the mystery of artistic recombination and interpretation. The Monarchs, who have "been photographed—*immensely*" (37), frustrate the illustrator's alchemical artistry with looks suited much better for the photographer's lens. It is Mrs. Monarch's accommodation to the photographic situation that proves the greatest weakness of her modeling. The artist relates: "Do what I would with it my drawing always looked like a photograph or a copy of the photograph" (201). Taking his cue from such passages, Richard A. Hocks characterizes the tale's central theme as the "distinguishing of 'photographic' realism from a more valid rendering that allows the artist sufficient freedom to transform his or her material" (49).

These aesthetic controversies are related to the tale's social and moral dimensions, which Earl Labor considered in the 1960s. In the story's opposition of lower- and upper-class figures (the name Monarch seems overtly symbolic), James offers an allegory of social transformation. Just as the Monarchs' claim to embody the image of British propriety is usurped by Miss Churm and Oronte, older and more fixed structures of class and privilege were giving way to market forces that valued the ability to adapt and transform social types; thus, when the cheeky cockney and Italian immigrant become raw material out of which the narrator depicts the stereotypic image of upper-class Britain, James calls the reader's attention to the transformative capacity of realism in its claim to document the real thing.

The story's artist dismisses the Monarchs because they are inadequate models, but their relationship lingers beyond their initial contract. The story raises a moral question of how to treat others in the process of negotiating social categories. The story begins with the artist's act of seeing and classifying the Monarchs: "I had immediately seen them. I had seized their type" (34). The narrator means that the Monarchs offer an example of a British lady and the gentleman whose genteel appearance offers a screen for him to project their entire lives: "It was in their faces, the blankness, the deep intellectual repose of the twenty years of country-house visiting" (37).

While contemporary philosophers and psychologists such as Charles Sanders Peirce, John Dewey, and the novelist's brother WILLIAM JAMES argued that generalized categories or types were necessary in ordering perceptions of the world, Stuart Burroughs argues that "stereotyping" hinders rather than helps the artist in reaching a full perception and adequate depiction of the social world. The story's artist is blind to how the Monarchs potentially break with an aristocratic type, and despite the evidence of the Monarchs' potential destitution, the artist cannot revise his impression of them

as the literal embodiment of a certain type. This makes the Monarchs' actions at the conclusion of the tale—their willingness to act "heroically" as servants—all the more surprising and ultimately instructive. As Earle puts it, the narrator achieves in his lingering relationship to the failed models "a new awareness of what constitutes 'the real thing' in human relationships: compassion" (32).

Sam Whitsitt argues that "The Real Thing" is less an allegory of writing than "a lesson in reading" (304). For him, the conclusion suggests that the artist has read the Monarchs incorrectly. Indeed, the artist's perception has essentially produced the same fixity and flatness that he critiques in photography. This contradiction undercuts the narrator's authority; David Toor suggests that the artist is an unreliable narrator. Thus readers should not simply take his pronouncements on art at face value or automatically interpret them as views held by James. Indeed, as Toor sees it, the tale prompts readers to question whether the overly photographic drawings are the failure of the Monarchs or of the artist. Perhaps, Toor posits, "It is the painter who is not the real thing" (39).

In a similar reading, Catherine Veilledent stresses the "paradoxical" dimension that the narration brings to the parable (37). Through the retrospective telling of the tale, the narrative involvement is actually split: The artist participates in the action of the story and recalls it. This means that the views expressed within the story are not necessarily the ones which the artist holds when he tells the story. With this in mind, the text does not offer a finished lesson but rather suggests a learning process. The concluding lines of the tale contradict the artist's previous comments about the Monarchs and their photographic fixity. Whereas his friend claims that the Monarchs have done the artist "permanent harm," the artist does cherish having gained some sort of insight, and he claims that "if it be true I'm content to have paid the price—for the memory" (57).

The price of memory is not reducible to a monetary amount and offers an aesthetic insight of value that is worth a commercial failure. The memory of these models' failure and of their perseverance in the face of this failure suggests the mysterious alchemy of artistry that stands behind the realist enterprise—an alchemy of art after which the artist in this tale strives. In remembering Mrs. Monarch's willingness to serve the models whom the artist can transform into a realist image, the narrator cherishes the breakdown of the narrow stereotypes that had enabled his aesthetic process. This may be the Monarch's final lesson, and the narrator notes: "I confess I should have liked to paint *that*" (56).

CHARACTERS

Artist, the   The unnamed narrator of the tale makes his living by illustrating popular fiction.

Churm, Miss   The cockney model outshines the Monarchs in her modeling skills.

Monarch, Major and Mrs.   A former British army officer and his wife have lost their fortune and are reduced to seeking employment as models for illustrations of the British upper class.

Oronte   A poor Italian immigrant, he is an ideal model for the artist, thus emphasizing the Monarch's inadequacies.

ADAPTATIONS

Numerous adaptations of the story were broadcast on U.S. television in the late 1940s and 1950s.

FURTHER READING

Bogardus, Ralph F. *Pictures and Texts: Henry James, A. L. Coburn, and New Ways of Seeing in Literary Culture.* Ann Arbor, Mich.: UMI Research Press, 1984.

Burroughs, Stuart. "Stereotyping Henry James." *Henry James Review* 23, no. 3 (2002): 255–264.

Cady, Edwin H. *The Realist at War.* Syracuse, N.Y.: Syracuse University Press, 1958.

Hocks, Richard A. *Henry James: A Study of the Short Fiction.* Boston: Twayne, 1990.

Howells, William Dean. *Norton Anthology of American Literature,* vol 2. Edited by Nina Baym, 266–282. New York: Norton, 1989.

James, Henry. "The Real Thing." In *The Complete Stories 1892–1898,* 32–57. New York: Library Classics, 1996.

———. *The Notebooks of Henry James.* Edited by F. O. Matthiessen and Kenneth B. Murdock. New York: Oxford University Press, 1947.

———. "The Art of Fiction." *Norton Anthology of American Literature,* 456–470.

Labor, Earle. "James's 'The Real Thing': Three Levels of Meaning." In Tompkins, 29–32.

Orvell, Miles. *The Real Thing: Imitation and Authenticity in American Culture.* Chapel Hill: University of North Carolina Press, 1989.

Todorov, Tzvetan. *The Poetics of Prose.* Translated by Richard Howard. Ithaca, N.Y.: Cornell University Press, 1977.

Tompkins, Jane, ed. *Twentieth Century Interpretations of "The Turn of the Screw" and Other Tales.* Englewood Cliffs, N.J.: Prentice Hall, 1970.

Toor, David. "Narrative Irony in Henry James's 'The Real Thing.'" In Tompkins, 33–39.

Veilledent, Catherine. "Representation and Reproduction, a Reading of Henry James's 'The Real Thing.'" In *Interface: Essays on History, Myth and Art in American Literature,* edited by Daniel Royot, 31–49. Montpellier: Université Paul Valéry, 1984.

Whitsitt, Sam. "A Lesson in Reading: Henry James's 'The Real Thing.'" *Henry James Review* 16, no. 3 (1995): 304–314.

MaryAnn Snyder-Koerrber,
Freie Universitaet (Berlin)

"The Story of a Year"   (1865)

First published in March 1865 in *Atlantic Monthly,* the story is the earliest short story to which James's name is affixed. The work never appeared in any subsequent collection published by James.

SYNOPSIS

(Section 1) The story opens in a fictional New England town called Glenham. The unnamed narrator addresses the reader directly in a retrospective telling of events. The "romance" begins with two lovers taking an evening stroll in the springtime air of May. (See ROMANCE/REALISM/NATURALISM.) Lieutenant John (Jack) Ford wears a Union uniform as he muses with his fiancée, Elizabeth (Lizzie) Crowe, about his impending service in the CIVIL WAR. Jack's protective mother is also Lizzie's guardian. Together, the two lovers observe a sunset that suggests warfare to Jack; he calls the scene an "allegory" and warns Lizzie that they should keep their betrothal a secret. Returning home from their walk, Jack finds his marching orders, which send him in two days' time to serve in Virginia. Jack confesses his and Lizzie's engagement to his mother. Mrs. Ford expresses her disapproval, faulting his fiancée as too shallow, but assures her son that she will keep his confidence.

(Section 2) In Glenham, Lizzie seeks ways of staying connected to Jack in his absence. After reading romances about Scottish chiefs, she collects her lover's old college books, which include a copy of Goethe's *Faust*. She imagines herself in the role of a lover deserted by her man. Mrs. Ford disapproves of Lizzie's fanciful nature. Lizzie keeps up her correspondence with Jack during the summer and into fall. When she receives a photograph of Jack with a new beard, she finds it ugly. Lizzie tires of her romance and grows bored with pining for Jack.

(Section 3) In February, with her engagement still a secret, Lizzie travels to Leatherborough, a town two hours south of Glenham by train. Mrs. Littlefield offers to help with Lizzie's debut into society. A whirlwind of dressmaking ensues. At her hostess's home, Lizzie meets the very attractive Robert Bruce, a tall and well-to-do gentleman. They dance, much to Lizzie's delight. Days after the debut, Lizzie runs into Robert at the train station on her return home. He settles her into her train car and sits across from her with a newspaper. Sharing war reports, Robert announces that a John Ford, second lieutenant, has been severely wounded. Shaken, Lizzie returns home to learn that Mrs. Ford is leaving to help care for Jack. Lizzie halfheartedly offers to go, but Mrs. Ford rejects the suggestion.

(Section 4) After a week, Lizzie receives details about Jack's injuries in letters from his mother. With three very serious wounds, Jack endures in the "midst of horrible scenes." Lizzie suffers a disagreeably premonitory dream. Torn between her loyalty to Jack and her attraction to Robert,

Lizzie imagines herself going mad. When she meets the sister of Jack's doctor, Miss Cooper, Lizzie's appearance has changed; she looks "pale, thin, and worn out." Later, she again sees Miss Cooper, who informs her that Robert Bruce has come to town with his sister. Lizzie later arrives at Dr. Cooper's for a visit and seems to regain her color and liveliness in the company of Robert, who seems similarly enraptured by her.

(Section 5) Three weeks later, Lizzie sits in Dr. Cooper's parlor as the Coopers prepare to attend a lecture called "A Year of the War." Lizzie complains of being tired of the war and declines an invitation to join them. She receives news of Jack's deterioration and expected death. Alone and in the dark, Robert appears. With the Lizzie's engagement to Jack still a secret, Robert and Lizzie discuss Jack's condition. Robert confesses his love and proposes MARRIAGE. Rattled and still contemplating Jack's state, Lizzie nevertheless accepts. A week later, a gravely wounded Jack returns. Lizzie catches only glimpses of the patient, managing just a brief exchange with her former lover. Finally, Jack asks to see her and confirms that he is dying. He gives his blessing to her to seek a new lover, careful not to mention Robert by name. He dies in her presence. The next day, Lizzie crosses paths with Robert outside the Ford home on her return from a walk. She spurns Robert, forbidding him to follow her into the house. Robert enters anyway.

CRITICAL ANALYSIS

"The Story of a Year" appeared during the last year of the Civil War to address the irrevocable damage to conventional romance caused by warfare. Given the effects of neurasthenia (a medical term applied to soldiers suffering from what later became known as "shell shock"), the issue of being wounded, both physically and mentally, held fascination for James, who secretly nursed what he called in his autobiography an "obscure hurt" of his own.

During the course of the story, John (Jack) Ford changes from an idealistic young man to a severely wounded adult who dies contemplating his sacrifice as a soldier and his failure to become a husband and father. His name "Ford" suggests his transition from youth to maturity, from idealism to disappointment, and from life to death. Initially, Jack seems to possess a confident and even heroic MASCULINITY, with a "swinging stride which often bespeaks . . . the answering consciousness of a sudden rush of manhood" (259). Yet he fears that his love for Lizzie will make him unable to face the challenge of war. As if training himself to feel courageous, he jests that if he should find his memory of love interfering with his duty then he will hide her picture and think of her only on Sundays.

Recent scholarly work on masculinity in the writing of James suggests the importance of understanding the story in relation to Walt Whitman's understanding of "comradeship"—which stems from the ancient Greek form of education and military training, based in a relationship between an older, possibly bearded adult mentor and a clean-faced young student. By juxtaposing Jack Ford and Robert Bruce (whose name alludes to the fierce Scottish warrior king Robert the Bruce), James investigates two contrasting manifestations of masculinity. Certainly, Jack forever changes as a result of warfare; a "rough camp-photograph" of his "newly bearded visage" revolts Lizzie, who calls the image "too ugly for anything" and thrusts it "out of sight" (266). The war destroys Jack, whose wounds make him sickly pale and fair. Conversely, the civilian Robert may initially appear as a "tall, sallow man," but he survives and woos Lizzie away from Jack. Lizzie herself sees her suitors as two alternative knights, "the black and the white," on the "great chess-board of fate" (272). In a prophetic dream, Lizzie foresees her future with a "tall, dark-eyed man," instead of with a man so covered with wounds and so deathly pale that he resembles an unburied corpse. The symbolism of Lizzie's own darkness (her last name is "Crowe") links her to Robert. Is he a true man or just someone lacking courage and spared by his unwillingness to serve as a romantic hero would?

Adrian Hunter emphasizes the importance of Jack's "wish to belong to the 'tragic fellowship' of War veterans," citing the soldier's "obscure injury" as equally mental and physical. Hunter links "The Story of a Year" to James's own desire to participate vicariously in "homosocial relationships with fighting men" (283). Sheldon Novick suggests that the

figure of Jack reflects qualities of Oliver Wendell Holmes, Jr., whom Novick claims was James's first love (106). In Jack's "jokes about looking like a lady when he returns from the Civil War" (15), Wendy Graham infers James's anxiety over his own obscure injury that prevented him from serving in the war as his two younger brothers had.

CHARACTERS

Bruce, Robert A tall, sallow, and successful businessman from Leatherborough, he pursues and proposes to Lizzie Crowe, whose betrothed is away at war.

Crowe, Elizabeth (a.k.a. Lizzie) A dark-haired young woman from Glenham, the ward of Mrs. Ford (Jack's mother), she becomes engaged to Jack Ford, a lieutenant in the Union Army. When her fiancé leaves for Virginia, she remains home, keeping a vigil for his return. Her commitment wavers, and she meets a new man, Robert, whom she also agrees to marry.

Ford, Lieutenant (a.k.a. John, Jack) A second lieutenant in the Union Army, he goes to Virginia to fight in the Civil War, leaving behind his mother and betrothed. In a skirmish on the Rappahannock, Jack is severely injured, with three unspecified but fatal wounds. He eventually returns home to die but not before telling Lizzie to find a new love.

Ford, Mrs. Jack's mother is austere and protective of her son. She is also the guardian of Lizzie, of whom she does not think so highly. Upon hearing news of her son's injuries, she travels to the hospital and nurses him until he is able to be moved home, where he will die. She cares for Jack until his death, guarding him from Lizzie.

FURTHER READING

Cannon, Kelly. *Henry James and Masculinity: The Man at the Margins.* New York: St. Martin's Press, 1994.

Graham, Wendy. *Henry James's Thwarted Love.* Palo Alto, Calif.: Stanford University Press, 1999.

Horne, Philip, ed. *Henry James: A Life in Letters.* New York: Viking, 1999.

Hunter, Adrian. "Obscured Hurts: The Civil War Writing of Henry James and Ambrose Bierce." *War, Literature, and the Arts: An International Journal of the Humanities* 14, nos. 1–2 (2002): 280–299.

Kaplan, Fred. *Henry James: The Imaginative of Genius.* New York: William Morrow, 1992.

Long, Robert Emmet. "Henry James's Apprenticeship—the Hawthorne Aspect." *American Literature* 48, no. 2 (1976): 194–216.

Martin, W. R. "*Hamlet* and Henry James's First Fiction." *ANQ: A Quarterly Journal of Short Articles, Notes and Reviews* 4 (October 2, 1989): 137–138.

McElderry, Jr., B. R. "The Uncollected Stories of Henry James." *American Literature* 21, no. 3 (1949): 279–291.

Novick, Sheldon. *Henry James: The Young Master.* New York: Random House, 1996.

Sharon Kehl Califano, *University of New Hampshire*

"The Turn of the Screw" (1898)

"The Turn of the Screw" has its origins in an anecdote James heard during a social call to the archbishop of Canterbury, E. W. Benson, in 1895. The story was first serialized in *Collier's Weekly* between January 27 and April 16, 1898. Later that same year, it appeared in *The Two Magics*, alongside the tale "Covering End." A decade later, James revised the tale substantially for inclusion in Volume 12 of the NEW YORK EDITION. Quotations in this entry are taken from Library of America volume *Henry James: Complete Stories 1892–1898*, which reprints the text of the English edition of *The Two Magics*, published by Heinemann.

SYNOPSIS

(Prologue) It is Christmas Eve, and the assembled guests at a country house party are sharing ghost stories. A nameless narrator relates that one guest, Douglas, offers to tell a story of "uncanny ugliness and horror and pain" (636) involving two children. The party is intrigued, but the story cannot be told immediately. Douglas needs to have the manuscript sent down from LONDON, which he promises to do. On the next night, still waiting for the manuscript, he offers a few preliminary remarks, explaining that the manuscript was written by his sister's former governess, and that the story it tells was her own. He further explains how the governess, with whom he was clearly in love himself, came to be employed by a charming bachelor to look after the nephew and niece left to his charge at their parents' death. There are mysterious circumstances relating to the job, notably the children's residence in their uncle's country house, the death of their former governess, and the bachelor's stipulation that he not be bothered over any detail relating to their care. But, despite many reservations, Douglas says, the governess took the job—her first. Douglas finally begins to read the story itself on the fourth night. The narrator lets readers know, however, that Douglas has died since he told the story and that the version of the story being given is actually a copy of the manuscript transcribed by the narrator himself.

(Chapter 1) The governess relates her arrival at Bly on a fine June day. She is equally impressed by the house and her female charge, Flora, calling her "the most beautiful child I had ever seen" (642). Mrs. Grose, the housekeeper, seems remarkably pleased by her arrival and shares her delight in Flora. She promises, moreover, that if the governess is taken by the girl, she will be even more so by the boy, Miles. Flora conducts her on a tour of the house, and the governess marvels at being in charge.

(Chapter 2) On her first evening at Bly, the governess receives a cursory note from her employer, simply forwarding a letter from Miles's headmaster. It tells her that Miles will not be welcome to return to his school after the forthcoming holiday. The governess questions Mrs. Grose about Miles and is told that, like any boy, he is capable of being bad. A further question about the former governess receives an ambiguous response. Is Mrs. Grose implying that there was a bigger scandal than their employer's preference for young, pretty help.

(Chapter 3) The governess meets Miles and sees in him "something divine that I have never found to the same degree in any child" (650). She and

Mrs. Grose decide to keep the headmaster's letter to themselves, and they share an intimate, conspiratorial moment over the decision. The governess settles into a happy, playful routine with the children, but her reverie is interrupted when, out walking the grounds alone, she catches sight of an unknown, hatless man at the top of one of Bly's towers.

(Chapter 4) The agitated governess refrains from telling Mrs. Grose about her shock. She continues to wonder who the man on the tower could have been, but she is comforted by her time with the angelic children until a second shock. Coming into the dining room on a Sunday, she sees the same male figure gazing at her through a window. She runs out of the house to the spot where she saw him, but he has disappeared. Mrs. Grose is then frightened when she sees the governess staring back into the house through the same window.

(Chapter 5) Mrs. Grose justifies her fear by saying that the governess is "white as a sheet" (659). The governess tells her about seeing a man through the window and on the tower. She says the man is certainly not a "gentleman" (660), calls him a "horror" (661), and describes his red hair, red whiskers, and long pale face. Mrs. Grose recognizes the description as that of Peter Quint, the master's former valet, whom she reveals is now dead.

(Chapter 6) The governess learns that Quint had been "clever," "deep," and definitely "bad" (666), but that nobody had dared tell the master. He had also been friendly with Miles. Quint was eventually found dead in the road, apparently having slipped and knocked his head on the way back from the pub, and the governess becomes convinced his dead spirit has returned to continue his communion with the boy. She revels in her task of protecting the children but acknowledges that her fears might well have led to "something like madness" (668) had they not been accompanied by what she feels were demonstrable "horrible proofs" (668). One of these comes almost immediately when she sees a figure that she takes to be that of Miss Jessel, her late predecessor, while playing with Flora by the lake.

(Chapter 7) The governess tells Mrs. Grose that she is sure Flora saw Miss Jessel too, though the girl is determined to keep her secret. Mrs. Grose explains that Miss Jessel and Quint were "infamous" (673) lovers. Believing that the former governess has come back for Flora just as Quint has returned for Miles, the governess breaks down: "I don't save or shield them! It's far worse than I dreamed—they're lost!" (674).

(Chapter 8) The governess grows ever more enraptured by the children and even admires what she perceives as their secrecy and deception about Quint and Jessel. On questioning Mrs. Grose further, she discovers that Quint and Miles had been "perpetually together" (677) for some time before Quint's death and that Mrs. Grose had herself spoken to Miles about this inappropriate relationship with a servant, only to be insulted by the boy. The governess comes to the conclusion that Miles was party to Quint's relationship with Miss Jessel.

(Chapter 9) The governess spends long summer days waiting for further developments, meanwhile relishing the company of the children. The three play together "in a cloud of music and love and success and private theatricals" (681), which the governess enjoys despite the growing sense that she is being "practised upon" (681). The notion of Miles going away to school again is shelved, and at times one child distracts the governess while the other disappears. Then, one night, she again encounters Quint, this time on the stairs inside the house.

(Chapter 10) After seeing Quint, the governess returns to the nursery to find Flora's bed empty. But Flora appears from behind the curtains and accuses the governess of having left her alone in the room. Flora claims to have been looking out the window in search for the governess but to have seen no one, which the governess takes to be a lie. The governess begins keeping watch at night, and on one occasion she sees Miss Jessel in the house. On the 11th night, she again finds Flora out of bed, looking out of the window. The governess looks out herself from a different room and sees Miles out on the lawn, apparently looking up at something or someone on the tower.

(Chapter 11) The next day, the governess tells Mrs. Grose what had happened during the night, but she keeps to herself the details of her exchange with Miles in his room. Once put back to bed and pressed to explain his actions, Miles says that he wanted the governess to "'Think me—for a change—*bad!*'" (691). He then kisses her.

(Chapter 12) While admitting that it makes her sound "crazy" (692), the governess insists to Mrs. Grose that the children are consorting with their dead attendants. Mrs. Grose suggests that they appeal to the children's uncle, but mindful of her promise never to bother her employer, the governess rejects this proposal and threatens to leave immediately if Mrs. Grose should try to contact him herself.

(Chapter 13) Autumn arrives during an awkward period between the children and their governess. There are no further sightings of the dead servants, but avoiding talking about them puts a strain on her conversations and lessons with Miles and Flora. The governess knows that to be the first to raise the issue of ghosts with them would be a scandal and professional disgrace. At the same time, she is absolutely convinced that the children continue to see the ghosts and are just waiting for her to say something about it.

(Chapter 14) On the way to church one Sunday morning, Miles raises the question of his going back to school, a subject the governess has so far avoided. He is clearly keen to go, suggesting he is too old to be taught by a governess. When the governess does not answer, he reminds her of how bad he is capable of being, and like Mrs. Grose before him, talks of asking his uncle to intervene. He then goes ahead of her into the church.

(Chapter 15) The governess waits outside the church, concerned that Miles has got the better of her. Now she must either deal directly with the matter of his education, and the reasons he is not allowed to return to his school, or face breaking the vow made to the uncle not to involve him in the children's affairs. She thinks of running away and gets as far as returning alone to Bly. She goes up to the schoolroom and sees Miss Jessel sitting at her desk and writing a letter. She calls out, "You terrible, miserable woman!" (705), but gets no response, and Miss Jessel disappears.

(Chapter 16) The children return from church and surprise the governess by not mentioning her desertion. Later, she tells Mrs. Grose that she had

returned to the house to see a friend, and Mrs. Grose in turn explains that the children had asked her not to say anything about the governess's decision not to go into the church. The governess then claims to have had an exchange with Miss Jessel, which has made her determined to send for the children's uncle after all. Mrs. Grose offers to contact the uncle through the local bailiff, but reminded of some of the complexities of the situation, she willingly consents that the governess should do it herself.

(Chapter 17) The governess starts the letter at night, but she pauses to look in on Miles, who is awake and engages her in conversation. They talk vaguely of "this queer business" (709), a phrase that could just as easily refer to the way Miles is being educated as to his consorting with ghosts. The governess admits that he should go away to school but, still not admitting that she knows he has been expelled, says that returning to his old one is out of the question. He again says that he wants his uncle to settle the matter, and the governess once more probes him to tell her everything, pleading with him, "I just want you to help me to save you!" (712). At this outburst, she hears and feels a cold blast of air blow through the room. Miles screams, and his candle is extinguished, but the governess looks up to find the window still closed. Miles says it was he who blew out the candle.

(Chapter 18) The next day, the governess, with the completed letter in her pocket, finds her pupils unusually cooperative and brilliant. Miles in particular charms her by offering to play the piano in the schoolroom. She loses track of time, then suddenly realizes that Flora is nowhere to be seen. Miles claims not to know where his sister is, and a search begins. After looking around the house and confirming that Flora is not with Mrs. Grose or any of the other servants, the governess decides that she must have gone out to meet Miss Jessel. Miles, meanwhile, has absconded, and the governess quickly concludes that he is in the schoolroom with Quint. She leaves her letter on the hall table to be posted before going in search of Flora.

(Chapter 19) The governess and Mrs. Grose head for the lake, where Flora seems to have taken out the boat. They find the boat moored up and partly hidden a little way around the lake. They then find Flora, apparently happy, safe, and alone. Mrs. Grose embraces her, but the governess holds back, convinced that the children have played a trick. When Flora asks the apparently guileless question, "Where's Miles?" (718), the governess replies, "I'll tell you if you'll tell *me* . . . Where, my pet, is Miss Jessel?" (719). The subject of the ghosts has been raised explicitly for the first time.

(Chapter 20) The mention of Miss Jessel's name is like "the smash of a pane of glass" (719). Mrs. Grose shrieks, but the governess gasps, having suddenly seen Miss Jessel herself on the opposite shore of the lake. She is overjoyed at what she sees as proof of her suspicions—"I was neither cruel nor mad" (719)—but Flora seems not to see Miss Jessel, staring fixedly at the governess herself, and Mrs. Grose also claims not to see anything. The latter tries to defend Flora from the governess and from the idea that it is possible to see dead people. Flora herself attacks the governess, saying, "I see nobody. I see nothing. I never *have*. I think you're cruel. I don't like you!" (721). The governess can still see Miss Jessel, but she acknowledges that she has lost Flora and allows Mrs. Grose to take her back to the house. That night, Flora sleeps with Mrs. Grose while the governess keeps company with Miles.

(Chapter 21) Having come down with a fever and taken sides against her governess, Flora is escorted by Mrs. Grose to her uncle's, apparently without having had a chance to communicate with Miles about the events at the lake. Mrs. Grose is more than willing to leave, having heard Flora speak about the governess in the vilest of terms. Despite her claim of not having seen anybody at the lake, Mrs. Grose now concedes that she does believe in what she rather vaguely terms "such doings" (727). She also tells the governess that her letter to the uncle seems not to have been posted, perhaps because it was removed by Miles. Mrs. Grose concludes that it was stealing letters that led Miles to be expelled from school.

(Chapter 22) The governess is left alone at Bly with Miles. There is no pretense at schooling on the first day, and the two manage to avoid each other in the large house and grounds. They meet, finally, at dinner, where Miles inquires about

Flora's health. The governess reassures him, and they eat in silence. Only after all the servants have departed does Miles announce "Well—so we're alone!" (732).

(Chapter 23) They talk of being alone except for "the others" (732), a phrase the governess takes to refer to the ghosts but which might just as easily indicate the Bly servants. Miles stares out of the window while the governess engages in some needlework. They begin to talk, and Miles concludes that the governess has stayed on to get him to tell her something. She acknowledges this and asks him to tell her that moment. But he resists: "You'll stay on with me, and we shall both be all right and I *will* tell you—I *will*. But not now" (735). She takes this as the preliminary to a confession about the ghosts and presses him further. He claims that he has to see Luke, the servant, but she responds that he can only go once he has told her whether he stole her letter the day before.

(Chapter 24) As Miles takes in this question, the governess grabs him and pushes his back against the window, through which she can suddenly see Peter Quint approaching the house. She has the sensation of fighting with Quint for the boy's soul. Miles confesses to stealing the letter, and she embraces him. He says he wanted to read what she had written about him, but as the letter was a simple request for a meeting with the uncle, he has learned nothing. She asks him if he had stolen things at school, and she finally tells him that she knows he has been expelled. He replies he did not steal but "said things" (738) that were then repeated around the school and eventually to teachers. These things were "too bad" (739) to be repeated in a letter home, but this does not prevent the governess from wanting to know what they were. She asks him again, still pressing him to her as Quint's face rears once more. Miles sees her horror and asks, oddly, if it is Miss Jessel at the window. She says no, and he guesses again, finally naming Peter Quint but looking around the room as if he himself does not see anybody. The governess is triumphant, crying, "*I* have you . . . but he has lost you for ever!" (740). Miles, though, has "jerked straight round, stared, glared again, and seen but the quiet day" (740). He cries and falls. The governess catches him, realizing simultaneously that they are alone and that his heart has stopped.

CRITICAL ANALYSIS

In the prologue to "The Turn of the Screw," those gathered around a Christmas fire, as well as the story's readers, are promised nothing more or less than a generic ghost story. It may prove to be particularly "dreadful" in terms of its "general uncanny ugliness and horror and pain" (636), but it is to differ in degree, not in kind, from the stories its first audience have already heard. Indeed, Douglas's wish to tell his tale is inspired by a previous story involving a single child, a detail its hearers agree adds "another turn of the screw" (635) to the general run of ghost stories. Introducing a second child is just to turn the same screw twice.

James himself often spoke of the tale in slighting terms. In his 1908 preface to the NEW YORK EDITION of the tale, he dismisses it as "a fairy-tale pure and simple" (*Art of the Novel* 171) and a "pure romance" (175). In the same essay, he refers to Peter Quint and Miss Jessel as "demon-spirits" (175) and says his most taxing artistic challenge was to make them appear "sufficiently bad" (176). He even played down the qualities of the story when others praised it, responding to a letter from Louis Waldstein by calling it a "bogey-tale" (qtd. in Beidler 177) and explaining to H. G. WELLS that it should be regarded as merely "a pot boiler and a *jeu d'esprit*" (178). Similar terms were used in a letter to Frederic Myers, where James calls the tale "mechanical" and a "shameless pot-boiler" (178). For James, it appears, "The Turn of the Screw" was no more sophisticated, subtle, or mysterious a ghost story than any of the others he wrote during his career.

The story's earliest commentators were kinder. Of the five 1898 reviews Peter Beidler reprints in his very useful critical edition, four are in no doubt that the tale justifies the buildup it is given by Douglas in the prologue. Only the *Bookman* reviewer demurs, refusing, like many others after him, to believe that the ghosts are really haunting the children, but putting this down to James's poor execution and concluding that the story is "cruel and untrue" (Beidler 173). Most interesting is the review in the *Critic*, which offers a tantalizing glimpse of future readings of the story in its comments on the governess: "[T]he reader who begins by questioning whether she is supposed to be sane ends by accepting her conclusions and thrilling over the horrors they involve" (173). The question of whether or not the governess is to be believed is one that would come to dominate responses to the tale.

There is little in James's comments or in the responses of contemporary readers that foreshadows the later critical debate surrounding the story, which has been the subject of more controversy than almost any other work in his oeuvre, and it is certainly the best known and most discussed of his more than 100 tales. Much of this must be put down not to what the story includes but to what it leaves out, the gaps in readers' knowledge that leave room for speculation and disagreement. So many questions remain unanswered at the end of the tale that there is almost endless scope for discussion. How did Miss Jessel die? What was the nature of Miles's relationship with Quint? Or Flora's with Miss Jessel? What did Miles do to be expelled from school? Does Mrs. Grose really believe in the ghosts? Of what does Miles die? How did the governess recover and go on to look after other children? Do those gathered around the fire think the story was worth waiting for? The biggest of these, of course, is the one touched on by the reviewer in the *Critic*, the question of whether the ghosts of Quint and Jessel are to be taken as real or as figments of the governess's own overheated imagination.

The problem with all these questions, and especially the last one, is that almost everything the reader knows about the story is presented by the governess herself. In choosing to tell the tale from her point of view—the only perspective offered, which is not hers, is Douglas's brief testimony—James exposes readers solely to what the governess herself sees, hears, feels, and believes. Readers are not asked to consider how events look from other points of view. This formal choice was James's most significant break with the notes he made for the story on the night he first heard it, January 12, 1895. He wrote that the story would be "told—tolerably obviously—by an outside spectator, observer" (*Notebooks* 109). This is a technique he had used successfully in other stories. Many of his tales of literary life, for instance "The NEXT TIME" (1895) and "The DEATH OF THE LION" (1894), have the careers of writers narrated by a character only marginally involved in them. But for "The Turn of the Screw," as well as for "The ASPERN PAPERS" (1888) a decade earlier, he ultimately decided to have the tale told by a figure who could not possibly be further "inside" the situation. The governess does not just tell the story; she is implicated in it. Indeed, given the death of one of her charges and the horrors experienced by the other, she has a lot of explaining to do.

This raises questions of credibility, and every reader will wonder how far to believe the account of events given by the governess. Some will conclude that she is not at all to be trusted, that the ghosts are entirely in her imagination and that she herself is the most dangerous figure in the children's lives. Such readers will point out that nobody except the governess ever fully acknowledges seeing the ghosts and that the only evidence for their appearance comes from her. They will also point to the many occasions when the words of others are interpreted by the governess in a way that confirms her theories, when their rather vague expressions leave the possibility for alternative interpretations. Accordingly, the experience of reading "The Turn of the Screw" is to realize, for instance, that Miles could just as easily be talking about his education as about ghosts when he refers to this "queer business" (709). Thus, the merit of the story lies in the active role it demands of readers, requiring them not just to accept everything the governess says and interprets but to question and reinterpret for themselves. Rather than a conventional ghost story, "The Turn of the Screw" becomes in this reading a subtle piece of psychological profiling, with James using the first-person narrative to expose the governess as a fantasist. Much of the language James gives to the governess supports this theory. She has a tendency for hyperbole and polarized thinking, with the children as angels or devils but never as anything in between. She even admits on a number of occasions that her ideas make her seem crazy, and when she believes she sees the ghosts, she is torn between fear and celebration that external evidence appears to bear her theories out.

Such skepticism with regard to the governess's version of events has a distinguished critical history going back to the early decades of the 20th century. Though preempted by Harold Goddard and Edna Kenton, Edmund Wilson is usually credited with inaugurating the Freudian school of commentary on the tale. In his 1934 essay, "The Ambiguity of Henry James," Wilson argues that the governess is sexually repressed, reading the ghosts as hallucinations, and the tower and lake as obvious symbols for the male and female genitalia. This psychoanalytical interpretation was followed and developed in the 1965 book An Anatomy of "The Turn of the Screw," by Thomas Cranfill and Robert Clark, as well as by many others. Leon Edel presents the view that it is "the governess herself who haunts the children" (195) and that much of the behavior of the children and Mrs. Grose can be explained as an attempt to placate and pacify her.

At the opposite extreme, many readers, like most of the tale's initial reviewers, believe that the governess is to be taken at her word and that the ghosts are both real and malevolent. Robert Heilman was among the first to counter Wilson's arguments in his 1947 essay, "The Freudian Reading of 'The Turn of the Screw,'" which argues that the children are indeed haunted and that the efforts of the governess to save them are heroic, if flawed by naïveté. Following this essay, and again with Wilson in mind, J. A. Waldock asked how if she imagines the ghosts the governess is able to describe them so accurately that Mrs. Grose recognizes them as Quint and Jessel. In response, Wilson was forced to amend his views slightly, though he maintained his basic belief that the governess is not to be trusted. An important consideration for many like-minded critics is the question of where narrative unreliability stops. As Tim Lustig points out, once one questions whether or not to believe the governess about the ghosts, there is no reason not to question her about everything else. Perhaps she made up Bly, the children, and their uncle too. Perhaps she herself was made up by Douglas. Of course, with a little help from the archbishop of Canterbury, James himself made the whole story up. To claim that the ghosts are not real is to imply that there could be such a thing as "real" in something that is wholly a fiction.

During the middle years of the 20th century, much ink was spilled over the question of whether the governess was mad or the ghosts real; the assumption was that only one of these two positions had to be the truth and that, as Lustig again has it, "to read 'The Turn of the Screw' is to establish *the* reading and if necessary to defeat other readings" (xiii). Alternative positions, such as the ghosts are real but not harmful, gained little credence or attention during this time. More recently, however, much commentary has focused on the very inconclusiveness of such debates and suggested that the tale's strength is not so much in its brilliance as either a generic ghost story or a psychological portrait as that it manages to be both at the same time. For a structuralist critic like Tzvetan Todorov, for instance, the permanently unresolved nature of the mystery at the heart of this tale makes it successful. Such readers point to the many deliberate ambiguities and gaps James includes, as well as to the odd absence of an epilogue to match the prologue and to tie up any loose ends. Readers never know what those who hear Douglas tell the story make of it, nor do many quite know what to make of it themselves. Just as Douglas regularly did with correspondents who asked him about the fate of a fictional character beyond the close of the novel in which they figured, James refuses to offer any guidance. "What you know, you know," as Shakespeare's Iago says, "from this time forth I never will speak word." Making a virtue of this open-endedness, many commentators view "The Turn of the Screw" as an early postmodern text, a playful study in precisely the kind of ambiguity the governess herself is unable to accept.

Like the similar discussions about Hamlet's sanity, debate about whether or not the governess is mad for a long time overshadowed other avenues of critical inquiry. However, with a sort of stalemate on this point and with a growing body of James criticism concerned with subjects of gender and class, recent studies bring new and interesting approaches. Several Marxist critics, among them Bruce Robbins, have emphasized that "The Turn of the Screw" is a story almost wholly populated by the socially dispossessed (though told one Christmas for the entertainment of the leisured elite).

The children and servants at Bly are left to fend for themselves because they have been abandoned by a well-to-do master who, for a number of readers, represents the whole of his irresponsible and self-indulgent ruling class. While it is set apart from the social world, Bly is by no means a democratic retreat. Many have pointed to the traditional superiority of governesses to other ranks of domestic servant, using this insight in order to throw light on the relationship between the governess and Mrs. Grose, as well as to pose questions about her response to Quint in particular. What is worse for her, given this figure's apparent relations with Miles: that he is dead or that he is a mere servant?

For Marxist critics, "The Turn of the Screw" engages late Victorian (see VICTORIANISM) attitudes to class and service, but for feminist critics it is usefully understood as a response to attitudes to women during that same period and, indeed, since. One feminist claim has been that a male narrator would never have been subjected to the same accusations of hysteria and unreliability as the governess or put through the same critical mauling. In any case, the debate has moved well beyond the stage of simply deciding whether or not to believe the governess. "The Turn of the Screw," like the rest of James's fiction, has been opened up to the full range of theoretical and contextual readings, including homoerotic readings of the relationships between Quint and Miles, and Jessel and Flora; studies of Miles and Flora that consider attitudes to children and infant sexuality; and genre studies comparing the tale with James's other horror stories or his many tales of country house life. Still, there is little consensus on the tale; the only point on which almost all critics agree is that it is certainly no mere "pot-boiler."

CHARACTERS

Douglas   He claims to have known the governess after the events at Bly as she served in that same role to his sister. He is the direct source of some of the reader's information about how the governess came to be employed by the children's uncle. The story as read is supposedly based on that given in the manuscript written by the governess, which Douglas leaves to the narrator on his death. He admits to having been in love with the governess as a young man.

Flora The orphaned young girl the governess is employed to look after, she immediately views her as "the most beautiful child [she] had ever seen" (642). Flora was apparently close to Miss Jessel, and the governess is convinced that this relationship continues after Miss Jessel's death. The governess's eventual confrontation with Flora results in no confession, however, just stupefaction and disgust. This is the last time Flora appears. She comes down with a fever and is taken by Mrs. Grose to London.

Governess, the The youngest of several daughters of a Hampshire parson, she takes up her profession at the age of 20. The position at Bly is her first. She falls in love with the children's uncle, and her desire to follow his instructions and impress him with her professionalism seems to motivate many of her actions and decisions. She is also driven, however, by clear fascination and delight in her wards, whom she tends to view as either angels or devils. If Douglas is to be believed, she carries on as a governess after the events at Bly and eventually records these events in a manuscript on which the story is based.

Grose, Mrs. The apparently illiterate Bly housekeeper forges an uneasy alliance with the governess in protection of the children. Mrs. Grose relays the little information the reader learns about the relationship between Peter Quint and Miss Jessel and their connection with Miles and Flora. She claims not to see the ghosts herself, even when the governess points to Miss Jessel by the lake, but does finally admit to believing in "such doings" (727). She is eventually relieved to quit the house with Flora.

Jessel, Miss The "infamous" (673) predecessor to the governess, she was Quint's lover before leaving the house to die. She appears to the governess, dressed in mourning clothes, by the lake and in the schoolroom. The governess believes she has come for Flora, with whom she was apparently close.

Luke A Bly servant one of whose jobs is to take out letters; Miles claims he needs to speak to Luke just before his death.

Miles Flora's brother returns from school to spend the summer at Bly under the care of the governess. Despite his angelic appearance, Mrs. Grose admits that he is capable of being "bad" (648). A letter from his headmaster implies that he has also been bad at school and says he may not return, though the governess does not discuss this matter with him. As summer draws to a close, his desire to return to school precipitates a confrontation with the governess, which culminates in his death.

Narrator An unnamed figure among the party to whom Douglas reads the manuscript written by the governess, has inherited the manuscript and, for reasons never explained, makes a copy of it. It is this transcript, apparently, that the reader is offered.

Quint, Peter The uncle's former valet, he is characterized by Mrs. Grose as a thief and a drunk. He was left at Bly the year before the story takes place, and during this time he became Miss Jessel's lover and perhaps engaged in an inappropriate relationship with Miles. He died, apparently, from a blow to the head sustained during a fall on the way back from the public house. The governess sees him on one of Bly's towers, through its windows, and in the house itself. She believes he has returned for Miles.

Uncle, the A wealthy and handsome London bachelor, he lives in Harley Street and seldom visits his family seat in Essex. After the death of his brother in India, he finds himself the unwilling guardian to two small children. He houses them at Bly and employs servants to look after them. The death of Miss Jessel leads him to take on a new governess, charming her into accepting the unusual stipulation that she deal with all concerns herself without bothering him. He goes so far as to forward to her a letter from Miles's school without so much as opening it. During the course of the story, writing the uncle is repeatedly presented as a possibility, but the governess manages to keep her vow until Mrs. Grose takes Flora to London toward the end.

ADAPTATIONS

The Turn of the Screw (1954) was Benjamin Britten's last completed chamber opera. The opera has been filmed on numerous occasions, most recently in a 2004 BBC Wales version.

The Turn of the Screw (1959), directed for TV by John Frankenheimer, was most notable for the appearance of Ingrid Bergman as the governess. There have been many subsequent TV versions, a full list of which can be found in Susan Griffin's *Henry James Goes to the Movies*.

The Innocents (1961) was directed by Jack Clayton, a superior cinematic version with Deborah Kerr as the governess (here named Miss Giddens). Not only is it one of the best film adaptations of James's work, but it is also one of the most effective psychological horror movies ever made.

The Nightcomers (1971) was directed by Michael Winner, a "prequel" to the story, with Marlon Brando as Peter Quint.

The Turn of the Screw (1974) was directed by Dan Curtis for television with a screenplay by William F. Nolan.

The Turn of the Screw (1983) is the original tale rewritten as a play by Ken Whitmore.

The Turn of the Screw (1990) was directed for television by Graeme Clifford.

The Turn of the Screw (1994) was directed by Rusty Lemorande. It was updated to the 1960s, with a group therapy session standing in for the fireside telling of ghost stories. Patsy Kensit stars.

The Haunting of Helen Walker (1995), directed by Tom McLoughlin, was another notable made-for-TV version, with Valerie Bertinelli as the governess (renamed Helen Walker) and Diana Rigg as Mrs. Grose.

The Turn of the Screw (1999) was directed for television by Ben Bolt.

Presence of Mind (1999), directed by Antoni Aloy, was a poorly distributed Spanish version with an intriguing cast including Sadie Frost, Harvey Keitel, Jude Law, and Lauren Bacall.

The Others (2001), directed by Alejandro Amenabar, was not strictly an adaptation of "The Turn of the Screw" but certainly borrowed its atmosphere. The same title was in fact used for a 1957 TV version of the tale in the *Matinee Theatre* series.

In a Dark Place (2006), directed by Donato Rotunno, was the most recent attempt to film the story, with Leelee Sobieski as the governess, this time going by the name Anna Veigh.

FURTHER READING

As already noted, criticism and commentary on "The Turn of the Screw" is not in short supply. Indeed, the tale's reception history (up to 1979, at least) has itself been the subject of a Ph.D. dissertation, made public by its author, Dr. Edward J. Parkinson, at http://www.turnofthescrew.com. This site includes a very useful bibliography, as does Peter G. Beidler's fine edition of the tale (2004) in the *Case Studies in Contemporary Criticism Series*. The comments presented above are deeply indebted to the latter, which also houses a very useful selection of responses and contextual documents, from mid-Victorian essays on the conduct of governesses to recent critical commentaries that offer psychoanalytical readings, or those that consider issues of gender and class. The list below does not include these individual pieces, but it gives details of the articles mentioned in the critical analysis section and those of major book-length studies, as well as those of Joyce Carol Oates's retelling of the tale and Hilary Bailey's sequel, which may appeal to some readers. The best way to start, though, would be by reading some of James's other ghost stories, a list of which I have also included.

Bailey, Hilary. *Miles and Flora: A Sequel to Henry James's "The Turn of the Screw."* London: Touchstone Books, 1997.

Banta, Martha. *Henry James and the Occult: The Great Extension.* Bloomington: Indiana University Press, 1972.

Beidler, Peter G., ed. *Ghosts, Demons, and Henry James: "The Turn of the Screw" at the Turn of the Century.* Columbia: University of Missouri Press, 1989.

———. *The Turn of the Screw.* Boston/New York: Bedford/St. Martin's, 2004.

Brooke-Rose, Christine. *A Rhetoric of the Unreal.* Cambridge: Cambridge University Press, 1981.

Cranfill, Thomas Mabry, and Robert Lanier Clark, Jr. *An Anatomy of "The Turn of the Screw."* Austin: University of Texas Press, 1965.

Edel, Leon. *Henry James: The Treacherous Years, 1895–1901.* London: Rupert Hart-Davis, 1969.

Felman, Shoshana. "Turning the Screw of Interpretation." *Yale French Studies* 55/56 (1977): 94–207.

Goddard, Harold C. "A Pre-Freudian Reading of *The Turn of the Screw.*" *Nineteenth-Century Fiction* 12 (1957): 1–36.

Griffin, Susan, ed. *Henry James Goes to the Movies.* Lexington: University Press of Kentucky, 2002.

Heilman, R. B. "The Freudian Reading of *The Turn of the Screw.*" *Modern Language Notes* 62 (1947): 433–445.

Heller, Terry. *"The Turn of the Screw": Bewildered Vision.* Boston: Twayne, 1989.

James, Henry. *The Art of the Novel: Critical Prefaces.* Edited by R. P. Blackmur. 1934. Reprint, New York: Scribner's, 1962.

———. *The Complete Notebooks of Henry James.* Edited by Leon Edel and Lyall H. Powers. New York and Oxford: Oxford University Press, 1987.

———. "Covering End." In *Henry James: Complete Stories 1892–1898,* 741–834. New York: Library of America, 1996.

———. "The Jolly Corner." In *Henry James: Complete Stories 1898–1910,* 697–731. New York: Library of America, 1996.

———. "Owen Wingrave." In *Henry James: Complete Stories 1892–1898,* 256–290. New York: Library of America, 1996.

———. "Sir Edmund Orme." In *Henry James: Complete Stories 1884–1891,* 851–878. New York: Library of America, 1999.

———. "The Real Right Thing." In *Henry James: Complete Stories 1898–1910,* 121–134. New York: Library of America, 1996.

———. "The Turn of the Screw." In *Henry James: Complete Stories 1892–1898,* 635–740. New York: Library of America, 1996.

———. "The Way It Came." (a.k.a. "The Friends of the Friends"). In *Henry James: Complete Stories 1892–1898,* 609–634. New York: Library of America, 1996.

Kenton, Edna. "Henry James to the Ruminant Reader: *The Turn of the Screw.*" *The Arts* 4 (1924): 245–255.

Lustig, T. J. *Henry James and the Ghostly.* Cambridge: Cambridge University Press, 1994.

———. Introduction to *"The Turn of the Screw" and Other Stories,* vii–xxv. Oxford and New York: Oxford University Press, 1992.

Oates, Joyce Carol. "Accursed Inhabitants of the House of Bly." In *Haunted Tales of the Grotesque.* New York: Dutton, 1994.

Rimmon, Shlomith. *The Concept of Ambiguity: The Example of James.* Chicago: University of Chicago Press, 1977.

Robbins, Bruce. "Shooting Off James's Blanks: Theory, Politics, and *The Turn of the Screw.*" *Henry James Review* 5, no. 3 (1984): 12–18.

Rowe, John Carlos. *The Theoretical Dimensions of Henry James.* Madison: University of Wisconsin Press, 1984.

Sheppard, E. A. *Henry James and "The Turn of the Screw."* Auckland, New Zealand: Auckland University Press, 1974.

Siegel, Eli. *James and the Children: A Consideration of Henry James's "The Turn of the Screw."* New York: Definition Press, 1968.

Todorov, Tzvetan. *The Fantastic: A Structural Approach to a Literary Genre.* Translated by Richard Howard. Ithaca, N.Y.: Cornell University Press, 1977.

Walton, Priscilla L. *The Disruption of the Feminine in Henry James.* Toronto: University of Toronto Press, 1992.

Willen, Gerald, ed. *A Casebook on Henry James's "The Turn of the Screw."* New York: Crowell, 1969.

Rory Drummond, *Framlingham College/ University of Cambridge*

Nonfiction

The American Scene (1907)

Many of the essays that eventually made up *The American Scene* were first published in the *North American Review* or *Harper's Magazine*. Four selections ("New York: Social Notes I," "Boston," "Philadelphia," and "Richmond, Virginia") also appeared in the British *Fortnightly Review*. *The American Scene* itself was first published in LONDON by Chapman and Hall on January 30, 1907; the American edition came out from Harper and Brothers a week later. The two editions are almost identical, but there are two very important differences. First, James provided descriptive headings (e.g., "The Tall Buildings," "The Alien at Home," "The Car Window") that appeared at the top of every right-hand page of the London edition but were omitted, presumably for reasons of economy, from the American. Second, and much more important, the American edition omitted the final section of the text (part VII of chapter 14, "Florida") with its strong, even bitter indictment of the conversion of the "large and noble sanities" of the American land "to crudities, to invalidities, hideous and unashamed" (735). The reasons for this omission remain obscure, but it seems likely that they had more to do with penny-pinching and sloppy editing at Harper's than any kind of censorship on the PUBLISHER's part (Hewitt [1983] 46–47). Whatever the cause, the effect was a weaker ending.

After these first editions, nearly 40 years went by before another was published. In 1946 Scribner's brought out a new edition with an introduction by the poet W. H. Auden, including three additional American essays from the earlier *Portraits of Places* (1883) along with some of the original headings and the omitted last section. The original English edition was reprinted by Horizon Press in NEW YORK in 1967, with an introduction by Irving Howe, and the 1946 Scribner's edition, without the three earlier essays, was reprinted by the Indiana University Press with an introduction and notes by Leon Edel in 1968. The complete text appeared again in the Library of America edition of James's *Collected Travel Writings: Great Britain and America*, with notes by Richard Howard (New York, 1993). This is now the definitive edition. There is also a Penguin paperback, edited and with an introduction by John F. Sears (New York, 1994).

SYNOPSIS

The American Scene is a highly self-conscious literary text built on a simple, easily recognizable generic foundation. It looks like a conventional travel book, beginning on the dock at Hoboken, New Jersey, and following its author's progress up and down the Atlantic seaboard. It is in fact both a simplified and a complicated adaptation of this model. Rather than exhaustively chronicling his travels, James reduced his many comings and goings to an easily graspable narrative, roughly half of which is devoted to a northeastern circuit taking in New Hampshire, New York, NEWPORT, Boston, and Concord with intermediate stops and excursions, and half to a journey south from Philadelphia to Florida, with a concluding section written from the Pullman carrying him back north. Rather than simply reporting what he saw, he provided an account of the "impressions" (353) that his observations made upon him and their effect on his developing understanding of the United States and his relation to it (or, perhaps better, them). Rather than furnishing his readers with "information" (354), he deployed his lifelong concern "with the human subject . . . with the appreciation of life itself, and with the consequent question of literary representation" (354) to produce a work of art whose interest lies not only in its subject but in its analytical acuity and its literary power. James gives himself many titles in the course of this book: "the ancient contemplative person" (366); "the visionary tourist" (444); "the palpitating pilgrim" (655), but he most commonly presents himself as "the restless analyst" (361, 383, 384, and passim), seeking to understand the scenes that he surveys and to represent his understanding in artistic terms.

(Chapter 1: New England: An Autumn Impression) After a quick visit to Deal Beach, New Jersey, with its "chain of big villas" (362), the seaside retreats of the newly rich, where "the expensive" asserted itself as "a power by itself" (363), James joins his brother WILLIAM JAMES's family at their presumably more modest summer house at Chocorua, New Hampshire, on the southern edge of the White Mountains. Here he contemplates the pastoral scene, savoring the pictorial, even the painterly, aspect of the landscape. The farms and villages suit him less well, however. He finds their appearance disorderly, a fault he attributes to the absence of those inescapable features of English country life, "the squire and the parson" (375).

After a short trip to Cape Cod, James travels to Farmington, Connecticut, which he finds surprisingly cultured and aristocratic. From there he proceeds to the novelist EDITH WHARTON's summer place in the Berkshires, the starting point for wide and exciting rambles in that grand and liberating novelty, the motorcar.

He then returns to CAMBRIDGE, MASSACHUSETTS, where he comments on the interesting anomaly of the enclosed College Yard "in the land of the 'open door'" (407) and the pervasiveness of the "'business man' face" (409) in America. This leads him to remark on the respective roles of men and women in American life, suggesting a much clearer distinction than in England between the realm of men in "the world" of business and that of women as participants in a "society" that this world makes possible (410) (see WOMEN'S ISSUES). In Cambridge, too, he passes the houses of James Russell Lowell and Henry Wadsworth Longfellow, which leads him to comment on what he sees as the decline of interest in literature at the university, and he walks to Fresh Pond, haunt in his day of Harvard youth but now barely there at all, its transformation balanced in part at least by the creation of a country club—an institution about which James will have more to say later on—and Boston's noted system of parks.

(Chapter 2: New York Revisited) James begins his account of New York with a memorable description of Manhattan seen from a Pullman car as it is conveyed by barge from a station on the west bank of the Hudson River around the Battery and up the East River to Harlem, to be added to a train to Boston. He writes of the power of the city, of the tall buildings, "triumphant payers of dividends" that flash in the sun like the "lamps of some general permanent 'celebration'" (419). He then travels to Ellis Island, where he begins his famous and sustained analysis of the immigrant—whom he always

calls the "alien"—in American life. His search for remnants of his own New York childhood reveals that his first home and birthplace (on Washington Place, just east of Washington Square) has been torn down.

In the next section, James makes his way Uptown, commenting in passing on the "original sin" (439) of the city's relentlessly rectangular grid of streets, to the Waldorf-Astoria, in those days a colossal French chateau-style pile on Fifth Avenue at 33rd Street. Here he broaches another of the themes he will pursue throughout the book, "the amazing hotel-world" (440) and its congruence with American society at large, which values extravagant display, a gregarious life led largely in public places, and a "promiscuous" social life mediated not by class but by money (441). The chapter concludes with a walk up Fifth Avenue past the enormous stone mansions of the day, extravagantly expensive, gilded "as many inches thick as may be" (447), but for all that manifestly temporary, doomed to be replaced by 50-story buildings as surely as lovely old staircases must, in the American way of things, be replaced by the latest in elevator technology (449).

(Chapter 3: New York and the Hudson) James's New York observations continue with his visits to immigrant neighborhoods and further ruminations on "the ubiquity of the alien" (455). There is no doubt that James is shocked by this aspect of American life, but it is also clear that he accepts it as a given condition, asking what it means rather than how it can be reversed. He visits an Italian neighborhood and then proceeds to the Jewish Lower East Side, whose inhabitants seem more truly "alien" to him since he has not seen them on their home ground nor does he speak their language. He persists in his exploration, however, visiting beer halls and cafés, listening to accented conversations and predicting with total inaccuracy that whatever languages the American of the future may come to speak, "we shall not know it for English" (471).

From the Lower East Side James travels to the Upper West Side, to Riverside Drive, the recently relocated Columbia University, and Grant's Tomb, all of which he finds symptomatic of the publicity and impermanence of the New York scene. (The idea of moving a university seems particularly shocking to him.) In the last sections of the chapter James moves farther and farther away from the city, describing first the view of the Hudson River from a train window, then the aesthetic and geographical appeal of West Point, and finally, a "charming old historic house" on a "golden Sunday" (482), a retreat in space and almost in time, rivaled only by a subsequent visit to "the 'little' American literary past" itself, as embodied in Washington Irving's home at Sunnyside (484).

(Chapters 4 and 5: New York: Social Notes; The Bowery and Thereabouts) These relatively brief chapters elaborate on some of the themes James raised in earlier sections. There is further discussion of the Fifth Avenue mansions, of the place of men and women in American society, and of the suppression of the private in social and family life as well as domestic and commercial architecture. James describes Central Park as an accommodating "hostess" to "polyglot" visitors, an accomplished "actress" who plays a variety of different parts in succession (500–502). He comments on the general air of ambition and hard-earned prosperity and invokes the public evidence of shoemaking and dentistry in the populace at large, presumably in contrast to the toothless, shoeless hordes of Europe (and perhaps in private allusion to his own long ordeal at the hands of a Boston dentist). He celebrates the grand, unfinished Public Library, both as a temple of learning and as a comparatively low-rise gesture of defiance against "the great religion of the Elevator," that "packed and hoisted basket" (509) that he takes as yet another emblem of the crowded publicity of American life.

Downtown again on the Bowery, James goes to the theater and observes the Jewish and Irish spectators contentedly watching the melodrama while munching on large quantities of candy. After the play, he is taken on a tour of some "'characteristic' evening resorts" (520), where he has the chance to observe both the vulgarity, as he defines it, of the beer-cellar, and the refinement of a working-class German café. The chapter concludes with a description of an anonymous nightspot that is, for James, representative of the whole New York experience: "[M]atching, in its mixture, with nothing else one had elsewhere known [i]t breathed its simple 'New York! New York!' at every impulse of inquiry; so that I can only echo contentedly, with analysis for once quite agreeably baffled, 'Remarkable, unspeakable New York!'" (527).

(Chapter 6: The Sense of Newport) The title of this chapter hints at its multiple purposes. James wants to give his readers a *sense* of Newport as it was in his youth, when he and his family lived there for several years, and in his early manhood before the monstrous palaces had arisen. In the glow of nostalgia, he sees this old Newport as a pastoral Arcadia in which a small colony of the modestly privileged shared their leisure, their common experiences of Europe, and their "critical habit" (538), discussed the latest French fiction, and enjoyed the natural setting on genteel pedestrian rambles. He also wants to provide a *sense* of early 20th-century Newport where, as he writes, the "shallow Arcadian summer-haunted valleys" have been "violated" (530) by "things . . . of many ugly, and of more and more expensive, sorts," when the landscape has been "heap[ed]" with "gold . . . to an amount so oddly out of proportion to the scale of nature and of space" (529–530). Finally, he wants to *make sense* of Newport and use it to help him make sense of a generation of wealthy Americans for whom conspicuous consumption had replaced modest refinement. What he finds, however, is not sense but a kind of nonsense, the thoughtless proliferation of large and useless houses whose owners "wonder what in the world is to be done with them" (540).

(Chapter 7: Boston) James begins his description of Boston by recounting two more nostalgic visits, this time to the house in Ashburton Place on Beacon Hill, where the family had moved after their time in Newport. On the first visit, he finds the house still standing and is moved to think of the years he spent there toward the end of the CIVIL WAR, at the time of his own tentative literary beginnings. On the second visit, a month later, the house has been demolished, and he feels a kind of personal and historic vertigo "as if the bottom had fallen out of one's own biography, and one plunged backward into space without meeting anything" (544).

James's Ashburton Place experience sets the tone for his Boston observations, which combine reflections on changes in architecture, institutions, and society. He finds the Boston Athenaeum brutally dwarfed by the tall buildings surrounding it, and the Park Street Church bravely holding "the note of the old felicity" (551) in the face of its increasingly commercial setting, where "pecuniary gain" now "sets the tune" (549–550). Passing the house where Annie Fields, the writer and literary hostess, entertained such great mid-century figures as Thackeray and Dickens, RALPH WALDO EMERSON and Stowe, he contrasts its modest charms and near-"mediaeval" (557) setting with the "rich and prosperous" (557) streets and houses of the reclaimed Back Bay, where "a bourgeoisie without an aristocracy" (558) is leading a new kind of life on what is emblematically known as "the new land." Even the new Public Library at Copley Square disturbs James with its magnificence and its very publicness, its lack, as he puts it of "penetralia" (560), of privacy and mystery, of depth, of an interior that is not at the same time a "thoroughfare" (561). He has similar feelings about the Boston Art Museum, at the time also located at Copley Square, where he admires the antiquities but deplores the prospect of a bigger and grander building, the core of the modern Museum of Fine Arts on Huntington Avenue. It is not surprising, then, that he ends the chapter with a tribute to a very different sort of project, the private museum of his old friend Isabella Stewart Gardner, which had opened in a reproduced Venetian palazzo on the Fenway just a year before his visit.

(Chapter 8: Concord and Salem) Concord is a symbolic site for James, an American epitome, defined and limited by its past—"the little old Concord Fight, essentially, and Emerson and Hawthorne and Thoreau" (567)—never threatening, like modern cities, to "spread, on the map, like irremediable grease-spots" (565) (see HAWTHORNE). He visits with a sense of reverence and contemplative leisure, using the occasion to develop an unusual comparison with the German town of Weimar, and comparing its two most famous literary residents, Goethe and Schiller, to Emerson and Thoreau.

What James found or imagined in Concord was a relic of what he calls "the New England homogeneous" (573). When he looks for it in Salem, however, he is confronted once again with the "polyglot air" (574) of the "flagrant foreigner" (572), in this case an Italian of whom he vainly asks directions to the House of the Seven Gables made famous by Hawthorne's romance. James wonders briefly what such a man from such a place can make of New England's relatively recent antiquities, and he is gratefully relieved to be taken in charge by a local boy who knows all about his native town and its literary history. When the lad shows James a house that he claims is the Seven Gables, James finds it hard to associate the structure with the novel, and he uses the occasion to meditate on the arbitrary and illusory relations between art and the "real" places that inspire it.

(Chapter 9: Philadelphia) James likes Philadelphia. Unlike New York, Chicago, and even Boston, it does not "bristle" (580) with the tall buildings he is coming more and more to despise. Like Concord, it is redolent of history, and it also seems to James more homogeneous than the other cities he has visited, marked less by foreignness than by "consanguinity," "common knowledge," "common consciousness," and "the state of infinite cousinship" (584). He is shocked to learn, however, that such a pleasant, congenial "Society" coexists with a "City" best known for political corruption, and he goes on to draw parallels between "social Philadelphia" "dancing, all consciously, on the thin crust of a volcano" and some "old order," an *ancien régime* doomed, perhaps, but brave while it lasts (588–589).

He is pleased with Philadelphia's historic buildings—Independence Hall and Carpenters' Hall in particular—and their little neighborhood, devoid of skyscrapers, and exerting, in his view, a social, moral, and aesthetic influence on the residents. It feels a little like architect Christopher Wren's London to him, a pleasant jumble of history, religion, and society, pervaded by the cosmopolitan humanity of the city's great father, Benjamin Franklin. He visits the Pennsylvania Academy of Fine Arts, admiring works by his friends Whistler and JOHN SINGER SARGENT and spends an hour at the university. Following in Dickens's footsteps, he goes out to the Pennsylvania Penitentiary, where he indulges in a novelist's reflections on the association between criminality and character, between the immoral deed and the fundamentally base or perhaps otherwise innocent perpetrator.

(Chapter 10: Baltimore) From Philadelphia, James turns definitively southward. It is early February. Snow follows him nearly as far as Charleston, and he finds its ability to erase differences in the landscape quite consistent with the American tendency to avoid discriminations whenever possible. His first stop after Philadelphia was actually Washington, D.C., but in *The American Scene* he inserts his impressions of visits to Baltimore in their geographical rather than their chronological place. So he shows readers Baltimore in June, commenting on the charming squares but also "the huge shadow of the [Civil] War" (609) that loomed so large for him even 40 years later. He visits important Baltimore institutions—notably the relatively new Johns Hopkins University and its hospital—and enjoys its modest buildings and suburban vistas. His most notable comments, though, and those most often held against him by critical readers, are on the country club, which he calls "one of the great garden-lamps in which the flame of Democracy burns whitest and steadiest" (619). What James means by this, as it turns out, is not that the country club accepts all comers—its membership is limited, for example, to "the disembarked" (623) as opposed to the "alien"—but rather that it is based on the family as a single social unit so that all members are treated equally, unlike in societies where membership is based on a hierarchy of sons and daughters, older and younger, and where primogeniture is the rule and titles are at stake. James's comments on this subject provide a particularly striking example of the limits of his Europeanized perspective on American society.

(Chapter 11: Washington) James's Washington chapter actually begins at Mount Vernon, one of the places in America where he feels genuinely moved. It is distinguished for him not by its architecture, which is unremarkable, or even by its lovely setting, but by the way it is pervaded by the first president—"not his invention and his property, but his presence and his person" (630). If in Concord James felt proud of his New England literary forebears, at Mount Vernon he feels truly patriotic and

expresses his feeling in a memorable image of "the star-spangled banner itself, in the folds of which I had never come so near the sense of being positively wrapped" (632).

James's visit to Washington itself was socially and personally gratifying. He stayed with his old friend the writer, historian, and celebrated Washington figure, Henry Adams. At Adams's, he met other old friends, including Secretary of State John Hay and the painter JOHN LA FARGE. The architect Charles McKim invited James, La Farge, and sculptor Augustus Saint-Gaudens to a dinner of the American Institute of Architects. The French ambassador, whom he had known in London, gave a dinner for him, as did Secretary Hay, and President Roosevelt invited him to a diplomatic reception and dinner, despite his reservations about his snobbery and lack of manliness (Edel 265–266).

Not surprisingly, then, James finds that the social life in Washington more than compensates for the slightly provisional air of the place. It is "the City of Conversation pure and simple," he writes (634), the home of "the so fresh experiment of constitutive, creative talk" (637). One of the distinguishing features of this talk for James is that *men* in Washington actually take part in it, carrying on serious conversations about subjects other than business. In other parts of the country, James observes, the admirable American woman—the subject of much of his fiction—dominates the social world, but in Washington "the victim of effacement, the outcast at the door has . . . *talked himself* back" (642), and a healthy social balance has been reestablished.

James's remaining comments on Washington are primarily cultural and aesthetic. He praises the Library of Congress and comments that in the United States libraries and universities have taken the place that the church still holds in Europe. He admires the newly enlarged White House, remarks in a typical Jamesian fashion on the relatively large proportion of monuments to history, and provides a thorough, amused, and amusing account of the Capitol as a kind of stage where America plays out its sense of itself. The last figures to appear on this stage, however, are perhaps the most striking and surprising in the whole chapter. Three Native Americans, or, as he more romantically puts it, "a trio of Indian braves" (652), dressed in shabby American style, cross his path at the Capitol, reminding him of one of the most shameful aspects of American history ("the bloody footprints of time" [653]) as well as the tendency of "aliens" of all sorts to assimilate to what he sees as the vulgar American norm.

(Chapter 12: Richmond) In Richmond, the former capital of the Confederacy, James confronts the South in earnest. It is for him at this stage in his life as romantic and mysterious as Europe had been in his youth and potentially as deeply imbued with history. His attitude toward the South is at the same time condescending and oddly sympathetic. He characterizes the "old Southerners" as "benighted" but "innocent," "passive . . . victims of fate," "untouched by any intellectual tradition of beauty or wit" (661, 662). He treats "the negro" as both an exotic feature of the scene and a social problem, describing "a group of tatterdemalion darkies [who] lounged and sunned themselves within range" and suggesting that their presence implied a "question, which rose suddenly like some beast that had sprung from the jungle" (662). He describes a young Virginian whom he meets in the Confederate Museum as friendly, charming, and inveterately, dangerously racist (673).

Richmond also provides James with another occasion to comment on the disappointing thinness of American culture, the blankness of the snow-clad city, its failure to adequately embody and represent the complexities of its history. Once again, he blames an obsession with money for overpowering more spiritual and aesthetic concerns, converting "an ancient treasure of precious vessels" "into the small change, the simple circulating medium of dollars and 'nickels'" (668).

(Chapter 13: Charleston) James arrives in Charleston after a detour to Biltmore, George Vanderbilt's "strange, colossal, heartbreaking house" (*Letters* 346) in the North Carolina mountains. Charleston's street doors and enclosed gardens suggest "a finer feeling for the enclosure" (686) than he had found in the North, but as a transient visitor he must rely on the relative publicity of the hotel. On the Battery, across the harbor from Fort Sumter, he thinks again about the Civil War,

but he spends most of his Charleston visit enjoying the streets and gardens, soft southern air, and the feminine charm of the place, while regretting the absence of men and of consequential action. (It is interesting to note in this regard James's reference to Massachusetts-born W. E. B. DuBois's *The Souls of Black Folk* as "the only 'Southern' book of any distinction published for many a year" [697].)

(Chapter 14: Florida) The long railroad journey from Charleston to Palm Beach with an overnight stop at Jacksonville gives James the opportunity to reflect on several aspects of American travel. There is, first of all, the ubiquitous traveling salesman, the "bagman" or "drummer" who dominates the Pullman. There is the terrifyingly unregulated American child and, once again, the American girl, exposed to public view in ways that the Europeanized James still finds shocking. There is more on the hotel world and the hotel spirit, which reaches its apotheosis in South Florida, and there are insightful comments on the Pullman itself as both containing a traveling show and framing a passing one, depending on whether one is looking into or out of its windows.

Palm Beach itself is a disappointment. There are pleasures, of course—"the air, the sea, the sky, the sunset, the orange . . . the divine bougainvillea" (717–718)—but there is too little art, too little taste, and too much mere affluence. James amuses himself by observing his fellow hotel guests as they parade their "ability to spend and purchase" (726) in the gardens, corridors, and endless shops of the great hotels. A final Florida stop in St. Augustine disappoints as well, for the promise of history in this—for North America—ancient town goes unfulfilled, but James ends by admitting to a certain vague charm in the faintly Spanish, sweetly scented air of the place.

The last section of the chapter, and of the book as a whole, is the one omitted from the first American edition. It finds James seated again by the Pullman window, lamenting the depredations of capital and technology, greed and rapacious development, to the land and its original people.

CRITICAL ANALYSIS

On August 30, 1904, the 61-year-old Henry James returned to America for the first time in

Max Beerbohm imagines James addressing an audience of American caricatures and stereotypes who talk among themselves and ignore James's convoluted reflections on the extent to which he feels alienated from the country where he was born. Max Beerbohm, "Mr. Henry James (in America)," *A Book of Caricatures* (Methuen: London, 1907), plate 48

22 years. James had spent several years of his childhood and youth in Europe and had moved there definitively in 1875. When he returned to America for a six-month visit in December 1881 and again for nearly eight months when his father died in December 1882, he was already a celebrated writer, the main exponent of the INTERNATIONAL THEME in American fiction in works such as "DAISY MILLER: A STUDY" (1878), *The AMERICAN* (1877), and *The PORTRAIT OF A LADY* (1881). When he came back again at the beginning of the 20th century, he was widely acknowledged as the principal American novelist of his day. His departure in 1883 had drawn little notice; his return and his 10-month sojourn in the land of his birth were chronicled in newspapers, described in popular weekly magazines, and discussed in literary journals (Novick 383).

James's ship, the *Kaiser Wilhelm II*, docked at Hoboken, New Jersey. After pausing briefly in New York City, he traveled to the North Jersey shore, where his PUBLISHER, George Harvey, was entertaining his fellow author Samuel Clemens ("poor dear old Mark Twain," as James called him in a letter to his brother William [*Letters* 319]). He spent the fall and early winter with family and friends, visiting William and his wife, Alice, in Chocorua, New Hampshire, and Cambridge, Massachusetts, spending time with the novelist Edith Wharton in the Berkshires and New York City, and making side trips to Newport and Cape Cod. As the new year began and winter came on in earnest, he headed south, beginning his career as a public speaker in Philadelphia, then proceeding rapidly through Washington, where he stayed with Henry Adams and dined with President Theodore Roosevelt, and on to Richmond, Charleston, Jacksonville, Palm Beach, and St. Augustine. By the end of February, he was back in Cambridge for a round of painful dentistry, followed by a busy and exhausting progress west with lectures and visits in St. Louis, Chicago, Indianapolis, Los Angeles, San Diego, Monterey, San Francisco, Portland, and Seattle before returning east at the end of April. In spring and early summer, he traveled up and down the East Coast from Washington to Maine, speaking, among other places, at the Bryn Mawr College commencement, visiting the novelist WILLIAM DEAN HOWELLS, and spending a few more days with Edith Wharton. On July 5, he left his homeland, boarding the Cunard liner *Ivernia* in Boston for the eight-day trip to Liverpool.

James had several purposes in returning to the United States after so long an absence. He wanted to visit his family and friends on their home ground; he wanted to see for himself what America had become while he was away; he felt "a passion of nostalgia," a need to revisit the scenes of his youth "before senile decay sets in" (Edel 225). He was contemplating what would become the NEW YORK EDITION of his fiction, a grand collection to rival Balzac's great *La comédie humaine,* and he wanted to discuss it with American publishers. There was also the prospect of lucrative lecturing, which he found both alluring and intimidating, and the promise that

Harper and Brothers would publish his impressions, first in the *North American Review* and then in book form, with perhaps one volume devoted to the East and another to the Midwest and West. And there was, supremely as always for James, the challenge of transforming the raw material of observed life into the highest, most perceptive literary art. He had thought of calling his book *The Return of the Native,* but Thomas Hardy had preempted that title, so he settled provisionally on *The Return of the Novelist,* appropriate, as he wrote to his publisher, because "it *describes* really my point of view . . . I'm so very much more of a Novelist than of anything else and see all things *as* such." "I can't 'knock off' things," he wrote. "I want to produce a work of art, and shall." "I . . . believe that I shall be able not only to write the best book (of social and pictorial and, as it were, human observation) ever devoted to this country, but one of the best—or why 'drag in' one *of,* why not say frankly *the* Best?—ever devoted to any country at all" (*Letters* 327–328). The result was *The American Scene,* one of James's most controversial works when it was first published (Hewitt [1980] 179), and the subject of spirited debate in recent years.

Making Sense

James begins the Philadelphia chapter of *The American Scene* with some remarks on the relations between things in the world and their sense or meaning. There is a "superstition," he writes, that

> objects and places . . . have a sense of their own, a mystic meaning proper to themselves to give out: to give out, that is, to the participant at once so interested and so detached as to be moved to a report of the matter. That perverse person is obliged to take it for a working theory that the essence of almost any settled aspect of anything may be extracted by the chemistry of criticism, and may give us its right name, its formula, for convenient use. From the moment the critic finds himself sighing, to save trouble in a difficult case, that the cluster of appearances can *have* no sense, from that moment he begins, and quite consciously, to go to pieces; it being the prime business and the high honour of the painter of life always to *make* a sense—and to

make it most in proportion as the immediate aspects are loose or confused. (579)

James is himself, of course, an observer and a participant both interested in and detached from the scenes around him. He is an American, and so a part of his own subject; he is also a resident of England, and so a kind of foreigner, even, to use his own favorite term, an "alien." He is a relatively detached observer and reporter, traveling from place to place, stopping for brief visits with friends or in hotels, but he is also an interested party who has a stake in the objects and places of his native land. He fits, then, his own definition of the "perverse person," whom he goes on to describe as a critical chemist intent on "extracting" the "essence" of the scene before him and deriving a "formula" for its use. In the next sentence, however, he changes metaphors and switches verbs. Confronted with "a cluster of appearances" that seems to "*have* no sense," he transforms himself from a scientific analyst intent on *extracting* meaning into a creative artist—"the painter of life"— whose "prime business" and "high honour" is to "*make* sense" of what he sees (579).

This ambition is consistent with James's view of himself as an artist and a meaning-maker throughout his career. In the preface to *The American Scene,* he had disavowed any documentary ambitions, declaring his interest in "features of the human scene" that do not lend themselves to representation by reports and statistics, by mere "information," and demand instead the meaning-making skills of the literary artist.

Critics and scholars have frequently noted this aspect of James's project, suggesting the many very different ways it appears in *The American Scene.* Ross Posnock argues that James valued the aesthetic precisely because it substitutes the ongoing meaning-making activity of the artist-perceiver for any given preexisting sense. Beverly Haviland analyzes James's meaning-making process in terms of the semiotic theories of the pioneering American philosopher Charles Sanders Peirce. Sharon Cameron suggests that James is interested above all in making sense of his own thought processes. "The journey across the country," she argues, "is less the occasion for exploring aspects of places than it is for examining aspects of consciousness" (2).

I want to suggest that James made conscious, artful use of the resources of language to generate meaning from the complex interaction between the perceiving, imagining mind and its object. Meaning, in this view, cannot be understood, does not indeed exist independent of language; it is not embedded in the American scene but created by *The American Scene*. In this book as throughout his works, James made sense of the world by putting it into words and by elaborating those words into simple or extended figures of speech—similes, metaphors, synecdoches. Some of his subjects lent themselves easily to this treatment, producing verbal formulations characterized by wit and insight; others were more resistant, leading James to try many different words, comparisons, and figures to make sense of them.

James made meaning on the simplest level by *naming* what he saw. Using the word *boarders* for the guests at the most exclusive and luxurious Palm Beach hotels suggests their very temporary relation to the place and relates them to far humbler vacationers on New England farms and at seaside boardinghouses (722). Calling the vast and pretentious Newport mansions "white elephants" not only implies that they were superfluous pieces of property, hard to get rid of and hard to know what to do with, it also conjures the image of a line of enormous marble and limestone structures lumbering trunk to tail along the strip of land between Bellevue Avenue and the sea cliffs (540). Referring to New York's "sky-scrapers and league-long bridges" as "monsters of the mere market" (422) combines in a single alliterative phrase implications of vast size and malevolence (monsters), triviality and insignificance (mere), and the suggestion that their worth is defined not by their beauty or even their utility but by their price. Naming Washington the City of Conversation opens the way for an appreciation of a social scene that includes men and women alike in good serious talk (635).

He also made meaning by repeating in different contexts words and images from a particular realm of experience. His belief that American was obsessed with money—making it, spending it, having it—is reflected in his descriptions of New Jersey summer houses ("here was the expensive as a power by itself" [363]), the commercial life of the city ("rank with each variety of the poison-plant of the money-passion" [403]) as opposed to the contemplative life of the university, and what he called "the main American formula": "to make so much money that you won't, that you don't 'mind,' don't mind anything" (550). He describes the "pecuniary power" of wealthy New Yorkers as a great bird, soaring in the "void" with no sense of "the possible awkwardness or possible grace" of its flight (486–487). He devotes a remarkable two pages to tiaras, which in America, unlike Europe, stand for not for the wearer's rank in aristocratic society but merely for the size of their husbands' bank accounts (490–492).

His repeated variations on the vocabulary of inside and outside, belonging and exclusion, reveal his anxiety about a changing America, where the old values of privacy and social and ethnic homogeneity are threatened by the culture of publicity and the rising tide of immigration. He adopts the phrase "open door," used at the time to refer to certain free trade policies advocated by his old friend John Hay, to stand for the general openness of American society, which he thinks may be good for the country at large but bad for individual "places" (407). The new Boston Public Library is a case in point for him, an indispensable institution but a building that is more like a railway station than a temple of learning and lacks those secret quiet places—"penetralia," he calls them—so essential for study and contemplation (560). Across the river in Cambridge, Harvard Yard seems to him a fairer compromise, which, though its "palings" may be "insufficiently high," still demonstrates the way in which "the formal enclosure of objects at all interesting immediately refines upon their interest, immediately establishes values" (407).

The very title of his book, finally, alludes to the theme of spectatorship and performance in American life. The American scene is on one level just a picture, a panorama of what James saw. James the dramatist also knew that *scene* refers to a stage set or a theatrical spectacle, and to a unit of dramatic action, and he used it and related words to insist on his own role as viewer and critic of American life. There is "something splendidly scenic" about the White Mountains, he writes, with Mount Washington "its most eminent object holding exactly the middle of the stage and the grand effect stretching without a break to either wing" (381). In New York, he characterizes himself as a "picture-seeker" (520) and sees the immigrant neighborhoods he visits as "picturesque" scenes (Johnson 156). When he visits a New York theater, he uses his position in "a curtained corner of a private box" as a vantage point for viewing the spectacle of the audience as much as the action of the play (516). On his southern travels, he experiences the Pullman as both a moving theater, "a positive temple of the drama" where he can observe "the comedy and the tragedy of manners" acted out by his fellow travelers (713), and an auditorium on wheels, whose windows act as a "great moving proscenium" (709), framing the passing scene.

In addition to employing particular vocabularies to create and convey his sense of American life, James also uses figurative language—simile, metaphor, personification, synecdoche—to generate meaning. On the most basic level, he uses comparisons to embody and communicate his sense of the scene. He describes what he sees as the random and overwhelming array of New York's skyscrapers "standing up to the view . . . like extravagant pins in a cushion already overplanted" (419). A few sentences later, he sums up their showiness, their artificiality, and their planned obsolescence by calling them a "nosegay" not just of "architectural flowers" but specifically of the "'American beauty,' rose of interminable stem," bred to be "'picked,' in time, with a shears," when the interests of the market dictate (420).

James also often relies on personification to distinguish the characters of places. New York is a hoyden, a "bold bad charmer," a "bad bold beauty," unfailingly seductive, repeatedly forgiven, yet never finally serious about anything except money (445–447). Concord, in contrast, is a respectable widow, a "grave, refined New England matron of the 'old school,'" wise and discreet, knowing much and revealing little, sitting placidly on the bank of her river that flows quietly "with the purr of a mild domesticated cat who rubs against the family and the furniture" (567, 569). He finds Baltimore neither loose nor deep but rather strikingly inoffensive, sitting amid its leafy suburbs "as some quite robust but almost unnaturally good child might sit on the green apron of its nurse, with no concomitant crease or crumple, no uncontrollable 'mess,' by the nursery term, to betray its temper" (616).

In his quest to make sense of America, James is particularly drawn to synecdoche, the figure in which a part is made to stand for the whole and acutely observed details stand in for larger meanings. The difference between European and American poverty can be seen, for example, in the fact that "every one, without exception, no matter how 'low' in the social scale, wore the best and the newest, the neatest and the smartest, boots" (504). The American obsession with appearance and display is embodied in the frequently bold, gold-toothed "'Californian' smile" of the lower classes and the "good, handsome, pretty," "cherished and tended teeth" of "society" (505). More important, James sees the audience at a popular Bowery theater as a fair, and to him disconcerting, sample of the new American people, "the [predominantly Irish] representatives of the races we have nothing 'in common' with," at home in this new environment, taking their ease "as naturally, as comfortably, as munchingly, as if the theatre were their constant practice" (517).

The Hotel Spirit

In addition to deploying individual figures of speech for the insight they can provide, James develops elaborate metaphors as tools of perception, inviting readers to understand American society in their terms. Probably the most celebrated of these is his description of the spectacle of life in the great hotels—particularly the Waldorf-Astoria in New York and the Breakers in Palm Beach—which he sees as an emblem for much of what fascinates and sometimes repels him in American life. Americans, he argues, have made this "amazing hotel-world" into "a synonym for civilization" (440), the kind of collective national fantasy people now associate with theme parks, "a gorgeous golden blur, a paradise peopled with unmistakable American shapes"

(443). At his most extravagant, he goes on to claim that hotel life is the most highly developed feature of American culture, and that "the hotel-spirit is an omniscient genius, while the character of the tributary nation is still but struggling into relatively dim self-knowledge" (715).

What does he mean by this? What is there about hotel life that makes it an appropriate figure for American life as a whole? Hotel life is, first of all, life lived in public, open ostensibly to the view of all, catering to the pleasures of spectacle and display, seeing and being seen, performing and witnessing acts of conspicuous consumption. It is also a life of "promiscuous" mingling—James chooses his words carefully—in which European distinctions of rank and class have been replaced by simple distinctions of wealth. Hotel life is open to anyone who can pay for it. On one level, then, the life of American hotels is freer, looser, and more democratic than the life of European courts and drawing rooms. On another level, though, James finds it oppressively leveling, hostile to both art and individuality, tending to blandness and boredom.

The grand hotel is the splendid theater of privileged American public life, where "huge-hatted ladies" "seated under palms and by fountains" preside over the rites of fashion, evoking, perhaps a little ironically, "the shade of Marie Antoinette" at Versailles or the Trianon (443). Whether they like it or not, all hotel guests become public performers, objects of the curious gaze, "thrown upon . . . the general painted scene over which the footlights of publicity play" (688). Even the bedrooms are stage sets, done up like chambers in a rococo palace, possible scenes of lurid if somewhat more private dramas.

Americans come to hotels to mingle with their social likes and betters, ostensibly protected from contact with their inferiors by the high cost of the arrangements and the insistence upon a superficial kind of respectability that represses the very appearance of "pursued or desired adventure" (441). The result is a kind of gregarious promiscuity that the fastidious James finds striking, if not appalling. In a memorable passage, he describes "promiscuity" itself as a magnificent hotel guest, walking, talking, reveling, roaming, parading through 20th-century American public rooms masquerading as the "halls and saloons" of historic European palaces (441). Hotel culture reminds James of some grand and public Vanity Fair, played out "in a single huge *vitrine* [glass display case] which there would be nothing to prevent one's flattening one's nose against for days of delight" (723).

On one level, then, hotel life is a kind of carnival, a scene of sanctioned freedom within conventionally defined safeguards and limits. James also sees it, though, as a scene of more ominous social control, a performance "controll[ed] and command[ed]" by "some high-stationed orchestral leader," or perhaps a puppeteer who controls every movement of his "army of puppets" while finding "the means to make them think of themselves as delightfully free and easy" (444). A number of critics have called attention to this aspect of James's text. In an analysis influenced by the thinking of Michel Foucault, Mark Seltzer calls the reader's attention to the way the "art" of James's hotel spirit "muffles the violence of the hotel world and covers its power of management" (112). In a brief essay connecting James's description of hotels, hospitals, country clubs, and even the famous Philadelphia Penitentiary, Martha Banta emphasizes the ways in which all of these institutions impose a certain bland and governable uniformity, leaving their inhabitants, as James himself writes of the guests at "the universal Waldorf-Astoria," "captured and governed," "beguiled and caged" (717).

If, as James suggests, "the hotel spirit may . . . just *be* the American spirit most seeking and finding itself" (440), readers can be fairly sure that he does not take a lot of comfort in the association. His extended description of the hotel world has served as a vehicle for a profound criticism of American culture as combining brash social exhibitionism with an underlying conformity and a pecuniary standard of values.

The Ubiquitous Alien

As already suggested, James was particularly struck on his return to his native country by the inescapable presence of the immigrant. Walking alone in the New Hampshire countryside, for example, the recently disembarked traveler lost his way.

Encountering a young man who has just emerged from a neighboring wood, he asked directions but received no answer. Looking more closely, James noticed that the man "had a dark-eyed 'Latin' look," decided that he must be Canadian, and repeated his question in French. When this did not work, he tried Italian, also to no avail. He reverted at last to English, asking not where he was or how to get home, but rather more bluntly, "'What *are* you then?'" The rude challenge produced a direct reply: "'I'm an Armenian,' he replied, as if it were the most natural thing in the world for a wage-earning youth in the heart of New England to be—so that all I could do was to try and make my profit of the lesson" (455).

James uses this anecdote to illustrate what he called "the ubiquity of the alien" (455), the presence of immigrants not just in the cities but in the remote "heart" of a quintessentially "American" landscape. It is not easy to decide, however, who is the more "alien" figure in this story, the native-born but totally Europeanized gentleman lost on a pleasant walk during a visit or the foreign-born youth at home in the land where he earns his wages. That James is himself aware of this conundrum becomes clear in his reflections on his fellow passengers in a New York trolley who, "foreign as they might be, newly inducted as they might be, . . . were *at home*, . . . [and] he was at home too, quite with the same intensity" (460). "Who and what is an alien," he asks, "in a country peopled . . . by migrations at once extremely recent, perfectly traceable, and urgently required?" (459). It is as if he were repeating Crèvecoeur's famous question—"What then is the American, this new man?"—and finding it difficult to come up with an answer that included himself, the "palpitating pilgrim" (655) from London and Rye, his family and friends, and the immigrants he encountered not just at Ellis Island and the Lower East Side of Manhattan but everywhere in his travels.

James reacts to the "alien" in two ways. His initial response is a kind of fastidious nativism, as distasteful then as it is now. Faced with an Armenian in the New Hampshire woods, incommunicative Italian workers on the Jersey shore (who appear to have lost the inclination, so charming on their native soil, to pass the time of day with a condescending, Italian-speaking gentleman), Irish spectators devouring candy in the theater, and above all the Jews of New York, James longs for "the small homogeneous Boston of the more interesting time" (545) or perhaps "the luxury of some such close and sweet and *whole* national consciousness as that of the Switzer and the Scot" (428). Exploring a Jewish neighborhood in New York, he permits himself a series of metaphors that dehumanize the immigrants. First he compares them to bees, seeing them not as individuals but as a swarm ("there is no swarming like that of Israel" [464]). Then he imagines them as "innumerable fish, of over-developed proboscis," swimming in "some vast sallow aquarium" (464). His likening them to "small strange animals, known to natural history, snakes or worms, I believe" that preserve their life and their identity when cut into pieces is more complicated in its reference to their proud and persistent Jewishness but just as offensively animalizing and deindividualizing (465). His most extended metaphor, finally, compares their whole neighborhood to "some great zoological garden" where the metal fire escapes at once suggest the bars of the cages and provide "a little world of bars and perches and swings for human squirrels and monkeys" (466–467).

Passages like these betray an undeniable (and, to modern readers, inexcusable) sense of superiority to the ethnic other, but they do not exhaust James's views on the subject. If his first, unexpected, encounters prompted him to distance the immigrants by exoticizing them, patronizing them, or turning them into a picturesque or grotesque spectacle, his further reflections on the changing nature of Americanness suggest a more positive, even progressive view of their future role in American life. The "drama" of Ellis Island, he writes, must inevitably transform "the spirit of any sensitive citizen who may have happened to 'look in'" (426). Like seeing a ghost in "his supposedly safe old house," it chills his heart and unsettles his sense of possession. One possible reaction—and readers have seen that James is tempted by it—is to long for a comfortable homogeneity. The other, though, the one that James advocates, is to "regain lost ground" by redefining it, to go "*more than* half-way to meet them," transforming the sense of "dispossession" generated by the presence of the alien into a new form of shared possession (426–427). Ross Posnock describes the result as a form of "pragmatist pluralism" ([1998] 232) that redefines American identity as a constantly evolving, "perpetually provisional" notion ([1998] 233). James affirms this idea in at least two ways. While he finds the idea of "brotherhood" with the newly landed difficult to conceive, he enthusiastically applauds the effects of "the political and social habit, the common school and the newspaper" on their children. "*They* are the stuff of whom brothers and sisters are made," he writes, "and the making proceeds on a scale that really need leave nothing to desire" (455). It is not only the children of the immigrants who must be educated, though, and James undertakes an educational project of his own. He visits a Jewish home for dinner (464; Edel 291) and explores the cafés of the Lower East Side, learning to see the "intelligence" and "civility" of individuals distinct from the "mob" (470), listening with alarm to what he hears as a threat to the English language but recognizing it all the same as "the Accent of the Future" (471). The result of this education can be seen in James's view of "polyglot" Central Park, with its "Hebraic crowd of pedestrians in particular" as "New York at its best," an inclusive, evolving society in which the "alien" would not be alien for long (501–502).

There is something missing from this picture, however. James is careful to refer to European immigrants as "ethnic," not racial, others and to imagine their "ingurgitation" into "our body politic and social" in distinctly physical terms (426; Blair 173). These aliens, or their children, are to be literally incorporated into, made part of, the undifferentiated body of "our" nation and the culture, the America they have chosen to join. A different fate is in store for racial others: the Native American "aliens" whom "we" have displaced and those long-standing inhabitants of North America, the descendants of African-American slaves. Both enter James's narrative only briefly—an indication, perhaps, of the failure of his Europeanized perspective to understand their important place in the national picture.

The "braves" James describes at the Capitol make a sorry sight, denatured and Americanized in their "neat pot-hats, shoddy suits and light overcoats, with their pockets, I am sure, full of photographs and cigarettes" (652). They are apparently school-Indians, "specimens, on show, of what the Government can do with people with whom it supposed able to do nothing" (652). What the government can do, James suggests, is turn original peoples into poor copies of their conquerors, turning "the bloody footsteps of time" into the fiction of "a single smooth stride" (653) from barbarianism to civilization.

Aside from W. E. B. DuBois, whose work James admired, African Americans fare no better. I have mentioned the "tatterdemalion darkies" outside the Richmond station. Kenneth Warren in his book *Black and White Strangers* points out that James habitually *saw* African Americans as servants while deploring their failure to serve *well* (122). James himself contrasts "the old Southern tradition, the house alive with the scramble of young darkies for the honour of fetching and carrying" with the ineptitude of "the negro waiter at the hotel" (702). In his contribution to a published exchange on the issue, Ross Posnock asks a pointed and one assumes intentionally simplistic question: "[I]s *The American Scene* a brief against racism, and if not why not?" ([1995] 275). The answer to the first part of this question is clearly "no." *The American Scene* is not a "brief" against or for anything: It is an analysis, not a polemic; its purpose is to complicate perception not to denounce injustice. James caught some important features of the American scene, but he missed others. His failure to grasp the fundamental importance of race in American culture and society is clear and regrettable. But if, as Posnock argues, his literary techniques and complex intentions facilitated "an elaborate evasion of moral/ethical responsibility about Jim Crow America" ([1995] 275), they also enabled a profound and stimulating analysis of other aspects of the American scene, which readers understand better today than if *The American Scene* had not been published 100 years ago.

Conclusion

The American Scene is just what James wanted it to be: a work of art. As such, it offers the reader both pleasure and insight. The writer Henry James creates a character, "Henry James," "the visionary tourist," "the restless analyst," a traveler-narrator with certain well-defined preferences and prejudices that resemble but do not duplicate his own. He places this character in a landscape—the American scene—and sets him to exploring. Like novel readers, people come to know this character, to anticipate his views and judgments, to share and sometimes to criticize them. Readers participate vicariously in his adventures and discoveries, imagining themselves in the position of a 61-year-old white American male of Irish descent (who believed with pride that he had English ancestry), unmarried, almost certainly homosexual, mightily cultivated, a little snobbish, temperamentally if not artistically conservative, but open to new impressions and accepting that change is inevitable.

This James describes the American scene in aesthetic and analytic terms. He offers verbal landscapes and sketches of daily life; he allows himself flights of metaphoric fancy; he makes memorable phrases and spins seemingly interminable sentences, enticing readers into the "penetralia" of his own mind and perception. He makes meaning by analyzing aspects of American culture that remain of crucial importance today: moneymaking, architecture, urban planning, the destruction of the natural world, the roles of men and women, immigration, conspicuous consumption, public display. The result is a supreme example of artistic travel writing as a source of pleasure and as a tool for making sense of the world.

FURTHER READING

Banta, Martha. "'Strange Deserts:' Hotels, Hospitals, Country Clubs, Prisons, and the City of Brotherly Love." *Henry James Review* 17, no. 1 (1996): 1–10.

Blair, Sara. *Henry James and the Writing of Race and Nation*. Cambridge: Cambridge University Press, 1996.

Cameron, Sharon. *Thinking in Henry James*. Chicago: University of Chicago Press, 1989.

Edel, Leon. *Henry James: 1901–1916: The Master*. New York: Lippincott, 1972.

Haralson, Eric. "The Person Sitting in Darkness: James in the American South." *Henry James Review* 16, no. 3 (1995): 249–256.

Haviland, Beverly. *Henry James's Last Romance: Making Sense of the Past and* The American Scene. Cambridge: Cambridge University Press, 1997.

Hewitt, Rosalie. "Henry James, The Harpers, and *The American Scene*." *American Literature* 55, no. 1 (1983): 41–47.

———. "Henry James's *The American Scene*: Its Genesis and Its Reception, 1905–1977." *Henry James Review* 1, no. 3 (1980): 179–196.

James, Henry. *Letters*, vol. 4. Edited by Leon Edel. Cambridge, Mass.: Harvard University Press, 1984.

Johnson, Kendall. *Henry James and the Visual*. Cambridge: Cambridge University Press, 2007.

Novick, Sheldon M. *Henry James: The Mature Master*. New York: Random House, 2007.

Posnock, Ross. "Affirming the Alien: The Pragmatist Pluralism of *The American Scene*." In *The Cambridge Companion to Henry James*, edited by Jonathan Freedman, 224–246. Cambridge: Cambridge University Press, 1998.

———. "Henry James and the Limits of Historicism." *Henry James Review* 16, no. 3 (1995): 273–277.

Seltzer, Mark. *Henry James and the Art of Power*. Ithaca, N.Y.: Cornell University Press, 1984.

Warren, Kenneth W. *Black and White Strangers*. Chicago: University of Chicago Press, 1993.

William W. Stowe, *Wesleyan University*

"The Art of Fiction" (1884)

James's essay first appeared in the September 1884 issue of *Longman's Magazine* and was reprinted later that same year in an unauthorized publication alongside Walter Besant's "Fiction as One of the Fine Arts," the essay to which James responds. James later revised "The Art of Fiction" and published it in a collection of essays entitled *Partial Portraits* (1888). "The Art of Fiction" remains a seminal essay about the novel and is regularly reprinted in numerous anthologies, particularly those specializing in American literature and literary theory and criticism.

SYNOPSIS

"The Art of Fiction" marks a significant transition in the critical examination of the English novel. James wrote it in response to Besant's essay, which he considered too narrow and too prescriptive. James feared that Besant's essay did not sufficiently persuade readers of the deeper significance of the art of fiction. Indeed, the English novel often met with suspicion from its readers, usually due to the perception that novels lacked morality or contributed to idleness. With "The Art of Fiction," James tries to lift such concerns by inviting readers to consider the deeper reasons for the novel, especially the complex relationship between the novel and lived experience. "The Art of Fiction" challenges the commonplace understanding of the English novel and introduces the terms of modern scholarly discussion on the nature and purpose of the novel. Even though other writers commented on the novel's significance, James's discussion widened the discourse so that novelists could become much more conscious about what they were trying to accomplish.

James begins by defending the position that the novel is a legitimate art form, one that must necessarily be free from social suspicions and religious scruples. Such concerns, James suggests, limit the possibilities of the novel because they do not invite proper reflection on the reading experience. Most people, even those who read novels, saw them as distractions, things that could be held in the same category as "pudding" (44). James challenges such indifference by suggesting that art, including the novel, "lives upon discussion, upon experiment, upon curiosity, upon variety of attempt, upon the exchange of views and the comparison of standpoints" (44–45).

James next presses the reader to consider the ways in which novels speak to the great diversity of lived experience. In fact, he asserts that "the only reason for the existence of a novel is that it does attempt to represent life" (46). James does not imply that the novel represents life the way a photograph captures a single moment in time. Instead, James argues that the novel is more analogous to one's experiences, including one's impressions of life. James writes, for example, that "a novel is in its

broadest definition a personal, a direct impression of life: that, to begin with, constitutes its value, which is greater or less according to the intensity of the impression" (50). In other words, the quality of a novel largely depends on the keenness of the observer. Because of this, the novelist must be able to search as broadly and as deeply into lived experience as he or she possibly can.

"The Art of Fiction" likewise provides a model through which writers may begin to think about their craft beyond the basic prerequisites of skill and ambition. James argues against writers like Besant who limit their advice to young writers to overly prescriptive suggestions that try to dictate what they must and must not do. Instead, James writes that the key to strong writing is to follow one's own observations carefully. Successful writers, in other words, need to "try to be one of the people on whom nothing is lost" (53). One of the most important discussions concerns James's views on the nature of life and consciousness. James focuses particularly on the necessity of paying very careful attention to the matters of life itself. For example, he writes that "it goes without saying that you will not write a good novel unless you possess the sense of reality; but it will be difficult to give you a recipe for calling that sense into being" (52). James's refusal to define reality simply for his readers suggests that he wants them to understand that they must take a certain responsibility for coming to terms with reality itself. All James can suggest, then, is that "Humanity is immense, and reality has a myriad forms" (52). Most important, James writes that "Experience is never limited, and it is never complete; it is an immense sensibility a kind of huge spider-web of the finest silken threads suspended in the chamber of consciousness, and catching every airborne particle in its tissue" (52). James writes that "A novel is in its broadest definition a personal, a direct impression of life" (50).

"The Art of Fiction" is central to James's work, largely because it serves as the moment in which James begins to formulate his theory of the novel beyond the more evaluative comments he made in earlier reviews. Here James imagines a legitimate theory of the novel, one based on the varieties of

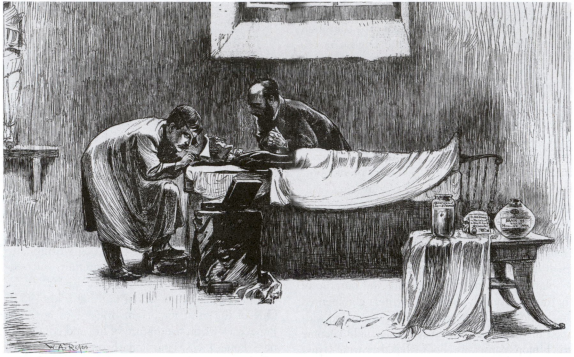

THE MODERN NOVEL
Do these gentlemen find what they are hunting for?
Oh, yes.
What is it?
Nothing.
W. A. Rogers, "The Modern Novel," *Life* 17, no. 176 (May 1886). "Gentlemen" refers to William Dean Howells and Henry James; the patient is the modern novel.

conscious experience. But James does not mean for his theory to lead to a narrowly defined practice. Instead, James wants readers to understand that the nature of his theory is to invite discussion. According to James, most commentary on the novel, like Besant's, relies on commonplace advice and does not help writers understand the larger purposes of the novel. Although Besant recognizes that a novelist ought to write from experience, he limits such experiences to commonly held social norms and restraints. He suggests, for example, that "a young lady brought up in a quiet country village should avoid descriptions of garrison life" (51). James disagrees with such claims by inviting writers to write from the broadest possible sense of what experience means. Doing so will not limit a writer's stories to perceived expectations of race,

class, or gender. James's essay widens the discussion by helping readers understand that the art of the novel develops in proportion to the writer's ability to see truly.

CRITICAL COMMENTARY

Most evaluations of "The Art of Fiction" focus on the question of James's overall status as a literary critic. On the one hand, many readers turn to James's essay hoping to discover a precise theoretical description of the role of the novelist. Others refer to "The Art of Fiction" as something much more suggestive than rigorous. Sarah Daugherty, for example, argues that readers should avoid seeing James's essay as a single declarative "statement of theory" (113). This is because "The Art of Fiction" sometimes "seems confusing and self-contradictory" and does not always help readers understand all of its points clearly (113). Perhaps this is why some readers prefer to read "The Art of Fiction" more generally as an essay filled with useful but broad literary insights. Rene Wellek, for example, suggests that James is "the best American critic of the nineteenth century," someone who is "brimful of ideas and critical concepts" (213). In other words, readers might turn to James for new insights into ways of reading the novel.

One way to read "The Art of Fiction" is to see it as an argument about the responsibility of the artist. Indeed, James urges readers to explore the diversity of reality further by bringing to their art the same kind of constant activity that is required for a productive life. James argues that without such diligence art suffers from stagnation. James explains further that "Art lives upon discussion, upon experiment, upon curiosity, upon variety of attempt, upon the exchange of views and the comparison of standpoints" (44–45). According to James, art is analogous to the organic growth and life of nature. He writes that "[A] novel is a living thing, all one and continuous, like any other organism, and in proportion as it lives will it be found, I think, that in each of the parts there is something of each of the other parts" (54). Unlike nature, art will not always grow spontaneously. It requires the constant efforts of the writer to create work that can "catch the colour of life itself" (65). In order to do that, the artist must become carefully aware of life, including the fleeting impressions that usually pass unnoticed. As James cautions, "No good novel will ever proceed from a superficial mind" (64). F. R. Leavis suggests that James's purpose was to argue for a "general full recognition among the educated that creative talent—creative genius—was at least as likely to go into the novel as into any mode of art, and that for the critic and the 'educated' reader to be innocent of their corresponding obligation was ignoble" (111–112). Leavis appeals to his readers' sense of responsibility, an idea that further helps to understand James's essay. In fact, Leavis goes on to write that "in respect of any art one takes seriously one *has* to make value-judgments, since a real response entails this; it entails forming an implicit critical

sense of the human significance of the art in question" (113, emphasis in text).

"The Art of Fiction" therefore deals with the larger ethical responsibilities of the artist and the reader. In this sense, James's essay asks readers to make the same kinds of careful choices that he asks writers to make. James's point that would-be novelists need to be "one of the people on whom nothing is lost" implies an active sense of responsibility (53). An artist must not fail to observe his or her world directly. This means that art is something more concerned with praxis or doing more than anything else. Indeed, writers must learn to "guess the unseen from the seen, to trace the implication of things, to judge the whole piece by the pattern, the condition of feeling life in general so completely that you are well on your way to knowing any particular corner of it" (53). Such comments are typical of James's "The Art of Fiction." He readily admits that he has no interest in creating a list of things to do. Instead, he invites his readers (and future writers) to learn to observe deeply and to take careful notes so that they will come to understand the importance of recognizing that the significant things in life lie all around them and that these things do not require any special act of fortune or of plot to become significant. If readers turn the act of observation into a lifelong practice, James suggests, they will then understand the true diversity of life.

FURTHER READING

Daugherty, Sarah B. *The Literary Criticism of Henry James*. Athens: Ohio University Press, 1981.

James, Henry. "The Art of Fiction." In *Henry James: Essays on Literature, American Writers, English Writers*. New York: Library of America, 1984.

Jones, Vivien. *James The Critic*. New York: St. Martin's Press, 1985.

Leavis, F. R. *The Critic as Anti-Philosopher: Essays and Papers by F. R. Leavis*, edited by G. Singh. Athens: University of Georgia Press, 1983.

Miller, J. Hillis. *The Ethics of Reading: Kant, de Man, Trollope, James, and Benjamin*. New York: Columbia University Press, 1987.

Rawlings, Peter. *American Theorists of the Novel: Henry James, Lionel Trilling, Wayne C. Booth*. New York: Routledge, 2006.

Wellek, Rene. *A History of Modern Criticism: 1750–1950, vol. 4. The Later Nineteenth Century.* New Haven, Conn.: Yale University Press, 1965.

Carl Sederholm, *Brigham Young University*

autobiographies

The autobiography of Henry James is actually a series of three books. Charles Scribner's Sons published the first, *A Small Boy and Others*, in NEW YORK CITY on March 29, 1913. Macmillan and Company published the LONDON edition on April 1, 1913. The second book, *Notes of a Son and Brother*, was published a year later, in 1914, by the same New York and London publishers, on March 7 and March 13, respectively. The last book of James's autobiography, *The Middle Years* (not to be confused with his tale bearing the same title), was an unfinished fragment when James died on February 28, 1916. Edited by Percy Lubbock, this last installment of James's story of his life was published posthumously in London, Glasgow, Melbourne, and Auckland by W. Collins Sons on October 18, 1917, and on November 23, 1917, in New York City by Charles Scribner's Sons. In 1956, the three texts were published as a single volume called *Henry James: Autobiography*. Edited and with an introduction by Frederick W. Dupee, it was published by Criterion Books in New York City. This volume contains an index that makes it possible to research specific references, names, and subjects mentioned in the autobiography. The original three volumes did not have indices.

SYNOPSIS

This section is limited to discussion of general themes and selected landmark events in each volume.

A Small Boy and Others (1913)

The first edition of *A Small Boy and Others* features a Matthew Brady frontispiece of James and his father, HENRY JAMES, SR. The younger Henry is wearing the brass-buttoned coat for which William Makepeace Thackeray, whom he once met,

nicknamed him "Buttons." This first volume begins with James's memory of his development from a small, passive boy into a strongly creative, well-known literary figure. The book's 29 chapters cover James's visits with his father's family in Albany, his childhood in New York City, his first experiences with the theater and literature, and his early experiences of traveling with his family in Europe, where he begins his education.

When Henry was barely six months old, his parents had moved to England and France for two years, before returning and setting up house in Albany. The volume offers James's memories of "infantile Albany" (4) as the seat of his father's well-to-do family. James's Welsh-Irish paternal great-grandfather, William, had emigrated from Ireland and settled in Albany in the 1790s. His maternal great-grandparents, the Barbers, were Scottish-Irish and had been actively involved in the Revolutionary War.

Sharing memories of leisurely summer afternoons in Albany, when he was "yet beginning to be bedless, or cribless" (4), James offers the image of his grandmother, the "joyless" Catherine Barber, reading the fiction of the day. This grandmother took in orphaned relatives while having many children of her own, but she wanted to remove herself through fiction from interacting with them. James likes this position of an observer who stands apart from the action, and he finds himself increasingly on the outskirts of activities, watching others.

The volume introduces us to members of James's immediate family: his father, Henry James, Sr., a well-known thinker and philosopher of the American 19th-century transcendentalist period; his mother, Mary Robertson Walsh of Washington Square, New York City (although James does not speak of her in any detail in this volume); her sister, James's Aunt Kate, who lived with the family except for a short-lived MARRIAGE; his three brothers—elder brother WILLIAM JAMES and younger brothers Wilky (Garth Wilkerson) and Bob (Robertson); and the youngest of the siblings, Alice. The memoir takes readers up to the time when Henry James reached 14 years old and contracted typhus while the family was living in PARIS.

During the course of his childhood, because of Henry James, Sr.'s, involvement with the radical cultural and intellectual scene, James met such illustrious men as American transcendentalists RALPH WALDO EMERSON and Bronson Alcott, as well as the novelists Thackeray and Charles Dickens. The Jameses lived in New York City for 10 years. James writes of the 14th Street neighborhood of his early boyhood and such places as the "torture chamber" of his dentist, Dr. Parkhurst. In New York City begins a long line of "instructresses" and tutors to whom Henry and his older brother William were sent. Their father seems to have taken charge of their education and enrolled the boys at about a dozen schools in their early days. *A Small Boy and Others* details the friendship between the two brothers as they made their way to Barnum's Museum and to stage performances of *Uncle Tom's Cabin*. Henry depicts his brother William as a rough-and-tumble boy and himself as being more reticent and contemplative.

In 1851, James, Sr., moved the family to Europe. They lived in France, where their educations were no more stable than they had been in New York. Henry and William went to one school in 1851, another in 1852, and yet another in 1854. Then the family moved to SWITZERLAND and then back to France, on to England, and by 1856 they were back in France again.

In a section close to the end of *A Small Boy and Others*, James brings readers forward in time to a dream that he had as a young man. It takes place in the Galerie d'Apollon of the Louvre Museum in Paris. A dark shadow chases Henry, who suddenly turns to face and then pursue the shadow. Henry recalls his bout with typhus, and the volume comes to a close.

Notes of a Son and Brother (1914)

This second volume of James's autobiography covers the author's life from his adolescence and young adulthood through the years of the CIVIL WAR, then to his early writing and his friendship with his cousin MARY TEMPLE ("Minny"), who died at a young age from tuberculosis.

In this second phase of the autobiography, James draws from—but edits and revises—the letters between members of his immediate family and friends. Henry recalls his brother William's

strong interest in visual art as a young adult. Henry remains the focus of the book. The 13 chapters are sprinkled with line drawings, portraits, and sections of correspondence that help build a connection with the reader.

James picks up his narrative in Geneva in 1855. James, Sr., insists that Henry study math at a polytechnical school, but he "feared and abhorred mathematics" (240), concluding that his parents hoped to cure him of the vice of reading too many novels. As in *A Small Boy and Others*, James details further rapid changes in schooling situations. In 1858, the family moves to NEWPORT, Rhode Island, an affluent, upper-class community to which many of the Boston intelligentsia and wealthy society had ties. Despite the fact that the James children seemed content in this setting, Henry, Sr., moved them back to Europe a year later and enrolled Henry, Jr., at the Institution Rochette to study engineering. James tells of his despair. Finally, Henry, Sr., relents, and the family goes briefly to Germany, and in 1860 James, Sr., moves the family back to Newport, where William is to study painting under William Morris Hunt.

In Newport, the Jameses were reunited with their orphaned cousins, the Temples. Henry's favorite was Minny. James's two younger brothers, Wilky and Bob, attended the school of Frank Sanborn in Concord. Sanborn, a friend of Emerson from their days at Harvard College, had opened the Concord Academy and instructed the children of Emerson, Nathaniel Hawthorne (see HAWTHORNE), and Horace Mann, as well as the daughter of the abolitionist John Brown. Sanborn's school was closed when authorities sought the collaborators of John Brown, who raided Harpers Ferry in his stand against slavery in 1859.

A landmark event in *Notes of a Son and Brother* is the 1861 incident in which Henry received "a horrid even if an obscure hurt" (415). Fighting a stable fire, he apparently received some injury that could never be corroborated by doctors. James himself emphasizes the debilitating effect of the enigmatic injury.

When the Civil War broke out, William James enrolled at Harvard College to study chemistry, having abandoned the idea of pursuing art. Henry, as a consequence of his wound, did not go into service either. Instead, he enrolled in Harvard Law School and discovered he was unsuited for the law. At this juncture, Henry James decides to devote himself to writing.

During this period, his two younger brothers enlisted in the Union Army. Wilkerson was 17, and he ultimately served in the 54th Massachusetts Regiment, the first black regiment, led by Robert Gould Shaw. Wilkerson sustained injuries in the battle at Fort Wagner and returned home seriously wounded. Robertson, 16, enlisted with the 55th Massachusetts Regiment, the second black regiment. He suffered sunstroke and was sent home to Massachusetts, where the Jameses had moved to return to their 1864 home in order to be near the older boys at Harvard.

Notes of a Son and Brother moves forward and backward in time, and it is difficult to recreate Henry's style of interweaving accounts of remembered associations in a richly narrated life story. Suffice it to say that historic and notable events take shape in the background. At school, James met a range of young men, such as Oliver Wendell Holmes, who would become notable figures on the American scene. He had also met Hawthorne, about whom James would eventually write a literary biography. In the midst of the Civil War, on James's 22nd birthday, Abraham Lincoln succumbed to his mortal wounds. James submitted an "attempt at literary criticism" to Charles Eliot Norton, who had taken over the *North American Review* (Dupee 1956, 476). Meanwhile, William had gone to the Amazon to study with the famous naturalist Louis Agassiz, who had been Georges Cuvier's student in Paris and was now William's mentor at Harvard. In 1865, James met and became friends with WILLIAM DEAN HOWELLS, who was already a well-known author and had begun working on the *Atlantic Monthly*. Recovered from their service in the Civil War, James's younger brothers attempted yet failed to build a plantation in Florida manned by freed slaves.

And finally, in 1869, James sailed to England, where he was admitted into the high cultural circles where he met the Pre-Raphaelite poet/artist Dante Gabriel Rossetti, the novelist GEORGE ELIOT (Mary

Photograph of Henry James, 1910, George Grantham Bain Collection *(Library of Congress)*

Ann Evans), and artistic savant William Morris. The ending of *Notes of a Son and Brother* focuses on the death of Minny Temple. Though James moves well past this point as he follows his siblings and friends into the future, he pulls back to the year 1870. The closing chapter is devoted not only to Minny's strong, personal character and James's affection for her but also to her death and, finally, her last letter in 1870. James gives the impression that Minny's love was lost too soon.

The Middle Years (1917)

The little collection of memories (52 pages in the Dupee edition) published as *The Middle Years* follows James's practice of writing as if in the process of remembering and sifting through the past. The narrative is loosely chronological in its associative style as Henry relates the deep impressions of his young adult life. The fragment begins with Henry recalling the injury he had described in the first volume as preventing him from serving in the

Civil War. In England, James seeks his fortune as a writer in his beloved Europe. Readers glimpse the dreary Liverpool port where James arrived, then travel with him to London and into his first rented rooms at 7 Half-Moon Street. James introduces his landlord, then tells of his excursions as he is introduced into high English society, where he meets the novelist George Eliot, Alfred Lord Tennyson, and others of their stature.

CRITICAL ANALYSIS

Henry James's autobiographies present several challenges to readers. First, they are written in James's "late" style, once characterized in a letter from his brother William as "crustaceous," and indeed it is an elaborate and hard-to-follow narrative style, quite different from the simple, straightforward style James had used when he began writing short stories early in his career. By the time he began writing *A Small Boy and Others,* he had begun the practice of dictating from memory to his typist THEODORA BOSANQUET. Much of the autobiographies read as if spoken aloud, and that style, coupled with James's habit of embedding clauses in his sentences to help dramatize a narrative, is sometimes demanding to the reader.

Autobiographies generally unfold chronologically, often beginning with the author's childhood and ending with an important turning point or when the author reaches a moment of notoriety that makes his or her life a subject of interest to a reading audience. Henry James follows this narrative pattern, but only as its most basic structure. That is, though the three autobiographical texts generally move forward in time, they are so replete with details and associations that move forward and backward in time, projections, memories, and literary segues, that it is sometimes challenging for the reader to chart the precise when and where of Henry James's life. A related challenge is the way James narrates the story from multiple viewpoints at once.

Finally, James began writing *A Small Boy and Others* in 1910, after the deaths of his younger brother Robertson and his elder brother, William. William's children were still alive, but all of the members of James's immediate family had died

when he undertook the memoirs. *A Small Boy and Others* was originally conceptualized as an homage to William; however, it is, in fact, a retracing of James's own first 15 years of life, augmented, edited, reorganized, and sometimes fictionalized to bring the events in line with the way James wanted to be remembered. Henry directs the spotlight on his brother and father, but it is Henry himself who is the key player in the autobiography.

In general, James's autobiographies challenge an image of him as a literary master who controlled life through his ability to represent human experience in his fiction. In his autobiographies, he seems vulnerable to life's experiences and in his attempts to rescue poignant memories from the decades long passed, as when he comments in *A Small Boy and Others:* "I confess myself embarrassed by my very ease of recapture of my young consciousness; so that I perforce try to encourage lapses and keep my abundance down. The place for the lapse consents with difficulty, however, to be any particular point of the past at which I catch myself (easily caught as I am) looking about me" (288). James's embarrassment manifests itself in a complex literary style that is as much about screening the abundance of historical detail as it is about revealing how he truly felt.

In many ways, James's autobiographies are an act of fiction that conforms to popular expectations about an autobiography. James uses the form in the autobiography to protect the mystery of his creative powers and to cultivate his legacy as an artist. James goes so far as to tamper with such "facts," including excerpts of some of his family's letters. For example, in *Notes of a Son and Brother,* James liberally revised many of William's letters, later defending himself to his nephew for doing so. James justified the alterations of the texts by saying that those materials from the past were "my truth, to do what I could with" (*Letters* II: 346–348).

In another instance, when reporting the date of the intimate wound, James contradicts his childhood friend THOMAS SERGEANT PERRY's timetable of the events by six months. This suggests that James used and shifted actual dates to create a novelistic flow to his life. Thus, while there is a factual basis to his representation of events, readers should approach the autobiography in part as one would a work of fiction or a psychological map of James's "life."

A Small Boy and Others and *Notes of a Son and Brother* are goldmines of information about the historical, cultural, and political contexts within which Henry James grew up. Many of the events of his life and the lives of his family actually helped shape the United States as known today. The Jameses of Albany, for example, were involved in the high society, politics, and economic development of New York State, and many of the young cousins and relations to whom James refers in his memoir were connected to the Van Burens and DeWitt Clintons, who enjoyed great prestige in the late 18th and early 19th centuries. The extended James and Walsh families helped form towns, governments, and industries in a number of New York and New Jersey areas. Their activities contributed to the development of international trading circuits, and their enterprises reached as far west as Illinois and as far south as South Carolina and Florida. From participation in the abolitionist movement, to active duty in the Civil War, and to Henry's own emotional involvement in the Spanish-American War and WORLD WAR I, tracing the lives of the James family reflects the national concerns of a rapidly changing nation as it survived the Civil War and asserted its manufacturing might on a global scale.

The autobiography also demonstrates a deep and at times tense intimacy between Henry and his older brother, William. In *A Small Boy and Others,* James shares the well-known anecdote about Emerson, a friend of his father, visiting the James household to bless the newborn William. Instead of launching into a narrative of William's life, Henry remarks that he is "interested for the moment . . . in identifying" his "very own perceptions." He continues, reflecting that his brother occupied:

> a place in the world to which I couldn't at all aspire to any approach. . . . I quite definitely and resignedly thought of him as in the most exemplary manner already beforehand with me, already seated at his task when the attempt to drag me crying and kicking to the first hour

of my education failed on the threshold of the Dutch House in Albany. . . . That failure of my powers [to be educated] or that indifference to them . . . was to leave him once for all already there an embodied demonstration of the possible . . . I never for all the time of childhood and youth in the least caught up with him or overtook him. He was always round the corner and out of sight. . . . [T]his relation alike to our interests and to each other seemed proper and preappointed. (7)

Thus, James characterizes William as the achiever and himself as the passive little onlooker. In *A Small Boy and Others,* James frequently positions himself at his father's side, looking on at the great world of culture and arts and biding his time until he can get there. This position provides a forward-looking narrative through which James molds and shapes the memory of his observant childhood into the dedicated pursuance of writing. The first two volumes lend an air of inevitability to James's authorial power, suggesting a kind of classical destiny in his literary achievement. *The Middle Years* continues this arc in the suggestion of a literary apprenticeship. Perhaps the finished volume would have depicted James's growing recognition of himself as an author who enjoyed an international reputation of high regard.

CHARACTERS

Emerson, Ralph Waldo (1803–1882)   He was a leading figure of the 19th-century American transcendentalism movement that climaxed in the early 1840s. Margaret Fuller and Henry David Thoreau are the two writers most closely associated with Emerson, though Bronson Alcott, Henry James, Sr., and others were actively engaged with the ideas of transcendentalism as well. Emerson was a poet, essayist, lecturer, and mentor to a large number of thinkers in his day. Emerson hailed Walt Whitman as the voice of the next generation. He died in the same year as Henry James's parents.

James, Alice (1850–1892)   The youngest of the James siblings and the only girl, Alice had a strong intellect and vibrant interest in learning. Despite her father's iconoclasm in other regards, he prescribed a narrower educational curriculum for Alice than for his sons. Alice spent much of her life battling hypochondria. She had friends in New England society and became involved in some limited activities during the Civil War. She lived with her parents until their deaths in 1882, and thereafter she came under her brother Henry's guidance. Her longtime companion, Katherine Loring, died of breast cancer in 1892. Alice's diary was published posthumously in 1934, and since then she has become a symbol of the oppressive weight of Victorian (see VICTORIANISM) gender roles. Her insightful entries have been appreciated for their intelligence and for offering yet another window into the life of the Jameses.

James, Garth Wilkerson (1845–1883)   The third son of Henry James, Sr., Wilky served in the Civil War and was severely wounded in the battle at Fort Wagner. After the war, he lost a great amount of family money in a plantation venture in Florida that used the labor of former slaves. He eventually moved to Milwaukee, Wisconsin, where he started a family. Henry, Sr., had financially supported Wilky in various professional ventures, but upon his death he left nothing for Wilky. Henry James, Jr., executor of his father's will, joined with his siblings to make certain that Wilky was not disinherited. Wilky died young at 38 years of age of Bright's disease, a kidney ailment.

James, Henry Sr. (1811–1882)   A dynamic and idiosyncratic religious philosopher, he was a rebel in his well-to-do family from Albany. As a boy, he lost a leg after kicking a burning hay-ball in a childhood game. A member of the Boston cognoscenti, James was a close friend of Bronson Alcott, father of American novelist Louisa May Alcott, and of Ralph Waldo Emerson, the American transcendentalist leader. Through Emerson, he came to know Frank Sanborn, the Peabody sisters, Henry David Thoreau, Margaret Fuller, Nathaniel Hawthorne, and others involved with the utopian movement of early 19th-century America. He was also a follower of the ideas of spiritual philosopher EMANUEL SWEDENBORG. James, Sr., shaped the peripatetic educa-

tion of the James children. After his wife's death, James followed her shortly thereafter, essentially by refusing to eat.

James, Mary Robertson (1810–1882)   Henry James's mother called him "Angel," and although he barely addresses her in the autobiographies, he refers to her as the life of the family home.

James, Robertson (1846–1910)   The youngest of the James boys, Bob had an artistic impulse but never was able to turn it into a notable life's work. Like his older brother Wilky, he served as a soldier in the Civil War. He followed his brother to Milwaukee and tried his hand as a railroad clerk and a curator of the minuscule Milwaukee Art Museum. Eventually, battling alcoholism and depression, he returned east, never realizing any of his literary or artistic ambitions.

James, William (1842–1910)   A key figure in the development of the field of American psychology, William was a celebrated Harvard professor and philosopher who promoted the idea of PRAGMATISM. His *The Varieties of Religious Experience* (1902) remains a classic text in the psychology of religious faith.

Sanborn, Franklin Benjamin (1831–1917)   An educator and abolitionist who ran the Concord Academy, he associated with a veritable who's who of Massachusetts intelligentsia and political figures. James's two younger brothers attended school there until Sanborn's political involvement with the revolutionary abolitionist John Brown resulted in the closing of his school.

FURTHER READING

Allen, Gay Wilson. *William James: A Biography*. New York: Viking, 1967.

Bosanquet, Theodora. *Henry James at Work*. London: Hogarth Press, 1924.

Burr, Anna Robeson. *Alice James: Her Brothers; Her Journal*. Cornwall, N.Y.: Dodd, 1934. Includes letters and expurgated journal.

Dupee, F. W. *Henry James*. New York: Sloane, 1951.

———, ed. *Henry James: Autobiography*. New York: Criterion Books, 1956.

Edel, Leon. *Henry James: The Conquest of London, 1870–1881*. Philadelphia: Lippincott, 1962.

———. *Henry James: A Life*. New York: Harper, 1985.

———. *The Life of Henry James*. 2 vols. London: Penguin, 1977.

———. *Henry James: The Master, 1901–1916*. Philadelphia: Lippincott, 1972.

———. *Henry James: The Middle Years, 1882–1895*. Philadelphia: Lippincott, 1969.

———. *Henry James: The Treacherous Years, 1895–1901*. Philadelphia: Lippincott, 1969.

———. *Henry James: The Untried Years, 1843–1870*. Philadelphia: Lippincott, 1953.

Feinstein, Howard. *Becoming William James*. Ithaca, N.Y., and London: Cornell University Press, 1984.

James, Alice. *The Death and Letters of Alice James*. Edited by Ruth Bernard Yeazell. Berkeley, Los Angeles, London: University of California Press, 1981.

———. *The Diary of Alice James*. Edited by Leon Edel. New York: Dodd, 1964.

James, Henry. *The Letters of Henry James*. Edited by Percy Lubbock. 2 vols. New York: Scribner's, 1920.

———. *The Middle Years*. New York: Charles Scribner's Sons, 1917.

———. *The Notebooks of Henry James*. Edited by F. O. Matthiessen and Kenneth Murdock. New York: Oxford University Press, 1947.

———. *Notes of a Son and Brother*. New York: Scribner's, 1920.

———. *A Small Boy and Others*. New York: Scribner's, 1913; London: Macmillan, 1913.

James, Henry, Sr. *The Literary Remains of Henry James*. Edited by William James. Boston: Osgood, 1884.

James, William. *The Letters of William James*. Edited by Henry James, III. 2 vols. Boston: Atlantic Monthly Press, 1920.

———. *The Thought and Character of William James: Briefer Version*. Cambridge, Mass.: Harvard University Press, 1935.

Keynes, Geoffrey. *Henry James in Cambridge*. Cambridge: Heffer, 1967.

Lewis, R. W. B. *The Jameses: A Family Narrative*. New York: Farrar, Straus & Giroux, 1991.

Maher, Jane. *Biography of Broken Fortunes: Wilkie and Bob, Brothers of William, Henry and Alice James*. Hamdon, Conn.: Archon, 1986.

Matthiessen, F. O. *The James Family: A Group Biography*. New York: Vintage, 1980.

Perry, Ralph Barton. *The Thought and Character of William James*. 2 vols. Boston: Little, Brown, 1936.

Rosenberg, Ellen. "The Crucible of the Imagination: Psychobiographical and Family Systems Theory and Application to the Creative Process of Henry James and Family." Dissertation Indiana University: Ann Arbor, Mich., 1991.

Strouse, Jean. *Alice James: A Biography*. Boston: Houghton, 1980.

Ellen Rosenberg, *North Carolina School of the Arts*

correspondence

The first publication of James's letters appeared in 1920, four years after James's death, and was edited by Percy Lubbock. Letter collections were customary of the age, commonly presenting a benign glimpse of notable individuals. When Lubbock solicited friends to submit letters for the volumes, most sent business-related or nondescript missives. James's family in turn sent hand-transcribed copies of original letters, omitting any passages deemed too personal, controversial, or unflattering of James. The result became a two-volume collection of mostly professional correspondence and highly excised family letters.

Leon Edel's four-volume selection is the current standard edition of James's letters. The broad range of 1,092 letters accounts for roughly 10 percent of the total extant correspondence. The silent emendations of the Edel edition have been criticized by those who cite instances when entire passages of letters have been omitted (Horne 141). Subsequent editions have been published, including the letters between James and WILLIAM DEAN HOWELLS, James and EDITH WHARTON, James and THOMAS SERGEANT PERRY, and between Henry and WILLIAM JAMES (a three-volume collection). The first two volumes of *The Complete Letters of Henry James* are also in print. This inclusive plain-text edition presents deletions, overwriting, and insertions that James made during the compositional process.

SYNOPSIS

Henry James was a prolific letter writer. Although he encouraged recipients to burn his letters, 10,424 are extant as identified by Steve Jobe in his *Calendar of the Correspondence of Henry James* (http://jamescalendar.unl.edu). More than 3,000 letters have been published to date. James wrote to more than 1,000 correspondents, including Wharton, Isabella Stewart Gardner, JOHN SINGER SARGENT, Howells, H. G. WELLS, FANNY KEMBLE, and Émile Zola. The letters are scattered in various libraries; the largest collection (3,917) is held in the Houghton Library at Harvard University.

Henry James's first extant letter was written at an early, although undetermined, age. While living in NEW YORK from 1845 to 1855, he enclosed a postscript with a letter from his brother William to Eddie Van Winkle agreeing to join a proposed theater to which he "would like very much to belong" (*Complete Letters* I: 3). Subsequent letters of James's adolescence are addressed primarily to his boyhood friend Thomas Sergeant Perry, beginning when the James family travels abroad in 1859 to 1860. This correspondence reveals James's homesickness for the United States but also includes detailed accounts of his travel experience and anecdotes of the people whom he encountered. Of the German family with whom he was studying, James remarked, "I don't believe that between them they can muster, Germanlike, more than half a dozen teeth" (51). Returning to NEWPORT, his correspondence with Perry matures as the two debate notions of prejudice ("it is hard to know when we deceive or violate ourselves" [82]); discuss the writings of Taine, Feuillet, Cherbuliez, Sand, and Arnold; and forecast their own literary futures ("one of these days we shall have certain persons *on their knees*, imploring for contributions" [107]).

Early letters also document the beginning of James's professional writing. In 1864, he contacted Charles Eliot Norton, editor of the *North American Review*, regarding a review of Nassau Senior's *Essays on Fiction*. James's article was accepted, along with others for *Emily Chester*, *Azarian*, and *Lindisfarn Chase*, which were also published the same year. James also corresponded with William Conant Church and his brother, Francis Pharcellus Church, coeditors of the *Galaxy*, who published his first story, "A Day of Days," in 1866. Letters to the Churches convey an initial authorial control that James would practice throughout his career with editors and critics. He argues, "As for adding a paragraph I should strongly object to it. It doesn't seem to me necessary" (187). The letter firmly concludes by stating "the story closes in a more dramatic manner, to my apprehension, just as I have left it" (187).

Convincing his parents that travel was necessary for his health, education, and career, James embarked on a European tour in 1869. Letters during this period relate an aggressive sightseeing agenda. He frequently visited the National Gallery in London, met friends at Queen's Gate Terrace, and strolled through St. James's Park. James regularly attended dinner engagements with Victorian notables, although the letters show a certain modicum of modesty in his description of these encounters: "The dinner this evening is to be at the [Leslie] Stephen's. . . . I breakfasted yesterday at the Nortons along with Frederic Harrison and Professor Beesly—the politico-economists of the *Fortnightly Review*. . . . I was asked to dine to day at the N.'s with [John] Ruskin and John Morley, editor of the Fortnightly, but this dinner prevents" (248). When overcome by back pain and indigestion, he retreated to the spas of Malvern, summarizing the therapeutic day as "Breakfast at 8.30: Bath at noon. Another reactionary walk. Dinner at 2. 'Running' sitz-bath at 5. Walk number 3. Tea at seven. Bed early" (275). After recovering his good health, James traveled throughout the Continent, following the recommended routes for SWITZERLAND, Austria, Germany, and Italy, as outlined in the Baedeker and Murray tourist guides.

Although these letters were addressed to his parents, sister, or brother, they were commonly read aloud for the entire family. Following this pattern, James developed a lifelong practice of sharing letters within certain circles and an acute awareness that his letters would also be shared. It was not uncommon for James to navigate financial matters with his brother William, knowing the information would be read by his parents. Furthermore, William would sometimes relay parental appeals that Henry spend his money more conservatively. During this time, Henry also relied on William's cross-Atlantic medical advice regarding his intestinal problems and would signal when the letter was intended only for William. For example, in the April 8, 9, [1869] letter to William, James stresses, "Here my letter becomes *private* and unfit for the family circle" (274). Henry's sister, Alice, also proved to be an effective collaborator; attempting to persuade his parents to extend his yearlong trip, James writes to his sister, "I hope to be able, in walking, to get so much diversion and to save so much money that I may strike out freely at certain times and places. I already have distant visions of doing England in bits, next summer on foot" (*Complete* II: 86).

James returned to Europe in 1872 and was later joined by his sister, Alice, and their aunt, Catharine Walsh. The letters from this period echo James's extensive travel and serve as preliminary drafts for essays that would appear in the *Nation* and *Atlantic Monthly*. These letters, full of cultural and geographical descriptions, travel routes, and his discriminating observations, lent themselves to multiple uses. In a letter to his father, James relates:

> We sat out the service in the Cathedral—nestling, so to speak, in the old brown stalls of the choir—and heard Canon Kingsley preach. The service and the *mise en scène* were most agreeable but poor Kingsley is in the pulpit a decidedly weak brother. His discourse (on the Athanasian Creed) was, intellectually, flat and, sentimentally, boyish. (*Henry James Letters* I: 287)

A fuller description of this sequence appears in his July 1872 *Nation* article "A European Summer. I. Chester." Of the Kingsley sermon, James writes:

> Canon Kingsley's discourse was one more example of the familiar truth—not without its significance to minds zealous for the good old fashion of "making an effort"—that there is an odd link between large forms and small emanations. The sermon, beneath that triply consecrated vault, should have had a builded majesty. It had not; and I confess that a tender memory of ancient

obligations to the author of "Westward Ho!" and "Hypatia" forbids my saying more of it. (9)

Accompanying the ladies, writing letters, and submitting weekly articles proved exhausting, but these were necessary components in James's plan to extricate himself from parental constraints and maintain financial independence. Always concerned about economic resources, he asks his father, "*À propos* of *money* above, has the *Nation* ever sent you any cheques? I suppose not, or you would mention them. I can't as yet suspect you of secreting the gains of your toiling and loving child" (*Henry James Letters* I: 298).

Alice and Aunt Kate returned to CAMBRIDGE, freeing James to travel to Switzerland, Germany, and Italy during the next year. He continued a rigorous writing schedule, vowing to Howells, "Suffice it that I promise you some tall writing. My only fear is that it may turn out taller than broad" (444). Letters reveal that James does not spend the entire year working. Writing to his parents, Sarah Butler Wister, and Grace Norton, James details his new interest in horseback riding and advocates the advantages to his health: "the Campagna, with its great stretches of turf, its slopes and holes and ditches, being a capital place to acquire vigilance and firmness" (366). He takes riding lessons in Italy with Elizabeth Boott, Alice Bartlett, and Alice Mason (Sumner). When Boott is visiting the United States, James laments, "Rome is as yet very empty, and I hear of no one coming to chase away last winter's ghosts. So be it: I prefer the ghosts: I'm afraid even my rides will be ghostly" (419) (see ROME).

Letters note the dramatic increase in the number and intensity of James's literary and personal relationships: the diplomatic exchanges with *Tribune* editor Whitelaw Reid; the flattery of Isabella Stewart Gardner; the complicated friendship with Henry Adams; the wooing by publisher James Osgood; the sympathy toward Ivan Turgenev; the admiration for Émile Zola; and approbation for bibliophile Lord Richard Milnes Houghton, a frequent interlocutor for young artists, with whom James met regularly. He was also acquainted with Matthew Arnold, GEORGE ELIOT, Longfellow, William and Jane Morris, John Ruskin, William Wetmore Story, and Robert Browning.

During no other time in his life is James's career so fully recorded in letters as from 1876 to 1880. He learns how to navigate the professional terrains of publishing, to propose new novels, and to negotiate payment. Contacting rival PUBLISHERS, James suggests:

> The vision of a serial in Scribner does not, I may frankly say, aesthetically delight me; but it is the best thing I can do, so long as having a perpetual serial running has defined itself as a financial necessity for me. When my novels (if they ever do) bring me enough money to carry me over the intervals I shall be very glad to stick to the *Atlantic*. Or I would undertake to do this if I could simply have money down for my MS., leaving the Magazine to publish at its leisure. My novel is to be an *Americana*—the adventures in Europe of a female Newman, who of course equally triumphs over the insolent foreigner. (*Henry James Letters* II: 70–71)

Howells serialized *The American* in the *Atlantic Monthly*, and Macmillan published the novel. Success of the publication also brought criticism from his correspondents. The letter Elizabeth Boott wrote to James no longer exists, but its praising and questioning contents can be extricated from his jocular yet firm response to her:

> Generous, admirable, sublime you are, both of you, & I kiss the hem of your garments: that, namely, of Miss Bartlett's riding-habit, & of your (Miss Boott's) painting-blouse. Such readers are worth having—readers who really care what one does & who pay one the divine compliment of taking things hard. I will dedicate my next novel to both of you under the emblem of a mahl-stick & a riding whip intertwined. I feel, indeed, as if I had been rapped about the head with each of these instruments; but, as I say, the pleasure & honor were greater than the pain. Of course I hold you mortally wrong, & deem my dénoûement the only possible one. (*A Life in Letters* 91)

After the death of his parents in the early 1880s, James's sister, Alice, moves to London, thus decreasing his American connections. Correspondence with his brother William, Grace Norton, and Howells is habitual, but the focus of letter writing is redirected to his European associations, including MRS. MARY HUMPHRY WARD, EDMUND GOSSE, Lady Louisa Wolseley, and Henrietta Reubell. With Ward, James discusses her fiction writing—characteristic of his early exchanges with Howells—offering high praise in regard to character description and plot development:

> The whole book has inspired me with a very great awe, as a large, full picture of life, overflowing with experience, with atmosphere, with multitudinous touches and intentions of a kind I relish. The interest of any novel, in the last analysis, is as a view of the world, and your view is a great sweep on which I congratulate you. (*Henry James Letters* III: 236–237)

In correspondence with Gosse and Reubell, James exchanges pieces of gossip and literary criticism. In letters to Lady Wolseley, James cultivates a close friendship; he provides companionship while her husband travels on various military campaigns and often advises her on bookbindings:

> The said Fontaine is the biggest "swell," as a dealer in books, in Europe, & has *treasures* in the way of antiquities, rare copies, rare bindings &c, & I am sure that his shop would be worth your visit. I ought to mention that his *prices* are colossal, but for that reason it is *d'usage* to go & look, to again & again. Tell him frankly who you are & what you want. (*Dear Munificent Friends* 245)

In turn, Lady Wolselely is instrumental in brokering a half-truce between James and Violet Paget (Vernon Lee) after James is satirized in Paget's short story "Lady Tal." Learning of the publication, James writes to William Fullerton: "I believe (as I have been told,) the said Vernon has done something to me ('Lady Tal'?) but I don't know what it is and if I should know I shld. have to take upon myself the burden of 'caring' in some way or other established of men, or of women—and oh, I don't *care* to care (*Henry James Letters* III: 399). Through much cajoling on Lady Wolseley's part,

James sends an abrupt note seven years later to Paget: "I hold that we *shall* meet again—let us by all means positively do so; at some time of full convenience" (*Henry James Letters* IV: 155).

As James settles into European life, letters no longer reflect the interests of a tourist visiting unfamiliar terrains and meeting notable individuals; he instead details complicated friendships and new acquaintances. Traveling regularly to France and Italy, James sees Daniel and Ariana Curtis at the Palazzo Barbaro in VENICE, he visits the Bootts at Bellosguardo in FLORENCE, and also stays at the Palazzo Brichieri with his close friend CONSTANCE FENIMORE WOOLSON, the grandniece of James Fenimore Cooper. James wrote affectionately about her to his brother William, Francis and Elizabeth Boott, Grace Norton, and Florence Bell. Learning of Woolson's suicide in 1894, he grieves in a letter to Lady Margaret Brooke, "A close & valued friend of mine—a friend of many years with whom I was extremely intimate and to whom I was greatly attached (Miss Fenimore Woolson the American novelist, a singularly charming + distinguished woman,) died last Wednesday, in Venice, with dreadful attendant circumstances" (January 28, 1894). The typically articulate mourning letters James sent to his brother William, Charles Eliot Norton, Grace Norton, Elizabeth Gaskell Norton, Francis Boott, and Sarah Butler Wister when close friends or family members died are noticeably absent after Woolson's death. Instead, James grapples with a justification for her suicide. In a letter to Anna Grace Carter he writes:

Unquestionably she had become actively insane under the influence of her illness and her fever, but I seem to see, now, in the light of the event, how far that depression of spirits to which she was at all times so tragically liable had progressed in her mind, and what a morbid obsession it had become. Other signs and symptoms come to me which I didn't fully read at the time. She was intensely unhappy, by her natural disposition (her deafness greatly increased it,) and unhappy in a way that no one, I think, however much fighting, as it were, on her side—I mean even in the closest sympathy with her—could effectually or permanently combat. But she

had got much worse this winter—I now feel sure—and quite in spite of any external cause. (February 2, 1894)

As James entered the major phase of his writing career, he no longer entertained book ideas with longtime editor Howells but negotiated payments, through his agent James Pinker, with Scribner's, and Macmillan. Similarly, letters to fellow literary friends also assume a different tone. Casual self-effacement gradually replaced critical sensitivity. In a tone of diarylike introspection, he writes to Mary Ward about *The GOLDEN BOWL* (1904):

Likewise I think it heroic of you to plough through the *Golden Bowl* which nothing could have induced *me* to do if I hadn't been its author. The work has merit, but it's too long and the subject is pumped *too* dry, even; that is, the pump is too big for it (it isn't itself so big), and tends thereby to *usurp* space in it. I shall never again do anything so long-winded. I find, myself, as I go on, that I can't read new fiction, and am lost in wonder at the strange law that condemns me to write it—and to assume, to that extent, a reading of same *by* others—unlike myself! (*Henry James Letters* IV: 415)

James met Wharton in 1904, shortly after the publication of *The Golden Bowl*. Mutual interest in the literary profession accounted for the beginning of their friendship as did their mutual friendship with writer Paul Bourget and his wife Minnie (*Henry James and Edith Wharton Letters* 2). Before meeting formally, Wharton and James exchanged letters, starting with her congratulatory note to him prior to the opening of *Guy Domville* in 1895. Their early correspondence resembles one between the master and an apprentice, and Wharton affectionately addressed James as "Cher Maître," or "Dear Master," in her letters to him. He advised her to write from her own societal experience:

I mean I value, I egg you on in, your study of the American life that surrounds you. Let yourself go in it and *at* it—it's an untouched field, really: the folk who try, over there, don't come within miles of any civilized, however superficially, any "evolved" life. And use to the full your remarkable ironic and valeric gift; they form a most valuable, (I hold,) and beneficent engine. (*Henry James Letters* IV: 171)

Within the next year, James became more emphatic: "All the same DO NEW YORK! The 1st-hand account is precious" (*Henry James and Edith Wharton Letters* 34). Following James's advice, Wharton wrote *The House of Mirth*.

Their 20-year friendship is recorded in the 173 extant letters to Wharton. James introduced Wharton to English society, and Wharton became the witty, intellectual friend he missed after Woolson's death. They discussed their shared circle of American friends (including Grace and Sara Norton, Walter Berry, and HOWARD STURGIS) and determined how to extricate MORTON FULLERTON from a blackmail scheme. Letters to Wharton continued even as James was on his deathbed; his secretary THEODORA BOSANQUET wrote to Wharton, keeping her informed of James's health status.

The late letters of James's life (1914–1915) are dominated by the devastation of WORLD WAR I. To lifelong friend and author Rhoda Broughton, James writes, "Black and hideous to me is the tragedy that gathers, and I'm sick beyond cure to have lived on to see it. You and I, the ornaments of our generation, should have been spared this wreck of our belief that through the long years we had seen civilization grow and the worst become impossible. . . . I avert my face from the monstrous scene!" (*Henry James Letters* IV: 713). Recipients such as Brander Matthews, Rhoda Broughton, Lilla Cabot Perry, Edmund Gosse, Margaret Mary James (Peggy), Harry James, Frederic Harrison, Clare Sheridan, Hugh Walpole, Walter Berry, even his agent James Pinker cannot escape James's growing outrage. Frustrated by the United States's delayed response to the war, he writes to American friend Lilla Cabot:

> I could wish the U.S. government were not, as in this last note, buttering so with assurances of its "friendship" the power that is perpetrating all the dastardly barbarities piled up now by Germany to her credit—the Zeppelins are all over the place even as I write, with their peculiarly unerring instinct for poor old women and young children. That, on the whole, is the

heaviest strain to bear—the irrepressible amiability of Mr. Wilson in conditions that call for it so little. (758)

To other recipients, James relates his visits to the combat hospital and his admiration for Wharton's wartime charitable work.

Disconcerted with the United States, James became a British subject on July 26, 1915. Anticipating the reaction of the American public, James wrote to artist John Singer Sargent:

> Yes, I daresay many Americans *will* be shocked at my "step"; so many of them appear in these days to be shocked at everything that is not a reiterated blandishment and slobberation of Germany, with recalls of ancient "amity" and that sort of thing, by our Government. I waited long months, watch in hand, for the latter to show some sign of intermitting these amiabilities to such an enemy—the very smallest would have sufficed for me to throw myself back upon it. But it seemed never to come, and the misrepresentation of *my* attitude becoming at last to me a thing no longer to be borne, I took action myself. It would really have been *so* easy to the U.S. to have "kept" (if they had cared to!). (774)

James is not so forthcoming with fellow American Wharton. Predicting her scathing reaction, James writes to Wharton on the day he was granted citizenship; he neglects to mention this event to Wharton.

In regard to the literal look of James's handwriting, it appears round and legible at first glance. Generally, the letters contain few misspellings, omissions, or other errors, but they were not infrequently misread. The long *ess* (now written as *ss*) was easily confused for a *p* as revealed in the transcription of the nonextant letter to Mary Holton James, dated July 8, 1873: "Here is a little Roman crop which I hope will help you to think of me sometimes until the day comes when we may know each other and I can speak for myself." James actually sent his sister-in-law a cross that she wore on a necklace. James's contemporaries also struggled with his handwriting; editors often misread handwritten emendations. In a letter to William, James reports an inaccuracy in a *Nation* article: "I got a nation with my letter from Pisa &c. What do you think of this for a misprint:—'idle vistas and melancholy nooks'—*'idle sisters and melancholy monks!!'* In the article on *Siena* the sense of two or three good sentences was also ruined" (*Henry James Letters* I: 456). Editors had corrected the text in the subsequent publishing of *Transatlantic Sketches* to read "How grass-grown it seemed, how drowsy, how full of idle vistas and melancholy nooks!" (*Transatlantic* 326). Throughout his epistolary life, French, Italian, and German phrases appear regularly. Slowed by rheumatism, James began dictating letters to a typist in 1896 while still handwriting the larger share of his correspondence. The dictated letters often include additional handwritten insertions or comments to the recipients that James was not willing to share with the typist.

FURTHER READING

Horne, Philip. "The Editing of Henry James's Letters." *Cambridge Quarterly* 15, no. 2 (1986): 126–141.

James, Henry. *The Complete Letters of Henry James, 1855–1872.* Edited by Pierre Walker and Greg Zacharias. 2 vols. Lincoln: University of Nebraska Press, 2007.

———. *The Correspondence of Henry James and Henry Adams: 1877–1914.* Edited by George Monteiro. Baton Rouge: Louisiana State University Press, 1992.

———. *The Correspondence of Henry James and the House of Macmillan: 1877–1914.* Edited by Rayburn S. Moore. Baton Rouge: Louisiana State University Press, 1993.

———. *Dear Munificent Friends: Henry James's Letters to Four Women.* Edited by Susan Gunter. Ann Arbor: University of Michigan Press, 1999.

———. *Dearly Beloved Friends: Henry James's Letters to Younger Men.* Edited by Susan Gunter and Steven Jobe. Ann Arbor: University of Michigan Press, 2001.

———. "A European Summer. I. Chester." *Nation* 15 (July 4, 1872): 7–9.

———. *Henry James: A Life in Letters.* Edited by Philip Horne. New York: Viking, 1999.

———. *Henry James and Edith Wharton Letters: 1900–1915.* Edited by Lyall H. Powers. New York: Scribner's, 1990.

———. *Henry James and John Hay: A Record of a Friendship.* Edited by George Monteiro. Providence, R.I.: Brown University Press, 1963.

———. *Henry James Letters.* Edited by Leon Edel. 4 vols. Cambridge, Mass.: Harvard University Press, 1974–84.

———. "Letter to Anna Grace Carter." February 2, 1913. University of Virginia, MSS 6251-AC (Box 2, #108).

———. "Letter to Lady Margaret Alice Lili de Windt, Brooke Ranee of Sarawak." January 28, 1894. Columbia University, Spec. MsColl: James, H.

———. "Letter to Mary Holton James" July 8, 1873. Edel Archive.

———. *Letters, Fictions, Lives: Henry James and William Dean Howells.* Edited by Michael Anesko. New York: Oxford University Press, 1997

———. *The Letters of Henry James.* 2 vols. Edited by Percy Lubbock. London: Macmillan, 1920.

———. *Selected Letters of Henry James to Edmund Gosse, 1882–1915: A Literary Friendship.* Edited by Rayburn S. Moore. Baton Rouge: Louisiana State University Press, 1988.

———. *Thomas Sergeant Perry: A Biography and Letters to Perry from William, Henry, and Garth Wilkinson James.* Edited by Virginia Harlow. Durham, N.C.: Duke University Press, 1950.

———. *Transatlantic Sketches.* Boston: Osgood, 1875.

James, William. *The Correspondence of William James.* Vols. 1–3. Edited by Ignas K. Skrupskelis and Elizabeth M. Berkeley. Charlottesville: University Press of Virginia, 1992–1994.

Jobe, Steven. *A Calendar of the Letters of Henry James.* Lincoln: University of Nebraska Press. Available online. URL: http://jamescalendar.unl.edu.

Maher, Jane. *Biography of Broken Fortunes.* New York: Archon, 1986.

Tara Knapp, *Creighton University*

criticism

Henry James published his first critical essay, a review of Nassau W. Senior's *Essays on Fiction*, in October 1864. "We opened this work with the hope of finding a general survey of the nature and principles of the subject of which it professes to treat," he writes. "We had long regretted the absence of any critical treatise upon fiction" (*LC* I: 1,196). From that moment until his death 52 years later, James would answer his own call.

Today James is best known for his creative work. But he is also considered one of the most important and influential English-language literary critics of his era. He argued for fiction to be regarded as a fine art in an era when the novel was routinely dismissed as secondary. He convincingly established the connections between continental realism and its younger Anglo-American counterparts. As the print media of the Gilded Age exploded all around him, James labored to position the literary artist and the critic in a rapidly expanding marketplace in meaningful ways. And, finally, he presented a theory of artistic composition and production that profoundly altered how scholars and authors discuss the creative practice of writing.

Certain of James's critical works, such as "The ART OF FICTION" or the PREFACES TO THE NEW YORK EDITION, have received generous attention from literary scholars. The rest of them, however, has not received nearly as much attention. The prime reason for this is ease of access. Most of James's criticism was published in journals and magazines of the period, and a good portion of it was unsigned (a common practice in the 19th century). James collected and reprinted only a fraction of his criticism during his lifetime. The major volumes of literary criticism published during James's lifetime are *French Poets and Novelists* (1878), *Partial Portraits* (1888), *Essays in London and Elsewhere* (1893), and *Notes on Novelists* (1914). Other important works include HAWTHORNE (1879) and the prefaces to the New York Edition (1907–09), discussed elsewhere in this study. In short, the bulk of this work was unread and uncollected for most of the 20th century. This lapse was corrected in 1984, when Leon Edel and Mark Wilson published their two-volume edition of James's collected literary criticism, a great boon to readers. Perhaps a less daunting starting point for newcomers is James E. Miller's edited selection, *Theory of Fiction: Henry James*. To date, four full-length scholarly studies of the literary criticism have been published: Morris

Roberts, *Henry James's Criticism* (1929); Sarah B. Daugherty, *The Literary Criticism of Henry James* (1981); Vivien Jones, *James the Critic* (1985); and Rob Davidson, *The Master and the Dean: The Literary Criticism of Henry James and William Dean Howells* (2005) (see WILLIAM DEAN HOWELLS).

The aims and purposes of James's criticism were diverse and complex. Generally speaking, he abhorred abstract treatises on art; such essays as "The Art of Fiction" (1884) or "The Science of Criticism" (1891) while extremely important, are rare. Rather, James preferred to select a "case"— usually a single author or text—and to use it as the starting point for an extended consideration of a particular series of questions. And so his essays on George Sand, Ivan Turgenev, and Honoré de Balzac (among others) contain his most cogent literary criticism. Occasionally, James's essays appear to stray from their purported subject into related if distinctly different areas. The "Introduction to *The Tempest*" has less to do with Shakespeare's final play than it does with broader questions about the nature of an author's relation to the text and its reader; an essay on Robert Browning, "The Novel in *The Ring and the Book*," can be read as a meditation on the nature of artistic inspiration. The reader of James's criticism learns to appreciate such diversions, as they often constitute his best work.

It is important to put James's criticism in context with that of his contemporaries. First, English literary criticism of the late 19th century was, broadly speaking, a practical exercise designed to test a given work against a given set of a priori aesthetic or moral codes. Consequently, the work of a controversial author like Émile Zola might be dismissed as obscene solely on the basis of the chosen subject matter (e.g., prostitutes, thieves, and drunkards). Second, the novel itself was not considered one of the finer arts; rather, it was considered by many to be a lower art, a kind of vulgar entertainment (Jones 108–161). James, a careful student of avant-garde literature and aesthetic theory, worked against these prejudices. Much of his criticism—particularly his earliest work—is a response, direct or indirect, to the insular school of English critics that dominated his era. Important essays such as "The Art of Fiction" would in time fundamentally reconfigure the conversation concerning the state of the novel in Britain and the United States. Among his fellow American critics, only William Dean Howells could rival James for the scope, the importance, and the influence of his work.

The following examines a selection of important themes and concepts that James returned to frequently in his criticism: the role of the critic in the literary marketplace of the late 19th and early 20th centuries; French realism and the question of propriety in fiction; the state of the novel and prose aesthetics; contemporary British literature; and James's thoughts on American literature and America as a literary subject.

DEFINING THE CRITIC

American literary society before the CIVIL WAR was primarily a salon culture, the domain of an intellectual aristocracy firmly rooted in New England. All of that changed after the Civil War. The country's population exploded in the late 19th century; Americans were increasingly literate, had more disposable income for books and magazines, and had more leisure time for reading than at any prior moment in the nation's history. The rapid growth of the literary marketplace during the Gilded Age brought many changes to the world of publishing, and these changes presented professional, high-minded literary artists such as Henry James with new audiences—and new challenges.

One such challenge was to define the role of the literary critic in the new print media culture. In the late 19th century, the practices of literary criticism and book reviewing were not as clearly distinguished from each other as they are today. Criticism was typically published in newspapers and magazines intended to reach a general audience. In the United States, it was in such forums as *Harper's, Atlantic Monthly,* and *North American Review* that much of the century's literary debate was enacted. Henry James entered the discussion early, publishing his first book review at the age of 21.

One of James's earliest reviews concerned Harriet Elizabeth Prescott Spofford's novel *Azarian* (1864). James is not subtle in his assessment. Spofford possesses a "venturesome, unprincipled literary spirit, defiant alike of wisdom and taste." He

proceeds to catalog the author's numerous "aberrations of taste," chief among them a cast of shallow, overcontrolled characters—all style and no substance. "She fingers her puppets to death," he intones. "This bad habit of Miss Prescott's is more than an offense against art. Nature herself resents it." In the second half of the review, James lectures his readers on the virtues of "the famous realistic system." Rather than employing idealized, flat caricatures, the realist author presents complex, emotive characters who resonate with verisimilitude. James insists that the novel's "foremost claim to merit . . . is its *truth*," and offers the example of Honoré de Balzac, whose work "is literally real: he presents objects as they are. The scene and persons of his drama are minutely described." What Balzac chooses to describe is always somehow linked to the dramatic action of the story: "[T]hese things are all described *only in so far as they bear upon the action,* and not in the least for themselves." In his conclusion, James playfully pleads with Spofford to abandon her "flimsy conceptions" and "verbal superlatives." Rather, "We would earnestly exhort Miss Prescott to be *real,* to be true to something" (*LC* I: 603, 606–608, 612).

This review exemplifies James's earliest critical practice. Adamant about his preferences, he is unafraid to deliver a sermon. Occasionally, he was harsh and overly dismissive; two noteworthy instances are James's 1865 reviews of Walt Whitman's *Drum-Taps* (*LC* I: 629–634) and Charles Dickens's *Our Mutual Friend* (*LC* I: 853–858). But he would quickly develop a cooler, more judicious critical stance, partly in response to the example of certain European critics. One of them was the English poet and critic Matthew Arnold. In an 1865 review of Arnold's *Essays in Criticism*, James praises the Englishman's "sensitive and generous" spirit and his "delicate perceptions." The function of criticism, as Arnold exemplifies it, "is simply to get at the best thought which is current,—to see things in themselves as they are,—to be disinterested" (*LC* I: 712–713, 715). In Arnold, James found a worthy role model, a keenly sensitive reader unafraid to include personal, unique thoughts and feelings on the page. Above all, he found in Arnold the model of a "disinterested" critic—that is, one who abhorred a priori judgment, formulating an opinion only after prolonged and careful consideration of the work in question. It was a style that would profoundly shape the young Henry James.

The same held true for certain French literary critics, one of the more influential models being Edmond Schérer. Other important French models for James include Charles Augustin Sainte-Beuve (see James's review of Taine's *History of English Literature, LC* II: 841–848) and Francisque Sarcey (see "The Théatre Français," reprinted in *French Poets and Novelists,* 316–344, and *The Scenic Art,* 68–91). In an 1865 study, James finds in Schérer "plenty of theories, but no theory. We find—and this is the highest praise, it seems to us, that we can give a critic—none but a moral unity: that is, the author is a liberal." James continues:

> The age surely presents no finer spectacle than that of a mind liberal after this fashion; not from a brutal impatience of order, but from experience, from reflection, seriously, intelligently, having known, relished, and appropriated the many virtues of conservatism; a mind inquisitive of truth and of knowledge, accessible on all sides, unprejudiced, desirous above all things to examine directly, fearless of reputed errors, but merciless to error when proved, tolerant of dissent, respectful of sincerity, content neither to reason on matters of feeling nor to sentimentalize on matters of reason, equitable, dispassionate, sympathetic. M. Schérer is a solid embodiment of Mr. Matthew Arnold's ideal critic. (*LC* II: 803)

James sees in Schérer—as he saw in Arnold—a deep intellectual integrity, a willingness to forgo prefigured truths, aesthetic standards, and moral judgments, relying instead on his own sensibilities and judging each work on a case-by-case basis. In this deep appreciation, there is a developing sense of what James thought a literary critic could and should do. Like many critics of his era, James initially saw the role of the critic as secondary, or subservient to the literary artist. That is, it was the critic's job to respond to the initial, or primary, effort of the artist. As he matured, James would struggle to find creative ways to establish the authority and autonomy of the critic within this otherwise restrictive paradigm. James writes:

> Of all men who deal with ideas, the critic is essentially the least independent; it behooves him, therefore, to claim the utmost possible incidental or extrinsic freedom. His subject and his stand-point are limited beforehand. He is in the nature of his function *opposed* to his author, and his position, therefore, depends upon that which his author has taken. If, in addition to his natural and proper servitude to his subject, he is shackled with a further servitude, outside of his subject, he works at a ridiculous disadvantage. This outer servitude may either be to a principle, a theory, a doctrine, a dogma, or it may be to a party; and it is against this latter form of subordination, as most frequent in his own country, that Mr. Arnold more especially protests. But as a critic, quite as much as any other writer, must have what M. Schérer calls an inspiration of his own, must possess a *unit* of sincerity and consistency, he finds it in his conscience. It is on this basis that he preserves his individuality, or, if you like, his self-respect. (*LC* II: 804)

In this passage one finds a clear articulation of James's earliest conception of the critic's role in relation to the artist: the critic as subservient to the artist, and limited in the sense that all commentary must be directed at the work in question. Schérer's "independence" and "individuality" are marked by his ability to write criticism that, while still focused on the primary text in question, nevertheless demonstrates a kind of unique, creative freedom. Schérer resists received or prefigured theories of literature, relying instead on his own original insights. Schérer is free to think and to feel, to articulate new ideas in response to new works of art. Inspired by Schérer's example, James struggles to articulate how a critic can meet his practical obligations without compromising his intellectual freedom. He is beginning to sense that the critical act itself may be akin to the creative act: an imaginative opportunity for a fine mind to express itself.

That said, James believed there were certain principles the critic must observe. First among them was the idea that one ought to judge a work of art on its own terms, rather than with some prefigured set of artistic standards. This is a central idea in "The Art of Fiction" (1884), but James continued to address the topic throughout his career. In an 1888 essay on Guy de Maupassant, James argues that what is most important in a work of fiction is the quality of the artist's "impression," the total articulation of a writer's subject, style, and form. "The value of the artist resides in the clearness with which he gives forth [his] impression. His particular organism constitutes a *case*, and the critic is intelligent in proportion as he apprehends and enters into that case. To quarrel with it because it is not another, which it could not possibly be without a wholly different outfit, . . . [would be] a deplorable waste of time" (*LC* II: 524). It is worth noting that James quotes liberally from Maupassant's writings on the art of fiction in this essay; close study confirms that Maupassant's theories on fiction fundamentally shaped James's views (Jones 82–92). In essence, James repeats the crucial point he put forward in "The Art of Fiction": that a critic must grant the author his *donnée*, or subject, and restrict his evaluation to the quality of execution. Quarreling over a given subject, why an author chose to depict this or that, is beside the point. The only salient question is how fully realized that subject is on the page, how distinct the "impression." It is by means of this argument that James successfully sidestepped the narrow English method of applying rigid a priori moral standards to a book, often judging it on the basis of content rather than quality of execution.

James clarified his conception of the critic's role in his essay "The Science of Criticism" (1891). James begins by noting the prodigious flood of book reviewers in the popular press: "If literary criticism may be said to flourish among us at all, it certainly flourishes immensely, for it flows through the periodical press like a river that has burst its dikes." This gives James cause for worry. In his opinion, most reviewers lack intellectual depth or rigor. "The vulgarity, the crudity, the stupidity" of these amateurs puts a sophisticated, professional critic in a sour mood. At stake is the very nature of art itself. "Literature lives essentially," James writes, "in the sacred depths of its being, upon example, upon perfection wrought; that, like other sensitive organisms, it is highly susceptible of demoralization, and that nothing is better calculated than irresponsible pedagogy to make it close its ears and lips" (*LC* I: 95–97). Here James articulates a delicate, symbiotic relationship between the artist and the critic: The artist relies on the critic for direction and guidance, for inspiration and counsel. As depicted by James, the mass-market reviewer, so crass and untutored, risks doing more harm than good to the "sensitive organism" that is art.

James proposes that the art of criticism is every bit as difficult as art itself: "It is in reality the most complicated and the most particular" of endeavors, he writes. The finest critics are "absolutely rare" and offer a gift "inestimably precious and beautiful." The true critic is "the real helper of the artist, a torch-bearing outrider, the interpreter, the brother." Indeed, "There is something sacrificial in his function. . . . To lend himself, to project himself and steep himself, to feel and feel till he understands, and to understand so well that he can say, to have perception at the pitch of passion" are all signal qualities of this ideal critic (*LC* I: 97–98). James depicts the artist and the critic in a quasi-feudalistic paradigm akin to that of a lord and his knight: The critic is immensely powerful, a person of the highest standards, but always serving the aim and mission of the lord of the house, the creative writer. Whereas he has not exactly emancipated his critic from bondage, James has significantly revised the critic's role, arguing that whereas the critic must always labor within a limited playing field of the work in question, there is within that framework the freedom to feel and to say. He expects the critic, like the artist depicted in "The Art of Fiction," to express a direct and personal vision. In short, James has configured the critic as an artist in his own right, albeit one with certain important restrictions. More important, he has explained the delicate, dynamic interrelationship between criticism and literary art. Art, that "sensitive organism," can be helped or hindered by criticism; in the worst case, poorly executed criticism can "kill" it.

In "The Science of Criticism," James offers a plea for the highest standards in both art and criticism for the mutual health of both disciplines. Underlying the exercise is his awareness of a growing body of readers in need of guidance and instruction; great artists must produce their great art, and great critics are needed to interpret and position that art in the marketplace. In a sense, this is one key motivation behind the prefaces to the New York Edition; building on some of these ideas, James took the unusual step of writing a book about himself, as it were, in an effort to reintroduce his work to a new generation of readers. James's writings on the nature and function of the literary critic were always, to some extent, an effort to develop his own readership. That is, James considered himself to be an ideal critic—sensitive, intelligent, liberal, and so forth. And while he wanted to be valued and respected for these qualities, his larger aim and purpose was essentially didactic: He wanted to create a readership with keen taste and sensitivities, a readership inclined to appreciate his own particular brand of fiction. This impulse is explicitly articulated in the prefaces to the New York Edition, but it is implicitly present in much of his earlier criticism too. With characteristic prescience, James understood that audiences are made, not found, and he used his literary criticism in support of that mission.

FRENCH REALISM AND THE QUESTION OF PROPRIETY

No writers were more important to Henry James than the French. Gustave Flaubert, Guy de Maupassant, Émile Zola, George Sand, and above all, Honoré de Balzac represented in many ways the best of contemporary literature. But the French also tested James's scruples as a reader, for he often found their subject matter distasteful—poverty, drunkenness, prostitution, adultery, and so forth. Either way, the French were central to James's thinking on questions of aesthetics and morality in literature.

For James, morality in fiction had less to do with rules of behavior or didacticism than with questions of execution and form in art—a decidedly French idea. It was in Flaubert's PARIS salon that James learned "that art and morality are two perfectly different things, and that the former has no more to do with the latter than it has with astronomy or embryology. The only duty of a novel was to be well written; that merit included every other of which it was capable" (*LC* II: 1,014). It was a lesson taken dearly to heart.

Flaubert was an extremely important figure to James, and *Madame Bovary* (1857) would always be an important book. To the English, and to some of the French, the novel was considered shocking for two reasons. First, for its storyline: A wife and mother who, drowning in romantic illusions, abandons her family for a pair of lovers who, in turn, abandon her. The second and larger offense, however, concerned Flaubert's seemingly objective, nonjudgmental tone, which some readers mistook for tacit acceptance of Emma Bovary's behavior. James, following his own critical dictum, took the book first on its own terms. Acknowledging the "sufficiently vulgar elements" of the novel, he nevertheless considers it "a great work, and capable really of being applied to educational purposes." Essentially, the novel would teach by indirection, by showing the young what not to do. But that is not its chief virtue. That would be the novel's form, its overall quality of artistic execution. "The form is in *itself* as interesting, as active, as much of the essence of the subject as the idea. . . . The work is a classic because the thing, such as it is, is ideally *done,* and because it shows that in such doing eternal beauty may dwell" (*LC* II: 290, 325). *Madame Bovary* would always be a prime example of French realism for James, but not because Flaubert dared to write of "vulgar" topics (see ROMANCE/REALISM/NATURALISM). Rather, the novel was a classic because it was so exquisitely executed.

The same line of thinking illuminates James's important 1888 essay on Guy de Maupassant. James finds Maupassant's subject matter distasteful. "If he is a master of his art," James writes, then "it is discouraging to find what low views are compatible with mastery." Nevertheless, Maupassant is "a writer with whom it [is] impossible not to reckon." To ignore him because he is "vulgar" would be a gross mistake. In his best work, Maupassant's mastery of form demands close examination. There is an "essential hardness" and clarity in Maupassant's vision; his work is forceful, compelling, and ultimately convincing because it expresses a unique, personal truth, distinct from that of any other writer (*LC* II: 547, 522).

It is important to remember that James was almost always directing his criticism to an English-speaking audience, an audience that had very particular tastes. Unlike the French, 19th-century English authors avoided frank treatment of sexual matters (see SEXUALITY). James saw this as both a blessing and a curse. "It may be said that our English system is a good thing for virgins and boys," he writes in 1880, "and a bad thing for the novel itself, when the novel is . . . considered as a composition that treats of life at large and helps us to *know*" (*LC* II: 869). James saw this cultural bias as a limitation on the progress of English literature. In an 1899 essay on "The Future of the Novel," he notes that the English had, to that point, always wanted a novel to be "safe" for any reader, young or old. Such restrictions on content are dangerous, he warns. "By what [the novel] shall decide to do in respect to the 'young' the great prose fable will, from any serious point of view, practically see itself stand or fall." Interestingly, James himself could never cross that line in his own fiction, nor could he wish that the history of English literature had been anything other than what it was. Acknowledging that "there is an immense omission in our fiction," he nevertheless prefers to take Dickens, Scott, and the giants of an earlier era "as they are." In a noteworthy conclusion, he suggests that the next generation of writers, and in particular the women of that generation, might revolutionize the English novel: It is they who will "smash with final resonance the window all this time most superstitiously closed" (*LC* I: 107–109).

Despite his relatively liberal appreciation for the French, James often found them testing the limits of good taste. Nevertheless, he was prone to reconsider his own opinions—and sometimes to reverse them. In 1876, a young James accuses Émile Zola of "brutal indecency," lamenting not only the Frenchman's focus on "the unclean" but also the manner of presentation: "[H]e utters his crudities with an air of bravado which makes them doubly intolerable." Four years later, the frustration is still present: "On what authority does M. Zola represent nature

to us as a combination of the cesspool and the house of prostitution?" James asks. "Never surely was any other artist so dirty as M. Zola!" The crucial difference in 1880 is that James wants to reconsider the grounds for his dissatisfaction. "Zola's attempt is an extremely fine one," he writes, "it deserves a great deal of respect and deference . . . we could, at a pinch, go a long way with it without quarreling." James struggles to articulate a middle ground. "Reality is the object of M. Zola's efforts, and it is because we agree with him in appreciating it highly that we protest against its being discredited." In other words, James recognizes and respects Zola as a fellow realist writer; he cannot base his critique solely on aesthetic grounds. The theory is pure. Rather, James will examine how Zola uses (or debases) that theory; the author's chosen subject cannot be the matter in dispute: "[T]he thing remains always a question of taste," James observes, anticipating a point he would soon make in "The Art of Fiction." Rather, he continues, "the matter reduces itself to a question of application" and Zola, "allied to the impure," is clearly found wanting (*LC* II: 861, 866–868). James wants to praise Zola as a realist but cannot move past an essential dislike for the subject matter.

James goes even further in his final essay on Zola, published in 1903. The controversial author, who "had appeared for so long to fail us," now presents a "new impression . . . a *case*." In fact, James humbly concedes, Zola "was always there to be had, but we ourselves [had to] throw off an oblivion, an indifference for which there are plenty of excuses." He now understands that if Zola chose to examine only a selected aspect of human experience, he nevertheless managed to do so with great force and depth. James likens the novelist to a harp player who, despite having an array of strings available for making music, chooses to "throw himself on the strings he might thump with effect, and . . . work them, as our phrase is, for all they [are] worth." In short, it is a question of the novelist selecting his material and then completely immersing himself in it—the Jamesian definition of creative success. Anything less would only have weakened the affair: "[W]ho cannot see to-day how much a milder infusion of it would have told against the close embrace of the subject aimed at?" James is not quite willing to grant Zola everything; Zola's best work is forceful and convincing, but when it fails it fails due to a lack of taste (*LC* II: 871, 879–880, 888). Despite these reservations, James has essentially come full circle. The "dirty" Frenchman who initially struck James as "intolerable" was, 27 years later, a "case" of the highest order. The 1903 essay on Zola is perhaps the quintessential Jamesian exercise: The critic essentially grants the author his chosen subject, or *donnée*, restricting his analysis only to matters of execution. It was as much as James could ever hope to give another author, and it was certainly what he wished from his own readers.

PROSE AESTHETICS AND THE STATE OF THE NOVEL

James was an early proponent of realism in Anglo-American literature. Along with his friend and fellow critic William Dean Howells, James traced the connections between precedent-setting European authors and their English-speaking counterparts. In the process, he clarified and championed several key tenets of the realist aesthetic. Some of James's most important early work on these questions concerned George Sand, Ivan Turgenev, and Honoré de Balzac.

Questions of form and character in the novels of George Sand were, for a young James, a kind of measuring stick. "Her novels have a great many faults," he writes in 1876. "They lack three or four qualities which the realistic novel of the last thirty or forty years, with its great successes, has taught us to consider indispensable. They are not exact nor probable; they contain few living figures; they produce a limited amount of illusion. . . . Her people are usually only very picturesque, very voluble, and very 'high-toned' shadows." Furthermore, Sand's didacticism is the product of "a decidedly superficial moralist." A year later, James crystallizes his own developing prose aesthetic when he observes that "It has been said that what makes a book a classic is its style. We should modify this, and instead of style say *form*. Madame Sand's novels have plenty of style, but they have no form" (*LC* II: 706–707, 730). In conclusion, James finds Sand an important but deeply flawed novelist whose overoptimistic

didacticism, shallow characters, and lack of form relegate her to the second tier of literary achievement. It should be noted that, despite the reservations noted here, James found many strengths in Sand (see Daugherty 88–94 and Jones 67–74).

In Turgenev, James found a kind of counterpoint to Sand. Turgenev offers "a view of the great spectacle of human life more general, more impartial, more unreservedly intelligent, than that of any novelist we know." In his fiction, character is paramount: "Our author *feels* the Russian character intensely." More important, Turgenev "has an eye for all our passions, and a deeply sympathetic sense of the wonderful complexity of our souls." The aim of his work is "that of finding an incident, a person, a situation, *morally* interesting" (*LC* II: 972–973, 975). Turgenev manages to combine deep character with penetrating moral analysis and exquisite form—a genuinely "moral" example in every Jamesian sense of the term.

But when it comes to the ultimate power and force of the novel, no author was more important to James than Honoré de Balzac. Characteristically, James found much to praise and to blame. In a landmark 1875 essay, he notes that Balzac was "morally and intellectually . . . superficial. . . . The moral, the intellectual atmosphere of his genius is extraordinarily gross and turbid; it is no wonder that the flower of truth does not bloom in it. . . . He had no natural sense of morality, and this we cannot help thinking a serious fault in a novelist" (*LC* II: 47). But these reservations are dwarfed by Balzac's strengths, which include both a broad social scope and minute attention to detail. In *La comédie humaine,* James notes, Balzac attempted "to illustrate by a tale or a group of tales every phase of French life and manners during the first half of the nineteenth century." This required an "encyclopaedic" knowledge of French society, but then "Balzac's strongest side is his grasp of actual facts. . . . His accuracy, so far as we can measure it, is extraordinary" (39–40). Balzac conveys a "mighty passion for *things*—for material objects, for furniture, upholstery, bricks and mortar," and his attention to place in fiction is unparalleled: "The place in which an event occurred was in his view of equal moment with the event itself; it was part of the action; it was not a thing to take or to leave, or to be vaguely and gracefully indicated; it imposed itself; it had a part to play; it needed to be made as definite as anything else" (48–50). For James, Balzac was a writer of paradox: He could be both grand and crude; he lacked a certain charm or intellectual depth, but he more than made up for it in the sheer force and power of his work. "Our last word about him is that he had incomparable power," James concludes (68).

Many consider "The Lesson of Balzac," written for a 1905 lecture tour of the United States, one of James's finest efforts. Much of the essay is a loving homage to an old mentor. From Balzac, James learned "more of the lessons of the engaging mystery of fiction than from any one else." One such teaching is that "The Poet is most the Poet when he is preponderantly lyrical, when he speaks, laughing or crying, most directly from his individual heart, which throbs under the impressions of life. It is not the *image* of life that he thus expresses, so much as life itself, in its sources—so much as his own intimate, essential states and feelings" (LC II: 121). This idea—a revision of the "direct, personal vision" called for in "The Art of Fiction"—is a fundamental Jamesian tenet. The power of the individual vision, the unique aesthetic projection, is the fundamental quality of literary achievement. "It is a question," James argues, "of *penetrating* into a subject." He expresses his wonder, indeed his "envy" (127–128) that Balzac was able to examine, to assimilate, to penetrate such a wide range of data, subjects, and characters in his fiction. "The mystic process of the crucible, the transformation of the material under aesthetic heat" is how James describes the conversion of such raw material into art. In Balzac, the transformation is "intenser . . . completer, and also finer" than anywhere else, and this is a vital point, for "When saturation fails no other presence really avails." In Balzac, "the fusion of all the elements of the picture . . . is complete—of what people are with what they do, of what they do with what they are, of the action with the agents, of the medium with the action, of all the parts of the drama with each other" (130–131, 135). A late-period reconsideration of an important early influence, "The

Lesson of Balzac" confirms that many of James's mature aesthetic stances date back to his earliest criticism.

BRITISH VIEWPOINTS

James was also a careful student of British literature. Characteristically, he saw in its authors much to praise and to condemn. The work of GEORGE ELIOT and Anthony Trollope are noteworthy in this regard. In the final analysis, both writers stood central in James's conception of English realism (see ROMANCE/REALISM/NATURALISM).

Reviewing George Eliot's novel *Felix Holt* in 1866, James labels it the product "of a secondary thinker and an incomplete artist." James found that Eliot's story lines are baggy and mismanaged, with secondary characters enjoying a disproportionate amount of attention in a novel; furthermore, Eliot is guilty of a kind of excess optimism—or at least of avoiding a truly comprehensive account of her chosen milieu, the "average humanity" (i.e., the lower and middle classes) of England: "There are no pictures of vice or poverty or squalor. There are no rags, no gin, no brutal passions. That average humanity which she favors is very *borné* [limited] in intellect, but very genial in heart." Despite these reservations, James is fond of Eliot's work and sees in it many worthy qualities. He admires Eliot's "firm and elaborate delineation of individual character"; above all, he admires the strength of her vision, her own particular, direct impression of English society. "George Eliot's humanity colors all her other gifts—her humor, her morality, and her exquisite rhetoric" (LC I: 907–908, 914). In her best work—for James, *Romola* and *Middlemarch*, in that order—the quality of moral observation and the depth of character combine to create a uniquely powerful fiction:

> We feel in her, always, that she proceeds from the abstract to the concrete; that her figures and situations are evolved . . . from her moral consciousness. . . . Her preoccupation with the universe helped to make her characters strike you as also belonging to it; it raised the roof, widened the area, of her aesthetic structure. Nothing is finer, in her genius, than the combination of her

love of general truth and love of the special case. (*LC* I: 1003)

This aesthetic principle is of central interest to Henry James. In praising Eliot's ability to ground her acute moral and philosophical observations in concrete, firmly delineated characters, he avails himself of yet another opportunity to celebrate an aesthetic close to his own novelistic heart. As the author of *The Portrait of a Lady* (1881) and other novels criticized for their slow-moving plots and overly psychological characters, James happily claims Eliot as a precedent of sorts.

A similar pattern emerges with James's studies of Anthony Trollope. His earliest reviews are biting and harsh. Trollope's *Belton Estate* is "a *stupid* book," James growls in 1866. "It is without a single idea. It is utterly incompetent to the primary functions of a book, of whatever nature, namely—to suggest thought" (*LC* I: 1,325–1,326). *Can You Forgive Her?* is overwritten and full of filler; and while James praises *Linda Tressell* for its air of reality, he also finds it dull. James revised his opinions in an 1883 essay; Trollope may not have espoused a polished theory of the novel, but his "inestimable merit was a complete appreciation of the usual . . . the familiar, the actual." He respects Trollope's use of character-driven story lines: "Character, in any sense in which we can get at it, is action, and action is plot." And James singles out *The Warden* for high praise: "It is simply the history of an old man's conscience," he notes. "A motive more delicate, more slender, as well as more charming, could scarcely be conceived" (*LC* I: 1,333, 1,336, 1,340–1,341).

But perhaps the most surprising passage comes when James uses Trollope as a foil against the French. Like Zola, Trollope sought to "describe the life that lay near him." But Trollope and Zola chose quite different subjects, and James notes "the difference in the application" of each author's realist method. Though Trollope lacked Zola's theoretical focus and "systematic" application, "I think he tells us, on the whole, more about life than the 'naturalists' in our sister republic." Once again, James has found a way to grant the French their avant-garde aesthetic theory, criticizing not the approach but the execution. Trollope, rather surprisingly, is trumpeted as a successful realist author because, though his work is "inferior in audacity" to the racier French, he nevertheless captures the English character so completely. "His natural rightness and purity are so real that the good things he projects must be real," James concludes. "A race is fortunate when it has a good deal of the sort of imagination—of imaginative feeling—that had fallen to the share of Anthony Trollope; and in this possession our English race is not poor" (*LC* I: 1,347–1,348, 1,354).

James was also a keen student of younger British authors. His 1888 essay on Robert Louis Stevenson is a noteworthy example. Stevenson had published a number of essays on the state of the novel, and James appreciated Stevenson's serious tone and critical openness. "Mr. Stevenson has a theory of composition in regard to the novel on which he is to be congratulated," James writes, "as any positive and genuine conviction of this kind is vivifying so long as it is not narrow. The breath of the novelist's being is his liberty, and the incomparable virtue of the form he uses is that it lends itself to views innumerable and diverse, to every variety of illustration" (*LC* I: 1,248). It is this diversity of example that James praises in Stevenson's creative work, expressing wonder that the author of *Dr. Jekyll and Mr. Hyde* also wrote *Treasure Island,* books so apparently dissimilar. And yet Stevenson's fiction is united in that it is "personal, expressive, [and] renewed at each attempt." In Stevenson, James recognizes a fine artistic mind: "He feels, as it seems to us, and that is not given to every one" (1,234–1,235). But it is on the question of the romance novel as a literary genre that Stevenson is most illustrative; whereas the French and Italian romances of the day rely on exotic locales and overly idealized characters, Stevenson's romances are firmly rooted in the commonplace and the plausible—perhaps to a fault. James's strongest criticism of *Dr. Jekyll,* for instance, concerns the overly detailed description of the doctor's transformative combination of medicinal powders: "[T]his uncanny process would be more conceivable . . . if the author had not made it so definite" (1,253). Setting aside this minor complaint, James praises Stevenson's plausible, well-rounded fictional characters, a welcome addition to the storied tradition of the romance—and a force of revitalization. "A tradition is kept alive only by something being added to it," James observes. "Stevenson has added psychology" (1,250).

Some of James's later essays on British authors demonstrate how he continued to use criticism in increasingly creative ways. The 1907 "Introduction to *The Tempest*" is a noteworthy example. Less an analysis of Shakespeare's play, this essay examines the process of an author's personal investment in a creative text, and the question of whether or not, through reading a text, a reader can touch the mind of its creator. For James, deeply immersed in the revisions for the New York Edition, these were not idle questions. He differentiates the Artist from the Man (i.e., the historical Shakespeare), positing that the Man is "effectually locked up and imprisoned in the artist," who is, in turn, locked up in the characters he creates. It is impossible to touch the "real" Shakespeare through the work; rather, the reader deals only with traces of the artist as rendered in the text. The Man is, in a sense, "protected" from reach: "[W]e shall never touch the Man *directly* in the Artist," James concludes (*LC* I: 1,209, 1,220). For James, this is as it should be. In a surprising conclusion, he likens the critics to Hamlet and the artists to Polonius, hiding behind his arras. If the comparison gives one pause for thought, the essential idea seems clear. In Shakespeare's play, Hamlet murders the hidden Polonius, mistaking him for Claudius, Hamlet's uncle and stepfather. Of course, Polonius is generally regarded as a dangerous meddler and a provider of specious, self-serving advice. Consequently, James's provocative metaphor seems uncharacteristically strained. In "The Science of Criticism," James had written of the "sensitive organism" of art, which "is highly susceptible of demoralization." Poor criticism, he had warned, could literally and figuratively "kill" an artist (*LC* I: 97). It comes as little surprise, perhaps, to find the author, in the "Introduction to *The Tempest*," safely out of reach.

With this thought in mind, the prefaces to the New York Edition—written concurrently with the "Introduction to *The Tempest*"—take on new meaning. As James described them in the preface to *Roderick Hudson*, the prefaces are "a safe paradise of self-criticism," where he, "the artist, the prime creator," can saunter about a "sweet old overtangled walled garden" of his own design (*LC* II: 1,045). James is more than a little disingenuous here, though the metaphor rings true in other respects: James maintains a kind of protective distance throughout the prefaces, sharing almost no biographical or personal information whatsoever; the reader deals only with the artist, the "monster and magician of a thousand masks," as he is depicted in the "Introduction to *The Tempest*" (*LC* I: 1,209). If James had his reasons for protecting his personal life from a curious public, it was partly because he wanted the reader always to deal with the text, not the author of the text. That was, as he put it, the "real and right relation" (*LC* I: 1,206) between an author and his audience. That is the lesson he drew from Shakespeare, and it is one of the key ideas behind the prefaces to the New York Edition.

Related questions inform a 1912 essay on Robert Browning, "The Novel in *The Ring and the Book*." The essay begins with the conceit of approaching the "literary monument" that is Browning's great poem, which James likens to a cathedral. How best to enter the holy structure? Which perspective is best? On one level, James is asking how a living author comes to grips with the powerful legacy of a highly influential author of a previous generation. He confesses a need to "push our chair back, from the table he so tremendously spreads, just to see a little better what is on it" (*LC* I: 791, 801). This pose of humility quickly gives way to a bolder, more creative response. After quickly recounting the plot of Browning's narrative poem, James openly wonders how he might rewrite it as a novel. He would first choose none of the dozen or more viewpoint characters employed by Browning, but just one: Canon Caponsacchi, the heroic priest who aids the beleaguered Pompilia. Choosing a central consciousness is a matter of selecting "the point at which the various implications of interest [in a novel], no matter how many, *most* converge and interfuse." Caponsacchi, as James imagines him, would be "a large lucid reflector" illuminating numerous dimensions of the story (*LC* I: 798, 806).

James continues, openly meditating on changes he would make to the story line and even sketching out a scene or two.

It is a fascinating exercise, and anything but idle speculation. Nor is it a backhanded compliment intended to denigrate Browning. Rather, this complex essay stages a dialectical process of reading and writing as a dynamic exchange, an idea James promotes in the prefaces to the New York Edition. In "The Novel in *The Ring and the Book*," he demonstrates how the work of an older artist inspires a younger artist to create anew in response to his example: "Browning works the whole thing over—the whole thing as originally given him—and we work *him*," James explains, "helpfully, artfully, boldly, which is our whole blest basis." It is, in its own way, the ultimate homage to Browning; such is clearly the tone when, in closing his discussion, James observes that "Browning's great generous wings are over us still and even now, more than ever now . . . they shake down on us his blessing" (*LC* I: 807, 810–811).

AMERICA AFTER *HAWTHORNE*

Henry James's relationship to his homeland was complex. He left the United States in 1875, living most of his adult life in England. He would die a British subject in 1916. Early in his career, James declared his literary sympathies in his book-length study *Hawthorne* (1879), a volume criticized by many for its cool dismissal of American literature.

James continued to study and comment on American writers and literature throughout his career. After *Hawthorne*, his next major essay on America as a literary subject was an 1887 study of RALPH WALDO EMERSON. James strikes early in "Emerson," recalling in the sage of Concord a "singular impression of paleness. . . . Emerson's personal history is condensed into the single word Concord, and all the condensation in the world will not make it look rich." Emerson was, James freely grants, distinct: "The genius itself it seems to me impossible to contest." Nevertheless, if Emerson stood out, it was because "New England fifty years ago offered to the observer . . . a kind of achromatic picture, without particular intensifications" (*LC* I: 250, 254). James intensifies his

critique as he addresses Emerson's conception of the American scholar:

In truth, by this term he means simply the cultivated man, the man who has had a liberal education, and there is a voluntary plainness in his use of it—speaking of such people as the rustic, or the vulgar, speak of those who have a tincture of books. . . . An American reader may be excused for finding in it a pleasant sign of that prestige, often so quaintly and indeed so extravagantly acknowledged, which a connection with literature carries with it among the people of the United States. There is no country in which it is more freely admitted to be a distinction—*the* distinction; or in which so many persons have become eminent for showing it even in a slight degree. Gentlemen and ladies are celebrated there on this ground who would not on the same ground, though they might on another, be celebrated anywhere else. (*LC* I: 262–263)

The trivializing, condescending tone is clear. Like *Hawthorne* eight years prior, "Emerson" rewrites the legacy of antebellum New England, making it appear weak, timid, and second-rate. James's condescension peaks when he broadens his attack to include all of Emerson's generation, undermining the legacy of their accomplishments:

Nothing is more perceptible to-day than that their criticism produced no fruit—that it was little else than a very decent and innocent recreation—a kind of Puritan carnival. The New England world was for much the most part very busy, but the Dial and Fruitlands and Brook Farm were the amusement of the leisure-class. Extremes meet, and as in older societies that class is known principally by its connection with castles and carriages, so at Concord it came, with Thoreau and Mr. W. H. Channing, out of the cabin and the wood-lot. (*LC* I: 267)

James had his reasons for belittling the American authors who had preceded him. Clearly, he felt that the older, more "sophisticated" atmosphere of Europe was more conducive to the art he labored to create. James considered himself erudite, sophisticated, worldly, and complex, and he promoted such values in his own fiction. To denigrate New England as provincial, narrow-minded, and lacking in distinction was, in part, an attempt to distinguish himself as a different type of American and to draw a clear line between the work that he offered and the work of those who had preceded him. Also, some measure of professional jealousy was likely an issue. Emerson and Hawthorne had, by the 1880s, been elevated to iconic status. Henry James desired nothing less for himself.

On other occasions, James saw much to celebrate in American literature. In 1898, he published an important essay entitled "The Question of the Opportunities," in which he forecasts where American literature might head in the new century. The question of cultural and social diversity is first on his list. America, with its "huge, homogenous and fast-growing population," has grown into a "great common-schooled and newspapered democracy" filled with a "variety of faces and idioms." Idiomatic English, James suggests, might be a great "opportunity" in the new American literature. The sheer size and magnitude of the growing nation—ever more diverse culturally and ethnically—is surely a recipe for change: "It is impossible not to entertain with patience and curiosity the presumption that life so colossal must break into expression at points of proportionate frequency. These places, these moments will be the chances" (*LC* I: 651–653).

But, for the novelist, it is the world of commerce that seems most ripe. "The typical American figure is above all that 'business man' whom the novelist and the dramatist have scarce yet seriously touched," James observes.

> Even more important is the extraordinary, the unique relation in which [the businessman] for the most part stands to the life of his lawful, his immitigable womankind, the wives and daughters who float, who splash on the surface and ride the waves, his terrific link with civilization, his social substitutes and representatives, while, like a diver for shipwrecked treasure, he gasps in the depths and breathes through an air-tube. This relation, even taken alone, contains elements that strike me as only yearning for their interpreter—elements, moreover, that

> would present the further merit of melting into the huge neighboring province of the special situation of women in an order of things where to be a woman at all—certainly to be a young one—constitutes in itself a social position. (*LC* I: 655)

James never sounded more clairvoyant. The question of the "new woman" in the 20th century would preoccupy American writers such as EDITH WHARTON, Ellen Glasgow, and F. Scott Fitzgerald. (See WOMEN'S ISSUES.) And in predicting that the American businessman should be at the heart of the affair, James all but names Theodore Dreiser, Sinclair Lewis, and John Dos Passos. In doing so, however, he seems to have overlooked the work of his contemporaries, some of whom had already begun to address this very question.

One such contemporary was William Dean Howells, a close friend and an influential editor (who had helped see, among others, a young Henry James into print). Howells was also a leading novelist, and in such major works as *A Modern Instance* (1882), *The Rise of Silas Lapham* (1885), and *A Hazard of New Fortunes* (1890), he had addressed a range of questions concerning the American businessman. Whereas James may have missed this opportunity to celebrate Howells's achievement, there were other occasions. James's essays on Howells are among his best work on American literature. And characteristically they reflect back on James in interesting ways. James's most important essay on Howells appeared in *Harper's Weekly* in 1886. The rhetorical occasion of "William Dean Howells" requires contextualization.

In 1882, Howells published an essay entitled "Henry James, Jr.," in which he provocatively claimed that the novel as written by Dickens and Thackeray was "of the past." Realism was the school "of the future as well as the present," and Henry James was "its chief exemplar . . . it is he who is shaping and directing American fiction" (Howells 322). Though it was not his intention, Howells's essay sparked a transatlantic barrage of heated responses and counterresponses concerning the future of the novel. Initially pleased to be the subject of so much attention, James eventually wearied of the affair; there was a perception, in the eyes of some, that he and Howells were members of a self-serving fraternity of upstart, radical authors. Like it or not, James had been pulled into the fray. He felt he had no choice but to respond. His first effort was "The Art of Fiction." The seemingly deferential, humble tone of that essay is, in part, a response to the hyperbolic rhetoric of the debate thus far.

James's second response came in "William Dean Howells," the tone of which is decidedly mixed. To be sure, James offers praise, noting his friend's "unerring sentiment of the American character. . . . Other persons have considered and discoursed upon American life, but no one, surely, has *felt* it so completely as he" (LC I: 500). In a well-known passage, he eloquently catalogs Howells's realist aesthetic:

> He is animated by a love of the common, the immediate, the familiar and vulgar elements of life, and holds that in proportion as we move into the rare and strange we become vague and arbitrary; that truth of representation, in a word, can be achieved only so long as it is in our power to test and measure it. He thinks scarcely anything too paltry to be interesting, that the small and the vulgar have been terribly neglected, and would rather see an exact account of a sentiment or a character he stumbles against every day than a brilliant evocation of a passion or a type he has never seen and does not even particularly believe in. He adores the real, the natural, the colloquial, the moderate, the optimistic, the domestic, and the democratic; looking askance at exceptions and perversities and superiorities, at surprising and incongruous phenomena in general. . . . Mr. Howells hates an artificial fable and a *dénouement* that is pressed into the service; he likes things to occur as they occur in life, where the manner of a great many of them is not to occur at all. He has observed that heroic emotion and brilliant opportunity are not particularly interwoven with our days, and indeed, in the way of omission, he *has* often practised in his pages a very considerable boldness. It has not, however,

made what we find there any less interesting and less human. (LC I: 502–503)

Here James proves himself to be as careful and astute a reader as Howells could hope for. But such praise is offset by other passages that are at best lukewarm assessments and in some cases pointed criticisms. The chief complaint is that Howells's work is overly optimistic and perhaps naive:

> If American life is on the whole, as I make no doubt whatever, more innocent than that of any other country, nowhere is the fact more patent than in Mr. Howells's novels, which exhibit so constant a study of the actual and so small a perception of evil. . . . Purity of life, fineness of conscience, benevolence of motive, decency of speech, good-nature, kindness, charity, tolerance (though, indeed, there is little but each other's manners for the people to tolerate), govern all the scene; the only immoralities are aberrations of thought, like that of Silas Lapham, or excesses of beer, like that of Bartley Hubbard. (LC I: 504)

James is more than a little reductive in this assessment. Nevertheless, he has a valid point, and this complaint of "excessive optimism" has followed Howells ever since.

James intended "William Dean Howells" to be a tepid endorsement. Concerned that his own reputation and status had suffered as a result of the fray surrounding "Henry James, Jr.," he responded by publicly distancing himself from his friend. This fact reminds one that, for James, literary criticism was often a personal exercise. Several of his most important critical works, including "William Dean Howells," "The Art of Fiction," and the prefaces to the New York Edition, were designed to position himself and his fiction in the literary marketplace. That is not to say that James's criticism was exclusively self-serving; clearly, "The Art of Fiction" and the prefaces go beyond such a narrow scope. But a complete understanding of what James wrote includes careful consideration of the uniquely personal reasons for which he wrote it.

In 1908, James wrote to Howells that his prefaces to the New York Edition "ought, collected together ... to form a sort of comprehensive manual or *vade-mecum* for aspirants in our arduous profession" (qtd. in Anesko 426). He might have expanded this self-assessment to include the entire body of his work as a critic. If James began his career lamenting "the absence of any critical treatise upon fiction," he could rest secure in the knowledge that no one of his generation did more to correct that lapse in English letters. James's influence on his contemporaries was great; his influence on 20th-century literature would prove seminal; at the beginning of a new millennium, his legacy stands strong.

FURTHER READING

Anesko, Michael. *Letters, Fictions, Lives: Henry James and William Dean Howells*. New York: Oxford University Press, 1997.

Borus, Daniel H. *Writing Realism: Howells, James, and Norris in the Mass Market*. Chapel Hill: University of North Carolina Press, 1989.

Cady, Edwin H. *The Road to Realism: The Early Years, 1837–1885, of William Dean Howells*. Syracuse, N.Y.: Syracuse University Press, 1956.

Chilton, Neil. "Conceptions of a Beautiful Crisis: Henry James's Reading of *The Tempest*." *Henry James Review* 26, no. 3 (2005): 218–228.

Davidson, Rob. *The Master and the Dean: The Literary Criticism of Henry James and William Dean Howells*. Columbia: University of Missouri Press, 2005.

Daugherty, Sarah B. *The Literary Criticism of Henry James*. Athens: Ohio University Press, 1981.

Hale, Dorothy J. "James and the Invention of Novel Theory." In *The Cambridge Companion to Henry James*, edited by Jonathan Freedman, 79–101. Cambridge: Cambridge University Press, 1998.

———. *Social Formalism: The Novel in Theory from Henry James to the Present*. Palo Alto, Calif.: Stanford University Press, 1998.

Horne, Philip. *Henry James and Revision*. Oxford: Oxford University Press, 1990.

Howells, William Dean. *Selected Literary Criticism, Volume I: 1859–1885*. Edited by Ulrich Halfmann. Bloomington: Indiana University Press, 1993.

Jacobson, Marcia. *Henry James and the Mass Market*. Tuscaloosa: University of Alabama Press, 1983.

James, Henry. *Essays in London and Elsewhere*. London: James R. Osgood, McIlvaine, 1893.

———. *French Poets and Novelists*. London: Macmillan, 1878.

———. *Literary Criticism, Volume I: Essays on Literature, American Writers, English Writers*. Edited by Leon Edel and Mark Wilson. New York: Library of America, 1984. Abbreviated as *LC I*.

———. *Literary Criticism, Volume II: French Writers, Other European Writers, The Prefaces to the New York Edition*. Edited by Leon Edel and Mark Wilson. New York: Library of America, 1984. Abbreviated as *LC II*.

———. *Notes on Novelists*. New York: Scribner's, 1914.

———. *Partial Portraits*. London: Macmillan, 1888.

———. *The Scenic Art: Notes on Acting & the Drama: 1872–1901*. Edited by Allan Wade. New Brunswick, N.J.: Rutgers University Press, 1948.

Jones, Vivien. *James the Critic*. New York: St. Martin's Press, 1985.

Miller, James E., ed. *Theory of Fiction: Henry James*. Lincoln: University of Nebraska Press, 1972.

Posnock, Ross. *Henry James and the Problem of Robert Browning*. Athens: University of Georgia Press, 1985.

Roberts, Morris. *Henry James's Criticism*. Cambridge, Mass.: Harvard University Press, 1929.

Rowe, John Carlos. *The Theoretical Dimensions of Henry James*. Madison: University of Wisconsin Press, 1984.

Salmon, Richard. *Henry James and the Culture of Publicity*. Cambridge: Cambridge University Press, 1997.

Shi, David E. *Facing Facts: Realism in American Thought and Culture, 1850–1920*. New York: Oxford University Press, 1995.

Smith, Janet Adam, ed. *Henry James and Robert Louis Stevenson: A Record of Friendship and Criticism*. London: Rupert Hart-Davis, 1948.

Tanner, Tony. "Henry James and the Art of Criticism." In *Henry James and the Art of Nonfiction*, 27–57. Athens: University of Georgia Press, 1995.

Tucker, Herbert F. "James's Browning Inside Out." *Henry James Review* 26, no. 3 (2005): 210–217.

Rob Davidson, *California State University, Chico*

Hawthorne (1879)

Henry James completed his study of Nathaniel Hawthorne's life and works in PARIS in the fall of 1879, and the book appeared later the same year. Part of Macmillan's "English Men of Letters" series, *Hawthorne* was issued first in LONDON and then in the United States. The work received favorable reviews in England and howls of outrage in the United States. James was 36 years old when he wrote the study, and he began work on *The POR-TRAIT OF A LADY* (1881) soon after completing it.

SYNOPSIS

(Chapter 1) James explains the goals of the work, stressing that his will be a critical essay rather than a biography because the tranquility of Hawthorne's life does not readily lend itself to study. Hawthorne's importance to American culture derives from the fact that his work is the best and most representative literature yet produced in the United States, displaying deep connections to Hawthorne's native New England. Arguing that history is necessary for art, James traces Hawthorne's Puritan ancestors and links their stern moralizing to the author's delicate genius. The chapter follows Hawthorne's life to graduation from Bowdoin College.

(Chapter 2) This chapter covers Hawthorne's life from 1826 until 1838. These years, which "had an altogether peculiar dreariness" (338), were a period of incubation for Hawthorne, who lived at home in Salem and spent much of his time alone. James points to Hawthorne's *Note-Books* to justify his characterization of the author as a shy man of serene and simple character. Given the cultural pressures to be "in business" (342) and the country's limited interest in literature, Hawthorne's decision to be an author shows "great courage" (343). This period of solitude motivated Hawthorne's genius as he produces a steady stream of remarkable short stories, collected in *Twice-Told Tales* (1845) and *Snow Image* (1852). Nevertheless, these stories were insufficient to support Hawthorne and did not garner him the fame he deserved.

(Chapter 3) Hawthorne continues to write short stories, which appear in the second volume of *Twice-Told Tales* (1845). The same year he also edits *The Journals of an African Cruiser*, written by his college friend Horatio Bridge. In considering Hawthorne's writing, James groups his tales into three categories: fantasy and allegory; tales of New England history; and sketches of actual scenes. James admits his own bias against allegory, even as he acknowledges that Hawthorne's works shine most brightly when the author's fancy is fully engaged. James argues against the assessment of M. Émile Montégut, a French critic, particularly his claim that Hawthorne is bitter and pessimistic. Some brief biographical details are included— Hawthorne's engagement at the age of 35 and his 1839 appointment by the Van Buren administration as an employee in the Boston Custom-house. The chapter ends in April 1841 as Hawthorne joins the community at Brook Farm.

(Chapter 4) *The Blithedale Romance* (1852) is the product, James explains, of Hawthorne's tenure at Brook Farm, a utopian community organized according to socialist principles. Despite this direct experience, Hawthorne writes a romance rather than a more realistic work, and this choice provides a clue to the "Arcadian and innocent" (385) life Hawthorne led there. The Brook Farm experience opens a discussion of Hawthorne's acquaintances with various members of the transcendentalist circle, including Margaret Fuller, RALPH WALDO EMERSON, and Henry David Thoreau. After his marriage to Sophia Peabody in July 1842, Hawthorne moves to Concord.

(Chapter 5) Owing to his ongoing connections with the Democratic Party and the administration of President Polk, Hawthorne receives another political appointment, this time to the Custom-house in Salem; he returns to his hometown in 1846 and seems to stop writing until 1849. This fallow time provides the experience for what James calls "one of the most perfect of Hawthorne's compositions," the "Custom-House," the introductory section of *The Scarlet Letter* (1850), a critical success that brings fame to its author (398). James calls particular attention to Hawthorne's approach of capturing the past through a literary tone and a quality of vision rather than through extensive detail. Despite the praise, James finds numerous faults in the book.

From the summer of 1850 to the early months of 1851, Hawthorne writes *The House of the Seven Gables* (1851). This work is "larger and more various" than its predecessor but neither as "rounded" nor as "complete" (411). In addition, Hawthorne publishes two collections of children's stories (*The Wonder-Book* [1852] and *Tanglewood Tales* [1853]) and *The Blithedale Romance,* for James the most charming of Hawthorne's three American novels. In 1853, Hawthorne's friend Franklin Pierce, for whom he had written a campaign biography, is elected president, and he appoints Hawthorne to the consulate in Liverpool, England. Hawthorne leaves the United States later in the year and remains abroad until 1860. Hawthorne's political involvement allows James to reflect on the general attitudes of his generation, particularly their optimism and faith in the special destiny of the United States, soon to be shattered by the CIVIL WAR.

(Chapter 6) Because Hawthorne is almost 50 when he goes abroad, his experience in Europe has little effect on his creative development. He records some of his observations in a beautifully written series of magazine pieces, collected in *Our Old Home* (1863). In 1857, Hawthorne resigns his consulate and departs for the Continent, traveling through France and Italy, pausing in ROME and FLORENCE. These experiences motivate Hawthorne's last completed novel, entitled *The Transformation* (1860) in the first, British edition and *The Marble Faun: or The Romance of Monte Beni* (Hawthorne's preferred title) in the American edition. James gripes that although the novel suffers from an "almost fatal vagueness," it is the most popular of Hawthorne's works (447).

(Chapter 7) Hawthorne returns to the United States in the summer of 1860 and takes up residence again in Concord. Despite his critical success, he is plagued by financial worries and anguish over current events. The Civil War, which begins in April 1861, devastates Hawthorne's sense of the nation and brings all Democrats under suspicion of disloyalty. Hawthorne remains true to his Democratic friends, refusing to withdraw the dedication of *Our Old Home* to conciliate readers. Hawthorne writes a controversial essay entitled "Chiefly About War Matters" (July 1862) for the *Atlantic Monthly* under the pseudonym "A Peaceable Man." Hawthorne's spirits and writing suffer from the national turmoil. While traveling in New Hampshire with Pierce, Hawthorne dies in his sleep on May 18, 1864, leaving two unfinished works: *The Dolliver Romance* and *Septimius Felton.*

CRITICAL ANALYSIS

In 1878, John Morley launched the "English Men of Letters" series, which was supposed to show that authors were "representative men, representatives of great social, historical, or philosophical forces" (Caramello 21). Morley approached Henry James about writing a study of Nathaniel Hawthorne, and James agreed, with some reluctance. The aims of the series clearly shaped the work James produced, which alternates between biography and criticism. As much as the series guidelines influenced James's work, however, *Hawthorne* also provided him with the opportunity to express his own ideas about what matters in artistic creation, especially about the kind of novel an American author should or could write. Although the book is a critical study of Hawthorne, it is also "James's effort to discover his own relation to New England and to the American past" as well as his own career path as an artist (Poirier 94).

In writing *Hawthorne,* James did not seek out new factual information on his subject, relying instead on George Parson Lathrop's *Study of Hawthorne* (1876) and informal conversations with Hawthorne's son Julian. James's critical perspective is also informed by Émile Montégut, whose work he references. Even as James rejects Montégut's conclusions, especially his claim that Hawthorne was a pessimist, James's choice of a French perspective points to his basic commitment to an international perspective on the debates over the generic categories of romance, realism, and naturalism (see ROMANCE/REALISM/NATURALISM). A rejection of provincialism is at the core of his essay and is James's main consideration in assessing Hawthorne and the country of which he was a representative.

By the time James wrote the work, Hawthorne had been established as one of the most important authors yet produced by the United States. American readers rebelled when the young Henry James opined from Paris that this American master was "provincial" and that "it takes a great deal of history to produce a little literature" (320)—history that the nation lacked. In a February 1880 review of *Hawthorne* in the influential *Atlantic Monthly*, WILLIAM DEAN HOWELLS observed, "We foresee, without any powerful prophetic lens, that Mr. James will be in some quarters promptly attainted of high treason" (qtd. in Edel 389). Howells reasserted the respectability of American provincialism, arguing that "If it is not provincial for an Englishman to be English or a Frenchman French, then it is not so for an American to be American; and if Hawthorne was 'exquisitely provincial,' one had better take one's chance of universality with him than with almost any Londoner or Parisian of his time" (qtd. in Edel 389). James was stung by the negative reaction, but he jauntily exclaimed in an 1880 letter that "The whole episode projects a lurid light upon the state of American 'culture,' and furnishes me with a hundred of wonderful examples, where, before, I had only more of less vague impressions" (*Letters* 274).

Ironically, the remarks by James that drew the most serious complaints from critics are based on similar observations that Hawthorne himself makes in the preface to *The Marble Faun* (1860):

No author, without a trial, can conceive of the difficulty of writing a Romance about a country where there is no shadow, no antiquity, no mystery, no picturesque and gloomy wrong, nor anything but a common-place prosperity, in broad and simple daylight, as is happily the case with my dear native land. It will be very long, I trust, before romance-writers may find congenial and easily handled themes, either in the annals of our stalwart Republic, or in any characteristic and probable events of our individual lives. Romance and poetry, ivy, lichens, and wall-flowers, need Ruin to make them grow. (3)

James revises this list for *Hawthorne* and changes its argument. In his well-known rephrasing of Hawthorne, James outlines the all-encompassing set of obstacles facing a potential American author, asserting that the nation has:

No State, in the European sense of the word, and indeed barely a specific national name. No sovereign, no court, no personal loyalty, no aristocracy, no church, no clergy, no army, no diplomatic service, no country gentlemen, no palaces, no castles, nor manors, nor old country-houses, nor parsonages, nor thatch cottages nor ivied ruins; no cathedrals, nor abbeys, nor little Norman churches; no great Universities nor public schools—no Oxford, nor Eton, nor Harrow; no literature, no novels, no museums, no pictures, no political society, no sporting class—no Epsom nor Ascot! (351–352)

Without such "items of high civilization," the American author is left with few resources out of which to create great art (351). In other words, for James it is of little surprise that Hawthorne's writing would be provincial. While Hawthorne worried that there was insufficient material for the romance writer, James concludes that the only kind of novel one could write under such conditions would be a romance, which depends more on the author's inspired reworking of familiar plot devices and turns of plot rather than on established cultural manners and sturdy social distinctions. Also noteworthy is the authors' differing opinions about American innocence. Hawthorne's preface to *The Marble Faun*, written before the Civil War, describes the nation as "stalwart," "broad and simple." But this innocence was destroyed by the war, which, James explains "introduced into the national consciousness a certain sense of proportion and relation, of the world being a more complicated place than it had hitherto seemed, the future more treacherous, success more difficult" (427–428). Prosperity might have been commonplace to Hawthorne's generation, but postwar Americans would find the world more precarious.

In James's view, this new world would require a new kind of novel. Whereas Hawthorne's romances might have been appropriate for the innocence of antebellum America, they were an inadequate vehicle for representing the transformation of "proportion and relation" in the postbellum United States. James notes that Hawthorne himself dismissed abolition as "the mistiness of a philanthropic theory" in his campaign biography of Franklin Pierce and that he judged slavery a "respectable institution" (427). James regards this limited point of view as likewise evident in the kind of art Hawthorne produced. As noted, James divides Hawthorne's tales into fantasy and allegory; "little tales" of New England history (361); and "slender sketches of actual scenes" (362). Of these three, Hawthorne is "most original" when working from the fancy or imagination (361).

Even though James praises the "simple genius" and "quality of imagination" in Hawthorne's writings and celebrates how he "reflect[s] the hue" of Puritan morality (362), James concludes that allegory "is quite one of the lighter exercises of the imagination" (366). What does he mean by this? An allegory is a literary form in which the plot is designed to illustrate a moral maxim and tell a second, related story. A very popular allegory, and one Hawthorne had read, is John Bunyan's *Pilgrim's Progress* (1678), in which the journey of Christian to the Celestial City shows the kinds of challenges a faithful person might encounter while living a Christian life. According to James, however, an allegory "is apt to spoil two good things— a story and a moral, a meaning and a form" (366). Only when "extremely spontaneous," as in some of Hawthorne's best tales, does allegory work. All too often its "machinery" is clumsy and distracting (366).

Most of James's complaints about Hawthorne's style are related to a crisis in allegory. When James suggests that the people in *The Scarlet Letter* (1850) are "representatives, very picturesquely arranged, of a single state of mind" rather than complicated characters (404), his remark suggests that, like figures in an allegory, Hester Prynne and Arthur Dimmesdale are interesting because of their "moral situation" (403). "After the first scene," James argues, Hester is almost "an accessory figure" (403). Many of Hawthorne's characters suffer, in short, from "a want of reality" (405). A heavy use of symbolism also weakens the longer works, contributing to their insufficient reality. James omits a precise definition of realism, preferring to hint at what art should be through statements of how Hawthorne fails to achieve it. A few years later, in "The Art of Fiction" (1884), James moves even further away from the attempt to delineate romance and realism, saying that such "clumsy separations" do more harm than good (55–56).

James's unflattering comparison of *The Scarlet Letter* to the forgotten novel *Adam Blair* by John Gibson Lockhart might suggest that Hawthorne had little influence on James. On the contrary, Hawthorne's novels had a potent effect on James's creative development. *The* BOSTONIANS (1886) shares many plot details with Hawthorne's fictional representation of Massachusetts reformers in *The Blithedale Romance* (1852). James's various treatments of American artists in Europe (as in RODERICK HUDSON [1875]) demonstrate a debt to Hawthorne's *The Marble Faun*. Raymond J. Wilson claims that "The FIGURE IN THE CARPET" (1896) echoes Hawthorne's image from "The Custom-House." Hawthorne's novels provide for James a rich "intertext," or a set of references upon which James builds and comments in his writing.

The question of authorial influence has offered a fruitful field for critical inquiry, as commentary by Michael Anesko, Richard Brodhead, F. O. Matthiessen, Richard Poirier, and John Carlos Rowe makes clear. To understand *Hawthorne*, Rowe explains, the reader must realize that it expresses James's desire "to find a tradition of which he might be the proper heir" (32). In Rowe's view, James's INTERNATIONAL THEME develops from his reading of Hawthorne and is his antidote to the provincialism that characterizes his predecessor's works (34). James's confrontation with Hawthorne provided James with the perspective necessary to "swerve from his precursor's dominant influence" (48) and to write his own masterpiece, *The Portrait of a Lady* (1881), which owes much to *The Scarlet Letter*.

FURTHER READING

The interpretive work on James's criticism is extensive, although *Hawthorne* has received less scholarly attention than the prefaces to the New York Edition.

Anesko, Michael. *"Friction with the Market": Henry James and the Profession of Authorship*, 61–77. New York: Oxford University Press, 1986.

Brodhead, Richard. *School of Hawthorne*, 134–155. New York: Oxford University Press, 1989.

Caramello, Charles. *Henry James, Gertrude Stein, and the Biographical Act*, 21–56. Chapel Hill: University of North Carolina Press, 1996.

Edel, Leon. "Provincial Storm." In *Henry James: the Conquest of London, 1870–1881*, 383–360. Philadelphia: Lippincott 1962.

———, ed. *Henry James Letters*. Vol. 2, 274–275. Cambridge, Mass.: Harvard University Press, 1975.

Freedman, Jonathan. "Introduction: The Moment of Henry James." In *Cambridge Companion to Henry James*, edited by Jonathan Freedman, 1–21. Cambridge: Cambridge University Press, 1998.

Hawthorne, Nathaniel. *The Marble Faun. The Centenary Edition of the Works of Nathaniel Hawthorne*, vol. 4. Edited by William Charvat, Roy Harvey Pearce, et al. Columbus: Ohio State University Press, 1968.

James, Henry. *Hawthorne*. In *Literary Criticism: Essays on Literature, American Writers, English Writers* (1879). New York: Library of America, 1984.

Matthiessen, F. O. *American Renaissance: Art and Expression in the Age of Emerson and Whitman*, 351–368. New York: Oxford University Press, 2002.

Poirier, Richard. *World Elsewhere: The Place of Style in American Literature*, 93–143. New York: Oxford University Press, 1966.

Rowe, John Carlos. *The Theoretical Dimensions of Henry James*, 30–57. Madison: University of Wisconsin Press, 1984.

Saint-Amour, Paul K. "Transatlantic Tropology in *Roderick Hudson*." *Henry James Review* 18, no. 1 (1997): 22–42.

Wilson, Raymond J., III. "The Possibility of Realism: 'The Figure in the Carpet' and Hawthorne's Intertext." *Henry James Review* 16, no. 2 (1995): 142–152.

Elizabeth Duquette, *Gettysburg College*

prefaces to the New York Edition (1905–1909)

After experiencing a sales slump around the turn of the century, Henry James spent the years from 1905 to 1909 preparing a collected edition of his novels and tales that included a new series of 18 substantial prefaces. Originally published from 1907 to 1909 as part of the NEW YORK EDITION, the prefaces were later collected by R. P. Blackmur as *The Art of the Novel* (1934). This edition, which includes Blackmur's seminal introduction, had been the standard source for the prefaces before the publication of the Library of America edition of James's *Literary Criticism* (vol. 2, *French Writers, Other European Writers, the Prefaces to the New York Edition*, 1984; subsequent references are to this edition). While nominally attached to their respective volumes and not intended as a sustained critical exegesis, the prefaces do contain an extended discussion of James's ideas of art and novel-writing.

SYNOPSIS

(Preface to RODERICK HUDSON, 1907): Ostensibly beginning with the origin of *Roderick Hudson*, James subtly shifts to announce his conception of the project of the prefaces as a whole: "the private history" that records "the growth of his whole operative consciousness" (1,039–1,040). Employing metaphors of sailing and embroidery, James confronts the problem of art as representation: How does one foster a sense of the infinite whole while containing it within a finite fictional framework. In one of his more famous descriptions that prefigures much of James's structural description, he proposes, "Really, universally, relations stop nowhere, and the exquisite problem of the artist is eternally but to draw, by a geometry of his own, the circle within which they shall happily *appear* to do so" (1,041). In regard to *Roderick Hudson*, James admits having failed in this respect, and in the central consciousness of Rowland Mallett, his house of fiction "totters and refuses to stand square" (1,051).

(Preface to The AMERICAN, 1907): James again begins with the germ of the novel, remembering how the story came to him as he sat in an American "horse-car." As with *Roderick Hudson*, James identifies a significant fault to the novel, confessing to "plotting arch-romance without knowing it." In defining romance, James distinguishes the real, which "represents to my perception the things we cannot possibly *not* know, sooner or later, in one way or another" (1,063), and the romantic, which accounts for "the things that, with all the facilities in the world, all the wealth and all the courage and all the wit and all the adventure, we never *can* directly know" (1,063). In an often-cited image, he describes how the "balloon of experience is in fact of course tied to the earth, and under that necessity we swing, thanks to a rope of remarkable length, in the more or less commodious car of the imagination" (1,064). The successful romancer severs the cable so subtly that the reader never notices. The problem with *The American* is that because James predetermined Christopher Newman's renunciation of revenge, the novel lacks verisimilitude; in reality, the Bellegardes would never have sacrificed Newman's wealth to their aristocratic principles.

(Preface to *The* PORTRAIT OF A LADY, 1908): Unlike *The American,* whose germ resides in a certain action, the germ of *The Portrait of a Lady* lies within the conception of a particular character, the unattached Isabel Archer. The challenge of this novel was in representing that character. Here James composes what is likely the most remembered passage from all of the prefaces, describing the novel as the "house of fiction" that "has in short not one window, but a million. . . . [T]he pierced aperture, either broad or balconied or slit-like and low-browed, is the 'literary form'; but they are, singly or together, as nothing without the posted presence of the watcher—without, in other words, the consciousness of the artist" (1,075). The architectural metaphors of this description run throughout the prefaces, but here Isabel Archer is the "corner-stone" (1,076) of the novel; he identifies her all-night vigil in chapter 42 as "obviously the best thing in the book" (1,084). Whereas James calls Isabel Archer the "central consciousness" of the novel, he develops the word *ficelle* (the French word for string) in referring to characters like Henrietta Stackpole here and Maria Gostrey in *The Ambassadors,* whose purpose is simply to advance the plot. The *ficelles* are the "wheels to the coach" (1,082), neither part of the coach nor seated inside with the hero or heroine.

(Preface to *The* PRINCESS CASAMASSIMA, 1908): Where James identifies the importance of VENICE and PARIS in the previous prefaces, in *The Princess Casamassima* he ascribes similar importance to LON-

DON, noting how Hyacinth Robinson "sprang up for me out of the London pavement" (1,087). James emphasizes the "degrees of feeling" imparted to characters, who are "interesting only in proportion as they feel their respective situations" (1,088). Like Hamlet and Lear, their consciousness of their situations is what captures the audience's interest. James remarks on the importance of "notes," his "gathered impressions and stirred perceptions" (1,101) that allow him to penetrate imaginatively the subject or setting in multiple ways and, in this case, to describe Hyacinth's "subterraneous politics and occult affiliations" (1,101). According to James, this ability is at the heart of the novelist's art.

(Preface to *The* TRAGIC MUSE, 1908): James does not recall the origin of *The Tragic Muse,* characterizing it as a story of the artist's life. James notes the absence of the novel's center, or the lack of an artistic design, exemplified by the "large loose baggy monsters," those 19th-century novels marked by "the accidental and the arbitrary" (1,107). James attempts to allay this problem by presenting the novel entirely in the "pictorial." Additionally, he elaborates on his notion of "foreshortening," in which representation is achieved not by additional detail but "by the art of figuring synthetically, a compactness into which the imagination may cut thick, as into the rich density of a wedding-cake" (1,110).

(Preface to *The* AWKWARD AGE, 1908): In his usual fashion, James begins with relating the origin of the novel, confessing that he can easily remember the germ but declining to delineate it at first. He recalls that he had originally planned a short treatment, but it somehow grew, somewhat organically, to "monstrous" proportions. He had also planned to treat it lightly with some irony in the manner of "Gyp," or Sibylle de Riquetti-Mirabeu, the French author of social comedies written almost entirely in dialogue as is *The Awkward Age.* This heavy use of dialogue lends itself to the dramatic structure of the novel and is reinforced by James's analogizing the composition to constructing a play. The theatrical metaphor also informs the structure, described by James as that of concentric circles surrounding a central subject. In this case, however, that situation is not a character but the situation dramatized by the novel through a series of social scenes. Of the earlier novels presented in the edition, James is least critical of this one.

(Preface to The SPOILS OF POYNTON, "A LONDON LIFE," "The Chaperon," 1908): James provides his most comprehensive account of the germ here: "the stray suggestion, the wandering word, the vague echo" (1,138). For James, the main problem of the germ is that it should only be a hint; giving too much information ruins the germ's ability "to penetrate as finely as possible" (1,138). James continues to expand on the definition of art, describing it as a conscious act of "discrimination and selection" in the face of life's "inclusion and confusion" (1,138). Unlike his earlier discussions of "central consciousnesses" such as Isabel Archer and Rowland Mallett, here James identifies the material objects (the spoils) collected by the Gereths as the heart of the novel's conflict. James also expands on his character types, introducing his idea of the "free spirit" as Fleda Vetch, who "both sees and feels" (1,147), in contrast with the "figure" of Mrs. Gereth, who is clever but not intelligent. At stake here is James's consistent concern with the "appreciation" of his work in its various forms and from various perspectives of reading.

(Preface to WHAT MAISIE KNEW, "The PUPIL," "IN THE CAGE," 1908): Focusing primarily on the narrative viewpoint, James describes the composition of What Maisie Knew and his choice of telling the story through the child's perspective. He describes Maisie's "vivacity of intelligence by which she indeed does vibrate in the infected air" (1,164). As in earlier prefaces, James points to particular passages that represent the "associational magic" of Maisie's consciousness upon which the reader depends. Similarly, he discusses the point of view of the young child in "The Pupil," illustrative of James's self-admitted "incorrigible taste for gradations and superpositions of effect" in conveying "truth diffused, distributed and, as it were, atmospheric" (1,168). In references to "In the Cage," James outlines what he calls the "scenic law," the succession of "little constituted dramas" (1,171), and how that scenic structure leads to an organic sense of plot.

(Preface to "The ASPERN PAPERS," "The TURN OF THE SCREW," "The Liar," "The Two Faces," 1908): James's main concern with "The Aspern Papers" is the story's invention of Jeffrey Aspern, a distinguished American literary figure without a basis in fact. James responds by recalling his discussion of romance (see ROMANCE/REALISM/NATURALISM) and by marking the difference between the historian and the dramatist. As with the concept of the germ, too much information is fatal for the dramatist. Conversely, the historian revels in documents and facts: "[N]ine tenths of the artist's interest in them [facts] is that of what he shall add to them and how he shall turn them" (1,176). With "The Turn of the Screw," James theorizes the modern ghost story, again recalling the idea of romance. In this case, Peter Quint and Miss Jessel, while not typical ghosts, convey the story's sense of the sinister. In not making the story too specific, James hopes to draw the reader into a contemplation of story's elusive sense of evil.

(Preface to "The Reverberator," "Madame de Mauves," "A Passionate Pilgrim," "The Madonna of the Future," "Louisa Pallant," 1908): Discussing this collection of early stories, James defends the slightness of the stories by defining the "anecdote" as "something that has oddly happened to some one" (1,193). James emphasizes how the trivial nature of the action contrasts with the enlargement of the subject, like an "insidious grease-spot" (1,192). The remainder of the preface discusses the INTERNATIONAL THEME, earlier mentioned in prefaces to The American and The Portrait of a Lady. James contrasts the American's and European's awareness of life and explains his predilection for stories about the young American girl, like Francie Dosson and Daisy Miller, as opposed to the American businessman or older woman.

(Preface to "Lady Barbarina," "The Siege of London," "AN INTERNATIONAL EPISODE," "The Pension Beaurepas," "A Bundle of Letters," "The Point of View," 1908): James again picks up the international theme and considers its pervasiveness in his work, concluding that "one never really chooses one's general range of vision . . . so that whatever it 'gives,' whatever it makes us feel and think of, we regard very much as imposed and inevitable" (1,210). In discussing Lady Barbarina, James notes the story's reversal of the usual pattern in his fiction of an older European male marrying a young American woman. In a turn on the "house of fiction" metaphor, James relates the composition of "The Siege of London," recalling a large house blocking the view of London from his study, "like the most voluminous of curtains" (1,220).

(Preface to "The LESSON OF THE MASTER," "The DEATH OF THE LION," "The NEXT TIME," "The FIGURE IN THE CARPET," "The Coxon Fund," 1909): Recalling his association with the *Yellow Book* periodical, James expounds on the differences between the short story and the novella, criticizing the former for its "rude prescription of brevity at any cost" (1,227). James rues the effects on public taste of such constraints. James then defines his concept of operative irony, which "implies and projects the possible other case, the case rich and edifying where the actuality is pretentious and vain" (1,229). In the context of this preface, operative irony becomes another tool to critique the literary marketplace, just as his discussion of "correspondences" between fictional characters and real people addresses the public's sensationalist curiosity.

(Preface to "The AUTHOR OF 'BELTRAFFIO,'" "The MIDDLE YEARS," "GREVILLE FANE," "Broken Wings," "The Tree of Knowledge," "The Abasement of the Northmores," "The GREAT GOOD PLACE," "Four Meetings," "Paste," "Europe," "Miss Gunton of Poughkeepsie," "Fordham Castle," 1909): In the shortest of the prefaces, James returns to the idea of the "concise anecdote" (1,238) and describes the foreshortening necessary to treat a theme in such a form. James uses the term *bristle,* a favorite term found throughout the prefaces, to capture the essence of the anecdote as well as his personal sense of the work of literature. He compares the form of the anecdote to the sonnet in its "indestructible" nature (1,244).

(Preface to "The ALTAR OF THE DEAD," "The BEAST IN THE JUNGLE," "The Birthplace," "The Private Life," "OWEN WINGRAVE," "The Friends of the Friends," "Sir Edmund Orme," "The Real Right Thing," "The JOLLY CORNER," "Julia Bride," 1909): James ties together the stories collected in this volume by addressing the issue of the "wonderful" or the "fairy-tale" (1,257), which induces a reader to wonder. In these stories, the "ghost-story"

fulfills this function, but the key thing that remains is the question of representation, particularly of the supernatural, which for James is best done by showing the way things are felt rather in providing explicit graphic description; for James, "in art economy is always beauty" (1,260).

(Preface to "DAISY MILLER: A STUDY" "The Patagonia," "The Marriages," "The REAL THING," "BROOKSMITH," "The Beldonald Holbein," "The Story in It," "Flickerbridge," "Mrs. Medwin," 1909): James begins by recounting the germ of "Daisy Miller," its composition, and a prospective publisher's rejection of the story as "an outrage on American girlhood" (1,269). He also provides his most extensive treatment of the concept of foreshortening, touching on again the idea of representation. How does one capture the intense truth of a situation in the space of a short story or novella? For James, foreshortening is a "controlled and guarded acceptance, in fact a perfect economic mastery of that conflict" and is instrumental in the story's production of a "rich effect" (1,278). By addressing the question of dialect, James suggests the other stories all represent James's solution to the problem of representing the American social system, the "dilemma formed by the respective discouragement of down-town, of up-town and of the great dialectic tracts" (1,280).

(Preface to The WINGS OF THE DOVE, 1909): In the preface to *The Wings of the Dove,* James addresses the challenge of developing the novel's central consciousness and related subjects. In order of composition, this preface was written somewhere in the middle, around the time of the prefaces to *What Maisie Knew* and "The Aspern Papers." Milly Theale represents a subject in which James had always been interested: a young person knowing she would shortly die and attempting to gain an awareness of having lived. Such was the case of James's cousin Minny (MARY TEMPLE), who died when she was 24. James uses two metaphors similar to the "house of fiction" in describing this subject: first, a medal hanging free in the middle of and reflected in a series of concentric rings (suggesting the dynamics of indirect presentation outlined in the preface to *The Awkward Age*); and second, two series of solid blocks, reaching to the center from each side of an uncompleted arch, an analogy of the novel as comprising unequal halves, connected by the artist in a "makeshift middle" (1,299). Here he defines two more important terms: The picture is narrated or told, whereas the scene is shown or dramatized, either through the interaction of characters or delineation of consciousness.

(Preface to *The* AMBASSADORS, 1909): James commends *The Ambassadors* as "frankly, quite the best, 'all round,' of my productions" (1,306). The principal object of the preface is to delineate Lambert Strether as the central consciousness and to outline the limitations imposed upon a narrative when it is restricted to the first-person point of view, "the darkest abyss of romance . . . foredoomed to looseness" (1,315). He returns to the concept of the *ficelle,* first introduced in the preface to *The Portrait of a Lady,* to exemplify Maria Gostrey as a solution to the narrative problem of providing sufficient information on Strether. James considers the way the picture and the scene interact to provide the foundational structure of the novel. He concludes the preface with a generalization about the novel as "the most independent, most elastic, most prodigious of literary forms" (1,321).

(Preface to *The* GOLDEN BOWL, 1909): In the final preface, James attends to one of the more significant material aspects of the New York Edition, Alvin Langdon Coburn's frontispiece photographs. James applauds Coburn's work, even as he famously warns: "Anything that relieves responsible prose of the duty of being, while placed before us, good enough, interesting enough, and, if the question be of picture, pictorial enough, above all *in itself,* does it the worst of services, and may well inspire in the lover of literature certain lively questions as to the future of that institution" (1,326). For James, the frontispiece photographs function much as his prose in expressing the idea or impression of a thing rather than the thing itself. James's second major concern is over the matter of revision. James describes revision not as rewriting but as rereading: "[T]o revise is to see, or to look over, again—which means in the case of a written thing neither more nor less than to re-read it" (1,332). Recent critics have picked up on this comment to argue that the edition—and the prefaces—are James's attempt to

recreate himself as his own best reader in reaction to the public's misreading.

CRITICAL ANALYSIS

Despite the economic failure of the New York Edition, Henry James's prefaces have consistently received much critical attention, becoming both figuratively and literally James's "art of the novel." Critics have interpreted the prefaces as offering a poetics of the novel that would establish it as a legitimate literary form in the 20th century, particularly with the New Critics. From the beginning, James regarded his prefaces as critical essays. In a letter to WILLIAM DEAN HOWELLS, he describes them as "a sort of plea for Criticism, for Discrimination, for Appreciation on other than infantile lines. . . . They ought, collected together, none the less, to form a sort of comprehensive manual or *vademecum* for aspirants in our arduous profession" (Horne 463).

In 1921, Percy Lubbock published *The Craft of Fiction,* drawing heavily on James's prefaces for his technical language. Leon Edel (1931) was another crucial early voice in establishing them as James's statement on his method of writing novels. R. P. Blackmur also regarded the prefaces as a sort of aesthetic manifesto, presenting them as *The Art of the Novel* in 1934. Influential in reasserting James's reputation, Lubbock, Edel, and Blackmur clearly established the aesthetic nature of the prefaces, an attitude that held sway until the 1970s.

In the 1970s and 1980s, critics began to turn away from viewing the prefaces as either keys to particular novels or as a cohesive theory of the novel, considering instead the importance of the prefaces' autobiographical tone. William Goetz treats the prefaces as extensions of James's earlier works, noting such factors as first-person narrative and dialogue construction. Although he argues for an autobiographical reading, he concludes that the prefaces try to be both formalist criticism and autobiographical reflection, thus mingling the intrinsic and extrinsic criticism without attempting to reconcile the two. Mutlu Blasing also reads the prefaces autobiographically, identifying James's stance in the prefaces as "precisely the position of the author in autobiography," exhibiting both retrospective recollection and inwardly directed self-conscious criticism (313). Blasing points out that because of their autobiographical nature, the prefaces are inherently works of fiction, recreating James's life, not just his career.

Informed by poststructuralist theory, more recent interpretations have considered the prefaces as commentary on the notion of reading. Walter Benn Michaels, writing in 1976, compares the self-reading tactics of James and T. S. Eliot and concludes that with Eliot the reader submits to the text, whereas with James textual meaning depends on the reader, motivating James to offer himself as an ideal reader. John Pearson, in one of the few book-length studies dedicated solely to the prefaces, argues that "James creates the modern reader by assuming authority over his work both as its creator and ideal consumer and then overtly and covertly instructs his readers how to appreciate and discriminate Jamesian literary art" (2).

Another strand of recent criticism contextualizes the prefaces as part of the material production of the New York Edition. In 1993, Herschel Parker took issue with the iconic status of Blackmur's collection, noting that "the mere existence of the wonderfully convenient *The Art of the Novel* subtly and insidiously robbed the prefaces of their volume-specific qualities . . . [and has] all but stopped us from reading them as prefatory" (305). Parker warns against viewing *The Art of the Novel* as one more work *by* James or as a codified statement of his aesthetic and literary conceptions, and he calls above all for a study of "a reading of the prefaces the way the purchasers of the New York Edition were privileged to read them—one at a time, prefaced to individual novels and to groups of shorter fictions" (303). More recently, Michael Anesko and David McWhirter have historicized the publication of the New York Edition, a deluxe edition in which the prefaces framed James's revised masterpieces. Many of the essays in McWhirter's collection represent the variety of contemporary theoretical approaches applied specifically to the prefaces. Paul Armstrong, for instance, demonstrates a poststructural approach by calling for a "doubled reading" of the prefaces: "James's prefaces are at their best as introduction to James when they

refuse to specify what his fiction means" (137). In her reading of the prefaces, Eve Sedgwick coins the term *queer performativity*, thereby linking James's shame over his theatrical failures to his complex negotiation of gender codes as manifested in the dense literary style of his late period.

It is important to remember the context of his intended readers, who expected an intimate connection to the author through the prefaces. James played along, at least on one level. In a memorandum to Scribner's, he describes the prefaces to his PUBLISHER, not as a critical exposition, but as a conversation: "I desire to furnish each book . . . with a freely colloquial and even, perhaps, as I may say, confidential preface or introduction, representing, in a manner, the history of the work or the group" (367). The contrast between a "comprehensive manual" and a "freely colloquial," "confidential" talk indicates the difficult position in which James found himself as he prepared the edition and wrote the prefaces. The prefaces provide a key vantage point to read James himself as he attempts to respond to these contradictory expectations.

As a product of the marketplace, the preface to the novel has a history intricately intertwined with the novel. One of the most common strategies used in prefaces is to describe the origin of the story in order to ground it in reality. With James, the relating of the story's genesis comes through in his theory of the germ, or the *donnée*. Many of his prefaces begin with a description of where and when the story was originally composed: "'Roderick Hudson' was begun in Florence in the spring of 1874, designed from the first for serial publication in 'The Atlantic Monthly,' where it opened in January 1875" (1,039) (see FLORENCE); "'The American,' which I had begun in Paris early in the winter of 1875–76" (1,053); or "The simplest account of the origin of 'The Princess Casamassima' is, I think, that this fiction proceeded quite directly, during the first year of long residence in London, from the habit and interest of walking the streets" (1,086). James uses this strategy in the first several prefaces, but in the subsequent prefaces the detailed description of the *where* and *when* of composition gives way to a description of the germ alone. Whereas, for example, in the preface to *The American*, he describes both where and when he began the composition and recalls the anecdote of the "horse-car," which gave him the idea of the novel, the preface to *The Ambassadors* begins directly with the germ. Although the veracity of the germ is often questioned, such as when Gregory Pfitzer explores James's sudden memory lapse in regard to the genesis of *The Tragic Muse*, that problem is not so critical since it is the gesture alone that is vital to the prefatory function. In fact, bringing up his inability to remember works tends to endear James to the reader—exposing his own faults and exhibiting his humanness.

James also draws upon the self-effacing style of the preface when he calls attention to the mistakes or flaws in his books. For example, he remarks of *Roderick Hudson*: "My mistake on Roderick's behalf—and not in the least of conception, but of composition and expression—is that, at the rate at which he falls to pieces, he seems to place himself beyond our understanding and our sympathy" (1,047). Likewise, of *The American*, he reveals: "What I have recognized then in 'The American,' much to my surprise and after long years, is that the experience here represented is the disconnected and uncontrolled experience—uncontrolled by our general sense of 'the way things happen'—which romance alone more or less successfully palms off on us" (1,064–1,065). Not only does James (the Master) admit a mistake here, but he subtly ingratiates himself to readers by inserting such phrases as "much to my surprise." Culminating in his discussion of romance and reality, this passage legitimates the genre of the novel. However, James also alters the conception of the author, analogizing it variously as a bricklayer, builder, conjurer, craftsman, creator, critic of life, dramatist, fabulist, magician, painter, and parent. An odd collection of metaphors, they all insist in some way on the author's role as creator.

Unlike prefaces of earlier authors, for example those by Henry Fielding, which almost always subordinate the writer to the reader (intentionally or not), James openly reveals his attitude toward the reader who, in his mind, does not properly read his novels. Many critics agree that James wrote the prefaces because he felt misunderstood, and

it is these statements that reveal this relationship to the reader. In *The American*, the same preface in which he reveals his "greatest flaw," he writes that "ninety-nine readers in a hundred have no use whatever" for "intimate appreciations" (1,062). Similarly, in *The Tragic Muse*, he complains that "there would be more still to be said . . . could I fondly suppose as much of the interest of the book 'left over' for the reader as for myself" (1,117). One of the more scathing comments appears in the preface to *What Maisie Knew*. Describing the method in which the reader "feels" the scene, James writes: "That is, we feel it when, in such tangled connexions, we happen to care. I shouldn't really go on as if this were the case with many readers" (1,172). Other examples include: "the dire paucity of readers ever recognizing or ever missing positive beauty" (1,315); the reader as "monster" (1,233); and reader's "extraordinary benightedness . . . perverse and inconsequent" (1,127). Vivien Rundle states that "James's ambivalence toward his audience prompted him to use the New York Edition for the particular purpose of redefining his own literary career, deliberately creating in the prefaces a 'heroic narrative'" (68). This heroic narrative, however, is often at the expense of the reader.

As the genre of the novel became more accepted by the mid-19th century, the legitimating function of the preface became unnecessary, and many of the realist writers in America in the late 19th century such as William Dean Howells and Frank Norris did not pen prefaces. If writers of this period attached prefaces, they were often for different reasons than legitimating the genre, which had by now been accepted and had even surpassed poetry as a literary genre. With this change then, James's claims to legitimacy may have seemed out of place. As necessities changed, the preface may have disappeared had it not been for a relatively new publishing phenomenon now appearing and culminating in the 1890s, the collected edition. The standard, uniform library edition of works of different authors can be traced to the 18th century, but the collected edition, or more relevant to James, the deluxe edition of a single living novelist, appears to be a 19th-century invention, one that also reflects the changing notion of the author and the commodification of both the author and the book itself. Issued in uniform size and fine binding, featuring an engraving or photograph of the author as a frontispiece and often a facsimile signature, these deluxe editions almost without fail featured prefaces written by the author, all attesting to the authenticity of the edition, again tying into the growing commodity culture. The collected edition perpetuated the use of prefaces and slightly altered their purpose. The collected edition serves as, in Michael Millgate's terms, a testamentary act, a way "in which writers famous in their own times have sought in old age to exert some degree of posthumous control over their personal and literary reputation" (2). The preface, then, often became the site of the author's personal "testament" to the work. It was the combination of physical appearance and authorial commentary provided in the preface that allowed this. Contemporary critics and reviewers generally applauded James's preface to the edition; yet most looked in them for what they had grown accustomed to: personal memoirs and explanations of problems.

Whatever theoretical aims James may have had for the prefaces, there was from the beginning an undercurrent that developed from their use in the collected edition. James said of the prefaces that they were first a marketing ploy:

> This staleness of sensibility, in connection with them [the prefaces], blocks out for the hour every aspect but that of their being all done, and of their perhaps helping the Edition to sell two or three copies more! They will have represented much labour to this latter end—though in that they will have differed indeed from no other of their fellow manifestations (in general) whatever; and the resemblance will be even increased if the two or three copies *don't*, in the form of an extra figure or two, mingle with my withered laurels. (qtd. in McWhirter 3–4)

James here aligns the preface with the commodity of the collected edition and recognizes that he is following an established tradition. James's prefaces offer a certain poignancy as witness to his attempt to establish his authority as author through a form that implicitly erases the author. The loss of the edition's power as a commodity does not fully explain the economic failure of the New York Edition. Neither do economic problems of production or distribution. James's concern with the production of the edition, investing not only his time and effort but, even more important, his hopes of public acclaim, appears as a critical issue with him.

As late as 1913, James was still relying on the edition's power. In responding to Fanny Prothero's query asking which of his books a friend should read, James writes that his suggestions "are all on the basis of the Scribner's (or Macmillan's) collective and revised and prefaced Edition of my things" (Edel, *Letters* 683). He chides his correspondent that "if he is not minded somehow to obtain access to *that* form of them, ignoring any other, he forfeits half or much more than half, my confidence" (683). How much self-deprecating humor should be ascribed to the statement (James adds, "So I thus amicably beseech him—!") is debatable, but he continues to promote the edition even after recognizing its failure. The issue of critical acclamation versus commercial success seems to be a fundamental problem with James's conception of the purpose of the New York Edition and is integrally linked to the changing conception of public and private. As Marcia Jacobson points out, "[W]riting [for James] becomes a vocation instead of a business" (10). Yet there is a strong urge apparent in James to want to be recognized in the popular realm. It is curious as to why James invested so much in the economic return—why he judged his success in market "business" terms instead of artistic "vocational" terms. On the other hand, Vivienne Rundle's comparison between James and JOSEPH CONRAD suggests how James's edition might not have fit into the current notion of public. Rundle argues that the difference between the two sets of prefaces is one of rhetoric, that Conrad's prefaces "grant the reader a place and a role, allowing the prefaces to function as living texts, while James' prefaces are transfixed and petrified because of the exclusion of any real readerly contribution from their narrative system" (69). James sees himself above most of his readers, sees himself as an artist, as the poet, far different from the mass consumers of the commercial public. James fervently resists becoming a fixture, and this resistance is finally what works against the plan of the edition—nowhere is this better seen than in the prefaces.

The preface as part of the collected edition had certain functions different from what had been commonplace before and different also from what James intended. By the early 1900s, the collected edition was also losing its power as commodity, and James had relied upon that power to reestablish his literary stature. When Jacobson notes that James spoke "with an authority more akin to that of his Victorian predecessors than his peers of the eighties" (15), she suggests that James's conception of the author and the market was several years out of date, although it can be argued that he was also ahead of his time with his arch-critical prefaces.

FURTHER READING

Anesko, Michael. *"Friction with the Market": Henry James and the Profession of Authorship.* New York: Oxford University Press, 1986.

Armstrong, Paul B. "Reading James's Prefaces and Reading James." In McWhirter, 125–137.

Blackmur, R. P., ed. *The Art of the Novel: Critical Prefaces of Henry James.* New York: Scribner's, 1934.

Blasing, Mutlu. "The Story of the Stories: Henry James's Prefaces as Autobiography." In *Approaches to Victorian Autobiography*, edited by George P. Landow, 311–332. Athens: Ohio University Press, 1979.

Cameron, Sharon. *Thinking in Henry James.* Chicago: University of Chicago Press, 1989.

Culver, Stuart. "Ozymandias and the Mastery of Ruins: The Design of the New York Edition." In McWhirter, 39–57.

———. "Representing the Author: Henry James, Intellectual Property and the Work of Writing." In *Henry James: Fiction as History*, edited by Ian F. A. Bell, 114–137. London: Vision, 1984.

Davidson, Rob. "James's Prefaces to the New York Edition." In *The Master and the Dean: The Literary Criticism of Henry James and William Dean Howells*, 193–223. Columbia: University of Missouri Press, 2005.

Edel, Leon, ed. *Henry James: Letters, vol. 4: 1895–1916.* Cambridge, Mass.: Harvard University Press, 1984.

———. *The Prefaces of Henry James.* Paris: Jouve, 1931.

Goetz, William R. "The Prefaces: Criticism and Autobiography." *Henry James and the Darkest Abyss of Romance*, 82–110. Baton Rouge: Louisiana State University Press, 1986.

Holland, Laurence B. "The Prefaces." In *The Expense of Vision: Essays on the Craft of Henry James*, 155–182. Princeton, N.J.: Princeton University Press, 1964.

Horne, Philip. *Henry James: A Life in Letters.* New York: Viking, 1999.

Jacobson, Marcia. *Henry James and the Mass Market.* Tuscaloosa: University of Alabama Press, 1983.

James, Henry. *French Writers, Other European Writers, the Prefaces to the New York Edition.* Edited by Leon Edel and Mark Wilson. New York: Library of America, 1984.

Kimball, Jean. "A Classified Subject Index to Henry James's Critical Prefaces to the New York Edition (Collected in *The Art of the Novel*)." *Henry James Review* 6, no. 2 (1985): 89–135.

Leuschner, Eric. "'Utterly, insurmountably, unsaleable': Collected Editions, Prefaces, and the 'Failure' of Henry James's New York Edition." *Henry James Review* 22, no. 1 (2001): 24–40.

Margolis, Ann. *Henry James and the Problems of Audience: An International Act.* Ann Arbor: UMI Research Press, 1985.

McWhirter, David, ed. *Henry James's New York Edition: The Construction of Authorship.* Palo Alto, Calif.: Stanford University Press, 1995.

Michaels, Walter Benn. "Writers Reading: James and Eliot." *Modern Language Notes* 91 (1976): 827–849.

Miller, J. Hillis. *The Ethics of Reading: Kant, de Man, Eliot, Trollope, James, and Benjamin.* New York: Columbia University Press, 1987.

Millgate, Michael. *Testamentary Acts: Browning, Tennyson, James, Hardy.* Oxford, U.K.: Clarendon, 1992.

Parker, Herschel. "Deconstructing the Art of the Novel and Liberating James's Prefaces." *Henry James Review* 14, no. 3 (1993): 284–307.

Pearson, John H. "The Art of Self-Creation: Henry James in the New York Edition Prefaces." In *Marketing the Author: Authorial Personae, Narrative Selves and Self Fashioning 1880–1930*, edited by Marysa Demoor, 40–53. Basingbroke, England: Palgrave, 2004.

———. *The Prefaces of Henry James: Framing the Modern Reader.* University Park: Pennsylvania State University Press, 1997.

Pfitzer, Gregory M. "Sins of Omission: What Henry James Left Out of the Preface to *The Tragic Muse* and Why." *American Literary Realism* 25, no. 1 (1992): 38–53.

Ross, Melanie H. "'The Mirror with a Memory': Tracking Consciousness in the Preface to *The Golden Bowl.*" *Henry James Review* 26, no. 3 (2005): 246–255.

Rowe, John Carlos. *Theoretical Dimensions of Henry James.* Madison: University of Wisconsin Press, 1984.

Rundle, Vivienne. "Defining Frames: The Prefaces of Henry James and Joseph Conrad." *Henry James Review* 16, no. 1 (1995): 66–92.

Sedgwick, Eve Kosofsky. "Shame and Performativity: Henry James's New York Edition Prefaces." In McWhirter, 206–239.

Eric Leuschner, *Fort Hays State University*

travel writings

Few, if any, American writers have shown as much preoccupation and fascination with the Old World of Europe as Henry James. This INTERNATIONAL THEME figures in many of James's most well-known works, and one can easily say that his experiences both in America and Europe animate his work. James was well traveled, especially during his formative years of the 1870s, producing a large body of work documenting his experiences traveling in England and on the European continent, and continuing to do so, albeit more sporadically, throughout his career. While these travel writings have not received the same level of attention as his fiction, they are nonetheless satisfying in their own right and make a significant contribution to the Jamesian canon. They offer an intimate look into James's personal and intellectual development as he struggles to absorb and to find adequate forms to represent the sheer magnitude and complexity of Europe. In this respect, moreover, they expand the scope and potential of the genre of travel writing.

SYNOPSIS

It is difficult to track the full publication history of James's travel writings since many of the individual essays first came into print as magazine articles, appearing in PERIODICALS such as the *Nation* and the *Atlantic Monthly*. Many of the essays were revised by James before their final inclusion in the NEW YORK EDITION, sometimes more than once, and in some instances quite drastically, to the point that the final versions say and mean something very different from the originals. Furthermore, volumes of collected travel essays appeared throughout James's career, beginning in 1875 with *Transatlantic Sketches*, which was then republished in 1883 under the title *Foreign Parts*. This was followed in 1884 by *Portraits of Places*. The sketches devoted to James's travels throughout the French countryside, after first appearing in serial form in the *Atlantic Monthly* in 1883–84, were released in book form as *A Little Tour in France* (1884). *English Hours* came out in 1905, adding two new pieces to the older sketches written about England from the 1875 and 1884 collections. Similarly, *Italian Hours* (1909) collected the revised versions of all the previously published Italian travel writings, along with a few retrospective pieces written specifically for that volume. The critical analyses below will concentrate on these last three titles since they give individual focus to James's most important destinations of France, England, and Italy and also represent the most finished editions of the travel writings.

CRITICAL ANALYSIS

A Little Tour in France (1884)

In the preface to *A Little Tour in France*, James explains that these travel essays will be written as a series of impressionistic sketches, as opposed to a sustained exposition of the finer or deeper elements of the French experience:

> The expectation had been that [these writings] should accompany a series of drawings, and they themselves were altogether governed by the pictorial spirit. They made . . . no pretensions

to any other; they are impressions, immediate, easy, and consciously limited; if the written word may ever play the part of brush or pencil, they are sketches on "drawing paper" and nothing more. (3)

The traveler James thus goes in search of "the largest cluster of curious things that presents itself to his sight" (86). He finds this, for instance, in his quick impressions of Provence; it appears to him as a picturesque "land where the silver-grey earth is impregnated with the light of the sky," imbued with "the Provençal charm which . . . glowed in the sweet sunshine and the white rocks and lurked in the smoke-puffs of the little olives" (187). Similarly, in Le Mans, in that "idle half-hour in front of the café, in the mild October afternoon suffused with human sounds," James revels in the pleasure of simple, yet evocative sensations:

> The afternoon was warm and still; the air was admirably soft . . . . [M]y ear was soothed by the fine shades of French enunciation, by the detached syllables of that perfect tongue. There was nothing in particular in the prospect to charm; it was an average French view. Yet I felt a charm, a kind of sympathy, a sense of the completeness of French life and of the lightness and brightness of the social air . . . . (112)

At the same time, however, these quick impressions are tempered by the realization that the past is fleeting and that modernization is encroaching upon the old Europe. A visit to a wine exposition in Bordeaux, for example, occasions a lament for the lost arts of the past. At the geographical and spiritual center of French winemaking, rather than sharing in what he calls the essential distillation of the French "soul," James instead tastes vintages that are "all machine made and expressionless, in spite of the . . . conscious smartness of the 'last new thing,' that was stamped on all of them" (145). The town of Angers disappoints James since it has joined "the disagreeable class of old towns that have been, as the English say, 'done up.' Not the oldness, but the newness, of the place is what strikes the sentimental tourist today, as he wanders with irritation along second-rate boule-vards, looking vaguely about him for absent gables" (114). The town has been "'[s]tupidly and vulgarly modernised'" to the extent that it has become a "victim" of its own "improvements" (114). At Azay-le-Rideau, James takes a "particular fancy to the roof, high, steep, old, with its slope of bluish slate, and the way the weather-worn chimneys seemed to grow out of it—living things in a deep soil" (79). Yet, while the organicism of the scene animates, enlivens, and harmonizes his vision of this world, it is nonetheless marred by "the blankness and bareness of the walls, which have none of that delicate parasitic deposit that agrees so well—to the eye—with the surface of old dwellings" (79). The nostalgic preference for the untainted, unrestored past here takes form as the desire for the past to cling literally to or coat the surface of the European world. In this, James argues for the physicality or substantiality of time itself, a quality that is needed in order for an American truly to experience European travel.

While James's entire corpus of travel writings makes some attempt to reckon with this fleeting or disappearing "sense of the past," A Little Tour is especially marked by James's continual, and at times startling or emotionally wrenching, realization of the violent history of France. The sketches fuse their impressions with reflections triggered by confrontations with France's often bloody history, and the legacy of suffering and conflict is an inseparable part of the envisioned scenes, penetrating and infusing the visible terrain of the present as a kind of atmosphere or ambience. Amboise, for example, confronts the observer with "the ineffaceable stain" that "[t]he wars of religion have left here . . . wherever they passed. An imaginative visitor at Amboise to-day may fancy that the traces of blood that are mixed with the red dust on the crossed iron bars of the grim-looking balcony . . ." (64). The social pleasantries of France always seem to exist against the dark background of past war, turmoil, and most tragically, the Revolution. The nostalgic revelry in the charm of the scene seems often, if not always, tempered by the recognition that the famous sights in France, for all their architectural and picturesque splendor, were sites as well of tragedy and suffering. For every positive historical event, there is in the same breath the recollection of unspeakable brutalities:

> The most hideous episode of the Revolution was enacted at Nantes, where hundreds of men and women, tied together in couples, were set afloat upon rafts and sunk to the bottom of the Loire. The tall eighteenth-century house, full of the *air noble,* in France always reminds me of those dreadful years—of the street scenes of the Revolution . . . . [W]henever I have a vision of prisoners bound on tumbrels that jolt slowly to the scaffold, . . . I see in the background the well-ordered features of the architecture of the period—the clear grey stone, the high pilasters, the arching lines of the *entresol,* the classic pediment, the slate covered attic. (122)

Despite the stated intent in the preface, this seems already to venture far beyond the limitations of the impressionistic sketch. Rather, this wants to become a commentary on the Enlightenment and, perhaps by extension, on the United States, whose own revolutionary origins are of a piece with the French. Why or how, James seems to be asking does brutality come hand in hand with the most enlightened and rational expressions of humanity? How can a culture capable of building such perfectly designed and measured architecture also build the guillotine? Or perhaps, the question is, how can a culture dedicated to order create one and *not* create the other?

English Hours (1905)

In the depictions of the towns and countryside of England, *English Hours* shares many of the same themes and attitudes of the French and Italian essays, again because most of them were composed in the decade of the 1870s, James's most prolific period of travel. English towns are "full of that delightful element of the crooked, the accidental, the unforeseen," a novelty to "American eyes, accustomed to our eternal straight lines and right angles" (56). Yet, much like the French countryside, rural England seems burdened with the heavy, foreboding sense of the past. Everything seems "cruelly quaint," and "dreadfully expressive," and "seems fairly to reek with mortality"

(60). "Every stain and crevice seems to syllable some human record—a record of lives airless and unlighted, . . . peopled by victims of dismal old-world pains and fears" (60).

Perhaps the most intriguing chapters in *English Hours,* however, are those devoted to James's travels in LONDON. James has a complex and contradictory experience of London, introducing it to his readers as a "murky modern Babylon," as a city that is at once "dreadful" and "delightful," one that "evokes as many associations of misery as of empire" (13, 18, 30). On one hand, "[a]ll history appeared to live again, and the continuity of things to vibrate through my mind . . . . It appeared to me to present phenomena and to contain objects of every kind, of an inexhaustible interest" (16). On the other hand, without much provocation other than sitting in a hotel in the "fading daylight," James makes note of how a "sudden horror of the whole place" descends upon him, "like a tiger-pounce of homesickness" (18). London is "hideous, vicious, cruel, and above all overwhelming" (18). If London "is the particular spot in the world which communicates the greatest sense of life," it is nevertheless "as indifferent as Nature herself to the single life" of each of its individual inhabitants (18, 21).

Here the travel essay becomes a more deeply considered meditation on the growth or establishment of the modern city. London is the paradigmatic or emblematic city in the English-speaking world, if not in the world itself; it is for James, "the capital of the human race" (21). It is the testing ground or laboratory for a new kind of social organization in which life is lived on a massive scale. The "idea and the name" of London becomes not so much a designation of a "place" per se but an abstract expression of "extent and number," and it is this "mere immensity" of the city that ultimately forms the "large part of its savour" (18, 19). "One has not the alternative of speaking of London as a whole, for the simplest reason that there is no such thing as the whole of it. It is immeasurable . . . ." (35). The true inhabitant of London "fancies himself . . . for being a particle in so unequalled an aggregation; and its immeasurable circumference, even though unvisited and lost in smoke, gives him the sense of a social, an intellectual margin" (19).

Whereas in France and Italy James seeks out and delights in what might be called a "vertical" connection to some very deep, unspoiled, and authentic vision of the past, in London he celebrates his anonymity, if not his disappearance, into the vast horizontal spread of the present-day metropolis. The "London lover loses himself" in the city's "swelling consciousness," in the "dusky mantle" that it "spreads . . . over innumerable races and creeds" (20). This quality of sprawl is reflected in the "scenes" or impressions that present themselves to James's eye. London unfolds as a "tremendous chapter of accidents," as "miles upon miles of the dreariest, stodgiest commonness" (24). Whereas other great European cities offer an abundance of picturesque sights, the observer of London is left to contemplate "[t]housands of acres . . . covered by low black houses of the cheapest construction, without ornament, without grace, without character or even identity" (24). And yet, this dreary vision itself becomes transformed into something magnificent, and even sublime; the vastness of the city extending everywhere in all directions elevates even the poorest of perspectives, infusing every "shabby corner" with the energy of importance that derives from being a part of some much larger entity. It is as if the city of London takes on the creative, elemental force of Nature itself; it is a city that "makes everything," even "its own system of weather and its own optical laws," one whose very "atmosphere, with its magnificent mystifications . . . flatters and superfuses, makes everything brown, rich, dim, vague, magnifies distances and minimises details" (24). Despite or perhaps because of this realization, James is moved to argue that London "is immensely democratic, and that, no doubt, is part of the manner in which she is salutary to the individual; she teaches him his 'place' by an incomparable discipline, but deprives him of complaint by letting him see that she has exactly the same lash for every other back" (32). "[F]rom the moment you *are* of [London], . . . you belong to a body in which a general equality prevails. However exalted, however able, however rich, however renowned you may be, there are too many people at least as much so for your own idiosyncrasies to count" (33). Here the generalized and undiffer-

entiated extension of the city generates an ethic. In a city whose primary virtue is its formlessness, which is to say its "poverty" of beautiful sensory impressions, "economic" poverty—which, as James quickly comes to find out, is an enormous social problem in 19th-century London—ceases to be a "disgrace" (33).

This may seem to be an equivocal or ambivalent perspective upon such a problematic social issue, although one senses that the disparities between the rich and the poor in English society, more than anything else he encounters in his travels, disillusion him, ruling out the "impressionistic" or highly aestheticized stance he adopts in the Italian and French excursions. Rather than "close one's eyes upon the immense misery," James, in the end, will advise the enlightened traveler to remain "irremediably conscious of that dark gulf" between social and economic classes (35).

Italian Hours (1909)

Italian Hours seems richer, more textured and complex than James's other travel writings, in part perhaps because Italy, more than any other place in the world, looms largest in James's imagination. Nathalia Wright has argued that James's entire career was in fact a "retrospective engagement with the Italian scene," an observation confirmed by James himself in writings such as the PREFACE to RODERICK HUDSON (1875): "[T]he loved Italy was the scene of my fiction—so much *more* loved than one has ever been able, even after fifty efforts to say!" (248, viii).

Readers of James's fiction will undoubtedly notice the frequent references to the visual sense. So much of what happens to James's characters depends upon or proceeds from what and how they "see" or, tragically, what they fail to see. Similarly, *Italian Hours* seems, above all, to be an extended exercise or exploration of the capacities of vision. Bonney MacDonald goes so far as to argue that Italy was, in fact, where James "learned to see," even to the point of his becoming "overpowered by the direct force of visual experience" (3, 2).

This is dramatically realized in the group of essays devoted to the city of VENICE, the most "picturesque" of Italian cities. They exemplify a painterly style of writing in their colorful descriptions, their playful use of light and shadow, their careful attention to the compositional arrangement and "framing" of objects and scenes. "The mere use of one's eyes in Venice is happiness enough," begins James in the essay "Venice: An Early Impression" (337). "Sea and sky seem to meet half-way, to blend their tones into a soft iridescence, a lustrous compound of wave and cloud and a hundred nameless local reflections . . . ." (337). The mundane, concrete reality of Venice, the "slimy brick, marble battered and befouled," the "rags, dirt [and] decay" becomes visible, and knowable, through this "inscrutable flattery of the atmosphere," this "clear tissue" of light that is flung "against every object of vision" (337). Finally, there is "nothing but the light to see," and one's experience of the city becomes simply a "longing for pure radiance" (337). The city itself follows the same visual logic as a painted image: Venice is both "model and painter"; it is "both the picture and the point of view" (304, 317). The paintings that are on display in Venice are so radiant and aesthetically rich because the city that contains, inspires, and produces them is itself possessed of these same qualities:

> Nowhere, not even in Holland, where the correspondence between the real aspects and the little polished canvases is so constant and so exquisite, do art and life seem so interfused and, as it were, so consanguineous. All the splendor of light and color, all the Venetian air and the Venetian history are on the walls and ceilings of the palaces; and all the genius of the masters, all the images and visions they have left upon canvas, seem to tremble in the sunbeams and dance upon the waves. That is the perpetual interest of the place—that you live in a certain sort of knowledge as in a rosy cloud. (303)

Yet, if James writes of Italy as if it appears to him as a stream of brief and delightful sensory impressions, this is both exceeded and tempered by an abiding consciousness that what he sees are merely repetitions of past impressions from previous travelers. James, in fact, believed that he "could never absorb Italy as he had appropriated London and Oxford, and indeed all of England," for example,

"where he had felt himself breathing the air of home" (Edel 298–299). Italy, as James wrote in an 1892 letter to Grace Norton did not "reveal itself easily, or ever completely" (Tuttleton 44). James addresses this difficulty in the preface to "The ASPERN PAPERS" (1888) as well: Italy is "beyond our ken and escap[es] our penetration." "The great historic complexity" of Italy renders one's perceptive faculties impotent: "penetration fails; we scratch at the extensive surface, we meet the perfunctory smile, we hang about in the golden air" (27–28). The creative, impulsive force of Italy always overruns the limits of one's own senses, and yet at the same time leaves one incomplete, unfulfilled. As Sergio Perosa writes: "[T]he beauty and enticement of Italy prove a double-edged menace. Her sunny atmosphere harbors mischief; her magnificence can be a blight; her exuberance proves destructive" (60–61). "The 'portrait of Italy,'" adds Agostino Lombardo, "is always incomplete, always 'in progress'; it is always in the end unreachable, and if it *represents* anything at all, it is the limitation, if not the failure of the act of representation itself" (233). "Italy is solitude and renunciation; Italy is a stage where men and objects wear masks, creating a show in the presence of which the American 'dreamers' find themselves . . . face to face with history" (Lombardo 236).

The *Italian Hours* essays thus exhibit something of a dualistic quality, reflecting both this love of Italy and the sense of resignation that this longing will always remain, in the end, unfulfilled. In this, these travel essays speak to, or from, the larger metaphoric significance of Italy in Western literature. The "meaning" of Italy is its duality, its placement both at the center of Western cultural and artistic achievement and again beyond the margins, as the embodiment of sensual excess that leads to mental and moral corruption and decay amid the heavy, overdetermined ornamentations of the Italian cityscape. Italy represents the not always reconcilable duality of a rational civilization resting on the still visible remnants—the catacombs, the half-buried relics—of the classical past that extrude through the "barriers" of time onto the field of the present.

As a result, these texts reflect an anxiety about the status or meaning of the past relative to the present and future. The past literally haunts James as he travels throughout Italy, and at times, the essays seem to have that same preternatural attraction to the ghostly that one finds in such stories as "The TURN OF THE SCREW" (1898) or "The JOLLY CORNER" (1908). At the site, for example, of Jean-Jacques Rousseau's former lodgings at Les Charmettes, James makes the unsettling observation that "the place generally, in so far as some faint ghostly presence of its famous inmates seems to linger there, is by no means exhilarating. . . . Les Charmettes is haunted by ghosts unclean and forlorn. The place tells of poverty, perversity and distress" (366).

It is not only the past that haunts James, however. If anything, the notion that Italy, a country whose meaning and value derive from its historicity, might in fact have a *future* is, for James, a source of great concern. This is voiced most poignantly in the 1892 essay "The Grand Canal":

Venetian life, in the large old sense, has long since come to an end, and the essential present character of the most melancholy of cities resides simply in its being the most beautiful of tombs. Nowhere else has the past been laid to rest with such tenderness, such a sadness of resignation and remembrance. Nowhere else is the present so alien, so discontinuous, so like a crowd in a cemetery without garlands for the graves. (314)

The commentaries on the Italian Carnival in the essay "A Roman Holiday" and again in "Florentine Notes" express this lament for Italy's modernization as well:

[N]ow that Italy is made, the Carnival is unmade . . . . The spectacle on the Corso has seemed to me, on the whole, an illustration of that great breach with the past of which Catholic Christendom felt the somewhat muffled shock in September, 1870. A traveller acquainted with the fully Papal Rome, coming back any time during the past winter, must have immediately noticed that something momentous had happened—something hostile to the elements of picture and colour and "style." (413)

James continues:

Yesterday that languid organism known as the Florentine Carnival put on a momentary semblance of vigour, and decreed a general *corso* through the town. The spectacle was not brilliant . . . . [T]here was an almost ludicrous incongruity in seeing Pleasure leading her train through these dusky historic streets . . . . [A]s the carriages crept solemnly along they seemed to keep a funeral march—to follow an antique custom, an exploded faith, to its tomb. The Carnival is dead, and these good people who had come abroad to make merry were funeral mutes and grave-diggers. (542)

In these brief observations, there already is a rupture in what James calls the Carnival's "brilliant promise of legend" (413). The historical process of Italy actually forming itself as a modern nation corrupts and diminishes what is by rights the sacred ritual of the Carnival—not so much to the Italians themselves but to the foreign tourist who has come to Italy in search of authentic expressions of the past. James, with no small degree of regret, if not sarcasm, identifies this as the "march of progress" (413).

Such an attitude may strike the reader as excessively reactionary. The reader, moreover, cannot help but notice the curious *absence* of actual Italians from the otherwise beautifully observed, highly detailed renderings of the Italian cityscapes. Where people do appear, they are seldom more than ornamentation to the larger picturesque scenes that James presents to his readers. James's Italy is rather one of the imagination, one in which the physical matter of the observed scene becomes an occasion for his reflecting, ironically enough, on just how it has become such an occasion. One can perhaps redeem this by observing that, at their best, the *Italian Hours* essays become more than mere travelogues and seem in some way to be meditations on art making, on writing, and on consciousness in general. They are not mere collections of fragmentary impressions, whose only organization is the sequence of their occurrence. Rather, when read carefully, a narrative form begins to emerge, and it becomes clear that James is using the occasions of travel to meditate upon moral or philosophical questions of considerable weight. The sketches in this sense approach the quality of fiction; along with setting, they have a plot, a conflict, a main character (the traveler/narrator James), and a constellation of meanings that emerges from the interplay of these elements. The pieces have great value and interest as travel writings but also in their attempt to "giv[e] the supreme right accent or final exquisite turn to the immense magnificent phrase" (as James writes in the closing lines of the collection), they ultimately illuminate the processes by which James comes to craft his fiction (618).

FURTHER READING

Bailey, Brigitte. "Travel Writing and the Metropolis: James, London, and *English Hours*." *American Literature* 67 (1995): 201–232.

Bradbury, Nicola. "'While I Waggled My Small Feet': Henry James's Return to Paris." *Yearbook of English Studies* 34, no. 1 (2004): 186–193.

Buzard, James. *The Beaten Track: European Tourism, Literature, and the Ways to Culture, 1800–1918.* Oxford: Oxford University Press, 1993.

Caesar, Terry. "Counting the Cats in Zanzibar: American Travel Abroad in American Travel Writing to 1914." *Prospectus* 13 (1988): 95–127.

Collister, Peter. "Levels of Disclosure: Voices and People in Henry James's Italian Hours." *Yearbook of English Studies* 34, no. 1 (2004): 194–213.

Edel, Leon. *Henry James: The Untried Years, 1843–1870.* Philadelphia: Lippincott, 1953.

James, Henry. *Collected Travel Writings: Great Britain and America: English Hours, The American Scene, Other Travels.* Edited by Richard Howard. New York: Library of America, 1993.

———. *Collected Travel Writings: The Continent: A Little Tour in France, Italian Hours, Other Travels.* Edited by Richard Howard. New York: Library of America, 1993.

———. *Roderick Hudson.* New York Edition, vol. 1. New York: Scribner's, 1907.

———. *The Turn of the Screw and The Aspern Papers.* London: Penguin Books, 1984.

Hulme, Peter, and Tim Youngs. *The Cambridge Companion to Travel Writing.* Cambridge: Cambridge University Press, 2002.

Lombardo, Agostino. "Italy and the Artist in Henry James." In Tuttleton and Lombardo, 228–240.

MacDonald, Bonney. *Henry James's Italian Hours: Revelatory and Resistant Impressions.* Ann Arbor, Mich.: UMI Research Press, 1990.

Perosa, Sergio. "Italy in Henry James's International Theme." In Tuttleton and Lombardo, 48–65.

Rawlings, Peter. "Grotesque Encounters in the Travel Writing of Henry James." *Yearbook of English Studies* 34, no. 1 (2004): 171–185.

Rowe, John Carlos. "Hawthorne's Ghost in Henry James's Italy: Sculptural Form, Romantic Narrative, and the Function of Sexuality." *Henry James Review* 20, no. 2 (1999): 107–134.

Salmoni, Steven. "Ghosts, Crowds, and Spectacles: Visions of Venetian Travel in Henry James's *Italian Hours*." *Journal of Narrative Theory* 35 (2005): 277–291.

Smith, Carl. "James's Travels, Travel Writings, and the Development of His Art." *Modern Language Quarterly* 38 (1977): 367–380.

Stowe, William W. *Going Abroad: European Travel in Nineteenth-Century American Culture.* Princeton, N.J.: Princeton University Press, 1994.

Tanner, Tony. *Henry James and the Art of Nonfiction.* Athens: University of Georgia Press, 1995.

Tuttleton, James W. "Dipped in the Sacred Stream: The James Family in Italy." In Tuttleton and Lombardo, 22–47.

Tuttleton, James, and Agostino Lombardo, eds. *The Sweetest Impression of Life: The James Family and Italy.* New York: New York University Press, 1990.

Wright, Nathalia. *American Novelists in Italy, The Discoverers: Allston to James.* Philadelphia: University of Pennsylvania Press, 1965.

Ziff, Larzer. *Return Passages: Great American Travel Writing, 1780–1910.* New Haven, Conn.: Yale University Press, 2000.

Steven Salmoni, *Pima Community College*

PART III

Related People, Places, and Topics

the Aesthetic movement   The Aesthetic movement was a broad-based literary, artistic, philosophical, social, and cultural movement that emerged in England in the late 1860s around the time that James began to publish his first short stories. Also known as the "Art for Art's Sake Movement," it was premised upon the controversial notion of detaching the art object from any moral or political function. The Aesthetic movement valued the aesthetic or the beautiful over the functional or natural object, and it encouraged a very particular form of fin-de-siècle cultural elitism.

As members of a deliberately cultivated and highly self-conscious movement, aesthetes of the 1880s and 1890s were recognizable for their extravagant posing, excessive preoccupation with dress, and meticulous attention to the decorative elements of objects and interiors. James's considerable reserve and his distaste for the showiness of rivals such as OSCAR WILDE (on whom he purportedly based the character of Gabriel Nash in The TRAGIC MUSE [1890]) led him to disassociate himself publicly from the identity of aesthete. However, his prolific art reviews and the frequent allusions to visual art, decoration, costume, and the all-important question of taste in his fiction are all testament to a sophisticated aesthetic sensibility.

The Aesthetic movement was profoundly influenced by the publication of essays by the prominent Oxford lecturer Walter Pater, who suggested that the sensual appreciation of art could transcend the experience of everyday life. His Studies in the History of the Renaissance (1873) became the iconic text for aesthetes of the late 19th century. The origins of aestheticism are also traceable to the Arts and Crafts movement of the mid-19th century, which was initiated and advanced by such figures as William Morris and John Ruskin, who advocated fine, archaic workmanship over emerging methods of mass production and industrialization. While the Aesthetic movement abandoned many of the moral principles of its mid-century antecedents, the focus upon exquisite design and the rejection of the bourgeois taste for cheap fabrication and reproduction remained.

In spite of its elitist principles, from 1875 aestheticism was effectively popularized and commercialized by Liberty and Co. in London, which made aesthetic design available to a far broader selection of consumers. The late 1870s saw the emergence of aesthetic dress, which was characterized by loose, flowing fabric and borrowed heavily from medieval and so-called oriental design principles. It provided women with a desirable alternative to the tight corseting of contemporary Victorian fashion (see VICTORIANISM) and as a consequence came to be associated with early advocates of women's rights. James clothed several of his female protagonists in aesthetic dress, most notably Milly Theale in The WINGS OF THE DOVE (1902).

The representation and manipulation of gender and SEXUALITY were significant themes within aestheticism. The movement facilitated recognition of figures such as the Dandy and the New Woman, who threatened the conventional Victorian perceptions of gender and sexuality, and it was aestheticism's apparent promotion of such figures and their associated behaviors that was to provoke the most heated accusations of immorality. (See MASCULINITY and WOMEN'S ISSUES.) However, James remained ambivalent about the movement's interrogation of gender, favoring a more subdued version of the aesthetic sensibility premised upon ideals of refinement rather than subversion.

Despite conservative criticism, aestheticism continued to flourish, and the publication of critic Walter Hamilton's book The Aesthetic Movement in England (1882) established the movement as a cultural phenomenon. Significant figures within the Aesthetic movement included members of the Pre-Raphaelite Brotherhood (in particular William Michael Rossetti and Dante Gabriel Rossetti), Algernon Charles Swinburne, James Abbott MacNeill Whistler, Wilde, Arthur Symonds, Aubrey Beardsley, and the Victorian satirist Max Beerbohm. James was integrally involved in London's artistic and cultural life during this period, attending and reviewing exhibitions (in particular at the Grosvenor Gallery) and incorporating details of aesthetic culture into much of his fiction.

Although aestheticism is viewed as a predominantly British movement, it also had a substantial influence upon contemporary American culture. Wilde's 1882–83 tour of the United States was the most publicized importation of British aestheticism to America; however, it was by no means the first. By the 1870s, aspects of British aestheticism were already present in American fine and decorative arts. There were several significant participants in the transatlantic dissemination of aestheticism, including James's friend Whistler, a painter who was born in Massachusetts, educated in England, and made his name in American society, from which he drew many of his most lucrative commissions. Boston was renowned for its version of aestheticism; it was the home of Ruskin's close friend Charles Eliot Norton, who founded an American branch of Morris's Arts and Crafts movement.

Mid-century American writers such as Nathaniel Hawthorne (see HAWTHORNE) and Edgar Allan Poe took as their subjects the interactions and conflicts of art, beauty, morality, and morbidity in a manner that seemed to foreshadow many of the central concerns of British aestheticism. Several of James's early short stories followed the baroque model of stories by Hawthorne or Poe, interweaving aesthetic doctrine with ghostliness and sinister eroticism. These include "The Last of the Valerii" (1874), in which an Italian count falls passionately and unwholesomely in love with a marble statue of Juno, and "The Romance of Certain Old Clothes" (1867), in which a treasured chest of exquisite clothing is guarded by the ghost of its owner. These stories offer invaluable insights into the development of James's aesthetic sensibility and contain some of his most exquisite decorative descriptions. James's later novels demonstrate a profound engagement with the subtle interrelationship of aestheticism, art, and psychology. The PORTRAIT OF A LADY (1881), The SPOILS OF POYNTON (1897), and The GOLDEN BOWL (1904) detail the lives of obsessive collectors whose activities and relationships are governed largely by aesthetic principles of beauty.

James's exploration of morality in relation to aesthetics was a fraught one, in which no ultimate solutions were offered. He proclaimed himself apathetic to the "inane" question of morality and immorality in art and proposed instead that one should ask "is it valid, in a word, is it genuine, is it sincere, the result of some direct impression or perception of life?" (*PPL* 6). This vision of art *as* morality, rather than art in conflict with morality, was a characteristically Jamesian one. Repeatedly, James employed art and decoration as means of expressing character and of directing plot; they could even function as revelatory forces, most notably in *The Golden Bowl,* in which the crack in the eponymous artifact becomes a metaphor for the novel's flawed relationships. Yet James rarely offered clearly delineated heroes and villains, and the amoral aesthetes in his stories and novels were frequently no less sympathetically portrayed than seemingly more "moral" characters. There is a recurrent implication in James's work that the aesthetic life will be lived at the expense of traditional familial and marital relationships; however, it is never truly evident whether James considered human relationships to be preferable to the romance of styles and objects. The year before his death, James proclaimed in a letter to H. G. WELLS, "It is art that makes life, makes interest, makes importance, and I know of no substitute whatever for the force and beauty of its process" (*Letters* IV: 536).

Further Reading

James, Henry. *The Golden Bowl.* New York: Popular Library, 1904.
———. *Preface to The Portrait of a Lady, New York Edition.* New York, London: Norton, 1995. Abbreviated as *PPL*.
———. *The Letters of Henry James.* Edited by Leon Edel. 4 vols. Cambridge, Mass.: Harvard University Press, 1974.

Angela Hesson, *University of Melbourne*

Andersen, Hendrik Christian (1872–1940) Andersen was a Norwegian-American artist, specializing in idealized, monumental sculptures of the human figure. Although born in Norway, he immigrated as an infant with his family to NEWPORT, Rhode Island, a town James knew well and particularly loved. As an adult, Andersen began his work as a sculptor in Newport, moving among that city's well-known circle of prosperous and prominent Americans; at one point, he was an art teacher to Gertrude Vanderbilt Whitney (granddaughter of

Cornelius Vanderbilt and patroness of the Whitney Museum of American Art). In 1893, he settled in ROME to study art, meeting other artists as well as wealthy Americans living in Rome. In 1897, Andersen became for a time the protégé of Lord Glower, the English sculptor and art critic who was known for his homosexual relationships; Glower was thought to be the model for OSCAR WILDE's Lord Henry Wotton in *The Picture of Dorian Gray*.

In 1899, the tall, blond, handsome young 27-year-old Andersen met 56-year-old Henry James in Rome in the drawing room of Maude Howe Eliot, the writer and feminist. In a striking coincidence, Andersen strongly resembled the title character of James's novel RODERICK HUDSON (1875). James's fictional character Roderick Hudson was also a young American sculptor living as an expatriate in Italy. In addition to Andersen's remarkable physical beauty, James was also moved by Andersen's sincere wish to do his best in a difficult family situation, which eventually required him to support his derelict alcoholic father and a menage of family members, including his mother. James was also highly sympathetic to Andersen's ambitions to accomplish great things as an artist.

Although James was almost 30 years senior of Andersen, the two men began that day a friendship that was to last to the end of James's life. That same year, Andersen stayed for three days with James at LAMB HOUSE, his recently purchased retreat in Sussex. They spent time walking in the gardens and bicycling as James planned to renovate his studio so that Andersen could work there on his return from the United States. Andersen paid visits to Lamb House on an annual basis in the first five years of their friendship, but these days were only brief, and James's plans to have Andersen work and live for significant lengths of time at Lamb House were never realized. The last face-to-face meeting between the two was in Rome in 1907.

The relationship of Andersen and James thrived mainly through their frequent personal letters; whereas James burned his correspondence from Andersen, Andersen kept his, which were finally published many years after Andersen's death, and which demonstrate the warmth and intimacy of their epistolary relationship. James's letters are filled with a freely expressed tenderness and passion. The intimate tone of the letters, some of which James describes as having been written "long past midnight" and which refer to Andersen as "Belovedest" and "Darling darling," suggest that James was, indeed, in love with the young artist. Referring to Andersen as both brother and lover, James wrote of their separation as an ache and a torment, and although always elegantly written, the letters revealed a frank longing for close physical intimacy. James's correspondence with Andersen was coterminous with what is considered the major phase of James's writing; the letters' open references to the body and to touching and embracing are consonant with the last novels' undercurrents of eroticism.

In addition to the overflow of affection in the letters, James also offered paternal advice and encouragement to Andersen, from corrections of spelling to information about train schedules. Despite his affection for Andersen, James became increasingly unenthusiastic about Andersen's work. In addition to his dedication to public sculptures of monumental nudes, Andersen held the optimistic conviction that the construction of a central World City could shape human consciousness in such a way that new heights of international peace and harmony would also follow. While Andersen's ambitions for art and architecture were often considered naive, his belief in the socially transformative power of architecture anticipated the ideas of later urban planners such as Le Corbusier. James remained skeptical of Andersen's utopian aspiration. Quoting Voltaire, James counseled Andersen instead to cultivate his garden; he persisted in advising him to abandon his public work and concentrate on smaller and more manageable projects intended for private use. James did purchase from Andersen for his dining room mantel a portrait bust of a beautiful young boy, Count Alberto Bevilacqua, which seem to personify for James Andersen's youth and beauty; additionally, he hung a photograph of Andersen in his home to console himself over Andersen's absence.

As James failed to appreciate Andersen's art and ambitions as an urban planner, Andersen failed to understand James's later complex work. James's emphasis on life's flawed reality continued to elude Andersen, who possessed a far more uncomplicated faith in progress. Despite these differences, the affection between the two was unwavering, and loving letters continued to the end of James's life. After James's death, Andersen expressed his gratitude for a friendship with a man whom he felt understood him as no one else could.

James's relationship with Andersen developed simultaneously with friendships with other young men such as the British writer Hugh Walpole, fellow American Howard Sturgis, and Jocelyn Persse. James's letters to these young men show him reaching out for comfort and affection in his old age, as well as giving advice, encouragement, and constructive criticism. These letters suggest that James in his later years became less inhibited about building homoerotic bonds and less restrained in openly expressing his affection for the young men with whom he corresponded.

Further Reading

Gunter, Susan, and Steven Jobe, eds. *Dearly Beloved Friends: Henry James's Letters to Younger Men.* Ann Arbor: University of Michigan Press, 2002.

Person, Leland. *Henry James and the Suspense of Masculinity.* Philadelphia: University of Pennsylvania Press, 2003.

Zorzi, Roselli Mamoli, ed. *Beloved Boy: Letters to Hendrik Andersen.* Charlottesville: University of Virginia Press, 2004.

Margaret Boe Birns, *New York University*

anti-Semitism   While historians disagree on the exact role that anti-Semitism has played in American history, most agree that its modern birth was signaled by the DREYFUS AFFAIR in France in the 1890s and contemporaneous responses to the influx of Jewish immigrants from eastern Europe and Russia into the United States that began in the 1880s and lasted through the first decades of the 20th century. In this period, overlapping with the arc of James's career, the number of Jews in the United States rose to approximately 4 million (Rischin 19–33, 270). By 1924, the National Origins Act singled out eastern and southern Europeans for exclusion.

According to David Gerber in *Anti-Semitism in American History* (1986), anti-Semitism includes a combination of the following: a belief in a fundamental difference in the religious belief, physical makeup, and psychological experience of Jews; a tendency to see Jews as materialistic, aggressive, dishonest, clannish; a fear and dislike of Jews based on their presumed alienness; and the willingness to subject Jews to social and legal discrimination on these bases (3). Jonathan Sarna contends that prior to 1945 historians in the United States were more concerned with figuring out how to fit Jews into mainstream society, characterizing anti-Semitism as part of a European past whose force would wane as a process of assimilation into American culture ran its course (Gerber 9). However, postwar historians such as John Higham, Oscar Handlin, and Cary McWilliams focused more on late 19th-century cases of Jews being used as scapegoats by populist farmers, disaffected workers, and nativist patricians in the United States (7–9). Jacob Rader Marcus moves further back to the colonial era, when Jews were limited in their rights of settlement, naturalization, suffrage, and office holding. After 1776, Jews generally enjoyed relative civil and political equality and religious freedom under the U.S. Constitution and Bill of Rights, unlike the governmentally sanctioned anti-Semitism in Europe (Gerber 10–11, 13–15).

Anti-Semitism was prevalent among James's influential friends and mentors such as the poet and editor James Russell Lowell, the Harvard scholar Charles Eliot Norton, and the French writer and strident anti-Dreyfusard Paul Bourget (Carter 82; see also Harap). Henry Adams, the distinguished grandson of President John Quincy Adams, was well known for his prejudice against Jews, whom he characterized as parvenus embodying material ambition and threatening to level social standards in their accumulation of money. As Everett Carter and others note, James's prejudices were never as vicious as Adams's; James was sympathetic to Dreyfus and thought the Dreyfus affair sinister. Certainly, James wrote too many negative representations of Jews to ignore, but simply to label James as anti-Semitic and catalogue examples, as Eli Ben-Joseph does in his book

Aesthetic Persuasion (1996), overlooks how James engaged in satirical critique by staging characters' prejudices and other characters' reactions to these prejudices (Carter 82–83). Bryan Cheyette's influential *Constructions of 'the Jew' in English Literature and Society: Racial Representations, 1875–1945* (1993) shifts emphasis toward what he calls "semitic discourse" at the center of English literary studies. For Cheyette, "lethal" postwar charges of literary anti-Semitism (like Geismar's) rely too easily on the Holocaust as a means of concentrating the criticism (Cheyette 3). To counter this, he argues, one should regard the figure of the Jew in its complexity, as "*both* the embodiment of liberal progress *and* as the vestiges of an outdated medievalism . . . as the ideal economic man *and* the degenerate plutocrat *par excellence; as* the modern alienated artist *and* the incarnation of corrupt worldliness" (9).

Furthermore, the revived interest in James during the 1940s and '50s was inspired by the first generation of Jewish academics, scholars, and critics such as Philip Rahv, Lionel Trilling, and Clifton Fadiman, as well as James biographer Leon Edel. Yet as Maxwell Geismar complains in *Henry James and the Jacobites* (1962), they all but ignored James's negative representations of Jews.

For example, in his 1907 travelogue, *The AMERICAN SCENE*, James recalls the "poignant and unforgettable" drama of Ellis Island, where he encounters the "inconceivable alien," more at home than he himself feels as the alienated expatriate (James 82). He notably remarks upon "the intensity of the material picture in the dense Yiddish quarter" (99) and the "great swarming" of the Lower East Side (100). "There is no swarming like that of Israel when once Israel has got a start," he writes, describing "a Jewry that had burst all bounds" (100). Geismar argues that these phrases—"inconceivable" and "ubiquitous alien"—suggest James's "nightmarish fantasies of prejudice and doom" (348), that his "worst fears are confirmed, since these new Americans were not only gross and greasy, but apparently they were almost all Jewish" (Geismar 349). Like Geismar, Louis Harap (1974) claims that the Jews were "alien" to James (375). He finds James's reaction

"not humane and compassionate and comprehending, but rather disgusted and dehumanized" (375), such as when he compares Jews to "small, strange animals, known to natural history, snakes or worms . . . who, when cut into pieces, wriggle away and live in the snippet as completely as in the whole" (*The American Scene* 100).

Taking a view more attuned to the implications of Jewishness in *The American Scene*, Cheyette notes that James's depiction of the "unsurpassed strength of the [Jewish] race" could potentially help distinguish an unfolding United States culture (6). Similarly, Ross Posnock in *The Trial of Curiosity* (1998) sees *The American Scene* enacting James's "pragmatist pluralism," preferring a democratic openness to heterogeneity, miscegenation, and hybridity over a "quixotic at best" ideology of "melting pot" Americanism (232). "To affirm the alien is to affirm one's own Americanness, to embrace the immigrant in oneself," argues Posnock (240). Jonathan Freedman (1996) resists both Geismar's dismissal of James and Posnock's recuperation of the obvious anti-Semitic slurs in *The American Scene*. Freedman sees the figure of the Jew as a "vexing other," a scapegoat to absolve James of charges of artistic degeneracy, and as a "receptacle: a figure onto which can be loaded all the sources of his inchoate anxieties and unacknowledged terrors" (67, 78). In *Temple of Culture* (2000), Freedman further argues that the generation of mid-century Jewish scholars used their mastery of James to secure the cultural capital necessary in assimilating into the United States academy. Reinventing James in their own image, they overlooked James's potentially anti-Semitic portraits.

Following Posnock's lead, Greg Zacharias (1996) argues that in "the Jew" James finds the identity of the future: "the ideal cosmopolitanism James sought for himself" (193); and Sara Blair (1996) has claimed that Miriam Rooth, the part-Jewish actress heroine of *The TRAGIC MUSE* (1890), "achieves a power of cosmopolitan self-invention that James himself embraces" (496). Gert Buelens (2002), too, has argued for a relation of identity between James and "the Jew": a likeness based on the shared experience of alienation.

In addition to *The American Scene,* James's novel *The GOLDEN BOWL* (1904) complicates an easy charge of anti-Semitism and has also divided generations of critics. Everett Carter argues that James found prejudice wrong and tasteless, that representations of anti-Semitism in this novel work to redirect the reader's sympathies toward Maggie and Adam Verver (87). Other characters' reactions to the Jewish characters, in other words, serve to measure their own moral sensibilities, whether "democratic" and "sympathetic" like Maggie or "aristocratic" and "disdainful" like the Prince (89). Jonathan Freedman (1996) sees Jewish characters in the novel as abject figures of degeneration, "uncanny mocking double" figures for James himself (149). They are linked to what the novel values—in the case of Gutterman-Seuss, this being family, high culture, "spoils" of empire, capitalist accumulation—but as the potentially corrupting force that emerges from within society (141). Even though the Jewish shopkeeper is ethically superior to the Prince, Freedman argues that "the novel oddly endorses the Prince's vision," only to reverse it later when the shopkeeper repents and gets "converted" (143–144). Elsewhere, Sharon Oster reads the shopkeeper as a revised Jewish pawnbroker, an unlikely stereotypical figure who captures for James not an identity but the social function of value production. Both modern writer and pawnbroker create and unleash different types of value—economic, aesthetic, and ethical value—from objects through ritual acts of exchange.

Another much debated example of James's ambivalent views on Jews manifests itself in the early critical piece "*Daniel Deronda*: A Conversation," published in the December 1876 *Atlantic Monthly.* Here James stages a conversation between three fictional personae: Theodora, a philo-Semite; Pulcheria, a polite anti-Semite; and Constantius, a critic like James himself. In contrast with Pulcheria's revulsion for Deronda—whom she calls the "solemn, sapient young man" with an undoubtedly "horrid big Jewish nose" (James 121, 104)—Constantius reads Deronda as an idea: "All the Jewish part is at bottom cold; that is my only objection . . . It is admirably studied, it is imagined, it is understood, but it is not embodied" (116). Overlooking

how James constructs the exchange as a provocative conversation, Harap claims that James simply assumes the "conventional social attitude toward the Jews" (368). However, for Cheyette the Jew in this piece is a complex vector of the intersecting discourses of aesthetics and race. These disparate readings typify the sticky generational, theoretical, and ideological factors in ongoing debates over James and anti-Semitism.

(See also RACE AND ETHNICITY.)

Further Reading

Arendt, Hannah. *Antisemitism: Part One of the Origins of Totalitarianism,* vol. 1. New York: Schocken, 1951.

Ben-Joseph, Eli. *Henry James, the Jews, and Race.* Lanham, Md.: University Press of America, 1996.

Blair, Sara. "Henry James, Jack the Ripper, and the Cosmopolitan Jew: Staging Authorship in *The Tragic Muse.*" ELH 63, no. 2 (1996): 489–512.

Boyarin, Daniel, and Jonathan Boyarin, eds. *Jews and Other Differences: The New Jewish Cultural Studies.* Minneapolis: University of Minnesota Press, 1997.

Buelens, Gert. *Henry James and the "Aliens" in Possession of the American Scene.* Amsterdam, New York: Rodopi, 2002.

Carter, Everett. "Realists and Jews." *Studies in American Fiction* 22, no. 1 (1994): 81–91.

Cheyette, Bryan. *Constructions of 'the Jew' in English Literature and Society: Racial Representations, 1875–1945.* Cambridge: Cambridge University Press, 1993.

Dinnerstein, Leonard. *Antisemitism in America.* New York: Oxford University Press, 1994.

———, ed. *Antisemitism in the United States.* New York: Holt, Rinehart and Winston, 1971.

Dobkowski, Michael. *The Tarnished Dream: The Basis of American Anti-Semitism.* Westport, Conn.: Greenwood Press, 1979.

Freedman, Jonathan. "Henry James and the Discourses of Antisemitism." In *Between 'Race' and Culture: Representations of 'the Jew' in English and American Literature,* edited by Bryan Cheyette, 62–83. Palo Alto, Calif.: Stanford University Press, 1996.

———. *The Temple of Culture: Assimilation and Anti-Semitism in Literary Anglo-America.* New York: Oxford University Press, 2000.

Geismar, Maxwell. *Henry James and the Jacobites*. 1962. Reprint, New York: Hill and Wang, 1965.

Gerber, David A., ed. *Anti-Semitism in American History*. Urbana: University of Illinois Press, 1986.

Handlin, Oscar. *Adventure in Freedom: Three Hundred Years of Jewish Life in America*. New York: McGraw Hill, 1954.

Harap, Louis. *The Image of the Jew in American Literature from the Early Republic to Mass Immigration*, 2d ed. 1974. Reprint, Syracuse, N.Y.: Syracuse University Press, 2003.

Higham, John. *Send These to Me: Jews and Other Immigrants in Urban America*. New York: Atheneum, 1975.

———. "American Anti-Semitism, Historically Reconsidered." In *Jews in the Mind of America*, edited by Charles Herbert Stember, 237–258. New York: Basic Books, 1966.

James, Henry. *The American Scene*. 1907. Reprint, New York: Penguin, 1994.

———. *The Critical Muse: Selected Literary Criticism*. Edited by Roger Gard. New York: Penguin, 1988.

Marcus, Jacob Rader. *The Colonial American Jew, 1492–1776*. Vols. 1–3. Detroit, Mich.: Wayne State University Press, 1970.

McFarlane, I. D. "A Literary Friendship—Henry James and Paul Bourget." *Cambridge Journal* 4 (1951): 144–161.

McWilliams, Carey. *A Mask for Privilege: Anti-Semitism in America*. Boston: Little, Brown, 1948.

Oster, Sharon. "The Shop of Curiosities: Henry James, 'the Jew,' and the Production of Value." *ELH*, forthcoming.

Posnock, Ross. "Affirming the Alien: the Pragmatist Pluralism of *The American Scene*." In *The Cambridge Companion to Henry James*, edited by Jonathan Freedman, 224–246. Cambridge: Cambridge University Press, 1998.

———. *The Trial of Curiosity*. New York, Oxford: Oxford University Press, 1991.

Rischin, Moses. *The Promised City: New York City's Jews, 1870–1914*. Cambridge, Mass.: Harvard University Press, 1962.

Whitfield, Stephen. "The Presence of the Past: Recent Trends in American Jewish History." *AJH* 70 (December 1980): 150–151.

Zacharias, Greg. "Henry James' Fictional Jew." In *Representations of Jews through the Ages*, edited by Leonard Jay Greenspoon and Bryan F. Le Beau. Omaha, Neb.: Creighton University Press, 1996.

Sharon B. Oster, *University of Redlands*

Bosanquet, Theodora (1880–1961) James's last secretarial typist, Bosanquet had two predecessors, William MacAlpine and Mary Weld. By 1897, James suffered from chronic rheumatism in his right wrist and began dictating his works and personal letters to a typist, or "amanuensis" as he preferred to call her. Bosanquet worked for James from 1907, when he was busy preparing the NEW YORK EDITION, until his death in 1916.

Bosanquet was born the only daughter to Frederick Charles Tindal Bosanquet, a curate, and Gertrude Bosanquet in Sandown, Isle of Wight, Hampshire, on October 3, 1880. She attended Cheltenham Ladies' College, then moving to University College, LONDON, she earned a bachelor of science degree. After graduation, she worked as a proofreader at Miss Petheridge's Secretarial bureau briefly around 1907. Soon hearing at the bureau that James was searching for a new typist, she taught herself typing and got the job. James was very satisfied with Bosanquet's performance from the beginning; in a letter to his brother WILLIAM JAMES on October 17, 1907, he happily reports about his "excellent amanuensis, a young boyish Miss Bosanquet, who is worth all the other [females] that I have had put together" (qtd. in *Letters* 370). Their relationship as a whole was more than a mere businesslike one, imbued with mutual respect and friendliness. According to Leon Edel, James was pleased with Bosanquet's quick understanding of his intentions and directions during the dictation (635). They often spent time together, having dinner or going to the theater. Bosanquet took James's last dictation during December 1915, while he was bedridden in a state of mental confusion. The dictation is famous for James's Napoleonic mumblings, in which his memories of his own family and himself are frequently intermingled with the legend of Napoleon Bonaparte. Edel reports that in January 1916, just before James died, Bosanquet looked through his incomplete typescripts and made lists of them at the request of Harry James, James's nephew and executor (714).

After James's death, Bosanquet declined an offer from EDITH WHARTON, whom she came to know through James, to work as her secretary, and she started her own writing career; as noted by Pamela Thurschwell, Bosanquet expressed her desire to be an author in her diary several times while working for James (14). Her novel *Spectators*, coauthored by Clara Smith, appeared in 1916. The following year, her essay "Henry James" came out in the June issue of the *Fortnightly Review*. The essay consists of two parts; Bosanquet first talks about her reading experience of James's works, such as *The EUROPEANS*, "The TURN OF THE SCREW," and *Covering End* (*The Two Magics*), before being hired by him; she then presents her personal observations on James's dictating styles and working habits, on his modest reticence about his writing in front of friends, and on his single-minded devotion to his profession. Another essay on James, "The Revised Edition," was issued in the *Little Review* in August 1918. This one focuses on explaining the basic principles of James's revision for the New York Edition. Bosanquet later combined the second half of "Henry James" with "The Revised Edition" and expanded it into a pamphlet, *Henry James at Work*, published in 1924 by the Hogarth Press of Virginia and Leonard Woolf. The pamphlet gives an additional account of James's sense of uncertainty about being an American in Europe and his condemnation of tyranny in human relations. She also points out some misunderstandings about James by contemporary reviewers and tries to rectify them. Bosanquet proceeded to write critical biographies of British writer and philosopher Harriet Martineau (in 1927) and French poet and essayist Paul Valéry (1933).

Bosanquet was also a practicing journalist. In 1920, she cofounded a weekly PERIODICAL, *Time and Tide*, with feminist activist Margaret Haig Thomas, also known as Lady Rhondda, and she served as its literary editor from 1935 to 1943 and as its director from 1943 to 1958. *Time and Tide* initially aimed to support women's rights by providing political information and literary works to enlighten and empower its women readers. Even

though it eventually lost its original liberal radicalism and went conservative, the periodical marks a milestone in the early feminist movement, with the contribution of a number of renowned literary figures, including E. M. Delafield, Graham Greene, Aldous Huxley, George Orwell, George Bernard Shaw, and Virginia Woolf, to name a few. Bosanquet herself wrote reviews and poetry for it. *Time and Tide* ceased publishing in 1979.

Even as she followed the path of a writer, Bosanquet never gave up her secretarial career. She acted as an assistant to the War Trade Intelligence Department between 1917 and 1918 and then to the Ministry of Food between 1918 and 1920. After receiving the Member of the Order of the British Empire (MBE) in 1919, she went on to officiate as an executive secretary to the International Federation of University Women from 1920 to 1935.

Throughout her life, Bosanquet was deeply intrigued by extrasensory perception (ESP) and paranormal phenomena. She frequently attended séances and practiced automatic writing in the 1930s and 1940s, when she was a member of the Society for Psychical Research.

Bosanquet's diaries, letters, photographs, and other papers are currently at the Houghton Library, Harvard College Library, Harvard University. *Paul Valéry*, initially brought out by Hogarth, was reprinted by Haskell House in 1974. *Henry James at Work*, edited by Lyall H. Powers, was reprinted by the University of Michigan Press in 2006.

Further Reading

Edel, Leon. *Henry James: A Life*. New York: Harper & Row, 1985

James, Henry. *Henry James Letters, volume 4: 1895–1916*. Edited by Leon Edel. Cambridge, Mass.: Harvard University Press, 1984.

Thurschwell, Pamela. "Henry James and Theodora Bosanquet: on the Typewriter, *In the Cage*, at the Ouija Board." *Textual Practice* 13, no. 1 (1999): 5–23.

Kiyoon Jang, *Texas A&M University*

Cambridge, Massachusetts Located just west of Boston, Massachusetts, along the Charles River,

Cambridge began as a small town established in the early 17th century where Harvard College was founded.

HENRY JAMES, SR., moved his family to Cambridge in 1866, where they resided until 1872. In 1875, James made Europe his permanent home. He revisited Cambridge in 1904 while touring the United States to write articles that would become *The AMERICAN SCENE* (1907). He returned to Cambridge again in 1910 to mourn the death of his brother WILLIAM JAMES, who had died in New Hampshire.

While in Cambridge during the late 1860s, James wrote his first novel, *Watch and Ward* (1871). Although *Watch and Ward* was serialized in the *Atlantic Monthly* during James's stay in Cambridge, the story bears closer relation to Boston. Cambridge was often boring for James. In a letter to William, Henry claims that his evenings were typically tiresome. Biographer Leon Edel noted that in Cambridge James would pass his days at "the writing desk, the book, the occasional play, the rare and usually disappointing social call, the journey by horse-car from Cambridge to Boston a full and chilly evening's adventure among the city's deep snows or irksome and exhausting in the summer's heat" (248). While in Cambridge, Massachusetts, James corresponded with notable figures, including THOMAS SERGEANT PERRY, WILLIAM DEAN HOWELLS, and Grace Norton.

During his Cambridge years, James spent a great deal of time reflecting on the time he had spent in Europe and dreamed of spending more. Frequent walks from Cambridge to Boston and back allowed him to contemplate what to chronicle in his next journal entry. The locale played a significant role in James's middle years because Cambridge Cemetery was where his father, Henry James, Sr., and mother were buried. When James visited the family plot on December 31, 1882, he read aloud with great sorrow and love his brother William's letter to their father—a letter dated December 14, 1882, which unfortunately arrived after his father's death. Henry struggled with the question that his family had been contemplating for decades: What would life be like without Henry James, Sr.? William's letter stated that the death was not a great shock given his long

illness and that he hoped he was now reunited with his wife, Mary. He promised to compile a collection of his father's writings in memoriam to a long life of letters. Henry James would be named the sole executor of his father's family estate, which he later divided among the surviving family members.

New England remained an important source of inspiration for Henry throughout his career. He requested that his remains be returned to Cambridge after his death, and he is buried in his family's plot in Cambridge Cemetery at Prospect Avenue, Lot 1222.

Further Reading

Edel, Leon. *Henry James: 1882–1895, The Middle Years*. Philadelphia & New York: Lippincott, 1962.

———. *Henry James: 1843–1870, The Untried Years*. Philadelphia & New York: Lippincott, 1953.

Heimer, Jackson W. *The Lesson of New England: Henry James and His Native Region*. Muncie, Ind.: Ball State University, 1967.

Gerardo Del Guercio, *Independent Researcher*

the Civil War (1861–1865)   In December 1860, a month after Republican Abraham Lincoln won the presidential election, South Carolina seceded from the United States of America; Mississippi, Alabama, Georgia, Louisiana, Texas, Virginia, Tennessee, Arkansas, and North Carolina followed. By the summer of 1861, Richmond, Virginia, was the capital of the Confederate States of America.

The causes for the Civil War were the political and social accommodations of slavery. Although the actual word *slavery* does not appear in the U.S. Constitution (1787), slavery's profound impact resonates in the formula of counting the enslaved as "three fifths of all other Persons" (art. 1, sec. 2) to estimate the population in apportioning congressional representation; in the prohibition on legislation regulating "the Migration or Importation of such Persons as any of the States now existing shall think proper to admit" (art. 1, sec. 9) until at least 1808; and, in the so-called Fugitive Slave Clause (art. 4, sec. 2), which demanded that all states—even those in which slavery had been outlawed—return an escaping person "held to Service or Labour" in another state. In the first half of the 19th century, a series of tense compromises extended the accommodation of slavery in lands acquired through the Louisiana Purchase of 1803. To maintain the balance between slave and free states in Congress, the Missouri Compromise of 1821 enabled the admission of Missouri as a slave state and Maine as a free state, while stipulating the latitude of 36°30′ as the boundary above which slavery would be prohibited in future additions of states.

In the aftermath of the Mexican War (1846–48) the nation's compromises crumbled. Sparking explosive protest in the North, the Fugitive Slave Act (1850) demanded anew that all states meet the constitutional responsibility of tracking and returning fugitives to the South. The Kansas and Nebraska Act (1954) opened the question of slavery in the territories to popular sovereignty, unleashing waves of intimidation and bloodshed. In the *Dred Scott* decision (1857), the Supreme Court opined that the plaintiff, Dred Scott (who had sued for his freedom based on his prior residence in the free state of Illinois), and by extension all blacks, whether enslaved or free, lacked the civic standing that the Constitution's framers had intended solely for white men. John Brown's 1859 raid on the armory at Harpers Ferry in Virginia foreshadowed the coming war. In June 1858, unsuccessful Senate candidate Lincoln of Illinois had predicted that such "a house divided against itself can not stand." However, in his inaugural address of March 1861, President Lincoln was willing to overlook slavery to preserve a national union by appealing to the nation's "mystic chords of memory" in order to reach "the better angels of our nature." His eloquence could not prevent the war.

On the early morning of April 12, 1861, Confederate troops fired on federal troops at Fort Sumter in South Carolina, and from 1861 to 1865 battles were fought in more than 10,000 places through the fractured nation. When the war began, there were approximately 31 million people in the United States, 21 million in the North and 9 million in the South, including 4 million enslaved. Approximately 3.5 million men fought as soldiers and militia in the war. More than 600,000 died of battle wounds and disease. Technological innova-

tions in weaponry made battle wounds particularly horrific, foreshadowing the carnage of trench warfare in WORLD WAR I. Union victory was eventually secured through the development of a total war strategy targeting the South's infrastructure and its social capacity to wage war. William T. Sherman famously concluded: War is "all hell". On April 12, 1865, General Robert E. Lee surrendered to General Ulysses S. Grant at Appomattox. Two days later, on April 14, Lincoln was shot in the head during an evening at a theater in Washington, D.C. He died early the next morning.

In September 1862, Lincoln had issued the Emancipation Proclamation, liberating on January 1, 1863, all those enslaved in the Confederate states, while not mentioning the five neutral border states of Delaware, Kentucky, Maryland, Missouri, and West Virginia. After the war, the Thirteenth Amendment to the Constitution abolished slavery. The Fourteenth and Fifteenth Amendments enfranchised blacks and guaranteed their equal protection under the law—legal guarantees that the policy of Reconstruction was supposed to make a social and economic reality. However, an ensuing compromise ended the controversial election standoff of 1876 by abandoning the Reconstruction policy, recalling all federal troops from the South in exchange for the Republican presidency of Rutherford B. Hayes. With the end of Reconstruction, the federal government tacitly sanctioned the discriminatory Jim Crow laws that would intensify and block the economic and political enfranchisement of the formerly enslaved. Furthermore, in 1896 the Supreme Court's majority opinion of *Plessy v. Ferguson* established the "separate but equal" standard, ruling that existing racial segregation was a matter of local concern, the consequence of natural antipathies between the races, and beyond the pale of federal authority.

Whereas the battle for civil rights continued well beyond 1865 into the 20th century, the Civil War did represent a fundamental shift in national consciousness. Thirty years after its conclusion, Supreme Court Justice Oliver Wendell Holmes summarized in a Harvard commencement address the war's effect on those who had served: "We have shared the incommunicable experience of war; we have felt, we still feel, the passion of life to its top" (269). Throughout his literary career, Henry James struggled to outline a sense of national identity in the wake of the war and to understand his personal relation to a crisis in which he had not participated as a soldier.

HENRY JAMES, SR., was a fierce critic of slavery. However, he shielded his two older sons, WILLIAM JAMES and Henry from enlisting. His younger sons, Wilkerson (or Wilky) and Robertson, did join and served in, respectively, the 54th and 55th Massachusetts Volunteer Infantries, all-black regiments with white officers. Wilky was seriously wounded in the 54th's brutalizing assault on Fort Wagner, South Carolina, during which a great many in the regiment, including the commander, Colonel Robert Gould Shaw, were killed. As Henry watched his brothers and friends endure war's "incommunicable experience," he followed his brother William to Harvard and tried to study law. In his AUTOBIOGRAPHY, *Notes of a Son and Brother* (1914), he recalls a practical impediment to soldiering in an "obscure hurt" he suffered in the summer of 1861. Biographers and literary historians have speculated on the exact nature of this hurt, nominally a sprained back, interpreting it as a tangle of mental and physical anxiety through which James negotiated the expectations of conventional MASCULINITY.

The Civil War is a vital context for his work and a frequent theme in his fiction. "The STORY OF A YEAR" (1865) considers the fate of romance in relation to the wounds of war. Civil War veterans are important characters in the novels *RODERICK HUDSON* (1875), *The AMERICAN* (1877), and *The PORTRAIT OF A LADY* (1881). The postwar tension between Northern and Southern culture is central to Basil Ransom's winning of Verena Tarrant in *The BOSTONIANS* (1886). In *The AMERICAN SCENE* (1907), James tours the South, writing chapters on Charleston and Florida in which he weighs the national and regional legacy of the war. In an anecdote from his autobiography, *Notes of a Son and Brother* (1914), James unknowingly foreshadowed his WORLD WAR I advocacy for the Ambulance Corp. He remembers an afternoon's excursion to Portsmouth Grove, where he visited soldiers of the Rhode Island regiments, following in the footsteps of Walt Whitman, who nursed and comforted so many dying young men of the North and South with a dedicated practical sympathy that Henry grew to admire.

Further Reading

Holmes, Oliver Wendell. "An Address Delivered on Memorial Day, May 30, 1895." In *The Written Wars: American War Prose through the Civil War,* edited by Joseph T. Cox. North Haven, Conn.: Archon Books, 1996.

Menand, Louis. *The Metaphysical Club.* New York: Farrar, Straus & Giroux, 2001.

Wilson, Edmund. *Patriotic Gore: Studies in the Literature of the American Civil War.* Boston, New York: Oxford University Press, 1962.

Kendall Johnson, *Swarthmore College*

Coburn, Alvin Langdon (A. L. Coburn) (1882–1966)   Alvin Langdon Coburn was a pioneering and innovative photographer. He is considered one of the most influential photographers of the 20th century, a leading figure in the struggle for the recognition of photography as a means of artistic expression, and the father of abstract photography.

Coburn was born in Boston into a middle-class family and received his first Kodak camera as a gift when he was only eight years old. In 1899, he visited LONDON and his cousin Fred Holland Day, who organized an exhibition at the Royal Photographic Society. In 1901, he studied in PARIS with Edward Steichen and Robert DeMachy. The following year, he opened a studio in NEW YORK CITY, entered the "Photo-Secession Group," and studied with Gertrude Kasebier (1832–1934), one of the founding members of the group, whose leader was the American-born photographer Alfred Stieglitz. In 1903, he was elected to the prestigious avant-garde English photo group "The Linked Ring" (founded in 1892), whose members did not share the tendencies of the Royal Photographic Society and were attracted by mysticism and symbolism. The period from 1905 to 1910 is generally considered Coburn's symbolist phase. Both groups expressed a growing dissatisfaction with the photographic establishment in England and in America. Coburn opened his first solo

"The Court of the Hotel," by A. L. Coburn, frontispiece to *The Reverberator,* in Volume 13, the New York Edition

exhibition at the Camera Club of New York; one of his photogravures was published in *Camera Work,* the quarterly magazine founded by Alfred Stieglitz, where many of Coburn's photographs appeared.

In 1904, Coburn returned to London, where he met and photographed George Bernard Shaw, who called him "one of the most accomplished and sensitive artist-photographers now living" and introduced him to other notable sitters, including Henry James, Arthur Symons, and Maurice Maeterlinck (Coburn 36). In 1905, Coburn met James in New York and photographed him for the *Century Magazine.* The year 1906 was the year of his important one-man exhibition at the Royal Photographic Society in London; the preface to the show catalog was written by Shaw. After viewing this show, James met Coburn at the Reform Club in London in May 1906; this meeting probably led to the novelist's first sitting for the portrait used as the frontispiece of volume 1 in the collected deluxe NEW YORK EDITION (1907–09).

James also invited him to LAMB HOUSE for more photographing. Twenty-four of Coburn's photos appear as the frontispieces in the New York Edition. In his autobiography, Coburn writes that it was "one of the most interesting experiences of my photographic career" (52). He was then only 24, and James did not refrain from instructing the photographer on where and what to photograph. James, Coburn writes, "was like a boy, always displaying unquenchable and contagious enthusiasm over every detail concerning these illustrations" (54). He dispatched Coburn to the Continent, to the cities of his fiction, and promised that he would himself guide him in London.

In his preface to *The GOLDEN BOWL* (1904), where James discusses the issue of illustrations, he characterizes their search as amusing. James, who generally disliked illustrations, decided for photographic frontispieces probably because he wanted to make the edition more attractive to the American audience. Perhaps James thought that the photographs might present him as a modern writer and enhance the edition, considering the interest in photography in early 20th-century America. According to Coburn, James decided on photographs as illustration for his novels because photographs were a medium as different as possible from James's literary work.

The year 1909 was a turning point in Coburn's artistic development: He broke with Stieglitz and the experience of *Camera Work.* In 1909–10, he produced photogravures for two books, *London* and *New York,* which mark the passage from pictorialism to the influence of MODERNISM with its abstract and geometric forms (1909 was also the year of the first Futurist Manifesto). Coburn's attention turned to form, and his main subjects became the city, the machine, and the technological conquests of modern humankind. In 1912, Coburn married Edith Wightman Clement from Boston, and they moved to England. In 1913, he published his first famous collection of portraits, *Men of Mark,* which would be followed in 1922 by a companion volume, *More Men of Mark.*

A new phase in Coburn's career began in 1916, when he met Ezra Pound and the avant-garde group of painters—Wyndham Lewis, Henry Gaudier-Brzeska, Charles Nevinson, William

Roberts—whom Pound called Vorticists. On the model of a kaleidoscope, Coburn developed a device of prisms and mirrors, the Vortoscope, which allowed him to produce the first abstract pictures called Vortographs. But in 1919 he was already tired of Vorticism and resumed taking photos with a traditional camera. In 1916, he had visited Harlech, in Wales, at the invitation of his friend George Davison, who was managing director of Kodak Ltd in Britain. Two years later, he built a house there and called it Cae Besi. In 1920, he published *The Book of Harlech*, for which he provided illustrations and text. After that date, he became increasingly interested in mysticism and involved in esoteric groups in search of spiritual fulfilment.

For the last 40 years of his life, Coburn was an active Freemason, writer and lecturer on Masonic philosophy. In 1931, he was elected honorary fellow of the Royal Photographic Society, to which he donated his collection of photographs; in 1932, he became a naturalized British subject. In 1945, he moved from Harlech to Rhos-on-Sea owing to the failing health of his beloved wife, who died in 1957. In 1962, the largest solo exhibition of his life was presented at Reading University, and in 1966, he published his autobiography. He died in November in the same year, 13 days after the opening of his final exhibition at Colwyn Bay Library.

Further Reading

Coburn, Alvin Langdon. *Alvin Langdon Coburn, Photographer: An Autobiography with over 70 Reproductions of His Works*. Edited by Helmut and Alison Gernsheim. 1966. Reprint, New York: Dover, 1978.

James, Henry. "Preface to *The Golden Bowl*." In *Henry James, Literary Criticism: French Writers, Other European Writers, The Prefaces to the New York Edition*, edited by Leon Edel and M. Wilson. New York: The Library of America, 1984.

Edel, Leon, *Henry James. A Life*. London: Collins, 1987.

Vittoria Intonti, *University of Bari*

Conrad, Joseph (1857–1924) Józef Teodor Konrad Korzeniowski was born on December 3, 1857, in Berdyczów, a predominantly Polish part of Ukraine. Conrad's father was Apollo Korzeniowski, a minor writer in Poland who was also involved in revolutionary activities, which resulted in his exile to a remote part of Russia in 1862. Conrad accompanied his mother and father into exile, where his mother died a few years later. Shortly after being allowed to return to Poland in 1869, Conrad's father died. Conrad was then raised by his maternal uncle, Tadeusz Bobrowski. As a youth, Conrad decided that he wanted to pursue a life at sea, and at 17 he was allowed to move to France to spend the next four years training for that profession. Being fluent in French, Conrad planned to join the French Merchant Marine service, but because of problems regarding working papers, that became impossible, so Conrad decided to join the British Merchant Marine service, knowing no English at the time.

Conrad would spend the next 16 years traveling to Southeast Asia, South America, Africa, and many other parts of the world. He rose from the position of seaman eventually to captain a ship. In 1889, on holiday, he began writing what would become his first novel, *Almayer's Folly* (1895), and Conrad chose to write the novel in English despite it being his third language. In 1890, he traveled to the Congo, an experience that would change him forever and would become the basis for his most famous fictional work, *Heart of Darkness* (1899). In 1895, Conrad gave up his life at sea and became a full-time writer when *Almayer's Folly* was published. Over the next several years, Conrad made a number of important literary friendships with Ford Madox Hueffer (Ford), R. B. Cunninghame Graham, Arnold Bennett, Stephen Crane, H. G. WELLS, and Henry James. For nearly the next 20 years, Conrad produced a remarkable number of masterpieces, including *The Nigger of the "Narcissus"* (1897), "Youth" (1898), *Heart of Darkness* (1899), *Lord Jim* (1900), "Typhoon" (1902), *Nostromo* (1904), *The Secret Agent* (1907), "The Secret Sharer" (1910), and *Under Western Eyes* (1911). Despite his critical success, however, Conrad found life as a writer trying. The writing process itself was painful and difficult, often leading to emotional breakdowns. To make matters worse, his works did not achieve commercial success, and he was in constant financial difficulties. The 1913 publication of *Chance,* however, brought him financial success, and by the time of his death in 1924, Conrad was one of the most important literary figures in England.

Conrad's relationship with Henry James is particularly interesting. Conrad and James first met in the winter of 1897 and remained friends until James's death in 1916. Conrad admired James more than any other living writer and consistently sought James's approval. In "Henry James: An Appreciation," Conrad wrote, "The critical faculty hesitates before the magnitude of Mr. Henry James' work" (102), going on to refer to James as a "great artist" (108). James also seems to have appreciated Conrad's work. In a letter to EDMUND GOSSE dated June 26, 1902, he remarks that he finds Conrad to be "one of the most interesting & striking of the novelists of the new generation. His production . . . has all been fine, rare & *valid*. . . . *The Nigger of the Narcissus* is in my opinion the very finest & strongest picture of the sea and sea-life that our language possesses—the masterpiece in the whole great class; & *Lord Jim* runs it very close." The mutual admiration of James and Conrad results in part from similar views on the art of fiction, and if one compares James's essay "The Art of Fiction" (1884) to Conrad's famous "Preface" to *The Nigger of the "Narcissus,"* one can see affinities between the two literary manifestos. Nevertheless, neither author seems to have directly influenced the other in the traditional sense.

Although Conrad and James admired each other's work and appreciated each other's friendship, their relationship was always somewhat distant. Conrad initiated their friendship and appears to have taken the greater efforts to maintain the relationship, with James often apologizing for his tardy replies to Conrad's letters or for their infrequent meetings. In many ways, their relationship was more like that between a master and his student. In fact, Conrad habitually addresses James in his letters as "*Très cher Maître.*" Although he appreciated Conrad's friendly feelings toward him, James's feelings toward Conrad seem to have never progressed beyond a comfortable warmth. A slight strain in their relationship occurred in 1914 with

publication of James's article "The Younger Generation" in the *Times Literary Supplement,* in which he ranks the work of EDITH WHARTON above that of Conrad and subtly criticizes *Chance* by praising its technical virtuosity while implying a corresponding lack of content. James likely never felt a strain in their relationship, but Conrad was hurt by the article. In a letter to John Quinn dated May 24, 1916, Conrad admitted that "this was the *only time* a criticism affected me painfully" (595). Nonetheless, Conrad continued to approach James with warmth and appreciation in his later letters, and in that same letter to Quinn, Conrad wrote that James was "always warmly appreciative and full of invariable kindness. I had a profound affection for him. He knew of it and he accepted it as if it were something worth having" (595–596).

Further Reading

Conrad, Joseph. *The Collected Letters of Joseph Conrad, 1912–1916.* Edited by Frederick R. Karl and Laurence Davies. Vol. 5. Cambridge: Cambridge University Press, 1996.

———. "Henry James: An Appreciation." *North American Review* 180 (January 1905): 102–108.

James, Henry. "The Younger Generation: Part II." *Times Literary Supplement* 637 (April 2, 1914): 157–158.

John G. Peters, *University of North Texas*

critical reception   In his lifetime, James's works did not sell very well although he was highly respected by many of his peers. James helped set the terms of his own literary-critical reception with the prefaces he wrote to the NEW YORK EDITION. Early treatments by the British writers Ford Maddox Hueffer (Ford) in *Henry James: A Critical Study* (1913) and Rebecca West in *Henry James* (1916) established James's critical reputation as a challenging writer who demanded much from his reader in emphasizing the characters' impressions of their European and American worlds. The British author Percy Lubbock, a personal friend of James and the editor of *The Letters of Henry James* (1920), put a spotlight on James's New York Edition prefaces in *The Craft of Fiction* (1921). Hogarth Press, started and run by Virginia and Leonard Woolf, published *Henry James at Work* (1924), written by James's last secretary, THEODORA BOSANQUET, in the same year that the press published the first edition of T. S. Eliot's *The Waste Land*.

Meanwhile, in the United States James's posthumous reputation was off to a rockier start. American critic Van Wyck Brooks in *The Pilgrimage of Henry James* (1925) characterized James's expatriation as a wayward deracination that cut him off from the vital elements of his American culture. Vernon Parrington's assessment of James in *The Beginnings of Critical Realism in America* (1930) similarly paints James as solipsistic in transforming "a suppositious [European] culture into an abstract *tertium quid*, something apart from social convention or physical environment" (240). For Brooks and Parrington, James's art was a symptom of his being caught between the Old and New Worlds. Granville Hicks passed similar judgments in *The Great Tradition: An Interpretation of American Literature since the Civil War* (1933).

In the 1930s, Constance Rourke reconsidered James, appreciating in her *American Humor: A Study of the National Character* (1931) his novel *The* AMERICAN for its comedic capacity to use the subject of American identity as a foundation for internal character development in an international context (see INTERNATIONAL THEME). James's reputation was further cultivated by men on the political left such as Stephen Spender in England and C. Hartley Grattan in the United States. The 1934 issue of *Hound & Horn* included an influential contribution by R. P. Blackmur, who praised James's resistance to conventions of genre and literary formulation. Blackmur's 1946 essay, "The Loose Baggy Monsters of Henry James: Notes on the Underlying Classic Form in the Novel," argued for appreciating an organic quality to the way in which the perception of the world by James's characters is a matter of moral conscience. Edmund Wilson, also a contributor to the *Hound & Horn* issue, offered a Freudian reading of "The TURN OF THE SCREW" that implied a critique of the repressive nature of Victorian society (see VICTORIANISM).

In *The American Renaissance* (1941), F. O. Matthiessen considered James as a bridge figure from the canonical five of (RALPH WALDO) EMERSON, Thoreau, Hawthorne (see HAWTHORNE), Melville, and Whitman to T. S. Eliot. He emphasized Hawthorne's fundamental influence on James and pondered why James's fiction seemed aloof to contemporaneous political crises. Matthiessen continued to publish on James, including *Henry James: The Major Phase* (1944) and *The James Family: Including Selections from the Writings of Henry James, Senior, William, Henry, and Alice James* (1947) (see HENRY JAMES, SR.; WILLIAM JAMES; ALICE JAMES). He also edited (with Kenneth Murdock) the first edition of James's notebook in 1947.

In the mid-1940s, the *Partisan Review* group of NEW YORK intellectuals, including Phillip Rahv, Saul Rosenzweig, and Lionel Trilling, further resuscitated James from Brooks, Parrington, and Hicks's negative judgments. Rahv's essays in the early 1940s, later collected in *Image and Idea: Fourteen Essays on Literary Themes* (1949), reconsidered James as expressing elements crucial to American character; for example, the conservatism of Basil Ransom's reaction to contemporary society in *The* BOSTONIANS (1886). In 1948, Trilling reread Hyacinth Robinson's suicide in *The PRINCESS CASAMASSIMA* (1886) as depicting an important moral crisis in the relationship between art and politics. Quentin Anderson's 1946 article in the *Kenyon Review* tied James to the spiritual philosophies of his father, Henry James, Sr., particularly those insisting on the sanctity of the individual's spiritual vision; Anderson followed up his ideas in *The American Henry James* (1957). In 1948, F. R. Leavis's *The Great Tradition: George Eliot, Henry James, Joseph Conrad* (see GEORGE ELIOT; JOSEPH CONRAD) appreciated the way James expanded the potential of the novel to represent the awakening of human awareness. Leavis valued James's mid-career works such as *The* PORTRAIT OF A LADY (1881) and thought less of James's later novels. In *The American Novel and Its Tradition* (1957), Richard Chase pointed to *The Portrait of a Lady* as a tour de force in which James reworks the notion of romance to present Isabel Archer's struggle to understand her world (see ROMANCE/REALISM/NATURALISM).

In the 1950s, Leon Edel's immensely influential five-volume biography of James began to appear

(1953–72). Mixing Freudian analysis, scrupulous research (plus control over James's letters), and sensitivity to James's style, Edel's work shaped a generation of scholarship in emphasizing the sibling tension between William and Henry. Meanwhile, the independent scholar Adeline Tintner collected a massive trove of James material in her Manhattan apartment, upon which she based several books on James. After the publication of his biography's final volume, Edel published a more complete collection of James's letters than that assembled by Lubbock.

In 1962, Maxwell Geismar's *The Cult of Henry James* (republished in the United States as *Henry James and the Jacobites* [1963]) revived the assessments of Brooks, Parrington, and Hicks in his debunking of James as a great writer and charged critics for remarkably overestimating the small-minded, prejudicial James. In *The Comic Sense of Henry James* (1960), Richard Poirier extended the work of Constance Rourke and considered how comedy enabled James to develop a sense of dramatic freedom in his characters. In *The Novels of Henry James* (1961), Oscar Cargill claimed that James had virtually invented the international novel with plot development that relied on characters' changing self-perception in the experience of cultural conflict. Dorothea Krook's *The Ordeal of Consciousness in Henry James* (1962) responded to the criticisms of Geismar and Leavis, insisting that James's characters experience moral struggles on par with characters of Shakespeare and the Greek tragedies. Lawrence Holland's influential *The Expense of Vision: Essay on the Craft of Henry James* (1964) analyzed the form of James's writing and narration to emphasize the reader's role in responding to the characters' struggles to attain self-understanding in their connection to those around them.

In the 1970s, influential works by Peter Brooks, Martha Banta, William Stowe, Philip Weinstein, and Ruth Bernard Yeazell considered ways in which the structural elements of James's fiction (reworking of genre, nesting of narrative frames, techniques of free indirect discourse) were integral to James's exploration of his characters' self-perception. Feminist critics such as Nina Baym, Judith Fetterley, and Sara de Saussure Davis read James both in terms of the female characters in his work and the women writers who were his contemporaries and friends. Richard Hocks, in *Henry James and Pragmatist Thought: A Study of the Relationship between the Philosophy of William James and the Literary Art of Henry James* (1974), laid the groundwork for reassessments of James that probe the philosophical significance of his writing. Ross Posnock's *The Trial of Curiosity: Henry James, William James, and the Challenge of Modernity* (1991) further developed the intersecting influences of philosophy and literature to consider James in relation to John Dewey and Theodor Adorno. Michael Anesko's "*Friction with the Market*": *Henry James and the Profession of Authorship* (1986) pushed the critical attention to the rhetorical style of James to encompass the profession and process of serial and book publication; David McWhirter edited a collection of essays in *Henry James's New York Edition: The Construction of Authorship* (1995) that pay keenly insightful attention to James's process of writing and publishing in the early 20th century.

In 1979, Daniel Mark Fogel founded the immensely influential *Henry James Review*, and under the editorship of Susan Griffin from the 1990s on the *Henry James Review* has embraced new critical and historical methodologies in examining James's work and has continued to proliferate beyond the scope of any short summary. The attention paid by feminist critics to gender dynamics in James's work has led to considerations of James's own SEXUALITY. Unfettered from the Freudian premise of Edel's biography, queer theory helped critics explore the ambiguities of James's private life in ways that increased the flexibility of gender signifiers in his oeuvre. Recent critics—whose works are listed in the bibliography of this *Companion*—have further developed interpretations of James's work bearing on social contexts of gender and sexuality (Graham, Habegger, Haralson, Moon, Pigeon, Sedgwick, Stevens); of RACE and culture (Bentley, Blair, Boelhower, Buelens, Freedman, Haviland, Johnson, McKee, Michaels, Warren); and of the politics integral to the 19th- and early 20th-century transatlantic world of print publication (Habegger, Jacobson, Salmon) as well as to the genre of realism (Bentley, Bersani, Seltzer, Thomas).

Since the completion of Edel's biography, subsequent biographers have taken advantage of wider access to James's letters to offer different versions of his life. Millicent Bell and H. Montgomery Hyde offered less Freudian views of James in their respective books *Edith Wharton & Henry James: The Story of Their Friendship* (1965) and *Henry James at Home* (1969). Fred Kaplan's major biography *Henry James: The Imagination of Genius: A Biography* (1992) developed the theme of James's intimacy with his male friends, and Sheldon Novick's two-volume biography, *Henry James The Young Master* (1996) and *Henry James: The Mature Master* (2007), interpreted James's letters and autobiography as hinting at physical intimacies that Edel had denied. Philip Horne edited the excellent *Henry James: A Life in Letters* (2001). Work by Lyndall Gordon, Susan Gunter, Steven Jobe, and Rosella Mamoli Zorzi have recast James by exploring the terms of intimacy in James's relationships with men and women. In 2006, Pierre Walker and Greg Zacharias began the multivolume publication of James's entire correspondence, which includes thousands of letters unavailable to, or overlooked and excluded by, Lubbock and Edel. Finally, James has proven a vibrant subject in the fiction of contemporary authors such as Alan Hollinghurst, David Lodge, and Colm Tóibín.

Further Reading
As the selected bibliography to this *Companion* demonstrates, there is a prodigious amount of criticism written on James. Useful reference guides published by Boston's G. K. Hall include: *Henry James, 1866–1916: A Reference Guide* (1982; edited by Linda J. Taylor); *Henry James, 1917–1959* (1979; edited by Kristin Pruitt McColgan); *Henry James, 1960–1974* (1979; edited by Dorothy McInnis Scura); *Henry James, 1875–1987: A Reference Guide* (1991; edited by Judith E. Funston). For an overview of criticism on James, see Linda Simon's *The Critical Reception of Henry James: Creating a Master* (Rochester, N.Y.: Camden House, 2007).

Nicholas Birns, *The New School*

drama   James's relation to the theater was highly conflicted, and the failure of his plays to gain popu-

lar acclaim was one of the central disappointments of his life. The theater and theatricality, however, would prove central themes and structuring principles of his narrative work.

James's sense of the theater's mystery and glamour preceded his actual attendance of theatrical productions. With great anticipation Henry, at the age of eight, attended his first show, recalled as *A Comedy of Errors*. In his early years in NEW YORK, James saw much Shakespeare, popular farces of the day by Dion Boucicault and others, adaptations of Dickens and *Uncle Tom's Cabin*, and Broadway spectacles. In addition, WILLIAM JAMES mounted homegrown theatricals in which Henry participated as actor, then playwright and scenic director. When James was 13, his family traveled to Europe, and James recounts Europe as "perceptibly more theatrical" than the United States (Edel 25). However, the adult themes of much European drama meant that the James children were exposed to little of it. He would long rue the lost opportunity to see French acting at its fabled height. During his time at Harvard Law School in the 1860s, he frequently escaped to Boston to see plays. A critique of one of these plays was the first writing he would submit for publication. While James's first decade as a professional writer was dominated by other genres, drama remained in the forefront of his consciousness. Following Francisque Sarcey, he praised the rigid formalism of classical drama, as exemplified in the current day by the "well-made" French play. He abhorred the messy license, by contrast, of the Anglo-American stage. He held dramatic "compactness" and "passion" as essential to narrative, taking several novelists, including GEORGE ELIOT and Louisa May Alcott, to task for the lack of it, and maintained drama as "of all literary forms, the noblest" (qtd. in Edel 33–34). The theater often appears in his narrative works, most notably in *The* TRAGIC MUSE (1890) and the short story "Nona Vincent" (1892).

James's first theatrical efforts were light sketches: the one-act *Pyramus and Thisbe* (1869) and *Still Waters* (1871)—composed for a charity event—and the 15-scene play *A Change of Heart* (1872), all small-cast and concerned with courtship themes. He attempted no full plays until over age

40, when he was approached to adapt his novella "DAISY MILLER: A STUDY" (1878) for the stage. The result, however, was rejected as too wordy. He published it (1882) but returned, chastened, to fiction. In 1890, asked to dramatize his 1877 novel *The AMERICAN*, he tarried, torn between the prospects of audience acclaim and the high earnings successful playwrights commanded and the indignities of the production process and bourgeois audiences bent on light entertainment. James published the unproduced romantic dramas *Tenants* (1890) and *Disengaged* (1892) as the volume *Theatricals* (1894), with a wry, chagrinned preface about his attempts to bring them to the stage. *Theatricals* was followed by *Theatricals: Second Series* (1895) containing two unproduced farces, *The Album* (1891) and *The Reprobate* (1891), with a preface regarding the sacrifices required in writing for the public. James held high hopes for a major production of *Guy Domville* (1895), a ponderous meditation upon religion and renunciation. However, at the close of the premiere—which James had spent watching OSCAR WILDE's smash hit *An Ideal Husband*—James was booed, and *Guy Domville* closed early. This humiliation plunged him into the deepest depression of his life.

Guy Domville was followed by the one-act *Summersoft* (1895)—written at the request of actress Ellen Terry but never, finally, produced by her. James converted *Summersoft* first into a short story, "Covering End," to be published as a complement to "The TURN OF THE SCREW" (1898), and then further expanded for the light, favorably received production *The High Bid* (1907). In 1908, *The Saloon* (1908), a dramatized version of James's ghost story "OWEN WINGRAVE" (1892), appeared. *The Saloon* received mixed reviews. *The Other House* (1908), a murder story inspired by Ibsen's *Hedda Gabler* and adapted from James's serial of the same title, remained unproduced after James rejected changes. *The Outcry* (1909), James's final play, regarding the ethics of art collection, was written for a London program conceived by J. M. Barrie and featuring the work of Shaw, Somerset Maugham, John Galsworthy, and others. This, however, was canceled due to the death of Edward VII. *The Outcry* was produced only after James's own death.

While in fiction, as Leon Edel explains, James "made his own laws," in his plays he "bowed to a whole series of laws other playwrights ignored," including "a minuteness of exposition" and "a constant fear that the audience would not understand him and therefore the need to explain every detail" (Edel 36). He was, at the same time, hampered and irritated by these bounds, complaining that he "never sat down to write a play without a feeling that a thousand devils were besetting him from all sides." In Edel's words, "[H]is plays became the prisoners of his theories" (Edel 36). Seeking to reconcile his veneration for dramatic form with the pain of his work's unpopularity, James formulated a palliative compromise: "I may have been meant for the drama—God Knows!—but I certainly wasn't made for the theatre" (qtd. in Edel 53). In his final years, James found himself composing narrative in "scenario" form and outlining dramatic structures in advance of writing novels, including *The AMBASSADORS* (1903) and *The GOLDEN BOWL* (1904), works considered among his finest. In this sense, his theatrical experiments, however doomed, may have strengthened his narrative abilities.

Further Reading

Edel, Leon. *The Complete Plays of Henry James*. New York: Oxford University Press, 1990.

Greenwood, Christopher. *Adapting to the Stage: Theatre and the Work of Henry James*. London: Ashgate, 2000.

James, Henry. *A Small Boy and Others*. New York: Scribner's, 1913.

S. I. Salamensky, *University of California, Los Angeles*

the Dreyfus affair   This was the name the French press used to refer to events from 1894 to 1906 surrounding the legal case of Captain Alfred Dreyfus, a French Jewish officer wrongfully charged with treason against France. The case polarized Europe and Great Britain, producing camps of "Dreyfusards" and "anti-Dreyfusards." This was particularly true after January 13, 1898, when French author Émile Zola published his famous letter to the president of the French Republic, "J'Accuse!"—a vituperative denunciation of the French military, government, and press for their dishonesty regarding the Dreyfus case and a public call for justice and truth. After Georges Clemenceau printed Zola's letter in his paper, *L'Aurore*, Zola was charged with libel, fined, and sentenced to the maximum penalty of one year imprisonment. Before his appeal, he fled for LONDON. All his property was confiscated, and he did not return to France until June 4, 1899.

To many historians, the Dreyfus affair marked the birth of modern ANTI-SEMITISM. Accused by Lieutenant-Colonel du Paty-de-Clam of selling French military secrets to a German military attaché, Maximilian von Schwartzkoppen, Dreyfus was arrested on October 15, 1894, without explanation. He was isolated and imprisoned for three months, denied contact with his family, and then tried by a secret court-martial on December 19–22, 1894. Unanimously convicted, he was sentenced to a life of solitary confinement in a specially constructed prison camp on Devil's Island, a penal colony off the coast of French Guiana, in northeast South America.

Within weeks of Dreyfus's arrest, anti-Semitic French newspapers like Édouard Drumont's *La Libre Parole* printed news of his arrest, proclaimed his guilt, and named him a Jew, falsely claiming that he had confessed to the charges. On January 5, 1895, Dreyfus endured a public ceremony of military degradation. His buttons and stripes were torn from his uniform, and his sword and scabbard broken and thrown contemptuously at his feet. He was forced to march before those under his command. All this took place before a crowd of 20,000 citizens howling "Death to the traitor!" "Kill him!" "Vive la France!" and "Dirty Jew!" The only thing that saved Dreyfus from being executed was article 5 of the 1848 Constitution, which had abolished the death penalty for political prisoners.

The flimsy case against Dreyfus was based on one document containing secret information known as "the *bordereau*." Although du Paty-de-Clam tried to pin its authorship on Dreyfus, handwriting experts disagreed. The case took a turn in Dreyfus's favor when the young Major Georges Picquart discovered that, in spite of Dreyfus's isolation, sensitive documents were still being sent to Germany. Picquart's

investigation uncovered an express letter-card, called a *petit bleu*, sent from Colonel von Schwartz-koppen to a Major Esterhazy. Upon studying the handwriting, Picquart became convinced that Esterhazy had authored the *bordereau*. Immediately, Esterhazy demanded an investigation to prove the "falsity" of the charges against him. When Dreyfus's brother, Mathieu, publicly denounced Esterhazy, the latter ordered a court-martial granted on January 11, 1898, a farce that produced a unanimous acquittal. Esterhazy emerged from the courtroom to cheers of "Long live France!" "Down with the Jews!" This provoked international outrage: Two days later, Zola published "J'Accuse!" Eight months later, Esterhazy fled France and confessed to writing the *bordereau*, but Dreyfus had already suffered four years' imprisonment on Devil's Island, developing severe physical, mental, and nervous disorders. Dreyfus was recondemned in a second court-martial in Rennes in September 1899, and then pardoned on September 19, 1899, but without honor.

When the Dreyfus case exploded, Henry James was living in LAMB HOUSE, where he resided from 1898 until his death in 1916. It was not until Zola published "J'Accuse!" that James emerged as a Dreyfusard. James never spoke out publicly. In personal letters, however, he wrote of feeling as if he were "every a.m. in Paris by the side of the big brave Zola, whom I find really a hero." James regarded Zola's letter "one of the most courageous things ever done and an immense honor to our too-puling corporation! But his [Zola's] compatriots—!" (Edel 274). In another correspondence, James refers to a letter of support he wrote to Zola, which has never been found (274).

James was both saddened and fascinated by the Dreyfus case, writing to MRS. MARY HUMPHRY WARD, "What a bottomless & sinister *affaire* & in what a strange mill it is grinding the poor dear French" (Horne 308). Days later, he wrote to a friend, the French author Paul Bourget, an anti-Dreyfusard, that he didn't "understand" the unfortunate events in France. "Nothing here [in England] corresponds to them—neither the good relations which we maintain with the Jews, and, in sum, with one another, nor the supreme importance we attach to civil justice, nor the 'short work' which we would make of the military if they attempted to substitute their justice for it" (Edel 275). Although in February 1899 James wrote his nephew, Harry, that he thought the affair "a more or less mad panorama, phantasmagoria and dime museum" (Edel 239), in March 1899 James still visited the Bourgets on the Riviera, a commitment made long before the news exploded.

Shortly after this trip to France, James published an essay in the *North American Review* (1899), "The Present Literary Situation in France," in which he praises Zola and makes the one public reference to the Dreyfus affair. He begins the essay stating the difficulty he has acknowledging the "great particular debt" those "caring for the things of the mind" owe to France of the past 50 years because the current political moment is all wrong. "There has . . . been no crisis in France at which the things of the mind were so little the fashion. Practically suppressed and smothered, stricken and silent behind the bars of their hideous political cage, we must think of them as, at the worst, only living by the light of faith and biding their time" (PLS 488).

James found the Dreyfus affair not just a political crisis but a crisis of the mind. He was disgusted on Dreyfus's behalf, but ever the cosmopolitan, he saw France trapped within a "hideous political cage" of corrosive nationalism. James's Dreyfusard position distinguished him from such virulent anti-Semitic contemporaries as Henry Adams.

Further Reading

Edel, Leon. *Henry James: The Treacherous Years*. Philadelphia: Lippincott, 1969.

Horne, Philip, ed. *Henry James: A Life in Letters*. London: Penguin, 1999.

James, Henry. *Henry James Letters, vol. 4, 1895–1916*. Edited by Leon Edel. Cambridge, Mass.: Harvard University Press, 1984.

———. "The Present Literary Situation in France." *North American Review* 169 (1899): 488–500. Abbreviated as PLS.

Kaplan, Fred. *Henry James: The Imagination of Genius*. New York: William Morrow, 1992.

Kneeblatt, Norman L., ed. *The Dreyfus Affair: Art Truth and Justice*. Berkeley: University of California Press, 1987.

Moore, Rayburn S., ed. *Selected Letters of Henry James to Edmund Gosse, 1882–1915: A Literary Friendship*. Baton Rouge: Louisiana State University Press, 1988.

Snyder, Louis L. *The Dreyfus Case: A Documentary History*. New Brunswick, N.J.: Rutgers University Press, 1973.

Sharon B. Oster, *University of Redlands*

Du Maurier, George (George du Maurier)

(1834–1896) Professional cartoonist, amateur singer, and late-blooming novelist, George Du Maurier was a major figure in the artistic world of Victorian London (see VICTORIANISM). Now best remembered for his blockbuster novel *Trilby* (1894), Du Maurier was known in his lifetime primarily for the gently satiric cartoons he contributed for three decades to *Punch*, one of the most popular journals of his era.

Born on March 6, 1834, George Louis Palmella Busson Du Maurier was the first child of the English Ellen Clarke and the French Louis-Mathurin du Maurier. The latter, a scientist and inventor, was better at producing grand plans than financial stability. During Du Maurier's youth, his family moved back and forth across the Channel, leading Du Maurier to develop what Henry James—later a close friend—described as a "charming Anglo-French mind and temper" (letter to Grace Norton, September 30, 1888, in Horne 208). Indeed, Du Maurier's dual, sometimes conflicted sense of national identity is evident in his work, which often depicts habits and stereotypes of French and English life.

Following his father's wishes, Du Maurier briefly enrolled in the Birkbeck Chemical Laboratory at University College in London. But after his father's death in 1856, he opted to study art in PARIS. For roughly a year, he attended the atelier of Charles Gleyre in the Latin Quarter, which he would go on to romanticize in *Trilby*. Later, he studied in Antwerp and Düsseldorf. Unfortunately, in 1857, Du Maurier suddenly went blind in his left eye, an occurrence that prompted initial depression and lifelong anxiety about his health. Forced by poor vision to abandon painting, Du Maurier turned to black-and-white illustration—and to London.

THE NEW SOCIETY CRAZE

The New Governess (through her pretty nose). "Waall—I come right slick away from Ne'York City, an' I ain't had much time for foolin' around in Europe—you bet! So I can't fix up your Gals in the Eurôpean Languages, no-how!"
Belgravian Mamma (who knows there's a Duke or two still left in the Matrimonial Market). "Oh, that's of no consequence. I want my Daughters to acquire the American Accent in all its purity—and the Idioms, and all that. Now I'm sure *you* will do *admirably!*"
George Du Maurier, "The New Society Craze," *Punch* (December 1, 1888)

After struggling for a few years to master this increasingly professionalized and respected craft, his career took off in 1864, when he joined the staff of *Punch.* James, who had been fond of the middlebrow magazine since his childhood, wrote repeatedly about Du Maurier's work, including "Du Maurier and London Society" (1883) and an 1897 piece eulogizing him in *Harper's New Monthly Magazine.* In the former, he praised Du Maurier's *Punch* illustrations for "hold[ing] up a singularly polished and lucid mirror to the drama of English society" (Rawlings 385). Especially noteworthy were those cartoons exposing social snobbery and a series deriding what Du Maurier viewed as the excesses and foppery of the AESTHETIC MOVEMENT. He also contributed to periodicals such as the *Cornhill* and *Once a Week* and designed the illustrations for novels such as Elizabeth Gaskell's *Wives and Daughters* (1866), Thomas Hardy's *The Hand of Ethelberta* (1896), and an edition of Thackeray's *The History of Henry Esmond, Esq.* (1852).

As that list suggests, Du Maurier crossed paths with many of London's prominent artistic figures; he counted as friends the Pre-Raphaelite painter Edward Burne-Jones, the writers GEORGE ELIOT and G. H. Lewes, the future head of the Royal Academy, Edward Poynter, and the painter James McNeill Whistler. Du Maurier's relationship with the infamously contentious Whistler, whom he first met in Paris, deteriorated when Whistler nearly sued him for libel, claiming the minor character Joe Sibley in *Trilby* was based on a "mendacious recollection" of Whistler himself (Ormond 466). In response to Whistler's protests, Du Maurier reluctantly replaced Sibley with another character in the book version of the novel.

Du Maurier's relationship with James was more felicitous. Whereas neither was quite satisfied with the illustrations Du Maurier did for James's WASHINGTON SQUARE (1880), the two soon became devoted friends. In a letter, James described Du Maurier as "personally and conversationally the pleasantest creature" (Horne 208). On one of their many walks, Du Maurier offered James an idea for a new novel about a scheming musician who, using hypnosis, remakes a beautiful young woman into a dazzling cosmopolitan singer. James turned it down, urging Du Maurier to take it up himself, which he eventually did in *Trilby*. But his first venture as a novelist was *Peter Ibbetson* (1891); opening with nostalgic reflections of Du Maurier's Paris childhood, the novel traces the love between two characters who, separated by circumstance, continue their romance in a shared dream world by accessing the mind's "hidden capacities" (*Peter* 80).

Three years later, Du Maurier completed the writing and illustrations for *Trilby*, which was serialized in *Harper's Monthly Magazine*. Featuring the memorable character of Svengali (the sinister Jewish musician and mesmerist), the novel combines the original plot outlined to James with the tale of three young British artists enjoying "Paris! Paris!! Paris!!!" (*Trilby* 8). In doing so, it played upon late-Victorian curiosity about mesmerism, Jewishness, and French bohemian life. The novel became a transatlantic best seller and generated various spin-offs, from plays and films to Trilby hats, Trilby ice cream, and trick cards called a "Svengali Deck." James, with a tinge of envy, congratulated his friend on the "fame and flattery and flowers"—not to mention the funds—he was now receiving (Lubbock 213). Du Maurier wrote one more novel, *The Martian* (1897), which continued his interest in psychological and supernatural powers but failed to match *Trilby*'s success. He is also the author of the parodic poems "A Lost Illusion" and "A Legend of Camelot."

Just as important to Du Maurier as his work was his family. In 1863, he married Emma Wightwick, whom he semi-jokingly called "Miss Salvation," viewing her as a bulwark against the dangers of dissipation (Ormond 130). The two had five children: Beatrix, Guy, Sylvia, Marie-Louise (May), and Gerald. Although fond of evenings on the London social scene, with their storytelling, bantering, and singing, Du Maurier increasingly preferred to spend his time at the family home in Hampstead, where he lived until his death in 1896. Du Maurier was the grandfather of the novelist Daphne du Maurier. In *The Young George Du Maurier*, her collection of his early letters, she remembers her grandfather as "a bohemian at heart" who "mocked at many, but with a twinkle in his eye" (ix).

Further Reading

du Maurier, Daphne. *The Young George Du Maurier.* Garden City, N.Y.: Doubleday, 1952.

Du Maurier, George. *Peter Ibbetson.* New York: Harper and Brothers, 1891.

———. *Trilby.* Edited by Elaine Showalter. Oxford and New York: Oxford University Press, 1998.

James, Henry. "Du Maurier and London Society." Reprinted in *Henry James: Essays on Art and Drama.* Edited by Peter Rawlings. Aldershot, Hants, England, and Brookfield, Vt.: Scolar Press, 1996.

———. *Henry James: A Life in Letters.* Edited by Philip Horne. London and New York: Allen Lane Penguin Press, 1999.

———. *The Letters of Henry James,* vol. 1. Edited by Percy Lubbock. New York: Octagon Books, 1970.

Ormond, Leonée. *George Du Maurier.* Pittsburgh, Pa.: University of Pittsburgh Press, 1969.

Sarah Gracombe, Stonehill College

Eliot, George (1819–1880)

George Eliot is the pseudonym of Mary Ann Evans, a British journalist, fiction writer, and poet, whose work Henry James greatly admired, often criticized, and reviewed extensively. When Eliot published her first fiction in 1857 for *Blackwood's Edinburgh Magazine*, James was with his family in France, devouring libraries, as his father put it (Edel: 43).

Eliot was known for her psychological realism and concern with issues of morality and consciousness. In his 1866 review of *Felix Holt, the Radical* (1866), James praised Eliot's delineation of character through which she attempted to extend "human sympathy" with "her humor, her morality, and her exquisite rhetoric" (1996b: I, 461, 462). However, at the same time, he criticized her artificial plots, slow narrative pace, diffuse style, and anticlimactic endings, which threatened to reduce her to "a secondary thinker and an incomplete artist" (1996b: I, 461). In his own novels, James tried to overcome what he called the disproportion "between the meagre effect of the whole and the vigorous character of the different parts" in Eliot's novels.

Eliot began her career after a transformative tour of France, Italy, and SWITZERLAND in 1849–50, a journey coinciding with her growing agnosticism. In 1854, she risked scandal by eloping with George Henry Lewes. In a letter to a friend in November 1855, Eliot said that she had found in Lewes "a mind which I have every day more reason to admire and love" (qtd. in Ashton: 197–198). In the dedication of her first novel, *Adam Bede* (1859), she avers that it would never have been written without him. James praised Eliot for her "rich and complicated mind," but like many of her contemporaries, he was critical of her relationship with Lewes (1996a: I, 522). In an *Atlantic Monthly* review of J. W. Cross's biography of Eliot, James describes Lewes as "a versatile, hard-working journalist, with a tendency, apparently, of the drifting sort" (1996a: I, 526). James first met Eliot and Lewes at their LONDON home in May 1869. James praised her inner beauty, which emanated, as he wrote to his father, from the "hundred conflicting shades of consciousness and simpleness" of "her personality," which gave her an "admirable physiognomy" (1974: I, 116–117). It is important to note that James's visit followed his anonymous reviews of her early fiction for the *Atlantic Monthly*, of her political novel *Felix Holt, the Radical* for the *Nation* in 1866, and of her epic poem *The Spanish Gypsy* for the *North American Review* in 1868. These three reviews are important not only for marking the beginning of James's reviewing career but also for foreshadowing the overlaps and differences in their writing.

By the second time that James met Eliot and Lewes in London in April 1878, he was a travel writer, art critic, short story writer, and novelist. He was disappointed when "The Great G. E.," as he called her in a letter, did not praise his recently published RODERICK HUDSON (1875), *The AMERICAN* (1877) and *The EUROPEANS* (1878) (James 1920: I, 61). James was perhaps too self-absorbed to understand that Eliot's disengagement was due to Lewes's fatal illness. (He died only two weeks after James's visit.) Whereas a novel like *The PORTRAIT OF A LADY* (1881) shows James's indebtedness to Eliot, the fiction of his later phase (for instance, *The WINGS OF THE DOVE* [1902], *The AMBASSADORS* [1903] and *The GOLDEN BOWL* [1904]) marks his shift from social realism (see ROMANCE/REALISM/NATURALISM) to MODERNISM. The more his writing became metaphorical and symbolic through its exploration of the psychological analysis of character, the more James developed techniques such as the interior monologue, which Eliot only foreshadowed with her late plot-fragmenting narratives in *Daniel Deronda* (1876) and in the autobiographical essays *Impressions of Theophrastus Such*. James's unsigned *Galaxy* review in March 1873 characterizes *Middlemarch* (1879) as an "old-fashioned novel," suggesting his dissatisfaction with the kind of realist fiction that aimed to be an organic whole (Haight: 444).

James's reading of Eliot's poetry and novels were influential in defining her reputation in the early 20th century. The philosophical and aesthetic aspects of her narration were only recovered with scholarship that emerged after Gordon Haight had revived an interest in her authorial figure with the publication of her letters during 1954–78.

Further Reading

Ashton, Rosemary. *G. H. Lewes: A Life*. Oxford: Oxford University Press, 1991.

Edel, Leon. *Henry James: A Life*. New York: Harper and Row, 1985.

Haight, Gordon. *George Eliot: A Biography*. Oxford: Oxford University Press, 1968.

James, Henry. *Autobiography: A Small Boy and Others, Notes of a Son and Brother, the Middle Years*. Edited by F. W. Dupee. London: W. H. Allen, 1956.

———. *Letters of Henry James.* Edited by Percy Lubbock. 2 vols. London: Macmillan, 1920.

———. *Henry James Letters.* Edited by Leon Edel. 4 vols. London: Macmillan, 1974.

———. "Review of Cross's *George Eliot's Life, Atlantic Monthly,* LV, May 1885." In *George Eliot Critical Assessments,* edited by Stuart Hutchinson, vol. 1, 522–534. 4 vols. Hastings, England: Helm Information, 1996.

———. "Unsigned Review, '*Felix Holt, the Radical*', *Nation,* III, 16 August 1866." In *George Eliot Critical Assessments,* edited by Stuart Hutchinson, vol. 1, 461–464. 4 vols. Hastings, England: Helm Information, 1996.

Kyriaki Hadjiafxendi, *University of East Anglia*

Emerson, Ralph Waldo (1803–1882) One of the United States's most important thinkers of the 19th century, Emerson was a poet, essayist, and founder of transcendentalism. His most famous essays, including "Nature" (1836) and "Self-Reliance" (1841), articulated themes of American individualism and a transcendental relationship to the natural world. As a close friend of the James family, Emerson was a key figure in James's life, both personally and intellectually.

Emerson was born in Boston in 1803. The son of a Unitarian minister, he grew up in Massachusetts, eventually going on to Harvard Divinity School and graduating as a Unitarian minister in 1829. The same year, he married Ellen Louisa Tucker, who was already ill with tuberculosis and died in 1831 at the age of 19. Grieving for his wife, Emerson began to question core elements of his belief. He found fault with the more dogmatic principles of the Unitarian faith, leaving the ministry in 1832 due to his disagreement with the church's understanding of communion and public prayer.

After resigning, Emerson traveled to Italy, France, and England, meeting and exchanging ideas with such European writers as William Wordsworth, Samuel Coleridge, and especially Thomas Carlyle. Upon returning to Boston, he began lecturing, the vocation by which he would earn his living (helped by inheritance from his first wife's family). Living and lecturing in Boston, he married Lydia Jackson in 1835, with whom he would have four children. The eldest, Waldo, died at the age of five in 1842. The other children were Ellen (born 1839), Edith (1841), and Edward (1844). Emerson spent most of his life with his family in Concord and Boston.

Emerson came to dominate American intellectual life, becoming one of the "representative men" about which he wrote. He was a poet and scientist, lecturer and writer, philosopher and political activist. He helped establish transcendentalism in its American form, drawing from the English romantics, who had themselves borrowed ideas from Immanuel Kant and German idealism. Emerson's ideal of transcendentalism was that human knowledge and experience came from each individual's intuition and spiritual understanding. He privileged intuition and emotion above reason and empirical inspection of the material world. Thus, all individuals were capable of discerning truth through their own intuition and observations instead of having to rely on institutions (particularly religious ones) to do it for them. His philosophy of transcendentalism was notoriously unsystematic. Rather than laying out a clear scheme of ethics and philosophies, Emerson's lectures and essays tended to string together isolated observations and ideas, prompting HENRY JAMES, SR., to deem him a "man without a handle" (qtd. in Lewis 65).

Emerson was joined in his general beliefs by such 19th-century intellectuals as Margaret Fuller, Elizabeth Peabody, Bronson Alcott, Nathaniel Hawthorne (for a time) (see HAWTHORNE), and Henry David Thoreau. For many transcendentalists, the movement was a social or political one, and hopes for a utopian future were high. While he ardently opposed slavery and served as editor of the *Dial*, a transcendental journal, Emerson remained apart from formal political organizations and organized groups in general, holding to his belief in the spiritual integrity of the individual. Emerson hated feeling bullied into adopting a moral stance.

James had a deep personal respect for the elder Emerson. He was a close friend of James's father, Henry James, Sr., even agreeing to be the godfather of James's elder brother, WILLIAM JAMES. Henry, Jr., grew up listening to intellectual conversation at the

James and Emerson homes. In adolescence, Henry and William attended school with Emerson's son Edward. Up until Emerson's death, James would continue to meet him occasionally.

Intellectually, James felt both respect for and resistance to the spokesman of an older generation of American intellectuals. Along with Hawthorne, he saw Emerson as *the* "writer in whom the world at large has interested itself" (*Hawthorne* 66), keenly feeling Emerson's status as America's first internationally respected man of letters. Like his father, James respected Emerson's promotion of individual judgment over institutional decrees, especially with regard to religion.

However, James departed from Emerson's philosophies in several ways, expressing his differences in his critical essays and novels. While he appreciated Emerson's individualism, he often suggested that cultural and social forces could not—and should not—be ignored or subordinated. James casts Emerson's individualist, introspective philosophy as important for its moment, "thanks to a want of other entertainment" (*Hawthorne* 67), implying that individualism was necessary before the new country had "culture" about which to write. Several of James's novels, including *The* AMERI-CAN (1877) and *The* PORTRAIT OF A LADY (1881), include American characters who are stridently (and admirably) individualistic but whose individualism blinds them to the forces of culture or leads to unabated self-interest.

Also, Emerson and James had different ideas about what it meant to be an American. For Emerson, being American meant forging "an original relation to the universe" (*Nature* 27) and making a clean break with all that came before. James was also concerned with what being an "American" writer meant, but to him there could be no clean break with the European tradition since great art needed a great deal of history to inform it. James saw the ideal American as able to pick and choose which national traditions to use and which to discard: Americans were the inheritors of European legacies and yet not strictly limited to any single one.

Finally, James saw Emerson as too idealistic. He claimed that Emerson "had no great sense of wrong . . . no sense of the dark, the foul, the base" (qtd. in Lewis 561). In his novels, James specialized in naive American characters who entered situations and cultures idealistically only to be manipulated, taken advantage of, and disillusioned (see INTERNATIONAL THEME). For James, Emerson's idealism, his transcendentalism, and his strict definition of American identity distinguished him as a great, albeit flawed, genius.

Further Reading

Emerson, Ralph Waldo. *Nature. Emerson's Prose and Poetry*. Edited by Joel Porte and Saundra Morris. Norton Critical Edition, 27–55. New York: Norton, 2001.

James, Henry. *Hawthorne*. 1879. Reprint, Ithaca, N.Y.: Cornell University Press, 1967.

Lewis, R. W. B. *The Jameses: A Family Narrative*. New York: Farrar, Straus & Giroux, 1991.

Richardson, Robert D. *Emerson: The Mind on Fire: A Biography*. Berkeley: University of California Press, 1995.

Amanda Adams, *Miami University*

film adaptations   In his 1899 essay "The Future of the Novel," Henry James observed, "the future of fiction is intimately bound up with the future of the society that produces and consumes it" (*Essays* 106). Beneath this truism lies an anxious recognition that the fiction James himself wrote was becoming less compelling, perhaps too difficult, for distracted modern readers. "We live in a lonely age for literature or for any art but the mere visual," James lamented in a letter to WILLIAM DEAN HOWELLS in 1903, adding that newspapers and "picture magazines" were diminishing the very "*faculty of attention*" needed to make sense of complex works of fiction like his own (*Letters* 250). The novel clearly faced an uncertain future in an increasingly image-based visual culture.

James's fears were prescient. Writing at the beginning of the 20th century, he gave voice to what Kathleen Fitzpatrick has called the anxiety of obsolescence. While literary fiction continues to be written and read today, the culturally dominant forms of fictional narrative, more often than not, are supplied by film and television. Novels still have a place in culture, yet they play a diminished role in comparison to the enormous influence and popularity of film, notwithstanding the film industry's heavy reliance on literature for source material. The fate of James's novels is arguably a case in point: They tend to be read by graduate students or advanced undergraduates and by a relatively small cadre of teachers who assign them. Others are more likely to encounter him in one of many film adaptations of his work.

Early filmmakers did not regard James's fiction as well suited for adaptation. In contrast to EDITH WHARTON, who had four of her novels turned into silent films, there are no silent film adaptations of James's work. The first adaptations of Henry James's fiction came in the classical Hollywood studio era: *Berkeley Square* (1933, Frank Lloyd), an adaptation of his unfinished novel *The Sense of the Past*; and *The Lost Moment* (1947, Martin Gabel), adapted from his story "The ASPERN PAPERS." The most notable adaptation from the period, however, is *The Heiress* (1949), based on the novel WASHINGTON SQUARE. Olivia de Havilland won an Academy Award, her second, for her performance as Catherine Sloper. The prominent studio director William Wyler greatly accentuated the melodramatic potential of James's narrative, converting it into a revenge plot (Rivkin). Catherine's suitor, Morris Townsend, played by the gifted young actor Montgomery Clift, gives her up when he learns that her domineering father Dr. Austin Sloper (Ralph Richardson) will likely disinherit her if she elopes with him. Taking liberties with both chronology and characterization, *The Heiress* transforms the jilted Catherine into a steely spinster who will get her revenge.

Although there were several television versions of James's fiction in the 1950s, the next film adaptation came more than a decade later with *The Innocents* (1962), a brilliant reworking of "The TURN OF THE SCREW" by the British director Jack Clayton from a screenplay by William Archibald and Truman Capote. The film heightens the psychosexual tensions of James's tale; it has the look and feel of a Hitchcock thriller. Director of photography Freddie Francis uses the wide aspect ratio of Cinemascope to great effect from the remarkable opening credit

sequence: The anguished governess Miss Giddens (Deborah Kerr), her hands clasped as if in prayer, declares in a whispered voice-over, "I want to save the children, not destroy them." Like the tale on which it is based, *The Innocents* makes it virtually impossible to determine whether the ghosts at Bly are real or whether Miss Giddens is delusional. In a series of hallucinatory, even surrealistic sequences, made all the more terrifying by George Auric's masterful score, she comes to believe that the ghosts of Peter Quint (Peter Wyngarde) and the former governess, Miss Jessel, have possessed her charges, Flora and Miles, so that they can, in effect, carry on their clandestine affair after death. The film ends with an exorcism.

Not surprisingly, "The Turn of the Screw" has been adapted more frequently than any other James tale—all told there are five film versions and 10 television versions—but *The Innocents* remains by far the best. Marlon Brando plays Peter Quint in a little-known prequel to the tale titled *The Nightcomers* (1972, Michael Winner), which was no doubt overshadowed by the release a month later of *The Godfather* (1972). More recently, Alejandro Ammenabar's thriller *The Others* (2001), although not strictly an adaptation of "The Turn of the Screw," owes much to James's tale (interestingly, a 1957 television version of the tale was titled *The Others*).

One of the most celebrated French New Wave directors, François Truffaut, came out with his own James adaptation in 1978, *La chambre verte* (*The Green Room*), loosely based on "The ALTAR OF THE DEAD" and "The BEAST IN THE JUNGLE." The American director Peter Bogdanovich, coming off a string of successful films in the early 1970s, also tried his hand at James in *Daisy Miller* (1974), an adaptation of the James novella with the director's then-girlfriend, Cybill Shepherd, in the title role. In a striking scene shot at the Colosseum in ROME, Frederick Winterbourne encounters Daisy cavorting with the young Italian suitor Giovanni and admonishes her for "lounging away the evening in this nest of malaria." When James wrote the novella, the discovery that malaria is caused by mosquitoes was still some 20 years away; in a clever bit of dramatic irony, mosquitoes buzz in the background as Daisy responds indignantly, "I don't care whether I have Roman fever or not!" Daisy's defiance here and elsewhere surely struck a more resoundingly feminist note for movie audiences in the 1970s than it did for James's readers in the 1870s.

The Europeans (1979) was the first of three Henry James adaptations by director James Ivory with his longtime producing partner, Ismail Merchant. Another adaptation of James followed five years later, The Bostonians (1984), with a stellar cast highlighted by Vanessa Redgrave's nuanced performance as Olive Chancellor. Both films are Masterpiece Theater–style period treatments of the sort favored by art-house audiences. In fact, The SPOILS OF POYNTON and The GOLDEN BOWL had already been adapted for Masterpiece Theater broadcasts. Yet more than any other filmmakers, Merchant and Ivory deserve credit for bringing James to college-educated filmgoers who had been schooled in the French New Wave and the so-called New Hollywood. They helped create a niche market for their relatively low-budget adaptations that not only garnered awards but also proved to be quite lucrative. The Europeans received one Academy Award nomination; The Bostonians, two. A Room with a View (1985), an adaptation of E. M. Forster's novel, was their most successful yet, winning three Oscars. These films, with their international aura and literary cachet, offered a form of cultural capital that was simply unavailable from high-concept movies made for teens.

Merchant and Ivory were attached to an adaptation of The PORTRAIT OF A LADY before the New Zealand director Jane Campion took on the project, with stunning results. The Portrait of a Lady (1996), which came three years after her acclaimed film The Piano (1993), opens with voices of modern-day women discussing love and romance over a blank screen, followed by images of similar young women looking directly at the camera, as if to underscore the fact that "watching lovely women has become," in Nancy Bentley's apt phrase, "a central preoccupation of the celluloid world" (127). That Campion means to challenge the dominant male gaze of cinema in this opening sequence is confirmed when the film cuts to an extreme close-up shot of Isabel

Archer's eyes, the first glimpse of Nicole Kidman in what is arguably her finest performance as an actor. While imposing an overly schematic—and Freudian—explanation for Isabel Archer's crisis in the novel as a problem of sexual repression, Campion nonetheless poses searching questions about how female desires, not least the desire for self-determination, may (or may not) have changed since James's time (see WOMEN'S ISSUES).

Questions about female agency resurfaced in two James adaptations released the same year: Agnieszka Holland's Washington Square (1997), with Jennifer Jason Leigh as Catherine Sloper, and Iain Softley's The Wings of the Dove (1997), with Helena Bonham Carter as Kate Croy. Both films take liberties with their source texts in bold and mostly felicitous ways. Washington Square restores Catherine's European "grand tour" that had been omitted from The Heiress, for instance, yet it overplays the rivalry between Morris Townsend (Ben Chaplin) and Dr. Sloper (Albert Finney). With one of the bleakest endings of any film in recent memory, The Wings of the Dove was the more successful of the two—it surpassed all the recent James adaptations at the box office by a large margin (Bousquet 234). Softley includes an explicit sex scene that does not appear in the novel, but it does feel consistent with Carter's acute portrayal of Kate Croy as a reckless femme fatale.

Merchant and Ivory would go on to revisit James in The Golden Bowl (2000), starring Kate Beckinsale, Nick Nolte, Jeremy Northam, and Uma Thurman. This film is more innovative than their two previous James adaptations, juxtaposing lush cinematography shot on locations in England and Italy with actual newsreel footage of industrializing America—images of streetcars, coal mines, and railroads meant to convey the source of Adam Verver's newly acquired wealth. There is a telling moment toward the end of the film when Charlotte acts as a tour guide for her husband's extensive art collection before it all gets transported from Europe back to American City, a town Fanny Assingham (Anjelica Huston) likens to "some Indian trading post on the Oregon Trail." Charlotte calls attention not merely to the artifacts themselves but also to the social distinction they confer upon the

Ververs. For wealthy Americans in James's time, as Richard Brodhead points out, European high culture "became one of the chief ways of displaying upper-class prerogatives of wealth and leisure" (97), and no one was better placed to write about Americans abroad than James, whose self-styled INTERNATIONAL THEME instructed his readers in European manners. Film adaptations of Henry James's fiction trade upon a similar form of social distinction, for his work now bestows symbolic cultural capital upon readers and viewers alike.

Selected Filmography of Henry James Adaptations

The Bostonians was directed by James Ivory, screenplay by Ruth Prawer Jhabvala and James Ivory, cast included Vanessa Redgrave, Christopher Reeve, Jessica Tandy. Merchant Ivory Productions, 1984.

Daisy Miller was directed by Peter Bogdanovich, screenplay by Frederic Raphael, cast included Cybill Shepherd, Barry Brown, Eileen Brennan. Director's Company, 1974.

The Europeans was directed by James Ivory, screenplay by Ruth Prawer Jhabvala and James Ivory, cast included Lee Remick, Robin Ellis. Merchant Ivory Productions, 1979.

The Golden Bowl was directed by James Ivory, screenplay by Ruth Prawer Jhabvala, cast included Uma Thurman, Nick Nolte, Kate Beckinsale, Jeremy Northam. Merchant Ivory Productions, 2000.

The Heiress, based on *Washington Square,* was directed by William Wyler, screenplay by Ruth and Augustus Goetz, cast included Olivia de Havilland, Ralph Richardson, Montgomery Clift. Paramount Pictures, 1949.

The Innocents, based on "The Turn of the Screw," was directed by Jack Clayton, screenplay by William Archibald and Truman Capote, cast included Deborah Kerr, Michael Redgrave. CinemaScope Twentieth-Century Fox/Achilles, 1962.

The Portrait of a Lady was directed by Jane Campion, screenplay by Laura Jones, cast included Nicole Kidman, John Malkovich, Barbara Hershey. Gramercy Pictures, 1996.

Washington Square was directed by Agnieszka Holland, screenplay by Carol Doyle, cast included Jennifer Jason Leigh, Ben Chaplin, Albert Finney, Maggie Smith. Hollywood Pictures/Caravan Productions, 1997.

The Wings of the Dove was directed by Iain Softley, screenplay by Hossein Amini, cast included Helena Bonham Carter, Linus Roache, Alison Elliott. Miramax, 1997.

Further Reading

Anesko, Michael. *"Friction with the Market": Henry James and the Profession of Authorship.* New York and Oxford: Oxford University Press, 1986.

Bentley, Nancy. "Conscious Observation: Jane Campion's *Portrait of a Lady.*" *Henry James Goes to the Movies.* In Griffin, 127–146.

Bourdieu, Pierre. *Distinction: A Social Critique of the Judgment of Taste.* Translated by Richard Nice. Cambridge, Mass.: Harvard University Press, 1984.

———. *The Field of Cultural Production.* New York: Columbia University Press, 1993.

Bousquet, Marc. "Cultural Capitalism and the 'James Formation.'" *Henry James Goes to the Movies.* In Griffin, 210–239.

Bradley, John R., ed. *Henry James on Stage and Screen.* New York: Palgrave, 2000.

Brodhead, Richard H. *Cultures of Letters: Scenes of Reading and Writing in Nineteenth-Century America.* Chicago: University of Chicago Press, 1993.

Eaton, Mark A. "Driving Miss Daisy: Peter Bogdanovich's *Daisy Miller.*" In *Approaches to Teaching Henry James's* Daisy Miller *and* The Turn of the Screw, 177–185. Edited by Peter Biedler and Kimberly Reed. New York: MLA, 2005.

———. "'Exquisite Taste': The Recent Henry James Movies as Middlebrow Culture." In Bradley, 157–76.

———. "Miramax, Merchant Ivory, and the New Nobrow Culture: Niche Marketing *The Wings of the Dove* and *The Golden Bowl.*" *Literature/Film Quarterly* 34, no. 4 (2006): 257–266.

Fitzpatrick, Kathleen. *The Anxiety of Obsolescence: The American Novel in the Age of Television.* Nashville, Tenn.: Vanderbilt University Press, 2006.

Freedman, Jonathan, ed. *The Cambridge Companion to Henry James.* Cambridge: Cambridge University Press, 1998.

Griffin, Susan, ed. *Henry James Goes to the Movies.* Lexington: University Press of Kentucky, 2002.

Guillory, John. *Cultural Capital: The Problem of Literary Canon Formation.* Chicago: University of Chicago Press, 1995.

James, Henry. *Essays on Literature: American Writers, English Writers.* New York: Library of America, 1984.

———. *Henry James Letters.* Vol. 4. Edited by Leon Edel. Cambridge, Mass.: Harvard University Press, 1984.

Johnson, Kendall. *Henry James and the Visual.* Cambridge and New York: Cambridge University Press, 2007.

McGurl, Mark. *The Novel Art: Elevations of American Fiction after Henry James.* Princeton, N.J.: Princeton University Press, 2001.

Menand, Louis. "Not Getting the Lesson of the Master." *New York Review of Books* 44, no. 19 (1997): 19–20.

Rivkin, Julie. "'Prospects of Entertainment': Film Adaptations of *Washington Square.*" *Henry James Goes to the Movies.* In Griffin, 147–169.

Sadoff, Dianne F. "'Intimate Disarray': The Henry James Movies." *Henry James Review* 19, no. 3 (1998): 286–295.

Stewart, Garrett. "Citizen Adam: The Latest James Ivory and the Last Henry James." *Henry James Review* 23, no. 1 (2002): 1–24.

Walton, Priscilla. "The Janus Faces of James: Gender, Transnationality, and James's Cinematic Adaptations." In *Questioning the Master: Gender and Sexuality in Henry James's Writing,* edited by Peggy McCormack, 37–53. Newark: University of Delaware Press, 2000.

Mark Eaton, *Azusa Pacific University*

Florence, Italy With an origin in the Roman Empire dating back to the rule of Julius Ceasar, Florence boasts a ground of dense historical layers stretching more than 2,000 years. Haunted by the ghosts of his encounters in Florence and determined to evoke them in fiction and prose, James turned to the Tuscan capital as the third most significant Italian city in his work. Florence maintained its central place in James's consciousness to the end of his life, as evidenced by his writing in the NEW YORK EDITION preface to "The PUPIL" (1891) that, although the tale was set in Nice, VENICE, and PARIS, its characters were of "the special essence of the little old miscellaneous cosmopolite Florence, the Florence of other, of irrecoverable years, the restless yet withal so convenient scene of a society that has passed away for ever with all its faded ghosts and fragile relics" (xvi).

During seven visits to Florence between 1869 and 1907, James came to know intimately fellow American expatriates Francis Boott and his daughter, Lizzie; CONSTANCE FENIMORE WOOLSON; Dr. William Baldwin; the sculptor Horatio Greenough and his family; the Huntingtons and their daughter, Laura Huntington Wagniere; and Edith Story Peruzzi, daughter of expatriate sculptor William Wetmore Story, who introduced James to the aristocratic families of Corsinis, Antinaris, and Farinolas. He also associated with the English expatriate writer Vernon Lee and her family. During his extended stay in Florence in 1886–87, he wrote "The ASPERN PAPERS" (1888), "Louisa Pallant" (1888), and his essays on LONDON and ROBERT LOUIS STEVENSON. James used Florence as the setting for the short tales "The Madonna of the Future" (1874) and "Diary of a Man of Fifty" (1879) and as the nest of bachelor Gilbert Osmond and his daughter, Pansy, in *The PORTRAIT OF A LADY* (1881).

James's literary and artistic appreciation of Florence existed on at least three levels: in the deep history of its classical, medieval, and Renaissance periods; in its pre-Risorgimento days contemporaneous with pre–CIVIL WAR America; and in its later 19th-century phase, when Italy, united, began modernizing and became a well-trafficked tourist destination for the moneyed set of the Gilded Age (from 1865 until the early 1870s, Florence served as the capital of all of Italy). Deeply embedded to James's imagination, these layers enriched his fiction, adding a dark cast to his Florentine scenes that exude the intrigue and deception not only of Medici corruption and Dantesque irony but also of the more recent decadence and failures in the American expatriate world. From conversations with the Francis Boott, the Huntingtons, and the Greenoughs, James was acutely aware of the Anglo-American expatriates residing in their Florentine colony of the 1840s through 1860s. As related in *Notes of a Son and Brother* (1914) (see AUTOBIOGRA- PHIES), James understood Florence as the site where Hawthorne had set Donatello's family estate in *The Marble Faun* (1860) near the Tower Montuato on Bellosguardo (see HAWTHORNE). James's Florence was also the residence of Robert and Elizabeth Bar- rett Browning at Casa Guidi, where Elizabeth was buried after her premature death in 1861. The city implied Walter Savage Landor's ubiquitous pres- ence, and Margaret Fuller's last days before board- ing the ship *Elizabeth* that would founder tragically on the rocks of NEW YORK's Fire Island in 1850. James glimpsed the aristocratic society of Florence through Edith Story Peruzzi's marriage to a minor Medici. Her tragic downfall, brought about by her son Bindo's court-martial upon suspicions of homo- sexuality and his eventual suicide, was presaged by James's deprecating biography of her father, *Wil- liam Wetmore Story and His Friends* (1903).

Florence was often the stage in James's fiction for alienated expatriates from the United States. "The Madonna of the Future" tells the story of a tragically deluded and blocked American painter, and "Diary of a Man of Fifty" relates the sad tale of a lonely grand tourist whose emotional distance precludes his happiness. This bleak theme cul- minates in James's depiction of the warped and degenerate Florentine expatriate colony in *The Portrait of a Lady*. James's great novel uses Florence as the site of the narcissistic aunt Lydia Touchett's continental villa as well as the residence of Gil- bert Osmond and his sister, Countess Gemini, née Susan Osmond (with "Gemini" suggesting false doubleness or duplicity), and the perch of Madame Serena Merle, whose surname ominously connotes "blackbird" in French. James thereby suggests the decadence, corruption, and aristocratic pretension of hybrid American expatriates. Although Osmond and Isabel eventually set up their household in the Palazzo Roccanera in ROME, Florence's history and architecture establish a suffocating and ominous atmosphere and the taint of sexual intrigue tied to Madame Merle and Osmond's sister, the Countess Gemini, through whom James alludes to Americans who had married into Italian noble families, includ- ing Margaret Fuller and Edith Story. Although

James frequented the Uffizi and the Pitti Palace galleries, tombs of the Medicis, the churches, the various palazzos, and the Cascine, his deeper con- nection to Florence centered on the south side of the Arno River up the hill called Bellosguardo with its Villa Brichieri, where he lived with Con- stance Fenimore Woolson from December 1886 through the winter of 1887, and the neighboring Villa Castellani, owned by the Huntingtons and partly leased to the Boots. He mused nostalgically to Boott in 1897 that "Lamb House, in short, is *my* Bellosguardo" (James to Boott, December 28, 1898, Houghton) (see LAMB HOUSE). But James wrote to Boott in 1894 after Fenimore Woolson's tragic suicide, "[T]he whole place is now such a perfect cemetery of ghosts that there is little joy in it left for me—or rather there would be little if I had not deep-seated dispositions to find myself secretly, even whenever so sadly, fond of the company of the relics of the dead: Villa Brichieri seemed to stare down at one with unspeakably mournful eyes of windows" (*Letters*: 494). James was pleased with Duveneck's expressive and realistic funeral monu- ment of Lizzie Boott in Florence's Allori cemetery, writing to her father, "[O]ne is touched to tears by this particular example which comes home to one so—of the jolly great truth that it is *art* alone that triumphs over fate" (December 28, 1898).

Further Reading

James, Henry to Francis Boott (December 28, 1898), Francis Boott Papers, Houghton Library, Harvard University.

James, Henry. Preface to "The Pupil." *New York Edi- tion*, vol. 11. New York: Scribner's, 1908.

———. *Henry James Letters*, vol. 3. Edited by Leon Edel. Cambridge, Mass.: Harvard University Press, 1980.

Kathleen Lawrence, *George Washington University*

Fullerton, William Morton (1865–1952) Mor- ton Fullerton was a journalist for the London *Times* who befriended James in 1890 and whose affairs with sculptor Lord Ronald Gower and writer EDITH WHARTON brought him closer to James. James wrote many impassioned letters to Fullerton, enabled Fullerton's liaison with Wharton (he introduced them), and provided Fullerton with counsel when he was blackmailed by a former mistress with letters proving his tryst with Gower. Fullerton was well connected in the literary world. He was friends with OSCAR WILDE, who wrote to Fullerton asking for a loan when in prison. Fullerton's former lover Gower is said to have been the model for Lord Henry Wotton in *The Picture of Dorian Gray* (1891).

Born in Norwich, Connecticut, to the minister Bradford Morton Fullerton and his wife, Julia Ball Fullerton, "Morton" or "Will" demonstrated at a young age a natural charisma and attractiveness. A bright student, Fullerton attended Phillips Academy in Andover, Massachusetts, and later matriculated at Harvard, where he was classmates with the philosopher and writer George Santayana. According to Marion Mainwaring, Fullerton's relationships with men, especially those that were sexually charged, were motivated largely by his drive for power (see MASCULINITY). He aligned himself with men who were able to offer him valuable assistance—monetarily, socially, or professionally. These associations and connections led Fullerton to LONDON, where he established a career writing first for the *Times* for two years and then moving to the Paris *Times*, where he remained for another 15 years.

Several scholars claim that Fullerton and James were strongly drawn to each other when they initially met and that they maintained a flirtation in subsequent correspondence. Susan Gunter and Steven Jobe write that "they were instantly attracted to one another" (129), and Fred Kaplan notes that "the attraction was immediate and mutual" (406). Fullerton looked to the older author as an adviser on his literary, financial, and romantic affairs. James enjoyed Fullerton's attention.

When James confirmed that Fullerton had had sexual relationships with men, he wrote in a letter from November 14, 1907:

> I seem to feel now that if I had been nearer to you—by your admission of me (for I think *my* signs were always there) something might have been advantageously different, and I think of the whole long mistaken perversity of your averted *reality* so to speak, as a miserable *personal* waste, that of something—ah, so tender!—in *me* that was only quite yearningly ready for you, and something all possible, and all deeply and admirably appealing in yourself, of which I never got the benefit. (Edel, IV: 473)

Signaling to Fullerton his own regret of not having gotten "the benefit" of the journalist's sexual experience, James gestures toward the inner conflict he had long experienced when "longing," "yearning," or "gnashing" his teeth for younger men. Unable to satiate his desire for men like Fullerton physically (whether due to the "obscure hurt" he sustained in youth, as suggested by biographers, or to his "Puritan" upbringing, as noted by another favorite, Hugh Walpole), James did find a way to channel his desire for Fullerton through his "comrade" the novelist Edith Wharton.

In October 1907, James introduced Fullerton to his close friend Wharton, sending him to her home, The Mount, in Lenox, Massachusetts, with a letter of introduction. From that point forward, James acted as a "facilitator-voyeur" (as Susan Goodman has termed it) in the affair, arranging for meetings, encouraging the progression of the romance, and even becoming a confidant for Wharton, for whom this was an extramarital relationship. Known better for his friendships and sexual connections with authors and artists than for his own literary accomplishment, Fullerton stands as an alluring and mysterious man who influenced many creative persons around him. Scholars have suggested that Fullerton was the model for Merton Densher in *The WINGS OF THE DOVE* (1904) and inspired the character George Darrow in Wharton's *The Reef* (1912).

Further Reading

Goodman, Susan. *Edith Wharton's Inner Circle.* Austin: University of Texas Press, 1994.

Gunter, Susan E., and Steven H. Jobe. "Dearly Beloved Friends: Henry James's Letters to Younger Men." In *Henry James and Homo-Erotic Desire.* Edited by John R. Bradley, 125–135. New York: St. Martin's Press, 1999.

James, Henry. *Letters.* Edited by Leon Edel. 4 vols. Cambridge, Mass.: Harvard University Pres, 1984.

Kaplan, Fred. *Henry James: The Imagination of Genius.* New York: William Morrow, 1992.

Lee, Hermione. *Edith Wharton.* London: Chatto & Windus, 2007.

Mainwaring, Marion. *Mysteries of Paris: The Quest for Morton Fullerton.* Hanover, N.H.: University Press of New England, 2001.

Sharon Kehl Califano, *University of New Hampshire*

Gosse, Sir Edmund (1849–1928)   Edmund Gosse, a literary critic, translator, and poet, was one of the most influential English men of letters of the late 19th and early 20th centuries. After his mother died when he was nine, he moved from LONDON with his father, the naturalist Philip Henry Gosse, to Devon. Philip was a member of a fundamentalist Christian sect, and Edmund's upbringing, described in his best-known book, *Father and Son* (1907), was strict. He was not allowed to read fiction or nonreligious poetry, but he secretly developed a love for secular literature. After coming to London in 1867, Gosse established himself as one of the most eminent critics of the day, despite his lack of a university education. His wide-ranging critical and biographical works include *Seventeenth-Century Studies* (1883), *The Life of William Congreve* (1888), *Portraits and Sketches* (1912), and *Aspects and Impressions* (1922). A speaker of Norwegian and other Scandinavian languages, Gosse helped introduce the work of Henrik Ibsen to English readers in a series of articles, books, and translations. Although he began his literary career thinking of himself as a poet and nursed grand ambitions for his poetry for many years, his endeavors in verse had less effect than his criticism. Among his books of poetry are *On Viol and Flute* (1883), *In Russet and Silver* (1894), and *The Autumn Garden* (1907). Gosse first met Henry James in 1879, and the two had a close relationship from the early 1880s. In the last three decades of James's life, Gosse was probably James's most intimate friend.

Gosse never lived by his writing alone but worked in various bureaucratic jobs, pursuing his literary interests in his spare time. He worked first as a transcriber at the British Museum. In 1875, he

was appointed as a translator at the Board of Trade. In the same year, he married Nellie (Ellen) Epps, the daughter of a doctor and a talented painter. From 1885 to 1890, he was Clark Lecturer at Trinity College, Cambridge, a position that entailed giving 20 lectures a year on literary topics and which he combined with his duties at the Board of Trade. From 1904 to 1914, he was the librarian at the House of Lords. With Nellie, Gosse had three children, Sylvia, Philip, and Tessa.

From early in his adult life, Gosse cultivated the friendship of English, American, and European literary figures. He also had many friends in other fields, including politics, journalism, the visual arts, and the aristocracy. Gosse was able to give Matthew Arnold, Alfred Lord Tennyson, and Robert Browning as references in his first application for the Cambridge lectureship, and while at the House of Lords he became an intimate of the prime minister, Herbert Henry Asquith. Gosse was not a universally admired figure, however. In 1886, his book *From Shakespeare to Pope* (1885) was attacked in the *Quarterly Review* by a former friend, John Churton Collins, for shoddy scholarship. Although there was a widespread perception in literary circles that Collins's article was malicious in tone, many of the accusations were well founded, and a reputation for carelessness clung to Gosse until the end of his life and beyond. Even James, whose sympathetic letters to Gosse about what he called the "beastly business" (Moore 42) of the Collins scandal helped deepen their friendship, later said that Gosse had a "genius for inaccuracy" (*Letters* III: 338). After his death, Gosse's reputation as a critic and scholar went into swift decline, though *Father and Son* continues to be well regarded.

The James-Gosse correspondence was extensive. But while Gosse saved his letters from James, James apparently burned most of his letters from Gosse in his famous "gigantic bonfire," mentioned in a letter of 1910 (*Letters* IV: 541). Gosse's revelation about the unhappy marriage of JOHN ADDINGTON SYMONDS was the source of James's story "The AUTHOR OF 'BELTRAFFIO'" (1884). Gosse later told James about Symonds's homosexuality and showed James some of Symonds's private papers in which he defended homosexual desire. Gosse was also the recipient of a story from James about watching and waiting for a face at a window in an unnamed foreign town, which has been regarded by some as evidence of James's homoerotic desire. Some scholars have supposed that Gosse also had a homoerotic orientation, partly on the basis of a mention of repressed desires in a letter to Symonds, while others have argued that there is little or no evidence that Gosse was homosexual.

Gosse was an important facilitator of James's later career. In 1911, in his capacity as a member of the English Committee of the Nobel Prize, Gosse proposed James for that honor, which eventually went to Belgian author Maurice Maeterlinck. In 1913, along with Percy Lubbock, HUGH WALPOLE, and others, he issued an appeal to honor James on his 70th birthday. The appeal resulted in James being presented with an inscribed silver-gilt Charles II porringer and dish, a bust of James by the sculptor Derwent Wood, and a portrait by JOHN SINGER SARGENT. In 1915, James called upon Gosse to testify to his "knowledge of [James] as a respectable person, 'speaking and writing English decently' &c." in his application for British citizenship (Moore 308). At James's request, Gosse also appears to have helped secure the prime minister as a witness for James's application. In late 1915, shortly before James's death, Gosse was instrumental in ensuring that he was awarded the Order of Merit by King Edward VII. After James died, Gosse was proposed by Max Beerbohm as the editor of James's letters. This was opposed by Mrs. William (Alice) James, although Gosse consulted Percy Lubbock on the edition of letters that appeared in 1920. Gosse continued to use his influence to promote James's work until his own death. In a letter, Gosse wrote, "I always adored [James]. But now that he is gone, he seems to me almost supernatural in the beauty of his sympathy and intelligence" (Thwaite 470).

Further Reading

James, Henry. *Letters.* 4 vols. Edited by Leon Edel. Cambridge, Mass.: Harvard University Press, 1974–1984.

Moore, Rayburn S., ed. *Selected Letters of Henry James to Edmund Gosse, 1882–1915: A Literary Friendship.* Baton Rouge: Louisiana State University Press, 1988.

Thwaite, Ann. *Edmund Gosse: A Literary Landscape.* London: Secker and Warburg, 1984.

Guy Davidson, *University of Wollongong*

Howells, William Dean (1837–1920)   William Dean Howells was a well-known author, travel writer, poet, and an influential editor of the *Atlantic Monthly* (1871–81). His prolific authorship includes *Italian Journeys* (1867), *Their Wedding Journey* (1872), *A Chance Acquaintance* (1873), *The Undiscovered Country* (1880), *A Modern Instance* (1882), *The Rise of Silas Lapham* (1885), *A Hazard of New Fortunes* (1890), and *My Mark Twain* (1910).

Born in Ohio, Howells received little formal education because his family moved frequently in search of newspaper work for his father. Howells began to set type at the age of nine, an experience he shared with his future friend Mark Twain.

William Dean Howells, undated photo by T. E. Mort *(Library of Congress)*

A voracious reader, he learned Spanish, Latin, French, and German as a teenager. His intense self-education served him well; in 1861, he was appointed U.S. consul in VENICE, where he lived for the duration of the CIVIL WAR. While in Italy, Howells published travel pieces on Venice, which he later revised and collected in book form as *Venetian Life* (1866). On Christmas Eve 1862, he married Elinor Mead from Vermont, with whom he had three children. Family responsibilities necessitated financial security, which to a certain extent drove his profuse literary productivity.

Returning to the United States in 1865, Howells wrote for E. L. Godkin's *Nation* before moving to CAMBRIDGE, Massachusetts, in 1866 to serve as assistant editor of the *Atlantic Monthly*. He soon met James, though neither man would remember their first meeting, and they formed a lifelong friendship as they discussed "the true principles of literary art" (Howells, *Letters*, IV:271). As assistant editor (soon to be editor in chief) of one of the most influential periodicals of its day, Howells held a position of power in shaping the realist form of late 19th-century American literature. Howells enthusiastically supported James's work, accepting several of his early stories for the *Atlantic*, and the two frequently reviewed each other's work publicly and privately. In an often-quoted 1871 letter to Charles Eliot Norton, art professor at Harvard and coeditor of the *North American Review*, James both complimented and critiqued his friend:

> Howells edits, and observes & produces—the latter in his own particular line with more & more perfection. His recent sketches in the *Atlantic* . . . belong . . . to very good literature. He seems to have resolved himself, however, into one who can write solely of what his fleshly eyes have seen; & for this reason I wish he were "located" where they would rest upon richer and fairer things than this immediate landscape. (*Complete Letters* II: 390)

James concluded that America "will yield its secrets only to a really *grasping* imagination. This I think Howells lacks. (Of course I don't!)" (*Complete Letters* II: 390). Howells, too, privately complained to

James about the unhappy endings of novels like *The* AMERICAN (1877), but in public he praised his colleague's endeavors, as he did in an essay published in the November 1882 *Century*. Howells argued that the fiction of Dickens, Thackeray, and Trollope was outmoded. Defending a new school of realism that "studies human nature much more in its wonted aspects," he boldly asserted that "[t]his school, which is so largely of the future as well as the present, finds its chief exemplar in Mr. James; it is he who is shaping and directing American fiction, at least" (28) (see ROMANCE/REALISM/NATURALISM). The essay provoked a flurry of debate from the British press, which perceived the essay as an affront to their country.

In the 1880s, Howells declined professorships at Johns Hopkins and Harvard as he continued to produce novels. He also became interested in socialism, a position that is evident in his 1890 novel, *A Hazard of New Fortunes*. This work was in part a reaction to Chicago's Haymarket riot in 1886. Though he disagreed with the anarchists' position, Howells felt that the state of Illinois wrongly convicted the men accused, so he petitioned the governor to commute their death sentences. The novel, James wrote to his brother WILLIAM JAMES, was "so prodigiously good & able, & so beyond what [Howells] at one time seemed in danger of reducing himself to" (*Life in Letters* 223).

Howells moved his family to NEW YORK CITY in 1888, where, with the exception of a year in 1890 and time he spent in Europe, he lived until his death. During an 1894 trip to France, he briefly met with Jonathan Sturges, whom he passionately advised to live all he could. Sturges related this exchange to James, who recorded it in an October 1895 notebook entry as the germ for *The* AMBASSADORS (1903). Howells, like James, continued to write and publish through his later years, and in 1908 the American Academy of Arts and Letters elected him as its first president, a position he held for the remainder of his life. His continued affection and respect for James prompted him to join efforts with EDITH WHARTON and EDMUND GOSSE to nominate James for the 1911 Nobel Prize in literature. When James died five years later, Howells eagerly agreed to write a commemorative essay for *Monthly*, but he never completed it for publication. His last extant letter to James, however, sums up his feelings for his friend and colleague of 50 years: "I have somehow always looked to you as my senior in so many important things. You have greatly and nobly lived for brave as well as beautiful things, and your name and fame are dear to all who honor such things" (qtd. in Anesko 464–465).

Further Reading

Anesko, Michael. *Letters, Fictions, Lives: Henry James and William Dean Howells.* New York: Oxford University Press, 1997.

Howells, William Dean. "Henry James, Jr." *Century Magazine* 25 (November 1882): 25–29.

———. *Selected Letters, Volume 1: 1852–1872,* vol. 4. Edited by George Arms, et al. 32 vols. Boston: Twayne, 1979.

James, Henry. *The Complete Letters of Henry James: 1855–1872.* Edited by Peter Walker and Greg Zacharias. 2 vols. Lincoln: University of Nebraska Press, 2006.

———. *Henry James: A Life in Letters.* Edited by Philip Horne. New York: Viking Press, 1999.

Jennifer Eimers, *University of Georgia*

the international theme   One of the dominant subjects of his life as well as art, James's international theme has in reality a narrower transatlantic scope. Split between an American upbringing and an adulthood lived almost entirely in Europe, James based much of his fiction on both collisions and conjunctions between the two worlds. The subject resonated with readers on both continents. The early "DAISY MILLER: A STUDY" (1878), for instance, remained throughout the author's life one of his most popular works, and its theme echoes in subsequent writings: An adventurous American ingénue confronts a European society that presumes her to be unrefined and uncultured, and it is not accustomed to allowing women the freedoms she takes for granted back home.

James often reversed the direction of this critique, as in *The Reverberator* (1888). In that novel, the pressman George Flack stands for everything overbearing and self-righteous in the United States as he intrudes into the lives of a reclusive, inoffensive, albeit elite Parisian family, seeking scandal for his paper. James's major work, however, will usually encompass both his censure and celebration of each culture in its relation to the other. In *The PORTRAIT OF A LADY* (1881), for example, a refined, gentle, and privacy-loving English society, typified by Ralph Touchett (son of an American expatriate) and Lord Warburton, is threatened by the somewhat shallow, intrusive, and overly "familiar" American Henrietta Stackpole; yet her compatriots also have a bravery, artlessness, and good nature, as embodied in Isabel Archer, which ultimately become prey to the continental decadence and cynicism of the expatriated American Gilbert Osmond (146). As reflected in this scenario, James often exempts England from his general conception of Europe, especially when he is most critical. This could be attributed to the intensifying identification of James with his chosen home or, conversely, to the politic diplomacy that this extremely social author inevitably had to maintain with his adopted countrymen as a national guest. (James became a naturalized British subject in 1915, the year before his death.)

If there is any single work that develops the theme to its greatest depth, it may be *The AMBASSADORS* (1903). Many biographers see strong affinities between Lambert Strether, the novel's center of consciousness, and James himself, and thus the story can be seen as the most personal statement he would make about his own liminal international position. Strether, a middle-aged editor of a New England journal, comes to PARIS on a mission for Mrs. Newsome, who in many ways represents American culture in general. Strether's task is to rescue her son, Chad, from the Parisian life into which he has settled. For most Americans in the novel, a life on the Continent is by definition immoral and decadent, and they assume this corruption is embodied in Madame de Vionnet, the mature and cultured Parisian who has taken Chad under her wing. Strether is surprised to find that under de Vionnet's influence, Chad has matured and gained a great degree of polish and refinement. As Strether comes to admire the expansive potential of Parisian life, especially in contrast to the angry provincialism he sees in his compatriots, he realizes he is betraying his mission as an American "ambassador." Some readers might assume that the novel portrays the European contingent as having been truly deceitful, revealing an immorality endemic to their old-world cosmopolitanism. But this reading ignores the fact that James portrays Strether as having a certain naïveté that prevents him from understanding the diplomatic language with which the Europeans have been speaking the truth to him all along.

For James's Americans, the act of presenting a public "face" to the world in order to screen one's private erotic entanglements should be denounced as deceitful and immoral. James, however, strongly disagreed. One of the most persistent conflicts in his transatlantic fiction arises from an American insistence that one's life should be transparent, and that one ought not to maintain a privacy that is unavailable to public inspection. Privacy, in this view, is inimical to honesty and sincerity. Thus Henrietta Stackpole, who, as Isabel says in *Portrait*, is "a kind of emanation . . . of the nation" itself, alarms her English hosts as one who "walks in without knocking at the door," and who would consider any such knocker "a rather pretentious ornament" (146). In The AMERICAN SCENE (1907), which records James's impressions of his homeland after a 20-year absence, he is shocked to see that this antipathy to privacy has infiltrated the very architecture of the nation. The American house, James reports, has banished *"penetralia"* and areas of seclusion and interiority (250). "The custom rages like a conspiracy for nipping the interior in the bud, for denying its right to exist" (166). When every part of the house is "visitable, penetrable," the effect on the inhabitant is one of "positively serving you up for convenient inspection" (168). Perhaps more than anything else, it is this issue that eventually reversed the anti-European bent of his earlier writing. James would increasingly align himself not only with the European insistence on privacy's "right to exist" but also with the individual's right to maintain a separate "personal" narrative for public use, one that acts as an envoy or ambassador for oneself.

Further Reading

James, Henry. *The Portrait of a Lady.* 1881. Reprint, New York: Penguin, 1986.
———. *The American Scene.* 1907. Reprint, London: Rupert Hart-Davis, 1968.

Brian Artese, *Agnes Scott College*

the Irish question   For James's biographers, Ireland is pretty much where things begin. Nearly all major accounts of James's life and career emphasize the practical, cultural, and financial impact of his Presbyterian millionaire grandfather, William James, who left the village of Curkish, part of the townland of Bailieborough in County Cavan, about 50 miles northwest of Dublin, in 1789 with the twin aims of visiting the battlefields of the recently fought American War of Independence and of making his fortune (Lewis 3). He accomplished both objectives. The determined, astute, and religiously driven William died at aged 62 one of the richest men on the eastern seaboard of the United States. His strict and far-seeking will, which attempted to tame the excesses of HENRY JAMES, SR., was successfully contested, and the Jameses lived their lives, as Henry later wrote, "never in a single case . . . for two generations, guilty of a stroke of business" (qtd. in Lewis 13). When Ireland surfaces again in accounts of James's life and in his work, its status shifts from that of a troublingly albeit enabling foundation to a dangerous, contradictory, and sometimes erotic fascination. Whether foundational or dangerously fascinating, James's Irishness and his relationship thereto are difficult to know how to read or assimilate.

Without the levels of political opportunism that marked American-Irish relations in the revolutionary period, that first William James would have made neither the journey nor the money that enabled the James family to be as they were. Furthermore, Henry James's grandfather was Presbyterian, not officially part of the visibly oppressed religious Catholic majority of the island but practically disenfranchised in every way. These cultural forces are what, on profoundly formative and perhaps invisible levels, shaped Henry James into a writer. Key episodes in James's later career and adult life are impressed by his fascination with Ireland and Irishness, including his conflicted and uncomfortable position in relation to OSCAR WILDE, his fascination with Charles Stewart Parnell, and his later life-enhancing love for Jocelyn Persse. It is telling that in his attitudes toward Wilde and Persse, James's step from uncomfortable association to emotional, sexual expansion was a short one. Throughout his career, Ireland and its emergent personalities remain close but never contemplated, influential but without the same kinds of directness that mark his engagements with England, France, or Italy.

If readers do not know what to do with James's Irishness, that is because his own representation of Ireland is deeply conflicted. For example, James participates in casually racist scenarios right up until the end of his career. His notes for *The Ivory Tower* (1917) dismiss "Dublin" as an acceptable place-name on the grounds of its inherent, assumed, and uninterrogated ugliness. In the first half of his career, he partially equates Irish immigrants to the United States with libidinous and possibly menacing greed. For example, in WASHINGTON SQUARE (1880) Aunt Lavinia dismisses the Battery as a possible place for a conspiratorial rendezvous with Morris Townsend on the grounds that it "was rather cold and windy, besides being exposed to intrusion from Irish emigrants who at this point alight, with large appetites, in the New World" (109). It is interesting here that James uses the term *emigrants* rather then *immigrants*. These persons may, in James's prose, alight intrusively, but the foundational energy of their journey is *away* in flight, not forward in aspiration. And in attributing "large appetites" to these emigrants, James's prose suggests a 19th-century racist discourse equating Irishness with libidinous greed. It is also telling that *Washington Square*'s narrative method attributes this sentiment to Aunt Lavinia, a figure against whom the novel more than sharply defines intelligence and ethical consideration. Placed in the historical context with Ireland, *Washington Square* is a profoundly contemporary novel: It was published in the early 1880s, but the main bulk of its action takes place in the 1840s, when James's idyllic NEW YORK of childhood stood in stark contrast to the genocidal catastrophe of the famine unfolding in Ireland.

This ambivalent representation of Ireland registers elsewhere in James's fiction. Very early in *The* PORTRAIT OF A LADY (1881) Osmond cruelly chides the nuns who are bringing Pansy back from the formative school and eventual prison of her convent. He infers, with light sarcasm, that Pansy has been taught Irish—historically a "minority," déclassé, and politically oppressed language. The French nun returning Pansy tells Osmond that she speaks to her pupils in her own language. She continues:

> "But we have sisters of other countries—English, German, Irish. They all speak their proper language."
> The gentleman gave a smile. "Has my daughter been under the care of one of the Irish ladies?" (252)

Through this kind of joke, *The Portrait of a Lady* does three things: First, it announces its own cosmopolitanism and that of its author; second, it conveys an Anglo-American sense of culture that regards "Irishness" as an object of culturally formative derision and repudiation. But third, and most important, it subjects this enabling disrespect of Ireland to rather sharp interrogation. This is early in the novel's representation of the villainous Osmond, whose first act of verbal assault amounts to the ridicule of a shy nun and his daughter's education as he simultaneously gives voice to his anxieties about his own social standing.

This kind of tangential, ambivalent, and politically charged representation of Ireland also turns up in James's autobiographical and critical reflections on his career, as in this passage from the NEW YORK EDITION preface to Volume 10, which contained *The* SPOILS OF POYNTON (1897), "A LONDON LIFE" (1888), and a lesser-known story, "The Chaperon" (1891):

> I recapture perfectly again, in respect to "The Chaperon," both the first jog of my imagination and the particular local influence that presided at its birth—the latter a ramshackle inn on the Irish coast, where the table at which I wrote was of an equilibrium so vague that I wonder today how any object constructed on it

should stand so firm. The strange sad charm of the tearful Irish light hangs about the memory of the labour of which this small fiction—first published in two numbers of "The Atlantic Monthly" of 1891—was one of the fruits; but the subject had glimmered upon me, two or three years before, in an air of comedy comparatively free from sharp under-tastes. (1,154)

Here there are aspects of James's representation of Ireland that would be at home in any imperialist representation of Ireland—the "ramshackle inn," for example (this was, in fact, the rather swish Marine Hotel in Dun Laoghaire—Kingstown as it was then known—just outside of Dublin) or the comically off-balance table. And toward the passage's end, James is certainly as keen to distance Ireland as a source of inspiration for this story.

There are other instances of this ambivalent sort of representation of Ireland in James ("The JOLLY CORNER" [1908], for example, or *The AMERICAN* [1877]), but the text by James that gives the most full, intense, and telling representation of Irish legacies, politics, and forms of affect is "The Modern Warning," published along with "Louisa Pallant" in the same volume as "The ASPERN PAPERS" in 1888. In "The Modern Warning," the sound of an Irish first name—Macarthy—is an acoustic reminder of violent history that lies beneath the surface of the characters' friendly associations and familial attachments. This echo of historical memory in "The Modern Warning" provides an interesting context in which to consider the story's melodramatic excesses.

Further Reading

James, Henry. *Literary Criticism: French Writers, Other European Writers, The Prefaces to the New York Edition.* Edited by Leon Edel and Mark Wilson. New York: Library of America 1984.

———. *The Portrait of a Lady.* Edited by Nicola Bradbury. Oxford: Oxford University Press, 1998.

———. *Washington Square.* Edited by Brian Lee. Harmondsworth, England: Penguin, 1984.

Lewis, R. W. B. *The Jameses: A Family Narrative.* London: Andre Deutsch, 1991.

Denis Flannery, *University of Leeds*

James, Alice (1848–1892)   Alice James was the sister of Henry James and the only daughter of HENRY JAMES, SR., and Mary James. With four older brothers and a father who taught her to think independently but saw women as the inferior sex, she spent much of her adult life as an invalid, seeking love from her family and friends. Her brother Henry modeled his characters Catherine and Dr. Sloper in WASHINGTON SQUARE (1880) on Alice's relationship with her father.

Alice's life was not one of creative output, although her intellect matched that of her two older brothers, WILLIAM JAMES and Henry. In the late 1860s, she became friends with the reformer Elizabeth Peabody and became preoccupied with the poor and working-class conditions. In 1868, she joined the Female Humane Society of CAMBRIDGE, founded in 1814 for the relief of women, and in the late 1870s, she started work with the Society to Encourage Studies at Home, a correspondence school for women. In 1875, she started teaching history for the society. Perhaps her greatest achievement is her diary published in 1934. Started in 1890, two years before her death, she chronicled her thoughts, past and present, shining light on her childhood and that of her famous brother Henry. It is also a detailed description of her many breakdowns, showing considerable insight into her frustrations with the limited psychological theories at the time.

Born on August 7, 1848, she grew up in NEW YORK CITY with her parents, four elder brothers, and her Aunt Kate. In 1855, the family traveled to Europe, and Alice learned to speak French by the age of eight. She was later to use this to her advantage and read many French novels, not something usually done by the Victorian lady (see VICTORIANISM). Although her father was pleased with his daughter's intellect, he did not believe in formal education for girls, and Alice had to make do with a series of governesses. With four older brothers who would tease and taunt her, she learned to hide her emotions behind a biting wit, and in later life this wit would entertain and win her many friends. In the years 1858–59, the family moved to NEWPORT, Rhode Island, where Alice enjoyed riding, swimming, and walking. In 1860, at the age of only 12, her nervous manner had already been noted by her family. The events of the CIVIL WAR increased her isolation. While her older brothers enlisted or went to Harvard, she was expected to stay at home.

By the 1860s, the family had moved to Boston, and Alice started to make female friends, including Lizzie Boott and Clover Hooper (who later married Henry Adams). In 1866, she was sent to Dr. Charles Fayette Taylor, an orthopaedist who preached the benefits of limiting education for women. Alice's illness is not clear, but neurasthenia is presumed. She stayed in Taylor's care until May the following year. At the age of 19, she collapsed in one of her many breakdowns. At the time, Alice said little about her condition and would only remark on it later in her diary with the benefit of hindsight. She wrote in an entry for October 26, 1890: "As I used to sit immoveable reading in the library with waves of violent inclination suddenly invading my muscles taking some of their myriad forms such as throwing myself out of the window, or knocking off the head of the benignant pater as he sat with his silver locks, writing at his table . . ." (Edel 149). The only work she was able to do was charitable and light, so in 1868 she joined a sewing bee, set up originally to make hospital blankets and to sew for the soldiers of the war. By the 1870s, she became the president but was under no illusions as to its limited, purely social role. Her chance of freedom from her stifling family life came in 1872, when she traveled with Henry and Aunt Kate to Europe. Despite Henry's fears for her health, Alice proved a good traveling companion and was delighted and amazed at all she saw.

In 1875, she met Katherine Loring and developed the most important friendship of her life. When William got married in 1878, Alice plunged into a mental breakdown, the worst of her life. In her diary for February 2, 1892, she was later to describe this as "that hideous summer of '78 when I went down to the deep sea, its dark waters closed over me, and I knew neither hope nor peace . . ." (Edel 230). The following year, Katherine began to care for Alice, and she remained her nurse and constant companion until her death. This was seen by William and his wife, Alice, as a "Boston marriage," and Henry's uneasiness with this situation is reflected in his novel *The BOSTONIANS* (1886). Upon her mother's death, Alice took control of the household and nursed her father until his death in December 1882. Alice's loneliness was now palpable, and the following year she checked herself into the Adams Nervine Asylum, which promoted the so-called rest cure, forbidding reading, writing, and serious conversations. In 1884, she sailed to England with Katherine and would not see America again. Between her battles with mental disease, Alice was a social butterfly, and while in London she held a salon whose participants included Sara Sedgwick, FANNY KEMBLE, E. L. Godkin, and CONSTANCE FENIMORE WOOLSON. Inspired by the works of GEORGE ELIOT and George Sand, she began to keep a diary. Years later, upon reading this diary, Henry would remark, "her tragic health was in a manner the only solution for her of the practical problem of life" (qtd. in Strouse 284). In 1891, Alice was diagnosed with a tumor, and she died on March 5, 1892. In 1894, Katherine Loring published four copies of Alice's diary for the family.

Further Reading

Edel, Leon, ed. *The Diary of Alice James.* Boston: Northeastern University Press, 1999.

Kaplan, Fred. *Henry James, The Imagination of Genius: A Biography.* London: Hodder and Stoughton, 1992

Strouse, Jean. *Alice James: A Biography.* Cambridge, Mass., and London: Harvard University Press, 1999.

Laura Christie, *Roehampton University*

James, Henry, Sr. (1811–1882)   Henry James, Sr., was the father of the novelist Henry James, of the psychologist and philosopher WILLIAM JAMES, and of the diarist ALICE JAMES. He was the son of an Irish immigrant named William James, who came to America around 1789 and amassed a large fortune of around $3 million in business enterprises in Albany and upstate New York. His son Henry (the father of Henry James, Jr.) grew up in Albany, where he led something of a privileged and dissolute life as a young socialite; his share of William James's estate was a large parcel of real estate in

Syracuse that yielded an estimated income of about $10,000 per year for life (Edel 21).

The elder Henry spent much of his youth in Albany, rebelling against the stern Presbyterianism of his father. A sensitive but able-bodied young man, Henry enjoyed outdoor activities and sports. He also enjoyed great rambles in the countryside, away from home, where nearly every pleasurable activity (that is, any activity not related to study or industry) was forbidden. Henry's excursions allowed him to escape the Calvinistic regimen of his father's home. Henry, Sr., wrote late in his life, "I was never so happy at home as away from it" (qtd. in Edel 23).

The elder Henry James's life was framed by two events that bracketed and defined his spiritual life, and these events left an indelible mark on his children. The first occurred when Henry was 13 years old. He and some friends were participating in balloon flying, a popular sport among students at the Albany Academy. The balloons were propelled by a cloth wick saturated with turpentine. Henry saw that one of the balloons was drifting toward a nearby barn. He rushed to the barn to extinguish the flame, and in the process his trousers were soaked with turpentine and ignited. As a result, Henry's leg had to be amputated above the knee. During his two-year recovery, Henry became introspective, speculating on the nature of the accident, on his future without the strenuous physical activity he so enjoyed, and on the spiritual meaning of his misfortune. Thus, the elder Henry James confronted God seriously perhaps for the first time. With his physical activity limited, Henry's focus shifted inward on intense intellectual activity (Edel 24–25).

On the advice of his father, Henry entered Schenectady's Union College in 1828. In Schenectady, Henry, "liberated from his bed of sickness—and home—indulged himself freely in un-Presbyterian luxuries—cigars, smart clothes, books of an undevout character, oysters" (Edel 26). Henry charged the expenses to his father, who was convinced that Henry's lifestyle would "lodge him in a prison" (qtd. in Edel 27). Rather than face his father, Henry escaped to Boston. He eventually returned to Union College, where he graduated in 1830. Afterward, he attempted to study law (again to placate

his father), but he found no satisfaction and broke off his study.

"Seeking to understand his misgivings over religion and to comprehend his relationship with God" (and perhaps with his own father, the strict Presbyterian), Henry enrolled at the Princeton Theological Seminary in 1835, three years after his father died. While there, he felt that the conviction of God's supernatural being "was burnt into me as with a red-hot iron" (Edel 28). However, though the elder Henry James had escaped the feeling of anxiety over his juvenile behavior, he now found that he suffered anxiety in the form of religious guilt. Henry decided to leave the seminary.

In 1840, Henry married Mary Robertson Walsh, the sister of a fellow seminary student. In 1842, the couple named their first son William, after Henry's father. Henry and Mary eventually bought a home at No. 21 Washington Square, where Henry James Jr., was born on April 15, 1843. Shortly afterward, in England, the second major event in Henry James's life occurred.

One evening after dinner in May 1844, James experienced the sensation that he was not alone in the room, that he was in the presence of an invisible presence, "raying out from his fetid personality influences fatal to life . . . to all appearance it was a perfect insane and abject terror, without ostensible cause . . . the thing had lasted not ten seconds before I felt myself a wreck; that is, reduced from a state of firm, vigorous, joyful manhood to one of almost helpless infancy" (qtd. in Edel 30–31). Henry remained in the room until he was able to gather his faculties. His experience was diagnosed by doctors as an effect of nervous anxiety, or simple mental exhaustion. Edel writes, "[T]he second experience, twenty years after the first, was a collapse of his mental well-being. Evil, to put it in theological terms, in that shape that squatted invisible, had come to reveal to the elder Henry James that he must not question the word of God but await the Truth of Divine Revelation" (31).

Henry sought a water-cure to ease his body and mind. During this treatment, he encountered a woman known only as "Mrs. Chichester," to whom he related his experience. She explained to him that he had undergone the kind of experience EMANUEL

SWEDENBORG defined as a "vastation"—one of the regenerative stages in the evolution of human life. This process involves awakening, purgation, and illumination; such a new birth for man was the secret of Divine Creation (Edel 33). Henry sought out all the information he could find on Swedenborg. He claimed to have found in Swedenborg the truth already apparent in his heart. As Edel writes, the "Swedish seer provided the ailing man with a kind of mental healing that strengthened and saved and altered the whole course of his life" (33). In Swedenborg, Henry James found that "God's great work was wrought not only in the minds of individuals here and there, as my theology taught me, but in the very stuff of human nature itself, in the very commonest affections and appetites and passions of universal man, a transforming, redeeming, regenerating work, which shall lift all mankind into endless union with God" (qtd. in Edel 34).

Upon returning to America in 1838, the elder Henry complemented his study of Swedenborg with the theories of the French social reformer Charles Fourier. Fourier became the intellectual rage of early 19th-century New England. His practical social science claimed that all passions and appetites of man were good and that these passions might better serve a communal society in which strict organization and moral impetus served all. Fourier's ideas would play a role in inspiring experiments in communal living such as Brook Farm and Fruitlands. Henry James, Sr.'s, last book was titled *Society the Redeemed Form of Man and the Earnest of God's Omnipotence in Human Nature*; the title alone attests to his blend of Fourierist reform with Swedenborgian theology.

In his later years, the elder Henry James enjoyed the life of minor literary celebrity; through his friendship with RALPH WALDO EMERSON, he came to know the transcendentalists. He became an elder statesman in New England literary and spiritual circles, known both for his warmth, wit, and his writings on Swedenborg. Henry James, Sr., died in Boston on December 18, 1882.

Further Reading

Edel, Leon. *Henry James 1843–1870: The Untried Years*. New York: Lippincott, 1953.

Bill Scalia, *St. Mary's Seminary and University*

James, William (1842–1910)   William James was the oldest of the children of HENRY JAMES, SR., and the older brother of Henry James. William wrote books on psychology and religious experience, and he developed the philosophy known as PRAGMATISM, one of his major contributions to American philosophy. William was born in NEW YORK CITY. Their father was heir to a real estate fortune that enabled him to develop into an eccentric philosopher and Swedenborgian [see SWEDENBORG, EMANUEL] theologian who experimented with his children's education by means of much travel and many private tutors. The family made two trips to Europe; these extensive trips provided the children a multilingual and cosmopolitan education.

At first, William hoped to become a painter, leading to an early apprenticeship in the studio of William Morris Hunt in NEWPORT, Rhode Island. Less than a year later, he changed his mind and never returned to the art world; instead, he enrolled in the Lawrence Scientific School at Harvard College. This was the first time he spent time away from his parents, and after three terms at Harvard, he was forced to return home because of poor health. As a young adult, William suffered from numerous physical ailments and from bouts of depression, during which he considered suicide. Partly as a result of his own medical problems, William determined to become a physician, entering Harvard Medical School in 1864.

When James received an M.D. in 1869, he had already decided not to practice medicine. He continued to suffer from physical and psychological problems, including back pain, insomnia, digestive problems, and suicidal depression. A transformative experience—in which he felt an overwhelming terror and anxiety in confronting what he felt was the certain extinction of his personality—convinced him that his mind was the source of his difficulties. William's "soul-sickness" was significantly alleviated in 1872, when he became an instructor in physiology at Harvard. He quickly shifted his studies to psychology, helped found the department of psychology at Harvard, and established one of the first American laboratories of experimental psychology in 1875. In the early 1870s, James also became part of a philosophical discussion group,

"He stayed perhaps two hours, at times talking delightfully, and giving me the impression of having any amount of leisure to listen. He had the gift of seeming to be interested in another's point of view, whether you were the photographer or the scrub woman. Kindly and genial, essentially the gentleman, putting one at ease without one's being conscious this was so" (98). Alice Boughton, "William James," *Photographing the Famous* (New York: Avondale Press, 1928)

The Principles of Psychology (1890). This was a pioneering work on psychology, but it also marked the end of his research on the subject. James moved to the philosophy department of Harvard in 1880, devoting the rest of his life to the study of philosophy and religion.

Although William James was only one year older than his brother Henry, there were definite differences in their temperaments. Each brother developed expertise and interests outside the other's reach; William had relatively little interest in literature, and Henry was relatively uninterested in philosophy. William based his life and work at Harvard, whereas Henry made his home in England and continental Europe. Although each brother dutifully read the other's work, William especially had difficulty with James's later novels. At one point, he strongly advised Henry to abandon the complexity of his late style in favor of a more straightforward approach. William, whose own life experiences led him to believe in the efficacy of free will, was not able to embrace Henry's more receptive and aesthetic sensibility. As the oldest brother, William had the more responsible and self-serious personality, whereas Henry possessed the greater sense of humor and an artistic temperament. One school of thought emphasizes the sibling rivalry between the brothers, especially on the side of William. An alternative school of thought suggests that the rivalry between Henry and William inspired them both to achieve great things, and that in fact the two brothers liked and admired each other and were proud of each other's distinguished contributions to their respective fields. Both shared a devotion to their sister, ALICE (JAMES), and sustained throughout their lives a brotherly affection.

Despite their differences, there are also many similarities between the brothers. William's contributions to modern psychology and the nature of human consciousness complement Henry's development of the modern psychological novel. It was William James who coined the phrase *stream of consciousness*, which has also been used by critics in their examination of Henry James's later work. Both brothers, like their father, were prone to much introspection and soul-searching, and both felt compelled to correct their father's optimistic transcendentalism with a more

the Metaphysical Club, which is considered a source of many ideas that would shape America's future intellectual climate. Throughout his life, William James developed relationships with many writers and thinkers, including his godfather RALPH WALDO EMERSON, Louis Agassiz, Charles Sanders Peirce, Chauncey Wright, Oliver Wendell Holmes, Jr., Josiah Royce, and George Santayana.

In 1878, James married Alice Gibbons, a Boston schoolteacher, with whom he raised five children. At the time of his marriage, he contracted to write measured and complex view of things. Both brothers also became increasingly interested in aspects of the supernatural, especially following the deaths of their parents. William founded an American branch of the Society for Psychical Research, and he personally explored various paranormal phenomena. Contemporaneously, Henry produced a number of ghost stories, and in his novels he included the uncanny as an important aspect of life experience.

William's major work, *The Varieties of Religious Experience* (1902) appeared the same year as Henry's novel *The WINGS OF THE DOVE* (1902), a novel with a strong spiritual component. It has been suggested that Henry's *The AMERICAN SCENE* (1907) has its philosophical counterpart in William's *Pragmatism* (1907), often characterized as a definitive work of American philosophy.

Further Reading

Lamberth, David. *William James and the Metaphysics of Experience.* New York: Cambridge University Press, 1999.

Richardson, Robert D. *William James: In the Maelstrom of American Modernism.* Boston: Houghton Mifflin, 2006.

Simon, Linda. *Genuine Reality: A Life of William James.* Chicago: University of Chicago Press, 1998.

Margaret Boe Birns, *New York University*

Kemble, Frances (Fanny) (1809–1893)   Frances ("Fanny") Kemble was a celebrated British actress and writer who spent many years living in the United States, where she married Pierce Mease Butler, whose grandfather had signed the U.S. Constitution on behalf of South Carolina. Kemble published several memoirs, including the controversial *Journal of a Residence in America* (1835), *A Year of Consolation* (1847), *Journal of a Residence on a Georgia Plantation, 1838–39* (1863), *Records of a Girlhood* (1878), and *Records of Later Life* (1882), which, according to James, "form together one of the most animated autobiographies in the language" (1,089). In addition, she wrote poetry, plays, and, at the age of 80, the novel *Far Away and Long Ago* (1889). Beginning in the early 1870s, Fanny became a dear friend of Henry James, who men-

tions her as the source for stories such as "Georgina's Reasons" (1884), "The Pantagonia" (1888), "The Solution" (1889), and *WASHINGTON SQUARE* (1880). James reviewed Kemble's *Records of a Girlhood* (1878) in the *Nation* (December 12, 1878) and, upon her death, published a tribute in *Temple Bar* (April 1893), which was reprinted in *Essays in London and Elsewhere* (1893).

Fanny was the niece of Sarah Siddons, England's "Tragic Muse," and the Kemble family was a pillar of the British theater. Her father, Charles, was a notable actor who managed LONDON's Covent Garden, often to the detriment of his health and account books. While growing up, Fanny knew many of the era's great authors and thespians, such as Edmund Kean, Sheridan Knowles, and Mademoiselle Mars. In early 1829, Fanny, who never enjoyed acting, was a big hit with her lead performance in *Romeo and Juliet*, and she followed with widely acclaimed

Frances Anne Kemble, steel engraving after painting by Alonzo Chappel after painting by Sir Thomas Lawrence (1873) *(Library of Congress)*

performances as Shakespeare's Portia and Fazio's Beatrice. In 1832, she toured the United States, packing venues in Boston, NEW YORK, Philadelphia, and Washington, D.C., where she met President Andrew Jackson.

In 1834, she surprised many by moving to Philadelphia to marry Pierce Mease Butler, whose family wealth depended on vast plantations in Georgia, worked by hundreds of slaves, which Fanny's new husband stood to inherit. Except for their two daughters, Sarah and Fan, the MARRIAGE proved a bitter disaster. Kemble claimed to know nothing before her marriage of Butler's dependence on slavery. She became determined to witness the plantation business firsthand, and for 15 weeks, beginning in late 1838, Fanny and her two daughters lived with Pierce on the Georgia plantation. In the few years after, their marriage fell apart in arguments over money, slavery, Fanny's independence, and Butler's philandering. Kemble spent the next decade exiled from her family in England, where she reluctantly returned to the stage.

Deeply disturbed by what she had witnessed in Georgia, Kemble wrote letters to Elizabeth Sedgwick that would make up *Journal of a Residence on a Georgia Plantation, 1838–39* (1863), which James singled out as the "best" of her prose, offering "the most valuable account—and as a report of strong emotion scarcely less valuable from its element of parti-pris—of impressions begotten by that old Southern life which we are too apt to see today as through a haze of Indian summer" ("FAK" 1,089). The manuscript circulated privately in the abolitionist circuit and was eventually published 15 years after her 1849 divorce, when Pierce no longer had control over her daughters' or Fanny's purse strings.

As a young boy riding in a carriage in the 1840s, James first caught a glimpse of Kemble on horseback outside New York. He would later sit enraptured on several occasions by her dramatic readings of Shakespeare. In ROME during late 1872, Sarah Wister, Kemble's eldest daughter, formally introduced James to her mother. Sarah was James's riding companion to the Colonna Gardens near Rome in 1873, memorialized in the article "From a Roman Notebook" and included in *Italian Hours*

(1909). Sarah eventually reviewed RODERICK HUDSON (1875) for the *North American Review*.

After Rome, Fanny and the much younger James maintained a close friendship. In the centennial year of 1876, Fanny followed the serialized installments of *The AMERICAN* (1877) in Philadelphia, where she had relocated with Sarah and Sarah's husband, Owen Wister. (Pierce Butler had died in 1867.) In a March 30, 1877, letter to WILLIAM DEAN HOWELLS, James famously references Kemble's skepticism over Newman and Claire's marriage to defend the novel's unhappy ending. In 1877, Kemble left the United States for the last time to spend her remaining years traveling to SWITZERLAND and living in London. James kept in frequent contact with Kemble, often visiting her until she died on January 15, 1893. In a touching letter to Sarah on January 20, James described Fanny's funeral and sighed that her death seemed like "the end of some reign or the fall of some empire" (*Letters* III: 400). Fanny left James her traveling clock.

When James visited the United States in 1904–05 to write the articles later collected in *The AMERICAN SCENE* (1907), he stayed with the Wisters in Philadelphia. Sarah's son, also named Owen Wister and author of *The Virginian* (1902), guided James on a tour of the South. James describes him as "a Northerner of Southern descent . . . [who] knew his South . . . with an intimacy that was like a grabbag into which, for illustration, he might always dip his hand" (*AS* 302).

Further Reading

Clinton, Catherine. *Fanny Kemble's Civil Wars.* New York: Simon & Schuster, 2000.

Furnas, J. C. *Fanny Kemble: Leading Lady of the Nineteenth-Century Stage.* New York: Dial Press, 1982.

James, Henry. *The American Scene.* 1907. Reprint, New York: Penguin Books, 1994. Abbreviated as *AS*.

———. "Frances Anne Kemble." *Temple Bar* (April 1893). In *Literary Criticism: Essays on Literature, American Writers, English Writers,* 1,071–1,007. New York: Library of America, 1984. Abbreviated as "FAK."

———. *Henry James Letters.* Edited by Leon Edel. 4 vols. Cambridge, Mass.: Harvard University Press, 1974–84.

———. Review of *Records of a Girlhood*, *Nation* (December 12, 1878). In *Literary Criticism: Essays on Literature, American Writers, English Writers*, 1,069–1,071. New York: Library of America, 1984.

Kendall Johnson, *Swarthmore College*

Kipling, Rudyard (1865–1936) Rudyard Kipling was born on December 30, 1865, in Bombay, India, to a family closely connected to the arts. His mother, Alice Kipling, had one sister who married Edward Burne-Jones, the famous Pre-Raphaelite artist. Kipling's father, John Lockwood Kipling (1837–1911), accepted the position of principal and professor of architectural sculpture at the newly founded Jeejeebhoy School of Art and Industry in Bombay soon after his MARRIAGE. Rudyard, their first son, was born there.

Rudyard's beautiful childhood in India (Hindustani was his first language) came to an end when he and his younger sister, Alice (Trix), were taken to England and left with an English family in Southsea. Here the nearsighted, six-year-old Rudyard suffered brutal treatment and a disciplined regime imposed by his foster parents. Though in 1878 he was admitted to the United Services College, a boarding school for young men training for a military career, he did not continue, and in 1882, he returned to Lahore to work as a journalist for *Civil and Military Gazette* (1882–87). In 1888, he published his first collection, *Plain Tales from the Hills* (39 stories), and the next year six prose collections, *Soldiers Three, The Story of the Gadsbys, In Black and White, Under the Deodars, The Phantom Rickshaw*, and *Wee Willie Winkie* (41 stories). In 1889, he was sent as the *Pioneer*'s roving correspondent to Singapore, Hong Kong, and Japan, and then he visited several cities in the United States and Canada before returning to Liverpool.

In England, he found himself already famous, and the *Times* published an editorial on his work in 1890. He lived the next three years in LONDON and published *Life's Handicap* (1891) and a collection of poems, *Barrack-Room Ballads* (1892), in which he praised the virtues of British soldiers. He also met an American writer and editor, Wolcott Balestier, with whom he collaborated on the novel

Rudyard Kipling (New Amsterdam Book Company, 1899) *(Library of Congress)*

The Naulahka (1891). The same year he took another long journey to South Africa, Australia, and New Zealand. Hearing about Balestier's sudden death, he returned to London, where he married Balestier's sister, Carrie. Henry James gave the bride away. Kipling and his new bride embarked on a sea voyage and visited America (Brattleboro, Vermont, the Balestiers' residence, included) and Japan. Learning that their bank had failed, the Kiplings returned to America and settled not far from Carrie's family in Vermont, where their two daughters, Josephine and Elsie, were born. In 1896, the family left America to live in Torquay, England. The American years were prolific for he had published the famous *Jungle Books* (1894, 1895), written the novel *Captains Courageous* (published in 1897), and the volumes of poetry *Seven Seas*. In 1897, his son, John, was born in England. The next year, the family started what was to become their habit of spending winter holidays visiting South Africa.

In 1899, during a last visit to America, he and his elder daughter developed pneumonia and, unfortunately, the little girl died. The same year, Kipling was involved in a service charities campaign named after one of his poems *The Absent-Minded Beggar Fund,* and he continued writing in favor of the British cause in the Boer War. In 1901, he published the novel *Kim,* the most enduring of his works set in India. In 1902, the family settled in Burwash, Sussex, and he published the collection of fables *Just So Stories for Little Children.* In the next two years, Kipling published poems and stories about the Boer War.

His fame was at its peak, and in 1907 he was the first English author to be awarded the Nobel Prize in literature. The prize citation read: "[I]n consideration of the power of observation, originality of imagination, virility of ideas and remarkable talent for narration which characterize the creations of this world-famous author." He continued to publish *Puck of Pook's Hill* (1906), *Actions and Reactions* (1909), and *Rewards and Fairies* (1910), which contained the poem "If," declared in 1995 to be the favorite poem of England.

In 1915, his son was reported missing in action during the Battle of Loos, and as a consequence Kipling joined the Imperial War Graves Commission, which was responsible for all sites in the world where Commonwealth soldiers were buried. In 1923, he also wrote a two-volume history of the Irish Guards, his late son's regiment. He became a personal friend of King George V but declined most of the honors that were offered to him, including a knighthood, the poet laureateship, and the Order of Merit. In 1935, he wrote an autobiographical work, *Something about Myself,* published posthumously.

Kipling had suffered from a gastric ulcer since 1915, and on January 18, 1936, he died of a hemorrhage. His ashes were buried in the Poets' Corner of Westminster Abbey. Kipling showed his spark of genius in perfecting the art of the short story. However, his writings seem to glorify the white male figure of the British Empire whom Kipling depicts as energetic, enterprising, brave, and honest, and embracing a keen if paternalistic sense of responsibility toward the putatively less civilized. He has been accused of regarding nations other than Britain as inferior, incapable of spiritual development, and in need of Christian charity. Such attitudes seem to manifest themselves in lines from *Kim* such as, "He could lie like an Oriental." His controversial poem "The White Man's Burden" also presents non-European peoples and cultures as less civilized than European ones. His stories for children, *The Jungle Books,* and the novel *Kim,* along with collections of his best poetry, still have a strong effect on contemporary readers and are cherished worldwide.

Henry James read Kipling extensively, wrote an introduction for *Mine Own People* (1891), and mentions him in letters to friends. James generally praised the liveliness and freshness of Kipling's narratives, especially those set in India; however, in letters to friends James criticized Kipling's tendency toward heavy-handed brutality and violence in his fiction.

Further Reading

Carrington, Charles. *Rudyard Kipling—His Life and Work.* London: Macmillan, 1955.

Gale, Robert L. "Rudyard Kipling." In *A Henry James Encyclopedia,* 365–367. New York: Greenwood Press, 1989.

Ricketts, Harry. *The Unforgiving Minute: A Life of Rudyard Kipling.* London: Chatto and Windus, 1999.

Wilson, Angus. *The Strange Ride of Rudyard Kipling, His Life and Works.* New York: Viking Press, 1978.

Aloisia Sorop, *University of Craiova*

La Farge, John (1835–1910)   John La Farge was a painter, illustrator, author, lecturer, and stained glass window designer and manufacturer. Born in NEW YORK CITY, he was the child of wealthy French-Catholic immigrants who educated their eldest son well and introduced him to drawing and watercolor at an early age. In the early 1850s, he attended Mount Saint Mary's College in Maryland and Saint John's College (now Fordham University) in New York. Graduating in 1853, he spent the next three years studying law and painting before sailing for Europe, where he copied the work of old masters and painted landscapes. In PARIS, his mother's first cousin, the famous art critic Paul de

Saint-Victor, introduced him into French literary circles. His father's ill health in the autumn of 1857 recalled La Farge to New York, where he resumed the study of law and continued to study painting. His father's death in June 1858 left him with a substantial inheritance, and he decided on a career as an artist.

In 1859, he relocated to NEWPORT, Rhode Island, in order to study painting with William Morris Hunt. There he met the Jameses, with whom he remained lifelong friends, particularly with WILLIAM JAMES, who was also taking art lessons with Hunt, and with Henry, who soaked up La Farge's knowledge of French authors. Cortissoz described the artist as a great conversationalist whose personality was "a lambent flame of inspiration" (Cortissoz 262). La Farge fascinated the future novelist, who became a noted conversationalist in his own right. Henry later wrote in *Notes of a Son and Brother* (1913) (see AUTOBIOGRAPHIES) that "John La Farge became at once, in breaking on our view, quite the most interesting person we knew" (*NSB* 84–85). The artist, who painted a portrait of Henry in 1862, was the first to wholeheartedly encourage Henry's literary efforts, reminding him that if he lacked the talent to be a painter, the "arts were after all essentially one and that even with canvas and brush whisked out of my grasp I still needn't feel disinherited" (*NSB* 97).

In October 1860, La Farge married Margaret Perry, the sister of James's good friend THOMAS SERGEANT PERRY. By 1864, the James and the La Farge families had moved away from Newport, but they kept in close and friendly contact. La Farge continued painting and experimenting with color theory, but in the mid-1870s, he found the medium that would absorb most of his artistic efforts: stained glass windows. His early experiments were so successful that by 1879 he had established a glass manufacturing shop. He executed commissions for windows in many lavish houses, including those of J. Pierpont Morgan, William Henry Vanderbilt, and Cornelius Vanderbilt II. He also designed murals and windows for churches, most famously for Trinity Church in Boston, and for memorials such as the "Battle Window" and "Virgil" and "Homer" in Harvard's Memorial Hall.

In 1886, he traveled to Japan with Henry Adams, who was grieving after the recent suicide of his wife. La Farge had long been interested in the designs and concepts of Japanese art, and he learned much on the expedition. *Century Magazine* serialized his thoughts in "An Artist's Letters from Japan." Four years later, he took another trip with Adams, this time to tour the South Seas, where he painted landscapes and native life. The two men also visited ROBERT LOUIS STEVENSON. James was good friends with Stevenson and wrote to him in early 1891 that La Farge "is one of the two or three men now living whom (outside of my brotherhood), I have known longest since before the age of puberty. He was very remarkable then—but of late years I've seen less of him and I don't know what he has become. However, he never can have become commonplace—he is a strange and complicated product" (*Letters* III: 337). Later that year, La Farge briefly visited James in LONDON on his way back to New York.

After his return to America, La Farge continued to paint, lecture, and design windows. In 1898, he completed illustrations for James's "The TURN OF THE SCREW" (1898), published serially in *Collier's*. The two men met for the last time in Washington, D.C., in January 1905. La Farge fell ill in April 1910, and he died in November in Providence, Rhode Island. Days later, James, who was spending time in America following the death of his brother William in August, wrote to La Farge's daughter Margaret that "I think of him as one of the very small number of *truly* extraordinary men whom I've known. He was that rare thing—a *figure*—which innumerable eminent and endowed men (and particularly in this country) haven't been. And he was the intellectual or temperamental artist as no one else has ever been here" (qtd. in La Farge 190).

Further Reading

Cortissoz, Royal. *John La Farge: A Memoir and a Study.* Boston and New York: Houghton Mifflin, 1911.

James, Henry. *The Letters of Henry James.* Edited by Leon Edel. 4 vols. Cambridge, Mass.: Harvard University Press, 1974–84.

———. *Notes of a Son and Brother.* New York: Scribner, 1914. Abbreviated as *NSB*.

La Farge, John, Jr. "Henry James's Letters to the La Farges." *New England Quarterly* 22, no. 2 (1949): 173–192.

Jennifer Eimers, *University of Georgia*

Lamb House   Lamb House was James's beloved home from 1898 until his death in 1916. While he maintained a place in LONDON, Lamb House provided the space and peace he needed to write his later works.

Located in Rye, in the southeastern part of England, Lamb House was a relatively simple yet distinguished three-story red brick structure built in the Georgian style. It had an illustrious history from the time that James Lamb, a member of a powerful family, built the home in 1723; the family maintained ownership until the 1860s. The house gained early prestige after hosting King George I for several days when he had been driven ashore by a storm trying to cross the English Channel.

After the 1860s, the house had various owners. James initially leased it in 1897, and he was thrilled to purchase it in 1899. Rye was two miles from the sea, a distance easily traversed on the flat marshes where James enjoyed riding his bicycle in the afternoons. In the mornings, James worked on his novels. At the age of 55 when he moved in, he had acquired a "rheumatic" wrist, which made writing difficult. To avoid straining it, he hired various secretaries to whom he would dictate his novels in the mornings at Lamb House. In the winter months, he worked in a small "green room" on the second floor, with just enough space for him to pace as he dictated (Booth 223). In the summer months, he worked in the garden-house, which was adjacent to the main house and which was destroyed by a bomb during World War II.

Lamb House represented for James his first real home. Because he had moved around from house to house—and from nation to nation—Lamb House was especially important. The fact that this home was in England, not the United States, anticipated his naturalization as a British citizen toward the end of his life. He saw his acquisition of the house as fated, exclaiming to a friend that "It is exactly what I want and secretly and hopelessly coveted" (Edel IV: 57).

Lamb House would be a place of peace and serenity in his later years, when James's world was rapidly changing. At the turn of the last century, when England was engaged in the Boer War and Europe was generally politically agitated, James called his home "a quite adorable corner of the wicked earth. And the earth is *so* wicked just now. Only Lamb House is mild; only Lamb House is sane; only Lamb House is true" (qtd. in Kaplan 429).

James was well aware of the growing interest shown to the personal lives of authors, alive or dead. He usually portrayed it negatively, as in "The ASPERN PAPERS" (1888), and yet he was a literary tourist himself. Particularly toward the end of his life, during his preparation on the NEW YORK EDITION of his works, James was extremely conscious of his reputation and cultivated his status as "The Master" of the novel. Alison Booth has argued that the acquisition of Lamb House was part of this cultivation—creating a home that people could write about and visit after his death. His efforts were not unrewarded. Lamb House is still standing and is part of Britain's National Trust of historic sites, having been donated by James's nephew's wife in the years following James's death. Tourists can visit the home during the summer months. It still holds some of his furniture, portraits of the author, and part of his library.

Further Reading

Booth, Alison. "The Real Right Place of Henry James: Homes and Haunts." *Henry James Review* 25, no. 3 (2004): 216–227.

James, Henry. *Henry James Letters*. Edited by Leon Edel. 4 vols. Cambridge, Mass.: Belknap Press of Harvard University, 1974–1984.

Kaplan, Fred. *Henry James: The Imagination of Genius: A Biography*. New York: William Morrow, 1992.

The National Trust. "Lamb House." Available online. URL: http://www.nationaltrust.org.uk/main/wvh/w-visits/w-findaplace/w-lambhouse/. Accessed July 25, 2007.

Amanda Adams, *Miami University*

London, England   When ROME thrived as an imperial capital in the first century of the first millennium, London was a mere outpost of Roman conquest. In subsequent centuries, London would be conquered by the Celts, by the Anglo-Saxons, and by the Normans, before emerging in the 16th century as the capital of an initially anxious British Empire, which would reach its zenith of global power in the 19th century.

Henry James's decision to settle in London in the late fall of 1876 had profound consequences for his life and work. The city became his main locus of social and imaginative life from the age of 33 until his death. He had written to his brother WILLIAM JAMES that summer: "Easy and smooth-flowing as life is in Paris, I would throw it over tomorrow for an even very small chance to plant myself for a while in England. If I had a single good friend in London I would go thither" (Edel II: 59). Four months later, he was ensconced in his first London rooms at 3 Bolton Street, "small chambers in a small street that opened, at a very near corner, into Piccadilly and a view of the Green Park; I had dropped into them almost instantaneously, under the accepted heavy pressure of the autumnal London of 1876, and was to sit scribbling in them for nearly ten years" (xviii). James had wanted "to feed on English life and the contact of English minds" (Edel II: 59) and now found that the "big human rumble of Piccadilly (all human and equine then and long after) was close at hand." He wrote: "I liked to think that Thackeray's Curzon Street, in which Becky Sharp, or rather Mrs. Rawdon Crawley, had lived, was not much further off: I thought of it preponderantly, in my comings and going, as Becky's and her creator's; just as I was to find fifty other London neighborhoods speak to me almost only with the voice, the thousand voices, of Dickens" (xviii). James wrote to sister, ALICE JAMES, that "London seems—superficially—almost horrible; with its darkness, dirt, poverty and general unaesthetic cachet. I am extremely glad however to have come here and feel completely that everything will improve on acquaintance" (Edel II: 82).

James was right—he became a literary and social success in London as never before, dining out almost 100 times during his first season and filling the role for London hostesses of the engaging and intelligent bachelor. As much as London's soot and

fogs and constant social pressure weighed on James, he believed that to do serious work "one must live in an ugly country; and that is why, instead of lingering in that golden climate [of Italy], I am going back to poor, smutty, dusky, Philistine London" (Edel II: 144).

Socially and professionally well-established, James moved in March 1886 to an apartment at 34 De Vere Gardens, "within three minutes of Kensington Gardens" on a "spacious cul-de-sac"—an apartment "flooded with light like a photographer's studio," where he could "commune with unobstructed sky and have an immense bird's eye view of housetops and streets" (Edel III: 114, 7, 124). Robert Browning lived across the street from James at 29 De Vere Gardens, and Sir Leslie Stephen with his teenage daughter Virginia and her siblings resided a block away at 22 Hyde Park Gate. By 1895, however, with London's constant social pressures mounting, James searched for a "calm retreat

"31 Lowndes Square, Mr. Lowell's House while Minister to England," by A. L. Coburn, frontispiece to *The Sense of the Past*, Volume 26, the New York Edition (1917).

between May and November" (Edel IV: 62) and found it in Rye at LAMB HOUSE, leased in 1897 and possessed and inhabited by 1898, where he could make use of the "delightful little old architectural garden-house" (Edel IV: 63) to dictate his late great novels first to secretary Mary Weld and then to THEODORA BOSANQUET. But James maintained rooms in London at the Reform Club on Pall Mall, where "for my declining years I have already put my name down for one of the invaluable south-looking, Carlton-Gardens-sweeping bedrooms" (Edel IV: 74) to be near the "big Babylon, with its great spaces for circulation, for movement, and for variety" (Edel IV: 595) and "the blessed miles of pavement, lamplight, shopfront, apothecary's beautiful and blue jars and numerous friends' teacups and tales" (Edel IV: 597).

James returned to London more permanently in 1913 to a commodious flat at 21 Carlyle Mansions on Cheyne Walk with a view of the Thames, where he lived until his death. While there, he dictated to Miss Bosanquet his AUTOBIOGRAPHIES, *A Small Boy and Others* (1913) and *Notes of a Son and Brother* (1914). He resisted his sister-in-law's request that he return to CAMBRIDGE in the United States, because "my capital—yielding all my income, intellectual, social, associational, on the old investment of so many years—my capital is here" in London (Edel IV: 658). James died on February 28, 1916, at his Chelsea flat, and his funeral was held on March 3 at nearby Chelsea Old Church, recorded by a memorial plaque on the right-hand wall off the main aisle.

Using London as the scene of many short stories, novellas, and novels, James apprehended the subtle machinations of London society, writing a continuing moral history of the great Victorian (see VICTORIANISM) capital in significant short works and novellas such as "The Siege of London" (1882), "Lady Barberina," (1884), "A LONDON LIFE" (1888), "IN THE CAGE" (1898), and culminating in his novels *The PRINCESS CASAMASSIMA* (1886), *The TRAGIC MUSE* (1890), *The SPOILS OF POYNTON* (1897), *WHAT MAISIE KNEW* (1897), and *The AWKWARD AGE* (1899). His early short fiction about England, such as "A Passionate Pilgrim" (1871), centered on his discovery of sensual aspects

of an old civilization replete with all that America lacked. While Rome, FLORENCE, and VENICE stood in James's imaginative universe for the perversely hidden legacies of corrupt ancient societies, London represented for him the modern Babylon in which one is confronted with moral dilemmas generated by materialism, the frantic pace of life, and changing sexual mores.

Further Reading

James, Henry. *Henry James Letters*. Edited by Leon Edel. 4 vols. Cambridge, Mass.: Harvard University Press, 1974–1984.
———. *The Novels and Tales of Henry James*. Vol. 14. New York: Scribner's, 1907–1909.

Kathleen Lawrence, *George Washington University*

marriage   Much of Henry James's status as an American realist or protomodernist may be attributed to his treatment of what Prince Amerigo in *The GOLDEN BOWL* (1904) designates as the "monster" that is marriage (GB 58). Or as a character in the seminal *The PORTRAIT OF A LADY* (1881) puts it, "I never congratulate any girl on marrying; I think they ought to make it somehow not quite so awful a steel trap" (PL 300). Departing, as Joseph A. Boone notes, from 18th- and 19th-century literary traditions in which marriage was both the sentimentalized culmination of a romantic narrative and the catapult that launched the middle-class into respectability, James's works either satirize marriage or offer a scathing critique of its profound investment in capitalist hierarchies of social standing. *WHAT MAISIE KNEW* (1897), the novel that best exemplifies James's ability to demystify the illusions surrounding the sanctity of marriage and the family, depicts the misadventures of a young girl who is cynically used as a weapon and an alibi by her divorced parents and their subsequent lovers.

While *Maisie* is a beautiful critique of the Victorian (see VICTORIANISM) family's obsession with class rank, James's novels from the middle to late periods use marriage in a more expansive way. Challenging the American ideals of individual freedom and choice, *The BOSTONIANS* (1886), *The Portrait of a Lady*, and *The WINGS OF THE DOVE*

(1902) elucidate how marriage and, by extension, its supportive social structures of capitalism and patriarchy, reduce people to properties and greatly limit the individual.

The political satires *The Bostonians* and *The Portrait of a Lady* feature independent female characters whose attempts to imagine and cultivate lives outside the heteronormative marital sphere ultimately fail. In *The Bostonians*, Verena Tarrant, a young and gifted speaker for the women's movement, enjoys a Sapphic union with her mentor and financial sponsor, Olive Chancellor. Whereas the social and financial powers that Olive wields lend an ironic accent to her claim that theirs is a relationship based on mutuality and freedom, Olive does shrink from demanding what she views as inherently patriarchal marital vows from Verena: "I don't want your signature; I only want your confidence . . . I hope with all my soul that you won't marry; but if you don't it must not be because you have promised me" (*Bostonians* 106). Olive's assertion is countered by her rival, Basil Ransom, who, in asking Verena to marry him, demands that she relinquish her signature and her voice by retiring from her career as a speaker. After successfully wooing Verena, Ransom covers her in a fur cloak that both obscures her face from her prospective audience and symbolically announces that she is now his sexual possession. Silenced and effaced, Verena is led by Ransom into a marriage that, as the narrator warns, is to be "so far from brilliant" (*Bostonians* 350).

The shrouded figure of Verena mirrors the more subtle and sinister matrimonial veiling of Isabel Archer. At the start of *Portrait*, Isabel personifies for her cousin, Ralph Touchett, the modern, American ideal of independence. Declaring that a woman's life should not be determined by marriage, Isabel tells Ralph, "I don't want to begin life by marrying. There are other things a woman can do" (*PL* 133). Yet after Ralph furnishes her with a considerable inheritance to realize her aspirations, Isabel is "made a convenience of" and ensnared in a domestic situation that she hoped most to avoid. Her marriage to the treacherously mannered and conventional Gilbert Osmond results in a foreclosure of her possibilities; her pleas for freedom are usurped by Osmond's severe regard for decidedly patriarchal traditions. With her independence cruelly curtailed, Isabel becomes, as Ralph observes, a "representation . . . even an advertisement" for the social conventions that suffocate her. And while Isabel reflects that she must grapple with the one sacred decision she has made, she must also contend with the knowledge that that decision has been orchestrated by and for the material interests of her husband and his former lover, Madame Merle.

The trope of clandestine lovers who manipulate others in order to pursue their desires becomes the leitmotif in James's later novels, particularly *The Wings of the Dove* (1902) and *The Golden Bowl*. Both novels feature couples who for socioeconomic reasons are unable to marry and who must compromise their romantic relationships for more economically viable matches. In *The Wings of the Dove*, Kate Croy is painfully situated between the choice of marrying her lover, Merton Densher, a poor journalist, or ending their relationship and remaining under the dehumanizing shelter that her Aunt Maud's wealth provides. Haunted by the specter of her parents' failed marriage and the demands of her impoverished sister's family, Kate attempts to maintain her relationship with Densher and her aunt's patronage by convincing Densher to engage the affections of her friend, a terminally ill American heiress, Milly Theale. While Kate hopes that Milly, in death, will "cover" Densher with her affluent wings, Kate does not adequately anticipate how thoroughly Milly's wings will cover them both. After Milly's death, Densher, disillusioned by Kate's machinations and his concessions to them, seeks refuge in the memory of Milly's comparatively pure love. He can only ineffectually repeat his offer to Kate, to "marry . . . in an hour" on the condition that they relinquish any claim to Milly's wealth (*WD* 403). At this impasse, Kate and Densher arrive, regrettably late, at the realization that in commodifying themselves and their affections, they have lost their mutual love and esteem for one another. Their impasse crystallizes what is the quintessential hard truth for James about marriage: The ideals of romantic love and individual freedom are available only to those who can afford them.

Further Reading

Boone, Joseph A. "Modernist Maneuverings in the Marriage Plot: Breaking Ideologies of Gender and Genre in James's *The Golden Bowl*." *PMLA* 101 (1986): 374–388.

James, Henry. *The Bostonians*. New York: Penguin Classics, 2001.

———. *The Golden Bowl*. New York: Penguin Classics, 1987. Abbreviated as *GB*.

———. *The Portrait of a Lady*. Edited by Robert Bamberg. 2d ed. New York: W.W. Norton, 1995. Abbreviated as *PL*.

———. *What Maisie Knew*. New York: Penguin Classics, 1986.

———. *The Wings of the Dove*. Edited by J. Donald Crowley and Richard A. Hocks. New York: W.W. Norton, 1978. Abbreviated as *WD*.

Rachel Walsh, *Stony Brook University*

masculinity   Masculinity was a central concern for Henry James, both in his life and in his work. As a novelist, James always keenly felt the distance of his chosen career from the usual understanding, in both American and British cultures, of true manliness, and he frequently attempted to identify novel-writing as a properly masculine activity. At the same time, James repudiated or at least questioned certain aspects of conventional masculinity and explored alternative ways of being a man. James's complex relationship to orthodox masculinity was registered in criticism of him during his lifetime and, increasingly, throughout the 20th century. Unsympathetic critics have often attacked James for his supposed delicacy and effeminacy. His contemporary, the novelist George Moore, called James a "eunuch" who wrote "like a man to whom all action is repugnant" (qtd. in Henke 1), while the critic H. G. Dwight declared in 1907 that James was thought of as a "woman's writer; no man was able to read him" (438). Continuing in this vein, many scholars after the James revival of the 1930s saw in James's writing evidence of his failure to embody an orthodox masculine identity. For instance, Georges-Michel Sarotte argued that he was a "prototypical 'sissy'," who was "passive and feminine" (198), and Alfred Habegger claimed

he was a "boy who could not become a man" (256). Since the 1980s, influenced by feminism and queer theory, critics have produced more sympathetic discussions of James's engagement with unconventional forms of masculinity.

The favored attributes of men in the middle-class U.S. society of the mid-19th century in which James grew up included physical strength, aggressiveness, heterosexuality (ideally realized in marriage), and an active role in public life. Intellectual matters and the arts were less valued than in Europe, and a boy or man who displayed an interest in them—especially if he did not demonstrate a complementary interest in more conventional manly pursuits—was generally perceived as lacking in masculine vigor. In autobiographical accounts of his childhood (see AUTOBIOGRAPHIES), James consistently presents himself as enacting proper masculine behavior less successfully than his older brother, WILLIAM (JAMES), and he notes that, by comparison with his cousins, he could not help "feeling that as a boy I showed more poorly than [the] girls" (*Autobiography* 217). James felt he failed to meet his father's requirements of competitiveness and achievement, writing that "I never dreamed of competing—a business having in it at the best, for my temper, if not for my total failure of temper, a displeasing ferocity" (*Autobiography* 101).

In adulthood, James's nonnormative masculine identity was compounded by his failure to participate in the CIVIL WAR, by his bachelorhood, and by his choice of a career in art. In England, where James did most of his writing, the cultural ideal of masculinity was somewhat different from that of the United States. Whereas in America, the businessman in many ways embodied the ideals of manhood, there was not quite the same emphasis on commercial achievement in the English context. Nevertheless, literary activity was in some ways seen as somewhat effeminate, particularly in regard to novel-writing. In England in the 19th century, women constituted a significant proportion of novelists, often writing novels—like those of James—featuring young women as protagonists and focusing on courtship and marriage. James did not identify his work with that of women novelists, however, but tended, somewhat anxiously, to claim that novel-writing could be a serious, properly masculine business. In his writings on the novel form, he often aligned it with the more traditionally masculine genre of history (Douglas 260). James also tried to differentiate his own practice from those of women authors by frequently endorsing a view, widespread among male authors of the time, that women novelists and readers represented inferior standards of artistic achievement and taste. This view is evident in several of his stories from the 1880s and 1890s, such as "The AUTHOR OF 'BELTRAFFIO'" (1884), "The LESSON OF THE MASTER" (1888), and "The NEXT TIME" (1895), in which women are associated with poor taste or responsible for a serious male artist compromising his vision. However, James also respected the work of many women novelists—for instance, that of his friend EDITH WHARTON—and he continued to value women for their association with literary and artistic culture.

James departed from the conventional expectations of masculine behavior not only because he did not marry but also because of his homoerotic orientation. While the issue of whether James ever had sexual relations with men has been a source of debate among scholars and biographers, it is indisputable that he had a number of intense, erotically charged friendships with men. This was especially the case in the last two decades of his life, in which James was passionately involved with a number of younger men, including HENDRIK ANDERSEN, MORTON FULLERTON, and HUGH WALPOLE. During this period, many in James's circle of friends were either homosexual or departed in other ways from masculine norms. However, despite his interest in and ease with alternative forms of masculinity, James remained cautious with regard to the public expression of homosexual identity. He was shocked by what he saw as the flagrance of OSCAR WILDE and, earlier, by that of Paul Zhukovski, a friend of Ivan Turgenev (Stevens 131).

James's preoccupation with nonnormative masculine behavior and identities informs much of his fiction. Since the 1990s, critics have analyzed the ways in which intense relations between men are erotically charged or the ways in which unspecified secrets might indicate homosexual desires

in many of James's works, including RODERICK HUDSON (1875), "The PUPIL" (1891), and "The BEAST IN THE JUNGLE" (1903). James's exploration of homoeroticism is frequently, though not always, related to his interest in figures who fail to embody orthodox masculinity. Few if any of James's central male characters are conventional heroes. Hyacinth Robinson in The PRINCESS CASAMASSIMA (1886), for instance, is physically stunted and weak, speaks with a high-pitched voice, is preoccupied with art and beauty, and appears uninterested in sexual love. Despite these departures from orthodox masculinity, he is presented as a sympathetic character, and he is contrasted favorably with the robust working-class revolutionary Paul Muniment. Lambert Strether in The AMBASSADORS (1903) is also sympathetically presented by James but has been seen by some critics as passive and timid, faulted for his lack of responsiveness to heterosexual overtures and his tendency to observe rather than participate in the action of the novel. Other examples of the many male characters in James who resist or fail to embody masculine norms such as heterosexual involvement or active public life include Rowland Mallett in Roderick Hudson, Ralph Touchett in The PORTRAIT OF A LADY (1881), Nick Dormer and Peter Sherringham in The TRAGIC MUSE (1890), and the protagonists of the tales "The ALTAR OF THE DEAD" (1895), "The FIGURE IN THE CARPET" (1896), and "The JOLLY CORNER" (1908).

Even when James features male characters who are more conventionally masculine, he often presents them in such a way that normative manliness is critiqued or compromised. For instance, some critics have argued that Christopher Newman's embodiment in The AMERICAN (1877) of the go-getting businessman is undermined by the plot in which he is outdone and humiliated by the Bellegardes. Unlike Newman, the manly Basil Ransom in The BOSTONIANS (1886) seems to win out at the end of the novel, carrying Verena Tarrant away from his rival, Olive Chancellor. However, James stresses the anachronism and the intolerance intrinsic to Ransom's southern chivalry, making the treatment of him ambivalent at best. In The GOLDEN BOWL (1904), Amerigo seems to fulfill the requirements of manly attractiveness and virility, but James also emphasizes that because he has effectively been purchased by Adam and Maggie Verver, he has been removed from the masculine sphere of public life and is obliged to exist as a prized possession, much like the other works of art they own. In investigating these and other representations of masculinity in James's work, recent scholarship has drawn attention to the subtle ways in which James troubles 19th- and early 20th-century understandings of gender and SEXUALITY.

Further Reading

Banta, Martha. "Men, Women, and the American Way." In *The Cambridge Companion to Henry James*, edited by Jonathan Freedman. Cambridge: Cambridge University Press, 1998.

Cannon, Kelly. *Henry James and Masculinity: The Man at the Margins*. New York: St Martin's Press, 1994.

Douglas, Ann. *The Feminization of American Culture*. New York: Knopf, 1977.

Dwight, H. G. "Henry James—'In His Own Country.'" In *Henry James: The Critical Heritage*, edited by Roger Gard, 432–449. New York: Barnes and Noble, 1968.

Habegger, Alfred. *Gender, Fantasy, and Realism in American Literature*. New York: Columbia University Press, 1982.

Haralson, Eric. *Henry James and Queer Modernity*. Cambridge: Cambridge University Press, 2003.

Henke, Richard. "The Man of Action: Henry James and the Performance of Gender." *Henry James Review* 16, no. 2 (1995): 227–241.

James, Henry. *Autobiography*. Edited by Frederick W. Dupee. London: W. H. Allen, 1956.

Moon, Michael. "A Small Boy and Others: Sexual Disorientation in Henry James, Kenneth Anger, and David Lynch." In *Comparative American Identities: Race, Sex, and Nationality in the Modern Text*, edited by Hortense J. Spillers, 141–156. New York: Routledge, 1991.

Person, Leland S. *Henry James and the Suspense of Masculinity*. Philadelphia: University of Pennsylvania Press, 2003.

Sarotte, Georges-Michel. *Like a Brother, Like a Lover: Male Homosexuality in the American Novel and Theater from Herman Melville to James Baldwin.* Translated by Richard Miller. Garden City, N.Y.: Doubleday, 1978.

Sedgwick, Eve Kosofsky. "The Beast in the Closet: James and the Writing of Homosexual Panic." In *Epistemology of the Closet*, 182–212. Berkeley: University of California Press, 1990.

Stevens, Hugh. *Henry James and Sexuality*. Cambridge: Cambridge University Press, 1998.

Guy Davidson, *University of Wollongong*

modernism and modernity   Modernity is generally defined as a period in the history of Western European and American cultures beginning around the middle of the 19th century, whereas modernism is usually understood as an aesthetic response to the social conditions of modernity and most evident in the period of approximately 1890–1930. The terms have been contentious ones. Some critics have argued that modernity begins earlier than the 19th century with the intellectual developments of the Renaissance or the Enlightenment, while others have maintained that modernity is not confined to Western cultures but is also evident in 19th- and 20th-century colonial and postcolonial societies. Similarly, the precise features of modernism, and the issue of exactly which writers and other artists qualify as modernist, continue to be much debated.

Western European modernity is characterized by immense cultural, intellectual, and technological change. The second half of the 19th century and the early 20th century saw the rapid intensification of urbanization, the rise of mass industry and mass entertainment, the continued development of the consumer economy, and the further expansion of European global influence. Revolutionary technologies such as the telegraph, the radio, the phonograph, photography, and the cinema constituted dynamic forms of information processing, communication, and creativity. New kinds of transportation such as the railway, the car, and the airplane helped alter understandings of time and space. The writings of such groundbreaking thinkers as Charles Darwin, Karl Marx, Sigmund Freud, and Albert Einstein transformed orthodox understandings of nature, the individual, and culture, while the rise of the labor and suffragette movements challenged existing social hierarchies. So profound were these diverse developments that modernity is often thought of as a period of crisis, in which long-standing features of Western culture are disrupted or overturned.

In the field of literature, modernism responded to these cultural transformations by breaking away from the dominant Victorian (see VICTORIANISM) mode of realism (see ROMANCE/REALISM/NATURALISM). Literary realism, as practiced by mid-Victorian novelists such as Charles Dickens and GEORGE ELIOT, was characterized by authoritative and reliable narration, accessible language, linear plots generally set in the contemporary social world of their readers, and "closure," or the tying up of narrative and thematic concerns. Representative modernist authors such as William Faulkner, James Joyce, and Virginia Woolf thought that the realist style was inadequate for expressing the experience of modernity, and they favored writing characterized by unreliable narration, self-referentiality, disjointed temporality, fragmentation, technical experimentation, and irresolution. Rather than realism's "objective" view of narrative events, modernist writing often emphasizes the subjective interiority of characters and the partiality of their perspectives. An important consequence of this feature in modernist texts is uncertainty about the nature of "reality" and "truth"—the sense that these do not name a single, transcendent entity but rather refer to multiple, subjective, or competing accounts of experience or perhaps have no firm signification at all. Whereas modernism has been a major influence on later 20th-century literature and literary criticism, it was practiced by a very small minority of writers and generally reached a very small audience. The realist patterns of narrative development and resolution continued to be the most widely practiced literary modes throughout the modernist period and remain prominent today.

Henry James is a transitional figure in the development of literary modernism. He increasingly moved away from the 19th-century expectation that the novel should provide a realistic reflection of social manners, aiming instead to convey psychological realism through the detailed rendition of characters' thought processes and perceptions. Chapter 42 of *The PORTRAIT OF A LADY* (1881), which relates Isabel Archer's unspoken impressions as she stares silently into the fire, is seen by critics as a watershed in the development of this Jamesian tendency and, more generally, in the literary representation of interiority. Later novels such as *WHAT MAISIE KNEW* (1897) feature James's celebrated technique of the "centre of consciousness," in which the story is largely related from the point of view of one of the characters, with little in the way of qualifying commentary from an omniscient narrator. James's last three major novels, *The WINGS OF THE DOVE* (1902), *The AMBASSADORS* (1903), and *The GOLDEN BOWL* (1904), in which the story is filtered entirely through the consciousness of various characters, represent the culmination of this technique in James and anticipate the stream-of-consciousness technique practiced by such modernist writers as James Joyce and Dorothy Richardson.

James also foreshadowed modernism in his increasing interest in epistemological uncertainty. This can be seen, for instance, in the late novella "The TURN OF THE SCREW" (1898), in which the central question of whether or not the ghosts are real is unresolved and undecidable. The novella's ambiguity is compounded by the unreliability of the Governess's narration, which is in turn compounded by the elaborate mediation of her narrative set out in the frame-story. James here demonstrates a self-consciousness about narration and other fictional techniques that would become a hallmark of 20th-century modernism. Like "The Turn of the Screw," the tales "The DEATH OF THE LION" (1894) and "The FIGURE IN THE CARPET" (1896) feature unresolved enigmas, though in the tales the enigmas are more explicitly literary. "The Figure in the Carpet," with its titular metaphor standing in for literary artistry and a hermeneutic desire that is ultimately frustrated, has been seen as "the quintessential self-reflexive Modernist story" (Childs 85).

"The Figure in the Carpet" likens the relation between the novelist Vereker and the young critic to the relation between a priest and his acolyte, with literary criticism described as an "initiation" and Vereker's novels described as "only for the initiated" (White 51). This scenario resembles the relation developing between James and his own audience in his later career. After initial early best sellers such as "DAISY MILLER: A STUDY" (1878) and *The Portrait of a Lady* (1881), James's work sold less and less well. Although his lack of popular success distressed James, and although he never entirely gave up hope of reversing this situation from the 1890s and into the 20th century, he cultivated the persona of "the Master," a writer of difficult literary work who found a small, though often influential, audience. With their oblique and complex prose style, James's late novels provide interpretative challenges for the reader, who is required to tease out the precise nature of characters' motivations and interactions.

James's work of this period, along with the work of writers such as JOSEPH CONRAD and George Meredith, suggest the novel is a form of high art, an early indication of the split between elite and popular tastes that came to define 20th-century literary culture. By comparison with the mid-Victorian era, in which novelists such as Thackeray and Dickens enjoyed popular success as well as critical acclaim, in the late-Victorian period self-styled literary artists had little hope of reaching a wide audience. For James and other writers of self-consciously artistic novels, popular taste was pilloried, somewhat defensively, as crass and debased, and constituted the example against which their own demanding work was defined. James wrote about what he called the "vulgarization" of the novel form as early as 1884 in "The ART OF FICTION" and returned to this theme at length in "The Future of the Novel" (1899). In distinguishing his own challenging, painstakingly constructed novels from the allegedly formulaic rubbish that was flooding the literary market, James again anticipated the modernists, for whom popular literary taste constituted a necessary contrast for their own work.

Furthermore, James was a trenchant critic of the standard plot-oriented realism of his day, not only as it was exemplified in popular literature, but also as it was practiced by many of the serious writers who were regarded at the time as his peers. In his essay "The New Novel" (1914), he criticized younger novelists such as Arnold Bennett, H. G. WELLS, and D. H. Lawrence for amassing realist detail at the expense of aesthetic form. In his pursuit of an artistic perfection in which style and content are married, James was a key influence (though not always an uncritically celebrated one) on a number of important modernists, including Ezra Pound, T. S. Eliot, and Virginia Woolf.

Much James scholarship since the 1980s has sought to show the extent to which his work not only anticipates modernism on a formal level but also interacts with distinctive features of modernity. This view of James's work contrasts with earlier critical assessments, which tended to maintain that his narratives of upper-middle-class life exhibited little interest in the material conditions of late-Victorian and Edwardian civilization. As a cultural conservative, James's representation of the changes brought about by modernity is generally critical. For instance, he treats media, advertising, and celebrity satirically in *The BOSTONIANS* (1886) and *The TRAGIC MUSE* (1890), and he disparages the standardization of life evident in what he calls the "hotel-civilization" of the United States in *The AMERICAN SCENE* (1907). In his critical treatment of modernity, James again anticipated modernist literature, which was often (though by no means always) pessimistic about contemporary civilization.

Further Reading

Anesko, Michael. "O O O O that Ja-hamesian Rag/ It's so Elegant/So Intelligent: Tracing Appropriations of the Master's Aura in Modernist Critical Discourse." *Henry James Review* 27, no. 3 (2006): 264–274.

Boudreau, Kristin. "The Difficulty with Plain Answers: Introducing Modernism by Way of Henry James." In *Approaches to Teaching Henry James's* Daisy Miller *and* The Turn of the Screw, edited by Kimberley C. Reed and Peter G. Beidler, 18–27. New York: Modern Language Association of America, 2005.

Childs, Peter. *Modernism*. London: Routledge, 2000.

Freedman, Jonathan. *Professions of Taste: Henry James, British Aestheticism, and Commodity Culture*. Palo Alto, Calif.: Stanford University Press, 1990.

McGurl, Mark. *The Novel Art: Elevations of American Fiction after Henry James.* Princeton, N.J.: Princeton University Press, 2001.

Posnock, Ross. *The Trial of Curiosity: Henry James, William James, and the Challenge of Modernity.* New York: Oxford University Press, 1991.

Seltzer, Mark. *Henry James and the Art of Power.* Ithaca, N.Y.: Cornell University Press, 1984.

White, Allon. *The Uses of Obscurity: The Fiction of Early Modernism.* London: Routledge and Kegan Paul, 1981.

Guy Davidson, *University of Wollongong*

Newport, Rhode Island　A port town founded in the 17th century in what became the state of Rhode Island, Newport exerted an important influence on Henry James's life intellectually, aesthetically, socially, and morally. The James family returned to Newport from Europe briefly in 1858 and again for a longer period in 1860 for brother WILLIAM JAMES to study painting under the French-trained master William Morris Hunt. The James family stayed there to wait out the CIVIL WAR and became friends with many who would have a major influence on James's life and writing. In choosing Newport, the James family joined "a collection of the detached, the slightly disenchanted and casually disqualified" who were "united by three common circumstances, that of their having for the most part more or less lived in Europe, that of their sacrificing openly to the ivory idol whose name is leisure, and that, not least, of a formed critical habit" (*Harper's* 353). In Newport, James confronted "the hard American world" of "the great black ebony god of business" but learned that he could devote his life to art and become an artist with a critical and ironic approach (*Harper's* 353). Although the James family moved to CAMBRIDGE, Massachusetts, in late 1864, James's five years in Newport left an indelible imprint on his consciousness.

Three Newport figures stand out as major influences on James. First there was his beloved cousin MARY (Minny) TEMPLE, living "with the Albany cousins then gathered at Newport under their, and derivatively our, Aunt Mary's wing" (Dupee 293). She was to "count as a young and shining apparition" of "originality, vivacity, audacity, generos-

ity" (Dupee, 282) and served as the prototype for James's high-spirited, independent heroines, especially Milly Theale of *The* WINGS OF THE DOVE (1902). Second, there was painter JOHN LA FARGE, whose romantic Franco-American background supplied the "corrective or antidote" to New England by representing for James "the gospel of esthetics" (Dupee 292). La Farge introduced James to the *Revue des Deux Mondes*, to Browning's *Men and Women*, and to Balzac's *La comédie humaine*, initiations James cherished "as ineffaceable dates, sudden milestones, the first distinctly noted, on the road of so much inward or apprehensive life" (Dupee 292). And third, there was transcendentalist Caroline Sturgis Tappan, who "became fairly historic, with the drawing-out of the years, as almost the only survivor of that young band of the ardent and uplifted" (Dupee 364–365). She became for James the source of "vicarious exposure" to "comprehensive culture and awareness unafraid" (Dupee 364–

"On the Cliff Walk, Newport," by A. L. Coburn, frontispiece to *The Ivory Tower,* Volume 25, the New York Edition (1917)

365). Having been an intimate of RALPH WALDO EMERSON and Margaret Fuller, as well as a rebel against Boston conventionality, Sturgis Tappan provided yet another model of the artist and of the independent-minded American woman of "infinite freedom of inquiry and irony" (Dupee 364). Newport also introduced James to lifelong friends THOMAS SERGEANT PERRY, Julia Ward Howe, and her daughter, Maud Howe Elliott, whom James would reencounter in ROME in the 1890s. Henry James appears as a contemplative youth and late-adolescent devotee of art in Elliott's *This Was My Newport* (1944).

Newport also served as a significant setting in James's fiction and nonfiction, encapsulating America's postbellum shift from relative simplicity to Gilded Age grandeur and greed in its revolution from quiet watering-place of "the middle years" of the "fifties, sixties, and seventies" to a place that "bristles with the villas and palaces into which the cottages have all turned" as "monuments of pecuniary power" (*Harper's* 350–352). Newport appears first in James's early tale "AN INTERNATIONAL EPISODE" (1878), where during a hot August in the early seventies two traveling Englishmen confront the cultural differences between England and America, in particular the lack of an American leisure class, the overworked American male, and the forthright American girl. The story unfolds against the backdrop of "the beautiful old summer" of the "extinct life and joy, and of the comparative innocence" of old Newport (*Harper's* 352). James portrayed Gilded Age Newport in the first four books of his late unfinished novel *The Ivory Tower* (1917) as the scene now of "the dreadful American money-world" (*The Ivory Tower* 286). In this story, Newport supplies the backdrop for a moral conflict between meretricious and human values.

James began his nonfiction analysis of Newport in an early unsigned article "Newport," which appeared in the *Nation* in 1870 and introduced themes he would later explore in more depth, including the beauty of land, sea, and sky, the idleness of society, and the freedom of the American girl. James also wrote about Newport in his late nonfiction work, first in "The Sense of Newport" for *Harper's Monthly Magazine* (1906), which was reprinted in *The AMERICAN SCENE* (1907), and in the second volume of his AUTOBIOGRAPHY, *Notes of a Son and Brother* (1914), where he revealed Newport's disproportionate influence on his psyche and artistic development. It is in *Notes of a Son and Brother* that James divulges the origin of his "obscure hurt" sustained on October 28, 1861: "[B]y a turn of fortune's hand, in twenty odious minutes" while assisting as a volunteer firefighter during a serious fire in Newport, he supposedly weakened his back, disqualifying him from serving in the Union army (Dupee 414).

Some James family landmarks are still visible in Newport. In 1858, the James family rented two different houses, first at the corner of Old Beach Road and Tew's Court and next at 13 Kay Street, now 64 Kay Street, until they purchased in March 1862 the house that still stands at the northwest corner of Spring Street and Lee Avenue, presently the O'Neill-Hayes Funeral Home. Other significant landmarks include the Redwood Library, where James spent many hours reading, the Berkeley Institute, now the Masonic Temple at the northeast corner of Church and School Streets, where he attended school. The art studio of William Morris Hunt is no longer in existence but stood at the present-day site of the Hotel Viking swimming pool on Church Street.

Further Reading

James, Henry. *The Ivory Tower*. New York Edition, vol. 25. New York: Scribner's, 1917.

———. "Newport." *The Nation* (September 15, 1870): 170–172.

———. "The Sense of Newport." *Harper's Monthly Magazine* (August, 1906): 343–354.

———. *Autobiography*. Edited by Frederick W. Dupee. New York: Criterion Books, 1956.

Kathleen Lawrence, *George Washington University*

New York City   The United States's biggest city of the mid-19th century, New York's Manhattan, initially separate from Brooklyn and the rest of its contemporary boroughs, was first settled by the Dutch, who claimed to have purchased the land from the Lenni Lenape in the 17th century. By 1700, England had taken control. In 1789, George

Washington was inaugurated the first president of the United States at Federal Hall on Wall Street, in the southern part of Manhattan. During the CIVIL WAR in 1863, it was the site of riots in which African Americans became the target for the brutal violence of whites, many of them poor Irish and German immigrants who were angry over the unfairness of the draft. By the end of the 19th century and into the 20th, New York became the major center of immigration into the United States.

Henry James was born in New York City at 21 Washington Place, a building that was demolished in his lifetime. James wrote in The AMERICAN SCENE (1907) that the destruction of the home gave him the feeling of "having been amputated of half my history" (431). The Jameses lived in New York City at 58 West 14th Street from 1848 to 1855 (for Henry, between the ages of five and 12). James was close to an extended family, including his grandmother, who lived at 19 Washington Square North; this home was the setting for his later work WASHINGTON SQUARE (1880). The James family departed New York in 1855, living in Europe and elsewhere; James finally returned to visit New York in 1904–05.

James's relationship with the city is revealed in many of his tales. When a character calls New York home, it typically indicates that he or she is a part of upper-class society, as in the case of Miss Marian Everett in "The Story of a Masterpiece" (1868). In other tales, it indicates a kind of aspiration to such society; as Daisy Miller is at great pains to explain to Winterbourne, "I used to go to New York every winter. In New York I had lots of society" (246). New York is the sine qua non of American society; however, American society does not typically come off so well in James's stories.

The New York of many of the tales is a grimy, unpleasant place. In "A Most Extraordinary Case" (1868), the "case" opens in the squalor of a New York boarding hotel. The protagonist's aunt calls the place a "horrible hole" (265) and exclaims that the city "is enough to kill you outright—one Broadway outside of your window and another outside of your door!" (265–266). New York is portrayed as a place one would hope to escape on account of its population density, dirt, and disease. The terribly hot summers, as well as the rather brutal winters, are sources of discomfort for characters in James's New York stories.

James's narrator-protagonist in "The Impressions of a Cousin" (1883) provides a thorough critique of the aesthetic inadequacies of the city. The writer of the story's journal entries, set in 1870s New York, is an artist little impressed with the views she finds in the city: "[T]he vista seems too hideous: the narrow, impersonal houses, with the dry, hard tone of their brown-stone, a surface as uninteresting as that of sand-paper; their steep, stiff stoops, giving you such a climb to the door; their lumpish balustrades, porticoes, and cornices, turned out by the hundred and adorned with heavy excrescences—such an eruption of ornament and such a poverty of effect!" (650). The lack of beauty is compounded by the city's focus on numbers, whether matters of size generally or finance specifically. She feels that "The city of New York is like a tall sum in addition, and the streets are like columns of figures. What a place for me to live, who hate arithmetic!" (654). Both the people and the streets alike are a disappointment to the artist, who is dismayed by the city's focus on commerce. For his characters, as for James himself, New York has become an unpleasant and hard-edged place. In his essays appearing in The American Scene, James is similarly disappointed in and disturbed by the way the city has grown into an unrecognizable architectural and financial monster.

In numerous stories, James's characters return to New York after a long time away, much as James himself did. In these stories, characters typically differentiate between "Old" New York and "New" New York, the latter being completely inferior to the former. In "The JOLLY CORNER" (1908), a man returns to his home in New York after living abroad; he wonders how he might have turned out if he had remained in New York. His real or imagined encounter with this other self reveals extreme horror at the outcome of the "New York" version of himself. Likewise, "CRAPY CORNELIA" (1909) features a middle-aged man who is disturbed by the "New" New York; he sits in Central Park (called "the Park") in two scenes, observing New York and its residents. He distinguishes between the two different New Yorks as he contemplates a woman: "He could have lived on in *his* New York, that is in the sentimental, the spiritual, the more or less romantic visitation of it; but had it been positive for him that he could live on in hers?" (834). As evidenced by his return to Europe, James was sure he could not live in the "New" New York.

In his essay "New York Revisited," collected in *The American Scene* (1907), he describes what he sees as various objectionable parts of New York. The harbor, the skyscrapers, the business district, and even the people—particularly the immigrant populations—alternately fascinate, horrify, and captivate him. But despite his ambivalent feelings regarding the city, in 1905 he chose to name the edited collection of his works after it. He wrote to his PUBLISHER that calling the series the NEW YORK EDITION "refers the whole enterprise explicitly to my native city—to which I have had no great opportunity of rendering that sort of homage" (*Letters* 368). Both his stories and essays indicate that his native New York, thus honored, was a New York that no longer existed.

Further Reading

James, Henry. "Crapy Cornelia." In *Henry James: Complete Stories, vol. 5: 1898–1910*, 818–846. New York: Library of America, 1996.

———. "Daisy Miller: A Study." In *Henry James: Complete Stories, vol. 2: 1874–1884*, 238–295. New York: Library of America, 1999.

———. "The Impressions of a Cousin." In *Henry James: Complete Stories, vol. 2: 1874–1884*, 650–722. New York: Library of America, 1999.

———. *The Letters of Henry James: Volume IV, 1895–1916*. Edited by Leon Edel. Cambridge, Mass.: Harvard University Press, 1984.

———. "A Most Extraordinary Case." In *Henry James: Complete Stories, vol. 1: 1864–1874*, 263–303. New York: Library of America, 1999.

———. "New York Revisited." In *The American Scene. Collected Travel Writings: Great Britain and America*, 416–451. New York: Library of America, 1993.

———. "A Round of Visits." In *Henry James: Complete Stories, vol. 5: 1898–1910*, 896–924. New York: Library of America, 1996.

———. *Washington Square. Novels: 1881–1886*, 1–190. New York: Library of America, 1985.

Bridget M. Marshall, *University of Massachusetts, Lowell*

the New York Edition This is the popular appellation for *The Novels and Tales of Henry James*, a collection of James's fictions published by Charles Scribner's Sons in New York between December 1907 and July 1909. The name first showed up in James's letter to Scribner's of July 30, 1905: "I should particularly like to call it the New York Edition if that may pass for a general title of sufficient dignity and distinctness. My feeling about the matter is that it refers the whole enterprise explicitly to my native city—to which I have had no great opportunity of rendering that sort of homage" (*Letters* 368). At the peak of his career, James must have associated this first extensive collected edition of his works with his place of origin to define anew who he was as a writer and thus reaffirm his professional status. In this respect, the name "New York Edition" plays a significant role in understanding the whole edition as a representation of James's perspectives toward himself, his literary performance, and his life, and is accordingly used more widely than its official title.

The edition was originally published in 24 volumes, but Scribner's added posthumously two more volumes, including the uncompleted novels—*The Ivory Tower* and *The Sense of the Past*—in 1917 for a total of 26 volumes. The contents of the volumes, with the publication year of each in parentheses, are as follows:

Vol. 1 (1907)	*Roderick Hudson*
Vol. 2 (1907)	*The American*
Vol. 3 and 4 (1908)	*The Portrait of a Lady*
Vol. 5 and 6 (1908)	*The Princess Casmassima*
Vol. 7 and 8 (1908)	*The Tragic Muse*
Vol. 9 (1908)	*The Awkward Age*

Vol. 10 (1908)	"The Spoils of Poynton"; "A London Life"; "The Chaperon"
Vol. 11 (1908)	*What Maisie Knew*; "In the Cage"; "The Pupil"
Vol. 12 (1908)	"The Aspern Papers"; "The Turn of the Screw"; "The Liar"; "The Two Faces"
Vol. 13 (1908)	*The Reverberator*; "Madame de Mauves"; "A Passionate Pilgrim"; "The Madonna of the Future"; "Louisa Pallant"
Vol. 14 (1908)	"Lady Barbarina"; "The Siege of London"; "An International Episode"; "The Pension Beaurepas"; "A Bundle of Letters"; "The Point of View"
Vol. 15 (1908)	"The Lesson of the Master"; "The Death of the Lion"; "The Next Time"; "The Figure in the Carpet"; "The Coxon Fund"
Vol. 16 (1909)	"The Author of 'Beltraffio'"; "The Middle Years"; "Greville Fane"; "Broken Wings"; "The Tree of Knowledge"; "The Abasement of the Northmores"; "The Great Good Place"; "Four Meetings"; "Paste"; "Europe"; "Miss Gunton of Poughkeepsie"; "Fordham Castle"
Vol. 17 (1909)	"The Altar of the Dead"; "The Beast in the Jungle"; "The Birthplace"; "The Private Life"; "Owen Wingrave"; "The Friends of the Friends"; "Sir Edmund Orme"; "The Real Right Thing"; "The Jolly Corner"; "Julia Bride"
Vol. 18 (1909)	"Daisy Miller; A Study"; "Pandora"; "The Patagonia"; "The Marriages"; "The Real Thing"; "Brooksmith"; "The Beldonald Holbein"; "The Story in It"; "Flickerbridge"; "Mrs. Medwin"
Vol. 19 and 20 (1909)	*The Wings of the Dove*
Vol. 21 and 22 (1909)	*The Ambassadors*
Vol. 23 and 24 (1909)	*The Golden Bowl*
Vol. 25 (1917)	*The Ivory Tower* (unfinished)
Vol. 26 (1917)	*The Sense of the Past* (unfinished)

As the list of contents suggests, the New York Edition is arranged according to James's essential principle of keeping it "selective as well as collective" (James to Pinker, June 6, 1905, Beinecke Rare Book and Manuscript Library, Yale University). This exclusiveness enabled James to pour his energy into reviewing and revising the included works—especially his early works such as *The* AMERICAN (1877), "DAISY MILLER: A STUDY" (1878), and *The* PORTRAIT OF A LADY (1881)—continuously and tirelessly for almost five years. In the process of revision, moreover, he composed 18 new prefaces that contain his self-reflective reminiscence of the conception and development of each work, conjoined with the detailed elucidation of his philosophies and techniques of fiction writing. These prefaces are often discussed independently from the main texts of the edition, chiefly due to the influence of American literary critic R. P. Blackmur. In 1934, Blackmur wrote an article about the prefaces in the special Henry James issue of *Hound and Horn*, a modernist literary journal. Blackmur argued that James's prefaces can stand on their own to provide a comprehensive picture of James's artistic self-consciousness. Blackmur's article became the introduction to *The Art of the Novel*, a collection of the prefaces published by Scribner's.

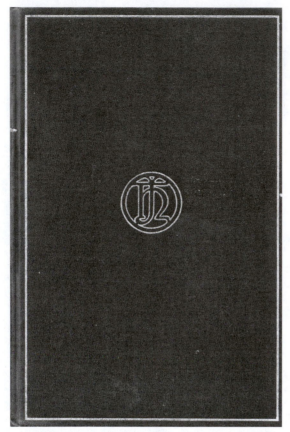

Book cover of the New York Edition by Charles Scribner's Sons

James also partook actively in the construction of the edition's physical appearance. He not only expressed his preferences strongly regarding the margins, types, page styling and design, and bindings of the edition, but he also collaborated in the production of 24 frontispieces with the photographer ALVIN LANGDON COBURN. All these enthusiastic efforts of James evince his wish to present the edition as his literary monument, as the "Edition Définitive of [his] writings" (James to Elizabeth Robins, March 28, 1906, qtd. in *Theater* 256). Nevertheless, contemporary responses to the edition were disappointing, both financially and critically. The effect of this failure on James is vividly described in his letter to his close friend, the British writer EDMUND GOSSE: "I remain at my age (which you know,) & after my long career, utterly, insur-

mountably, unsaleable. . . . The Edition is from that point of view really a monument (like Ozymandias) which has never had the least intelligent critical justice done it—any sort of critical attention at all paid it" (August 25, 1915, *Selected* 313).

The New York Edition was published in Great Britain by Macmillan starting in 1908 and was later reprinted by Augustus M. Kelley Publishers of New York in 1971, without the frontispieces. *The Art of the Novel* was reprinted by Northeastern University Press in 1984.

Further Reading

Anesko, Michael. *"Friction with the Market": Henry James and the Profession of Authorship.* New York and Oxford: Oxford University Press, 1986.

Horne, Philip. *Henry James and Revision: The New York Edition.* Oxford, U.K.: Clarendon, 1990.

James, Henry. *Henry James Letters, vol. 4: 1895–1916.* Edited by Leon Edel. Cambridge, Mass.: Harvard University Press, 1984.

———. *Selected Letters of Henry James to Edmund Gosse 1882–1915: A Literary Friendship.* Edited by Rayburn S. Moore. Baton Rouge and London: Louisiana State University Press, 1988.

———. *Theater and Friendship, Some Henry James Letters.* Edited by Elizabeth Robins. New York: Putnam, 1932.

McWhirter, David, ed. *Henry James's New York Edition: The Construction of Authorship.* Palo Alto, Calif.: Stanford University Press, 1995.

Kiyoon Jang, *Texas A&M University*

Paris, France "No two things could be more unlike than England and France," Henry James opined in 1877. He chose to make his permanent home in England, but France remained an important source of literary and aesthetic inspiration. James's French was, according to Harry Levin, "fluent to the point of encroaching on his English." Paris functions in his fiction both as a figure both for France and French culture, as well as an example of the bewildering and dazzling modern metropolis. It provides the central backdrop to *The AMBASSADORS* (1903) and *The AMERICAN* (1877), and it plays an important supporting role in *The TRAGIC MUSE*

(1890), The PRINCESS CASAMASSIMA (1886), and many of James's shorter works, such as "Madame de Mauves" (1874) and *The Reverberator* (1888).

Often the city figures as a testing ground or place of resolution, where James compares and weighs opposing cultures and ethical systems (commercial and artistic, Puritan and Catholic, material and sensuous, New World and Old World). James appreciated the city's beauty and sensuality but also wanted to represent Paris's everyday life, beneath its "stock-in-trade" of "brightness and gaiety" (*Occasional Paris* 723). He was always careful to separate himself from the inarticulate "hymn of praise" offered up by the average Anglo-American tourist. In *The Princess Casamassima,* he satirized this response by describing Hyacinth Robinson's breathless and repeated approbations—"Splendid Paris, charming Paris" (II: 124).

Henry James paid his first visit to Paris as an infant and was to claim in his autobiographical *A Small Boy and Others* (1913) (see AUTOBIOGRAPHIES) that one of his first and formative memories was seeing the Place Vendôme from a carriage window "as a baby in long clothes" (53). He returned as an adult in 1869–70 on his first extended trip to Europe and while he was composing his first novel, *Watch and Ward* (1871). In 1875, at the age of 32 and following a disappointing spell in NEW YORK CITY, he decided to make a more permanent move to Europe and to "take possession of the old world" (letter to the James family, November 1, 1895). After disembarking in Liverpool and spending a few days in LONDON, Paris was once again his first port of call.

He rented rooms in the rue de Luxembourg and found himself quickly assimilated into a rich intellectual and cultural milieu. Leon Edel argues after the solitude of CAMBRIDGE, "it seemed indeed as if Henry had suddenly been transported to some Olympus" (214). During the course of the winter 1875–76, he befriended a number of Russian expatriates, including the great novelist Turgenev, and he was introduced through this circle to some of the leading French writers, including Alphonse Daudet, Edmond Goncourt, and Gustave Flaubert. Before leaving America, James had arranged to write a series of Parisian letters for the *New York Tribune.* These letters give the impression of a very rich cultural life—opulent private salons, visits to the opera and theater, day trips outside the city—interspersed with a mixture of political and social reflections.

Originally, James had planned to stay in Paris on a semipermanent basis, but he tired of it more quickly than he imagined and was proclaiming himself "both satiated and dissatisfied" with the city by November 1876. From December 1876, he settled permanently in London; thereafter he visited Paris fairly infrequently. And yet the impressions formed during his bewildering first year abroad were to last for a lifetime. Peter Brooks has argued that James found himself exposed during this period to the crucible of literary MODERNISM, absorbing a welter of aesthetic influences that would be slowly digested and worked out over the next 40 years.

The first of James's fictions to be set in Paris is *The American,* which he began in 1875 shortly after his arrival in the city. In a letter to WILLIAM DEAN HOWELLS, he wondered, in fact, whether he had begun prematurely, before his materials could be fully digested. Indeed, compared to his later fiction, *The American* presents its cultural oppositions baldly, and James later revised it heavily for the NEW YORK EDITION. His hero, Christopher Newman, is a model American businessman, embodying energy, health, optimism, openness, and sincerity. His intended bride, Claire de Cintré, is by contrast "a supersubtle Parisian" (178), whose actions and free will are curtailed by tradition, dark family secrets, and an ancient religious tradition that Newman cannot begin to understand. Paris itself appears as a series of grand and sometimes rather artificial frames in the novel. The opening scene shows Newman reclining on a "great circular divan" at the very center of the Louvre, surrounded by artistic masterpieces; later the reader is introduced to the regimented modern city built by Haussman, where Newman's fellow expatriates live, the busy cafés and streets of a commercial center, and the more ancient city inhabited by the Bellegardes, "those grey and silent streets of the Faubourg" (59).

The Ambassadors, considered by James the most perfect of his novels, turns a more complex and cynical gaze on the city. Lambert Strether is sent to "rescue" his fiancée's son, Chad Newsome, from his debauched Parisian lifestyle. On arriving in Paris, however, Strether is also seduced by this "most interesting of great cities" (xiv). In the preface added for the New York Edition, James explained that he wanted to avoid "the dreadful little old tradition, one of the platitudes of the human comedy, that people's moral scheme *does* break down in Paris," arguing that "another surrounding scene would have done as well" (xiv). And yet James's glittering descriptions of the city, as a "vast bright Babylon, like some huge iridescent object," "all surface one moment [and] all depth the next" (89), have been universally admired and provide some of the most vivid depictions of place in all of his fiction.

Further Reading

Brooks, Peter. *Henry James Goes to Paris.* Princeton, N.J.: Princeton University Press, 2007.

Edel, Leon. *Henry James: The Conquest of London, 1870–1881.* Philadelphia: Lipincott, 1962.

James, Henry. *A Small Boy and Others.* New York: Scribner's, 1913.

———. "Occasional Paris." In *The Art of Travel, Scenes and Journeys in America, England, France and Italy from The Travel Writings of Henry James,* edited by Morton Dauwen Zabel. New York: Doubleday, 1958.

———. *The Ambassadors.* New York: Charles Scribner's, 1909.

———. *The American.* New York: Charles Scribner's, 1907.

———. *The Princess Casamassima.* New York: Scribner's, 1908.

Levin, Harry. Introduction to *The Ambassadors* by Henry James, 7–27. London: Penguin, 1986.

Hannah Sullivan, *Stanford University*

periodicals In the mid-19th century United States, a new wave of American periodicals played an important role in shaping what eventually became recognized in the 20th century as "American literature." The well-established British periodicals such as *Blackwood's Monthly Magazine* (founded 1817), the *Edinburgh Review* (founded 1802), *Quarterly Review* (founded 1809), and the *Westminster Review* (founded 1823) offered templates for extending the influence of the prestigious Boston-based the *North American Review* (founded 1815).

In Boston, NEW YORK CITY, and Philadelphia, a handful of influential editors and financiers had a major impact on the often mutual endeavors of book and periodical publication. For example, James Thomas Fields was an editor of the *North American Review,* the first editor of Boston-based *Atlantic Monthly* (founded 1857), and a partner in the Boston-based publishing house of Ticknor and Fields, which later purchased the major Boston-based publishing house of James Osgood. In 1865, as the CIVIL WAR ended, Fields helped Edwin L. Godkin start the *Nation,* in which appeared many of Henry James's TRAVEL WRITINGS and literary reviews. Other friends of James's family were also centrally influential. Charles Eliot Norton, a distinguished professor of art at Harvard University, and James Russell Lowell, the celebrated American poet, were both editors of the *North American Review* and cofounders of the *Atlantic Monthly.* In 1868, Norton offered the editorship of the *North American Review* to James, who turned it down. James's father's friendship with the major PUBLISHERS surely benefited his sons Henry and WILLIAM JAMES, who grew up in a culture of literary publication. However, most of the time Henry, Jr., submitted his early stories anonymously and without telling his family, anxiously watching the post to intercept letters of acceptance or rejection.

In the 1860s, James gained his footing as a writer in the United States by publishing reviews in the *North American Review.* In the later years of his career, this magazine also serialized *The* AMBASSADORS (1903) and printed many of the articles that became the book *The* AMERICAN SCENE (1907), including "Boston" (March 1906), "Philadelphia" (April 1906), "Baltimore" (August 1906), "New York and the Hudson: A Spring Impression" (December 1905), and "Washington" (May and June 1906). Sheldon Novick traces James's earliest review article to an anonymous review entitled "Miss Maggie Mitchell in 'Fanchon the Cricket,'" published in the Boston newspaper the *Daily Traveler*, January 6, 1863. In his biography, Leon Edel traces James's first-published major short story to "A Tragedy of Error," which appeared without attribution in New York's *Continental Monthly* in February 1864. The first signed story of "Henry James, Jr." was "The STORY OF A YEAR." It appeared in the March 1865 issue of the Boston-based *Atlantic Monthly*, whose circulation peaked in the 19th century at around 30,000.

The *Atlantic Monthly* enjoyed a high literary reputation and also featured articles by scientists and politicians who covered subjects mentioned in its full title: *The Atlantic Monthly: A Magazine of Literature, Science, Art, and Politics*. From 1871 to 1881, the magazine was edited by James's good friend WILLIAM DEAN HOWELLS, who promoted many of James's novels and short stories, including *Watch and Ward* (serialized August–December 1871), RODERICK HUDSON (January–December 1875), *The AMERICAN* (June 1876–May 1877), *The EUROPEANS* (July–October 1878), *The PORTRAIT OF A LADY* (November 1880–December 1881), *The PRINCESS CASAMASSIMA* (September 1885–October 1886), *The SPOILS OF POYNTON* (as *The Old Things*, April–October 1896), "The ASPERN PAPERS" (March–May 1888), "GLASSES" (February 1896), and *The TRAGIC MUSE* (January 1889–May 1890).

James's most "profitable publications" were "short stories, for which, between 1883 and 1888, he was being handsomely paid by American and British magazines" (Kaplan 285). After their initial appearance in periodicals, James would then collect his stories and novel installments for publication as books for which he negotiated related contracts with publishing houses that often published both periodicals and books. James also managed simultaneous or overlapping publication of some of his novels and short stories in American and British periodicals. Other important American periodicals in which James published include: the *Century* (New York, 1881), which serialized *The BOSTONIANS* in 13 installments from February 1885 to February 1886; the New York–based *Galaxy* (1866–79), edited by F. P. Church, which eventually folded into the *Atlantic Monthly* after publishing many of James's early short stories, including "A Day of Days" (June 1866), "A Light Man" (July

1869), and "Madame De Mauves" (February–March 1874); the Harpers Brothers periodicals, including *Harper's Monthly Magazine* (New York; 1850–present), in which James published WASHINGTON SQUARE in six installments (July–December 1880), and *Harper's Weekly*, in which appeared "BROOKSMITH" (May 1891) and *The AWKWARD AGE* (October 1898–January 1899).

In England, James was well respected by editors and regularly placed stories in the most prestigious journals. *Cornhill Magazine* was a very popular and respected British periodical founded in 1860 in which first appeared Matthew Arnold's essays that would become *Culture and Anarchy* (1869). *Cornhill's* first editor was the celebrated author William Makepeace Thackeray. In 1871, Sir Leslie Stephen became editor and published James's popular "DAISY MILLER: A STUDY" (June–July 1878) after the Philadelphia-based Lippincott rejected it. *Cornhill* also published *Washington Square* in six installments (June–November 1880), with illustrations by GEORGE DU MAURIER. The London-based *Macmillan's Magazine* (founded in 1859) published *The Portrait of a Lady* in installments running from October 1880 to November 1881. *Portrait's* British run overlapped with the novel's serialization in the *Atlantic Monthly*.

James also published short stories in the *Yellow Book: An Illustrated Quarterly* (London, 1894–97), a magazine dedicated to aestheticism edited by Henry Harland and with illustrations by Aubrey Beardsley (see AESTHETIC MOVEMENT). The first issue of April 1894 led with James's story "The DEATH OF THE LION"; the second issue included "The Coxon Fund"; and the sixth issue of July 1895 led with "The NEXT TIME." There are many other periodicals in which James published, including the *Anglo-American Magazine*, *Black and White*, the Chicago-based *Chap Book*, *Collier's Weekly*, *Cosmopolitan Magazine*, *Chapman's Magazine of Fiction*, the *English Illustrated Magazine*, the *English Review*, the *Fortnightly Review*, *Illustrated London News*, the *Independent*, *Longman's Magazine*, the *New Review*, the *New York Sun*, *New York Times Magazine*, *Pall Mall Gazette*, *Parisian*, *Scribner's Monthly*, the *Times Literary Supplement*, and the *Universal Review*.

Further Reading

Edel, Leon. *The Life of Henry James: 1843–89*, vol. 1. 1963. Reprint, Penguin Books, 1977.

Glazener, Nancy. *Reading for Realism: The History of a U.S. Literary Institution, 1850–1910*. Durham, N.C., and London: Duke University Press, 1997.

Horowitz, Floyd R. *The Uncollected Henry James: Newly Discovered Stories*. New York: Carroll & Graf, 2004.

Novick, Sheldon M. *Henry James: The Young Master*. New York: Random House, 1996.

Kendall Johnson, *Swarthmore College*

Perry, Thomas Sergeant (1845–1928)　Thomas Sergeant Perry was an educator, literary critic, translator, writer, and editor who championed the cause of realist fiction, along with WILLIAM DEAN HOWELLS and Henry James (see ROMANCE/REALISM/NATURALISM). Virginia Harlow writes that "[a]s a critic he can hold only a minor place" (235) despite his extremely productive period between 1871 and 1881, when he wrote 744 reviews and 67 articles for several literary magazines. The publication of *The Life and Letters of Francis Lieber* (1882) effectively marked the end of Perry's magazine contributions; he published only around 30 articles over the next 46 years of his life. His other works include *English Literature in the Eighteenth Century* (1883), *From Opitz to Lessing* (1885), *The Evolution of the Snob* (1886), *The Library of Universal Adventure by Sea and Land* (1888), *A History of Greek Literature* (1890), and *John Fiske* (1906). Throughout his life, Perry remained a fixture in academia and the publishing world largely through the power of his personal associations, most notably that with Henry James.

Born in NEWPORT, Rhode Island, on January 23, 1845, Perry could trace his paternal roots back to the Plymouth Colony, where Edward Perry had fled with the Society of Friends around 1650. Edward Perry left Plymouth shortly thereafter to help settle South Kingston on Narragansett Bay. Thomas Sergeant's grandfather, Oliver Hazard, famous for his victory on Lake Erie during the War of 1812, was the son of Christopher Raymond Perry and Sarah Alexander, a descendant of Scotland's William Wallace. Thomas Sergeant's father, Christopher Grant Perry, graduated from Brown University and began practicing law in 1836 (Harlow 4). From his mother's side, Thomas Sergeant was a distant relative, through marriage, to Benjamin Franklin (5). Perry's grandfather and namesake also served as secretary of the commonwealth, postmaster of Philadelphia, and a district and Supreme Court judge. His sister Margaret married his friend the artist JOHN LA FARGE, while his sister Fanny married Dr. William Pepper, the provost of the University of Pennsylvania.

Perry first met James in Newport at Rev. W. C. Leverett's school in 1858, after the James family returned "from one of their educational sessions in Europe" (Horne 2). Here, both young men studied "English, Classical, French, German, Spanish, Drawing, and Music" (qtd. in Harlow 8) in preparation for their transition to Harvard College. Perry also befriended the younger Wilky James, but "[c]ertainly the richest of his Newport friendships was that which he formed with Willie and Harry James" (Harlow 12) (see WILLIAM JAMES). When the James family left again for Europe in 1859, Henry and Perry began what turned into a lifelong correspondence. While away, Henry yearned for Newport and his friendship with Perry, whom he describes in *Notes of a Son and Brother* (1914) (see AUTOBIOGRAPHIES) as the "superexcellent and all-reading, all engulfing friend of those days and still, sole survivor, of these" (108).

Upon the recommendation of Rev. W. C. Leverett, Perry was admitted to Harvard College. Like many other students at Harvard at the time, Perry was disappointed with the quality of instruction, and the "failure to find congenial friends" (Harlow 17). Despite an improvement in collegiate associations by his second term, Perry still sought out the James children whenever in Boston (18). In 1864, Perry published an article in the *Harvard Magazine*, and later that year he was offered a position as its editor. During his senior year, Perry published his first review in the *North American Review* on J. G. Holland's *Plain Talks on Familiar Subject* (20–23). Perry graduated from Harvard in July 1866, and by August he had departed for Europe, where he spent two years traveling and studying. While in France,

Spain, SWITZERLAND, Germany, and Italy, among other places, Perry "visited the galleries, museums, theaters, and churches of the principal cities; ate and drank and talked with friends whom he met at every turn" (27).

He returned from Europe in August 1868 and began as a tutor of French and German at Harvard College (31). He served in this position for four years, each year being passed up for promotion to instructor. Perry began in 1871 to contribute to the *Atlantic Monthly* (now under Howells's editorship), the *Nation*, and the *North American Review*. Perry resigned from his post at Harvard in 1873 and assumed editorship of the *North American Review* while Henry Adams was abroad, from January 1873 to January 1874 (37). When Adams returned, Perry was excused from his position and left to support his new wife, Lilla Cabot Perry, whom he had married in April 1874 (39). Perry sought to supplement an annual allowance from his mother by increasing his writing output and translating. Howells was quick to offer him more opportunities to publish in the *Atlantic Monthly*, and James set up relationships between Perry and English publishers. In 1877, Perry again began work at Harvard as an English instructor, but the college again kept Perry on annual appointments. In 1881, Harvard refused to reappoint him, despite numerous requests by Perry and other public figures and his popularity among the student body.

The years following his dismissal were filled with numerous trips abroad with his family, several teaching engagements, work at the Boston Public Library, and writing. His financial insecurities were eased considerably in 1885, when the death of his father resulted in a substantial inheritance. Perry was at last able to support his wife and two children. From 1882 to 1883 and again from 1884 to 1887, Perry taught at what is now Radcliffe College. He donated to the Boston Public Library and served as a consultant, contributing volumes and recommending others for purchase (98). Between two lengthy trips abroad (April 1894–July 1897; October 1905–November 1909), Perry moved his family to Tokyo, where he taught at the University of Keiogijuku from 1898 to 1901 (153). Perry spent his remaining years making occasional contribu-

tions to journals and traveling extensively along the eastern seaboard and Europe. Late in his life, Perry's daughter was taken by a mental illness, and in 1923 Lilla Cabot suffered a serious, but not fatal, attack of diphtheria (228).

Throughout his life, Perry and James remained friends, and James's correspondence with others, such as Howells, reveals a genuine concern for Perry's often precarious financial position. Despite his periods of struggle, Perry was always aided by Howells and James, and the three men were referred to by the critic Van Wyck Brooks as "the triumvirate" (3). James had introduced Perry to Howells in the autumn of 1869, and Perry was indebted to Howells for the access that he provided to the *Atlantic Monthly* (50). Together, the three writers heralded the importance and primacy of realistic fiction (61). Perry died on May 7, 1928, at the age of 83, from pneumonia (229).

Further Reading

Harlow, Virginia. *Thomas Sergeant Perry: A Biography.* Durham, N.C.: Duke University Press, 1950.

Horne, Philip. *Henry James: A Life in Letters.* New York: Penguin, 1999.

James, Henry. *Notes of a Son and Brother.* New York: Scribner's, 1914.

Patrick Phillips, *University of Kansas*

pragmatism Pragmatism was a turn-of-the-century American philosophical movement that had a profound effect on 20th-century thought. The term *pragmatism* was first introduced to the general public in 1898 by WILLIAM JAMES, Henry James's older brother, though he gave credit for the term to his friend Charles Sanders Peirce. James, Peirce, and the philosopher and educational reformer John Dewey were central figures of this American philosophical movement, which influenced other disciplines, including history, legal theory, political theory, and art and literature, and it crossed national boundaries, affecting the direction of philosophy in Italy, England, France, and Germany.

Pragmatism hinged upon the claim that "Our beliefs are really rules for action" (*Pragmatism* 23). Marrying a skepticism toward metaphysical and transhistorical truths with an emphasis on the real-world application of ideas, pragmatism argued that what should matter most are the consequences of beliefs, not the beliefs themselves. It eschewed the dualisms that had characterized the study of philosophy up until that point: the split, for example, between mind and body, means and ends, subject and object, individual and society. "A pragmatist turns his back resolutely and once and for all upon a lot of inveterate habits dear to professional philosophers," explained James in *Pragmatism* (1907). "He turns away from abstraction and insufficiency . . . from fixed principles, closed systems, and pretended absolutes and origins. He turns towards concreteness and adequacy, towards facts, towards actions, and towards power" (25).

In his later years, Henry James read his brother's philosophical works with great interest and wrote to him enthusiastically of the deep affinities connecting their two intellectual projects. After reading *Pragmatism,* Henry wrote to William that he was "lost in the wonder of the extent to which all my life I have . . . unconsciously pragmatised" (*SL* 489). Responding to *A Pluralistic Universe* (1909), Henry wrote, "I am *with* you, all along the line—and can conceive of no sense in any philosophy that is not yours!" (*SL* 508).

Critics have interpreted such responses to his brother's philosophy in different ways. Early critics tended to dismiss them and to see little connection between William's philosophy and Henry's fiction, focusing instead on William's barbed criticisms of his brother's late style as evidence of the prickly and competitive relationship between the two. Both F. O. Matthiessen and Ralph Barton Perry see Henry as a disciple of pragmatism, influenced by William's philosophy without ever developing a sophisticated understanding of it. Perry goes so far as to claim that "Henry let William do his philosophizing for him . . . his mind was quite naïve on that side, and . . . his profession of pragmatism was an extension of that admiring pride with which he had from childhood viewed all of William's superior attainments" (429). Leon Edel sees the relationship between the two brothers primarily in terms of a "long buried struggle for power" (294), emphasizing

the submissive attitude with which Henry accepted William's criticisms of his work.

Later critics, beginning with Richard Hocks in *Henry James and Pragmatistic Thought* (1974), have argued for a much richer relationship between the work of the two brothers. Hocks's book attempts "to examine William's work through Henry's own eyes" ("Recollecting" 280), providing an analysis of Jamesian pragmatism as enacted and embodied in Henry's fiction. Hocks argues that "William James's pragmatism is literally actualized as the literary art and idiom of his brother, Henry James," continuing, "whereas William is the pragmatist, Henry is, so to speak, the pragmatism; that is, he possesses the very mode of thinking that William characteristically expounds" (Hocks 4–5).

In *The Trial of Curiosity: Henry and William James and the Challenge of Modernity* (1991), Ross Posnock expands Hocks's argument by claiming Henry as a philosopher and cultural theorist in his own right. Posnock emphasizes Henry's own embodiment of a selfhood—"vulnerable, defiant . . . improvisational" (4)—that achieves a pragmatist ideal. Putting Henry in dialogue not just with his brother but with later pragmatists such as John Dewey, Randolph Bourne, and Walter Lippman, as well as with Frankfurt School critics such as Theodor Adorno and Walter Benjamin, Posnock finds in Jamesian "curiosity" and "nonidentity" a model for how to "loosen emotional . . . constrictions and abandon oneself to the shocks of experience" (82).

There is no doubt that Henry's late novels, with their exquisitely detailed renderings of the processes of consciousness, offer a counterpart to William's description in his *Principles of Psychology* (1890) of experience as a "blooming, buzzing confusion" (486). If, according to James Livingston, pragmatism "emphasized the inadequacy of philosophers' attempts to freeze, split apart, and otherwise compartmentalize the dynamic continuities and multiple connections of life as we live it" (104), then Henry's novels dramatize this dynamism and multiplicity and repeatedly mark the limitations of preconceived notions and classifications. In James's late fiction especially, such "philosophical inadequacy" is frequently rendered as moral failure, as in The AMBASSADORS (1903) when Sarah Pocock comes to PARIS armed with her closed-minded notions about the corrupting influence of the French capital.

Many of James's protagonists—including Lambert Strether in *The Ambassadors*, Maggie Verver in *The GOLDEN BOWL* (1904), Milly Theale in *The WINGS OF THE DOVE* (1902), Isabel Archer in *The PORTRAIT OF A LADY* (1881), and Christopher Newman in *The AMERICAN* (1877)—embody a pragmatist ideal of openness, curiosity, and unwillingness to make decisions in advance. Such characters' troubles often stem from their encounters with a society ruled by more conventional values. For example, Christopher Newman, "a born experimentalist" (53), confounds and baffles a Unitarian minister named Babcock: "[Babcock] often tried . . . to infuse into Newman a little of his own spiritual starch, but Newman's personal texture was too loose to admit of stiffening. His mind could no more hold principles than a sieve can hold water." Such lines strikingly anticipate one of William's most memorable claims for pragmatism, made over 30 years *after* the publication of Henry's novel, that it "'unstiffens' our theories," (*Pragmatism* 38), and suggest that Henry's own version of pragmatism is worthy of consideration in its own right. In his construction of pragmatist characters, his fascination with the pragmatist concept of habit and his analyses of the complex webs of social norms and institutions that constitute collective experience, Henry emerges as a crucial figure in American pragmatism.

Further Reading

Edel, Leon. *The Life of Henry James.* 5 vols. Philadelphia: Lippincott, 1953–72.

Hocks, Richard A. *Henry James and Pragamtistic Thought.* Chapel Hill: University of North Carolina Press, 1974.

———. "Recollecting and Reexamining William and Henry." *Henry James Review* 18, no. 3 (1997): 280–287.

James, Henry. *The American.* New York: Penguin, 1986.

James, William. *Pragmatism: A New Name for Some Old Ways of Thinking.* 1907. Reprint, Buffalo, N.Y.: Prometheus Books, 1991.

———. *The Principles of Psychology.* 2 vols. New York: Henry Holt, 1918.

Livingston, James. *Pragmatism, Feminism, and Democracy.* New York: Routledge, 2001.

Perry, Ralph Barton. *The Thought and Character of William James.* 2 vols. Boston: Little, Brown, 1935.

Posnock, Ross. *The Trial of Curiosity: Henry James, William James, and the Challenge of Modernity.* New York: Oxford University Press, 1991.

Skrupskelis, Ignas K., and Elizabeth M. Berkeley, eds. *William and Henry James: Selected Letters.* Charlottesville: University of Virginia Press, 1997. Abbreviated as *SL*.

Lisi Schoenbach, *University of Tennessee*

publishers   In the United States and England, Henry James worked with several publishers who attempted to make money by publishing periodicals (such as the *Atlantic Monthly* in the United States and *Macmillan's* in England) and books of varying quality and prices. The publishers sold most books to individual buyers and the very popular lending libraries in England, such as Mudie's and W. H. Smith. To reach an audience, an author considered the oversight not only of book and magazine editors but also of librarians, most of them men who evaluated the propriety of reading material for the largely female audience of the 19th-century novel.

In the United States, James worked with a few other publishers: in Boston, Houghton, Mifflin and Company (founded in 1880) and Ticknor & Fields (1829); in Chicago, Herbert S. Stone (1896); in New York, Charles Scribner's Sons (1846) and Harper & Brothers (1817). With the exception of a few titles such as "Daisy Miller: A Study" (1878), *The EUROPEANS* (1878), *HAWTHORNE* (1879), *Confidence* (1879), *WASHINGTON SQUARE* (1880), and *The PORTRAIT OF A LADY* (1881), which sold approximately 7,000 copies in the United States, James's books did not sell very well during his life. His most lucrative arrangements involved first publishing his fiction in British and American periodicals and then compiling these tales and serial installments for publication as a book. His first two early collections of short stories were published by Boston's J. R. Osgood & Company (founded 1870).

They did not turn much of a profit. For *A Passionate Pilgrim and Other Tales* (1874), James received 10 percent royalties after the sale of first 1,000 copies paid off the book's production costs (Kaplan 155). For *Transatlantic Sketches* (1875), James paid $550 to Osgood (the cost of the printing plates) and negotiated for 15 percent of the book's royalties. Osgood published 1,500 copies of each title and priced them at $2 apiece; a year later, James had made $88 on *A Passionate Pilgrim* and nothing on *Transatlantic Sketches*.

In England, James published primarily with the Macmillan & Company (founded in 1843 by the brothers Daniel and Alexander Macmillan) and William Heinemann (1890), as well as with Archibald Constable & Company, Chapman and Hall, Chatto & Windus, J. M. Dent & Sons Limited, J. Miles & Co., James R. Osgood, McIlvane & Company, Methuen & Company, William Blackwood and Sons, all based in LONDON. James's friendship with Frederick Macmillan, the nephew of the company founder, Alexander Macmillan, helped facilitate the winter publication of 1,250 copies of *French Poets and Novelists* (1878). The following year, Macmillan published a collection of tales, including the very popular "Daisy Miller: A Study," which had first appeared in England's *Cornhill Magazine*. The first British edition of *The AMERICAN* followed in early 1879. Macmillan also signed a contract with James to write a biographical study of Hawthorne for the series "English Men of Letters" (Kaplan 205)—a contract that James later regretted because he received a mere 100 pounds for the book's British copyright and relinquished any stake in American royalties. In the ensuing decades, the book sold a very respectable 20,000 copies.

The unwillingness of the United States to abide by an international copyright agreement was a daunting challenge to writers who hoped to capitalize on their work in a transatlantic context. For example, although "Daisy Miller" was very popular after its British appearance, pirated editions in the United States, where copyright law did not yet protect works published abroad, greatly diminished James's profits. To protect a book from being pirated, authors, publishers, and agents had to secure independent copyrights in both the United States and England for each separate installment of a serialization and for the book as a whole (Novick 59).

When it came to business, James was not a savvy negotiator. Eventually, to his publishers' chagrin, James employed professional literary agents to negotiate his terms, to keep an eye on the profits, and to promote competition among publishers who bid for his work. In the late 1880s, on the advice of EDMUND GOSSE, James enlisted Alexander P. Watt to represent him. The year of 1888 was a particularly lucrative period, yielding approximately $9,000. Nevertheless, there were the customary bumps in the road. Whereas the *Atlantic Monthly* serialized *The TRAGIC MUSE* for a total payment of $4,400, no magazine in England took it on, and for the book edition Macmillan's stipulated that James pay a 250-pound subvention and relinquish rights to all profits for five years (Kaplan 330–331).

After Watt, James employed the young Wolcott Balestier, an American who encouraged James's growing interest in theater, facilitating negotiations with the Compton Theater Company, which produced *The American*. Balestier also collaborated with William Heinemann, under whose press James later published. After Balestier's sudden and sad death in 1891, James found his most effective agent and account manager, James Pinker, who more than 20 years later would be one of four to witness James's competence in the English language on his application for British citizenship. With Pinker, James eventually contracted with Charles Scribner's Sons for the NEW YORK EDITION, published from December 1907 to July 1909. Sales were disappointing, recalling a letter James had written to MORTON FULLERTON in October 1896: "The representation of my sales brings the blush to my cheek . . . . They have—publishers *always* have—the last word. . . . A little aesthetic book never does much. It does a little—that's all" (qtd. in Kaplan 410).

Further Reading

Kaplan, Fred. *Henry James, the Imagination of Genius: A Biography.* New York: William Morrow, 1992.
Novick, Sheldon. *Henry James: The Mature Master.* New York: Random House, 2007.

—————. *Henry James: The Young Master.* New York: Random House, 1996.

Kendall Johnson, *Swarthmore College*

race and ethnicity   During the 19th century, the concepts of race and ethnicity entered public discourse in striking new ways and helped to shape and reshape national policy, cultural practices, and social mores. Literature was very much part of the debate over the meaning and political implications of these terms. Henry James lived through the CIVIL WAR and its aftermath and saw the large-scale force on theories of humankind's origins, development, and scientific categorizations that followed upon the publication of Charles Darwin's *On the Origin of Species* (1859). These two seismic events (among many others) can help one understand how thinkers, writers, political actors, and the general populace in America and Europe began talking about and redefining race and ethnicity.

After the Civil War, the Thirteenth Amendment made slavery unconstitutional but did not diminish the importance of race to the national consciousness or literary culture. The social and economic legacy of slavery continued to plague the nation's conscience and polity and served as a constant reminder that the rights of citizenship were not a guarantee against forms of discrimination and prejudice that severely limited the life opportunities of those not considered "white." The discrepancy between the promise of "America" and what actually constituted the American experience became a prevailing theme in U.S. literature. In *Playing in the Dark: Whiteness and the Literary Imagination* (1992), Toni Morrison points out that race cannot be seen solely "in terms of its consequences on the victim," warning against "always defining [race] asymmetrically from the perspective of its impact on the object of racist policy and attitudes" (11). Rather, a productive definition of race in the United States should acknowledge that "black presence is central to any understanding of our national literature" (5).

In *The* AMERICAN (1877) Henry James introduces Christopher Newman, a wealthy American searching for a wife in Europe: "An observer, with anything of an eye for national types, would have had no difficulty in determining the local origin of this underdeveloped connoisseur . . . The gentleman on the divan was a powerful specimen of an American . . . He had a very well-formed head, with a shapely, symmetrical balance of the frontal and the occipital development, and a good deal of straight, rather dry brown hair . . ." (35). Implicitly, James links national type—the question of who best qualifies as "the" American—with certain racially associated physical qualities, leaving those who do not fit this ideal to define the "American" type in the margins. Details of Newman's characterization, from his acquired wealth to his admirable physique, circulate in a historical moment that defined people by their social status as well as their racial makeup.

Scientific words like *specimen* and attention to cranial proportions represent another cultural current, that of ethnography and biomedical anthropology. These pseudo-sciences held that biological traits determined character and fate and correlated skin color and other physical features with relative intellectual ability. While some of these ideas predated *On the Origin of Species*, Darwin's theory of evolution transformed the race conversation by proposing that races could evolve, change, and become extinct. For the British Empire at its peak and the American at its beginnings, the idea of a racially determined fate or doom produced much anxiety. In *The American*, when Valentin de Bellegarde refers to his brother as "a great ethnologist," Newman assumes he "collect[s] negroes' skulls, and that sort of thing" (185). Indirectly, James signals the importance of racial lineage to the narrative of his quest for a perfect wife. Newman is rejected by the Bellegarde family because he is not of noble blood.

James's *The* AMERICAN SCENE (1907) dealt profoundly with matters of race, ethnicity, the nation, and immigration. Sara Blair argues in *Henry James and the Writing of Race and Nation* (1996) that this and other works engage "scientific and popular anxieties about racial virility, national character, and the fate of the 'Anglo-Saxon' type" (16). One branch of racial "science," the eugenics movement, linked overreproduction of certain ethnic types with a purported decline in national health.

This became a focal point as James witnessed large waves of immigrants coming to America in the early 20th century. *The American Scene* clearly supplies his aesthetic principles with racial undertones in speaking from and for a distinctly "Anglo-Saxon" point of view: "a haunting wonder as to what might be becoming of us all, 'typically,' ethnically, and thereby physiognomically, linguistically, *personally*, was always in order" (64). For James, a change in the ethnic makeup of the United States meant a change in aesthetics and art. Literature was particularly vulnerable to this ethnic reshaping since language indicated national belonging.

The American Scene describes NEW YORK's slums and ghettos, which were home to America's Jewish population. James describes this population in terms that echo a larger immigration and eugenics debate, as a "vast sallow aquarium in which innumerable fish, of over-developed proboscis, were to bump together, for ever" (131). James's description of Jewish immigrants uses racial stereotypes about skin color and nose shape. James took ethnic difference to mean the possible demise of the dominant culture: "[F]or it was in the light of letters, that is in the light of our language as literature has hitherto known it, that one stared at this all-unconscious impudence of the agency of future ravage" (138). James foresees ethnicity permanently changing the cultural and national landscape.

Further Reading

Blair, Sara. *Henry James and the Writing of Race and Nation*. New York: Cambridge University Press, 1996.

James, Henry. *The American*. 1877. Reprint, New York: Penguin Books, 1981.

———. *The American Scene*. 1907. Reprint, Bloomington: Indiana University Press, 1968.

Morrison, Toni. *Playing in the Dark: Whiteness and the Literary Imagination*. New York: Vintage Books, 1992.

Warren, Kenneth. *Black and White Strangers: Race and American Literary Realism*. Chicago: University of Chicago Press, 1993.

Jessica S. Stock, *Stony Brook University*

romance/realism/naturalism   Romance, realism, and naturalism are genres of literature whose definitions have varied over time as writers in 19th-century England, France, the United States, and other countries have differentiated their own writing from both classical authors of the past and rival contemporary writers. In the 20th century, literary critics used these categories to identify and canonize books that would make up an American literary tradition.

The term *romance* has an interesting history. Etymologically, it implies the local languages that sprang up on the periphery of the Holy Roman Empire—vernacular languages that were different from Latin and through which distinct communities of people on the rim of the imperial pale began to communicate as separate groups. Contemporaneous technological innovations in the printing and dissemination of books enabled these vernacular languages to exert an influence that began to rival the scholastic authority implied by the official word of scribal or printed Latin. In this basic sense, the stories that became known as "romances" were notable for deviating from the classical course of epic narratives derived from Greek and Roman dominion. The "romance" introduced a new story and a hero with which people identified; later, literary critics recovered these romances such as that of *Beowulf*, the *Breton Lays*, the *Song of Roland*, *Morte Darthur*, and *Don Quixote*, and associated them with the rise of new people—"the French," "the British," or "the Spanish."

In the 19th-century United States, WILLIAM DEAN HOWELLS and Henry James criticized the romance as a relatively simplistic narrative pattern that wore thin a reader's patience with narrative clichés—knights in shining armor, damsels in distress, pirates on the high seas, holy grails and dragons, happy MARRIAGES—and in plot development—decisive action by the protagonist, social settings that are mere background to the hero's self-realization, the inevitable happy ending. Howells criticizes his contemporaries' embrace of romance's hackneyed narrative patterns in this way:

> It was still held that in order to interest the reader the characters must be moved by the old romantic ideals; we were to be taught that

'heroes' and 'heroines' existed all around us, and that these abnormal beings needed only to be discovered in their several humble disguises, and then we should see every-day people actuated by the fine frenzy of the creatures of poets. How false that notion was few but the critics, who are apt to be rather belated, need now be told. Some of these poor fellows, however, still contend that it ought to be done, and that human feelings and motives, as God made them and as men know them, are not good enough for novel-readers. (305)

As an editor who published a good amount of James's fiction, Howells looked for writers who pierced the fantasy of fantasy, daring to represent the real world.

The above quote is from Howell's book *Criticism and Fiction* (1891), which collected many of his articles first published in *Harper's Monthly* under the column "Editor's Study." In this column, he introduces realism by instructing the "young writer" (301) to "report the phrase and carriage of everyday life" and not to mimic the styles of great writers like Shakespeare, Dickens, Scott, Thackeray, and Balzac (301). He criticizes those who have become so enamored of literary tradition that they cannot see the world around them or discover new ways of expressing the social life in the United States. He continues:

> But it is no new thing in the history of literature; whatever is established is sacred with those who do not think. At the beginning of the century, when romance was making the same fight against effete classicism which realism is making to-day against effete romanticism, the Italian poet Monti declared that "the romantic was the cold grave of the Beautiful," just as the realistic is now supposed to be. The romantic of that day and the real of this are certain degree the same. Romanticism then sought, as realism seeks now, to widen the bounds of sympathy, to level every barrier against aesthetic freedom, to escape from the paralysis of tradition. It exhausted itself in this impulse; and it remained for realism to assert that fidelity to experience and probability of

motive are essential conditions of a great imaginative literature. (301–302)

Important here is the developmental tension between the genres: As the romantic corrected "effete classicism," a disciplined and democratically minded realism now widens the constraints of an exhausted romanticism.

Howells goes on to suggest the themes for American writers, including the "common-place" of "well-to-do-actualities" (339) that derive from an understanding of "the universal in the individual rather than the social interests." Oddly in his cheery description of the past, Howells seems to overlook the nation's bloody struggles over slavery, maintaining the Union, and Indian removal. As the book continues, he does advise that "the Arts must become democratic" if the "expression of America in art" is to distinguish itself (339). He concludes his book by virtually replacing "realism" with the term democracy, exhorting: "Democracy in literature . . . wishes to know and tell the truth, confident that consolation and delight are there; it does not care to paint the marvelous and impossible for the vulgar many, or to sentimentalize and falsify for the vulgar few" (354). Howell's realism seems unavoidably implicated in his desire to promote a "truth" based on his hope that the United States would become less stratified both economically and politically.

In addition to being a powerful editor of the *Atlantic Monthly* from 1871 to 1881, Howells was a longtime friend of Henry James. However, even these two did not agree on definitions for romance and realism. James's understanding of the terms are apparent in his biography of Hawthorne (1879), the 1907 prefaces to *The American* (1877) and *The Princess Casamassima* (1886), as well as in his essay "The Art of Fiction" (1884). To a greater extent than Howells, James looked to an international set of writers for examples of literary realism. James reported back to Howells his firsthand conversations with such French writers as Gustave Flaubert, Edmond Goncourt, Émile Zola, and the Russian Ivan Turgenev, whose novels intensified the putative realism of Balzac with greater emphasis on the predetermining influences of environment and heredity. In a post-Darwinian world of natural selection, was it credible to suggest that human beings had control over their lives? In a world where the promise of social and political revolutions seemed perpetually unfulfilled, are human beings motivated by ethical concerns or a determination to survive? In his Rougon-Macquart series of novels (1871–93) and *Le roman experimental* (1880), Zola answered this dilemma with a theory of the novel as a scientific exercise in which the author should observe the world like a naturalist dispassionately collecting notes on how inhabitants interact with their environments.

James did not embrace the French style of writing novels even though he read "a great deal of what he called their 'naturalism'" (Kaplan 269). For James, *naturalism* conveyed a sense of hard-fact reality that was inescapable, material, and quite often sordid. James admitted that Zola "seems to me to be *doing something*—which surely (in the imaginative line) no one in England or the U.S. is" (qtd. in F. Kaplan 217). Still, one can sense the limit to James's patience in a letter (February 3, 1876) to Howells: "They are all charming talkers. As editor of the austere *Atlantic* it would startle you to hear some of their projected subjects. The other day [Goncourt] said he had been lately working very well on his novel—he had gotten upon an episode that greatly interested him. . . . *Flaubert*: 'What is it?' E. de G.: 'A whorehouse *de province*'" (Edel II: 23). In the end, James moved to LONDON, giving up on art that focused on either the deprivation of working-class people or the exhausted, decadent stagnation of those stranded in the bored hedonism of the aristocratic classes.

In the 20th century, *naturalism* became a term with which American authors revised the previous generation's investment in realism. Literary critics defined a group of writing by authors such as Stephen Crane, Theodore Dreiser, and Frank Norris as naturalistic to the extent that forces of business seemed to condition characters into determined behaviors beyond any hope of romantic autonomy.

Further Reading

Davidson, Rob. *The Master and the Dean: The Literary Criticism of Henry James and William Dean Howells.* Columbia: University of Missouri Press, 2005.

Howells, H. D. *Selected Literary Criticism: Volume II: 1886–1897.* Bloomington and Indianapolis: Indiana University Press, 1993.

Kaplan, Amy. *The Social Construction of American Realism.* Chicago: The University of Chicago Press, 1988.

Pizer, Donald, ed. *The Cambridge Companion to American Realism and Naturalism.* Cambridge: Cambridge University Press, 1995.

Powers, Lyall H. *Henry James and the Naturalist Movement.* East Lansing: Michigan State University Press, 1971.

Stowe, William W. *Balzac, James, and the Realist Novel.* Princeton, N.J.: Princeton University Press, 1983.

Warren, Kenneth. *Black and White Strangers: Race and American Literary Realism.* Chicago: The University of Chicago Press, 1993.

Kendall Johnson, *Swarthmore College*

Rome, Italy   Once the capital of the mighty Roman Empire, Rome languished in the devastation of the empire's fifth-century fall and eventually became the seat of the pope's Catholic authority in Vatican City. Rome was sacked again in 1517, when Charles V of Spain was the Holy Roman Emperor, and for the next few centuries it took second seat to the rising commercial city-states such as Genoa and VENICE. Nathaniel Hawthorne and Henry James experienced a mid-19th century Rome that was a site of deep historical distress, occupied by France and yet soon to become the capital of a newly united Italy in 1871 under Victor Emmanuel II.

Upon reaching Rome on his first adult journey to Europe in 1869, his own grand tour, James wrote to his brother WILLIAM JAMES, "Here I am then in the Eternal City. . . . From midday to dusk I have been roaming the streets. *Que vous en dirai-je?* At last—for the first time—I live!" (Edel I: 160). Rome fed not only James's historic and aesthetic consciousness as he went "reeling and moaning thro' the streets, in a fever of enjoyment" but also his moral sense. It became the first capital city of his INTERNATIONAL THEME, manifesting itself in his early novel RODERICK HUDSON (1875), "DAISY MILLER: A STUDY" (1878), and The PORTRAIT OF

A LADY (1881), as well as the early tales "Traveling Companions" (1873), "Adina" (1874), "The Sweetheart of M. Briseaux" (1873), and "The Last of the Valerii" (1874). Rome was also the ancestral home of the Prince in "Miss Gunton of Poughkeepsie" (1899) and, more important, of Prince Amerigo in The GOLDEN BOWL (1904), implying depths of social and psychological complexity and intrigue. Rome figured prominently in both of James's nonfiction biographies, HAWTHORNE (1879) and William Wetmore Story and His Friends (1903). He criticized Hawthorne's indifference to art as another example of his provinciality, while conversely blaming another fellow expatriate, Story, for allowing the sensual aspects of Roman life to distract him from single-minded dedication to his art. Rome eventually seemed "commonplace and familiar" to James, but this familiarity "only prove[d] how thoroughly [he] had enjoyed and appropriated it in former years" (Edel II: 141). James returned to Rome eight more times in his life, in 1872–73, 1877, 1881, 1888, 1894, 1899, 1901, and for the last time in 1907.

James was alert to the painful ironies of a life lived amid the "golden Roman air" (WWS I: 328), especially for his naive, untutored American characters like Roderick Hudson, Daisy Miller, and Isabel Archer. Each of these fictional personae is undone by unsuspected duplicity and deception, reflected in layers of ancient, Renaissance, and baroque artifacts surrounding them. Referencing Hawthorne's travelogue tone of The Marble Faun (1860), James added another depth of meaning to Rome's famous architectural, pictorial, and sculptural facets: Roderick encounters the femme fatale Christina Light in the garden of the Villa Ludovisi after admiring the colossal antique head of the capricious goddess Juno; Daisy Miller conducts her intimate colloquy with Mr. Giovanelli in the secluded nook of the Palazzo Doria-Pamphili in front of Velasquez's great portrait of Innocent X; and Isabel Archer says good-bye to the vanquished Lord Warburton in front of the statue of the Dying Gladiator. Writing wistfully to Grace Norton that "When I next go to Italy it will be not for months but years" (Edel I: 241), James returned to Rome for an extended stay in 1872–73. Although he still inhaled "the influence of an atmosphere electrically charged with historic intimation and whisperings" (Edel I: 324), he also deepened and refined his apprehension of social and moral intricacies, especially those concerning the world of American expatriates. As he wrote to his mother, "The chapter of 'society' here—that is American society—opens up before me" (Edel I: 317), and indeed he was to meet significant lifelong friends during this visit, including Mrs. FANNY KEMBLE, the renowned British actress, her American-born daughter, Mrs. Sarah Butler Wister (James's constant companion during this sojourn), Mrs. Louisa Ward Crawford Terry and her son the future novelist F. Marion Crawford (one of James's popular rivals), and William Wetmore Story, the neoclassical sculptor and unofficial social head of American artists abroad. As James wrote to his father, "I have now (proud privilege) the entrée of three weekly receptions—the Terrys, Storys and Mrs. Wister's" (Edel I: 328). He also spent time with Francis Boott and his daughter, Lizzie, who were renting an apartment in the Palazzo Barberini next to the Storys. The Bootts were later his close associates and neighbors during his extended stay in FLORENCE in 1886.

Although James paid short visits to Rome in 1881 and 1894, his most significant later journeys there were in 1899 and 1907. In 1899, he went to examine William Wetmore Story's studio as well as the bulk of his correspondence, diaries, journals, and literary remains in preparation for a two-volume biography, William Wetmore Story and His Friends (1903). During his last return in 1907, he sat for the young sculptor HENDRIK ANDERSEN.

James's literary career began with fictional portrayals of the effects of Roman life on Americans abroad, and his late, commissioned biography of Story echoed this theme, describing Story as one of the "victims" of Rome who lived in "a rare state of the imagination, dosed and drugged" by "the effectual Borgia cup" (WWS I: 208–209) so that "he was not with the last intensity a sculptor" (WWS I: 83). In analyzing "the case of the permanent absentee or exile," James believed that the "moral seems to be that somehow, in the long-run, Story paid" and became "the prey of mere beguilement." James saw Story's career "as a sort of beautiful sacrifice to a noble mistake" because there "were always, for however earnest a man, some seed of danger in consciously planning for happiness" (*WWS* I: 224). Rome's deeply tragic aura echoed in James's depiction of those by whom he had been so fascinated upon his arrival as a young writer in 1869.

Further Reading

Edel, Leon. *Henry James Letters.* 4 vols. Cambridge, Mass.: Harvard University Press, 1974–84.

James, Henry. *William Wetmore Story and His Friends.* 2 vols. London: William Blackwood and Sons, 1903. Abbreviated as *WWS*.

Kathleen Lawrence, *George Washington University*

Sargent, John Singer (1856–1925)   Henry James and Sargent met each other for the first time in PARIS in February 1884. James reported the occasion to a friend: "The only Franco-American product of importance here strikes me as young John Sargent the painter, who has high talent, a charming nature, artistic and personal, and is civilized to his finger-tips. He is perhaps spoilable—though I don't think he is spoiled. But I hope not, for I like him extremely; and the best of his work seems to me to have in it something exquisite" (*HJL* III: 32).

Sargent was born in FLORENCE in 1856. His parents had left Philadelphia for a life in Europe, and he grew up in various cities in Italy, France, SWITZERLAND, and Germany. He received his artistic training in Paris, studying at the atelier of Émile Carolus-Duran, who specialized in portraiture. Duran greatly admired the 17th-century Spanish painter Velázquez, who also became an important figure for Sargent. *The Daughters of Edward D. Boit* (1882), in particular, pays homage to Velázquez's masterpiece, *Las Meninas* (1656). Its arrangement of space and placement of figures generate a mysterious psychological tension, which characterizes many of Sargent's powerful portraits. James considered it an "astonishing" work, noting "the sense it gives us as of assimilated secrets and of instinct and knowledge playing together" ("Sargent" 688).

In May 1884, Sargent exhibited his dazzling portrait of Virginie Gautreau, known as *Madame X* (1883–84), at the Paris Salon. The painting depicts a society beauty in a striking pose. She wears a black satin décolleté, and her lavender-powdered flesh glows against the dark background. The picture is elegant yet decisively provocative. It shocked many viewers at the time and caused an artistic scandal, which became one of the factors that led Sargent eventually to leave Paris for LONDON.

Sargent had visited London back in March of that year. James, who took a great interest in his friend's career, arranged visits to the studios of several important English artists and entertained him at a dinner, where the Pre-Raphaelite painter Edward Burne-Jones was among the guests. By March 1886, Sargent had made his decision to move permanently to London, and the following year, he signed a lease for his studio in Tite Street, which had previously belonged to the American expatriate painter James McNeill Whistler. In October 1887, *Harper's Magazine* published

Sketch of James by John Singer Sargent, 1886, frontispiece to *The Letters of Henry James,* volume 1 (Charles Scribners's Sons, 1920)

James's influential article on Sargent, which introduced the painter to an American audience and set him on the path to becoming one of the most important portraitists in the Edwardian age. This article was later revised and reprinted, along with James's other writings on art, in *Picture and Text* (1893).

James's admiration for Sargent can also be connected to his deep interest in the visual arts. In his youth, James had even tried his hand at becoming an artist, following his brother WILLIAM JAMES to his painting classes. Although James soon gave up this attempt, he remained fascinated with the world of painting and wrote a number of art reviews between 1868 and 1897. In addition, in his fiction James frequently incorporated references to artworks or employed characters who are artists. Portraits or portrait painters especially play a crucial role in many of his stories—ranging from an early tale such as "The Story of a Masterpiece" (1868) to his mid-career work *The TRAGIC MUSE* (1890) to his unfinished novel *The Sense of the Past* (1917).

One of the key elements that characterize a work of portraiture is that it depicts a person consciously presenting himself or herself to be looked at by other people. The sitter constructs and puts on a certain expression for the given occasion, as if acting out some part in a play. This dramatic quality of the genre is pronounced in many of Sargent's portraits, where the subject's facial expression hints at the presence of some story just beneath the painted surface, a story that is known to the sitters yet kept undisclosed to the viewers. In James's fiction, too, there is always something mysterious, something suggested but left unsaid about his characters. James's and Sargent's shared artistic sensibility is especially evident in their portrayal of children and women. The knowingness of James's child protagonists in *WHAT MAISIE KNEW* (1897) or "The TURN OF THE SCREW" (1898) is reminiscent of Sargent's child sitters in *The Pailleron Children* (1881) or the Boit portrait mentioned above. The self-possession and grace with which James's late heroines carry themselves are embodied in Sargent's great female portraits, such as *Mrs. Henry White* (1883) and *Lady Agnew of Lochnaw* (1892).

The dramatic element in James's and Sargent's work can be linked in part to their mutual interest in the theater. Sargent attended the opening night of James's (unsuccessful) *Guy Domville*. W. Graham Robertson notes that when James was led by actor-manager George Alexander to face the booing and jeering audience at the end of the performance, Sargent burst out in "violent eruption" with "one of his rare attacks of fury and seemed about to hurl his hat at Alexander and leap upon the stage to rescue his friend" (Robertson 269).

Yet there is perhaps no better tribute to their friendship than Sargent's portrait of James, painted in 1913. The plan was initiated by a group of James's friends who drew up a subscription to commemorate James's 70th birthday. James was very happy with the result and wrote to a friend: "Sargent at his very best and poor old H. J. not at his worst; in short a living breathing likeness and a masterpiece of painting" (*LHJ* II: 330). A photograph of the painting signed by both James and Sargent was sent to each of the subscribers, who were also invited to a private view at Sargent's Tite Street studio, which lasted several days. The portrait now hangs in the National Portrait Gallery in London.

Further Reading

Charteris, Evan. *John Sargent*. New York: Scribner's, 1927.

Edel, Leon. *Henry James: A Life*. New York: Harper & Row, 1985.

James, Henry. *Henry James Letters*. Edited by Leon Edel. London: Macmillan London Limited, 1980. Abbreviated as *HJL*.

———. "John S. Sargent." *Harper's New Monthly Magazine* LXXV (October 1887): 683–691.

———. *The Letters of Henry James*. Edited by Percy Lubbock. London: Macmillan, 1920. Abbreviated as *LHJ*.

———. *The Painter's Eye: Notes and Essays on the Pictorial Arts*. Edited by John Sweeney. 1956. Reprint, Madison: University of Wisconsin Press, 1989.

McCauley, Elizabeth Anne, et al. *Gondola Days: Isabella Stewart Gardner and the Palazzo Barbaro Circle*. Boston: Isabella Stewart Gardner Museum, 2004.

Ormond, Richard, and Elaine Kilmurray. *John Singer Sargent: Complete Paintings*. 4 vols. New Haven,

Conn. and London: Yale University Press, 1998–2006.

Robertson, W. Graham. *Time Was*. London: Hamish Hamilton, 1931.

Kyoko Miyabe, *Cambridge University*

sexuality   Images of sexuality abound in the works of Henry James and are firmly linked with issues of sexuality in his own life. Biographers vary as to his sexual history; some conclude that he never experienced a consummated sexual relationship, while others point to the affectionate letters written by James to both women and men as evidence of an active sex life. Famously ambiguous on the subject, James hid his sexual history—or lack of it—and critics are left with the problem of drawing conclusions from this ambiguousness.

Among women, James himself acknowledged the significance of an early relationship with his cousin MARY (Minny) TEMPLE. Her 1870 death is frequently cited as a major reason James never married (he immortalized Minny in several of his women characters, most notably Isabel Archer in *The PORTRAIT OF A LADY* [1881] and Milly Theale in *The WINGS OF THE DOVE* [1902]). James's correspondence with novelist Lucy Clifford, a New York friend named Mary Cadwalader Jones, and novelist CONSTANCE FENIMORE WOOLSON, whose 1894 suicide caused him significant distress (some biographers suggest the suicide resulted, in part, from the lack of a consummated relationship with James), was filled with declarations of deep affection but no definitive sense of his engagement in sexual activity.

In recent years, much attention has been given to repressed homosexual yearnings in James. These seem to have been mostly epistolary but ardent in their passionate declaration, a somewhat surprising aspect of an author whose works are often criticized for failing to evoke passion. Among the earliest objects of James's homosexual desires was Russian artist Paul Joukowsky, but there were apparently others, as evidenced by surviving correspondence with American artist HENDRIK ANDERSEN and an English friend, HOWARD STURGIS. Whether any of these relationships extended beyond erotic cor-

respondence remains open to speculation. James's attitudes on gender and sexuality seem largely to conform to the accepted social structures of his time; for example, he expressed shock over revelations of OSCAR WILDE's flamboyant homosexuality (and refused to sign an 1896 petition circulated among artists and writers in an attempt to secure a pardon for Wilde) and, according to HUGH WALPOLE, he reacted with horror to Walpole's expressed desire for a sexual relationship.

Regardless of James's personal sexual history, the discourse of sexuality in his work is present from his earliest novels and short stories, at the very least reflecting the growing visibility of sexual and gender themes in late Victorian literature and art (see VICTORIANISM). A century of criticism is firmly divided over James's depiction of sexuality; contemporary scholars suggest that his writing was daring for its time and features depictions of transgressive desires. Reflecting his own homosexual urges in the presentation of same-sex relationships makes James's writings appear radical when set against the work of his peers. If James's writings do not fully anticipate the queering of literature that began a generation later, there is no denying the heterosexual-homosexual binary he subtly explores.

Frequently praised for the emotional and intellectual complexity of his women characters, James demonstrated an antipathy toward certain women in his personal opinions. He opposed women's rights and often expressed dismissive attitudes toward women writers, but his intimate portrayals of women characters are consistently sympathetic, particularly regarding those suffering under either societal or familial repression, as with Catherine Sloper in *WASHINGTON SQUARE* (1880). James also depicts latent lesbianism in the relationship of two women, Olive Chancellor and Verena Tarrant, in *The BOSTONIANS* (1886), balancing (or unsettling) their relationship with Basil Ransom, a hypermasculine character, in order to preserve the story's normative heterosexuality by allowing him to take Verena away from Olive. Critics disagree in describing James as either a closeted pro-feminist in the creation of such women characters or as dismissive, even disdainful, of women in his expectation that they conform to socially normative expectations of the time; as such, the claim goes, he typically restricts them to domesticated circumstances. In fact, James's work is animated by the tensions he identifies between the hidden desires of his women characters and the constrained ways society views them.

James's portraits of male sexuality, from hypermasculinity to effeminacy, and particularly veiled depictions of homosexuality, begin with one of his first novels, RODERICK HUDSON (1875). Focused on the relationship of a wealthy art collector, Rowland Mallet, and his protégé, the title character, this novel builds to the concluding suicide of Hudson, an event that deeply affects Mallet and, more significant, reflects James's belief in the inherent futility of societally forbidden male relationships. Similarly, several James short stories depict homoerotic relations between older men and youthful protégés, as in "The AUTHOR OF 'BELTRAFFIO'" (1884), "The PUPIL" (1891), and "The MIDDLE YEARS" (1893). Cautious depictions of such relationships reflect James's unease despite his desire to explore them and further suggests the necessity for homosexuals to remain in the closet during this time, particularly those, like himself, who were well-known figures. Eve Kosofsky Sedgwick points to the homosexual panic she and other critics find in James's oeuvre, particularly in his stories "The BEAST IN THE JUNGLE" (1903) and "The JOLLY CORNER" (1908), in which the expatriate central character turns to heterosexual love as opposed to risking relations outside the social or sexual norms. James strives to insist upon the heterosexual norm in "The TURN OF THE SCREW" (1898), which some critics believe is a depiction of the sexual upheavals of Victorian England—as most obviously seen in the "gross indecency" trials of Oscar Wilde—in the enforcement of heterosexual dominance by the governess. Similarly, critics observe that James also examines the pervasiveness of gender normalcy in such novels as The TRAGIC MUSE (1890) and his travel narrative, The AMERICAN SCENE (1907).

James frequently employs a dispassionate male observer in his fiction, a character outside the social world depicted and occasionally a confidante to one or more of the central characters. The Jamesian observer provides a view of the surface normativity of heterosexuality, while James sets his subtle examination of transgressive behavior against it. Lambert Strether in James's most acclaimed novel, The AMBASSADORS (1903), is such a figure; watching over Chad Newsome, the feckless son of his fiancée in PARIS, Strether learns to live life more fully from this transgressive figure. Earlier, in his novel The SACRED FOUNT (1901), James depicts his observer character concluding that young men may be weakened through the reinvigorating energy they supply older men in elder-protégé relationships. A few critics find evidence of sadomasochistic qualities in the eroticism of James's The GOLDEN BOWL (1904), a novel in which James experiments with varied conceptions of maleness (see MASCULINITY).

As an American living in Europe for much of his life, and arguably as a deeply closeted gay man living in an officially heterosexual society, James may well have directed his feelings of marginality into the creation of characters such as Strether, a figure reflecting the cultural and sexual anxieties of his era. James's oeuvre often centers on the heterosexual-homosexual binary about which he seems, at best, ambivalent. His characters live in a sexually censorious time on either side of that division, but James, in imagining a more diverse and complex realm of gender than was typical in the writings of many of his contemporaries, may be viewed as something of a sexual pioneer—one less sensational than Wilde but one who served an essential role in opening the subject of sexuality to modernist writers (see MODERNISM AND MODERNITY).

Further Reading

Allen, Elizabeth. *A Woman's Place in the Novels of Henry James*. London: Macmillan, 1984.

Graham, Wendy. *Henry James's Thwarted Love*. Palo, Alto, Calif.: Stanford University Press, 1999.

Hall, Richard. "Henry James: Interpreting an Obsessive Memory." In *Literary Visions of Homosexuality*, edited by Stuart Kellogg. New York: Haworth Press, 1983.

Martin, Robert K. "'The High Felicity' of Comradeship: A New Reading of *Roderick Hudson*." *American Literary Realism 2* (1978): 100–108.

McCormack, Peggy, ed. *Questioning the Master: Gender and Sexuality in Henry James's Writings.* Newark: University of Delaware Press, 2000.

Moon, Michael. "Sexuality and Visual Terrorism in *The Wings of the Dove.*" *Criticism* 28, no. 4 (1986): 427–443.

Person, Leland S. "Henry James, George Sand, and the Suspense of Masculinity." *PMLA* 106 (1991): 515–528.

———. "Strether's 'Penal Form': The Pleasure of Imaginative Surrender." *Papers on Language & Literature* 23 (1987): 27–40.

Pippin, Robert B. *Henry James & Modern Moral Life.* Cambridge: Cambridge University Press, 2000.

Savoy, Eric. "Hypocrite Lecteur: Walter Pater, Henry James and Homotextual Politics." *Dalhousie Review* 72, no. 1 (1992): 12–36.

Sedgwick, Eve Kosofsky. *Epistomology of the Closet.* Berkeley: University of California Press, 1990.

Seltzer, Mark. *Henry James and the Art of Power.* Ithaca, N.Y.: Cornell University Press, 1984.

Stevens, Hugh. *Henry James and Sexuality.* Cambridge: Cambridge University Press, 1998.

Walton, Priscilla L. *The Disruption of the Feminine in Henry James.* Toronto: University of Toronto Press, 1992.

Winner, Viola Hopkins. "The Artist and the Man in 'The Author of "Beltraffio."'" *PMLA* 83 (1968): 102–108.

James Fisher, *The University of North Carolina at Greensboro*

Stevenson, Robert Louis (1850–1894)

A celebrity in his own time, Robert Louis Stevenson was a best-selling author of many adventure and travel books as well as poetry. His work represented a reaction against literary realism and a return to the values of fantasy and romance (see ROMANCE/REALISM/NATURALISM). Always drawn to tales of horror and the supernatural, he is perhaps most well known for a psychological mystery, *Dr. Jekyll and Mr. Hyde* (1886); this novella was a best seller and has ensured his place in the literary canon.

Stevenson was born in Edinburgh, Scotland, the son of Thomas Stevenson, an engineer and inventor, and Margaret Balfour, daughter of a Scottish clergyman and professor of moral philosophy. His father, grandfather, and great-grandfather were accomplished designers of lighthouses, and it is often said that it is this side of the family that gave him his love of adventure and of the sea. Stevenson, however, was not a robust child. Largely raised by his Christian fundamentalist nanny, Alison Cunningham, he suffered from tuberculosis or a similar lung ailment as a child; as a result, he spent much of his time alone in bed, dreaming, reading, and composing stories. In 1867, Stevenson entered Edinburgh University to study engineering, but he frequently preferred to walk the streets of Edinburgh, befriending the denizens of its seedier districts. Stevenson's father then encouraged him to study law, but by the time he was called to the Scottish bar in 1875, he had already begun to publish stories and essays for magazines. His freethinking bohemian lifestyle was also a source of conflict with his strict and puritanical father, who failed to comprehend his son's creative genius.

Stevenson was an inveterate traveler, constantly seeking venues for the benefit of his health and for the stimulation of new people and places. In the late 1870s, he made many trips to PARIS, where he became close friends with Andrew Lang, EDMUND GOSSE, and Leslie Stephen, and he began to develop his artistry and broaden the range of his experience. During one of these trips, Stevenson fell in love with Fanny Vandegrift Osbourne, an exotic-looking American woman who was 10 years Stevenson's senior, married, with two children. She was drawn to the occult and was said by her son's wife to be a clairvoyant. After Fanny won a divorce from her husband, Stevenson traveled to California to marry her in 1880.

Between 1880 and 1887, Stevenson traveled widely in search of a healthy climate. In 1881–82, he published his adventure novel *Treasure Island*, the success of which launched him on a career as a popular favorite with the reading public; this novel and others also received praise from the literary world, which immediately recognized his inventive genius. The author James Barrie went so far as to suggest that the initials "R.L.S." were the most beloved initials in the English language.

Stevenson developed a close relationship with Henry James in 1884. The two had met in 1879, just before Stevenson's departure for a trip to America; James dismissed him to friends as a raffish bohemian and a poseur, and Stevenson concluded, in turn, that James was a bit of a stuffed shirt. In 1885, however, James published an article that praised *Treasure Island,* inspiring Stevenson to write and invite James to visit him in Bournemouth. James wrote back to congratulate Stevenson on his talent as a writer, and when he later came to Bournemouth to visit his invalid sister, ALICE JAMES, he also called on Stevenson and his wife at their house, Skerrymore. This was the beginning of a warm, lifetime friendship between the two writers. James's first visit to Skerrymore, however, was not auspicious since he was at first taken for a carpet-layer and shown to the tradesmen entrance; but after sorting out the confusion, James immediately charmed the Stevensons, especially the wife, Fanny, who was struck by what she felt was James's resemblance to the Prince of Wales. James visited the Stevensons regularly for 10 weeks, making a habit of dropping by Skerrymore almost every evening after dinner, and even joining them for dinner on their wedding anniversary. A particular chair that had belonged to Stevenson's grandfather became known as the "Henry James chair" to the Stevensons, and it can be seen in the important portrait of the Stevensons by JOHN SINGER SARGENT. Stevenson also celebrated James's visits in a poem in which all James's fictional characters enter in a procession into his home, after which James himself arrives, welcomed as best of all.

Stevenson and his wife admired James's character and emotional intelligence, but Stevenson also found he shared with James much common ground with regard to their identity as artists, especially in their concern for the aesthetic, moral, and philosophical questions involved in the writing of fiction. James, who had publicly praised Stevenson as the only man in England who could write a decent sentence, encouraged him to continue to explore the complexities of character and motive in his fiction; Stevenson, on the other hand, encouraged James to move outside of the upper echelons of modern society and to engage with the lower depths, advice that led to James's *The PRINCESS CASAMASSIMA* (1886).

Another commonality between the two authors was their concern with issues of good and evil; while both were avowed freethinkers and free spirits, each also used his fiction as a way to explore and develop a moral philosophy and to explore especially the issue of spiritual evil. Each made a major contribution to the genre of the psychological/paranormal mystery. Stevenson's *Dr. Jekyll and Mr. Hyde* and James's later "The TURN OF THE SCREW" (1898) both addressed the issue of diabolical possession, but even more, the presence of such evil in those who present the appearance of unassailable innocence and virtue.

The final meeting between James and Stevenson was in the South Place hotel at Finsbury in 1887, where James, recently returned from Italy, came to bid the Stevensons farewell before they sailed for America. After his father died, Stevenson felt he could leave Scotland for healthier climes; he never returned to his homeland again. James's parting gift was a crate of champagne and a literary profile of Stevenson eventually published in *Century* magazine. Stevenson and James continued to correspond for the rest of Stevenson's short life.

After a brief period in the United States, Stevenson sailed from San Francisco to Hawaii and other islands in the Pacific with his family. In 1890, he built an estate named Vailima ("Five Rivers") on one of the islands of Samoa, where he soon became involved in local affairs, providing valuable advice and earning the loyalty of the native Samoans by favoring them over their colonial overlords. He was given the name "Tusitala," or storyteller, by the chief of the Samoans. Stevenson was buried on a mountaintop in Samoa, having died of a stroke suffered while opening a bottle of his favorite wine.

Further Reading

Harman, Claire. *Myself and the Other Fellow: A Life of Robert Louis Stevenson.* New York: HarperCollins, 2005.

Marías, Javier. *Written Lives.* Translated from the Spanish by Margaret Jull Costa. New York: New Directions, 2006.

Smith, Janet Adam. *Henry James and Robert Louis Stevenson: A Record of Friendship and Criticism.* New York: Hyperion Press, 1985.

Margaret Boe Birns, *New York University*

Sturgis, Howard Overing (1855–1920) Howard Sturgis was born to American parents in LONDON and educated at Eton and Cambridge University. He published only three novels, all strong indictments of the late 19th-century society of his adopted home of England. Henry James was both Sturgis's friend and literary mentor.

Sturgis's father, Russell Sturgis, a successful businessman, partnered with the firm of Baring Brothers in 1846 and began entertaining. James was introduced to the Sturgis family around 1878 and became a frequent visitor to Russell Sturgis's homes. Both of Sturgis's parents died in 1888, leaving Howard a vast fortune. He traveled to America, where he met EDITH WHARTON and his distant cousin George Santayana. Returning to England in 1889, he bought a villa called Queen's Acre (or Qu'Acre) outside Windsor Park and began a long tradition of entertaining friends such as Wharton and authors A. C. Benson and George Santayana. James was also a visitor to Qu'Acre, calling it a "sybarite sea," where he enjoyed Sturgis's hospitality (Posnock 75).

Tim: A Story of Eton (1891), Sturgis's first publication, was a commercial success. *All That Was Possible,* the story of an actress treated shabbily by two gentlemen, followed in 1895. In *Tim,* a novel that reworks Tennyson's *In Memoriam,* Sturgis emphasizes an adolescent love of one man for another. It is not clear that Sturgis was himself homosexual, but the writings of his friends do comment on his ambivalent SEXUALITY and affinity for conventionally feminine occupations, such as needlework, a sign of his refusal to conform to Edwardian gender roles. *All That Was Possible* again borrows from Tennyson, this time *Maud,* with the title referencing the line "Oh! That 'twere possible." Sibyl Croft, an actress and mistress, draws men to her wherever she goes, but with serious repercussions.

Sturgis's last novel, *Belchamber* (1903), uses the main character Sainty, earl of Belcamber, to highlight the hypocrisy and self-centeredness of other characters. Sturgis again sketches a character of ambivalent sexuality in Sainty, whom the novel contrasts to a villainous cousin Claude. This Victorian bildungsroman follows Sainty's development through an ambiguous conclusion. Henry James objected to the novel's failure to create "a constituted and intense imaginative life" for Sainty (Kirchhoff 439). James also took issue with Sainty's passivity in approaching his conflicts.

Although James acted as a mentor to Sturgis, his rejection of *Belchamber* is often cited as the reason that Sturgis quit writing. According to E. M. Forster, Sturgis "wrote to please his friends, and deterred by his failure to do so he gave up the practice of literature" (Borklund 256). However, several Sturgis stories were discovered posthumously, indicating that perhaps he had not given up writing in the face of James's criticisms.

Further Reading

Borklund, Elmer. "Howard Sturgis, Henry James, and *Belchamber.*" *Modern Philology* 58 (1961): 255–269.
Kirchhoff, Frederick. "An End to Novel Writing: Howard Overing Sturgis." *English Literature in Transition* 33, no. 4 (1990): 425–441.
Posnock, Ross. "Genteel Androgyny: Santayana, Henry James, Howard Sturgis." *Raritan: A Quarterly Review* 10, no. 3 (1991): 58–84.

Patricia Bostian, *Central Piedmont Community College*

Swedenborg, Emanuel (1688–1772) The spiritual philosophies of Emanuel Swedenborg were a primary influence on HENRY JAMES, SR. Swedenborg, the "Northern Plato," was born Emanuel Swedberg on January 29, 1688, in Stockholm, Sweden. In his lifetime, he mastered almost every field of scientific endeavor, from engineering, chemistry, mineralogy, physiology, astronomy, mathematics, and philosophy, to more esoteric fields of study such as epistemology, psychology, and spirituality.

Swedenborg's father, Jesper Swedberg, was a royal chaplain, and from his mother, Sara Behm Swedberg, he inherited holdings in Swedish ore mines (Synnestvedt 16). Swedenborg attended Uppsala University, where he proved himself a gifted scholar with a wide field of interests, mostly focused in the physical sciences. In 1716, Swedenborg published his first paper in the journal *Daedalus,* Sweden's first scientific journal, for which he later served as editor. His work at *Daedalus* so impressed King Charles XII that Swedenborg was called upon to solve a number of engineering problems; he crafted a new design for a dry dock, invented a system for moving large warships overland, and devised machinery for working salt springs (Synnestvedt 20–21). Also, at this time he produced designs for an airplane, a submarine, a steam engine, and an air gun. In 1716, he was appointed assessor in the Royal College of Mines. The Swedberg family was granted nobility in 1718; with this came the change of the family name to Swedenborg. The same year, Swedenborg assumed a seat in the House of Nobles in the Swedish Diet.

The year 1720 saw the publication of Swedenborg's first book, a philosophical work titled *Principles of Chemistry*. Swedenborg spent the years 1729–34 writing and publishing his most significant philosophical work, *Philosophical and Mineralogical Works*, in three volumes. Among Swedenborg's notable accomplishments in this phase of his life include his description of the importance of the cerebral cortex and the assignment of specific areas of the brain to control different physical activities, the function of ductless glands (including the pituitary gland), the composition of water, and the makeup of the Earth's atmosphere.

However, Swedenborg's two principal interests were cosmology and the nature of the soul. His work in the sciences and physiology led him to an investigation of the location of the soul in the body (Synnestvedt 22). By 1735, Swedenborg became heavily invested in an intense study on the nature of human existence, with specific interest on the concept of the soul. Swedenborg continued this period of study until 1744, the year he first experienced visions. This marks the point of Swedenborg's transition from philosopher to mystic, as his transcendent experiences intensified. Swedenborg described his mystical experiences, his inner visions, with great detail, always with the interest of a scientist. He came to understand that his inward journeys were a part of the cosmic whole, and that the gift of vision was given to him as a divine commission. He believed that all creative forces flow from a universal divine center of existence and find expression in both physical and spiritual kingdoms; this is the essential nature of the personal God.

Swedenborg dedicated the last 27 years of his life to the study of the symbolic substrata of the Bible (*Emanuel Swedenborg*, not paginated).

In April 1745, Swedenborg had the first of his profound visions. While at a LONDON inn where he often dined, Swedenborg had the impression that the room grew dark and an apparition spoke to him. He later returned to his room, where he had a similar experience; the same apparition spoke regarding the need of a human to serve as a vessel by which God would reveal Himself to the world. Thus Swedenborg experienced a "call" to become a revelator, and he resigned from the Swedish Board of Mines in order to concentrate on theological writing (Synnestvedt 25–26). From 1748 to 1758 Swedenborg produced his first major theological work, *Arcana Coelestia*, in 12 volumes. The work offers an exposition of the symbolic and allegorical nature of the books of Genesis and Exodus and expands Swedenborg's work on the symbolic underpinning of the language of the Bible.

In 1759, while dining with friends in Gothenburg, about 300 miles from Stockholm, Swedenborg became noticeably disturbed. He withdrew from the room and appeared later with the news that a great fire had broken out in Stockholm not far from his home. At 8:00 P.M., he revealed that the fire had been extinguished three houses away from his, saving several important manuscripts. When news of the fire arrived several days later, Swedenborg's vision was proved correct, to the level of details of the fire and the method by which it had been extinguished. Swedenborg demonstrated other clairvoyant gifts, and news of Swedenborg's visions spread rapidly, making him a public figure (Synnestvedt 27–28).

Swedenborg published what is generally considered his most important theological work, *Heaven and Hell*, in 1758. *Heaven and Hell* is a detailed, highly descriptive view of the afterlife, recorded and explained based on Swedenborg's own experiences in the spiritual realm.

In 1768, a country parson in Gothenburg introduced a resolution in the Gothenburg Consistory, calling for measures to stop the circulation of works at variance with the dogmas of Lutheranism, especially Swedenborg's writings. In 1769, Swedenborg answered charges of heresy leveled against him by some of the prelates of the Lutheran state church. His theological writings had become the subject of controversy. As a result, Swedenborg was charged with Socinianism, or refusal to accept the divinity of Christ. The nature of the debate caused the University of Uppsala, among other universities, to carry out detailed scrutiny of Swedenborg's ideas. The debate shifted to the political realm and was taken up in the national Diet. The Royal Council rendered its decision in April 1770: Swedenborg's work was effectively banned from public teaching. Swedenborg continued for three years to fight the decision, going so far as to petition the king himself. Most clergymen chose not to preach Swedenborg's ideas, though a few defied the council's decision. The affair eventually quieted down, and Swedenborg spent his last years concentrating on the completion of *True Christian Religion*, a broad examination of modern Christianity, published in two volumes in 1771–72 (Synnestvedt 31–32).

Accurately predicting the day of his own death, Swedenborg died in London on March 29, 1772, at the age of 84. Among the many writers and thinkers to borrow freely from his work are Thomas Carlyle, RALPH WALDO EMERSON, Samuel Taylor Coleridge, William Blake, and Henry James, Sr. Swedenborg's works have been translated into many languages and continue to be studied today (*Emanuel Swedenborg*). The principal center for Swedenborg studies in the United States is the Swedenborg Foundation of West Chester, Pennsylvania, founded in 1849.

Further Reading

Emanuel Swedenborg. West Chester, Pa.: The Swedenborg Foundation, n.d.

Synnestvedt, Sig. *The Essential Swedenborg.* West Chester, Pa.: The Swedenborg Foundation, 1977.

Bill Scalia, *St. Mary's Seminary and University*

Switzerland   In 1855, the James family decided to expatriate from the United States in order to allow Henry and his brothers to get a European education. It was in Geneva that Henry James, then a boy of 12, began to absorb the "European virus—the nostalgia for the old world that made

it impossible for him to rest in peace elsewhere" (*Letters* I: 4). After visiting other countries, the family returned to Switzerland in late 1859. Henry was first placed at a pre-engineering school before he was allowed to join his brother WILLIAM JAMES in attending courses at the Academy—the present University of Geneva.

In 1869, Henry James set sail for his first European tour on his own. Until 1910, he had visited Switzerland several times, mostly on the way to or returning from Italy. Although James dutifully inspected all the popular tourist haunts, the universally admired Alpine scenery of central Switzerland seemed to lack refinement in James's estimation, as he observes in "Swiss Notes," published in 1875 in his *Transatlantic Sketches*: "I have often thought it, intellectually speaking, indifferent economy for the American tourist to devote many of his precious summer days in Switzerland. Switzerland presents, generally, nature in the rough, and the American traveller in search of novelty entertains a rational preference for nature in the refined state" (*TS* 56). Very seldom did the Swiss countryside gratify James's sense of the past: "These little towns . . . with their desolate air of having been and ceased to be, their rugged solidity of structure, their low black archways, surmounted with stiffly hewn armorial shields, their lingering treasures in window-screen and gate of fantastically wrought-iron, they are among the things which make the sentimental tourist lean forth eagerly from his carriage" (*TS* 69). His pleasure derived from specifically pictorial elements; it was not nature that really counted.

Berne was the only Swiss town besides Geneva that James described at some length in his TRAVEL WRITINGS. It is interesting to note that his observations show a characteristic feature of his later writings; with intuitive boldness, he inferred from Berne's outward appearance the life inside the thick Bernese walls: "There are broad jokes made, I imagine, at the *abbayes* or headquarters of the old guilds . . . . They all look as if they had a deal of heavy plate on their sideboards—as if a great many schoppen [glasses] were emptied by the smokers in the deep red-cushioned window-seats" (*TS* 235).

As regards Switzerland, James's opinions were formed by 1874; it was mostly a "show country" already too well exploited: "I expect to live to see the summit of the Monte Rosa heated by steam-tubes and adorned with a hotel setting three tables d'hôte a day" (*TS* 231). Although he frequently returned in subsequent years, there is no evidence that he changed his opinion. In 1882, for instance, he wrote in a letter: "I am not particularly fond of Switzerland myself; would give it all for one hour of Italy" (*Life* 138).

James's travels through Switzerland nevertheless provided him with his first great theme of the American-European contrast. Early treatments of this subject can be found in the short stories "Travelling Companions" (1870) and "At Isella" (1871). James continued to draw on his experience, and his childhood vision of Switzerland echoes in novels such as The WINGS OF THE DOVE (1902) and The AMBASSADORS (1903). In a number of cases, he chose the Swiss countryside as the most suitable background for a story; "DAISY MILLER: A STUDY" (1878) contains autobiographical elements, as do "The Pension Beaurepas" (1879), "The LESSON OF THE MASTER" (1888), "The Private Life" (1892), and "Fordham Castle" (1904). Swiss scenery provides, for instance, the hostile background for the last chapters of RODERICK HUDSON (1875). In The AMERICAN (1877), the Alps have a more positive connotation. The Alpine atmosphere is at its sternest in WASHINGTON SQUARE (1880), where James uses it to underline a moment of great dramatic antagonism between father and daughter. Meetings incidental to the plot, and which are merely reported in conversation, usually take place in Switzerland, such as in "The Modern Warning" (1888): "[H]e met us first in the Engadine, three or four weeks ago, and came down here with us—it seemed as if we already knew him and he knew us" (*Stories* 1884–91, 383). In "Maud-Evelyn" (1900) James described another holiday acquaintance that would be rather unlikely on other terms and conditions. The same is true in the short story "CRAPY CORNELIA" (1909): "Two years ago in Switzerland when I was on a high place for an 'aftercure' . . . she was the only person . . . with whom I could have a word of talk. She and I were the only speakers of English, and were thrown together like castaways on a deserted island and in a raging storm"

(*Stories* 1898–1910, 832). Switzerland often seems a European crossroad where touring characters of different cultural identity and class standing intersect in incidental but significant ways.

Further Reading

Harden, Edgar F. *A Henry James Chronology*. Basingstoke, England: Palgrave Macmillan, 2005.

James, Henry. *Complete Stories 1884–1891*. New York: Library of America, 1999.

———. *Complete Stories 1898–1910*. New York: Library of America, 1996.

———. *The Letters of Henry James*. Edited by Percy Lubbock. 2 vols. London: Macmillan, 1920.

———. *Henry James: A Life in Letters*. Edited by Philip Horne. London: Penguin Press, 1999.

———. *Transatlantic Sketches*. 1875. Reprint, New York: Books for Libraries Press, 1972. Abbreviated as *TS*.

Andrea Heiglmaier, *University of Zurich*

Symonds, John Addington (1840–1893)   Henry James and John Addington Symonds shared a great deal, at least superficially, in their participation in elite literary circles of Victorian (see VICTORIANISM) England, their prominence as essayists on art and travel, their love of Italy, particularly of VENICE and Venetian painters, and their mutual friendships with EDMUND GOSSE, Leslie Stephen, Robert Browning, Vernon Lee (Violet Paget), and ROBERT LOUIS STEVENSON, among others. What divided them was a profound difference of temperament and opinion on questions of morality, particularly the expression of homosexuality.

By the turn of the last century, James had entered his later years and relaxed his usual emotional restraint to bestow demonstrative affections on a circle of younger men, including American sculptor HENDRIK ANDERSEN and acolytes in Great Britain such as Jocelyn Persse, HUGH WALPOLE, and HOWARD STURGIS, indulging at last in deep homosocial attachments denied or unexplored earlier in life. While James was profoundly ambivalent about Symonds's semipublic disclosure of his homosexuality, he was fascinated by the difficulties inherent in the situation of the married man in

Autographed "John Addington Symonds 1889 to Walt Whitman," Feinberg-Whitman Collection *(Library of Congress)*

Victorian England, fictionalizing Symonds's condition in "The AUTHOR OF 'BELTRAFFIO'" (1884).

James greatly admired Symonds's volumes on Italy and the Renaissance, acquiring nearly all of his works for his library at LAMB HOUSE. Conversely, Symonds was not a great admirer of James's work. James first showed his respect for Symonds as a scholar and writer about Italy in 1882, sending to Symonds his essay "Venice" from *Century*, XXV (reprinted in *Portraits of Places*, 1883) "because it was a constructive way of expressing the good will I felt for you in consequence of what you have written about the land of Italy—and of intimating to you, somewhat dumbly, that I am an attentive and sympathetic reader" (*HJL* III: 29–30). In addition to *Sketches in Italy and Greece* (1874), *Sketches and Studies in Italy* (1879), *Italian Byways* (1883), and the seven volumes of his *Renaissance in Italy*, (1875–86), Symonds published *Studies of the Greek Poets, Series One* (1873) and *Series Two* (1876), and the more privately circulated *A Problem in Greek Ethics* (1883). These appreciations of Greek culture obliquely celebrated what he called the "Hel-

lenic ideal," which combined physical love between men with a deeper and lasting companionship, thus dangerously flaunting his unconventional desires before the Victorian reading public.

After 1886, James began to visit Venice frequently to stay with Daniel and Ariana Curtis at their Palazzo Barbaro and to participate in the social world centered in Katherine Bronson's Casa Alvisi. Although James apparently never crossed paths with Symonds in Venice, he no doubt heard news and gossip at the Palazzo Barbaro's fireside or whenever the Curtises, Katherine Bronson, or Isabella Stewart Gardner visited LONDON. Beginning in 1881, Symonds became romantically involved with the handsome gondolier Angelo Fusato. The ensuing relationship evolved from infatuation into something close to Symonds's ideal of male comradeship. Symonds not only courted the young man with gifts and money but treated him with a kind of democratic equality and love inspired by Whitman's *Leaves of Grass*, Symonds's favorite poem. Symonds rented a small pied-à-terre on the Zattere facing the Guidecca canal; the apartment was attached to the house of his English friend and later biographer, Horatio Brown. Symonds hired Fusato as his gondolier and lived a sensual existence for one month a year in Venice until his death in 1893.

James converted an anecdote about Symonds told to him by Gosse into the tale "The Author of 'Beltraffio,'" recording in his notebook on March 26, 1884, "Edmund Gosse mentioned to me the other day a fact which struck me as a possible donnee. He was speaking of J.A.S., the writer (from whom, in Paris, the other day I got a letter), of his extreme and somewhat hysterical aestheticism, etc.... Then he said that, to crown his unhappiness, poor S.'s wife was in no sort of sympathy with what he [Symonds] wrote, disapproving of its tone, thinking his books immoral, pagan, hyperaesthetic, etc". (*Complete Notebooks* 25). James's notebook entry contains not only this key discord between the character Mark Ambient and his wife but also the central conflict in the tale over their son's exposure to his father's work and views. In his own life, James cherished his privacy and could not understand Symonds's desire to expose his condition publicly. Nevertheless, James was struck by the way Symonds led an outwardly conventional existence as an upper-class British man who was married with four daughters and concealed his intense inner passions, eventually revealing them obliquely in his writing.

After publication of Horatio Brown's two-volume biography of Symonds in 1895, two years after Symonds's death, James wrote to Gosse, "I have been reading with the liveliest—and almost painful—interest the two volumes on the extraordinary Symonds. They give me an extraordinary impression of his 'gifts'—yet I don't know what keeps them from being tragic" (qtd. in Grosskurth 321). When Ariana Curtis asked if he would be interested in writing an article on Symonds, James nervously answered, "There was in Symonds a whole side—tout au cote—that was strangely morbid & hysterical & which toward the end of his life coloured all his work & utterance. To write of him without dealing with it, or at least looking at it, would be an affectation; & yet to deal with it either ironically or explicitly would be a Problem—a problem beyond me" (Curtis Papers, Dartmouth). Alluding to what James judged as the mistake of public exposure, he concluded, "Yet, there are also in him—in his work—there were in him things I utterly don't understand; & the idea of taking the public into his intimissima confidence which seems to me to have been almost insane" (Curtis Papers, Dartmouth).

Further Reading

Curtis, Daniel and Ariana. Papers in Rauner Special Collections, Dartmouth College Library.

Grosskurth, Phyllis. *John Addington Symonds, A Biography.* London: Longmans, 1964.

James, Henry. *Henry James Letters,* vol. 3. Edited by Leon Edel. Cambridge, Mass.: Harvard University Press, 1980. Abbreviated as *HJL.*

———. *The Complete Notebooks of Henry James.* Edited by Leon Edel and Lyall H. Powers. New York and Oxford: Oxford University Press, 1987.

Kathleen Lawrence, *George Washington University*

Temple, Mary (1845–1870)

Mary Temple, called Minny by family and friends, was Henry James's cousin and an extremely vital source of inspiration for his works. She was the daughter of Colonel Robert Emmet Temple and Catherine Temple, HENRY JAMES, SR.'s younger sister. Her correspondence was used in Henry James's memoir, *Notes of a Son and Brother* (1914) (see AUTOBIOGRAPHIES), for which he received much acclaim, especially the chapter dedicated to Minny's letters. In a letter to his sister-in-law, James wrote: "I seem really to have . . . made her emerge and live on, endowed her with a kind of dim sweet immortality that places and keeps her" (March 29, 1914, qtd. in Gordon 352).

The most notable characters inspired by Minny's presence are Isabel Archer, in The PORTRAIT OF A LADY (1881), the protagonist of "DAISY MILLER: A STUDY" (1878), and Milly Theale in The WINGS OF THE DOVE (1902). Minny was vivid, possessed of a rebellious nature, and vivacious. In 1861, she cut her hair down to half an inch due to an illness and sent Henry's brother WILLIAM JAMES a photograph. Her love of bold conversation prompted Henry to name her the "amateur priestess of rash speculation" (Gordon 41). Minny would voice strong opinions regarding Henry's father's religious and political ideas, and Henry loved her for her fiery nature. Her often shocking personality prompted the James family to disapprove of Henry's close relationship with her, and so he felt impelled to hide his admiration and instead immortalized her in his art. It was a literary tradition to kill off difficult women such as Minny, and so in "Daisy Miller" James represses and eventually halts the free spirit of Daisy, showing also a desire to contain Minny, his muse. For his main character in *The Portrait of a Lady,* James said to his friend Grace Norton in a letter dated December 28, 1880, "You are right and wrong about Minny Temple. I had her in mind & there is in the heroine a considerable infusion of my impression of her remarkable nature" (qtd. in Gordon 139).

Her father died of tuberculosis in 1854, when Minny was nine years old, and her mother died three months later of the same disease. As orphans, she and her sisters, Elly, Kitty, and Henrietta, and her two brothers, Robert and William, were looked after by the Tweedy family in Albany for the early years of their lives. Minny's brother William became a captain in the CIVIL WAR and was fatally struck by a musket ball at the Battle of Chancellorsville in Virginia on May 1, 1863. Minny was devastated at this news and wrote to her friend Helena de Kay on May 12 of that year: "I have found out, I believe it now, that Willy is dead. Yes he is dead, and I am never going to see my boy again in this world. . . . I could not *breathe* when I thought of it; it seemed as if everything had been *torn* out of my life and yet I lived. He was *all, everything*—and it has left a great *void*; a vacancy that makes me feel like *dying* when I think of it" (Gordon 56). The Civil War affected Minny to the extent that she visited wounded soldiers at Portsmouth Grove, Rhode Island, and Henry followed her example.

Her most notable friendship other than Henry was with Helena de Kay, who was a student at a school for young ladies in Connecticut with Minny. Their friendship displeased Helena's mother, who thought Minny was a disruptive influence on the already free-spirited Helena. Their friendship and strong opinions caused the headmistress to send complaints back to the families of the girls in 1863. The following year, both girls stayed in NEWPORT under the tuition of George Bradford. Toward the end of Minny's life, their friendship had faltered, causing Helena to write in a letter to her friend Mary Foote: "Someone came between us . . . and it seemed to me as if death were better" (Spring 1870, qtd. in Gordon 92).

In 1866, the Tweedy family, who had acted as guardians to the Temple sisters, withdrew their support due to financial difficulties. In the summer of 1868, Kitty announced her engagement to Richard Stockton Emmet, who was 22 years older. This marriage would enable Kitty to provide a home for her sisters, but Minny was shocked by it. An other sister, Elly, also married an older man, Dr. Christopher Temple Emmet, prompting Minny to say that she would not marry unless it was on completely equal terms.

In 1868, Minny fell ill with consumption, and when James traveled to Europe in 1869, Minny wrote often, expressing her deep wish that she could join him in ROME. She asked him to meet and talk with GEORGE ELIOT for she was a great reader of her works. In November 1869, it was arranged that she would travel to California with the Emmets, which displeased Minny and put her plans for travel to Europe and see Henry further away. She wrote in a November letter to Henry: "When shall we meet again, /Dearest & best/ Thou going Easterly/I, to the West?' as the song saith" (qtd. in Gordon 111).

With Henry gone, Minny found solace in writing letters to her friend John Chipman Gray. He would provide the comfort and conversation she needed in the lonely hours spent in her bedroom at the Emmets' house. When she died on March 8, 1870, of tuberculosis, Henry James received the news in England and with great shock. To his mother he wrote: "It comes home to me with irresistible power, the sense of how much I knew her & how much I loved her" (March 26, 1870, *A Life in Letters* 36). His brother William said in a letter, "Few spirits were as free as hers" (qtd. in Gordon 65), and Henry attempted to capture this spirit in many female characters created from his own portrait of Minny.

Further Reading

Gordon, Lyndall. *A Private Life of Henry James: Two Women and His Art.* London: Random House, 1998.

James, Henry. *Henry James: A Life in Letters.* Edited by Philp Horne. London: Penguin Books, 1999.

Kaplan, Fred. *Henry James, The Imagination of Genius: A Biography.* London: Hodder and Stoughton, 1992.

Laura Christie, *University of Roehampton*

Venice, Italy   James first arrived at "these blessed isles," located on the northeast coast of Italy at the head of the Adriatic Sea, on September 15, 1869. In a letter to his father soon after, James describes his domestic situation as a "little heaven—within this larger heaven—about me" (ALS Houghton bMS Am 1,094 [1,763]). James may not have been instantly enchanted with this city, especially when compared with his reaction to ROME, yet he returned to Venice no less than eight times, generally staying for periods of two weeks. James's several TRAVEL WRITINGS on Venice include: "Venice: an

Early Impression" (1872, also published as "From Venice to Strassburg"), "Venice" (1882), and "The Grand Canal" (1892). It also served as a setting in several of James's fictional works, including "The ASPERN PAPERS" (1888) and *The WINGS OF THE DOVE* (1902). "A LONDON LIFE" (1888) and "The Aspern Papers" were written while James stayed at Daniel Sargent and Ariana Wormeley Curtis's Palazzo Barbaro.

Venice began as an independent republic in 421 C.E. From the ninth to 12th centuries, it served as a major center of trade between Western Europe and world markets. By the 18th century, however, the republic, which was once seen "as the possessor of a model government and as a state commanding economic power, . . . preferred carnival to trade, its government was effete and its policy of neutrality made [it] irrelevant in the politics of Europe" (Plant 9). Napoleon took advantage of this turn of events and conquered the republic in May 1797, with very little resistance from Venetian forces. Following the fall of the republic, there was rampant destruction and pillaging of Venice's richly artistic buildings, especially the extravagantly decorated palaces of rich Venetian families. Speculators "did not hesitate to sell off and disperse the memories of centuries of history, the family archives, paintings, art objects, [and] antique furniture" of these patrician houses (Zorzi 20). One palace that was saved from complete destruction at the hands of speculators was the Curtises' Palazzo Barbaro. By the 20th century, the old world of Venice regained a sort of romanticized aura and became a center of world travel. As Margaret Plant explains, "Venice was always a highlight of the aristocratic grand tour, but bourgeois tourism compelled the city's modernisation, even while the visitors were coming to see what was old" (4). This is undoubtedly what led James to Venice and also what led him to remark to his father that "Atmospherically [Venice] is a good deal like Newport" (ALS Houghton bMS Am 1,094 [1,763]).

When James first arrived in Venice, he stayed at the Casa Barbesi. Between 1869 and 1887, he stayed in several different hotels. It was not until 1887, after his first visit at the Curtis's Palazzo Barbaro that he settled upon it as his consistent

residence while in Venice. From his correspondence to family and friends, it is clear that Italy held a special place in James's heart; yet, at the same time, it is also clear that he was not as quickly taken by Venice as he was by Rome. In his first letter to WILLIAM JAMES upon arriving in Rome, he writes, "At last—for the 1st time—I live! It beats every thing: it leaves the Rome of your fancy—your education—nowhere. It makes Venice—Florence—Oxford—London—seem like little cities of paste-board" (30 Oct 1869, ALS Houghton bMS Am 1,094 [1938]). James later adds that "Venice is magnificently fair + quite, to my perception, the Venice of Romance + fancy. Taine, I remember, somewhere speaks of 'Venice + Oxford—the two most picturesque cities in Europe.' I personally prefer Oxford; it told me deeper + richer things + than any I have learned here" (25 Sept 1869, ALS Houghton bMS Am 1,094 [1,934]). Nonetheless, James's later correspondence from the Palazzo Barbaro evinces a deep appreciation of the city's art and society.

Staying at the Palazzo Barbaro positioned James within a society of American expatriates who appreciated Venice's artistic heritage and who were committed to continuing an artistic tradition. The Venetian society became largely composed of artists, poets, writers, and musicians (Zorzi 42). Being in Venice also exposed James to the work of Tintoretto, whose "use of viewpoint" would greatly affect the way in which James envisioned the modern novel (28).

While it may have been a slow realization, James grew to adore Venice, and as Zorzi writes, "Perhaps towards the end of the 1880s or at the beginning of the 1890s James really dreamed of having a small *pied-à-terre* in Venice. But in the summer of 1893 he acknowledged this wish was a mere dream, 'fading a little' when he was not there" (29). For James, there was also tragedy associated with Venice. On January 24, 1894, his close friend CONSTANCE FENIMORE WOOLSON committed suicide by jumping from a window of the Palazzo Semiticolo along Venice's Grand Canal. "Woolson's death," Rosella Mamoli Zorzi writes, "marked, for James, a period of detachment from Venice" (30). Despite the tragedy of Woolson's death, James would return to

Venice several months later. His correspondence shows that he visited Venice on two occasions in 1894, once in April/May, and again in June. He would return only twice more, for brief stays in 1899 and 1907.

Further Reading

Plant, Margaret. *Venice, Fragile City: 1797–1997.* New Haven, Conn.: Yale University Press, 2002.

Zorzi, Rosella Mamoli, ed. *Letters from the Palazzo Barbaro.* London: Pushkin, 1998.

Patrick Phillips, *University of Kansas*

Victorianism Victorianism refers to the period when Queen Victoria reigned in England (1837–1901). Queen Victoria grew into a symbol for the nation because she set a standard for domestic virtues and devotion to the family, and during her 60-year reign England became the most prosperous and powerful empire. By 1900, the British Empire covered 13 million square miles inhabited by nearly 370 million persons.

The Victorian era is generally divided into three periods. The first, from 1837 to 1851, was an age of both social unrest and economic growth with such hallmarks as the Reform Bill (1832), which marked the beginning of political and administrative changes in England; the Chartist movement (1837–48), which pointed to the growing social and political force of the working-class; and the Industrial Revolution, which transformed England from a predominantly rural and agricultural country into an urban and manufacturing one. During the second period, from 1851 to 1870, England enjoyed a period of steady prosperity, global power, and commercial influence, mainly due to great technological achievements; for example, steam power was used for railway transportation, printing presses, and an unparalleled merchant fleet. During the third period, from 1870 to 1901, England ceased to be the "workshop of the world" and turned into the "world's banker." During this stage, trade unions gained power and the Labor Party was formed, the Education Act (1870) established a state education system, and the Boer War in South Africa (1899–1901) ended with the absorption of

two independent republics into the British Empire. Some were skeptical of these material gains and unsettled by the corresponding shift in national moral standards.

In "Signs of the Times" (1829), Thomas Carlyle (1795–1881) characterized the era in the following terms: "Only the material, the immediately practical, not the divine and spiritual is important to us . . . . It is no longer a worship of the Beautiful and Good, but a calculation of the Profitable" (74). Charles Darwin's work *On the Origin of Species by Means of Natural Selection* (1859) also jolted Christian orthodoxy by challenging literal readings of Genesis; in the process, he helped to establish the discipline of modern biology. In the field of education, Matthew Arnold (1822–88), a famous poet and critic, advocated a democratization of national education. Primary education became compulsory. Modern sciences and languages were included in the curriculum, along with religion and moral philosophy. John Ruskin (1819–1900) exhorted his readers to engage art as a moral concern. Ruskin was also the patron of the Pre-Raphaelite Brotherhood (Dante Gabriel Rossetti [1828–82] was its leader), a group of poets and painters who admired the paintings made in the Middle Ages (before Raphael) and who were against technical skill devoid of inspiration. Another movement in the late 19th century was aestheticism [see AESTHETIC MOVEMENT], influenced by the Pre-Raphaelites' cult of art and the Oxford professor Walter Pater (1839–94), whose study of the Renaissance impressed aestheticism's most celebrated and controversial figure, OSCAR WILDE (1854–1900).

The Victorian era was a period of drastic social changes. Great urban communities developed as people relocated from the countryside to industrial towns. Whereas in 1832 LONDON had 2 million inhabitants, in 1901 it had 6.5 million. Slavery was abolished throughout the British Empire in 1833. The same year, the Factory Act established legal limits on the working hours of children and young persons. The movement for the emancipation of women won important changes in their status. Women's suffrage was introduced on the parliamentary agenda as early as the 1840s, even though it was not legislated until 1918. The Married Women's Property Acts (1870–1908) granted women the right to own their property after MARRIAGE. The University of London opened its degree examination to women in 1878.

During the Victorian era, the novel flourished, addressing a vast array of topics of concern to 19th-century readers. Novelists such as Charles Dickens (1812–70), William Makepeace Thackeray (1811–63), Elizabeth Gaskell (1810–65), Anthony Trollope (1815–82), Charlotte Brontë (1816–55), Emily Brontë (1818–48), and GEORGE ELIOT (1819–80) were critical of their era but also confident in humanity's capacity for improvement. Samuel Butler (1835–1902), George Meredith (1828–1909), and Thomas Hardy (1840–1928) were influenced by the European and Russian novels. Their approach was bleaker and more cynical.

Victorian poets extended the innovations of early 19th century romantic poets such as William Wordsworth, Samuel Taylor Coleridge, John Keats, and Percy Bysshe Shelley. Alfred Lord Tennyson (1809–92) rewrote the epic to express the uncertain times of England's rise to commercial power. Robert Browning (1812–89) and Gerard Manley Hopkins (1844–89) experimented with the dramatic monologue (Browning) and sprung rhythm (Hopkins). Victorians were great theatergoers and regarded DRAMA as a sophisticated yet popular form of entertainment. Dion Boucicault (1820?–90) and Oscar Wilde were among the lionized playwrights of the age. The Victorian era was an age of complex and often contradictory tendencies. Today it is remembered for the ascendancy of the British Empire.

Further Reading

Carlyle, Thomas. "Signs of the Times." In *Critical and Miscellaneous Essays*, 5 vols. Vol. 2, 56–82. Reprint, New York: AMS Press, 1969.

Gilmor, Robin. *The Victorian Period: The Intellectual and Cultural Context of English Literature*. London and New York: Longman, 1994.

Strachey, Lytton. *Eminent Victorians*. London: Chatto and Windus, 1934.

Wynne-Davies, Marion, ed. *Bloomsbury Guide to English Literature*. London: Bloomsbury, 1989.

Aloisia Sorop, *University of Craiova*

Walpole, Hugh (1884–1941)   A prolific writer of novels, short stories, and critical works, Hugh Walpole was dismissed by the modernists (see MODERNISM AND MODERNITY) as a mere storyteller but was much loved by the general reading public for his sprawling adventure stories. His Herries series, *Rogue Herries* (1930), *Judith Paris* (1931), *The Fortress* (1932), and *Vanessa* (1933), is set in Cumberland, England, and is still his most popular work. Walpole was a longtime correspondent and intimate friend of Henry James.

Born into a clerical family in Auckland, New Zealand, Walpole came to England in 1893. His early years in English public schools were miserable but led him to later write *Mr. Perrin and Mr. Traill* (1911), starting a trend of schoolroom novels. The criticism that his novels failed to have a controlling form was evidenced in James's letters:

> Don't let any one persuade you—there are plenty of ignorant and fatuous duffers to try to do it—that strenuous selection and comparison are not the very essence of art, and that Form is not substance to that degree that there is absolutely no substance without it. Form alone takes, and holds and preserves substance, saves it from the welter of helpless verbiage that we swim in as in a sea of tasteless tepid pudding. (*Letters* 237)

His first novel was *The Wooden Horse* (1909), but it was not until his 1913 release of *Fortitude* that he won widespread recognition. Later, after *The Duchess of Wrexe* was published in 1914, an essay by James entitled "The Younger Generation" appeared in the *Times Literary Supplement*, praising Walpole's novel yet still criticizing the author's sometimes careless form (142–145).

The boost to Walpole's career from James's mostly positive review contributed to his publishing a book almost every year from 1914 to his death in 1941. Walpole volunteered with the Russian Red Cross in WORLD WAR I, which provided him with material for *The Dark Forest* (1916) and *The Secret City* (1919). Several letters from James during this time reflect on Walpole's youth and James's aging as he implores the younger writer to come home safely (*Letters* 423). In 1924, Walpole bought a home in Cumberland and divided his time between Brackenburn and LONDON. He loved living in the country, and many of his books are set in the area. His self-proclaimed masterpiece is his Herries series. The four novels in the series are influenced by Sir Walter Scott, on whom Walpole was an authority. *Rogue Herries* is set during the period of the 1745 Jacobite rebellion. The final novel, *Vanessa*, follows the protagonist through the hard years of the Boer Wars. Walpole's sprawling chronicles rival Galsworthy's *Forsyte Saga* and were scorned by the modernists, whom Walpole in turn dismissed. He found the modernists cold and incapable of telling a good story. His 1928 *Wintersmoon* set forth his antimodernist ideas. In addition to his swashbuckling epics, Walpole wrote novels inspired by Anthony Trollope (another favorite author), such as *The Cathedral* (1922), and psychological suspense and horror fiction (*Portrait of a Man with Red Hair* [1925] and *The Killer & the Slain* [1942]) influenced by Nathaniel Hawthorne (see HAWTHORNE). He also produced critical works on James Branch Cabell, JOSEPH CONRAD, and Anthony Trollope.

Recent scholarship has focused on Henry James's relationships with younger men, including Hugh Walpole, who was openly homosexual (Gunter and Jobe). Whatever the relation between the two, James served as an important mentor to Walpole.

Further Reading

Gunter, Susan E., and Steven H. Jobe, eds. *Dearly Beloved Friends: Henry James's Letters to Younger Men.* Ann Arbor: University of Michigan Press, 2001.

James, Henry. "The Younger Generation." *Times Literary Supplement* (19 March/2 April 1914). Reprinted as "The New Novel" in *Henry James: Literary Criticism,* edited by Leon Edel, 127–159. New York: Library of America, 1984.

———. *The Letters of Henry James.* Vol. 2. Edited by Percy Lubbock. New York: Scribner's, 1920.

Patricia Bostian, *Central Piedmont Community College*

Ward, Mrs. Mary Humphry (1851–1920)

Mary Augusta Arnold was a popular novelist and memoirist, publishing under her married name of Mrs. Humphry Ward. She was born in Hobart, Tasmania, to literature professor Tom Arnold, brother of Matthew Arnold, and Julia Sorell. She married Thomas Humphry Ward and overshadowed his own literary career, to the point that some critics and journalists referred to her husband as "Mr. Mary Humphry Ward."

Her most famous novel was *Robert Elsmere* (1888), centered on her theological and religious ideas and written in the mode of psychological realism (see ROMANCE/REALISM/NATURALISM). She published *Marcella* in 1894 to wide acclaim, *Helbeck of Bannisdale* in 1898, and *Helena* (1919). Her novel *The Case of Richard Meynell* (1911), a sequel to *Robert Elsmere,* was unpopular, but *The Marriage of William Ashe* (1905) was a success. In 1918, she published her memoirs, *A Writer's Recollections,* in two volumes.

When she was still a small child, the family set sail for England from Tasmania on July 12, 1856. Mary's birth had been followed closely by that of five brothers, William (b. 1852), Arthur (b. 1854) who died within 24 hours, Theodore (b. 1855), another Arthur (b. 1856), and Frank (b. 1860), the black sheep of the family. Her sisters were Lucy (b. 1858), Julia (b. 1862), and Ethel (b. 1866). As the oldest child she was strong-willed, boisterous, and prone to tempers and fits. Upon arriving in England, the destitute family traveled immediately to Ireland, where Tom had a teaching position, leaving the disruptive Mary at Fox How with her grandmother and aunt. Her mother and father's marriage was marred by the constant disputes over religion. Her mother was an Anglican, and her father converted to Catholicism, provoking Julia Sorell to deliver him an ultimatum: either her or ROME. He converted back to Protestantism in 1867, and then again to Catholicism in 1876. This religious tug-of-war between her parents would form many of the ideas and stories for her later novels.

Until she was 16, she spent a nomadic existence at different boarding schools. Her lonely childhood forced her to write, and by the age of 13 she had written a Spanish romance, *A Tale of the Moors.* In 1865, she went to Clifton, under the tutelage of a Miss May, whom she used as a model for Miss Pemberton in *Marcella* and whom she idolized. In 1867,

Mrs. Mary Humphry Ward, no date, George Grantham Bain Collection *(Library of Congress)*

her family moved to Oxford, and Mary returned to live with them, studying Spanish at the Bodleian Library. Although nothing came of this venture, her status as "researcher" granted her access to academic society.

After her marriage in 1872 to Thomas Humphry Ward, who had been granted a fellowship at Oxford's Brasenose College and who would become part of a new wave of lecturers at Oxford, she set up a lectures for women committee, which led to the formation of the Association for the Education of Women in 1877. During this period, Mary worked herself to exhaustion, as would become a habit; she also gave birth to three children between 1874 and 1879.

In the 1870s, her literary career was going nowhere, and her only notable publications were "Plain Facts about Infant Feeding" (1874) and contributions to *The Dictionary of Christian Biography*. Their fortunes changed when Humphry Ward took up a position at the *Times*, and they moved to Bloomsbury, LONDON. Mary wrote for the *Times*, the *Saturday Review*, the *Pall Mall Gazette*, *Macmillan's Magazine*, and the *Oxford Chronicle*. She met Henry James in 1882, and their friendship lasted until his death in 1916. She was inspired by James's fiction to make new attempts at her own, and her novel *Miss Bretherton* (1884) pays homage to the master.

Robert Elsmere, her greatest success, brought two physical breakdowns; her health suffered badly from the pressure of delivering her three-volume baby, as she called it. The same day that Mary buried her mother, who had died of cancer, the novel received rave reviews in the press, leaving a taste of bittersweet success. In 1889, despite her previous work for women's rights, she mounted an attack on the women's suffrage cause, publishing an "appeal" against it.

In 1896, she published *Helbeck of Bannisdale*; her dilemma regarding her father's position over Catholicism required her to make many revisions, and the content upset the church. Her main protagonist, Laura Fountain, is brought up in Cambridge among atheists and is sent to live in the Lake District with her stepmother's brother, Alan Helbeck. He is a staunch Catholic, and when she falls in love with him, she must choose between his religion and that of her dead father, Protestantism. Unable to commit to Alan, she drowns herself. This novel, which probes the difficulties in her own family, is perhaps her finest.

At the turn of the last century, her health and popularity were waning, and she grew dependent on morphine. Her play *Eleanor* in 1902 was a failure, as was *Agatha* (1905). Like Henry James, who also failed with his play *Guy Domville* (1895), she turned again to novels. *The Marriage of William Ashe* (1905) was a success, and in 1908 she embarked on a lecture tour in North America. Meanwhile, she had set up a settlement program called the Passmore Edwards Settlement, which was the first day-care center in London for working-class children.

In 1916 in the midst of WORLD WAR I, Theodore Roosevelt encouraged her to write reports for the American people, and the *England's Effort* letters served as propaganda but also boosted her self-esteem at this time. On March 2, in Ypres, she was handed a telegram informing her of Henry James's death on February 28. In her letters, she wrote: "I was looking over ground where every inch was consecrated to the dead sons of England, dead for her; but even through their ghostly voices came the voice of Henry James, who, spiritually, had fought in their fight and suffered in their pain" (Ward II: 203–204). She was named a Commander of the Order of the British Empire in 1919, and she died on March 27, 1920.

Further Reading

Kaplan, Fred. *Henry James, The Imagination of Genius: A Biography*. London: Hodder and Stoughton, 1992.

Sutherland, John. *Mrs Humphry Ward: Eminent Victorian, Pre-eminent Edwardian*. Oxford: Oxford University Press, 1990.

Ward, Mary Humphry. *A Writer's Recollections*. 2 vols. London, 1918.

Laura Christie, *University of Roehampton*

Wells, Herbert George (1866–1946) Herbert George (commonly H. G.) Wells was a prolific and versatile essayist, novelist, short story writer, scientific popularizer, and amateur historian. Best known today as a father of science fiction, Wells also penned numerous realist (see ROMANCE/REALISM/NATURALISM) novels, essays, and a best-selling history textbook. Wells first met Henry James in 1898. For 17 years, in private correspondence, face-to-face meetings, and public reviews, they conducted a lively debate about whether the novel should be primarily a work of art or a vehicle for a social message. The rich and impassioned exchange essentially came to a halt following Wells's publication of a savage satire of James's style and ideas in *Boon* (1915), the year before James's death.

H. G.'s father, Joseph Wells, was a gardener turned shopkeeper and professional cricketer. His mother, Sarah Neal Wells, was a lady's maid at Uppark, a country house in Sussex, before she was married; she returned to this post in 1880, when H. G. was 14 years old. From 1881 to 1883, Wells was miserably indentured as a draper's apprentice. In 1884, he won a scholarship to the Normal School of Science in South Kensington, where he studied biology under T. H. Huxley, whose evolutionary teachings colored everything Wells wrote. He left in 1887 without a degree, serving as a schoolmaster for several years, before dedicating himself to a life of letters. In 1891, Wells married his cousin Isabel Mary Wells. In 1894, he left her for a student, Amy Catherine Robbins ("Jane"), whom he subsequently married. During their 30 years of marriage (until Jane's death in 1927), Wells had numerous affairs, including those with Dorothy Richardson, Violet Hunt, and, from 1913 to 1923, Rebecca West (each an accomplished author in her own right). In 1903, Wells became a short-lived member of the social-democratic Fabian Society, and in 1928, he joined PEN, an international club of writers of which he became president in 1933.

Wells published more than 100 books and pamphlets during his extremely varied career. From 1895 to 1900, he published a series of scientific romances, including *The Time Machine* (1895), *The Island of Dr. Moreau* (1896), *The Invisible Man* (1897), and *The War of the Worlds* (serialized 1897). This was followed by a series of largely autobiographical, social realist novels, including *Love and Mr. Lewisham* (1900), *Kipps* (1905), *Tono-Bungay* (1909), *Ann Veronica* (1909), and *The History of Mr. Polly* (1910). Beginning with *The New Machiavelli* (1911), Wells began to use fiction almost exclusively as a platform for ideas. His best-selling *The Outline of History* (1919–20) charted human history from the dawn of civilization to WORLD WAR I, earning Wells a world reputation as a popular educator. Wells died in 1946 at the age of 79.

Wells reviewed the first performance of James's *Guy Domville* in LONDON in 1895, calling it well conceived and beautifully written, though weakly developed and marred by bad acting. The two writers met in 1898 and began avidly reading and reviewing each other's work. James praised *Love and Mr. Lewisham* highly and called *The Time Machine* a "masterpiece" (January 29, 1900;

Edel and Ray 63). Reading *The First Men in the Moon* (1901) made him "sigh" to collaborate with Wells—to "intervene" as he put it (September 23, 1902; Edel and Ray 80–81). James later reiterated this wish to "*re*-compose" Wells; to serve, in other words, as his "faithful finisher" (October 7, 1902; Edel and Ray 81, 82). In 1900, Wells moved to Sandgate (cycling distance from James's home in Rye [see LAMB HOUSE]), where his literary circle included, along with James, JOSEPH CONRAD, Stephen Crane, George Gissing, and Ford Maddox Hueffer (Ford).

A turning point in their relationship occurred in 1912, when Wells declined James's entreaties to join the Academic Committee of the Royal Society of Literature, declaring an opposition to hierarchies in general and insisting that the world of literature was best left "anarchic" (March 25, 1912; Edel and Ray 162). To James, Wells's refusal to join signified the younger writer's "cutting loose" from literature (Edel and Ray 164). Wells professed "dazzled admiration" for James's technique (April 9, 1913; Edel and Ray 170). James's effusive praise for Wells's ideas and imagination was frequently counterbalanced by frustration with the younger writer's slapdash style. He admired the "life and force and temperament" of *The New Machiavelli* but was impatient with its crude execution and wrote that reading *Marriage* (1912) required "complete abdication" of the "canons of form" and the "sacred laws of composition" (October 18, 1912; Edel and Ray 166). Wells conceded both novels' faults, yet declared that he was "destined to be worse before . . . better; the next book is 'scandalously' bad in form" (October 19, 1912; Edel and Ray 169).

Even as Wells privately conceded his stylistic limitations, publicly he began to defend the view that the novel should be an instrument for probing social problems. In "The Scope of the Novel," a lecture delivered to the *Times* Book Club in 1911, Wells argued that the English novel should be free from the "fierce pedantries" of form, "a discursive thing; . . . not a single interest but a woven tapestry of interests" ("SN" 134, 136).

In his essay "The Younger Generation" (1914), James implicitly rebuked Wells's claims for the novel, accusing such authors as Arnold Bennett, Joseph Conrad, and Compton Mackenzie, along with Wells, of supersaturating the novel with details while neglecting form. Bennett stands as a particular offender, who has merely quarried and gathered material, heaping it before the reader without a shape ("YG" 188). James goes on to praise Wells's mind as extraordinarily various and reflexive yet undisciplined: Novels such as *The New Machiavelli* and *Marriage* are "much more attestations of the presence of material than of an interest in the use of it" ("YG" 190).

Wells retorted by caricaturing James and cruelly parodying his style in *Boon*, the supposed late essays of the fictional critic George Boon. James

H. G. Wells, no date, George Grantham Bain Collection *(Library of Congress)*

is portrayed in this work as "one of the strongest, most abundant minds alive . . . [yet with] the smallest penetration" (Edel and Ray 245). Boon argues that in aiming for artistic unity, or "the picture effect," James denies the "great complexity of life" (246). Through Boon, Wells mocks James for verbosity and circumlocution, as well as for his supposed vacancy of ideas, accusing him of eviscerating life.

James was deeply offended by this portrait, writing that the loss of the two writer's "common meeting-ground" was "like the collapse of a bridge which made communication possible" (July 6, 1915; Edel and Ray 262). Wells apologized for the gracelessness of *Boon*, but there is no evidence of James accepting this apology before passing away the following year. Nonetheless, they continued jousting in correspondence, and Wells's critique prompted James to a much-quoted declaration of his credo: "It is art that *makes* life, makes interest, makes importance, . . . and I know of no substitute whatever for the force and beauty of its process" (July 10, 1915; Edel and Ray 267). Still going over the ground of their debate nearly two decades later in *Experiment in Autobiography* (1934), Wells concludes, "I had a queer feeling that we were both incompatibly right" (488).

Further Reading

Edel, Leon, and Gordon N. Ray, eds. *Henry James and H. G. Wells: A Record of their Friendship, Their Debate on the Art of Fiction, and Their Quarrel.* Urbana: University of Illinois Press, 1958.

Hammond, John. *A Preface to H. G. Wells.* Essex, England: Pearson Education Limited, 2001.

James, Henry. "The Younger Generation." *Times Literary Supplement* (April 2, 1914). In Edel and Ray, eds., *Henry James and H. G. Wells,* 178–215. Abbreviated as "YG."

Wells, H. G. *Experiment in Autobiography: Discoveries and Conclusions of a Very Ordinary Brain.* New York: Macmillan, 1934.

———. "The Scope of the Novel" (Later published as "The Contemporary Novel"). In Edel and Ray, eds., *Henry James and H. G. Wells,* 131–156. Abbreviated as "SN."

Carey Snyder, *Ohio University*

Wharton, Edith (Edith Newbold Jones Wharton) (1862–1937)

In 1921, Edith Wharton became the first woman to win the Pulitzer Prize for fiction, for *The Age of Innocence* (1920), and in 1927 she was the first woman to receive an honorary doctorate from Yale. The author of more than 40 books, including *The House of Mirth* (1905), *Ethan Frome* (1911), *The Reef* (1912), and *The Custom of the Country* (1913), she wrote in several languages (French, German, and Italian) and across literary genres, including poetry, short stories, travel writing, memoir, novels, and critical essays. In 1916, she received the recognition of Chevalier of the Legion of Honour in France for her work during WORLD WAR I to raise money for homeless children with her literary compilation *The Book of the Homeless* (1916). After reading Henry James's *The PORTRAIT OF A LADY* (1881), Wharton sought the writer's friendship, and their close relationship had a profound effect on her writing career and personal life.

Born on January 24, 1862, in NEW YORK to George Frederick and Lucretia Rhinelander Jones, Edith entered the world of upper-crust lineage and old money about which she wrote. With a nervous sensibility and mild social anxiety from an early age, Wharton found in reading and writing an escape from the pressures of familial expectation, especially those of her domineering mother. Her father's library was a refuge. The year her father died, 1882, Wharton also experienced a serious romantic disappointment when her engagement to Harry Stevens abruptly ended after his mother objected to the marriage. A year later, a summer flirtation with Walter Berry waned. Although Berry, a cosmopolitan lawyer and diplomat, became a lifelong friend, Wharton felt even more disillusioned. In 1885, Wharton married her brother's friend Edward "Teddy" Wharton, whose high position in society secured the match despite the lack of any true affection between them. Wharton's marriage to Teddy allowed her freedom from the oppressive personality of her mother and gained for Wharton a measure of independence. However, Teddy suffered from mental instability and behaved erratically. They divorced in 1913.

The friendship between Wharton and James gained solid footing in 1903. James became a mentor to Wharton, despite their differences in literary style and Wharton's higher degree of popularity. A key moment in their friendship took place at Wharton's home, The Mount, in Lenox, Massachusetts, in October 1904, when James read aloud from Whitman's *Leaves of Grass*, a reading that revealed to Wharton a shared passion for the great American poet. James played a major role in the formation of her mature identity as a writer. James's complexity intrigued Wharton—his ability to fashion a publicly performed self, which concealed his private life of nuanced SEXUALITY and affection among friends.

When James sent the younger journalist MORTON FULLERTON to Wharton's door in 1907, he facilitated a relationship that forever changed her and acted as a catalyst for the development of a unique literary voice. Wharton and Fullerton carried on an affair that began in 1908 and ended in 1910. Depending upon James for courage and support, Wharton drew upon their shared passion for Whitman to describe her feelings for Fullerton, using Whitman's concept of "comradeship" to describe the kind of relationship she wanted. James's presence during pivotal meetings of the couple allowed Wharton to push through her fears and consummate her affair with Fullerton: "This was her first extramarital affair, and she confided to her journal that she often felt shy and awkward when left alone with Fullerton, but that 'with our dear H.J. I felt at my ease'" (qtd. in Novick 446).

Through James, Wharton met and then further drew together a close-knit circle of male friends who were largely bisexual, homosexual, or "queer" (in the sense that they never married and refused to formulate their desire in terms of heterosexuality). (See MASCULINITY.) The "Qu'acre Group"—named after HOWARD STURGIS's home Queen's Acre, in Windsor, England, where the set often met—provided their "Firebird" (as Wharton was lovingly called) with safety for self-discovery. When they gathered, Wharton and James shared a keen sense of humor, and their letters to each other were playfully affectionate and teasing.

Edith Wharton, no date *(Library of Congress)*

For Wharton, James became a father figure, a confidante, a mentor, and a dear friend whom she nurtured; his death in 1916 profoundly saddened her. In her memoir *A Backward Glance* (1934) she averred: "I cannot think of myself apart from the influence of the two or three greatest friendships of my life, and any account of my own growth must be that of their stimulating and enlightening influence" (169). James was one of her greatest friends.

Further Reading

Erlich, Gloria. *The Sexual Education of Edith Wharton*. Berkeley: University of California Press, 1992.

Goodman, Susan. *Edith Wharton's Inner Circle*. Austin: University of Texas Press, 1994.

Lee, Hermione. *Edith Wharton*. London: Chatto & Windus, 2007.

Lewis, R. W. B. *Edith Wharton: A Biography*. New York: Harper, 1975.

Lewis, R. W. B., and Nancy Lewis, eds. *The Letters of Edith Wharton.* New York: Collier, 1988.

Novick, Sheldon. *Henry James: The Mature Master.* New York: Random House, 2007.

Sharon Kehl Califano,
University of New Hampshire

Wilde, Oscar (1854–1900)   Wilde was a poet, essayist, fiction writer, playwright, editor, and public figure known best for his epigrammatic witticisms, his association with aestheticism (see AESTHETIC MOVEMENT), his outrageous flouting of social convention, and his 1895 conviction for "gross indecency," or homosexual acts, with other men.

During Wilde's 1882 speaking tour in the United States, Henry James was flattered by Wilde's remark to a reporter that "no living Englishman can be compared to Howells and James as novelists." James called on Wilde at his hotel to thank him. According to Wilde's principal biographer, Richard Ellmann, the visit was less than successful. James's polite remark about his own nostalgia for LONDON was met by Wilde's blithe retort: "Really? You care for places? The world is my home." Wilde's apparent sense of cosmopolitan superiority and rudeness left James "raging." Upon his return from the hotel, he conceded that his friend Mrs. Henry Adams, who disdained Wilde, was right: He was a "fatuous fool, tenth-rate cad," an "unclean beast," his sex suspiciously "undecided." According to Ellmann, "Wilde had no idea of the hostility he had aroused in James" (*Oscar Wilde* 170–179). James later sponsored Wilde's membership for the literary Savile Club yet distanced himself from him socially, referring to him in letters to friends as "the unspeakable one" (367). James expressed disgust at the treachery of the blackmailers and servants who had testified against Wilde in court, yet James refused to sign a petition urging the mitigation of Wilde's sentence to hard labor. His rationale was that the document would have no effect on the authorities and stand only as a statement of loyalty to Wilde by his friends; nevertheless, he thought the sentencing of Wilde too severe (Ellmann, *Oscar Wilde* 493). James's apparent repugnance would seem to be based, at least in part, in his envy of Wilde's popularity, as well as his conflicted feelings about what was becoming defined as "homosexuality" (see SEXUALITY).

There is evidence, however, that Wilde had an effect on James. Although other models for the character Gabriel Nash in James's 1890 *The TRAGIC MUSE* have been suggested—Leon Edel names James McNeill Whistler and the Count Robert de Montesquiou (Edel 255)—Wilde, as Eric Haralson argues, is commonly acknowledged as the model (Haralson 191). For instance, the opening encounter between Nash, the flamboyant, sexually ambiguous aesthete, and the novel's protagonist, the artistic yet bourgeois Nick Dormer, distinctly echoes James and Wilde's first private meeting: "[O]ur paths in life are so different," Nash tells Nick. "Different, yes, but not so different as that," rejoins Nick. "Don't we both live in London, after all, and in the nineteenth century?" "Ah my dear Dormer," Nash demurs. "I don't live in the nine-

Oscar Wilde, 1882 *(Library of Congress)*

teenth century." "Not in London either?" "Yes—
when I'm not at Samarcand!" (*The Tragic Muse*
13). Nick is drawn to the Wildean figure of Nash.
"You're not in London? One can't meet you there?"
Nick asks. "I rove, I drift, I float," his companion
replies. "I should like to get hold of you," Nick
persists, and his ardor is returned. *The Tragic Muse*
could well be read as James's exploration of Wilde
and the aesthetic and sexual freedom for which he
stood. Richard Ellmann has ventured, additionally,
that following Wilde's trials James wrote a series of
homosexually suggestive works that "took advantage of the freedom Wilde had won for art even
while losing his own freedom," notably the 1897
"The TURN OF THE SCREW," with its undertones of
lesbian desire and pedophilia (Ellmann, *A Long the
Riverrun* 10).

Two coincidental points of contact between
James and Wilde occurred in 1895 on the London stage. James's ponderous religious play, *Guy
Domville*, premiered at the St. James Theatre during the smash hit run of Wilde's buoyant comedy
An Ideal Husband at the Haymarket. Too nervous
to sit through his own show, James escaped to
Wilde's. Although he had long disparaged Wilde's
comedies—calling one, for instance, "infantine"
(Ellmann, *Oscar Wilde* 365)—Wilde's audience
adored the play. Returning to the St. James at the
end of his premiere, James stepped out to take a
curtain call only to be booed and jeered. When
actor-manager George Alexander closed *Guy Domville* ahead of schedule, Wilde hastily suggested to
him what became *The Importance of Being Earnest*.
Written in three weeks, it proved Wilde's greatest
success. *Earnest* was shut down some weeks later
when Wilde's trials began. Yet James was severely
affected by this blow. Although James privately
criticized Wilde's cruel prosecution, conviction,
and imprisonment, he remained distanced from his
case and would always carry resentment at the
sense of having been bested by him.

Further Reading

Edel, Leon. *Henry James: 1882–95*. New York: H.
Wolf, 1962.
Ellmann, Richard. *A Long the Riverrun*. New York:
Knopf, 1989.

————. *Oscar Wilde*. New York: Vintage, 1998.
Haralson, Eric. *Henry James and Queer Modernity*.
Cambridge: Cambridge University Press, 2003.
James, Henry. *The Tragic Muse*. 1890. Reprint, Lon-
don: Penguin, 1995.

S. I. Salamensky,
University of California, Los Angeles

women's issues   Changes in women's rights were
manifold over the course of Henry James's career,
ranging from improvements in education, employment, and marital legislation to the emergence of
the suffrage campaign. Yet, although the trend was
progressive, the limiting factors were many, and
James's work conveys a consistent ambivalence
surrounding the role of women. Many of his novels and stories take as their subjects the plight of
women constrained or confined by both legislation
and social expectation.

James's friendship and correspondence with a
number of highly educated and cultured women—
among them prominent authors such as Lucy Clifford and EDITH WHARTON—endowed him with a
detailed knowledge and awareness of contemporary
women's issues. He maintained a long and close
friendship with American novelist CONSTANCE FEN-
IMORE WOOLSON, and he suffered prolonged shock
and grief after her suicide in 1894. Woolson's tale
"Miss Grief" (1880) encapsulated the frustrations
she felt as a female artist subjected to masculine
condescension. Another close friend and correspondent was Isabella Stewart Gardner, an educated and independently wealthy art collector of
considerable influence. James's sister, ALICE JAMES,
was also to have a substantial influence upon his
work, in particular his focus upon feminine psychology, part of the emergent discipline of psychology in
which his brother WILLIAM JAMES was a pioneering
author. Alice did not receive the education granted
to her brothers, and she developed a series of psychological and physical problems with which she
suffered throughout her life, eventually being diagnosed with "female hysteria." This was commonly
diagnosed condition among 19th-century women,
which was arguably alluded to in James's tale "The
TURN OF THE SCREW" (1898).

James's transatlantic lifestyle exposed him to both English and American issues and events in the women's movement. This was a period in which much legal discrimination remained, and strict social restrictions were also imposed upon women. Decency and decorum were perceived as the most important aspects of feminine behavior, and the conflict inherent in trying to fulfil these requirements while also striving for greater independence was to become a central theme of much of James's fiction. The figure of the New Woman emerged in the early 1880s and reached a pinnacle of notoriety at the turn of the last century, when James was approaching the peak of his career. The New Woman became an icon of fin-de-siècle gender transformation, symbolizing an increase in women's education and independence and embodying many of the advances that culminated in the suffrage movement. With her readily identifiable iconography of spectacles, reading matter, bicycle, and "rational dress," the New Woman was an object of admiration for women's rights advocates and of derision for opponents of social change.

A number of James's novels explore the subject of unhappy MARRIAGE and its effect upon the modern female protagonist, whose desires and expectations fall outside the confines of 19th-century convention. The PORTRAIT OF A LADY (1881) details the fate of Isabel Archer, a young American woman who, after inheriting a fortune, marries the cold, elitist and manipulative American art collector Gilbert Osmond. The novel explores the theme of the feminine desire for freedom, the apparent granting of that freedom (through inheritance), and the painful and protracted loss of it (as Isabel enables, and then becomes a part of, Osmond's collection). The novel also addresses women's education (and lack of it), which was one of the central concerns of the early women's movement. The mid- to late 19th and early 20th centuries saw the emergence of a number of institutions to address the problem, including Queen's College in London, which was established for the education of women in 1848, followed by Girton College at Cambridge in 1869, and Newnham College, also at Cambridge, in 1871. Yet education remained inaccessible to many women whose families were either disinclined to educate their daughters or unable to afford the usually exorbitant fees required to do so. Isabel is not formally educated, and this heightens her vulnerability to the urbane Osmond. By contrast, her friend Henrietta Stackpole, who is an educated journalist and New Woman, ultimately makes a happy marriage in which her independence and intellectual integrity are not compromised. The character is thought to be based upon Kate Field, a prominent feminist journalist of the 1860s and 1870s.

The BOSTONIANS (1886) provided James's most direct exploration of the suffrage movement, which was without question the most highly publicized issue for women during James's lifetime. In 1869, Susan B. Anthony and Elizabeth Cady Stanton formed the National Woman Suffrage Association, the primary goal of which was to acquire voting rights for women by means of a congressional amendment to the Constitution. Similar movements occurred in Britain, led and publicized by such influential figures as moderate leader Millicent Fawcett and the more militant Pankhurst sisters. In 1869, unmarried British women householders were granted the right to vote in local elections, and in the same year, certain American states also extended voting rights to women. In 1894, the United Kingdom expanded women's voting rights such that married women could vote in local but not national elections. The Bostonians, which is set during a crucial phase of these changes in the post–CIVIL WAR United States, takes as its central protagonists a prominent member of the movement named Olive Chancellor and her charismatic protégée, Verena Tarrant, for whom, it is implied, Olive develops a lesbian attachment. The novel focuses upon the subsequent contest between Olive and her politically conservative cousin, Basil Ransom, to win the affection and allegiance of Verena. The Bostonians has been noted for its highly ambivalent treatment of fin-de-siècle feminism, ultimately concluding with Verena's abandonment of both Olive and her feminist principles yet refusing to idealize or romanticize the marriage that replaces them.

The SPOILS OF POYNTON (1897) addressed the issue of women's property rights, and in particular the fate of the widow under the custom of primogeniture, in which all inheritance was entailed through the male line. This was a period in which Victorian (see VICTORIANISM) property law, to which James referred as "the ugly English custom," frequently denied women "with a knowledge and adoration of artistic beauty, the tastes, the habits of a collector" the right to their own possessions (CN 79). In the United States in 1852, the issue of women's property rights had been presented to the Vermont Senate by Clara Howard Nichols and became a major issue for the suffragists. In England in 1870, the first Married Women's Property Act was passed and was revised in 1882. Under the terms of this act, married women had the same rights over their property as unmarried women, thereby allowing a married woman to retain ownership of property that she might have earned or inherited prior to or during marriage. At the time that The Spoils of Poynton was written, however, there existed no legal protection for widows, and it is the scheming and misery invoked by this lack of protection that governs the novel's narrative. Here James communicates the conflict inherent in a society of increasingly independent and aesthetically conscious women constrained by an outmoded legal system.

James also demonstrated a consistent interest in the theme of female respectability and romantic etiquette. From his early novella "DAISY MILLER: A STUDY" (1878), which addressed the dangers of flirtation to a woman's reputation, to The WINGS OF THE DOVE (1902), which traced the plotting of a young woman to acquire a fortune that would allow her to marry her lover, to his famous late novel The GOLDEN BOWL (1904), which examined marital infidelity, James detailed the manifold perils and pitfalls into which women might slip in their pursuit of romantic love. The loss of respectability and social status is as central to these women's downfall as any emotional trauma suffered; thus James effectively emphasizes the vulnerability of fin-de-siècle women to both legal and social/domestic forms of discrimination.

James died in 1916, two years before British women were granted the vote and four years before American women would receive the same right. He is identifiable neither as an advocate nor as an opponent of women's rights, although his awareness of the multifaceted issues surrounding the battle for these rights is unquestionable, and his writings contain some of the most complex and varied examples of late 19th- and early 20th-century feminine characterization.

Further Reading

James, Henry. The Complete Notebooks of Henry James. Edited by Leon Edel and Lyall H. Powers. New York: Oxford University Press, 1987. Abbreviated as CN.

Scharnhorst, Gary. Kate Field: The Many Loves of a Nineteenth-Century American Journalist. New York: Syracuse University Press, 2008.

Angela Hesson, University of Melbourne

Woolson, Constance Fenimore (1840–1894) Constance Fenimore Woolson was the great grandniece of the American novelist James Fenimore Cooper. An important realist (see ROMANCE/REALISM/NATURALISM) writer, Woolson published four novels, 57 short stories, poems, and travel essays. She met Henry James in April 1880 while living in Europe, and they maintained a literary acquaintance for 14 years (Boyd 191).

Born in New Hampshire in 1840, Woolson grew up in Ohio. She visited numerous states, including New York, Michigan, the Carolinas, Georgia, Kentucky, Pennsylvania, Tennessee, and Virginia. A pioneer of the "local color" or regionalist movement of the 1870s with stories such as "King David" and "Castle Nowhere," Woolson contributed to her era's understanding of the American South, where she lived after the CIVIL WAR, as well as the Midwest Great Lakes region and Europe. Woolson's regional literature "let readers experience how industrialization and development were changing the natural landscape" (Brehm and Dean xvii). In November 1879, Woolson moved to Europe. She lived primarily in FLORENCE, Italy, as well as in England, France, SWITZERLAND, Austria, Germany, and Egypt.

Woolson is renowned for her stories about women artists and writers. One of her most famous works, the 1880 story "Miss Grief," describes the frustrations of an impoverished woman writer whose work is apparently brilliant but who refuses to revise. The prideful narrator of the story, a successful yet average writer, gives her the nickname "Miss Grief," although her real name is Aaronna Moncrief. Ultimately, she dies without seeing any work published. Woolson wrote this story before she met James in person, but she already knew about him through his publications (Boyd 193). James probably picked up the metaphor "the figure in the carpet," which he used to title a story of his own after the death of Woolson, directly from this story (Brehm 8).

Woolson's death in January 1894 was caused by a fall from the window of a rented residence in Venice, Italy. Most scholars believe that her death was a suicide and that she ended her life due to a combination of factors such as failing physical health, near-deafness, depression, and other medical problems. There is no indication that writer's block was a reason since Woolson had a forthcoming novel and was already planning her next book (Moore 37). Although Leon Edel perpetuated a notion that Woolson killed herself due to unrequited love for James, there is no factual basis for this speculation.

With a biography of Woolson in 1989, Cheryl Torsney corrected the view of the relationship between James and Woolson and analyzed their literary friendship. This companionship was not romantic in character. Woolson, a self-described "loner," never married or had children (Boyd 204 n. 7). James was among the realist writers who influenced Woolson, and she affected him in return. Woolson was already a well-established writer when she met James, and the two published in several of the same magazines (Coulson 83). The relationship between James and Woolson has recently been reexamined in Lyndall Gordon's 1998 study, *A Private Life of Henry James: Two Women and His Art*, which suggests that James both exploited and memorialized Woolson and her image in his literature.

Although James probably burned many of Woolson's private letters and disposed of some personal effects immediately following her death, four remaining letters she wrote to him indicate how much Woolson admired James and his writing (Coulson 91). Anne Boyd reads this correspondence as showing "a striking mixture of almost groveling appreciation and envious resentment" (203 n. 3). James took Woolson's responses to his novels seriously but did not always answer her questions about literature (Boyd 202). Woolson had published two anonymous reviews of *The Europeans* (1878) for the *Atlantic* in 1879, praising him as an author for "the cultivated minority," and she felt herself to be among this elite group (Boyd 197). In a private letter to James in 1883, Woolson said of his writings: "They voice for me—as nothing else ever has—my own feelings; those that are so deep—so a part of me, that I cannot express them, and do not try to . . . they are my true country, my real home." In 1884, James remarked in a letter to William Dean Howells that he took the time to read only two contemporary writers in the English language, Howells and Woolson (Coulson 84).

James's essay "Miss Woolson," first published in the prestigious journal *Harper's Weekly* on February 12, 1887, is an important work of literary criticism about Woolson. The essay praises examples of Woolson's characterization and plotting, singling out the novel *East Angels* as particularly strong (181–182, 189). But in examining Woolson as a woman author, not simply as a writer, James characterizes her work as limited by feminine tact and discretion. Lyndall Gordon interprets James's essay as carrying "an armoury of stings in its velvet glove" (213). The essay does seem patronizing or arch at moments, such as when he names her first two collections of short stories and admits, "I may not profess an acquaintance with the former of these volumes, but the latter is full of interesting artistic work" (179).

Rather than reading James and Woolson as competitors, it is more useful to see them as complements. They addressed some of the same topics, including artistic integrity, the writer's life, American expatriates in Europe, and clashes among different cultures. Like James with his intellectually complex narratives, Woolson included subtexts that hid subversive meanings in her stories, although she did it to retain her readership and to make a living as a writer (Brehm and Dean xvii).

As Woolson suggests in her story "Miss Grief," she sought recognition as a writer, not as a woman. Her works have merit and interest for 21st-century readers. The appreciative reader of James would enjoy reading the literature of Constance Fenimore Woolson.

Further Reading

Boyd, Anne. "Anticipating James, Anticipating Grief." In Brehm, *Constance Fenimore Woolson's Nineteenth Century: Essays,* 191–206.

Brehm, Victoria. Introduction to *Constance Fenimore Woolson's Nineteenth Century: Essays,* Edited by Victoria Brehm, 7–17. Detroit, Mich.: Wayne State University Press, 2001.

Brehm, Victoria, and Sharon Dean. Introduction to *Constance Fenimore Woolson: Selected Stories and Travel Narratives,* edited by Victoria Brehm and Sharon Dean, xv–xxvi. Knoxville: University of Tennessee Press, 2004.

Coulson, Victoria. "Teacups and Love Letters: Constance Fenimore Woolson and Henry James." *Henry James Review* 26, no. 1 (2005): 82–98.

Dean, Sharon, and Gary Woolson. "Chronology of Constance Fenimore Woolson's Life." In Brehm, *Constance Fenimore Woolson's Nineteenth Century: Essays,* 241–243.

Gordon, Lyndall. *A Private Life of Henry James: Two Women and His Art.* New York: Norton, 1998.

James, Henry. "Miss Woolson." In *Partial Portraits.* 1888. Reprint. Westport, Conn.: Greenwood, 1970, 177–192.

Moore, Rayburn. *Constance Fenimore Woolson.* New York: Twayne, 1963.

Torsney, Cheryl. *Constance Fenimore Woolson: The Grief of Artistry.* Athens: University of Georgia Press, 1989.

Woolson, Constance Fenimore. Letter to James, May 7, 1883. *The Letters of Henry James,* vol. 3. Edited by Leon Edel, 550–551. Cambridge, Mass.: Harvard University Press, 1984.

Amy Cummins, *Fort Hays State University*

World War I (1914–1918)

In a March 22, 1915, letter to his house servant and valet Bugess Noakes, who was serving with the British Army in France, James wrote: "We go on as quietly here as all our public anxiety and suspense allow; and it helps us greatly that we believe in you all at the Front so thoroughly and are doing all we can, very great things in fact, to make you believe in *us*" (Edel 4: 739).

On June 28, 1914, in Sarajevo, a Serbian nationalist assassinated the archduke Franz Ferdinand, heir to the Austro-Hungarian throne, in what proved a misguided attempt to reunite Bosnia-Herzegovina and Serbia. The ensuing confrontation escalated to the point of Austria-Hungary declaring war on Serbia by the end of July. The standing alliances of the Triple Entente (Britain, France, Russia) and Triple Alliance (Austria-Hungary, Germany, Italy) resulted in warfront standoff on eastern and western fronts as Russia backed Serbia, and German backed Austria-Hungary. Anticipating French participation and hoping to prevent simultaneous fighting on two fronts, Germany attacked Belgium to invade France. (Italy backed out of the Triple Alliance and realigned itself against Austria-Hungary.) For the next four years, battles raged throughout the world, in Africa, Europe, India, and the Ottoman Empire.

In the run-up to the Great War, James hoped that England and the United States could remain above the potentially bloody fray on the Continent. However, when Germany invaded the neutral Belgium and England declared war on August 4, 1914, James condemned the German aggression and passionately supported the British war effort. As trench warfare set in and dragged on, he became impatient and even disgusted with President Woodrow Wilson's reluctance to enter the war, even after German submarine attacks in 1915 on passenger steamers resulted in the sinking of the *Lusitania,* claiming the lives of more than 100 Americans.

James recalled his initial reactions to the war in the posthumous essay "Within the Rim" (*Fortnightly Review* 1917), written in response to a request to aid the Arts Fund by the British prime minister Asquith's precocious teenage daughter, Elizabeth. In the essay, James strives to make sense of the initial stages of the war, recalling the dreadful and portentous U.S. CIVIL WAR 54 years before. He notes that previous continental wars, particularly the Franco-Prussian War of 1870, had left England both insulated from the brutality of ground warfare and yet very aware of the threat represented in the Prussian conquest of France. From his 1914 perspective in Chelsea, James broods over the looming threat of violence and the "unprecedented" (23) scale of this war's violence—"armaments unknown to human experience looming all the while larger and larger" (23).

From Rye (see LAMB HOUSE) and in LONDON, James worked with thousands of Belgian refugees. He held a morale-boosting social twice a week in Chelsea and visited St. Bartholomew's hospital, where many Belgian wounded recuperated in exile (Kaplan 555). He recalls these visits, reminiscent of poet Walt Whitman's tending of the wounded during the American Civil War, in the essay "Refugees in Chelsea" (*Times Literary Supplement* 1916):

> The strong young man (no young men are familiarly stronger) mutilated, amputated, dismembered in penalty for their defence of their soil against the horde, and now engaged at Crosby Hall in the making of handloom socks, to whom I pay an occasional visit—much more for my own cheer, I apprehend, than for theirs—express so in their honest concentration under difficulties the actual and general value of their people that just to be in their presence is a blest renewal of faith. (52–53)

As the war escalated, James became the honorary president of the American Volunteer Motor-Ambulance Corps, founded by archeologist Richard Norton, the son of Charles Eliot Norton. James promoted the endeavor in the pamphlet "The American Volunteer Motor-Ambulance Corps in France: A Letter to the Editor of an American Journal," signed and dated 25 November 1914, LONDON. The corps, which included recent graduates from Harvard University, worked with the British Red Cross, the St. John Ambulance Corps, and the French Army to remove tens of thousands of wounded from the battlefields, expediting their relay from the triage units near the warfront to the life-sustaining facilities at the base hospitals. James imagines the "rude field hospital," improvised from a "poor schoolhouse of a village," where the "man-

gled and lacerated" are first taken "on stretchers or on any rough handcart or trundled barrow"; once there, "*villageoises*, bereft of their men, full of the bravest instinctive alertness, not wincing at the sights of horror fit to try even trained sensibilities, handling shattered remnants of humanity with an art as extemporized as the refuge itself, and having each precarious charge ready of the expert transfer by the time the car has hurried up" (69–70). James appreciates the relationships of the corps with the villagers as equally important in the grim task of finding and identifying the dead. He concludes by encouraging his pamphlet's readers to donate money in order to support the volunteers who had been funding their lifesaving endeavors.

In a March 21, 1915, *New York Times* interview by Preston Lockwood, James continued to promote the corps. Considering the war's "enormous facts of destruction" he stated, "One finds it in the midst of all this hard to apply one's words as to endure one's thoughts." He then continued:

> The war has used up words; they have weakened, they have deteriorated like motor car tires; they have, like millions of other things, been more overstrained and knocked about and voided of the happy semblance during the last six months than all the long ages before, and we are now confronted with a deprecation of all our terms, or, otherwise speaking, with a loss of expression through increase of limpness, that may well make us wonder what ghosts will be left to walk. (145)

When Lockwood followed up with a question about the author's latest literary efforts, James responded by providing an address to which he urged the public to send checks in support of the corps.

Motivated in part by his wartime advocacy of relief projects, James applied for British citizenship in the summer of 1915. On his application, four sponsors attested to his competence in the English language, including his longtime friend EDMUND GOSSE, his literary agent James Pinker, Prime Minister Herbert Henry Asquith, and the historian and editor George Prothero. James did not live to see the war's end. In his declining invalid state of December 1915, he must have worried for his sister-in-law Alice's safety as she braved a transatlantic crossing to take care of him in his final weeks. After James's death, the war raged for nearly two more years. When the United States entered the war in 1917, Norton's Volunteer Motor-Ambulance Corps became part of the U.S. Army Ambulance Corps. An armistice ended fighting on the western front on November 11, 1918. Twenty million civilians and soldiers had been killed, and 20 million more wounded. Writers such as E. E. Cummings, Ernest Hemingway, Somerset Maugham, John Dos Passos, and Gertrude Stein drove ambulances or other aid vehicles during the Great War.

Further Reading

James, Henry. "Henry James's First Interview." In *Henry James on Culture: Collected Essays on Politics and the American Social Scene,* edited by Pierre A. Walker, 138–145. Lincoln: University of Nebraska Press, 1999.

———. *Letters.* Volume 4, 1895–1916. Edited by Leon Edel. Cambridge, Mass.: Harvard University Press, 1984.

———. *Within the Rim and Other Essays 1914–15.* London: W. Collins, 1918.

Kaplan, Fred. *Henry James, The Imagination of Genius: A Biography.* New York: William Morrow, 1992.

Kendall Johnson, *Swarthmore College*

PART IV

Appendices

CHRONOLOGICAL BIBLIOGRAPHY OF WORKS BY HENRY JAMES

The Library of America has published the most complete series of the writings by Henry James, including:

Collected Travel Writings: The Continent. Notes by Richard Howard. New York: Library of America, 1993.

Collected Travel Writings: Great Britain and America: English Hours, The American Scene, Other Travels. Notes by Richard Howard. New York: Library of America, 1993.

Complete Short Stories: 1864–1874. Notes by Jean Strouse. New York: Library of America, 1999.

Complete Short Stories: 1874–1884. Notes by William L. Vance. New York: Library of America, 1999.

Complete Short Stories: 1884–1891. Notes by Edward Said. New York: Library of America, 1999.

Complete Short Stories: 1892–1898. Notes by David Bromwich and John Hollander. New York: Library of America, 1996.

Complete Short Stories: 1898–1910. Notes by Denis Donoghue. New York: Library of America, 1996.

Literary Criticism: Essays on Literature, American Writers, English Writers. Notes and selections by Leon Edel. New York: Library of America, 1984

Literary Criticism: French Writers, Other European Writers, The Prefaces to the New York Edition. Notes and selections by Leon Edel. New York: Library of America, 1984.

Novels: 1871–1880. Notes and selections by William T. Stafford. New York: Library of America, 1983.

Novels: 1881–1886. Notes and selections by William T. Stafford. New York: Library of America, 1985.

Novels: 1886–1890. Notes and selections by Daniel Mark Fogel. New York: Library of America, 1989.

Novels: 1896–1899. Notes and selections by Myra Jehlen. New York: Library of America, 2003.

Novels: 1901–1902. Notes and selections by Leo Bersani. New York: Library of America, 2006.

Novels

1870s

Watch and Ward. Houghton, Osgood and Company: Boston, 1878. First published in *The Atlantic Monthly* (August–December 1871). Not included in the New York Edition.

Roderick Hudson. Boston: J. R. Osgood, 1875. First published in the *Atlantic Monthly* (January–December 1875). Included as Volume 1 of the New York Edition in 1907.

The American. Boston: J. R. Osgood, 1877. First published in the *Atlantic Monthly* (June 1876–May 1877). Included as Volume 2 of the New York Edition in 1907.

The Europeans. London: Macmillan and Co., 1878; Boston: Houghton, Osgood and Company, 1878. First published in the *Atlantic Monthly* (July–October 1878). Not included in the New York Edition.

Confidence. London: Chatto & Windus, 1879; Boston: Houghton, Osgood and Company, 1880. First published in *Scribner's* (August 1879–January 1880). Not included in the New York Edition.

1880s

Washington Square. New York: Harper & Brothers, 1880; London: Macmillan & Co., 1881. First published in *Cornhill Magazine* (June–November 1880). Not included in the New York Edition.

The Portrait of a Lady. Boston: Houghton, Mifflin and Company, 1881; London: Macmillan & Co., 1881. First appeared in *Macmillan's Magazine* (October 1880–November 1881) and the *Atlantic Monthly* (November–December 1881). Included as Volumes 3 and 4 of the New York Edition in 1908.

The Bostonians. London: Macmillan & Co., 1886; New York: Macmillan & Co., 1886. First published in the *Century Magazine* (February 1885–February 1886). Not included in the New York Edition.

Princess Casamassima. London: Macmillan & Co., 1886. First published in the *Atlantic Monthly* (September 1885–October 1886). Included as Volumes 5 and 6 of the New York Edition in 1908.

The Reverberator. London: Macmillan & Co., 1888. First published in *Macmillan's Magazine* (February–July 1888). Included in Volume 13 of the New York Edition in 1908.

1890s

The Tragic Muse. Boston: Houghton, Mifflin, 1890; London: Macmillan, 1890. First published in the *Atlantic Monthly* (January 1889–May 1890). Included as Volumes 7 and 8 of the New York Edition in 1908.

The Other House. London: William Heinemann, 1896. Not included in the New York Edition.

The Spoils of Poynton. London: William Heinemann, 1897; Boston: Houghton and Mifflin, 1897. First published as "The Old Things" in the *Atlantic Monthly* (April to October 1896). Included in Volume 10 of the New York Edition in 1908.

What Maisie Knew. Chicago: Herbert Stone, 1897; London: William Heinemann, 1897. First published in *The Chapbook* (January–August 1897) and *The New Review* (February–September 1897). Included in Volume 11 of the New York Edition in 1908.

The Awkward Age. London: William Heinemann, 1899; New York: Harpers Brothers Publishers, 1899. First published in *Harper's Weekly* (October 1898–January 1899). Included as Volume 9 of the New York Edition in 1908.

1900s

The Sacred Fount. New York: Charles Scribner's and Sons, 1901; London: Methuen, 1901. Not included in the New York Edition.

The Wings of the Dove. London: Archibald Constable & Co., 1902; New York: Charles Scribner's, 1902. Included as Volumes 19 and 20 of the New York Edition in 1909.

The Ambassadors. London: Methuen, 1903; New York: Harper's, 1903. First published in the *North American Review* (January–December 1903). Included as Volumes 21 and 22 of the New York Edition in 1909.

The Golden Bowl. New York: Charles Scribner's and Sons, 1904. Included as Volumes 23 and 24 of the New York Edition in 1909.

The Outcry. London: Methuen, 1911; New York: Charles Scribner's and Sons, 1911. Not included in the New York Edition.

The Ivory Tower (unfinished). New York: Charles Scribner's and Sons, 1917. Included posthumously as Volume 25 of the New York Edition in 1917.

A Sense of the Past (unfinished). New York: Charles Scribner's and Sons, 1917. Included posthumously as Volume 26 of the New York Edition in 1917.

Short Stories

1860s

"A Tragedy of Error." *Continental Monthly* (February 1964).

"The Story of a Year." *Atlantic Monthly* (March 1865).

"A Landscape Painter." *Atlantic Monthly* (February 1866). Collected in *Stories Revived.*

"A Day of Days." *Galaxy* (June 15, 1866). Collected in *Stories Revived.*

"My Friend Bingham." *Atlantic Monthly* (March 1867).

"Poor Richard." *Atlantic Monthly* (June 1867 and July–August 1867). Collected in *Stories Revived.*

"The Story of a Masterpiece." *Galaxy* (January–February 1868).

"The Romance of Certain Old Clothes." *Atlantic Monthly* (February 1868). Collected in *A Passionate Pilgrim* and collected in *Stories Revived.*

"A Most Extraordinary Case." *Atlantic Monthly* (April 1868). Collected in *Stories Revived.*

"A Problem." *Galaxy* (June 1868).

"De Grey: A Romance." *Atlantic Monthly* (July 1868).

"Osborne's Revenge." *Galaxy* (July 1869).

"A Light Man." *Galaxy* (July 1869). Collected in *Stories Revived.*

"Gabrielle de Bergerac." *Atlantic Monthly* (July–September 1869).

1870s

"Traveling Companions." *Atlantic Monthly* (November–December 1870).

"A Passionate Pilgrim." *Atlantic Monthly* (March–April 1871). Collected in *A Passionate Pilgrim* and collected in *Stories Revived.*

"At Isella." *Galaxy* (August 1871).

"Master Eustace." *Galaxy* (November 1871). Collected in *Stories Revived.*

"Guest's Confession." *Atlantic Monthly* (October–November 1872).

"The Madonna of the Future." *Atlantic Monthly* (March 1872). Collected in *A Passionate Pilgrim* and collected in *The Madonna of the Future and Other Tales.*

"The Sweetheart of M. Briseux." *Galaxy* (June 1873).

"The Last of the Valerii." *Atlantic Monthly* (January 1874). Collected in *A Passionate Pilgrim* and collected in *The Madonna of the Future and Other Tales.*

"Madame De Mauves." *Galaxy* (February–March 1874). Collected in *A Passionate Pilgrim* and collected in *The Madonna of the Future and Other Tales.*

"Adina." *Scribner's Monthly* (May–June 1874).

"Professor Fargo." *Galaxy* (August 1874).

"Eugene Pickering." *Atlantic Monthly* (October–November 1874). Collected in *A Passionate Pilgrim* and *Madonna of the Future and Other Tales.*

"Benvolio." *Galaxy* (August 1875). Collected in *Madonna of the Future and Other Tales.*

"Crawford's Consistency." *Scribner's Monthly* (August 1876).

"The Ghostly Rental." *Scribner's Monthly* (September 1876).

"Four Meetings." *Scribner's Monthly* (November 1877). Collected in *Daisy Miller: A Study, An International Episode, Four Meetings* and in *The Author of Beltraffio.* Included in the New York Edition.

"Rose-Agathe." *Lippincott's Magazine* (May 1878). Collected in *Stories Revived,* volume 2.

"Daisy Miller: A Study." *Cornhill Magazine* (June and July 1878). Collected in *Daisy Miller: A Study. An International Episode, Four Meetings.* Included in the New York Edition.

"Longstaff's Marriage." *Scribner's Monthly* (August 1878). Collected in *Madonna of the Future and Other Tales.*

"An International Episode." *Cornhill Magazine* (December 1878). Collected in *Daisy Miller: A Study, An International Episode, Four Meetings.* Included in the New York Edition.

"The Pension Beaurepas." *Atlantic Monthly* (April 1879). Collected in *Washington Square, The Pension Beaurepas, A Bundle of Letters* and in *The Siege of London, The Pension Beaurepas, and The Point of View.* Included in the New York Edition.

"The Diary of a Man of Fifty." *Harper's New Monthly Magazine* (July 1879) and *Macmillan's Magazine* (July 1879). Collected in *The Madonna of the Future and Other Tales* and in *The Diary of a Man of Fifty and A Bundle of Letters.*

"A Bundle of Letters." *Parisian* (December 18, 1879). Collected in *The Diary of a Man of Fifty* and in *Washington Square, The Pension Beaurepas, A Bundle of Letters.* Included in the New York Edition.

1880s

"The Point of View." *Century Magazine* (December 1882). Collected in *The Siege of London, The Pension Beaurepas, and The Point of View.* Included in the New York Edition.

"The Siege of London." *Century Magazine* (January–February 1883). Collected in *The Siege of London, The Pension Beaurepas, and The Point of View* and in *The Siege of London, Madame De Mauves.* Included in the New York Edition.

"The Impressions of a Cousin." *Century Magazine* (November–December 1883). Collected in *Tales of Three Cities.*

"Lady Barberini." *Century Magazine* (May–July 1884). Collected in both editions of *Tales of Three Cities.* Included in the New York Edition.

"Pandora." *New York Sun* (June 1 and 8, 1884). Collected in *The Author of Beltraffio* and in *Stories Revived.* Included in the New York Edition.

"The Author of 'Beltraffio.'" *English Illustrated Magazine* (June–July 1884). Collected in *The Author of Beltraffio* and *Stories Revived.* Included in the New York Edition.

"Georgina's Reasons." *New York Sun* (July 20 and 27, August 3, 1884). Collected in *The Author of Beltraffio* and in *Stories Revived.*

"A New England Winter." *Century Magazine* (August–September 1884). Collected in both editions of *Tales of Three Cities.*

"The Path of Duty." *English Illustrated Magazine* (December 1884). Collected in *The Author of Beltraffio* and in *Stories Revived.*

"Mrs. Temperly." *Harper's Weekly* (August 6, 13, and 20, 1887) as "Cousin Maria." Collected in *A London Life, The Patagonia, The Liar, Mrs. Temperly.*

"Louisa Pallant." *Harper's New Monthly* (February 1888). Collected in *The Aspern Papers, Louisa Pallant, The Modern Warning.* Included in the New York Edition.

"The Aspern Papers." *Atlantic Monthly* (March–May 1888). Collected in *The Aspern Papers, Louisa Pallant, The Modern Warning.* Included in the New York Edition.

"The Liar." *Century Magazine* (May–June 1888). Collected in *A London Life, The Patagonia, The Liar, Mrs. Temperly.* Included in the New York Edition.

"The Modern Warning." *Harper's New Monthly* (June 1888) as "Two Countries." Collected in *The Aspern Papers, Louisa Pallant, The Modern Warning.*

"A London Life." *Scribner's Magazine* (June, July–September 1888). Collected in *A London Life, The Patagonia, The Liar, Mrs. Temperly.* Included in the New York Edition.

"The Lesson of the Master." *Universal Review* (July–August 1888). Collected in *The Lesson of the Master.* Included in the New York Edition.

"The Patagonia." *English Illustrated Magazine* (August–September 1888). Collected in *A London Life, The Patagonia, The Liar, Mrs. Temperly.* Included in the New York Edition.

"The Solution." *New Review* (February 1889). Collected in *The Lesson of the Master.*

1890s

"The Pupil." *Longman's Magazine* (March–April 1891). Collected in *The Lesson of the Master.* Included in the New York Edition.

"Brooksmith." *Harper's Weekly* (May 2, 1891) and *Black and White* (May 2, 1891). Collected in *The Lesson of the Master.* Included in the New York Edition.

"The Marriages." *Atlantic Monthly* (August 1891). Collected in *The Lesson of the Master.* Included in the New York Edition.

"The Chaperon." *Atlantic Monthly* (November–December 1891). Collected in *The Real Thing and Other Tales.* Included in the New York Edition.

"Sir Edmund Orme." *Black and White* (November 25, 1891). Collected in *The Lesson of the Master.* Included in the New York Edition.

"Nona Vincent." *English Illustrated Magazine* (February–March 1892). Collected in *The Real Thing and Other Tales.*

"The Real Thing." *Black and White* (April 16, 1892). Collected in *The Real Thing and Other Tales.* Included in the New York Edition.

"The Private Life." *Atlantic Monthly* (April 1892). Collected in *The Private Life, The Wheel of Time, Lord Beaupré, The Visits, Collaboration, Owen Wingrave* and in *The Private Life, Lord Beaupré, The Visits.* Included in the New York Edition.

"Lord Beaupré." *Macmillan's Magazine* (April–June 1892). Collected in *The Private Life, The Wheel of Time, Lord Beaupré, The Visits, Collaboration, Owen Wingrave* and in *The Private Life, Lord Beaupré, The Visits.*

"The Visits." *Black and White* (May 28, 1892) as "The Visit." Collected in *The Private Life, The Wheel of Time, Lord Beaupré, The Visits, Collaboration, Owen Wingrave* and in *The Private Life, Lord Beaupré, The Visits.*

"Sir Dominick Ferrand." *Cosmopolitan Magazine* (July–August 1892) as "Jersey Villas." Collected in *The Real Thing and Other Tales.*

"Greville Fane." *Illustrated London News* (September 17 and 24, 1842). Collected in *The Real Thing and Other Tales.* Included in the New York Edition.

"Collaboration." *English Illustrated Magazine* (September 1892). Collected in *The Private Life, The Wheel of Time, Lord Beaupré, The Visits, Collaboration, Owen Wingrave* and in *The Wheel of Time, Collaboration, Owen Wingrave.*

"Owen Wingrave." *The Graphic, an Illustrated Weekly Newspaper* (November 28, 1892). Collected in *The Private Life, The Wheel of Time, Lord Beaupré, The Visits, Collaboration, Owen Wingrave* and in *The Wheel of Time, Collaboration, Owen Wingrave.* Included in the New York Edition.

"The Wheel of Time." *Cosmopolitan Magazine* (December 1892–January 1893). Collected in *The Private Life, The Wheel of Time, Lord Beaupré, The Visits, Collaboration, Owen Wingrave* and in *The Wheel of Time, Collaboration, Owen Wingrave.*

"The Middle Years." *Scribner's Magazine* (May 1893). Collected in *Terminations.* Included in the New York Edition.

"The Death of the Lion." *The Yellow Book* (April 1894). Collected in *Terminations.* Included in the New York Edition.

"The Coxon Fund." *The Yellow Book* (July 1894). Collected in *Terminations.* Included in the New York Edition.

"The Altar of the Dead." *Terminations.* London: William Heinemann, 1895; New York: Macmillan, 1895. Included in the New York Edition.

"The Next Time." *The Yellow Book* (July 1895). Collected in *Embarrassments.* Included in the New York Edition.

"Glasses." *Atlantic Monthly* (February 1896). Collected in *Embarrassments.*

"The Figure in the Carpet." *Cosmopolis* (January–February 1896). Collected in *Embarrassments.* Included in the New York Edition.

"The Way It Came." *Chapbook* (May 1, 1892) and *Chapman's Magazine of Fiction* (May 1896).

"The Turn of the Screw." *Collier's Weekly* (January 27–April 16, 1898). Collected in *The Two Magics.* Included in the New York Edition.

"Covering End." *The Two Magics.* London: William Heineman, 1898; New York: Macmillan, 1898.

"In the Cage." *In the Cage.* London: Duckworth & Co., 1898; Chicago: Herbert S. Stone & Co., 1898. Included in the New York Edition.

"John Delavoy." *Cosmopolis* (January–February 1898). Collected in *The Soft Side.*

"The Given Case." *Collier's Weekly* (December 31, 1898–January 7, 1899) and *Black and White* (March 11–18, 1899). Collected in *The Soft Side.*

"'Europe.'" *Scribner's Magazine* (June 1899). Collected in *The Soft Side.* Included in the New York Edition.

"The Great Condition." *The Anglo-Saxon Review* (June 1899). Collected in *The Soft Side.*

"The Real Right Thing." *Collier's Weekly* (December 16, 1899). Collected in *The Soft Side.* Included in the New York Edition.

"Paste." *Frank Leslie's Popular Monthly* (December 1899). Collected in *The Soft Side.* Included in the New York Edition.

1900s

"The Great Good Place." *Scribner's Magazine* (January 1900). Collected in *The Soft Side.*

"Maud Evelyn." *Atlantic Monthly* (April 1900). Collected in *The Soft Side.*

"Miss Gunton of Poughkeepsie." *Cornhill Magazine* (May 1900) and *Truth* (May–June 1900). Collected in *The Soft Side.* Included in the New York Edition.

"The Special Type." *Collier's Weekly* (June 16, 1900). Collected in *The Better Sort.*

"Broken Wings." *Century Magazine* (December 1900). Collected in *The Better Sort.* Included in the New York Edition.

"The Tree of Knowledge." *The Soft Side* (1900). Included in the New York Edition.

"The Abasement of the Northmores." *The Soft Side* (1900). Included in the New York Edition.

"The Third Person." *The Soft Side* (1900).

"The Faces." *Harper's Bazaar* (December 15, 1900); "The Two Faces." *Cornhill Magazine.* (June 1901). Collected in *The Better Sort.* Included in the New York Edition.

"Mrs. Medwin." *Punch* (August 28–September 18, 1901). Collected in *The Better Sort.* Included in the New York Edition.

"The Beldonald Holbein." *Harper's New Monthly Magazine* (October 1901). Collected in *The Better Sort*. Included in the New York Edition.

"The Story in It." *The Anglo-American Magazine* (January 1902). Collected in *The Better Sort*. Included in the New York Edition.

"Flickerbridge." *Scribner's Magazine* (February 1902). Collected in *The Better Sort*. Included in the New York Edition.

"The Birthplace." *The Better Sort* (1903). Included in the New York Edition.

"The Beast in the Jungle." *The Better Sort* (1903). Included in the New York Edition.

"The Papers." *The Better Sort* (1903).

"Fordham Castle." *Harper's Monthly Magazine* (December 1904). Included in the New York Edition.

"Julia Bride." *Harper's Monthly Magazine* (March–April 1908). Collected in *Julia Bride*. Included in the New York Edition.

"The Jolly Corner." *The English Review* (December 1908). Included in the New York Edition.

"The Velvet Glove." *The English Review* (March 1909). Collected in *The Finer Grain*.

"Mora Montravers." *The English Review* (August–September 1909). Collected in *The Finer Grain*.

"Crapy Cornelia." *Harper's Monthly Magazine* (October 1909). Collected in *The Finer Grain*.

"The Bench of Desolation." *Putnam's Magazine* (October 1909 to January 1910). Collected in *The Finer Grain*.

"A Round of Visits." *The English Review*. (April–May 1910). Collected in *The Finer Grain*.

Collections of Short Stories

A Passionate Pilgrim. Boston: James R. Osgood, 1875.

The Madonna of the Future and Other Tales. 2 vols. London: Macmillan, 1979.

Daisy Miller: A Study, An International Episode, Four Meetings. London: Macmillan, 1879.

The Diary of a Man of Fifty and A Bundle of Letters. New York: Harper and Brothers, 1880.

Washington Square, The Pension Beaurepas, A Bundle of Letters. 2 vols. London: Macmillan, 1881.

The Siege of London, Madame De Mauves. London: Macmillan, 1883.

The Siege of London, The Pension Beaurepas, and the Point of View. Boston: J. R. Osgood, 1883.

Tales of Three Cities. Boston: J. R. Osgood, 1884.

Tales of Three Cities. London: Macmillan, 1884.

The Author of Beltraffio. Boston: J. R. Osgood, 1885.

Stories Revived. 2 vols. London: Macmillan 1885.

The Aspern Papers, Louisa Pallant, The Modern Warning. London and New York: Macmillan, 1888.

A London Life, The Patagonia, The Liar, Mrs. Temperly. London and New York: Macmillan, 1889.

The Lesson of the Master. London and New York: Macmillan, 1892.

The Private Life, The Wheel of Time, Lord Beaupré, The Visits, Collaboration, Owen Wingrave. London: J. R. Osgood, McIlvaine & Co, 1893.

The Private Life, Lord Beaupré, The Visits. New York: Harper and Brothers, 1893.

The Real Thing and Other Tales. London and New York: Macmillan, 1893.

Terminations. London: William Heinemann, 1893; New York: Macmillan, 1893.

The Wheel of Time, Collaboration, Owen Wingrave. New York: Harper and Row, 1893.

Embarrassments. London: William Heinemann, 1896; New York: Macmillan, 1896.

In the Cage. London: Duckworth & Co., 1898; Chicago: Herbert S. Stone & Co., 1898.

The Two Magics. London: William Heineman, 1898; New York: Macmillan, 1898.

The Soft Side. London: Methuen & Co., 1900; New York: Macmillan, 1900.

The Better Sort. London: Methuen & Co., 1903; New York: Charles Scribner's Sons, 1903.

Julia Bride. New York: Harper and Brothers, 1909.

The Finer Grain. London: Methuen & Co., 1910; New York: Charles Scribner's Sons, 1910.

Plays

The Complete Plays of Henry James. Edited by Leon Edel. 1949. Reprint, New York: Oxford University Press, 1990.

Guy Domville. London: J. Miles & Co., 1894.

Theatricals. London: Osgood, McIlvaine & Co., 1894. Includes *Tenants* and *Disengaged*.

Theatricals: Second Series. New York: Harper & Brothers, 1895. Includes *The Album* and *The Reprobate*.

Cultural, Literary, and Visual Criticism

Over the span of his writing career from 1864 to 1916, James wrote more than 300 essays of various kinds, including 18 prefaces to the New York Edition. For the most comprehensive listing of these publications, consult the *Literary Criticism* volumes published by the Library of America. What follows is a list of James's major essays and his collections of literary criticism.

French Poets and Novelists. London: Macmillan and Co., 1878. Includes essays on: Alfred de Musset, Theophile Gautier, Charles Baudelaire, Honoré de Balzac, George Sand, Gustave Flaubert, Ivan Turgénieff, The Two Ampéres, Madame de Sabran, Mérimée's Letters, and the Théâtre Français.

Partial Portraits. London: Macmillan and Co., 1888. Includes essays on: Emerson, George Eliot, Anthony Trollope, Robert Louis Stevenson, Constance Fenimore Woolson, Alphonse Daudet, Guy de Maupassant, George du Maurier, Ivan Turgénieff, and "The Art of Fiction" (1884).

Essays in London and Elsewhere. London: James R. Osgood, McIlvane & Co., 1893; New York: Harper & Brothers, 1893. Includes essays on: London, James Russell Lowell, Frances Kemble, Gustave Flaubert, Pierre Loti, the Journal of the Brothers Goncourt, Browning in Westminster Abbey, Henrik Ibsen, Mrs. Humphry Ward, etc.

Picture and Text. New York: Harper and Brothers, 1893. Includes essays on "Black and White," Edwin A. Abbey, Charles S. Reinhart, Alfred Parsons, John Singer Sargent, Honoré Daumier, etc.

The Question of Our Speech, The Lesson of Balzac: Two Lectures. Boston: Houghton, Mifflin and Company, 1905.

Notes on Novelists. London: J. M. Dent & Sons; New York: Charles Scribner's Sons, 1914. Includes essays on: Robert Louis Stevenson, Émile Zola, Gustave Flaubert, Honoré de Balzac, George Sand, Gabriele D'Annunzio, Matilde Serao, "The New Novel" (1914), Dumas the Younger, "The Novel in 'The Ring and the Book,'" Charles Eliot Norton, and several essays on London.

Travel Writing

James published many travel pieces, many of which were never collected and published in book form. The following includes only the book collections of his travel writing:

Transatlantic Sketches. Boston: James R. Osgood and Company, 1875.

Portraits of Places. London: Macmillan and Company, 1883.

A Little Tour of France. Boston: James R. Osgood, 1884. First published in the *Atlantic Monthly* (July–November 1883) as *En Provence.*

English Hours. Boston: Houghton, Mifflin and Company; London: William Heinemann, 1905.

The American Scene. London: Chapman and Hall, Ltd.; Harper and Brothers: New York, 1907.

Italian Hours. London: William Heinemann; Boston: Houghton Mifflin Company, 1909.

Biographies

Hawthorne. London: Macmillan and Co., 1879; New York City: Harper & Brothers, 1880.

William Wetmore Story and His Friends. Boston: Houghton, Mifflin & Co., 1903.

Autobiographies

Autobiography. Edited by Frederick W. Dupee. New York: Criterion Press, 1956. Includes *A Small Boy and Others.* New York: Charles Scribner's Sons, 1913; *Notes of a Son and Brother.* New York: Charles Scribner's Sons, 1914; and *The Middle Years.* New York: Charles Scribner's Sons, 1917.

Correspondence

The Correspondence of Henry James and Henry Adams, 1877–1914. Edited by George Monteiro. Baton Rouge: Louisiana State University Press, 1992.

The Correspondence of Henry James and the House of Macmillan, 1877–1914. Edited by Rayburn S. Moore. Baton Rouge: Louisiana State University Press, 1993.

Henry James, Letters, 4 vols. Edited by Leon Edel. Cambridge, Mass.: Harvard University Press, 1974.

Selected Letters to Edmund Gosse, 1882–1915. Edited by Rayburn S. Moore. Baton Rouge: Louisiana State University Press, 1988.

WJ-HJ Letters—The Correspondence of William James, 3 vols. Edited by Ignas K. Skrupskelis and Elizabeth M. Berkeley. Charlottesville: University Press of Virginia, 1992–94.

The Complete Letters of Henry James, 1855–1872; 1872–1876, 2 vols. Edited by Pierre A. Walker and Greg W. Zacharias. Lincoln: University of Nebraska Press, 2006–2009.

Notebooks

The Complete Notebooks of Henry James. Edited by Leon Edel and Lyall H. Powers. New York: Oxford University Press, 1987.

The Notebooks of Henry James. Edited by F. O. Matthiessen and Kenneth B. Murdock. New York: Oxford University Press, 1947.

SELECTED BIBLIOGRAPHY OF SECONDARY SOURCES

For an overview of the criticism written about James, please see the entry CRITICAL RECEPTION.

Agnew, Jean-Christophe. "The Consuming Vision of Henry James." In *The Culture of Consumption: Critical Essays in American History, 1880–1980,* edited by Richard Wightman Fox and T. J. Jackson Lears, 65–100. New York: Pantheon, 1983.

Anderson, Charles R. *Person, Place, and Thing in Henry James's Novels.* Durham, N.C.: Duke University Press, 1977.

Anderson, Quentin. *The American Henry James.* New Brunswick, N.J.: Rutgers University Press, 1957.

———. "Henry James and the New Jerusalem: Of Morality and Style." *Kenyon Review* 8 (August 1945): 515–566.

Anesko, Michael. *"Friction with the Market": Henry James and the Profession of Authorship.* Oxford University Press, 1986.

———. *Letters, Fictions, Lives: Henry James and William Dean Howells.* New York: Oxford University Press, 1997.

Armstrong, Paul B. *The Phenomenology of Henry James.* Chapel Hill: University of North Carolina Press, 1983.

Banta, Martha. *Henry James and the Occult: The Great Extension.* Bloomington: Indiana University Press, 1972.

———, ed. *New Essays on* The American. Cambridge: Cambridge University Press, 1987.

Baym, Nina. "Revision and Thematic Change in *The Portrait of a Lady.*" *Modern Fiction Studies* 22 (1976): 183–200.

Bell, Millicent. *Edith Wharton & Henry James, the Story of their Friendship.* New York: G. Braziller, 1965.

———. *Meaning in Henry James.* Cambridge, Mass.: Harvard University Press, 1991.

Ben-Joseph, Eli. *Aesthetic Persuasion: Henry James, the Jews and Race.* Lanham, N.Y.: University Press of America, 1996.

Bentley, Nancy. *The Ethnography of Manners: Hawthorne, James, Wharton.* Cambridge: Cambridge University Press, 1995.

Bersani, Leo. *A Future for Astyanax: Character and Desire in American Literature.* Boston: Little, Brown, 1976.

Blackmur, Richard P. "The Critical Prefaces." *Hound and Horn* 7 (April–May): 444–477.

———. "The Sacred Fount." *Kenyon Review,* 4 (Autumn 1942): 328–352.

———. *Studies in Henry James.* New York: New Directions, 1983.

Blair, Sara. *Henry James and the Writing of Race and Nation.* Cambridge: Cambridge University Press, 1996.

Boelhower, William. *Through a Glass Darkly: Ethnic Semiosis in American Literature.* Oxford: Oxford University Press, 1987.

Bosanquet, Theodora. *Henry James at Work.* Edited and with an introduction by Lyall H. Powers. Ann Arbor: University of Michigan Press, 2006.

Bradley, John. *Henry James and Homo-Erotic Desire.* New York: St. Martin's Press, 1999.

———. *Henry James's Permanent Adolescence.* New York: Palgrave, 2000.

Brooks, Peter. *Henry James Goes to Paris.* Princeton, N.J.: Princeton University Press, 2007.

———. *The Melodramatic Imagination: Balzac, Henry James, Melodrama, and the Mode of Excess.* New Haven, Conn.: Yale University Press, 1976.

Brooks, Van Wyck. *The Pilgrimage of Henry James.* New York: E.P. Dutton, 1925.

Buelens, Gert, ed. *Enacting History in Henry James: Narrative, Power, and Ethics.* Cambridge: Cambridge University Press, 1997.

Cain, William E. "Criticism and Politics: F. O. Matthiessen and the Making of Henry James." *The New England Quarterly* 60, no. 2 (June 1997): 163–186.

Cameron, Sharon. *Thinking in Henry James.* Chicago: University of Chicago Press, 1989.

Cannon, Kelly. *Henry James and Masculinity: The Man at the Margins.* New York: St. Martin's Press, 1994.

Cargill, Oscar. *The Novels of Henry James.* New York: Macmillan, 1961.

Chase, Richard. "The Lesson of the Master." In *The American Novel and Its Tradition,* 148–165. Garden City, N.Y.: Doubleday, 1957.

Collister, Peter. *Writing the Self: Henry James and America.* London: Pickering and Chatto, 2007.

Coulson, Victoria. *Henry James, Women and Realism.* Cambridge: Cambridge University Press, 2007.

Crews, Frederick C. *The Tragedy of Manners: Moral Drama in the Later Novels of Henry James.* 1957. Reprint, Hamden, Conn.: Archon Books, 1971.

Daugherty, Sarah B. *The Literary Criticism of Henry James.* Athens: Ohio University Press, 1981.

Davidson, Rob. *The Master and the Dean: The Literary Criticism of Henry James and William Dean Howells.* Columbia: University of Missouri Press, 2005.

Davis, Sara deSaussure. "Feminist Sources in *The Bostonians.*" *American Literature* 50 (1978–79): 570–587.

Dupee, Frederick W. *Henry James: His Life and Writings.* 1951. Reprint, Garden City, N.Y.: Doubleday Anchor, 1956.

———. *The Question of Henry James: A Collection of Critical Essays.* New York: Henry Holt, 1944.

———, ed. *Henry James.* 1951. Reprint, Garden City, N.Y.: Anchor Book, 1965.

Edel, Leon. *Henry James: The Untried Years, 1843–1870.* Philadelphia: Lippincott, 1953.

———. *Henry James: The Conquest of London, 1870–1881.* Philadelphia: Lippincott, 1962.

———. *Henry James: The Middle Years, 1882–1895.* Philadelphia: Lippincott, 1962.

———. *Henry James: The Treacherous Years, 1895–1901.* London: Hart-Davis, 1969.

———. *Henry James: The Master, 1901–1916.* Philadelphia: Lippincott, 1972.

———. *Letters/Henry James.* Cambridge, Mass.: Belknap Press of Harvard University, 1974–84.

Edel, Leon, and Lyall H. Power, eds. *The Complete Notebooks of Henry James.* New York and Oxford: Oxford University Press, 1987.

Felman, Shoshana. "Turning the Screw of Interpretation." *Yale French Studies* 55/56 (1977): 94–207.

Fetterley, Judith. *The Resisting Reader: A Feminist Approach to American Fiction.* Bloomington: Indiana University Press, 1978.

Fisher, Paul. *House of Wits: An Intimate Portrait of the James Family.* New York: Henry Holt, 2008.

Flannery, Denis. *Henry James: A Certain Illusion.* Hampshire, England: Ashgate, 2000.

Fogel, Daniel Mark. *Henry James and the Structure of the Romantic Imagination.* Baton Rouge: Louisiana State University Press, 1981.

Follini, Tamara. "Habitations of Modernism: Henry James's New York, 1907." *Cambridge Quarterly* 37, no. 1 (2008): 30–46.

———. "James, Dickens, and the Indirections of Influence." *Henry James Review* 25, no. 3 (2004): 228–238.

Freedman, Jonathan, ed. *The Cambridge Companion to Henry James.* Cambridge: Cambridge University Press, 1998.

———. *Professions of Taste: Henry James, British Aestheticism, and Commodity Culture.* Palo Alto, Calif.: Stanford University Press, 1990.

———. *The Temple of Culture: Assimilation and Anti-Semitism in Literary Anglo-America.* Oxford: Oxford University Press, 1998.

Funston, Judith E. *Henry James: A Reference Guide, 1975–1987.* Boston: G. K. Hall, 1991.

Fussell, Edwin Sill. *The Catholic Side of Henry James.* Cambridge: Cambridge University Press, 1993.

———. *The French Side of Henry James.* New York: Columbia University Press, 1990.

Gale, Robert. *A Henry James Encyclopedia*. New York: Greenwood Press, 1989.

Geismar, Maxwell. *Henry James and the Jacobites*. 1962. Reprint, New York: Hill and Wang, 1965.

Gordon, Lyndall. *A Private Life of Henry James: Two Women and His Art*. New York: W.W. Norton, 1998.

Graham, Kenneth. *Henry James, The Drama of Fulfillment*. Oxford, U.K.: Clarendon Press, 1975.

———. *Henry James, a Literary Life*. New York: St. Martin's Press, 1996.

Graham, Wendy. *Henry James's Thwarted Love*. Palo Alto, Calif.: Stanford University Press, 1999.

Griffin, Susan M. *The Historical Eye: The Texture of the Visual in Late James*. Boston: Northeastern University Press, 1991.

Grover, Philip. *Henry James and the French Novel: A Study in Inspiration*. New York: Barnes & Noble, 1973.

Gunter, Susan E., ed. *Dear Munificent Friends: Henry James's Letters to Four Women*. Ann Arbor: University of Michigan Press, 1999.

Gunter, Susan E., and Steven H. Jobe, eds. *Dear Beloved Friends: Henry James's Letters to Younger Men*. Ann Arbor: University of Michigan Press, 2002.

Habegger, Alfred. *Henry James and the 'Woman Business'*. Cambridge: Cambridge University Press, 1989.

Hadley, Tessa. *Henry James and the Imagination of Pleasure*. Cambridge: Cambridge University Press, 2002.

Haralson, Eric. *Henry James and Queer Modernity*. Cambridge: Cambridge University Press, 2003.

Haviland, Beverly. *Henry James's Last Romance: Making Sense of the Past and the American Scene*. Cambridge: Cambridge University Press, 1997.

Hayes, Kevin J., ed. *Henry James: The Contemporary Reviews*. Cambridge: Cambridge University Press, 1996.

Hicks, Granville. *The Great Tradition: An Interpretation of American Literature since the Civil War*. New York: Macmillan, 1933.

Hocks, Richard A. *Henry James and Pragmatist Thought: A Study in the Relationship between the Philosophy of William James and the Literary Art of Henry James*. Chapel Hill: University of North Carolina Press, 1974.

Holland, Lawrence B. *The Expense of Vision: Essays on the Craft of Henry James*. Princeton, N.J.: Princeton University Press, 1964.

Hollinghurst, Alan. *The Line of Beauty*. London: Macmillan, 2004.

Holly, Carol. *Intensely Family: The Inheritance of Family Shame and the Autobiographies of Henry James*. Madison: University of Wisconsin Press, 1995.

Horne, Philip. *Henry James and Revision: The New York Edition*. Oxford, U.K.: Clarendon Press, 1990.

———, ed. *Henry James: A Life in Letters*. New York: Viking, 1998.

Howe, Irving. *Politics and the Novel*. Greenwich, Conn.: Fawcett, 1967.

Hueffer, Ford Maddox. *Henry James: A Critical Study*. London: Martin Secker, 1913.

Hutchison, Hazel. *Seeing and Believing: Henry James and the Spiritual World*. New York: Palgrave, 2006.

Hyde, Montgomery. *Henry James at Home*. New York: Farrar, Straus & Giroux, 1969.

Izzo, Donatella. *Portraying the Lady: Technologies of Gender in the Short Stories of Henry James*. Lincoln: University of Nebraska Press, 2001.

Jacobson, Marcia. *Henry James and the Mass Market*. Tuscaloosa: University of Alabama Press, 1987.

Johnson, Kendall. *Henry James and the Visual*. Cambridge: Cambridge University Press, 2007.

Jolly, Roslyn. *Henry James: History, Narrative, Fiction*. Oxford, U.K.: Clarendon Press, 1993.

Kaplan, Fred. *Henry James: The Imagination of Genius: A Biography*. New York: William Morrow, 1992.

Katz, Daniel. *American Modernism's Expatriate Scene: The Labour of Translation*. Edinburgh: Edinburgh Press, 2007.

Kress, Jill M. *The Figure of Consciousness: William James, Henry James, and Edith Wharton*. New York: Routledge, 2002.

Krook, Dorothea. *The Ordeal of Consciousness in Henry James*. New York: Cambridge University Press, 1962.

Leavis, F. R. *The Great Tradition: George Eliot, Henry James, Joseph Conrad*. Garden City, N.Y.: Doubleday, 1948.

Lewis, R. W. B. *The Jameses: A Family Narrative*. New York: Farrar, Straus & Giroux, 1991.

Lodge, David. *Author, Author.* New York: Viking, 2004.

Lubbock, Percy. *The Craft of Fiction.* New York: Scribner's, 1921.

———, ed. *The Letters of Henry James.* New York: Scribner's, 1920.

Lustig, T. J. *Henry James and the Ghostly.* Cambridge: Cambridge University Press, 1994.

Marshall, Adré. *The Turn of the Mind: Constituting Consciousness in Henry James.* London: Associated Universities Press, 1998.

Matthiessen, F. O. *The American Renaissance: Art and Expression in the Age of Emerson and Whitman.* New York: Oxford University Press, 1941, 351–368.

———. *Henry James: The Major Phase.* New York: Oxford University Press, 1944.

———. *The James Family: Including Selections from the Writings of Henry James, Senior, William, Henry, and Alice James.* New York: Knopf, 1947.

Matthiessen, F. O., and Kenneth Murdock, eds. *The Notebooks of Henry James.* New York: Oxford University Press, 1947.

McColgan, Kristin Pruitt. *Henry James 1917–1959.* Boston: G. K. Hall, 1979.

McCormack, Peggy, ed. *Questioning the Master: Gender and Sexuality in Henry James's Writings.* Newark: University of Delaware Press, 2000.

McGurl, Mark. *The Novel Art: Elevations of American Fiction after Henry James.* Princeton, N.J.: Princeton University Press, 2001.

McKee, Patricia. *Producing American Races: Henry James, William Faulkner, Toni Morrison.* Durham, N.C.: Duke University Press, 1999.

McWhirter, David. *Desire and Love in Henry James: A Study of the Late Novels.* Cambridge: Cambridge University Press, 1989.

———, ed. *Henry James's New York Edition: The Construction of Authorship.* Palo Alto, Calif.: Stanford University Press, 1995.

Meissner, Collin. *Henry James and the Language of Experience.* New York: Cambridge University Press, 1999.

Mendelssohn, Michèle. *Henry James, Oscar Wilde and Aesthetic Culture.* Edinburgh: Edinburgh University Press, 2007.

Michaels, Walter Benn. *Our America: Nativism, Modernism, and Pluralism.* Durham, N.C.: Duke University Press, 1995.

Miller, J. Hillis. *Literature as Conduct: Speech Acts in Henry James.* New York: Fordham University Press, 2005.

Moon, Michael. *A Small Boy and Others: Imitation and Initiation in American Culture from Henry James to Andy Warhol.* Durham, N.C.: Duke University Press, 1998.

Novick, Sheldon M. *Henry James: The Mature Master.* New York: Random House, 2007.

———. *Henry James: The Young Master.* New York: Random House, 1996.

Ohi, Kevin. *Innocence and Rapture: The Erotic Child in Pater, Wilde, James, and Nabokov.* New York: Palgrave Macmillan, 2005.

Parrington, Vernon L. *The Beginnings of Critical Realism in America (1860–1920).* Vol. 3 of *Main Currents in American Thought from the Beginnings to 1920.* New York: Harcourt, Brace, 1927–30.

Perosa, Sergio. *Henry James and the Experimental Novel.* Charlottesville: University Press of Virginia, 1978.

Person, Leland S. *Henry James and the Suspense of Masculinity.* Philadelphia: University of Pennsylvania Press, 2003.

Pigeon, Elaine. *Queer Impressions: Henry James's Art of Fiction.* New York: Routledge, 2005.

Pippin, Robert. *Henry James and Modern Moral Life.* Cambridge: Cambridge University Press, 2000.

Poirier, Richard. *The Comic Sense of Henry James.* New York: Oxford University Press, 1960.

Poole, Adrian. "Henry James and the Mobile Phone." *Henry James Review* 37, no. 1 (2008): 79–89.

———. "Nanda's Smile: Teaching James and the Sense of Humor." *Henry James Review* 25, no. 1 (2004): 4–18.

———. "James and the Shadow of the Roman Empire." In Buelens, 75–92.

Porter, Carolyn. *Seeing and Being: The Plight of the Participant Observer in Emerson, James, Adams, and Faulkner.* Middletown, Conn.: Wesleyan University Press, 1981.

Posnock, Ross. *The Trial of Curiosity: Henry James, William James, and the Challenge of Modernity.* New York: Oxford University Press, 1991.

Powers, Lyall H. *Henry James and the Naturalist Movement.* Lansing: Michigan State University Press, 1971.

Przbylowicz, Donna. *Desire and Repression: the Dialectic of Self and Other in the Late Works of Henry James.* Tuscaloosa: University of Alabama Press, 1986.

———. Introduction to *The Bostonians* by Henry James, v–ix. New York: Dial Press, 1945.

Rahv, Philip. "The Cult of Experience in American Writing." In *Literary Opinion in America,* edited by Morton D. Zabel. New York: Harper and Brothers, 1937.

———. *Image and Idea: Twenty Essays on Literary Themes.* 1949. Reprint, Norfolk, Conn.: New Directions Paperbacks, 1957.

Raw, Laurence. *Adapting Henry James to the Screen: Gender, Fiction, and Film.* Oxford, U.K.: Scarecrow Press, 2006.

Rawlings, Peter. *American Theorists of the Novel: Henry James, Lionel Trilling, Wayne C. Booth.* London and New York: Routledge, 2006.

———. *Henry James and the Abuse of the Past.* Basingstoke, Hampshire, and New York: Palgrave Macmillan, 2005.

———, ed. *Palgrave Advances in Henry James Studies.* Basingstoke, U.K.: Palgrave Macmillan, 2007.

Richardson, Robert. *William James: In the Maelstrom of American Modernism.* New York: Houghton Mifflin, 2007.

Rivkin, Julie. *False Positions: The Representational Logics of Henry James's Fiction.* Palo Alto, Calif.: Stanford University Press, 1996.

Rourke, Constance. *American Humor: A Study of National Character.* New York: Harcourt, Brace, 1931.

Rowe, John Carlos. *The Other Henry James.* Durham, N.C.: Duke University Press, 1998.

———. *The Theoretical Dimensions of Henry James.* Madison: University of Wisconsin Press, 1984.

Salmon, Richard. *Henry James and the Culture of Publicity.* Cambridge: Cambridge University Press, 1997.

Savoy, Eric. "Embarrassments: Figure in the Closet." *Henry James Review* 20, no. 3 (1999): 227–236.

———. "The Jamesian Thing." *Henry James Review* 22, no. 3 (2001): 267–277.

———. "The Jamesian Turn: A Primer on Queer Formalism." In *Approaches to Teaching Henry James's Daisy Miller and The Turn of the Screw,* 132–142. New York: Modern Language Association, 2005.

———. "The Queer Subject of the 'Jolly Corner.'" *Henry James Review* 20, no. 1 (1999): 1–21.

———. "Theory a tergo in 'The Turn of the Screw.'" In *Curiouser: On the Queerness of Children,* edited by Steven Bruhm and Natasha Hurley, 245–276. Minneapolis: University of Minnesota Press, 2004.

Scura, Dorothy McKinnis. *Henry James 1960–1974.* Boston: G.K. Hall, 1979.

Sears, Sallie. *The Negative Imagination: Form and Perspective in the Novels of Henry James.* Ithaca, N.Y.: Cornell University Press, 1986.

Sedgwick, Eve Kosofsky. "The Beast in the Closet: James and the Writing of Homosexual Panic." In *Epistemology of the Closet.* Berkeley: University of California Press, 1990.

———. *Tendencies.* Durham, N.C.: Duke University Press, 1993.

Segal, Ora. *The Lucid Reflector: The Observer in Henry James's Fiction.* New Haven, Conn.: Yale University Press, 1969.

Seltzer, Mark. *Bodies and Machines.* New York: Routledge, 1992.

———. *Henry James and the Art of Power.* Ithaca, N.Y.: Cornell University Press, 1984.

Simon, Linda. *The Critical Reception of Henry James: Creating a Master.* Rochester, N.Y.: Camden House, 2007.

Spender, Stephen. *The Destructive Element: A Study of Modern Writers and Beliefs.* Boston and New York: Houghton Mifflin, 1936.

Stadler, Gustavus. *Troubling Minds: The Cultural Politics of Genius in the United States, 1840–1890.* Minneapolis: University of Minnesota Press, 2006.

Stevens, Hugh. *Henry James and Sexuality.* Cambridge: Cambridge University Press, 1998.

Stowe, William W. *Balzac, James, and the Realist Novel.* Princeton, N.J.: Princeton University Press, 1983.

Strouse, Jean. *Alice James, A Biography.* Boston: Houghton Mifflin, 1980.

Tambling, Jeremy. *Lost in the American City: Dickens, James, Kafka.* New York: Palgrave, 2001.

Taylor, Andrew. *Henry James and the Father Question.* Cambridge: Cambridge University Press, 2002.

Taylor, Linda J. *Henry James, 1866–1916, A Reference Guide.* Boston: G.K. Hall, 1982.

Thomas, Brook. *American Literary Realism and the Failed Promise of Contract.* Berkeley: University of California Press, 1997.

Thurschwell, Pamela. *Literature, Technology and Magical Thinking, 1880–1920.* Cambridge: Cambridge University Press, 2001.

Tinter, Adeline. *Henry James's Legacy: The Afterlife of His Figure and Fiction.* Baton Rouge: Louisiana State University Press, 1988.

———. *The Museum World of Henry James.* Ann Arbor: University of Michigan Research Press, 1986.

Tóibín, Colm. *The Master.* New York: Scribner's, 2004.

Trilling, Lionel. *The Liberal Imagination: Essays on Literature and Society.* New York: Viking, 1950.

Veeder, William. *Henry James—the Lessons of the Master: Popular Fiction and Personal Style in the Nineteenth Century.* Chicago: University of Chicago Press, 1975.

Wagenknecht, Edward. *Eve and Henry James: Portraits of Women and Girls in His Fiction.* Norman: University of Oklahoma Press, 1978.

Walker, Pierre A., ed. *Henry James on Culture: Collected Essays on Politics and the American Social Scene.* Lincoln: University of Nebraska Press, 1999.

———. "Leon Edel and the 'Policing' of Henry James Letters." *Henry James Review* 21, no. 3 (2000): 279–289.

———. *Reading Henry James in French Cultural Contexts.* DeKalb: Northern Illinois University Press, 1995.

———, and Greg W. Zacharias, eds. *The Complete Letters of Henry James.* 2 vols. Lincoln: University of Nebraska Press, 2006.

Walton, Priscilla. *The Disruption of the Feminine in Henry James.* Toronto: University of Toronto Press, 1992.

Warren, Kenneth W. *Black and White Strangers: Race and American Literary Realism.* Chicago: University of Chicago Press, 1993.

Weinstein, Philip M. *Henry James and the Requirements of the Imagination.* Cambridge, Mass.: Harvard University Press, 1971.

West, Rebecca. *Henry James.* New York: Henry Holt, 1916.

Williams, Merle A. *Henry James and the Philosophical Novel.* Cambridge: Cambridge University Press, 1993.

Wilson, Edmund. "The Ambiguity of Henry James." *Hound and Horn* 7 (April–May, 1934): 385–406.

———. "The Last Phase of Henry James." *Partisan Review* 4 (February 1938): 3–8.

———. "The Pilgrimage of Henry James." In *The Shores of Light: A Literary Chronicle of the Twenties and Thirties,* 217–228. New York: Farrar, Straus, and Young, 1952.

Winner, Viola Hopkins. *Henry James and the Visual Arts.* Charlottesville: University Press of Virginia, 1970.

Winters, Yvor. "Henry James and the Relation of Morals and Manners." *American Review* 9 (October 1937): 482–503.

Wonham, Henry B. *Playing the Races: Ethnic Caricature and American Literary Realism.* Oxford: Oxford University Press, 2004.

Yeazell, Ruth B. *Language and Knowledge in the Late Novels of Henry James.* Chicago: University of Chicago Press, 1980.

Zorzi, Rosella Mamoli, ed. *Beloved Boy: Letters to Hendrik C. Andersen, 1899–1915.* Charlottesville: University of Virginia Press, 2004.

CHRONOLOGY OF HENRY JAMES'S LIFE

1843

Henry James is born in New York City on April 15 (older brother William born January 11, 1842).

James family leaves the United States to live in England and France.

1844

First public telegraph message sent between Baltimore and Washington.

1845

James family returns to the United States, lives briefly in Albany and mostly in Manhattan for the next 10 years.

Garth Wilkinson ("Wilky") James is born.

Frederick Douglass publishes *The Narrative of a Life of Frederick Douglass, an American Slave, Written by Himself.*

The Irish potato famine begins, leading to mass immigration to the United States.

1846

Mexican-American War begins, ending in 1848 with the Treaty of Guadalupe Hidalgo.

Robertson (Bob) James is born.

1848

Alice James is born.

The Communist Manifesto by Karl Marx and Friedrich Engels is published.

Revolutions sweep across Europe.

Second Republic is established in France when King Louis Philippe abdicates throne.

1850

Fugitive Slave Act passes into law.

Nathaniel Hawthorne publishes *The Scarlet Letter.*

1851

London's Great Exhibition is the first World's Fair, boasting the Crystal Palace.

1852

Napoleon III establishes the Second Empire in France, which will continue until 1870.

Harriet Beecher Stowe publishes the antislavery novel *Uncle Tom's Cabin.*

1853

In the Crimean War, Russia is defeated by an alliance of England, France, and the Ottoman Empire.

1854

Kansas-Nebraska Act allows settlers in these territories to decide on the legality of slavery, thus upsetting the Missouri Compromise of 1821.

1855

James family leaves for Europe, where they will live for the next three years.

1856

In retaliation for his speech against the Kansas-Nebraska Act, Massachusetts senator Charles Sumner is beaten nearly to death in the Senate chambers by Preston Brooks, a congressman from South Carolina.

John Brown executes the Pottawatomie Massacre in Kansas after the sacking of Lawrence, Kansas, by proslavery advocates.

1857
Economic crash of 1857 occurs.
The *Atlantic Monthly* is founded.
Supreme Court rules that descendants of slaves can never be United States citizens in *Dred Scott v. Sanford.*

1858
James family returns to the United States, settling for a year in Newport, Rhode Island.
Telegraph becomes transatlantic.

1859
James family spends a year in Geneva, Switzerland.
Abolitionist John Brown attempts to start a rebellion against slavery by raiding the federal armory in Harpers Ferry, Virginia (hanged in December).
Darwin publishes *On the Origin of Species.*

1860
James family returns to Newport.
Abraham Lincoln is inaugurated as U.S. president.

1861
Henry James is injured (an "obscure hurt") in helping to extinguish a stable fire in Newport.
William James enrolls at Harvard University.
U.S. Civil War begins.

1862
Henry enrolls in Harvard Law School but finds it unsatisfying and concentrates on his writing.
Younger brothers, Wilky and Bob, enlist to serve in the Civil War.
Older brother, William, continues his studies at Harvard's Lawrence Scientific Institute.

1862–63
Emancipation Proclamation begins process of freeing slaves.

1864
James anonymously publishes his first story, "A Tragedy of Error," in *Continental Monthly.*
Hawthorne dies.

1865
James's signed tale "The Story of a Year" appears in the *Atlantic Monthly* (March 1865).
Civil War ends.
Abraham Lincoln is shot on April 14. He dies early the next morning, on James's 22nd birthday.
Thirteenth Amendment to the United States Constitution abolishes slavery.

1866
James family moves to Cambridge, Massachusetts.
Austro-Prussian War occurs.

1868
Fourteenth Amendment defines rights of citizenship, guaranteeing equal protection of all citizens (including former slaves) under the law.
Benjamin Disraeli becomes prime minister of England.

1869
James embarks on his first unaccompanied European tour. His beloved cousin Minny Temple dies of tuberculosis.
The transcontinental railroad is completed.

1870
James returns to Cambridge, Massachusetts, where he will stay for the next two years.
Fifteenth Amendment guarantees voting rights to all male citizens without consideration of "race, color, or previous condition of servitude."
Third Republic of France established.

1870–71
Franco-Prussian War occurs.

1871
James's first novel, *Watch and Ward,* is serialized in the *Atlantic Monthly* (August–December).
The short-lived revolutionary Paris Commune exercises power in Paris.

1872
James returns to Europe to tour the Continent with his Aunt Kate and sister, Alice.

1874
James returns to live briefly in New York City.

First exhibition in Paris by the impressionists, *Société anonyme des artists, peintres, sculpteurs, graveurs,* including Claude Monet, August Renoir, Edgar Degas, and Camille Pissaro, opens on April 15.

1875

James goes to live in Paris, where he meets Gustave Flaubert, Émile Zola, Guy de Maupassant, Edmond de Goncourt, Ivan Turgenev, and many other writers.

James's novel *Roderick Hudson* is serialized in the *Atlantic Monthly.*

1876

James moves to London.

The American is serialized in the *Atlantic Monthly.*

Philadelphia Centennial of American Revolution draws millions.

Alexander Graham Bell invents the telephone.

1878

James publishes *The Europeans,* "Daisy Miller: A Study," and *French Poets and Novelists.*

1879

James publishes biography *Hawthorne.*

1880

Washington Square is published.

James meets American author Constance Fenimore Woolson.

1880–81

First Boer War occurs.

1881

The Portrait of a Lady is published.

1882

James's mother and father die, and Henry executes the will.

Longtime family friend Ralph Waldo Emerson dies.

1883

James returns to London.

Brother Wilky dies.

1884

Alice James moves to London.

1886

James publishes two long novels, *The Bostonians* and *The Princess Casamassima.*

James moves to 34 De Vere Gardens, Kensington, in London before spending eight months in Italy and visiting with Woolson.

1888

The Reverberator is published.

James hires Wolcott Balestier as his literary agent.

British poet and critic Matthew Arnold dies.

1890

The Tragic Muse is published.

William James publishes *The Principles of Psychology.*

Wounded Knee Massacre occurs.

1891

Play version of James's *The American* opens to lukewarm reviews in London.

1892

Alice James dies on March 6.

1893

World's Columbian Exhibition in Chicago opens.

Second Irish Home Rule Bill is rejected by House of Lords.

1894

James's play *Guy Domville* ends after a short five-week run in London.

Woolson dies in Venice, apparently by suicide.

1895

James serializes *The Awkward Age.*

Trials of Oscar Wilde end with conviction, and his two-year prison sentence begins.

1896

"The Turn of the Screw" and "The Figure in the Carpet" appear.

Supreme Court decision *Plessy* v. *Ferguson* upholds the constitutionality of racial segregation.

1897

What Maisie Knew is published.

James moves to Lamb House in Rye, England.

1898

James privately supports Zola's protest against the Dreyfus affair.

Spanish-American War begins.

1899

Boxer Rebellion in China occurs.

Second Boer War begins (ends 1902).

Philippine-American War begins (ends 1902).

1900

John Ruskin dies.

1901

The Sacred Fount is published.

Queen Victoria dies, having reigned over British Empire since 1837.

President William McKinley is assassinated at the Pan-American Exposition in Buffalo, New York.

1902

Wings of the Dove is published.

William James publishes *The Varieties of Religious Experience.*

Émile Zola dies.

1903

James publishes *The Ambassadors.*

1904

The Golden Bowl is published.

James returns to the United States after a 20-year absence to deliver lectures and gather impressions of American culture.

1905

James returns to England and begins working on the New York Edition of his works.

1906

The San Francisco earthquake strikes, worrying Henry over William's safety.

1907

The American Scene appears.

1908

James grows very disappointed with the poor sales of Scribner's 24-volume New York Edition of his works.

1910

Bob James dies.

William James dies, and Henry spends year (August 1910–July 1911) in the United States.

King Edward VII dies.

George V ascends to British throne.

Mark Twain dies.

1911

James returns to England, never again to see the United States.

1912–13

Balkan Wars occurs.

1913

A Small Boy and Others, the first volume of James's autobiography, appears.

Woodrow Wilson becomes U.S. president.

1914

Notes of a Son and Brother, the second volume of James's autobiography, appears.

World War I breaks out in August.

Panama Canal opens

1915

James becomes a British citizen out of loyalty to the war effort. He suffers a debilitating stroke in early December. His sister-in-law, Alice (widow of William James), arrives to care for him.

Germany sinks the *Lusitania.*

1916

James receives British Order of Merit.

James dies on February 28. His ashes are then returned to family burial plot in Cambridge, Massachusetts.

Easter Rebellion in Ireland occurs.

1917
United States declares war on Germany.
The Russian Revolution occurs.

1918
World War I ends.

1919
The Irish War of Independence begins.

1920
The Nineteenth Amendment to the U.S. Constitution prohibits restrictions on voting due to gender, allowing women to vote.

INDEX